ART LAW HANDBOOK

ART LAW HANDBOOK

Roy S. Kaufman, Editor

ASPEN LAW & BUSINESS
Aspen Publishers, Inc.
Gaithersburg New York

Printed in the United States of America

Library of Congress Cataloging-in-Publication Data

Art law handbook / Roy S. Kaufman, editor.
p. cm.
Includes index.
ISBN 0-7355-1641-3
1. Law and art--United States. I. Kaufman, Roy S.
KF4288 .A948 2000
344.73'097--dc21

00-056558

2 3 4 5 6 7 8 9

About Aspen Law & Business

Aspen Law & Business—comprising the former Prentice Hall Law & Business, Little, Brown and Company's Professional Division, and Wiley Law Publications—is a leading publisher of authoritative treatises, practice manuals, services, and journals for attorneys, financial and tax advisors, corporate and bank directors, and other business professionals. Our mission is to provide practical solution-based, how-to information keyed to the latest legislative, judicial, and regulatory developments.

We offer publications in the areas of banking and finance; bankruptcy; business and commercial law; construction law; corporate law; pensions, benefits, and labor; insurance law; securities; taxation; intellectual property; government and administrative law; real estate law; matrimonial and family law; environmental and health law; international law; legal practice and litigation; and criminal law.

Other Aspen Law & Business products treating intellectual property and communications law issues include:

The Commercial Law of Intellectual Property
The Computer Lawyer
Copyright
Drafting License Agreements
Epstein on Intellectual Property
Intellectual Property Litigation: Pretrial Practice
IP Litigator
The Journal of Proprietary Rights
Kohn on Music Licensing
The Law of Chemical and Pharmaceutical Invention
Libel & Privacy
The Licensing Journal
Patent Practice Handbook
Perle and Williams on Publishing Law
Protecting Trade Secrets, Patents, Copyrights, and Trademarks
Scott on Computer Law
Scott on Multimedia Law
Software Patents
Trade Dress Law
Trademark Law

ASPEN LAW & BUSINESS
A Division of Aspen Publishers, Inc.
A Wolters Kluwer Company
www.aspenpublishers.com

SUBSCRIPTION NOTICE

This Aspen Law & Business product is updated on a periodic basis with supplements to reflect important changes in the subject matter. If you purchased this product directly from Aspen Law & Business, we have already recorded your subscription for the update service.

If, however, you purchased this product from a bookstore and wish to receive future updates and revised or related volumes billed separately with a 30-day examination review, please contact our Customer Service Department at 1-800-234-1660, or send your name, company name (if applicable), address, and the title of the product to:

ASPEN LAW & BUSINESS
A Division of Aspen Publishers, Inc.
7201 McKinney Circle
Frederick, MD 21704

Dedication

To my dad, Harold Kaufman, who painted Lascaux.

SUMMARY OF CONTENTS

CONTENTS

Chapter 11 Auction Law by Jonathan A. Olsoff 899

ABOUT THE AUTHORS

Roy Kaufman (Editor) is a member of the Bar of the State of New York and co-chair of the Intellectual Property Subcommittee of the Art Law Committee, Association of the Bar of the City of New York. He has published and lectured extensively on the subjects of copyright, new media, artists' rights and art law, and has represented publishers, artists, dealers, curators, Web site providers and not-for-profit entities in connection with artist/gallery contracts, licensing, commissioned artwork agreements, theft, disputes and related issues. He is a graduate of Brandeis University (B.A., European cultural studies) and Columbia Law School (J.D.), where he served as Executive Notes Editor of the Columbia-VLA Journal of Law and the Arts. He is currently Assistant General Counsel to John Wiley and Sons, Inc., a global multinational publisher.

Jonathan Bloom (Chapter 5) is an associate in the New York office of Weil, Gotshal & Manges LLP, specializing in media law, art law, and intellectual property law. He holds a B.A. summa cum laude in art history from Princeton University (1984), an M.A. in art history from Yale University (1987), and a J.D. from New York University School of Law (1991).

Peter S. Canelias (Chapter 2) maintains a private practice in Manhattan, where he concentrates in the area of intellectual property law. He received his B.S. summa cum laude in physics from the Massachusetts State College at Bridgewater, including graduate work in mathematical physics and quantum mechanics, and his J.D. cum laude from Boston College Law School, where he served as a staff member and Executive Editor of the Boston College Law Review. After completing his legal education, he served as a law clerk to the Hon. Pauline Newman, Circuit Judge, United States Court of Appeals for the Federal Circuit. Currently, he chairs the Subcommittee for Improving the Rights of Patentees and the Rights of Employed Inventors of the American Bar Association Intellectual Property Law Section, and is an active member of numerous intellectual property organizations. He is also an instructor at the New York Paralegal School.

Richard E. Halperin (Chapters 13 and 15) received his B.A. in 1965 and his LL.B. in 1968 from the University of Pennsylvania. As counsel to the firm of Kay Collyer & Boose LLP in New York City, his practice encompasses a broad variety of domestic and international tax matters, many involving authors, composers, playwrights, screenwriters, photographers, cartoonists, and software designers. He is also a working photographer and teaches a workshop at the International Center of Photography in New York City.

William M. Hart (Chapter 1) is a partner in the New York office of Proskauer Rose, LLP, who specializes in intellectual property litigation and transactional matters, with a particular emphasis on copyright issues, focusing primarily on entertainment and literary property matters. A graduate of Carnegie-Mellon University and the University of Pittsburgh School of Law, and a 1981 recipient of the Burton Fellowship in 1981 from Columbia University Law School to pursue postgraduate studies in copyright law, he is a past member of the Committee on Copyright and Literary Property of the Association of the Bar of the City of New York and of the Federal Legislation Committee of the United States Trademark Association, and currently is a member of the United States Copyright Society.

Steven Johnson (Chapter 8) is a litigation attorney with the law firm of Paul, Hastings, Janofsky & Walker in New York, and has extensive experience litigating and arbitrating a wide variety of art, entertainment and general commercial matters. As a regular part of his practice, he also counsels clients in connection with dispute resolution. He received his B.A. cum laude from the University of Washington in 1982 and his J.D. cum laude from New York Law School in 1986.

Steven Mark Levy (Chapters 10 and 12) is a partner at Lewis, D'Amato, Brisbois & Bisgaard in Los Angeles. He received his B.A. magna cum laude from Claremont McKenna College, where his studies included advanced courses in art history, and his J.D. from the University of California at Berkeley, Boalt Hall. The author of several articles on art law and a lecturer to audiences in both the artistic and legal communities, he has had extensive experience advising artists, collectors, galleries, art publishers, appraisers, insurers, and others, and when necessary representing them in litigation.

Matthew A. McMurphy (Chapter 3) is a corporate associate in the Dallas, Texas office of Jackson Walker L.L.P. He graduated from Cornell University in 1994 with a B.S. in policy analysis and earned his J.D. from the University of Texas at Austin School of Law in 1999. His practice consists of representing issuers and purchasers in public and private offerings of debt and equity securities; SEC compliance matters; and mergers, acquisitions, and reorganizations. Additionally, he counsels business organizations with regard to contractual and procedural issues.

Rena Moulopoulos (Chapter 6) began her career as an associate in the New York office of the law firm of Sullivan & Cromwell. In 1989, she joined Sotheby's, Inc. in New York where she focused on issues involving Sotheby's in North America. In 1994, she moved to London as General Counsel for Sotheby's in Europe. She returned to New York in 1996, as Deputy General Counsel worldwide for Sotheby's Holdings, Inc. In October 1997, she was appointed Worldwide Director of Compliance, Business Practices Counsel and Senior Vice President of Sotheby's Holdings, Inc. In this position, she is focusing on issues arising from the international movement of works of art and the auction process. She served on the Committee on Art Law of the Association of the Bar of the City of New York. She received her B.A. in philosophy from Denison University and her J.D. from Washington College of Law, American University.

Jonathan A. Olsoff (Chapter 11) is Associate General Counsel and Senior Vice-President at Sotheby's, Inc., where he handles a variety of matters relating to the sale of art at auction, specializing in issues of title and authenticity. Previously, he was an associate at Berger & Steingut, and a partner at Berger Stern & Webb, where he worked on a variety of art-related litigation. He is a graduate of Tufts University and Washington College of Law, American University, where he served as Senior Articles Editor on the law review. He served as a clerk to Hon. James K. Logan of the United States Court of Appeals for the Tenth Circuit.

Jenifer DeWolf Paine (Chapter 1) practices in the area of intellectual property, focusing on copyright and trademark litigation, transactions, and prosecution. She earned her B.A. from Boston University and her J.D. from Northeastern University, and is admitted to the state bars of California, Massachusetts, and New York, as well as the Federal District of Massachusetts, the Southern District of New York, and the U.S. Court of Claims. She is a member of the American Bar Association's Intellectual Property Committee, the U.S. Copyright Society, and the International Trademark Association, and is the author of "Legal Issues in the Music Business from the Artist's Perspective," in *Lawyering for the Media and Entertainment Industries* (Massachusetts Continuing Legal Education 1996) and co-author of "Issues for Producers of Multimedia," in *Multimedia Licensing* (Massachusetts Continuing Legal Education 1995).

Van Kirk Reeves (Chapter 7), of the Paris office of Porter & Reeves, is admitted to the bar in both Paris and New York and has practiced law in France for more than 30 years. He has substantial experience in art-related disputes, counseling a number of museums as well as collectors and dealers in the U.S. and Europe. He is a member of the board of the Art Law Center of Geneva and was for many years vice-president and a member of the board of the International Council of Museums Foundation. He contributes regularly to specialized legal publications; recent speaking engagements (1999) include a discussion on the use of trusts and foundations for donations and legacies of art collections at "*L'Art et la Gestion de Patrimoine*," a conference organized by the *Club Parisien des Professions Financières*; a talk on tax aspects of the disposal of art and cultural property at "Cross-Border Planned Giving, a U.S. and European Survey," a London conference sponsored by the European Association for Planned Giving; and a discussion of art loans at "Art Loans," a conference organized by the Art Law Center in Lausanne, Switzerland. He is a graduate of Harvard College and Harvard Law School.

Laura Lee Stapleton (Chapter 3) is a partner in the Litigation, Appellate and Intellectual Property sections and a member of the Media Law, Technology, and Entertainment and Sports practice groups of Jackson Walker, L.L.P. in Texas. A graduate of the University of Texas, where she earned both her B.B.A. and J.D. degrees, she is a member of the bar in both Texas and California and is admitted to practice in all U.S. District Courts in Texas and the Fifth Circuit Court of Appeals. She has been a member of the Texas Association of Broadcasters Legislative Task force and serves as an on-call attorney for the Freedom of Information Foundation of Texas hotline, a member of the Board of Directors of Lifeworks, and a member of the Advisory Board of Artists Legal and Accounting Assistance. Her other publications include articles in the Media and the Law newsletter, the Texas Lawyer, and the LDRC Libel Letter, as well as "The Professional Athlete's Right of Publicity," in the Marquette Sports Law Journal, Fall 1999.

Erik K. Stapper (Chapter 14), of Stapper & Van Doren, has practiced tax law in New York City for more than 35 years, has successfully represented a number of artists before the IRS, and has formed and represented domestic and foreign tax-exempt organizations in the course of his estate planning practice. He has participated in art law panels of the International Academy of Estate and Trust Law in Paris (1997) and Sydney (1998), and on estate planning panels for that organization; the American Bar Association, for which he also has organized and chaired a program on international estate planning; and the Association of the Bar of the City of New York. He was a U.S. National Co-Reporter for the 1985 International Fiscal Association Congress in London on the topic of "International Double Taxation of Inheritances and Gifts." His publications include "Direct Investment in The Netherlands: The U.S. Perspective," 45 Bulletin Int'l Fiscal Documentation 41 (January 1991); "Valuation of Real Estate for Tax Purposes: A Personal and Practical Approach," 18 Tax Mgmt. Est., Gifts & Tr. J. 90 (May 13, 1993); and, as a contributor, *A Visual Artist's Guide to Estate Planning* (The Marie Walsh Sharpe Art Foundation).

Benjamin Straus (Chapters 4 and 9) is Vice-President and General Counsel of Javelin Technologies, Inc., the leading provider of electronic trading connectivity solutions. A graduate of Columbia College and New York University Law School, before joining Javelin Technologies, he helped found the Internet Practice Group at the entertainment law firm of Kay Collyer & Boose LLP, and began his legal career in the Intellectual Property Department at Paul, Hastings, Janofsky & Walker. He was also a founder of Peekaboo, Inc., a multimedia company that produced original music, theatre, and entertainment industry seminars that were broadcast on the Internet. He and a team of technologists produced a finalist entry for the New York Times's invitational competition to design a 2000-year time capsule. He is the author of "Where's the Next MTV®? Product Distribution Across Converging Media," in the NATAS Almanac for the 1999 Emmy® Awards, and is actively involved in leading multinational efforts to weave copyright protection into electronic commerce.

ACKNOWLEDGMENTS

There are more people to thank than I possibly can, so if I miss anyone, I apologize in advance. To begin with, I need to acknowledge the supreme efforts of Ira Hoch and Lauren Feeney, great researchers who helped out in more than one emergency. I would like to thank my employer, John Wiley & Sons, Inc., and particularly Marjorie Normand, Dick Rudick, and Danielle Jones for supporting this project in their own ways, and the team at Aspen Law and Business, especially Michelle Virzi, Maryann Young, Sue Gruesser, Matt Gallaway, Marc Gallant, and Rick Kravitz.

I also wish to thank those individuals and organizations that provided forms and/or critical advice, including Tim Burgard of John Wiley & Sons; Margaret Bodell; Robert Panzer of the Visual Artists and Galleries Association; Lee White Galvis, Esq., of Christie's; Susan Greenberg of St. Louis Volunteer Lawyers and Accountants for the Arts; Anna Kisluk of the Art Loss Register; Nancy Wolfe, Esq., attorney for the Picture Agency Council of America; Paul Basista of the Graphic Artist's Guild; Rachel Warren, Esq., of Davidoff and Malito; Sara Blotner, Esq., of Citicorp; Constance Lowenthal of the Art Recovery Fund of the World Jewish Congress; Sharon Flescher of the International Foundation for Art Research; Saskia Brown of the International Council of Museums; Robin Thornes of the Counsel for Protection from Art Theft; Joseph D. Ketner and John Rexine of the Rose Art Museum; Brandeis University; and Sotheby's, Inc.

I would be remiss not to recognize certain individuals and institutions responsible for creating an environment where art law can be studied and practiced, including Columbia Law School's Kernochan Center for Law, Media and the Arts, particularly Adria Kaplan and Professors John Kernochan and Jane Ginsberg; the Columbia-VLA Journal of Law and the Arts; and the Committee on Art Law of the Association of the Bar of the City of New York, in particular Herbert Hirsch and Barbara Hoffman, respectively the current and former chairpersons. It is also worth mentioning certain key works preceding this one: *Art Law*, by Ralph Lerner and Judith Bresler; *Art Law,* by Franklin Feldman, Stephen E. Weil and Susan Duke Biederman; *The Deskbook of Art Law*, by Leonard D. Duboff and Sally Holt Caplan; *Art Loans,* by Norman Palmer; and *Art, Law and Ethics,* by John Henry Merryman and Albert E. Elsen.

I also wish to thank my wife Cindy, and my sons Jordan and Caleb, who had to live with me through this project, and my friends and family, who cannot remember what I used to talk about. Lastly, I need to thank my diverse and multi-talented contributors, who are discussed individually in the introduction.

INTRODUCTION

At a recent due diligence conference sponsored by the International Foundation for Art Research, I was asked by the curator of a regional museum in rural New England why it seems that every lawyer now "specializes in art law." One answer is that many lawyers would tell a curator that they are "specialists" in order to try to obtain work, and "art law" sounds more interesting than "real estate closings." But I think there is also a real trend, arising from the fact that art is now actively transformative. We all know the story—artists seeking large spaces for low rents occupy an abandoned industrial downtown, followed by restaurants and dealers, maybe even a small museum. Next, expensive retail shops and businesses move in, rent goes up, and the artists move to the next abandoned area.[1] Art is also used for urban renewal in a less organic way as more city leaders, in their quest to draw people downtown, realize that it is easier to build an arts center or museum than to lure and pay for a professional sports team. With tens of thousands of people graduating from American universities each year with degrees in art history and fine arts who produce and consume art, the market for art lawyers can be understood.

At the same time, opportunities for lawyers have increased as a confluence of wealth, politics, and technology have recently conspired to change what were once simple rules of the art trade into complex, often incomprehensible transactions. Consider the examples of the following artists, *A* and *B*.

Artist *A*, as legend tells us, worked in the court of a great noble family (or in a lonely garret, if the legend is from the late nineteenth century). He (always *he* at the time, if we have a historical record) decided to create a painting, so he bought canvas, paint, and brushes (which he now owned), created a painting, and then sold or gave it to his patron.

Now consider artist *B*, who lives and works in the present, and wants to create a unique work of visual art in the most adaptable medium available today, the electronic. She goes to the local software store and buys some off-the-shelf software. She reviews, or more likely ignores, the densely worded shrink-wrap license, and by opening the package, agrees to the terms. She begins to build a Web site by herself (so as not to complicate the example unduly), downloads some plug-ins after agreeing to terms and conditions of use, clears rights in certain video and music clips, and sends the files to be hosted by an Internet Service Provider (one more agreement). She makes her work accessible via the Web after posting copyright notices for herself and the parties who granted permissions. She might also be required to include a notice for the owner of her authoring tools. Because she wants feedback from visitors to her site, she also posts a restrictive privacy policy designed to

[1] Roberta Brandes Gratz and Norman Mintz have labeled this process the "SoHo syndrome," and have chronicled it in their book Cities Back from the Edge: New Life for Downtown (Wiley 1998).

conform to recent European legislation. When she decides to sell the work, she must first acquire consent to assignment from all licensors whose work she incorporated, and then must negotiate the terms of the sale, including cost, hosting obligations of the purchaser, and the duties of the buyer and seller to update the work to conform to future technological shifts (an artwork prepared for a Commodore Vic 20 is not worth the cassette tape on which it is recorded). The purchaser, if he is savvy, will likely demand some form of moral rights waiver to protect himself from claims based on necessary modifications due to differing hosting environments.

New complications in art transactions are not limited to the rapidly changing world of the Internet. In the early 1800s, Thomas Bruce, Seventh Earl of Elgin, decided to purchase sculptures and inscriptions from the Parthenon in Athens. He completed some paperwork, paid some money, and shipped them to England. Today, if tourists visiting Canada want to purchase a $50 stone carving from a curio shop, they must first review the Canadian Cultural Property Export Control list, and then seek legal opinion as to the applicability of the Canadian/United States Bilateral Agreement on Archaeological and Ethnological Material in Canada, designed to protect against illicit trade in antiquities from certain aboriginal cultural groups native to Canada. There is a reasonable possibility that the carving will not be exportable.

Moreover, art disputes often result in odd rules. In what other field would a statute of limitation for the recovery of stolen property expire in three years for a thief, while extending indefinitely for a good faith innocent purchaser for value (see Chapter 5, "Stolen Art")?

Lawyers representing art clients must recognize that while on their face, transactions and litigations are concerned with money and ownership, behind these issues lie vanity, greed, desire, obsession, nationalism, fear, beauty, sexuality, and politics. Art's so-called uniqueness and its ability to confer status on its owner can elevate simple issues beyond any rational measure of their importance.

For example, on May 5, 2000, the Associate Press reported the following "breaking news": two small Picasso etchings valued at $12,000 each were stolen from a Boca Raton, Florida synagogue. The etchings, from 1933 and 1934, were each from editions of 250. Without minimizing the importance of the theft to the people involved, one might fairly ask why this deserves to be national news. If two computers, valued at $12,000 each and containing the sole copies of the synagogue's member/contributor list, had been stolen, the incident might have been reported in the local paper, but it would certainly not have been national news. What is the difference? The etchings were not "original" or "unique" in any real sense. It is also likely that they were insured, and that their theft will not affect the synagogue's ability to function. If the computers were stolen, on the other hand, critical records essential to day-to-day functioning would have been lost.

Another example of this tendency toward overemphasis is the extreme caution collectors and institutions now use in acquiring new works. This is a natural consequence of the excessive press coverage of cultural property lawsuits, spoliation, and art theft. While these are all major issues, when viewed in the context of any non-art-related for-profit business, the amount of money involved actually is trivial. The Seattle Art Museum, for instance, has been in the press lately in connection with ownership of a donated Matisse stolen from a Jewish owner's collection during World War II. The museum's permanent collection has over

23,000 pieces, yet the public has evidence of only one work being recently returned to a claimant. While growing public awareness of art theft in general and Holocaust-era spoliation in particular has placed an appropriate new focus on the review of provenance in art acquisitions, the downside is that an inappropriate chilling effect has settled on the market.

It is fair to ask how many quality works with provenance gaps or questionable export certificates need to be kept from the public because of the very occasional return of a Matisse or some Turkish coins. Indeed, if one in fifty works acquired by a museum by purchase or gift were eventually forfeited to a claimant, one could rationally think the museum was doing pretty well.

These days, a museum can lose works in two ways: a claim can be made against a work in its permanent collection, which, if publicized, will appear on the front page of the *New York Times* and lead to congressional hearings. On the other hand, a museum that feared this possibility could choose not to acquire a work with a provenance gap.[2] There is no adverse publicity in the second situation, but the museum's curators, scholars, members, and other constituents suffer the same loss. As attorneys we must be vigilant against encouraging theft and spoliation while recognizing the ultimate goals of our clients and the benefits of the art trade to the public.

Thus, the challenge for art lawyers today is to apply the cold rules of tax, customs, intellectual property and tort laws to cases that are often fraught with emotions more typically seen in family court. With this in mind, this book (1) explains art-related issues in more than 15 discrete legal areas, (2) notes cases where the conflict between common sense and difficult facts have produced odd results, and (3) suggests some practical solutions for lawyers, clients, and judges involved in art law cases.

The book's fifteen chapters are divided into three sections: "Artists and Rights," "The Business of Art," and "Death and Taxes." There is some overlap between the chapters, as the individual contributors and I have attempted to give the reader a thorough overview with minimal need for flipping back and forth.

Part One: Artists and Rights

When I was in law school, my professors were fond of stating that copyright was like virginity: Once it was lost, it could never be recovered. The duration of copyright was life plus 50 years, and formalities were eliminated only recently. Today, the United States applies the extended term of life plus 70 years that is prevalent throughout the industrialized nations (thereby ensuring that the great-grandchildren of famous artists will not be destitute) and the copyrights of certain foreign works that had lapsed into the public domain have been automatically resurrected. Perhaps even more surprising is that developments in the art world have led some artists and historians to turn against a scheme originally enacted for their benefit.[3] Chapter One, "Copyrights, Trademarks, and Moral

[2] I am not referring to works that are clearly stolen, or are being sold by the descendants of high-ranking SS officials, but rather of works the provenance of which was lost at a time when it was not considered "must-have" information.

[3] For example, a letter to the editor in the Monday May 22, 2000 New York Times by Eugene Dwyer, an art history professor at Kenyon College, echoes the complaints of many artists, namely that copyright stifles creativity by limiting access to works.

Rights," seeks to explain the bases of three related, and, in the context of art creation and protection, inseparable, fields. The authors, William Hart and Jenifer Paine, are both with the New York office of Proskauer Rose, LLP. Bill is one of those copyright lawyers who can site from memory the case and relevant chapters from *Nimmer* and *Goldstein* that are closest to any given fact pattern. Both Bill and Jennifer represent artists, entertainment industry personalities, and museums in matters of litigation, licensing, and other related matters.

Prior to the establishment of the Court of Appeals for the Federal Circuit in 1988, patents were the poor stepchildren of intellectual property. More often than not they were struck down by courts when they were asserted. At the time, design patents were the poor stepchildren of the poor stepchildren. Now that patents are issued and upheld for such unoriginal concepts as bargaining on the Internet, all forms of patents are being revisited as appropriate methods of protecting intellectual property. For many artists, "design work" for utilitarian objects is indistinguishable from "fine art." Museums now exhibit motorcycles and clothes, and on June 8, 2000, Christie's auctioned a life-sized clay model of the new Volkswagen Beetle along with Charles Rennie Mackintosh furniture. Accordingly, the second chapter, "Intellectual Property Protection for Useful Artices," covers the overlapping intellectual property schemes protecting artistic elements of utilitarian items, primarily under copyright and design patent laws. Peter Canelias, who wrote the chapter, is one of the few patent lawyers who also has an active arts practice, and his insights are certainly welcome in this arcane field.

When I originally commissioned Laura Stapleton and Matt McMurphy, entertainment and media specialists from the pan-Texas firm Jackson and Walker, to write the chapter entitled "The First Amendment and Related Issues," I told them that the focus would be on the evolving law of the limitations on free speech—specifically libel, obscenity, and publicity rights. I naïvely thought that, whereas the Supreme Court had already ruled that art is First Amendment speech and set clear rules for governmental funding and interference with art, such issues were of more academic than practical interest. But as long as art remains political, litigation will ensue, and the controversy in the fall of 1999 over the "Sensation" exhibit at the Brooklyn Museum demonstrates that, clear precedent notwithstanding, art and politics still have the power to create courtroom drama.

If the Internet makes everyone with a Web site into a publisher, then, at a minimum, every new publisher either becomes an artist or consumes art. When people think about the art market and the Internet, they usually think of all the new sites that sell art, as galleries, cooperatives or auctions. But those are a tiny part of art on the Internet. Each Web site is essentially an artwork. Most of these artworks include other artworks, such as photographs or animation clips, and are further connected to other artworks through the World Wide Web. Our relationships with these artworks are governed by a complex set of laws, expectations, and contracts. Chapter Four, "Introduction to New Media and Art," is the first of two new media chapters written by Benjamin Strouse, the vice president and general counsel of Javelin Technologies, Inc., and an early Internet entrepreneur and philosopher. In this chapter, he provides a clear explanation of the revolutionary and evolutionary legal aspects of applying digital technology to the creation and distribution of works of art.

Part Two: The Business of Art

Today, art theft, and particularly theft as related to World War II claims, is probably the most talked about topic in the "art world" (or, at least, it is the only topic currently giving the Internet a run for its money). It is curious that it took 50 years for museums and governments to address the issues of spoliation during World War II. One can debate endlessly about the cause of this seemingly newfound emphasis, although I attribute it to the convergence of three more or less contemporaneous incidents: first, the seizure by the New York City district attorney of two Egon Schiele works on loan from a museum in Austria on the basis of a nonexistent criminal investigation; second, the publication of Hector Feliciano's *The Lost Museum*, which added a human dimension to the literature on the topic;[4] and third, the recovery of works located or identified in that book. Jonathan Bloom, of Weil, Gotschal and Manges, has worked for such diverse clients as the American Association of Museum Directors and the American Association of Publishers. His chapter, "Stolen Art," discusses the conflicting rules, judicial missteps, and often confusing precedents in this field, and suggests some rules of practice to help both victims and purchasers in their efforts to protect their rights.

While Chapter 5 concerns thefts of known works from known victims, Chapter 6, "Cultural Property," addresses the international movement of fine arts and antiquities, particularly the regulations governing import, export, and nationalization of works upon creation, discovery, and export. Cultural property concerns the politicization of culture, nationalism, jingoism, and the notion that modern national boundaries should define ownership and regulate movement of great works of humanity. Rena Moulopoulos, the senior vice-president of compliance for Sotheby's, is a road warrior in the battle for a sane policy regarding art and antiquities. Her chapter provides practical lessons and a wealth of necessary information for those involved in the international trade.

The purchase and sale of artworks ultimately defines the art market. In the past, many transactions involved a transfer of funds in exchange for a work, with at most a bill of sale to set forth the terms. Today, a cautious buyer must be aware of issues relating to, *inter alia*, export, cultural patrimony, theft, moral rights, and authenticity. It is not unusual for a transaction to involve an American buyer and an Asian seller haggling over a work located in Switzerland, with four dealers or other middlemen each competing for their shares. Van Kirk Reeves of Porter and Reeves in Paris represents many renowned artists, and while his topic, "International Transactions in the Art Market," would require many volumes to be thoroughly covered, he has managed to draft a chapter highlighting all of the major issues that need to be addressed when a client is contemplating a purchase or sale.

An artist without a dealer is like an author without a publisher; she may be talented, creative, and energetic, but without the validation that comes with representation, she will not be perceived as "professional." Artworks, however, are not mere commodities. At their best, they are manifestations of an individual artist's self. However, to the dealer, even one who believes in his artists, artworks are chattel to be sold. As dealers and artists become stars, inevitably tensions arise, as can be seen in the lawsuits brought by Jenny Holzer

[4] *See also* Lynn Nicholas, The Rape of Europa (Vintage Books 1994).

against Barbara Gladstone and by the Mary Boone Gallery against David Salle, and the seemingly endless lawsuits against the Marlborough Gallery. Steven Johnson, of Paul, Hastings, Janofsky and Walker in New York, is an attorney for both artists and dealers, and his chapter, "Artist-Dealer Relations," recognizes that even when the goal is mutual, the interests often compete.

In Chapter 9, "E-Commerce," Ben Strouse, who introduced the varied concepts of "new media" in Chapter 4, provides guidance on how to transact business on the Internet, from negotiating agreements with developers and Internet Service Providers to clearing rights and managing sites. His discussion brings together the common legal concepts (such as contracting in the digital environment, rights and liabilities) necessary to run everything from a Net art site to an online gallery. Perhaps most important, he explains current new media practice and relevant issues of "netiquette."

Problems of authenticity and authentication are arguably the largest legal issue in art transactions. Many older works may have been copied innocently in workshops, forged, or "over-restored." Sellers often refuse to warrant authenticity, and even auction houses give limited guarantees. Still, authenticity matters. The proper attribution of a work can change its value from nothing to millions. Recently, an individual placed a work for sale on eBay that had a signature and style similar to that of artist Richard Diebenkorn. If the work is authentic, the alleged garage sale purchase may be worth millions. If not, it may be worth $10. But whether the painting is "real" or not, it is the same painting; the difference is expert opinion. However, finding an expert willing to testify to authenticity is becoming increasingly difficult in our litigious society. In Chapter 10, "Authentication and Appraisal of Artwork," Steven Mark Levy, a senior litigation partner in the Los Angeles office of Lewis, D'Amato, Brisbois and Bisgaard, analyzes the dramatic effect of the legal rules on both the market and art history research itself.

In the eighteenth century, auctions were something polite society tried to avoid. Auction houses were considered to be immoral, unethical places. Today, auctions have become a new national pastime. At this writing, there are currently over four million items for sale on eBay. Every e-commerce site now wants an auction. Venerable brick-and-mortar houses are joining with Internet companies to expand their reach: eBay and Butterfields; Sotheby's and Amazon.com; Skinner and Lycos. As auctions become more important, authenticity issues, duties to buyers and sellers, disclaimers, and other issues of liability become increasingly important. Chapter 11, "Auction Law," was written by Jonathan Olsoff, who litigated numerous seminal art cases before joining the legal department of Sotheby's and is uniquely qualified to explain both the regulations and business practices.

Like issues of theft, issues of restoration and conservation make news. Everyone has his own opinion as to whether works should be conserved, restored, or allowed to age. Certain academics would even give artworks standing to sue for improper restorations. Defamation suits in the United States and abroad result when famous works are altered from their late twentieth century appearance in an attempt to show the artists' original visions. Notwithstanding the numerous disputes, there is little case law, possibly because if a conservator is sued, any statements in court are protected from defamation claims by litigation privilege, and few professionals can withstand the fair or unfair damage to their reputation that would follow. Thus, most cases settle. In Chapter 12, "Conservation and

Restoration of Artwork," Steven Mark Levy explains the pertinent case law, professional standards, and certain legal controversies important to restoration professionals and their clients.

Part Three: Death and Taxes

The power to tax is the power to destroy, and artists who keep meticulous records of their sales and income from artworks can be notoriously lax when it comes to proper tax planning. Moreover, although there may be no answer to the metaphysical question "what is art?" the IRS is more than willing to define "artist," as well as "hobbyist," "dealer," "collector," and "investor," and apply its rules differently to each classification. Chapter 13, "Federal Income Tax Consequences of Creating, Owning, Selling and Donating Works of Art," was authored by Richard Halperin, counsel to the entertainment/media/arts/intellectual property firm Kay Collyer and Boose. In addition to being a seasoned tax lawyer, he is also an accomplished landscape photographer and instructor of photography at New York's International Center for Photography. His personal experience on all sides of the art world and commitment to art is evident.

Vita brevis, ars longa. Many view art as a way to earn immortality. For the collector, that might mean a name on a wing of the local art museum. For the artist, it could mean having a lasting influence on contemporary aesthetics—and a few works in the aforementioned wing. But for either one, an improper estate plan can end any chance at immortality. Chapter 14, "Trusts and Estates" is the one chapter relevant to every artist, dealer, collector, and lawyer. The controversies surrounding the estates of Andy Warhol, Mark Rothko, and Francis Bacon are just three well-publicized illustrations of the problems that arise in respect to estates and planning. Building upon his contributions to the book *A Visual Artist's Guide to Estate Planning* (produced in conjunction with the Marie Walsh Sharpe Art Foundation and the Judith Rothschild Foundation), Erik Stapper of New York's Stapper and Van Doren has prepared a chapter detailing the issues and explaining the proper considerations for a well-developed plan.

As artists become more savvy, many realize that the creation of entities such as S corporations, limited liability companies, and limited liability partnerships will provide them with benefits that lawyers routinely receive from such structures; for example, limited liability, employee benefits, and tax shelters. For creative artists, there are other advantages, including prevention of fragmentation of copyright ownership and beneficial treatment of gifts of minority interests. The final chapter of this book, Rich Halperin's "Structures for Holding and Transferring Copyrights," details the advantages and pitfalls of a number of structures that artists should consider.

New York, New York
September 2000

Roy S. Kaufman

ART LAW HANDBOOK

PART I

ARTISTS AND RIGHTS

CHAPTER 1

COPYRIGHTS, TRADEMARKS, AND MORAL RIGHTS

William M. Hart
Jenifer deWolf Paine

* Included on companion CD-Rom.

§ 1.01 INTRODUCTION

Intellectual property laws intended to protect works of authorship and artistic expression, such as copyright laws, trademark laws, and moral rights laws, would seem to have obvious applicability to protecting rights in works of art. However, these legal doctrines were developed in commercial and industrial settings and, as a result, are surprisingly inapt to the art world and its issues. On many occasions when intellectual property issues have been presented in the art world, the outcomes have often been anomalous and counterintuitive.

For example, while copyright is intended to protect the unauthorized taking of an author's expression,[1] there have been a number of cases involving sculpture where copyright has either been held inapplicable or forfeit because the author failed to comply with certain legalistic formalities.[2] Likewise, it was only in the last two decades that the U.S. Trademark Office recognized that an artist's signature can function as a trademark, even though the inscription of a creator on his or her work of art is historically one of the most obvious "trademarks," conveying as it does an identification of the source of the work,[3] which, historically, is the chief attribute of a trademark by any definition.

Finally, while there is much talk about so-called "moral rights" or *droit moral,* this doctrine has been virtually nonexistent in the United States, although its policy goals (of preventing mistaken attribution and/or unauthorized mutilation of artworks) have sometimes been vindicated through other, less obvious legal mechanisms.[4] Even now, there exists only limited recognition of moral rights in our national laws, and somewhat spotty treatment under state or local laws, which may themselves be deemed "preempted" by the very existence of a federal system that does not meaningfully recognize these rights. In short, the art world and the legal world operate in distinct spheres, even though some of the best recognized legal doctrines would seem to be rooted in the needs of artists to protect and control the multiplication and integrity of their works.

To appreciate the dichotomous world of intellectual property law and art, it is necessary to examine the most common intellectual property doctrines and look at how these legal principles in the areas of copyrights, trademarks, and moral rights have been applied, or misapplied, to works of art.

---

[1] "Expression" is discussed in § 1.02[B][3] *infra.*

[2] *See* discussion of Letter Edged in Black Press, Inc. v. Public Building Commission of Chicago, 320 F. Supp. 1303 (N.D. Ill. 1970), *infra* at § 1.02 [F][3][c].

[3] *See infra* discussion at § 1.03.

[4] *See infra* § 1.04 for a discussion of moral rights.

§ 1.02 COPYRIGHT

[A] Overview

Copyright is essentially a creature of statute. While there still persists in the public mind, if not in legal practice, notions of "common law" copyright, currently, all copyright law in the United States is provided for under one unified federal statute, 17 U.S.C. § 101 *et seq.*

Primarily two copyright statutes have relevance to copyright protection today in the United States: the 1909 Copyright Act and the 1976 Copyright Act, which largely replaced the 1909 Act, while carrying over some earlier formalities such as copyright notice and renewal, for previously published or registered works, as discussed below.

Under the 1909 Act, only published works enjoyed statutory copyright protection, with a few exceptions for unpublished works that could be registered and hence statutorily protected. Works that remained unpublished and/or unregistered enjoyed "common law" protection under state statute or general principles of unfair competition. Unlike federal statutory copyright, which only endures for a specified term,[5] common law protection lasted until the work was published. As explained in some of the cases discussed below, this dual system of statutory copyright (for published works) and common law protection (for unpublished works) converged at the point of "publication." Once a work was "published," it lost whatever common law protection it enjoyed. At the same time, if the work was published with a copyright notice (the copyright symbol, ©, accompanied by the date of publication and the name of the copyright owner), the work was *invested* with statutory copyright protection. The obvious stumbling block for many authors was an act of publication unaccompanied by the then requisite copyright notice. At that point, not only was common law protection lost, but so, too, was any possibility of securing statutory copyright. As could be expected, much litigation under the 1909 Act turned on whether an act of "publication" had occurred such that copyright notice was required (no notice was required on unpublished works). It did not help matters that the term "publication" was never defined in the statute itself, leaving it to the courts to develop myriad and sometimes conflicting definitions of a term of art that grew increasingly obscure despite its fundamental significance to statutory copyright protection.

When the copyright statute underwent a substantial overhaul (the so-called "1976 Act," which became effective on January 1, 1978), the significance of copyright notice was somewhat diminished, but not eliminated. Thus, omission of notice from a published work would not immediately put the work into the public domain, but eventually would if certain steps were not taken to "cure" that

[5] U.S. Const. art. I, § 8, cl. 8.

omission.[6] It was not until March 1, 1989, that U.S. copyright law finally came into conformity with the sort of "no formalities" approach that had been adopted by most other countries many years earlier. However, in eliminating the notice requirements, Congress only did so *prospectively* for works first published after March 1, 1989. Accordingly, for works published before that date, one still must look to the then applicable statute—in the case of works published before January 1, 1978, to the strict notice requirements of the 1909 Act, or if published after January 1, 1978, to the slightly more lenient provisions of the 1976 Act.

Thus there are three regimes of copyright that may be applicable, depending upon when a work was first published: the 1909 Act; the 1976 Act; or the so-called Berne amendments to the 1976 Act, which took effect on March 1, 1989. *When* a work was published will dictate which statutory regime applies and thus the degree to which an omission of notice, or other noncompliance with statutory formalities, might prove fatal. As explained below, merely displaying or exhibiting a work does not ordinarily constitute an act of "publication," although some courts seem to have concluded otherwise. Below, we will talk about the circumstances in which an absence of notice puts the copyright at risk.

One final "introductory" observation about our marvelously complex copyright system in the United States: when the 1976 Act came into effect, it purported to abolish all equivalent forms of common law protection in order to unify in a single federal statute all aspects of copyright. No longer was the published/unpublished distinction significant in determining whether statutory (as opposed to common law) protection was obtained. All works, published or unpublished, came under the aegis of the 1976 Act; this was true for earlier works which remained unpublished as well, thus subjecting them to the limited, rather than indefinite, term of protection afforded by statutory copyright.

[B] Copyrightability

The standards for copyrightability are fairly low, but that has still proven to be a barrier to protection for certain types of works. The 1909 Act provided for discrete categories of copyrightable matter such as books, newspapers, works of art, musical compositions, and motion pictures,[7] all stemming from the constitutional mandate that Congress enact laws to protect the "writings" of authors for limited times.[8] As the mode of artistic expression expanded to encompass motion pictures, computer programs and so forth, the copyright statute had to be augmented to cover additional classes of copyrightable works and, with limited exceptions,[9]

[6] 17 U.S.C. § 405 (before Berne Convention Implementation Act of 1988).

[7] 17 U.S.C. § 5 (repealed 1978).

[8] U.S. Const. art. I, § 1, cl. 8.

[9] 17 U.S.C. § 12 (repealed 1978).

the only works that qualified for statutory copyright protection under the 1909 Act were *published* works.

This "pigeonhole" approach in defining copyrightable subject matter changed with the advent of the 1976 Act, which defined copyrightable subject matter as that comprising "original works of authorship" "fixed in any tangible medium" or form.[10] Thus, a diorama of the Gettysburg battlefield molded out of cauliflower would be copyrightable, provided that it meets the basic requisites of originality and fixation described below.

[1] Fixation

The "fixation" requirement is derived from the Constitution, which gives Congress the authority to create copyright laws by authorizing Congress to secure for "authors" the rights to their "writings." The word "writings" has been liberally construed, and has come to mean any original work which is somehow "fixed" in a "tangible" form. Therefore, it applies to any original works of authorship that are written or drawn on paper, canvas, or any other material; anything that is sculpted out of tangible material; and any image on film, or any other tangible format. The 1976 Act allows for copyright to keep pace with emerging technologies by providing that copyright protection subsists "in original works of authorship fixed in any tangible medium of expression, now known or later developed, from which they can be perceived, reproduced, or otherwise communicated, either directly or with the aid of a machine or device."[11] The statute defines a work as "fixed" when it is embodied "in a tangible medium of expression . . . sufficiently permanent or stable to permit it to be perceived, reproduced or otherwise communicated for a period of more than transitory duration."[12]

Expressly *not* protected by the Copyright Act are *unfixed* works such as performances. Until such works are fixed, they are not subject to copyright protection. For example, a performance artist who simply delivers a performance onstage which consists of words and body language generally has no copyright protection in her performance. Often this is not the case, since speeches and the like are usually granted copyright protection because they are written down or recorded before being delivered. Similarly, choreography is subject to copyright protection because it is often "written" or notated in a special form called Labanotation or Kinetographic Laban (choreography can be fixed in other ways, though, for example, by being filmed, or written/recorded in narrated form).

If a performance artist has not written or otherwise reduced to a tangible form his performance before or during its performance, as in the case of an

---

[10] 17 U.S.C. § 102(a).

[11] *Id.*

[12] 17 U.S.C. § 101.

improvisation, there is no copyright protection available. If the performer has the performance filmed or taped, the fixation requirement will be met. However, if the performer does not arrange the recording but rather a member of the audience makes an unauthorized recording (a "bootleg"), then the fixation requirement has *not* been met, and the material will not be protected (note, however, that the making of "bootleg" or unauthorized recordings of certain performances is a criminal act under federal law).[13]

[2] Originality

Only "original" works of authorship are protected by copyright. This does not mean that the work must be the first of its kind. Unlike patent law, which requires that an invention be "new" in order to be patentable, there is no requirement under the Copyright Act that an author be the first to create a particular work. Theoretically, copyright law allows for two different authors to create identical works, provided that one author did not copy from the other. Early cases articulated originality as requiring no more than merely a prohibition against copying the works of another.[14] Each will own the copyright in her respective work, provided they each created their works independently of each other.

Later cases took a more stringent view of originality and excluded from protection that which is prosaic (at least insofar as it amounts to a standard device that all authors or artists must employ), while at the same time paying lip service to the notion that even the most common forms of artistic expression, however banal, deserve copyright protection. Although courts are admonished not to interject their subjective judgment in determining what is "original" in a copyright sense, there have been irreconcilable results that are hard to justify on any other grounds. Thus, copyright protection for a painstakingly exact miniature reproduction of a Rodin sculpture has been upheld,[15] while copyright in a plastic "Uncle Sam Bank" modeled on a cast-iron public-domain bank was denied due to lack of originality.[16] Similarly, one court held that inflatable three-dimensional costumes based on two-dimensional cartoon characters were not sufficiently original to be copyrightable as derivative works of the cartoon characters.[17] Yet in a different case, a different court concluded that animal costumes are simply "useful articles" and are not entitled to copyright protection at all.[18]

---

[13] 18 U.S.C.A. § 2319A.

[14] Alfred Bell & Co. v. Catalda Fine Arts Inc., 191 F.2d 99, 102-03 (2d Cir. 1951).

[15] Alva Studios, Inc. v. Winninger, 177 F. Supp. 265 (S.D.N.Y. 1959).

[16] L. Batlin & Son Inc. v. Snyder, 536 F.2d 486 (2d Cir.), *cert. denied*, 429 U.S. 857 (1976).

[17] Entertainment Research Group, Inc. v. Genesis Creative Group, Inc., 122 F.3d 1212 (9th Cir. 1997). *See also* Beaudin v. Ben & Jerry's Homemade, Inc., 95 F.3d 1 (2d Cir. 1996); Whimsicality, Inc. v. Battat, 27 F. Supp. 456 (S.D.N.Y. 1998).

[18] Wildlife Express Corp. v. Carol Wright Sales, Inc., 18 F.3d 502 (7th Cir. 1994). See Chapter 2 for a discussion of design protection for useful articles.

The standard for originality is completely separate from that of copyright infringement. In other words, a second creator may adapt or transform a previous artwork in a way that gives rise to a new and additional copyright interest in the new matter that was added. However, if that creator based his or her work upon the copyright matter of another, without permission from the author of the underlying matter, the second creator's efforts may infringe the rights in the underlying work even if the second creator could otherwise claim to have added "original" copyrightable work to the pre-existing material. The statute makes it clear in those instances that no new copyright can be claimed in such a derivative work to the extent that it infringes the copyright in the underlying matter.[19] In order for a work to be copyrightable (and copyrighted) under current U.S. law, it need not be registered (more about this subject below), nor comply with any other formalities; it is enough that it is "original" and "fixed" within the meaning of the statute as described above.

[3] Copyright Law Protects Expression, Not Ideas

Chief among copyright's limitations is that it protects only expression, not ideas. This distinction, however nebulous, existed in the case law[20] long before it was codified in the 1976 Act, which precludes copyright protection for any "idea, procedure, process, system, method of operation, concept, principle, or discovery."[21] Thus, the idea of a painting of a sunset over the Grand Canyon may not be protected by copyright, which thereby permits others to be "inspired by" such a work in the creation of their own work. At the same time, should someone copy too closely the particular shades, expressionistic lines of rock formations, reflections and overall perspective, they may well have crossed the line from the nonactionable copying of an idea into an invasive and actionable infringement of copyrighted expression.

Illustrative Example: Photography

Photography presents a particularly fertile area for testing the premises of originality and the so-called idea/expression dichotomy described immediately above. On the one hand, the act of making a photograph is almost purely mechanical; on the other, it also involves a series of aesthetic choices. Courts seem to recognize this in prohibiting others not just from straight duplication of photographs but also from creating imitative new photographs, that capture the style,

---

[19] 17 U.S.C. § 103.

[20] *See* Baker v. Selden, 101 U.S. 99 (1880).

[21] 17 U.S.C. § 102(b).

angle, lighting and other aesthetic choices made by the creator.[22] In one well-known case, *Rogers v. Koons*,[23] a sculptor was found liable for copyright infringement as a result of creating a sculpture entitled "String of Puppies" which recreated the plaintiff's photograph (consisting of a man and woman sitting next to each other, holding eight puppies lined up in a straight row). Koons's sculpture infringed the copyright because, in the photograph, he copied the photographer's "composition, poses, and expressions."[24] Koons's fair-use defense failed.[25]

By contrast, in a dispute over the famous photograph used on the cover of the book *Midnight in the Garden of Good and Evil*, a court held that a photograph of the "Bird Girl" statue in Savannah's Bonaventure Cemetery did not entitle the photographer to prevent Warner Brothers's recreation of that same subject in connection with a film based on the book. The court noted that "[p]laintiff may be correct in asserting that if it were not for his idea, the Bird Girl would not be associated with *Midnight in the Garden of Good and Evil*. Nevertheless, copyright law does not protect ideas."[26] In a similar vein, another court held that the literal photographic recreation of public domain artworks was undeserving of copyright protection since the photographer added nothing original in the process, but instead sought to capture exactly, without change or artistic coloration, the precise attributes of various underlying art works.[27] The court observed that "[t]here is little doubt that many photographs, probably the overwhelming majority, reflect at least the modest amount of originality required for copyright protection . . . [b]ut 'slavish copying,' although doubtless requiring technical skill and effort, does not qualify."[28] Central to the court's reasoning was the apparent use of the copyrights in the photographs as a means to extract a fee from others who wished to reproduce the public domain artworks depicted in those photographs, a practice sometimes endorsed by museums for works in their collections. In essence, the court did not permit the use of mechanical photographic depiction to invest copyright in the underlying art works which were otherwise free for anyone to copy.

[C] Ownership

Copyright ownership vests initially in the author (or authors) of a work.[29] However, this does not require "hands-on" work. As one court put it:

---

[22] Kisch v. Ammirati & Puris Inc., 657 F. Supp. 380 (S.D.N.Y. 1987).

[23] 960 F.2d 301 (2d Cir. 1992).

[24] *Id.* at 308.

[25] *See infra* § 1.02[H]. *See also* Woods v. Universal City Studios, Inc., 920 F. Supp. 62 (1996).

[26] Leigh v. Warner Bros., 10 F. Supp. 2d 1371, 1379 (S.D. Ga. 1998)

[27] Bridgeman Art Library, Ltd. v. Corel Corp., 36 F. Supp. 2d 191 (S.D.N.Y. 1999).

[28] *Id.* at 196.

[29] 17 U.S.C. § 201(a).

> A sculptor . . . might sit in a chair, never moving and never touching the materials, perhaps in part because he might be paralyzed or simply because the materials might be large and heavy. There are sculptors nowadays who work in huge materials, I-beams, storage tanks, things like that, that are welded together where the sculptor's contribution is rendered entirely by the giving of instructions to workmen to put a member in a certain position and bolt it to another member and so forth. I think it is clear without question that such participation is authorship . . . under the copyright law even if the author never places his hand on the material.[30]

Similarly, a writer might dictate his or her entire novel to a secretary—the writer would still be the author.[31] In one case, a court held that the person conceiving a compilation of material was entitled to authorship, rather than the amanuensis, or scribe, who merely implemented those instructions. This borders on affording authorship to the person conceiving of noncopyrightable ideas, a notion antithetical to copyright law.[32]

[1] Works For Hire

One of the most confounding areas of the copyright law is "work made for hire." Most people (we will include some lawyers here) believe that they have a pretty good commonsense understanding of the term. Thus, if a party has the idea for a particular work, commissions that work, pays for its production, and even provides the materials and facilities for its creation, one could assume that this party would also obtain the copyright as a work made for hire. That, however, is not the law. There are situations where an employer or commissioning party is deemed to be the author, but the circumstances in which this occurs are fairly well confined to traditional employment relationships or specific statutorily designated relationships involving particular kinds of works.

[a] Works For Hire Under the 1976 Act

Under the 1976 Act, there are only two ways a work can be considered a work for hire: either it is created by an employee "within the scope of his or her employment," or it is expressly agreed in a writing signed by both parties that the work is a work for hire *and* the work fits within one of nine categories listed in the statute: (1) a contribution to a collective work, (2) part of a motion picture or other audiovisual work, (3) a translation, (4) a supplementary work (a work designed to supplement a work by another author, such as a foreword, afterword,

---

[30] Fisher v. Klein, 16 U.S.P.Q.2d 1795, 1796 (S.D.N.Y. 1990).

[31] Andrien v. Southern Ocean County Chamber of Commerce, 927 F.2d 132 (3d Cir. 1991).

[32] 17 U.S.C. § 103. *Compare* Childress v. Taylor, 945 F.2d 500 (2d Cir. 1991).

illustrations, editorial notes, and others), (5) a compilation, (6) an instructional text, (7) a test, (8) answer material for a test, or (9) an atlas.[33]

Therefore, even if both parties agree in writing that a work is to be considered a work for hire, but it does not fall within one of the nine categories and the commissioned party is an independent contractor (rather than an employee creating the work within the scope of his or her employment), a work *cannot* be a work for hire. Conversely, if a work does not fall within one of the nine categories, but it is created by an employee within the scope of his or her employment, it *will* be a work for hire. As a result, much attention has been paid to what constitutes an employee, and when a work is created within the scope of employment.

Application: CCNV v. Reid

The Supreme Court resolved the issue of what constitutes an "employee" in the work-for-hire context in 1989 in a landmark decision called *Community for Creative Non-Violence v. Reid*[34] (*CCNV*).

The background of *CCNV* was as follows: CCNV commissioned Reid, a sculptor, to create a statue symbolizing the plight of the homeless. There was no written agreement between the parties respecting copyright ownership, and Reid did not sign an assignment or transfer of copyright to CCNV. After a life-sized model of the sculpture was completed, Reid refused to relinquish possession of the sculpture to CCNV, and CCNV sued, seeking return of the sculpture and a determination of copyright ownership.

Although CCNV was the motivating force behind the idea of the sculpture, provided the funds and personnel necessary to assist Reid in the completion of the sculpture, and contributed limited but arguably copyrightable elements to the completed work, the Court ultimately held that Reid, as the actual author of the sculpture, and not CCNV, was the copyright owner of the work.

The Court first noted that sculpture did not fit within any of the nine categories of "specially ordered or commissioned" works enumerated in the statute. Even if the parties had signed a written agreement purporting to make the sculpture a work for hire, it would not have met that qualification. Therefore, the determination depended on whether Reid was an "employee" within the meaning of the statute. The Court held that the word "employee" in the statute meant a conventional employee as defined by the law of agency, "Employee" status was to be determined by evaluating such factors as:

- the hiring party's right to control the manner and means by which the work is accomplished

---

[33] 17 U.S.C. § 101.

[34] 490 U.S. 730, 109 S. Ct. 2166 (1989).

- the skill required
- the source of the instrumentalities and tools
- the location of the work
- the duration of the relationship between the parties
- whether the hiring party has the right to assign additional projects to the hired party
- the extent of the hired party's discretion over when and how long to work
- the method of payment
- the hired party's role in hiring and paying assistants
- whether the work is part of the regular business of the hiring party
- whether the hiring party is in business
- the provision of employee benefits
- the tax treatment of the hired party

Because under this analysis Reid was not an "employee" of CCNV, his work did not fit within the work-for-hire provisions of the 1976 Act.

As a result of *CCNV* the rights in works created by persons other than salaried "employees" under the standard definition remain with the actual creator, not the commissioning party or putative "employer." This poses considerable difficulty in the fine arts, since the alternate "work made for hire" prong—the "specially owned or commissioned" works within the nine specified categories—does not directly cover works of art. Therefore, even if the parties agreed, in writing, that the work was to be "made for hire," the copyright would not pass to the commissioning party. The *only* way to convey the copyright in such instances is by a written assignment of the copyright.

Because works for hire are so narrowly confined, and because agreeing that a work is to be considered a work for hire does not make it so, it is wise to have "assignment" language in work-for-hire agreements. Therefore, if a work is determined not to be a work for hire, the hiring party will nonetheless own the copyright pursuant to the assignment. A suggested work-for-hire agreement with back-up assignment language is included here as Form 1-1.

Further, because the law of works for hire is different under the 1976 Act and the 1909 Act, it is very important to know when a work was created and/or published, in order to determine whether it is subject to the 1976 Act or the 1909 Act. The ownership results may differ significantly, depending upon which copyright statute governs.

[b] Work For Hire Under the 1909 Act

Under the 1909 Act, the work-for-hire doctrine was much less restrictive, and as a result it was much easier for a work created before January 1, 1978, to be considered a work for hire.

Independent contractors were often deemed "employees" for copyright purposes under the 1909 Act. Courts have held that where one party hires another to create a copyrightable work, under the 1909 Act there is a *presumption* that the employing party was the author of the work as a work for hire, absent an agreement to the contrary.[35] In the case of independent contractors, a work could be considered a work for hire if it was created at the hiring party's "instance and expense,"[36] which happens when the "motivating factor in producing the work [is] the employer who induced the creation."[37] The burden will be on the independent contractor to demonstrate by a preponderance of the evidence that there was an agreement to the contrary (either oral or written), and that the work was not intended to be a work for hire.[38] It has also been held (but not by all courts) that under the 1909 Act, "an essential element of the employer-employee relationship [is] the right of the employer 'to direct and supervise the manner in which the [creator] performs his work.' "[39]

Application: The Playboy/Nagel *Case*

A watershed case which construed the work-for-hire doctrine under both the 1909 Act and the 1976 Act involved the works of the artist Patrick Nagel, who created numerous drawings published in Playboy Magazine between 1974 and 1984.[40] The paintings produced before January 1, 1978 (the effective date of the 1976 Act) were governed by the 1909 Act, and the paintings produced after January 1, 1978 were governed by the 1976 Act.

As to the works governed by the 1909 Act, the court found that the "expense" factor was met simply by the fact that Playboy paid Nagel a fixed sum for each

---

[35] *See, e.g.,* Playboy Enters. v. Dumas, 53 F.3d 549, 533 (2d Cir. 1995); Forward v. Thorogood, 985 F.2d 604, 606 (1st Cir. 1993); Lin-Brook Builders Hardware v. Gertler, 352 F.2d 298, 300 (9th Cir. 1965).

[36] Brattleboro Publ'g Co. v. Winmill Pub. Corp., 369 F.2d 565, 567-68 (2d Cir. 1966).

[37] Picture Music Inc. v. Bourne, Inc., 457 F.2d 1213, 1216 (2d Cir.); *cert. denied*, 409 U.S. 997 (1972); Siegel v. National Periodical Publications, Inc., 508 F.2d 909, 914 (2d Cir. 1974).

[38] Real Estate Data, Inc. v. Sidwell Co., 809 F.2d 366, 371 (7th Cir. 1987); Yardley v. Houghton Mifflin Co., 108 F.2d 28, 31 (2d Cir. 1939), *cert. denied*, 309 U.S. 686 (1940).

[39] Picture Music, Inc. v. Bourne, 457 F.2d 1213, 1216 (2d Cir.), *cert. denied*, 409 U.S. 997 (1972) (quoting Donaldson Publ'g Co. v. Bregman, Vocco & Conn, Inc., 375 F.2d 639, 643 (2d Cir. 1967)).

[40] Playboy Enters., Inc. v. Dumas, 53 F.3d 549 (2d Cir. 1994), *cert. denied*, 116 S. Ct. 567 (1995).

of the works. The "instance" factor was satisfied by Playboy giving Nagel specific assignments and asking him to illustrate particular articles. The court also considered whether Playboy had the "right to control" Nagel's work, and concluded that it did because it controlled certain characteristics of the paintings by requesting that he illustrate certain articles and giving him specific instructions as to the content of the paintings.

Regarding the works created after January 1, 1978 and therefore subject to the 1976 Act, it was undisputed that Nagel was not an "employee" of Playboy under the standards articulated in *CCNV*, and therefore the works could only be works for hire if they fell within one of the nine categories set forth in the statute, and if there was a written agreement signed by both parties. The parties also agreed that Playboy Magazine is a "collective work," one of the nine categories, which left only the issue of the written agreement for determination.

The only written agreement between Nagel and Playboy was an endorsement legend on the checks Playboy wrote out to Nagel as payment for the drawings. It had previously been disputed by courts and commentators whether a writing had to be executed *before* the creation of the work in order to satisfy the work-for-hire doctrine. The *Playboy/Nagel* court held that the parties did have to agree that a work was to be considered a work for hire before creation of the work, but that the agreement did not have to be memorialized in writing at that time. Therefore, if the parties agreed orally that a work was to be a work for hire before creation, and confirmed that agreement in a written instrument after creation of the work, the writing requirement of the statute was satisfied.

The court held that check legends which stated that by endorsing the check, Nagel agreed that he was receiving "payment in full for services rendered on a work-made-for-hire basis" and confirmed ownership by Playboy "of all right, title, and interest . . . including all right of copyright" to the drawings, fulfilled the writing requirement of the work-for-hire doctrine. An even more recent case has held that the words "work made for hire" do not have to appear in the written agreement or confirmation of agreement in order to satisfy the statutory requirement that the parties embody their work-for-hire agreement in writing.[41]

[2] Joint Authorship and Its Ramifications

A "joint work" is defined in the 1976 Act as "a work prepared by two or more authors with the intention that their contributions be merged into inseparable or interdependent parts of a unitary whole."[42] The 1976 Act does not require a written agreement to establish the existence of a joint work. For that reason, courts

---

[41] Armento v. Laser Image Inc., 950 F. Supp. 719 (W.D.N.C. 1996), *aff'd*, 134 F.3d 362 (4th Cir. 1998).

[42] 17 U.S.C. § 101 (definition of "joint work").

faced with an unsuccessful work-for-hire argument[43] have been forced to consider the alternate possibility that a work involving two or more participants may be a "joint work."

To establish that the contributions of two or more authors constitutes a "joint work," it is essential that the contribution of each co-author itself be copyrightable. The contribution of uncopyrightable ideas, even if made by the party who first conceived the work and at whose instance the collaboration proceeds, is insufficient to qualify as a "contribution" giving rise to a joint interest in the copyright.[44]

It is also a prerequisite to finding a work to be a joint work that the parties *intend* the creation of a joint work. For this reason, a later dispute concerning the subjective intentions of the parties will likely destroy any possibility of joint authorship status.

A special case arises in connection with interviews. In the absence of an agreement, both the interviewer and the interviewee will own the copyright in their respective expressions.[45] This will usually not be affected by the fact that the interviewer tape-recorded the interview; while the existence of the tape (as with the writing down of the words) will satisfy the fixation requirement, it will not vest ownership of the interview in the interviewer.

Once it is determined that a work is a joint work, the following results:

1. each author acquires an undivided ownership interest in the entire work;
2. each author may license the *entire* work, at least on a nonexclusive basis, without the consent or approval of his or her co-author;
3. nevertheless, when licensing internationally, some countries may still require joinder of all co-authors; and
4. an action for infringement against a co-author (or its licensees) will not lie because an individual cannot infringe his own copyright;
5. the principal duty joint owners have to one another with respect to the joint work is to account for profits from its use;
6. no right of survivorship exists, absent an express agreement—joint authors are treated as tenants in common (which means that if one author dies, his or her interest does not pass to the remaining co-author(s), but rather, the deceased co-author's interest will pass to his or her heirs);
7. one co-author may assign his rights only to the extent of that co-author's interest in the joint work; his transferee becomes a co-tenant with the remaining (and nonassigning) joint author(s); and
8. all co-authors should be identified in the copyright notice.

---

[43] Including the Supreme Court in *CCNV*, discussed *supra* in § 1.02[C][1][a].

[44] *See, e.g.,* Childress v. Taylor, 945 F.2d 500 (2d Cir. 1991); S.O.S., Inc. v. Payday, Inc., 886 F.2d 1081 (9th Cir. 1989); M.G.B. Homes, Inc. v. Ameron Homes, Inc., 903 F.2d 1486 (11th Cir. 1990).

[45] Compendium of Copyright Office Practices II, 1984, § 317.

Note that one joint author cannot grant *exclusive* licenses without the other joint authors' approval. This can significantly devalue the licensing potential of works, as often the value of a license is its exclusivity. Because of the serious consequences of joint work status, and because one of the determinative tests for establishing joint authorship is the parties' intent, it is a good idea to have a written agreement between collaborating parties which establishes (or specifically denies) joint work status. In the absence of a written agreement, each co-author's share of the whole work is deemed to be equal irrespective of the relevant significance (or insignificance) of their respective contributions.[46]

[D] Transfers and Assignments of Copyright; Right of Physical Possession versus Copyright

Under the 1976 Act, a transfer of copyright ownership is only valid if in writing and signed by the owner of the rights conveyed.[47] This is a statutory requirement and cannot be overcome by any industry custom or course of dealing.[48] Within the copyright law any grant of rights that is *exclusive* in nature, however limited in medium, term, or territory, is considered a "transfer" or assignment of an ownership right to the extent of that grant.[49] Thus, the word "transfer" may refer to an assignment (generally understood to mean a transfer of all rights in the copyright) or exclusive license (which usually involves the transfer of something less than all of the rights). Whatever the characterization, all such transfers must be in writing, as discussed below. An intended transfer that does not satisfy this writing requirement may still constitute the grant of a nonexclusive license.

Nonexclusive licenses do *not* need to be in writing. It is not unusual for a court to rule that a party reasonably relying on an oral agreement (or an unenforceable assignment), industry custom, or course of dealing may have a nonexclusive license, especially when to rule otherwise would result in the reliance party receiving no value for that for which it bargained. Thus in *Effects Associates, Inc. v. Cohen,*[50] in which a film producer failed to obtain a transfer of rights in the film footage he commissioned from a special effects studio because he neglected to memorialize the transfer in writing, the court nonetheless found that the producer enjoyed a nonexclusive license to reproduce that footage in his film. The obvious downside of a nonexclusive license is plain: it does not prevent the grantor from

---

[46] *See, e.g.,* Papa's-June Music, Inc. v. McLean, 921 F. Supp. 1154 (S.D.N.Y. 1996).

[47] 17 U.S.C. § 204.

[48] *See* Effects Assocs., Inc. v. Cohen, 908 F.2d 555 (9th Cir. 1990), *cert. denied*, Danforth v. Cohen, 498 U.S. 1103 (1991).

[49] 17 U.S.C. § 201(d)(2).

[50] 908 F.2d 555 (9th Cir. 1990), *cert. denied*, Danforth v. Cohen, 498 U.S. 1103 (1991).

licensing others to exploit the same work in the same media in the same territory at the same time.

If a party expects to obtain exclusive rights in a work, it is thus crucial to enter into a written agreement. Two such instruments are included here as Forms 1-2 and 1-3. The transfer should plainly refer to copyright rights rather than rights in a particular named work, such as the title of a painting to avoid ambiguities over whether the transfer is merely of the physical object as opposed to the rights under copyright (see discussion below). More than once, litigation has ensued where no dispute should have been necessary, simply because a transfer was ambiguous in this regard.[51] Another trap may be sprung on the unwary if a copyright owner informally permits another party to make an adaptation of his or her work; the adaptor then becomes the owner of the copyright in the derivative work. The adaptor may thus be in a position to exploit the derivative work with impunity, despite the objections of the copyright holder of the underlying work. Rather than an informal permission, the copyright owner should grant the right in a written document that provides for an assignment of the derivative work back to the original copyright holder.

One common area of concern for visual artists is what rights they are transferring when they sell a work. Historically, transfer of physical possession of a work of art would often also transfer the copyright to that work. One such case arose in New York in 1942 and held that an artist who had sold a painting had relinquished the right to prevent duplication of the painting.[52] That case was overruled in New York by enactment of a state statute in 1966,[53] and the 1976 Act also specifically states that the right to the physical object is separate and distinct from the right to the copyright:

> Ownership of a copyright . . . is distinct from ownership of any material object in which the work is embodied. Transfer of ownership of any material object . . . does not of itself convey any rights in the copyrighted work embodied in the object; nor, in the absence of an agreement, does transfer of ownership of a copyright or of any exclusive rights under a copyright convey property rights in any material object.[54]

This is an important distinction, as often people believe that if they own a physical copy of a work of art, it is theirs to do with as they please. This is not so. If someone is shooting a film in your home, you do not have the right to

---

[51] *See, e.g.,* Friedman v. Stacey Data Processing Servs. Inc., 17 U.S.P.Q.2d 1858, Copyright L. Rep. (CCH) ¶¶ 26, 653 (N.D. Ill. 1990).

[52] Pushman v. New York Graphic Soc'y, Inc., 287 N.Y. 302, 39 N.E.2d 249 (N.Y. 1942).

[53] N.Y. Arts & Cult. Aff. L. § 14.03.

[54] 17 U.S.C. § 202.

allow the filmmaker to include works of art you "own"—this may constitute copyright infringement.[55]

What, then, does the purchaser of a work of art acquire along with the physical object? The purchaser acquires the right of physical possession of the material object, the right to publicly display that copy (to viewers in the place where the copy is located), and the right to further transfer the physical object without the copyright owner's permission.[56]

This becomes an issue for museums and galleries that wish to reproduce and in some way exploit a piece of artwork without having rights in the copyright. It may be one thing to have a photograph of a painting reproduced in a magazine or promotional materials of the museum to promote the presence of a particular artwork in a gallery (which *may* be permissible under the fair use doctrine[57]), but another thing to sell merchandise such as posters or postcards bearing the image of the piece (which is clearly *not* permissible without the copyright holder's permission).

[E] Licensing Copyright Rights

Because an exclusive license is actually considered a "transfer" of copyright (even if only for a limited time), any exclusive license must be in writing. As we have seen above in connection with work-for-hire scenarios gone wrong, nonexclusive licenses do not need to be in writing, and can be inferred from conduct.

However, even nonexclusive licenses ideally should be committed to writing. This avoids ambiguity as to the specific scope of the license. Because ambiguous licenses are breeding grounds for litigation, and also because most licensors (and, for that matter, licensees) do not want a court to interpret a license as being broader or narrower than intended, it is important both to commit licenses to writing and to be as specific as possible.

Unlike trademark licenses (to be discussed below in § 1.03[D]), copyright licenses have few formal requirements other than that exclusive licenses be in writing. However, the basic terms that are important to include in most copyright licenses are:

- the specific work being licensed (if possible, attach a copy, avoid confusion as to whether the license includes variations or later versions of the work
- the term or duration of the license

---

[55] *See, e.g.,* Ringgold v. Black Entertainment Television, Inc., 126 F.3d 70 (2d Cir. 1997).

[56] 17 U.S.C. § 109(a) and (c).

[57] *See infra* § 1.02[I].

- the specific rights granted (for example, is only the right of public performance granted, or is the right to copy or distribute granted as well? How about the right to edit the work or create derivative works?)

For samples of copyright licenses, see Forms 1-4 through 1-8.

Being as specific as possible in a grant of rights is crucial. In one dispute one of the authors was involved in, at issue were the rights to an old film adapted from a short story. The short story had been the basis for a famous musical play and later a movie version of the musical. The heirs of the story's author had, long after the musical and movie of the musical, granted a party rights to distribute the old film on a "quitclaim" basis—that is, refusing to represent that they had any rights to grant. Most of the parties to the dispute believed that this grant was indeed worthless, as the rights had been granted to the producers of the famous musical.

However, a close inspection of the license by which the author had granted rights to the producers of the musical revealed that very limited rights were granted—only the right to *create a derivative work* in the form of a dramatic-musical play *based on* the story. Then all rights in and to that musical work, in all media, were assigned to the producers. Thus, the rights to the original short story were retained, and nothing precluded the author (or, later, his heirs) from granting additional film adaptation rights based on the original story. This is just one illustrative example of how neatly copyright rights can be carved up, and how important those carve-ups can be.

[F] Formalities

There are now few, if any, formalities necessary to secure a copyright under current United States law. One need not register the copyright in the United States Copyright Office to claim a copyright; the copyright arises "automatically" and vests in the actual creator (unless work-for-hire considerations apply) upon fixation of an original work of authorship.

[1] Registration

Registration is obtained by submitting to the U.S. Copyright Office in Washington, D.C. an application for registration, the required fee, and deposit copies of the work to be registered.[58] Although registration is not necessary to acquire copyright rights, it is still required (except in the case of certain qualifying foreign authors) in order to bring suit for copyright infringement in the United States federal courts. The registration also affords certain presumptions of ownership

---

[58] *See* 37 C.F.C. § 201 *et seq.*; *see also* Appendices 1-A through 1-D.

and authorship, which ease the burden of establishing a claimant's rights in a work. Moreover, the right to certain extraordinary remedies (statutory damages and the right to reimbursement of attorney fees as the prevailing party in an infringement case) depends on having registered the work in the Copyright Office *before* the infringing acts at issue in a given dispute commence. Late registration of the work will enable the infringed party to commence suit and recover its proven, actual damages incurred before and after registration, but will not restore the right to any extraordinary remedies, such as statutory damages and the right to recover attorney fees, which are barred absolutely for the particular infringing activities at issue.[59]

There are also renewal registration requirements for works first published or registered before 1964. An important quirk of renewal law is that the rights to the renewal period vest in the parties designated by the copyright statute, which provides that the renewal passes to the author if the author is alive, and to the author's surviving spouse and children if the author is dead.[60] Thus, an assignment of both the first and renewal terms by the author will only be effective as to the renewal term if the author was alive when the renewal term vested; if the author died before the renewal term vested, his or her grant of the renewal term had no effect, as the right to the renewal term passed to the statutory heirs, and *not* to the author's estate.[61] The Copyright Act was amended in 1992 to effect an early vesting of the renewal right to reduce (but not eliminate) the risk resulting from a granting author not surviving into the 29th year of copyright.[62]

[2] Copyright Notice

Proper copyright notice consists of the copyright symbol, the date of first publication, and the name of the copyright holder. Notice is no longer mandatory for works first published after March 1, 1989 (the date when the United States acceded to and implemented the Berne Convention, the most significant international copyright treaty). However, the presence of a copyright notice on copies of a work precludes a defense of innocent infringement, which may affect the monetary relief awarded in an infringement case.[63]

For works first published *before* March 1, 1989, but *after* January 1, 1978, copyright notice was and remains effectively mandatory; its absence on published copies would not immediately invalidate the copyright, but would eventually do so—within, at most, five years of the date of publication of copies without notice—

---

[59] 17 U.S.C. § 412.

[60] 17 U.S.C. § 304(a).

[61] *Id.*

[62] *Id.*

[63] *See* 17 U.S.C. § § 402(d) and 405(b).

if certain affirmative steps were not taken by the copyright owner to "cure" the omission of notice on published copies.[64]

The 1909 Act imposed extremely harsh consequences on the omission of notice from published copies: in effect, the copyright was forfeited if copies (and in some cases, a single copy) of a work were published without a copyright notice. This law is still applicable to works first published before the January 1, 1978 effective date of the 1976 Act.

Practical Application of Notice Requirements

There are three different notice requirements which affect works first published at different times. For works first published before January 1, 1978, there is an absolute notice requirement, and failure to comply will result in forfeiture of the copyright. For works published between January 1, 1978 and March 1, 1989, there is a more lenient notice requirement, which permits a "cure" for omissions of notice within five years. For works first published after March 1, 1989, there is no notice requirement at all.

As applied to works of art, these requirements can play out in several ways. Because copyright notice was only ever required on *published copies* of a work, and the display of a work is not (at least under the 1976 Act) "publication," the omission of notice on a work of art displayed to the public should have no legal consequence. Under the 1909 Act, there were a few cases suggesting that public display was a publication,[65] and hence, if no copyright notice accompanied the displayed work, its copyright was vulnerable to divestiture. These cases are in the minority, but remain troublesome.

If copies of a work were publicly distributed (through such media as catalogues, posters, postcards, or newspaper photographs) those very likely would be "published" copies for which notice would have been required under either the 1909 Act or the 1976 Act (before accession to the Berne Amendment). The publication of such copies could have rendered the copyright in the work invalid immediately (under the 1909 Act) or eventually (under the 1976 Act). Such "divestive publication" is of particular importance when copies of the work in issue were first distributed without proper notice before March 1, 1989. Note that there have been some mitigating doctrines developed by the courts (for example, the copyright in a three-dimensional work, such as a sculpture, might not be

---

[64] 17 U.S.C. § 405(a).

[65] Pierce & Bushnel Mfg. Co. v. Werckmeister, 72 F. 54 (1st Cir. 1896); William A. Meier Glass Co. v. Anchor Hocking Glass Corp., 95 F. Supp. 264 (W.D. Pa. 1951); Morton v. Raphael, 334 Ill. App. 399, 79 N.E.2d 522 (1948); Scherr v. Universal Match Corp., 297 F. Supp. 107 (S.D.N.Y. 1967), *aff'd on other grounds*, 417 F.2d (2d Cir. 1969), *cert. denied*, 397 U.S. 936 (1970).

rendered invalid by the publication without notice of photographs of it in two-dimensional form).[66]

[3] Publication

[a] Generally

In light of the various requirements for copyright notice discussed above, all of which have traditionally depended upon an act of "publication" to trigger the need for notice, a definition of "publication" would be helpful. Unfortunately, the 1909 Act provided no such definition. Instead, courts were left to create their own definitions, which varied widely. As a result, a distribution of copies in one case might not be deemed an act of "publication" (requiring the presence of notice), whereas another court, on similar facts, could find "publication" and quite possibly a forfeiture of the copyright if the notice had been omitted.

To rectify this, the 1976 Act embodies a single statutory definition of "publication":

> "Publication" is the distribution of copies or phonorecords of a work to the public by rental, lease, or lending. The offering to distribute copies or phonorecords to a group of persons for purposes of further distribution, public performance, or public display, constitutes publication. A public performance or display of a work does not itself constitute publication.[67]

This definition is itself shaded by varied court interpretations, and, like prior law, is highly dependent upon the facts of the nature and scope of the dissemination of copies at issue. Technically, this definition is only applicable to events of alleged publication occurring *after* the January 1, 1978 effective date of the current Copyright Act; for events of publication that possibly occurred before that date, 1909 Act case law must be consulted.

[b] Publication Under the 1909 Act

Under the 1909 Act, there were two kinds of "publication"—"investive" publication and "divestive" publication. This is because before the 1976 Act, there were two systems of copyright protection—"common law" copyright protection and statutory protection. The 1909 Act, which provided statutory protection, generally only protected published works. Unpublished works were usually protected by common law copyright under state law (common law copyright had no finite duration; it could protect the work forever, as long as it remained unpub-

---

[66] *See* Academy of Motion Pictures Arts & Sciences v. Creative House Promotions, 944 F.2d 1446 (9th Cir. 1991).

[67] 17 U.S.C. § 101 (definition of "publication").

lished). Once copies of the work were published, the work lost common law protection. It also gained statutory protection under the 1909 Act upon publication with proper copyright notice. If, however, the work was published without notice (or with a defective notice), it not only lost common law protection on publication, but through failure to comply with statutory notice requirements, failed to gain statutory protection as well. As a result, the work went into the "public domain"; it lost all copyright protection, whether statutory or common law.

Hence the two different types of "publication" under the 1909 Act were conceived—"investive" publication, which was publication with proper notice which invested the work with statutory copyright protection, and "divestive" publication, without notice, which resulted in forfeiture of the copyright. The difference between these two types of publication is not merely the presence or absence of notice. Due to the harsh consequences of publication without notice, judges quickly developed the rule that it took a far greater "act" of publication to *divest* a work of copyright protection than it took to *invest* a work with copyright protection.[68] Additionally, only publication by the copyright holder or the copyright holder's authorized agent or licensee can qualify as a divestive publication. For example, if a painter created a work which was then featured in an advertisement and published, without notice, in a magazine during the reign of the 1909 Act, it would constitute a divestive publication *only* if the artist or copyright holder had authorized the use of the painting in the advertisement. If, however, such permission was contingent upon the use of proper copyright notice, then a publication without notice would be treated as a noncomplying use, hence a use without authorization of the copyright holder, and therefore not divestive.[69]

Also because of the harsh consequences of divestive publication, courts developed the doctrine of "limited publication" versus "general publication." Only a general publication, without notice, could divest a work of copyright protection. An early formulation of this concept defined a "limited" publication (which did not destroy copyright protection, even if made without notice) as a publication by which the copyright holder restricts the work's "use or enjoyment" to "definitely selected individuals" or a "limited, ascertained class."[70] By contrast, "general" publication occurs "when a work is made available to members of the public at large without regard to who they are or what they propose to do with it."[71]

---

[68] *See, e.g.,* Roy Export Co. v. Columbia Broad. Sys., 672 F.2d 1095, 1102 (2d Cir.), *cert. denied*, 459 U.S. 826 (1982).

[69] *See, e.g.,* National Comics Publications, Inc. v. Fawcett Publications, Inc., 191 F.2d 594 (2d Cir. 1951), *supplemented by* 198 F.2d 927 (2d Cir. 1952).

[70] Werckmeister v. American Lithographic Co., 134 F. 321, 326, 328 (2d Cir. 1904), *aff'd*, 207 U.S. 284 (1907).

[71] Burke v. N.B.C., 598 F.2d 688, 691 (1st Cir. 1979).

[c] *Practical Application of the 1909 Act*

The 1909 Act is still important today. It is applicable to all works published up through December 31, 1977, and thus applies to many works still in popular currency. Therefore it is important to understand how the notice and publication requirements apply.

One 1970 case from the Northern District of Illinois invalidated the copyright in a work by Picasso. In *Letter Edged In Black Press, Inc. v. Public Building Commission of Chicago*,[72] Picasso had donated a sculpture to the Art Institute of Chicago. A display of the sculpture without notice where the public was allowed to take pictures was held to have invalidated the copyright. The court rejected the copyright holder's limited publication argument. Although the Art Institute merely displayed the statue, it nonetheless allowed copies to be made by allowing the public, including the press, to photograph the statue and reproduce those photographs in newspapers. Hence, there was no restriction on who could "make copies" of the work, and no restriction on what could be done with those copies.

Thus, the notice requirement is not confined to the original work itself, but also applies to copies of the work reproduced in other media. In *Schatt v. Curtis Management Group, Inc.*,[73] a photographer who had taken numerous photographs of James Dean was found to have lost his copyright protection in the photographs by distributing them (without copyright notice) to fans of James Dean who visited the photographer's studio after Dean's death. The photographer argued that his distribution of the photographs was merely a limited publication, as only about 35 to 50 people came to his studio, and he sold photographs only to individuals who passed his subjective "test of cordiality." The court was unconvinced, and found that he did not meet the test for limited publication.

[G] Duration

Copyright protection, by constitutional mandate, can only last for a "limited" period of time. Exactly what that time period is has changed over the years. Thus, while the current law is simple to apply to works created today, duration under former law (which is far more complex) must also be understood, because it affects many works which are still in the marketplace.

Works created today are subject to the 1976 Act, as amended. Works that were first registered for copyright or published before January 1, 1978 are subject to the 1909 Act.

---

[72] 320 F. Supp. 1303 (N.D. Ill. 1970).

[73] 764 F. Supp. 902 (S.D.N.Y. 1991).

[1] Duration Under the Current Act (The 1976 Act)

The 1976 Act generally applies to works created on or after January 1, 1978. These works are protected for a term of the life of the author plus 70 years.[74] For joint works (works created by more than one author), the term is the life of the last surviving author plus 70 years.[75]

With respect to works for hire, anonymous works, and pseudonymous works, the duration of copyright is 95 years from the year of first publication, or 120 years from creation, whichever is shorter.[76]

[2] Duration Under the 1909 Act

The general term of protection under the 1909 Act was an initial term of 28 years, and then a renewal term (provided a renewal registration was timely obtained) of an additional 28 years, for a total of 56 years. However, the 1976 Act changed the term of protection for many works that were subject to the 1909 Act, so the duration of copyright for works subject to the 1909 Act depends on when the work was first published or registered.

[a] Works Created But Not Published or Registered Before January 1, 1978

Works created, but not published or registered, before January 1, 1978 are subject to the same "life plus 70" scheme as for 1976 Act works. However, there is a caveat: in no event will protection for a work which falls into this category expire before December 31, 2002; or if it is published before December 31, 2002, it will not expire before December 31, 2047.[77]

[b] Works Created Before January 1, 1978, and Either Published or Registered Before January 1, 1978

[i] Works in their first term of protection on January 1, 1978. Works that were in their *first* term (meaning the *initial* 28-year term provided for under the 1909 Act) on January 1, 1978, are entitled to an initial term of 28 years from either the date the work was first published or on the date of registration, if registered as an unpublished work.[78] After the expiration of the initial 28-year

---

[74] 17 U.S.C. § 302(a). Until recently, the term was life of the author plus 50 years. The Sonny Bono Copyright Term Extension Act, which went into effect on October 27, 1998, extended the term by an additional 20 years.

[75] 17 U.S.C. § 302(b).

[76] 17 U.S.C. § 302(c).

[77] 17 U.S.C. § 303.

[78] 17 U.S.C. § 304(a)(1)(A).

term, these works can be renewed for a renewal term of 67 years, for a total of 95 years.[79] In general, the 1909 Act required the copyright holder to apply to the U.S. Copyright Office for a renewal copyright in order to be entitled to the renewal term.

Copyrights secured (either by date of first publication or by date of registration, if registered as an unpublished work) between January 1, 1964, and December 31, 1977, are automatically entitled to the renewal term, without any formal renewal being secured by the holder (works secured after December 31, 1977, are subject to the 1976 Act and are therefore subject to the life-plus-70 term with no renewal). Therefore, after 1992 (28 years after 1964), it was no longer necessary to obtain formal renewal registrations of copyright in order to be entitled to the renewal period.[80]

[ii] Works in their renewal term on October 27, 1998. Works that were in their renewal term on October 27, 1998, are protected for a total of 95 years from the time the copyright was first secured.[81]

Additionally, by a series of interim laws, any work as to which the 28-year *renewal* term was set to expire under the 1909 Act anytime between September 19, 1962, and December 31, 1976, was granted an extension of such renewal term until December 31, 1976, and was (as of January 1, 1978) entitled to a 75-year term of protection. Works in this category that were still subsisting as of October 27, 1998, are now entitled to the 95-year term of protection.[82]

If a work's renewal term expired before September 19, 1962, the work has entered the public domain and is not entitled to any extension of the renewal term. Fifty-six years remains the total duration for works whose 56th year expired before September 19, 1962 (works created before 1906).

[3] Foreign Works

United States law does not specify different copyright terms for domestic and foreign works. Thus, the terms set forth above apply to *all* works, as far as exploitation in the United States is concerned. However, in some circumstances, copyright for works that might otherwise be in the public domain due to failure to comply with a formality (such as proper copyright notice or a failure to renew) *may* be restored if at least one author of the work was a national or domiciliary of a country that is a member of the Berne Convention or of the World Trade

[79] 17 U.S.C. § 304(a)(2)(A).

[80] 17 U.S.C. § 304(a) (as amended by the Copyright Renewal Act of 1992).

[81] 17 U.S.C. § 304(b).

[82] *See* Sonny Bono Copyright Term Extension Act of 1998, Pub. L. No. 105-298, 112 Stat. 2827 (codified as amended in scattered sections of 17 U.S.C.).

Organization.[83] Restoration for qualified works occurred automatically on January 1, 1996, but there are significant benefits to filing a Notice of Intent to Enforce Restored Copyright with the Copyright Office. The proper format for this notice appears below, as Form 1-9.

[4] Determining the Copyright Status of a Particular Work

Obviously, calculating the duration of copyright for any work requires some understanding of when the copyright was originally secured and, at least for works published or registered before 1964, whether renewal formalities were satisfied. Also, a copyright that may otherwise still be valid in that the term of protection has not expired may nonetheless have lost copyright protection due to failure to comply with copyright notice requirements. Typically, determining whether a particular copyright is valid requires a fair amount of fact research and, in some cases (such as in validating publications without notices), the facts may be difficult to ascertain.

Copyright registration in the United States is permissive, not mandatory. However, in order to enforce a copyright in U.S. courts, the work must ordinarily be registered. Also, because registration confers certain extraordinary remedies, most copyright-driven industries (typically music, motion picture and software) routinely secure registration to preserve those remedies. As a result, many works are registered, and therefore checking the records of the U.S. Copyright Office is a good place to start when trying to determine the status of a particular work.

It is important to remember that when the copyright in a given work expires or otherwise falls into the public domain, derivative works that were made from that work may still be protected. Therefore, it is important to make sure that even if a work has fallen into the public domain in the United States, it does not have later editions or arrangements which may still be protected.

[H] Infringement

[1] Generally

A copyright owner has exclusive rights "to do and to authorize" the following:

1. reproduce copies;
2. prepare derivative works;
3. distribute copies;

[83] 17 U.S.C. § 104(a).

4. perform the work; and
5. display the work.[84]

Anyone who violates any of these rights is an infringer. It is not a requirement that a defendant profit from his or her infringement in order to be liable for civil copyright infringement. Additionally, "innocence" is no defense. If a defendant copies from a third party without knowledge that the third party was infringing, the defendant is still liable for infringement.[85] However, a very limited exception exists for innocent infringement in reliance on an erroneous copyright notice. If a copyright notice identifies the wrong party as the copyright holder, and an infringer obtains a license from the party named in the notice, the infringer has a complete defense to a claim of copyright infringement by the true owner.[86]

Each of the above rights listed under § 106 of the Copyright Act can be infringed independently. For example, in *Agee v. Paramount Communications, Inc.*,[87] the Second Circuit held that a copyright owner's exclusive right to reproduce a copyrighted sound recording could be infringed by synchronizing the recording with a television program, without distribution and sale of copies of the infringing work. Thus, if an artist's painting were hanging in a gallery *without* the artist's permission (and assuming that the display was not authorized by the owner of the painting), it would be an infringement of the artist's right of public display (however, once the artist sells the physical painting, the limited right of display *only* is transferred to the purchaser). If someone were to come in and photograph the painting, that would be an infringement of the artist's right to reproduce copies. If someone were to then make duplicates of that photograph, that would be another violation of the artist's right to reproduce copies. And if someone were to then pass out those duplicates as flyers, or sell them to stores, it would be a violation of the author's right of distribution. If these acts were each performed by different people, the artist would have claims of copyright infringement against each of them.

In order to make out a prima facie case for copyright infringement, a plaintiff must establish two elements: ownership of a valid copyright, and copying by the defendant of constituent elements of the work that are original.[88] Because direct evidence of copying is often unavailable— rarely is there testimony from someone who stood over the defendant's shoulder and watched him copy the plaintiff's work—copying can be established by showing access and substantial similarity.[89]

---

[84] 17 U.S.C. § 106.

[85] *See* Lipton v. Nature Co., 71 F.3d 464, 471 (2d Cir. 1995).

[86] 17 U.S.C. § 406(a).

[87] 59 F.3d 317 (2d Cir. 1995).

[88] Feist Publications Inc. v. Rural Tel. Serv. Co., 499 U.S. 340, 361, 111 S. Ct. 1282, 1296, 113 L. Ed. 2d 358 (1991).

[89] Sid & Marty Krofft Television Prods., Inc. v. McDonald's Corp., 562 F.2d 1157 (9th Cir. 1977).

Access can be shown through circumstantial evidence, such as widespread dissemination. In one famous case against George Harrison over his song "My Sweet Lord,"[90] it was found that Harrison had copied the plaintiff's song "He's So Fine." Because the song "He's So Fine" had been number one in the United States on the Billboard Charts for five weeks, and was a top hit in England for seven weeks, access was inferred. The court found that Harrison "subconsciously" knew that the particular arrangement of notes he used in "My Sweet Lord" would work, because it had worked before in "He's So Fine."

In determining substantial similarity, traditionally the standard has been whether the "ordinary person" could detect without suggestion by others that the work was copied from another.[91] Increasingly, however, in cases involving more technical works such as computer programs or music, experts in the applicable field will be called on to testify as to substantial similarity.[92]

[2] Derivative Liability and New Technologies

As computers have become more and more a part of daily life, new infringement issues have arisen, and copyright law has been interpreted to respond accordingly. Courts have confirmed that certain computer uses constitute "copying," "distributing," or "public displays," and thus constitute copyright infringements. At the same time courts have recognized that the unique format of computers requires that certain activities be allowed without risking liability for infringement.

For example, interim copying (copying at an intermediate stage of a work's development) has traditionally been regarded as infringement even when the "final" product bears no trace of copied material.[93] However, in recent years, as courts have faced this concept in the context of computer programs, they have granted limited authority to make interim copies to the extent necessary to extract ideas, which are unprotectable matter, from another's work. For example, in *Sega Enterprises Ltd. v. Accolade, Inc.,*[94] the Ninth Circuit held that interim copying of software code can be a permissible fair use where such copying is the only access to those elements of a program that are unprotected. In that case, Accolade, a competitor of Sega's, created computer game cartridges that could run on Sega's machines. In order to make their cartridges compatible with Sega's machines,

---

[90] Bright Tunes Music Corp. v. Harrisongs Music, Ltd., 420 F. Supp. 177 (S.D.N.Y. 1976), *aff'd*, 722 F.2d 988 (2d Cir. 1983).

[91] Harold Lloyd Corp. v. Witwer, 65 F.2d 1, 18 (9th Cir. 1933).

[92] Plains Cotton Coop. Assoc. v. Goodpasture Computer Serv., Inc., 807 F.2d 1256, 1259 (5th Cir. 1987), *reh'g denied*, 813 F.2d 407 (5th Cir. 1987) (en banc), *cert. denied*, 484 U.S. 821 (1987); Gates Rubber Co. v. Bando Chem. Indus., Ltd., 9 F.3d 823, 835 (10th Cir. 1993); Q-Co Indus., Inc. v. Hoffman, 625 F. Supp. 608, 610, 613 (S.D.N.Y. 1985).

[93] Walt Disney Prods. v. Filmation Assocs., 628 F. Supp. 871 (C.D. Cal. 1986).

[94] 977 F.2d 1510 (9th Cir. 1992).

Accolade needed to disassemble Sega's code, which it did by printing out a copy of the code so that it could be read and understood by humans in order to analyze its contents. Although the ultimate Accolade product did not contain any of Sega's code, Sega contended that the interim step of printing out the code was an infringement. The Ninth Circuit disagreed, and held that the copying was a fair use.[95] However, it limited its holding to those situations where the functional attributes of a program are not readily discernible to the human eye.

Other computer-related uses of works have been found to constitute infringements. In *MAI Systems Corp. v. Peak Computer, Inc.*,[96] the Ninth Circuit held that the loading of software into a computer's random access memory (RAM) creates a "copy" for infringement purposes. The court rejected the defendant's argument that loading software does not constitute a copy because the so-called "copy" created in RAM is not "fixed" and disappears when the computer is turned off. Instead, the court, citing to 17 U.S.C. § 101, held that because the copy created in RAM can be "perceived, reproduced, or otherwise communicated," it qualifies as a copy under the Copyright Act. Following this reasoning, the District Court for the Northern District of Illinois in *Marobie-FL, Inc. v. National Assoc. of Fire Equipment Distributors*[97] found that a "copy" was created when defendants transmitted a copy of computer "clip art" in electronic form through its RAM and over the Internet to various users. The dispositive factor was the fact that the "copy" could be "perceived," albeit not with the naked eye, but with the aid of an Internet user's computer. The court rejected the defendant's argument that a "copy" was not created because the information does not remain in the RAM of defendants' computer, but rather is immediately transmitted over the Internet. According to the court, "[t]he fact that a copy is transmitted after it is created, or even as it is created, does not change the fact that once an Internet user receives a copy, it is capable of being perceived and thus "fixed."[98] The installation of software onto a computer as well as loading the software into RAM when the computer is "booted up," has also been held to be a "copy"[99] for infringement purposes.

The computer age has not only brought about new ways of infringing copyrights, but consequentially has created a new batch of infringers. Because the Internet is home to many small-time rogues and copyright anarchists who have a tendency to be either hard to track down, cash-poor, or both, plaintiffs have had to look for more established defendants with deeper pockets and easier methods of halting the infringing activity. As a result, many bulletin board operators

[95] *See infra* discussion of the fair use defense in § 1.02[H].

[96] 991 F.2d 511 (9th Cir. 1993), *cert. dismissed*, 510 U.S. 1033 (1994).

[97] 983 F. Supp. 1167 (N.D. Ill. 1997).

[98] *Id.* at 1178.

[99] Stenograph LLC v. Bossard Assoc., 114 F.3d 96 (D.C. Cir. 1998).

and service providers have found themselves on the wrong side of copyright infringement lawsuits.

Although the courts have begun to address electronic copying in the context of computer programs, there is as of yet little direct guidance on the potential liability of an artist who digitizes and manipulates copyrighted images as an interim step toward creating a new and substantially different artistic work. Technically, such interim copying still constitutes infringement even if the end product is dissimilar to the underlying copied matter.

Principles of Vicarious and Contributory Liability

Potential liability for any act of copyright infringement is not only to the direct actor, but also others who abet, facilitate or profit from infringement.

For example, In *Fonovisa, Inc. v. Cherry Auction, Inc.*,[100] the operator of a flea market or "swap meet" was held liable for the infringing acts of independent vendors because the operator had the ability to control access of customers to the swap meet area, received "direct" financial benefit from infringing sales (by way of rental fees from the defendant vendor, admission fees to the market, and "incidental" financial benefits such as parking fees, food sales, and so forth), and had been put on notice by the copyright owners that such infringing activities were occurring. Thus, a gallery owner may be liable for infringements committed by an artist whose work is being displayed.

These principles have, in recent years, been extended to Web site operators and others involved in Internet-related activities.[101] Recent amendments to the Copyright Act have codified vicarious and contributory liability principles insofar as Internet activities are concerned by making it clear that one who merely provides Internet access and has no control over content is ordinarily not liable unless it fails to take certain mitigating steps in response to a specific written notice calling the infringing activities to the access provider's attention, and follows certain statutory formalities.[102]

[I] Fair Use

There are numerous different kinds of defenses to infringement actions, but the majority of them break down into the following categories:

---

[100] 76 F.3d 259 (9th Cir. 1996).

[101] Marobie-FL, Inc. v. National Ass'n of Fire Equip. Distribs. & Northwest Nexus, Inc., 983 F. Supp. 1167 (N.D. Ill. 1997); Religious Tech. Ctr. v. Netcom On-Line Communications Servs., Inc., 907 F. Supp. 1361 (N.D. Cal. 1995).

[102] Digital Millennium Copyright Act of 1998, Pub. L. No. 105-304, 112 Stat. 2860 (Oct. 28, 1998).

1. access and copying are denied (often these are the "idea theft" cases brought by novelists or struggling screenwriters as a result of a film they claim infringes on their work);
2. access (and sometimes copying) is admitted, but it is claimed that either the plaintiff's work is unprotectable, or only unprotectable components were copied; and
3. access and copying are admitted, copyrightability is admitted, but the defendant claims its use is nonetheless not an infringement or is an excusable one.

Most often the third type of case involves a claim of "fair use." Fair use was not addressed in the 1909 Act itself, but is a doctrine developed by case law.[103] If applicable, it will excuse an unauthorized copy of a protected work that would otherwise constitute an infringement. The doctrine is now codified in § 107 of the 1976 Act. The defense applies to uses for purposes of criticism, commentary, news reporting, teaching, scholarship, or research.[104] In determining whether or not a particular use is a fair use, courts are to consider the following four factors:

1. the purpose and character of the use, including whether such use is of a commercial nature or is for nonprofit educational purposes;
2. the nature of the copyrighted work;
3. the amount and substantiality of the portion used in relation to the copyrighted work as a whole; and
4. the effect of the use upon the potential market for or value of the copyrighted work.[105]

One aspect of the "nature of the copyrighted work" is whether or not it has been published. An unpublished work will be subject to a greater degree of protection than a published work,[106] and thus a defense of fair use will be less likely to stand. Also to be considered under this factor is whether the work is factual or fictional; factual works are subject to less copyright protection, and therefore the use by another of a factual work is more likely to be considered a fair use.[107] Another very important aspect of the "nature of the copyrighted work" factor is whether or not the use is "transformative," that is, whether it "adds something new, with a further purpose or different character, altering the first with new expression, meaning or message."[108] For example, making a simple

[103] *See* Folsom v. Marsh, F. Cas. 342 (C.C.D. Mass. 1841).

[104] 17 U.S.C. § 107.

[105] *Id.*

[106] Harper & Row Publishers, Inc. v. Nation Enters., 471 U.S. 539, 105 S. Ct. 2218 (1985).

[107] American Geophysical Union v. Texaco Inc., 60 F.3d 913, 925 (2d Cir. 1995).

[108] Campbell v. Acuff Rose Music, Inc., 510 U.S. 569, 114 S. Ct. 1164, 127 L. Ed. 2d 500 (1994).

photocopy of a work is not transformative.[109] However, in one well-known case involving an advertisement for one of the *Naked Gun* movies, it was found that a photograph of actor Leslie Nielsen's head superimposed on the naked body of a pregnant woman, parodying the famous Demi Moore Vanity Fair cover, was a transformative use.[110]

The *Naked Gun* case falls into a separate subcategory of fair uses: cases involving parodies. Before 1994, the courts were split as to what constituted a proper parody; a line of cases held that a parody qualified as a fair use only if it parodied the work it was using, and did not qualify if it was simply a satire, using another work to comment on society at large.[111] In one such 1992 case, *Rogers v. Koons*, the Second Circuit held that a sculptor's three-dimensional replication of a photograph was an infringement, not a fair use. Koons created the sculpture as part of a show he called "The Banality Show." His intention was to comment upon the "commonplace." As the court summarized:

> [Koons] belongs to the school of American artists who believe the mass production of commodities and media images has caused a deterioration in the quality of society, and this artistic tradition of which he is a member proposes through incorporating these images into works of art to comment critically both on the incorporated object and the political and economic system that created it.[112]

The court noted the rule in the Second Circuit that in order to qualify as a parody, "the copied work must be, at least in part, an object of the parody, otherwise there would be no need to conjure up the original work," and thus held that "Koons' claim that his infringement of Rogers' work is fair use solely because he is acting within an artistic tradition of commenting upon the commonplace thus cannot be accepted."[113]

Another line of cases suggests that a parody need not comment upon the work being used in order to qualify for fair use protection.[114] However, the Supreme Court took up the question in *Campbell v. Acuff-Rose Music, Inc.*,[115] and suggested that a parody must comment (at least in part) on the work it is copying in order to qualify for fair use. It found that the disputed work, a scatological cover of the Roy Orbison song "Pretty Woman" by the hardcore rap band 2 Live Crew,

---

[109] *See* American Geophysical Union v. Texaco, Inc., 60 F.3d 913 (2d Cir.), *cert. dismissed*, 516 U.S. 1005, 116 S. Ct. 592 (1995).

[110] Leibovitz v. Paramount Pictures Corp., 137 F.3d 109 (2d Cir. 1998).

[111] *See, e.g.*, Rogers v. Koons, 960 F.2d 301, 310 (2d Cir.), *cert. denied*, 113 S. Ct. 365 (1992).

[112] *Id.* at 309.

[113] *Id.* at 310.

[114] Elsmere Music, Inc. v. National Broad. Co., 482 F. Supp. 741 (S.D.N.Y. 1980), *aff'd*, 623 F.2d 252 (2d Cir. 1980).

[115] 510 U.S. 569, 114 S. Ct. 1164 (1994).

qualified as a parody of the Roy Orbison song and a non-infringing fair use with rather humorous results.

After the *Campbell* case, courts considering parody cases must consider the parodist's commentary (or lack thereof) on the work being copied. In the *Naked Gun* case mentioned above concerning the photograph of Leslie Nielsen's head superimposed on the body of a pregnant woman,[116] the Second Circuit held that it qualified as a parody of Annie Leibovitz's photograph of Demi Moore "[b]ecause the smirking face of Nielsen contrasts so strikingly with the serious expression on the face of Moore, the ad may reasonably be perceived as commenting on the seriousness, even the pretentiousness, of the original."[117] In *Dr. Seuss Enterprises v. Penguin Books USA, Inc.*,[118] the Ninth Circuit held that a book about the O.J. Simpson murder trial entitled *The Cat Not in the Hat* which followed the format and style of Dr. Seuss' *The Cat in the Hat* was not a permissible parody, because it did not comment upon *The Cat in the Hat*, but rather used *The Cat in the Hat* as a vehicle to comment upon the murders. (The defendants' book satirized Dr. Seuss' famous "One Fish Two Fish Red Fish Blue Fish" by replacing it with "One Knife? Two Knife? Red Knife/Dead Wife," and featured a cartoon O.J. Simpson wearing The Cat's famous scrunched red and white stovepipe hat 13 times.)

[J] De Minimis Cases

In recent years, several cases have been brought under the rubric of fair use involving the use of an artist's work in a film or television show, which has caused courts to consider arguments that the use is "de minimis" and thus not an infringement. In one such case, *Ringgold v. Black Entertainment Television, Inc.*,[119] the plaintiff had designed a quilt that hung in a museum which created and sold (authorized) posters of the work. Defendant producers of a television show used a poster of plaintiff's quilt as part of a set decoration. The poster appeared in nine shots ranging from 1.86 to 4.16 seconds long, for a total of 26.75 seconds. Only parts of the poster were visible during the shots. The lower court concluded that the use was de minimis and a fair use. That determination was reversed on appeal.

In the process, the court distinguished between a de minimis defense to copyright infringement and a fair use defense. According to the court, "[i]f the allegedly infringing work makes such a quantitatively insubstantial use of the copyrighted work as to fall below the threshold required for actionably copying,

---

[116] Leibovitz v. Paramount Pictures Corp., 137 F.3d 109 (2d Cir. 1998).

[117] *Id.* at 114.

[118] 109 F.3d 1394 (9th Cir. 1997).

[119] 126 F.3d 70 (2d Cir. 1997).

it makes more sense to reject the claim on that basis and find no infringement, rather than undertake an elaborate fair use analysis in order to uphold a defense."[120]

Another case based on similar facts reached a different result while following the same legal principles. In *Sandoval v. New Line Cinema*,[121] the Second Circuit held that a fleeting and obscured use of ten copyrighted photographs appearing in a movie was a de minimis use (but *not* a fair use) under the standard set forth in *Ringgold*, and thus not an infringement.

Fair use is a difficult area, because establishing it depends almost entirely on fact, but often seems to turn on the subjective reaction of the judge or jury deciding the case. As a result, it is often difficult to advise clients as to a particular use. While lawyers often take comfort in precedent, it is difficult to see how the factual backgrounds of *Sandoval* and *Ringgold* were sufficiently different to warrant such different outcomes.

§ 1.03 TRADEMARKS AND ANALOGOUS RIGHTS

[A] Introduction

Trademark law, which also embraces trade names, service marks, and "trade dress" such as product and packaging design, is intended to protect virtually any word, name, symbol, device, or combination thereof which serves to *identify the source* of particular goods or services. Trademarks inform the relevant purchasing public that products or services originate from a single source, and serve to assure the public of a consistency of quality.

Trademarks would seem to have relatively little applicability to the art world. The most obvious trademark issue that arises in the art world is the identity of the artist, and an artist's name (and signature) can become a very valuable trademark. An artist's name or signature may be just as recognizable to the relevant public as commercial brand names such as "McDonald's" or "Marlboro" are to the masses. However, much less attention (and litigation) has been devoted to trademarks in the art world than to other areas of intellectual property and as a result, the literature of the law in this area is sparse. Nonetheless, there are certain areas of critical interest to the artist or artist's advisor, including the protectibility of the artist's trade indicia (and just how broadly that indicia can be defined) as well as potential infringement and fair use considerations in appropriating the trade indicia of others. For example, can a particular style of an artist be protected as a trademark? Conversely, to what extent does an artist's use of another's trade symbols in a work of art require permission (the Warhol Campbell's Soup can being the most obvious example)?

---

[120] *Id.* at 76.

[121] 147 F.3d 215 (2d Cir. 1998).

Before turning to particular topics affected by trademark law, we provide a very basic understanding of how trademarks function and how rights in them are obtained.

[1] What Constitutes a Trademark?

As mentioned above, a "trademark" in the broad sense of the term constitutes anything that serves to identify a source. It can be the shape of a bottle, the name of a musical band, the name of an individual artist, entertainment characters, the name of a film studio, the color scheme of a product's packaging, a distinctive sound (such as NBC's three chimes), or any word, symbol, design, logo, or other indicia that lets the public know that a particular source is standing behind the goods or services offered under the mark.

Federal trademark law, referred to as the "Lanham Act," is codified in 15 U.S.C. § 1051 *et seq.* Section 32 defines infringement of registered trademarks, but § 43(a) extends protection to a broad array of "marks," even if unregistered, which can go beyond the scope of traditional trademarks and be applied to

> [any] word, term, name, symbol, or device . . . or any false designation of origin, false or misleading description of fact, or false or misleading representation of fact, which (A) is likely to cause confusion, or to cause mistake, or to deceive as to the affiliation, connection, or association of such person with another person, or as to the origin, sponsorship, or approval of his or her goods, services, or commercial activities by another person, or (B) in commercial advertising or promotion, misrepresents the nature, characteristics, qualities, or geographic origin of his or her or another person's goods, services, or commercial activities . . .

Section 43(a) has been used to protect such untraditional "designations" as the design of a restaurant,[122] the look of a mail-order catalogue,[123] the design of the car used on the "Dukes of Hazzard" television show,[124] the cover of romance novels,[125] and comic book characters.[126] Section 43(a) is routinely used to protect "trade dress" or overall package designs of products.[127]

---

[122] Two Pesos Inc. v. Taco Cabana, Inc., 505 U.S. 763, *reh'g denied*, 505 U.S. 1244 (1992).

[123] Tools USA & Equip. Co. v. Champ Frame Straightening Equip., Inc., 87 F.3d 654, 658 (4th Cir. 1996).

[124] Warner Bros. v. Gay Toys, Inc., 658 F.2d 76 (2d Cir. 1981).

[125] Harlequin Enters., Ltd. v. Gulf & Western Corp., 644 F.2d 946 (2d Cir. 1981).

[126] *See* D.C. Comics, Inc. v. Filmation Assocs., 486 F. Supp. 1273 (S.D.N.Y. 1980).

[127] *See, e.g.,* Chevron Chem. Co. v. Voluntary Purchasing Groups, 659 F.2d 695 (5th Cir. 1981); AmBrit, Inc. v. Kraft, Inc., 812 F.2d 1531 (11th Cir. 1986), *cert. denied*, 481 U.S. 1041 (1987).

[2] How Trademark Rights Develop

Trademark rights are acquired through use.[128] The first person to "think up" a trademark or its equivalent will *not* have rights to it. It is the first person or entity to actually *use* the mark who will have rights to it.[129] However, those rights (absent a registration) will extend only to the extent of the use. For example, if someone who only does business in New York begins using a trademark in New York, but the use is limited to the state of New York, the trademark rights will only be enforceable in that area. Another user can come along and use the identical mark in all 49 other states, and the second user will have priority in those other states.[130]

Trademarks, unlike copyrights or patents, can last forever. There are famous brand names and company names that have been serving as trademarks for over 100 years. However, marks can be lost if they are "abandoned"—that is, if a party discontinues use of a mark and has no intention to resume use of the mark, the mark will be "abandoned" and thus no longer enforceable.[131]

[3] Protection Afforded

Owning a trademark does not entitle the owner to exclusive use of the mark on any and all goods and services. Generally, with a few exceptions, trademark rights will only extend to the particular category of goods and services in connection with which the owner uses the mark. This is because the crux of trademark infringement is "likelihood of confusion," meaning that consumers are likely to be confused into believing that the goods offered under the infringing mark emanate from the same source as the trademark holder.[132] For example, the name "Jackson Pollock," when applied to works of art, certainly has source-identifying significance and its appearance on or in connection with works of visual art would cause consumers to believe that the works emanate from the well-known artist.

---

[128] Although trademark rights are not dependent on registration, registration does have benefits. The intricacies of registration are covered in 15 U.S.C. § 1051 *et seq.*, and 37 C.F.R. § 2.1 *et seq. See also* the *Trademark Manual of Examining Procedure*, available on the USPTO's Web site at www.uspto.gov.

[129] G. & C. Merriam Co. v. Saalfield, 198 F. 369 (6th Cir. 1912); Walter Baker & Co. v. Delepenha, 160 F. 746 (C.C.D.N.J. 1908).

[130] *See, e.g.,* Hanover Star Milling Co. v. Metcalf, 240 U.S. 403, 412 (1916); United Drug Co. v. Theodore Rectanus Co., 248 U.S. 90, 100 (1918); Food Fair Stores, Inc. v. Square Deal Market Co., 206 F.2d 482 (D.C. Cir. 1953), *cert. denied*, 346 U.S. 937 (1954).

[131] 15 U.S.C. § 1127.

[132] Trademark infringement is the "use in commerce [of] any reproduction, counterfeit, copy, or colorable imitation of a registered mark in connection with the sale, offering for sale, distribution, or advertising of any goods or services on or in connection with which such use is likely to cause confusion, or to cause mistake, or to deceive." 15 U.S.C. § 1114.

However, if the name "Pollock" were used in connection with a fast-food chain, it is unlikely that anyone would seriously be confused into believing that the fast-food stores were in any way connected to the famous artist, and therefore there would be no infringement (although use of the full name in this manner might infringe upon the right of publicity, discussed below).

However, a junior user cannot always avoid a claim of infringement by using the mark in connection with different goods or services. Courts will protect not just the class of goods and services for which the trademark holder uses the mark, but also goods and services within the trademark holder's "natural zone of expansion."[133] For example, if the name "Pollock" were applied to paints or artist's supplies, one might conclude that those products were endorsed by or in some way connected with Pollock.

Comparing the goods and services is not the only step in analyzing a claim of infringement. Courts will evaluate several factors, usually (1) the strength of the mark, (2) the degree of similarity between the two marks, (3) the proximity of the products, (4) the likelihood that the prior owner will bridge the gap, (5) actual confusion, (6) defendant's good faith in adopting its own mark, (7) the quality of defendant's product, and (8) the sophistication of the buyers.[134]

There is another type of protection that is afforded trademarks that does not require that the goods and services be related. Trademark "dilution" protects against uses that are not competitive, and no likelihood of confusion is required. On January 16, 1996, the Federal Dilution Act went into effect.[135] Previously, dilution claims were governed exclusively by state dilution statutes.

Dilution action protects only famous marks[136] from uses that are likely to cause the trademark to lose its distinctive character, either by "blurring" or "tarnishment." Blurring occurs where famous marks are used on noncompeting goods. The use is therefore likely to diminish the value of the famous mark. Historical examples include the use of "Rolls Royce" on radio tubes,[137] "Kodak" on bicycles,[138] and "Tiffany" in connection with a restaurant.[139] "Tarnishment"

---

[133] Scarves by Vera, Inc. v. Todo Imports Ltd., 544 F.2d 1167 (2d Cir. 1976).

[134] Polaroid Corp. v. Polarad Elecs. Corp., 287 F.2d 492, 495 (2d Cir. 1961).

[135] 15 U.S.C. § 1125(c).

[136] Whether or not a mark is famous depends on: (1) the distinctiveness of the mark; (2) the duration and extent of use in connection with the goods with which the mark is used; (3) the extent of advertising and publicity involving the mark; (4) the geographical area in which the mark is used; (5) the channels of trade in which the mark is used; (6) the recognition of the marks within the channels of trade used by the owner and the person against whom an injunction is sought; (7) the extent of use of similar marks by third parties; and (8) whether the mark is registered. 15 U.S.C. § 43(c).

[137] Walls v. Rolls Royce of Am., Inc., 4 F.2d 233 (3d Cir. 1925).

[138] Eastman Kodak Co. v. Kodak Cycle Co., 15 Rep. Pat. Cas. 105 (1898).

[139] Tiffany & Co. v. Boston Club, Inc., 231 F. Supp. 836 (D. Mass. 1964).

occurs when a mark is used in a derogatory manner or setting, and can be of concern to pop or avant-garde artists who may use another's trademark in a less than flattering manner. Examples of uses which have been found to constitute tarnishment include "candyland.com"[140] and "Adults-R-Us"[141] for sexually explicit Internet sites, and "Buttweiser"[142] on t-shirts.

[B] Internet Uses

Traditional trademark remedies have been furiously applied to new types of infringements taking place on the Internet. The most prevalent misuse of a trademark is the practice of "cybersquatting"—when an entrepreneur registers a domain name that consists of or includes another's trademark. The Internet Corporation for Assigned Names and Numbers (ICANN) has recently enacted an arbitration procedure, but it is quite new and, at this writing, had not been tested. Additionally, on November 29, 1999, President Clinton signed into law the Anty-cybersquatting Consumer Protection Act, which creates a separate cause of action against one who registers a domain name that is identical or confusingly similar to another's trademark. The new statute also creates a separate cause of action against one who registers a living person's name as a domain name.

Another Internet-related problem is the use of metatags or search-engine spamming to attract users to a competing (or sometimes noncompeting) company's Web site. Metatags are encoded text that is invisible to the user but is coded into a Web site so that the Web site will show up on search results. For example, if XYZ Company sells widgets, a competitor, Widget Company, will embed metatags that say "XYZ" repeatedly in the Widget Company Web site. This has been held by one court to constitute trademark infringement,[143] although another court held that it is not actionable.[144]

For a more detailed discussion of the Internet and domain name disputes see Chapter 9.

[C] Trademarks as Applied to the Art World

The most obvious trademark applicable to the world of fine art is that of the artist's name. No other element more readily and obviously serves to identify the source of a work of art. Yet, interestingly, it was not until fairly recently that

---

[140] Hasbro Inc. v. Internet Entertainment Group Ltd., 40 U.S.P.Q.2d 1479 (1996).

[141] Toys "R" Us Inc. v. Akkaoui, 40 U.S.P.Q.2d 1836 (1996).

[142] Anheuser-Busch Inc. v. Andy's Sportswear Inc., 40 U.S.P.Q.2d 1542 (1996).

[143] Brookfield Communications, Inc. v. West Coast Entertainment Corp., 174 F.3d 1036 (9th Cir. 1999).

[144] Playboy Enters., Inc. v. Netscape Communications Corp., 55 F. Supp. 2d 1070 (C.D. Cal. 1999).

the courts recognized that an artist's signature on a painting served to function as a trademark. The issue was first presented to the Trademark Trial and Appeal Board in 1983 in *In re Wood*,[145] an appeal of the Trademark Office's refusal to register the name of an artist as a trademark. The Trademark Office cited an earlier opinion that refused to allow Samuel Clemens, a/k/a Mark Twain, from asserting a trademark right in his pseudonym to prevent the further publication of certain of his writings that were no longer protected by copyright.[146] The reasoning of the Trademark Office in *In re Wood* and that of the court in the Mark Twain case was that trademarks could not be used to extend the life of a copyright. However, in *In re Wood*, there was no such attempt; rather, the purpose of obtaining trademark protection for the name and signature was to prevent others from creating counterfeit works using the artist's name. In approving the registration of the name, the board noted "[w]e see no other practical yet aesthetically pleasing alternative" for identifying the source of a work of art.[147]

Even before *In re Wood*, Pablo Picasso's heirs granted exclusive merchandise licensing rights in the name "Picasso" to an organization called the Visual Artists and Galleries Association (VAGA). VAGA enforced its rights in the "Picasso" mark against t-shirt vendors during the Museum of Modern Art's Picasso retrospective exhibit in 1980.[148] Today artists ranging from Keith Haring to Charles Schulz regularly use trademark rights in addition to copyright rights to protect use of their works or elements of their works.

[1] "Style" as a Protectible Trademark

In addition to an artist's name serving as a trademark, an artist can create and use a particular style that may also be entitled to protection. Artists have been met with varied success in asserting a protectible trademark in their "style." One of the most successful claims of trade dress by an artist was in the case of *Romm Art Creations Ltd. v. Simcha International, Inc.*,[149] in which the licensee of the artist Itzchak Tarkay, licensed to distribute limited editions and fine art posters, brought a trade dress claim against the defendant who was distributing works that were "slavishly similar and entirely derivative" of Tarkay's works.[150] The court found that the Tarkay works presented a "distinctive visual impression"

---

[145] 217 U.S.P.Q. 1345 (T.T.A.B. 1983).

[146] Clemens v. Belford, Clark & Co., 14 Fed. 728 (C.C.N.D. Ill. 1983).

[147] 217 U.S.P.Q. at 1350.

[148] Jensen, The Selling of Picasso: A Look at the Artist's Rights in Protecting the Reputation of His Name, 4 Colum.-VLA J. L. & Arts 3 (1981). VAGA (phone number 212-736-6666) and Artists Rights Society (phone number 212-420-9160) remain two of the largest artist licensing collectives in the United States.

[149] 786 F. Supp. 1126 (E.D.N.Y. 1992).

[150] *Id.* at 1131.

and were thus protectible under the Lanham Act.[151] A less successful claim was made by the rights holders to the works of Salvador Dali against a counterfeiter in *Galerie Furstenberg v. Coffaro et al.*[152] Plaintiff claimed a protectible trade dress that consisted of "the particular lines, unique figural constellation, colors, stylistic features and design of a certain subject in an image created by Dali . . . the trademark is the image or the configuration of the drawing as applied to paper."[153] The court rejected this contention, holding that such a claim had to be based in copyright rather than trademark.

Similar claims have been made in the context of greeting cards. Such a claim was rejected by the Second Circuit, refusing to find protectible the creator's alleged style of "straight-on, strong photographic, glossy images of animals, persons or objects on die-cut cards that are cut without bleed of any kind;" the court found this to be an improper attempt to protect "an idea, a concept, or a generalized type of appearance."[154] However, other courts have granted protection to the "style" or "trade dress" of greeting cards.[155]

[2] Characters

Performing artists also create styles that may, under some circumstances, be protected from imitation by a careful application of trademark law. Elvis Presley's estate, which has been very active in protecting its trademarks, failed in its attempt to prohibit the production of a show patterned after an Elvis Presley show. The disputed show began with the theme music that Elvis traditionally used to introduce his show, and featured a performer who looked, dressed, sang, and posed like Elvis. The court held that absent proof that the public was deceived, the First Amendment allowed the production of such an imitative show. However, the court did find that the use of Elvis's logo and photos that resembled Elvis constituted trademark infringement.[156]

Entertainment characters can be the subject of trademark protection.[157] Disney has successfully asserted trademark protection in its numerous animated characters.[158] The owner of the rights to "The Lone Ranger" enjoined an actor who

---

[151] *Id.* at 1136.

[152] 697 F. Supp. 1282 (S.D.N.Y. 1988).

[153] *Id.* at 1289 (citing plaintiff's memorandum).

[154] Jeffrey Milstein, Inc. v. Greger, Lawlor, Roth, Inc., 58 F.3d 27, 33, 32 (2d Cir. 1995).

[155] Roulo v. Russ Berrie & Co., 886 F.2d 931 (7th Cir. 1989), *cert. denied*, 493 U.S. 1075 (1990); Hartford House, Ltd. v. Hallmark Cards, Inc., 846 F.2d 1268 (10th Cir.), *cert. denied*, 488 U.S. 908 (1988).

[156] Estate of Presley v. Russen, 513 F. Supp. 1339 (D.N.J. 1981).

[157] *See* D.C. Comics, Inc. v. Filmation Assocs., 486 F. Supp. 1273 (S.D.N.Y. 1980).

[158] *See, e.g.,* Walt Disney Productions, v. Air Pirates et al., 581 F.2d 751 (9th Cir. 1978).

played the role in a film from appearing in a circus dressed as the character.[159] Charlie Chaplin enjoined the imitation of his makeup, outfit, and mannerisms in a movie promoted as featuring "Charles Aplin."[160]

[3] Right of Publicity; Sound-Alikes and Imitations

For claims involving characters like Charlie Chaplin and the Marx Brothers,[161] who are not so much fictional characters as characters intertwined with the identity of an actual performer, a better basis than trademark violation is violation of the "right of publicity."

The right of publicity is a state law doctrine, codified in roughly half the states, that provides protection for identifiable elements of someone's persona. The right of publicity is similar to the law of unfair competition but requires no proof of falsity, deception, or confusion; a violation occurs simply upon use of a person's identity to draw attention to a product or advertisement.[162] Generally, in order to state a claim a plaintiff has to show an enforceable right in the identity of a human being, the use of some aspect of the identity or persona by the defendant in such a way that the plaintiff is identifiable from the use, and damage to the commercial value of that persona. A detailed discussion of the right of publicity is found in Chapter 3.

[4] Lanham Act Claims in Lieu of Copyright Claims

There is a limit to the extent to which a claimant can assert a claim under § 43(a) of the Lanham Act incidental to a copyright claim. Often, plaintiffs whose primary claim is in the nature of copyright infringement will try to add a § 43(a) claim for failure to properly credit the plaintiff as the true author of the infringed work. These claims are either asserted in addition to a copyright claim, or are asserted as the primary claim when for some reason a claim of copyright is unavailable.

While failure to properly credit a plaintiff is the subject of a proper § 43(a) claim, courts will often disallow such a claim when it is simply incidental to a claim of copyright infringement. The leading credit case is *Smith v. Montoro*,[163] which held that an actor who was not properly credited in advertising for a film in which he appeared had a viable § 43(a) claim. In this case, there was no copyright interest that should or could have been asserted—the actor was not the

---

159 Lone Ranger, Inc. v. Cox, 124 F.2d 650 (4th Cir. 1942).

160 Chaplin v. Amador, 93 Cal. App. 358, 269 P. 544 (1st Dist. 1928).

161 Groucho Marx Productions v. Day & Night Co., 523 F. Supp. 485 (S.D.N.Y. 1981); *rev'd on other grounds*, 689 F.2d 317 (2d Cir. 1982).

162 See Restatement (Third) of Unfair Competition, § § 46-49 (1995).

163 648 F.2d 602 (9th Cir. 1981).

author of the film, he simply rendered a performance for which he should have been credited. However, when there is a copyright-type interest, a § 43(a) claim will be superfluous.

This issue of credit arises most often in the context of a Lanham Act claim that is alleged as a result of an allegedly improper copyright notice (listing the defendant rather than the plaintiff). When an allegedly incorrect copyright notice is the only factor giving rise to a Lanham Act claim, courts have made it clear that no § 43(a) claim can be brought. Allowing such a claim "would simply transform virtually every copyright action into a Lanham Act action as well."[164] However, if some additional or affirmative representation is made regarding ownership or authorship of the disputed work, courts may allow such a claim.[165]

[5] Parody and Satire

While most cases involving parody and satire involve the use of works protected by copyright rather than trademark, often trademark issues come in to play as well. While courts have been mixed on accepting "parody" as a defense, overall the defense has been favored, often under the reasoning that the imitative work is so obviously a parody or satire there is no likelihood that consumers will be confused into believing it is affiliated with the trademark holder.

For example, the Seventh Circuit reversed an order of summary judgment in favor of Nike on its claim for infringement against a company making t-shirts with "Mike" used in conjunction with Nike's "swoosh" symbol, stating "[w]hen businesses seek the national spotlight, part of the territory includes accepting a certain amount of ridicule. The First Amendment . . . allows such ridicule in the form of parody."[166] Similarly, the Second Circuit reversed an order enjoining the distribution by the publisher of Spy Magazine of "Spy Notes," parodying the famous "CliffsNotes" study guides, stating "parody is a form of artistic expression, protected by the First Amendment" and finding that any slight risk of consumer confusion was outweighed by the public interest in free expression.[167] Others have

---

[164] Merchant v. Lymon, 828 F. Supp. 1048, 1060 (S.D.N.Y. 1993), *rev'd on other grounds*, 92 F.3d 51 (2d Cir. 1996).

[165] Kregos v. Associated Press, 937 F.2d 700, 711 (2d Cir. 1991) (no Lanham Act claim for allegedly improper copyright notice; however, the court also stated that "Kregos could complain, for example, if [defendant] unfairly competed with him by falsely claiming that its form was originated by some [third party]."). *See also* Lipton v. Nature Co., 71 F.3d 464 (2d Cir. 1995); Eden Toys, Inc. v. Florelee Undergarment Co., 697 F.2d 27, 37 (2d Cir. 1982); Banff Ltd. v. Express, Inc., 921 F. Supp. 1065 (S.D.N.Y. 1995)*; but see* Waldman Publ'g Corp. v. Landoll, Inc., 43 F.3d 775 (2d Cir. 1994).

[166] Nike, Inc. v. "Just Did It" Enters., 6 F.3d 1225, 1227 (7th Cir. 1993).

[167] CliffsNotes, Inc. v. Bantam Doubleday Dell Publ'g, 886 F.2d 490 (2d Cir. 1989).

successfully parodied the Budweiser beer can to promote a beach,[168] the "Miami Vice" television show to sell t-shirts featuring "Miami Mice,"[169] and the "The Black Dog" t-shirts promoting the famous tavern on Martha's Vineyard by making t-shirts containing "The Dead Dog" and "The Black Hog."[170]

Other parodists have not been so successful. For example, the Hard Rock Café enjoined the use of "Hard Rain Café" in conjunction with a logo similar to the Hard Rock Café logo on t-shirts sold in Seattle.[171] In response to the defendant's parody defense, the court held "parody is not a defense to trademark infringement, but rather is another factor to be considered in the likelihood of confusion equation . . . a defendant's claim of parody will be disregarded where the purpose of the similarity is to capitalize on a famous mark's popularity for the defendant's own commercial use."[172] Similarly, the insurance company Mutual of Omaha was successful in enjoining an individual from creating and selling merchandise that mimicked Mutual of Omaha's "Indian Head" logo with an emaciated human head and the words "Mutant Of Omaha" and "Nuclear Holocaust Insurance."[173] The Eighth Circuit dismissed the defendant's First Amendment defense in short order, finding it unimpressive in light of the finding of likelihood of confusion and the availability of other means of expression.

Most of the reported parody cases are from before the enactment of the federal dilution statute; because dilution does not require a likelihood of confusion, it will be interesting to see if more courts reject parody defenses to claims of trademark dilution, when they can no longer assert lack of likelihood of confusion as an absolute bar to a trademark claim.

Although the federal dilution statute was only enacted in 1996, there have been state dilution statutes in effect for years. Traditionally, courts have used dilution statutes to prevent parodies of an obscene or offensive nature.

For example, in *Dallas Cowboys Cheerleaders, Inc. v. Pussycat Cinema, Ltd.*,[174] the Second Circuit held that the outfit of the Dallas Cowboys Cheerleaders (consisting of a combination of white boots, white shorts, a blue blouse, and a star-studded white vest and belt) was a protectible trademark and could be asserted to enjoin the distribution of a pornographic film, "Debbie Does Dallas," which

---

[168] Anheuser-Busch Inc. v. L & L Wings, Inc., 962 F.2d 316 (4th Cir. 1992), *cert. denied,* 506 U.S. 872 (1992).

[169] Universal City Studios, Inc. v. Casey & Casey, Inc., 622 F. Supp. 201, *aff'd*, 792 F.2d 1125 (11th Cir. 1986).

[170] The Black Dog Tavern Co. v. Hall, 823 F. Supp. 48 (D. Mass. 1993).

[171] Hard Rock Café Licensing Corp. v. Pacific Graphics, Inc., 776 F. Supp. 1454 (W.D. Wash. 1991).

[172] *Id.* at 1462.

[173] Mutual of Omaha Ins. Co. v. Novak, 836 F.2d 397 (8th Cir. 1987), *cert. denied*, 488 U.S. 933 (1988).

[174] 604 F.2d 200 (2d Cir. 1979).

featured an actress wearing a similar uniform. The court rejected defendants' First Amendment defense, reasoning that "there are numerous ways in which defendants may comment on 'sexuality in athletics' without infringing plaintiffs' trademark."[175] As mentioned above, other examples of uses prohibited due to dilution in the form of "tarnishment" are "candyland.com"[176] and "Adults-R-Us"[177] for sexually explicit Internet sites, and "Buttweiser"[178] on t-shirts.

[6] Titles

Generally, titles are not entitled to trademark protection. The title of a film or book cannot be registered with the Trademark Office unless it is to designate a *series* of films or books. For example, "Gone With the Wind" could not be registered as a trademark, but "Nancy Drew" could, because there is a series of books that all use the Nancy Drew designation.

Needless to say, were someone to make a film or write a book entitled *Gone With the Wind*, it is quite likely that the heirs of Margaret Mitchell, or the successor to Selznick International Pictures, could prevent such a use. While it depends on the use, if enough factors were present to make it appear that the second *Gone With the Wind* were a sequel or somehow related to the first, § 43(a) could be invoked to prevent the use. This is because titles, although they cannot be registered and generally are not entitled to trademark protection, can obtain protection if they have acquired secondary meaning,[179] meaning that the mark is so well known that the public has come to identify the mark with the owner of the mark. Because *Gone With the Wind* is one of the most famous books and films of all time, it has certainly acquired secondary meaning.

[D] Licensing

A trademark or trademark rights (including the right of publicity) can be licensed to third parties.[180]

Trademark rights can be licensed in any number of ways; nonexclusive or exclusive rights can be granted, or rights can be granted for only certain products or services (t-shirts but not coffee mugs, posters for only a specific event, to terminate after a given time period, and so on).

---

[175] *Id.* at 206.

[176] Hasbro Inc. v. Internet Entertainment Group Ltd., 40 U.S.P.Q.2d 1479 (1996).

[177] Toys "R" Us Inc. v. Akkaoui, 40 U.S.P.Q.2d 1836 (1996).

[178] Anheuser-Busch Inc. v. Andy's Sportswear Inc., 40 U.S.P.Q.2d 1542 (1996).

[179] *See, e.g.,* International Film Serv. Co. v. Associated Producers, Inc., 273 F. 585 (S.D.N.Y. 1921); In re National Council Books, Inc., 121 U.S.P.Q. 198 (T.T.A.B. 1959).

[180] *See* Form 1-10.

[1] Quality Control

The primary consideration in trademark licensing is that the licensor must retain what is called "quality control" over any goods or services that are offered under the licensed mark. Quality control is crucial, as the function of trademarks is to identify the source of goods and assure consumers of their consistent quality. As stated by one court:

> Courts have long imposed upon trademark licensors a duty to oversee the quality of licensees' products. The rationale for this requirement is that marks are treated by purchasers as an indication that the trademark owner is associated with the product. Customers rely upon the owner's reputation when they select the trademarked goods. If a trademark owner allows licensees to depart from his quality standards, the public will be misled, and the trademark will cease to have utility as an informational device. A trademark owner who allows this to occur loses its right to use the mark.[181]

Without sufficient quality control, a license is considered a "naked" license, and can result in abandonment of the trademark.[182] Thus, it is not just crucial that a license agreement specifically calls for quality control, but that the licensor actually exercise quality control. Typical quality control provisions call for the following:

- general obligation of the licensee not to use the licensed mark in a manner that would be "offensive to good taste" or would injure the reputation of the licensor or the licensed mark
- a requirement that the licensee make its facilities where the goods are manufactured and sample goods (and packaging or promotional materials) available to the licensor for inspection at regular intervals, and an agreement to remedy any deficiency in quality found by the licensor
- prohibition of the sale or offer for sale of any new line of goods or changed goods (and packaging or promotional materials) without the licensor's prior approval
- prohibition of the sale of any damaged, defective, or nonconforming goods

Sometimes, a license will include an attached exhibit illustrating a pre-approved format for use of the mark, or a pre-approved product manufactured

---

[181] Kentucky Fried Chicken Corp. v. Diversified Packaging Corp., 549 F.2d 368, 387 (5th Cir. 1977) (citations omitted).

[182] Stanfield v. Osborne Indus., Inc., 52 F.3d 867, 871 (10th Cir. 1995).

under the mark. Any deviation from the pre-approved form must then be approved by the licensor in advance.

[2] Other License Provisions

Other typical provisions in a trademark license include:

- an acknowledgment that the licensor is the owner of the mark, and that the license gives licensee no rights to the mark other than as expressly set forth in the license
- the "territory" of the license (the geographic location in which licensee is licensed to use the mark)
- the type of license, whether exclusive or non-exclusive
- the specific rights granted (exactly what goods or services licensee is allowed to sell or render under the mark)
- a requirement that licensee use the ®, ™, or ℠ (whichever is appropriate) symbols in connection with uses of the mark, and provide an acknowledgment that the mark is licensed by the licensor
- a covenant by the licensee not to use, adopt, or register a mark similar to the licensed mark, and not to challenge licensor's rights in the mark
- an agreement by licensee to notify licensor of any infringement, and to cooperate with licensor in the prosecution of any infringement

A sample license agreement, covering these provisions and others, is included as Form 1-10.

§ 1.04 MORAL RIGHTS

[A] Introduction

Moral rights, or *droit moral*, stem from an entirely different aspect of intellectual property than the purely economic rights that we commonly associate with U.S. copyright law. Those economic rights generally entitle the author or copyright holder to be compensated for reproduction, distribution, or other exploitation of the copyrighted work. Moral rights, by contrast, address issues of integrity and attribution and go to the core of those privileges naturally associated with the rights of any creator. The right of "attribution" is the right to receive credit for those uses of an artist's work that the artist and the public should rightly associate with the artist, and conversely, to avoid derogating associations with versions of a work that are not truly representative of the artist's efforts. The moral right of "integrity" essentially underlies the preservation of the artist's work in its authentic and unadulterated form. Poor reproductions or adaptations of a work, even if otherwise "licensed" for the purposes of economic rights, may nonetheless simultaneously offend principles of attribution *and* integrity.

Although these rights are well recognized in one form or another in a number of European countries (particularly in France), they infrequently apply in the U.S., subject to a number of exceptions discussed below. That does not mean, however, that the work of a United States author may not be subject to the moral rights of another country such as France. In perhaps what is the most famous recent case, the heirs of John Huston, the director of *The Asphalt Jungle*, along with the screenwriter of the film, brought suit in France against a French television channel to prevent the broadcast of a colorized version.[183] Their claim was recognized by the French courts, even though none of the plaintiffs held a copyright interest in the work under U.S. law, because each of them had undertaken their contributions as a work made for hire. That, however, did not preclude a moral rights claim under French law. Moreover, because moral rights are generally inalienable and may last well beyond the life of the copyright in a work, the issues of attribution and integrity remain significant for any work that may be subject to exploitation outside the United States. Even within the United States, moral rights have occasionally been recognized by courts fashioning equitable remedies, and have some limited statutory basis under federal and state law. The following discussion considers some of the sources for moral rights or their nearest equivalent under U.S. law.

[B] What Are Moral Rights?

In addition to the rights of attribution and integrity discussed above, the basic moral rights afforded in France and other European countries include the right of publication (to control if and when a work is published, including the right to withdraw a work from publication), and the right to control the use of the author's name (to publish a work anonymously or pseudonymously).

These rights are significant, because they impose severe limitations on what a party other than the author can do with a work. Because moral rights are generally inalienable (they cannot be assigned or waived), if a third party acquires an author's entire right under copyright to a particular work, that party's hands may still be tied with respect to certain uses of the work. Imagine the consequences if a software developer hired a programmer to write code, acquired the programmer's entire copyright to the code, but then could not make changes to it. Under regular business practices in the United States, the outcome would be disastrous.

[183] Huston v. la Cinq, 1991 Bull. Civ. No. 89-19.522.

[C] Moral Rights in the United States

[1] Berne Convention

Because moral rights have been perceived in the United States to impose significant if not insurmountable hurdles to the commercial exploitation of a variety of copyrightable works, there has been considerable resistance to any effort to recognize such rights under U.S. law.

For this reason, the United States has resisted implementing moral rights. This became a significant issue when the United States acceded to the Berne Convention (the most important international copyright treaty) in 1989. Article 6*bis* of the Berne Convention provides as follows:

> (1) Independently of the author's economic rights, and even after the transfer of the said rights, the author shall have the right to claim authorship of the work and to object to any distortion, mutilation, or other modification of, or other derogatory action in relation to, the said work, which would be prejudicial to his honor or reputation
>
> (2) The rights granted to the author in accordance with the preceding paragraph shall, after his death, be maintained, at least until the expiry of the economic rights, and shall be exercisable by the persons or institutions authorized by the legislation of the country where protection is claimed . . .[184]

Ultimately, a compromise was effected by Congress declaring (despite several judicial proclamations to the contrary[185]) that existing U.S. law adequately provided for the rights required by Article 6*bis*, and therefore no special legislation was required to implement this Article. Because Article 6*bis* also provides (in a later provision not quoted above) that the enforcement of moral rights is left to the laws of each member country, courts have a great deal of flexibility in granting or denying the rights provided for in Article 6*bis*. Even though the 1994 Uruguay Round of the General Agreement on Tariffs and Trade (GATT), signed into law April 15, 1994, required each member country (including the United States) to more effectively comply with Articles 1 through 21 of the Berne Convention, Article 6*bis* was excluded from this requirement.[186]

[2] Other Methods of Creating Moral Rights Under U.S. Law

There are methods under U.S. law of attempting to secure the rights provided in Article 6*bis*. A selection of copyright law, unfair competition under the Lanham

---

[184] The Berne Convention (Paris Text—July 24, 1971), Article 6*bis*.

[185] Vargas v. Esquire, Inc., 164 F.2d 522 (7th Cir. 1947); Crimi v. Rutgers Presbyterian Church, 194 Misc. 570, 89 N.Y.S.2d 813 (Sup. Ct. 1949).

[186] Act of Dec. 8, 1994, Pub. L. No. 103-465, 103d Cong., 2d Sess., 108 Stat. 4809.

Act, defamation, or various state laws may help achieve the desired goals. However, artists historically have had mixed luck using these methods.

[a] Reverse Passing Off

In general, U.S. copyright law does not grant authors a right of attribution, that is, the right to be identified as the author of a particular work (or, conversely, the right *not* to be associated with a mutilated, distorted, or altered work). There are exceptions, such as the right of attribution afforded by the Visual Artists Rights Act (discussed below in § 1.04[C][3]) and under state statutes (discussed below in § 1.04[C][4]). However, these rights are limited in their application to specified works of art or works of "fine art."

One way for an author to attempt to enforce a right of attribution is through § 43(a) of the Lanham Act,[187] discussed above in § 1.03. These attempts have met with varied degrees of success.

The leading case in which § 43(a) was used to secure a right of attribution is *Smith v. Montoro.*[188] In *Smith,* an actor brought suit against a film distributor for deleting his name from the credits of a film in which he had starred, and inserting the name of another actor in its place. The Ninth Circuit held such conduct constituted a "false designation of origin" under § 43(a).

Others have tried to use § 43(a) to provide a claim for "misattribution" of authorship when a plaintiff claims that the defendant used his work and called it his own. Often such claims are disallowed. Several courts have held that if the crux of a party's claim is copyright infringement, he cannot assert an additional § 43(a) claim based on failure to identify him as the author of the allegedly infringing work. For example, in *Merchant v. Lymon,*[189] plaintiffs sought a declaration that they were co-authors of the song "Why Do Fools Fall In Love." Plaintiffs' copyright claim was barred by the statute of limitations. In dismissing plaintiffs' § 43(a) and state law unfair competition claims for failure to be credited as the authors of the song, the court noted that "plaintiffs' position that the Lanham Act covers circumstances where an author has not been properly credited for his authorship role would simply transform virtually every copyright action into a Lanham Act action as well."[190] Note that in *Smith,* there was no copyright claim (an actor's performance itself is not copyrightable), and thus the Lanham Act claim was not being used to substitute for a failed copyright claim.

In general, courts have held that statements of copyright ownership (or similar "proprietary" claims, such as labels or copyright notices), even if false,

---

[187] 15 U.S.C. § 1125(a).

[188] 648 F.2d 602 (9th Cir. 1981).

[189] 828 F. Supp. 1048 (S.D.N.Y. 1993), *rev'd on other grounds*, 92 F.3d 51 (2d Cir. 1996).

[190] 828 F. Supp. at 1060.

do not give rise to a § 43(a) claim, insofar as they only state to the public that the person or entity identified has the right to sell the work or the goods (even if that claim is wrong, the remedy is still a copyright action).[191] However, if an affirmative statement is made about the *creator* or *author* of a work that leaves out the alleged "true" creator or author, then a § 43(a) claim may be brought in addition to the copyright claim.[192]

Other unsuccessful attempts to use § 43(a) of the Lanham Act to create rights similar to moral rights have included: a claim that advertisement of a film rated PG as rated R constituted a false representation (no claim survived, because the defendant movie theater was not competitive with the plaintiff, and thus there was no unfair competition);[193] a claim that the placement of commercial advertisements at the beginning of a home video of plaintiff's film constituted a false designation of origin (no likelihood of consumer confusion as to the source or sponsorship of the commercials was found).[194] Trying a different approach, a professor brought a claim under 47 U.S.C. § 1983 as a result of being listed third rather than first in connection with an academic article written with two other professors, claiming that the failure to list him first deprived him of a property right without due process.[195] This claim was, somewhat predictably, rejected.

[b] Attribution of Authorship to Altered Version of Work

The landmark case *Gilliam v. American Broadcasting Co.*[196] held that material unauthorized alterations to a work constitute copyright infringement and that attributing authorship of the altered work to the original author constitutes false designation of origin. At issue was plaintiffs' "Monty Python's Flying Circus" television show, which had been licensed to the defendant, the American Broadcasting Corporation (ABC). ABC edited the program and removed 24 minutes, including elements the plaintiff regarded as essential to the humor and integrity of the original program. In addition to finding that copyright encompasses the right to make changes to a work, the *Gilliam* court also recognized under § 43(a) "the right of the artist to have his work attributed to him in the form in which he created it."[197] The court found that "the edited version broadcast by ABC

---

[191] *See* Kregos v. Associated Press, 937 F.2d 700 (2d Cir. 1991); Lipton v. Nature Co., 71 F.3d 464 (2d Cir. 1995); Banff Ltd. v. Express, Inc., 921 F. Supp. 1065 (S.D.N.Y. 1995).

[192] *See* Waldman Publ'g Corp. v. Landoll, Inc., 43 F.3d 775 (2d Cir. 1994); Kregos v. Associated Press, 937 F.2d 700 (2d Cir. 1991); Banff Ltd. v. Express, Inc., 921 F. Supp. 1065 (S.D.N.Y. 1995).

[193] Halicki v. United Artists Communications, Inc., 812 F.2d 1213 (9th Cir. 1987).

[194] Paramount Pictures Corp. v. Video Broad. Sys., Inc., 724 F. Supp. 808 (D. Kan. 1989).

[195] Weinstein v. University of Ill., 811 F.2d 1091 (7th Cir. 1987).

[196] 538 F.2d 14 (2d Cir. 1976).

[197] 538 F.2d at 24.

impaired the integrity of appellants' work and represented to the public as the product of the appellants what was actually a mere caricature of their talents."[198]

This "false designation of origin" theory was also applied in *King v. Innovation Books, Div. of Innovative Corp.*,[199] in which the Second Circuit considered whether a film very loosely derived from a Stephen King short story entitled "The Lawnmower Man" could be advertised as "Stephen King's *The Lawnmower Man*." The only points of similarity between the two stories are the presence of an unusual person (in one case simple-minded, in the other a servant of a pagan god) who is hired to mow the lawn, and the psychokinetic movement of a lawnmower resulting in murder, leaving the victim's remains in a backyard birdbath. Beyond that, the stories are entirely different, with the film being primarily about a doctor's scientific experiments to improve human intelligence through the use of virtual reality (a theme nowhere present in King's story), with the lawnmower incident a mere detail. The court held that the film could not be advertised as "Stephen King's *The Lawnmower Man*," but could be billed as "based upon" the Stephen King story.

In the course of determining such claims, courts often make subjective determinations as to a particular work's value. While tampering with "Monty Python" was considered a violation, the shoddy printing of a law review article riddled with both substantive and nonsubstantive errors was not. In *Choe v. Fordham University School of Law*,[200] a law student was unsuccessful in claiming that the printing of a "mangled" version of his law review article and identifying him as the author constituted a § 43(a) violation. The court disagreed, framing the issue as "whether the published Comment departed so substantially from the original work that Choe may be said not to be its author,"[201] and answering the question in the negative due to the fact that a reader of the Comment would not be so confused as to "fail to understand his argument." While this ruling may make sense when dealing with academic subject matter, when dealing with art it is less comforting to the artist, who wants not simply to have his story or plot "understood" but presumably to have his artistic vision recognized. The same result was reached in *Lish v. Harper's Magazine Foundation*,[202] in which plaintiff, a well-known and secretive writer who wrote a letter to students of his upcoming class, objected to Harper's Magazine publishing the letter after removing approximately 40 percent of its contents and doing nothing to indicate that the letter had been edited. The court found that while the nature of the magazine's activity

[198] 538 F.2d at 25.

[199] 976 F.2d 824 (2d Cir. 1992).

[200] 920 F. Supp. 44 (S.D.N.Y. 1995).

[201] 920 F. Supp. at 48.

[202] 807 F. Supp. 1090 (S.D.N.Y. 1992).

could give rise to a Lanham Act claim, there had not been "substantial distortion" sufficient to make the claim successful.

[3] Visual Artists Rights Act

The most significant "moral rights" statute in the United States is the Visual Artists Rights Act of 1990 (VARA), embodied in §§ 106A and 113(d) of the Copyright Act. VARA grants an "author of a work of visual art" rights of "attribution and integrity" distinct from those rights of a copyright owner. These rights allow an author to object to a use or distortion of his work if such use or distortion would damage the reputation or honor of the author.[203] The right of attribution entitles an artist to "claim authorship" of her work by demanding that the artist's name be used in conjunction with the work.[204] Conversely, this right empowers an author to prevent the use of her name as the author of a work that she did not in fact create (for example, an author might sue for damage to her reputation resulting from attributing to her a distorted work of visual art).[205]

The right of integrity enables an author to "prevent any intentional distortion, mutilation, or other modification of that work which would be prejudicial to his or her honor or reputation."[206] In addition, the right of integrity permits an author to prevent the destruction of "a work of recognized stature."[207] While an author cannot transfer these dual rights of attribution and integrity, she can waive them. For a waiver to be effective, however, VARA requires that the author expressly agree to such a waiver in a writing which identifies "the work, and uses of that work, to which the waiver applies."[208]

These rights are similar to the moral rights recognized abroad in that they protect authors regardless of whether they presently own the copyright. However, VARA is limited to protecting authors of paintings, sculptures, or photographs produced for exhibition only, or such works in a signed or numbered series of no more than 200[209] (the requirement that a series of works number less than 200 may be a formality that is inconsistent with the Berne Convention's prohibition on formalities).[210] VARA does not protect, *inter alia*, works made for hire, books,

---

[203] 17 U.S.C. § 106A(a)(2). *See generally* Carter v. Helmsley-Spear, Inc., 861 F. Supp. 303 (S.D.N.Y. 1994), *rev'd and vacated in part, aff'd in part*, 71 F.3d 77 (2d Cir. 1995), *cert. denied*, 116 S. Ct. 1824 (1996).

[204] 17 U.S.C. § 106A(a)(1).

[205] 17 U.S.C. § 106A(a)(2).

[206] 17 U.S.C. § 106A(a)(3)(A).

[207] 17 U.S.C. § 106A(a)(3)(B).

[208] 17 U.S.C. § 106A(e).

[209] 17 U.S.C. § 101 (definition of "work of visual art").

[210] *See* Roy S. Kaufman, The Berne Convention and American Protection of Artists' Moral Rights: Requirements, Limits, and Misconceptions, 15 Colum.-VLA J.L. & Arts, No. 3 (Spring 1991) at 429-30.

magazines, motion pictures, newspapers, posters, or advertising materials.[211] Moreover, the Act excludes from infringement the distortion of a work resulting from the "passage of time or the inherent nature of the materials" or that results from conservation efforts or public presentation (unless caused by gross negligence).[212] Additionally, an exception applies to works that are incorporated into or made part of a building. If the work's incorporation into the building is such that "removing the work from the building will cause the destruction, distortion, mutilation, or other modification of the work,"[213] the integrity right is inapplicable, provided that the artist appropriately (pursuant to the statutory scheme) consented to the installation of the work in the building.[214] Additionally, if a work of art is present in a building without permission (the artist was trespassing, as in the case of most graffiti murals), then there is no VARA right.[215]

[4] State Laws

Several states have enacted statutes which provide some form of moral right protection. Statutes in California,[216] Connecticut,[217] Louisiana,[218] Maine,[219] Massachusetts,[220] New Jersey,[221] New Mexico,[222] New York,[223] Pennsylvania,[224] and Rhode Island[225] all restrict uses of works of fine art in altered or mutilated forms and grant authors a right of attribution. Other state statutes, such as those of Utah,[226] Georgia,[227] and Montana,[228] grant certain protections to artists who create works on commission for state-sponsored programs. Some of the rights created by these statutes may be preempted, however, by the Copyright Act or by VARA. The Copyright Act preempts state laws which create "all legal or

---

[211] *Id.*

[212] 17 U.S.C. § 106A(c).

[213] 17 U.S.C. § 113(d).

[214] *Id. See generally* Martin v. City of Indianapolis, 982 F. Supp. 625 (S.D. Ind. 1997).

[215] English v. BFC & R East 11th Street LLC, 1997 WL 746444 (S.D.N.Y. 1997), *aff'd*, 198 F.3d 233 (2d Cir. 1999) (table).

[216] Cal. Civ. Code § 987.

[217] Conn. Gen. Stat. § § 42-116s and 42-116t.

[218] La. Rev. Stat. tit. 51, § § 2151-2156.

[219] Me. Rev. Stat. tit. 27 § 303.

[220] Mass. Gen. Laws ch. 231, § 85S.

[221] N.J. Stat. Ann. tit. 2A, § § 24A-1 to 24A-8.

[222] N.M. Stat. Ann. ch. 13. art. 4B.

[223] N.Y. Arts & Cult. Aff. Title C, art. 11-14.

[224] Pa. Stat. Ann. tit. 73, § § 2101-2110.

[225] R.I. Gen. Laws § § 5-62-2 to 5-62-6.

[226] Utah Code Ann. tit. 9, ch. 6 § § 401-409.

[227] Ga. Code Ann. § § 8-5-1–8-5-9.

[228] Mont. Code Ann. tit. 22, ch. 2 § § 401-408.

equitable rights that are equivalent to any of the exclusive rights"[229] afforded by the Copyright Act. Any state statute that places limitations on a person's right to reproduce, modify, distribute, perform, or publicly display[230] a work that is fixed in a tangible form will be preempted by the Copyright Act. Therefore, if a state statute restricts the right to publicly display a work in altered form, that may be preempted by the Copyright Act's exclusive right of public display and the right to create derivative works. In such a case, the author would likely *not* have a right or remedy under the state statute, but would have to bring an action for copyright infringement.

However, there are clear gaps left by copyright and trademark laws that can be filled by these state statutes. One such case involved an artist, David Wojnarowicz, whose work was targeted by an organization called the American Family Association as "indecent." The AFA produced a pamphlet, entitled "Your Tax Dollars Helped Pay For These 'Works of Art.' " The AFA included in the pamphlet fragments of various of Wojnarowicz's works, taken from a recent exhibit, and identified Wojnarowicz as the artist. Wojnarowicz brought suit for copyright infringement, Lanham Act violations, and violation of the New York Artist's Authorship Rights Act.[231]

Wojnarowicz's copyright claims were dismissed because the AFA's use was held to be a fair use, a rationale similar to the holding in a suit brought by Hustler Magazine against the Moral Majority.[232] Wojnarowicz's Lanham Act claims were dismissed because the use was not employed in the advertising or promotion of goods or services, which the court found to be a requirement for a Lanham Act violation.

However, Wojnarowicz was able to enjoin the AFA's distribution of the pamphlet containing fragments of his work, under the New York Artists' Authorship Rights Act. The Southern District of New York held (1) that the New York claim was not preempted by the Copyright Act because the right to prevent attribution to an artist of an altered or modified version of his work was an "extra element" that took the right out of the realm of copyright; and (2) that the defendant's photocopying of "cropped" images of Wojnarowicz's works, as well as excerpting and reproducing only small portions of Wojnarowicz's works, thereby reducing the multi-imaged works to solely sexual images, constituted an "altered,

[229] 17 U.S.C. § 301.

[230] *See* 17 U.S.C. § 106.

[231] Wojnarowicz v. American Family Ass'n, 745 F. Supp. 130 (S.D.N.Y. 1990).

[232] Hustler Magazine, Inc. v. Moral Majority, Inc., 796 F.2d 1148 (9th Cir. 1986). Hustler had published a cartoon depiction of Jerry Falwell that referred to him having sex with his mother in an outhouse. Falwell sued for defamation and lost. In the meantime, however, the Moral Majority reproduced the cartoon in a fundraising mailer, and Hustler sued for copyright infringement. The Moral Majority's use was found to be a "fair use" under the Copyright Act. For a further discussion on fair use, see § 1.02[I]).

defaced, mutilated, or modified" form of the work and thus violated the New York statute.

[5] Emerging Technologies and Moral Rights

Due to the limitations of the Visual Artists Rights Act and the spotty nature of the moral rights protection afforded under state laws, there may be a movement for stronger moral rights legislation to protect artists due to developing technologies. Computer imaging allows for distortions and new uses of works which the authors of those works likely never intended. While some may argue that this makes the need for moral rights legislation all the stronger, others will argue that legislation which restricts such activity will put a damper on creativity. This tension has so far been reconciled under U.S. law by giving short shift to moral rights-type claims except in the most egregious cases.

FORMS AND APPENDICES

Form 1-1: Work-for-Hire Agreement

Form 1-2: Short Form Assignment—Assignor's Form

Form 1-3: Long Form Assignment—Assignee's Form

Form 1-4: Simple Non-Exclusive Copyright License

Form 1-5: Sample Letter—Permission for Image in a Book—Narrow Grant

Form 1-6: Permission Request Form—Broad Grant

Form 1-7: Contract for Use of Art as Set Dressing in a Movie

Form 1-8: Stock Agency License

Form 1-9: Notice of Intent to Enforce a Restored Copyright

Form 1-10: Trademark License Agreement

Appendix 1-A: United States Copyright Office Circular 40—Copyright Registration for Works of the Visual Arts

Appendix 1-B: United States Copyright Office Circular 40a—Deposit Requirements for Registration of Claims to Copyright in Visual Arts Material

Appendix 1-C: Application Form VA*

Appendix 1-D: Instructions and Short Form VA*

Appendix 1-E: Selections from 1976 Copyright Law Act as Amended

---

* Included on companion CD-Rom.

FORM 1-1

Work-For-Hire Agreement (With Backup Assignment Language)

AGREEMENT

This Agreement is entered into between ____________ ("[Name]") on the one hand, and ______________________ ("Company") on the other.

Company has engaged __[Name]__ to create for Company certain __[describe general nature of work]__ and other related works to be incorporated into the __[type of work, such as "audio/visual"]__ work "______________" (referred to collectively herein as the "Works").

For good and valuable consideration, the receipt and sufficiency of which ____[Name]__ hereby acknowledges, __[Name]__ hereby acknowledges and agrees that the Works are and/or were created as works made for hire for Company under the United States Copyright Act, and that Company is to be considered the author of the works for purposes of copyright. To the extent that the Works may be ineligible for work-for-hire status, __[Name]__ hereby irrevocably sells, transfers, and assigns to Company all present and future right, title and interest in and to the Works, in any and all media now known or hereafter developed, including but not limited to worldwide copyright rights therein (and all renewals and extensions thereof) along with all causes of action, including those for infringement, known or unknown, which have accrued or will accrue, from the conception or creation of each such work.

Without limiting the foregoing, Company will have the sole and exclusive right to reproduce, publish, display, publicly perform, sell, and otherwise the Works, or to refrain therefrom, and to grant such rights to others.

__[Name]__ agrees to take such further steps and execute such further documents as Company may deem necessary or appropriate to confirm, implement or enforce the rights granted and/or confirmed hereunder, and this obligation will remain in effect following cessation, for any reason, of __[Name]__'s engagement by, or relationship with, Company. Should ____[Name]____ fail to take such further steps or execute such further documents promptly upon request, Company may, in the name of, and on behalf of, Assignee, take such steps or execute such documents and make appropriate disposition of the same, and Assignee hereby irrevocably appoints Company as his or her lawful attorney-in-fact with full power to do so. This power of attorney is coupled with an interest and is irrevocable. Nothing herein may be construed to limit any of the rights or remedies of Company in any respect. This Agreement will be effective upon the earlier of Company's initial engagement of __[Name]__ and/or the first creation of the Works.

This Agreement constitutes the parties' entire understanding with respect to the subject matter hereof, and all prior or contemporaneous agreements, whether oral or written, are hereby merged herein. This Agreement is entered into in the State of ___________, and is governed by the laws thereof pertaining to the making and performing of contracts. Both parties waive any objection to the personal jurisdiction or venue of the state or federal courts of the State of _________________.

[NAME]	COMPANY
______________________	______________________________
Signature	By ____________________
Date signed:___________	Title: ____________________
	Date signed:______________

FORM 1-2

Short Form Assignment—Assignor's Form

I, Jane Artist, for $1.00 and other good and valuable consideration, do hereby assign to Joe Publisher all of my rights, title and interest in and to the copyrights of my painting entitled "Moonlight Over Cambodia" (the "Work", a copy of which is attached hereto) [and my rights, title and interest in and to the copyright registrations pertaining thereto]. The Work is [not] registered in the United States Copyright Office [, Registration # ________]. For the avoidance of doubt, this document does not transfer title to the Work itself.

____

Signature

FORM 1-3

Long Form Assignment—Assignee's Form

COPYRIGHT ASSIGNMENT

WHEREAS, Jane Artist, an individual residing at ____ (the "Assignor"), owns certain copyrights which are associated with the work entitled "Moonlight Over Cambodia," a copy of which is attached hereto (the "Work"); and

WHEREAS, John Publisher, an individual residing at ____ (the "Assignee") is desirous of acquiring all said copyrights;

NOW, THEREFORE, in consideration of One Dollar ($1.00) and other good and valuable consideration, the receipt and sufficiency of which are hereby acknowledged, the Assignor does hereby sell, assign and the transfer to the Assignee, its successors and assigns, with full title guarantee, all right, title and interest in all the copyrights associated with the Work, and all of the Assignor's rights in copyright registrations related thereto, if any, and all individual rights comprised in the copyrights which exist or may exist in any nation throughout the world, and the right to apply for copyright registrations and renewals and extensions thereof, for the full term of copyright and any renewals and extensions thereof in all media now known or hereafter devised, together with all rights of action and claims for damages and benefits arising because of past or future infringements of said copyrights. Assignor hereby waives any claims to the fullest extent permissible by law for damages based upon reproduction of the Work in its current or any modified form, and any so-called moral rights or their equivalents arising with respect to the reproduction of the Work.

Assignor shall promptly, upon the written request of Assignee, execute such other documents of conveyance as Assignee shall reasonably require to confirm or record this assignment of rights. If Assignor fails to do so in a timely manner upon written request of Assignee, Assignee shall have the full right and authority to execute such documents in the name of Assignor.

IN WITNESS WHEREOF, the Assignor has executed this instrument as of the 1st day of January, 2000.

Jane Artist

____

STATE OF ____________)
) ss.:
COUNTY OF ________)

On this ___ day of ____________ 20__, before me personally appeared Jane Artist, to me personally know, who, being duly sworn, did execute the foregoing instrument in her name.

____

Notary Public

FORM 1-4

Simple Non-Exclusive Copyright License

This license (the "License"), granted by ____________ (the "Licensor") to ______________ (the "Licensee") as of the ____ day of _______ 2000, covers the following terms:

1. The Work. The work (the "Work") subject to this license is "__________" performed by / written by ______________.

2. The Use. Licensee's use (the "Use") covered by this License is ______________________.

3. Territory. The "Territory" covered hereby is worldwide.

4. License to ________________. In consideration of the sum of __________($___.00), Licensor hereby grants to Licensee the non-exclusive right, license, privilege, and authority to [copy, distribute, record, use, publicly perform, display, create a derivative work, etc.] the Work in the Territory.

5. License Limited to Express Provisions Herein Stated. This License does not authorize or permit any use of the Work not expressly set forth herein.

6. Duration of License. This License in its entirety will be for __________ from the date hereof.

7. Warranty. Licensor warrants and represents that it is the owner of and/or authorized agent for one hundred percent (100%) of the rights in the Work, that it has the full right and authority to enter into this License and grant the rights herein described; that the Work is original and does not and will not constitute an infringement of any copyright; that the use by Licensee of the Work is expressly authorized herein and will not infringe upon or violate the rights of any third party; no other rights, permission or consent are necessary for Licensee's use of the Work; and no fees, royalties, or reuse payments of any kind will be due in connection with the rights granted to Licensee hereunder, other than as provided in Paragraph 4 above. Licensor agrees to indemnify and hold harmless Licensee (and its employees, directors, officers, shareholders, and agents) from any claim, loss, liability, damage or expense (including reasonable attorneys' fees) arising out of any claim, lawsuit or demand which is inconsistent with the warranties, covenants, and representations herein.

8. Non-Exclusive License. All rights granted hereunder to Licensee are granted on a non-exclusive basis.

9. Transfers, Assignments, etc. This License is binding upon and will inure to the benefit of the respective successors, licensees, heirs, administrators, and assigns of the parties hereto.

10. Applicable Law. This License is governed by the laws and in the state and federal courts of the State of New York and both parties waive any objections to the personal jurisdiction and venue of such courts.

IN WITNESS WHEREOF, the parties have set their hands and seals to the foregoing as of the day and year first set forth above.

LICENSOR	LICENSEE
By:____________________	By: ____________________
Title: ____________________	Title: ____________________

FORM 1-5

Sample Letter—Permission for Image in a Book—Narrow Grant

Permission is granted for one-time, non-exclusive English language rights to reproduce William Goodartist's painting, *True Blue*, in the forthcoming book entitled, Rights: How to Protect Them, to be published by Best Book Co. in 1999. The reproduction will be ½ page in color. **Distribution of the book is limited to 10,000 copies.**

These rights are limited to the specific media and number of copies detailed above. This means that if additional copies or new editions are to be printed/published in the media above, or new versions created in any other media whatsoever, including, but not limited to, electronic and multimedia, then VAGA's prior written authorization MUST be obtained. All reproductions must be full-toned black and white or full color and may not be reproduced on colored paper stock. There shall be no alteration of the image, including, but not limited to, cropping, overprinting and bleeding off the page. VAGA shall take all actions necessary to police and enforce these requirements.

Permission is given on condition that the following copyright credit line appear below or adjacent to the image along with the name of artist, title, year, size, media and owner (if applicable) unless otherwise authorized by VAGA. The copyright credit line listed below must appear with the image and may not be placed solely on a separate credit page.

Failure to insert the proper copyright credit line and caption information as set forth herein shall result in a revocation of this license and a 100% surcharge on the invoice amount.

© William Goodartist /Licensed by VAGA, New York, NY

VAGA requires that upon publication 1 copy of the book be sent for its archives or for distribution to the artist. Failure to provide the required samples shall result in a 100% surcharge on the invoiced amount.

An invoice ( ) is enclosed for this use.

Sincerely,

Robert Panzer
Executive Director

encl.

Please sign below and return by fax to VAGA to confirm your receipt and acceptance of the above requirements.

By (Signature): ______________________________

Print Name: ________________________________

FORM 1-6

Permission Request Form—Broad Grant

[Date]

To:

I am preparing a manuscript for a book to be published by __________ on the subject of ____________. The book, which is tentatively entitled ______________________, has an estimated publication date of ______________.

I request your permission to include the following artworks in this and all subsequent editions of the above-referenced book, including versions made by nonprofit organizations for use by blind or physically handicapped persons, and in all foreign language translations and other derivative works in all media of expression now know or later developed, published or prepared by ___________, or its licensees, for distribution throughout the world.

Name of Artwork(s) ____

Artist(s) ____

Copyright date(s) _______________________

(If necessary attach continuation sheet)

Please indicate agreement by signing and returning the enclosed copy of this letter. In signing, you warrant that you are the sole owner of the rights granted and that your material does not infringe upon the copyright or other rights of anyone. If you do not control these rights, I would appreciate your letting me know to whom I should apply.

Thank you

Name

AGREED TO AND ACCEPTED:
by: ____
Signature   Title   Date
Credit and/or copyright notice:____________________________________
____
____
____

FORM 1-7

Contract for Use of Art as Set Dressing in a Movie

Dated as of , 1999. Agreement between VAGA at 350 Fifth Avenue, Suite 6305, New York, NY 10118 and [producer/studio, etc.] at Contact: Tel:

This is with reference to your motion picture currently entitled ("Picture") and the agreement between you and VAGA relating to the right to reproduce a work of art entitled " " ("Art") by ("Artist") in featured use as set decoration in said Picture.

VAGA hereby grants you, your successors, assigns and licensees the non-exclusive right to use said Art (or a reproduction of said Art) as set decoration in the Picture in connection with the exhibition of the Picture in all media, and all manner including but not limited to videocassette, videotape, videodisc, or other technology, now or hereafter known, at any time throughout the universe. This includes the right to reproduce a portion of the Picture for trailers and for still photographs. The Art may not be used except as set decoration as filmed.

Uses of the Art for promotion, advertising, merchandise or for any other use whatsoever are prohibited.

All reproductions must be at least 15% larger or smaller than the original Art.

Permission is given on the condition that the following credit line appear on-screen in the credit sequence at the beginning or end of the film:

Art by is:
© /Licensed by VAGA, New York, NY

The following notice shall be prominently and permanently placed on a tag on the front of each reproduction of the Art prior to storage:

"See Reverse"

The following notice shall be prominently placed on the reverse of each reproduction of the Art.

> "This is a reproduction of a work of art protected by copyright. All uses of this reproduction must first be cleared in writing from:
>
> VAGA
> 350 Fifth Avenue
> Suite 6305
> New York, NY 10118
> Tel: 212-736-6666
> Fax: 212-736-6767"

VAGA represents and warrants that it is the authorized representative for the Artist or Artist's Estate and has the full right and authority to grant the rights herein, and that no one else's permission is required.

To the extent that the Picture is made into a videocassette, then one courtesy copy of the Picture on videocassette shall be sent to VAGA, when available to the general public. It is expressly agreed that such courtesy video is for personal use only by recipient and may not be commercially exploited in any manner whatsoever. Failure to provide the videocassette shall result in a 100% penalty fee.

In consideration for the rights granted herein to you, upon execution of this agreement, you shall pay to the undersigned the sum of . (Invoice # enclosed.) Should you notify VAGA in writing that you have chosen not to use said Art, and such notice is sent to VAGA within 90 days of the date of this agreement, then VAGA shall refund 75% of the invoiced amount per work of art. If notification is sent to VAGA after the 90 day period, VAGA shall refund 50%. An invoice (#) is enclosed.

ACCEPTED AND AGREED TO: VAGA	ACCEPTED AND AGREED TO:
By:________________________	By:________________________
Name: Robert Panzer	Name:
Executive Director	Title:

FORM 1-8

Stock Agency License

We recommend placing a logo, if any, in the upper left or right of this page, aligning with the left or right hand side of this column as shown here. Copy should begin 2 inches from the top of the page. To place a logo, put your cursor where you want to insert the logo and select "picture" from the "insert" menu. Find the logo you want to place. **If you do not wish to include a logo simply select and delete this copy from the form.**

INVOICE

To: ----

Our Invoice Number: ----

Our Delivery Contract: ----

Your Purchase Order Number: ----

Your Job Number: ----

Your Client Product: ----

Date of Billing: ----

Image Description and Number	Rights Granted	Amount
----	----	----
----	----	----
----	----	----
----	----	----
----	----	----
----	----	----
----	----	----
----	----	----
----	----	----
----	----	----
	Subtotal	
	Delivery Fee	----
	Total Due	----

Unless otherwise stated rights granted above expire one year from the date on this invoice.
All rights not specifically granted are reserved for copyright holder.

The materials listed above must be returned in the same condition as delivered.
A service charge of 2% per month will be added on all balanced over 30 days past due.
The terms and conditions set forth on the reversed side are deemed incorporated herein and made a part thereof.

SUBJECT TO TERMS BELOW

Submission of images for examination or use is conditioned upon recipient agreeing to all the terms contained herein. If you object to any of these terms, including the arbitration or stipulated damage provisions, you must return the images immediately.

Terms Relative to Submission and Use

1. Transparencies, negatives, prints or digital images (hereafter "images") may be held for fourteen (14) days' approval. Unless a longer period is requested and granted by [Agency, Inc.], (hereafter " "), in writing, a holding fee of Five ($5.00) Dollars per week per image will be charged after such 14-day period and up to the time of return.
2. Images may not be used in any way, including layouts, sketches, scans or photostats, until submission of and payment of an invoice indicating Recipient's right to use same, or indicating purchase of the Images outright, which shall be only on terms of use hereinafter specified.
3. Recipient is responsible for loss or damage to the Images delivered to it, from time of receipt until their return to [Agency]. Recipient shall be responsible for safe delivery and return of Images to [Agency] and shall indemnify [Agency] against any loss or damage to Images in transit or while in the possession of Recipient. This agreement is not considered a bailment and is specifically conditioned upon the item so delivered being returned to [Agency] in the same condition as delivered. Projection of transparencies is not permitted. Recipient assumes an insurer's liability herein for the safe and undamaged return of the Images to [Agency]. Such Images are to be returned by bonded messenger or by registered mail (return receipt requested), prepaid and fully insured.
4. The monetary damage for loss or damage of an original color transparency or photograph shall be determined by the value of each individual photograph. Recipient agrees, however, that the reasonable value of such lost or damaged photograph or transparency shall be Fifteen Hundred ($1,500.00) Dollars. [Agency] agrees to the delivery of the goods herein only upon the express covenant and understanding by Recipient that the terms contained in this Paragraph 4 are material to this agreement. Recipient assumes full liability for its employees, agents, assigns, messengers and free-lance researchers for the loss, damage or misuse of the Images.
5. (a) Unless otherwise specifically stated, Images remain the property of [Agency] or the particular photographers. Upon submission of and payment of an invoice by [Agency], a license only is granted to use the Images for the use specified on the invoice and for no other purpose, unless such Images are purchased outright. Such use is granted for the United States only, unless otherwise specified. Recipient does not acquire any right, title or interest in or to any image, including, without limitation, any electronic reproduction or promotional rights, and will not make, authorize or permit any use of the particular photograph(s), plate(s) or digital files made therefrom other than as specified herein. Full credit and copyright information must remain with file. (b) Images are to be returned within 4 months after date of invoice, except in cases of outright purchase. Recipient agrees to pay, as reasonable charges, the sum of $5.00 per week per Image after such 4-month period to date of return.
6. No model releases or other releases exist on any Images unless the existence of such release is specified in writing by [Agency]. Recipient shall indemnify [Agency] against all claims arising out of the use of any Images where the existence of such release has not been specified in writing by [Agency]. In any event, the limit of liability of [Agency] shall be the sum paid to it per the invoice for the use of the particular photograph involved. User will hold [Agency] harmless from all claims for the use of the Images, including defamatory use. Agency gives no rights or warranties with respect to the use of names, trademark, logo types, registered or copyrighted designs or works of art depicted in any picture, and the client must satisfy himself that all necessary rights, consents or permission as may be required for reproduction are secured.
7. This agreement is not assignable or transferable on the part of Recipient.
8. This contract contains all the terms of the agreement between us (agency and recipient) concerning delivery and review of images, and no term or conditions may be added or deleted unless made in writing and signed by both of us. These terms and the terms of any subsequent invoice/copyright license supersede any and all terms of the client's purchase order. Any subsequent invoice/copyright license you may issue, may contain additional terms relating to the rights granted and the type of use allowed.
9. Time is of the essence in the performance by Recipient of its obligations for payments and return of Images hereunder. No rights are granted until payment is made to [Agency], even though Recipient has received an invoice.
10. Payment herein is to be net thirty (30) days. A service charge of two (2%) percent per month on any unpaid balance will be charged thereafter. Any claims for adjustment or rejection of terms must be made to [Agency] within ten (10) days after receipt of invoice. In the event that any Images are used by Recipient in publications, then Recipient shall send to [Agency], on a semiannual basis (June 30th and December 31st), a certified statement setting forth the total number of sales, sublicenses, adaptations, translations and

any other uses. Recipient shall provide [Agency] with two (2) free copies of such publication immediately upon printing.

11. Rights are being reserved to recipient when an invoice is created. If recipient does not use the invoiced image, it must notify Agency] within five (5) days from receipt of the invoice. If recipient fails to do so, it is responsible for full payment on the invoice.
12. Images used editorially should bear a credit line as indicated by [Agency]. Recipient must register copyright in their name to afford protection to the photograph. Such copyright shall be immediately reassigned upon request, without charge.
13. All rights not specifically granted herein to Recipient are reserved for [Agency's] use and disposition without any limitations whatsoever.
14. Recipient agrees that the above terms are made pursuant to Article 2 of the UNIFORM COMMERCIAL CODE and agrees to be bound by same. Objection to any terms must be made in writing within ten (10) days.

Disputes or Claims Arising out of Submission and/or Use

15. Any and all disputes, with the exception of copyright claims, arising out of, under or in connection with this agreement, including, without limitation, the validity, interpretation, performance and breach hereof, shall be settled by arbitration in [Agency's City], pursuant to the rules of the American Arbitration Association. Judgment upon the award rendered may be entered in the highest court of the forum, State or Federal, having jurisdiction. This agreement, its validity and effect, shall be interpreted under and governed by the laws of the State of [ ]. If recipient of this contract is an agent for or an employee of a non-U.S. company but operates in a place of business in the United States or its territories, said recipient expressly agrees that any dispute regarding this contract shall be adjudicated within the United States in the manner described here.
16. Copyright claims shall be brought in the Federal Court having jurisdiction.
17. If [Agency] is caused to present claims or suit as a result of any breach of the above terms set forth, it shall be made whole for such reasonable legal fees or costs by recipient or user herein.

FORM 1-9

Notice of Intent to Enforce a Restored Copyright

Notice of Intent to Enforce a Restored Copyright Restored under the Uruguay Round Agreements Act (URAA):

1. Title:____________________________________ (If this work does not have a title, state "No title.")

OR

Brief description of work (for untitled works only):

____

2. English translation of title (if applicable):

____

3. Alternative title(s) (if any):____________________

____

4. Type of work:________________________________
(e.g. painting, sculpture, music, motion picture, sound recording, book)

5. Name of author(s):____________________________

____

6. Source country:_______________________________

7. Approximate year of publication:_____________________

8. Additional identifying information:____________________

____

(e.g. for movies: director, leading actors, screenwriter, animator; for photographs: subject matter; for books: editor, publisher, contributors, subject matter).

9. Name of copyright owner:___________________________
(Statements may be filed in the name of the owner of the restored copyright or the owner of an exclusive right therein.)

10. If you are not the owner of all rights, specify the rights you own:

____

(e.g. the right to reproduce/distribute/publicly display/publicly perform the work, or to prepare a derivative work based on the work)

11. Address at which copyright owner may be contacted:

____

____

____

(Give the complete address, including the country and an "attention" line, or "in care of" name, if necessary.)

12. Telephone number of owner:________________________________

13. Telefax number of owner:__________________________________

14. Certification and Signature: I hereby certify that, for each of the work(s) listed above, I am the copyright owner, or the owner of an exclusive right, or the owner's authorized agent, the agency relationship having been constituted in a writing signed by the owner before the filing of this notice, and that the information given herein is true and correct to the best of my knowledge.

Signature:____
Name (printed or typed):___________________________
As agent for (if applicable):_________________________
Date:____

NOTE: Notices of Intent to Enforce must be in English, except for the original title, and either typed or printed by hand legibly in dark, preferably black, ink. They must be on 8- by 11-inch white paper of good quality, with at least a 1-inch (or 3 cm) margin.

FORM 1-10

Trademark License Agreement

This Agreement is made this day of , 20__, between ______________, ("Licensor") and ______________________ ("Licensee").

WHEREAS, Licensor is the owner of certain trademarks; and

WHEREAS, Licensee wishes to obtain a non-exclusive license to use certain specified trademarks of Licensor under the terms and conditions of this Agreement;

NOW THEREFORE, for mutual considerations, the receipt and sufficiency of which are severally acknowledged, Licensor and Licensee agree as follows:

1. Trademark Ownership

(a) Licensee acknowledges and agrees that Licensee is the sole and exclusive owner of the entire right, title, and interest (including any and all accompanying goodwill) in and to the trademarks described in Exhibit A, collectively referred to as the "Licensed Marks".

(b) Licensee agrees that this Agreement gives it no rights whatsoever to the Licensed Marks except as specifically provided hereunder.

2. Territory

The Territory for this Agreement is the United States.

3. Trademark License

Licensor grants to Licensee a nonexclusive limited license to (a) use the Licensed Marks as trademarks in the applicable Territory only in connection with the following goods and services: ________________________________, subject to the following conditions:

(a) Licensee is not in default of any term or condition of this Agreement;

(b) Licensee will acknowledge in all usages of a Licensed Mark that each Licensed Mark (if registered in the Territory) is "a registered trademark of ___________" and that each Licensed Mark is "licensed by ______________" to Licensee. Licensee will include the above acknowledgment in conjunction with all usages of the Licensed Marks. Licensee will also cause the □ symbol to appear next to each of the Licensed Marks registered in the applicable Territory (or in any country of usage within the Territory) at least once in all published usages of such Licensed Marks; and to use the □ or □ (whichever is applicable) next to each of the Licensed Marks unregistered in the applicable Territory (or in any country of usage within the Territory) at least once in all published usages of such Licensed Marks.

(c) Except for its licensed use of the Licensed Marks hereunder, Licensee will not adopt or use any mark, logo, insignia, or design that is or is likely to be confusingly similar to or cause deception or mistake with respect to any of the Licensed Marks;

(d) Licensee may use the Licensed Marks only in connection with ________________ and

(e) Licensee may not ship goods or provide services under any of the Licensed Marks without the prior written consent of Licensor.

4. Quality Control

(a) Licensee agrees that it will not use the Licensed Marks in a manner that would be offensive to good taste or would injure the reputation of Licensor and/or the Licensed Marks.

(b) Licensee agrees to permit Licensor and its designated representatives, at any time, to inspect the operations of Licensee at Licensee's place of business during normal working hours to ensure that the products and services provided under the Licensed Marks are up to Licensor's quality standards. If, in the judgment of Licensor, an inspection reveals deficiencies in quality of services, products, or materials bearing the Licensed Marks, Licensee agrees promptly to rectify all such deficiencies in quality to the satisfaction of Licensor.

5. No Trademark Registration by Licensee

Licensee agrees that it will not, during the term hereof or at any time thereafter, make application for or aid or abet others to seek trademark registrations or recordings of trade names or company names in any state of the United States, in the United States Patent Office or other United States governmental agencies or in any foreign country of any mark or design which includes the Licensed Marks, or variations thereof, or limitations thereof, alone or in combination, except with the express prior written permission of Licensor, nor to contest Licensor's rights thereto. All goodwill and uses by Licensee of the Licensed Marks will inure to the benefit of Licensor. If Licensor deems it advisable to obtain design or trademark protection in connection with this Agreement, Licensee agrees to supply Licensor with all material it may request for such purposes and to give Licensor its full cooperation in connection therewith.

6. Infringement

Licensee agrees to notify Licensor promptly of any adverse claim and will fully cooperate in any proceeding or settlement Licensor deems advisable. Licensee will have no right or obligation to proceed against or make any settlement with infringers and Licensor will have sole control thereof; unless Licensor agrees otherwise in writing. Further, Licensee will notify Licensor of any suspected or actual infringements of Licensor's trademarks, unfair competition, "palming off", or other intellectual property rights violations.

7. Remedies

All remedies under this Agreement and under law are intended to be cumulative and not exclusive. Licensee acknowledges that Licensor has no adequate remedy hereunder or at law for Licensee's use of the Licensed Marks in violation of this Agreement and Licensor will be entitled to injunctive relief or other equitable remedies therefor.

8. No Assignment

This Agreement will bind and benefit the parties hereto and their respective successors and permitted assigns. The rights granted herein are personal to Licensee and may not be assigned, sub-licensed, or transferred, in whole or in part, by Licensee in any manner whatsoever, except with the prior written consent of Licensor. Any attempted assignment, transfer or sublicense of this Agreement, in whole or in part, in violation of the foregoing prohibition will be null and void, unless specifically ratified by Licensor. This license may be assigned by Licensor.

9. Warranty and Indemnity

(a) Licensee warrants and represents that it will respect all the Licensed Marks; that it will not claim or apply for registration of any Licensed Mark or a mark similar thereto; and that it will not violate the trademark, unfair competition, or the intellectual property right of Licensor or any third party.

(b) Licensee agrees at its own cost and expense to defend, indemnify and hold harmless Licensor (including, without limitation, Licensor's subsidiaries, affiliates, stockholders, directors, officers, employees, and agents), harmless from and against any and all loss, liability, claims, suits, actions, proceedings, judgments, awards, damages, and expense (including, without limitation, attorneys' fees) that they, or any of them, may incur or suffer which arise out of or is claimed by the claimant to arise out of any state of facts which would constitute a breach by Licensee of any representation, warranty, covenant, or term of this Agreement or by reason of the operation of Licensee's business. Licensor agrees to notify Licensee promptly of any claim hereunder. Licensor may, at its own expense, have counsel of its own choice represent Licensor or its affiliates in such matters. However, if Licensee fails promptly and diligently to defend, Licensor may, but will have no obligation to, defend, or settle the same without Licensee's consent and Licensee agrees to pay the costs of defense and/or settlement, including, without limitation, counsel fees, and any judgments, awards and settlements incurred by Licensor and its affiliates related thereto. Notwithstanding the foregoing, Licensor will have sole control of such proceedings and settlements at Licensee's expense if (i) the same would adversely affect the Licensed Marks, or (ii) an adverse result would irreparably damage Licensor's goodwill, or (iii) Licensee fails to provide Licensor, at its request, with proof satisfactory to Licensor of the financial responsibility of Licensee or its insurers for any judgments which may be entered or, absent such proof, with a satisfactory surety bond to assure such payment.

10. Insurance

Licensee will maintain liability insurance covering claims of trademark infringement, unfair competition, copyright infringement, and "palming off" in an amount determined by Licensor in its discretion.

11. Applicable Law

This Agreement will be construed under the laws and in the state and federal courts of the State of New York. Licensor and Licensee waive any objection to the personal jurisdiction and venue of such courts.

12. Notices

The written communications permitted or required by this Agreement are sufficiently conveyed to the other party if mailed first class by certified or registered mail, return receipt requested, postage prepaid, to the other party at the last known mailing address of the other party or to such other address as such other party may designate by written notice hereunder. All written communications given in compliance herewith will be effective on the date of mailing.

13. Severability

Any provision of this Agreement found to be invalid, unenforceable, or prohibited by law will be ineffective only to the extent of such invalidity, unenforceability, or prohibition without invalidating the rest of this Agreement.

14. Modifications

This Agreement may not be modified, except by written instrument signed by an authorized officer or partner of the party to be charged. This Agreement constitutes the complete understanding of the parties with respect to the subject matter hereof and supersedes all prior agreements and understandings.

15. Captions

The headings and captions in this Agreement are for the convenience of the parties and will have no effect on the interpretation of this Agreement.

16. Termination

(a) Licensor may terminate this Agreement and all of the rights licensed to Licensee hereunder, upon written notice to Licensee.

(b) Paragraphs 1(a), 5, 6, 7, 9, 11, 12, 13, 15, and this Paragraph 16(b) will survive termination of this Agreement for any reason.

IN WITNESS WHEREOF, the parties hereto have set their hands and seals to this Agreement as of the day and year above written.

____

By:______________________________

Title:______________________________

Date Signed:______________________________

____

By:______________________________

Title:______________________________

Date Signed:______________________________

EXHIBIT A

The Licensed Marks

APPENDIX 1-A

United States Copyright Office Circular 40

40

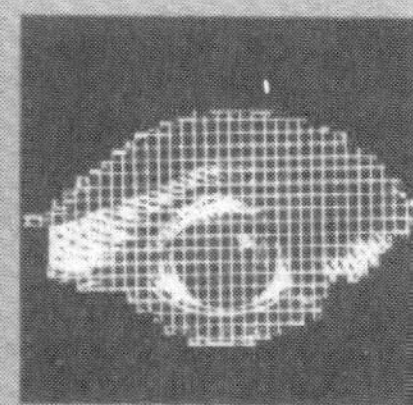

United States Copyright Office

Circular

Copyright Registration for Works of the Visual Arts

GENERAL INFORMATION

Copyright is a form of protection provided by the laws of the United States to the authors of "original works of authorship," including "pictorial, graphic, and sculptural works." The owner of copyright in a work has the exclusive right to make copies, to prepare derivative works, to sell or distribute copies, and to display the work publicly. Anyone else wishing to use the work in these ways must have the permission of the author or someone who has derived rights through the author.

Copyright Protection Is Automatic

Under the present copyright law, which became effective Jan. 1, 1978, a work is automatically protected by copyright when it is created. A work is created when it is "fixed" in a copy or phonorecord for the first time. Neither registration in the Copyright Office nor publication is required for copyright protection under the present law.

Advantages to Copyright Registration

There are, however, certain advantages to registration, including the establishment of a public record of the copyright claim. Copyright registration must generally be made before an infringement suit may be brought. Timely registration may also provide a broader range of remedies in an infringement suit.

Copyright Notice

Before March 1, 1989, the use of a copyright notice was mandatory on all published works, and any work first published before that date should have carried a notice. For works first published on or after March 1, 1989, use of the copyright notice is optional. For more information about copyright notice, request Circular 3, "Copyright Notice."

PUBLICATION

The copyright law defines "publication" as: the distribution of copies of a work to the public by sale or other transfer of ownership or by rental, lease, or lending. Offering to distribute copies to a group of persons for purposes of further distribution or public display also constitutes publication. A public display does not of itself constitute publication.

A work of art that exists in only one copy, such as a painting or statue, is not regarded as published when the single existing copy is sold or offered for sale in the traditional way, for example, through an art dealer, gallery, or auction house. A statue erected in a public place is not necessarily published.

When the work is reproduced in multiple copies, such as reproductions of a painting or castings of a statue, the work is published when the reproductions are publicly distributed or offered to a group for further distribution or public display.

Publication is an important concept in copyright because, among other reasons, whether a work is published or not may affect the number of copies and the type of material that must be deposited when registering the work. In addition, some works published in the United States become subject to mandatory deposit in the Library of Congress. These requirements are explained elsewhere in this circular.

WORKS OF THE VISUAL ARTS

Copyright protects original "pictorial, graphic, and sculptural works," which include two-dimensional and three-dimensional works of fine, graphic, and applied art. The following is a list of examples of such works:[1]

- Advertisements, commercial prints, labels
- Artificial flowers and plants
- Artwork applied to clothing or to other useful articles
- Bumper stickers, decals, stickers
- Cartographic works, such as maps, globes, relief models
- Cartoons, comic strips
- Collages
- Dolls, toys
- Drawings, paintings, murals
- Enamel works
- Fabric, floor, and wallcovering designs
- Games, puzzles
- Greeting cards, postcards, stationery
- Holograms, computer and laser artwork
- Jewelry designs
- Models
- Mosaics
- Needlework and craft kits
- Original prints, such as engravings, etchings, serigraphs, silk screen prints, woodblock prints
- Patterns for sewing, knitting, crochet, needlework
- Photographs, photomontages
- Posters
- Record jacket artwork or photography
- Relief and intaglio prints
- Reproductions, such as lithographs, collotypes
- Sculpture, such as carvings, ceramics, figurines, maquettes, molds, relief sculptures
- Stained glass designs
- Stencils, cut-outs
- Technical drawings, architectural drawings or plans, blueprints, diagrams, mechanical drawings
- Weaving designs, lace designs, tapestries

[1]Copyright protection extends to the design of a building created for the use of human beings. Architectural works created on or after Dec.1, 1990, or that on Dec. 1, 1990, were either unconstructed or embodied only in unpublished plans or drawings are eligible. For registration of architectural works, use Form VA. Request Circular 41, "Copyright Claims in Architectural Works," for more information.

Copyright protection for an original work of authorship does not extend to the following:

- Ideas, concepts, discoveries, principles
- Formulas, processes, systems, methods, procedures
- Words and short phrases, such as names, titles, and slogans
- Familiar symbols or designs
- Mere variations of typographic ornamentation, lettering, or coloring

USEFUL ARTICLES

A "useful article" is an article having an intrinsic utilitarian function that is not merely to portray the appearance of the article or to convey information. Examples are clothing, furniture, machinery, dinnerware, and lighting fixtures. An article that is normally part of a useful article may itself be a useful article, for example, an ornamental wheel cover on a vehicle.

Copyright does not protect the mechanical or utilitarian aspects of such works of craftsmanship. It may, however, protect any pictorial, graphic, or sculptural authorship that can be identified separately from the utilitarian aspects of an object. Thus, a useful article may have both copyrightable and uncopyrightable features. For example, a carving on the back of a chair or a floral relief design on silver flatware could be protected by copyright, but the design of the chair or flatware itself could not.

Some designs of useful articles may qualify for protection under the federal patent law. For further information, contact the Patent and Trademark Office at Commissioner of Patents and Trademarks, Washington, D.C. 20231 or via the Internet at www.uspto.gov. The telephone number is (800) 786-9199 and the TTY number is (703) 305-7785. The automated information line is (703) 308-4357.

Copyright in a work that portrays a useful article extends only to the artistic expression of the author of the pictorial, graphic, or sculptural work. It does not extend to the design of the article that is portrayed. For example, a drawing or photograph of an automobile or a dress design may be copyrighted, but that does not give the artist or photographer the exclusive right to make automobiles or dresses of the same design.

REGISTRATION PROCEDURES

If you choose to register a claim in your work, package together the following materials in the same envelope:

1. A properly completed application form
2. A nonreturnable deposit of the work to be registered, and
3. A nonrefundable filing fee of $30* in the form of a check or money order payable to the **Register of Copyrights** with each application

*NOTE: Filing fees are effective through June 30, 2002. For information on the fee changes, please write the Copyright Office, check the Copyright Office Website at www.loc.gov/copyright, or call (202) 707-3000.

Send the items to:

Library of Congress
Copyright Office
101 Independence Avenue, S.E.
Washington, D.C. 20559-6000

Application Form

Form VA is the appropriate form for registration of a work of the visual arts. The form should be completed legibly with black ink or type. Do not use pencil or send a carbon copy. All pertinent information should be given on the basic application form.

If you photocopy our forms, be sure that they are legible and printed head-to-head so that when you turn the sheet over, the top of page 2 is directly behind the top of page 1. Do not send two-page photocopies. The application must bear an original signature in ink. A continuation sheet supplied by the Copyright Office should be used only when all necessary information cannot be recorded on the basic form. No other attachments will be accepted. For information on ordering application forms and circulars, see "For Further Information" on page 6 of this circular.

DEPOSIT REQUIREMENTS

Circular 40a, "Deposit Requirements for Registration of Claims to Copyright in Visual Arts Material," provides a basic guide about material that should be sent when register-

3

ing a claim. Circular 40a also defines basic terms such as "complete copy," "best edition," and "identifying material." The following is a general outline of the deposit requirements:

Two-Dimensional Works

If unpublished, send one complete copy or identifying material.

If first published in the United States **on or after** Jan. 1, 1978, generally send two complete copies of the best edition.

If first published in the United States **before** Jan. 1, 1978, send two complete copies of the best edition as first published. Where identifying material is permitted or required, the identifying material must represent the work as first published.

If first published outside the United States **before March 1, 1989,** send one complete copy of the work as first published. Where identifying material is permitted or required, the identifying material must represent the work as first published.

If first published outside the United States **after March 1, 1989,** send one complete copy of either the first published edition or the best edition of the work.

Three-Dimensional Works and Two-Dimensional Works Applied to Three-Dimensional Objects

For published and unpublished works, send identifying material, such as photographs. **Do not** send the three-dimensional work.

Special Provisions

For some works first published in the United States, only **one copy** is required instead of two. These include:

- Greeting cards, picture postcards, stationery, business cards
- Games
- Pictorial matter or text on a box or container (where the contents of the container are not claimed)
- Contributions to collective works. The deposit may be either one complete copy of the best edition of the entire collective work, the complete section containing the contribution, the contribution cut from the collective work in which it appeared, or a photocopy of the contribution itself as it was published in the collective work.

For some works, identifying material is permitted, not required. For example, either identifying material or actual copies may be deposited for some unpublished works and for limited editions of posters or prints with certain qualifying conditions.

For all works that exceed 96 inches in any dimension, identifying material is required.

For additional information on what is permitted or required for registration of certain kinds of visual arts works, request Circular 40a and Circular 96, Sections 202.19, 20, and 21, which contains the deposit regulations of the Copyright Office.

Deposits cannot be returned.

REGISTRATION FOR TWO OR MORE WORKS WITH ONE APPLICATION AND FEE

Two or more individual works may be registered with one application and fee as follows:

Unpublished Works

A group of unpublished works may be registered as a collection if **all** the following conditions are met.

- The elements of the collection are assembled in an orderly form.
- The combined elements bear a single title identifying the collection as a whole.
- The copyright claimant or claimants for each element in the collection are the same.
- All the elements are by the same author, or if they are by different authors, at least one author has contributed copyrightable authorship to each element.

NOTE: Works registered as an unpublished collection will be listed in the records of the Copyright Office only under the collection title.

Published Works

All copyrightable elements that are included in a single unit of publication and in which the copyright claimant is the same may be considered a single work for registration pur-

4

poses. An example is a game consisting of playing pieces, a game board, and game instructions.

Group Registration of Contributions to Periodicals

A single registration may be made for a group of contributions to periodicals if **all** the following conditions are met.

- All the works have the same copyright claimant.
- All the works are by the same author.
- The author of each work is an individual, not an employer or other person for whom the work was made for hire.
- Each work was first published as a contribution to a periodical (including newspapers) within a 12-month period.
- The application identifies each contribution separately, including the periodical containing it and the date of its first publication.

In addition to the above conditions, if first published before March 1, 1989, a contribution as first published must have borne a separate copyright notice, and the name of the owner of copyright in the work (or an abbreviation or alternative designation of the owner) must have been the same in each notice.

Such contributions are registered on Form VA accompanied by Form GR/CP (group registration of contributions to periodicals). Examples of works eligible for such a group registration include cartoon strips, newspaper columns, horoscopes, photographs, drawings, and illustrations.

No Blanket Protection

Registration covers only the particular work deposited for the registration. It does not give any sort of "blanket" protection to other works in the same series. For example, registration of a single cartoon or comic strip drawing does not cover any earlier or later drawings. Each copyrightable version or issue must be registered to gain the advantages of registration for the new material it contains. However, under the conditions described above under **"Published Works"** and **"Group Registration of Contributions to Periodicals,"** certain group registrations may be made with one application and fee.

MANDATORY DEPOSIT FOR WORKS PUBLISHED IN THE UNITED STATES

Although a copyright registration is not required, the 1976 Copyright Act establishes a mandatory deposit requirement for works published in the United States. In general, the owner of copyright or the owner of the exclusive right of publication in the work has a legal obligation to deposit in the Copyright Office within 3 months of publication in the United States **two** complete copies or phonorecords of the best edition. It is the responsibility of the owner of copyright or the owner of the right of first publication in the work to fulfill this mandatory deposit requirement. Failure to make the deposit can result in fines and other penalties but does not affect copyright protection.

Some categories of pictorial, graphic, and sculptural works are exempt from this requirement, and the obligation is reduced for other categories. The following works are **exempt** from the mandatory deposit requirement:

- Scientific and technical drawings and models
- Greeting cards, picture postcards, and stationery
- Three dimensional sculptural works, except for globes, relief models, and similar cartographic works
- Works published only as reproduced in or on jewelry, toys, games, textiles, packaging material, and any useful article
- Advertising material published in connection with articles of merchandise, works of authorship, or services
- Works first published as individual contributions to collective works (but not the collective work as a whole)
- Works first published outside the United States and later published without change in the United States, under certain conditions (**see** Circular 96, Sections 202.19, 20, and 21)

Copies deposited for the Library of Congress under the mandatory deposit provision may also be used to register the claim to copyright but only if they are accompanied by the prescribed application and fee for registration. For further information about mandatory deposit, request Circular 7d, "Mandatory Deposit of Copies or Phonorecords for the Library of Congress."

5

EFFECTIVE DATE OF REGISTRATION

A copyright registration is effective on the date the Copyright Office receives all the required elements in acceptable form, regardless of how long it then takes to process the application and mail the certificate of registration. The time the Copyright Office requires to process an application varies, depending on the amount of material the Office is receiving.

If you apply for copyright registration, you will not receive an acknowledgment that your application has been received (the Office receives more than 600,000 applications annually), but you can expect

- A letter or a telephone call from a Copyright Office staff member if further information is needed or

- A certificate of registration indicating that the work has been registered, or if the application cannot be accepted, a letter explaining why it has been rejected.

If you want to know the date that the Copyright Office receives your material, send it by registered or certified mail and request a return receipt.

MORAL RIGHTS FOR VISUAL ARTISTS

For certain one-of-a-kind visual art and numbered limited editions of 200 or fewer copies, authors are accorded rights of attribution and integrity. The right of attribution ensures that artists are correctly identified with the works of art they create and that they are not identified with works created by others. The right of integrity allows artists to protect their works against modifications and destructions that are prejudicial to the artists' honor or reputation. These rights may not be transferred by the author, but they may be waived in a written instrument. Transfer of the physical copy of a work of visual art or of the copyright does not affect the moral rights accorded to the author.

For works of visual art incorporated in a building, special rules apply. If the owner of a building desires to remove such a work from the building and removal is possible without destruction, the owner is required to accord the author the opportunity to make the removal himself. A registry is established within the Copyright Office to record information relevant to this obligation. Both owners of buildings and authors of visual art incorporated in buildings may record statements in the registry. For further information, request Circular 96, Section 201.25, "Visual Arts Registry."

FOR FURTHER INFORMATION

To request Copyright Office circulars and application forms, write to:

Library of Congress
Copyright Office
Publications Section, LM-455
101 Independence Avenue, S.E.
Washington, D.C. 20559-6000

Or, if you know which circulars you want, request them from the **Forms and Publications Hotline** at (202) 707-9100 24 hours a day. Leave a recorded message.

Selected circulars and other information (but not application forms) are available from **Fax-On-Demand** at (202) 707-2600 if you have a touchtone phone.

Circulars, announcements, regulations, related material, and all copyright application forms are available via the Copyright Office **Website** at www.loc.gov/copyright.

For general information about copyright, call the **Copyright Public Information Office** at (202) 707-3000. The TTY number is (202) 707-6737.

Library of Congress • Copyright Office • 101 Independence Avenue, S.E. • Washington, D.C. 20559-6000
www.loc.gov/copyright

November 1999—50,000
WEB REV: June 1999

PRINTED ON RECYCLED PAPER

☆ U.S. GOVERNMENT PRINTING OFFICE: 2000-461-113/83

APPENDIX 1-B

United States Copyright Office Circular 40a

40a

Circular

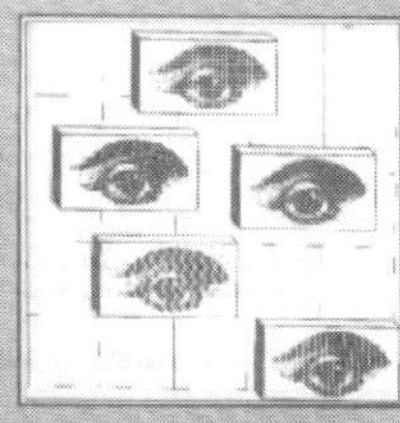

United States Copyright Office

Deposit Requirements for Registration of Claims to Copyright in Visual Arts Material

IN GENERAL

To register a claim to copyright in a work of the visual arts, submit a properly completed application Form VA, a nonrefundable filing fee of $30*, and an appropriate deposit, generally one complete copy of the work if unpublished, two complete copies of the best edition if the work was first published in the United States, or, for certain types of works, identifying material instead of actual copies.

This circular presents a simplified version of the deposit requirements for registration of claims to copyright in visual arts material. It should be viewed only as a basic guide. The items given on pages 2, 3, and 4 are only examples and are not meant to be restrictive. For more detailed information, write for a copy of Circular 96, Sections 202.19, 202.20, and 202.21, which contains the deposit regulations of the Copyright Office. (See "For More Information" on back page.)

BASIC DEFINITIONS

Complete Copy

A "complete copy" of an **unpublished** work is a copy that represents the complete copyrightable content of the work being registered. A complete copy of a **published** work is one that contains all elements of the unit of publication, including those which, if considered separately, would not be copyrightable subject matter. The copies deposited for registration should be physically undamaged. *(Continued on page 3)*

*NOTE: Registration filing fees are effective through June 30, 2002. For information on the fee changes, please write the Copyright Office, check the Copyright Office Website at www.loc.gov/copyright, or call (202) 707-3000.

TWO-DIMENSIONAL WORKS

Nature of Work	Required Deposit: Published	Required Deposit: Unpublished
Advertisements (pictorial)	1 copy as published or pre-publication camera-ready copy	1 photocopy, proof, drawing, copy, or layout
Artwork for bed, bath, and table linens or for wearing apparel (For example: heat transfers or decals already applied to T-shirts)	I.D. material preferred in all cases; I.D. material *required* if copy cannot be folded to 4" thickness or less; 1 copy permitted if it can be folded to 4" thickness or less	same as published
Blueprints, architectural drawings, mechanical drawings, diagrams	1 complete copy	1 copy
Book jackets or record jackets	1 complete copy	1 copy
Commercial print published in newspaper or other periodical	1 copy of entire page or pages	
Commercial print or label (For example: flyers, labels, brochures, or catalogs used in connection with the sale of goods or services)	1 complete copy	1 copy
Contributions to collective works (photographs, drawings, cartoons, etc., published as part of a periodical or anthology)	1 complete copy of the best edition of entire collective work, complete section containing contribution if published in newspaper, entire page containing contribution, contribution cut from the newspaper, or photocopy of contribution as it was published	
Fabric, textile, wallpaper, carpeting, floor tile, wrapping paper, yard goods (If applied to a three-dimensional work, see below)	1 complete copy (or swatch) showing the design repeat and copyright notice, if any	1 complete copy (or I.D. material if the work has not been fixed in repeat)
Fabric emblems or patches, decals or heat transfers (not applied to clothing), bumper stickers, campaign buttons	1 complete copy	1 copy or I.D. material
Greeting cards, picture postcards, stationery, business cards, calendars	1 complete copy	1 copy or I.D. material
Holograms	1 actual copy if image is visible without the aid of a machine or device; otherwise 2 sets of display instructions and 2 sets of I.D. material showing the displayed image	1 copy or display instructions and I.D. material of image
Maps or cartographic material	1 copy of CD-ROM if work published in that format; otherwise, 2 complete copies	1 copy of CD-ROM if work fixed in that format; otherwise, 1 complete copy or I.D. material
Patterns, cross-stitch graphs, stitchery brochures, needlework and craft kits	1 complete copy	1 copy or I.D. material
Pictorial or graphic works (For example: artwork, drawings, illustrations, paintings)	2 complete copies	I.D. material
Pictorial or graphic works fixed only in machine-readable form	I.D. material	1 copy or proof, photocopy, contact sheet
Posters, photographs, prints, brochures, exhibition catalogs	2 complete copies	
"Limited edition" posters, prints, or etchings (published in quantities of fewer than 5 copies, or 300 or fewer numbered copies if individual author is owner of copyright)	1 copy or I.D. material	
Oversize material (exceeding 96" in any dimension)	I.D. material	I.D. material

THREE-DIMENSIONAL WORKS

Nature of Work	Published	Unpublished
Artwork or illustrations on 3-D objects (For example: artwork on plates, mugs)	I.D. material	I.D. material
Fabric or textile attached to or part of a 3-D object (such as furniture)	I.D. material	I.D. material
Games	1 complete copy if container is no larger than 12"x24"x6"; otherwise, I.D. material	1 copy if container is no larger than 12"x24"x6" or I.D. material★
Globes, relief models, or relief maps	1 complete copy including the stand (I.D. material *not* acceptable)	1 complete copy or I. D. material★
Jewelry	I.D. material or 1 copy if fixed only in the form of jewelry cast in base metal not exceeding 4" in any dimension	same as published
Pictorial matter and/or text on a box or container that can be flattened (contents of container are not claimed)	1 copy of box or container if it can be flattened or 1 paper label	1 copy or I. D. material★
Prints or labels inseparable from a three-dimensional object (For example: silk screen label on a bottle)	I.D. material	I. D. material
Sculptures, toys, dolls, molds, relief plaques, statues	I.D. material	I. D. material
Sculpture (For example: doll) in a box with copyrightable pictorial and/or textual material; claim in sculpture and artwork/ text	I.D. material for sculpture plus 1 copy of box and any other printed material	I. D. material for sculpture plus copy of box or I.D. material★
Oversize material (exceeding 96" in any dimension)	I. D. material	I.D. material

ARCHITECTURAL WORKS

	Unconstructed Building	Constructed Building
To be eligible for copyright protection, an architectural work must have been created on or after December 1, 1990, or have been unconstructed and embodied only in unpublished drawings as of that date. (Request Circular 41, "Copyright Claims in Architectural Works," for more information.)	1 complete copy of an architectural drawing or blueprint showing the overall form of the building and any interior arrangement of spaces and/or design elements in which copyright is claimed	1 complete copy as described at left plus I.D. material in the form of photographs clearly identifying the architectural work being registered

★ Because storage space is limited, the Copyright Office prefers I.D. material rather than a copy in these cases.

(continued from page 1)

Best Edition

The "best edition" is the edition published in the United States at any time before the date of deposit in the Copyright Office that the Library of Congress determines to be most suitable for its purposes. Generally, when more than one edition is available, the best edition is: larger rather than smaller; color rather than black and white; and printed on archival-quality rather than less-permanent paper. Request Circular 7b, "'Best Edition' of Published Copyrighted Works for the Collections of the Library of Congress," for additional information.

Identifying Material (I.D. Material)

"Identifying material" or "I.D. material" generally consists of two-dimensional reproduction(s) or rendering(s) of a work in the form of photographic prints, transparencies, photocopies, or drawings that show the complete copyrightable content of the work being registered.

SPECIFICATIONS FOR VISUAL ARTS IDENTIFYING MATERIAL

Copyright Office regulations require the deposit of identifying material instead of copies for three-dimensional works and for works that have been applied to three-dimensional objects. Examples of such works include sculpture, toys, jewelry, artwork on plates, and fabric or textile attached to or part of a three-dimensional object such as furniture. Identifying material must also be submitted for any pictorial, graphic, or sculptural work that exceeds 96 inches in any dimension.

In certain cases, identifying material is permitted; in other cases, it is required. (See chart.) Identifying material should meet the following specifications:

- **Type of identifying material:** The material should consist of photographic prints, transparencies, photocopies, drawings, or similar two-dimensional reproductions or renderings of the work, in a form visually perceivable without the aid of a machine or device.
- **Color or black and white:** If the work is a pictorial or graphic work, the material should reproduce the actual colors employed in the work. In all other cases, the material may be in black and white or may consist of a reproduction of the actual colors.
- **Completeness:** As many pieces of identifying material should be submitted as are necessary to show clearly the entire copyrightable content of the work for which registration is being sought.
- **Number of sets:** Only one set of complete identifying material is required. **NOTE:** With respect to three-dimensional holograms, please write the Copyright Office for additional information.
- **Size:** Photographic transparencies must be at least 35 mm in size and, if 3 x 3 inches or less, must be fixed in cardboard, plastic, or similar mounts; transparencies larger than 3 x 3 inches should be mounted. All types of identifying material other than photographic transparencies must be not less than 3 x 3 inches and not more than 9 x 12 inches, but preferably 8 x 10 inches. The image of the work should show clearly the entire copyrightable content of the work.
- **Title and dimension:** At least one piece of identifying material must give the title of the work on its front, back, or mount and should include an exact measurement of one or more dimensions of the work.

Copyright Notice

Before March 1, 1989, the use of copyright notice was mandatory on all published works, and any work first published before that date should have carried a notice. For works first published on and after March 1, 1989, use of the copyright notice is optional.

For a work published with notice of copyright, the notice and its position on the work must be clearly shown on at least one piece of identifying material. If necessary because of the size or position of the notice, a separate drawing or similar reproduction may be submitted. Such reproduction should be no smaller than 3 x 3 inches and no larger than 9 x 12 inches and should show the exact appearance and content of the notice and its specific position on the work. For more information about copyright notice, request Circular 3, "Copyright Notice."

FOR FURTHER INFORMATION

- **Information via the Internet:** Frequently requested circulars, announcements, regulations, other related materials, the Document Cover Sheet, and all copyright registration forms are available via the Internet. You may access these from the Copyright Office homepage at *www.loc.gov/copyright,* or the Library of Congress home page at *www.loc.gov.*
- **Information by fax:** Selected circulars and other information including the Document Cover Sheet (but not application forms) are available from **Fax-on-Demand** at **(202) 707-2600**.
- **Information by telephone:** For general information about copyright, call the Copyright Public Information Office at **(202) 707-3000**. The TTY number is **(202) 707-6737.** Information specialists are on duty from 8:30 a.m. to 5:00 p.m., eastern time, Monday through Friday, except federal holidays. Recorded information is available 24 hours a day. Or, if you know which forms and circulars you want, request them from the Forms and Publications Hotline at **(202) 707-9100** 24 hours a day. Leave a recorded message.
- **Information by regular mail:** To request Copyright Office publications including the Document Cover Sheet, application forms, and circulars, write to:

  Library of Congress
  Copyright Office
  Publications Section, LM-455
  101 Independence Avenue, S.E.
  Washington, D.C. 20559-6000

Library of Congress • Copyright Office • 101 Independence Avenue, S.E. • Washington, D.C. 20559-6000

www.loc.gov/copyright

November 1999 — 50,000
WEB REV: June 1999

PRINTED ON RECYCLED PAPER

☆U.S. GOVERNMENT PRINTING OFFICE: 2000-461-113/84

APPENDIX 1-C

Application Form VA

Application Form VA

Detach and read these instructions before completing this form.
Make sure all applicable spaces have been filled in before you return this form.

BASIC INFORMATION

When to Use This Form: Use Form VA for copyright registration of published or unpublished works of the visual arts. This category consists of "pictorial, graphic, or sculptural works," including two-dimensional and three-dimensional works of fine, graphic, and applied art, photographs, prints and art reproductions, maps, globes, charts, technical drawings, diagrams, and models.

What Does Copyright Protect? Copyright in a work of the visual arts protects those pictorial, graphic, or sculptural elements that, either alone or in combination, represent an "original work of authorship." The statute declares: "In no case does copyright protection for an original work of authorship extend to any idea, procedure, process, system, method of operation, concept, principle, or discovery, regardless of the form in which it is described, explained, illustrated, or embodied in such work."

Works of Artistic Craftsmanship and Designs: "Works of artistic craftsmanship" are registrable on Form VA, but the statute makes clear that protection extends to "their form" and not to "their mechanical or utilitarian aspects." The "design of a useful article" is considered copyrightable "only if, and only to the extent that, such design incorporates pictorial, graphic, or sculptural features that can be identified separately from, and are capable of existing independently of, the utilitarian aspects of the article."

Labels and Advertisements: Works prepared for use in connection with the sale or advertisement of goods and services are registrable if they contain "original work of authorship." Use Form VA if the copyrightable material in the work you are registering is mainly pictorial or graphic; use Form TX if it consists mainly of text. **NOTE:** Words and short phrases such as names, titles, and slogans cannot be protected by copyright, and the same is true of standard symbols, emblems, and other commonly used graphic designs that are in the public domain. When used commercially, material of that sort can sometimes be protected under state laws of unfair competition or under the federal trademark laws. For information about trademark registration, write to the Commissioner of Patents and Trademarks, Washington, D.C. 20231.

Architectural Works: Copyright protection extends to the design of buildings created for the use of human beings. Architectural works created on or after December 1, 1990, or that on December 1, 1990, were unconstructed and embodied only in unpublished plans or drawings are eligible. Request Circular 41 for more information. Architectural works and technical drawings cannot be registered on the same application.

Deposit to Accompany Application: An application for copyright registration must be accompanied by a deposit consisting of copies representing the entire work for which registration is to be made.

Unpublished Work: Deposit one complete copy.

Published Work: Deposit two complete copies of the best edition.

Work First Published Outside the United States: Deposit one complete copy of the first foreign edition.

Contribution to a Collective Work: Deposit one complete copy of the best edition of the collective work.

The Copyright Notice: Before March 1, 1989, the use of copyright notice was mandatory on all published works, and any work first published before that date should have carried a notice. For works first published on and after March 1 1989, use of the copyright notice is optional. For more information about copyright notice, see Circular 3, "Copyright Notice."

For Further Information: To speak to an information specialist, call (202) 707-3000 (TTY: (202) 707-6737). Recorded information is available 24 hours a day. Order forms and other publications from the address in space 9 or call the Forms and Publications Hotline at (202) 707-9100. Most circulars (but not forms) are available via fax. Call (202) 707-2600 from a touchtone phone. Access and download circulars, forms, and other information from the Copyright Office Website at:

www.loc.gov/copyright

LINE-BY-LINE INSTRUCTIONS

Please type or print using black ink. The form is used to produce the certificate.

1 SPACE 1: Title

Title of This Work: Every work submitted for copyright registration must be given a title to identify that particular work. If the copies of the work bear a title (or an identifying phrase that could serve as a title), transcribe that wording *completely* and *exactly* on the application. Indexing of the registration and future identification of the work will depend on the information you give here. For an architectural work that has been constructed, add the date of construction after the title; if unconstructed at this time, add "not yet constructed."

Publication as a Contribution: If the work being registered is a contribution to a periodical, serial, or collection, give the title of the contribution in the "Title of This Work" space. Then, in the line headed "Publication as a Contribution," give information about the collective work in which the contribution appeared.

Nature of This Work: Briefly describe the general nature or character of the pictorial, graphic, or sculptural work being registered for copyright. Examples: "Oil Painting"; "Charcoal Drawing"; "Etching"; "Sculpture"; "Map"; "Photograph"; "Scale Model"; "Lithographic Print"; "Jewelry Design"; "Fabric Design."

Previous or Alternative Titles: Complete this space if there are any additional titles for the work under which someone searching for the registration might be likely to look, or under which a document pertaining to the work might be recorded.

2 SPACE 2: Author(s)

General Instruction: After reading these instructions, decide who are the "authors" of this work for copyright purposes. Then, unless the work is a "collective work," give the requested information about every "author" who contributed any appreciable amount of copyrightable matter to this version of the work. If you need further space, request Continuation Sheets. In the case of a collective work, such as a catalog of paintings or collection of cartoons by various authors, give information about the author of the collective work as a whole.

Name of Author: The fullest form of the author's name should be given. Unless the work was "made for hire," the individual who actually created the work is its "author." In the case of a work made for hire, the statute provides that "the employer or other person for whom the work was prepared is considered the author."

What is a "Work Made for Hire"? A "work made for hire" is defined as: (1) "a work prepared by an employee within the scope of his or her employment"; or (2) "a work specially ordered or commissioned for use as a contribution to a collective work, as a part of a motion picture or other audiovisual work, as a translation, as a supplementary work, as a compilation, as an instructional text, as a test, as answer material for a test, or as an atlas, if the parties expressly agree in a written instrument signed by them that the work shall be considered a work made for hire." If you have checked "Yes" to indicate that the work was "made for hire," you must give the full legal name of the employer (or other person for whom the work was prepared). You may also include the name of the employee along with the name of the employer (for example: "Elster Publishing Co., employer for hire of John Ferguson").

"Anonymous" or "Pseudonymous" Work: An author's contribution to a work is "anonymous" if that author is not identified on the copies or phonorecords of the work. An author's contribution to a work is "pseudonymous" if that author is identified on the copies or phonorecords under a fictitious name. If the work is "anonymous" you may: (1) leave the line blank; or (2) state "anonymous" on the line; or (3) reveal the author's identity. If the work is "pseudonymous" you may: (1) leave the line blank; or (2) give the pseudonym and identify it as such (for example: "Huntley Haverstock, pseudonym"); or (3) reveal the author's name, making clear which is the real name and which is the pseudonym (for example: "Henry Leek, whose pseudonym is Priam Farrel"). However, the citizenship or domicile of the author **must** be given in all cases.

Dates of Birth and Death: If the author is dead, the statute requires that the year of death be included in the application unless the work is anonymous or pseudonymous. The author's birth date is optional but is useful as a form of identification. Leave this space blank if the author's contribution was a "work made for hire."

Author's Nationality or Domicile: Give the country of which the author is a citizen or the country in which the author is domiciled. Nationality or domicile **must** be given in all cases.

Nature of Authorship: Catagories of pictorial, graphic, and sculptural authorship are listed below. Check the box(es) that best describe(s) each author's contribution to the work.

3-Dimensional sculptures: fine art sculptures, toys, dolls, scale models, and sculptural designs applied to useful articles.

2-Dimensional artwork: watercolor and oil paintings; pen and ink drawings; logo illustrations; greeting cards; collages; stencils; patterns; computer graphics; graphics appearing in screen displays; artwork appearing on posters, calendars, games, commercial prints and labels, and packaging, as well as 2-dimensional artwork applied to useful articles, and designs reproduced on textiles, lace, and other fabrics; on wallpaper, carpeting, floor tile, wrapping paper, and clothing.

Reproductions of works of art: reproductions of preexisting artwork made by, for example, lithography, photoengraving, or etching.

Maps: cartographic representations of an area, such as state and county maps, atlases, marine charts, relief maps, and globes.

Photographs: pictorial photographic prints and slides and holograms.

Jewelry designs: 3-dimensional designs applied to rings, pendants, earrings, necklaces, and the like.

Technical drawings: diagrams illustrating scientific or technical information in linear form, such as architectural blueprints or mechanical drawings.

Text: textual material that accompanies pictorial, graphic, or sculptural works, such as comic strips, greeting cards, games rules, commercial prints or labels, and maps.

Architectural works: designs of buildings, including the overall form as well as the arrangement and composition of spaces and elements of the design.

NOTE: Any registration for the underlying architectural plans must be applied for on a separate Form VA, checking the box "Technical drawing."

3 SPACE 3: Creation and Publication

General Instructions: Do not confuse "creation" with "publication." Every application for copyright registration must state "the year in which creation of the work was completed." Give the date and nation of first publication only if the work has been published.

Creation: Under the statute, a work is "created" when it is fixed in a copy or phonorecord for the first time. Where a work has been prepared over a period of time, the part of the work existing in fixed form on a particular date constitutes the created work on that date. The date you give here should be the year in which the author completed the particular version for which registration is now being sought, even if other versions exist or if further changes or additions are planned.

Publication: The statute defines "publication" as "the distribution of copies or phonorecords of a work to the public by sale or other transfer of ownership, or by rental, lease, or lending"; a work is also "published" if there has been an "offering to distribute copies or phonorecords to a group of persons for purposes of further distribution, public performance, or public display." Give the full date (month, day, year) when, and the country where, publication first occurred. If first publication took place simultaneously in the United States and other countries, it is sufficient to state "U.S.A."

4 SPACE 4: Claimant(s)

Name(s) and Address(es) of Copyright Claimant(s): Give the name(s) and address(es) of the copyright claimant(s) in this work even if the claimant is the same as the author. Copyright in a work belongs initially to the author of the work (including, in the case of a work make for hire, the employer or other person for whom the work was prepared). The copyright claimant is either the author of the work or a person or organization to whom the copyright initially belonging to the author has been transferred.

Transfer: The statute provides that, if the copyright claimant is not the author, the application for registration must contain "a brief statement of how the claimant obtained ownership of the copyright." If any copyright claimant named in space 4 is not an author named in space 2, give a brief statement explaining how the claimant(s) obtained ownership of the copyright. Examples: "By written contract"; "Transfer of all rights by author"; "Assignment"; "By will." Do not attach transfer documents or other attachments or riders.

5 SPACE 5: Previous Registration

General Instructions: The questions in space 5 are intended to find out whether an earlier registration has been made for this work and, if so, whether there is any basis for a new registration. As a rule, only one basic copyright registration can be made for the same version of a particular work.

Same Version: If this version is substantially the same as the work covered by a previous registration, a second registration is not generally possible unless: (1) the work has been registered in unpublished form and a second registration is now being sought to cover this first published edition; or (2) someone other than the author is identified as a copyright claimant in the earlier registration, and the author is now seeking registration in his or her own name. If either of these two exceptions applies, check the appropriate box and give the earlier registration number and date. Otherwise, do not submit Form VA; instead, write the Copyright Office for information about supplementary registration or recordation of transfers of copyright ownership.

Changed Version: If the work has been changed and you are now seeking registration to cover the additions or revisions, check the last box in space 5, give the earlier registration number and date, and complete both parts of space 6 in accordance with the instruction below.

Previous Registration Number and Date: If more than one previous registration has been made for the work, give the number and date of the latest registration.

6 SPACE 6: Derivative Work or Compilation

General Instructions: Complete space 6 if this work is a "changed version," "compilation," or "derivative work," and if it incorporates one or more earlier works that have already been published or registered for copyright, or that have fallen into the public domain. A "compilation" is defined as "a work formed by the collection and assembling of preexisting materials or of data that are selected, coordinated, or arranged in such a way that the resulting work as a whole constitutes an original work of authorship." A "derivative work" is "a work based on one or more preexisting works." Examples of derivative works include reproductions of works of art, sculptures based on drawings, lithographs based on paintings, maps based on previously published sources, or "any other form in which a work may be recast, transformed, or adapted." Derivative works also include works "consisting of editorial revisions, annotations, or other modifications" if these changes, as a whole, represent an original work of authorship.

Preexisting Material (space 6a): Complete this space **and** space 6b for derivative works. In this space identify the preexisting work that has been recast, transformed, or adapted. Examples of preexisting material might be "Grunewald Altarpiece" or "19th century quilt design." Do not complete this space for compilations.

Material Added to This Work (space 6b): Give a brief, general statement of the **additional** new material covered by the copyright claim for which registration is sought. In the case of a derivative work, identify this new material. Examples: "Adaptation of design and additional artistic work"; "Reproduction of painting by photolithography"; "Additional cartographic material"; "Compilation of photographs." If the work is a compilation, give a brief, general statement describing both the material that has been compiled **and** the compilation itself. Example: "Compilation of 19th century political cartoons."

7,8,9 SPACE 7, 8, 9: Fee, Correspondence, Certification, Return Address

Deposit Account: If you maintain a Deposit Account in the Copyright Office, identify it in space 7a. Otherwise, leave the space blank and send the fee of $30 (effective through June 30, 2002) with your application and deposit.

Correspondence (space 7b): This space should contain the name, address, area code, telephone number, email address, and fax number (if available) of the person to be consulted if correspondence about this application becomes necessary.

Certification (space 8): The application cannot be accepted unless it bears the date and the **handwritten signature** of the author or other copyright claimant, or of the owner of exclusive right(s), or of the duly authorized agent of the author, claimant, or owner of exclusive right(s).

Address for Return of Certificate (space 9): The address box must be completed legibly since the certificate will be returned in a window envelope.

PRIVACY ACT ADVISORY STATEMENT Required by the Privacy Act of 1974 (P.L. 93 - 579)
The authority for requesting this information is title 17, U.S.C., secs. 409 and 410. Furnishing the requested information is voluntary. But if the information is not furnished, it may be necessary to delay or refuse registration and you may not be entitled to certain relief, remedies, and benefits provided in chapters 4 and 5 of title 17, U.S.C.
The principal uses of the requested information are the establishment and maintenance of a public record and the examination of the application for compliance with the registration requirements of the copyright code.
Other routine uses include public inspection and copying, preparation of public indexes, preparation of public catalogs of copyright registrations, and preparation of search reports upon request.
NOTE: No other advisory statement will be given in connection with this application. Please keep this statement and refer to it if we communicate with you regarding this application.

FEE CHANGES

Fees are effective through June 30, 2002. After that date, check the Copyright Office Website at www.loc.gov/copyright or call (202) 707-3000 for current fee information.

FORM VA

For a Work of the Visual Arts
UNITED STATES COPYRIGHT OFFICE

REGISTRATION NUMBER

VA VAU

EFFECTIVE DATE OF REGISTRATION

Month Day Year

DO NOT WRITE ABOVE THIS LINE. IF YOU NEED MORE SPACE, USE A SEPARATE CONTINUATION SHEET.

1

TITLE OF THIS WORK ▼

NATURE OF THIS WORK ▼ See instructions

PREVIOUS OR ALTERNATIVE TITLES ▼

Publication as a Contribution If this work was published as a contribution to a periodical, serial, or collection, give information about the collective work in which the contribution appeared. **Title of Collective Work ▼**

If published in a periodical or serial give: **Volume ▼** **Number ▼** **Issue Date ▼** **On Pages ▼**

2

a **NAME OF AUTHOR ▼**

DATES OF BIRTH AND DEATH
Year Born ▼ Year Died ▼

Was this contribution to the work a "work made for hire"?
☐ Yes
☐ No

Author's Nationality or Domicile
Name of Country
OR { Citizen of ▶ / Domiciled in ▶

Was This Author's Contribution to the Work
Anonymous? ☐ Yes ☐ No
Pseudonymous? ☐ Yes ☐ No
If the answer to either of these questions is "Yes," see detailed instructions.

NATURE OF AUTHORSHIP Check appropriate box(es). **See instructions**

☐ 3-Dimensional sculpture ☐ Map ☐ Technical drawing
☐ 2-Dimensional artwork ☐ Photograph ☐ Text
☐ Reproduction of work of art ☐ Jewelry design ☐ Architectural work

NOTE

Under the law, the "author" of a **"work made for hire"** is generally the employer, not the employee (see instructions). For any part of this work that was "made for hire" check "Yes" in the space provided, give the employer (or other person for whom the work was prepared) as "Author" of that part, and leave the space for dates of birth and death blank.

b **NAME OF AUTHOR ▼**

DATES OF BIRTH AND DEATH
Year Born ▼ Year Died ▼

Was this contribution to the work a "work made for hire"?
☐ Yes
☐ No

Author's Nationality or Domicile
Name of Country
OR { Citizen of ▶ / Domiciled in ▶

Was This Author's Contribution to the Work
Anonymous? ☐ Yes ☐ No
Pseudonymous? ☐ Yes ☐ No
If the answer to either of these questions is "Yes," see detailed instructions.

NATURE OF AUTHORSHIP Check appropriate box(es). **See instructions**

☐ 3-Dimensional sculpture ☐ Map ☐ Technical drawing
☐ 2-Dimensional artwork ☐ Photograph ☐ Text
☐ Reproduction of work of art ☐ Jewelry design ☐ Architectural work

3

a **Year in Which Creation of This Work Was Completed** ◀ Year **This information must be given in all cases.**

b **Date and Nation of First Publication of This Particular Work** **Complete this information ONLY if this work has been published.** Month ▶ Day ▶ Year ▶ ◀ Nation

4

See instructions before completing this space.

COPYRIGHT CLAIMANT(S) Name and address must be given even if the claimant is the same as the author given in space 2. ▼

Transfer If the claimant(s) named here in space 4 is (are) different from the author(s) named in space 2, give a brief statement of how the claimant(s) obtained ownership of the copyright. ▼

DO NOT WRITE HERE OFFICE USE ONLY

APPLICATION RECEIVED

ONE DEPOSIT RECEIVED

TWO DEPOSITS RECEIVED

FUNDS RECEIVED

MORE ON BACK ▶ • Complete all applicable spaces (numbers 5-9) on the reverse side of this page. • See detailed instructions. • Sign the form at line 8.

DO NOT WRITE HERE

Page 1 of ____ pages

EXAMINED BY | FORM VA

CHECKED BY

☐ CORRESPONDENCE Yes

FOR COPYRIGHT OFFICE USE ONLY

DO NOT WRITE ABOVE THIS LINE. IF YOU NEED MORE SPACE, USE A SEPARATE CONTINUATION SHEET.

PREVIOUS REGISTRATION Has registration for this work, or for an earlier version of this work, already been made in the Copyright Office? 5

☐ **Yes** ☐ **No** If your answer is "Yes," why is another registration being sought? (Check appropriate box.) ▼

a. ☐ This is the first published edition of a work previously registered in unpublished form.

b. ☐ This is the first application submitted by this author as copyright claimant.

c. ☐ This is a changed version of the work, as shown by space 6 on this application.

If your answer is "Yes," give: **Previous Registration Number** ▼ **Year of Registration** ▼

DERIVATIVE WORK OR COMPILATION Complete both space 6a and 6b for a derivative work; complete only 6b for a compilation. 6

a. Preexisting Material Identify any preexisting work or works that this work is based on or incorporates. ▼ a

See instructions before completing this space.

b. Material Added to This Work Give a brief, general statement of the material that has been added to this work and in which copyright is claimed. ▼ b

DEPOSIT ACCOUNT If the registration fee is to be charged to a Deposit Account established in the Copyright Office, give name and number of Account. 7

Name ▼ **Account Number** ▼ a

CORRESPONDENCE Give name and address to which correspondence about this application should be sent. Name/Address/Apt/City/State/ZIP ▼ b

Area code and daytime telephone number ▶ ( ) Fax number ▶ ( )

Email ▶

CERTIFICATION* I, the undersigned, hereby certify that I am the 8

check only one ▶
- ☐ author
- ☐ other copyright claimant
- ☐ owner of exclusive right(s)
- ☐ authorized agent of ______
  Name of author or other copyright claimant, or owner of exclusive right(s) ▲

of the work identified in this application and that the statements made by me in this application are correct to the best of my knowledge.

Typed or printed name and date ▼ If this application gives a date of publication in space 3, do not sign and submit it before that date.

Date ▶

Handwritten signature (X) ▼

X ______

Certificate will be mailed in window envelope to this address: 9

Name ▼
Number/Street/Apt ▼
City/State/ZIP ▼

YOU MUST:
- Complete all necessary spaces
- Sign your application in space 8

SEND ALL 3 ELEMENTS IN THE SAME PACKAGE:
1. Application form
2. Nonrefundable filing fee in check or money order payable to *Register of Copyrights*
3. Deposit material

As of July 1, 1999, the filing fee for Form VA is $30.

MAIL TO:
Library of Congress
Copyright Office
101 Independence Avenue, S.E.
Washington, D.C. 20559-6000

*17 U.S.C. § 506(e): Any person who knowingly makes a false representation of a material fact in the application for copyright registration provided for by section 409, or in any written statement filed in connection with the application, shall be fined not more than $2,500.

June 1999—100,000
WEB REV: June 1999

PRINTED ON RECYCLED PAPER

☆U.S. GOVERNMENT PRINTING OFFICE: 1999-454-879/71

APPENDIX 1-D

Instructions and Short Form VA

Instructions for Short Form VA

For pictorial, graphic, and sculptural works

USE THIS FORM IF—

1. You are the **only** author and copyright owner of this work, *and*
2. The work was **not** made for hire, *and*
3. The work is completely new (does not contain a substantial amount of material that has been previously published or registered or is in the public domain).

If any of the above does not apply, you must use standard Form VA.
NOTE: Short Form VA is not appropriate for an anonymous author who does not wish to reveal his or her identity.

HOW TO COMPLETE SHORT FORM VA

- Type or print in black ink.
- Be clear and legible. (Your certificate of registration will be copied from your form.)
- Give only the information requested.

NOTE: You may use a continuation sheet (Form __/CON) to list individual titles in a collection. Complete Space A and list the individual titles under Space C on the back page. Space B is not applicable to short forms.

1 Title of This Work

You must give a title. If there is no title, state "UNTITLED." If you are registering an unpublished collection, give the collection title you want to appear in our records (for example: "Jewelry by Josephine, 1995 Volume"). Alternative title: If the work is known by two titles, you also may give the second title. If the work has been published as part of a larger work (including a periodical), give the title of that larger work instead of an alternative title, in addition to the title of the contribution.

2 Name and Address of Author and Owner of the Copyright

Give your name and mailing address. You may include your pseudonym followed by "pseud." Also, give the nation of which you are a citizen or where you have your domicile (i.e., permanent residence).

Please give daytime phone, fax numbers, and email address, if available.

3 Year of Creation

Give the latest year in which you completed the work you are registering at this time. A work is "created" when it is "fixed" in a tangible form. Examples: drawn on paper, molded in clay, stored in a computer.

4 Publication

If the work has been published (i.e., if copies have been distributed to the public), give the complete date of publication (month, day, and year) and the nation where the publication first took place.

5 Type of Authorship in This Work

Check the box or boxes that describe your authorship in the material you are sending. For example, if you are registering illustrations but have not written the story yet, check only the box for "2-dimensional artwork."

6 Signature of Author

Sign the application in black ink and check the appropriate box. The person signing the application should be the author or his/her authorized agent.

7 Person to Contact for Rights/Permissions

This space is optional. You may give the name and address of the person or organization to contact for permission to use the work. You may also provide phone, fax, or email information.

8 Certificate Will Be Mailed

This space must be completed. Your certificate of registration will be mailed in a window envelope to this address. Also, if the Copyright Office needs to contact you, we will write to this address.

9 Deposit Account

Complete this space only if you currently maintain a deposit account in the Copyright Office.

MAIL WITH THE FORM

- A $30 filing fee (effective through June 30, 2002) in the form of a check or money order *(no cash)* payable to "Register of Copyrights," **and**
- One or two copies of the work or identifying material consisting of photographs or drawings showing the work. See table (right) for the requirements for most works. **Note:** Request Circular 40a for more information about the requirements for other works. Copies submitted become the property of the U.S. Government.

Mail everything **(application form, copy or copies, and fee)** ***in one package*** to:

Library of Congress
Copyright Office
101 Independence Avenue, S.E.
Washington, D.C. 20559-6000

QUESTIONS? Call (202) 707-3000 [TTY: (202) 707-6737] between 8:30 a.m. and 5:00 p.m. eastern time, Monday through Friday. For forms and informational circulars, call (202) 707-9100 24 hours a day, 7 days a week, or download them from the Internet at www.loc.gov/copyright. Selected informational circulars but not forms are available from Fax-on-Demand at (202) 707-2600.

If you are registering:	And the work is *unpublished/published* send:
• 2-dimensional artwork in a book, map, poster, or print	**a. And the work is *unpublished*, send** one complete copy or identifying material **b. And the work is *published*, send** two copies of the best published edition
• 3-dimensional sculpture, • 2-dimensional artwork applied to a T-shirt	**a. And the work is *unpublished*, send** identifying material **b. And the work is *published*, send** identifying material
• a greeting card, pattern, commercial print or label, fabric, wallpaper	**a. And the work is *unpublished*, send** one complete copy or identifying material **b. And the work is *published*, send** one copy of the best published edition

PRIVACY ACT ADVISORY STATEMENT Required by the Privacy Act of 1974 (P.L. 93-579)

The authority for requesting this information is title 17 U.S.C., secs. 409 and 410. Furnishing the requested information is voluntary. But if the information is not furnished, it may be necessary to delay or refuse registration and you may not be entitled to certain relief, remedies, and benefits provided in chapters 4 and 5 of title 17 U.S.C.

The principal uses of the requested information are the establishment and maintenance of a public record and the examination of the application for compliance with the registration requirements of the copyright law.

Other routine uses include public inspection and copying, preparation of public indexes, preparation of public catalogs of copyright registrations, and preparation of search reports upon request.

NOTE: No other advisory statement will be given in connection with this application. Please keep this statement and refer to it if we communicate with you regarding this application.

FEE CHANGES
Fees are effective through June 30, 2002. After that date, check the Copyright Office Website at www.loc.gov/copyright or call (202) 707-3000 for current fee information.

SHORT FORM VA

For a Work of the Visual Arts
UNITED STATES COPYRIGHT OFFICE

Registration Number

VA VAU

Effective Date of Registration

Application Received

Examined By

Deposit Received
One Two

Correspondence ❑

Fee Received

TYPE OR PRINT IN BLACK INK. DO NOT WRITE ABOVE THIS LINE.

Title of This Work: Alternative title or title of larger work in which this work was published:	**1**	
Name and Address of Author and Owner of the Copyright: Nationality or domicile: Phone, fax, and email:	**2**	Phone ( ) Fax ( ) Email
Year of Creation:	**3**	
***If work has been published,* Date and Nation of Publication:**	**4**	a. Date ______ Month ______ Day ______ Year ______ *(Month, day, and year all required)* b. Nation
Type of Authorship in This Work: Check all that this author created.	**5**	❑ 3-Dimensional sculpture ❑ Photograph ❑ Map ❑ 2-Dimensional artwork ❑ Jewelry design ❑ Text ❑ Technical drawing
Signature: Registration cannot be completed without a signature.	**6**	*I certify that the statements made by me in this application are correct to the best of my knowledge.** Check one: ❑ Author ❑ Authorized agent **X** ______________________________
OPTIONAL **Name and Address of Person to Contact for Rights and Permissions:** Phone, fax, and email:	**7**	❑ Check here if same as #2 above. Phone ( ) Fax ( ) Email

8 **Certificate will be mailed in window envelope to this address:**

Name ▼
Number/Street/Apt ▼
City/State/ZIP ▼

9 **Complete this space only if you currently hold a Deposit Account in the Copyright Office.**

Deposit Account # ______
Name ______

DO NOT WRITE HERE Page 1 of ____ pages

*17 U.S.C. § 506(e): Any person who knowingly makes a false representation of a material fact in the application for copyright registration provided for by section 409, or in any written statement filed in connection with the application, shall be fined not more than $2,500.

June 1999—100,000
WEB REV: June 1999

PRINTED ON RECYCLED PAPER

☆U.S. GOVERNMENT PRINTING OFFICE: 1999-454-879/54

APPENDIX 1-E

Selections from 1976 Copyright Law Act as Amended

U.S. Code Title 17

§ 101. Definitions (Selected)

A "derivative work" is a work based upon one or more preexisting works, such as a translation, musical arrangement, dramatization, fictionalization, motion picture version, sound recording, art reproduction, abridgment, condensation, or any other form in which a work may be recast, transformed, or adapted. A work consisting of editorial revisions, annotations, elaborations, or other modifications which, as a whole, represent an original work of authorship, is a "derivative work."

A "joint work" is a work prepared by two or more authors with the intention that their contributions be merged into inseparable or interdependent parts of a unitary whole.

"Pictorial, graphic, and sculptural works" include two-dimensional and three-dimensional works of fine, graphic, and applied art, photographs, prints and art reproductions, maps, globes, charts, diagrams, models, and technical drawings, including architectural plans. Such works shall include works of artistic craftsmanship insofar as their form but not their mechanical or utilitarian aspects are concerned; the design of a useful article, as defined in this section, shall be considered a pictorial, graphic, or sculptural work only if, and only to the extent that, such design incorporates pictorial, graphic, or sculptural features that can be identified separately from, and are capable of existing independently of, the utilitarian aspects of the article.

"Publication" is the distribution of copies or phonorecords of a work to the public by sale or other transfer of ownership, or by rental, lease, or lending. The offering to distribute copies or phonorecords to a group of persons for purposes of further distribution, public performance, or public display, constitutes publication. A public performance or display of a work does not of itself constitute publication.

A "useful article" is an article having an intrinsic utilitarian function that is not merely to portray the appearance of the article or to convey information. An article that is normally a part of a useful article is considered a "useful article."

A "work of visual art" is—

(1) a painting, drawing, print, or sculpture, existing in a single copy, in a limited edition of 200 copies or fewer that are signed and consecutively numbered by the author, or, in the case of a sculpture, in multiple cast, carved, or fabricated sculptures of 200 or fewer that are

consecutively numbered by the author and bear the signature or other identifying mark of the author; or

(2) a still photographic image produced for exhibition purposes only, existing in a single copy that is signed by the author, or in a limited edition of 200 copies or fewer that are signed and consecutively numbered by the author. A work of visual art does not include—

(A)

(i) any poster, map, globe, chart, technical drawing, diagram, model, applied art, motion picture or other audiovisual work, book, magazine, newspaper, periodical, data base, electronic information service, electronic publication, or similar publication;

(ii) any merchandising item or advertising, promotional, descriptive, covering, or packaging material or container;

(iii) any portion or part of any item described in clause (i) or (ii);

(B) any work made for hire; or

(C) any work not subject to copyright protection under this title.

A "work made for hire" is—

(1) a work prepared by an employee within the scope of his or her employment; or

(2) a work specially ordered or commissioned for use as a contribution to a collective work, as a part of a motion picture or other audiovisual work, as a translation, as a supplementary work, as a compilation, as an instructional text, as a test, as answer material for a test, or as an atlas, if the parties expressly agree in a written instrument signed by them that the work shall be considered a work made for hire. For the purpose of the foregoing sentence, a "supplementary work" is a work prepared for publication as a secondary adjunct to a work by another author for the purpose of introducing, concluding, illustrating, explaining, revising, commenting upon, or assisting in the use of the other work, such as forewords, afterwords, pictorial illustrations, maps, charts, tables, editorial notes, musical arrangements, answer material for tests, bibliographies, appendixes, and indexes, and an "instructional text" is a literary, pictorial, or graphic work prepared for publication and with the purpose of use in systematic instructional activities.

The terms "WTO Agreement" and "WTO member country" have the meanings given those terms in paragraphs (9) and (10), respectively, of section 2 of the Uruguay Round Agreements Act. A "computer program" is a set of statements or instructions to be used directly or indirectly in a computer in order to bring about a certain result.

§ 102. Subject matter of copyright: In general

(a) Copyright protection subsists, in accordance with this title, in original works of authorship fixed in any tangible medium of expression, now known or later developed, from which they can be perceived, reproduced, or otherwise communicated, either directly or with the aid of a machine or device. Works of authorship include the following categories:

(1) literary works;
(2) musical works, including any accompanying words;
(3) dramatic works, including any accompanying music;
(4) pantomimes and choreographic works;
(5) pictorial, graphic, and sculptural works;
(6) motion pictures and other audiovisual works;
(7) sound recordings; and
(8) architectural works.

(b) In no case does copyright protection for an original work of authorship extend to any idea, procedure, process, system, method of operation, concept, principle, or discovery, regardless of the form in which it is described, explained, illustrated, or embodied in such work.

§ 103. Subject matter of copyright: Compilations and derivative works

(a) The subject matter of copyright as specified by section 102 includes compilations and derivative works, but protection for a work employing preexisting material in which copyright subsists does not extend to any part of the work in which such material has been used unlawfully.

(b) The copyright in a compilation or derivative work extends only to the material contributed by the author of such work, as distinguished from the preexisting material employed in the work, and does not imply any exclusive right in the preexisting material. The copyright in such work is independent of, and does not affect or enlarge the scope, duration, ownership, or subsistence of, any copyright protection in the preexisting material.

§ 106. Exclusive rights in copyrighted works

Subject to sections 107 through 120, the owner of copyright under this title has the exclusive rights to do and to authorize any of the following:

(1) to reproduce the copyrighted work in copies or phonorecords;
(2) to prepare derivative works based upon the copyrighted work;

(3) to distribute copies or phonorecords of the copyrighted work to the public by sale or other transfer of ownership, or by rental, lease, or lending;

(4) in the case of literary, musical, dramatic, and choreographic works, pantomimes, and motion pictures and other audiovisual works, to perform the copyrighted work publicly;

(5) in the case of literary, musical, dramatic, and choreographic works, pantomimes, and pictorial, graphic, or sculptural works, including the individual images of a motion picture or other audiovisual work, to display the copyrighted work publicly; and

(6) in the case of sound recordings, to perform the copyrighted work publicly by means of a digital audio transmission.

§ 106A. Rights of certain authors to attribution and integrity

(a) Rights of Attribution and Integrity.—Subject to section 107 and independent of the exclusive rights provided in section 106, the author of a work of visual art—

(1) shall have the right—

(A) to claim authorship of that work, and

(B) to prevent the use of his or her name as the author of any work of visual art which he or she did not create;

(2) shall have the right to prevent the use of his or her name as the author of the work of visual art in the event of a distortion, mutilation, or other modification of the work which would be prejudicial to his or her honor or reputation; and

(3) subject to the limitations set forth in section *113*(d), shall have the right—

(A) to prevent any intentional distortion, mutilation, or other modification of that work which would be prejudicial to his or her honor or reputation, and any intentional distortion, mutilation, or modification of that work is a violation of that right, and

(B) to prevent any destruction of a work of recognized stature, and any intentional or grossly negligent destruction of that work is a violation of that right.

(b) Scope and Exercise of Rights.—Only the author of a work of visual art has the rights conferred by subsection (a) in that work, whether or not the author is the copyright owner. The authors of a joint work of visual art are coowners of the rights conferred by subsection (a) in that work.

(c) Exceptions.—(1) The modification of a work of visual art which is a result of the passage of time or the inherent nature of the materials is not a distortion, mutilation, or other modification described in subsection (a)(3)(A).

(2) The modification of a work of visual art which is the result of conservation, or of the public presentation, including lighting and placement, of the work is not a destruction, distortion, mutilation, or other modification described in subsection (a)(3) unless the modification is caused by gross negligence.

(3) The rights described in paragraphs (1) and (2) of subsection (a) shall not apply to any reproduction, depiction, portrayal, or other use of a work in, upon, or in any connection with any item described in subparagraph (A) or (B) of the definition of "work of visual art" in section *101*, and any such reproduction, depiction, portrayal, or other use of a work is not a destruction, distortion, mutilation, or other modification described in paragraph (3) of subsection (a).

(d) Duration of Rights.—(1) With respect to works of visual art created on or after the effective date set forth in section 610(a) of the Visual Artists Rights Act of 1990, the rights conferred by subsection (a) shall endure for a term consisting of the life of the author.

(2) With respect to works of visual art created before the effective date set forth in section 610(a) of the Visual Artists Rights Act of 1990, but title to which has not, as of such effective date, been transferred from the author, the rights conferred by subsection (a) shall be coextensive with, and shall expire at the same time as, the rights conferred by section 106.

(3) In the case of a joint work prepared by two or more authors, the rights conferred by subsection (a) shall endure for a term consisting of the life of the last surviving author.

(4) All terms of the rights conferred by subsection (a) run to the end of the calendar year in which they would otherwise expire.

(e) Transfer and Waiver.—(1) The rights conferred by subsection (a) may not be transferred, but those rights may be waived if the author expressly agrees to such waiver in a written instrument signed by the author. Such instrument shall specifically identify the work, and uses of that work, to which the waiver applies, and the waiver shall apply only to the work and uses so identified. In the case of a joint work prepared by two or more authors, a waiver of rights under this paragraph made by one such author waives such rights for all such authors.

(2) Ownership of the rights conferred by subsection (a) with respect to a work of visual art is distinct from ownership of any copy of that work, or of a copyright or any exclusive right under a copyright

in that work. Transfer of ownership of any copy of a work of visual art, or of a copyright or any exclusive right under a copyright, shall not constitute a waiver of the rights conferred by subsection (a). Except as may otherwise be agreed by the author in a written instrument signed by the author, a waiver of the rights conferred by subsection (a) with respect to a work of visual art shall not constitute a transfer of ownership of any copy of that work, or of ownership of a copyright or of any exclusive right under a copyright in that work.

§ 107. Limitations on exclusive rights: Fair use

Notwithstanding the provisions of sections *106* and 106A, the fair use of a copyrighted work, including such use by reproduction in copies or phonorecords or by any other means specified by that section, for purposes such as criticism, comment, news reporting, teaching (including multiple copies for classroom use), scholarship, or research, is not an infringement of copyright. In determining whether the use made of a work in any particular case is a fair use the factors to be considered shall include—

(1) the purpose and character of the use, including whether such use is of a commercial nature or is for nonprofit educational purposes;

(2) the nature of the copyrighted work;

(3) the amount and substantiality of the portion used in relation to the copyrighted work as a whole; and

(4) the effect of the use upon the potential market for or value of the copyrighted work. The fact that a work is unpublished shall not itself bar a finding of fair use if such finding is made upon consideration of all the above factors.

§ 109. Limitations on exclusive rights: Effect of transfer of particular copy or phonorecord

(a) Notwithstanding the provisions of section 106(3), the owner of a particular copy or phonorecord lawfully made under this title, or any person authorized by such owner, is entitled, without the authority of the copyright owner, to sell or otherwise dispose of the possession of that copy or phonorecord. Notwithstanding the preceding sentence, copies or phonorecords of works subject to restored copyright under section *104A* that are manufactured before the date of restoration of copyright or, with respect to reliance parties, before publication or service of notice under section *104A*(e), may be sold or otherwise disposed of without the authorization of the owner of the restored copyright for purposes of direct or indirect commercial advantage only during the 12-month period beginning on—

(1) the date of the publication in the Federal Register of the notice

of intent filed with the Copyright Office under section 104A(d)(2)(A), or

(2) the date of the receipt of actual notice served under section 104A(d)(2)(B), whichever occurs first.

(c) Notwithstanding the provisions of section *106*(5), the owner of a particular copy lawfully made under this title, or any person authorized by such owner, is entitled, without the authority of the copyright owner, to display that copy publicly, either directly or by the projection of no more than one image at a time, to viewers present at the place where the copy is located.

(d) The privileges prescribed by subsections (a) and (c) do not, unless authorized by the copyright owner, extend to any person who has acquired possession of the copy or phonorecord from the copyright owner, by rental, lease, loan, or otherwise, without acquiring ownership of it.

§ 113. Scope of exclusive rights in pictorial, graphic, and sculptural works

(a) Subject to the provisions of subsections (b) and (c) of this section, the exclusive right to reproduce a copyrighted pictorial, graphic, or sculptural work in copies under section *106* includes the right to reproduce the work in or on any kind of article, whether useful or otherwise.

(b) This title does not afford, to the owner of copyright in a work that portrays a useful article as such, any greater or lesser rights with respect to the making, distribution, or display of the useful article so portrayed than those afforded to such works under the law, whether title 17 or the common law or statutes of a State, in effect on December 31, 1977, as held applicable and construed by a court in an action brought under this title.

(c) In the case of a work lawfully reproduced in useful articles that have been offered for sale or other distribution to the public, copyright does not include any right to prevent the making, distribution, or display of pictures or photographs of such articles in connection with advertisements or commentaries related to the distribution or display of such articles, or in connection with news reports.

(d) (1) In a case in which—

(A) a work of visual art has been incorporated in or made part of a building in such a way that removing the work from the building will cause the destruction, distortion, mutilation, or other modification of the work as described in section *106*A(a)(3), and

(B) the author consented to the installation of the work in the building either before the effective date set forth in section 610(a) of the Visual Artists Rights Act of 1990, or in a written instrument executed on or after such effective date that is signed by the owner of the building and the author and that specifies that installation of the work may subject the work to destruction, distortion, mutilation, or other modification, by reason of its removal,

then the rights conferred by paragraphs (2) and (3) of section 106A(a) shall not apply.

(2) If the owner of a building wishes to remove a work of visual art which is a part of such building and which can be removed from the building without the destruction, distortion, mutilation, or other modification of the work as described in section 106A(a)(3), the author's rights under paragraphs (2) and (3) of section 106A(a) shall apply unless—

(A) the owner has made a diligent, good faith attempt without success to notify the author of the owner's intended action affecting the work of visual art, or

(B) the owner did provide such notice in writing and the person so notified failed, within 90 days after receiving such notice, either to remove the work or to pay for its removal.

For purposes of subparagraph (A), an owner shall be presumed to have made a diligent, good faith attempt to send notice if the owner sent such notice by registered mail to the author at the most recent address of the author that was recorded with the Register of Copyrights pursuant to paragraph (3). If the work is removed at the expense of the author, title to that copy of the work shall be deemed to be in the author.

(3) The Register of Copyrights shall establish a system of records whereby any author of a work of visual art that has been incorporated in or made part of a building, may record his or her identity and address with the Copyright Office. The Register shall also establish procedures under which any such author may update the information so recorded, and procedures under which owners of buildings may record with the Copyright Office evidence of their efforts to comply with this subsection.

§ 120. Scope of exclusive rights in architectural works

(a) Pictorial Representations Permitted.—The copyright in an architectural work that has been constructed does not include the right to prevent the making, distributing, or public display of pictures, paintings, photographs, or other pictorial representations of the work, if the building in which the work is embodied is located in or ordinarily visible from a public place.

(b) Alterations to and Destruction of Buildings.—Notwithstanding the provisions of section *106*(2), the owners of a building embodying an architectural work may, without the consent of the author or copyright owner of the architectural work, make or authorize the making of alterations to such building, and destroy or authorize the destruction of such building.

§ 201. Ownership of copyright

(a) Initial Ownership.—Copyright in a work protected under this title vests initially in the author or authors of the work. The authors of a joint work are coowners of copyright in the work.

(b) Works Made for Hire.—In the case of a work made for hire, the employer or other person for whom the work was prepared is considered the author for purposes of this title, and, unless the parties have expressly agreed otherwise in a written instrument signed by them, owns all of the rights comprised in the copyright.

(c) Contributions to Collective Works.—Copyright in each separate contribution to a collective work is distinct from copyright in the collective work as a whole, and vests initially in the author of the contribution. In the absence of an express transfer of the copyright or of any rights under it, the owner of copyright in the collective work is presumed to have acquired only the privilege of reproducing and distributing the contribution as part of that particular collective work, any revision of that collective work, and any later collective work in the same series.

(d) Transfer of Ownership.—

(1) The ownership of a copyright may be transferred in whole or in part by any means of conveyance or by operation of law, and may be bequeathed by will or pass as personal property by the applicable laws of intestate succession.

(2) Any of the exclusive rights comprised in a copyright, including any subdivision of any of the rights specified by section *106*, may be transferred as provided by clause (1) and owned separately. The owner of any particular exclusive right is entitled, to the extent of that right, to all of the protection and remedies accorded to the copyright owner by this title.

(e) Involuntary Transfer.—When an individual author's ownership of a copyright, or of any of the exclusive rights under a copyright, has not previously been transferred voluntarily by that individual author, no action by any governmental body or other official or organization purporting to seize, expropriate, transfer, or exercise rights of ownership with respect to the copyright, or any of the exclusive rights under a copyright, shall be given effect under this title, except as provided under title 11.

§ 202. Ownership of copyright as distinct from ownership of material object

Ownership of a copyright, or of any of the exclusive rights under a copyright, is distinct from ownership of any material object in which the work is embodied. Transfer of ownership of any material object, including the copy or phonorecord in which the work is first fixed, does not of itself convey any rights in the copyrighted work embodied in the object; nor, in the absence of an agreement, does transfer of ownership of a copyright or of any exclusive rights under a copyright convey property rights in any material object.

§ 401. Notice of copyright: Visually perceptible copies

(a) General Provisions.—Whenever a work protected under this title is published in the United States or elsewhere by authority of the copyright owner, a notice of copyright as provided by this section may be placed on publicly distributed copies from which the work can be visually perceived, either directly or with the aid of a machine or device.

(b) Form of Notice.—If a notice appears on the copies, it shall consist of the following three elements:

(1) the symbol © (the letter C in a circle), or the word "Copyright", or the abbreviation "Copr."; and

(2) the year of first publication of the work; in the case of compilations, or derivative works incorporating previously published material, the year date of first publication of the compilation or derivative work is sufficient. The year date may be omitted where a pictorial, graphic, or sculptural work, with accompanying text matter, if any, is reproduced in or on greeting cards, postcards, stationery, jewelry, dolls, toys, or any useful articles; and

(3) the name of the owner of copyright in the work, or an abbreviation by which the name can be recognized, or a generally known alternative designation of the owner.

(c) Position of Notice.—The notice shall be affixed to the copies in such manner and location as to give reasonable notice of the claim of copyright. The Register of Copyrights shall prescribe by regulation, as examples, specific methods of affixation and positions of the notice on various types of works that will satisfy this requirement, but these specifications shall not be considered exhaustive.

(d) Evidentiary Weight of Notice.—If a notice of copyright in the form and position specified by this section appears on the published copy or copies to which a defendant in a copyright infringement suit had access, then no weight shall be given to such a defendant's interposition of a defense based on innocent infringement in mitigation of actual or statutory damages, except as provided in the last sentence of section 504(c)(2).

§ 501. Infringement of copyright

(a) Anyone who violates any of the exclusive rights of the copyright owner as provided by sections 106 through 118 or of the author as provided in section 106A(a), or who imports copies or phonorecords into the United States in violation of section 602, is an infringer of the copyright or right of the author, as the case may be. For purposes of this chapter (other than section 506), any reference to copyright shall be deemed to include the rights conferred by section 106A(a). As used in this subsection, the term "anyone" includes any State, any instrumentality of a State, and any officer or employee of a State or instrumentality of a State acting in his or her official capacity. Any State, and any such instrumentality, officer, or employee, shall be subject to the provisions of this title in the same manner and to the same extent as any nongovernmental entity.

(b) The legal or beneficial owner of an exclusive right under a copyright is entitled, subject to the requirements of section *411*, to institute an action for any infringement of that particular right committed while he or she is the owner of it. The court may require such owner to serve written notice of the action with a copy of the complaint upon any person shown, by the records of the Copyright Office or otherwise, to have or claim an interest in the copyright, and shall require that such notice be served upon any person whose interest is likely to be affected by a decision in the case. The court may require the joinder, and shall permit the intervention, of any person having or claiming an interest in the copyright.

(c) For any secondary transmission by a cable system that embodies a performance or a display of a work which is actionable as an act of infringement under subsection (c) of section *111*, a television broadcast station holding a copyright or other license to transmit or perform the same version of that work shall, for purposes of subsection (b) of this section, be treated as a legal or beneficial owner if such secondary transmission occurs within the local service area of that television station.

(d) For any secondary transmission by a cable system that is actionable as an act of infringement pursuant to section *111*(c)(3), the following shall also have standing to sue: (i) the primary transmitter whose transmission has been altered by the cable system; and (ii) any broadcast station within whose local service area the secondary transmission occurs.

(e) With respect to any secondary transmission that is made by a satellite carrier of a primary transmission embodying the performance or display of a work and is actionable as an act of infringement under section *119*(a)(5), a network station holding a copyright or other license to transmit or perform the same version of that work shall, for purposes of subsection (b) of this section, be treated as a legal or beneficial owner if such secondary transmission occurs within the local service area of that station.

§ 502. Remedies for infringement: Injunctions

(a) Any court having jurisdiction of a civil action arising under this title may, subject to the provisions of section *1498* of title 28, grant temporary and final injunctions on such terms as it may deem reasonable to prevent or restrain infringement of a copyright.

(b) Any such injunction may be served anywhere in the United States on the person enjoined; it shall be operative throughout the United States and shall be enforceable, by proceedings in contempt or otherwise, by any United States court having jurisdiction of that person. The clerk of the court granting the injunction shall, when requested by any other court in which enforcement of the injunction is sought, transmit promptly to the other court a certified copy of all the papers in the case on file in such clerk's office.

§ 503. Remedies for infringement: Impounding and disposition of infringing articles

(a) At any time while an action under this title is pending, the court may order the impounding, on such terms as it may deem reasonable, of all copies or phonorecords claimed to have been made or used in violation of the copyright owner's exclusive rights, and of all plates, molds, matrices, masters, tapes, film negatives, or other articles by means of which such copies or phonorecords may be reproduced.

(b) As part of a final judgment or decree, the court may order the destruction or other reasonable disposition of all copies or phonorecords found to have been made or used in violation of the copyright owner's exclusive rights, and of all plates, molds, matrices, masters, tapes, film negatives, or other articles by means of which such copies or phonorecords may be reproduced.

CHAPTER 2

INTELLECTUAL PROPERTY PROTECTION FOR USEFUL ARTICLES

Peter Canelias

§ 2.01 INTRODUCTION

The intellectual property protection afforded to the appearance of two- and three-dimensional utilitarian objects creates unique issues for attorneys representing artists and designers. Copyright law generally denies protection to the design of "useful articles" where the design is not "separable" from the utility, or, in the words of the Bauhaus School, where the form follows the function. Of course, the utilitarian aspect of an object is often in the eye of the beholder. A three-dimensional figure may be protected by copyright if it is prepared as a sculpture, but not if it is prepared as a useful object.[1] Furthermore, as discussed below, determining whether a design is "separable" from an object is a fact-dependent inquiry, and is sometimes incapable of certain resolution absent a court decision.

Copyrights are not the only form of intellectual property protection implicated by the appearance of useful articles. Design patents can provide some degree of protection for creative designs embodied in useful articles, such as a Bauhaus chair, a pen,[2] or almost any other example of industrial design. Design patents, however, offer protection for a more limited time than do copyrights (14 years from the date of issue of the patent, as opposed to the author's life plus 70 years), and at a higher cost. Another important consideration for attorneys is that design patents may be applied for only by the creator(s) of the design, that is, a natural person, even though the employer or other entity may be the owner of the patent through an assignment. The creator of the design (or his or her assignee) may be represented during the patent application process only by patent lawyers registered to practice before the United States Patent and Trademark Office (PTO). It is, however, important that attorneys representing artists and designers understand the fundamentals of design patents as well as copyrights so as to properly advise their clients.

§ 2.02 COPYRIGHT PROTECTION FOR USEFUL ARTICLES

[A] Definition of "Useful Article"

A "useful article" is defined by the copyright statute as "an article having an intrinsic utilitarian function that is not merely to portray the appearance of the article or to convey information. An article that is normally a part of a useful article is considered a 'useful article.' "[3] In defining "pictorial, graphic and sculp-

---

[1] *See, e.g.*, Brandir Int'l Inc. v. Cascade Pac. Lumber Co. 834 F.2d 1142, 1145, 5 U.S.P.Q.2d 1089, 1093 (2d Cir. 1987) (bicycle rack, inspired from wire sculptures created originally by designer for nonfunctional purposes, is not copyrightable).

[2] *See, e.g.*, U.S. Des. Patent No. 392,317, titled "Writing Instrument," appended to the end of this chapter as Appendix 2-B.

[3] 17 U.S.C. § 101 (1999).

tural works," the copyright statute also provides that "the design of a useful article, as defined in this section, shall be considered a pictorial, graphic, or sculptural work only if, and only to the extent that, such design incorporates pictorial, graphic, or sculptural features that can be identified separately from, and are capable of existing independently of, the utilitarian aspects of the article."[4]

Before addressing separability of the design, however, it is necessary to decide first whether an article is a "useful article" as that term is used in the copyright statute. Again, the determination is not simple, because all artistic works possess at least some potential for utility. For example, a purely "aesthetic" painting can be a jigsaw puzzle. A sculpture of a hand (a maquette) can be a sculpture admired for its intrinsic aesthetic worth or it can be used as a mold for forming gloves. Almost any two-dimensional design can be used to cover a wall (wallpaper), or a floor (carpeting), and almost any small three-dimensional work may be employed as a paperweight.

However, a copyrighted work of art does not lose is protected status merely because it subsequently is put to a functional use.[5] Generally courts have held articles to be "useful" only where the utility of the article is its primary purpose, or where the utilitarian aspects are marginal in view of the aesthetic content.[6] For example, in *Gay Toys, Inc. v. Buddy L Corp.*[7] the court held that a toy airplane was not primarily a "useful article," noting that "a toy airplane is to be played with and enjoyed, but a painting of an airplane, which is copyrightable, is to be looked at and enjoyed. Other than the portrayal of a real airplane, a toy airplane, like a painting, has no intrinsic utilitarian function."[8] The uncertainty of this inquiry into the nature of an article, however, suggests that the prudent course is to first allow that a particular article is useful, and then seek protection to the extent that the design elements are separable from the utilitarian aspects.[9]

[B] Separability of Design

As seen from the statutory language, useful articles are not subject to a blanket disqualification from copyright protection. The key to the availability of

---

[4] *Id.*

[5] Mazer v. Stein, 347 U.S. 201, 100 U.S.P.Q. 325 (1954). *But see Brandir*, 834 F.2d 1142, 5 U.S.P.Q.2d 1089 (bicycle rack, which was inspired from wire sculptures created originally by designer for nonfunctional purposes, is not copyrightable, since form of rack is influenced in significant measure by utilitarian concerns and thus any aesthetic elements are not conceptually separate from its utilitarian elements, even though sculptures which inspired rack may have been copyrightable).

[6] *See* Paul Goldstein, Copyrights § 2.5.3.1a. (Aspen L. & Bus. 1999).

[7] 703 F.2d 970, 973, 218 U.S.P.Q. 13 (6th Cir. 1983).

[8] *Id.*

[9] *See* Goldstein, *supra* note 6, § 2.5.3.1a.

copyright protection lies in the separability of the design from the useful article. What is and is not separable, however, is a distinction not easy to make. Courts are split as to the nature of separability. The views can be divided into (1) the narrow view of many courts (and the Copyright Office) that, to be "separable" means that the artistic elements must be capable of physical separation from the useful article in question,[10] and (2) the broader view that those artistic elements that are conceptually separable from the function of the article are copyrightable.[11]

Where the aesthetic elements have merely been applied to an article, as in the case of a decal, separability of the design from the object is obvious, and would comport with the requirements of both the broad and narrow view. Physical separability (the narrow view) exists when (1) a pictorial, graphic or sculptural feature may be physically removed without impairing the utility of the article, and (2) the removed feature could stand alone as a work of art. As an example and illustration of the limitations of the doctrine of physical separability, it would be useful to contrast two case decisions that concern the copyrightability of related items. In the first decision, *Ted Arnold Ltd. v. Silvercraft Co.*,[12] the court upheld the copyrightability of a miniature sculpture of an eagle welded to an outdoor light fixture, based on the obvious physical separability of the two major constituent parts—that they had been physically joined.

In the second case, *Esquire, Inc. v. Ringer*,[13] the court upheld a determination by the Copyright Office that the shape of an outdoor lighting fixture was not copyrightable because it was not physically separable from the lighting fixture itself.[14] The distinction between the decisions in *Ted Arnold* and *Ringer* appears to be that attaching a separate design, as in *Ted Arnold*, is copyrightable, whereas the merger of a design into the shape of an existing object, as in *Ringer*, is not copyrightable.

The test of conceptual separability is less clear than that of physical separability, and has been the subject of different articulations.[15] A proposed synthesis of the various theories states that "a pictorial, graphic or sculptural feature incorporated in the design of a useful article is conceptually separable, if it can stand on its own as a work of art traditionally conceived, and if the useful article in which it is

[10] *See* Esquire, Inc. v. Ringer, 591 F.2d 796, 803-04, 199 U.S.P.Q. 1 (D.C. Cir. 1978), *cert. denied*, 440 U.S. 908, 201 U.S.P.Q. 256, *reh'g denied*, 441 U.S. 917 (1979).

[11] *See, e.g.*, Brandir Int'l Inc. v. Cascade Pac. Lumber Co. 834 F.2d 1142, 5 U.S.P.Q.2d 1089 (2d Cir. 1987) (" 'Conceptual separability' is thus alive and well, at least in this circuit.").

[12] 259 F. Supp. 733 (S.D.N.Y. 1966).

[13] 591 F.2d. 796 (D.C. Cir. 1978).

[14] *Id.* at 803-04.

[15] *See, e.g.*, Carol Barnhart Inc. v. Economy Cover Corp., 773 F.2d 411, 419, 228 U.S.P.Q. 385 (2d Cir. 1985) (Newman, J., dissenting) (setting out four possible tests of conceptual separability before articulating his own).

embodied would be equally useful without it."[16] Thus, the "idea" of the article and the "idea" of the design become separable in the abstract, such as the separation of the ornamental design of a belt buckle from the buckle itself, because the buckle without the design would remain useful and the design could exist on its own as a work of art.[17] In some respects, this theory parallels the patent law doctrine that the availability of alternative designs for the same article of manufacture indicates that the design is ornamental rather than purely functional.[18]

The Second Circuit, in *Brandir International Inc. v. Cascade Pacific Lumber Co.*,[19] articulated the test (as adopted from a law review article) as "if design elements reflect a merger of aesthetic and functional considerations, the artistic aspects of a work cannot be said to be conceptually separable from the utilitarian elements. Conversely, where design elements can be identified as reflecting the designer's artistic judgment exercised independently of functional influences, conceptual separability exists." The above test was derived as follows:

> Perhaps the difference between the majority and the dissent in *Carol Barnhart* might have been resolved had they had before them the Denicola article in *Applied Art and Industrial Design: A Suggested Approach to Copyright in Useful Articles*, *supra*.[20] There, Professor Denicola points out that although the Copyright Act of 1976 was an effort " 'to draw as clear a line as possible,' " in truth "there is no line, but merely a spectrum of forms and shapes responsive in varying degrees to utilitarian concerns." 67 Minn. L. Rev. at 741. Denicola argues that "the statutory directive requires a distinction between works of industrial design and works whose origins lie outside the design process, despite the utilitarian environment in which they appear." He views the statutory limitation of copyrightability as "an attempt to identify elements whose form and appearance reflect the unconstrained perspective of the artist," such features not being the product of industrial design. Id. at 742. "Copyrightability, therefore, should turn on the relationship between the proffered work and the process of industrial design." Id. at 741. He suggests that "the dominant characteristic of industrial design is the influence of nonaesthetic, utilitarian concerns" and hence concludes that copyrightability "ultimately should depend on the extent to which the work reflects artistic expression uninhibited by functional considerations."[21]

---

[16] Goldstein, *supra* note 6, § 2.5.3, 109.

[17] Kieselstein-Cord v. Accessories by Pearl, Inc., 632 F.2d 989, 993, 208 U.S.P.Q. 1 (2d Cir. 1980). *See also Carol Barnhart*, *supra* note 15, 773 F.2d at 419 (copyright denied for mannequins where human torso configurations were so simple that few if any mannequins would be useful without them).

[18] *See infra* § 2.05 [C].

[19] 834 F.2d 1142, 1145, 5 U.S.P.Q.2d 1089, 1091-92 (2d Cir. 1987).

[20] Denicola, Applied Art and Industrial Design: A Suggested Approach to Copyright in Useful Articles, 67 Minn. L. Rev. 707, 709-17 (1983).

[21] *Id.* Professor Denicola rejects the exclusion of all works created with some utilitarian application

Even this synthesis, however, is not without its detractors. Dissenting in part from the majority decision, Circuit Judge Winter remarked: "[M]y colleagues' adaptation of Professor Denicola's test diminishes the statutory concept of 'conceptual separability' to the vanishing point."[22]

§ 2.03 DESIGN PATENTS

In addition to limited copyright protection[23] for useful articles, patent protection is available particularly for those artistic works that may be classified as industrial design. Although the term "patent" usually suggests a useful invention, rather than an artistic creation, ornamental designs also may qualify for patent protection, subject to statutory requirements, via design patents. A design patent differs fundamentally from a utility patent (a patent on the useful features of a device or process), in that a design patent covers only the ornamental or decorative aspects of an article of manufacture, and does not extend to purely functional aspects.

Section 171 of the patent statute provides for the grant of patents on designs: "Whosoever invents any new, original and ornamental design for an article of manufacture may obtain a patent therefor, subject to the conditions and requirements of this title."[24] A patentable design may consist of surface ornamentation, the configuration of an article, or some combination of both. To be ornamental, a design must present a pleasing aesthetic appearance[25] and must not be dictated solely by functional considerations.[26] As set forth in the statute, a design patent

---

in view, for that would not only overturn *Mazer v. Stein*, 347 U.S. 201 [100 U.S.P.Q. 325] (1954), on which much of the legislation is based, but also "a host of other eminently sensible decisions, in favor of an intractable factual inquiry of questionable relevance." 67 Minn. L. Rev. at 741. He adds that "[a]ny such categorical approach would also undermine the legislative determination to preserve an artist's ability to exploit utilitarian markets." *Id.* (citing 17 U.S.C. § 113(a) (1976)).

[22] Brandir Int'l Inc. v. Cascade Pac. Lumber Co. 834 F.2d 1142, 5 U.S.P.Q.2d 1089 (2d Cir. 1987) (Winter, C.J., dissenting in part).

[23] *See* Landscape Forms Inc. v. Columbia Cascade Co., 113 F.3d 373, 42 U.S.P.Q.2d 1641 (2d Cir. 1997) ("Those who would seek monopolistic protection for industrial design, but are unable to obtain a design patent, have had little success under the law of copyright even with the 'conceptual separateness' gloss provided by the 1976 Act.").

[24] 35 U.S.C. § 171 (1999). For the application of regulations, 37 C.F.R. § 1.151 provides that, "the rules relating to applications for patents for other inventions or discoveries are also applicable to applications for patents for designs except as otherwise provided."

[25] Note that although the Court used the term "pleasing," it is established that " 'ornamental' does not always mean artistic or pleasing to the eye." Best Lock Corp. v. Ilco Unican Corp., 94 F.3d 1563, 1567, 40 U.S.P.Q.2d 1048 (Fed. Cir. 1996) (Newman, J. dissenting) (*citing* In re Koehring, 37 F.2d 421, 422 (CCPA 1930)).

[26] *See* Bonito Boats Inc. v. Thunder Craft Boats Inc., 489 U.S. 141, 9 U.S.P.Q.2d 1847, 1851 (1989) ("To qualify for protection, a design must present an aesthetically pleasing appearance that is not dictated by function alone, and must satisfy the other criteria of patentability.").

must comply with the ordinary requirements applicable to utility patents, unless such requirements would clearly be irrelevant. This means, briefly, that the design (1) must be novel or new, and (2) would not have been obvious at the time the design was created to a designer of ordinary skill who designs articles of that type. A design patent is enforceable for a 14-year period from the date of issue.[27] In addition, no maintenance fees are required to keep a design patent in force.

[A] Contrast with Copyright Protection

The design patent and copyright laws partially overlap in terms of subject matter.[28] Under the design patent statute, a patent may issue for an "ornamental design for an article of manufacture." Under the Copyright Law, as revised in 1976, a copyright may be secured for "the design of a useful object" (that is, "an article having an intrinsic utilitarian function that is not merely to portray the appearance of the article or to convey information") "if, and only to the extent that, such design incorporates pictorial, graphic, or sculptural features that can be identified separately from, and are capable of existing independently of, the utilitarian aspects of the article."[29]

Copyrights have the advantage in a number of comparisons with design patents. Copyrights are much less expensive to register than design patents. Copyrights last for much longer periods of time. Copyright registration is faster than obtaining a design patent. Timely registration of a copyright permits the award of statutory damages, whereas none are allowed under the patent law.[30]

The one real advantage of design patent protection for an otherwise copyrightable object is that a design patent allows the patentee to exclude others from making, using, selling, offering to sell or importing the patented article. Copying, whether shown by direct evidence or indirectly through access and substantial similarity, is not required for design patent infringement. Indeed, a later, independent development of the same design is not a defense to patent infringement. For a noncopyrightable artistically designed object such as a Bauhaus chair, or the lighting fixture in *Esquire v. Ringer*, discussed above, design patenting is the only way to protect the artist's rights.

[B] Doctrine of Election

There has been a basic question as to whether one may obtain both a copyright registration and a design patent for the same design, or whether one must "elect"

---

[27] *See* 35 U.S.C. § 173 (1999).

[28] *See* Schnadig Corp. v. Gaines Mfg. Co., 620 F.2d 1166, 206 U.S.P.Q. 202 (6th Cir. 1980) ("[W]here copyright is available, it is more popular than the design patent largely because copyrights are far easier and less expensive to obtain than the design patents.").

[29] 37 U.S.C. § 101, § 102(a) (1999).

[30] 35 U.S.C. § 289 does provide for a minimum of $250 damages.

one or the other form of protection. The present answer is that an artist may obtain both.

The most common situation is where a design patent is sought after obtaining a copyright registration. In *In re Yardley,*[31] the applicant sought a design patent on a "Spiro Watch" upon which a copyright registration had already been obtained. The PTO, in refusing to grant a design patent based on the prior copyright registration, contended that there was a "failure of adequate consideration for grant of a design patent" since the disclosed subject matter would not, because of the copyright's greater duration, fall into the public domain upon expiration of the patent. The court rejected the PTO's position, reasoning that "a patent is not a contract" and neither the copyright and patent statutes nor the Constitution supported a doctrine of election.

The other situation, obtaining a copyright registration for a work that is already the subject of an issued design patent, occurs less frequently because it is faster, cheaper and easier to secure and register a copyright than it is to obtain a design patent. In *Korzybski v. Underwood & Underwood, Inc.,*[32] the Second Circuit applied the doctrine of election to invalidate a copyright on a work that was already the subject of a design patent. Consistent with the decision in *Korzybski,* the now-replaced regulations of the Copyright Office provided that a copyright registration would not be granted for a design where the design patent had issued. The new regulation, however, provides:

> **§ 202.10 Pictorial, graphic, and sculptural works.**
>
> (a) In order to be acceptable as a pictorial, graphic, or sculptural work, the work must embody some creative authorship in its delineation or form. The registrability of such a work is not affected by the intention of the author as to the use of the work or the number of copies reproduced. The availability of protection or grant of protection under the law for a utility or design patent will not affect the registrability of a claim in an original work of pictorial, graphic, or sculptural authorship.[33]

A cautious lawyer representing an artist whose work is either utilitarian or whose work will be incorporated into a utilitarian object will apply for both

[31] 493 F.2d 1389, 181 U.S.P.Q. 331 (CCPA 1974). *See also* Comment, "Dual Copyright and Design Patent Protection: Works of Art and Ornamental Designs," 49 St. John's L. Rev. 543 (1975). The PTO amended its rules, effective January 1, 1989, to allow inclusion of copyright notices in patent specifications and drawings. 37 C.F.R. §§ 1.71(d), (e); § 84(o). The applicant must include a specific authorization allowing "facsimile reproduction by anyone of the patent document or the patent disclosure, as it appears in the Patent and Trademark Office patent file or records, ..."

[32] 36 F.2d 727, 3 U.S.P.Q. 242 (2d Cir. 1929).

[33] 37 C.F.R. § 202.10(a) (1999).

copyright registration (assuming the work is not clearly excluded from copyright protection), which costs virtually nothing, and also for a design patent. If granted both, the client would be given a minimum of 14 years of protection, with the possibility of being protected for the full term of the copyright. This "belt and suspenders" approach will also work for those items that serve contemporaneously as artistic works and, with some modification, as utilitarian objects, such as a sculpture that is also adapted and marketed as a mannequin.[34]

§ 2.04 PATENTABLE DESIGNS

[A] Inseparability of Design and Object

The Manual of Patent Examining Procedure ("MPEP") defines a design as follows:

> The design of an object consists of the visual characteristics or aspects displayed by the object. It is the appearance presented by the object which creates an impression, through the eye upon the mind of the observer.
>
> Since a design is manifested in appearance, the subject matter of a design patent application may relate to the configuration or shape of an object, to the surface ornamentation on an object, or both.
>
> Design is inseparable from the object to which it is applied and cannot exist alone merely as a scheme of surface ornamentation. It must be a definite, preconceived thing, capable of reproduction and not merely the chance result of a method.[35]

A design rests on appearance created by the configuration of the article, surface ornamentation, or some combination of configuration and ornamentation. A patentable design must theoretically be inseparable from the object and cannot exist alone, and this particular requirement has led to much uncertainty of what is and is not patentably inseparable. For example, in *Pioneer Photo Albums Inc. v. Holson Co.*,[36] the district court noted that the patentee "has not cited the Court to any case or other authority which even suggests that adding mere graphics to the surface of the 'article' can render patentable an otherwise unpatentable 'design for an article of manufacture.' " Contrast this statement with the patentability of computer-generated fonts, or with designs for wallpaper.[37] The Board of Patent

[34] Goldstein, *supra* note 6, § 2.5.3.1.

[35] MPEP § 1502.

[36] 654 F. Supp. 87, 2 U.S.P.Q.2d 1638 (C.D. Cal. 1987).

[37] *See, e.g.*, the design patent for a wallpaper, no. 337,662 issued to Lagomarsino on July 27, 1993, appended to the end of this chapter as Appendix 2-C. *See also* the design patent for a decorative glass panel, no. 305,364 issued to Shaffer, also appended to the end of this chapter as Appendix 2-D.

Appeals and Interferences (an administrative tribunal within the PTO) stated: "[A] picture standing alone is not protectable by a design patent."[38] Despite this stance, however, design patents have been obtained for posters containing artwork,[39] where the affixing of the picture to a poster sufficed for patentability (though the fate of such patents in litigation is unclear). Despite the apparent inconsistencies, however, articles of manufacture with surface ornamentation qualify as patentable subject matter. For example, design patents have been issued (and litigated) for trash bags with jack-o'-lantern patterns.[40]

Because the key to patentability is the ornamental or decorative aspects of the design, it follows that designs that are never actually seen do not qualify for design patent protection. A number of cases have disallowed patents for designs that are hidden or obscured while in use or where the appearance of the article "could be a matter of concern to no one."[41] On the other hand, a design for an article that is hidden in its final use may be patentable because, during some point in its life, its appearance is a "matter of concern."[42]

[B] Computer-Generated Images

Many artists today work with computer design programs to produce their work. Ordinarily, if the computer generated design qualifies as protectable subject matter under the copyright laws, a copyright registration may be obtained for the work. However, some forms of computer-generated art are not protectable by copyright; for example, fonts.[43] When a computer-generated image is not clearly copyrightable, design patent protection is usually available. To continue the example given above, fonts are protectable by design patent,[44] whether the patent is

[38] Ex parte Donaldson, 26 U.S.P.Q.2d 1250 (Bd. Pat. App. & Int'f 1992).

[39] Design patent no. 290,100 titled "Poster or the Like" and issued to Brown et al. on June 2, 1987 and design patent no. 361,733 titled "Poster" and issued to Masuda on August 29, 1995, both of which are appended to this chapter as Appendices 2-E and 2-F.

[40] *See, e.g.*, Sun Hill Indus. Inc. v. Easter Unlimited Inc. 48 F.3d 1193, 33 U.S.P.Q.2d 1925 (Fed Cir. 1995) (design patent on trash bags decorated with lines and facial features, allowing the bag, when filled with trash or leaves, to resemble a Halloween pumpkin, or jack-o'-lantern).

[41] In re Cornwall, 230 F.2d 457, 109 U.S.P.Q. 57 (CCPA 1956) ("It is well settled that patentability of a design cannot be based on elements which are concealed in the normal use of the device to which the design is applied."); *see also* KeyStone Retaining Wall Sys. Inc. v. Westrock Inc. 997 F.2d 1444, 27 U.S.P.Q.2d 1297 (Fed Cir. 1993) ("We agree that generally concealed features are not proper bases for design patent protection because their appearance cannot be a 'matter of concern.' ") (*citing* In re Stevens, 173 F.2d 1015, 1016, 81 U.S.P.Q. 365, 365-66 (CCPA 1949)).

[42] In re Webb, 916 F.2d 1553, 1557, 16 U.S.P.Q.2d 1433, 1435 (Fed. Cir. 1990) (design for prosthesis patentable).

[43] *See* Adobe Sys. Inc. v. Southern Software Inc., 45 U.S.P.Q.2d 1827, 1830-31 (N.D. Cal. 1998); 57 Fed. Reg. 35 at pp. 6201-2 (February 12, 1992) (computer programs that generate typefaces registrable even though typefaces are not protected by copyright).

[44] *See, e.g.*, *id.*

for the print block containing the font design[45] or for a computer-generated font.[46] The PTO's guidelines issued March 20, 1996[47] state:

> The PTO considers designs for computer-generated icons embodied in articles of manufacture to be statutory subject matter eligible for design patent protection under Section 171. Thus, if an application claims a computer-generated icon shown on a computer screen, monitor, other display panel, or a portion thereof, the claim complies with the "article of manufacture" requirement of section 171.
>
> * * *
>
> Traditionally, type fonts have been generated by solid blocks from which each letter or symbol was produced. Consequently, the PTO has historically granted design patents drawn to type fonts. PTO personnel should not reject claims for type fonts under Section 171 for failure to comply with the "article of manufacture" requirement on the basis that more modern methods of typesetting, including computer-generation, do not require solid printing blocks.

§ 2.05 REQUIREMENTS FOR PATENTABILITY

Generally, the requirements for patenting a design are as follows:

1. the design must be novel,[48]
2. the design must be non-obvious (at the time made) to a person of ordinary skill,[49] and
3. the design must be ornamental, rather than functional.[50]

[A] Novelty

Whether a design is "new" within the meaning of the patent law is determined by reference to 35 U.S.C. § 102, which provides that:

> A person shall be entitled to a patent unless—
>
> (a) the invention was known or used by others in this country, or patented or described in a printed publication in this or a foreign country, before the invention thereof by the applicant for patent, or
>
> (b) the invention was patented or described in a printed publication in this or a foreign country or in public use or on sale in this country, more

---

[45] For example, Des. 305,437, appended to this chapter as Appendix 2-G.

[46] For example, Des. 337,604, appended to this chapter as Appendix 2-H.

[47] 61 Fed. Reg. 11380, 11381-82.

[48] 35 U.S.C. § 102(a)-(g) (1999).

[49] 35 U.S.C. § 103 (1999).

[50] 35 U.S.C. § 171 (1999).

than one year prior to the date of the application for patent in the United States, or

(c) he has abandoned the invention, or

(d)[51] the invention was first patented or caused to be patented, or was the subject of an inventor's certificate, by the applicant or his legal representatives or assigns in a foreign country prior to the date of the application for patent in this country on an application for patent or inventor's certificate filed more than twelve months before the filing of the application in the United States, or

(e) the invention was described in a patent granted on an application for patent by another filed in the United States before the invention thereof by the applicant for patent, or on an international application by another who has fulfilled the requirements of paragraphs (1), (2), and (4) of section 371(c) of this title before the invention thereof by the applicant for patent, or

(f) he did not himself invent the subject matter sought to be patented, or

(g) before the applicant's invention thereof the invention was made in this country by another who had not abandoned, suppressed or concealed it. In determining priority of invention there shall be considered not only the respective dates of conception and reduction to practice of the invention, but also the reasonable diligence of one who was first to conceive and last to reduce to practice, from a time prior to conception by the other.[52]

[1] Section 102(a)—Restriction on Old Design

Section 102(a) prohibits the grant of a patent (and may provide the basis to invalidate an issued patent) where the invention was (1) known or used by others in this country, (2) patented, or (3) described in a printed publication anywhere, where any of the foregoing occurred before the applicant invented the design in issue. The essence of § 102(a) is that no patent may be secured for a design that is old, that is, has been done before by someone else, as evidenced by one or more of the recited acts. Section 102(a) does not apply to the artist's own work, in that the entire paragraph assumes that these acts are done by someone other than the patent applicant.

[2] Section 102(b)—Grace Period

Section 102(b) essentially provides for a one-year grace period, starting from the day that the design was (1) patented, (2) described in a printed publication

---

[51] 35 U.S.C. § 172 expressly alters § 102(d) by reducing the period to six months (rather than twelve months) for design patents.

[52] 35 U.S.C. § 102 (1999).

anywhere, (3) in public use in the United States, or (4) on sale in the United States, to file a patent application. It is important to realize that the provisions of § 102(b) apply to the inventor's own work, unlike the provisions of §§ 102(a) and (g). Thus, a potential applicant should be aware that a public display, publication (such as a copyright registration or trademark registration), or *offer* for sale of the design will start the one-year period, and if no patent application is filed within this period, the inventor will be permanently barred from seeking a patent.[53]

[3] Section 102(c)—Invention Abandonment

Section 102(c) provides that the artist or designer may not receive a patent if he or she has abandoned the invention. In other words, if a designer gives up on a particular design, he may not obtain a patent. At what point such abandonment occurs is subject to the particular situation; a mere lapse of time is insufficient to show abandonment.

[4] Section 102(d)—Foreign Patents

Section 102(d) addresses the situation where foreign patents are filed for the same design. Section 102(d) bars issuance of a United States design patent if the design was first patented in a foreign country where (1) the foreign patent issues before the United States patent is applied for, and (2) the foreign application was filed in the foreign country more than six months before the filing of the United States application.

[5] Section 102(e)—Patent Already Issued

Section 102(e) concerns applications where the design is described in an issued patent that was applied for before the present applicant "invented" his or

[53] This is subject to the factual determination as to the actual first date of public display, publication, or offer for sale. The applicability of the "experimental use" exception concerning design patents is doubtful, especially in the context of the "on sale" bar to patentability. *See* Continental Plastic Containers Inc. v. Owens-Brockway Plastic Prods. Inc., 141 F.3d 1073, 46 U.S.P.Q.2d 1277 (Fed. Cir. 1998) (experimental negation does not apply to design patents in context of on-sale bar). *See also* Tone Bros., Inc. v. Sysco Corp., 28 F.3d 1192, 31 U.S.P.Q.2d 1321 (Fed. Cir. 1994) (distinguishing In re Mann, 861 F.2d 1581, 8 U.S.P.Q.2d 2030 (Fed. Cir. 1988) in the context of public use). *Mann* held that there was "no way in which an ornamental design for an article of manufacture can be subject to the 'experimental use' exception applicable in the case of functioning machines, manufactures, or processes." 861 F.3d at 1582, 8 U.S.P.Q.2d at 2031. *See generally* Rooklidge & Weil, The Application of Experimental Use to Design Patents: A Square Peg in a Round Hole, 77 J. Pat. & Trademark Off. Soc'y 921 (1995). The applicant should also be aware that the patent laws of many foreign countries do not even extend such a one-year grace period; any nonconfidential disclosure of the invention may irrevocably bar a patent.

her design. Note that the additional provisions of § 102(e) relating to international treaty-based applications are not applicable to design patents.

[6] Section 102(f)—Derivation Restriction

Section 102(f) provides that an applicant may not receive a patent if he or she did not invent the subject matter sought to be patented. This requirement embodies one of the unique distinctions of United States patent law, which is that, in the first instance, only the first and true inventor (designer) may obtain a patent on the design. To take the work of another and present it as one's own is termed "derivation," and would bar the issuance of a patent to the person who derived the subject matter from another.

[7] Section 102(g)—Priority Requirement

Section 102(g) bars the grant of a patent if, before the applicant made his or her invention, the invention was made in the United States by another who had not abandoned, suppressed or concealed it. Thus, § 102(g) outlines the requirements for priority, namely, who invented a particular design first. In determining priority, invention is measured by the dates of conception (the complete idea of the design) and reduction to practice (embodiment of the design or the filing of a patent application), and the competing claimants' respective diligence between the two dates.

[B] Non-Obviousness

A design patent must meet a requirement of non-obviousness comparable to that for utility patents.[54] It is hardly surprising that the courts admit that any assessment of obviousness is necessarily subjective.[55] Despite the conceptual difficulties, non-obviousness remains a statutory requirement for patentability. Specifically, a patent may not be obtained (and an issued patent may be held invalid) "if the differences between the subject matter sought to be patented and the prior art are such that the subject matter as a whole would have been obvious at the time the invention was made to a person having ordinary skill in the

---

[54] Section 103 applies to designs because of the provision in § 171 that design patents are "subject to the conditions and requirements of this title." *See* Durling v. Spectrum Furniture Co., 101 F.3d 100, 103, 40 U.S.P.Q.2d 1788, 1790 (Fed. Cir. 1996) (design patent applicant "must satisfy the patentability requirement of 35 U.S.C. § 103 (1994)").

[55] *See* In re Bartlett, 300 F.2d 942, 944, 133 U.S.P.Q. 204 (CCPA 1962) ("[T]he determination of patentability in design cases must finally rest on the subjective conclusion of each judge."); In re Johnson, 175 F.2d 791, 792, 82 U.S.P.Q. 199 (CCPA 1949) (determination is a "subjective standard in the mind of the judge").

art to which said subject matter pertains."[56] For design patents, obviousness is determined from the standpoint of the "designer of ordinary capability who designs articles of the type presented in the application."[57]

In the case of design patents, although § 103 applies to designs as it does to utility inventions, the claimed design must contain novel and non-obvious ornamental features, as opposed to functional limitations. In order for a design to be obvious, there must first be some prior art reference that shows the same fundamental design as the new design. This reference is referred to as the "primary reference." A primary reference is one that creates "basically the same" visual impression as the claimed or patented design.[58]

The ultimate question of obviousness or non-obviousness is one of law, meaning that ultimately, the court decides. The predicate inquiry under § 103, however, is based upon the factors set forth in *Graham v. John Deere Co.*:[59]

- the scope and content of the prior art
- the differences between the prior art and the claims at issue
- the level of ordinary skill in the art
- objective evidence of non-obviousness[60]

These "*Graham* factors," together with the statutory language, provide the basic legal framework for obviousness determinations.

[1] Scope and Content of the Prior Art

This first factor simply means that any things or references that precede the applicant's design (as measured by the subparagraphs of § 102), are evaluated for all that they disclose. The obviousness inquiry turns on the "differences" between the prior art and the claimed invention. If there are no differences between the claimed invention and a single prior art reference, then the invention is

---

[56] 35 U.S.C. § 103(a) (1999).

[57] *See Durling*, 101 F.3d at 103, 40 U.S.P.Q.2d at 1790 ("In the design patent context, the ultimate inquiry under section 103 is whether the claimed design would have been obvious to a designer of ordinary skill who designs articles of the type involved."); In re Borden, 90 F.3d 1570, 1574, 39 U.S.P.Q.2d 1524, 1526 (Fed. Cir. 1996) ("[C]entral inquiry in analyzing an ornamental design for obviousness is whether the design would have been obvious to 'a designer of ordinary skill who designs articles of the type involved.' "); L.A. Gear, Inc. v. Thom McAn Shoe Co., 988 F.2d 1117, 1124, 25 U.S.P.Q.2d 1913, 1917 (Fed. Cir. 1993) (obviousness "is reviewed from the viewpoint of a designer of ordinary skill or capability in the field to which the design pertains.").

[58] *See Durling*, 101 F.3d at 103, 40 U.S.P.Q.2d at 1790. *See also* In re Borden, 90 F.3d at 1574, 39 U.S.P.Q.2d 1524.

[59] 383 U.S. 1, 148 U.S.P.Q. 459 (1966).

[60] *See also* MPEP § 2141.

anticipated under § 102. Assuming some difference, however, the determination of whether the invention is obvious is neither terribly clear nor certain. By definition, obviousness requires some alteration or combination of prior art features, present at the time the invention was made, where such combination or alteration would have been obvious to one of ordinary skill in the art.

[2] Differences Between the Prior Art and the Claims

According to statute, the predicate for the obviousness inquiry is that there are at least some differences between any single reference and the claimed subject matter. Having first determined what is and what is not prior art under § 102, and analyzed its scope and content, including whether the references are properly combinable as analogous, the differences between the prior art and the claims are identified. This is largely a factual inquiry based on the particular claims and the prior art.

[3] The Level of Ordinary Skill in the Art

As § 103 states, obviousness occurs at the time the invention was made. This applies as well to the determination of what level of skill a person of ordinary skill possessed at the time.[61] It is a way of maintaining objectivity, a way of excluding the present technical art, which may include many advances now taken for granted, from intruding on and contaminating the consideration of obviousness. In general, a person of ordinary skill in the art is "one who thinks along the lines of conventional wisdom in the art and is not one who undertakes to innovate."[62] Unlike the familiar retort to the question of what "obscenity" means—"I know it when I see it"—for obviousness, the test might be phrased as "I know it when I've seen it."

Many factors may be considered to assess the level of ordinary skill, including education and experience. A helpful list is provided in *Custom Accessories, Inc. v. Jeffrey-Allan Industries, Inc.*[63] "Factors that may be considered in determining level of skill include: type of problems encountered in art; prior art solutions to those problems; rapidity with which innovations are made; sophistication of the technology; and education level of active workers in the field."

---

[61] Stewart-Warner Corp. v. City of Pontiac, 767 F.2d 1563, 226 U.S.P.Q. 676 (Fed. Cir. 1994).

[62] Standard Oil Co. v. American Cyanamid Co., 774 F.2d 448, 227 U.S.P.Q. 293 (Fed. Cir. 1985).

[63] 807 F.2d 955, 1 U.S.P.Q.2d 1196 (Fed. Cir. 1986) (cited in In re GPAC, Inc., 57 F.3d 1573, 35 U.S.P.Q.2d 1116 (Fed. Cir. 1995)).

[4] Objective Evidence of Non-Obviousness

The objective evidence referred to in *Graham* is usually referred to as "secondary considerations." Secondary considerations may come in many forms, but the most common types include commercial success of the design, satisfying a long-felt need, unexpected results, expressions of disbelief by experts, the failure of others to find a solution to the design problem at hand, and copying of the design by others. Of the various secondary considerations, allegations of commercial success are the most common in determining the obviousness of a design. Copying by the accused infringer can also be given weight since design patents "encourage ornamentation and beautification in manufactured articles so as to increase their salability and satisfy the aesthetic sense of the purchasers."[64] However, it must be clear that the commercial success is attributable to the patented design and not to other factors such as functional improvement.[65]

Evaluating commercial success for design patents "presents a special difficulty."[66] Evidence of commercial success should clearly establish that the success is attributable to the design, and not to some other factor.[67] Secondary considerations, however, do apply in the design patent context and can provide probative evidence of non-obviousness.[68]

[C] Ornamentality

[1] Contrast With Function

A design or shape that is entirely functional, without ornamental or decorative aspect, does not meet the statutory criteria of a design patent.[69] It is sometimes difficult, however, to separate the "useful" and "ornamental" aspects of an article of manufacture. Articles of manufacture usually possess both functional and ornamental characteristics. Although the design patent is directed to the ornamental aspect of a useful article, the fact that the design of a particular article is related to the article's use may not defeat patentability. When the design is primarily

---

[64] In re Rosen, 673 F.2d 388, 213 U.S.P.Q. 347 (CCPA 1982) ("[C]lear-cut imitation is indicative of the commercial appeal of the design of an article and should be given proper consideration.").

[65] Litton Sys., Inc. v. Whirlpool Corp., 728 F.2d 1423, 221 U.S.P.Q. 97 (Fed. Cir. 1984).

[66] *Id.*

[67] *Id. See also* Petersen Mfg. Co. v. Central Purchasing Inc., 740 F.2d 1541, 222 U.S.P.Q. 562 (Fed. Cir. 1984) (no evidence that acceptance of patented tool was due to ornamental appearance rather than filling need for quality tool of its type).

[68] *See, e.g.,* L.A. Gear, Inc. v. Thom McAn Shoe Co., 980 F.2d 1117, 25 U.S.P.Q.2d 1913 (Fed. Cir. 1993) (commercial success and copying relevant to analysis of obviousness of design).

[69] *Id.* at 1123, 25 U.S.P.Q.2d at 1917. *See* Lee v. Dayton-Hudson Corp., 838 F.2d 1186, 1188-89, 5 U.S.P.Q.2d 1625, 1627 (Fed. Cir. 1988) (the design patent protects the nonfunctional aspects of a useful article); In re Rosen, 673 F.2d at 391, 213 U.S.P.Q. at 350.

ornamental, although it also serves a utilitarian purpose, this design patent condition is met. As explained in *Bonito Boats, Inc. v. Thunder Craft Boats, Inc.*,[70] to qualify for design patent protection, a design must have an ornamental appearance that is not dictated by function alone. In determining whether the statutory requirement that the design be "ornamental" is met, it is relevant whether functional considerations demand only this particular design or whether other designs could be used, such that the choice of design is made for primarily aesthetic, non-functional purposes.[71] In other words, the availability of alternative designs for an article of manufacture indicates that the primary purpose of a particular design is ornamental.

To further illustrate the distinction between form and function, both design and utility patents (patents on functional aspects of an article of manufacture) may be obtained on the same article if invention resides both in its utility (function) and ornamental appearance. It follows that elements of a design may be functional. In *Avia Group International, Inc. v. L.A. Gear California, Inc.*,[72] the Federal Circuit held that the district court did not err in finding that patents which claimed the ornamental designs of an athletic shoe outer sole and an athletic shoe upper were not invalid for functionality:

> There is no dispute that shoes are functional and that certain features of the shoe designs in issue perform functions. However, a distinction exists between the functionality of an article or features thereof and the functionality of the particular design of such article or features thereof that perform a function. Were that not true, it would not be possible to obtain a design patent on a utilitarian article of manufacture, . . . or to obtain both design and utility patents on the same article.

It is only the design that is dictated *solely* by functional considerations that is not a proper subject for a design patent.[73] Of course, in the examples of a pen or the Bauhaus chair, where there is no functional improvement, the configuration would be entitled only to a design patent, and not a utility patent.

[2] Article of Manufacture

A design is patentable only insofar as it is embodied in an article of manufacture. A broad definition has been given to the phrase "article of manufacture" in

---

[70] 489 U.S. 141, 148, 9 U.S.P.Q.2d 1847, 1851 (1989).

[71] *See, e.g.*, L.A. Gear v. Thom McAn Shoe Co., 988 F.2d at 1123-24, 25 U.S.P.Q.2d at 1917 ("When there are several ways to achieve the function of an article of manufacture, the design of the article is more likely to serve a primarily ornamental purpose."); In re Carletti, 328 F.2d 1020, 1022, 140 U.S.P.Q. 653, 654 (CCPA 1964) (determining whether the appearance is "directed by" the use of the article).

[72] 853 F.2d 1557, 1563, 7 U.S.P.Q.2d 1548, 1553 (Fed. Cir. 1988).

[73] *See* Best Lock Corp. v. Ilco Unican Corp., 94 F.3d 1563, 1566, 40 U.S.P.Q.2d 1048, 1049-

the PTO and in the courts. An article of manufacture includes tools and machines,[74] as well as what would be considered a "manufacture" within the meaning of § 101. For the artist, the phrase "article of manufacture" can mean almost any material with which the artist chooses to work. For example, in *In re Hruby*,[75] the court held that a water fountain display, including the configuration of the spraying water, was patentable subject matter for a design patent. The court stated that "designs depend upon outside factors for the production of the appearance which the beholder observes. The design of a lampshade may not be apparent unless the lamp is lighted. The design of a woman's hosiery is not apparent unless it is in place on her legs. The designs of inflated articles such as toy balloons, water toys, air mattresses, and now even buildings are not apparent in the absence of the compressed air which gives them form, as the water pressure here gives shape to the fountain."[76]

Current PTO practice requires the design applicant to "designate the particular article" as to which a patent is sought.[77] The PTO does permit, however, the addition of the phrase "or similar article" in order "to allow latitude of construction."[78] It is not necessary to actually make the article in order to obtain a patent, though embodiment of the design in the article of manufacture may show reduction to practice.[79]

§ 2.06 ELEMENTS OF A DESIGN PATENT APPLICATION

A design patent may be applied for by the actual inventor of the design (or, in certain circumstances, by the inventor's heirs). Although a design patent may be assigned to another person or to a company, the application must be made by the inventor (or joint inventors, if more than one). A design patent may be submitted and pursued by the inventor, or by a registered patent attorney or registered patent agent as designated by the inventor.

---

50 (Fed. Cir. 1996) ("[I]f the design claimed in a design patent is dictated solely by the function of the article of manufacture, the patent is invalid because the design is not ornamental.").

[74] *See* In re Koehring, 37 F.2d 421, 4 U.S.P.Q. 169 (CCPA 1939).

[75] 373 F.2d 997, 1000-01, 153 U.S.P.Q. 61 (CCPA 1967).

[76] *Id.*

[77] 37 C.F.R. § 1.153(a) (1999).

[78] MPEP § 1503.01.

[79] As to what constitutes actual reduction to practice of a design, see Continental Plastic Containers Inc. v. Owens-Brockway Plastic Prods. Inc., 141 F.3d 1073, 46 U.S.P.Q.2d 1277 (Fed. Cir. 1998); Fitzgerald v. Arbib, 268 F.2d 763, 122 U.S.P.Q. 530 (CCPA 1959). *See also* Dieterich v. Leaf, 89 F.2d 226, 33 U.S.P.Q. 237 (CCPA 1937). Note that a three-dimensional design is actually reduced to practice when affixed in three-dimensional form, and that a two-dimensional design (such as for fabric, carpeting or wallpaper) is actually reduced to practice when affixed in two-dimensional form.

The general requirements of adequate disclosure[80] and definite claiming found in the first two paragraphs of § 112 apply to design patents:

> The specification shall contain a written description of the invention, and of the manner and process of making and using it, in such full, clear, concise, and exact terms as to enable any person skilled in the art to which it pertains, or with which it is most nearly connected, to make and use the same, and shall set forth the best mode contemplated by the inventor of carrying out his invention.[81]
>
> The specification shall conclude with one or more claims particularly pointing out and distinctly claiming the subject matter which the applicant regards as his invention.[82]

A design patent application should include the following:[83]

1. a preamble, stating the name of the applicant, the descriptive title of the design, and setting out a brief description of the nature and intended use of the article in which the design is embodied;
2. a description of the figure(s) of the drawings;
3. description, if any;
4. a single claim;
5. drawings or photographs; and
6. an executed oath or declaration.

In addition, the filing fee set forth in 37 C.F.R. § 1.16(f) is also required. If the applicant is a small entity (an independent inventor, a small business concern, or a nonprofit organization) and the inventor is not obligated to assign his or her rights to a large entity, the filing fee is reduced by half if the small entity files a Statement Claiming Small Entity Status.[84] Also, if a patent is ultimately allowed, an issue fee must be paid for the patent to issue. As of October 1999, the fees for design patents are: for large entities, a filing fee of $310 and an issue fee of $430; for small entities, a filing fee of $155 for filing and an issue fee of $215.

---

[80] *E.g.*, In re Salmon, 705 F.2d 1579, 217 U.S.P.Q. 981 (Fed. Cir. 1983).

[81] 35 U.S.C. § 112, ¶ 1 (1999). *But see* Racing Strollers Inc. v. TRI Indus. Inc., 878 F.2d 1418, 11 U.S.P.Q.2d 1300, 1301 (Fed. Cir. 1989) ("In the case of an 'ornamental design for an article of manufacture,' . . . the 'best mode' requirement of the first paragraph of § 112 is not applicable, as a design has only one 'mode' and it can be described only by illustrations showing what it looks like (though some added description in words may be useful to explain the illustrations).").

[82] 35 U.S.C. § 112 ¶ 2 (1999).

[83] Questions regarding an application and its forms may be directed to the Patent Assistance Center at 1-800-786-9199. Additional information may be obtained from the PTO Web site at http://www.uspto.gov.

[84] Forms PTO/SB/09 (independent inventor), PTO/SB/10 (small business concern) and PTO/SB/11 (nonprofit organization), are appended to the end of this chapter. *See* Forms 2-3 through 2-5.

[A] Figure Descriptions

The figure descriptions indicate what each view of the drawings represents—front elevation, top plan, perspective view, and so on. Any description of the design in the specification, other than a brief description of the drawing, is generally not necessary since, as a general rule, the drawing is the design's best description. However, a special description, while not required, is not prohibited.

In addition to the figure descriptions, the following types of statements are permissible in the specification:

1. description of the appearance of portions of the claimed design which are not illustrated in the drawing disclosure (for example, "the right side elevational view is a mirror image of the left side");
2. description disclaiming portions of the article not shown, that form no part of the claimed design;
3. statement indicating that any broken line illustration of environmental structure in the drawing is not part of the design sought to be patented; and
4. description denoting the nature and environmental use of the claimed design, if not included in the preamble.

[B] Single Claim

A design patent application may include only a single claim. The claim defines the design that the applicant wishes to patent in terms of the article in which it is embodied or applied. The claim must be in formal terms to "[t]he ornamental design for (the article which embodies the design or to which it is applied) as shown." The description of the article in the claim should be consistent in terminology with the title of the invention.

When there is a properly included special description of the design in the specification, or a proper showing of modified forms of the design, or other descriptive matter has been included in the specification, the words "and described" should be added to the claim following the term "shown," and the claim should read "The ornamental design for (the article which embodies the design or to which it is applied) as shown and described."

[C] Drawings and Photographs

The drawing disclosure is the most important element of the application. Every design patent application must include either a drawing or a photograph of the claimed design. As the drawing or photograph constitutes the entire visual disclosure of the claim, it is of utmost importance that the drawing or photograph be clear and complete, that nothing regarding the design sought to be patented is left to conjecture. Normally, drawings are required to be in black ink on white paper.

[1] The Views

The drawings or photographs should contain a sufficient number of views to disclose completely the appearance of the claimed design (ordinarily six views of the article, i.e., front, rear, right and left sides, top and bottom).[85] Nothing regarding the shape, configuration and surface ornamentation of the article for which the patent is sought may be left to conjecture.[86] If the drawings are insufficient in this respect, the design patent will be invalid under § 112.[87]

[2] Surface Shading

The drawing should be provided with appropriate surface shading which shows clearly the character and contour of all surfaces of any three-dimensional aspects of the design. Surface shading is also necessary to distinguish between any open and solid areas of the design. Solid black surface shading is not permitted except when used to represent the black color as well as color contrast. Lack of appropriate surface shading in the drawing as filed may render the design non-enabling under 35 U.S.C. § 112, first paragraph. Additionally, if the shape of the design is not evident from the disclosure as filed, the addition of surface shading after filing may be viewed as new matter. New matter is anything that is added to, or deleted from, the claim, drawings or specification that was neither shown nor suggested in the original application.[88]

[3] Broken Lines

A broken line is understood to be for illustrative purposes only and forms no part of the claimed design. Structure that is not part of the claimed design but is considered necessary to show the environment in which the design is used may be represented in the drawing by broken lines. This includes any portion of an article in which the design is embodied or applied to that is not considered part of the claimed design.

---

[85] 37 C.F.R. § 1.152 (1999).

[86] MPEP § 1503.02.

[87] *See, e.g.,* In re Salmon, 705 F.2d 1579, 217 U.S.P.Q. 981 (Fed. Cir. 1983) (drawing of stool with seat and support in solid lines gives no indication, for purposes of description requirement of § 112, that invented design resides in the support and not in the shape of the seat).

[88] *See* 35 U.S.C. 132 (1999); 37 C.F.R § 1.121 (1999).

[4] Photographs

The PTO will accept high quality black-and-white photographs in design patent applications only after the granting of a petition filed under 37 C.F.R. § 1.84(b)(1) requesting that photographs be accepted (photographs are not acceptable if filed together with drawings). The petition must include the appropriate fee set forth in 37 C.F.R. § 1.17(h) and the three sets of photographs required under 37 C.F.R. § 1.84(b)(1)(ii). If other provisions of 37 C.F.R. § 1.84(b) for photographs have not been complied with—for example, the photographs are not on double-weight photographic paper, the photos are not properly mounted, or details are not adequately reproducible—such lack of compliance will not bar the grant of a petition to accept the photographs but rather will form the basis of subsequent objection to the quality of the photographic disclosure.

Color drawings and color photographs will be accepted as formal drawings in design applications as long as they meet the requirements set forth in 37 C.F.R. § 1.84(a)(2). If color photographs are submitted as informal drawings and the applicant does not consider the color to be part of the claimed design, a disclaimer must be added to the specification as follows: "The color shown on the claimed design forms no part thereof." In the absence of a disclaimer filed with the original application, color will be considered an integral part of the disclosed and claimed design. If no disclaimer has been included, the omission of color in the later-filed formal drawings will be treated as introducing new matter into the claim, as stated in 35 U.S.C. § 132. A disclaimer may be used only when filing informal drawings, because 37 C.F.R. § 1.152(a)(2) requires that the disclosure in formal photographs be limited to the design for the article claimed.

[D] Oath or Declaration

The oath or declaration required of the applicant must comply with the requirements set forth in 37 C.F.R. § 1.63. A sample PTO form is included at the end of this chapter. It is important to note that the applicant declares compliance with Rule 56,[89] which requires that all persons involved in the application and prosecution disclose to the PTO all material prior art references of which they are aware.

[E] Sample Specification

The following is a sample specification which concludes with a formal claim appropriate for a design patent application:

---

[89] 37 C.F.R. § 1.56 (1999).

To the Commissioner of Patents and Trademarks:
Your petitioner, (Name) ____________ a citizen of (Country) ____________ and a resident of (City, State) ____________, prays that letters patent may be granted for the design for a (Title) ____________ as set forth in the following specification:
FIG. 1 is a ____________view of a ____________ showing my new design;
FIG. 2 is a ____________view thereof;
FIG. 3 is a ____________view thereof;
FIG. 4 is a ____________view thereof;
FIG. 5 is a ____________view thereof; and
FIG. 6 is a ____________view thereof.

I claim: the ornamental design for a ____________ as shown.

§ 2.07 THE DESIGN PATENT APPLICATION PROCESS

Preparing a design patent application and conducting the proceedings in the PTO to obtain the patent requires knowledge of patent law and rules and PTO practice and procedures. When a complete design patent application, with the appropriate filing fee, is received by the PTO, it is assigned an Application Number and a Filing Date. A "Filing Receipt" containing this information is sent to the applicant. The application is then assigned to an examiner. Applications are examined in order of their filing date.[90]

[A] Examination of the Application

The actual "examination" entails checking for compliance with formalities, ensuring completeness of the drawing disclosure, and comparing the claimed subject matter with the "prior art." In the context of patent examination, "prior art" consists of issued patents and published materials that are either disclosed by the applicant under the duty of disclosure or uncovered by the examiner during the examiner's search. If the claimed design is found to be patentable, the application will be "allowed" and the applicant will receive instructions for completing the process to permit issuance as a patent.

The examiner may reject the claim in the application if the disclosure cannot be understood or is incomplete, or if a reference or combination of references found in the prior art shows the claimed design to be unpatentable. The examiner will then issue an Office Action detailing the rejection and addressing the substantive matters that affect patentability, and which also may contain the examiner's suggestions for amendments to the application.

---

[90] *See* 37 C.F.R. § 1.101 (1999). The exception to this rule may be accomplished under certain circumstances by a Petition to Make Special, which, based upon certain grounds (such as infringement) can "bump" the application to the head of the line. *See* 37 C.F.R. § 1.102 (1999).

If, after receiving an Office Action, the applicant chooses to continue prosecution of the application, he or she must submit a timely reply to the action. This reply, which must be made in writing, should include a request for reconsideration or further examination of the claim, along with any amendments desired by the applicant; must distinctly and specifically point out the supposed errors in the Office Action; and must address every objection and/or rejection in the action.

If the examiner has rejected the claim over prior art, a general statement by the applicant that the claim is patentable, without specifically pointing out how the design is patentable over the prior art, does not comply with the rules. In all cases where the examiner has said that a reply to a requirement is necessary, or where the examiner has indicated patentable subject matter, the reply must comply with the requirements set forth by the examiner, or specifically argue each requirement as to why compliance should not be required.

[B] Responding to an Office Action

In any communication with the PTO, applicant should include the following items to identify the case:

1. application number (checked for accuracy);
2. group art unit number (copied from filing receipt or most recent Office Action);
3. filing date;
4. name of the examiner who prepared the most recent Office Action; and
5. title of invention.

When a reply to an Office Action is submitted, the application will be reconsidered and further examined in view of the applicant's remarks and any amendments with the reply. The examiner will then either withdraw the rejection and allow the application or, if not persuaded, repeat the rejection and make it final. After a final rejection or after a claim has been rejected twice, the applicant may file an appeal with the Board of Patent Appeals and Interferences. Applicant may also file a new application prior to the abandonment of the original application, claiming benefit of the earlier filing date. This will allow continued prosecution of the claim.

The PTO's designated time period for reply is set to run from the "Date Mailed," which is indicated on the first page of the Office Action. If the reply is not received within this period, the application will be considered abandoned. If the applicant cannot reply within the time period set in the Office Action, he or she may prevent abandonment by filing a reply within six months from the mail date of the Office Action, provided a petition for extension of time and the fee set forth in 37 C.F.R. § 1.17(a) are filed. The fee is determined by the amount of time requested, and increases as the length of time increases. These fees are set by rule and are subject to change. An "Extension of Time" does not have to be obtained prior to the submission of a reply to an Office Action; it may be mailed along with the reply.[91]

§ 2.08 INFRINGEMENT

To determine whether a design patent claim has been infringed, first, as with utility patents, the claim must be properly construed to determine its meaning and scope. Second, the claim as properly construed must be compared to the subject designs to determine whether there would be an infringement under the appropriate standards for design patents.[92] In construing the claim of a design patent, "[d]esign patents have almost no scope. The claim [of a design patent application] . . . is limited to what is shown in the application drawings."[93]

A design patent contains little or no written description; the drawings are the claims to the patented subject matter. To infringe a design patent the accused article must appropriate the features of the patented design and its overall appearance.[94] Infringement is determined from the viewpoint of the ordinary observer, whereby the observer would be led to believe that the accused article is that shown in the patent, due to the similarities in design.[95]

[A] The Ordinary Observer Test

The Supreme Court decided the seminal design patent infringement case of *Gorham Manufacturing Co. v. White,*[96] which remains the law today. *Gorham* concerned the question of infringement of a patent on a design for the handles of tablespoons and forks. The Court stated the proper standard for infringement of design patents as follows:

> We hold, therefore, that if, in the eye of an ordinary observer, giving such attention as a purchaser usually gives, two designs are substantially the same, if the resemblance is such as to deceive such an observer, inducing him to

---

[91] Note that an extension of time cannot be obtained when responding to a "Notice of Allowance."

[92] *See* Elmer v. ICC Fabricating Inc., 67 F.3d 1571, 1577, 36 U.S.P.Q.2d 1417 (Fed. Cir. 1995) (design patent claim construed first, citing Markman v. Westview Instruments, Inc., 52 F.3d 967, 976, 34 U.S.P.Q.2d 1321, 1326) (Fed. Cir. 1995) (en banc), *aff'd*, 517 U.S. 370, 116 S. Ct. 1384, 38 U.S.P.Q.2d 1461 (1996)).

[93] In re Mann, 861 F.2d 1581, 1582 8 U.S.P.Q.2d 2030 (Fed. Cir. 1988).

[94] L.A. Gear, Inc. v. Thom McAn Shoe Co., 988 F.2d 1117, 1125, 25 U.S.P.Q.2d 1913, 1918 (Fed. Cir. 1993); Litton Sys., Inc. v. Whirlpool Corp., 728 F.2d 1423, 1444, 221 U.S.P.Q. 97, 109 (Fed. Cir. 1984).

[95] *See* Gorham Co. v. White, 81 U.S. (14 Wall.) 511, 528 (1871).

[96] *Id.*

purchase one supposing it to be the other, the first one patented is infringed by the other.[97]

In analyzing the visual similarity, where the patented design is composed of functional as well as ornamental features, infringement must be shown by establishing that an ordinary observer would be deceived by the common ornamental features in the claimed design and the subject product.[98] The presence of a "deceiving resemblance" between the claimed design and the accused product, however, is only the first part of the test for infringement.

[B] The Point of Novelty Test

Once an accused design appears to infringe under the ordinary observer test of *Gorham*, the next step is to analyze the patented design to determine its "points of novelty"; those design aspects that differ from those found in the prior art. To infringe a design patent, the accused design must incorporate the points of novelty found in the patented design.[99]

In *Sun Hill Industries, Inc. v. Easter Unlimited, Inc.*,[100] the Federal Circuit held that the district court erred in failing to consider whether the accused product appropriated the specific novel features of the claimed design. The patented design was for bags decorated with lines and facial features which allowed the bag, when filled with trash or leaves or lawn clippings, to resemble a Halloween-style pumpkin, or jack-o'-lantern. The prior art design was a yellow plastic Halloween trick-or-treat bag with two identical happy jack-o'-lantern faces on either side, which, with vertical stripes, resembled a pumpkin when the bag was filled. Contrasting this description with the claimed design in the patent, the Federal Circuit noted that there were, at most, four points of novelty in the claimed design when compared with prior art design: contrasting (non-identical) jack-o'-lantern faces, the bottom closure of the bag, the specific features of the jack-o'-lantern faces,

---

[97] 81 U.S. at 527-28.

[98] Read Corp. v. Portec, Inc., 970 F.2d 816, 825, 23 U.S.P.Q.2d 1426 (Fed. Cir. 1992).

[99] *See* Sun Hill Indus., Inc. v. Easter Unlimited, Inc., 48 F.3d 1193, 1199, 33 U.S.P.Q.2d 1925 (Fed. Cir. 1995); Oakley, Inc. v. International Tropic-Cal, Inc., 923 F.2d 167, 169 17 U.S.P.Q.2d 1401 (Fed. Cir. 1991); Winner Int'l Corp. v. Wolo Mfg. Corp., 905 F.2d 375, 376, 15 U.S.P.Q.2d 1076 (Fed. Cir. 1990) ("To consider the overall appearance of a design without regard to prior art would eviscerate the purpose of the 'point of novelty' approach, which is to focus on those aspects of a design which render the design different from prior art designs"); Litton Sys., Inc. v. Whirlpool Corp., 728 F.2d 1423, 1444, 221 U.S.P.Q. 97, 110 (Fed. Cir. 1984) ("[E]ven though the court compares two items through the eyes of the ordinary observer, it must nevertheless, to find infringement, attribute their similarity to the novelty which distinguishes the patented device from the prior art.").

[100] 48 F.3d 1193, 33 U.S.P.Q.2d 1925 (Fed Cir. 1995).

and the shiny surface. The court then reversed the finding of infringement, holding that none of the points of novelty were incorporated into the accused product.

§ 2.09 REMEDIES FOR INFRINGEMENT

[A] Damages

[1] General Damages

The general damages provision is found in 35 U.S.C. § 284. Damages for infringement may be had for (1) the patentee's lost profits, or (2) no less than a reasonable royalty. The patentee may also recover interest and costs: "Upon finding for the claimant the court shall award the claimant damages adequate to compensate for the infringement, but in no event less than a reasonable royalty for the use made of the invention by the infringer, together with interest and costs as fixed by the court."[101]

[2] Special Damages for Design Patent Infringement

Section 289 of the patent law does provide a special remedy for infringement of a design patent: "Whoever during the term of a patent for a design, without license of the owner, (1) applies the patented design, or any colorable imitation thereof, to any article of manufacture for the purpose of sale, or (2) sells or exposes for sale any article of manufacture to which such design or colorable imitation has been applied shall be liable to the owner to the extent of his total profit, but not less than $250, recoverable in any United States district having jurisdiction of the parties."

The statute also provides: "Nothing in this section shall prevent, lessen, or impeach any other remedy which an owner of an infringed patent has under the provisions of this title, but he shall not twice recover the profit made from the infringement." In other words, a patentee may recover the usual patent infringement relief such as injunctive relief and damages (either the patentee's lost profits or a reasonable royalty), and may recover the infringer's profits, subject to the prohibition against double recovery.

[B] Injunctive Relief

Injunctive relief against patent infringement is available under § 283: "The several courts having jurisdiction of cases under this title may grant injunctions

---

[101] 35 U.S.C. § 284 (1999).

in accordance with the principles of equity to prevent the violation of any right secured by patent, on such terms as the court deems reasonable."[102]

[C] Treble Damages and Attorney Fees

Section 284, second paragraph, provides: "When the damages are not found by a jury, the court shall assess them. In either event the court may increase the damages up to three times the amount found or assessed." This provision gives the court the ability to increase damages up to three times for "willful" infringement.[103] Willfulness measures the infringing behavior, in the circumstances in which the infringer acted, against an objective standard of reasonable commercial behavior in the same circumstances.[104] To willfully infringe a patent, the infringer must have knowledge of the issued patent and subsequently act with disregard of the patentee's rights under the circumstances.[105]

In addition to being able to increase damages up to three times, "[t]he court in exceptional cases may award reasonable attorney fees to the prevailing party."[106] Exceptional circumstances include misconduct during litigation, inequitable conduct during prosecution of the patent, vexatious or unjustified litigation, or a frivolous lawsuit.[107] Willful infringement is a sufficient basis for finding a case exceptional, but not every exceptional case warrants the award of attorney fees.[108]

---

[102] 35 U.S.C. § 283 (1999).

[103] *See* Cybor Corp. v. FAS Tech., Inc., 138 F.3d 370, 46 U.S.P.Q.2d 1169 (Fed. Cir. 1998) (en banc).

[104] *See* Hoechst Celanese Corp. v. BP Chemicals Ltd., 78 F.3d 1575, 38 U.S.P.Q.2d 1126 (Fed. Cir. 1996).

[105] *See* National Presto Indus., Inc. v. West Bend Co., 76 F.3d 1185, 37 U.S.P.Q.2d 1685 (Fed. Cir. 1996).

[106] 35 U.S.C. § 285 (1999).

[107] *See* Bayer Aktiengesellschaft v. Duphar Int'l Research B.V., 738 F.2d 1237, 222 U.S.P.Q. 649 (Fed. Cir. 1984).

[108] L.A. Gear, Inc. v. Thom McAn Shoe Co., 988 F.2d 1117, 25 U.S.P.Q.2d 1913 (Fed. Cir. 1993).

FORMS AND APPENDICES

FORM 2-1

Design Patent Application Transmittal

Please type a plus sign (+) inside this box → ☐

PTO/SB/18 (1/98)
Approved for use through 9/30/2000. OMB 0651-0032
Patent and Trademark Office: U.S. DEPARTMENT OF COMMERCE

DESIGN PATENT APPLICATION TRANSMITTAL *(Only for new nonprovisional applications under 37 CFR 1.53(b))*	
Attorney Docket No.	
First Inventor or Application Identifier	
Title	
Express Mail Label No.	

ADDRESS TO:

Assistant Commissioner for Patents
Box Design
Washington, DC 20231

DESIGN V. UTILITY: *A "design patent" protects an article's ornamental appearance (e.g., the way an article looks) (35 USC 171), while a "utility patent" protects the way an article is used and works (35 USC 101). The ornamental appearance of an article includes its shape/configuration or surface ornamentation upon the article, or both. Both a design and a utility patent may be obtained on an article if invention resides both in its ornamental appearance and its utility. For more information see MPEP 1502.01.*

APPLICATION ELEMENTS

See MPEP chapter 1500 concerning utility patent application

1. ☐ *Fee Transmittal Form (e.g., PTO/SB/17)
   (Submit an original, and a duplicate for fee processing)
2. ☐ Specification *[Total Pages ____]*
   (preferred arrangement set forth below, MPEP 1503.01)
   - Preamble
   - Cross References to Related Applications
   - Statement Regarding Fed sponsored R & D
   - Description of the figure(s) of Drawings
   - Description, if any
   - Claim (only one (1) claim permitted, MPEP 1503.03)
3. ☐ Drawing(s) *(35 U.S.C. 113)* *[Total Sheets ____]*
4. Oath or Declaration *[Total Pages ____]*
   a. ☐ Newly executed (original or copy)
   b. ☐ Copy from a prior application (37 C.F.R. 1.63(d))
   (for continuation/divisional with Box 15 completed)
   [Note Box 5 below]
      i. ☐ DELETION OF INVENTOR(S)
      Signed statement attached deleting inventor(s) named in the prior application, see 37 C.F.R. 1.63(d)(2) and 1.33(b).
5. ☐ Incorporation By Reference *(usable if Box 4b is checked)*
   The entire disclosure of the prior application, from which a copy of the oath or declaration is supplied under Box 4b, is considered to be part of the disclosure of the accompanying application and is hereby incorporated by reference therein.

ACCOMPANYING APPLICATION PARTS

6. ☐ Assignment Papers (cover sheet & document(s))
7. ☐ 37 C.F.R. 3.73(b) Statement *(when there is an assignee)* ☐ Power of Attorney
8. ☐ English Translation Document *(if applicable)*
9. ☐ Information Disclosure Statement (IDS)/PTO-1449 ☐ Copies of IDS Citations
10. ☐ Preliminary Amendment
11. ☐ Return Receipt Postcard (MPEP 503)
    (Should be specifically itemized)
12. ☐ * Small Entity Statement(s) *(PTO/SB/09-12)* ☐ Statement filed in prior application, Status still proper and desired
13. ☐ Certified Copy of Priority Document(s)
    (if foreign priority is claimed)
14. ☐ Other: ....

** A new statement is required to be entitled to pay small entity fees, except where one has been filed in a prior application and is being relied upon.*

15. If a CONTINUING APPLICATION, *check appropriate box, and supply the requisite information below and in a preliminary amendment:*

☐ Continuation ☐ Divisional of prior application No.: ____ / ________

Prior application information: *Examiner* ________ *Group / Art Unit* ________

16. CORRESPONDENCE ADDRESS

☐ *Customer Number or Bar Code Label* *(Insert Customer No. or Attach bar code label here)* *or* ☐ *Correspondence address below*

Name					
Address					
City		*State*		*Zip Code*	
Country		*Telephone*		*Fax*	

Name (Print/Type)		*Registration No. (Attorney/Agent)*	
Signature		*Date*	

Burden Hour Statement: This form is estimated to take 0.2 hours to complete. Time will vary depending upon the needs of the individual case. Any comments on the amount of time you are required to complete this form should be sent to the Chief Information Officer, Patent and Trademark Office, Washington, DC 20231. DO NOT SEND FEES OR COMPLETED FORMS TO THIS ADDRESS. SEND TO: Assistant Commissioner for Patents, Box Design, Washington, DC 20231.

FORM 2-2

Declaration for Utility or Design Patent Application

Please type a plus sign (+) inside this box → ☐

PTO/SB/01 (12-97)
Approved for use through 9/30/00. OMB 0651-0032
Patent and Trademark Office; U.S. DEPARTMENT OF COMMERCE
Under the Paperwork Reduction Act of 1995, no persons are required to respond to a collection of information unless it contains a valid OMB control number.

DECLARATION FOR UTILITY OR DESIGN PATENT APPLICATION (37 CFR 1.63)

☐ Declaration Submitted with Initial Filing OR ☐ Declaration Submitted after Initial Filing (surcharge (37 CFR 1.16 (e)) required)

Attorney Docket Number	
First Named Inventor	
COMPLETE IF KNOWN	
Application Number	
Filing Date	
Group Art Unit	
Examiner Name	

As a below named inventor, I hereby declare that:

My residence, post office address, and citizenship are as stated below next to my name.

I believe I am the original, first and sole inventor (if only one name is listed below) or an original, first and joint inventor (if plural names are listed below) of the subject matter which is claimed and for which a patent is sought on the invention entitled:

(Title of the Invention)

the specification of which
☐ is attached hereto
OR
☐ was filed on (MM/DD/YYYY) ____ as United States Application Number or PCT International Application Number ____ and was amended on (MM/DD/YYYY) ____ (if applicable).

I hereby state that I have reviewed and understand the contents of the above identified specification, including the claims, as amended by any amendment specifically referred to above.

I acknowledge the duty to disclose information which is material to patentability as defined in 37 CFR 1.56.

I hereby claim foreign priority benefits under 35 U.S.C. 119(a)-(d) or 365(b) of any foreign application(s) for patent or inventor's certificate, or 365(a) of any PCT international application which designated at least one country other than the United States of America, listed below and have also identified below, by checking the box, any foreign application for patent or inventor's certificate, or of any PCT international application having a filing date before that of the application on which priority is claimed.

Prior Foreign Application Number(s)	Country	Foreign Filing Date (MM/DD/YYYY)	Priority Not Claimed	Certified Copy Attached? YES	NO
			☐	☐	☐
			☐	☐	☐
			☐	☐	☐
			☐	☐	☐

☐ Additional foreign application numbers are listed on a supplemental priority data sheet PTO/SB/02B attached hereto:

I hereby claim the benefit under 35 U.S.C. 119(e) of any United States provisional application(s) listed below.

Application Number(s)	Filing Date (MM/DD/YYYY)	
		☐ Additional provisional application numbers are listed on a supplemental priority data sheet PTO/SB/02B attached hereto.

[Page 1 of 2]

Burden Hour Statement: This form is estimated to take 0.4 hours to complete. Time will vary depending upon the needs of the individual case. Any comments on the amount of time you are required to complete this form should be sent to the Chief Information Officer, Patent and Trademark Office, Washington, DC 20231. DO NOT SEND FEES OR COMPLETED FORMS TO THIS ADDRESS. SEND TO: Assistant Commissioner for Patents, Washington, DC 20231.

Please type a plus sign (+) inside this box → ☐

PTO/SB/01 (12-97)
Approved for use through 9/30/00. OMB 0651-0032
Patent and Trademark Office; U.S. DEPARTMENT OF COMMERCE
Under the Paperwork Reduction Act of 1995, no persons are required to respond to a collection of information unless it contains a valid OMB control number.

DECLARATION — Utility or Design Patent Application

I hereby claim the benefit under 35 U.S.C. 120 of any United States application(s), or 365(c) of any PCT international application designating the United States of America, listed below and, insofar as the subject matter of each of the claims of this application is not disclosed in the prior United States or PCT International application in the manner provided by the first paragraph of 35 U.S.C. 112, I acknowledge the duty to disclose information which is material to patentability as defined in 37 CFR 1.56 which became available between the filing date of the prior application and the national or PCT international filing date of this application.

U. S. Parent Application or PCT Parent Number	Parent Filing Date (MM/DD/YYYY)	Parent Patent Number *(if applicable)*

☐ Additional U.S. or PCT international application numbers are listed on a supplemental priority data sheet PTO/SB/02B attached hereto.

As a named inventor, I hereby appoint the following registered practitioner(s) to prosecute this application and to transact all business in the Patent and Trademark Office connected therewith: ☐ Customer Number [ ] → *Place Customer Number Bar Code Label here*
OR
☐ Registered practitioner(s) name/registration number listed below

Name	Registration Number	Name	Registration Number

☐ Additional registered practitioner(s) named on supplemental Registered Practitioner Information sheet PTO/SB/02C attached hereto.

Direct all correspondence to: ☐ Customer Number or Bar Code Label [ ] *OR* ☐ Correspondence address below

Name					
Address					
Address					
City		State		ZIP	
Country		Telephone		Fax	

I hereby declare that all statements made herein of my own knowledge are true and that all statements made on information and belief are believed to be true; and further that these statements were made with the knowledge that willful false statements and the like so made are punishable by fine or imprisonment, or both, under 18 U.S.C. 1001 and that such willful false statements may jeopardize the validity of the application or any patent issued thereon.

Name of Sole or First Inventor: ☐ A petition has been filed for this unsigned inventor

Given Name (first and middle [if any])	Family Name or Surname

Inventor's Signature						Date	
Residence: City		State		Country		Citizenship	
Post Office Address							
Post Office Address							
City		State		ZIP		Country	

☐ Additional inventors are being named on the ___ supplemental Additional Inventor(s) sheet(s) PTO/SB/02A attached hereto

[Page 2 of 2]

FORM 2-3

Statement Claiming Small Entity Status—Small Business Concern

PTO/SB/10 (1-99)
Approved for use through 9/30/2000. OMB 0651-0031
Patent and Trademark Office; U.S. DEPARTMENT OF COMMERCE
Under the Paperwork Reduction Act of 1995, no persons are required to respond to a collection of information unless it displays a valid OMB control number.

STATEMENT CLAIMING SMALL ENTITY STATUS (37 CFR 1.9(f) & 1.27(c))--SMALL BUSINESS CONCERN	Docket Number (Optional)

Applicant, Patentee, or Identifier: ______________________
Application or Patent No.: ______________________
Filed or Issued: ______________________
Title: ______________________

I hereby state that I am
☐ the owner of the small business concern identified below:
☐ an official of the small business concern empowered to act on behalf of the concern identified below:

NAME OF SMALL BUSINESS CONCERN ______________________

ADDRESS OF SMALL BUSINESS CONCERN ______________________

____

I hereby state that the above identified small business concern qualifies as a small business concern as defined in 13 CFR Part 121 for purposes of paying reduced fees to the United States Patent and Trademark Office. Questions related to size standards for a small business concern may be directed to: Small Business Administration, Size Standards Staff, 409 Third Street, SW, Washington, DC 20416.

I hereby state that rights under contract or law have been conveyed to and remain with the small business concern identified above with regard to the invention described in:

☐ the specification filed herewith with title as listed above.
☐ the application identified above.
☐ the patent identified above.

If the rights held by the above identified small business concern are not exclusive, each individual, concern, or organization having rights in the invention must file separate statements as to their status as small entities, and no rights to the invention are held by any person, other than the inventor, who would not qualify as an independent inventor under 37 CFR 1.9(c) if that person made the invention, or by any concern which would not qualify as a small business concern under 37 CFR 1.9(d), or a nonprofit organization under 37 CFR 1.9(e).

Each person, concern, or organization having any rights in the invention is listed below:
☐ no such person, concern, or organization exists.
☐ each such person, concern, or organization is listed below.

Separate statements are required from each named person, concern or organization having rights to the invention stating their status as small entities. (37 CFR 1.27)

I acknowledge the duty to file, in this application or patent, notification of any change in status resulting in loss of entitlement to small entity status prior to paying, or at the time of paying, the earliest of the issue fee or any maintenance fee due after the date on which status as a small entity is no longer appropriate. (37 CFR 1.28(b))

NAME OF PERSON SIGNING ______________________

TITLE OF PERSON IF OTHER THAN OWNER ______________________

ADDRESS OF PERSON SIGNING ______________________

SIGNATURE ______________________ DATE ______________________

Burden Hour Statement: This form is estimated to take 0.2 hours to complete. Time will vary depending upon the needs of the individual case. Any comments on the amount of time you are required to complete this form should be sent to the Chief Information Officer, Patent and Trademark Office, Washington, DC 20231. DO NOT SEND FEES OR COMPLETED FORMS TO THIS ADDRESS. SEND TO: Assistant Commissioner for Patents, Washington, DC 20231.

FORM 2-4

Statement Claiming Small Entity Status—Independent Inventor

PTO/SB/09 (12-97)
Approved for use through 9/30/00. OMB 0651-0031
Patent and Trademark Office; U.S. DEPARTMENT OF COMMERCE
Under the Paperwork Reduction Act of 1995, no persons are required to respond to a collection of information unless it displays a valid OMB control number.

STATEMENT CLAIMING SMALL ENTITY STATUS (37 CFR 1.9(f) & 1.27(b))--INDEPENDENT INVENTOR	Docket Number (Optional)

Applicant,Patentee, or Identifier: ______________________

Application or Patent No.: ______________________

Filed or Issued: ______________________

Title: ______________________

As a below named inventor, I hereby state that I qualify as an independent inventor as defined in 37 CFR 1.9(c) for purposes of paying reduced fees to the Patent and Trademark Office described in:

☐ the specification filed herewith with title as listed above.

☐ the application identified above.

☐ the patent identified above.

I have not assigned, granted, conveyed, or licensed, and am under no obligation under contract or law to assign, grant, convey, or license, any rights in the invention to any person who would not qualify as an independent inventor under 37 CFR 1.9(c) if that person had made the invention, or to any concern which would not qualify as a small business concern under 37 CFR 1.9(d) or a nonprofit organization under 37 CFR 1.9(e).

Each person, concern, or organization to which I have assigned, granted, conveyed, or licensed or am under an obligation under contract or law to assign, grant, convey, or license any rights in the invention is listed below:

☐ No such person, concern, or organization exists.

☐ Each such person, concern, or organization is listed below.

Separate statements are required from each named person, concern, or organization having rights to the invention stating their status as small entities. (37 CFR 1.27)

I acknowledge the duty to file, in this application or patent, notification of any change in status resulting in loss of entitlement to small entity status prior to paying, or at the time of paying, the earliest of the issue fee or any maintenance fee due after the date on which status as a small entity is no longer appropriate. (37 CFR 1.28(b))

NAME OF INVENTOR	NAME OF INVENTOR	NAME OF INVENTOR
Signature of inventor	Signature of inventor	Signature of inventor
Date	Date	Date

Burden Hour Statement: This form is estimated to take 0.2 hours to complete. Time will vary depending upon the needs of the individual case. Any comments on the amount of time you are required to complete this form should be sent to the Chief Information Officer, Patent and Trademark Office, Washington, DC 20231. DO NOT SEND FEES OR COMPLETED FORMS TO THIS ADDRESS. SEND TO: Assistant Commissioner for Patents, Washington, DC 20231.

FORM 2-5

Statement Claiming Small Entity Status—Nonprofit Organization

PTO/SB/11 (12-97)
Approved for use through 9/30/00. OMB 0651-0031
Patent and Trademark Office; U.S. DEPARTMENT OF COMMERCE
Under the Paperwork Reduction Act of 1995, no persons are required to respond to a collection of information unless it displays a valid OMB control number.

STATEMENT CLAIMING SMALL ENTITY STATUS (37 CFR 1.9(f) & 1.27(d))--NONPROFIT ORGANIZATION	Docket Number (Optional)

Applicant , Patentee, or Identifier: ______________________________
Application or Patent No.: ______________________________
Filed or Issued: ______________________________
Title: ______________________________

I hereby state that I am an official empowered to act on behalf of the nonprofit organization identified below:
NAME OF NONPROFIT ORGANIZATION ______________________________
ADDRESS OF NONPROFIT ORGANIZATION ______________________________
____

TYPE OF NONPROFIT ORGANIZATION:
☐ UNIVERSITY OR OTHER INSTITUTION OF HIGHER EDUCATION

☐ TAX EXEMPT UNDER INTERNAL REVENUE SERVICE CODE (26 U.S.C. 501(a) and 501(c)(3))

☐ NONPROFIT SCIENTIFIC OR EDUCATIONAL UNDER STATUTE OF STATE OF THE UNITED STATES OF AMERICA
(NAME OF STATE ______________________________)
(CITATION OF STATUTE ______________________________)

☐ WOULD QUALIFY AS TAX EXEMPT UNDER INTERNAL REVENUE SERVICE CODE (26 U.S.C. 501(a) and 501(c)(3)) IF LOCATED IN THE UNITED STATES OF AMERICA

☐ WOULD QUALIFY AS NONPROFIT SCIENTIFIC OR EDUCATIONAL UNDER STATUTE OF STATE OF THE UNITED STATES OF AMERICA IF LOCATED IN THE UNITED STATES OF AMERICA
(NAME OF STATE ______________________________)
(CITATION OF STATUTE ______________________________)

I hereby state that the nonprofit organization identified above qualifies as a nonprofit organization as defined in 37 CFR 1.9(e) for purposes of paying reduced fees to the United States Patent and Trademark Office regarding the invention described in:

☐ the specification filed herewith with title as listed above.
☐ the application identified above.
☐ the patent identified above.

I hereby state that rights under contract or law have been conveyed to and remain with the nonprofit organization regarding the above identified invention. If the rights held by the nonprofit organization are not exclusive, each individual, concern, or organization having rights in the invention must file separate statements as to their status as small entities and that no rights to the invention are held by any person, other than the inventor, who would not qualify as an independent inventor under 37CFR 1.9(c) if that person made the invention, or by any concern which would not qualify as a small business concern under 37 CFR 1.9(d) or a nonprofit organization under 37 CFR 1.9(e).

Each person, concern, or organization having any rights in the invention is listed below:

☐ no such person, concern, or organization exists.
☐ each such person, concern, or organization is listed below.

I acknowledge the duty to file, in this application or patent, notification of any change in status resulting in loss of entitlement to small entity status prior to paying, or at the time of paying, the earliest of the issue fee or any maintenance fee due after the date on which status as a small entity is no longer appropriate. (37 CFR 1.28(b))

NAME OF PERSON SIGNING ______________________________

TITLE IN ORGANIZATION OF PERSON SIGNING ______________________________

ADDRESS OF PERSON SIGNING ______________________________

SIGNATURE ______________________________ DATE ______________________________

Burden Hour Statement: This form is estimated to take 0.2 hours to complete. Time will vary depending upon the needs of the individual case. Any comments on the amount of time you are required to complete this form should be sent to the Chief Information Officer, Patent and Trademark Office, Washington, DC 20231. DO NOT SEND FEES OR COMPLETED FORMS TO THIS ADDRESS. SEND TO: Assistant Commissioner for Patents, Washington, DC 20231.

APPENDIX 2-A

35 U.S.C. §§ 171-173

Chapter 16: Designs.

§ 171. Patents for designs

Whoever invents any new, original and ornamental design for an article of manufacture may obtain a patent therefor, subject to the conditions and requirements of this title. The provisions of this title relating to patents for inventions shall apply to patents for designs, except as otherwise provided.

§ 172. Right of priority

The right of priority provided for by subsections (a) through (d) of section 119 of this title and the time specified in section 102(d) shall be six months in the case of designs. The right of priority provided for by section 119 of this title shall not apply to designs.

§ 173. Term of design patent

Patents for designs shall be granted for the term of fourteen years from the date of grant.

APPENDIX 2-B

Rüffer Patent

US00D392317S

United States Patent [19]
Rüffer

[11] **Patent Number: Des. 392,317**
[45] **Date of Patent: **Mar. 17, 1998**

[54] **WRITING INSTRUMENT**

[75] Inventor: **Heinz Rüffer**, Rastatt, Germany

[73] Assignee: **Zeppelin Museum Friedrichshafen GmbH**, Friedrichshafen, Germany

[**] Term: **14 Years**

[21] Appl. No.: **66,117**

[22] Filed: **Feb. 5, 1997**

[30] **Foreign Application Priority Data**

Aug. 5, 1996 [DE] Germany .... M 96 06 696.2

[51] **LOC (6) Cl.** **19-06**
[52] **U.S. Cl.** **D19/51**; D19/47; D19/43; D19/56; D19/57
[58] **Field of Search** D19/35, 36, 41–50, D19/51, 53–58, 81–85; 401/99, 100, 104, 115, 116, 209, 221, 222, 243–247

[56] **References Cited**

U.S. PATENT DOCUMENTS

D. 269,530	6/1983	Luntz	D19/47
D. 327,621	7/1992	Heller	D19/51 X
D. 328,611	8/1992	Longarzo	D19/49
D. 329,461	9/1992	Katami	D19/51
D. 359,982	7/1995	Rosenbaum	D19/49
D. 362,682	9/1995	Pittloud	D19/48
D. 367,076	2/1996	Boix Gacia	D19/56 X
2,777,447	1/1957	Gossler	401/195 X

Primary Examiner—Martie Thompson
Attorney, Agent, or Firm—Robert W. Becker & Associates

[57] **CLAIM**

The ornamental design for a writing instrument, as shown and described.s

DESCRIPTION

FIG. **1** is a front elevational view of a writing instrument in the form of a fountain pen showing my new design;
FIG. **2** is a rear elevational view;
FIG. **3** is a left side elevational view;
FIG. **4** is a right side elevational view;
FIG. **5** is a left side elevational view in an exploded condition;
FIG. **6** is a bottom plan view;
FIG. **7** is a top plan view;
FIG. **8** is a front elevational view of a second embodiment of my design of FIG. **1** in the form of a pen or pencil;
FIG. **9** is a rear elevational view of FIG. **8**;
FIG. **10** is a left side elevational view of FIG. **8**;
FIG. **11** is a right side elevational view of FIG. **8**;
FIG. **12** is a bottom plan view of FIG. **8**; and,
FIG. **13** is a top plan view of FIG. **8**.

1 Claim, 7 Drawing Sheets

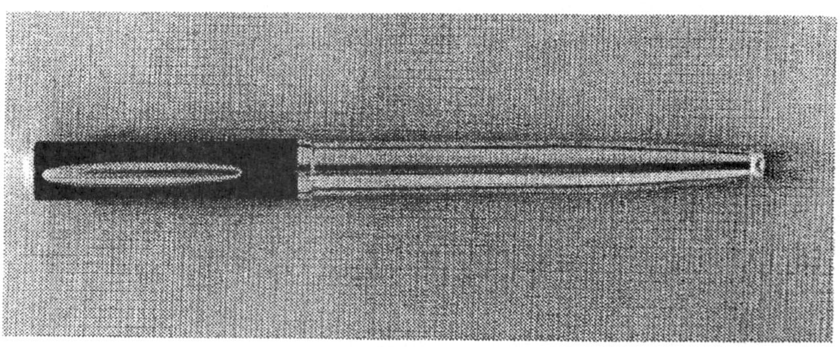

U.S. Patent Mar. 17, 1998 Sheet 1 of 7 Des. 392,317

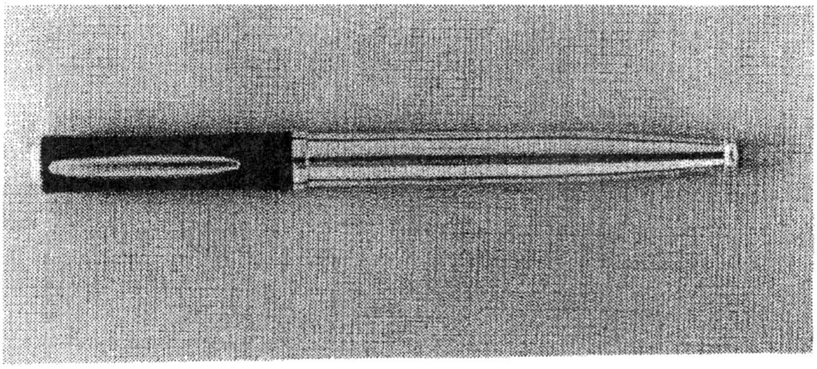

Fig. 1

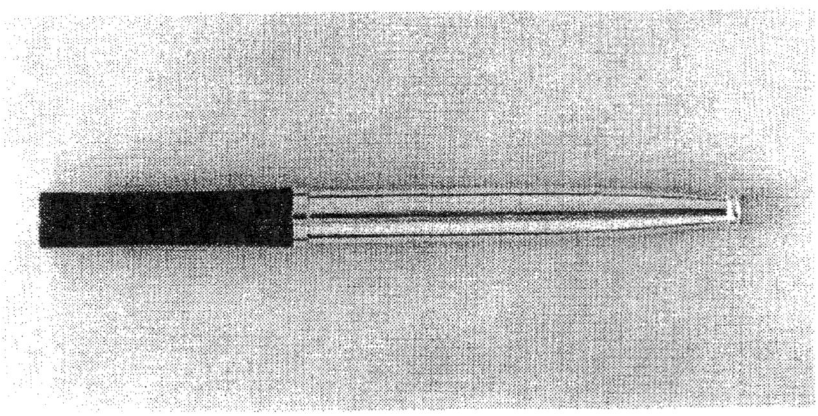

Fig. 2

U.S. Patent Mar. 17, 1998 Sheet 2 of 7 Des. 392,317

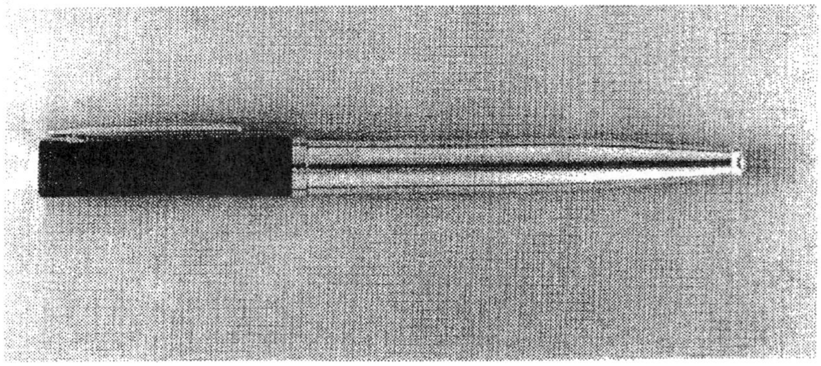

Fig. 3

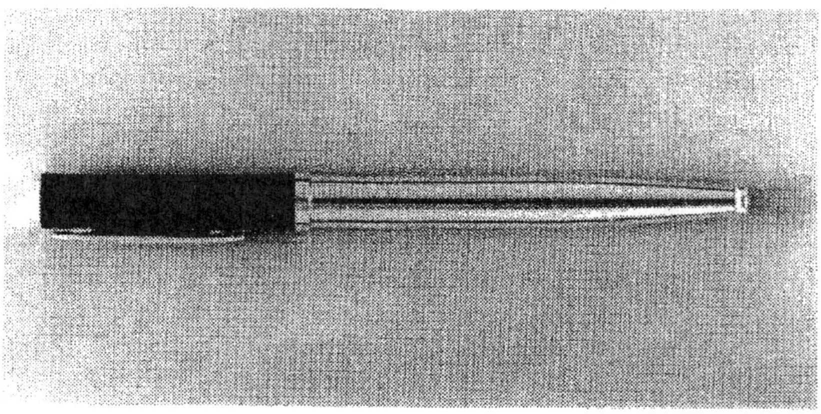

Fig. 4

U.S. Patent Mar. 17, 1998 Sheet 3 of 7 Des. 392,317

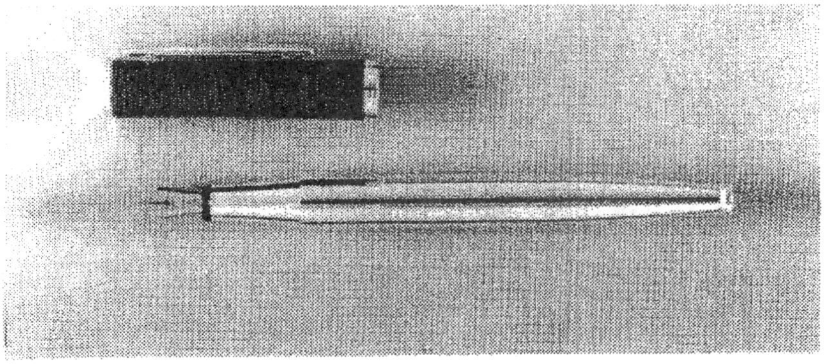

Fig. 5

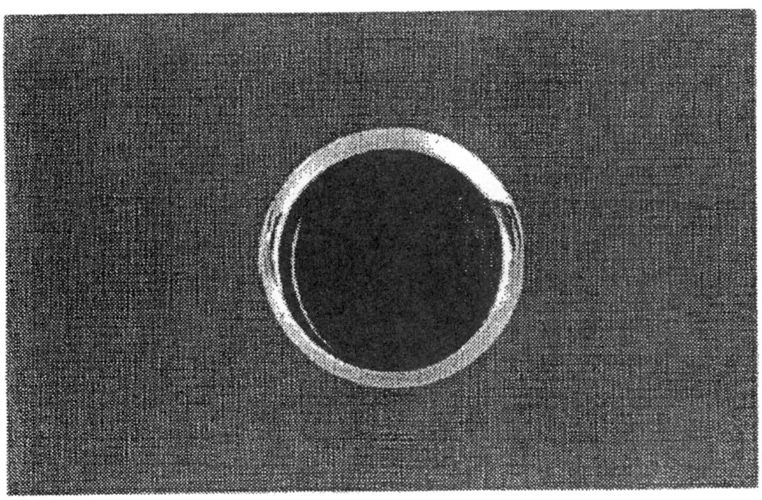

Fig. 6

U.S. Patent Mar. 17, 1998 Sheet 4 of 7 Des. 392,317

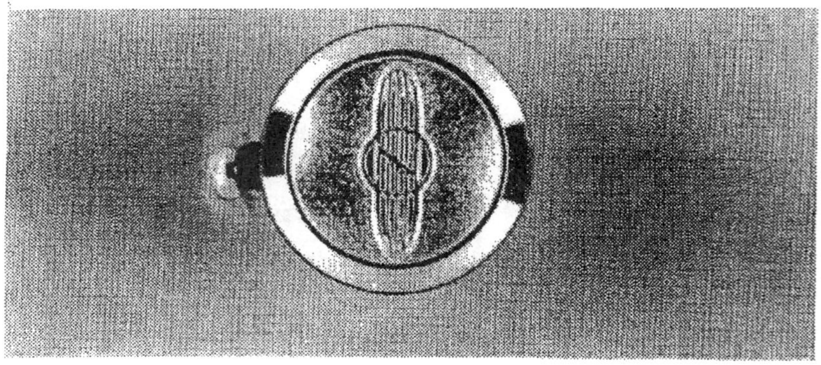

Fig. 7

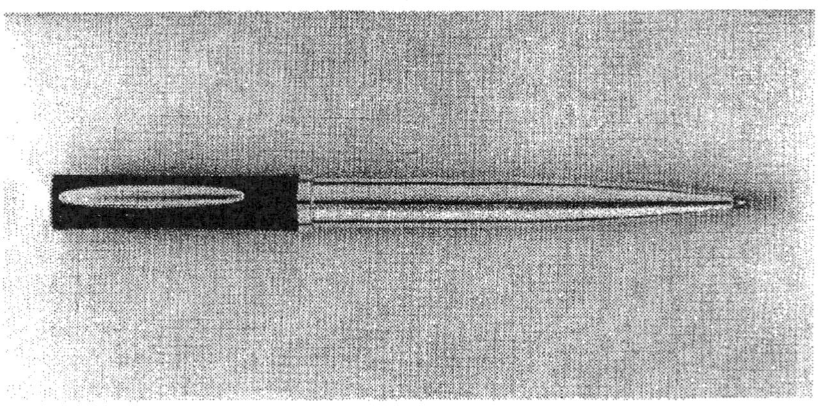

Fig. 8

U.S. Patent Mar. 17, 1998 Sheet 5 of 7 Des. 392,317

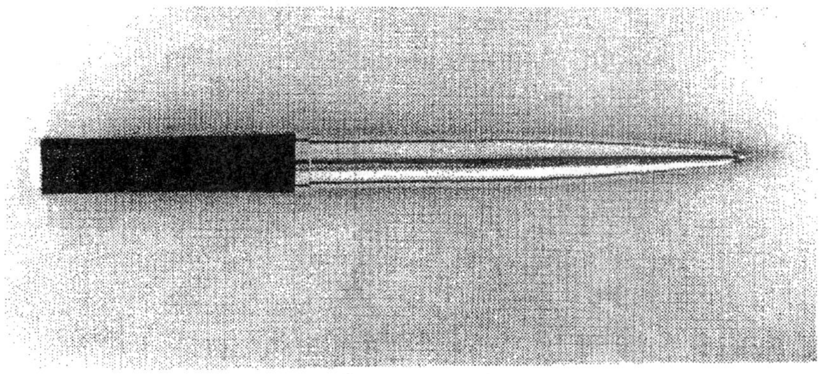

Fig. 9

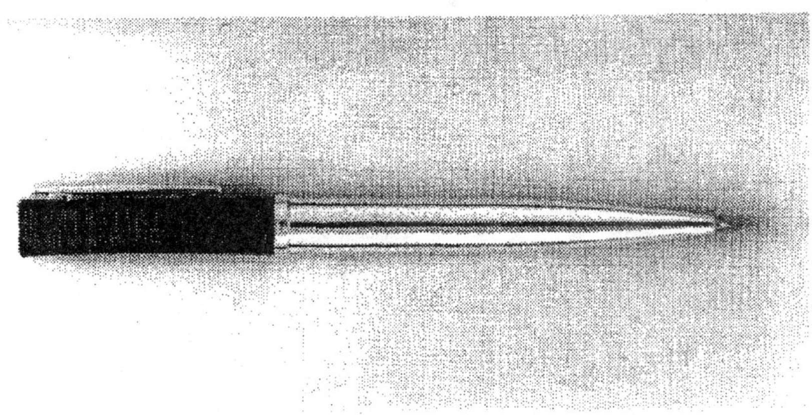

Fig. 10

U.S. Patent Mar. 17, 1998 Sheet 6 of 7 Des. 392,317

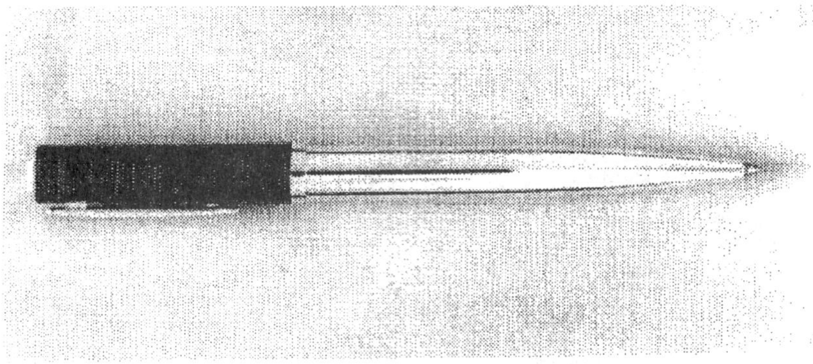

Fig. 11

Fig. 12

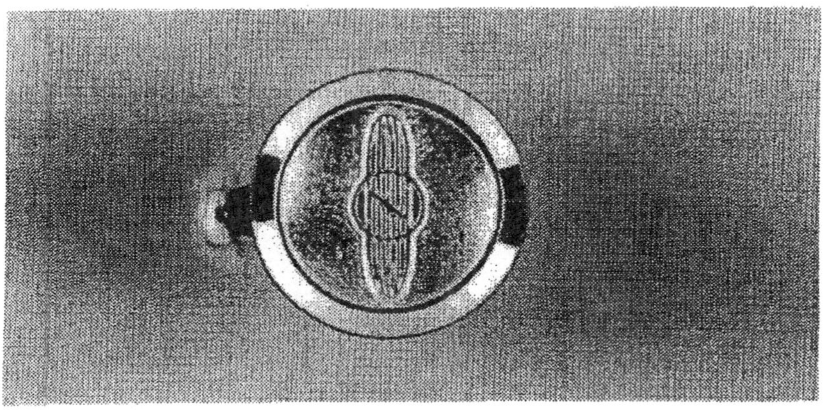

Fig. 13

APPENDIX 2-C

Lagomarsino Patent

US00D337662S

United States Patent [19]

Lagomarsino

[11] **Patent Number: Des. 337,662**

[45] **Date of Patent: ** Jul. 27, 1993**

[54] **WALLPAPER**

[76] Inventor: **Donald Lagomarsino,** 50 Lambert Ave., Mastic, N.Y. 11950

[**] Term: **14 Years**

[21] Appl. No.: **473,714**

[22] Filed: **Feb. 2, 1990**

[52] **U.S. Cl.** **D5/27; D5/8**

[58] **Field of Search** D5/5, 26, 27, 14, 64, D5/99, 65, 21; D2/506; D11/83, 101, 174; D20/25; D9/311

[56] **References Cited**

U.S. PATENT DOCUMENTS

D. 111,872	10/1938	Cable .	
D. 142,919	11/1945	Urschel .	
D. 146,690	4/1947	Southwick	D5/65
D. 151,482	10/1948	Wilson .	
D. 177,371	4/1956	Finkelstein .	
D. 212,733	11/1968	Thompson	D5/65
D. 325,708	4/1992	O'Malley	D11/83

OTHER PUBLICATIONS

Trophy Headquarters, 1941, p. 57, (5181) Man Softball Batter, center right.
The School Arts, Mar. 1932, p. 415, Rodeo Panel.

Primary Examiner—Alan P. Douglas
Assistant Examiner—Ann Hunt

[57] **CLAIM**

The ornamental design for a wallpaper, as shown and described.

DESCRIPTION

FIG. 1 is a perspective view of wallpaper showing my new design;
FIG. 2 is a top plan view; and,
FIG. 3 is a side elevational view thereof, the other side views being identical.
The bottom is plain and unadorned.

APPENDIX 2-H

Slimbach Patent

US00D337604S

United States Patent [19]

Slimbach

[11] **Patent Number: Des. 337,604**

[45] **Date of Patent: ** Jul. 20, 1993**

[54] TYPE FONT

[75] Inventor: **Robert J. Slimbach**, Mountain View, Calif.

[73] Assignee: **Adobe Systems Incorporated**, Mountain View, Calif.

[**] Term: **14 Years**

[21] Appl. No.: **734,332**

[22] Filed: **Jul. 19, 1991**

[52] **U.S. Cl.** **D18/28**

[58] **Field of Search** D18/24–32

[56] **References Cited**

U.S. PATENT DOCUMENTS

D. 25,389	4/1896	Schraubstadter	D18/28
D. 35,777	2/1902	Ihlenburg	D18/28
D. 47,554	7/1915	Benton	D18/24
D. 51,951	4/1918	Benton	D18/24
D. 327,903	7/1992	Slimbach	D18/28

OTHER PUBLICATIONS

The Mergenthaler Type Library; ©1987; p. 120—Medici Script.

Letraset Graphic Arts Materials Reference Manual; ©1983; p. 32—Bookman Bold Italiac; p. 44—Caslon Swashes.

Primary Examiner—A. Hugo Word
Assistant Examiner—Cathy Anne MacCormac
Attorney, Agent, or Firm—Roger S. Borovov; David J. Larwood

[57] **CLAIM**

The ornamental design for a type font, as shown and described.

DESCRIPTION

FIG. 1 is a face view of a type font showing my new design;

FIG. 2 is a face view of a modified form of the type font shown in FIG. 1; and,

FIG. 3 is a face view of a second modified form of the type font shown in FIG. 1.

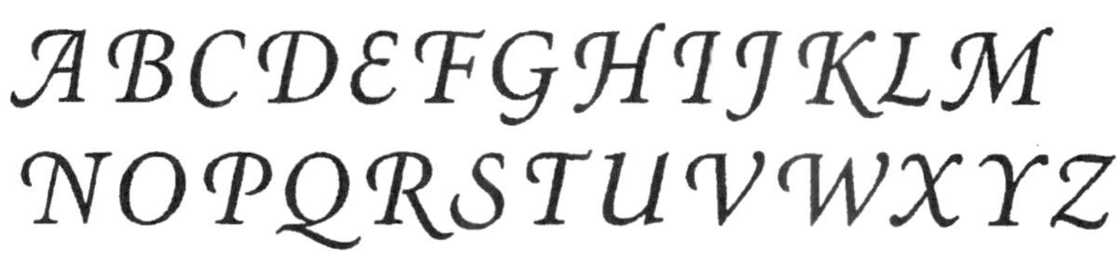

U.S. Patent **July 20, 1993** **Des. 337,604**

ABCDEFGHIJKLM
NOPQRSTUVWXYZ

Figure 1

ABCDEFGHIJKLM
NOPQRSTUVWXYZ

Figure 2

ABCDEFGHIJKLM
NOPQRSTUVWXYZ

Figure 3

CHAPTER 3

THE FIRST AMENDMENT AND RELATED ISSUES

Matthew A. McMurphy
Laura Lee Stapleton

---

* Included on companion CD-Rom.

§ 3.01 INTRODUCTION

Over two years ago, Rick Rush, who paints sports scenes, went to the Masters golf tournament to catch a glimpse of greatness, literally. He hoped to paint Tiger Woods, the young gun who won the Masters in his first attempt as a professional, in action, and add the painting to the list of other great athletes he has painted including Michael Jordan, Magic Johnson and Jack Nicklaus.[1] Rush, 52, has been painting famous sports heroes and the events they are a part of for 23 years. His activities at the Masters in 1997 led to a heated legal dispute. Rush produced a series of numbered prints that were signed by him and called "The Masters of Augusta."[2] He planned to sell a limited edition of 250 serigraphs for $700 each. He also planned to produce 5,000 smaller lithographs to be priced at $15 apiece.[3]

However, ETW Corporation[4] brought suit against Rush's company, Jireh Publishing, Inc. on dual theories of trademark infringement and right of publicity. The case raises many interesting legal questions involving art law, the right of publicity, and the conflict between an artist's First Amendment rights and the right of publicity. Some of the interesting questions involved include whether the court will find that the artist's paintings are entitled to full First Amendment protection, whether the court will consider the 250 limited-edition serigraphs a limited sale by the artist,[5] whether the limited sale theory will even apply in federal court in Cleveland, what test the court will use to determine the relative strengths of Rush's First Amendment protections versus Woods's rights of publicity, whether Woods's likeness will be considered newsworthy by the court in the context of Rush's art, whether the court will consider Rush's paintings to be communicative or commercial in nature, and numerous other issues.

On September 22, 1999, New York City Mayor Rudolph Giuliani threatened to eliminate all city subsidies to the Brooklyn Museum of Art unless the museum discontinued its plans to display an art exhibit entitled "Sensation: Young British Artists From the Saatchi Collection." The mayor remarked that the exhibit was offensive, saying, "you don't have a right to a government subsidy for desecrating somebody else's religion . . . And therefore we will do everything that we can to remove funding for the Brooklyn Museum until the director comes to his senses and realizes that if you are a government-subsidized enterprise, then you can't

---

1 Marcia Chambers, Lawsuit Pits Artists' Rights vs. Athletes, N.Y. Times, Feb. 16, 1999.

2 *Id.*

3 *See id.*

4 ETW's president is Earl Woods, Tiger's father. ETW's address in Cleveland is exactly the same as that of International Management Group, the entity that represents Tiger Woods. *See id.*

5 Another interesting question is whether the court would potentially consider just the 250 serigraphs when determining whether the sale of the artwork was incidental to any protected speech interest the artist might have, or whether the court would consider all 5,250 works of art in making its decision.

do things that desecrate the most personal and deeply held views of people in society."[6] The exhibit included such controversial pieces as a portrait of the Virgin Mary stained with elephant dung,[7] a pig sliced in half and suspended in a tank of formaldehyde,[8] and a bust of a man made from nine pints of his own frozen blood.[9] When the first of October came around, Giuliani withheld the museum's $497,554 city subsidy check.[10] The Mayor's Office also suggested that the museum could be in violation of its lease with the city because the museum was considering closing the exhibit to children under 17 without an adult companion.[11] The Brooklyn Museum responded by filing suit against the City of New York alleging three counts: (1) that the City violated the First Amendment by withholding public funds from the museum and by beginning eviction proceedings when the museum refused to withdraw the disputed art; (2) that by singling out the museum for punishment, the City violated the Constitution's guarantee of equal protection under the law; and (3) that the City violated the State Constitution and the City Charter by refusing to release money already appropriated to the museum by the City Council.[12]

These two vastly different situations, recently in the news, accentuate many of the different issues that arise in connection with the First Amendment and art. Both stories are teeming with interesting questions of law in relatively unsettled areas. Though seemingly emerging from very different fact patterns, both stories relate to the First Amendment protections that are afforded to artists and their artwork. This chapter will attempt to provide the background knowledge necessary to understand more about the interrelation of these issues.

§ 3.02 IS ART PROTECTED SPEECH UNDER THE FIRST AMENDMENT?

The extent to which fine art should be protected as core First Amendment speech has been considered in a number of court cases. Currently, the courts of appeals are split regarding whether art is entitled to full protection under the First

---

[6] Dan Barry & Carol Vogel, Giuliani Vows to Cut Subsidy Over "Sick" Art, N.Y. Times, Sept. 23, 1999.

[7] Abby Goodnough, Mayor Threatens to Evict Museum Over Exhibit He Dislikes, N.Y. Times, Sept. 24, 1999.

[8] *Id.*

[9] *Id.*

[10] Ralph Blumenthal, City Administration Official Opposes Giuliani on Museum, N.Y. Times, Oct. 9, 1999.

[11] *See* David M. Herszenhorn, Brooklyn Museum Accused of Trying to Spur Art Value, N.Y. Times, Sept. 30, 1999.

[12] *See* David Barstow, Art Museum Bolsters Lawsuit Against Giuliani, N.Y. Times, Oct. 2, 1999.

Amendment as visual speech. The modern trend appears to be to accord the arts full protection under the First Amendment. However, there is a decision in the First Circuit that holds otherwise. The following subsections analyze the First Amendment protection of so-called visual speech.

[A] First Circuit: Art Is Not Entitled to Full First Amendment Protection

The First Circuit Court of Appeals has held that art does not deserve the same level of First Amendment protection that other types of speech enjoy. In *Close v. Lederle*,[13] Chuck Close, a University of Massachusetts art instructor, accepted the invitation of a superior to display his paintings on the walls of a hallway in the Student Union. The hallway was used for this purpose from time to time.[14] As the court noted, "the exhibition, which had been arranged for but not seen by the superior in charge, proved to be controversial."[15] Several of the paintings displayed by the art instructor were male or female nudes.[16] The genitalia of the nudes were depicted in what was described as clinical detail.[17] One painting was titled, "I'm only 12 and already my mother's lover wants me."[18] Another was titled, "I am the only virgin in my school."[19]

Following several meetings of the school's administration regarding the paintings, the exhibition was removed five days into its scheduled twenty-four day period. The art instructor claimed that the removal of the exhibition violated his constitutional rights. He sued for a mandatory injunction ordering university officials to make the space available to his exhibition for the equivalent of the unexpired period.[20] In refusing to grant the art instructor his desired relief, the court remarked:

> There is no suggestion, unless in its cheap titles, that plaintiff's art was seeking to express political or social thought . . . Even as to verbal communication the extent of the protection may depend upon the subject matter . . . We consider plaintiff's constitutional interest minimal.[21]

The court dismissed the complaint.[22]

---

[13] 424 F.2d 988 (1st Cir. 1970), *cert. denied*, 400 U.S. 903 (1970).

[14] *Id.* at 989.

[15] *Id.*

[16] *See id.*

[17] *Close*, 424 F.2d at 990.

[18] *Id.*

[19] *Id.*

[20] *See id.* at 989.

[21] *Id.* at 989-90.

[22] In closing the opinion, the court remarked, "With all due respect, this is a case that should never have been brought." *Close*, 424 F.2d at 991.

[B] The Modern Trend: Art Fully Protected as Speech

The Second Circuit has extended full First Amendment protection to visual speech. In *Bery v. City of New York*,[23] artists, painters, sculptors and an artists' advocacy organization called Artists for Creative Expression on the Sidewalks of New York sought to enjoin enforcement of the New York City General Vendors Law which barred visual artists from exhibiting, selling or offering their work for sale in public places in New York City without first obtaining a general vendor's licence.[24] The Second Circuit reversed the New York federal district court's decision that the plaintiffs' constitutional rights had not been violated. In the process, the Second Circuit held that art, as a form of expression, is entitled to the highest level of First Amendment protection.

At the time the suit was filed, the General Vendors Law required general vendors selling nonfood goods or services in public areas of the City to obtain a license. The General Vendors Law limited the total number of licenses outstanding at any time to 853 licenses—the number of licenses outstanding on September 1, 1979. However, the General Vendors Law exempted vendors of newspapers, books, and other written matter from the licensing requirement. Any veteran who qualified for a vending license was exempt from both the license requirement and the 853-license limit.

In ruling for the City, the district court found that the General Vendors Law was a content-neutral municipal ordinance of general application which violated neither the First nor the Fourteenth Amendment, although its incidental effect was to restrict the sale of art on the sidewalks of New York.[25] As the Second Circuit noted:

> Stating that the precise nature of First Amendment protection for painting and sculpture with no verbal elements has not been addressed by the federal courts, the district court likened appellants' fine art to applied or decorative art and found that it rated only limited constitutional protection, in the absence of evidence of government censorship.[26]

Subjecting the General Vendors Law to a more lenient level of scrutiny than would have been required had the court found the restriction to be content-based, the district court found the incidental restrictions on plaintiffs' constitutional rights to be permissible.

The Second Circuit reversed the district court's decision in no uncertain terms. Initially calling the district court's understanding of the reach of the First

---

[23] 97 F.3d 689 (2d Cir. 1996), *cert. denied*, 520 U.S. 1251 (1997).

[24] *Id.* at 691.

[25] *Id.* at 693.

[26] *Id.*

Amendment more restricted than the jurisprudence warrants,[27] the Second Circuit then discussed the breadth of First Amendment coverage. The Second Circuit pointed out that the First Amendment's protections extend beyond political speech and verbal expression to such areas as entertainment,[28] theater,[29] and music without regard to words.[30]

The Second Circuit described the First Amendment's fundamental purpose as protecting all forms of peaceful expression in its many different manifestations. Calling visual art as wide-ranging in its depiction of ideas, concepts and emotions as any book, treatise, pamphlet or other writing,[31] the Second Circuit stated that paintings, photographs, prints and sculptures always communicate some idea or concept to those who view it, and as such are entitled to full First Amendment protection.[32]

Next, the Second Circuit turned to the issue of the proper level of scrutiny to apply to the General Vendors Law. As discussed earlier, the district court had determined that the restriction was content-neutral. Accordingly, the district court analyzed the General Vendors Law with more lenient scrutiny than would have been applied otherwise. The Second Circuit questioned the district court's classification of the General Vendors Law as a content-neutral restriction, based on the fact that the ordinance's effective bar on the sale of artwork in public places raised concerns that an entire medium of expression was being lost.[33] However, the Second Circuit elected not to decide whether the regulation was in fact content-neutral, since the Second Circuit determined that the restriction failed even under the lesser degree of scrutiny.

The Second Circuit noted that when a content-neutral regulation restricts the time, place, and manner of protected speech, it must be narrowly tailored to serve a significant governmental interest and leave open ample alternative channels for communication.[34] The Second Circuit next applied the following balancing test:

> The City certainly has a significant interest in keeping its public spaces safe and free of congestion. The license requirement as it relates to appellants,

---

[27] *Id.* at 694.

[28] 97 F.3d at 694 (citing Winters v. New York, 333 U.S. 507 (1948); Joseph Burstyn, Inc. v. Wilson, 343 U.S. 495 (1952)).

[29] *See id.* (citing Southeastern Promotion, Ltd. v. Conrad, 420 U.S. 546 (1975)).

[30] *See id.* (citing Ward v. Rock Against Racism, 491 U.S. 781 (1989)).

[31] *Id.* at 695.

[32] *Id.* at 696.

[33] *Id.* at 697 (citing City of Ladue v. Gilleo, 512 U.S. 43 (1994); United States v. National Treasury Employees Union, 513 U.S. 454 (1995)).

[34] *Id.* at 697 (quoting *Ward*, 491 U.S. at 791; Clark v. Community for Creative Non-Violence, 468 U.S. 288, 293 (1984)).

> however, which effectively bars them from displaying or selling their art on the streets, is too sweeping to pass constitutional muster.[35]

The Second Circuit found the district court's failure to properly consider the issues of narrow tailoring and alternative channels was an abuse of discretion.

The Second Circuit found that the city ordinance was not narrowly tailored. It pointed out that when the licensing exceptions for veterans and vendors of written material were taken into account, the regulation did not limit the number of people who could obtain licenses. The Second Circuit concluded that the city's control over congestion was obtained through means other than the General Vendors Law.

The Second Circuit also found that adequate alternative channels did not exist for the artists' expression. The Second Circuit did not agree with the city's contention that appellants' First Amendment rights were not violated because they could sell and display their artwork in private forums such as their homes, restaurants and street fairs. The Second Circuit found that displaying and selling artwork on the street is an attempt at communication with an entirely separate audience from the audience that can be reached through displaying artwork in galleries and museums.[36] The Second Circuit concluded that the sidewalks of the city must be available for appellants to reach their public audience.[37] Accordingly, the Second Circuit enjoined enforcement of the New York City General Vendors Law.

§ 3.03 ART IN PUBLIC SPACES

First Amendment analysis in any area of the law is convoluted. There are many balancing tests that the courts apply. The application of these tests is not an exact science. In cases that involve First Amendment issues and art, the outcome of a particular test seems to depend more often on the judges' subjective feelings for the art in question than on any truly objective standard. It is easy to see why predicting the outcome of First Amendment cases involving visual speech is extremely difficult. The best way to gain an understanding of the way courts handle these cases is to start with the basics. An analysis of the way that courts

---

[35] *Id.* at 697. Later in the opinion, the Second Circuit noted, "The City may enforce narrowly designed restriction as to where appellants may exhibit their works in order to keep the sidewalks free of congestion and to ensure free and safe public passage on the streets, but it cannot bar an entire category of expression to accomplish this accepted objective when more narrowly drawn regulations will suffice." 97 F.3d at 697.

[36] The Second Circuit noted that displaying and selling artwork on the street "reaches people who might not choose to go into a gallery or museum or who might feel excluded or alienated from these forums." 97 F.3d at 697.

[37] 97 F.3d at 698.

have traditionally handled First Amendment cases provides a good foundation for an analysis of the way that the courts approach First Amendment cases involving visual speech.

[A] The Public Forum Doctrine

In *Perry Education Ass'n v. Perry Local Educators' Ass'n*,[38] the Supreme Court laid out its approach to First Amendment questions that arise on government property. The Court described what has come to be known as the public forum doctrine. The public forum doctrine restricts the government's ability to regulate speech on certain types of government property. The Court divided government property into three categories: traditional public forums, limited purpose public forums, and nonpublic forums.[39] The Court explained that each of these forums is treated differently for First Amendment purposes.

The Court described traditional public forums as places which by long tradition or by government fiat have been devoted to assembly and debate.[40] The Court placed streets and parks in this category because they have immemorially been held in trust for the use of the public and, time out of mind, have been used for purposes of assembly, communicating thoughts between citizens, and discussing public questions.[41] In a traditional public forum, the rights of the government ("State") to limit expressive activity are sharply circumscribed.[42] The government cannot prohibit all communicative activity.[43] The State will only be permitted to enforce content-based restrictions that the government can demonstrate are necessary to serve a compelling State interest[44] and that are narrowly drawn to achieve that end.[45] The State can enforce time, place, and manner[46] restrictions as long as they are content-neutral, are narrowly tailored to serve a significant government interest,[47] and leave open ample alternative channels of communication.[48]

In the limited public forum category, the Court placed public property which the State has opened for use by the public as a place for expressive activity.[49]

---

[38] 460 U.S. 37 (1983).

[39] *See id.* at 45.

[40] *Perry*, 460 U.S. at 45.

[41] Hague v. CIO, 307 U.S. 496, 515 (1939).

[42] *Perry*, 460 U.S. at 45.

[43] *Id.*

[44] *Id.*

[45] *Id.*

[46] *Id.*

[47] *Id.*

[48] *Id.*

[49] *Id.*

The Court noted that a State is not required to keep the limited public forum open to communication indefinitely. However, as long as the State does keep the facility open to communication, the State is bound by the same standards as apply in a traditional public forum.[50]

The *Perry* Court described a nonpublic forum as "[p]ublic property which is not by tradition or designation a forum for public communication[.]"[51] In creating the nonpublic forum, the Court noted that the "First Amendment does not guarantee access to property simply because it is owned or controlled by the government."[52] The Court added that "[the] State, no less than a private owner of property, has power to preserve property under its control for the use to which it is lawfully dedicated."[53] Based on this justification, the State is not as limited in the restrictions it can place upon communication in nonpublic forums. In a nonpublic forum, the State is not limited to time, place, and manner regulations. The State may also reserve the forum for its intended purposes, communicative or otherwise, as long as the regulation on speech is reasonable and not an effort to suppress expression merely because public officials oppose the speaker's view.[54]

[B] Application of the Public Forum Doctrine to Visual Speech

[1] Private Works on Government Property

Claudio v. United States[55] demonstrates the application of the public forum doctrine to art works. The case illustrates the approach courts use when disputes arise involving private artwork displayed on government property.

In March, 1992, Dayton Claudio of California contacted Steven Grant, the Field Office Manager for the General Services Administration (GSA) in Raleigh, North Carolina. Claudio requested that he be allowed to display an art exhibit in the Raleigh Federal Building pursuant to the Public Buildings Cooperative Use Act.[56] Based on his discussion with Grant, Claudio requested permission to display his artwork on the wall in the main lobby of the Federal Building. Claudio was never asked to describe the nature of his exhibit. He received a revocable license to display an art exhibit in the main lobby May 4-29, 1992.[57]

---

[50] *Perry*, 460 U.S. at 46.

[51] *Id.*

[52] *Id.* (quoting United States Postal Service v. Council of Greenburgh Civic Assns., 453 U.S. 114, 129 (1981)).

[53] *Id.* (quoting United States Postal Service v. Council of Greenburgh Civic Assns., 453 U.S. 114, 129 (1981)).

[54] *Id.*

[55] 836 F. Supp. 1230 (E.D.N.C. 1993).

[56] 40 U.S.C. §§ 490.601a, 606, 611, 612.

[57] 836 F. Supp. at 1232.

At the unveiling ceremony, Claudio revealed his painting: a larger-than-life depiction of a nude woman, a coathanger, and a fetus,[58] entitled "Sex, Laws & Coathangers." Within a very short period of time, defendant Grant revoked Claudio's revokable license. Grant quickly prepared a written notice of revocation which stated:

> Although your display may be in the form of art it is more properly described as a political expression concerning the highly controversial issue of abortion . . . Since your work is considered to be political in nature it is not permitted on federal property and your license is hereby revoked.[59]

The painting was taken down.

Claudio appealed the decision to revoke the permit to David H. Jameson, the Director of the Real Property Management and Safety Division for the Federal Building in question. Jameson affirmed the decision to revoke the permit, but on different grounds than Grant had given. Jameson upheld the revocation because the U.S. Courts in the building "are part of the judicial system now hearing cases specifically on [the] subject [matter] of abortion and the exhibition interfered with security in the building and could cause disruption and damage to Government property."[60]

Claudio then filed suit in federal court asserting, among other things, that the revocation of the license violated his rights under the First Amendment, the Equal Protection clause, and the Due Process clause. Claudio sought an injunction requiring that his permit be reinstated and his artwork shown in the Federal Building without any further interference.

The district court's analysis began:

> Stripped to the bone and devoid of all extraneous legalese, plaintiff's position is as follows: any person is entitled by the United States Constitution to exhibit in any manner designated by anyone as art, any rendition of any subject, idea or issue in or on any federal building.[61]

The court disagreed with plaintiff's argument that the government should be forced to provide a forum for paintings of a political nature.

---

[58] *Id.*

[59] *Id.* at 1233.

[60] *Id.* at 1234.

[61] *Id.* (The court went even further, stating, "It would not stretch plaintiff's interpretation of the First Amendment to extend constitutional protection to the product of a citizen's decision to paint a mural realistically depicting the crimes of murder and rape along the outer facade of the Supreme Court Building in Washington, D.C., or to display a 'living sculpture' enacting a suicide by violent means in the lobby of the U.S. Courthouse, housing the Fourth Circuit Court of Appeals in Richmond.")

As a preliminary issue, the court looked into the nature of the forum involved in the dispute.[62] Claudio argued that the Federal Building was a limited public forum, and the defendants contended the Federal Building was a nonpublic forum. The court listed a number of factors which should be examined by courts in determining the government's intent as to forum determination. Those factors include the policy and practice of the government, the nature of the property,[63] the compatibility of the property with expressive activity, and the extent of the use granted.[64] Furthermore, the court noted that it should consider whether the facility is open to all or whether access has been limited by well-defined standards tied to the nature and function of the forum.[65]

The court concluded that the Federal Building's lobby had minimal compatibility with expressive activity. Supporting its conclusion, the court pointed out that the lobby was very small and its primary purpose was security of the building. The court also found that the Government has a legitimate interest in preserving a certain level of decorum within (and upon) the walls of a building which houses federal judicial, executive, and administrative offices.[66]

Next, the court considered the extent-of-use-granted factor.[67] The court found that in this case, the government's policy with regard to use of the Federal Building was governed by the Federal Buildings Cooperative Use Act and the Federal Real Property Management Regulations, which stated an intent to provide access to the public for the occasional use of public areas for cultural, educational and recreational activities.[68] The court found the extent of the use granted by the permit to be nearly unrestricted. However, the court tempered this finding by noting that a permit to display art in the lobby had never before been granted. The court seemed to feel that the defendants' lack of experience in granting permits of this type caused them to overlook the fact that some restrictions might be necessary. The court reasoned that because the defendants had no idea what the painting would look like until the unveiling, there was no reason for the defendants to consider additional restrictions prior to the hanging of the painting. In other words, the court did not feel that this factor carried much weight in this case, because the fact that no restrictions were placed upon the permit holder did not implicate an intention not to restrict, but rather a lack of experience in granting permits. Therefore, while this factor initially appeared to be resolved in Claudio's favor, the court downplayed its value in this particular situation.

---

[62] Claudio v. United States, 836 F. Supp. 1219, 1223 (E.D.N.C. 1993).

[63] *See id.* at 1224 (citing Cornelius v. NAACP Legal Defense & Educational Fund, 473 U.S. 788, 802 (1984)).

[64] *See id.* at 1224 (citing *Perry*, 460 U.S. at 46-47).

[65] *Id.* (quoting Gregoire v. Centennial School Dist., 907 F.2d 1366, 1370-71 (3rd Cir. 1990).

[66] *Id.* at 1225.

[67] *Id.*

[68] *Id.* (quoting 41 C.F.R. §§ 101.20-400).

After weighing the factors, the court concluded that the lobby of the Federal Building was a nonpublic forum. The court found that the Federal Building had been dedicated to use for either communicative or noncommunicative purposes but [had] never been designated for indiscriminate expressive activity by the general public.[69] The court held that in revoking Claudio's revocable permit, the defendants were acting in a discretionary capacity with regard to a nonpublic forum.[70] The court pointed out that in a nonpublic forum, the defendants have a good deal of latitude, noting that in such a forum "control over access . . . can be based on subject matter and speaker identity so long as the distinctions drawn are reasonable in light of the purpose served by the forum and are viewpoint neutral."[71]

The court, noting that mere "common sense" is sufficient to uphold agency action under the reasonableness standard that is applied to actions taken in a nonpublic forum,[72] dispensed with the remaining issues rather easily. The court did not even bother trying to determine whether the government's stated reasons for its action in the case were sufficient. Instead, the court stated, "The facts as developed during discovery unequivocally describe a 'common sense' reaction by government agents to the plaintiff's attempt to display a vulgar and inappropriate painting in the entrance lobby to the state capital's Federal Building."[73] Furthermore, the court made it clear that it did not see the government's actions as suppressing a viewpoint, since the government was never sure what viewpoint the painting in question was trying to get across. On these grounds, the court concluded that the government's actions were proper as part of the government's right to maintain the dignity and aesthetic quality of a building dedicated to administration of justice and public service.[74] Accordingly, the court granted defendants' motion for summary judgment.

As *Claudio* illustrates, the real battle in controversies over private art displayed on public property is now fought over whether or not the public property in question is a public or a nonpublic forum. If the court determines that the property is a public forum, the scrutiny the court must apply to the restriction in question will, in almost all situations, be too tough to overcome. If the court determines that the property is a nonpublic forum, the government's reasons for restricting the speech in issue will almost always be good enough to pass muster. Along these lines, the public forum doctrine has been criticized on the grounds

---

[69] *Id.* (quoting *Gregoire*, 907 F.2d at 1370-71).

[70] *Id.*

[71] *Id.* (quoting *Cornelius*, 473 U.S. at 806).

[72] *Claudio*, 836 F. Supp 1230, 1236 (E.D.N.C. 1993).

[73] *Id.*

[74] *Id.* at 1237.

that it enables judges to engage in result-oriented jurisprudence.[75] Some argue that the public forum doctrine is consistently misapplied in cases dealing with restrictions on private art in public spaces, generally at artistic expression's expense.[76] They feel that the misapplication is caused by the fact that as long as the court determines that the forum is a nonpublic forum, it is very easy for the court to uphold the government restriction in question.

[2] "Offensive" Art[77]

Offensive art is least likely to gain full First Amendment protection. As discussed above, some think that courts formulate their analysis of the public forum issue disingenuously to ensure that the art in question is denied First Amendment protection. If a court decides that the dispute involves a nonpublic forum, the restriction in question is virtually certain to pass constitutional muster, so courts are more likely to find a nonpublic forum when they are offended by the art in question. While this view may be cynical, *Piarowski v. Illinois Community College District 515*[78] demonstrates that decisions involving the public use doctrine can be confusing. At times, the correct forum determination may get lost in the confusion. Coincidentally or not, the confusion seems to be more frequent in cases involving offensive art.

Piarowski v. Illinois Community College District 515 involved a dispute between an Illinois state college and Albert Piarowski, the chairman of its art department. The president and other top officials of the college asked Piarowski to remove three of his works of art from a public exhibit at the college. Piarowski claimed that the action by the defendants violated his First Amendment rights, applicable to the states through the Fourteenth Amendment.[79]

Each year, the school held an annual faculty exhibition to which all four of the members of the art department were invited to contribute. Each member decided which of his works would be in the exhibit. Piarowski contributed eight stained-glass windows to the exhibit. Five of the windows were abstract, and three of them were representational.

---

[75] Daniel Mach, Note: The Bold and the Beautiful: Art, Public Spaces, and the First Amendment, 72 N.Y.U. L. Rev. 383, 403 (1997).

[76] *See id.* ("The courts engage[] in result-oriented jurisprudence, capitalizing on the inherently ambiguous nature of art speech to permit government officials, and the judges themselves, to substitute their personal moral judgments for more neutral, objective criteria.")

[77] The authors have placed the word "offensive" in quotation marks because it is a subjective term. What is "offensive" to one person may be a well conceived challenge to the status quo to another. With that concept in mind, it does appear that if the court itself is offended by the art in question, the art is less likely to receive full constitutional protection.

[78] 759 F.2d 625 (7th Cir. 1985), *cert. denied*, 474 U.S. 1007 (1985).

[79] Another aspect of this case, the application of captive-audience theory, will be considered in § 3.04[C][3], *infra*.

The three representational windows became the subject of this controversy. The Seventh Circuit described the three subject works of art as follows:

> One depicts the naked rump of a brown woman, and sticking out from (or into) it a white cylinder that resembles a finger but on careful inspection is seen to be a jet of gas. Another window shows a brown woman from the back, standing naked except for stockings, and apparently masturbating. In the third window another brown woman, also naked except for stockings and also seen from the rear, is crouching in a posture of veneration before a robed white male whose most prominent feature is a grotesquely outsized phallus (erect penis) that the woman is embracing.[80]

The three windows were displayed in the portion of the college referred to by the Court as the gallery, which was in an alcove off of the mall area of the college (the college's main thoroughfare). The three windows were visible from the mall area. The college received a number of complaints from students, cleaning women, and black clergymen regarding the three paintings. After the paintings had been up for 10 days, the defendants responded to the multiple complaints by asking Piarowski to remove the paintings. The college gave Piarowski the option of displaying the windows in another room on campus. When Piarowski declined to move the windows, the defendants removed them for him.

The Seventh Circuit began its analysis of the case by analyzing whether the gallery was a public forum. The court noted, "[i]f the college had opened up the gallery to the public to use as a place for expression it could not have regulated that expression anyway it pleased just because the gallery was its property."[81] However, the Seventh Circuit determined that the gallery was not a public forum. The court pointed out that the public was not allowed to exhibit in the gallery.[82] The court did not find the fact that Piarowski sometimes invited artists not affiliated with the college to display their work in the gallery to be enough to make the gallery into a traditional, or even a limited, public forum.[83]

At this point, the Seventh Circuit left the traditional constitutional analysis behind and considered a potpourri of extra-constitutional considerations. The court did not feel that the exhibit's artistic integrity would be violated by moving three

---

[80] *Id.* at 627.

[81] Perry Education Ass'n v. Perry Local Educators' Ass'n, 460 U.S. 37 (1983).

[82] *Piarowski*, 759 F.2d at 629.

[83] *See id.* ("Occasional use by outsiders, which is all that this record shows, is not enough to make a college art gallery a public forum . . . Faculty, unlike students, are employees, and it would make nonsense of the concept of public forum to say that because the employees of a public employer naturally have the use of the employer's property, which is where they work, it is a public forum.").

of the works elsewhere in the college.[84] The court did not want to limit the ability of the school to manage its affairs as it saw fit. Therefore, the court was swayed by the college's desire not to make it more difficult to recruit students.[85] Furthermore, the court gave much weight to the fact that Piarowski himself had been in charge of putting the exhibit together. The court did not feel that Piarowski should be allowed to put the show together without specifically getting approval for the offensive works from anyone else in the administration, and then complain when the college second-guessed his judgment.[86] The court's decision was also based in part on captive-audience theory.[87]

The court also considered where within the spectrum of free speech protection the art in question belonged. The court noted that sexually explicit though nonpornographic art can be regulated more broadly than political speech.[88] Based on this concept, the court concluded that relocation is not the equivalent of suppression, and therefore is not forbidden if reasonable. The Seventh Circuit further decided that even if it had been wrong in its decision that the gallery in question was not a public forum, the conclusion that the relocation of the artwork did not violate plaintiff's First Amendment rights would still hold. In that case the public forum could be considered to consist of all rooms on campus. Moving sexually explicit art from one portion of a public forum to another would be a reasonable relocation rather than suppression, and would not be a constitutionally suspect decision. The court stated that "[a] decision as to where within a public forum to display sexually explicit art is less menacing to artistic freedom than a decision to exclude it altogether."[89]

The court demonstrated the sheer number of different factors that went into its analysis when it concluded its opinion. In a single sentence that is informative precisely for its length and confusion of the issues, the court stated:

---

[84] The Court declared, "Since the exhibit was simply a group of self-selected works by the members of the department, it is not obvious that it had an artistic integrity to be violated." *Id.* at 631.

[85] The Court explained, "The college authorities were worried that Piarowski's stained-glass windows, created by the chairman of the college's art department and exhibited in an alcove off the college's main thoroughfare, would convey an image of the college that would make it harder to recruit students, especially black and female students." *Id.*

[86] *See id.* at 632 ("It cannot be right that if any authority whatever is delegated to a curator, the owner of the museum, the college in this case, is helpless to correct the curator's errors of taste.").

[87] *See* § 3.04[C][3].

[88] *Piarowski*, 759 F.2d at 630. *See also* Young v. American Mini Theatres, Inc., 427 U.S. 50 (1976) (plurality opinion). Of course, it is sometimes impossible to draw a distinction between sexually explicit speech and political speech. Few would conclude that images of black sexuality and white dominance in the work of Carrie Mae Weems or Kara Walker are not political. Thus, one could conclude that the distinction between sexually explicit speech and political speech turns not on content, but on the race and sex of the artist.

[89] *Piarowski*, 759 F.2d at 630.

> When we consider that the expression in this case was not political, that it was regulated rather than suppressed, that the plaintiff is not only a faculty member but an administrator, that good alternative sites may have been available to him, and that in short he is claiming a First Amendment right to exhibit sexually explicit and racially offensive art work in what amounts to the busiest corridor in a college that employs him in a responsible administrative as well as academic position, we are driven to conclude that the defendants did not infringe the plaintiff's First Amendment rights merely by ordering him to move the art to another room in the same building.[90]

[3] Art with a Clearly Political Message

Whether art is afforded full protection under the First Amendment may in fact depend on the content of the art, though courts are reluctant to admit it. While art that is sexually explicit is likely to have trouble passing muster under the constitutional tests,[91] art that does not include sexual references has a better chance of gaining full constitutional protection from the courts. The two cases that follow illustrate the point that art as visual speech gets the benefit of the doubt in purely political free speech cases.

In *Sefick v. City of Chicago*,[92] an artist named John Sefick brought suit seeking monetary damages and hoping to force the City of Chicago to display his environmental sculpture at the Richard J. Daley Civic Center. Sefick was an employee of the United States Probation and Parole Office. He also had done some considerable artwork in the installation or environmental sculpture genre, which had been exhibited in a number of public and private forums throughout Chicago. Sefick contacted Rose Farina of the Chicago Council on Fine Arts regarding showing some of his work at the Daley Center. Farina, who had exclusive authorization to schedule exhibits at the Daley Center, granted Sefick a permit to display three of his tableaux in the Daley Center without requiring him to provide so much as a picture or a description of the tableau he planned to exhibit. The three works were each scheduled to be displayed for one week.

Once Sefick learned that he had been granted a permit, he provided more information regarding the tableaux to Farina, in hopes of having the Daley Center issue press releases hyping the tableaus. He referred to the particular tableau that was the subject of this dispute as a depiction of Grant Wood's "American Gothic," using life-size figures representing contemporaries of Chicago Society. Sefick further commented that most of his artwork was based on critical social commentary.

---

[90] *Id.* at 632-33.

[91] *See Piarowski* discussion, *supra.*

[92] 485 F. Supp. 644 (N.D. Ill. 1979).

The first two tableaux were shown as scheduled. The third tableau, entitled "The Bilandics," satirized then-mayor Michael Bilandic's handling of Chicago's snow removal emergency of 1979. The tableau depicted Bilandic and his wife sitting on a chair in front of the fireplace. A recording of a man's voice, meant to be Bilandic talking to wife, was consistently playing a confused message about heavy snowfall, throwing logs on the fire, and not knowing what to do about all the snow.

Upon seeing the tableau for the first time, Farina informed Sefick that it was not suitable for display in the Daley Center. She draped a cover over the tableau and asked Sefick to remove the piece from the Daley Center. She sent him a letter explaining that the decision to revoke Sefick's permit was based on his failure to provide complete and accurate information about the works he would be displaying and on the fact that the tableau singled out and ridiculed particular individuals. Sefick removed "The Bilandics." He later reconsidered his decision to cooperate with Farina's request, and he sued the city for violation of his First Amendment rights.

As a preliminary matter, the court determined whether the tableau in question was speech worthy of First Amendment protection. The court decided that the art in this case was constitutional speech protected by the First Amendment because it consisted not only of figures depicting a fireplace scene but also included a tape recording of a conversation between the figures.[93]

Next, the court analyzed whether Farina's decision to cover "The Bilandics" and revoke Sefick's permit violated the First Amendment. The court noted that the Daley Center had voluntarily opened areas to art exhibits. While the defendants were under no obligation to provide a public forum, the court stated that once a public forum is provided, constitutional guarantees come into play.[94] Therefore, the court determined that the revocation of Sefick's permit was subject to First Amendment principles.

The court noted that whenever the speech in question does not involve obscenity, libel, creation of a clear and present danger to other individuals, or time, place and manner restrictions, a governmental unit cannot discriminate on the basis of content or viewpoint. The government argued, primarily, that its decision to revoke the permit was based on the difference between Sefick's description of the third tableau, and the actual nature of the tableau. The court did not find this argument convincing. First, the court countered that the difference between Sefick's description and the actual tableau was not very large. Second, the court noted that even though the actual appearance of the first two tableaux

---

[93] *Id.* at 648. Notice that use of this language by the court leaves open the possibility that, if the recording had not been part of the tableau, the court would not have afforded the piece the same full First Amendment protection.

[94] *Id.* at 649.

were not exactly like the description that Sefick gave to Farina, she did not cover them and ask that they be moved. The court found no substantial government interest that would be furthered by the removal of "The Bilandics." On the contrary, the court found the government's defenses to be disingenuous, and concluded that Farina's decision to revoke Sefick's permit was based predominantly if not exclusively on the content of that tableau.[95] Accordingly, the court ordered the city to display the tableau at the Daley Center for five days.

[C] Quasi-Governmental Property

Certain cases address the issues of government regulation of speech in museums situated on government-owned land. *Cuban Museum of Arts & Culture, Inc. v. City of Miami*[96] involved a situation where the controversy surrounded the identity of the artists, as well as the art itself. The Miami City Commission passed a resolution refusing to renew the Cuban Museum's lease at the end of the term. The museum brought suit alleging that the decision not to renew the museum's lease was a violation of the museum's First Amendment rights, in an unlikely fact pattern that was, surprisingly, to repeat itself in the City of New York.

In early 1988, the museum was planning its second art auction. An auction committee chose which works would be sold at auction. The committee chose a number of artworks that were created by artists who either had not forsworn Fidel Castro's government or had continued to live in Communist Cuba. An anonymous letter listing the names of the artists whose works would be shown at the auction and alleging their Communist leanings was sent to members of the media. At the auction, one of the paintings in question was purchased and burned in the street. A group of people demonstrated at the auction, displaying their disapproval of the inclusion of the allegedly Communist artists' work. The pressure increased following the auction when board members who had voted to include the unpopular artists' work in the auction were asked to step down. A number of the museum's board members were pressured to resign. Those who stayed were subjected to McCarthy-esque treatment.

A substantial number of people in the local Cuban community were against the actions taken by the museum in allowing the controversial artists' work to be included in the auction. They came to a meeting of the Miami City Commission and demanded that action be taken against the museum. The commission was asked to find a way to unseat the museum's unpopular board of directors. The commission looked into a number of ways to eliminate the museum's board. The commission unearthed a number of minor violations of the museum's lease, and ordered the city attorney to begin eviction proceedings. The city attorney advised

[95] *Id.* at 650.

[96] 766 F. Supp. 1121 (S.D. Fla. 1991).

that eviction proceedings would probably be unsuccessful based on the information he was given. The commission then passed a resolution not to renew the lease with the sitting board of directors of the museum. The plaintiffs filed an action in federal court alleging that the resolution not to renew the lease was based on considerations that violated the museum's First Amendment rights, and the city countered by filing eviction proceedings in state court.

Since the government "may not deny a benefit to a person on a basis that infringes his constitutionally protected interests—especially his interest in freedom of speech,"[97] the court initially noted that the fact that the museum did not necessarily have a right to renew the lease was not dispositive in this case. Instead, the court focused on whether the City of Miami denied the museum possession of the property in question because the museum chose to exercise its First Amendment rights.

The court's first task was to determine whether the plaintiffs had exercised any cognizable First Amendment right on which the city could have based its decision not to renew the lease. The burden of proof on this issue was on the plaintiff.[98] The court considered whether the museum's decision to exhibit the artwork created by Cuban artists who either lived in Cuba or had not denounced the Castro regime was constitutionally protected. The court stated that "[t]he decision made and the ideas conveyed by the Museum and its directors were that art should be exhibited and made available to the public regardless of the political beliefs and ideology of the artist."[99] The court determined that the decision in question was constitutionally protected.[100]

Subsequently, the court examined whether the city's refusal to renew the lease was based on the fact that the museum engaged in the constitutionally protected conduct discussed above. The city did have evidence that the museum had violated its lease in a few different ways. However, the mere existence of valid reasons for refusing to renew the lease did not of itself ensure that the city's decision would pass constitutional muster in this case. In order for the city's decision not to violate the plaintiffs' First Amendment rights, the court stated that the city had to prove by a preponderance of the evidence that its decision

[97] *Id.* at 1125.

[98] *See id.* ("Initially, plaintiffs bear the burden of showing that their conduct was constitutionally protected and that the conduct was a substantial or motivating factor in the governmental decision to deny a benefit.")

[99] *Id.* at 1125.

[100] The court also considered some defenses offered by the defendant that were based on the Trading with the Enemy Act. The court dismissed these defenses. For the full discussion, see 766 F. Supp. at 1125.

not to renew the museum's lease was based on the reasons the city gave, and not on the museum's decision to display the controversial artwork.[101]

As discussed earlier, the city gave the court a number of reasons for its refusal to renew the lease. However, the court concluded that if the board of directors had not decided to exhibit the controversial works, the city would not have denied the museum a new lease. This conclusion was based on the court's determination that the commission did not really want the museum to lose its location; it just wanted a new set of directors for the museum. The court observed:

> The conduct of the City Commission with respect to the asserted grounds for the denial of continued possession reveals that the reasons asserted were either minor concerns or a pretextual basis upon which to remove the Cuban Museum and its present directors. The reason behind the City's decision was the controversial and highly unpopular views that the plaintiff had advanced.[102]

The court concluded that by basing its decision not to renew the museum's lease on the museum's protected constitutional conduct, the city had in fact violated plaintiffs' constitutional rights.

In considering whether to issue an injunction requiring the city to allow the museum to renew its lease, the court noted that for an injunction to be appropriate, the plaintiffs have to demonstrate that there will be continuing irreparable injury if the injunction does not issue and that there is no adequate remedy at law for the First Amendment violation that is occurring.[103] The court found that both parts of the test had been satisfied. First, an ongoing injury was occurring because the city was still continuing to take steps to punish the plaintiffs for exercising their First Amendment rights. Second, there was no adequate remedy at law because the site on which the museum was situated had become uniquely associated with the Cuban Museum, so much so that groups opposing the museum and its current administration were unwilling to settle for an alternative city-owned site for a competing museum.[104] Since both tests were satisfied, the court enjoined the city from evicting the museum.

More recently, a very similar fact pattern arose in *The Brooklyn Institute of Arts and Sciences v. The City of New York and Rudolph W. Giuliani.*[105] The museum decided to display an exhibit entitled, "Sensation: Young British Artists and the Saatchi Collection," which included approximately 90 works by roughly

---

[101] *See* 766 F. Supp. at 1125 (citing Mount Healthy City School District Board of Education v. Doyle, 429 U.S. 274 (1977).

[102] *Id.* at 1127. *See* 766 F. Supp. at 1127-29 for the court's analysis justifying this finding.

[103] 766 F. Supp. at 1129.

[104] *Id.* at 1130.

[105] 64 F. Supp. 2d 184 (E.D.N.Y. 1999).

forty British contemporary artists. Opening day was scheduled for October 2, 1999. The exhibit, first shown at London's Royal Academy of Art in 1997, included works by Chris Ofili, Damien Hirst, and Rachel Whiteread, all recipients of the Turner Award from the Tate Gallery. Ofili's work, particularly his painting titled "The Holy Virgin Mary," was at the center of the controversy. The painting was made in part with elephant dung (as were all of his works included in the exhibit), and the background included buttocks and female genitalia.

On September 22, Mayor Giuliani objected to the museum showing the exhibit. He stated that Ofili's "Holy Virgin Mary" offended him and that it was sick.[106] He further referred to a work made up of two pigs in formaldehyde, by Damien Hirst, as sick stuff.[107] Giuliani decided to terminate all city funding of the museum until the museum canceled the exhibit. Initially, the mayor defended his decision by stating:

> You don't have a right to a government subsidy to desecrate someone else's religion. And therefore we will do everything that we can to remove funding from the [museum] until the director comes to his senses. And realizes that if you are a government subsidized enterprise then you can't do things that desecrate the most personal and deeply held views of the people in society.[108]

The mayor was not finished. The next day he charged that the museum had violated its lease with the city by staging an exhibition which was inaccessible to schoolchildren and by failing to obtain his permission to restrict access to the exhibit, which he made clear he would not give because of his view that taxpayer-funded property should not be used to "desecrate religion" or "do things that are disgusting with regard to animals."[109] On September 24, the mayor said he would not have any compunction about trying to put them out of business, meaning the "Museum's board of directors."[110] A city press release that day called the exhibit an insult to the community.[111] On October 1, 1999, the city withheld its monthly payment of $497,554.

The museum responded to the city's threats by commencing an action against the city and the mayor in federal district court, seeking declaratory and injunctive relief to prevent the defendants from punishing or retaliating against the museum for displaying the exhibit in violation of the museum's First Amendment Rights. The city reacted by filing an action for ejectment against the museum in New York Supreme Court, Kings County.

---

[106] *Id.* at 191.

[107] *Id.*

[108] *Id.*

[109] *Id.*

[110] *Id.*

[111] *Id.*

The district court sided with the museum. The court noted portentously, "[t]here is no federal constitutional issue more grave than the effort by government officials to censor works of expression and to threaten the vitality of a major cultural institution, as punishment for failing to abide by governmental demands for orthodoxy."[112] The court laid out the standards that the party seeking a preliminary injunction must meet. The party must demonstrate irreparable harm and either (1) likelihood of success on the merits or (2) questions going to the merits that are serious enough to be a fair ground for litigation and a balance of hardships that tips decidedly in its favor.[113] Defendants argued that the higher standard applied to them as government actors. The court found that the museum clearly was likely to be successful on the merits. This finding meant that the museum met the higher standard and rendered the defendants' argument moot.

The city and the mayor acknowledged that the art in question and the ideas expressed by the art were protected by the First Amendment.[114] However, the defendants argued that their decision to withhold the museum's appropriation check did not violate the museum's First Amendment rights because, rather than being prevented from exercising its rights, the museum was merely denied taxpayer support for the exhibit.

The court disagreed with the defendants' position. In an explanation worth quoting in its entirety, the court stated:

> The cases establishing the principle that the government cannot avoid the reach of the First Amendment by acting indirectly rather than directly also illustrate the fallacy in the claim of the Mayor and the City that, while the Exhibit can be shown privately, the taxpayers don't have to pay for it. Federal taxpayers in effect pay for the mailing of periodicals that many of them find objectionable; and they subsidize all manner of views with which they do not agree, indeed, which they may abhor, through tax exemptions and deductions given to other taxpayers. State taxpayers pay the salary for the professor whom the State wants to fire for speaking out against the State college. In sum, where the denial of a benefit, subsidy or contract is motivated by a desire to suppress speech in violation of the First Amendment, that denial will be enjoined. That is all that is involved here.[115]

The controlling consideration in cases like these is whether viewpoint discrimination has occurred.[116] The court found that such viewpoint discrimination existed by the defendants' own admission. The city initially claimed that the

[112] *Id.* at 193.
[113] *See id.* at 196.
[114] *See id.* at 199.
[115] *Id.* at 200.
[116] *See id.* at 200 (citing Ward v. Rock Against Racism, 491 U.S. 781, 791 (1989)).

museum had violated its lease and contract with the city. However, when the mayor called different works in the exhibit sick stuff, it was apparent to the court that the city's purpose in suing to evict the museum and in withholding the appropriation check was directly related to both the content of the exhibit and to the particular viewpoints expressed.[117]

The court emphasized the importance of First Amendment protection, stating: "If there is any fixed star in our constitutional constellation, it is that no official, high or petty, can prescribe what shall be orthodox in politics, nationalism, religion, or other matters of opinion."[118] The court expanded on that principle by noting that the First Amendment prevents government officials from censoring offensive, sacrilegious, morally improper and even dangerous works. Ideas may not be suppressed based on the fact that society finds them disagreeable or offensive.[119]

In determining whether to grant the injunction, the court noted that "[t]he loss of First Amendment freedoms, for even minimal periods of time, unquestionably constitutes irreparable injury."[120] The court stated that in the context of seeking an injunction to protect First Amendment rights, it has sometimes been said that irreparable harm and likelihood of success on the merits are combined into one threshold requirement.[121] By cutting off the museum's funding and suing in state court to evict the museum, the city had intentionally inflicted direct harm on the museum in response to the museum's exercise of its First Amendment rights. The court further found that the mayor and the city had engaged in an ongoing effort to coerce the museum into relinquishing its First Amendment rights.[122] The court found that the museum had established both irreparable harm and a likelihood of success on its First Amendment claim, and accordingly granted the museum's motion for a preliminary injunction.

§ 3.04 LIMITATIONS ON FIRST AMENDMENT PROTECTION FOR ARTWORK

The extent to which visual speech is protected by the First Amendment is not entirely settled. However, many courts do treat the limitations upon the First Amendment protections of art similarly. There are a number of different ways that a court might decide a particular piece of artwork falls outside of the traditional First Amendment analysis. This section reviews some of the alternative ways that courts dispose of art cases involving First Amendment issues.

---

[117] *See id.* at 200.

[118] *Id.* at 198.

[119] *Id.*

[120] *Id.* at 197 (citing Elrod v. Burns, 427 U.S. 347, 373 (1976) (plurality opinion); Bery v. City of New York, 97 F.3d 689, 693 (2d Cir. 1996), *cert. denied*, 520 U.S. 1251 (1997)).

[121] *Id.*

[122] *Id.*

[A] Obscenity

Obscenity, in the legal sense, is not protected by the First Amendment.[123] Therefore, it is very important that artists know what is, and what is not, obscene. Otherwise, artists run the risk of unwittingly creating a work of art that lands them in jail. The current test for obscenity was laid out by the Supreme Court in *Miller v. California*,[124] a case in which California attempted to prosecute a man under the California criminal obscenity statute for launching an aggressive sales campaign involving adult material in which sexually explicit materials were shipped to people who had not indicated any desire to receive the materials.

In determining the permissible scope of state obscenity statutes, the Court noted that state statutes designed to regulate obscene materials must be carefully limited due to the inherent dangers of any type of speech regulation.[125] Accordingly, the Court limited the allowable scope of obscenity regulation to works depicting or describing sexual conduct. Only sexual conduct can be defined by the states as legally obscene. The Court further required the states to specifically define which sexual conduct would be considered obscene.

The Court created guidelines for the trier of fact to consider when deciding whether a particular state statute is constitutional. Those guidelines include:

1. whether the average person, applying contemporary community standards,[126] would find that the work, taken as a whole, appeals to the prurient interest;
2. whether the work depicts or describes, in a patently offensive way,[127] sexual conduct specifically defined by the applicable state law; and
3. whether the work, taken as a whole, lacks serious literary, artistic, political, or scientific value.[128]

The Court explicitly announced that if a state law regulating obscene material is limited in the ways described above, First Amendment values applicable to the states by virtue of the Fourteenth Amendment are sufficiently protected, since

---

[123] *See* Kois v. Wisconsin, 408 U.S. 229 (1972); United States v. Reidel, 402 U.S. 351, 485 (1971); Roth v. United States, 354 U.S. 476 (1957).

[124] 413 U.S. 15 (1973).

[125] *Id.* at 23-24.

[126] The Court decided to apply community standards to the test for obscenity because "our Nation is simply too big and too diverse for this Court to reasonably expect that such standards could be articulated for all 50 States in a single formulation, even assuming the prerequisite consensus exists." *Miller*, 413 U.S. at 30.

[127] The Court explained that "no one will be subject to prosecution for the sale or exposure of obscene materials unless these materials depict or describe patently offensive 'hard core' sexual conduct specifically defined by the regulating state law." 413 U.S. at 27.

[128] *Id.* (citations omitted).

appellate courts have the power to conduct an independent review, when necessary, for constitutional claims.[129]

The Court gave two examples of the kinds of things that states could include in their definitions of obscene without violating the First Amendment: "patently offensive representations or descriptions of ultimate sexual acts, normal or perverted, actual or simulated,"[130] and "[p]atently offensive representations or descriptions of masturbation, excretory functions, and lewd exhibition of the genitals."[131]

[B] Government as Speaker

In *Serra v. United States*,[132] the Second Circuit was faced with the question of whether the removal of government-owned artwork from federal property violates the free expression and due process rights of the artist. The court decided that the removal of the artists' work did not violate the artists' constitutional rights.

In 1979, the General Services Administration (GSA) was looking for someone to design an outdoor sculpture for the space on the plaza next to the federal office complex at 26 Federal Plaza in lower Manhattan (the Plaza). The GSA chose Richard Serra, an artist whose sculptures have been put on display in famous locations all over the world. Serra was famous for so-called site-specific sculptures, which are conceived and created in relation to the particular conditions of a specific site[133] and are not meant to be displayed in more than one location.

Serra and the GSA signed a contract guaranteeing Serra $175,000 for erecting a sculpture at the Plaza. The terms of the contract called for all designs, sketches, models, and work produced under the agreement to be property of the United States government. The contract did not include any restrictions whatsoever on the government's use of the painting once the agreement was fulfilled.

The sculpture, titled "Tilted Arc," was installed in the Plaza in 1981. "Tilted Arc" was an arc of steel 12 feet high, 120 feet in length, and several inches thick. It was constructed out of a substance called Cor-Ten steel, which oxidizes naturally over time. The court noted that "[c]onsequently, the work is now coated with what the artist refers to as 'a golden amber patina' and what the sculpture's critics refer to as 'rust.' "[134] The sculpture divided the Plaza.

---

[129] *See id.* at 24. The Court specifically noted that the previous obscenity test required the prosecution to affirmatively establish that the material in question is "utterly without redeeming social value." *Miller*, 413 U.S. at 22. The Court changed the standard in this opinion because of the virtual impossibility of a prosecutor being able to prove a negative under American criminal standards of proof. *Miller*, 413 U.S. at 22.

[130] *Id.* at 25.

[131] *Id.*

[132] 847 F.2d 1045 (2nd Cir. 1988).

[133] *Id.* at 1047 (quotations omitted).

[134] *Id.* at 1047.

As soon as "Tilted Arc" was completed, it became the object of intense public criticism.[135] The GSA received numerous letters complaining about the way the sculpture looked and the way it obstructed the previously open area in the Plaza. When the criticism continued for many years, the GSA held a hearing to consider relocating the beleaguered sculpture. More than 150 people spoke at the hearing, including employees who worked at the Plaza, community residents, artists, and civic leaders. Serra declined the opportunity to speak at the hearing in order to present his views regarding the site-specific nature of "Tilted Arc." Following the hearing, the GSA decided to relocate the sculpture. In determining that "Tilted Arc" should be relocated, the GSA emphasized the fact that it obstructed the Plaza, interfering with public use of the area for recreational activities. The GSA expressly did not base its view on the aesthetic quality of the sculpture.

In response to the GSA's decision to relocate "Tilted Arc," Serra filed suit alleging that by removing the sculpture, the GSA was violating his First Amendment right to free speech and his Fifth Amendment right to due process. Serra sought an injunction against the removal of the sculpture, but also damages of $300,000. The district court granted summary judgment to the GSA on Serra's constitutional claims on the grounds that the decision to relocate "Tilted Arc" was a content-neutral determination made to further significant government interests and that the hearing provided all the process that was due.[136]

The Second Circuit opened with its analysis of the First Amendment claims: "While we agree that artwork, like other non-verbal forms of expression, may under some circumstances constitute speech for First Amendment purposes, we believe that the First Amendment has only limited application in a case like the present one where the artistic expression belongs to the Government rather than a private individual."[137] The Second Circuit based its decision in this case on its determination that the case did not involve government suppression of the speech of a private citizen, but rather government suppression of its own speech. The court stated:

> In this case, the speaker is the United States Government. Tilted Arc is entirely owned by the Government and is displayed on Government property. Serra relinquished his own speech rights in the sculpture when he voluntarily sold it to GSA; if he wished to retain some degree of control as to the duration and location of the display of his work, he had the opportunity to bargain for such rights in making the contract for sale of his work . . . . [T]he Government's action in this case is limited to an exercise of discretion with respect to the display of its own property.[138]

---

[135] *Id.*

[136] *Id.* at 1048.

[137] *Id.* (citations omitted).

[138] *Id.* at 1049.

The court concluded that, since "Tilted Arc" belonged to the government, nothing the GSA did infringed on any of Serra's First Amendment rights.[139]

The court's analysis of Serra's First Amendment claim affected its decision regarding the Due Process claim. Serra claimed that he was denied due process because the GSA administrator in charge of the hearing regarding whether to relocate "Tilted Arc" prejudged the removal issue and drummed up support among federal employees for the sculpture's removal. The court concluded that the Due Process claim failed as a matter of law. The Second Circuit's conclusion was based on the court's earlier finding that the contract between Serra and the GSA made the sculpture the government's property, rather than Serra's. Therefore, the court reasoned, Serra did not have a protected property interest in "Tilted Arc" remaining at the Plaza. Without a property or liberty interest in the sculpture's continued existence at the Plaza, there could be no cognizable deprivation of property or liberty,[140] even if there was injury to Serra's reputation as a result of the GSA's decision to move the sculpture. Without any deprivation of property or liberty, Serra had no right to a hearing before the removal of the sculpture. The court concluded that even if the hearing was biased, it was more process than what was due.[141] The Second Circuit affirmed the decision of the district court with regard to both the First Amendment and the Fifth Amendment claims.

[C] Captive Audience

Captive-audience theory embraces the idea that, although individuals have a protected right to express themselves, sometimes that right runs up against a more powerful countervailing force—the substantial privacy interests of the people that are forced to listen. In some circumstances, courts will find that the time or place the plaintiff has chosen for expressing himself is so inconsiderate of other people that the plaintiff's right to express himself must yield to the freedom of others not to listen.[142] Captive-audience theory may be best explained as a kind of default time, place, or manner restriction placed on a plaintiff by a court when no time, place, or manner restrictions had been explicitly adopted by the defendant prior to the conflict.

---

[139] The court went on to state that even if it Serra did somehow retain some First Amendment interest in "Tilted Arc's" continued display at the Plaza, the decision by GSA to remove the sculpture was also a permissible time, place, and manner restriction. However, for purposes of the current discussion, it is sufficient to note that the Court did not actually need to engage in the First Amendment analysis as such, since it dispatched Serra's claim on other grounds. *See Serra*, 847 F.2d at 1049. Of course, if the case were decided today, Serra might well have a cause of action under the Visual Artists Rights Act of 1990, discussed in Chapter 1, *supra*.

[140] *Serra*, 847 F.2d at 1052.

[141] *Id.*

[142] *See* Close v. Lederle, 424 F.2d 988, 991 (1st Cir. 1970) ("Freedom of speech must recognize, at least within limits, freedom not to listen.").

[1] *Close v. Lederle*

In *Close v. Lederle*,[143] discussed above, the First Circuit, after concluding that plaintiff had minimal constitutional rights in the paintings in question, noted that the university was entitled to consider the corridor's primary purpose when deciding whether to remove the offending paintings. The court stated:

> On the basis of the complaints received [regarding the explicit paintings], and even without such, defendants were warranted in finding the exhibit inappropriate to that use [as an art gallery for sexually explicit art]. Where there was, in effect, a *captive audience*, defendants had a right to afford protection against assault upon individual privacy, short of legal obscenity.[144]

The court found that the plaintiff's overdone, selfish concern with his own personal rights caused him to view his interest in self-expression as more important then the interests of his unwilling audience.[145] The court dismissed the plaintiff's complaint.

[2] *Cohen v. California*

The Supreme Court appeared to significantly limit the application of captive-audience theory in *Cohen v. California*.[146] In 1968, Paul Robert Cohen wore a jacket with an offensive message on the back.[147] He was convicted in Los Angeles Municipal Court of violating § 415 of the California Penal Code, which prohibits "maliciously and willfully disturb[ing] the peace or quiet of any neighborhood or person . . . by . . . offensive conduct . . ."[148] The Court found that the conviction was based upon the offensiveness of the words Cohen used when communicating his antiwar message to the public. The Court held that as long as Cohen did not intend to incite disobedience to or disruption of the draft,[149] he could not be punished for asserting the position that the draft was immoral or had no utility.

The Court analyzed the captive-audience theory in some depth, initially noting that much has been made of the claim that Cohen's distasteful mode of expression was thrust upon unwilling or unsuspecting viewers, and that the state might therefore legitimately act as it did in order to protect the sensitive from otherwise unavoidable exposure to his crude form of protest.[150] The Court stated

---

143 424 F.2d 988 (1st Cir. 1970). *See supra* § 3.02[A].

144 *Close*, 424 F.2d at 990 (citations omitted) (emphasis added).

145 *Id.*

146 403 U.S. 15 (1971).

147 The back of his jacket read, "Fuck the Draft." *See id.* at 16.

148 *Id.* at 16.

149 *Id.* at 18.

150 *Id.* at 21.

that the mere presence of unsuspecting listeners does not immediately justify prohibiting all potentially offensive speech.

> While this Court has recognized that government may properly act in may situations to prohibit intrusion into the privacy of the home of unwelcome views and ideas which cannot be totally banned from the public dialogue, we have at the same time consistently stressed that we are often "captives" outside the sanctuary of the home and subject to objectionable speech. The ability of government, consonant with the Constitution, to shut off discourse solely to protect others from hearing it is in other words, dependent upon a showing that *substantial privacy interests* are being invaded in an essentially intolerable manner.[151]

The Court was careful not to infringe upon Cohen's First Amendment rights when "[t]hose in the Los Angeles courthouse could effectively avoid bombardment of their sensibilities simply by averting their eyes."[152] In this manner, the Court attempted to curtail use of the captive audience theory as a means of suppressing otherwise free speech.

[3] *Piarowski v. Illinois Community College District 515*

However, captive audience theory never truly died. It has been employed since the Supreme Court's decision in *Cohen v. California*[153] as a tool for defeating artists' First Amendment claims in a few cases, though sometimes courts discuss the concept in terms of a fear that offensive material will be attributed to the defendants.[154] In *Piarowski*,[155] the Seventh Circuit seemed to rely at least partially on a derivation of the captive-audience theory, without actually mentioning the theory by name. The court noted that the area used as a gallery was a very prominent location at the college; that the stained-glass windows were visible to many people on campus, since they were in a window overlooking one of the college's main thoroughfares; and that the location of the stained-glass windows in this instance implied college approval. The court placed much weight on the fact that unless the school was allowed to move the stained glass windows, there was a likelihood that "the sexually explicit and racially offensive art work"[156]

---

[151] *Id.* (citations omitted) (emphasis added) (citing Rowan v. Post Office Dept., 397 U.S. 728, 738 (1970)).

[152] *Id.*

[153] 403 U.S. 15 (1971).

[154] Conceptually, it might be more in tune with the public forum analysis to say that restrictions placed on artwork in nonpublic forums will be considered reasonable if the impetus behind them was a desire by the government not to appear to endorse offensive art.

[155] 759 F.2d 625 (7th Cir. 1985). *See supra* § 3.03[C].

[156] *Id.* at 632.

would be attributed to the college. In this context, the Seventh Circuit held, "there is no constitutional right to exhibit sexually graphic works of art in a gallery that is missing an outside wall."[157]

[4] *Claudio v. United States*

In *Claudio v. United States*,[158] the district court considered an artist's claim that his First Amendment rights were violated when the GSA removed his painting from the entry hall of a federal building. The court noted that *Cohen v. California*[159] was a very similar case which seemed to dictate that the court had to rule for the artist on his First Amendment claims. The artist's argument was that, like in *Cohen*, anyone offended by the painting in question could avert his eyes.

However, the court distinguished the case before it from *Cohen* in a few ways. First, the court noted that no one who saw the jacket in *Cohen* could have attributed its sentiment to the government. The jacket was on Cohen's person, and as such the message on the back of the jacket was clearly the message of the wearer, and not of the government. In contrast, the court found that in *Claudio*, the offensive expression literally was physically attached to the courthouse itself, and it was so large and situated in such a location that anyone entering the Federal Building had to look at it.[160]

The court also found that in this case an element of compulsion existed that had not been present in *Cohen*. Claudio's huge painting was displayed where everybody who entered the building would definitely have to see it, and many of those people entered the building involuntarily.[161] The court remarked:

> Equally as precious as is our right to express ourselves is our right to be left alone. The court is unaware of any Constitutional requirement that we involuntarily endure the expression of someone else's artwork, regardless of its subject matter.[162]

While the court never actually used the words "captive audience," the court's analysis certainly resembled captive-audience analysis. However, the court never discussed whether the privacy interests of individuals were being violated in an essentially intolerable manner, as required by the Supreme Court in *Cohen*, for captive-audience theory to apply. However, it may be safe to say, based on the

---

[157] *Id.* at 630.

[158] 836 F. Supp. 1230 (E.D.N.C. 1993). *See supra* § 3.03[B].

[159] 403 U.S. 15 (1971).

[160] 836 F. Supp. at 1235.

[161] In using the word "involuntarily," the court was referring to the people who went to the Federal Building as prospective jurors, probationers reporting under court order, witnesses under subpoena, etc. *See id.* at 1235.

[162] *Id.* at 1235.

court's opinion of the painting in question,[163] that the court did in fact think that the situation in *Claudio* met the *Cohen* test.

[D] Defamatory Speech

As will be illustrated by the cases that follow, artistic speech is not influenced a great deal by defamation law. This lack of influence is due to the premium courts have placed on the free exchange of ideas and the requirement to prove all of the elements of defamation in the context of art, the difficulty of which is increased when the plaintiff is a public figure or a public official rather than a private figure. In addition to the other elements of defamation, public figure and public official plaintiffs must prove that the particular statement was made with actual malice, which the U.S. Supreme Court has defined as a "statement made with knowledge that it was false or with reckless disregard of whether it was false . . ."[164] Some examples of defamation cases as they apply to the art world follow.

In *Hustler Magazine v. Falwell*,[165] Jerry Falwell, a nationally known minister, brought a defamation claim in federal district court against Hustler Magazine.[166] The jury verdict favored the defendants, and eventually that verdict was upheld by the Supreme Court. The case started in November of 1983, when Hustler Magazine published an ad parody that contained Jerry Falwell's face and picture, entitled "Jerry Falwell talks about his first time." The Campari Liqueur ad campaign on which it was based involved interviews with celebrities regarding their "first times," meaning the first time they drank Campari, but playing on the double entendre. Hustler Magazine's parody included an interview with Falwell in which he admitted that his "first time" was during a drunken incestuous rendezvous with his mother in an outhouse.[167] The magazine's table of contents listed the ad as "Fiction; Ad and Personality Parody."[168]

In upholding the decision of the district court and of the court of appeals in the defendant's favor, the Court noted that Falwell was a public figure. It found that speech that is patently offensive and intended to cause emotional injury is protected by the First Amendment, even when the speech could not have been reasonably interpreted as stating actual facts about the public figure involved. The Court noted that freedom of expression "requires breathing space, which can only be fully protected by a constitutional rule which lets public figures recover

[163] At one point, the court referred to the painting in question as a visual horror. *Id.* at 1232.

[164] New York Times Co. v. Sullivan, 376 U.S. 254 (1964).

[165] 485 U.S. 46 (1988).

[166] Falwell also brought claims based on invasion of privacy and intentional infliction of emotional distress. Those claims are not the focus of this discussion.

[167] *Hustler Magazine*, 485 U.S. at 48.

[168] *Id.* at 48.

for defamation only when they can prove both that the statement was false and that the statement was made with the requisite level of culpability."[169] In defamation cases involving public figures, the requisite level of culpability is actual malice. This rule makes it especially difficult for an artist to lose a defamation suit when the subject of the artwork is a public figure.

Silberman v. Georges[170] offers an example of the difficulty that private figure plaintiffs encounter when trying to sue artists for defamation. The two plaintiffs and the defendant were artists. They had been friends for some time, and parted ways over a difference of opinion as to certain aspects of their art. The defendant painted a picture, entitled "The Mugging of the Muse," which he claimed was meant to allegorically portray his belief that the plaintiffs had killed art. The painting was set on a city street corner. Three males, armed with knives, were apparently attempting to assassinate a woman with bare feet who was dressed only in a small red cloth. A blue-winged cherub, standing between a brick wall and a fire hydrant that gushed red liquid, was watching the entire scene. Two of the assassins were wearing masks which resembled the plaintiffs clearly enough that the jury had no trouble recognizing them and identity was not in issue.

The plaintiffs claimed that "The Mugging of the Muse" held them up to scorn and ridicule. They sued the defendant in New York state court on the theory that the painting was defamatory because it portrayed the plaintiffs as muggers and liars and accused them of criminal conduct. The court did not think the plaintiffs' view of the meaning of the painting was reasonable. The court found that, at its worst, the painting accused the plaintiffs of destroying the arts. The court stated that "[i]n the context provided by the factual background and the use of the word 'Muse,' the [bare-footed woman] could be representative only of the arts; therefore, the painting states that plaintiffs' artistic beliefs and activities are destructive of the arts."[171] The court found that the defendants had suffered no injury. The court conceded that the painting may have caused the plaintiffs much embarrassment, but found that such embarrassment, while the intended result of such criticism, was not cognizable injury. Furthermore, the court noted that the fact that defendant intended for the plaintiffs to be recognized was not enough to justify a finding of malice on the part of the defendant. Therefore, the court ruled in favor of the defendant, dismissing the case.

Khawar v. Globe International, Inc.[172] involved a dispute over photographs published in a book written by Robert Morrow. The book alleged that Robert Kennedy was not killed by Sirhan Sirhan, but instead was assassinated by a young Pakistani man named Ali Ahmand, hired by the Iranian Shah's secret police and

---

[169] *Id.* at 52.

[170] 456 N.Y.S.2d 395 (N. Y. 1982).

[171] *Id.* at 397.

[172] 965 P.2d 696 (Cal. 1998).

the Mafia. The Morrow book contained four pictures of a man it identified as Ahmand standing in a group of people near Kennedy shortly before Kennedy was killed.

In its April 4, 1987, issue, Globe International, Inc., publisher of a weekly tabloid newspaper, published an uncritical summary of the allegations set forth in Morrow's book. The article included an enlarged photo from the book, with an arrow identifying one of the men in the photo as Ahmand. In August, 1989, Khalid Iqbal Khawar brought suit claiming that he was the person identified by Globe as Ahmand, and that Globe's false and defamatory depiction of him as the assassin had caused him substantial injury. The evidence at trial showed that Khawar had been a Pakistani citizen and freelance photojournalist at the time the photo was taken, working on assignment for a Pakistani periodical. He stood on the podium next to Kennedy in order to have his picture taken with Kennedy, and was not in the same room with Kennedy when Kennedy was killed.

Globe argued that because Morrow's book drew Khawar into the controversy surrounding Kennedy's death, he was a limited public figure and, as such, had to demonstrate that Globe acted with actual malice in order to prevail. The court disagreed. The court noted that the United States Supreme Court imposed the actual malice standard in defamation actions by public figures and public officials for two reasons: (1) such public individuals have access to the media which allows them to effectively defend their reputations in the public arena; and (2) such public individuals, by entering public controversies, can be said to have voluntarily subjected themselves to comment and criticism. The court found that Khawar did not have to prove actual malice because neither of the two reasons for requiring the plaintiff to prove actual malice applied to Khawar. In support of its conclusion, the court noted that nothing in the trial record suggested that Khawar had acquired a significant level of media access. The court also noted that when Khawar stood next to Kennedy to have a souvenir photo taken, he did not know, nor should he have known, that Kennedy would be assassinated moments later, much less that a book would be published 20 years thereafter containing the theory proposed by Morrow.[173]

Globe next argued that it should prevail based on the neutral-reportage privilege, under which accurate and disinterested reporting of serious charges made against a public figure by a responsible, prominent organization are protected by the First Amendment.[174] In considering whether such a privilege should exist in California, the court noted that "the theory underlying the privilege is that the reporting of defamatory allegations relating to an existing public controversy

[173] *See id.* at 703.

[174] The court noted that the U.S. Supreme Court has not taken a stance on the neutral-reportage privilege. 965 P.2d at 705. The privilege was first espoused in Edwards v. National Audubon Society, Inc., 556 F.2d 113 (2d Cir. 1977).

has significant informational value for the public regardless of the truth of the allegations."[175]

Since the court decided that the neutral-reportage privilege would not apply to private figures such as Khawar, in any event, the court never actually decided whether such a privilege existed in California. The court reasoned that if the neutral-reportage privilege included the defamation of private figures, it would eliminate any distinction between private- and public-figure plaintiffs whenever the defamation was reported neutrally. The court opined that eliminating this distinction would be inconsistent with the Supreme Court's emphasis on the need to balance the First Amendment interest in promoting the broad dissemination of information relevant to public controversies against the reputation interests of private figures.[176] The court denied Globe's claim that the neutral-reportage privilege protected it from being liable to Khawar for defamation.

[E] False Light

False-light invasion of privacy is often confused with defamation. The torts are seemingly quite similar. Therefore, many cases involving claims for false-light invasion of privacy also involve defamation claims, and it becomes difficult to find examples of cases involving artwork which focus primarily on the false-light claim.

According to the *Restatement (Second) of Torts*:

> One who gives publicity to a matter concerning another that places the other before the public in a false light is subject to liability to the other for invasion of his privacy if:
>
> (a) the false light in which the other was placed would be highly offensive to a reasonable person, and
>
> (b) the actor has knowledge of or acted in reckless disregard as to the falsity of the publicized matter and the false light in which the other would be placed.[177]

The biggest difference between false light and defamation is that defamation requires a showing of greater harm. Unlike defamation claims, false-light claims do not have to rise to the level of being injurious to the victim's reputation.[178] It is thus easier for a plaintiff to succeed on a false-light claim than on a defamation claim. Judges are leery of claimants who attempt to win through a false-light claim what they could not win on a defamation claim. The current trend is for

[175] *See Khawar*, 965 P.2d at 704.

[176] *Id.* at 707.

[177] Restatement (Second) of Torts § 652E (1977).

[178] *See* Rodney A. Smolla, Law of Defamation § 10:21, at 10-24 (2d ed. 1999).

judges to be more careful in awarding damages for false light, so as not to reward plaintiffs who bring actions that are really just second-rate defamation cases.[179] So, false-light cases are more likely to arise where the particular falsehood depicted is very offensive.

A number of false-light claims have been reported that are based on photographs. In *Brown v. Capricorn Records, Inc.*,[180] Rev. Pearly Brown[181] brought suit against members of the rock and roll group Wet Willie based on a photo of Brown used on one of the group's album covers. Members of the group recognized Rev. Brown on the street where the group was doing a photo shoot for an album cover, and the reverend agreed to allow his picture to be taken. The upper front corner of the album cover included a small photograph of Wet Willie, in front of the W. E. Brown Liquor Store. The album cover also included a larger photo of Rev. Brown playing guitar and singing by himself in front of the same liquor store.

Rev. Brown brought suit against the band's record label, Capricorn Records, alleging among other claims that Capricorn Records had published a photograph of Brown which placed him in a false light in the public eye. Brown argued that because he was a preacher, sang only religious songs and never drank any liquor in his life, the depiction of him on the Wet Willie album cover placed him in a false light by associating him with rock and roll and liquor. The court found that the album cover did not hold Brown out in a false light. At trial, the evidence revealed that Rev. Brown and W. E. Brown, the owner of the liquor store on the cover of the album, were close friends, and that Rev. Brown would stay at the hotel next to the liquor store when he was in town. Rev. Brown often took phone calls at the store, and sang on the sidewalk in front of the store. Moreover, Rev. Brown had performed at many festivals where numerous types of music other than religious music were played, and Rev. Brown even claimed that he had taught Duane Allman of the Allman brothers his style.[182] From this information, the court of appeals concluded that Rev. Brown was associated with the liquor store in ways unrelated to the photo and that the association of the plaintiff with rock and roll music was not false either. Since the court found that the falsity element of Brown's claim had been negated by the defendant, the court dismissed Brown's claim for false-light invasion of privacy.

---

[179] *Id.* at 10-24.

[180] 222 S.E.2d 618 (Ga. Ct. App. 1975).

[181] Rev. Brown was an elderly preacher and minstrel who was born blind. From the time he was a young boy, Rev. Brown supported himself and his family by singing in the streets of Americus and Macon, Georgia. Later in life, he also sang at folk festivals and occasionally performed on college campuses. 222 S.E.2d at 619.

[182] 222 S.E.2d at 620.

§ 3.05 GOVERNMENT INTERFERENCE WITH ARTWORK DISPLAYED ON PRIVATE PROPERTY

The First Amendment applies to government action. In most instances disputes over the First Amendment arise when art is displayed on public property, when government subsidies are involved, or when a government passes a law that arguably infringes upon First Amendment rights. However, government officials have been known to actually go onto private property and remove artwork they find offensive.

In *Nelson v. Streeter*,[183] the controversy surrounded a painting that a student at the Art Institute of Chicago entered in the school's annual fellowship competition. The artist, David Nelson, claimed that the painting was intended to portray the recently deceased Harold Washington, Chicago's first black mayor, in a more human light. Washington had become a revered figure within Chicago's black community. Apparently, Nelson did not share the sentiment. In response to a rumor that, upon arriving at the hospital following his fatal heart attack, Washington had been wearing female underwear, Nelson's painting, entitled "Mirth and Girth," depicted Washington in a white bra, G-string, garter belt, and stockings.

"Mirth and Girth" was placed in an exhibition, which was not open to the public, but only to students, faculty, and invited guests. The picture outraged many who saw it. A security guard was placed in front of the painting in order to make sure nothing happened to it.

In response to the uproar, the City Council passed two resolutions, signed by two of the defendants. One threatened to cut off the Art Institute's City funding unless the school issued an apology for "Mirth and Girth." The other demanded that the school remove the painting from the exhibition immediately.

The defendants, three city aldermen, went to the school, removed the painting from the exhibit, and tried to take it off campus. A school official stopped them and convinced them to go to the office of the president of the Art Institute, Anthony Jones. By the time the painting arrived at the president's office, it had a one-foot gash in it, although the court was unsure as to whether the defendants caused the gash. The aldermen explained that they had come to the school to carry out the city council's resolution that the painting be removed.

The aldermen covered the painting with brown paper to prevent anyone from seeing it. One alderman not involved in the removal of the painting called the police and explained to them what was happening. The chief of police called a lieutenant who was in the president's office and ordered him to take the painting into police custody. The police, accompanied by the three defendants, took the covered painting to a waiting police car. The scene was captured by television cameras.

---

[183] 16 F.3d 145 (7th Cir. 1994).

Nelson's suit alleged that the defendants, acting under color of state law, violated his rights under the First and Fourth Amendments, made applicable to the states through the Fourteenth Amendment. The court was not analyzing the case on the merits. Rather, the issue before it was the validity of the defendant's official-immunity defense. However, in its analysis of the official-immunity defense, the court made some relevant observations.

The court first remarked that it considered the legal issues to be straightforward. It noted that if the city had owned the Art Institute, it would have had some power to regulate offensive displays,[184] though the court declined to opine on how much regulation would be tolerable. However, the court found that since the city did not own the Art Institute, the city's officials

> have no more right to enter it uninvited and take the art off its walls than they would have to enter a private home and take offensive art off its walls. It has been clear since long before 1988 that government officials are not permitted to burn books that offend them, and we do not see any difference between burning an offensive book and burning an offensive painting.[185]

The court decided that the law was so settled in this area that the defendants were not entitled to government immunity.[186] This case was a clear victory for artists' First Amendment Rights.

Another finding by the court is relevant to this discussion. One of the aldermen's defenses was a type of public-necessity defense. The defendants argued that their actions should be protected because, in removing the painting from the Art Institute, they helped the city avoid a potential riot. In ruling on the issue, the court distinguished between a situation in which a speaker, writer, or artist intends to incite a riot and a situation in which a riot erupts because his message is offensive or unpopular.[187] The court placed this case in the second category. In such a situation, the court explained, "[t]he rioters are the culpable parties, not the artist whose work unintentionally provoked them to violence."[188] The court found that public officials are not allowed to protect the mob at the expense of the artist by removing the painting rather than arresting the rioters.

---

[184] *Id.* at 148.

[185] *Id.* (citations omitted).

[186] The court stated that, "A public official is not answerable in damages for a violation of the Constitution unless, at the time he acted, the law was clear that what he was doing really did violate the Constitution." 16 F.3d 145, 148 (7th Cir. 1994) (citing Harlow v. Fitzgerald, 457 U.S. 800 (1982); Anderson v. Creighton, 483 U.S. 635 (1987)). The court also noted, "The purpose of the doctrine of official immunity is to protect officials from legal surprises. The defendants could not have been surprised to learn that they were not free to take down paintings from the walls of the Art Institute."16 F.3d 145, 148, 151 (7th Cir. 1994).

[187] 16 F.3d at 150.

[188] *Id.*

§ 3.06 GOVERNMENT SUBSIDIES FOR ART AND THE FIRST AMENDMENT

The National Endowment for the Arts (NEA) was established in 1965 as part of a broadly conceived national policy of support for the arts in the United States.[189] The idea was to provide funds to help create and sustain not only a climate encouraging freedom of thought, imagination, and inquiry, but also the material conditions facilitating the release of creative intent.[190] As the Supreme Court has noted, "the enabling statute vests the NEA with substantial discretion to award grants; it identifies only the broadest funding priorities, including 'artistic and cultural significance,' giving emphasis to 'American creativity and cultural diversity, professional excellence, and the encouragement of public knowledge, education, understanding, and appreciation of the arts.' "[191]

Congress put certain procedures in place to guard against the potential for partisan influence on the NEA. NEA funding applications are first examined by an advisory panel made up of experts in the relevant area of the arts.[192] According to the 1990 Amendments to the enabling statute, the panels must reflect "diverse artistic and cultural points of view" and include "wide geographic, ethnic, and minority representation," as well as "lay individuals who are knowledgeable about the arts."[193] The panels make suggestions to a 26-member body called the National Council on the Arts. The council advises the NEA chairperson as to which artists deserve grants.[194] The chairperson has the final word in approving the recommendations, but cannot approve a grant that the council has not recommended.[195]

In the NEA's history, complaints regarding particular NEA-funded works of art have been few. But in 1989, two provocative displays stirred up a national controversy. The first controversial exhibit was a retrospective of photographer Robert Mapplethorpe's work, entitled "The Perfect Moment." The Institute of Contemporary Art at the University of Pennsylvania used $30,000 of an NEA visual-arts grant to fund the project. Several members of Congress condemned the exhibit, which included homoerotic photographs, as pornographic. The second controversial piece was Andres Serrano's photograph of a crucifix immersed in urine, titled "Piss Christ." For the project, Serrano received a $15,000 grant

[189] 20 U.S.C. § 953(b).

[190] 20 U.S.C. § 951(7).

[191] National Endowment v. Finley, 524 U.S. 569, 573 (1998) (citing 20 U.S.C. § 954(c)(1)-(10)).

[192] *See id.*

[193] *Id.* at 573 (citing 20 U.S.C. § 959(c)(1)-(2)).

[194] The 26 members of the council and the NEA chairperson are all appointed by the President, "by and with the advice and consent of the Senate." Finley v. National Endowment, 100 F.3d 671 (9th Cir. 1994).

[195] 524 U.S. 569 at 573.

from an organization that received NEA funds. In reaction to the controversy surrounding the exhibits described above, Congress eliminated $45,000 from the NEA's budget in 1990, the exact amount of money that the two controversial exhibits had received in NEA funds.[196]

In further response to the controversy, Congress enacted an amendment in the 1990 appropriations bill providing that no NEA funds "may be used to promote, disseminate, or produce materials which in the judgment of [the NEA] may be considered obscene, including but not limited to, depictions of sadomasochism, homoeroticism, the sexual exploitation of children, or individuals engaged in sex acts and which, when taken as a whole, do not have serious literary, artistic, political, or scientific value."[197] In response to the new mandate, the NEA decided to require applicants for NEA grants to certify in writing that none of the funds they might potentially receive would be used "to promote, disseminate, or produce materials which in the judgment of the NEA . . . may be considered obscene."[198]

This new requirement was challenged in federal district court in California in *Bella Lewitzky Dance Foundation v. Frohnmayer.*[199] The court found the new language in the NEA grant application unconstitutional for two reasons: the written certification requirement violated the Fifth Amendment because it was unconstitutionally vague,[200] and it violated the First Amendment due to the chilling effect the vague requirement would have on protected speech.[201]

The NEA attempted to avoid all of the First and Fifth Amendment analysis. It argued that the obscenity ban in the certification requirement was merely a government decision not to subsidize the exercise of particular protected expression. As such, the NEA contended, the obscenity ban did not violate the First or Fifth Amendments. The court responded that the outcome would be the same under government subsidy analysis as it was under constitutional analysis:

> In simple terms, the government may well be able to put restrictions on who it subsidizes, and how it subsidizes, but once the government moves to subsidize, it cannot do so in a manner that carries with it a level of vagueness that violates the First and Fifth Amendments.[202]

---

[196] *See id.* at 574.

[197] *Id.* at 575 (quoting Department of the Interior and Related Agencies Appropriations Act, 1990, Pub. L. 101-121, 103 Stat. 738, 738-42).

[198] Bella Lewitzky Dance Found. v. Frohnmayer, 754 F. Supp. 774, 776 (C.D. Cal. 1991) (citations omitted).

[199] 754 F. Supp. 774 (C.D. Cal. 1991).

[200] *See id.* at 781-82.

[201] *See id.* at 782-85.

[202] *Bella Lewitzky Dance Found.*, 754 F. Supp. at 784-85. *Cf.* Cuban Museum of Arts & Culture, Inc. v. City of Miami, 766 F. Supp. 1121 (S.D. Fla. 1991); Brooklyn Institute of Arts & Sciences v. City of New York and Rudolph W. Giuliani, 64 F. Supp. 2d 184 (E.D.N.Y. 1999); *see also supra* § 3.03[C].

Therefore, the court granted summary judgment in favor of the plaintiffs.

In response to legal attacks on the NEA's new application requirements, and at the suggestion of an Independent Commission of constitutional law scholars, Congress decided in the fall of 1990 to amend NEA grant guidelines again. As a compromise measure, Congress enacted 20 U.S.C. § 954(d), which provides:

> No payment shall be made under this section except upon application therefor which is submitted to the National Endowment for the Arts in accordance with regulations issued and procedures established by the Chairperson. In establishing such regulations and procedures, the Chairperson shall ensure that—
>
> (1) artistic excellence and artistic merit are the criteria by which applications are judged, taking into consideration *general standards of decency and respect* for the diverse beliefs and values of the American public; and
>
> (2) applications are consistent with the purposes of this section. Such regulations and procedures shall clearly indicate that obscenity is without artistic merit, is not protected speech, and shall not be funded.[203]

The National Council on the Arts then adopted a resolution to implement the new regulations merely by ensuring that the members of the advisory panels that conduct the initial review of grant applications represent geographic, ethnic, and aesthetic diversity.[204] The new regulations and the new policy landed the NEA in court yet again.

Four performance artists—Karen Finley, John Fleck, Holly Hughes, and Tim Miller—applied for NEA funding before new § 954(d)(1) was enacted. Initially, they filed suit claiming that the NEA had rejected their applications on political grounds in violation of the First Amendment.[205] The district court ruled against the NEA on its motion for summary judgment as to the claim that the NEA had refused the plaintiffs' applications on political grounds, and the NEA agreed to settle the claims with the artists.

Once § 954(d)(1) was passed, the plaintiffs amended their complaint, claiming that the new section was unconstitutional on its face. The district court granted summary judgment in favor of the plaintiffs on their facial constitutional challenge to § 954(d)(1) and issued an injunction against the statute's enforcement. In ruling that the new requirement violated the Fifth Amendment Due Process clause, the

---

[203] 524 U.S. 569 at 576 (emphasis added).

[204] *Id.*

[205] *See* Finley v. National Endowment, 795 F. Supp. 1457 (C.D. Cal. 1992). The four plaintiffs also claimed that the NEA had "failed to follow statutory procedures by basing the denial on criteria other than those set forth in the NEA's enabling statute, and had breached the confidentiality of their grant applications through the release of quotations to the press, in violation of the Privacy Act of 1974." 524 U.S. 569 at 577.

court noted that the provision "fail[ed] adequately to notify applicants of what is required of them or to circumscribe NEA discretion."[206] The NEA did not seek a stay of the district court's injunction, so § 954(d)(1) was not enforced by the NEA following the district court's decision. A divided panel of the Ninth Circuit affirmed the district court's ruling.[207]

The Supreme Court granted certiorari and reversed the decision of the Court of Appeals.[208] The Court first considered the burden that the plaintiffs had to overcome in their facial challenge of the statute. The Court noted that facial invalidation is a drastic measure that should be used rarely and only as a last resort.[209] The Court found that in order to prevail, the plaintiffs were required to demonstrate a substantial risk that application of the provision would lead to the suppression of speech.[210]

The majority opinion[211] found that the plaintiffs had not met their burden for a number of different reasons, and accordingly reversed the decision of the Court of Appeals that the statute was unconstitutionally vague and violated the Due Process clause of the Fifth Amendment. The plaintiffs argued that § 954(d)(1) was "an archetypical instance of viewpoint discrimination because it reject[ed] any artistic speech that either fail[ed] to respect mainstream values or offend[ed] standards of decency."[212] The NEA argued that the provision was merely advisory, and contended that the formulation of diverse advisory panels[213] was sufficient to fulfill the purposes of the statute. While the Court did not embrace the NEA's position regarding advisory panels, the Court rejected the plaintiffs' argument that the statute constituted "archetypical" viewpoint discrimination. The Court found that the statute's requirement that the NEA consider general decency and respect for the diverse beliefs and values of the American public[214] imposed no categorical requirement[215] on the NEA. Instead, the Court found that § 954(d)(1) merely urged the NEA to take "decency and respect" into consideration.[216] Since the Court did not feel that the decency and respect criteria silenced speakers by expressly "threatening censorship of ideas,"[217] the Court did not perceive a realistic

---

[206] 524 U.S. 569 at 578.

[207] *See* Finley v. National Endowment, 100 F.3d 671 (9th Cir. 1996).

[208] *See* National Endowment v. Finley, 524 U.S. 569 (1998).

[209] *See id.* at 580 (citing Broadrick v. Oklahoma, 413 U.S. 601 (1973); FW/PBS, Inc. v. Dallas, 493 U.S. 215, 223 (1990) (noting that "facial challenges to legislation are generally disfavored")).

[210] *Id.*

[211] The majority opinion was written by Justice O'Connor. Justices Rehnquist, Stevens, Kennedy, and Breyer joined in the opinion. *See id.* at 571.

[212] *Finley*, 524 U.S. at 580.

[213] *Id.* at 581.

[214] *Id.* at 576.

[215] *Id.* at 581.

[216] *Id.* at 582.

[217] *Id.* at 582 (citing R.A.V. v. St. Paul, 505 U.S. 377 (1992)).

danger that First Amendment values would be compromised by § 954(d)(1). The Court determined that since § 954(d)(1) was aimed at reforming procedures rather than precluding speech,[218] the plaintiffs could not convincingly argue that the provision would inevitably be utilized as a tool for invidious viewpoint discrimination.[219]

The Court viewed the plaintiffs' argument that § 954(d)(1) was unconstitutional on its face as an argument that the criteria set forth were subjective enough to enable the NEA to engage in viewpoint discrimination. In response, the Court commented that the determination of artistic excellence was itself subjective, and that the obligation to consider the decency and respect criteria would not make the process any more subjective. The Court pointed out that while the statute may in fact enable the NEA to practice viewpoint discrimination while hiding behind the subjective nature of the decency and respect provision, the plaintiffs made no allegations of discrimination in any specific funding decision. The Court refused to invalidate § 954(d)(1) as unconstitutional before the NEA actually used it in a manner that involved the suppression of disfavored viewpoints.[220]

The Court further found that the lower courts had erred in finding § 954(d)(1) to be unconstitutionally vague. The Court reasoned that the provision was vague, but not unconstitutionally so.[221] While recognizing that § 954(d)(1) would potentially have some chilling effect on artists' speech since artists might conform speech to what they perceived as the decision-making criteria of the NEA, the Court held that when the government is acting as patron rather than as sovereign, the consequences of imprecision are not constitutionally severe.[222] In closing, the Court observed:

> In the context of selective subsidies, it is not always feasible for Congress to legislate with clarity. Indeed, if this statute is unconstitutionally vague, then so too are all government programs awarding scholarships and grants on the basis of subjective criteria such as excellence. . . . Section 954(d)(1) merely adds some imprecise considerations to an already subjective selection process. It does not, on its face, impermissibly infringe on First or Fifth Amendment rights.[223]

---

[218] *Id.* at 582.

[219] *Id.* at 582.

[220] *See id.* at 587 (citing Red Lion Broadcasting Co. v. FCC, 395 U.S. 367, 396 (1969) ("We will not now pass upon the constitutionality of these regulations by envisioning the most extreme applications conceivable, but will deal with those problems if and when they arise").

[221] *See id.* at 588 ("The terms of the provision are undeniably opaque, and if they appeared in a criminal statute or regulatory scheme, they could raise substantial vagueness concerns. It is unlikely, however, that speakers will be compelled to steer too far clear of any 'forbidden area' in the context of grants of this nature.")

[222] *Id.* at 589.

[223] *Id.*

Therefore, the Court reversed the opinion of the Ninth Circuit Court of Appeals.

§ 3.07 RIGHTS OF PUBLICITY AND PRIVACY

[A] Relevance of the Rights of Publicity and Privacy to the Art World

Rights of publicity and privacy are rights of individuals, often famous and newsworthy, to control dissemination of information. As such, they are a form of defense against free speech. The rights of privacy and publicity are extremely relevant to the art community in the current legal environment. As noted earlier, the ongoing right-of-publicity case stemming from Rick Rush's portrayal of Tiger Woods at the Masters has potentially far-reaching consequences for artists' ability to express themselves.

Additionally, rights of privacy and publicity have an enormous impact upon the growing market for art licensing. For example, a party wishing to reprint copies of Grant Wood's "American Gothic" is well advised to clear the publicity rights of the artist's sister, who posed for the painting, through the Visual Artists and Galleries Association. Moreover, as technology has revolutionized the stock photo industry, publicity and privacy rights have become more important. In the past, publishers of catalogues, advertisements and other media received many of the images they used through agencies. If the agency providing the photo did not get the proper legal release from the individual whose image was being used, liability ensued, generally for the agency. However, it was rare that an improper use of an image would expose an agency to huge damages, because many agencies were localized and thus may have been more familiar with the graphic designers and ad agencies that used their product.[224] Therefore, the scope of the misuse was usually not large enough to yield much liability. That has now changed dramatically, thanks to digitization, which has enabled the exchange of large compilations of images across the country by means of Internet connections and CDs.[225] While this development makes it much easier for agencies with many images to grab a share of the national market,[226] it also opens agencies up to far greater potential liability when model releases are defective, because the images are widely and quickly distributed, and agencies have less say in how the images are used.[227] The amount of potential damages arising out of claims of this sort increases with the number of impressions made of the image.

---

[224] Tim W. Ferguson, Shutter Bugs, Forbes, November 2, 1998, at 88.

[225] *Id.*

[226] One example is PhotoDisc, whose image library exceeds 75,000 pictures. *Id.*

[227] David Walker, Royalty-Free Discs Create Model Release Meltdown, PDN, January, 1999.

PhotoDisc is in the royalty-free digital image business.[228] It produces images on CD-Rom and disseminates them to companies across the country to be used in advertising and editorial. One disk with up to 300 images can cost as little as $300.[229] In 1989, a commercial photographer took a picture of Victoria and Keith Simon and their baby daughter.[230] The picture was intended only for private use, but the photo ended up on PhotoDisc's "Volume 2: People and Lifestyles."[231] The photo was used by many different advertisers for diverse purposes:

> The Christian Coalition used the photo in a calendar; [the] retailer Costco used it to promote Rogaine, a baldness remedy; the *San Diego Union-Tribune* used it with personal ads for single parents; Macy's used the picture in a mailer; and it appeared on packaging for Quicken Family Layer, a software product. The photo also illustrated ads for drug counseling services and articles about chronically ill children.[232]

The Simons brought suit against PhotoDisc for violating their right to privacy. PhotoDisc ended up settling with the Simons for more than $1 million.[233] For stock photo agencies, the faulty model release has become a major concern. The rights of publicity and privacy will have a major influence on this industry as it reacts to the problem.

[B] Prosser's Four Torts of Privacy

In 1890, Samuel D. Warren and Louis Brandeis wrote an article in the Harvard Law Review titled "The Right to Privacy,"[234] which suggested that the common law creates a "common zone" in each person's life that is immune from the prying of neighbors, the press, and the public.[235] The article suggested that the law should protect people's feelings from public intrusion, and not just protect individuals from physical harm.[236] One commentator has noted that Warren and Brandeis viewed the right of privacy as preventing truthful but intrusive and embarrassing disclosures by the press,[237] separate from the protections that already existed for false intrusions.

---

[228] Tim W. Ferguson, Shutter Bugs, Forbes, November 2, 1998, at 88.

[229] *Id.*

[230] *Id.*

[231] David Walker, Royalty-Free Discs Create Model Release Meltdown, PDN, January, 1999.

[232] *Id.*

[233] *Id.*

[234] Samuel D. Warren & Louis Brandeis, The Right to Privacy, 4 Harv. L. Rev. 193 (1890).

[235] Martin P. Hoffman, The Rights of Publicity and Privacy, SC68 ALI-ABA 217, 219 (1998).

[236] *See id.*

[237] 4 J. Thomas McCarthy, McCarthy on Trademarks & Unfair Competition § 28:3, at 28-4 (1996).

In the early twentieth century, many cases involved a variation on the theme of the 1890 Warren and Brandeis article: the use of a person's name or picture in advertising without permission.[238] A split of authority quickly developed regarding the applicability of the right of privacy in such cases.[239] The cases that did grant redress for the unauthorized use of a person's name or picture in advertising did so based on traditional tort law concepts such as personal injury to dignity or state of mind.[240] In such cases, damages were typically measured by amount of mental distress.[241] Recovery in these cases was based on the concept that when a person's photograph is used for purposes of selling a product against his consent, it affronts his humanity, and damages his dignity.[242] Granting relief based on these grounds, the courts were still focusing on Warren's and Brandeis's concept of the right to be left alone.[243]

Dean William Prosser divided the amorphous collection of civil wrongs falling within the category called "invasion of privacy"[244] into four categories:

1. intrusion upon the plaintiff's physical solitude;
2. public disclosure of embarrassing private facts;
3. placing the plaintiff in a false light in the public eye; and
4. appropriation for commercial benefit of the plaintiff's name or likeness.[245]

These four categories make up Prosser's oft-cited Four Torts of Privacy, which courts almost universally follow.[246] Remedies for infringement of these rights was cast in the mental distress mode, meaning that damages were based on the mental suffering the plaintiff experienced due to not having been left alone.[247] Although all four torts of privacy are applicable to the art world, the rest of this discussion will focus primarily on the right of publicity, which, as a commercial right, has generated the most relevant cases.

[C] The Right of Publicity

The right of publicity was born out of the right of privacy. Whenever high-profile individuals sought redress for unauthorized use of their picture in advertising, courts were less willing to grant damages. The rationale for the courts'

---

[238] *Id.* § 28:3, at 28-4.
[239] *See id.* § 28:3, at 28-4.
[240] *See id.* § 28:3, at 28-4.
[241] *See id.* § 28:3, at 28-4.
[242] *See id.* § 28:3, at 28-4, 28-5.
[243] *Id.* § 28:3, at 28-5.
[244] *Id.* § 28:5, at 28-7.
[245] *Id.*
[246] *Id.*
[247] *See id.* § 28:4, at 28-5.

refusal to apply the right of privacy to celebrity figures in these situations was that celebrities should not be allowed to receive mental distress damages for being thrust into the limelight when they became celebrities precisely because they sought such attention and profited from it.[248] Due to conservative judicial interpretation, the right of privacy could not protect the ability of individuals to determine the use of their own name and likeness in advertising, and this shortcoming laid the foundation for a new approach to questions of commercial appropriation, one based on a property theory rather than a mental-anguish theory.

In 1953, in the case of *Haelan Laboratories v. Topps Chewing Gum*,[249] Judge Jerome Frank was the first to introduce the phrase "right of publicity." Haelan entered into a contract with a baseball player for the exclusive right to use his photograph in connection with the sale of its gum packs, which included baseball cards. Topps knew of the agreement, but convinced the ballplayer to give Topps a similar right to the use of his photograph for purposes of selling its gum. Haelan brought an action against Topps for inducement to breach contract.

Topps argued that because the New York right of privacy was personal in nature, it could not be assigned. Since the contracts with the ballplayers had not vested any property rights in Haelan, Topps argued that Haelan had no action against Topps, attempting to take advantage of the limitations of the right of privacy in New York and gain access to ballplayers with whom its competitor had already contracted.[250]

Judge Frank, writing for the majority in a divided decision, rejected Topps's position. He held that a common law assignable right of publicity did exist in addition to the statutory right of privacy in New York. In an opinion worth quoting, Judge Frank held:

> [I]n addition to and independent of that right of privacy (which in New York derives from statute), a man has a right in the publicity value of his photograph, i.e., the right to grant the exclusive privilege of publishing his picture, and that such a grant may validly be made in gross, i.e., without an accompanying transfer of a business or of anything else. Whether it be labelled [sic] a property

[248] Paul C. Weiler & Gary R. Roberts, Sports and the Law 422 (2d ed. 1998) ("There were serious doubts about whether this personal protection against the psychological injury (hurt feelings) from having such intrusion upon their lives extended to athletes (or entertainers) who had actively sought to make themselves into celebrated public figures."); *see also* McCarthy, *supra* note 237, § 28:4, at 28-5 ("[W]hen a plaintiff whose identity was already well known sued under [a right of privacy theory], judges were unable to see how there could be 'indignity' or 'mental distress' to a plaintiff whose identity was already in widespread circulation in the news media.").

[249] 202 F.2d 866 (2d Cir. 1953).

[250] *Id.*; *see also* Weiler & Roberts, *supra* note 248, at 423 ("Topps' defense was that both sets of contracts amounted to no more than the players giving Haelan a release from liability for invasion of the privacy right not to have their feelings hurt by unconsented-to publication: under the governing New York law there was no separate right in the commercial value of one's name and likeness.").

> right is immaterial; for here, as often elsewhere, the tag property simply symbolizes the fact that courts enforce a claim which has pecuniary worth.
>
> This right might be called a right of publicity. For it is common knowledge that many prominent persons (especially actors and ballplayers), far from having their feelings bruised through public exposure of their likenesses, would feel sorely deprived if they no longer received money for authorizing advertisements popularizing their countenances, displayed in newspapers, magazines, buses, trains and subways. This right of publicity would usually yield them no money unless it could be made the subject of an exclusive grant which barred any other advertiser from using their pictures.[251]

Because the court held that the ballplayer did have a property interest in the use of the player's photograph, the court was able to recognize the exclusive nature of the agreement between Haelan and the ballplayer. The court noted that Haelan's interest in the exclusive right to the photograph was entitled to protection against third parties inducing breach. The judicial ruling in *Haelan* gave an entirely different *property* twist to the traditional *tort* slant to privacy doctrine.[252]

The right of publicity protects a property right, whereas Prosser's fourth privacy tort only protected the right of a person to be let alone or to live his life in seclusion without mention in the media.[253] As Professor McCarthy indicates, the differences between the protections provided by the right of privacy and those provided by the right of publicity are relatively simple and straightforward.[254]

> Privacy rights are personal rights. Damage is to human dignity. Injury caused by an invasion of privacy is measured primarily by mental distress and damages causally connected to mental distress.
>
> On the other hand, the right of publicity is a property right. Damage is commercial injury to the business value of personal identity. For example, damages for infringement of the right of publicity can include the fair market value of the plaintiff's identity; unjust enrichment and the infringer's profits; and damage to the business of licensing plaintiff's identity.[255]

Courts do not always find this distinction as straightforward as Professor McCarthy finds it. While the majority of jurisdictions that discuss the right of publicity do seem to view it as a property right, some still see it as a subset of

---

[251] 202 F.2d at 868.

[252] Weiler & Roberts, *supra* note 248, at 423.

[253] J. Thomas McCarthy, The Human Persona as Commercial Property: The Right of Publicity, 19 Colum.-VLA J.L. & Arts 129, 134.

[254] *See id.*

[255] *Id.*

the right of privacy, based on the fact that it initially developed in right-of-privacy cases and that Dean Prosser includes it as the fourth of his Four Torts of Privacy.[256]

For example, in New York, the New York Court of Appeals[257] ruled that "[s]ince the 'right of publicity' is encompassed under the Civil Rights Laws as an aspect of the right of privacy, which, as noted, is exclusively statutory in this state, the plaintiff cannot claim an independent common law right of publicity."[258] Because there is no New York common law right of publicity, and the statutes mentioned by the court were not specifically designed to accommodate the right of publicity, the right of publicity is somewhat different in New York from that of other states. The right of publicity does exist in New York, and has many of the same basic elements as elsewhere. However, it does not specifically address a number of property features found in other versions, such as assignability and descent.[259]

The U.S. Supreme Court has recognized the distinction between the right of publicity and the right to privacy. In *Zacchini v. Scripps-Howard Broadcasting Co.*,[260] the Supreme Court acknowledged that violation of the right of publicity and invasion of the right of privacy were two distinct torts.[261] "[W]hile this new property right (and its tortious invasion) was born in the 'right of privacy' family, it has gradually matured since 1953 into an independent legal right with its own distinct characteristics. It is entitled to its own descriptive and distinctive name: the 'right of publicity.' "[262] In 1995, the right of publicity was included for the first time in the *Restatement (Third) of the Law of Unfair Competition*,[263] and the right of publicity now exists in some form in 24 states.[264]

---

[256] One such jurisdiction is New York, which sees the right of publicity as merely an aspect of the New York statutory right of privacy. *See* McCarthy, *supra* note 253, at 134 (citing Stephano v. News Group Publications, Inc., 474 N.E.2d 580, 584 (N.Y. 1984)).

[257] The New York Court of Appeals is the state's highest appellate court.

[258] Stephano v. News Group Publications, Inc., 64 N.Y.2d 174, 183 (1984). *See also* J. Thomas McCarthy, The Rights of Publicity and Privacy, § 6.9[D] at 6-67 (Rev. 1998).

[259] *See* McCarthy, *supra* note 258, § 6.9[D] at 6-67.

[260] Zacchini v. Scripps-Howard Broadcasting Co., 433 U.S. 562, 571-72 (1977)

[261] 433 U.S. 562, 571-72 (1977) (noting that the case the Ohio Supreme Court relied on dealt with a claim under the New York "Right of Privacy," which it characterized as "an entirely different tort from the 'right of publicity' recognized by the Ohio Supreme Court.")

[262] McCarthy, *supra* note 237, § 28:7, at 28-9.

[263] Restatement (Third) of the Law of Unfair Competition, § 46-49 (1995).

[264] McCarthy, *supra* note 258, § 6.1[B] at 6-6 to 6-8, 6-15; *see also infra*, Appendix 3-A, a chart summarizing information contained therein, for a brief analysis of the statutes which exist, and the extent to which they have adopted the right of publicity. In fact, the right of publicity is becoming so popular that its development has prompted one judge to note, "I find no reason to believe that Connecticut would buck the apparent trend in the law towards recognizing the right of publicity." Jim Henson Prods. v. John T. Brady & Assocs., 867 F. Supp. 175, 34 U.S.P.Q.2d 1001 (S.D.N.Y. 1994).

[D] The Right of Publicity Defined

The right of publicity protects every person's ability to control his identity's commercial use.[265] The right of publicity makes it illegal for one person to use another's identity as a means of attracting attention to an advertisement or product without first obtaining a license.[266] One commentator has characterized the right of publicity in the following manner:

> The right of publicity protects athletes' and celebrities' marketable identities from commercial misappropriation by recognizing their right to control and profit from the use of their names and nicknames, likenesses, portraits, performances (under certain circumstances), biographical facts, symbolic representations, or anything else that evokes this marketable identity.[267]

Under this description, any trait that uniquely identifies celebrities or athletes implicates their marketable identities[268] and should therefore be protected.

[E] The Elements of a Right-of-Publicity Claim

[1] Summary

The elements of a violation of the right of publicity are relatively straightforward. In order to make out a prima facie case for a violation of the right of publicity, the complaining party must prove one validity element and two infringement elements:

1) Validity
    a. Plaintiff owns an enforceable right in the identity of a human being.
2) Infringement
    a. Defendant, without permission, has used some aspect of identity or persona in such a way that plaintiff is identifiable from defendant's use.

---

[265] McCarthy, *supra* note 237, § 28:1, at 28-3.

[266] McCarthy, *supra* note 253, at 130.

[267] Pamela Edwards, What's the Score?: Does the Right of Publicity Protect Professional Sports Leagues?, 62 Alb. L. Rev. 579, 581 (1998) (citations omitted).

[268] *Id.*

b. Defendant's use is likely to cause damage to the commercial value of that persona.[269]

The right of publicity, like any other right, has its limitations. As Professor McCarthy notes:

> It can give every person the right either to prevent or to permit for a fee, the use of his or her identity in an advertisement to help sell someone's product. But the right of publicity cannot be used to prevent someone's name or picture in news reporting. It cannot be used to prevent the use of identity in an unauthorized biography. It cannot prevent use of identity in an entertainment parody or satire, such as that of Rich Little or Saturday Night Live.[270]

In order to better understand the strengths and weaknesses of the right of publicity as a tool for protecting the commercial value of identity, one needs to understand the derivation of the right of publicity.

[2] Validity

In order to bring a valid claim for infringement of the right of publicity, the plaintiff must first meet the validity element. However, it is thought that the validity of the right asserted will not usually be a material issue in right-of-publicity cases.[271] The argument is that as long as the plaintiff asserts a right of identity in a human being, the existence of the right will not be an issue unless the applicable state law does not recognize commercial rights in human identity.[272]

The validity element is connected very closely to the concept of standing to sue. In the context of the right of publicity, enforceable right means that either the plaintiff's own identity is at issue or that plaintiff is an assignee or exclusive licensee of someone else's right of publicity.[273] Therefore, a plaintiff will not have standing to sue unless his own identity is at issue or he has been assigned or licensed the right to use the identity or persona at issue.[274]

---

[269] McCarthy, *supra* note 237, § 28:7, at 28-10.

[270] McCarthy, *supra* note 253, at 131 (citations omitted).

[271] *See* McCarthy, *supra* note 258, § 3.1[C], at 3-4.

[272] *See id.* (noting that validity will be an issue if the right of publicity is claimed in something other than a human being, such as a corporation, partnership, institution or animal). *But see* Edwards, *supra* note 267 (arguing that the National Basketball Association should be able to assert a right of publicity, and further asserting that it probably can assert a right of publicity in states with statutes that do not explicitly prohibit entities from making such claims).

[273] McCarthy, *supra* note 258, § 3.1[B], at 3-3.

[274] Even when the plaintiff has been assigned or licensed the right of publicity in question, standing to sue may be an issue. McCarthy notes:

> An exclusive licensee of a Right of Publicity has standing to sue for infringement of the rights which it owns. Defendant may challenge "standing" in two senses: that plaintiff does not in fact hold any exclusive license; or that while plaintiff is a valid

[3] Infringement

[a] Use of Identity or Persona in Identifiable Way

The second element of the right of publicity is infringement. The test for this element is identifiability. For this element to be satisfied, the defendant must use some aspect of the plaintiff's identity or persona in such a way that the plaintiff is identifiable. Statutory versions of the right of publicity, including those that derive a right of publicity from a statute based on the right of privacy, such as New York, generally will spell out which aspects of the persona are protected.

It is important to emphasize that the test for infringement is identifiability, and not confusion as to endorsement by the person. Deception and false endorsement are not needed for a violation of the right of publicity.[275] Professor McCarthy notes:

> Identity can be stolen and used to attract attention to an advertisement or product without giving rise to a valid claim of false endorsement. The identity of a famous person is used to cut through the clutter of advertising and to merely draw attention to the advertisement. It is common in advertising just to use the picture or name of a celebrity or a person prominent in a certain field without any hint of endorsement.[276]

An example of this type of advertising would be a poster on which an artist has painted Jack Nicholson, with the caption, "Jack Nicholson has played the Joker, but he's never played poker with Joker brand playing cards."

The number of people that need to be able to recognize that the infringing use of identity or persona is that of the plaintiff is not set in stone. In *Ali v. Playgirl, Inc.*[277] Playgirl Magazine included in its February 1978 issue a cartoon of a nude black man seated in the corner of a boxing ring, with both hands taped and resting on the ropes. The picture was captioned "Mystery Man," and the identification of the portrayed individual was further implied by an accompanying reference to the Greatest. Ali claimed that it bore an unmistakable resemblance to him, and that the picture violated his right of publicity. The court took judicial notice of the fact that Ali had regularly claimed that appellation for himself and that his efforts to identify himself in the public mind as the Greatest "[had] been

---

exclusive licensee, defendant's use does not infringe upon any rights which the licensee-plaintiff possesses.

See McCarthy, *supra* note 258, § 3.1[C], at 3-4.

275 McCarthy, *supra* note 253, at 135.

276 *Id.*

277 447 F. Supp. 723 (S.D.N.Y. 1978).

so successful that he [was] regularly identified as such in the news media."[278] The court further commented, "[t]he cheekbones, broad nose and widest brown eyes, together with the distinctive smile and close cropped black hair are recognizable as the features of the plaintiff, one of the most widely known athletes of our time."[279] The court noted that recognition is the proper standard regarding whether there has been a violation of the right of publicity.[280] Finding a clear resemblance between the cartoon and Ali, the court concluded that Ali's right of publicity had been violated.

Motschenbacher v. Reynolds Tobacco Co.[281] was another case discussing the level of recognition necessary to infringe upon the right of publicity. The infringing representation was not as recognizable as the picture of Ali. This case involved Lothar Motschenbacher's appeal of the district court's decision that he was not recognizable in the advertisement in question. Motschenbacher was a professional race car driver known to racing fans internationally. His solid red car with a narrow white pinstripe and white oval surrounding the number 11 was equally well known to car racing enthusiasts. R.J. Reynolds Tobacco Co. produced and televised a commercial which included an altered version of Motschenbacher's car in the foreground. Rather than an 11, the car now had a 71, and the producers of the commercial made it look as if the car had a spoiler on the back with the word "Winston" on it. Defendants made no other changes to the car. After concluding that California courts would afford legal protection to an individual's proprietary interest in his own identity, the court turned to the issue of identifiability.[282] The court of appeals agreed with the district court that Motschenbacher's likeness itself was unrecognizable, but it determined that the district court had erred in concluding that the driver of the car was not identifiable as Motschenbacher because it "fail[ed] to attribute proper significance to the distinctive decorations appearing on the car. . . . [T]hese markings were not only peculiar to the plaintiff's cars but they caused some persons to think the car in question was plaintiff's and to infer that the person driving the car was the plaintiff."[283] Based on the uniquely distinguishing features that the court found, it determined that it was an issue for the jury whether Motschenbacher's proprietary interest in his own identity had been violated.

---

[278] *Id.* at 727 (noting that the cover of the February 27, 1978 issue of Time Magazine featured a photograph of Ali, captioned "The Greatest is Gone").

[279] *Id.* at 726.

[280] *See id.* at 726 (citing Negri v. Schering Corp., 333 F. Supp. 101, 104 (S.D.N.Y. 1971) for the proposition that the New York statute in question applies to any representations that are "recognizable as likenesses of the complaining individual").

[281] 498 F.2d 821 (9th Cir. 1974).

[282] *See id.* at 826.

[283] *Id.* at 827.

In a recent case in California, the court stretched the concept of recognition to its furthest reach yet.[284] In *White v. Samsung Electronics America, Inc.*,[285] Vanna White of "Wheel of Fortune" fame sued Samsung alleging that Samsung had violated her statutory and common law rights of publicity under California law. The dispute in this case arose out of an ad campaign that Samsung ran. Each ad was set in the twenty-first century and conveyed the idea that Samsung products would last that long. The commercial that led to this action depicted a robot, dressed in a wig, gown, and jewelry which "[had been] consciously selected" to resemble White's hair and dress. The robot was posed next to a game board "which [was] instantly recognizable as the Wheel of Fortune game show set. . . . The caption of the ad read: 'Longest running game show. 2012 A.D.' "[286] This ad was referred to by Samsung as the Vanna White ad, and unlike the other celebrities depicted in the ad campaign, White did not consent to the ad and was not paid for it.

The court first dismissed White's statutory right-of-publicity claim, because Samsung's use of the robot did not rise to the level of a likeness as contemplated by the California publicity statute. However, as the court had done on previous occasions, it held that the common law right-of-publicity claim could survive even though the statutory claim had been dismissed.[287] The court then held that, unlike the statutory right which is limited to the appropriation of name or likeness, the common law right of publicity is based on the use of any indicia by which the plaintiff is identifiable.[288]

The court concluded that Vanna White is the only one that dresses like the robot, turns letters, and appears on the "Wheel of Fortune" game show. Based on this conclusion, the court held that White had alleged facts showing that Samsung had appropriated her identity and her claim should accordingly survive the motion for summary judgment.

[b] Commercial Value of Identity or Persona

The third element of a violation of the right of publicity requires a plaintiff to prove that the defendant used the plaintiff's identity or persona in a way that is likely to cause damage to the commercial value of that identity or persona. This element was discussed in *Gautier v. Pro-Football, Inc.*[289] The court found

---

[284] *See* McCarthy, *supra* note 253, at 136 ("This discussion of identification brings us to the 1992 Vanna White case in California, which pushed the issue of identifiability to the limit.").

[285] 971 F.2d 1395 (9th Cir. 1992).

[286] *Id.* at 1396.

[287] *See also* Midler v. Ford Motor Co., 849 F.2d 460 (9th Cir. 1988); Carson v. Here's Johnny Portable Toilets, Inc., 698 F.2d 831 (6th Cir. 1983).

[288] McCarthy, *supra* note 253, at 136.

[289] 107 N.E.2d 485 (N.Y. App. 1952).

that a broadcast of an animal trainer's halftime show by a sports league, contrary to his contract, did not violate his New York statutory right of privacy. Although there had been a commercial announcement immediately preceding plaintiff's performance and immediately following the performances after the plaintiff's, the plaintiff's name and picture were in no way connected with the commercials. The commercials were presented at usual and appropriate intervals. The court gleaned that it was nothing more than coincidence that one commercial, at the close of the first half, occurred immediately prior to his act. No visual, oral or other reference connected him with the product, and no issue of fact was created by the physical juxtaposition of the single announcement prior to his performance.[290] The court concluded that his name or picture had not been used for advertising purposes within the meaning of the New York right-of-privacy statute.

[F] Defenses to the Right-of-Publicity Claim

There are two main defenses available to the defendant when the plaintiff asserts a right-of-publicity claim. The first defense is consent, and the second is the First Amendment.

[1] Consent

The consent defense is really just an offshoot of the validity element. If the defendant has the consent of the person whose right of publicity is in question, then there is no violation of that right of publicity. Discussion of this issue generally centers around whether the defendant had consent to take the particular actions in question.[291]

[2] First Amendment Defense

[a] Freedom of Speech and of the Press

[i] Communicative speech.[292] The most difficult defense to deal with in a right-of-publicity case is the assertion of the First Amend-

[290] *Id.* at 488.

[291] Consent is typically, but not always, manifested by a signed release, consent or waiver. Appended to this chapter as Forms 3-1 through 3-4 are some brief examples of such documents.

[292] One scholar on right-of-publicity law explains the difference between communicative and commercial speech as follows:

> [I]n general, with a balancing between the property right of the right of publicity and the policy of free speech, a given unauthorized use of a person's identity will fall within one of two categories: the challenged use is either "communicative" or "commercial." A "communicative" use is one in which the policy of free speech predominates over the right of a person to his identity, and no infringement of the right of publicity takes place. A "commercial" use is one in which the right of publicity is infringed because, while there are overtones of ideas being communicated, the use is primarily commercial.

ment.[293] Freedom of speech and of the press, as protected by the First Amendment, can limit the application of the right of publicity. Discussing the limitations imposed on the right of publicity by the First Amendment, a New York court stated:

> [W]here the right to publicity is recognized, it does not invest a prominent person with the right to exploit financially every public use of name or picture. What is made actionable is the unauthorized use for advertising purposes in connection with the sale of a commodity. The right of publicity, therefore, like that of privacy . . . would be held to have no application where the use of a name or picture . . . is in connection with a matter of public interest. That such use is constitutionally protected and must supersede any private pecuniary considerations is conceded even by those who urge more widespread recognition of a distinct right of publicity.[294]

In *Zacchini v. Scripps-Howard Broadcasting Co.*,[295] Hugo Zacchini was a daredevil whose human cannonball act involved his being shot out of a cannon into a net some 200 feet away. The act took approximately 15 seconds to complete. A reporter covering the county fair where Zacchini was performing videotaped the entire 15-second act over Zacchini's objection and played it on his television station's 11 o'clock news program that night. The reporter admonished the television audience that they really needed to see the act in person to appreciate it. Zacchini brought an action against the television station claiming that his right of publicity had been violated. A divided Supreme Court decided, five to four, that granting relief to Zacchini on the state law right-of-publicity claim would not infringe on the television station's First Amendment rights. The United States Supreme Court noted that Zacchini's right-of-publicity claim would not prevent the television station from reporting the newsworthy aspects of Zacchini's act. However, the Court held that when a member of the media broadcasts a performer's entire act without his consent, the First and Fourteenth Amendments do not immunize his conduct. In a famous passage, the Court explained the rationale for its decision:

> The medium used will often determine the result. For example, the unpermitted use of a person's identity on a product such as a coffee mug or a T-shirt will be "commercial" and require a license. But the unpermitted use of a person's identity and picture to illustrate a story in a newspaper, magazine or television news program will be "communicative" and immune.

McCarthy, *supra* note 237, § 28:41, at 28-49 to -50 (citations omitted).

[293] McCarthy, *supra* note 258, § 3.1[F], at 3-5.

[294] Paulsen v. Personality Posters, Inc., 299 N.Y.S.2d 501, 508 (1968). New York, as the home of many media industries, tends to decide many publicity claims in favor of the defendants. *See, e.g.*, Messenger v. Gruner & Jahr Printing and Publishing, 208 F.3d 122 (2d Cir. 2000).

[295] 433 U.S. 562 (1977).

> The broadcast of a film of [Zacchini's] entire act poses a substantial threat to the economic value of that performance. . . . [T]his act is the product of [Zacchini's] own talents and energy, the end result of much time, effort, and expense. Much of its economic value lies in the right of exclusive control over the publicity given to his performance; if the public can see the act free on television, it will be less willing to pay to see it at the fair. The effect of a public broadcast of the performance is similar to preventing petitioner from charging an admission fee . . . [and] goes to the heart of petitioner's ability to earn a living as an entertainer.[296]

The opposing principles that collided in this landmark right-of-publicity case were both important. On one hand, emphasized by the dissent, this case involved a newscast, worthy of far greater constitutional protection than commercial marketing. On other, focused on by the majority, this broadcast was not simply an "appropriation of an entertainer's reputation to enhance the attractiveness of a commercial product, but the appropriation of the very activity by which the entertainer acquired his reputation in the first place."[297] In *Zacchini*, the delicate balancing act tipped in favor of the right of publicity.

However, the First Amendment does not often play second fiddle to the right of publicity in cases involving communicative uses of a person's persona. Consider *Montana v. San Jose Mercury News, Inc.*,[298] a California state court case decided in 1995, in which Joe Montana sued the *San Jose Mercury News* on common law and statutory commercial misappropriation claims. On January 22, 1989, Montana led the San Francisco 49ers to a last-minute victory, 20-16, over the Cincinnati Bengals in Super Bowl XXIII. The next day, the *Mercury News* ran a front-page story paying homage to the accomplishment and depicting four players, including Montana, celebrating on the field. The very next year, after Montana's 49ers defeated the Denver Broncos 55-10 in Super Bowl XXIV, the *Mercury News* once again ran stories celebrating San Francisco's success, accompanied by pictures of Montana during the game. In 1990, Joe Montana and the 49ers won yet another Super Bowl, giving them an unparalleled four championships in the decade prior to 1990. This time, the *Mercury News* commemorated all four victories by issuing a special Souvenir Section in its Sunday, February 4, 1990, edition, devoted exclusively to the 49ers. The souvenir section, titled 'Trophy Hunters,' carried an artist's rendition of Montana on the front page. Within two weeks, each of the newspaper pages from the Souvenir Section was reproduced in poster form and made available for sale to the general public.[299]

---

[296] *Id.* at 575, 576.

[297] Weiler & Roberts, *supra* note 248, at 425.

[298] 40 Cal. Rptr. 2d 639 (Ct. App. 1995).

[299] *Id.* at 639-40.

Almost two years after production of the posters was completed, Montana brought suit against the *Mercury News* alleging common law and statutory misappropriation of his name, photograph, and likeness. The court noted that no cause of action will lie for the "publication of matters in the public interest, which rests on the right of the public to know and the freedom of the press to tell it . . . ," and that a matter in the public interest is not restricted to current events but may extend to the reproduction of past events.[300] Montana conceded that the articles themselves were entitled to First Amendment protection. However, he argued that the reproduction of the newspaper pages in poster form was not entitled to First Amendment protection.

The court granted the *Mercury News*'s motion for summary judgment on two First Amendment grounds. First, the court found that Montana's name and likeness appeared in the posters for precisely the same reason they appeared on the original newspaper front pages: because Montana was a major player in contemporaneous newsworthy sports events. Therefore, the *Mercury News* had a worthy purpose, other than merely extracting the commercial value from Montana's face and name. Second, the court found that a newspaper has a constitutional right to promote itself by reproducing its own news stories.

[ii] Commercial speech. The cases thus far discussed have dealt with communicative speech. When the right of publicity finds itself opposite to First Amendment rights in commercial speech cases, the right of publicity usually triumphs. Therefore, the determination by the court of whether speech is commercial or communicative can have a huge impact on the decision the court makes, as illustrated by the next case.

In *Hoffman v. Capital Cities/ABC, Inc.*,[301] Dustin Hoffman[302] brought a number of claims against ABC, Inc., the parent corporation of Los Angeles Magazine, Inc., stemming from the magazine's use of Hoffman's image in an article titled "Grand Illusions" in its March, 1997 issue. The article used computer technology to merge famous still photographs of famous actors and actresses from classic films, many of whom were deceased, with photographs of body models wearing spring 1997 fashions, identifying the designers of the articles of clothing used in the cannibalized photographs.[303] Many of the famous brand names displayed in the spread were also major advertisers in the magazine at the time of publication.

[300] *Id.* at 640.

[301] 33 F. Supp. 2d 867 (C.D. Cal. 1999).

[302] In the opening paragraph of the court's findings of fact, the court listed Hoffman's many accomplishments, including two Academy Awards and six Academy Award nominations. The court then stated, "[I]t can be said that Mr. Hoffman is truly one our [sic] country's living treasures, joining the ranks of an exclusive handful of motion picture talent." *Id.* at 869. At that point in the opinion, the result became obvious.

[303] *Id.* at 870.

The photograph at the center of this conflict was a famous still shot of Hoffman, dressed in a long red dress in front of an American flag, from the film *Tootsie*.[304] In the "Grand Illusions" article, the image was manipulated so that Hoffman's head and face and the American flag were still visible, but Hoffman's head was on top of the body of a model who was wearing a silk gown by Richard Tyler and high-heel shoes designed by Ralph Lauren.[305] Another section of the same article stated, "104 GRAND ILLUSIONS. By using state-of-the-art digital magic, we clothed some of cinema's most enduring icons in fashions by the hottest designers."[306]

Hoffman's claim was based on the theory that the magazine's computerized manipulation of the *Tootsie* image and subsequent publication of that image amounted to an unauthorized use of Hoffman's name and likeness under California law. In analyzing the claim, the court noted that the magazine did not attempt to get nor obtain Hoffman's permission to use his image in the article. Furthermore, the court found that the defendant did not get Hoffman's consent to act as pitchman for any fashion designer or advertiser or the magazine. The court also found that the magazine decided to use famous actors to model the clothes, but never intended to pay the fair market value of obtaining their consent. In fact, the court determined that the magazine decided not to ask the actors for their endorsement because the magazine either knew or should have known that the endorsement would not be given, or that the actors would demand payment for their services.[307]

Based on the foregoing factual conclusions, the court determined that the magazine had violated Hoffman's right of publicity in connection with its unauthorized use of his name to endorse and promote designers Richard Tyler and Ralph Lauren and use of his image as a runway model.

The magazine argued that its use of Hoffman's image was protected by the First Amendment, but the court dismissed the argument summarily and forcefully. The court stated, "The First Amendment does not protect the exploitative commercial use of Mr. Hoffman's name and likeness." In defending its finding that the magazine was engaged in commercial speech, the court stated that the article in question provided no commentary on fashion trends and no coordinated or unified view of current fashions.[308] The court further ruled that the magazine's First Amendment defense failed because the First Amendment does not protect speech

[304] The original photograph was a full-length shot of Hoffman as Tootsie in a long red dress, standing in front of an American flag, with the printed caption, "What do you get when you cross a hopelessly straight starving actor with a dynamite red sequined dress?" and "You get America's hottest new actress." *Id.* at 870.

[305] *Id.*

[306] *Id.*

[307] *See id.* at 872.

[308] *Id.* at 874.

that is knowingly false, and the magazine published the pictures of Hoffman knowing he had never worn the clothing he was depicted as wearing in the article.

This case is troubling because it is hardly a clear case of commercial speech. As noted earlier, the right of publicity protects against the unauthorized use for advertising purposes in connection with the sale of a commodity.[309] However, the images that the court determined to have violated the right of publicity were not in advertisements for the clothing designers. It appears that the "Grand Illusions" article was attempting to pique the interest of readers through the use of an amusing and creative spin on the fashion of the day, rather than trying to sell the clothes displayed in the magazine's pages. Such speech would be better characterized as communicative speech, subject to the highest level of protection, than as commercial speech, since in other contexts, courts have held that speech with entertainment value is as deserving of First Amendment protection as is informative speech.[310]

The *Hoffman* decision is also subject to criticisms similar to the criticisms leveled against courts applying the public use doctrine. In much the same approach that courts sometimes seem to use to resolve cases involving offensive art, the *Hoffman* decision appears to apply a results-oriented approach. Rather than engaging in a discussion regarding the key determination of whether the speech in question was communicative or commercial, the court summarily stated, "The First Amendment does not protect the exploitative commercial use of Mr. Hoffman's name and likeness." This sentence was the court's one and only reference to the most important decision before the court. It does not seem to be entirely coincidental to the decision that, as the footnotes to this section suggest, the court was in awe of Hoffman.

Abdul-Jabbar v. General Motors Corp.[311] is a more clear-cut case of commercial speech. Kareem Abdul-Jabbar, the former L.A. Lakers center, was born Ferdinand Lewis (Lew) Alcindor. He retained that name throughout his college career and into the early years of his career in the National Basketball Association. The dispute arose due to a GMC television commercial aired during the 1993 National Collegiate Athletic Association (NCAA) men's basketball tournament. It asked who held the record for being voted the most outstanding player of the tournament. The answer to the question, as shown on the television screen, was Lew Alcindor, UCLA, '67, '68, '69. The commercial drew an analogy of that feat with the fact that the Oldsmobile '88 had made the best-buy list more than

[309] Paulsen v. Personality Posters, Inc., 299 N.Y.S.2d 501, 508 (1968).

[310] *See* Cardtoons, L.C. v. Major League Baseball Players Association, *infra*, note 320, in which the court noted, "Speech that entertains, like speech that informs, is protected by the First Amendment because '[t]he line between the informing and the entertaining is too elusive for the protection of that basic right.' "

[311] 75 F.3d 1391 (9th Cir. 1996).

once. Abdul-Jabbar brought a state law right-of-publicity claim against GMC prompted by the mention of his former name in the commercial.

The court discussed defendant General Motors' contention that its use of the name Lew Alcindor was incidental and therefore not actionable.[312] The court distinguished *Montana*.[313] In dismissing General Motors' position, the court noted that while the basketball record of Lew Alcindor may be said to be newsworthy, it is not automatically privileged. The court held that because General Motors used the information in the context of an automobile advertisement (a commercial use), rather than in a sports or news account, the use was not privileged under the First Amendment.[314]

[b] Parody

A controversial issue currently in the forefront of discussions regarding the right of publicity involves the role that parody should play in the courts' First Amendment analysis. *White v. Samsung Electronics America, Inc.*,[315] discussed earlier for its analysis of identifiability, explored the extent to which parody should be considered a defense in right of publicity cases involving commercial speech. The court recognized that the purpose of the advertisement in question was to sell Samsung VCRs. In that context, the court remarked, "The ad's spoof of Vanna White and Wheel of Fortune is subservient and only tangentially related to the ad's primary message: 'buy Samsung VCRs.' "[316] Therefore, the court held that Samsung's parody arguments were better suited to noncommercial parodies, where the First Amendment hurdle is higher,[317] cautioning, "the difference between a 'parody' and a 'knock-off' is the difference between fun and profit."[318]

As demonstrated by the Ninth Circuit's decision in *White*, the parody defense may not be very effective when the court classifies the use in question as commercial, rather than communicative. However, it should be apparent even to the casual observer that the issue of whether a particular use is commercial or communicative is not set in stone. Courts apply a highly fact-sensitive analysis to this determination, which is subjective. It stands to reason, then, that when embroiled in a right-of-publicity suit, defendants will want to convince the court that for one reason or another, the use they are being sued for is in fact communicative and worthy

---

[312] 371 N.Y.S.2d 10 (Sup. Ct. 1975).

[313] 40 Cal. Rptr. 2d 639 (Ct. App. 1995).

[314] 75 F.3d at 1401.

[315] 971 F.2d 1395 (9th Cir. 1992).

[316] *Id.* at 1401.

[317] *See id.* at 1401 n.3.

[318] *Id.*

of the highest level of First Amendment protection.[319] Fueling this speculation is *Cardtoons, L.C. v. Major League Baseball Players Association,*[320] in which the court determined that defendant's use of parody should be subject to the highest level of protection.

In that case, Cardtoons, L.C. represented to the court that it was organized in late 1992 to produce parody trading cards that caricatured major-league baseball players. Cardtoons contracted a sports artist, a political cartoonist, and a sports author and journalist to design a set of 130 cards.[321] The cards lampooned various aspects of baseball and its players, including the players' substantial salaries,[322] player vanity,[323] and the physical characteristics of the players.[324] When the Major League Baseball Players Association (MLBPA), which acts as the assignee of the individual publicity rights of all active players,[325] discovered Cardtoons's plans to distribute the cards in question, it wrote a cease-and-desist letter to Cardtoons. In response, Cardtoons filed suit seeking declaratory judgment that its cards did not violate the publicity rights of the players or the MLBPA, and that it could distribute its parody baseball cards without the consent of the MLBPA.

The court employed a three-part test to figure out whether Cardtoons should be granted the relief it sought: (1) determining whether the cards infringed upon MLBPA's right of publicity, (2) determining whether the cards were protected by the First Amendment, and (3) balancing the relative importance of the rights at stake if both parties have been determined to have cognizable rights.[326] The court initially noted that all of the elements of the Oklahoma right-of-publicity

---

[319] For many years, some commentators have called for courts to apply a copyright fair-use analysis to right-of-publicity cases for consistency reasons. *See* Kym Carrier, Right of Publicity: Cardtoons, L.C. v. Major League Baseball Players Association, 51 Okla. L. Rev. 159, 162 (citing Randall T.E. Coyne, Toward a Modified Fair Use Defense in Right of Publicity Cases, 29 Wm. & Mary L. Rev. 781, 782 (1988); H. Lee Hetherington, Direct Commercial Exploitation of Identity: A New Age for the Right of Publicity, 17 Colum.-VLA J.L. & Arts 1, 28-30 (1992)). In 1994, the U.S. Supreme Court upheld the use of parody as a valid defense to commercial use in a copyright case, applying the fair-use doctrine. *See* Campbell v. Acuff-Rose Music, Inc., 510 U.S. 569 (1994). If courts begin to apply the Supreme Court's analysis in that case to right-of-publicity cases, it will not be as harmful to defendants to have the use in question characterized as commercial.

[320] 95 F.3d 959 (10th Cir. 1996).

[321] *Id.* at 962.

[322] One card referred to San Francisco Giants outfielder Barry Bonds as "Treasury Bonds of the Gents," noting that he "plays so hard he gives 110 percent, compounded daily, and always cashes in on the payoff pitch." *See id.* at 962-63.

[323] One card referred to Ricky Henderson, who played for the Oakland Athletics at the time, as "Egotisticky Henederson" of the "Pathetics," and described a scene in which he accepted the "Me-Me Award" at a fan club banquet. *See id.* at 963.

[324] One card referred to the 6′ 10″ Randy Johnson, who then played for the Seattle Mariners, as "Cloud Johnson" of the "Mari-Nerds." *See id.* at 963.

[325] *Id.*

[326] *See id.* at 966.

statute in question had been met, and that the only possibility of relief for Cardtoons was a First Amendment defense.[327] Therefore, the court moved to the second step in its analysis.

The court, unexpectedly, found that baseball cards receive full protection under the First Amendment.[328] The court referred to baseball cards as commentary on an important social institution[329] and an education in baseball.[330] It further held that the cards were not subject to a lesser degree of protection based on the fact that they were humorous. To the contrary, the court noted that "[s]peech that entertains, like speech that informs, is protected by the First Amendment" because "[t]he line between the informing and the entertaining is too elusive for the protection of that basic right."[331] The court specifically addressed the issue of commercial speech, noting that it is afforded a lower level of First Amendment protection, but found that Cardtoons's trading cards did not fall within the commercial speech category because they do not merely advertise another unrelated product.[332]

Since the court found that the MLBPA's right of publicity had been violated, and that Cardtoons's free speech had been implicated, it proceeded to the third step of its analysis, weighing the two rights against each other to determine which should prevail. The court found that Cardtoons could not have achieved its purpose through less invasive means, noting that "Cardtoons's expression requires use of player identities because, in addition to parodying the institution of baseball, the cards also lampoon individual players. Further, Cardtoons's use of the trading card format is an essential component of the parody because baseball cards have traditionally been used to celebrate baseball players and their accomplishments."[333] The court concluded that the First Amendment right of Cardtoons trumped the right of publicity because, otherwise, Cardtoons would have to get the MLBPA's consent to distribute the cards. The court thought such consent was unlikely,

---

[327] *See id.* at 968.

[328] *Id.* at 969. It has been said that the court took this unexpected step in an attempt to avoid the commercial use problem. *See* Carrier, *supra* note 319, at 170 (raising the possibility that by avoiding the commercial use problem, the court may have opened the door for nonparodic baseball card producers to distribute cards without seeking a licensing agreement, because if baseball cards are "education[s] in baseball," licenses may no longer be required).

[329] *Cardtoons*, 95 F.3d at 969 ("The cards provide social commentary on public figures, major league baseball players, who are involved in a significant commercial enterprise, major league baseball [sic]. While not core political speech (the cards do not, for example, adopt a position on the Ken Griffey, Jr., for President campaign), this type of commentary is an important social institution.").

[330] *Id.*

[331] *Id.* at 969 (citing Winters v. New York, 333 U.S. 507, 510 (1948)).

[332] *Id.* at 970.

[333] *Id.* at 971.

effectively preventing the cards from entering the public discourse.[334] The court decided that such censorship of player criticism was clearly undesirable,[335] and accordingly granted Cardtoons declaratory judgment.

If courts would apply this sort of analysis to all right-of-publicity cases that involve artists as defendants, artists would most likely be encouraged. A court that affords baseball cards full protection under the First Amendment would likely grant that same protection to art. The three-step analysis also seems to be a positive development from an artist's point of view. Under the three-step analysis, courts would have to find that artists' First Amendment rights had been implicated almost every time that a case involving art was involved, since under this approach art would most likely be considered entitled to full First Amendment protection. If the publicity rights of the subject were also implicated, then the court would have to move to step three. Under step three, it would appear, the court would usually favor the artists' First Amendment rights and that in the balancing test, art accorded full protection would never win out over the publicity interest.

Since the majority in *Cardtoons* cited the dissent in *White*, this probably is not the end of the parody argument. Furthermore, the courts have yet to address, in a meaningful way, the situation where commercial speech is implicated and a parody defense is asserted. Commentators who hoped that the Tenth Circuit would carve out a parody defense for commercial speech are probably disappointed by the fact that the court did not address that issue.[336] Commercial speech is not afforded the same level of protection as fully protected speech, but courts have not yet developed a test that would balance rights of publicity against commercial free speech. This is an issue that will surely arise again.

[G] Limited Art Sales

In the New York case of *Simeonov v. Tiegs*,[337] the court had to determine whether an artist's First Amendment rights superseded the right of publicity of

---

[334] The response to Carrier's concern that by avoiding the commercial use problem, the court may have opened the door for nonparodic baseball card producers to distribute cards without seeking a licensing agreement, *see* Carrier, *supra* note 319, at 70, may lie in this portion of the court's decision. The court's fear of censorship would not seem to apply to traditional baseball card distributors. Therefore, in a case involving nonparodic baseball cards, the court's balancing step analysis could swing in favor of the MLBPA.

[335] *See* 95 F.3d at 972-73 (quoting Judge Kozinski's dissent in White v. Samsung Elecs. Amer., Inc., 989 F.2d 1395, 1519 (9th Cir. 1992) ("The last thing we need, the last thing the First Amendment will tolerate, is a law that lets public figures keep people from mocking them.").

[336] *See* Carrier, *supra* note 319, at 170 (citing Michal E. Hartmann & Daniel R. Kelly, Parody (of Celebrities, in Advertising), Parity (Between Advertising and Other Types of Commercial Speech), and (the Property Side of) Publicity, 17 Hastings Comm. & Ent. L.J. 633, 687 (1995)).

[337] 602 N.Y.S.2d 1014 (1993).

the subject of his artwork. In 1979, defendant Cheryl Tiegs was a trustee of a wildlife preservation organization which planned to create a sculpture of an elephant. The sculpting process involved tranquilizing the elephant and making its impression in a quick-drying substance called alignate while it was sleeping. Some members of the organization had reservations about the possible effect of the technique on the elephant's health. In order to dispel their fears, Tiegs agreed to allow the defendant to apply alignate to her face, her throat, and a portion of her neck. Her demonstration was successful and the project was completed as planned.

During the ensuing two-year period, Simeonov recast Tiegs's alignate impression, creating a plaster cast of her head in deep repose upon a pillow.[338] Simeonov never received Tiegs's written consent to create the plaster cast. Simeonov planned to exhibit the sculpture, as well as to sell ten limited-edition bronze copies at $20,000 each. The sculpture was to be titled "Sleeping Beauty."

The plaster cast was taken to Tiegs's apartment in November, 1981. While the piece was at defendant's apartment, maintenance workers accidentally broke the plaster cast while attempting to install a television set.

Upon learning of the damage, Simeonov filed a civil suit in the City of New York for $200,000, the amount of money that he was denied due to his inability to sell the ten bronze copies of the plaster casting. Tiegs asserted a defense to the action for damages based on §§ 50 and 51 of the Civil Rights Law, which create a statutory cause of action for invasion of privacy. Section 51, which applies to civil cases, reads:

> Any person whose name, portrait or picture is used within this state for advertising purposes or for the purposes of trade without the written consent . . . may maintain an equitable action in the supreme court of this state against the person, firm or corporation so using his name, portrait or picture, to prevent and restrain the use thereof; and may also sue and recover damages for any injuries sustained by reason of such use. . . .[339]

Tiegs argued that by making the plaster casting without her consent, with the intent to sell copies of the sculpture, the plaintiff had violated her right of publicity, as encompassed in the statutory right of privacy in New York. Therefore, Tiegs argued, she would have been able to enjoin plaintiff from selling the sculptures, and could have been granted damages. Tiegs reasoned that the plaintiff could not sue her for lost profits, since she would have prevented him from selling the bronze sculptures and he never would have received any. Simeonov countered, in relevant part, that his actions fell outside the scope of §§ 50 and 51 because to hold otherwise would infringe upon his right to free speech under the First Amendment.

---

[338] *Id.* at 1015.
[339] *Id.* at 1016.

The court noted that some artwork is protected speech under the First Amendment,[340] and attempted to balance the right of privacy granted by §§ 50 and 51 against the First Amendment protection of free speech. The court further noted that the terms "portrait" and "picture" in § 51 include any representation, whether by photographing, painting or sculpture.[341] Therefore, § 51 did cover the plaster casting. However, because the sculpture was "plaintiff's creative expression which grew out of [the] impression [of Tiegs],"[342] the court found that the plaintiff did not use the plaster casting for advertising or trade purposes as required by the statute. The court reasoned that "[j]ust because he incidentally intended to sell *a limited number* of copies of his creation, that does not mean that he was acting for the purposes of trade [as required by the statute]."[343]

The court concluded that the constitutionally protected right to free speech outweighs a person's right of privacy. The court found that creative expression will not be considered for the purposes of trade, even when accompanied by incidental pecuniary interest. The court noted that "[a]n artist may make a work of art that includes a recognizable likeness of a person without her or his written consent and sell *at least a limited number of copies* thereof without violating Civil Rights Law §§ 50 and 51."[344]

This case was a victory for artists' rights. However, the victory was not complete. The fact that the court included the italicized language is cause for concern. While an artist may safely sell a limited number of copies, and, *a fortiori*, a single work, without being subject to §§ 50 and 51, it is not clear what happens if the number of copies sold by the artist exceeds a limited number, what that limited number should be, or why selling artwork should be considered any different than selling other media of expression, such as newspapers or magazines. Certainly, Rick Rush should be concerned.[345]

---

[340] *Id.* (citing Serra v. United States Servs. Admin., 847 F.2d 1045, 1048 (2nd Cir. 1988); Contemporary Arts Ctr. v. Ney, 735 F. Supp. 743, 744 (S.D. Ohio 1990); Sefick v. City of Chicago, 485 F. Supp. 644, 648 (N.D. Ill. 1979)).

[341] *Id.* at 1017 (citing Young v. Greneker Studios, Inc., 26 N.Y.S.2d 357 (1941).

[342] *Id.* at 1017, 1018 (emphasis added) (citing Time, Inc. v. Hill, 385 U.S. 374, 397 (1967) ("That books, newspapers, and magazines are published and sold for profit does not prevent them from being a form of expression whose liberty is safeguarded by the First Amendment.")).

[343] *Id.* at 1017, 1018 (emphasis added) (citing Time, Inc. v. Hill, 385 U.S. 374, 397 (1967) ("That books, newspapers, and magazines are published and sold for profit does not prevent them from being a form of expression whose liberty is safeguarded by the First Amendment.")).

[344] *Id.* at 1018 (emphasis added). The peculiar facts of the case may have also had some bearing on the decision. For the court to have accepted Tiegs's position would have been to absolve her from the damage caused to a plaster cast she had allowed to be taken of her and which was harmed while in her care.

[345] *See supra* § 3.01.

[H] Post-Mortem Rights of Privacy and Publicity

The right to privacy does not last beyond a person's death.[346] As discussed earlier, the right to privacy is a personal right. The damages are based on mental suffering or emotional trauma. Since the right of privacy protects things such as human dignity and reputation, it makes sense that once an individual is dead, the potential injury is also gone. A dead person can no longer suffer damage to his dignity or reputation.[347]

Whether or not any post-mortem rights exist with respect to the right of publicity depends on state law. As Appendix 3-A illustrates, states take many different approaches in this area. Even in states that recognize a post-mortem right, it can vary in duration from life plus 40 years (but only for the spouse and children)[348] to indefinite rights, if used.[349]

---

[346] Restatement (Second) of Torts § 6521 (1977); Prosser on Torts, § 117 at p. 815 (4th ed. 1971).

[347] *See* McCarthy, *supra* note 258, § 9.1 at 9-3.

[348] *See* Fla. Stat. ch. 540.08.

[349] *See* Tenn. Code Ann. §§ 47-25-1101 through 47-25-1108.

FORMS AND APPENDICES

* Included on companion CD-Rom.

FORM 3-1

Model Adult Release Form—Professional Model, Extended Version

ADULT RELEASE

In consideration of my engagement as a model, upon the terms hereinafter stated I hereby grant , his legal representatives and assigns agents these for whom is acting, and those acting with his authority and permission, the absolute right and permission to copyright and use, re-use and publish, and republish photographic portraits or pictures of me or in which I may be included, in whole or in part, or composite or distorted in character or form, without restriction as to changes or alterations from time to time, in conjunction with my own or a fictitious name, or reproduction thereof in color or otherwise made through any media at his studios or elsewhere for art, advertising, trade, or any other purpose whatsoever.

I also consent to the use of any printed matter in conjunction therewith.

I hereby waive any right that I may have to inspect or approve the finished product or products or the advertising copy or printed matter that may be used in connection therewith or the use to which it may be applied.

I hereby release, discharge and agree to save harmless, , his legal representatives or assigns, agents and all persons acting under his permission or authority or those for whom he is acting, from any liability by virtue of any blurring, distortion, alteration, optical illusion, or use in composite form, whether intentional or otherwise, that may occur or be produced in the taking of said picture or in any subsequent processing thereof, as well as any publication thereof even though it may subject me to ridicule, scandal, reproach, scorn and indignity.

I hereby warrant that I am of full age and have every right to contract in my own name in the above regard. I state further that I have read the above authorization, release and agreement, prior to its execution, and that I am fully familiar with the contents thereof.

Dated:

______________________________(L.S.)

____

____

(Address)________________________
(Witness)

FORM 3-2

Model Adult Release Form—Non-Professional, Simpler Version

ADULT RELEASE

For valuable consideration, I hereby give ______ the absolute and irrevocable right and permission, with respect to the photographs that he has taken of me or in which I may be included with others:

(a) To copyright the same in his own name or any other name that he may choose:

(b) To use, re-use, publish and re-publish the same in whole or in part, severally or in conjunction with other photographs, in any medium and for any purpose whatsoever, including (but not by way of limitation) illustration, promotion and advertising, and trade; and

(c) To use my name in connection therewith if he so chooses.

I hereby release and discharge ______ from any and all claims and demands arising out of or in connection with the use of the photographs, including any and all claims for libel and invasion of privacy.

This authorization and release shall enure to the benefit of the legal representatives, licenses and assigns of ______, as well as the person(s) for whom he took the photographs.

I am over the age of majority. I have read the foregoing and fully understand the contents thereof.

____

Witnessed by:

____

FORM 3-3

Model Minor Release Form—Extended Version

MINOR RELEASE

In consideration of the engagement as a model of the minor named below and upon the terms hereinafter stated, I hereby grant , his legal representatives and assigns agents those for whom the absolute right and permission to copyright and use, re-use and publish, and republish photographic portraits or pictures of the minor or in which the minor may be included, in whole or in part, or composite or distorted in character or form, without restriction as to changes or alterations from time to time, in conjunction with the minor's own or a fictitious name, or reproductions thereof in color or otherwise made through any media at his studios or elsewhere for art, advertising, trade, or any other purpose whatsoever.

I also consent to the use of any printed matter in conjunction therewith.

I hereby waive any right that I or the minor may have to inspect or approve the finished product or products or the advertising copy or printed matter that may be used in connection therewith or the use to which it may be applied.

I hereby release discharge and agree to save harmless, his legal representatives or assigns agents and all persons acting under his permission or authority or those for whom he is acting, from any liability by virtue of any blurring, distortion, alteration, optical illusion, or use in composite form, whether intentional or otherwise, that may occur or be produced in the taking of said picture or in any subsequent processing thereof, as well as any publication thereof even though it may subject the minor to ridicule, scandal, reproach, scorn and indignity.

I hereby warrant that I am of full age and have every right to contract for the minor in the above regard. I state further that I have read the above authorization, release and agreement, prior to its execution, and that I am fully familiar with the contents thereof.

Dated:

______________________	______________________
(Minor's Name)	(Father) (Mother) (Guardian)
______________________	______________________
______________________	______________________
______________________	______________________
(Minor's Address)	(Address)
______________________	
(Witness)	

FORM 3-4

Model Minor Release Form — Simpler Version

MINOR RELEASE

For valuable consideration, I hereby give the absolute and irrevocable right and permission, with respect to the photographs that he has taken of me, or in which I may be included with others:

(a) To copyright the same in his own name or any other name that he may choose;
(b) To use, re-use, publish and re-publish the same in whole or in part, severally or in conjunction with other photographs, in any medium and for any purpose whatsoever, including (but not by way of limitation) illustration, promotion and advertising, and trade; and
(c) To use my name in connection therewith if he so chooses.

I hereby release and discharge from any and all claims and demands arising out of or in connection with the use of the photographs, including any and all claims for libel.

This authorization and release shall enure to the benefit of the legal representatives, licensees and assigns of , as well as the person(s) for whom he took the photographs.

I have read the foregoing and fully understand the contents thereof.

Witnessed by:

____________________________ ____________________________

I represent that I am the (father), (mother), (guardian) of , the above-named model. For value received, I hereby consent to the foregoing on (his) (her) behalf.

Dated: ____________________________

Witnessed by:

____

FORM 3-5

Property Release

PROPERTY RELEASE

For good and valuable consideration herein acknowledged as received, the undersigned being the legal owner of, or having the right to permit the taking and use of photographs of certain property designated as ____ does grant to ________________, his agents or assigns, the full rights to use such photographs and copyright same, in advertising, trade or for any purpose.

I also consent to the use of any printed matter in conjunction therewith.

I hereby waive any right that I may have to inspect or approve the finished product or products or the advertising copy or printed matter that may be used in connection therewith or the use to which it may be applied.

I hereby release, discharge and agree to save harmless, ________________, his legal representatives or assigns, and all persons acting under his permission or authority or those for whom he is acting, from any liability by virtue of any blurring, distortion, alteration, optical illusion, or use in composite form, whether intentional or otherwise, that may occur or be produced by the taking of said picture or in any subsequent processing thereof, as well as any publication thereof even though it may subject me to ridicule, scandal, reproach, scorn and indignity.

I hereby warrant that I am of full age and have every right to contract in my own name in the above regard. I state further that I have read the above authorization, release and agreement, prior to its execution, and that I am fully familiar with the contents thereof.

Dated:

____

____

________________________ ________________________________

Witness

____

(Address)

Appendix 3-A

Sources of Law for Right of Publicity

State	Statute	Statutory Post Mortem Rule	Statutory Aspects of Identity (see key)	Statutory Remedies (see key)	Common Law	Common Law Post Mortem Rule	Common Law Aspects of Identity	Statute of Limitation (yrs)
Alabama					Yes	L, I, N, P		
Alaska								
Arizona								
Arkansas								
California	Cal. Civ. Code §§ 990, 3344	50 years; registration required	L, N, P, S, V	A[C], C, D, P, Pr	Yes	No	I, L, N, P, V	1
Colorado								
Connecticut					Yes	Yes	L, N	
Delaware								
Florida	Fla. Stat. ch. 540.08	40 years; right inheres only in surviving spouse and children	L, N, P, Pt	D, I, P	Yes	Undetermined	N, P	4 or 2
Georgia					Yes	Yes	L, N, P	
Hawaii					Yes	Undetermined	N, P	
Idaho								
Illinois					Yes	Undetermined	I, N, P	
Indiana	Ind. Code Ann. §§32-13-1-1 through 32-13-1-20	100 years	I, L, N, O, P, S, V	A[C], C, D, I, P, Pr , 3X	No			2
Iowa								
Kansas								

State	Statute	Statutory Post Mortem Rule	Statutory Aspects of Identity (see key)	Statutory Remedies (see key)	Common Law	Common Law Post Mortem Rule	Common Law Aspects of Identity	Statute of Limitation (yrs)
Kentucky	Ky. Stat. Ann. §391.170	50 years	L, N		Yes	Undetermined	L, N, P	5
Louisiana								
Maine								
Maryland								
Massachusetts	Mass Gen. Laws ch. 214 §§1 B, 3A	None	L, N, P, Pt	D, I, 3X	No			3
Michigan					Yes	Undetermined	I, L, N, P, S	
Minnesota					Yes	Undetermined	I, L, N	
Mississippi								
Missouri					Yes	Undetermined	L, N, P	
Montana								
Nebraska	Neb. Rev. Stat. §§ 20-201 to 20-211; 25-840.01	Unlimited	L, N, P, Pt	[C]	No			1
Nevada	Nev. Rev. Stat. §§ 597.770 to 597.810	50 years; registration required	L, N, P, S, V	D, I, P[C]	No			3
New Hampshire								
New Jersey					Yes	Yes	L, N, P	
New Mexico								
New York	N.Y. Civ. Rights Law §§ 5051	None	L, N, P, Pt (V for civil, not criminal)	Cr, D, I, P	No			1
North Carolina								
North Dakota								
Ohio					Yes	No	I, L, N	

State	Statute	Statutory Post Mortem Rule	Statutory Aspects of Identity (see key)	Statutory Remedies (see key)	Common Law	Common Law Post Mortem Rule	Common Law Aspects of Identity	Statute of Limitation (yrs)
Oklahoma	Okla. Stat. tit. 21, §§ 839.1 to 839.3; Okla. Stat. tit. 12, §§ 1448,1449	100 years; registration required	I, L, N, P, Pt, S, V	A, C, Cr, D, I, P, Pr	No			2 or 1
Oregon								
Pennsylvania					Yes	Undetermined	N, P	
Rhode Island	R.I. Gen.	None	L, N, P, Pt	D, I, 3X	No			3 or 10
	Laws § 9-1-28							
South Carolina								
South Dakota								
Tennessee	Tenn. Code Ann. §§ 47-25-1101 to 47-25-1108	10 years + indefinite if exploited with first twelve years	L, N, P	D[C], I	Yes	Yes	L, N, P	3
Texas	Tex. Prop. Code §§ 26.001,26.015	50 years; registration required	L, N, P, S, V	A[C], C, D , P, Pr	Yes	Yes	L, N	2
Utah	Utah Code Ann. §§ 45-3-1 to 45-3-6	None	L, N, P, Pt, T	A, C, D, I, P	Yes	Yes	L, N	3
Vermont					Yes		I, P, L, N	
Virginia	Va. Code Ann. §§ 8.01-40; 18.2-216.1		L, N, P, Pt	Cr, D, I, P	No			5
Washington	Wash. Rev. Code §63.60	50 years	N, V, S, P, L	I, P, A, C, I, P I, P				
West Virginia								
Wisconsin	Wis. Stat. § 895.50	None	L, N, P, Pt	A, D, I, (Profit or Licensing Fee)	Yes	Undetermined	I, L, N, P	3 or 6 or 2
Wyoming								

Key:

[C] — Comment

Statutory Aspects of Identity

I — identity
L — likeness (including "picture")
N — name
O — other[1]
P — photograph
Pt — portrait
S — signature
Sl — slogan or identifying phrase
T — title
V — voice

Statutory Remedies

A — reasonable attorney fees
C — court costs
Cr — criminal liability; misdemeanor and/or fine
D — damages
F — forfeiture of infringing property
I — injunction
P — punitive/exemplary damages
Pr — profits of defendant
3X — treble damages

COMMENTS:

Cal. — Also provided for greater of $750 minimum or actual damages and profits
Fla. — Damages may include a "reasonable royalty"
Ind. — Also provides for recovery of profits of the unauthorized use and provides for minimum damages of $1,000, and for impoundment and destruction orders
Neb. — Merely says a person has a "legal remedy"
Nev. — Also provides for minimum damages of $750
Tenn. — Includes defendant's profits and impounding and destruction orders
Tex. — Also provides for greater of $2,500 minimum or actual damages and also provides for profits

See also J. Thomas McCarthy, The Rights of Publicity and Privacy § 6 (Rev. 1998). Certain material in this chart was adapted from a useful chart contained therein.

---

[1]Other = Directive appearance, gestures, and mannerisms

CHAPTER 4

INTRODUCTION TO NEW MEDIA AND ART

Benjamin Strouse

* Included on companion CD-Rom.

§ 4.01 NEW MEDIA AND ART

It is popular wisdom that new media are changing the world. They change the way we communicate with each other, and with the machines surrounding us. They change the ways we do business. They empower us to try new things, and they alienate us from a familiar world.[1] While philosophers and historians wrestle with the grandest implications of these phenomena, new media are steadily transforming the means and manner of artistic expression, as well as art law and business.

We focus here, in two chapters, on the latter changes. This chapter is designed to set forth the basic parameters of the intersection of new media and the law by explaining the phenomenon of new media, its impact, and the efforts of our current legal system to adapt to its challenges, particularly with respect to intellectual property. The chapter is explanatory and may be read in conjunction with Chapter 9, which emphasizes the more mundane issues of actually conducting business on the Internet.

[A] Underpinnings of New Media

Most people use the term "new media" to describe systems, devices and products with certain common technologies or technological characteristics. The Internet, high-definition television, CD-Roms, DVDs (digital versatile discs) and video games (which have been around in many forms for decades) are a few examples of "new media" today. The term "new media" is used here, as it is generally in common parlance, as a *popular* concept, not an *artistic* one.[2] Specifically, the term "new media" is used in this chapter most frequently to refer, either individually or collectively, to digital technology, computer networks such as the Internet, and multimedia works of art.

[1] Digital Technology

Digitization is the armature of new media, and the technology that challenges how we conduct business. Digital technology enables the making of virtually perfect copies of copyrighted works for little or no money, which threatens to

---

[1] One observer has noted that new media force artists to develop new skills in order to manage their emotions simply to survive professionally among computers, as well as the resourcefulness to consult documentation and to experiment when trying to accomplish a new result. Dr. Timothy Binkley, former Chair, Graduate Computer Art Department, School of Visual Arts, Workshop: Core Curriculum: Basic Training for Artists, March 28, 1998: www.circuitsnys.org/reports/corecurriculum.html.

[2] Unlike "media art" and "computer art," "new media" describes a loose-knit collection of pervasive technologies that have permeated our popular culture.

increase unauthorized use of copyrighted works and to undermine current product distribution systems (music, movies, books, periodicals and, of course, art). On the other hand, the same core technologies facilitate widespread access to creative media, permitting purveyors to create and distribute products of all kinds in a single (digital) format.

Technologically speaking, we can understand digital technology as the interchange of information between computers in sequences comprised of only two "symbols" or "phases" (each of which is usually represented as "0" or "1," and which can also be thought of as "off" or "on").[3] In industry lingo, each place in the sequence is known as a "bit." Computers today process and render these series of bits, or strings of "off/on" patterns, in formats that are intelligible to us, such as shapes and colors, sound and music, and voice and text.[4] For instance, images such as the "Mona Lisa" or an advertisement for laundry detergent are systematic collections of colors. Sounds, such as the music of R.E.M. or the crashing of waves are systematic collections of tones at different volumes.

Imagery that is rendered on monitors (such as computer screens) is divided into a grid of tiny squares called "pixels." To continue for the moment with the visual manifestation of digital technology, each pixel is assigned one color, created by a combination of "bits" of information (each bit represents varying amounts of primary colors, so pixels with more bits can represent more colors).[5] One observer aptly noted that viewing a digital image is like a painting by George Seurat, as each uses small dots rather than large strokes to create complex images.[6]

We perceive—that is, our brains automatically interpret—blocks of colors with their shadings as shapes. If those shapes and colors are recognizable, we give them meaning: what is in reality patches of colored oil on a canvas, we perceive as a person. An oval of light-colored oils surrounded by dark-colored oils to the human mind is the "Mona Lisa"[7] (analogously, we perceive collections of tones as music, speech or noise).

---

[3] Digital technology is, by nature, not specific to any media. That is, sounds, pictures (both still and moving images) and text can all be rendered as a series of 1s and 0s. The appropriate hardware translates them back into their familiar forms. By contrast, analog and print are technologies that achieve similar results from the standpoint of our final perceptions, but are based entirely on their own discrete manipulation of the immediate physical environment (etchings in wax, ink on paper, etc).

[4] Computer memory, at this writing, is simply an arrangement of electronic (or magnetic) devices with two modes: on and off. The numerals one and zero represent the status of the electronic current as either pulsing or not. Mike Morrison, The Magic of Image Processing 8 (1993).

[5] For example, a computer that uses eight bits of memory for each color component can provide approximately 16.7 million shades of color. Adele D. Greenberg & Seth Greenberg. Digital Images: A Practical Guide II, at 54 (1995).

[6] Jeanne English Sullivan, Copyright for Visual Art in the Digital Age: A Modern Adventure in Wonderland, 14 Cardozo Arts & Ent. L.J. 563, 570 (1996).

[7] *Id.* at 569.

Images (and sounds) in digital form are essentially sequences of code; they have no physical integrity and can be altered freely. This is why, by using commercially available imaging software, we can change blocks of colors, add and erase drawings, insert images from other sources, and modify the scale of pictures and their components.[8]

Furthermore, all digital media (again, as it exists as lines of software code) can be transmitted, copied and, theoretically, recorded an infinite number of times with complete integrity; that is, with total accuracy and no loss of quality (unless there are imperfections in the recording process or storage media). Thus, as we shall discuss below, when works of art (or other forms of content) are digitized, they "become more susceptible to copying or altering, making it harder to enforce copyrights on creative works,"[9] and to some extent inhibiting the investment of time and money in the underlying businesses.

[2] The Internet

Perhaps our first association to the concept of new media is the Internet.[10] All information on the Internet is transmitted and rendered in digital form.[11] Enough has already been written elsewhere about the Internet that it should not be necessary to say much more here, other than simply that the Internet is made up of a global network of computers that communicate with each other. Some of those computers (called "servers") are used to store ("host") content or complex sets of instructions. Other computers like the ones most of us use (called "clients" in this context) are used to experience the programming that resides on "servers" around the world in the form of text, graphics, audio and video.[12]

The reservoir of most multimedia content, the "World Wide Web," is probably the most famous part of the Internet (the term "Web" is often mistakenly used synonymously with "Internet," although "Internet" also includes other tech-

---

[8] One author's example of this phenomenon is Richard W. Maile's work "Birth of Elvis," a digital combination of a reproduction of Botticelli's "The Birth of Venus" and the image of Elvis Presley. *Id.* at 572.

[9] *Id.*

[10] The Internet evolved from the Advanced Research Project Agency Network, created in 1969 by the Department of Defense as a decentralized national communications network designed to withstand nuclear attack.

[11] All content on the Internet is digital because the network consists of computers talking to each other, and computers only talk "digital." Confusion arises because digital content (such as a song) can seem identical to the same version of the content in nondigital (in this case, analog) form.

[12] Most of the computers that comprise and access the Internet are essentially the same kind of machine, with greater or lesser amounts of power and other features, devoted by their owners to specific purposes.

nologies or applications, such as e-mail, which are distinct).[13] To visitors with Internet access[14] and the appropriate basic browser software, various Web sites serve up media (music is very popular; so is pornography) or services (such as shopping for just about anything). Each Web site (and each of the individual pages, graphics and media files on it) is today identified by a discrete "domain name" —an identifier analogous to a telephone number or street address,[15] usually starting with the by-now-familiar letters "www" (again, standing for the "World Wide Web" portion of the Internet), followed by a brand or name, such as "Sony," and ending with popular suffixes like ".com."[16] In a very real sense, the Internet's domain name network[17] constitutes a parallel, powerful identity system that must be resolved with strictures of trademark law.

---

[13] The Internet itself consists of several technologically distinct areas, which may nevertheless appear seamless to visitors, including the World Wide Web (about which more is written here); bulletin board services (BBS), which are repositories of specialized files that users with niche interests "upload" (transmit to the servers) and "download" (copy from the servers); and electronic mail (e-mail), which is a form of communication that has outstripped the telephone by many measures.

[14] The computers that most of us use are able to access the Internet through "Internet Service Providers," which provide different kinds of Internet connectivity (usually for a monthly fee, but increasingly free of charge to the consumer). Most ISPs supply the basic software that is required to "surf the Net" when one signs up for their service: namely, a browser (which acts as a window onto Web sites, translating their code into the text, images, audio and video that we seek) and an e-mail application (for receiving, sending and managing e-mail messages). Thousands of ISPs provide "dial-up" connectivity, which is still the most common means of accessing the Internet, and requires a modem. It can also be an unsatisfying experience, because it is relatively slow (that is, it passes information back and forth more slowly), compared to other kinds of more expensive connections that support information-intensive ("rich") content like movies and music.

[15] Brookfield Communications, Inc. v. West Coast Entertainment Corp., 174 F.3d 1036, 50 U.S.P.Q.2d 1545 (9th Cir. 1999).

[16] The suffix, which is known as the "top-level" domain, is intended to indicate something about the nature of the Web site. The suffix ".com" (pronounced "dot com") means "commercial," and today is the most popular top-level domain, because it is perceived to have the greatest *cachet*. Other top-level names include ".net" (originally intended for ISPs, and now for anybody—especially those that find their brand with the dot-com identifier already taken by another entity); ".org" (for nonprofit and not-for-profit organizations), ".gov" for federal governmental entities (www.white house.gov is the Website for the White House and President, for instance; www.whitehouse.com is—as of this writing—a pornography site); and ".edu" (for educational institutions). It is expected that a host of new top-level domain names will shortly be added to the Internet registry system, although the expansions have been repeatedly delayed. The second-level domain is the brand that people associate with the owners of the Web site, such as the word "sony" in www.sony.com. The public expectation is therefore that the second-level domain name is the primary identification of a business, product or service related to the owner of the Web site. Frequently, for this reason, users today attempt to find a company's Web site by guessing at its domain name, using the company's trademark or other identifiers (such as product names or company acronyms) as the second-level domain name, followed by ''.com'' (or ".org", etc. as appropriate).

[17] Congress had passed legislation granting control over the regulation and supervision of the

General activity on the Web is based on the concept of links (also called "hyperlinks"), which are the primary means for users to branch out to information. The first of three basic kinds of links is known as a "hypertext link," and sends visitors away from the then-current Web page to the destination page (which may or may not be within the same Web site), or opens a new browser window for viewing the target. The second kind of link, known as an "in-line link," calls up audio, video or graphic content from another Web site and integrates it seamlessly (for display or play purposes only) within the then-current page. The third kind of link is known as "framing," which allows the creation of subwindows within the then-current Web page for displaying other content from other pages (which are usually located on other sites).[18]

Finally, "metatags" are text embedded in a Web page but not generally visible to visitors (that is, the metatags do not render while the visitor's Web browser is in its default viewing mode). Instead, metatags are written into a site in order to define and promote its identity *vis-à-vis* search engines that scour the Web, and are used by most people surfing the Net as a means of locating information. While metatags are a powerful means of shaping and communicating identity on the Internet, unchecked, they can also be used as tools for stealing, passing off and diluting the identities of competitors.

[B] Art and the Web

Through the Internet, artists and purveyors of art have worldwide access to all manner and form of resources worldwide, from the attention of patrons to the exhibitions of works, the offerings of galleries, and the ruminations of colleagues. As evidenced by the growing number of galleries presenting digital images of their offerings, and the frenzied atmosphere of online auctions, the Internet is

---

Internet to the National Science Foundation (NSF). In 1993 exclusive naming authorities for the top-level domain names (.com, .net, .org, .edu, and .gov) were granted by the NSF to Network Solutions, Inc. ("NSI"). Since 1993, NSI has registered several million "names" in the .com top-level domain. As recently as November of 1999, the Internet's governing board, the Internet Corporation for Assigned Names and Numbers (ICANN) helped to end this monopoly by opening up the registration process to more than 80 companies around the world, which will include the registration by competitors of the popular .com, .net and .org suffixes. Jeri Clausing, Internet Group Approves Domain Registration Rules, N.Y. Times, Nov. 5, 1999, at C2. Nevertheless, the perceived value of NSI became so great that a private acquisition of it for approximately $21 billion in stock is currently underway by VeriSign, Inc., a provider of digital certificates for confirming online identities.

[18] Each of the three kinds of links can also be further subdivided into two different categories: "invoke-to-load" and "auto-load," where, respectively, the link is presented in some form (*e.g.*, "click here to view") to the user, who has the option of selecting it, or the link simply executes without the user's direct knowledge based on associated actions (*e.g.*, visiting a new page may trigger the playing of an in-line song).

factoring into distribution and sales opportunities of art works. Likewise, aficionados can peruse both eclectic and grand collections of art around the world. It is no surprise to most that the Internet is also facilitating an evolution of new forms of art, such as Web art, that challenge notions of how art is to be perceived, valued, and sold.

[1] Benefits to Artists

On a rudimentary level, like any new field requiring design and creative services, the Internet has meant employment opportunities for many artists. The designs of millions of Web sites reflect the efforts of graphic artists using essentially the same computers that contemporary artists have for years used as a means of self-expression, instead as tools of commerce to meet demand for their skills as craftspersons.[19]

Artists seeking input about their work are using the Internet to generate feedback from around the world.[20] Artists and academicians seeking specialized knowledge use the Web for formal research through distant professional institutions,[21] as well as a window onto art that is often marginalized in conventional physical settings and might otherwise be inaccessible.[22]

In entrepreneurial terms, the Internet also empowers artists to be more involved in the business of art by breaking down barriers between art and the process of selling it. By creating a Web site, artists can display their work and achieve some measure of exposure, or bolster and embellish more traditional marketing methods. This new reality means, however, that artists availing themselves of such resources must also grapple with the tactics of traditional art commerce.[23]

[2] Art Sales Online

At this moment, perhaps the best-known example of selling art on the Internet is Web-based auctions. This phenomenon has captured the attention of the general public, and the favor of the financial markets, through such brand-name virtual

---

[19] Not surprisingly, there are members of the art community who perceive this commercialism as an affliction. John S. Johnson, Jr., quoted in "Groundbreaking Developments in Electronic Art," Matthew Mirapaul, http://www.nytimes.com/library/text/98/12/cyber/artsatlarge/24artsatlarge.html

[20] Belleville Artist Sets Up Web Site To Show Her Work, St. Louis Post-Dispatch, Mar. 8, 1999.

[21] The Web site www.artsconnected.org, which is operated jointly by the Walker Art Center (www.walkerart.org) and the Minneapolis Institute of Arts (www.artsmia.org is one of many examples of art research resources.

[22] For example, the Cunningham Dax Collection of Psychiatric art (http://www.ozemail.com.au/~ecdax) displays art made by patients in psychiatric hospitals and clinics that expresses the disturbances of mental illness.

[23] The State of Web Commerce, March 28, 1998, http://www.circuitsnys.org/reports/webcommerce.html

businesses as eBay (www.ebay.com); Yahoo (www.yahoo.com), which purchased the 134-year old California auction house Butterfield & Butterfield in 1999; and Amazon (www.amazon.com), which essentially provides the Web infrastructure for the operations of Sothebys.com, the Web-based arm of the auction house of the same name.[24]

By some estimates, the world has over 7,500 high-end dealers in art, antiques and collectibles, and 200 high-end auction houses,[25] which have cultivated their reputations over many years based on taste and reliability. Yet these days many of them are setting up a storefront on the Internet[26] alongside purveyors that lack any "brick-and-mortar" presence[27]—and its overhead. In short, the potential of selling art on the Internet portends a dramatic shift in the *status quo*.

It may be that art auctions will have the kind of impact on corresponding business methods and transaction fees that Internet day trading has had on the stock market and brokerage houses. Already, for example, while sellers at auction today pay up to a 20 percent seller's fee, and buyers may pay a 15 percent "buyer's premium,"[28] major art auction Web sites have had plans to offer auctions with no seller's commission and a buyer's fee of only 6 percent.[29]

[3] Art Exhibitions and Museums on the Internet

Web-based museums range in breadth, style, and identity from homemade collections of images focusing on a category of objects, such as quilts, to elaborate representations of a physical museum (including floor plans, tours, exhibits and new collections unavailable at the physical location).[30] Reportedly, there are more than ten thousand museums of one sort or another based in the 120 nations with a presence today on the Internet,[31] presenting works to an audience that would

---

[24] That the Internet does not provide the close contact with potential purchasers to which traditional art buyers are accustomed is not dissuading investors or entrepreneurs.

[25] Robert Goff, Auctions: Independence Day, The Forbes Life Sotheby's (Feb. 22, 1999).

[26] Reportedly, for example, Sotheby's has invested $25 million in Sothebys.com, and has been aggressively courting high-end art dealers and galleries for two- and three-year exclusive Internet selling relationships (for goods in excess of $300), in part by offering to waive the customary seller's fee.

[27] For example, the Web site www.nextmonet.com., like other online art retailers, claims to offer a wide variety of art objects, paintings and pictures.

[28] Robert Goff, Auctions: Independence Day, The Forbes Life (Feb. 22, 1999).

[29] See, for example, the art auction Web site www.artnet.com, which claims to be one of the first commerce sites geared toward fine-art buyers and is aggressively entering the art auction market. *Id.*

[30] Many museums boast impressive art sites; the Israel Museum's online tour (http://www.imj.org.il), for instance, offers one example of how online museums attempt to deliver complex experiences.

[31] The Elsas Producties Web site (www.elsas.demon.nl), which tallies museum links, claims that a new museum is added to its lists, on average, once a day. Steven Henry Madoff, Spotlight, reported in Fresno Bee (Jan. 17, 1999) (New York Times News Service).

otherwise be cut off by distance and limited resources.[32]

What is especially significant to the art industry is that many of the greatest museums in the world now boast very impressive sites, which some use for relatively bold and idiosyncratic ends.[33] Similarly, the medium permits museums to economically exhibit portions of their collections that might not otherwise be displayed to the general public.[34] Behind the scenes, museums are also using the Internet as a tool to share resources, both online and off.[35]

Yet, while it might be true, as one publication has noted, that the Internet is an ideal extension of the museum,[36] the issues inherent in creating a museum Web site can be tricky. For instance, museums must face the prospect of making electronic images of their most valuable assets freely available for the taking.[37]

[4] Web Art

A new discipline of digital art created specifically for the Web has been evolving since about 1995.[38] Known by some as "net.art,"[39] it involves a complex

---

[32] For example, one of the most comprehensive exhibitions of twentieth century American art ever assembled in New York City at the Whitney Museum of American Art was made available the day the exhibition opened at www.artmuseum.net, an Internet-based museum gallery presented by the Intel Corporation.

[33] *See, e.g.*, www.guggenheim.org/exhibitions/virtual/virtual-museum.html.

[34] See, *e.g.*, www.whitney.org.

[35] *See* the Museum Educational Site Licensing Project (http://www.gii.getty.edu/mesl/home.html) and the Art Museum Image Consortium (AMICO) (www.amico.org). AMICO members include 26 of the nation's top art museums, including New York's Metropolitan Museum of Art, the Art Institute of Chicago, the Museum of Fine Arts in Boston, and the Museum of Contemporary Art, San Diego. Its mission is to provide an authoritative, public, nonprofit, educationally focused, online database of art. Pam Dixon, Museums join forces to protect cyber rights to art, San Diego Union-Tribune, at E3 (Jan. 31, 1999).

[36] *See* Art Review Magazine, www.culturenet.ca/artbusiness/artreview5.html:

> To see art on the Net, from Vasari to Viola, Hobbema to Hill, is to experience it within an over-determined, ambivalent media. The Web has no intrinsic values or hierarchies to sustain. It has no taste, no political agenda. It's the ultimate clean slate, a democratic space where the symbols and structures evolved over thousands of years can be juxtaposed arbitrarily but instructively. The signifiers in Gauguin, Gentilleschi, and an ad for Givenchy, can be arranged for analysis, cut out for context, and re-presented for reading

[37] Computer Link, Simson Garfinkel, Creating a Web Site Especially Challenging for Museums, San Diego Union-Tribune (Dec. 29, 1998).

[38] While this subsection discusses only art forms arising out of the Internet, it should be noted that platform-based technology art has, for many more years than this, combined physical and digital resources to explore art in video, moving image, CD-Rom/DVD installation, film, two-, and three-dimensional digital imaging, and sound. Among many important institutions, including the Soho branch of the Guggenheim Museum, the Chelsea Facility (www.eyebeam.org/digital__mus__frmsrc.html) offers public space for the exhibition of such works.

[39] Pam Dixon, Art For the Web, San Diego Union-Tribune (Apr. 4, 1999). Another name,

use of the Web as a primary medium to communicate an artistic concept. The Walker Art Center in Minneapolis, the Guggenheim, the Museum of Modern Art in New York, and other institutions have significant net.art galleries on their Web sites.[40] Net.art is developing rapidly both in Europe and the United States, making it possibly the first new distinctive art to emerge out of the Internet and have an international impact.[41]

Like more traditional art works, net.art can be bought, sold and displayed.[42] However, unlike traditional art objects, net.art tends to be continuously changing, or inherently unstable, widely accessible, and relatively easy to duplicate, so valuing and transferring it can be challenging. Currently, it is more often licensed as an intellectual property on an exclusive or nonexclusive basis,[43] or as an expectation of relationship, similar to conceptual art, and in such ways it is slowly gaining acceptance from museums and other arbiters of cultural taste. While Web versions of pay-per-view are hardly unique,[44] the notion of springing such a business model upon the business of art[45] would be a major challenge to the status quo.

"Neen," was recently developed by artist Miltos Manetas in conjunction with Lexicon Branding and the Art Production Fund. *See* www.neen.org.

[40] Other prominent sites devoted to net.art as of this writing include Rhizome (www.rhizome.org), devoted to the movement and the literature, and exhibiting multiple artists; jodi.org (www.jodi.org), the work of a single group; the Museum of Web Art (www.mowa.org), a straightforward introduction with a section for children; arts-net (www.arts-net.org), the source of net.art contests; and the collections at Beyond Interface. *Also see generally* the Internet Public Library—IPL Pathfinder: Net Art (http://ipl.lub.cu.se/ref/QUE/PF/netart.html/searching.

[41] Lev Manovich, Avant-Garde as Software (www.crac.org/htmls/levavant.html) (visited November 1999).

[42] For example, art.teleportacia (http:\\art.teleportacia.org) bills itself as a gallery for the sale of Web art to individuals and corporations.

[43] For instance, at CyberArt99 Symposium held in New York, the director of the Whitney Museum of American Art, Maxwell L. Anderson, proposed a scenario involving the payment of royalties to digital artists displaying their pieces on a members-only site. Mirapaul, May 13, 1999, There May Be Money In Internet Art After All. Similarly, the director of Intel Productions suggested that it would be possible to sell digital works through Intel's ArtMuseum.Net Venture just as one might download a song from a music industry site.

[44] Many major newspapers, from The New York Times to The Christian Science Monitor charge a fee to view a specific archived article, and companies are even beginning to charge for audiovisual events. At one point, highly creative art sites such as "Hell.com" and BindiGirl charged visitors a credit card fee of a few dollars to view the works and performances during a limited period of time. Mirapaul, May 13, 1999, There May Be Money In Internet Art After All.

[45] As mentioned elsewhere in this book, the business of traditional art is fundamentally based on the first-sale doctrine of copyright law: once a copyrighted work is sold, the buyer (with a few exceptions based largely on laws of moral rights, discussed below and elsewhere in this book) gains total interest in and complete control of the single version of the purchased work. This control, however, conveys no interest in its copyright, so the buyer still may not reproduce copies or otherwise exploit it, other than simply to display, resell or lend that version.

§ 4.02 THE EVOLUTION OF ART LAWS

New media are colliding hard with the agglomeration of legal principles known as art law. More than a few art-related activities on the Internet, for instance, are today associated with some degree of uncertainty. This section opens by outlining some of the basic legal principles of art law, and reviews some relevant aspects of digital technology and the Internet. After pointing out some concrete examples of new media activities that raise legal questions, we will survey some of a few authoritative legal conclusions.

[A] Basic Legal Principles

Using digital technology to produce artworks is an area of unpredictability in the laws of the U.S. and other countries.[46] It is important to recognize that while there are some new legislative initiatives that specifically relate to the Internet, in general the laws applied to the Internet are the same laws that apply to the rest of human activities. This chapter focuses primarily on U.S. copyright and trademark, which are longstanding bodies of law with a large corpus of decisions and are at the heart of most analyses of creative activities in new media.

[1] Copyright[47]

As has been stated elsewhere in this book (and will only be reiterated briefly here), the purpose of copyright law is to encourage creativity through economic incentives by giving to the creator a monopoly on the use of the creation for a limited time. Therefore, during the copyright term, the creator has the right to demand payment from those who wish to copy, publish, perform, display, adapt, or distribute the creation or elements of it.[48]

United States copyright attaches to creative elements of an original creation upon its fixation in a tangible medium. Unless the work is a "work made for hire,"[49] all copyright in it resides in the creator(s). After the term of copyright ends, the formerly protected creation becomes freely available, as part of the public domain.[50]

---

[46] While this chapter focuses on the laws and legal principles of the United States, activity on the Internet theoretically can subject art sites and their owners to the laws of foreign countries and states, as discussed below in the Foreign Jurisdiction subsection.

[47] *See generally* Chapter 1.

[48] Copyright Act of 1976, 17 U.S.C. § 106 (1994).

[49] The definition of "work made for hire" is discussed extensively in Chapter 1.

[50] Once a work is "public domain," it can be exploited by anyone (although there may still be restrictions related to the "moral rights" of the creator under certain legal doctrines, *e.g.*, trademark law, as discussed in Chapter 1). In the context of new media, however, it is worth noting that "public domain" is a legal concept that does not confer the right of access to a work, which

The owner's right to reproduce the copyrighted work is broadly defined to include all forms of reproduction and distribution, including digital ones, and to be otherwise unqualified in terms of use. During transfers of creative work, unless expressly provided to the contrary and, generally, in writing, all exclusive rights to exploit the creation under U.S. copyright law are reserved to the copyright owner.[51] This means that, for instance, the sale of a work of visual art by the creator (or more commonly, an agent) does not by itself transfer to the buyer all of the rights of copyright in it—that is, the buyer will not have rights of reproduction in the work.[52]

Merely using an original work as a model, a template or inspiration does not by itself constitute an infringement,[53] because copyright law permits slight or trivial similarities between works, and allows de minimis copying from the original creation. Generally speaking, only *substantial* similarities between portions of the works would violate the copyright in the original, especially if the copied portions represent significant parts of the original, creative expression of the copyrighted work.[54] Under such circumstances, copyright infringement includes the unauthorized reproduction, publication, performance, display, adaptation or distribution of protected elements of a copyrighted work.[55]

Infringement can therefore occur, for instance, by virtue of an unauthorized posting of an object on an art site, or from appropriation art (despite the fact that

---

can be restricted (generally for business reasons) using encryption and other technology devices, notwithstanding the absence of copyright protection.

[51] A "transfer of copyright ownership," which by definition does not include nonexclusive licenses, must be by written instrument. 17 U.S.C.A. § 204. *See* I.A.E., Inc. v. Shaver, 74 F.3d 768, 775 (7th Cir. 1996); Pinkham v. Sara Lee Corp., 983 F.2d 824, 831 (8th Cir. 1992) (unlike an exclusive license, an authorization can be given orally or implied from conduct).

[52] Such a sale, however, is generally a transfer of all rights in the physical copy of the particular work of art that is sold, under what is known as the "first-sale doctrine" of the Copyright law, thereby extinguishing the artist's right of public display. 17 U.S.C.A. § 109(c).

[53] Wallace Computerserve, Inc. v. Adams Business Forms, Inc., 837 F. Supp 1413, 1416 (N.D. Ill. 1993).

[54] *See* Harper & Row Publishing, Inc. v. The Nation Enterprises, 471 U.S. 539 (1985).

[55] Part of the Copyright Act, known as the Visual Artists Rights Act (VARA), also confers to the creator the rights to "prevent any intentional distortion, mutilation, or other modification of that work which would be prejudicial to his or her honor or reputation, and any intentional distortion, mutilation, or modification of that work is a violation of that right." 17 U.S.C. § 116(a). These rights, sometimes called "moral rights," are distinct from other aspects of copyright in a number of ways. For instance, even if the copyright in the work has been transferred completely to another, under a moral rights rule, enforcement and ownership need not go hand in hand, and the artist can still sue the current owner of the work or of the copyright for moral rights violations. Notably, these rights are limited to paintings, drawings, prints, sculptures or still photographic images existing in a single copy, or in a limited edition of 200 copies or fewer that are signed and consecutively numbered by the author. Thus, its application to the Web is limited.

it may be the form of expression of the appropriating artist).[56] Understandably, one of the trickiest copyright analyses relates to the distinction between insubstantial copying (which is permissible) and substantial similarity (which is unlawful),[57] and the ever-increasing subtleties of digital technology threaten to add layers of complexity.[58]

[2] Trademark

As set forth in Chapter 1, a trademark or service mark is essentially the legal term for a brand or other form of identity of a product, service or business. In commerce, an entity cannot use any reproduction of a registered mark in a way that is "likely to cause confusion, or to cause mistake, or to deceive" a customer.[59] The determination of whether or not the use is likely to cause consumer confusion is based on certain factors:

1. the degree of similarity between the marks in both appearance and suggestion;
2. the similarity of products or services for which the mark is being used;
3. the area (automobiles, software) and manner (direct marketing, TV advertising) of concurrent use;
4. the degree of care likely to be exercised by potential customers;
5. the strength of the original mark;
6. any evidence of actual confusion; and
7. any intent by the alleged infringer to "palm off" its products as identified with another party.[60]

In addition, the Federal Trademark Dilution Act of 1995 created a cause of action that entitles the owner of a "famous" mark to injunctive relief against the

---

[56] Copyright law does not rely on aesthetics; where issues of originality and creative expression arise as part of an infringement dispute, the identical analyses are applied to the graphics of a Web site, the composition of an advertisement in a glossy magazine, and to a Georgia O'Keefe watercolor. *See* Geanne English Sullivan, Copyright For Visual Art in the Digital Age: A Modern Adventure in Wonderland, 14 Cardozo Arts & Ent. L.J. 563, at 585-89.

[57] *See* Peter Pan Fabrics, Inc. v. Martin Weiner Corp., 274 F.2d 487, 489 (2nd Cir. 1960).

[58] In an effort to address just one aspect of this problem, the National Conference on Fair Use (CONFU) has laid out guidelines for the fair use of digital images, which apply only to educational institutions, educators, scholars, students and image collection curators engaging in instructional, research, or scholarly activities at educational institutions for educational purposes.

[59] Simple trademark infringement (§ 32(1) of the Lanham Act, 15 U.S.C. §§ 1051-1127) allows a plaintiff to recover if he can prove that the defendant used a reproduction, counterfeit, copy, or colorable imitation of a registered mark in connection with the sale, offering for sale, distribution, or advertising of any goods or services without consent of the mark's owner, and which causes or is likely to cause confusion.

[60] 15 U.S.C. § 1114 (West 1996).

commercial use of a competing mark if that use "begins after the mark has become famous and causes dilution of the distinctive quality of the mark."[61] The concept of "dilution" means "the lessening of the capacity of a famous mark to identify and distinguish goods or services, regardless of the presence or absence of (1) competition between the owner of the famous mark and the other parties, or (2) likelihood of confusion, mistake, or deception,"[62] and can generally be traced through blurring[63] or tarnishment.[64]

The Lanham Act also creates a statutory claim for false designations of origin and false representations[65] (for both registered and unregistered marks[66]) where conduct is likely to cause confusion,[67] or, used in commercial advertising or promotion, "misrepresents the nature, characteristics, qualities, or geographic origin of her or another person's goods, services, or commercial activities."[68] In practice, false representation claims arise when a trademark (or other distinguishing characteristic of a product or service) is used in a false or deceptive manner,[69] and has been used by artists to give them "moral rights like" protection.[70] This last cause of action is frequently invoked in connection with misuse of marks on the Internet, especially the misuse of metatags[71] and other electronic mechanisms for identifying goods and services.

[B] Art Law and Technology

We speak of digital technology as a "paradigm shift" because, for so many years, legislators, judges, and business leaders understood the management of

---

[61] 15 U.S.C.A. § 1125(c) (West 1996).

[62] 15 U.S.C.A. § 1127 (West 1996).

[63] Blurring may be found to exist where "the defendant uses or modifies the plaintiff's trademark to identify the defendant's goods and services, raising the possibility that the mark will lose its ability to serve as a unique identifier of the plaintiff's product." Deere v. MTD Prods., 41 F.3d 39, 43 (2d Cir. 1994).

[64] Tarnishment may be found to exist where the plaintiff's famous mark is threatened by negative associations from a defendant's use of the mark in connection with poor-quality goods or services, or lewd or obscene activities. *See* Hormel Foods Corp. v. Jim Henson Prods., Inc., 73 F.3d 497, 507 (2d Cir. 1996).

[65] 15 U.S.C.A. § 1125(a) (West 1996).

[66] *See* Warner Brothers, Inc. v. Gay Toys, Inc., 658 F.2d 76, 78 (2d Cir. 1982); New West Corp. v. NYM Co. of Cal., Inc., 595 F.2d 1194, 1198 (9th Cir. 1979).

[67] 15 U.S.C.A. § 1125(a)(1)(a) (West 1996).

[68] 15 U.S.C.A. § 1125(a)(1)(b) (West 1996).

[69] *See* Dallas Cowboys Cheerleaders, Inc. v. Pussycat Cinema, Ltd., 604 F.2d 200 (2d Cir. 1979) (defendants Pussycat Cinema prohibited from distributing the film Debbie Does Dallas, featuring a performer in a uniform similar to plaintiff cheerleading group's outfit, as the association resulted in confusion that tended to impugn the group's services and injure its reputation).

[70] *See* Gilliam v. ABC, 538 F.2d 14 (2d Cir. 1976).

[71] Metatags are coded, often invisible references that can be found by search engines providing

creative media according to the characteristics of print and analog technologies, which were basically the only means of presenting copyrightable works. The earliest architects of copyright and trademark law probably never anticipated the technology-driven possibilities that exist today for manipulation and reproduction of creative media. In essence, digital technology affects every aspect of the creative work—creation, its dissemination and protection—and, as discussed below, the potential legal repercussions are enormous.[72]

[1] New Challenges

[a] Copying

Digital technologies and the Internet have conferred the power to be an author, a publisher, or an artist (talent aside) on almost everyone, through the manipulation of images on an electronic screen. Copiers of images can intentionally change an existing image sufficiently in order to avoid copyright infringement. Therefore, defining the threshold at which similarity becomes non-de minimis—and therefore infringing—is increasingly significant in the context of digital alteration.[73]

Put another way, new media is forcing the issue of how copyright law in a digital medium can honor an artist's need to borrow from existing idioms and still guard the integrity and uses of their expression.[74] In particular, the scope of copyright law as it relates the Internet specifically is very much an open question,[75]

---

a response to a searcher's query. By using a competitor's metatags, a competitor can ensure that a search based on the competitor's trademark can yield a response ("hit") to his site.

[72] Furthermore, works expressed in digital code can be copied perfectly and distributed to the public on an enormous scale, making possible entertainment products that previously would have been unimaginable, so the business consequences are equally gigantic. The Harvard Law Review Association, Note, Visual Artist's Rights in a Digital Age, 107 Harv. L. Rev. 1977 (1994).

[73] For instance, multimedia art could theoretically be infringing if a protected image is briefly shown during metamorphosis into another image. Likewise, it may be argued that scanning a representational work and then using a graphics program to render it abstract in order to change the composition or to add additional features may be an infringement, not only because the first step would involve the reproduction right, Copyright for Visual Art in a Digital Age: A Modern Adventure In Wonderland, 14 Cardozo Arts & Ent. L.J. 563 at 586 (1996), but also because the derivative-work right grants copyright owners the exclusive right to control the abridgment, adaptation, revision or other transformation of their works. 17 U.S.C. § 106(2) (West 1996).

[74] *See generally* Margaret Chon, Symposium: Innovation and the Information Environment, New Wine Bursting From Old Bottles: Collaborative Internet Art, Joint Works, And Entrepreneurship, Oregon L. Rev. (Spring 1996).

[75] That meeting the challenge of effectively applying established copyright laws to new media is of interest to businesses should be of little surprise, as filmmakers, publishers, visual artists, and especially record companies increasingly compete online with infringing copies or derivatives. The initiatives seeking to alleviate this problem range from using encryption technologies—which bypasses copyright law altogether—to attempting to expand copyright electronically through the

because "transmitting" information and viewing it or listening to it on a computer involves numerous strands in a copyright owner's bundle of rights—public performance, display, and reproduction, among others.

While, as one professor of law recently said, "the ethos of the Internet is that anything on it may be downloaded, cut, copied, and sent along to others,"[76] courts have held that, under certain circumstances, the copying of copyrighted work onto a computer's memory (such as copying to the hard disk, floppy disk or other storage device) or from one computer to another (such as downloading a digital image from a server, or transferring it between Internet users) infringes upon the right of reproduction.[77]

On the other hand, although hyperlinking requires the making of a copy, it is probably correct to assume that this copy either constitutes a fair use[78] (discussed briefly below) or is made under an implied license.[79] Either way, the essence of the professor's statement—the Internet is affecting copyright law—seems true. It has become necessary to search for new analyses in order to reconcile ordinary conduct with the letter of the law,[80] which suggests that further change to the latter is forthcoming.[81]

[b] Identity

In the art world, identity is a highly charged issue, both for works of art ("originals" versus "knock-offs") as well as for artists (who may be identified

---

assignment of perpetual identifiers to original creative works. One example of the latter methodology is promulgated by a group, founded by leading publishers of scientific, technical and medical texts, called the International DOI ("Digital Object Identifier") Foundation (IDF). *See* http://www.dlipb.org and www.doi.org.

[76] Marci Hamilton, Features, Christian Science Monitor, Feb. 25, 1999.

[77] U.S. Department of Commerce, Intellectual Property and National Information Infrastructure: Report of the Working Group on Intellectual Property Rights, at 65-67 (the White Paper). *See* MAI Sys. Corp. v. Peak Computer, Inc., 991 F.2d 511, 519 (9th Cir. 1993); Playboy Enters., Inc. v. Frena, 839 F. Supp. 1552 (S.D. Fla. 1993); Sega Enters. Ltd. v. Maphia, 948 F. Supp. 923 (1996).

[78] Alternatively, one might argue where the document is made freely available for copying in the first place, it is not necessary to inquire whether private copying was a fair use, as fair use excuses prima facie infringements. *See* Jane C. Ginsburgh, Putting Cars on the "Information Superhighway": Authors, Exploiters and Copyright in Cyberspace, 95 Colum. L. Rev. 1466, 1477-78 (1995).

[79] Nonexclusive licenses may be granted orally or implied from conduct of the parties. *See* 3 M. Nimmer & D. Nimmer, Nimmer On Copyright § 10.03[A] (1997), and the existence of any license, whether exclusive or nonexclusive, creates an affirmative defense to a claim of copyright infringement. *Id.*; *Effects Associates*, 908 F.2d at 559; Avtech Sys., Inc. v. Peiffer, 21 F.3d 568, 574 n.12 (4th Cir. 1994).

[80] In order to view a copyrighted document on the Web, a copy of it must be transmitted to the viewer's computer, placed in its memory, interpreted by the browsing software, and displayed on the viewer's video display (and frequently cached by a local server as well).

[81] In fact, in 1998 Congress passed the Digital Millennium Copyright Act, discussed below,

according to styles and methods of implementation).[82] Digital art can be copied perfectly; "originals" can be altered; "fakes" can be enhanced. While one might think that digital images therefore have little intrinsic value, that conclusion would be incorrect; the owner of digital-image rights controls access to those works on the Internet and through the world of electronic publishing in general.[83]

For the artist or designer, too, professional identity on the Internet is complicated by the characteristics of that medium. As discussed previously, the domain name is a primary means of conveying information to the world at large about the entity represented on it.[84] But domain names are unique, and problems arise when the second-level domain name—the "brand"—intrinsically identifies more than one entity. For example, the imaginary design firm of Syzygy, Inc. built a successful business over 15 years (although never registered its brand name as a trademark) but was dismayed to find out that "www.syzygy.com" was already registered to someone selling black-velvet Elvis posters, unwilling to sell the domain name at a reasonable price.[85]

In late 1999, Congress passed an amendment to the Trademark Act known as the Anticybersquating Law[86] to provide the owners of a trademark with rights against those who register or traffic in bad faith in domain names[87] that are

---

which among other things altered the potential for copyright infringement liability of providers of Internet hosting services. 17 U.S.C. 512(c)(2)(1998).

[82] *See generally*, Peter Landesman, A 20th-Century Master Scam, N.Y. Times Mag., July 18, 1999.

[83] Pam Dixon, Museums Join Forces to Protect Cyber Rights to Art, San Diego Union-Tribune, E-3, Jan. 31, 1999 ("In the mid-'90s some of the best art museums in the world started selling electronic rights to the greatest works of art they owned. Before anyone knew any better, major museums—like the Philadelphia Museum of Art and the National Gallery, London—had lost control of their digital visual heritage. And chief among those hauling in the catch was Corbis, a company founded and owned by Bill Gates.").

[84] Although it is the largest, the URL system is not the only proprietary online identity system. America Online's "key word system" and the relatively recent "real name system" of the company of the same name (www.realnames.com) are managed by private companies that would like to control the keys to Internet identity.

[85] Trademark law is slowly shaping the management of various forms of online identity. The domain name registration agency Network Solutions, for instance, has amended its dispute resolution policies to recognize all trademarks—not only federally registered ones, but state and common marks as well—and to permit complainants to seek to enjoin the use of domain names that are confusingly similar to their trademark (previously, only claims against URLs that were identical to the mark were permitted). *See* http://www.domainmagistrate.com/.

[86] 15 U.S.C. § 1125(d), as amended (West 2000).

[87] One example of bad faith would be the registration of a domain name without the intention of any legitimate use by the seller and for the sole purpose of selling it to the "rightful" trademark owner for a profit. Proof of bad faith can be inferred from such factors as whether the domain name owner has a history of trafficking in domain names, whether the domain name owner has provided material and misleading false contact information when applying for the domain name, whether the domain name owner's intent is to divert consumers from the trademark owner's online

identical or confusingly similar to distinctive trademarks. The same section also includes provisions, which govern the dilution of the distinctiveness of those marks that are considered famous. However, the law only applies to bad-faith "cybersquatting," and provides little guidance with respect to resolution of legitimate disputes.[88]

[2] Evolving Conduct

Digital media and the Internet have given rise to new activities that present challenges not only to the enforcement of intellectual property rights, but also to legal doctrines from privacy[89] to contract law.[90] In the absence today of clear legal authority in several areas we must infer what constitutes appropriate conduct based on existing legal principles.[91]

[a] Fair Use

The response to allegations of direct[92] copyright infringement on the Internet

---

location to a site that could harm the goodwill of the trademark owner for commercial gain with the intent to tarnish or disparage the mark, and whether the domain name owner offered to sell the name back to the "rightful" owner. Of course, this last factor makes settlement discussions extremely problematic.

[88] The law also does not address misdeeds involving other kinds of online identity such as metatags.

[89] For example, with respect to the issue of privacy, the European Union has developed strict codes of conduct that apply to the Internet, which prohibit the transfer of personally identifying information between any EU state and any country with privacy laws that are less protective, including, at present the U.S. European Union Directive on Data Protection, Directive 95/96/EC (1995), Official Journal of the European Communities, No. L. 281, p. 31 (Nov. 23, 1995).

[90] While many pre-Internet legal precepts apply today to the Internet with the same effect as they apply to other kinds of media and communication—for example, child pornography is illegal whether in print or online—it becomes increasingly unclear from a legal perspective where to draw the line with unprecedented scenarios, such as computer-generated (or "fake") child pornography that does not involve the direct exploitation of children.

[91] For a relatively up-to-date synopsis (as of this writing) in areas from intellectual property to privacy to contracts of Internet case law see the Internet Digest at www.perkinscoie.com/resources/ecomm/netcase/cases%2D08.html (12/1999).

[92] Direct infringement is infringement by an entity that is authorized to carry out, carries out, or authorizes the infringing activity. Religious Tech. Ctr. v. Netcom Online Communication Servs., Inc., 907 F. Supp. 1361, 1370 (N.D. Cal. 1995). However, copyright infringement claims can be brought under theories of "contributory" and "vicarious" liability as well. Contributory infringement involves direct infringement by an entity that results in liability for a third party that knowingly induces or participates in the direct infringer's activity. Fonovisa, Inc. v. Cherry Auction, Inc., 76 F.3d 259, 264 (9th Cir. 1996). Vicarious liability for infringing activity essentially occurs when a third party has the right or authority to supervise and has a direct financial benefit in a direct infringer's activity. Kathryn C. Spellman, Current Developments in Copyright Law, Online and

may be that the conduct was "fair use,"[93] which is an affirmative defense under § 107 of the Copyright Act. One court has observed, "absent a commercial or profit-depriving use, digital browsing is probably a fair use."[94] In adjudicating allegations of other forms of online misconduct courts have rejected assertions of fair use, concluding that the potential market for a plaintiff's product could be adversely affected by distribution in an online forum.[95]

Unlike the copy made during simple browsing that is only necessary because humans cannot otherwise perceive digital information the act of unauthorized linking (discussed further below) itself might implicate more blatant commercial interests. This makes a fair use defense much less likely to be successful in some linking scenarios, since of the four fair use factors, the effect of the use upon the potential market may be the most important,[96] and the unauthorized link might not conform to the intended revenue generation scheme that the author of the original work had in mind.[97] But as of this writing, no courts have definitively addressed the issue.

Recognizing the complexities inherent in conducting a fair use analysis in an Internet context, Congress passed the No Electronic Theft Act (NET Act) in 1997,[98] which criminalizes the making of electronic or photographic copies of copyrighted material[99] even when the person giving away the material does not

---

Internet Law—1998, 302 (1998). The importance of indirect infringement is especially marked in the online context, because the Internet is evolving as a culture that borrows and shares freely.

[93] The "fair use" provision of the copyright law of the United States was drafted to allow the reproduction of parts of copyrighted works for purposes such as criticism, comment, news reporting, teaching, scholarship and/or research, without the user having to fear any legal repercussions. There are four basic statutory elements to a fair use defense: (1) the purpose and character of the use, including whether the use is commercial or noncommercial; (2) the nature of the copyrighted (original) work; (3) the amount or proportion that was taken or copied; and (4) the economic impact of the use on the copyright owner of the original work. 17 U.S.C.A. § 107.

[94] Religious Tech. v. Netcom Online Communication Servs., Inc., 907 F. Supp. 1361, 1378 n.25 (N.D. Cal. 1995).

[95] *See* Sega Enters. Ltd. v. Maphia, 857 F. Supp. 679, 687-88 (N.D. Cal. 1994).

[96] For a quick analysis of the fair use factors, see www.utsystem.edu/ogc/intellectualproperty/copypol2.htm/ (12/1999).

[97] For instance, one could imagine a museum placing advertising material for its gift shop or licensing services on its home page but not on the images. This is a viable revenue generator only if the users peruse the pages in order (they at least need to see the first page to see the ads). An unauthorized link directly to a subsequent image, however, would display the content without exposing the user to the front page's advertisements. It could also have the effect of bypassing a Web site's terms and conditions of use, which would ostensibly govern the use of the Web site by end users.

[98] The law was passed after a Massachusetts college student posted a copy of commercial software on the Internet for others to download free of charge. H.R. 2265, 143 Cong. Rec. S12689, and H9883-01, modifying titles 17 and 18 of the U.S. Code.

[99] 17 U.S.C. §§ 101, 506 & 507, 18 U.S.C. §§ 2319, 2319A & 2320.

profit.[100] This has an obvious impact for those artists who would use copyrighted material for their own artistic reasons without expecting profit.

[b] Linking, Framing, and Identity

Linking controversies have been among the most famous early Internet disputes,[101] which have begun to define the manner in which links are to be formed and maintained.[102] Unauthorized linking scenarios not only involve potential copyright infringement, but also potential trademark liability if the linking party's site incorporates marks belonging to the party that controls the target of the link. For instance, invoke-to-load type links are usually designated by an icon or link-text that tells the user about what can be found when the link is actually invoked, and if the icon is a copy or imitation of a trademark, a user may be confused about the association between the linking party and the object party.

Unlike trademark infringement and dilution, the false-designation provision of the Lanham Act may have the flexibility to encompass unauthorized linking activities like those described above. Where an unauthorized link involves framing, for instance, it seems very possible that, absent clear disclaimers, confusion might

---

[100] The NET Act further improves copyright protection by amending federal copyright law to define "fiscal gain" to include the receipt of anything of value, including other copyrighted works.

[101] *Ticketmaster* and *TotalNEWS* are emblematic. In Ticketmaster v. Microsoft Corp., Case No. 97-3055 DDP (C.D. Cal. complaint filed Apr. 28, 1997), for instance, the defendant Microsoft established a hypertext link from event listings within its site to the corresponding area on the Ticketmaster site where tickets could be purchased. Ticketmaster objected, arguing that the link enabled visitors to circumvent its home page, and layers of advertising, and thereby deprived it of value. Microsoft replied that any person could establish such a link on their own, presumably by using the "favorites" function of any browser software. Ticketmaster also argued that the hyperlink represented unfair competition and passing off, two Lanham Act claims. The case was settled, and Microsoft removed the links. In Washington Post v. TotalNEWS.com, 97 Civ. 1190 (S.D.N.Y., filed Feb 2, 1997), a Web-based clearinghouse called TotalNEWS used frame technology to display content from different news sources, allowing the user to continue to see the TotalNEWS Logo and associated advertisements. The TotalNEWS site divided the window into frames featuring sources such as CNN, CBS and USA Today. A number of the news entities filed suit, alleging that their copyrighted content was being passed off as belonging to someone else. The defendant entered into a stipulation requiring it to cease all framing of plaintiffs' Web sites. *Also see* http://eon.law.harvard/edu/property/library/mainlib.html/.

[102] SportsLine, an affiliate of CBS, has recently undertaken to redirect Internet users trying to access the "sports" heart of a competitor's site by typing in a competitor's name, such as ESPN, CNN/SI and USA TODAY, followed by ".sports.com" (for example, ESPN.sports.com), to be instantly rerouted to SportsLine instead. However, the company backed away from this marketing scheme in the face of threatened legal action, stating that "the law is unclear in this area." In fact, wide-ranging interpretations of the applicable law compelled SportsLine to refer to its aborted attempt as "creative," while a competitor called it "deception." Michael Hiestand, Internet Competition Tough, USA Today (Oct. 28, 1999).

occur. A visitor to the linking site could easily have the impression that they were actually at the other site. Approximately the same trademark analysis would apply to the misuse of metatags, such as encoding a competitor's trademark on a third-party Web site to divert the competitor's audience.[103]

[103] Cases such as Playboy Enterprises, Inc. v. Calvin Designer Label, Civ. No. C-97-3204 CAL (N.D. Cal. 1997) supported the efforts of Playboy Enterprises to enjoin the use of its trademark by defendants who were using the ''Playboy'' mark in both the second level domain name and in "metatags," based on the fact that the defendants were attempting to make their site appear to be sanctioned by Playboy or confuse customers into thinking that theirs was a Playboy-related site. *But see* Playboy Enters., Inc. v. Universal Tel-A-Talk, Inc., 48 U.S.P.Q.2d 1779 (E.D. Pa. 1998).

FORMS AND APPENDICES

---

* Included on companion CD-Rom.

APPENDIX 4-A

Online Art Exhibitions and Museums[104]

http://metalab.unc.edu/louvre
www.aec.at
www.artmuseum.net
www.asianart.com
www.barakatmuseum.com
www.counterart.com/counter/index.html
www.culturalbridge.com/cnadd.htm
www.damnet.demon.nl/
www.diarioelpais.com/muva2
www.geocities.com/SoHo/3165/
www.getty.edu
www.guggenheim.org
www.lacma.org
www.mav.cl
www.moca.org
www.moma.org
www.mowa.org/
and www.mowa.org/constant/wallpaperii/wllpprii_enter.html
www.neen.org
www.newmusem.org
www.parnasse.com/net.in.arcadia.html
www.sfmoma.org
www.si.edu
www.si.edu/ndm
www.thetech.org
www.walkerart.org
www.zonezero.com

[104] These online resources are not intended to be either definitive or exhaustive but merely as jumping-off points in each category.

APPENDIX 4-B

Web Art Sites

www.absolutdj.com
http://adaweb.walkerart.org
www.aec.at
www.altoids.com
www.antirom.com
www.antropica.com
www.bmadesign.com
http://chaos.newmediacentre.com
www.hell.com
www.jodi.org
www.misterpants.com/clients/redline
www.mtv.com/sendme.tin?page=/mtv/tubescan/vma99
www.net-art.org
www.one38.org
www.rhizome.org
www.rozdimon.com
www.schlepper.com
www.shiseido.co.jp/cygnet
www.superbad.com
www.teleportacia.org
www.three.org
http://vodka.ru
www.volumeone.com
www.walkerart.org
and www.walkerart.org/gallery9/
www.zkm.de

APPENDIX 4-C

Auction and Gallery Web Sites

www.agnewsgallery.com
www.artfact.com
www.artnet.com
http://auctions.yahoo.com
www.auctionuniverse.com
www.bonhams.com
www.christies.com
www.circline.com
www.ebay.com
www.ehammer.com
www.ewolfs.com
www.guild.com
www.newel.com
www.nicklebys.com
www.photoarts.com
www.sothebys.com
www.tajan.com

APPENDIX 4-D

Online Art News and Resources

www.artresources.com
www.adaweb.com
www.archimuse.com/mw98/beyondinterface
www.artbyteonline.com
www.Artfact.com
www.artforum.com
www.artnet.com
www.artnewsonline.com
www.artonthenet.net
www.artquest.com
www.artsconnected.org
www.bc.edu/bc_org/avp/cas/fnart/Artweb.html
www.commarts.com
www.entropy8.com
www.fischer.com.au
www.museumlink.com

PART II

THE BUSINESS OF ART

CHAPTER 5

STOLEN ART

Jonathan Bloom

Forms and Appendices

Form 5-1: Stolen Art Data Sheet, National Stolen Art File

Form 5-2: Wartime Losses Report Form, Art Loss Register, Inc.

Appendix 5-A: Object ID Checklist

Appendix 5-B: Object ID Summary

Appendix 5-C: Registration of Stolen Objects Form, Art Loss Register, Inc.

Appendix 5-D: National Stolen Art File (FBI) Summary

Appendix 5-E: ICOM Code of Professional Ethics

Appendix 5-F: Holocaust Claims Processing Office—Art Claim Information and Form

Appendix 5-G: Commission for Art Recovery of the World Jewish Congress—Information and Form

Appendix 5-H: Report of the AAMD Task Force on the Spoliation of Art during the Nazi/World War II Era (1933-1945)

§ 5.01 OVERVIEW

It is unfortunate that stolen art is such an important topic in the field of art law, but art theft is an extremely widespread international phenomenon. Press estimates vary widely, and definitions of "stolen" art vary too, but most estimates peg the value of art thefts at more than $1 billion annually.[1] Art theft has been ranked by some behind only drug trafficking and illegal arms dealing among the most lucrative international crimes,[2] and each year tens of thousands of art thefts occur worldwide.[3] Only 10 to 15 percent of stolen art is recovered.[4]

Factors that motivate art thefts include the high and increasing value of art and antiquities,[5] the attractiveness for organized crime of stolen art as a means of laundering illegal profits from other sources, the reluctance of many owners[6] (including museums) to report thefts or press charges, the lure of owning unique and beautiful objects, and the light sentences associated with art theft. Art thefts are masterminded by organized crime figures, dishonest art dealers, avaricious collectors, and professional thieves,[7] among others. Transactions involving stolen art are said to constitute as much as 5 percent of the entire art market.[8]

---

[1] Some experts estimate that $4.8 billion worth of art and antiquities is stolen each year. *See* Sarah Lyall, Art World Nightmare: Made-to-Order Theft: Stolen Works Like Oxford's Cézanne Can Vanish for Decades, N.Y. Times, Feb. 3, 2000, at E1.

[2] Jennifer Sultan, Comment: Combating the Illicit Art Trade in the European Union: Europol's Role in Recovering Stolen Artwork, 18 N.W. J. Int'l L. & Bus. 759, 760 (1998). *See also* A. Hawkins, R. Rothman & D. Goldstein, A Tale of Two Innocents: Creating An Equitable Balance Between the Rights of Former Owners and Good Faith Purchasers of Stolen Art, 64 Fordham L. Rev. 49 (1995); John Conklin, Art Crime 119 (1994). Such rankings fail to take into account the theft of intellectual property and other proprietary information, which has mushroomed with the proliferation of the Internet and other computer information systems. *See* Society for Industrial Security International & PriceWaterhouseCoopers LLP, Proprietary Information Loss Survey Report (1999) (estimating that Fortune 1000 companies sustained losses of more than $45 billion from thefts of proprietary information in 1999).

[3] Foutty, *Autocephalous Greek-Orthodox Church of Cyprus v. Goldberg & Feldman Fine Art, Inc.*: Retrenchment of the Due Diligence Requirement in Replevin Actions for Stolen Art, 48 Vand. L. Rev. 1839, 1840 (1990). One good source of brief reports on art stolen around the world may be found on the Internet at http://www.artnewsroom.com.

[4] *See* Sultan, *supra* note 2, at 764.

[5] *See* Sultan, *supra* note 2, at 767-69; Monique Olivier, Comment, The Unidroit Convention: Attempting to Regulate the International Trade and Traffic of Cultural Property, 26 Golden Gate U. L. Rev. 627, 629 (1996) (noting that skyrocketing value of art has made art theft more attractive). The high value and easy transportability of stolen art is believed to make it a popular means of laundering money in the criminal underworld. *See* Lyall, *supra* note 1. For a good discussion of the motives and techniques of art theft, *see generally* Conklin, *supra* note 2.

[6] Throughout this chapter, "owner" is used to refer to the original owner (the theft victim).

[7] *See* Conklin, *supra* note 2, at 119-85.

[8] *See* Sultan, *supra* note 2, at 760.

Such statistics must be approached with caution, however, because they fail to distinguish between art that is stolen from museums, churches, collectors, and auction houses, which constitutes only about 10 percent of the so-called illicit art trade, and the looting and illegal export of antiquities, which comprises the bulk of what is commonly categorized as art "theft,[9] and which, by some definitions, may not be "stolen" at all.[10] This chapter deals only with art stolen from a known possessor who held undisputed title.

Victims of art theft include galleries, museums, private collections, religious institutions, and archaeological sites.[11] In addition, the massive confiscation and looting of works of art during World War II, principally, but not exclusively, by the Nazis and their allies, continue to be a source of title disputes in U.S. courts as well as between nations, notably Russia and Germany.

The trade in stolen art, like the legitimate art market, is international. Stolen art sometimes is smuggled across international borders by organized rings of brokers and middlemen who may create a false provenance and "launder" the works through jurisdictions such as Switzerland whose laws favor bona fide (good-faith) purchasers[12] by enabling them to acquire good title to stolen art after a prescribed period of years.[13] After a "cooling-off" period, the art may return to the market, generally in another country from that in which it was stolen, where it may be acquired for value by a good-faith purchaser who often is unaware of the theft, which may have occurred years earlier.[14] The extent to which the illicit and the legitimate art markets are interconnected, and the historically lax (although now more conscientious) approach among members of the art trade toward investigation of provenance, has created the possibility that purchasers—particularly unsophisticated collectors—would pay large sums to a reputable dealer for a stolen work of art or an antiquity without having any reason to believe it was stolen.

Suits to recover stolen art pose unique and complex legal issues that are attributable, in part, to the special characteristics of art and to the nature of the art market. Unlike other forms of personal property, most art is irreplaceable and valued for its rarity, aesthetic merit, cultural and historical significance, and prestige attaching to ownership. Owners often develop a powerful emotional attachment to art objects, which imbues those objects with significant nonmonetary

---

[9] *See* Conklin, *supra* note 2, at 119.

[10] As explained in Chapter 6, the ownership of found-in-the-ground antiquities in countries with broad cultural property laws is a hotly disputed issue.

[11] A high proportion of art thefts in the United States is from galleries; one in every nine reported thefts is from a museum, a location that tends to be better protected. Conklin, *supra* note 2, at 121.

[12] This chapter uses the terms "bona fide purchaser" and "good-faith purchaser" interchangeably.

[13] *See* Conklin, *supra* note 2, at 181, 201-02 (art thieves often create false sale documents and move stolen art across international borders, eluding law enforcement and moving the works to the market where the best possible price can be obtained).

[14] *See* Foutty, *supra* note 3, at 1840.

value. Art collectors "see their possessions as extensions of themselves, as a way to measure and present themselves to the world."[15] In addition, much art is portable, easily concealed, and readily identifiable, and it tends to increase dramatically in value over time.[16] Because famous works of art are so readily identifiable (unlike, say, diamonds), in order to make them marketable they typically must be kept underground, and far from the place of the theft, for long periods of time. It is thus not surprising that stolen art often surfaces years after the theft,[17] and may be displayed openly—and unwittingly—in the home of a good-faith purchaser for years before coming to the attention of the original owner. Thus, it is also that the original owners or their heirs seek to recover the art rather than settling for insurance proceeds or its fair market value.[18]

A civil action in *replevin* is the principal legal means by which theft victims seek to recover stolen art once it is located.[19] A replevin action to recover personal property seeks to determine which party has superior possessory interest in the property.[20] As with all causes of action, replevin actions are subject to a statute of limitations that is between three and six years in most U.S. jurisdictions. Although it is a fundamental principle of Anglo-American common law that a thief cannot pass good title to a good-faith purchaser,[21] either a thief or a good-faith purchaser for value can acquire title superior to that of the original owner if the expiration of the statute of limitations extinguishes the original owner's cause of action to recover the art or if the defendant can establish *laches* (prejudicial delay in bringing an action) on the part of the original owner.

Because stolen art often is not located by even a diligent owner until long after the limitations period (calculated either from the time of the theft or from the

[15] Conklin, *supra* note 2, at 22.

[16] *See* Hawkins, Rothman & Goldstein, *supra* note 2, at 50.

[17] For example, a still life by Cézanne recently was sold at auction more than 20 years after having been stolen from a private collection in Massachusetts. *See* Lyall, *supra* note 1. Many famous works of art, whose notoriety is such that they never could be offered for public sale, never surface on the legitimate market. *See id.* (noting missing works by Degas, Rodin, Rembrandt, Kandinsky, Turner, Caravaggio, Vermeer, and Van Gogh).

[18] Insurance companies pay between $3 billion and $5 billion a year on stolen art claims. *See* Sultan, *supra* note 2, at 763.

[19] Of course, art thieves also may be subject to criminal penalties. *See* 18 U.S.C. § 2314 (providing for fine, imprisonment for up to ten years, or both, for interstate transport of property known to have been stolen, converted, or taken by fraud); 18 U.S.C. § 668 (providing for fine, imprisonment for up to ten years, or both, for stealing or obtaining by fraud an "object of cultural heritage" from a museum or knowingly receiving, concealing, exhibiting, or disposing of such an object). Section 668 has been upheld against constitutional challenge. *See* United States v. O'Higgins, 55 F. Supp. 2d 172 (S.D.N.Y. 1998).

[20] David D. Siegel, New York Practice § 337 (2d ed. 1991); DeWeerth v. Baldinger, 658 F Supp. 688, 695 (S.D.N.Y.), *rev'd on other grounds*, 836 F.2d 103 (2d Cir. 1987).

[21] *See DeWeerth*, 658 F. Supp. at 696; O'Keefe v. Snyder, 83 N.J. 478, 488, 416 A.2d 862, 867 (1980).

time a good-faith purchaser acquired the work) would have expired, overcoming a good-faith purchaser's statute of limitations defense is often the owner's most significant hurdle. Absent some basis for tolling the statute of limitations or postponing the time of accrual of the cause of action, a high percentage of claims for the recovery of stolen art would be time-barred. In response to this problem, courts have employed various theories regarding when the owner's cause of action accrues to avoid depriving him of the right to sue for the return of his stolen art.

The purposes of statutes of limitations are to eliminate stale claims, penalize undiligent plaintiffs, and afford repose to defendants, As we will see, in order to protect victims of art theft, some accrual theories undermine these purposes. Whether judicial solicitude for original owners is wise as a matter of policy is subject to debate. It is unclear, however, that the lack of uniformity as to the principles applied in this area has promoted uncertainty regarding the obligations of original owners and purchasers, although this may be changing as more effective means of accessing and disseminating information on stolen art—in particular, computerized databases of stolen art—become more accessible to both purchasers and theft victims.

Of course, the differing laws of the countries involved in international stolen art transactions, as well as the varying laws within the United States, make choice of law an issue that may be as important as the statute of limitations in an art replevin action. Depending upon the applicable statute of limitations law, important subsidiary issues may include whether the purchaser acted in good faith and whether the original owner exercised due diligence in seeking to locate and claim the work.

§ 5.02 STATUTES OF LIMITATIONS AND LACHES

[A] Statutes of Limitations

Statutes of limitations set "maximum time periods during which certain actions can be brought or rights enforced."[22] The primary purpose of statutes of limitations is to protect defendants by cutting off stale claims.[23] Other policies

---

[22] Black's Law Dictionary 927 (6th ed. 1990).

[23] *See* Developments in the Law—Statutes of Limitations, 63 Harv. L. Rev. 1177, 1185 (1950) ("The primary consideration underlying [statutes of limitations] is undoubtedly one of fairness to the defendant. There comes a time when he ought to be secure in his reasonable expectation that the slate has been wiped clean of ancient obligations, and he ought not to be called on to resist a claim when "evidence has been lost, memories have faded, and witnesses have disappeared."). *See also* Duffy v. Horton Mem. Hosp., 66 N.Y.2d 473, 476-77 (1985) ("the primary purpose of a limitations period is fairness to a defendant") (*citing* Flanagan v. Mount Eden Gen. Hosp., 24 N.Y.2d 427, 429 (1969); Burnett v. N.Y. Central R.R., 380 U.S. 424, 428 (1965)); DeWeerth v. Baldinger, 836 F.2d 103, 109 (2d Cir. 1987). *See also* Hawkins, Rothman & Goldstein, *supra* note 2, at 60 n.61; John G. Petrovich, The Recovery of Stolen Art: Of Paintings, Statues, and Statutes of Limitations, 27 UCLA L. Rev. 1122, 1127 (1980).

animating statutes of limitations are to punish a party who does not assert his legal claim promptly and to promote certainty and stability in human affairs.[24] Statutes of limitations promote commerce by assuring those who have dealt in good faith that they will be secure in their property after the passage of a certain period of time.[25]

Statutes of limitations themselves are clear. The length of the limitations period is determined by the legislature and hence is not open to interpretation. What is often not clear, however, is when the limitations period begins to run. Typically, the limitations period begins to run when the cause of action accrues. Accrual, however, often is not statutorily defined.[26] It thus falls to the courts to develop rules for determining the point at which the cause of action could and should have been brought so as to begin the ticking of the clock against the potential plaintiff. There are several different approaches to this question that courts have taken in the context of art replevin claims.

[1] New York—The Demand and Refusal Rule and Laches

New York, the undisputed center of the U.S. art market and the forum for many art title disputes, stands out in applying the so-called "demand and refusal" rule in determining whether the statute of limitations has run against the owner of stolen art.[27] Pursuant to this rule, the statute of limitations does not begin to run until the owner locates her stolen art, demands its return from the current possessor, and is refused. By delaying the commencement of the limitations period in this manner, the rule, if strictly applied, favors theft victims by potentially preserving claims many years after a theft.

[a] Origins: Menzel v. List

The demand and refusal rule was first applied to a stolen art replevin claim in *Menzel v. List*,[28] which established the rule that the statute of limitations does not begin to run until the original owner has demanded return of stolen art and a good-faith purchaser has refused the demand. *Menzel* involved a replevin claim to recover a painting by Marc Chagall that was confiscated by the Nazis after the Menzels fled their Brussels apartment in 1941. The painting surfaced in Paris

---

[24] *See* Petrovich, *supra* note 23, at 1127-28; Wood v. Carpenter, 101 U.S. 135, 139 (1879).

[25] *See* Petrovich, *supra* note 23, at 1128.

[26] *Id.*

[27] In New York, the statute of limitations for the recovery of chattel is three years from the time the cause of action accrues. N.Y. Civ. Prac. L. & R. 214(3).

[28] 22 A.D.2d 647, 253 N.Y.S.2d 43 (1st Dep't 1964), *on remand*, 49 Misc. 2d 300, 267 N.Y.S.2d 804 (Sup. Ct. N.Y. County 1966), *modified as to damages*, 28 A.D.2d 516, 279 N.Y.S.2d 608 (1967), *rev'd as to modifications*, 24 N.Y.2d 91, 246 N.E.2d 742, 298 N.Y.S.2d 979 (1969).

in 1955 at the Galerie Art Moderne, where it was purchased by New York art dealer Klaus G. Perls. Albert A. List, a well-known collector, purchased the painting from Perls in New York in October 1955. The Menzels, who moved to the United States in 1941, had searched for the painting since the end of the war but were unable to locate it. In 1962, after Mr. Menzel's death, Mrs. Menzel came across an art book reproduction that identified List as the owner. She demanded its return, and List refused.

List moved to dismiss Menzel's replevin action, contending that he was a good-faith purchaser and that the claim was barred by the statute of limitations, whether the statute began running in 1941, when the painting was stolen, or 1955, when List acquired it. The New York state trial court rejected List's statute of limitations defense, holding that a replevin cause of action against a bona fide purchaser of chattel accrues upon the defendant's refusal to convey the chattel (until which the bona fide purchaser is not a wrongdoer), not upon the theft or the acquisition of the chattel by the defendant.[29] The court recognized that "one of two innocent parties must bear the loss"[30] and the practical effect of this "substantive demand requirement" in the context of art replevin actions was to protect the rights of the original owner as against those of the bona fide purchaser.[31]

That holding was affirmed on appeal.[32] In so holding, the Appellate Division refused to apply New York Civil Practice Law and Rules § 206(a), which provides that "where a demand is necessary to enable a person to commence an action, the time within which the action must be commenced shall be computed from the time when the *right* to make the demand is complete."[33] On its face, § 206(a) appears to commence the running of the limitations period from the time the

---

[29] 49 Misc. 2d at 304, 267 N.Y.S.2d at 809.

[30] *Id.*

[31] As the court put it: "Throughout the course of human history, the perpetration of evil has inevitably resulted in the suffering of the innocent, and those who act in good faith." 49 Misc. 2d at 314, 267 N.Y.S.2d at 819.

[32] 22 A.D.2d 647, 253 N.Y.S.2d 43 (1st Dep't 1964). The Appellate Division held that under New York law "with respect to a bona fide purchaser of personal property a demand by the rightful owner is a substantive, rather than a procedural, prerequisite to the bringing of an action for conversion by the owner." 22 A.D.2d 647, 253 N.Y.S.2d at 44. Thus, the court reasoned, the cause of action did not accrue, and the statute of limitations did not begin running, until Menzel's demand and List's refusal. By the same reasoning, the court held that List's cause of action against Perls for breach of warranty also did not accrue until, at the least, a demand had been made, and thus refused to dismiss on the pleadings List's third-party complaint. *Id.* The Court of Appeals eventually ruled that List was entitled to recover from Perls the value of the painting at the time of trial ($22,500), not the $4,000 purchase price (as the Appellate Division had ruled), so as to place List in the same position he would have been in had the Perls Gallery transferred good title. *Menzel*, 298 N.Y.2d at 97, 298 N.Y.S.2d at 983.

[33] N.Y. Civ. Prac. L. & R. 206(a) (emphasis added).

current possessor assumes possession in a manner inconsistent with the original owner's rights, not from the time when the demand is actually made.[34]

By transforming the demand requirement from a prerequisite to commencing an action against a bona fide purchaser into a prerequisite for commencing the running of the statute of limitations,[35] *Menzel* went a long way toward eliminating the statute of limitations for replevin claims involving works of art.[36]

Menzel's demand and refusal rule effectuates the common law rule that a thief cannot convey good title.[37] Because the bona fide purchaser of a stolen work cannot acquire good title, even where, as in *Menzel*, he purchased the work from another bona fide purchaser, the bona fide purchaser can prevail against the original owner only through expiration of the statute of limitations (or a successful laches defense). Unfortunately, *Menzel* does little to protect the bona fide purchaser, even against an undiligent original owner.

---

[34] Because it focused solely upon when the demand was made, the trial court did not scrutinize the adequacy of the Menzels' search or expressly require that their demand not have been unreasonably delayed, although it noted that the Menzels had searched for the painting "ever since the end of the war" to no avail until 1962. 49 Misc. 2d at 301, 267 N.Y.S.2d at 807.

[35] Prior to *Menzel*, New York courts had not required a demand in order to begin the running of the limitations period. Rather, the act of conversion was held to occur at the time of an exercise of dominion over the property inconsistent with the rights of the owner, thus commencing the limitations period against either a thief, a bad-faith purchaser, or a good-faith purchaser. *See* Cutler-Hammer, Inc. v. Troy, 283 A.D. 123, 125, 126 N.Y.S.2d 452, 454 (1st Dep't 1953) (demand not necessary if converter takes possession with knowledge of plaintiff's claim to the property); Del Piccolo v. Newburger, 9 N.Y.S.2d 512, 513 (1st Dep't 1939) (demand not necessary "when holder exercises an act of ownership inconsistent with the ownership and dominion of the true owner"); Watkins v. Madison County Trust & Deposit Co., 24 F.2d 370 (2d Cir. 1928) (applying New York law and holding that statute of limitations for conversion commenced against a good faith recipient of property from time of possession, not from date of demand and refusal); *see also* Hawkins, Rothman & Goldstein, *supra* note 2, at 70.

[36] *Menzel*'s interpretation of the demand and refusal rule has not been uniformly accepted by courts applying New York law. In Stroganoff-Scherbatoff v. Weldon, 420 F. Supp. 18, 22 n.5 (S.D.N.Y. 1976), a case that turned on the Act of State doctrine, the court noted in dicta that the right to make a demand for artworks appropriated by the Soviet government in 1921 and sold at auction in 1931 was complete at the time of the sale in 1931. The plaintiff's ancestors had known about the sale, but an action to recover the works was not commenced until 1974 by a claimed descendant of the original owner. Had the court reached the statute of limitations issue, it would have found the action time-barred; under *Menzel*, on the other hand, the action would have been timely despite the passage of over 50 years from when the works were seized.

[37] *See* Restatement (Second) of Torts § 229 & cmt. d (1965); U.C.C. § 2-403(1) ("a purchaser of goods acquires all title which his transferor had or had power to transfer . . . .").

[b] Menzel *refined:* Kunstsammlungen Zu Weimar v. Elicofon

The Court of Appeals for the Second Circuit, following *Menzel*, applied the demand and refusal rule in *Kunstsammlungen Zu Weimar v. Elicofon*,[38] to affirm a ruling awarding to a German museum title to two paintings by Albrecht Dürer in the possession of a collector in Brooklyn. *Elicofon* made clear, however, that a party may not unreasonably delay making a demand once it discovers the location of the stolen art.

The paintings, purchased by Elicofon in 1946 for $450 from an American ex-serviceman, had been exhibited in the Staatliche Kunstsammlunger Zu Weimar, the predecessor to the plaintiff museum, until 1943, when they were removed for safekeeping to a nearby castle in anticipation of an Allied bombardment. They were stolen from the castle in 1945 when the American occupation forces withdrew. The theft, discovered by the director of the museum, was reported, and diligent but fruitless efforts were undertaken to locate the paintings. Meanwhile, Elicofon displayed the works in his home, where over the years they were "viewed by many people, including some who were knowledgeable about art."[39] The location of the works was not known to the claimants until 1966, when a friend of Elicofon's saw the paintings in a German book listing art treasures stolen during World War II. Only by this happenstance did Elicofon learn the identity of the works. The New York Times featured the discovery in a front-page story on May 30, 1966. In September 1966, the museum demanded return of the paintings; in October 1966, Elicofon refused.[40] The Federal Republic of Germany commenced a replevin action in January 1969.[41]

Among Elicofon's defenses was that the statute of limitations barred the museum's claim. The district court rejected the defense, holding that under New York law the museum's claim did not accrue until 1966, when Elicofon refused the museum's demand, and that the museum's claim was therefore timely.[42] Noting that under New York law a party may not unreasonably delay making a demand that starts a limitations period, the court found that the museum had "made a

---

[38] 678 F.2d 1150 (2d Cir. 1982).

[39] 678 F.2d at 1156.

[40] The Federal Republic of Germany (FRD) and the Grand Duchy of Saxony-Weimar claimed ownership of the paintings.

[41] The museum moved to intervene in 1969 as "an arm and agency" of the government of the German Democratic Republic (GDR). The trial court denied the motion on the ground that the GDR was not then recognized by the United States and thus was barred from maintaining an action in our courts. In 1975, however, after the United States formally recognized the GDR, the court permitted the museum to intervene. 678 F.2d at 1156.

[42] In the alternative, the court held that even if the claim accrued in 1946, when Elicofon acquired possession, the six-year statute of limitations then applicable was tolled until 1974, when recognition of the GDR first permitted the museum to intervene. 678 F.2d at 1161.

diligent although fruitless effort to locate the paintings," and thus had not unreasonably delayed in making the demand.[43] The Second Circuit, relying on *Menzel*, affirmed.[44]

[c] Current Formulation: Solomon R. Guggenheim Foundation v. Lubell

The *Menzel* rule was reaffirmed, with a twist, in what is today the leading New York demand and refusal case, *Solomon R. Guggenheim Foundation v. Lubell.*[45] In that decision, the New York Court of Appeals removed the uncertainty as to the law of New York with respect to the accrual of art replevin claims, created by the Second Circuit's ruling in *DeWeerth v. Baldinger*, discussed below. The *Guggenheim* court firmly entrenched New York's commitment to protect the rights of art theft victims as against innocent purchasers even where the owner fails actively to search for the work.

At issue in *Guggenheim* was a gouache study by Marc Chagall that disappeared in the late 1960s from the collection of the Solomon R. Guggenheim Museum. Although the precise date the museum discovered the theft was disputed, at the end of an inventory that was completed in April 1970, the museum concluded that the work had been stolen. However, the museum did not notify any law enforcement agency or any museum, gallery, or art expert of the theft, ostensibly to avoid driving it underground and diminishing the odds of recovery (although the museum may have been motivated by a desire to avoid negative publicity).[46]

In May 1967, the Lubells purchased the work from the Robert Elkon Gallery in New York for $17,000. It later turned out that the "private collector" listed on the receipt as the prior owner was a Guggenheim mailroom employee who was suspected of having stolen the work. The Lubells openly exhibited the work twice, in 1967 and 1981, in exhibitions at the Elkon Gallery. In 1985, when the Lubells were exploring the possibility of selling the work through Sotheby's, a Sotheby's

---

[43] Kunstsammlungen Zu Weimar v. Elicofon, 536 F. Supp. 829, 849 (E.D.N.Y. 1981), *aff'd*, 678 F.2d 1150 (2d Cir. 1982).

[44] The Second Circuit agreed with *Menzel* that a demand is a substantive element of a conversion claim and held that N.Y. Civ. Prac. L. & R. 206(a) applied only to procedural, not to substantive, demands. The court rejected Elicofon's argument that § 206(a) applied to causes of action where a right to possession existed before the demand. The court held that accepting that argument would "eviscerate the undisputed distinction in New York law between substantive and procedural demands," since substantive demands typically are made by an owner who holds title to the property whose return he is demanding. 678 F.2d at 1162.

[45] 550 N.Y.S.2d 618 (1st Dep't 1990), *aff'd*, 77 N.Y.2d 311, 569 N.E.2d 426, 567 N.Y.S.2d 623 (1991).

[46] Indeed, in 1974 the museum's board voted to deaccession the work and remove it from the museum's records.

employee who formerly had worked at the Guggenheim recognized the work from the transparency and notified the museum. The museum wrote to Mrs. Lubell demanding return of the work. She refused. In September 1987, the museum commenced an action in New York state court seeking return of the work or its market value of $200,000. Lubell asserted as affirmative defenses the expiration of the three-year statute of limitations, laches, adverse possession, and her status as a good-faith purchaser for value. The statute of limitations defense was premised on the museum's failure to seek diligently to recover the painting. The trial court, relying upon the Second Circuit's ruling in *DeWeerth v. Baldinger*,[47] granted Lubell's summary judgment on the ground that the museum's efforts to locate the painting were not "reasonably diligent."[48]

A detour here to discuss *DeWeerth* is in order. In *DeWeerth*, the Second Circuit, applying New York law, was given the opportunity to predict how the New York Court of Appeals would determine whether the claim of the original owner of a painting that was stolen during World War II was time-barred as against a conceded bona fide purchaser in the United States. The court guessed—wrongly, as it turned out—that New York would abandon the demand and refusal rule.

The work in question, an 1879 Monet landscape, had evidently been stolen in 1945 by American soldiers from a castle in Germany, where DeWeerth had sent it for safekeeping. DeWeerth made some occasional efforts to locate the painting over the years, but did nothing after 1957. Meanwhile, in December 1956, Wildenstein & Co., Inc., a prominent New York art gallery, acquired the work on consignment from a Swiss art dealer. Baldinger purchased the painting from Wildenstein in June 1957 and thereafter kept it in her New York apartment. DeWeerth did not learn of Baldinger's possession until 1981, when her nephew identified the work in a Monet *catalogue raisonné* that had been published in 1974. In December 1982, DeWeerth demanded its return from Baldinger, who refused.

DeWeerth commenced a replevin action in federal court in New York. Baldinger asserted both laches and statute of limitations defenses, based on DeWeerth's long delay in bringing her claim and her lack of diligence in searching for the painting. The district court awarded the painting to DeWeerth, finding she had superior title and had exercised reasonable diligence in locating the work.[49]

On appeal, the Second Circuit, evidently finding DeWeerth less sympathetic, reversed. The court observed that under the demand and refusal rule, the good-faith purchaser is not considered a wrongdoer until demand and refusal "even though this rule somewhat anomalously affords the owner more time to sue a good-

[47] 836 F.2d 103 (2d Cir. 1987).

[48] 153 A.D.2d at 145.

[49] DeWeerth v. Baldinger, 658 F. Supp. 688 (S.D.N.Y.), *rev'd*, 836 F.2d 103 (2d Cir. 1987).

faith purchaser than a thief."[50] The court explained that even though DeWeerth had instituted the action within three years of Baldinger's refusal to return the painting, it was necessary to inquire further whether DeWeerth's demand had been "unreasonably delayed."[51] Extending the "unreasonable delay" rule to situations in which the plaintiff could be charged with *constructive*, rather than actual, knowledge of the location of the stolen property, the court concluded that the New York Court of Appeals would impose "a duty of reasonable due diligence in attempting to locate stolen property consistent with New York's policy of protecting the good-faith purchaser."[52]

Whereas *Menzel* apparently was animated by a desire to protect the original owner *as against* a bona fide purchaser, *DeWeerth* turned that analysis on its head. Although the purpose of the demand and refusal rule is to protect an innocent purchaser from being held liable until being informed of the true owner's claim, its strict application has precisely the opposite effect: it protects the rights of the original owner by preserving his right to sue. The *DeWeerth* court correctly recognized the unfairness to the bona fide purchaser if demand is delayed indefinitely, thus exposing him to a suit long after an action against a thief would be time-barred.[53] But that is precisely the result contemplated by *Menzel*. Accordingly, when the court concluded that implying an obligation of "reasonable effort to locate the property" on the part of the original owner "will prevent unnecessary hardship to the good-faith purchaser, the party intended to be protected,"[54] the Second Circuit may have developed a more equitable means of balancing the interests of two innocent parties, but it did so only by misinterpreting New York law.[55]

The *DeWeerth* court's imposition of a due diligence requirement also was motivated by its concern with effectuating the policies underlying statutes of limitations: protecting defendants from having to defend against stale claims and

---

[50] 836 F.2d at 106-07.

[51] *Id.* at 107.

[52] *Id.* at 108.

[53] *Id.*

[54] *Id.* at 109.

[55] *See* Drum, "Comment: *DeWeerth v. Baldinger*: Making New York a Haven for Stolen Art?" 64 N.Y.U. L. Rev. 909 (1989). In evaluating DeWeerth's due diligence, the Second Circuit found her efforts to locate the painting "minimal," specifically noting her failure to utilize any of several available listings of stolen art and her failure to conduct any search from 1957 to 1981. 836 F.2d at 111-12. The district court, on the other hand, had been far more lenient, refusing to hold DeWeerth, an elderly individual, to the standard of diligence that could be expected of a museum, with its greater resources, knowledge, and experience. *See* 658 F. Supp. at 694-95. Although it concluded that DeWeerth's action was time-barred, the Second Circuit did not specify when her cause of action accrued, merely identifying accrual as "the point where the plaintiff had an opportunity to use due diligence in locating the property and making a demand [but] failed to do so." 836 F.2d at 107 n.4.

penalizing plaintiffs for sleeping on their rights. In that case, DeWeerth's sister, from whom the painting had been stolen, had died; key documents were missing; and DeWeerth's claim was supported "largely by hearsay testimony of questionable value."[56] The court reasoned that "[t]o require a good-faith purchaser who has owned a painting for 30 years to defend under these circumstances would be unjust."[57]

Although *DeWeerth* is a compelling attempt to reconcile more equitably the conflicting interests of a theft victim and a good-faith purchaser, its somewhat disingenuous "prediction" as to whether New York's highest court would impose a diligence requirement on art theft victims was soon proven wrong. On appeal in *Guggenheim*, the Appellate Division reversed the trial court's dismissal of the action. A close analysis of *DeWeerth* led the court to conclude that, without acknowledging it, the Second Circuit had actually engaged in a laches analysis, arriving at a rule grounded in equity.[58] Opting for laches as the appropriate analysis of the original owner's diligence in searching for stolen property, the Appellate Division stated that its reason for doing so was to clarify that the defendant must demonstrate prejudice to himself as well as unreasonable delay by the plaintiff in order to protect against an undiligent owner.[59]

The Appellate Division disagreed with the Second Circuit that delay alone could make an action untimely, even when the plaintiff knows the whereabouts of the property. In its view, "the relative possessory rights of the parties cannot depend upon the mere lapse of time, no matter how long."[60]

Under a laches inquiry, the court pointed out, "defendant's vigilance is as much in issue as plaintiff's diligence" such that "[t]he reasonableness of both parties must be considered and weighed."[61] In that regard, the court noted many remaining factual issues, including when the museum first noticed the gouache was missing, when it should have concluded that it was stolen, the reasonableness of the museum's "passive" approach to locating the work, when the museum first learned of Lubell's possession, and, finally, whether the work was stolen or, as Lubell argued, disposed of by sale, in which case Lubell, as a good-faith purchaser, would have superior title.[62] The court therefore reversed the grant of summary

[56] *Id.* at 112.

[57] *Id.*

[58] 153 A.D.2d at 149.

[59] *Id.*

[60] *Id.*

[61] *Id.* at 152.

[62] *Id.* at 152-53. As to the issue of whether the work was stolen, the court placed on Lubell the burden of proving that it was not. *Id.* at 153. Denver Art Museum recently lost a claim for the return of a classic Navajo blanket from Sotheby's for "fail[ing] to establish that [the blanket] was stolen or improperly removed from the museum" by a curator. Denver Art Museum v. Adelaide de Menil, Edmund S. Carpenter, and Sotheby's Inc., 98 Civ. 3153 (NRB), slip op. at 18 (S.D.N.Y. June 2, 1999). The court found that the museum had treated the blanket as "missing" (due to faulty

judgment for Lubell and dismissed her statute of limitations defense, since the action was brought within three years after Lubbell refused the museum's demand.

The Court of Appeals affirmed, holding that the timing of the museum's demand and Lubell's refusal were the only factors relevant to the merits of Lubell's statute of limitations defense and that Lubell's contention that the museum did not act with reasonable diligence was relevant only to her laches defense. The court began its analysis by noting that New York law "has long protected the right of the owner whose property has been stolen to recover that property, even if it is in the possession of a good-faith purchaser for value."[63] Starting from this premise, the court stated that while the demand and refusal rule was not the only method of determining when a replevin claim accrued, "it does appear to be the rule that affords the most protection to the true owners of stolen property."[64] The court concluded that although the true owner, "having discovered the location of its lost property, cannot unreasonably delay making demand upon the person in possession,"[65] there was no basis for modifying the demand and refusal rule, with

recordkeeping) rather than as stolen and that the blanket had in fact been transferred by the curator to a dealer in a bona fide exchange for equivalent value. *See id.* at 15-18.

[63] 77 N.Y.2d at 317, 569 N.E.2d at 428, 567 N.Y.S.2d at 625.

[64] *Id.* at 318, 569 N.E.2d at 430, 567 N.Y.S.2d at 627. The court noted that in 1986 the governor had vetoed legislation that would have modified the demand and refusal rule in replevin actions brought against certain not-for-profit institutions by providing that the three-year statute of limitations would run from the time the institutions gave notice that they were in possession of a particular object. 77 N.Y.2d at 319, 569 N.E.2d at 430, 567 N.Y.S.2d at 627. In his veto message, Governor Cuomo expressed concern that potential private and governmental claimants would not have adequate opportunity to receive notice and institute action to recover their property. He stated further that he had been advised by the State Department that the bill, if enacted, would make New York "a haven for cultural property stolen abroad . . . ." *Id.*

[65] An unusual New York case in which an art replevin claim was disposed of on statute of limitations grounds is Hutchinson v. Horowitz, No. 604942/97, slip op. (S. Ct. New York County, Jan. 8, 1999). The court, in a decision by Justice Stephen G. Crane, granted summary judgment to dismiss a claim brought by descendants of the heirs of American Impressionist painter Theodore Robinson to recover a painting they claimed had been stolen in 1896. The defendants had bought the painting, "Low Tide—Riverside Yacht Club," at Parke Bernet Galleries in 1964. In October 1968, defendant Raymond Horowitz wrote to the father of plaintiff Thomas Hutchinson and informed him that he owned the painting and was interested in purchasing others, but plaintiffs did not demand the return of the painting until 1994. (The demand was refused on Sept. 28, 1994, and the action was commenced on Sept. 26, 1997.) Relying not on laches but on the rule that the plaintiff may not unreasonably delay making a demand for the return of stolen property, the court found that the plaintiffs' delay in demanding return of the paintings was unreasonable as a matter of law and that the action was therefore barred by the statute of limitations. Slip op. at 7. The court based this finding on the fact that the documents on which plaintiffs relied to prove that the work was stolen were written in 1926 and the plaintiffs had had access to them since the late 1940s. *Id.* The court also noted that similar actions brought by the plaintiffs had been pending since 1980. *Id.* In light of these facts, the court was unmoved by the plaintiffs' argument that they first discovered in 1992 that the painting had been stolen and had demanded its return promptly thereafter. *Hutchinson*

its "straightforward protection of true owners," by creating a duty of reasonable diligence.[66]

The court further articulated a preference for minimizing judicial scrutiny of the adequacy of steps taken by owners to retrieve stolen art. Noting the judgment by the Guggenheim not to publicize the theft of the gouache allegedly out of concern for driving it underground, as well as the numerous factors that might affect the conduct of an owner in searching for stolen art, the court stated that it would be inappropriate to "spell out arbitrary rules of conduct that all true owners of stolen art work would have to follow to the letter if they wanted to preserve their right to pursue a cause of action in replevin."[67]

Finally, the court forcefully articulated its desire to advance the policy of discouraging the illicit art market:

> . . . New York enjoys a worldwide reputation as a preeminent cultural center. To place the burden of locating stolen artwork on the true owner and to foreclose the rights of that owner to recover its property if the burden is not met would, we believe, encourage illicit trafficking in stolen art . . . . In our opinion, the better rule gives the owner relatively greater protection and places the burden of investigating the provenance of a work of art on the potential purchaser.[68]

Guggenheim is open to criticism on several grounds: (1) it eviscerates the statute of limitations by postponing indefinitely accrual of the owner's cause of action; (2) it discourages owners from diligently searching for their property; (3) it unfairly subjects bona fide purchasers to replevin suits many years after the theft, when critical evidence may have disappeared, and imposes on bona fide purchasers the difficult burden of proving both unreasonable delay by the plaintiff and resulting prejudice to the defendant in order to prevent a laches defense; (4) it treats thieves more favorably than bona fide purchasers; and (5) it threatens to impede legitimate commerce in art. It is perhaps for these reasons that the demand and refusal rule remains the minority view; in fact, New York is the only state to have applied it to art replevin claims.[69]

---

demonstrates that in a case of extreme neglect by a claimant in bringing an action once it has the facts necessary to do so, the demand and refusal rule does not wholly eviscerate the statute of limitations.

[66] 77 N.Y.2d at 319, 569 N.E.2d at 430, 567 N.Y.S.2d at 627.

[67] 77 N.Y.2d at 320, 569 N.E.2d at 431, 567 N.Y.S.2d at 628.

[68] *Id.*

[69] For a persuasive and detailed critique of *Guggenheim*, *see generally* Hawkins, Rothman & Goldstein, *supra* note 2. Subsequent to *Guggenheim*, the Second Circuit had occasion to apply the new rule (rather than its "hypothesized" *DeWeerth* rule) in Hoelzer v. City of Stamford, 933 F.2d 1131 (2d Cir. 1991). In *Hoelzer* (which did not involve stolen art), the restorer and current possessor of a WPA mural painted by James Daugherty for Stamford High School, which had been removed in 1970 from the school premises during a renovation brought an action against the City of Stamford

[d] New York Laches in Action: The Greek Orthodox Patriarchate of Jerusalem v. Christie's, Inc.

Before discussing alternative statute of limitations rules, it is important to look more closely at the laches doctrine and how it has been applied in the art replevin context since *Solomon R. Guggenheim Found. v. Lubbell.*[70] Laches is a common law equitable defense that "asks whether the plaintiff in asserting her rights was guilty of unreasonable delay that prejudiced the defendants."[71] It is based upon the principle that those who "slumber on their rights"[72] are not entitled to equitable relief. However, the plaintiff's lack of diligence or delay is not sufficient to establish laches; a party pleading laches also must establish that it was prejudiced by the delay.[73] Prejudicial harm, for purposes of laches, occurs where the delay "causes the defendant a disadvantage in asserting and establishing a claimed right or defense or other damage caused by detrimental reliance."[74] Laches is addressed to the court's discretion and may not be interposed in an action at law.[75] Although laches is an equitable defense, and replevin actions are generally considered legal, not equitable, New York courts permit equitable defenses in "equitable replevin" actions involving unique chattel.[76]

---

seeking a declaratory judgment that he held superior title to the work. He claimed that the city, which did not demand return of the work until 1986, had unreasonably delayed its demand and that the statute of limitations therefore had run on its title claim. Applying *Guggenheim*, the Second Circuit held that the city's claim did not accrue until 1986, when the city made its demand and the restorer (Hoelzer) refused. Although Hoelzer had not asserted a laches defense, the court stated that even if he had it would not have prevailed because he would not have been able to establish prejudice. *Id.* at 1138.

[70] 77 N.Y.2d 311, 569 N.E.2d 426, 567 N.Y.S.2d 623 (1991). For a discussion of *Guggenheim*, *see supra* § 5.02[A][1][c].

[71] Stone v. Williams, 873 F.2d 620, 623 (2d Cir.), *cert. denied*, 110 S. Ct. 377, *opinion vacated on rehearing*, 891 F.2d 401 (2d Cir. 1989). *See also* DeWeerth v. Baldinger, 836 F.2d 103, 110 (2d Cir. 1987) ("Laches is an equitable defense that requires a showing of delay and prejudice to the defendant, whereas the unreasonably prompt demand principle involved in this case is a legal doctrine based exclusively on an unexcused lapse of time.").

[72] Black's Law Dictionary 875 (6th ed. 1990).

[73] *See, e.g.,* Marcus v. Mamaroneck, 283 N.Y. 325, 331 (1940); Foley Machinery Co. v. Amaco Constr. Corp., 125 A.D.2d 603, 604, 511 N.Y.S.2d 40, 42 (2d Dep't 1987); Majorrea, S.A. v. R. H. Macy & Co., Inc., 762 F.2d 7, 8 (2d Cir. 1985).

[74] Cruz v. Hauck, 762 F.2d 1230, 1238 (5th Cir. 1985).

[75] *See, e.g.*, Brown v. Lockwood, 76 A.D.2d 721, 729, 432 N.Y.S.2d 186, 193 (2d Dep't 1980); Goodfarb v. Freedman, 76 A.D.2d 565, 572, 431 N.Y.S.2d 573, 578 (2d Dep't 1980).

[76] *See* N.Y. Civ. Prac. L. & R. Practice Commentaries, § C206:1 (McKinney 1999); Hawkins, Rothman & Goldstein, *supra* note 2, at 66 n.16. With respect to "unique chattels," New York law also provides that a court may grant a preliminary injunction or temporary restraining order barring disposition of the chattel until further order of the court, N.Y. Civ. Prac. L. & R. 7109(a), and may direct the party in possession to deliver the chattel to the party entitled to possession. *Id.* § 7109(b). Damages for wrongful taking or for injury to or depreciation of a chattel may be awarded in addition

In an appropriate case, a laches defense may well successfully defeat a replevin claim brought long after the theft. In *The Greek Orthodox Patriarchate of Jerusalem v. Christie's, Inc.*,[77] the Greek Orthodox Patriarchate of Jerusalem sought to recover a tenth-century manuscript, known as the Archimedes Palimpsest, that contained a copy of two of Archimedes' most significant works. The manuscript, allegedly stolen in the 1920s from a monastery in Constantinople belonging to the Patriarchate, was acquired under unknown circumstances in the 1920s by a M. Sirieix, a French civil servant, who kept it in his home in Paris until his death in 1956. Beginning in 1947, the manuscript was cared for by Sirieix's daughter, Mme. Anne Guersan, and her family, who had it restored in the early 1960s, and offered it for sale beginning in the early 1970s. The Guersans eventually consigned the manuscript to Christie's, which informed Greece on August 13, 1998, that a public auction of the Palimpsest was planned. One week before the October 22, 1998, auction, the patriarchate notified Christie's of its claim, the day before the auction, the patriarchate sought a temporary restraining order to prevent the auction of the Palimpsest. A New York district court denied the motion for a temporary restraining order, and the Palimpsest was sold for $2 million. The patriarchate thereafter amended its complaint to add Mme. Guersan and the purchaser as defendants.

Ruling on the defendants' summary judgment motion, the district court held that the law of France, as the situs of the transfer from the patriarchate to M. Sirieix, should govern the dispute, and that, under French law, the Guersan family had acquired title to the manuscript by prescriptive possession for more than the requisite 30 years.[78] The court went on to find, however, that even if it were to apply New York law, the defendants would prevail on their laches defense. The court noted that the principle of laches generally is applied "where it is clear that a plaintiff unreasonably delayed in initiating an action and a defendant was unfairly prejudiced by a delay."[79] In the context of claims to stolen art, the laches doctrine "safeguards the interests of a good faith purchaser . . . by weighing in the balance of competing interests the owner's diligence in pursuing his claim."[80] Under *Guggenheim*, the court emphasized, the laches defense contemplates an analysis of the owner's due diligence.[81]

---

to possession of the chattel. *See* N.Y. Civ. Prac. L. & R. 7108(a). A replevin judgment also must provide, in the alternative, for a money award based on the value of the chattel. *Id. See also* N.Y. Civ. Prac. L. & R. Practice Commentaries, § 7101 (McKinney 1998).

[77] No. 98 Civ. 7664 (KMW), 1999 WL 673347 (S.D.N.Y. Aug. 30, 1999).

[78] 1999 WL 673347, at *5.

[79] *Id.* at *7 (*citing* Robbins Island Preservation Fund, Inc. v. Southold Dev. Corp., 959 F.2d 409, 423 (2d Cir. 1992)).

[80] *Id.* (*citing* Czartoryski-Borbon v. Turcotte, N.Y.L.J., Apr. 28, 1999, at 27, col. 2 (Sup. Ct. N.Y. Co. 1999).

[81] *Id.*

While the fact-intensive question of whether the owner took reasonable steps to locate missing artwork typically cannot be resolved on summary judgment,[82] the court found that the patriarchate's total lack of diligence in seeking to recover the Palimpsest left no factual dispute as to that issue.[83] The court also readily concluded that the patriarchate's 70-year delay in coming forward to claim ownership of the Palimpsest "renders it virtually impossible for the Guersans to prove ownership."[84] The court cited the facts that M. Sirieix had died, memories had faded, and key documents were missing.[85] Because those same factors are likely to exist in many cases brought by owners who fortuitously learn the whereabouts of stolen art after having done nothing for years to track it down, the *Greek Orthodox Patriarchate* case, although it presents an extreme set of facts, suggests that defendants litigating art replevin cases under New York law have at least one potentially powerful (although costly and time-consuming) defense at their disposal.[86]

[2] The Discovery Rule

[a] The Discovery Rule Articulated: O'Keefe v. Snyder

The discovery rule was first articulated in an art replevin action by the Supreme Court of New Jersey in *O'Keefe v. Snyder.*[87] *O'Keefe* involved a replevin claim by artist Georgia O'Keefe to recover three of her paintings allegedly stolen

---

[82] *See Czartoryski-Borbon*, N.Y.L.J., Apr. 28, 1999, at 27, col. 2 (denying cross-motions for summary judgment in suit by Polish prince to recover painting by Jan Mostaert allegedly stolen by Nazis on ground that there were "conflicting facts as to whether plaintiff's family availed itself of numerous resources available in the west to locate stolen art); Republic of Turkey v. Metropolitan Museum of Art, 762 F. Supp. 44 (S.D.N.Y. 1990) (denying museum's summary judgment motion, finding genuine issue of material fact as to whether museum was prejudiced by plaintiff's delay in making a demand for stolen artifacts).

[83] *Greek Orthodox Patriarchate*, 1999 WL 673347, at *9.

[84] *Id.*

[85] *Id.*

[86] Hutchinson v. Horowitz, No. 604942/97, slip op. (S. Ct. New York County, Jan. 8, 1999), the court held that in addition to prevailing on their statute of limitations defense, the defendants were entitled to summary judgment on their laches defense. Slip op. at 8-10. The court found that plaintiffs' delay in asserting a claim to a Theodore Robinson painting allegedly stolen in 1896 was unreasonable and that the defendants were prejudiced by a lack of living witnesses with personal knowledge of the events surrounding the disposition of the painting. The court pointed out that had Robinson's heirs raised their claim in a timely manner, the matter would have been resolved before the defendants purchased the painting. *Id.* at 9. The court also noted that allowing the claim to proceed, a century after the alleged theft, "would place an onerous burden on anyone owning old artwork," as such works could always be subject to decendants' unverifiable claims of improper transfer. *Id.* at 9-10.

[87] 83 N.J. 478, 416 A.2d 862 (1980).

in 1946 from An American Place, a New York gallery run by her husband, Alfred Stieglitz. O'Keefe failed to search for the works, beyond discussing them with art world associates, until 1972, when she reported the theft to the Art Dealers Association of America, which kept a registry of stolen paintings. In February 1976, she learned that Ulrich A. Frank had sold the paintings to defendant Barry Snyder. She demanded their return from Snyder and commenced a replevin action in New Jersey state court following his refusal. Frank claimed to have received the paintings from his father in 1965 and that he had seen the paintings in his father's apartment in New Hampshire in 1941-43, prior to the alleged theft. Frank had kept the paintings in his residences in Yardley, Pennsylvania, and Princeton, New Jersey, and exhibited two of them in a one-day art show in Trenton in 1968. Frank admitted selling the paintings to Snyder. Neither Frank nor Snyder could trace the provenance of the works back to O'Keefe.

Snyder moved for summary judgment on the ground that O'Keefe's claim was barred by the statute of limitations and that Frank had acquired title by adverse possession. The trial court granted summary judgment for Snyder on the ground that O'Keefe's action was time-barred under New Jersey's statute of limitations because it was not commenced within six years of the theft. The Appellate Division reversed, finding that statute of limitations and adverse possession defenses were identical and that Snyder had not proved the elements of adverse possession. Because it also found that the paintings had been stolen, the court entered judgment for O'Keefe.[88]

The New Jersey Supreme Court reversed and remanded for trial on the ground that factual questions existed as to, among other issues, whether the paintings were stolen. However, the court went on to address at length the question of when O'Keefe's cause of action accrued. After determining that New Jersey's statute of limitations law applied to O'Keefe's claim, the court noted that under a discovery rule, a cause of action does not accrue "until the injured party discovers, or by exercise of reasonable diligence and intelligence should have discovered, facts which form the basis of a cause of action."[89] It is, the court noted, a rule of equity intended to "mitigate unjust results that might otherwise flow from strict adherence to a rule of law."[90] Originally developed in the medical malpractice area, it had since been extended to other types of claims, including the wrongful detention of shares of stock.[91]

---

[88] O'Keefe v. Snyder, 170 N.J. Super. 75, 405 A.2d 840 (1979), *rev'd*, 83 N.J. 478, 416 A.2d 862 (1980).

[89] 83 N.J. at 491, 416 A.2d at 869 (*citing* Burd v. New Jersey, 76 N.J. 284, 291-92, 386 A.2d 1310 (1978)).

[90] *Id.*

[91] 83 N.J. at 492, 416 A.2d at 869. In analysis similar to that adopted by the Second Circuit in *DeWeerth*, the court explained that, properly interpreted, the discovery rule "becomes a vehicle for transporting equitable considerations into the statute of limitations for replevin." However, whereas

Applying the discovery rule, the court stated that unless O'Keefe could demonstrate that her cause of action had not accrued more than six years prior to commencement of the action, the bona fide purchaser would acquire title by expiration of the statute of limitations without having to demonstrate adverse possession. The court held that adverse possession, which requires visible, open, and notorious possession for the statutory period in order for title to vest in the possessor, is unsuited to property like art that often is displayed out of public view, and that adverse possession therefore should not be required of bona fide purchasers of stolen art.[92] Rather, "the expiration of the statute of limitations bars the remedy to recover possession and also vests title in the possessor."[93] In rejecting adverse possession as a means of acquiring title to stolen art, *O'Keefe* announced that the focus of the inquiry would shift from whether the possessor could demonstrate adverse possession to whether the owner had acted with due diligence.[94]

Whereas in *Guggenheim*, New York's highest court adhered to the demand and refusal rule in order to better protect the rights of original owners, the *O'Keefe* court favored the discovery rule on the very different ground that it would "fulfill the purposes of a statute of limitations and accord greater protection to the innocent owner of personal property whose goods are lost or stolen."[95] The statute of limitations, modified by the discovery rule, would encourage owners to pursue their stolen works diligently. At the same time, because a thief acquires no title and therefore transfers no title to subsequent good-faith purchasers, a purchaser from a private party "would be well-advised to inquire whether a work of art has been reported as lost or stolen."[96]

DeWeerth placed the focus exclusively upon the owner's diligence—a reflection, perhaps, of the court's lack of sympathy for DeWeerth—*O'Keefe* held that in determining whether the discovery rule should apply in a given case, the court should "identify, evaluate and weigh the equitable claims of all parties." *Id.* at 498, 416 A.2d at 872.

92 *Id.* at 497, 416 A.2d at 872.

93 *Id.* at 500, 416 A.2d at 874.

94 *Id.* at 497, 416 A.2d at 872.

95 *Id.* at 499, 416 A.2d at 873.

96 *Id.* at 499, 416 A.2d at 873. As if to answer *Guggenheim*'s concern that imposing a diligence requirement would be tantamount to setting "arbitrary rules of conduct" for true owners to follow in order to preserve their rights, the *O'Keefe* court outlined a flexible, fact-specific inquiry as to whether the owner had acted with due diligence, which would vary depending on factors such as the nature and value of the property. It may be reasonable to expect an owner do more, for instance, with respect to a work of greater value. For the benefit of the trial court, the Supreme Court set out a nonexhaustive list of factors to be considered in determining whether O'Keefe was entitled to benefit from the discovery rule, including (1) whether O'Keefe used due diligence to recover the paintings, (2) whether at the time of the theft there was an effective method for O'Keefe to alert the art world to the theft, and (3) whether registering the painting with the Art Dealers Association or any other organization "would put a reasonably prudent purchaser of art on constructive notice that someone other than the possessor was the true owner." 83 N.J. at 493-94, 416 A.2d at 870.

O'Keefe, like *DeWeerth*, sought to equitably balance the rights of the owner and the bona fide purchaser so as to afford the owner adequate opportunity to assert his rights without unduly interfering with good-faith transactions in the legitimate art market. The result in both cases—a rule requiring a fact-specific inquiry into the reasonableness of the owner's efforts to recover the stolen art—has the virtue of fairness in its allocation of the respective burdens but lacks the degree of predictability needed to provide guidance to owners with regard to their obligations or certainty with relation to bona fide purchasers.[97]

[b] The Discovery Rule Applied: Autocephalous Greek-Orthodox Church of Cyprus v. Goldberg & Feldman Fine Arts, Inc.

Autocephalous Greek-Orthodox Church of Cyprus v. Goldberg & Feldman Fine Arts, Inc.[98] solidified a discovery rule with a due diligence requirement as the majority rule in stolen art cases. Although it involved a claim by a foreign government to recover cultural property, *Goldberg* is, analytically, a straightforward stolen art case with compelling facts for the plaintiff.

At issue in *Goldberg* were conflicting claims to four sixth-century Byzantine mosaics that vandals ripped from the apse of the Church of the Panagia Kanakaria in Lythrankomi, Cyprus, in the late 1970s during the Turkish occupation of northern Cyprus. After learning of the loss of the mosaics in November 1979, the Republic of Cyprus immediately took steps to recover them by contacting numerous international organizations such as the United Nations and UNESCO, international auction houses, museums, Byzantine curators and scholars, and the press. These efforts paid off when two dealers seeking buyers for the mosaics contacted Dr. Marion True of the Getty Museum. True contacted the directors of Cyprus's Department of Antiquities, who initiated an investigation that led to the discovery of the mosaics in the possession of Peg Goldberg, an art dealer and gallery operator, in Indianapolis.

While in the Netherlands, Goldberg had learned of the mosaics from Robert Fitzgerald, another Indiana art dealer. At a meeting in Amsterdam, Fitzgerald introduced Goldberg to Michel van Rijn, a Dutch art dealer who Goldberg learned had been convicted in France for art forgery, and Ronald Faulk, a California attorney. They showed Goldberg pictures of the mosaics and told her that the seller, a Turkish antiquities dealer who had found the mosaics the rubble of an "extinct" church while working as an archaeologist in northern Cyprus, wanted $3 million for them. Goldberg instructed Faulk to tell the seller she was interested; Faulk did so and, on his return from Munich, told Goldberg that the export

[97] The same criticism applies to the demand and refusal rule combined with laches (the New York rule).

[98] 717 F. Supp. 1374 (S.D. Ind. 1989), *aff'd*, 917 F.2d 278 (7th Cir. 1990).

documents he had seen appeared to be in order. He showed Goldberg copies of some of these documents, none of which were genuine. The next day, Goldberg, van Rijn, Fitzgerald, and Faulk agreed to acquire the mosaics for $1.08 million and to split the profits from any resale according to agreed upon percentages. Goldberg arranged for a loan to cover the cost of the mosaics and expenses.

On July 5, 1988, a meeting took place in the "free port" area of the Geneva airport, which is reserved for items that have not passed through Swiss customs. The seller, Aydin Dikman, arrived from Munich with the mosaics in crates; Dikman briefly introduced himself, then left. In the ensuing days, as Goldberg waited for the money from the bank, she made some telephone inquiries, including to UNESCO's offices in Germany, to determine whether the mosaics had been reported stolen and whether any treaties would prevent her from bringing them into the United States. At trial, she claimed to have called the International Center for Art Research (IFAR)[99] and customs officials in the United States, Switzerland, Germany, and Turkey, although there was no proof of such calls. She did not contact the Republic of Cyprus or Interpol, the European police agency. On July 7, Goldberg paid Faulk and Fitzgerald for the mosaics in $100 bills; the next day, she returned to the United States with the mosaics.

Ruling on Cyprus's replevin claim after a full trial, the district court awarded the mosaics to the Church of Cyprus.[100] Finding that Indiana law, not Swiss law, governed the title dispute, the district court looked to Indiana cases in which the courts had applied a "discovery rule" to postpone accrual of the cause of action until the plaintiff had, or reasonably should have, discovered the cause of action. Applying that rule, the court concluded that Cyprus's claim did not accrue until it learned from Dr. True that the mosaics were in Goldberg's possession in Indiana.[101] As to Cyprus's due diligence—a prerequisite to benefiting from the discovery rule—the district court found that Cyprus's efforts to locate the mosaics, which the court characterized as "an organized and systematic effort to notify those who might assist them and to seek the return of the mosaics," had been reasonable.[102]

On appeal, the Seventh Circuit affirmed. After affirming the district court's conclusion that Indiana law, not Swiss law, should govern the action, the appellate court turned to the "dispositive determination," that is, when Cyprus's cause of action accrued within the meaning of Indiana's statute of limitations. On this issue, the court affirmed the district court's holding that "discovery" required

---

[99] IFAR's stolen art database is now maintained by the Art Loss Register, Inc. Its Web site is found at http://www.artloss.com.

[100] 717 F. Supp. 1374 (S.D. Ind. 1989), *aff'd*, 917 F.2d 278 (7th Cir. 1990).

[101] 717 F. Supp. at 1388-93. Alternatively, the court held that the statute was tolled as a result of fraudulent concealment until at least the end of 1983. *Id.* at 1391-92.

[102] 717 F. Supp. at 1389-91.

knowledge of the identity of the holder of the mosaics because absent that knowledge the owner would lack an adequate factual basis to bring a claim.[103] As to Cyprus's due diligence, the court found the district court's analysis not clearly erroneous, despite Cyprus's failure to contact IFAR or Interpol. Cyprus had taken "substantial and meaningful steps, from the time it first learned of the disappearance of the mosaics, to locate and recover them."[104]

[c] The Discovery Rule as Equitable Tool: Erisoty v. Rizik

The flexibility with which courts apply to the discovery rule, taking into account the relative sophistication of the theft victim, is illustrated by *Erisoty v. Rizik.*[105] *Erisoty* is unusual in that the plaintiff was not the original owner but rather the bona fide purchaser of a stolen Corrado Giaquinto painting. The painting, one of five stolen from the home of Souraya Rizik in 1960, was sold at auction in 1989 to the Erisotys, from whom the FBI seized it in 1993 and returned it to the Riziks without commencing an interpleader action. After the Riziks refused the Erisotys' demand for return of the painting, the Erisotys commenced an action in Pennsylvania district court seeking declaratory and injunctive relief awarding them title to and possession of the paintings.

The facts adduced before the district court showed that immediately after the theft, the Riziks notified the FBI, which commenced an investigation. The FBI informed them that it also had notified Interpol of the theft. However, the Riziks did not report the theft to IFAR until 1992, shortly after learning of the agency's existence, and they did not provide any museum or auction house with photographs of the missing paintings until 1993. The court nevertheless found that the Riziks had exercised reasonable due diligence in their search.[106] Relying principally upon *Goldberg*, the court interpreted the discovery rule as "flexible" and "fact-sensitive," thus permitting the court to "adjust the level of scrutiny as appropriate in light of the identity of the parties" and to "consider the relative equities of the rival claimants to the art work."[107] In light of its finding that the Riziks were not art collectors and were not familiar with the art world, the court held that their reliance on law enforcement agencies constituted reasonable diligence.[108] (Query: what would the *DeWeerth* court have concluded on the same facts?) The court emphasized the Riziks' diligence in reporting the theft after

[103] 917 F.2d at 289.

[104] *Id.* at 290.

[105] No. Civ. A. 93-6215, 1995 WL 91406 (E.D. Pa. 1995), *aff'd without opinion*, 1996 U.S. App. LEXIS 14999 (3d Cir. May 7, 1996).

[106] The court held that the Riziks, as the party seeking the benefit of the discovery rule, bore the burden of proof as to their due diligence. 1995 WL 91406, at *11.

[107] *Id.* at *12, 14.

[108] *Id.* at *13.

learning of IFAR's existence rather than their failure to learn of its existence until 1992, noting that IFAR was not created until 16 years after the theft.[109]

Treating the issue before it as equitable, rather than legal (consistent with *O'Keefe*), the court further noted that the balance of the equities favored the Riziks. The Erisotys had purchased the painting without inquiring as to its prior ownership, even though it had been cut into five pieces—"suspicious circumstances" in the court's view[110]—and therefore assumed the risk that an original owner would surface. The Riziks, on the other hand, had been victimized, had worked with the FBI over the course of many years, and had helped bring about its discovery by reporting the theft to IFAR, thus demonstrating "continuing vigilance."[111] The standard, the court noted, is not "whether defendants did everything that might have been done with the benefit of hindsight, but whether their efforts were reasonable given the facts of the case."[112] In this regard, the court noted that "what efforts are reasonable for an individual who is relatively unfamiliar with the art world may not be reasonable for a savvy collector, a gallery, or a museum."[113] Accordingly, the court held that the Riziks' claim was not time-barred and awarded them possession and ownership of the painting.[114]

[3] Summary

All of the accrual rules currently developed are open to similar criticism, which reflects the fact that the differences between the rules are narrowing. The demand and refusal rule is flawed because it subverts the statute of limitations in order to prolong indefinitely the rights of the owner, so long as the owner does not unreasonably delay making a demand after discovering the location of the artwork. A laches defense engenders even greater uncertainty in the form of additional fact-specific issues to be litigated regarding both the reasonableness of the owner's delay and any resulting prejudice to the defendant.

A strict (actual) discovery rule, such as that codified in California,[115] is open to the same criticism as the demand and refusal rule. A discovery rule modified

---

[109] *Id.* at *13.

[110] *Id.* at *14.

[111] *Id.* With respect to the balance of the equities, the court distinguished *DeWeerth* on the ground that, unlike the Riziks, DeWeerth was a sophisticated collector who nevertheless had failed to contact law enforcement or post-war art recovery agencies or to search at all for a 24-year period. *Id.* at *14 n.7.

[112] *Id.* at *14.

[113] *Id.*

[114] The court permitted the Erisotys to pursue a quantum meruit claim (which it later dismissed on the Riziks' motion for summary judgment) for recovery of the value of the restoration performed on the painting by Steven Erisoty over a four-year period. *Id.* at *15.

[115] Section 338(c) of the California Code of Civil Procedure (as amended in 1983) imposes a three-year statute of limitations for actions to recover stolen or detained property and provides that, in the case of theft, the cause of action is not deemed to have accrued "until the discovery of the

by a due diligence requirement, on the other hand, seems to more equitably balance the obligations of owner and good-faith purchaser: the owner must demonstrate that he took reasonable steps to locate the stolen property, while the good-faith purchaser must establish that he acquired the work in good faith and for fair market value. Yet despite its advantages as a means of balancing the rights of two innocent parties, the discovery rule suffers from the very flexibility that is its most attractive feature.

The results in *DeWeerth* and *Erisoty* demonstrate the lack of certainty the discovery rule provides to a good-faith purchaser because the court has such wide discretion to reward sympathetic and penalize unsympathetic owners for taking or not taking particular steps to locate their property. For instance, even if the Erisotys had consulted IFAR's Art Loss Register at the time they purchased the stolen painting in 1989, they would not have discovered that it was stolen because the Riziks did not report the theft to IFAR until 1992. By then, Steven Erisoty already had spent three years restoring the work. The court viewed the Riziks' ignorance of the art world as justification for excusing the lapses in their diligence, but those lapses clearly seem to have prejudiced the Erisotys. The court criticized the Erisotys for failing to inquire as to the painting's prior ownership or the identity of the consignor or to check with law enforcement agencies, but other than the fact that Steven Erisoty was a painting conservator, the court gave no indication that the Erisotys were any more sophisticated as to the workings of the art market than the Riziks. Moreover, the court failed to explain why it was not reasonable for the Erisotys to presume that a work offered by a reputable auctioneer was not stolen, notwithstanding the boilerplate disclaimers in the auction catalogue.[116]

---

whereabouts of the article by the aggrieved party, his or her agent, or the law enforcement agency which originally investigated the theft." In Naftzger v. American Numismatic Soc'y, 42 Cal. App. 4th 421, 425, Cal. Rptr. 2d 784, 786 (Ct. App., 2d Dist. 1996), the court held that under the prior version of the statute, which did not specify when the cause of action accrued, the cause of action accrued when the owner discovered "the identity of the person in possession of the stolen property, without regard to the owner's diligence or lack thereof." The court reasoned that a suit to recover property is meaningless until the identity of the possessor is known. In Society of California Pioneers v. Baker, 43 Cal. App. 4th 774, 784, 50 Cal. Rptr. 865, 871 (Ct. App., 1st Dist. 1996), the court disagreed with *Naftzger* and held that prior to the 1983 amendment to § 338, the statute began running anew from the time a subsequent purchaser obtained possession of the stolen object. 43 Cal. App. 4th at 782, 783 n.10, 50 Cal. Rptr. 2d at 869 n.10. (*O'Keefe* held, to the contrary, that subsequent transfers of stolen property do not restart the running of the limitations period on the ground that such a rule "would tend to undermine the purpose of the statute in quieting titles and protecting against stale claims." *O'Keefe*, 83 N.J. at 503, 416 A.2d at 875.) The *Baker* court declined to decide whether the proper standard was actual or constructive notice of the location of the property, as it found that the owner could not have been charged with knowledge of its whereabouts more than three years prior to commencement of the action.

[116] The auction catalogue provided that the auctioneer assumed "no risk, liability or responsibility for the authenticity of the authorship of any property identified in this catalogue. All merchandise

Surely it is asking a great deal for every purchaser of art to conduct an independent investigation into its provenance. In many cases, the reluctance of dealers and auctioneers to disclose their sources, and the practice by art thieves of constructing fraudulent provenances,[117] would prevent the purchaser from discovering that a work was stolen.

While the best course of action for the original owner obviously is to avail himself of all available resources for tracking down stolen art, the varying limitations periods and accrual rules from state to state, and the inherent subjectivity involved in application of both the discovery rule and the demand and refusal rule as modified by laches, makes it difficult for an owner to predict how a court will evaluate his conduct. The owner has no way of knowing where the art might eventually turn up. A more significant problem is that the good-faith purchaser who has not undertaken an extensive independent investigation of the provenance of her purchase remains exposed to claims years or even decades after the purchase. Moreover, even where the purchaser has made inquiries reasonably calculated to turn up evidence that a work is stolen, such as checking with the Art Loss Register or Interpol, he still has no assurance that a claim will not be made many years after the purchase—and be held not time-barred—where an unsophisticated owner is held to a low standard of diligence.[118]

The difficulties confronting both owners and good-faith purchasers were recognized by *O'Keefe*:

> There does not appear to be a reasonably available method for an owner of art to record the ownership or theft of paintings. Similarly, there are no reasonable means readily available to a purchaser to ascertain the provenance of a painting. It may be time for the art world to establish a means by which a good faith purchaser may reasonably obtain the provenance of a painting. An efficient registry of original works of art might better serve the interests of artists, owners of art, and bona fide purchasers than the law of adverse possession with all of its uncertainties.[119]

The *Erisoty* court likewise observed "numerous vagaries associated with the discovery rule"[120] and added that it

> would be helpful to resolution of these dispute if a more definite approach were adopted, such as . . . a rule providing that statutes of limitations do not

is sold as is, where is, with no warranties or guaranties, whether specified or not." *Erisoty*, 1995 WL 91406, at *5.

[117] *See* Conklin, *supra* note 2, at 181-82.

[118] *See, e.g*, *Erisoty*, 1995 WL 91406, at *14.

[119] 83 N.J. at 497, 416 A.2d at 872.

[120] 1995 WL 91406, at *14.

apply to art theft victims who promptly report thefts to the police and a computerized theft database.[121]

Today, the existence of comprehensive stolen art registries such as the Art Loss Register, which lists more than 100,000 stolen works of art, as well as a number of other databases of stolen art in the U.S. and Europe, offers the prospect of more uniform and effective steps that both owners and purchasers can be expected to take if they are to protect their rights.[122] While courts can take into account the existence and availability of stolen art databases in evaluating the diligence of owners and purchasers, they are ill equipped to implement the sort of bright-line rules that would eliminate or simplify litigation over stolen art and more equitably balance the interests of owners and bona fide purchasers.[123]

Toward this end, commentators have proposed legislation under which the act of registering stolen art with a centralized, user-financed art loss database, such as the Art Loss Register, would toll the running of the statute of limitations until the original owner learned who had acquired the object, provided she continued to diligently attempt to locate it. Correspondingly, a purchaser who checked the database and found that his prospective purchase was not listed would start the clock on a three-year statute of limitations. Works stolen before implementation of the registry would be subject to a discovery rule.[124]

Regardless of which accrual rule applies, the following steps, if taken, should adequately protect any art theft victim against having his replevin claim time-barred:

- record the collection using Project ID parameters[125]

---

[121] *Id.*

[122] The Art Loss Register and other stolen art registries increasingly are contacted as a matter of course by art merchants seeking to determine whether works offered for sale are stolen. *See, e.g.*, Mindy Sink, Web Sites Make It Hard to Peddle Hot Renoirs, N.Y. Times, June 22, 2000, at G7 (dealer able to identify Navajo rugs offered for sale as stolen by consulting Antique Tribal Art Dealers Association Web site (www.atada.org), and also noting Art Loss Register, FBI National Stolen Art File, and Interpol's Cultural Property Program site as useful sources of information on stolen art); Daniel Costello, Art & Money: Who Owns the "Marcos Picasso," Wall St. J., June 18, 1999, at W9 (Christie's contacted the Art Loss Register and discovered that a 1954 Picasso painting offered for consignment had been reported missing by the Republic of the Philippines); United States v. Barry Trupin, No. 95 CR. 450 (PKL), 1998 WL 106146 (S.D.N.Y. Mar. 10, 1998) (art dealer learned from IFAR that Chagall painting offered for sale was stolen and helped FBI organize a "sting" operation to apprehend conspirators); Lyall, *supra* note 1 (Lloyd's underwriter who checked database discovered Cézanne still life sold at auction to be stolen goods).

[123] *See O'Keefe*, 83 N.J. at 497, 416 A.2d at 872 (justifying discovery rule as "more responsive to the needs of the art world than the doctrine of adverse possession" but noting "we cannot mandate the initiation of a registration system").

[124] *See* Hawkins, Rothman & Goldstein, *supra* note 2, at 88-95; Tarquin Preziosi, Note, Applying a Strict Discovery Rule to Art Stolen in the Past, 49 Hastings L. J. 225, 247-51 (1997).

[125] *See* Appendices 5-A and 5-B.

- report thefts in a timely manner to the Art Loss Register[126]
- report thefts in a timely manner to the FBI or other relevant police agency, such as Interpol[127]

It is highly unlikely that a court would conclude that a theft victim who took the preceding steps to document his collection and notify the authorities of a theft would be found insufficiently diligent under either a discovery rule or a laches analysis.[128]

§ 5.03 THE ROLE OF BONA FIDE PURCHASER STATUS

[A] Implications of Bona Fide Purchaser Status

A bona fide purchaser is an innocent party who acquires stolen property for fair market value and is unaware that it was stolen. Bona fide purchaser status presumes that the party has acted in good faith.[129]

The relevance of the purchaser-defendant's good faith, or lack thereof, in a replevin action depends upon the substantive law applicable to the action. In a number of European civil law jurisdictions, good-faith acquisition by the defendant is a necessary element of the statutory defenses available to purchasers of stolen art.[130]

---

126 *See* Appendix 5-C.

127 *See* Appendix 5-D and Form 5-1. If reporting a theft to a local police agency, a victim should inform the local police about the National Stolen Art File maintained by the Federal Bureau of Investigation and ensure that the local police record the theft in that database.

128 The practice of victims in reporting thefts individually to dealers and auction houses may look good to the courts, but generally is unnecessary today. However, this should not prevent the victim from contacting certain experts (*e.g.*, the compiler of a *catalogue raisonné*) where appropriate.

129 The Uniform Commercial Code adopts a subjective test of good faith which requires only that a non-merchant purchaser have acted honestly. 3A Anderson, Uniform Commercial Code, § 2-103(1)(b). Such a purchaser is entitled to rely upon a merchant's apparent good title without any obligation to investigate suspicious circumstances, absent an affirmative indication that the merchant cannot convey good title. *See* Gerstenblith, Cultural Property and World War II: Some Implications for American Museums: A Legal Background, SC40 ALI-ABA 17, 24 (1998).

130 *See* Greek Orthodox Patriarchate of Jerusalem v. Christie's, Inc., No. 98 Civ. 7664 (KMW), 1999 WL 673347, at *6 (S.D.N.Y. Aug. 30, 1999) (Article 2262 of French Civil Code permits acquisition of good title by prescriptive possession for 30 years provided acquisition was in good faith); Kunstsammlungen Zu Weimar v. Elicofon, 536 F. Supp. 829, 845 (E.D.N.Y. 1981) (under German law doctrine of *Ersitzung*, codified in BGB §§ 937-945, title to movable property may be obtained by good-faith acquisition plus possession without notice of defect in title for ten years from time owner loses possession), *aff'd*, 678 F.2d 1150 (2d Cir. 1982); Autocephalous Greek-Orthodox Church of Cyprus v. Goldberg & Feldman Fine Arts, Inc., 717 F. Supp. 1374, 1400 (S.D. Ind. 1989) (under Swiss law, purchaser of stolen property acquires title superior to that of original owner only if he purchases the property in good faith), *aff'd*, 917 F.2d 278 (7th Cir. 1990).

Under U.S. law, the relevance and implications of the purchaser's good faith is less clear. Anomalously, both the demand-and-refusal and the discovery rules place a good-faith purchaser in a *worse* position than a thief, since when the property remains in the possession of the thief, the statute of limitations begins running from the time of the theft, even if the owner did not discover the theft until much later.[131] By contrast, under the New York rule, when the property is held by an innocent purchaser, the statute of limitations does not begin running until there has been a demand and refusal,[132] while under the discovery rule, it commences either when the owner did or should with reasonable diligence have discovered the theft. There is an exception when the thief actively conceals the theft, an act that tolls the statute of limitations during the period of concealment.[133]

However, where the thief has not concealed the fact of the theft, such as by replacing the stolen painting with a copy, the statute of limitations will expire on an action against the thief before it would on an action against even an undiligent good-faith purchaser. The Second Circuit in *Elicofon* asserted that this apparently unjust outcome would not occur because a thief would be estopped from asserting a statute of limitations defense.[134] To be sure, a thief should not have the right to invoke a statute of limitations defense. A bad-faith purchaser—one who acquires stolen art with knowledge that it was stolen—likewise should be estopped from asserting a statute of limitations or laches defense. A contrary rule unjustly would place a bad-faith purchaser on the same footing as a good-faith purchaser. But a recent Second Circuit decision, while noting the anomaly, held that New York's three-year statute of limitations had run against a foundation alleged to have converted artwork entrusted to it by the artist but not against an art gallery that also held works by the artist but was not alleged to have stolen or converted them.[135]

What, then, is the advantage, if any, of being a good-faith purchaser under U.S. law? In the context of stolen cultural property, as to which the claimant is a foreign government, establishing good-faith purchaser status is an element of a defense to seizure under the Convention on Cultural Property Implementation

---

[131] *See* Solomon R. Guggenheim Found. v. Lubell, 77 N.Y.2d 311, 318, 569 N.E.2d 426, 429, 567 N.Y.S.2d 623, 626 (1991) (citing Sporn v. MCA Records, 58 N.Y.2d 482, 487-88, 448 N.E.2d 1324, 462 N.Y.S.2d 413 (1983); Varga v. Credit-Suisse, 5 A.D.2d 289, 292-93, 171 N.Y.S.2d 674, 676-77 (1st Dep't 1958), *aff'd*, 5 N.Y.2d 865, 155 N.E.2d 865, 182 N.Y.S.2d 17 (1958). *See also* Hawkins, Rothman & Goldstein, *supra* note 2, at 58.

[132] *See* Golden Budha Corp. v. Canadian Land Co. of America, N.V., 931 F.2d 196, 201 (2d Cir. 1991) (citing *Guggenheim*).

[133] *See* General Stencils, Inc. v. Chiappa, 18 N.Y.2d 125, 128, 219 N.E.2d 169, 171, 272 N.Y.S.2d 337 (1966); Hawkins, Rothman & Goldstein, *supra* note 2, at 58 n.53.

[134] *Elicofon*, 678 F.2d at 1163 and nn.23-24.

[135] *See* Johnson v. Smithsonian Inst., 189 F.3d 180, 188 n.6 (2d Cir. 1999).

Act.[136] In the context of a private civil replevin action governed by the New York demand and refusal rule, the laches defense is a traditional equitable doctrine that cannot be invoked by a party with "unclean hands." Thus, one who is not an innocent purchaser for value has no defense to a replevin claim brought within three years after refusal of the original owner's demand. In such cases, the manner in which the demand and refusal rule prolongs the owner's time to commence an action, does not unfairly prejudice the current possessor. By contrast, a good-faith purchaser can, as in *Greek Orthodox Patriarchate*, plead and prove laches and thereby establish superior title.[137]

Under the discovery rule, the relevance of the purchaser's good faith depends upon the extent to which the court focuses on the owner's diligence, as in *Goldberg* and *DeWeerth,*[138] or engages in balancing the equities, as in *Erisoty*.[139] In *Erisoty*, for instance, the court's finding that the Erisotys (the dispossessed purchasers) had ignored "suspicious circumstances," including the fact that the painting had been cut into five pieces,[140] led it to favor the Riziks (the theft victims) in balancing the equities. *Erisoty* suggests, then, that whether or not (or the degree to which) the current possessor of stolen art acquired the work in good faith enters into the court's evaluation of the relative strength of the parties' respective ownership claims under the discovery rule. As the court in *O'Keefe v. Snyder*[141] put it, the discovery rule is "a vehicle for transporting equitable considerations into the statute of limitations for replevin" and the court should "identify, evaluate and weigh the equitable claims of all parties."[142]

---

[136] *See* 19 U.S.C. § 2611. *See also* United States v. An Original Manuscript Dated November 19, 1778 Bearing the Signature of Junipero Serra, Located at Sotheby's 1334 York Avenue, New York, New York, No. 96 Civ. 6221 (LAP) (S.D.N.Y. Feb. 19, 1999) (purchaser who acquired a stolen Mexican manuscript for $16,000 cash in a hotel room without inquiring into or seeing documentation of its provenance was not entitled to innocent owner defense to seizure pursuant to the Convention on Cultural Property Implementation Act).

[137] *See supra* § 5.02[A][1][d].

[138] 717 F. Supp. at 1388-93.

[139] No. Civ. A. 93-6215, 1995 WL 91406 (E.D. Pa. Feb. 23, 1995), *aff'd without opinion*, 1996 U.S. App. LEXIS 14999 (May 7, 1996).

[140] *Erisoty*, 1995 WL 91406, at *13.

[141] 83 N.J. 478, 416 A.2d 862 (1980).

[142] *Id.* at 498, 416 A.2d at 872. Another possible defense available to a bona fide purchaser is to prove that the work in question was not, in fact, stolen, but rather was acquired by fraud, sold, or otherwise voluntarily transferred by the original owner. Under UCC § 2-403(1), one with voidable title (e.g., one who has acquired a chattel by fraud) has the power to transfer good title to a good-faith purchaser for value. *See* Solomon R. Guggenheim Found. v. Lubell, 153 A.D.2d 143, 153, 550 N.Y.S.2d 618, 623 (1st Dep't 1990) ("[I]f defendant is a good-faith purchaser and the gouache was not stolen, then [Lubell's] title is superior to [the Guggenheim's]."), *aff'd*, 77 N.Y.2d 311, 569 N.E.2d 426, 567 N.Y.S.2d 623 (1991). The bona fide purchaser bears the burden of proving that the work was not stolen. *See Guggenheim*, 77 N.Y.2d at 321, 569 N.E.2d at 431, 567 N.Y.S.2d at 628.

[B] Who Is a Bona Fide Purchaser?

For merchants, the good faith standard requires honesty in fact and observance of "reasonable commercial standards of fair dealing."[143] Under this standard, one who acquires art, even for fair market value, with knowledge that it is stolen is not a bona fide purchaser. Obviously, this disqualifies dealers and collectors who commission art thefts and dealers who knowingly traffic in stolen art from acquiring good title.[144]

---

[143] Anderson, *supra* note 129, at §§ 2-403:37, 2-403:39. *See also* Note, Title Disputes in the Art Market: An Emerging Duty of Care for Art Merchants, 51 Geo. Wash. L. Rev. 443, 444-45 (1983). One New York case, Porter v. Wertz, 68 A.D.2d 141, 416 N.Y.S.2d 254 (1979), *aff'd on other grounds*, 53 N.Y.2d 696, 421 N.E.2d 500, 439 N.Y.S.2d 105 (1981), which involved fraud rather than theft, held that the failure of the defendant art gallery to verify the authority of a seller to transfer title to a painting prevented the gallery from claiming bona fide purchaser status. Porter had lent a painting by Maurice Utrillo to Harold Von Maker, a con artist who used the alias Peter Wertz, so that Von Maker could decide whether to buy it. Von Maker then employed the real Peter Wertz to sell the painting to the Feigen Gallery, which, in turn, sold it to a private purchaser. Porter sued Wertz and the Feigen Gallery to recover the painting or its value. The gallery claimed that because it had reasonably assumed that Wertz (actually a delicatessen employee) was an art merchant, it took good title pursuant to the entrustment provision of the Uniform Commercial Code (§ 2-403(2)), which provides that the "entrusting of possession of goods to a merchant who deals in goods of that kind gives [the merchant] power to transfer all rights of the entruster to a buyer in the ordinary course of business." The court held that the gallery's indifference as to the work's provenance was inconsistent with the reasonable commercial standards that must be observed by a merchant acting in good faith. 68 A.D.2d at 148, 416 N.Y.S.2d at 258. Accordingly, the court concluded that the gallery did not qualify as a buyer in the ordinary course of business under U.C.C. § 2-403.

[144] In *Goldberg*, *supra* § 5.02[A][2][b], notes 98-104 and text accompanying them, the district court found it unnecessary under Indiana law to reach the question of whether Goldberg had acquired the mosaics in good faith because the mosaics were stolen and Goldberg had no valid statute of limitations defense because the plaintiff had been reasonably diligent in its search. However, in its alternative analysis of the case under Swiss law, the court concluded that Goldberg's failure to heed "the suspicious circumstances surrounding the sale," *id.* at 1402, and her failure to make a diligent inquiry into the seller's capacity to convey good title, *see id.* at 1403-04, were such that she did not purchase the mosaics in good faith. Among the facts the court cited with respect to Goldberg's lack of diligence were (1) the fact that all of her alleged inquiries took place after she had signed an agreement to split the profits from resale of the mosaics; (2) her failure to ask UNESCO whether the mosaics were stolen; (3) her failure to request a search of its records of stolen art by IFAR; (3) her failure to contact customs offices in the United States, Switzerland, Germany, and Turkey, despite her claim that she did so; (4) her failure to contact the Republic of Cyprus or the Church of Cyprus, even though she was told that the mosaics had come from a church in northern Cyprus, or the Turkish Republic of Northern Cyprus; (5) her failure to contact Interpol, the international police organization headquartered in France; and (6) her failure to contact any expert in Byzantine art. The court also noted that Goldberg, a dealer in nineteenth- and twentieth-century American and European art, was not an expert on Byzantine art. *Id.*

The question of how deeply an art merchant must probe in investigating the provenance of works acquired or accepted on consignment depends on a number of factors, including the value of the work, familiarity with the source, and the existence of any suspicious circumstances, such as disfigurement of the work or the refusal of the seller to disclose its source. At a minimum, checking the Art Loss Register should be required with respect to any work of significant value that has a provenance with conspicuous gaps or one which appears possibly to be falsified. A European modernist painting that cannot be accounted for during and after World War II should certainly arouse suspicion. There are, however, legitimate reasons why art merchants and collectors may wish to withhold provenance information. For collectors, security concerns often motivate them to avoid publicizing their ownership of valuable artwork. Dealers, for their part, have valid business reasons for treating their sources like trade secrets, identifying them generically ("from a private collection") rather than specifically.[145]

At the same time, a self-serving reluctance on the part of collectors,[146] dealers,[147] museum curators,[148] and auction houses[149] to ask too many questions

[145] It has been noted that "most dealers, legitimate or otherwise, do not tell law enforcement agents and the public everything that they know about the trade in stolen art. Their reluctance to reveal all they know, even to press charges against those who have sold them stolen art, is linked to their unwillingness to talk openly about the sources of the art they have for sale." Conklin, *supra* note 2, at 195. Of course, a statement like this is, by definition, impossible to verify.

[146] Collectors generally are a safer market for stolen art than museums or auction houses because they tend to ask fewer questions, are not constrained by formal acquisition or consignment policies, and are less scrutinized by the press. *See* Conklin, *supra* note 2, at 191.

[147] The conduct of Peg Goldberg in acquiring the stolen Cypriot mosaics is a good example of greed prevailing over ethical judgment. *See Goldberg*, 717 F. Supp. at 1400-04. Conklin notes that "[e]ven when dealers become suspicious of a price they are offered, they often do not check very closely into its origin." Conklin, *supra* note 2, at 195. Some unscrupulous dealers are actively complicitious in trafficking stolen art. One startling example is Paul Petrides, a French dealer and the leading expert on Maurice Utrillo, who was convicted of receiving nineteen paintings that had been stolen in four burglaries. Petrides falsified the titles and dimensions of the pictures in his records and recorded fake names for those from whom he claimed to have purchased the works. The judge, who sentenced him to three years in prison (later lengthened to four), commented, "Specialist art thieves only act because they are assured of getting rid of their booty with the complicity of go-betweens and receivers of stolen property." *See Conklin* at 137-38.

[148] Thomas Hoving, former director of the Metropolitan Museum of Art, has observed: "Aggressive collecting curators were more than a little larcenous. To land something great, they were perfectly willing to deal with shady characters." Thomas Hoving, Making The Mummies Dance 69 (1993). Describing the acquisition by the Metropolitan Museum of the calyx krater, a sixth-century B.C. painted Greek vase, Hoving wrote of the curator responsible for the acquisition: "He didn't want to know anything. If he knew anything, he didn't want me to know what he knew. We established an unspoken understanding. We would consciously avoid knowledge of the history of the vase." *Id.* at 310.

[149] One example of the once-cavalier attitude of auction houses toward the legal status of works offered for consignment is a teenager who consigned for sale at the Parke-Bernet auction house in

concerning provenance, and willful disregard of warning signs, has over the years facilitated the marketing of stolen art through legitimate channels.[150] More recently, however, heightened awareness of the stolen art problem has led those in the art trade to pay greater attention to diligence issues. The revelations concerning the trade in art stolen during World War II, and the increased accessibility of stolen-art databases, which has enhanced the ability of anyone contemplating an acquisition to determine whether it has been reported stolen, have combined to make the innocent acquisition of stolen art both less common and less excusable.

Just as courts applying the discovery rule have done so in a flexible manner to accommodate, among other factors, an owner's unfamiliarity with the art world,[151] it has been suggested that museums and auction houses should be held to a higher standard of due diligence than private purchasers, as a means of combating the illicit art market.[152] In reality, museums and auctions houses are poor places to dispose of stolen art, since they are highly public and are most likely to consult the Art Loss Register or other databases. Recognizing their responsibility in this regard, most major museums have agreed voluntarily to be bound by the International Code of Professional Ethics of the International Council of Museums,[153] and most also have adopted internal acquisition codes requiring the museum to determine that the provenance and history of an artwork prove, among other things, that the seller had good title.

As museums have more carefully scrutinized both new acquisitions and their existing collections, many in the United States and Europe have voluntarily returned works that had been identified as stolen, both out of a sense of moral obligation and a desire to avoid protracted litigation.[154]

New York a group of paintings and decorative objects that had been stolen from the DeShong Museum in Pennsylvania in the late 1970s, claiming to have inherited them. The teenager commented, "They don't ask any questions about who you are or where you got the paintings or anything." *See* Conklin, *supra* note 2, at 141.

[150] *See id.* at 195.

[151] *See* Erisoty v. Rizik, No. Civ. A. 93-6215, 1995 WL 91406, at *14 (E.D. Pa. 1995) (noting that the discovery rule is "fact-sensitive so as to adjust the level of scrutiny as is appropriate in light of the identity of the parties").

[152] *See* Julia A. McCord, Note, The Strategic Targeting of Diligence: A New Perspective on Stemming the Illicit Trade in Art, 70 Ind. L. J. 985 (Summer 1995). Among the impractical proposals in this regard are mandatory reporting of acquisitions to a central art registry and public disclosure of the provenance of new acquisitions. *Id.*

[153] *See* Appendix 5-E.

[154] *See, e.g.*, Museum Sending Artworks to Italy, Orlando Sentinel, Feb. 7, 1999, at A14 (reporting voluntary return by J. Paul Getty Museum of fragment of marble statue of god Mithra that museum determined had been stolen from Italian private collection); John Marks, Doing the right thing: a half-century later, art stolen by the Nazis is returned to the heirs of the owners, U.S. News & World Report, June 28, 1999, at 42 (reporting return by Seattle Art Museum of $2 million Matisse painting to family of French art dealer Paul Rosenberg and decision by Berlin National Gallery to return

Museums have the sophistication to set acquisition policies; however, bright-line recommendations are harder to formulate for individual purchasers. Courts must realize, as some have, that the standards of investigation are not, and should not be, the same for all purchasers.[155] The following are suggested factors that courts should consider in evaluating the good faith (or lack thereof) of a purchaser:

- For purchasers in the primary market, such as those buying works from dealers who claim to represent the artist or the artist's estate, no investigation generally should be required.
- Some bargains exist, others are too good to be true. While a substantially discounted price does not necessarily indicate a title problem, a purchase for market value does provide some indication that the purchaser did not suspect title problems.
- All auction catalogues for many major auction houses, including Sotheby's, Christie's, Phillips, and Bonhams, are vetted by the Art Loss Register prior to the sale. This has two implications. First, a purchaser may presume that the auction house has checked title and may forbear his own investigation. Second, while a truly unsophisticated thief might attempt to sell a work at auction, most people with knowledge of the art world understand that this is a good way to get caught.
- Be suspicious of cash purchases, but recognize that a $1,500 cash purchase is different from a $1 million cash purchase.
- Anonymity is not always nefarious.
- Attempts to avoid income taxes and import duties, while perhaps illegal, are not probative as to issues of good faith with respect to title.
- Transactions with out-of-town dealers will almost always occur in one of four places: (1) a private home, (2) an airport, (3) a hotel, or (4) an art fair. None of these, taken by itself, indicates a problem with title.

§ 5.04 CHOICE OF LAW

[A] Importance of Choice-of-Law Determination

The international character of the art market, and the significant substantive differences between U.S. law and that of civil law jurisdictions through which

$5 million van Gogh drawing to Gerta Silberberg, daughter-in-law of Max Silberberg, a German machine-tool magnate and collector of Impressionist paintings).

[155] *See, e.g.*, *Erisoty*, WL 91406, at *13 (citing original owners' "lack of familiarity with the art world" as factor in finding that delay in reporting theft to IFAR was not unreasonable).

stolen art sometimes passes en route to the United States, may make choice-of-law issues significant in an art replevin action. As we have seen, U.S. law protects the rights of a reasonably diligent original owner. By contrast, in civil law jurisdictions, good-faith purchasers (and subsequent transferees) can acquire good title notwithstanding the original owner's diligence.[156]

To be sure, the facts may so clearly favor one party or the other that the result would be the same regardless of the substantive law applied. For instance, in *Greek Orthodox Patriarchate of Jerusalem v. Christie's, Inc.*,[157] the court's decision to apply the law of France, where the initial transfer of the stolen manuscript had taken place, rather than the law of New York, where the manuscript was located at the time the action was commenced, did not determine the outcome of the case, as the court expressly found that it would have reached the same result under New York law.[158] Likewise, in *Autocephalous Greek-Orthodox Church of Cyprus v. Goldberg & Fine Arts, Inc.*,[159] where the plaintiff prevailed, the district court determined that the result would have been the same had the law of Switzerland, where the transfer took place, not that of Indiana, where the property was located, been applied. In both cases, however, the substantive differences between the respective bodies of law were significant and, under different factual circumstances, could well have dictated different outcomes.

[B] *Lex Loci*

The traditional choice of law rule is the *lex loci delicti commissi* rule, pursuant to which, in the context of title disputes, "questions relating to the validity of a transfer of personal property are governed by the law of the state where the property is located at the time of the alleged transfer."[160] In *Elicofon*, the district court stated that there was no anomaly in applying the *lex loci* rule notwithstanding New York's adoption of a "significant relationship" test into its actions[161] because the rule "incorporates the concept of a 'significant relationship.' "[162] In applying

[156] *See supra* note 132.

[157] No. 98 Civ. 7664 (KMW), 1999 WL 673347 (S.D.N.Y. Aug. 30, 1999).

[158] 1999 WL 673347, at *3.

[159] 717 F. Supp. 1374 (S.D. Ind. 1989), *aff'd*, 917 F.2d 278 (7th Cir. 1990).

[160] *Greek Orthodox Patriarchate*, 1999 WL 67347, at *4; (citing Kunstsammlungen Zu Weimar v. Elicofon, 536 F. Supp. 829, 845-46 (E.D.N.Y. 1981) (citing Wyatt v. Fulrath, 16 N.Y.2d 169, 264 N.Y.S.2d 233 (1965); Restatement (Second) of Conflict of Laws § 246 (1971)); Zendman v. Harry Winston, Inc., 305 N.Y. 180 (1953); Hutchinson v. Ross, 262 N.Y. 381 (1933); Goetschius v. Brightman, 245 N.Y. 186 (1927). *See* Gerstenblith, *supra* note 129, at 26.

[161] *See* Babcock v. Johnson, 12 N.Y.2d 473 (1963).

[162] *Elicofon*, 536 F. Supp. at 846. The court also noted the comment to § 246 of the Restatement, which states: "The state where a chattel is situated has the dominant interest in determining the circumstances under which an interest in chattel will be transferred by adverse possession or by prescription." *Id.* The "significant relationship" test, also know as the "significant contacts," test is discussed *infra* § 5.04[C].

the *lex loci* rule, the relevant transfer is the acquisition of the work by the first alleged good-faith purchaser, not the theft or subsequent transfers by the good-faith purchaser.[163]

Thus, the law of the forum will not necessarily apply. In *Greek Orthodox Patriarchate*, for example, the relevant "locus" was France, where Sirieix acquired the Palimpsest, while in *Elicofon* it was New York, where Elicofon acquired the Dürer paintings. Accordingly, in *Greek Orthodox Patriarchate*, the court applied French law and held that the Guersan family had acquired title by prescriptive possession, that is, continuous, uninterrupted, peaceful, public and unequivocal ownership for 30 years.[164] In *Elicofon*, the court applied New York law and therefore did not reach Elicofon's argument that he had acquired title by *Ersitzung*, the German law doctrine under which "title to movable property may be obtained by a good faith acquisition of the property plus possession of it in good faith, and without notice of a defect in title, for the statutory period of ten years from the time the rightful owner loses possession."[165]

[C] Most Significant Contacts Test

Courts in a number of states, including New York, have rejected or modified the traditional *lex loci* rule and adopted instead a "most significant contacts" choice-of-law test in tort and contract actions.[166] Rather than following the Restatement, as New York courts have, other courts have looked to the choice-of-law rules applied

---

[163] *See Greek Orthodox Patriarchate*, 1999 WL 673347, at *4; *Elicofon*, 536 F. Supp. at 846.

[164] *Greek Orthodox Patriarchate*, 1999 WL 673347, at *5-*7. The court rejected the plaintiff's argument that New York law should apply because the Guersans had consigned the manuscript for auction in New York and thereby availed themselves of the benefits of New York's law. The court held that public policy considerations dictate the resolution of a choice of law question only where the application of foreign law would violate "fundamental notions of justice or prevailing concepts of good morals." 1999 WL 673347, at *4-*5 (quoting Curley v. AMR Corp., 153 F.3d 5, 12 (2d Cir. 1998) (citation omitted)). The court held that New York's public policy interests did not rise to this level, as the 30-year period for prescriptive possession under French law would not implicate the concern that insufficient deference to the rights of owners would facilitate traffic in stolen art. *Id.* at *5. The court also noted that the "enhanced protection for original owners as against good faith purchasers" announced by the New York Court of Appeals in Solomon R. Guggenheim Found. v. Lubell, 77 N.Y.2d 311, 569 N.E.2d 426, 567 N.Y.S.2d 623 (1991), was "a relatively recent development" and thus could not be characterized as a fundamental notion of justice or a prevailing concept of good morals. *Id.*

[165] *Elicofon*, 536 F. Supp. at 845.

[166] *See, e.g.*, Fort Collins v. Rostak, 182 Colo. 437, 514 P.2d 314 (1973); Holder v. Elg, 151 Or. App. 329, 948 F.2d 763 (1997); Weiner v. Weiner, 84 Wash. 2d 360, 526 P.2d 370 (1974); Fox v. Morrison, 25 Ohio St. 2d 193, 267 N.E.2d 405 (1971); Issendorf *v.* Olson, 194 N.W.2d 750 (N.D. 1972). *See also* Gerstenblith, *supra* note 129, at 26; Jean F. Rydstrom, Annotation; Modern Status of Rule That Substantive Rights of Parties to a Tort Action Are Governed by the Law of the Place of the Wrong, 29 A.L.R.3d 603, 625-59 (1970) and 1999 Supp.

to tort actions to determine the most appropriate choice-of-law rule in art replevin actions. In *Goldberg*, the district court, applying the Indiana "significant contacts" choice-of-law rule applicable to tort claims, compared the contacts of Indiana and Switzerland to determine which jurisdiction had the most significant contacts with the dispute.[167] The court noted that under Indiana law, if the place where the wrong was committed (in that case, Switzerland) had significant contact, its law would apply.[168] But the court found that Switzerland's contacts were "fortuitous and transitory" and that Switzerland had "no significant interest in the application of its law" to the suit.[169] The court noted that none of the parties were citizens of Switzerland, no Swiss citizen owned an interest in the mosaics, the mosaics never entered the stream of commerce in Switzerland, the mosaics were on Swiss soil for no more than four days and never passed through Swiss customs, and most of the negotiations for the sale occurred in the Netherlands, not in Switzerland.[170]

Next, the court weighed Switzerland's contacts against those of Indiana and found Indiana's contacts to be more significant. Goldberg was a citizen of Indiana, as were others who held a financial interest in the mosaics; Goldberg's gallery, also a defendant, was an Indiana corporation with its principal place of business in Indiana; the resale agreement stipulated that disputes would be governed by Indiana law; the purchase was financed by a loan from an Indiana bank; and the mosaics were located in Indiana.[171]

Application of the "most significant contacts" test can prevent a good-faith purchaser from enjoying the benefits of the more favorable law of jurisdictions like Switzerland that have traditionally been transfer sites for stolen art. For a non-good-faith purchaser like Goldberg, on the other hand, choice of law is immaterial.[172]

---

[167] The *Goldberg* court noted that although the Indiana courts had not addressed choice of law in the context of a replevin action, in Hubbard Mfg. Co., Inc. v. Greeson, 515 N.E.2d 1071, 1073 (Ind. 1987), the Indiana Supreme Court had modified the traditional *lex loci delicti commissi* rule in the area of torts and instead adopted the "most significant contacts" analysis. Goldberg, 717 F. Supp. at 1393. The fact that replevin is a similar cause of action to conversion, which is a tort, persuaded the court that a "most significant contacts" test was the appropriate analysis under Indiana law. *Id.*

[168] 717 F. Supp. at 1393.

[169] *Id.* at 1394.

[170] *Id.*

[171] *Id.* The court found that even applying the Swiss choice of law rules, Indiana law would apply. Although the Swiss *lex loci situs* rule applies the law of the place where the property was located at the time of its transfer, the court found that the "in transit" exception for goods which have only a fortuitous or transitory connection with the jurisdiction applied to the mosaics, thus making the application of Swiss substantive law inappropriate. *See id.* at 1395.

[172] In Goldberg's case, choice of law did not matter because under Swiss law, a purchaser of stolen property acquires title superior to that of the original owner only if she purchases the property in good faith. *See Goldberg*, 717 F. Supp. at 1400. The court held that, even if Swiss law applied,

§ 5.05 WORLD WAR II ART CLAIMS

In the wake of the controversy surrounding the secreting of looted bank accounts and gold in Switzerland, governments, the art world, and the legal profession have begun shining the spotlight on the subject of art stolen or otherwise improperly acquired—primarily, but not exclusively—by the Nazis during World War II. The Nazi leaders had a voracious appetite for works of fine art, which were systematically confiscated on a massive scale principally from Jewish collectors to fill the private collections of Hitler, Goering, and other Nazi leaders and to serve as testimony to the greatness of the Third Reich.[173] The Nazis are said to have stolen about one-fifth of the world's art treasures—100,000 works of art from France alone, mostly from Jews and political opponents, one-quarter of which is still missing.[174] One expert on Nazi art confiscation believes that there are 20,000 to 100,000 art objects worldwide that were stolen by the Nazis from Jewish families and have not been located.[175]

Such art is, as a purely legal matter, no different from other stolen art. It is subject to the same rules regarding statutes of limitations; a purchaser of such art is entitled to plead the same defenses as the purchaser of any other stolen art. The same is true of works stolen from Germany by American servicemen during the occupation, as *DeWeerth v. Baldinger*[176] demonstrates.[177] One recent case

---

Goldberg would not have prevailed because she did not acquire the mosaics in good faith. *See id.* at 1400-04.

[173] *See* Michael J. Kurtz, Nazi Contraband: American Policy On The Return Of European Cultural Treasures 1-49 (1985) for a discussion of the goals and methods of Nazi art looting. *See also* Stephan Wilske, The Claims for Repatriation of Art Removed from Germany by the Soviet Army During or as a Result of World War II, 3 UCLA J. Int'l L. & Foreign Aff. 223, 227-29 (1998).

[174] Brian Burnes, Expert describes hunt for stolen artwork, Kansas City Star, Feb. 23, 1999, at B1.

[175] *Id.* Nazi art plunder was not, of course, limited to Jewish collections. The Nazis set out to eliminate Slavic culture through wholesale destruction and theft of artworks from homes, museums, and churches in Russia. In all, the U.S. government estimates that the Nazis stole some 220,000 artworks. It is estimated that half of that total, worth between $10 billion and $30 billion, is still missing. Michael Dougan, Nazi Art thievery haunts ex-S.F. buyer, San Francisco Examiner, Jan. 25, 1999, at A1.

[176] 658 F. Supp. 688 (S.D.N.Y.), *rev'd*, 836 F.2d 103 (2d Cir. 1987) (awarding bona fide purchaser title to Monet painting stolen from castle in Germany in which American soldiers were quartered in 1945).

[177] Following the war, as American forces in Germany inventoried millions of objects stolen by the Nazis in order to restore them to their rightful owners, many works were reportedly taken by American troops and mailed home for later sale through art galleries. *See* Conklin, *supra* note 2, at 221. Perhaps the most notorious case of art treasures stolen from Germany by an American serviceman is the theft by Lieutenant Joe T. Meador from Texas of a ninth-century illuminated manuscript with jewel-encrusted bindings (the "Samuhel Gospels"), a sixteenth-century manuscript, and other precious artifacts belonging to the St. Servatius Church of Quedlinburg from their hiding place in a cave near the German city of Quedlinburg. The treasures were stolen while the cave was

involving a claim to art stolen by the Nazis that found its way to the United States is the hard-fought two-year litigation brought by the heirs of Friedrich and Louise Gutmann, wealthy Dutch Jews and major art collectors who died at Auschwitz, to recover from a claimed good-faith purchaser a Degas pastel monotype print that was stolen by the Nazis from a Paris antiques dealer to whom the Gutmanns had sent several works for safekeeping.[178] The work passed to Hans Wendland, a German art dealer in Paris during World War II who was the Nazi's principal conduit for stolen art.[179] It eventually was located by one of Gutmann's grandsons in the book "Degas Landscapes" after years of searching by the family on both sides of the Atlantic. By then, it belonged to pharmaceutical magnate Daniel C. Searle, who had purchased it from a New York dealer in 1987 for $850,000.[180] Searle had lent the work to the Art Institute of Chicago, of which he was a trustee.[181]

The Gutmann heirs filed suit against Searle in federal court in New York in 1996. The suit was later transferred to Chicago.[182] Searle raised a statute of limitations defense, contending that he was a good-faith purchaser and that the heirs had not been diligent in searching for the work. Searle argued that he had no reason to suspect the work was stolen: the role of Wendland as a Nazi collaborator was not exposed until 1994 in Lynn Nicholas's book *The Rape of Europa*, and the work had been shown in two Degas exhibitions and had been listed in catalogues dating back to 1946. The heirs claimed that Searle should have questioned where the work was during World War II.[183]

---

being guarded by U.S. forces in 1945. In 1990, the Cultural Settlement Foundation of the States in Berlin agreed to purchase the Samuhel Gospels from Meador's heirs for $3 million. *See* United States v. Meador, 138 F.3d 986, 988 (5th Cir. 1998). In July 1990, the Church sued the heirs in federal court seeking the return of the rest of the treasures; the German government paid $2.75 million for the objects to settle the suit. Conklin, *supra* note 2, at 223. A suit by the federal government charging Meador's brother and sister with violating the National Stolen Property Act was dismissed on statute of limitations grounds. *See* United States v. Meador, *supra*. For a detailed discussion of the Quedlinburg saga, *see* Elizabeth Simpson, ed., The Spoils of War (1997); Hans Kennan, Take A Picture, It May Last Longer If *Guggenheim* Becomes the Law of the Land: The Repatriation of Fine Art, 8 St. Thomas L. Rev. 373, 376-78 (1996). *See also* Conklin, *supra* note 2, at 222-23.

178 *See* Ron Grossman, Art Stolen by Nazis Pits 2 Families in Suit, Bergen Record, Apr. 13, 1997, at A28.

179 *Id.*

180 *Id.*

181 *Id.*

182 Goodman v. Searle (Docket #96C6459, U.S. District Court, Northern District of Illinois, Eastern Division).

183 Grossman, *supra* note 178. Under the settlement reached weeks before the trial was to begin, the parties agreed to give the print to the Art Institute of Chicago, which will display it with a plaque explaining the ownership history; in return, the museum paid the heirs $243,750—half the

But if works looted by the Nazis have no special legal status, they do present special moral claims that have been recognized and increasingly acted upon by governments, museums, and organizations devoted to assisting in the recovery of art lost during World War II, as scholars have shed light on the widespread channeling of looted art through neutral countries like Switzerland to the United States.[184] One historian has noted that between the two World Wars, the United States became "the major market for European art, especially for Impressionist and modern paintings that the Nazis considered degenerate."[185]

More of this plundered art has begun surfacing on the market as the collectors who acquired the works have died.[186] Many works made their way to the United States, then as now a preeminent market for fine art, and often found their way to eager private collectors by way of opportunistic galleries. Willi Korte, a leading U.S. investigator into art looted by the Nazis, commented that "the chapter yet to be written about Nazi plundering is the one about dealers and collectors who clearly took advantage of the situation at the expense of Jewish victims of the Holocaust."[187]

The dissolution of the Soviet Union and the declassification of World War II-era documents have paved the way for hitherto impossible research necessary to trace ownership histories and document claims. The growing number of claims by the heirs of the original owners, in many cases assisted by research by organizations such as the Holocaust Art Restitution Project (HARP), the World Jewish Congress's Commission for Art Recovery, and the Holocaust Claims Processing Office of the State of New York Banking Department, has exposed a large number of works stolen during World War II now in public collections.[188] Governments and museums both in Europe and the United States have agreed to return works found to have been stolen by the Nazis and to undertake extensive research into the provenance of paintings whose known histories, and gaps in those histories,

---

work's appraised value. Searle donated his stake in the work to the museum. Andy Davis, War-Loot Degas Goes on Museum Display, Chicago Tribune, June 12, 1999, at 5.

[184] Important books on the subject include Lynn Nicholas, The Rape of Europa (1994) and Hector Feliciano, The Lost Museum: The Nazi Conspiracy to Steal the World's Greatest Works of Art (1995).

[185] It was these works that the Nazis sold off through collaborationist dealers. *See* Walter V. Robinson, Paradox of Peace: Artworks taken as reparations pose U.S. dilemma, Boston Globe, Aug. 1, 1997, at A1.

[186] *See* Dougan, *supra* note 175.

[187] Walter V. Robinson, US tracked WWII influx of looted art; Government did little to prevent sale of works here, files suggest, Boston Globe, May 9, 1997, at A1.

[188] *See* Constance Lowenthal, An Annotated Checklist of Cases and Disputes Involving Art Wrongfully Taken During the Nazi Era and Its Aftermath, 40 ALI-ABA 11 (1998), for a partial list of World War II-era art restitution claims.

render them suspect.[189] Many works stolen by the victorious Allies from Germany at the end of the war also should, as a legal matter, be returned, despite the fact that the moral claim for restitution of such works arguably is somewhat weaker.[190]

Notable recent returns of art by U.S. art museums include the return in June 1999 by the Seattle Art Museum of a Matisse "Odalisque," worth $2 million to the heirs of the prominent French art dealer Paul Rosenberg, less than a year after the heirs filed a lawsuit in federal court in Seattle—the first such suit against an American museum. According to the museum, its decision was based on a report on the painting's provenance by HARP that showed that the work had been stolen by the Nazis from Rosenberg's storage vault.[191] In April 1999, Monet's "Water Lilies 1904" was belatedly returned by the French government to Rosenberg's

---

[189] For example, a triptych by Count Leopold von Kalckreuth that was on loan to the Royal Academy of Arts in London is to be returned to the heirs of the original owner after research by the Bavarian State Collections in Munich and the Commission for Looted Art in Europe showed that the work had been taken illegally by the Nazis after its owner left it behind in Vienna when she fled the Nazis in 1938. *See* Sarah Lyall, Heirs Regain a Painting Taken by the Nazis in 1938, N.Y. Times, Mar. 14, 2000, at E8.

[190] Lloyd P. Goldenberg, a Washington art law specialist, has noted that "looted German museums have the same rights as Holocaust victims to recover works of art." Robinson, *supra* note 185. The works at issue in *Elicofon* and *DeWeerth* are just a few examples of works that have surfaced in the United States that were stolen from Europe at the end of the war. A Rubens painting that was purchased by the Allbright-Knox Art Gallery in Buffalo, New York from a New York dealer in 1952 was taken from a German museum in Gotha, in what became part of East Germany. In 1984, East Germany sought unsuccessfully to persuade the U.S. State Department to intervene with the museum. The museum did not learn that the work might have a tainted past until 1997, when the Boston Globe contacted the director. *Id.* In February 1995, the Dresden Museum filed a claim against the Philadelphia Museum of Art for the return of five pieces of ceremonial armor donated to the museum in 1977 by a New York tobacco magnate. *Id.* In April 1997, the German state of Kassel sued a Brookline, Massachusetts antique rug dealer in Massachusetts federal court seeking the return of seven 16th-century Flemish miniature paintings that disappeared from a Kassel library collection at the end of the war. *Id.* A Monet donated to the Metropolitan Museum of Art in 1994 allegedly was taken from a German civilian, which the museum did not know when it acquired the work. *Id.*

[191] Museum Returns Looted Matisse, News and Observer (Raleigh, N.C.), June 20, 1999, at G3; Jo Ann Lewis, Museums to Return Looted Artworks, Washington Post, June 17, 1999, at C1. Rosenberg was forced to abandon 300 of his works after the Germans marched into Paris in 1940. John Marks, Doing the right thing: A half-century later, art stolen by the Nazis is return to the heirs of its owners, U.S. News & World Report, June 28, 1999, at 42. *See also* Mary Jo Palumbo, Lost and found—Jewish art dealer's struggle is rediscovered thanks to MFA's Monet exhibit, Boston Herald, Dec. 17, 1998, at Arts & Life p. 75. The work had been given to the museum as a gift from lumber barons Virginia and Prentice Bloedel, who had purchased it in 1954 from Knoedler & Co., a New York gallery. Lewis, *supra*. In August 1998, the museum sued Knoedler & Co. for fraud, negligent misrepresentation and breach of warranty of title in selling the painting to the Bloedels, seeking $2 million, the painting's fair market value at the time of the sale. *Id. See* Rosenberg v. Seattle Art Museum, 42 F. Supp. 2d 1029 (W.D. Wash. 1999) (finding personal jurisdiction over gallery as to museum's tort claims).

heirs after it was identified as Nazi plunder while on exhibition at the Museum of Fine Arts in Boston.[192]

Germany also has acknowledged its moral obligations with respect to art stolen by the Nazis. In June 1999, the National Gallery of Berlin announced that it would return a Van Gogh drawing worth more than $5 million to the last surviving heir of Max Silberberg, a German collector who was forced to sell off more than 150 paintings and drawings in the 1930s before he and his wife were sent to Auschwitz.[193] The president of the Foundation for Prussian Cultural Heritage, the umbrella organization for Berlin's museums, acting pursuant to negotiating authority voted by the board of the foundation to enable claims to be settled without lengthy court battles, emphasized that the decision was made on moral, not legal grounds:[194] "The expiration of legally set deadlines can't be a reason that injustices are not set right."[195]

Some claims to art looted by the Nazis have called into question the good faith of reputable U.S. museums and dealers. A lawsuit filed in July 1999 in New York State Supreme Court by the heirs of Alphonse Kann, a French collector whose 1,200 artworks were seized by the Nazis in 1940, seeks the return from Wildenstein & Co. and its owners of eight rare fifteenth- to seventeenth-century illuminated manuscripts allegedly looted by the Nazis or compensation of $15 million.[196] The suit alleges that the works surfaced at Wildenstein & Co. in New York in 1996 bearing a Nazi inventory marking plus a number indicating that they were from the Kann collection.[197]

In June 1999, Wildenstein lost a libel claim before the Paris Tribunal de Grande Instance in which the gallery sought $1 million in damages from Hector Feliciano, the author of a book about Nazi art theft that contended that the gallery

---

[192] Mary Jo Palumbo, Monet Painting Returned to Heirs, Boston Herald, Apr. 30, 1999, at S18. Rosenberg registered a claim to the work in 1945 after escaping to the United States. The painting was returned to France from Germany after the war and was displayed at the Jeu de Paume in Paris until 1973. In 1975 it was given to the Fine Arts Museum of Caen, Normandy, which lent it to the Museum of Fine Arts for the exhibition. The French Culture Minister said that only recently had research, including matching a serial number revealed by infrared analysis to an inventory number in the collection of Nazi Foreign Minister Joachim von Ribbentrop, enabled French museum officials to establish Rosenberg's ownership. *Id.*

[193] *See* Lewis, *supra* note 191.

[194] *Id.*

[195] Frieder Reimold, Way cleared for return of lost art to Holocaust victim's heirs, Associated Press, June 4, 1999.

[196] Ken Bensinger, Wildenstein Is Sued By Collector's Heirs Over 'Spoils of War,' Wall St. J., July 28, 1999, at B2.

[197] Wildenstein claims that the manuscripts were from the Wildenstein family collection, which also was seized by the Nazis. *Id.*

had wartime links to the Nazis.[198] Evidence presented at trial reportedly suggests that Georges Wildenstein was directly involved in numerous sales of Jewish-owned art in France to Hitler, Goering, and their art agency.[199] Wildenstein (if the allegations are true) was not alone, however. A document compiled in 1946 by the art looting unit of the U.S. Office of Strategic Services (OSS, the predecessor of the CIA), and rediscovered in November 1998 by the World Jewish Congress, lists some 2,000 dealers and collectors—not all necessarily Nazi collaborators—who handled objects stolen by the Nazis.[200]

American museums may find themselves caught in the middle when claims are made to works on loan for exhibitions. The Museum of Modern Art in New York was forced to litigate to establish its right to return two paintings by Egon Schiele to the lender, the Leopard Foundation in Vienna, after the close of an exhibition. After the museum informed the heirs of the original owners that it intended to return the works to the foundation, the New York County District Attorney's office subpoenaed the works pursuant to a grand jury investigation into the theft of the paintings during the German annexation of Austria. The museum moved to quash the subpoena, citing § 12.03 of New York's Arts and Cultural Affairs Law, which exempts from "any kind of seizure" works lent by nonresidents for exhibition in New York. The Supreme Court granted the museum's motion,[201] but the Appellate Division reversed.[202] The Court of Appeals reversed again, holding that the plain language of the statute exempted the works from seizure even in a criminal proceeding and that the subpoena effectuated a seizure by interfering with the Leopold Foundation's possessory interests.[203] In support of its statutory interpretation, the court noted that the legislative history

---

[198] Godfrey Barker, Body Blow to the Pride of Wildenstein, Evening Standard, Aug. 2, 1999, at 50.

[199] *Id.* In one deal with Karl Haberstock, a member of Hitler's Committee for the Exploitation of Degenerate Art, Wildenstein allegedly agreed to exchange old masters from his gallery for "degenerate" art—French Impressionism and German Expressionism—much of it stolen from Jewish owners, which was to be sold through Wildenstein in New York. *Id.* The gallery denies the allegations and is appealing the ruling. *Id.*

[200] Jay Rayner, Document on Nazi art trade sheds new light on looting, Milwaukee J. Sentinel, Jan. 24, 1999, at 7. The list was assembled as an index to the reports prepared by OSS officers on the looting of art in Europe and as a reference source for the restitution process. *See* Jay Rayner, Rogues' gallery: The full list of art treasures looted by the Nazis has been suppressed for 50 years. Finally, it's been published. And now the trouble really begins . . . , The Observer, Jan. 17, 1999, at 1.

[201] In the Matter of the Application to Quash Grand Jury Subpoena Duces Tecum Served on the Museum of Modern Art, 177 Misc. 2d 985, 677 N.Y.S.2d 872 (Sup. Ct. N.Y. Co. 1998).

[202] In re Application to Quash Grand Jury Subpoena Duces Tecum, etc.: The People of the State of New York v. The Museum of Modern Art, 253 A.D.2d 211, 688 N.Y.S.2d 3 (1st Dep't 1999).

[203] In re Application to Quash Grand Jury Subpoena Duces Tecum, etc.: The People of the State of New York v. The Museum of Modern Art, No. 139, 1999 WL 740365 (Sept. 21, 1999).

"reveals a consistent, unyielding legislative intent to promote artistic and cultural exchanges by creating a climate in New York free from the threat of seizure by judicial process and by encouraging nonresidents to share their works of art with the public."[204]

The growing publicity concerning World War II art claims, and a strong push by the United States to address World War II restitution issues since the end of the Cold War opened up previously unavailable sources of information, has led to collective action by the U.S. and foreign governments as well as by museums in the United States and Europe. A four-day conference on Holocaust-era assets in Washington, D.C. from November 30 to December 3, 1998, organized by U.S. Undersecretary of State Stuart Eizenstat and attended by representatives of 44 countries and 13 organizations, focused on establishing principles for the restitution of art and property.[205] The conference produced an agreement to compile a master list of art stolen by the Nazis and to open up public and private archives relating to the Holocaust.[206]

The Holocaust Victims Redress Act[207] authorizes $25 million for distribution to organizations devoted to assisting survivors of the Holocaust and $5 million for archival research and translation services to assist the restitution of assets looted or extorted during the Holocaust. The Act also declares the "sense of Congress" that all governments should undertake "good faith efforts to facilitate the return of private and public property, such as works of art, to the rightful owners in cases where assets were confiscated from the claimant during the period of Nazi rule and there is reasonable proof that the claimant is the rightful owner." On June 30, 1998, in a session at the Holocaust Museum in Washington, the United States and 38 other countries announced an initiative to identify art stolen from Holocaust victims and to compensate their heirs.[208]

---

[204] *Id.* In a strange twist, the day after the Court of Appeals issued its decision, United States District Attorney Mary Jo White issued a seizure warrant for one of the paintings, "Portrait of Wally," the night before the museum was to return them to the Leopold Foundation. *See* Bruce Balestier, Return of Painting Blocked by U.S. Attorney, N.Y.L.J., Sept. 23, 1999, at 1, col. 6. The painting remains at the museum pending a determination of ownership in a civil proceeding. *See* Judith H. Dobrzynski, Modern Is Focus of a New Dispute Over a Painting, N.Y. Times, Feb. 10, 2000, at E3. In reaction to the Court of Appeals's decision, the New York State Legislature, over the opposition of the museum community, amended § 12.03 to confer immunity only from civil seizures. The amendment was signed into law by Governor George Pataki on May 24, 2000.

[205] *See* Carole Landry, US leads drive to return Nazi-confiscated art, property, Agence France Presse, Nov. 29, 1998.

[206] *See* Brigid O'Hara Forster, What Has Been Looted? The West's art museums face a daunting task as they search for the remnant of Nazi pillaging, Time, Mar. 15, 1999, at 58; Daniel Kurtzman, Focus on Issues: Drive for restitution prompts doubts about Holocaust legacy, Ethnic NewsWatch, Dec. 8, 1998, at 3.

[207] Pub. L. 105-158, 112 Stat. 15, 105th Cong., 2d Sess. (1998).

[208] Barry Schweid, 39 nations to search for Nazi art loot, Associated Press, July 1, 1998.

In January 1998, the Association of American Museum Directors (AAMD), reacting to recent controversies involving art alleged to have been stolen by the Nazis and seeking to stave off congressional action,[209] formed a nine-member Task Force on the Spoliation of Art during the Nazi/World War II Era (1933-1945), chaired by Philippe de Montebello, Director of the Metropolitan Museum of Art, to address Holocaust-era art restitution claims. On June 4, 1998, the Task Force released an admirable but vague statement of principles (reaffirmed in February 1999) that "recognizes and deplores the unlawful confiscation of art that constituted one of the many horrors of the Holocaust and World War II."[210] It calls upon American art museums to review the provenance of works in their collections to determine whether any of them were unlawfully confiscated during the Holocaust/World War II era and never restituted and to contact "established archives, databases, art dealers, auction houses, donors, art historians and other scholars and researchers" who may be able to provide provenance information.[211] The report urges member museums to request the seller to provide as much World War II-era provenance information as possible before acquiring a work. If a work is found to have been unlawfully confiscated and not restituted, the museum is urged not to acquire the object and to take "appropriate further action," including making the information public. Museums that receive documented claims for restitution of illegally confiscated works are to "offer to resolve the matter in an equitable, appropriate, and mutually agreeable manner," and mediation is recommended for resolving such claims. Finally, the report recommends the creation of databases by third parties to facilitate research into the histories of their collections. (The Commission for Art Recovery, the Art Loss Register, and HARP have, in fact, undertaken to assemble such databases.)[212] According to the AAMD, almost all member museums with collections that include the type of art

---

[209] *See* Lee Rosenbaum, Will museums in U.S. purge Nazi-tainted art?, 86 Art in America, No. 11 (Nov. 1998), at 37.

[210] *See* Appendix 5-E.

[211] De Montebello has made a point of distinguishing U.S. museums, which, if they acquired looted works, did so "most often as gifts or bequests from collector/philanthropists who are often the last in a long chain of innocent good-faith purchasers," from various European museums that knowingly acquired large numbers of works soon after they were seized by the Nazis. *See* Rosenbaum, *supra* note 209. In conformity with the AAMD policy, the Metropolitan Museum of Art reportedly is reviewing its entire collection "to determine whether there are any pictures whose provenance has questions or holes in it during the period 1933 to 1945." Group Says Met Painting May Have Been Nazi Loot, N.Y. Times, Mar. 12, 2000, at 49 (quoting museum spokesman Harold Holzer).

[212] For selected forms for claim filing, see Appendices 5-F and 5-G, and Form 5-1. We recommend filing with (1) the Art Loss Register because their records are searched by the major auction houses and dealers, (2) the Commission for Art Recovery because of their focus on research and help in tracking lost works, and (3) the State of New York Banking Department, which helps non-New York residents, and which has more political and economic clout than any private litigant would ever be able to acquire on his own.

stolen by the Nazis are researching their collections in compliance with the guidelines.[213] On March 9, 2000, the Art Institute of Chicago became the first major U.S. museum to announce that it would release a list of works in its collection for which there are gaps in provenance during the Nazi era.[214]

The moral force of claims to art looted by the Nazis, the large number of such works that still have not been restituted, and the high cost of suing to recover the works all compel resort to alternatives other than litigation to restore the works to their rightful owners. In this regard, the AAMD guidelines recommend "using mediation wherever reasonably practical to help resolve claims regarding art illegally confiscated during the Nazi/World War II era and not restituted."

It is important to stress with respect to art plundered during World War II that the possessors of the works, and particularly museums and other "public" institutions, should evaluate claims not purely on legal grounds but also on moral grounds, recognizing that such cases, as with other stolen art cases, often involve two innocent parties. Works could have been stolen by the state or by individuals, for public or private collections, by Nazis, Russians, or Americans. Sales occurred under implied threat of force—"sell me the works and you live"—or under the economic duress of needing to flee. The facts surrounding these cases are often difficult, if not impossible, to establish, and cooperation is not always forthcoming. In many cases, those who knew the facts have died or were murdered, or their memories have faded. The varying circumstances presented by World War II-era claims may have differing legal consequences, but, as the governments and institutions that have restituted such works have recognized, they are morally indistinguishable. Resolving these disputes on the basis of statutes of limitations, laches, jurisdiction, or other legal defenses in a court of law should be a last resort.

---

[213] AAMD press release, Feb. 9, 1999. *See* Appendix 5-F. European museums have also undertaken to research the World War II-era provenance of works in their collections. *See* Brigid O'Hara Forster, What Has Been Looted? The West's art museums face a daunting task as they search for the remnant of Nazi pillaging, Time, Mar. 15, 1999, at 58 (reporting that in response to a government directive to all major British museums to check the provenance of their collections between 1933 and 1945, the National Gallery of Art in London had launched a study of all of its paintings, including by contacting dealers, auction houses, previous owners, and the Art Loss Register and that museums across Europe were engaged in similar research). French museums have been reported to hold over 2,000 works known to have been stolen pending the recommendations of a commission investigating looting from French Jews. *Id. See also* Nick Fielding, Hunt for Secret Nazi Loot in Britain's Top Institute of Art, Mail on Sunday, Mar. 7, 1999, at 28 (London's Courtauld Institute of Art investigating whether some 120 paintings for which full provenances do not exist may have come from collections looted by the Nazis).

[214] *See* Kirsten Scharnberg, Art Institute Takes Initiative on Works Looted in Nazi Era, Chicago Tribune, Mar. 10, 2000, at 1.

FORMS AND APPENDICES

Form 5-1

Stolen Art Data Sheet, National Stolen Art File

FD-531 (Rev. 3-31-98)

STOLEN ART DATA SHEET

☐ Add to National Stolen Art File ☐ Search National Stolen Art File

Field Office/Agency: ____________________ File/Case Number: ____________________

Agent/Officer: ____________________ Date: ____________________

Special Agents and law enforcement officers are requested to ask the following questions when interviewing victims of art theft, or questioning sources about suspicious art. Please answer questions as fully as possible and submit to the National Stolen Art File, Interstate Theft/Government Reservation Crimes Unit (IT/GRCU), FBI Headquarters. **Explanations of categories on reverse.**

Type of Object ____________________

Title ____________________

____

Maker ____________________

____

Materials & Techniques ____________________

____

Subject ____________________

____

Inscriptions & Markings ____________________

____

Measurements ____________________

Date or Period ____________________

Distinguishing Features and Short Description ____________________

____

____

____

____

Value ____________________

Attach additional sheets if needed.

Please include a copy of the theft report, or other information relevant to the investigation, including descriptions and images of suspects. This information will be added to the National Stolen Art File to develop art theft statistics.

Include Photograph(s) if Available

Object ID is an international standard for describing art and cultural artifacts. It is a series of questions developed by the Getty Information Institute through the collaboration of museums, cultural heritage organizations, law enforcement agencies, the art and antiques trade, appraisers, and the insurance industry.

Type of Object

What kind of object is it (i.e., painting, sculpture, clock, mask)?
For a coin, what denomination is it (i.e., five cents, two and a half dollars)?

Title

Does the object have a title by which it is known and might be identified?

Maker

Do you know who made the object? This may be the name of a known individual (i.e., Pablo Picasso), a company (i.e.,Tiffany), or a cultural group (i.e., Navajo). If the specific maker is unknown, do you know the country where it was made?

Materials & Techniques

What materials is the object made of (i.e., bronze, wood, oil on canvas)?
How was it made (i.e., carved, cast, etched)?

Subject

What is pictured or represented (i.e., landscape, battle, woman holding child)?
For abstract art, are there any particular shapes or dominant colors used?

Inscriptions & Markings

Is the work signed? If so, where is the signature located (i.e., signed lower left)? Are there any identifying markings, numbers, or inscriptions on the object (i.e., dedication, maker's marks, coin mint marks)?

Measurements

What is the size and/or weight of the object? Specify which unit of measurement is being used (i.e., inches or centimeters) and to which dimensions the measurements refer (i.e., height, width, depth).

Date or Period

When was the object made (i.e., 1893, early 17th century, Ming Dynasty)?

Distinguishing Features and Short Description

Does the object have any physical characteristics that could help to identify it (i.e., damage, repairs, or manufacturing defects)? Include any additional information which helps to identify the object.

The criteria for an object to be eligible to be entered into the National Stolen Art File are as follows: 1. The object must be of artistic or historical significance, and uniquely identifiable; this includes fine arts, decorative arts, antiquities, Asian art, Islamic art, ethnographic objects (i.e. African, Native American, or Aboriginal art), archaeological material, textiles, books and manuscripts, clocks and watches, coins, stamps, musical instruments, and scientific instruments; 2. The object should have an estimated value of $2,000 or more; or lesser value if associated with a major crime.

For questions regarding this form or the National Stolen Art File, please contact:

Federal Bureau of Investigation
Art Theft Program
Interstate Theft Unit, Room 5096
935 Pennsylvania Avenue, N.W.
Washington, D.C. 20535
(202) 324-4192; fax (202) 324-1504

Form 5-2

Wartime Losses Report Form, Art Loss Register, Inc.

THE ART LOSS ■ REGISTER

Wartime Losses Report Form

This is a report to The Art Loss Register's Stolen & Missing Art Database.

The object(s) herein will be added to our database of stolen & missing art and will be searched for until an identification occurs. Identifications are made as we screen the auction market internationally and as we check the provenance of items for dealers, collectors and museums and international law enforcement agencies.

The Art Loss Register is committed to working with the Commission for Art Recovery of the World Jewish Congress and the New York State Banking Department Holocaust Claims Processing Office in order to build as comprehensive a database as possible of Holocaust and World War II art losses. Please be advised that, unless you indicate otherwise, information provided on this form will be forwarded to these organizations for inclusion in their own databases.

Please complete this form and return it to our address in New York or London :

NEW YORK

The Art Loss Register, 666 Fifth Avenue, 21st Floor, New York, NY 10103
Telephone: 212 262 4831 Fax: 212 262 4838 E-mail: alrnewyork@aol.com

LONDON

The Art Loss Register, 12 Grosvenor Place, London SW1X 7HH
Telephone: 0171 235 3393 Fax: 0171 235 1652 E-mail: artloss@artloss.com

Our form can also be found on the Internet at: www.artloss.com.

Please note that there is no charge to enter a wartime theft onto The Art Loss Register's Database. Recovery contingency fees are also waived.

Claimant Information

This section seeks biographical information about the claimant. This is the individual who claims to have ownership rights to the work of art that was stolen. Each separate claimant must complete a copy of this section.

Name ....

Current Address ....

....

Telephone Number .... Fax Number ....

E-mail address ....

Nationality (Include all previous nationalities) ....

....

Place(s) of residence up to May 1945 (if outside the USA) ....

....

....

Victim's Name ....

Claimant Representative Information *(Where applicable)*

Where the person submitting the claim is a representative of the claimant and is not entitled to inherit, this section must be completed. Written and notarized authorisation or power of attorney from the claimant providing authorisation to the named representative must also be submitted. Information about the claimant must also be supplied under the section **Claimant Information**

Name of Representative ....

Address of Representative ....

....

Telephone Number .... Fax Number ....

E-Mail Address ....

Representative's relationship to claimant (if applicable) ....

Documentation to support this relationship? ....

Representative's law firm, company or other organisation (where applicable) ....

Circumstances Of Theft

Circumstances and approximate date of theft of the item(s). Please attach any relevant documentation

....

....

Documentary Evidence to Support Registration? ....

Has Loss Been Reported to Any Post War Restitution Body? ....

Please provide any relevant documentation ....

Was the Item Covered by Insurance? ....

If yes, please supply name of insurer, name of policy holder and policy number ....

....

Statement of Accuracy

The following statement provides that the information supplied to The Art Loss Register is true and accurate. All claimants and representatives must acknowledge this statement so that the claim can be added to The Art Loss Register's Database.

I hereby state that the information provided is true and accurate to the best of my knowledge.

Claimants Signature .... Date ....

Representative's Signature .... Date ....

FORM 5-2

Descriptions Of Items Stolen

Please include as much information as possible. **Photographs are of foremost importance.**
Please include a written description or sketch. Please include provenance etc, in the space provided.

Artist/Maker/Jeweller *(if applicable)*: ....
Period: ....
Nationality: ....
Title/Subject/Type: ....
Dimensions *(Height, width, depth)*: ....
Exact Date or Century of Manufacture: ....
Medium/Material: ....

DISTINCTIVE MARKINGS *(Please specify position)*

....

Signature: ....
Edition No: ....
Inscriptions: ....
Condition: ....
Other Marks: ....

DESCRIPTION
Please describe the object below.

Value: ....

Artist/Maker/Jeweller *(if applicable)*: ....
Period: ....
Nationality: ....
Title/Subject/Type: ....
Dimensions *(Height, width, depth)*: ....
Exact Date or Century of Manufacture: ....
Medium/Material: ....

DISTINCTIVE MARKINGS *(Please specify position)*

....

Signature: ....
Edition No: ....
Inscriptions: ....
Condition: ....
Other Marks: ....

DESCRIPTION
Please describe the object below.

Value: ....

Artist/Maker/Jeweller *(if applicable)*: ....
Period: ....
Nationality: ....
Title/Subject/Type: ....
Dimensions *(Height, width, depth)*: ....
Exact Date or Century of Manufacture: ....
Medium/Material: ....

DISTINCTIVE MARKINGS *(Please specify position)*

....

Signature: ....
Edition No: ....
Inscriptions: ....
Condition: ....
Other Marks: ....

DESCRIPTION
Please describe the object below.

Value: ....

Descriptions Of Items Stolen *(Continued)*

Artist/Maker/Jeweller *(if applicable)*: ....
Period: ....
Nationality: ....
Title/Subject/Type: ....
Dimensions *(Height, width, depth)*: ....
Exact Date or Century of Manufacture: ....
Medium/Material: ....

DISTINCTIVE MARKINGS *(Please specify position)*

....
Signature: ....
Edition No: ....
Inscriptions: ....
Condition: ....
Other Marks: ....

DESCRIPTION
Please describe the object below.

Value: ....

Artist/Maker/Jeweller *(if applicable)*: ....
Period: ....
Nationality: ....
Title/Subject/Type: ....
Dimensions *(Height, width, depth)*: ....
Exact Date or Century of Manufacture: ....
Medium/Material: ....

DISTINCTIVE MARKINGS *(Please specify position)*

....
Signature: ....
Edition No: ....
Inscriptions: ....
Condition: ....
Other Marks: ....

DESCRIPTION
Please describe the object below.

Value: ....

Artist/Maker/Jeweller *(if applicable)*: ....
Period: ....
Nationality: ....
Title/Subject/Type: ....
Dimensions *(Height, width, depth)*: ....
Exact Date or Century of Manufacture: ....
Medium/Material: ....

DISTINCTIVE MARKINGS *(Please specify position)*

....
Signature: ....
Edition No: ....
Inscriptions: ....
Condition: ....
Other Marks: ....

DESCRIPTION
Please describe the object below.

Value: ....

Once this form has been completed and signed by the relevant parties, please ensure that it is returned as soon as possible to either our London office or our New York office (see address on front of form).

APPENDIX 5-A

Object ID Checklist

Take Photographs

Photographs are of vital importance in identifying and recovering stolen objects. In addition to overall views, take close-ups of inscriptions, markings, and any damage and repairs. If possible, include a scale or object of known size in the image.

Answer These Questions:

Type of Object. What type of object is it (*e.g.*, painting, sculpture, clock, mask)?

Materials & Techniques. What materials is the object made of (*e.g.*, brass, wood, oil on canvas)? How was it made (*e.g.*, carved, cast, etched)?

Measurements. What is the size and/or weight of the object? Specify which unit of measurement is being used (*e.g.*, cm., in.) and to which dimension the measurement refers (*e.g.*, height, width, depth).

Inscriptions & Markings. Are there any identifying markings, numbers or inscriptions on the object (*e.g.*, a signature, dedication, title, maker's marks, purity marks, property marks)?

Distinguishing Features. Does the object have any physical characteristics that could help to identify it (*e.g.*, damage, repairs, or manufacturing defects)?

Title. Does the object have a title by which it is known and might be identified (*e.g.*, "The Scream")?

Subject. What is pictured or represented (*e.g.*, landscape, battle, woman holding child)?

Date or Period. When was the object made (*e.g.*, 1893, early seventeenth century, Late Bronze Age)?

Maker. Do you know who made the object? This may be the name of a known individual (*e.g.*, Thomas Tompion), a company (*e.g.*, Tiffany), or cultural group (*e.g.*, Hopi).

Write a Short Description. This can also include any additional information which helps to identify the object (*e.g.*, colour and shape of the object, where it was made).

Keep it Secure

Having documented the object, keep this information in a safe place.

APPENDIX 5-B

Object ID Summary

Object ID is an international standard for describing art, antiques, and antiquities. It has been developed through the collaboration of museums, cultural heritage organizations, police and customs agencies, the art and antiques trade, appraisers, and the insurance industry.

The Importance of Documentation to the Protection of Cultural Objects

The illicit trade in cultural objects is now widely recognized as one of the most prevalent categories of international crime. There is widespread agreement that documentation is crucial to the protection of cultural objects, for stolen objects that have not been photographed and adequately described are rarely recoverable by their rightful owners. Unfortunately, very few objects have been documented to a level that can materially assist in their recovery in the event of theft. Even for objects that have been so documented, the information recorded is extremely variable. It is important, therefore, that efforts be made to increase awareness of the need to make adequate, standardized descriptions of cultural objects in both public and private collections.

It is one thing to encourage the compilation of descriptions of objects as a security measure, but quite another to develop effective means of circulating this documentation to organizations that can assist in the recovery of the objects if they are stolen. Ideally, the information that can identify a stolen or illegally exported object should be able to travel at least as fast as the object itself. This will mean that the information may have to cross national borders and be circulated among a number of organizations. The development of electronic networks makes this effort technically possible. But the existence of digital information and computer networks to transmit information solves only part of the problem; also needed are standards that will make it possible to exchange information in a form that is intelligible to both systems and people.

The Project

Discussions between the Getty Information Institute and leading national and international umbrella agencies and government bodies in 1993 established that there was a consensus on the need to collectively address issues relating to documentation practices and the implementation of international standards. In July of that year the Institute convened a meeting in Paris to discuss the possibility of developing an international collaborative project to define documentation standards for identifying cultural objects. The meeting was attended by representatives of the Conference for Security and Co-operation in Europe (now the

Organisation for Security and Co-operation in Europe), the Council of Europe, the International Council of Museums, Interpol, UNESCO, and the U.S. Information Agency. The participants agreed on the need for such an initiative and recommended that it should focus on developing a standard for the information required to identify cultural objects, and on the mechanisms for encouraging the implementation of the standard. As a result of these consultations, a project was defined and initiated, with the following primary objectives:

- To provide a collaborative forum for organizations that have demonstrated an interest in the protection of cultural objects.
- To recommend an international "core" documentation standard for the identification of cultural objects.
- To encourage the implementation of the standard.

The new standard is not seen as an alternative to existing standards, but rather as a minimum standard created for a specific purpose—that of describing objects to enable them to be identified. As such it can be incorporated into existing systems and nested within existing standards. It is a type of standard sometimes called a "core" standard: core because it comprises certain minimum categories of essential information that are common to a number of documentation systems, making it easier to record, use, and exchange information across systems. An important aspect of a core standard is that it provides the key to further information held in the database, both within an individual organization or elsewhere, but does not seek to make organizations conform to systems which are incompatible with their own needs. Moreover, these standards are designed to be capable of being implemented in traditional, non-computerized ways of making inventories and catalogues as well as in sophisticated computerized databases.

Developing the Standard

Threats to cultural objects are of concern to organizations charged with their management, interpretation, and protection, as well as those bodies responsible for their recovery in the event of theft. Museums, law-enforcement and customs agencies, commercial art theft databases, the art trade, appraisers, and insurance companies around the world all create and hold documentation on cultural objects. From the outset, the project has recognized the need to work collaboratively with organizations in six key communities:

- Cultural heritage organizations (including museums, national inventories, and archaeological organizations)
- Law enforcement agencies

- Customs agencies
- The art trade
- Appraisers
- The insurance industry

The information needs of these organizations inevitably vary, but all need documentation that makes it possible to identify objects. Building broad consensus across these communities on the categories of information needed to identify objects has been the essential precondition to a successful outcome for this initiative, for a universally applicable standard can be developed only by understanding and responding to the specific needs of these different communities.

The first step toward establishing consensus on this core information was to identify and compare the information requirements of each of these communities, to gain an understanding of the purposes for which their information is collected, and to determine how it is used and with whom it is shared. These requirements were identified by a combination of background research, interviews, and, most importantly, major international questionnaire surveys. The first of these surveys, carried out between July and December 1994 by the Getty Information Institute, was endorsed by the Council of Europe, the International Council of Museums, and UNESCO. The survey elicited responses from organizations in 43 countries, including many major museums and galleries, heritage documentation centers, Interpol, and a number of national law enforcement agencies. The survey also took account of existing standards and standards-making initiatives in the museum world, including those of the International Council of Museums, the Museum Documentation Association (UK), the Canadian Heritage Information Network, and the Getty Information Institute.

The results of this preliminary survey—published in July 1995 in *Protecting Cultural Objects Through International Documentation Standards: A Preliminary Survey*—demonstrated that there did, indeed, exist a broad consensus on many of the categories of information that are candidates for inclusion in the proposed standard. Encouraged by these findings, the project went on to survey the information needs of other key communities, namely the art trade; appraisers of personal property; art insurance specialists; and customs agencies. Over 1,000 responses were received from organizations in 84 countries and dependencies, making this survey the largest of its kind ever carried out.

The findings of the questionnaire surveys were used to inform a series of roundtable meetings of experts drawn from the communities concerned. The first of these was a meeting of conservation specialists, held in Washington, D.C. in August 1994. This was the first meeting of an international Conservation Specialists Working Group organized jointly by the Getty Information Institute and the Getty Conservation Institute. It was followed by a meeting of museum documentation experts, held in Edinburgh in November 1995. The third meeting was with art-insurance specialists, and was held at Lloyd's of London in March 1996. The fourth meeting—held at the Winterthur Museum in Delaware—brought together organizations representing dealers and appraisers of art, antiques and antiquities. The final meeting, held in Prague in November 1996, was for representatives of law-enforcement agencies and commercial organizations that operate computerized art theft databases. It was organized in partnership with UNESCO and the Czech Ministry of Culture.

The surveys and consultations established that there is strong agreement on the categories of information that should constitute the standard. The resulting standard—or Object ID, as it will be known—has been developed in response to an identified need, and is simple to understand and easy to implement. Moreover, it represents a true consensus because it reflects current opinion and practice in the communities responsible for protecting cultural objects.

Implementing the Standard

Object ID is best defined in terms of the ways in which it can be implemented:

- It provides a checklist of the information that is required to identify stolen or missing objects.
- It is a documentation standard that establishes the minimum level of information needed to describe an object.
- It is a key building block in the development of information networks that will allow diverse organizations to exchange descriptions of objects rapidly.
- It provides a solid basis for training programs that teach the documentation of objects.

An international conference held in Amsterdam in May 1997 gave an enthusiastic welcome to Object ID. Speakers included representatives of the Council of Europe, the International Council of Museums, Interpol, the Italian Carabinieri Artistico, the UK's Metropolitan Police, the Appraisers Association of America, the Incorporated Society of Valuers and Auctioneers (UK), and the Art Dealers Association of America. Participants at the conference heard of the many ways in which Object ID is already being implemented, and many of those present declared their intention to promote its use.

Around the world there is growing, broad-based support for the new standard. The Object ID checklist has already been translated into Arabic, Chinese, Czech, Dutch, French, German, Hungarian, Italian, Korean, Persian, Russian, and Spanish.

The Arabic, Chinese and Russian translations have been made by UNESCO, which has also reproduced it in its recent handbook: *Preventing the Illicit Traffic in Cultural Property: A Resource Handbook for the Implementation of the 1970 UNESCO Convention* (UNESCO, 1997). The tenth meeting of UNESCO's Intergovernmental Committee for Promoting the Return of Cultural Property (Paris, January 1999) endorsed Object ID "as the international standard for recording minimal data on movable cultural property," and in November 1999 Object ID was endorsed by the General Conference of UNESCO.

The Council of Europe has collaborated with the Getty Information Institute on a publication: *Documenting the Cultural Heritage*. This book, which is available in English and French, brings together the Council of Europe's core data standard for historic buildings, the Council of Europe/ICOM core data standard for archaeological sites, and Object ID.

Law enforcement agencies around the world assisted in the development of Object ID and a number of agencies are already using the standard. At the international level, the project is working with Interpol to develop a manual of guidance that will enable staff at Interpol National Central Bureaus around the world to translate information received in Object ID format into Interpol's Crigen format. In addition, Interpol is to include the Object ID checklist—together with an explanatory text—on a CD-ROM of stolen art. In the USA, the Federal Bureau of Investigation has adopted Object ID for its art theft database—the National Stolen Art File. In the UK, the Metropolitan Police is now using the Object ID checklist to compile descriptions of stolen art and, along with a number of regional forces, is using it in crime prevention initiatives.

It has been established that the Object ID checklist is compatible with the majority of art theft databases, including those of Interpol, the Italian Carabinieri, the Czech Republic, and the International Art Loss Register.

The United States Information Agency (USIA)—one of the original partners in the project—has adopted Object ID for its web site database of types of illicitly traded objects.

The involvement of the museum community, and of ICOM, in particular, has been very important for the project. In August 1997, the Executive Council of ICOM adopted a resolution put forward by the Council's Documentation Committee (CIDOC) stating that

> A museum should be able to generate from its collection information system such data (preferably according to the 'Object ID' standard) that can identify an object in case of theft or looting.

This statement has since been accepted by ICOM's 19th General Assembly as part of Resolution No. 4: Consolidation of the Movement Against Illicit Traffic in Cultural Property, during its triennial meeting in Melbourne, Australia, October 1998.

In the Netherlands, the Inspectorate of Museums is promoting Object ID, and the standard is also being used in a Dutch project that has developed a museum documentation system for use in museums in Mali and Vietnam. In the UK, the Museum Documentation Association—a participant in the project—has made small changes to the SPECTRUM standard in order to make it compatible with Object ID.

A number of insurance companies in Europe and North America are now promoting the standard, including AXA Nordstern Art Insurance, Chubb & Son, General Reinsurance Corporation, Hiscox Insurance, Mannheim Insurance, and Swiss Re.

In 1998 AXA Nordstern Art Insurance, in collaboration with General & Cologne RE (Kölnishen Rück) and the Getty Information Institute, organized a one-day conference on Object ID in Cologne.

The Object ID checklist has been circulated by a number of organizations representing the art trade, including CINOA, the London and Provincial Art Dealers Association, Private Art Dealers Association of Canada, the Association of Dealers in American Art, and the British Antique Dealers Association. Object ID has also attracted support from organizations representing appraisers, and it has already been endorsed by the Appraisers Association of America, the American Society of Appraisers, the Royal Institute of Chartered Surveyors in the UK, and the Incorporated Society of Valuers and Auctioneers (UK).

To increase the use of Object ID, the Getty Information Institute has published a training Manual—*Object ID: Guidelines for Making Records that Describe Art, Antiques, and Antiquities*. The book summarizes the evolution of Object ID, explains the Object ID categories, and gives guidance on their use. It also sets out guidelines for photographing cultural objects, including choosing viewpoints, selecting backgrounds, and positioning lighting.

Recent Developments

On 1 July 1999 the Getty Information Institute established a new home for Object ID at the Council for the Prevention of Art Theft (CoPAT) in the United Kingdom. CoPAT has been involved in the project from an early stage, playing a significant role in the development of Object ID, and being one of the first organizations to formally endorse the standard.

Established in 1992 as a not-for-profit organization, CoPAT's mission is to promote crime prevention in the fields of art, antiques, antiquities and architecture. At present it works through five specialist subcommittees: Trusts and Associations, Professions and Trade, Law Reform, Law Enforcement, and

Insurance. Members of the committees are drawn from the law-enforcement community, experts in various aspects of crime prevention, heritage organizations, historic house owners, the insurance industry, and the art trade.

For more information about Object ID contact the Council for the Prevention of Art Theft, The Estate Office, Warminster, BA12 6QD, United Kingdom.

APPENDIX 5-C

Registration of Stolen Objects Form, Art Loss Register, Inc.

THE ART LOSS REGISTER, INC.

666 Fifth Avenue, 21st Floor
New York, New York 10103

Telephone: 212-262-4831
Facsimile: 212-262-4838

REGISTRATION OF STOLEN OBJECT(S)

This is an application and agreement for registration of one or more works stolen works of art (the "Object(s)" with The Art Loss Register ("ALR"). The Object(s) reported and described herein will be recorded and maintained by The Art Loss Register. The Register will be available for appropriate inquiries such as those from subscribers, art dealers, museums, law enforcement agencies, auction houses and private citizens who may seek to determine whether certain specific objects may have been reported stolen. There is a one-time registration fee and a recovery service fee if the ALR plays a role in the recovery of the Object(s), described herein.

The Art Loss Register may publish information regarding the objects reported herein if such publication may enhance the chances for recovery of the stolen objects. Unless disclosure is specifically permitted as set forth below, the identity of the owner/insured of the objects shall be kept strictly confidential.

INFORMATION ABOUT REGISTRANT

Name ____________________

Address ____________________ Telephone ____________________

____________________ Fax ____________________

Registrant is: ☐Owner of Object(s) ☐Authorized agent of Owner ☐Law enforcement agency

☐Institution ☐Other: Specify ____________________

OWNER OF STOLEN OBJECT(S) (if different from Registrant)

Name ____________________

Address ____________________ Telephone ____________________

____________________ Fax ____________________

INSURANCE INFORMATION

Are the object(s) insured? No ☐ Yes ☐ Insured value (aggregate for all objects reported herein) ____________

Name of Insurance Company ____________________ Policy # ____________

Claim # ____________ Insurance Co. Contact ____________________

Name and Telephone if available

INFORMATION ABOUT THE THEFT

Date of Theft ________ Place of Theft ____________________

Circumstances of Theft ____________________

____

Police Report # ____________ Date of Report ________

Name, Organization and Address of Officer making report ____________________

____

Is a reward being offered for information leading to recovery? No ☐ Yes ☐ Amount ____________

CONFIDENTIALITY OF OWNER

Permission is granted to publish the identity (name only) of the Owner Yes ☐ No ☐

By signing and submitting this Registration, I declare that the information set forth herein is accurate and complete to the best of my current knowledge and belief and I agree to abide by the Rights and Rules set forth at the back of this document.

____________________ Signature

____________ Date

PERS1098

APPENDIX 5-C

Examples of Objects with Guidelines for Report Completion

Use the following questions to help describe the object(s) you are registering as completely as possible.

	Pictures & drawings	Garden Statuary & Sculpture	Jewelry	Clocks & Watches	Objects	Silver	Ceramics, China & Glassware	Furniture
Type of Object What kind of object is it?	Drawing, print, painting, lithograph, icon.	Fountain, statue, sundial, garden furniture.	Ring, bracelet, necklace, brooch.	Mantel, longcase (grandfather), carriage, bracket, wristwatch, pocket watch (lady's or gentleman's?); also, barometers.	Snuff box, cigarette case, trinket/pill box.	Liturgical items, center piece, tray, wine cooler, trophy, candelabra.	Figurine, vase, tableware, box.	Table, bureau, desk.
Materials & Techniques What material(s) is the object made of?	Oil on canvas, oil on panel, watercolor, gouache, pencil, pen & ink, pastel.	Stone, marble, lead, cast iron, wrought iron, bronze. Cast, carved.	Type, cut and number of stones, color, clarity, carat, type of gold/metal; style (*e.g.* art deco).	Type of wood, enamel, lacquer, metal, brass, marble, silver, gold (plated).	Gold, silver, enamel, glass, tortoiseshell.	Silver, silver gilt, silver plate, repousse (molded), engraved, beaten.	Porcelain, bone china, earthenware, stoneware.	Type of wood, mountings and inlay, brass, gilt, ormolu.
Measurements	What is the size (height, width, depth, diameter) and/or weight of the object?							
Inscriptions & Markings	Are there any crests, inscriptions, commemorative markings, carvings, signature, initials, foundry marks, edition no., coat of arms, date, religious symbols, hall marks and inscriptions, pattern?							
Distinguishing Features Does the object have any physical characteristics that could help to identify it?	Visible damage (stains, torn canvas, repairs, chipped paint), labels/stamps. (Including back of object).	Signs of restoration, weathering, corrosion/rust, cracks, chipped paint.	Missing stones, dents, scratches, repairs.	Visible damage, marks, missing parts (esp. movement mechanism), serial/movement numbers.	Loss of veneer, fading, scratches, staining, repairs and renovation.	Dents, scratches. Hall mark (maker – letter, date – letter & place of manufacture – symbol)	Chips, fading colors, loss of guilding, visible repairs, maker's mark.	Chipping, dents, missing stones.
Title	Does the object have a title by which it is known and might be identified? *e.g. The Scream*							
Subject	What is pictured or represented? *e.g.* "Abstract figure on bridge with open mouth as if screaming with hands either side of mouth," portrait or landscape?							
Date or Period	When was the object made? Estimated, if exact date unknown. Position of date if on object. Type of maker's marking may indicate date.							
Maker/Artist	If unavailable, nationality or school (in the style of a particular nationality).	If unavailable, nationality.	Tiffany & Co, Cartier, Boucheron, Marina B, Schlumberge.	Name of clock maker, town where made (may be inscribed on clock face).	Maker's name with position. Usually branded on wood or paper label (may be on metallic fixtures).	Identifiable from maker's name or initials.	Sevres, Meissen, Derby Worcester, Wedgewood, Dresden (indicated on base).	Faberge, *etc.*
Description Any additional information which helps to identify the object.	Details of subject.	Rams heads, gargoyles, dolphin shells.	Color, shape.	Shape of face, scenes (which may be present in arches or spandrels).	Shape and/or style, legs/feet.	History of item.		Hinges, fastenings, colors, pictorial scenes.

RIGHTS AND RULES GOVERNING
REGISTRATION WITH THE ART LOSS REGISTER ("ALR")

1. The Service. Subject to its right to withdraw any listing, the service provided by ALR under this agreement is to register the Object(s) and the information provided herein and other than this registration, no warranties, promises or undertakings are being made to the Owner through this Agreement. At the same time ALR will use its best efforts to respond to requests for information. However, ALR shall have no liability or responsibility of any kind, nature or description to the Owner or any heirs, executors, administrators, successors and assigns of the Owner for any act or omission of ALR.

2. Discretion to Register. ALR has the right at all times to determine in its sole discretion whether any object shall be included in the Register. Accordingly ALR may decline to register or delete a registration for any reason.

3. Recovery Service Fee and Costs. Either party shall promptly notify the other in the event that any recovery of the Object(s) occurs. In the event of any recovery of an Object(s) where ALR has played a role, ALR shall be entitled to a recovery service fee based on the fair market value of the Object(s) at the time of recovery. In the event that the Owner recovers property which was not registered but nevertheless recovered by or identified by the Owner as a consequence of efforts and/or information from ALR, a recovery service fee shall also be paid to ALR by the Owner. The fee, which shall be paid to ALR within thirty days from the determination of the fair market value, shall be calculated as follows: fifteen percent (15%) of the first $75,000 in value plus ten percent (10%) of any value in excess of $75,000. This obligation to pay a recovery service fee based on the fair market value of the Object or property at the time of recovery shall not be affected or altered by any post-recovery disposition of the Object or property or by any events or agreements occurring prior to recovery. Accordingly, in the event of any recovery from which a recovery service fee is due to ALR, the Owner grants ALR a security interest in the Object to the extent of or for the amount of the recovery service fee. In addition to this fee, if ALR has incurred any costs or made any expenditures directly in connection with any successful recovery of an Object (such as by way of example, packing, transportation, insurance, rewards or appraisals), the Owner will reimburse ALR for such costs or expenditures.

4. Fair Market Value. ALR will promptly seek a qualified appraisal of the fair market value of any recovered Object or property as of the date of recovery and the Owner agrees to cooperate and respond to reasonable requests for pertinent information. ALR will submit this appraisal to the Owner. Within thirty days the Owner will accept or contest this appraisal and a failure to respond will be deemed an acceptance of the appraisal and an account stated for the recovery service fee based on that appraisal. Timely written notice is required to contest the appraisal submitted by ALR, and in such event, the parties will jointly apply to the Appraisers Association of America for an appraisal. The cost of this procedure shall be charged to the Owner and the determination of the Appraisers Association of America shall be conclusively binding on both parties. The recovery service fee shall be payable fifteen days from receipt of this final determination and shall constitute an account stated for this amount.

5. Indemnity. The Owner agrees to indemnify and hold ALR harmless from any claim or expense whatsoever (including reasonable legal fees in defending any such claim against ALR) arising out of or relating to the use of information contained in the Register by a third party where such information has been made available to that third party by the Owner or at the request of the Owner.

6. Arbitration/Applicable Law. Any controversy or claim arising out of or relating to this agreement shall be submitted to arbitration in New York, New York in accordance with the Rules, then obtaining, of the American Arbitration Association. The fees of the arbitrators and of the American Arbitration Association, as the case may be, shall be advanced equally by the parties during the arbitration and chargeable against the non-prevailing party at the conclusion of the arbitration. Any award concurred in by a majority of the arbitrators or rendered by the sole arbitrator (as the case may be) shall be binding and conclusive on the parties; and a judgment thereon may be entered in any court having jurisdiction thereof. The performance and application of this Registration Agreement and the rights and obligations of the Owner and ALR shall be governed exclusively by the laws of the State of New York.

APPENDIX 5-C

DESCRIPTION OF OBJECT(S) TO BE REGISTERED

Along with a detailed description, a photograph or a sketch should be provided if at all possible. The more details you provide, the greater the chances for recovery. Use the chart on the opposite page to complete the object description below.

Type of Object ______________________

Materials & Techniques ______________________

Measurements ______________________

Inscription & Markings ______________________

____

Distinguishing Features ______________________

____

Title ______________________

Subject ______________________

Date or Period ______________________

Maker/Artist ______________________

Prior Owners ______________________

Further Description and/or Sketch

Photograph enclosed? Yes ☐ No ☐

To be returned? Yes ☐ No ☐

Type of Object ______________________

Materials & Techniques ______________________

Measurements ______________________

Inscription & Markings ______________________

____

Distinguishing Features ______________________

____

Title ______________________

Subject ______________________

Date or Period ______________________

Maker/Artist ______________________

Prior Owners ______________________

Further Description and/or Sketch

Photograph enclosed? Yes ☐ No ☐

To be returned? Yes ☐ No ☐

APPENDIX 5-D

National Stolen Art File (FBI) Summary

National Stolen Art File

Federal Bureau of Investigation

Criminal Investigative Division
Violent Crimes and Major Offenders Section
Major Theft/Transportation Crimes Unit

The illicit trade in art and cultural artifacts is a major category of international crime. This includes theft of individual works of art, illegal export of objects protected by international laws, and pillaging of archaeological sites. Art theft is an international problem requiring cooperation at all levels of law enforcement. To aid in this endeavor, the FBI established the National Stolen Art File (NSAF) to assist law enforcement agencies in resolving this ever increasing problem.

The National Stolen Art File is a computerized index of stolen art and cultural property as reported to the Federal Bureau of Investigation by law enforcement agencies throughout the United States and internationally. The NSAF consists of images and physical descriptions of stolen and recovered objects, in addition to investigative case information. The primary goal of the National Stolen Art File is to serve as a tool to assist investigators in art and cultural artifact theft cases and to function as an analytical database providing law enforcement officials with information concerning art theft.

The criteria for an object to be eligible to be entered into the National Stolen Art File are as follows:
1) The object must be uniquely identifiable and have historical or artistic significance; this includes fine arts, decorative arts, antiquities, Asian art, Islamic art, Native American art, ethnographic objects, archaeological material, textiles, books and manuscripts, clocks and watches, coins, stamps, musical instruments, and scientific instruments.
2) The object must be valued at $2,000 or more; or less if associated with a major crime.
3) The request must come through a law enforcement agency accompanied by a physical description of the object, a photograph of the object, if available, and a copy of any police reports or other information relevant to the investigation.

All requests for searches of the National Stolen Art File must be made through a law enforcement agency in support of a criminal investigation. Individuals or organizations in the United States wanting to access the NSAF should contact their local FBI office; foreign organizations should contact a Federal Bureau of Investigation Legal Attaché office.

The Federal Bureau of Investigation has no art theft unit specializing exclusively in the investigation of art cases. Art crime investigations are conducted by agents in the field who are assigned cases involving interstate or international thefts for which the federal government has investigative jurisdiction. Squads that are responsible for investigating interstate theft cases are located in each of the 56 field offices of the FBI. In addition, the FBI has more than 30 Legal Attaché offices worldwide.

APPENDIX 5-D

The Federal Bureau of Investigation has primary investigative jurisdiction for all federal criminal laws except cases in which responsibility is, by statute or otherwise, specifically assigned to another agency. The FBI has responsibility for the following federal statutes:

Title 18, United States Code, Section 659 - Theft From Interstate Shipment

Makes it a federal offense to steal or obtain by fraud anything from a conveyance, depot or terminal, any shipment being transported in interstate or foreign commerce. The statute also prohibits the "fencing" of such stolen property.

Title 18, United States Code, Section 1951 - Interference with Commerce by Threats of Violence (Hobbs Act)

Makes it a federal offense to obstruct interstate commerce by robbery or extortion or to use or threaten to use violence against any person or property in interstate commerce.

Title 18, United States Code, Section 2314 and 2315 - Interstate Transportation of Stolen Property

Prohibits the transportation in interstate or foreign commerce of any goods with a value of $5,000 or more knowing the goods to be stolen. These statutes also prohibit the "fencing" of such goods.

Title 18, United States Code, Section 668 - Theft of Major Artwork

Makes it a federal offense to obtain by theft or fraud any object of cultural heritage from a museum. The statute also prohibits the "fencing" or possession of such objects, knowing them to be stolen.

Title 18, United States Code, Section 1170 - Illegal Trafficking in Native American Human Remains and Cultural Items

Prohibits the sale of the human remains or cultural artifacts of Native Americans without the right of possession of those items in accordance with the Native American Graves Protection and Repatriation Act.

Title 18, United States Code, Section 641 and 2114 - Theft of Government Property

Makes it illegal to steal or embezzle any government property or to commit robbery of government property.

Prosecutive guidelines are established by the United States Attorney in each federal judicial district.

What to do when an art theft has been discovered:
Protect the scene of the crime and do not let staff or visitors into the area to disturb evidence.
Notify your local police department immediately.
Determine the last time the objects were seen and what happened in the area, or to the objects, since that time.
Gather documents, descriptions and images of the missing objects and provide to the police.
Follow-up on police actions and investigations to ensure that everything possible is being done.

National Stolen Art File
Federal Bureau of Investigation
MT/TCU, Room 5096
935 Pennsylvania Avenue, N.W.
Washington, D.C. 20535
(202)324-4192
Fax (202)324-1504

Information regarding the Art Theft Program can also be accessed on the Internet at www.fbi.gov

APPENDIX 5-E

ICOM Code of Professional Ethics

ICOM Code of Professional Ethics

I. Preamble

The ICOM *Code of Professional Ethics* was adopted unanimously by the 15th General Assembly of ICOM meeting in Buenos Aires, Argentina on 4 November 1986.

It provides a general statement of professional ethics, respect for which is regarded as a minimum requirement to practise as a member of the museum profession. In many cases it will be possible to develop and strengthen the Code to meet particular national or specialized requirements and ICOM wishes to encourage this. A copy of such developments of the Code should be sent to the Secretary General of ICOM, Maison de l'UNESCO, 1 rue Miollis, 75732 Paris Cedex 15, France.

For the purposes of Articles 2 para. 2, 9 para. 1(d), 14 para. 17(b), 15 para. 7(c), 17 para. 12(e) and 18 para. 7(d) of the ICOM *Statutes*, this Code is deemed to be the statement of professional ethics referred to therein.

1. Definitions

1.1. The International Council of Museums (ICOM)

ICOM is defined in Article 1 para. 1 of its *Statutes* as "the international non-governmental organization of museums and professional museum workers established to advance the interests of museology and other disciplines concerned with museum management and operations."

The objectives of ICOM, as defined in Article 3 para. 1 of its *Statutes*, are:

(a) To encourage and support the establishment, development and professional management of museums of all kinds;

(b) To advance knowledge and understanding of the nature, functions and role of museums in the service of society and of its development;
(c) To organize co-operation and mutual assistance between museums and between professional museum workers in the different countries;
(d) To represent, support and advance the interests of professional museum workers of all kinds;
(e) To advance and disseminate knowledge in museology and other disciplines concerned with museum management and operations.

1.2. Museum

A museum is defined in Article 2 para. 1 of the *Statutes* of the International Council of Museums as:

a non-profit making, permanent institution in the service of society and of its development, and open to the public which acquires, conserves, researches, communicates and exhibits, for purposes of study, education and enjoyment, material evidence of people and their environment.

(a) The above definition of a museum shall be applied without limitation arising from the nature of the governing body, the territorial character, the functional structure or the orientation of the collections of the institution concerned.
(b) In addition to institutions designated as `museums' the following qualify as museums for the purposes of this definition:
(i) natural, archaeological and ethnographic monuments and sites of a museum nature that acquire, conserve and communicate material evidence of people and their environment;
(ii) institutions holding collections of and displaying live specimens of plants and animals, such as botanical and zoological gardens, aquaria and vivaria;
(iii) science centres and planetaria;
(iv) conservation institutes and exhibition galleries permanently maintained by libraries and archive centres;
(v) nature reserves;
(vi) international or national or regional or local museum organizations, ministries or departments or public agencies responsible for museums as per the definition given under this article;
(vii) non-profit institutions or organizations undertaking research, education, training, documentation and other activities relating to museums and museology;
(viii) such other institutions as the Executive Council, after seeking the advice of the Advisory Committee, considers as having some or all of the characteristics of a museum, or as supporting museums and professional museum workers through museological research, education or training.

1.3. The Museum Profession

ICOM defines the members of the museum profession, under Article 2, para. 2 of its *Statutes*, as follows:

Professional museum workers include all the personnel of museums or institutions qualifying as museums in accordance with the definition in Article 2 para. 1 (as detailed under para. 1.2 above), having received specialized training, or possessing an equivalent practical experience, in any field relevant to the management and operations of a museum, and independent persons respecting the ICOM *Code of Professional Ethics* and working for museums as defined above, either in a professional or advisory capacity, but not promoting or dealing with any commercial products and equipment required for museums and services.

1.4. Governing Body

The government and control of museums in terms of policy, finance and administration etc., varies greatly from one country to another, and often from one museum to another within a country according to the legal and other national or local provisions of the particular country or institution.

In the case of many national museums, the Director, Curator or other professional head of the museum may be appointed by, and directly responsible to, a Minister or a Government Department, whilst most local government museums are similarly governed and controlled by the appropriate local authority. In many other cases the government and control of the museum is vested in some form of independent body, such as a board of trustees, a society, a non-profit company, or even an individual.

For the purposes of this Code the term "Governing Body" has been used throughout to signify the superior authority concerned with the policy, finance and administration of the museum. This may be an individual Minister or official, a Ministry, a local authority, a Board of Trustees, a Society, the Director of the museum or any other individual or body. Directors, Curators or other professional heads of the museum are responsible for the proper care and management of the museum.

II. Institutional Ethics

2. Basic Principles for Museum Governance

2.1. Minimum Standards for Museums

The governing body or other controlling authority of a museum has an ethical duty to maintain, and if possible enhance, all aspects of the museum, its collections and its services. Above all, it is the responsibility of each governing body to ensure that all of the collections in their care are adequately housed, conserved and documented.

The minimum standards in terms of finance, premises, staffing and services will vary according to the size and responsibilities of each museum. In some countries such minimum standards may be defined by law or other government regulation, and, in others, guidance on and assessment of minimum standards is available in the form of "Museum Accreditation" or similar schemes. Where such guidance is not available locally, it can usually be obtained from appropriate national and international organizations and experts, either directly or through the National Committee or appropriate International Committee of ICOM.

2.2. Constitution

Each museum should have a written constitution or other document setting out clearly its legal status and permanent, non-profit nature, drawn up in accordance with appropriate national laws in relation to museums, the cultural heritage, and non-profit institutions. The governing body or other controlling authority of a museum should prepare and publicize a clear statement of the aims, objectives and policies of the museum, and of the role and composition of the governing body itself.

2.3. Finance

The governing body holds the ultimate financial responsibility for the museum and for the protecting and nurturing of its various assets: the collections and related documentation, the premises, facilities and equipment, the financial assets, and the staff. It is obliged to develop and define the purposes and related policies of the institution, and to ensure that all of the museum's assets are properly and effectively used for museum purposes. Sufficient funds must be available on a regular basis, either from public or private sources, to enable the governing body to carry out and develop the work of the museum. Proper accounting procedures must be adopted and maintained in accordance with the relevant national laws and professional accountancy standards.

2.4. Premises

The board has especially strong obligations to provide accommodation giving a suitable environment for the physical security and preservation of the collections. Premises must be adequate for the museum to fulfil within its stated policy its basic functions of collection, research, storage, conservation, education and display, including staff accommodation, and should comply with all appropriate national legislation in relation to public and staff safety. Proper standards of protection should be provided against such hazards as theft, fire, flood, vandalism and deterioration, throughout the year, day and night. The special needs of disabled people should be provided for, as far as practicable, in planning and managing both buildings and facilities.

2.5. Personnel

The governing body has a special obligation to ensure that the museum has staff sufficient in both number and kind to ensure that the museum is able to meet its responsibilities. The size of the staff, and its nature (whether paid or unpaid, permanent or temporary), will depend on the size of the museum, its collections and its responsibilities. However, proper arrangements should be made for the museum to meet its obligations in relation to the care of the collections, public access and services, research, and security.

The governing body has particularly important obligations in relation to the appointment of the director of the museum, and whenever the possibility of terminating the employment of the director arises, to ensure that any such action is taken only in accordance with appropriate procedures under the legal or other constitutional arrangements and policies of the museum, and that any such staff changes are made in a professional and ethical manner, and in accordance with what is judged to be the best interests of the museum, rather than any personal or external factor or prejudice. It should also ensure that the same principles are applied in relation to any appointment, promotion, dismissal or demotion of the personnel of the museum by the director or any other senior member of staff with staffing responsibilities.

The governing body should recognize the diverse nature of the museum profession, and the wide range of specializations that it now encompasses, including conservator/restorers, scientists, museum education service personnel, registrars and computer specialists, security service managers, etc. It should ensure that the museum both makes appropriate use of such specialists where required and that such specialized personnel are properly recognized as full members of the professional staff in all respects.

Members of the museum profession require appropriate academic, technical and professional training in order to fulfil their important role in relation to the operation of the museum and the care for the heritage, and the governing body should recognize the need for, and value of, a properly qualified and trained staff, and offer adequate opportunities for further training and re-training in order to maintain an adequate and effective workforce.

A governing body should never require a member of the museum staff to act in a way that could reasonably be judged to conflict with the provisions of this Code of Ethics, or any national law or national code of professional ethics.

The Director or other chief professional officer of a museum should be directly responsible to, and have direct access to, the governing body in which trusteeship of the collections is vested.

2.6. Educational and Community Role of the Museum

By definition, a museum is an institution in the service of society and of its development, and is generally open to the public (even though this may be a restricted public in the case of certain very specialized museums, such as certain academic or medical museums, for example).

The museum should take every opportunity to develop its role as an educational resource used by all sections of the population or specialized group that the museum is intended to serve. Where appropriate in relation to the museum's programme and responsibilities, specialist staff with training and skills in museum education are likely to be required for this purpose.

The museum has an important duty to attract new and wider audiences within all levels of the community, locality or group that the museum aims to serve, and should offer both the general community and specific individuals and groups within its opportunities to become actively involved in the museum and to support its aims and policies.

2.7. Public Access

The general public (or specialized group served, in the case of museums with a limited public role), should have access to the displays during reasonable hours and for regular periods. The museum should also offer the public reasonable access to members of staff by appointment or other arrangement, and full access to information about the collections, subject to any necessary restrictions for reasons of confidentiality or security as discussed in para. 7.3 below.

2.8. Displays, Exhibitions and Special Activities

Subject to the primary duty of the museum to preserve unimpaired for the future the significant material that comprises the museum collections, it is the responsibility of the museum to use the collections for the creation and dissemination of new knowledge, through research, educational work, permanent displays, temporary exhibitions and other special activities. These should be in accordance with the stated policy and educational purpose of the museum, and should not compromise either the quality or the proper care of the collections. The museum should seek to ensure that information in displays and exhibitions is honest and objective and does not perpetuate myths or stereotypes.

2.9. Commercial Support and Sponsorship

Where it is the policy of the museum to seek and accept financial or other support from commercial or industrial organizations, or from other outside sources, great care is needed to define clearly the agreed relationship between the museum and the sponsor. Commercial support and sponsorship may involve ethical problems and the museum must ensure that the standards and objectives of the museum are not compromised by such a relationship.

2.10. Museum Shops and Commercial Activities

Museum shops and any other commercial activities of the museum, and any publicity relating to these, should be in accordance with a clear policy, should be relevant to the collections and the basic educational purpose of the museum, and must not compromise the quality of those collections. In the case of the manufacture and sale of replicas, reproductions or other commercial items adapted from an object in a museum's collection, all aspects of the commercial venture must be carried out in a manner that will not discredit either the integrity of the museum or the intrinsic value of the original object. Great care must be taken to identify permanently such objects for what they are, and to ensure accuracy and high quality in their manufacture. All items offered for sale should represent good value for money and should comply with all relevant national legislation.

2.11. Legal Obligation

It is an important responsibility of each governing body to ensure that the museum complies fully with all legal obligations, whether in relation to national, regional or local law, international law or treaty obligations, and to any legally binding trusts or conditions relating to any aspect of the museum collections or facilities.

3. Acquisitions to Museum Collections

3.1. Collecting Policies

Each museum authority should adopt and publish a written statement of its collecting policy. This policy should be reviewed from time to time, and at least once every five years. Objects acquired should be relevant to the purpose and activities of the museum, and be accompanied by evidence of a valid legal title. Any conditions or limitations relating to an acquisition should be clearly described in an instrument of conveyance or other written documentation. Museums should not, except in very exceptional circumstances, acquire material that the museum is unlikely to be able to catalogue, conserve, store or exhibit, as appropriate, in a proper manner. Acquisitions outside the current stated policy of the museum should only be made in very exceptional circumstances, and then only after proper consideration by the governing body of the museum itself, having regard to the interests of the objects under consideration, the national or other cultural heritage and the special interests of other museums.

3.2. Acquisition of Illicit Material

The illicit trade in objects destined for public and private collections encourages the destruction of historic sites, local ethnic cultures, theft at both national and international levels, places at risk endangered species of flora and fauna, and contravenes the spirit of national and international patrimony. Museums should recognize the relationship between the market place and the initial and often destructive taking of an object for the commercial market, and must recognize that it is highly unethical for a museum to support in any way, whether directly or indirectly, that illicit market.

A museum should not acquire, whether by purchase, gift, bequest or exchange, any object unless the governing body and responsible officer are satisfied that the museum can acquire a valid title to the specimen or object in question and that in particular it has not been acquired in, or exported from, its country of origin and/or any intermediate country in which it may have been legally owned (including the museum's own country), in violation of that country's laws.

So far as biological and geological material is concerned, a museum should not acquire by any direct or indirect means any specimen that has been collected, sold or otherwise transferred in contravention of any national or international wildlife protection or natural history conservation law or treaty of the museum's own country or any other country except with the express consent of an appropriate outside legal or governmental authority.

So far as excavated material is concerned, in addition to the safeguards set out above, the museum should not acquire by purchase objects in any case where the governing body or responsible officer has reasonable cause to believe that their recovery involved the recent unscientific or intentional destruction or damage of ancient monuments or archaeological sites, or involved a failure to disclose the finds to the owner or occupier of the land, or to the proper legal or governmental authorities.

If appropriate and feasible, the same tests as are outlined in the above four paragraphs should be applied in determining whether or not to accept loans for exhibition or other purposes.

3.3. Field Study and Collecting

Museums should assume a position of leadership in the effort to halt the continuing degradation of the world's natural history, archaeological, ethnographic, historic and artistic resources. Each museum should develop policies that allow it to conduct its activities within appropriate national and international laws and treaty obligations, and with a reasonable certainty that its approach is consistent with the spirit and intent of both national and international efforts to protect and enhance the cultural heritage.

Field exploration, collecting and excavation by museum workers present ethical problems that are both complex and critical. All planning for field studies and field collecting must be preceded by investigation, disclosure and consultation with both the proper authorities and any interested museums or academic institutions in the country or area of the proposed study sufficient to ascertain if the proposed activity is both legal and justifiable on academic and scientific grounds. Any field programme must be executed in such a way that all participants act legally and responsibly in acquiring specimens and data, and that they discourage by all practical means unethical, illegal and destructive practices.

3.4. Co-operation between Museums in Collecting Policies

Each museum should recognize the need for co-operation and consultation between all museums with similar or overlapping interests and collecting policies, and should seek to consult with such other institutions both on specific acquisitions where a conflict of interest is thought possible and, more generally, on defining areas of specialization. Museums should respect the boundaries of the recognized collecting areas of other museums and should avoid acquiring material with special local connections or of special local interest from the collecting area of another museum without due notification of intent.

3.5. Conditional Acquisitions and other Special Factors

Gifts, bequests and loans should only be accepted if they conform to the stated collecting and exhibition policies of the museum. Offers that are subject to special conditions may have to be rejected if the conditions proposed are judged to be contrary to the long-term interests of the museum and its public.

3.6. Loans to Museums

Both individual loans of objects and the mounting or borrowing of loan exhibitions can have an important role in enhancing the interest and quality of a museum and its services. However, the ethical principles outlined in paras. 3.1 to 3.5 above must apply to the consideration of proposed loans and loan exhibitions as to the acceptance or rejection of items offered to the permanent collections: loans should not be accepted nor exhibitions mounted if they do not have a valid educational, scientific or academic purpose.

3.7. Conflicts of Interest

The collecting policy or regulations of the museum should include provisions to ensure that no person involved in the policy or management of the museum, such as a trustee or other member of a governing body, or a member of the museum staff, may compete with the museum for objects or may take advantage of privileged information received because of his or her position, and that should a conflict of interest develop between the needs of the individual and the museum, those of the museum will prevail. Special care is also required in considering any offer of an item either for sale or as a tax-benefit gift, from members of governing bodies, members of staff, or the families or close associates of these.

4. Disposal of Collections

4.1. General Presumption of Permanence of Collections

By definition, one of the key functions of almost every kind of museum is to acquire objects and keep them for posterity. Consequently, there must always be a strong presumption against the disposal of specimens to which a museum has assumed formal title. Any form of disposal, whether by donation, exchange, sale or destruction requires the exercise of a high order of curatorial judgement and should be approved by the governing body only after full expert and legal advice has been taken.

Special considerations may apply in the case of certain kinds of specialized institutions such as "living" or "working" museums, and some teaching and other educational museums, together with museums and other institutions displaying living specimens, such as botanical and zoological gardens and aquaria, which may find it necessary to regard at least part of their collections as "fungible" (i.e. replaceable and renewable). However, even here there is a clear ethical obligation to ensure that the activities of the institution are not detrimental to the long-term survival of examples of the material studied, displayed or used.

4.2. Legal or other Powers of Disposal

The laws relating to the protection and permanence of museum collections, and to the power of museums to dispose of items from their collection vary greatly from country to country, and often from one museum to another within the same country. In some cases no disposals of any kind are permitted, except in the case of items that have been seriously damaged by natural or accidental deterioration. Elsewhere, there may be no explicit restriction on disposals under general law.

Where the museum has legal powers permitting disposals, or has acquired objects subject to conditions of disposal, the legal or other requirements and procedures must be fully complied with. Even where legal powers of disposal exist, a museum may not be completely free to dispose of items acquired: where financial assistance has been obtained from an outside source (e.g. public or private grants, donations from a Friends of the Museum organization, or private benefactor), disposal would normally require the consent of all parties who had contributed to the original purchase.

Where the original acquisition was subject to mandatory restrictions these must be observed unless it can be clearly shown that adherence to such restrictions is impossible or substantially detrimental to the institution. Even in these circumstances the museum can only be relieved from such restrictions through appropriate legal procedures.

4.3. De-accessioning Policies and Procedures

Where a museum has the necessary legal powers to dispose of an object the decision to sell or otherwise dispose of material from the collections should only be taken after due consideration, and such material should be offered first, by exchange, gift or private treaty sale, to other museums before sale by public auction or other means is considered. A decision to dispose of a specimen or work of art, whether by exchange, sale or destruction (in the case of an item too badly damaged or deteriorated to be restorable) should be the responsibility of the governing body of the museum, not of the curator of the collection concerned acting alone. Full records should be kept of all such decisions and the objects involved, and proper arrangements made for the preservation and/or transfer, as appropriate, of the documentation relating to the object concerned, including photographic records where practicable.

Neither members of staff, nor members of the governing bodies, or members of their families or close associates, should ever be permitted to purchase objects that have been de-accessioned from a collection. Similarly, no such person should be permitted to appropriate in any way items from the museum collections, even temporarily, to any personal collection or for any kind of personal use.

4.4. Return and Restitution of Cultural Property

If a museum should come into possession of an object that can be demonstrated to have been exported or otherwise transferred in violation of the principles of the UNESCO Convention on the Means of Prohibiting and Preventing the Illicit Import, Export and Transfer of Ownership of Cultural Property (1970) and the country of origin seeks its return and demonstrates that it is part of the country's cultural heritage, the museum should, if legally free to do so, take responsible steps to co-operate in the return of the object to the country of origin.

In the case of requests for the return of cultural property to the country of origin, museums should be prepared to initiate dialogues with an open-minded attitude on the basis of scientific and professional principles (in preference to action at a governmental or political level). The possibility of developing bilateral or multilateral co-operation schemes to assist museums in countries which are considered to have lost a significant part of their cultural heritage in the development of adequate museums and museum resources should be explored.

Museums should also respect fully the terms of the Convention for the Protection of Cultural Property in the Event of Armed Conflict (The Hague Convention, 1954) and in support of this Convention, should in particular abstain from purchasing or otherwise appropriating or acquiring cultural objects from any occupied country, as these will in most cases have been illegally exported or illicitly removed.

4.5. Income from Disposal of Collections

Any moneys received by a governing body from the disposal of specimens or works of art should be applied solely for the purchase of additions to the museum collections.

III. Professional Conduct

5. General Principles

5.1. Ethical Obligations of Members of the Museum Profession

Employment by a museum, whether publicly or privately supported, is a public trust involving great responsibility. In all activities, museum employees must act with integrity and in accordance with the most stringent ethical principles as well as the highest standards of objectivity.

An essential element of membership of a profession is the implication of both rights and obligations. Although the conduct of a professional in any area is ordinarily regulated by the basic rules of moral behaviour which govern human relationships, every occupation involves standards, as well as particular duties, responsibilities and opportunities that from time to time create the need for a statement of guiding principles. The museum professional should understand two guiding principles: first, that museums are the object of a public trust whose value to the community is in direct proportion to the quality of service rendered; and, secondly, that intellectual ability and professional knowledge are not, in themselves, sufficient, but must be inspired by a high standard of ethical conduct.

The Director and other professional staff owe their primary professional and academic allegiance to their museum and should at all times act in accordance with the approved policies of the museum. The Director or other principal museum officer should be aware of, and bring to the notice of the governing body of the museum whenever appropriate, the terms of the ICOM *Code of Professional Ethics* and of any relevant national or regional codes or policy statements on museum ethics, and should urge the governing body to comply with these. Members of the museum profession should also comply fully with the ICOM Code and any other codes or statements on museum ethics whenever exercising the functions of the governing body under delegated powers.

5.2. Personal conduct

Loyalty to colleagues and to the employing museum is an important professional responsibility, but the ultimate loyalty must be to fundamental ethical principles and to the profession as a whole.

Applicants for any professional post should divulge frankly and in confidence all information relevant to the consideration of their applications, and if appointed should recognize that museum work is normally regarded as a full-time vocation. Even when the terms of employment do not prohibit outside employment or business interests, the Director and other senior staff should not undertake other paid employment or accept outside commissions without the express consent of the governing body of the museum. In tendering resignations from their posts, members of the professional staff, and above all the Director, should consider carefully the needs of the museum at the time. A professional person, having recently accepted a new appointment, should consider seriously his/her professional commitment to his/her present post before applying for a new post elsewhere.

5.3. Private Interests

While every member of any profession is entitled to a measure of personal independence, consistent with professional and staff responsibilities, in the eyes of the public no private business or professional interest of a member of the museum profession can be wholly separated from that of the professional's institution or other official affiliation, despite disclaimers that may be offered. Any museum-related activity by the individual may reflect on the institution or be attributed to it. The professional must be concerned not only with the true personal motivations and interests, but also with the way in which such actions might be construed by the outside observer. Museum employees and others in a close relationship with them must not accept gifts, favours, loans or other dispensations or things of value that may be offered to them in connection with their duties for the museum (see also para. 8.4 below).-

6. Personal Responsibility to the Collections

6.1. Acquisitions to Museum Collections

The Director and professional staff should take all possible steps to ensure that a written collecting policy is adopted by the governing body of the museum, and thereafter reviewed and revised as appropriate at regular intervals. This policy, as formally adopted and revised by the governing body, should form the basis of all professional decisions and recommendations in relation to acquisitions.

Negotiations concerning the acquisition of museum items from members of the general public must be conducted with scrupulous fairness to the seller or donor. No object should be deliberately or misleadingly identified or valued, to the benefit of the museum and to the detriment of the donor, owner or previous owners, in order to acquire it for the museum collections, nor should be taken nor retained on loan with the deliberate intention of improperly procuring it for the collections.

6.2. Care of Collections

It is an important professional responsibility to ensure that all items accepted temporarily or permanently by the museum are properly and fully documented to facilitate provenance, identification, condition and treatment. All objects accepted by the museum should be properly conserved, protected, and maintained.

Careful attention should be paid to the means of ensuring the best possible security as a protection against theft in display, working or storage areas, against accidental damage when handling objects, and against damage or theft in transit. Where it is the national or local policy to use commercial insurance arrangements, the staff should ensure that the insurance cover is adequate, especially for objects in transit and loan items, or other objects, which are not owned by the museum but which are its current responsibility.

Members of the museum profession should not delegate important curatorial, conservation, or other professional responsibilities to persons who lack the appropriate knowledge and skill, or who are inadequately supervised, in the case of trainees or approved volunteers, where such persons are allowed to assist in the care of the collections. There is also a clear duty to consult professional colleagues within or outside the museum if at any time the expertise available in a particular museum or department is insufficient to ensure the welfare of items in the collections under its care.

6.3. Conservation and Restoration of Collections

One of the essential ethical obligations of each member of the museum profession is to ensure the proper care and conservation of both existing and newly-acquired collections and individual items for which the member of the profession and the employing institutions are responsible, and to ensure that as far as is reasonable the collections are passed on to future generations in as good and safe a condition as practicable having regard to current knowledge and resources.

In attempting to achieve this high ideal, special attention should be paid to the growing body of knowledge about preventative conservation methods and techniques, including the provision of suitable environmental protection against the known natural or artificial causes of deterioration of museum specimens and works of art.

There are often difficult decisions to be made in relation to the degree of replacement or restoration of lost or damaged parts of a specimen or work of art that may be ethically acceptable in particular circumstances. Such decisions call for proper co-operation between all with a specialized responsibility for the object, including both the curator and the conservator or restorer, and should not be decided unilaterally by one or the other acting alone.

The ethical issues involved in conservation and restoration work of many kinds are a major study in themselves, and those with special responsibilities in this area, whether as director, curator, conservator or restorer, have an important responsibility to ensure that they are familiar with these ethical issues, and with appropriate professional opinion, as expressed in some detailed ethical statements and codes produced by the conservator/restorer professional bodies.

6.4. Documentation of Collections

The proper recording and documentation of both new acquisitions and existing collections in accordance with appropriate standards and the internal rules and conventions of the museum is a most important professional responsibility. It is particularly important that such documentation should include details of the source of each object and the conditions of acceptance of it by the museum. In addition, specimen data should be kept in a secure environment and be supported by adequate systems providing easy retrieval of the data by both the staff and by other bona fide users.

6.5. De-accessioning and Disposals from the Collections

No item from the collections of a museum should be disposed of except in accordance with the ethical principles summarized in the Institutional Ethics section of this Code, paras. 4.1 to 4.4 above, and the detailed rules and procedures applying in the museum in question.

6.6. Welfare of Live Animals

Where museums and related institutions maintain for exhibition or research purposes live populations of animals, the health and well-being of any such creatures must be a foremost ethical consideration. It is essential that a veterinary surgeon be available for advice and for regular inspection of the animals and their living conditions. The museum should prepare a safety code for the protection of staff and visitors which has been approved by an expert in the veterinary field, and all staff must follow it in detail.

6.7. Human Remains and Material of Ritual Significance

Where a museum maintains and/or is developing collections of human remains and sacred objects, these should be securely housed and carefully maintained as archival collections in scholarly institutions, and should always be available to qualified researchers and educators, but not to the morbidly curious. Research on such objects and their housing and care must be accomplished in a manner acceptable not only to fellow professionals but also to those of various beliefs, including particular members of the community, ethnic or religious groups concerned. Although it is occasionally necessary to use human remains and other sensitive material in interpretative exhibits, this must be done with tact and with respect for the feelings for human dignity held by all peoples.

6.8. Private Collections

The acquiring, collecting and owning of objects of a kind collected by a museum by a member of the museum profession for a personal collection may not in itself be unethical, and may be regarded as a valuable way of enhancing professional knowledge and judgement. However, serious dangers are implicit when members of the profession collect for themselves privately objects similar to those which they and others collect for their museums. In particular, no member of the museum profession should compete with their institution either in the acquisition of objects or in any personal collecting activity. Extreme care must be taken to ensure that no conflict of interest arises.

In some countries and many individual museums, members of the museum profession are not permitted to have private collections of any kind, and such rules must be respected. Even where there are no such restrictions, on appointment, a member of the museum profession with a private collection should provide the governing body with a description of it, and a statement of the collecting policy being pursued, and any consequent agreement between the curator and the governing body concerning the private collection must be scrupulously kept. (See also para. 8.4 below).

7. Personal Responsibility to the Public

7.1. Upholding Professional Standards

In the interests of the public as well as the profession, members of the museum profession should observe accepted standards and laws, uphold the dignity and honour of their profession and accept its self-imposed disciplines. They should do their part to safeguard the public against illegal or unethical professional conduct, and should use appropriate opportunities to inform and educate the public in the aims, purposes and aspirations of the profession in order to develop a better public understanding of the purposes and responsibilities of museums and of the profession.

7.2. Relations with the General Public

Members of the museum profession should deal with the public efficiently and courteously at all times, and should in particular deal promptly with all correspondence and enquiries. Subject to the requirements of confidentiality in a particular case, they should share their expertise in all professional fields in dealing with enquiries, subject to due acknowledgement, from both the general public and specialist enquirers, allowing bona fide researchers properly controlled but, so far as possible, full access to any material or documentation in their care, even when this is the subject of personal research or special field of interest.

7.3. Confidentiality

Members of the museum profession must protect all confidential information relating to the source of material owned by or loaned to the museum, as well as information concerning the security arrangements of the museum, or the security arrangement of private collections or any place visited in the course of official duties. Confidentiality must also be respected in relation to any item brought to the museum for identification and, without specific authority from the owner, information on such an item should not be passed to another museum, to a dealer, or to any other person (subject to any legal obligation to assist the police or other proper authorities in investigating possible stolen or illicitly acquired or transferred property).

There is a special responsibility to respect the personal confidences contained in oral history or other personal material. Investigators using recording devices such as cameras or tape recorders or the technique of oral interviewing should take special care to protect their data, and persons investigated, photographed or interviewed should have the right to remain anonymous if they so choose. This right should be respected where it has been specifically promised. Where there is no clear understanding to the contrary, the primary responsibility of the investigator is to ensure that no information is revealed that might harm the informant or his or her community. Subjects under study should understand the capacities of cameras, tape recorders and other machines used, and should be free to accept or reject their use.

8. Personal Responsibility to Colleagues and the Profession

8.1. Professional Relationships

Relationships between members of the museum profession should always be courteous, both in public and in private. Differences of opinion should not be expressed in a personalized fashion. Notwithstanding this general rule, members of the profession may properly object to proposals or practices which may have a damaging effect on a museum or museums, or the profession.

8.2. Professional Co-operation

Members of the museum profession have an obligation, subject to due acknowledgement, to share their knowledge and experience with their colleagues and with scholars and students in relevant fields. They should show their appreciation and respect to those from whom they have learned and should present without thought of personal gain such advancements in techniques and experience which may be of benefit to others.

The training of personnel in the specialized activities involved in museum work is of great importance in the development of the profession and all should accept responsibility, where appropriate, in the training of colleagues. Members of the profession who in their official appointment have under their direction junior staff, trainees, students and assistants undertaking formal or informal professional training, should give these the benefit of their experience and knowledge, and should also treat them with the consideration and respect customary among members of the profession.

Members of the profession form working relationships in the course of their duties with numerous other people, both professional and otherwise, within and outside the museum in which they are employed. They are expected to conduct these relationships with courtesy and fair- mindedness and to render their professional services to others efficiently and at a high standard.

8.3. Dealing

No member of the museum profession should participate in any dealing (buying or selling for profit), in objects similar or related to the objects collected by the employing museum. Dealing by museum employees at any level of responsibility in objects that are collected by any other museum can also present serious problems even if there is no risk of direct conflict with the employing museum, and should be permitted only if, after full disclosure and review by the governing body of the employing museum or designated senior officer, explicit permission is granted, with or without conditions.

Article 7 para. 5 of the ICOM Statutes provides that membership of ICOM shall not be available, under any circumstances, to any person or institution that is dealing (buying or selling for profit) in cultural property.

4. Other Potential Conflicts of Interest

Generally, members of the museum profession should refrain from all acts or activities which may be construed as a conflict of interest. Museum professionals by virtue of their knowledge, experience, and contacts are frequently offered opportunities, such as advisory and consultancy services, teaching, writing and broadcasting opportunities, or requests for valuations, in a personal capacity. Even where the national law and the individual's conditions of employment permit such activities, these may appear in the eyes of colleagues, the employing authority, or the general public, to create a conflict of interest. In such situations, all legal and employment contract conditions must be scrupulously followed, and in the event of any potential conflict arising or being suggested, the matter should be reported immediately to an appropriate superior officer or the museum governing body, and steps must be taken to eliminate the potential conflict of interest.

Even where the conditions of employment permit any kind of outside activity, and there appears to be no risk of any conflict of interest, great care should be taken to ensure that such outside interests do not interfere in any way with the proper discharge of official duties and responsibilities.

8.5. Authentication, Valuation and Illicit Material

Members of the museum profession are encouraged to share their professional knowledge and expertise with both professional colleagues and the general public (see para. 7.2 above).

However, written certificates of authenticity or valuation (appraisals) should not be given, and opinions on the monetary value of objects should only be given on official request from other museums or competent legal, governmental or other responsible public authorities.

Members of the museum profession should not identify or otherwise authenticate objects where they have reason to believe or suspect that these have been illegally or illicitly acquired, transferred, imported or exported.

They should recognize that it is highly unethical for museums or the museum profession to support either directly or indirectly the illicit trade in cultural or natural objects (see para. 3.2 above), and under no circumstances should they act in a way that could be regarded as benefiting such illicit trade in any way, directly or indirectly. Where there is reason to believe or suspect illicit or illegal transfer, import or export, the competent authorities should be notified.

8.6. Unprofessional Conduct

Every member of the museum profession should be conversant with both any national or local laws, and any conditions of employment, concerning corrupt practices, and should at all times avoid situations which could rightly or wrongly be construed as corrupt or improper conduct of any kind. In particular no museum official should accept any gift, hospitality, or any form of reward from any dealer, auctioneer or other person as an improper inducement in respect of the purchase or disposal of museum items.

Also, in order to avoid any suspicion of corruption, a museum professional should not recommend any particular dealer, auctioneer or other person to a member of the public, nor should the official accept any "special price" or discount for personal purchases from any dealer with whom either the professional or employing museum has a professional relationship.

'The Conservator-Restorer: A Definition of the Profession'. *ICOM News*, Vol. 39, No. 1, 1986, pp. 5-6.

APPENDIX 5-F

Holocaust Claims Processing Office—Art Claim Information and Form

New York State Banking Department

HOLOCAUST CLAIMS PROCESSING OFFICE
Art Claim Information

On June 25, 1997 Governor George E. Pataki authorized the creation of the Holocaust Claims Processing Office of the New York State Banking Department. As part of its function, this office will assist individuals of all backgrounds seeking to recover art that was lost, looted or stolen prior to and during World War II.

The Holocaust Claims Processing Office will accept claims and provide assistance in the preparation of the claim form. Information provided on the claim form will be entered into a computer database and compared with provenance data, insurance company and museum records, Nazi confiscation lists, auction catalogues, and other resources in an effort to locate stolen art and aid in its recovery. Whenever possible and appropriate, we will forward information about missing items to other organizations that can be helpful in the recovery of stolen art. The Office will maintain contact with these bodies on a regular basis regarding the status of the claims and all search efforts. Similarly, claimants will be kept informed about these efforts.

It is important to note that the submission of a claim does not in any way guarantee the return of any art object. We believe, however, that through the talent and expertise of our staff, under the auspices of the New York State Banking Department, the burdens and costs encountered by claimants proceeding on their own will be alleviated.

In filling out a claim form, it is important to provide as much information as possible along with any documentation that may exist. If photographs of objects are available, please submit copies of these with the claim form. We understand that documentation may not be available in many cases. Although the claim form seeks detailed information, incomplete information is perfectly acceptable.

Individuals who need additional information or require assistance in the preparation of a claim form can contact the Holocaust Claims Processing Office. You do not need to retain the services of an attorney or other representative. **We will provide any and all assistance you may need free of charge.**

For the purposes of filing a claim, the individual filling out a claim form is referred to as the "claimant." This is the individual who claims to have ownership rights to the work of art that was stolen. Where the person submitting the claim is a representative of the claimant, such person must also submit the appropriate authorization or power of attorney. This documentation must be notarized by the person on whose behalf the representative is acting.

Download Claim Form

Contact Information:

Address:
State of New York Banking Department
Holocaust Claims Processing Office
2 Rector Street
New York, NY 10006

Telephone:
(800) 695-3318 (in the U.S.)
(212) 618-6983 (outside the U.S.)
(212) 618-6908 (fax)

E-mail Address:
claimsques@banking.state.ny.us

Internet Address:
http://www.claims.state.ny.us

Last Updated July 08, 1998

ART CLAIM FORM

1. Claimant Information

This section seeks biographical information about the claimant. This is the individual who claims to have ownership rights to the work of art that was stolen.

Last name ______________________________

First name ______________ Middle name ______________

Maiden name (where applicable) ______________________

Current address ______________________________

City ______________ State _____ Zip Code _______ Country ________

Telephone numbers:

Home ______________ Work ______________

Fax ______________

E-mail address ______________________________

Date of birth ______________

Place of birth (town, village, country) ______________________

Nationality (include all previous nationalities) ______________

Previous places of residence up to and including May 1945 (if outside the U.S.)

____

____

Father's full name ______________________________

Mother's full name ______________________________

Mother's maiden name ______________________________

Page 1 of 7

Revised 5/26/98

2. Claimant Representative Information (where applicable)

Where the person submitting the claim is a representative of the claimant and not someone entitled to inherit, this section must be filled out. Written and notarized authorization or a power of attorney from the claimant providing authorization to the named representative must also be furnished. All information regarding the claimant (the individual who has granted the power of attorney or other authorization) must still be provided in Section 1 of this form.

Representative's last name ______________________________

Representative's first name ______________________________

Representative's middle name ______________________________

Representative's relationship, if any, to claimant ____________________

____

Do you have documentation confirming this relationship? [ ] Yes [ ] No

If so, what is it? (please include a **copy** with this form) ________________

Representative's law firm, company, or other organization name (where applicable) ______________________________________

____

Representative's address ______________________________

City ____________________ State ________ Zip Code __________

Country ______________

Representative's telephone numbers:

Home ____________ Work ______________ Fax ____________

Representative's e-mail address ______________________________

Additional information ______________________________________

____

____

Revised 5/26/98

3. List of Objects

Please list the objects on which you are making a claim. Please include as much information as possible. **Photographs are of foremost importance**, but if you cannot provide them, please include a written description or sketch.

TYPE

Title/Titles ______________________________

____

Artist/Attributed to ______________________________

Country of origin______________ Period ______________

Date of execution ______________ Medium ______________

Dimensions: Height _____ Width _____ Depth _____ Framed? [ ] Yes [ ] No

DISTINCTIVE MARKINGS

Signature ______________________________

Date ______________ Edition number ______________

Inscriptions ______________________________

Condition ______________________________

Other identifying marks ______________________________

____

Description ______________________________

____

____

Last known location of the object ______________________________

Describe the time, place, and circumstances of seizure ______________

____

____

____

Leads as to where the object might presently be located ______________

____

INSURANCE INFORMATION

Was the object insured? [ ] Yes [ ] No

If yes, name insurance company

____

Was the object shipped? [ ] Yes [ ] No

If yes, was it insured? [ ] Yes [ ] No

If yes, name insurance company

____

Revised 5/26/98

List of Objects (Continued)

TYPE

Title/Titles ____

____

Artist/Attributed to ______________________________________

Country of origin__________________ Period ______________________

Date of execution _____________________ Medium __________________

Dimensions: Height _____ Width _____ Depth _____ Framed? [ ] Yes [ ] No

DISTINCTIVE MARKINGS

Signature ____

Date ______________________ Edition number ________________________

Inscriptions ____

Condition ____

Other identifying marks ___________________________________

____

Description ____

____

____

Last known location of the object ___________________________

Describe the time, place, and circumstances of seizure ________________

____

____

____

Leads as to where the object might presently be located ________________

____

INSURANCE INFORMATION

Was the object insured? [ ] Yes [ ] No

If yes, name insurance company

____

Was the object shipped? [ ] Yes [ ] No

If yes, was it insured? [ ] Yes [ ] No

If yes, name insurance company

____

Revised 5/26/98

List of Objects (Continued)

TYPE

Title/Titles ____

____

Artist/Attributed to ____

Country of origin__________________ Period ____________________

Date of execution ____________________ Medium ____________________

Dimensions: Height _____ Width _____ Depth _____ Framed? [ ] Yes [ ] No

DISTINCTIVE MARKINGS

Signature ____

Date ______________________ Edition number ____________________

Inscriptions ____

Condition ____

Other identifying marks ____

____

Description ____

____

____

Last known location of the object ____

Describe the time, place, and circumstances of seizure ____________________

____

____

____

Leads as to where the object might presently be located ____________________

____

INSURANCE INFORMATION

Was the object insured? [ ] Yes [ ] No

If yes, name insurance company

____

Was the object shipped? [ ] Yes [ ] No

If yes, was it insured? [ ] Yes [ ] No

If yes, name insurance company

____

(Please attach additional pages if space is insufficient)

4. Basis for Your Claim

5. Previous Claims or Inquiries Made

If any previous claims or inquiries have been made to any organization or government body, please identify them and include all details. Note: The filing or denial of a claim in the past does not preclude filing with the Holocaust Claims Processing Office. This information is requested only for the purpose of collecting as much information as possible.

6. Other Relevant Information

Use this section to provide any other information which you think may be important to your claim or which may assist in the search efforts.

____

____

____

____

____

____

____

____

I hereby state that the information provided herein is accurate to the best of my knowledge.

________________________ ________________________
Signature Date

Revised 5/26/98

APPENDIX 5-G

Commission for Art Recovery of the World Jewish Congress—Information and Form

Commission for Art Recovery
of the World Jewish Congress

Ronald S. Lauder, Chairman

Organization | Purpose | What We Do | Mediation | Cooperation | Filing a Claim
Claim Form | Contact Us | Links | About Us | Home

Organization

The Commission for Art Recovery is part of the World Jewish Congress, American Section, New York, and is affiliated with the World Jewish Restitution Organization, Jerusalem.

Purpose and Mission

The Commission for Art Recovery is dedicated to reuniting works of art looted by the Nazis before and during World War II with their rightful owners and/or their heirs.
Our mission is to:

- Identify and locate art stolen by the Nazis and their collaborators.
- Register claims for the victims of Nazi art theft.

What We Do

Our researchers comb many resources (including archival documents, books, and museum catalogues) in search of works of art whose provenances contain the names of individuals or institutions known to have bought, sold, or traded in art stolen by the Nazis,names of families whose works were confiscated or works whose provenances exhibit suspicious wartime gaps. Information from insurance records, Nazi confiscation lists, and postwar Allied restitution organizations is also compiled.

Our claims department collects information from the victims of Nazi art looting and their heirs. Our claim form, which may be downloaded from this website, seeks information regarding the person filing the claim (the claimant), the person from whom art was actually stolen (the victim), the art objects themselves, and the circumstances of the theft. Although the claim form seeks detailed information (which might not always be available in full), incomplete information is perfectly acceptable.

In a computer database, the information collected from our claimants is then compared to information gathered by our researchers. The powerful data-processing capabilities of the computer allow it to search through the thousands of works looted by the Nazis quickly and effectively. When a claimed work matches a looted work, information regarding the status and current whereabouts of the work is turned over to the claimant so that he or she may proceed in the pursuit of his or her claim. The Commission will advise claimants; the best way to proceed will depend on many factors and circumstances.

Mediation

At the present time, the Commission for Art Recovery does not provide mediation services in ownership disputes regarding art stolen by the Nazis. In the future, the Commission may take on such a role. The Commission does participate in the ongoing effort to establish appropriate guidelines for the restitution of art looted by the Nazis and to develop solutions to the complex problems of international law, institutional policy and government practice as they bear on these disputes.

Cooperation

The Commission for Art Recovery works in conjunction with other organizations such as the Holocaust Claims Processing Office of the New York State Banking Department,the

Art Loss Register, and the Holocaust Art Restitution Project (HARP). We also work with scholars, museums, and members of the art trade in a cooperative effort to build the largest possible base of claims and losses. The Commission for Art Recovery shares only art object information, not the names of claimants or victims associated with specific works.

Claimants may also indicate that they wish all information provided to remain confidential to the Commission for Art Recovery.

Filing a Claim

Please proceed to the claim form section and follow the instructions to fill out the form. The form should be printed out, completed by the claimant, and sent to us by mail or facsimile.

Contact Us

If you have further questions, or wish to receive a copy of the claim form by mail, please contact us at:

Commission for Art Recovery
767 Fifth Avenue
Suite 4600
New York, NY 10153
tel: 212-521-0102
fax: 212-319-8681
e-mail: car@rslmgmt.com

Commission for Art Recovery
of the World Jewish Congress

in affiliation with
the World Jewish Restitution
Organization

CLAIM FORM
Part I-A Claimant

Commission for Art Recovery

This is a claim form for the Commission for Art Recovery. Information provided on this form will be entered into a computer database and compared with provenance data, insurance company and museum records, Nazi confiscation lists, and other resources in an effort to locate stolen art and aid in its recovery.

Whenever possible and appropriate we will forward information about missing items to other organizations which can be helpful in the recovery of stolen art.

Please print out and fill in all sections of this claim form as thoroughly as possible. Although this form seeks detailed information (which might not always be available in full), incomplete information is perfectly acceptable.

I Case Information

I-A Claimant Information

(confidential to the Commission for Art Recovery)

This section seeks biographical information about the claimant. This is the individual who claims to have ownership rights to the work of art that was stolen. If there is more than one claimant, each individual claimant must complete a copy of this section. (This section may be reproduced as needed.)

OFFICE USE ONLY
Claimant ID # ____________________
Claimant type ____________________
Original ID # ____________________
Entry by ____________________

1. Last name ____________________
2. First name ____________________
3. Middle name ____________________
4. Maiden name (if applicable) ____________________
5. Previous name(s) (include date of name change ____________________
6. Current address ____________________
7. City ____________________
8. State/Province ____________________
9. Zip/Postal code ____________________
10. Country ____________________

Next Page

Back to Home Page

Commission for Art Recovery
of the World Jewish Congress

in affiliation with
the World Jewish Restitution
Organization

CLAIM FORM
Part I-A Claimant

11. Home telephone ______________________

12. Work telephone ______________________

13. Fax number ______________________

14. E-mail address ______________________

Victim(s) Information

15. Victim(s) last name ______________________

16. Victim(s) first name ______________________

17. Victim(s) middle name ______________________

18. Victim(s) date of birth ______________________

Victim(s) Place of Birth ______________________

19. City ______________________

20. State ______________________

21. Country ______________________

22. Nationality (including all previous) ______________________

____

23. Places of residence and/or home addresses from 1937-1945

____

____

____

____

____

24. Additional information about the victim (please attach additional page if necessary)

____

____

____

____

Next Page

Back to Home Page

Commission for Art Recove
of the World Jewish Congress

in affiliation with
the World Jewish Restitution
Organization

CLAIM FORM
Part I-B Rep Info

I-B Representative Information

This section seeks information about the representative of the claimant. If the person submitting the claim form is not someone entitled to inherit, this section must be filled out. Written and notarized authorization or power of attorney from the claimant providing authorization to the named representative must also be attached. All information regarding the claimant (the individual who has granted power of attorney or other authorization) must still be provided in Section I-A above. If there is more than one representative, each individual representative must complete a copy of Section I-B of this form. (This section may be reproduced as needed.)

25. Representative's last name ________________

26. Representative's first name ________________

27. Representative's middle name ________________

28. Representative's relationship to claimant ________________

29. Do you have documentation confirming this relationship?
[ ] Yes [ ] No 30. If so, what is it? (please include a copy with this form)

____

31. Representative's legal firm, company, or other organization
(where applicable) ________________

32. Representative's business address ________________

33. City ________________

34. State/Province ________________

35. Zip/Postal code ________________

36. Country ________________

Next Page

Back to Home Page

CLAIM FORM

Part I-B Rep Info

37. Representative's home address

38. City

39. State/Province

40. Zip/Postal code

41. Country

42. Home telephone

43. Work telephone

44. Fax number

45. E-mail address

Next Page

Back to Home Page

Commission for Art Recovery
of the World Jewish Congress

in affiliation with
the World Jewish Restitution
Organization

CLAIM FORM
Part II-A Art Objects

II Art Objects II-A Object Information

This section seeks information about art objects claimed. Please complete separate copies of this section for each object claimed OR you may attach information for each object and our staff will complete this form. (This section may be reproduced as needed, or we can send you additional copies.) If photographs of objects are available, please submit copies of these with the claim form. Even if photographic reproductions are submitted, please provide all available information on each object in the appropriate section of the claim form. Incomplete information is perfectly acceptable.

OFFICE USE ONLY
Parent record type ______________________________
Claimant/Source ID # ______________________________
Sequence # ______________________________

46. Artist: Attributed to [ ] Known [ ]

____

47. Title(s)

____

48. Subject

____

49. Date of execution (i.e. 1675)

____

50. Country/Place of origin

____

51. Object type (i.e. painting, sculpture, print)

____

52. Medium (i.e. oil, marble, ink)

____

53. Measurements: [ ] Exact [ ] Approximate [ ] Inches [ ] Centimeters

54. Height __________ 55. Width __________ 56. Diameter __________

Next Page

Back to Home Page

Commission for Art Recovery
of the World Jewish Congress

in affiliation with
the World Jewish Restitution
Organization

CLAIM FORM
Part II-A Art Objects

Distinctive markings:

57. Signature ______

58. Date ______

59. Edition or number ______

60. Inscription(s) ______

61. Other identifying marks (i.e. labels, repairs) ______

62. Present [ ] or last known [ ] location ______

63. Additional description (attach additional page if necessary) ______

64. Photo or other image available? [ ] Yes (if yes please attach) [ ] No

65. May we keep the photo(s)? [ ] Yes [ ] No

66. Was the art insured? [ ] Yes [ ] No [ ] Don't know

67. Name of policy holder ______

68. Insurance company name (if known) ______

69. Insurance policy number (if known) ______

70. Insurance city (if known) ______

Next Page

Back to Home Page

Commission for Art Recovery
of the World Jewish Congress

in affiliation with
the World Jewish Restitution
Organization

CLAIM FORM
Part II-B Circmstantial Info

II-B Circumstantial Information

This section seeks details concerning the theft of the art object.

71. Please describe what you know about the circumstances of the theft of the object. For example: Was the victim present at the seizure of the object? Did the victim flee his/her home? Was the object lost in transit? Attach additional page(s) if necessary. (Please include copies of any documents you have pertaining to circumstances of theft.)

72. Does this apply to all the art in this claim? [ ] Yes [ ] No (If yes you need only describe these circumstances once.)

73. If you have made any previous claims or inquiries to any other organization or government body, please identify them and include all details and copies of any pertinent documents. Note: Whatever happened before does not stop you from filing your claim with the Commission for Art Recovery. We are requesting this only for the purpose of collecting as much information as possible.

Next Page

Back to Home Page

Commission for Art Recovery
of the World Jewish Congress

in affiliation with
the World Jewish Restitution
Organization

CLAIM FORM
Part II-B Circmstantial Info
Part III Statement of Accuracy

Documentation

This section seeks information about documentation, if available, of the claimant's rightful ownership of the art claimed and its past or present whereabouts.

74. Do you have any appraisals, storage or transport records, or published materials referring to the art which you are claiming?

[ ] Yes Please attach copies of all relevant documents.
[ ] No

75. Use this section to provide any other information which you think may be important to your claim or which may assist in our efforts to locate your art.

____

____

____

____

____

III Statement of Accuracy

The following statement insures that the information received by the Commission for Art Recovery is true and accurate.

All claimants and representatives must acknowledge this statement with a signature before this claim is processed. Failure to do so will result in a delay processing this claim.

I promise that the information given in this claim form is true and accurate to the best of my knowledge.

Claimant name ______________________________

Claimant signature ______________________________

Date ______________________________

Representative's name ______________________________

Representative's signature ______________________________

Date ______________________________

Back to Home Page

APPENDIX 5-H

Report of the AAMD Task Force on the Spoliation of Art during the Nazi/World War II Era (1933-1945)

Report of the AAMD Task Force on the Spoliation of Art during the Nazi/World War II Era (1933-1945)

June 4, 1998

AAMD Statement of Purpose: "The purpose of the AAMD is to aid its members in establishing and maintaining the highest professional standards for themselves and the museums they represent, thereby exerting leadership in increasing the contribution of art museums to society."

I. Statement of Principles

A. AAMD recognizes and deplores the unlawful confiscation of art that constituted one of the many horrors of the Holocaust and World War II.

B. American museums are proud of the role they, and members of their staffs, played during and after World War II, assisting with the preservation and restitution of hundreds of thousands of works of art through the U.S. Military's Monuments, Fine Arts and Archives section.

C. AAMD reaffirms the commitment of its members to weigh, promptly and thoroughly, claims of title to specific works in their collections.

D. AAMD urges the prompt creation of mechanisms to coordinate full access to all documentation concerning this spoliation of art, especially newly available information. To this end, the AAMD encourages the creation of databases by third parties, essential to research in this area, which will aid in the identification of any works of art which were unlawfully confiscated and which of these were restituted. Such an effort will complement long-standing American museum policy of exhibiting, publishing and researching works of art in museum collections in order to make them widely available to scholars and to the general public. (See III. below.)

E. AAMD endorses a process of reviewing, reporting, and researching the issue of unlawfully confiscated art which respects the dignity of all parties and the complexity of the issue. Each claim presents a unique situation which must be thoroughly reviewed on a case-by-case basis.

II. Guidelines

AAMD has developed the following guidelines to assist museums in resolving claims, reconciling the interests of individuals who were dispossessed of works of art or their heirs together with the fiduciary and legal obligations and responsibilities of art museums and their trustees to the public for whom they hold works of art in trust.

A. Research Regarding Existing Collections

1. As part of the standard research on each work of art in their collections, members of the AAMD, if they have not already done so, should begin immediately to review the provenance of works in their collections to attempt to ascertain whether any were unlawfully confiscated during the Nazi/World War II era and never restituted.

2. Member museums should search their own records thoroughly and, in addition, should take all reasonable steps to contact established archives, databases, art dealers, auction houses, donors, art historians and other scholars and researchers who may be able to provide Nazi/World-War-II-era provenance information.

3. AAMD recognizes that research regarding Nazi/World-War-II-era provenance may take years to complete, may be inconclusive and may require additional funding. The

AAMD Art Issues Committee will address the matter of such research and how to facilitate it.

B. Future Gifts, Bequests, and Purchases

1. As part of the standard research on each work of art:

(a) member museums should ask donors of works of art (or executors in the case of bequests) to provide as much provenance information as possible with regard to the Nazi/World War II era and

(b) member museums should ask sellers of works of art to provide as much provenance information as possible with regard to the Nazi/World War II era.

2. Where the Nazi/World-War-II-era provenance is incomplete for a gift, bequest, or purchase, the museum should search available records and consult appropriate databases of unlawfully confiscated art (see III below).

(a) In the absence of evidence of unlawful confiscation, the work is presumed not to have been confiscated and the acquisition may proceed.

(b) If there is evidence of unlawful confiscation, and there is no evidence of restitution, the museum should not proceed to acquire the object and should take appropriate further action.

3. Consistent with current museum practice, member museums should publish, display or otherwise make accessible all recent gifts, bequests, and purchases thereby making them available for further research, examination and study.

4. When purchasing works of art, museums should seek representations and warranties from the seller that the seller has valid title and that the work of art is free from any claims.

C. Access to Museum Records

1. Member museums should facilitate access to the Nazi/World-War-II-era provenance information of all works of art in their collections.

2. Although a linked database of all museum holdings throughout the United States does not exist at this time, individual museums are establishing web sites with collections information and others are making their holdings accessible through printed publications or archives. AAMD is exploring the linkage of existing sites which contain collection information so as to assist research.

D. Discovery of Unlawfully Confiscated Works of Art

1. If a member museum should determine that a work of art in its collection

was illegally confiscated during the Nazi/World War II era and not restituted, the museum should make such information public.

2. In the event that a legitimate claimant comes forward, the museum should offer to resolve the matter in an equitable, appropriate, and mutually agreeable manner.

3. In the event that no legitimate claimant comes forward, the museum should acknowledge the history of the work of art on labels and publications referring to such a work.

E. Response to Claims Against the Museum

1. If a member museum receives a claim against a work of art in its collection related to an illegal confiscation during the Nazi/World War II era, it should seek to review such a claim promptly and thoroughly. The museum should request evidence of ownership from the claimant in order to assist in determining the provenance of the work of art.

2. If after working with the claimant to determine the provenance, a member museum should determine that a work of art in its collection was illegally confiscated during the Nazi/World War II era and not restituted, the museum should offer to resolve the matter in an equitable, appropriate, and mutually agreeable manner.

3. AAMD recommends that member museums consider using mediation wherever reasonably practical to help resolve claims regarding art illegally confiscated during the Nazi/World War II era and not restituted.

F. Incoming Loans

1. In preparing for exhibitions, member museums should endeavor to review provenance information regarding incoming loans.

2. Member museums should not borrow works of art known to have been illegally confiscated during the Nazi/World War II era and not restituted unless the matter has been otherwise resolved (e.g., II.D.3 above).

III. Database Recommendations

A. As stated in I.D. (above), AAMD encourages the creation of databases by third parties, essential to research in this area. AAMD recommends that the databases being formed include the following information (not necessarily all in a single database):

1. claims and claimants

2. works of art illegally confiscated during the Nazi/World War II era

3. works of art later restituted

B. AAMD suggests that the entity or entities creating databases establish professional advisory boards that could provide insight on the needs of various users of the database. AAMD encourages member museums to participate in the work of such boards.

CHAPTER 6

CULTURAL PROPERTY

Rena Moulopoulos*

---

* The views expressed in the article are the author's and not necessarily those of Sotheby's. The author thanks Roy Kaufman, editor of this book, for his patience and kind support. In addition, sincere appreciation is extended to Jonathan A. Olsoff and Daniel Shapiro for providing constructive criticism on the drafts of this chapter, and to Gina Driscoll who, as a law student, provided research support.

§ 6.01 THE INTERNATIONAL MOVEMENT OF CULTURAL PROPERTY

Rules on the international movement of cultural property will vary widely not only between exporters and importers but within both of those categories. If property is not absolutely banned, it may require special permits, licenses, or certificates prior to export, or in simpler cases, complete descriptions of the property with accurate valuations. This chapter focuses primarily on the various types of international, regional, and national controls on the export of cultural property, with emphasis on the import and export controls that affect United States commerce.

§ 6.02 CULTURAL PROPERTY: A WORKING DEFINITION

[A] Types of Cultural Property: Antiquities and Objects of Artistic Importance

Definitions[1] of "cultural property"[2] are often inconsistent and conflicting. Much of the debate regarding the sale of cultural property may stem from a lack of consistent definitions. In the practical world, because no standard international definition of what constitutes cultural property exists, specific laws must always be consulted when considering the international movement of a work of art. However, in general there are two basic types of cultural property: antiquities and objects of artistic importance.

"Antiquities" are broadly defined as items predating the Middle Ages that may have been found in the ground or collected or traded since their creation.[3]

---

[1] There are seemingly endless definitions of what constitutes "cultural property". *See, e.g.*, City University, Arts Policy and Management, Patrick Boylan's Arts, Museums and Heritage Organizations Policy Statements Series, Definitions of "Cultural Property," http://www.city.ac.uk/artspol/cult-def.html. Commonly used phrases in the international art market include the generic "work of art," which may include such diverse categories as fine arts, decorative arts, collectibles and antiquities. Fortunately, there is no need, for purposes of this chapter, to arrive at the ultimate definition; the terms "cultural property" and "works of art" will be used interchangeably throughout and, unless otherwise specified, will have the broadest meaning.

[2] In the context of governmental laws and regulations, variations on the phrase "cultural property" are often used. *See, e.g.*, Native American Grave Protection and Repatriation Act 25 U.S.C. §§ 3001 *et seq.* ("cultural patrimony"); French export control laws (Law 92-1477, "national treasures" and "national heritage"); Venezuelan laws, Law for the Protection of Public Patrimony (Art. 6(4), "national patrimony"); Spanish law (Historic Patrimony Law 16/85, 25 June 1985, "historic patrimony movables").

[3] As used herein, antiquities do not include immovables, such as an archaeological site or monument. However, an ancient site or monument as well as the decorative, architectural elements of the building or monument, including the sculpture attached to it, may be protected by legislation or treaty. *See, e.g.*, Pre-Columbian Monumental or Architectural Sculpture or Mural Statute, 19 U.S.C. § 2095(3)(A)(ii) (statute offers protection not only to the original immobile structures, but to any object that was a part of, or affixed to such structures).

The objects may include such archaeological materials as coins, objects used in ancient religious rituals, images of worship such as deities, and ancient objects of an everyday, utilitarian nature, such as eating and cooking implements, tools, jewelry, or weapons. Statutory definitions often require an object be at least 100 years old to be an antiquity.[4]

"Objects of artistic importance"[5] generally refers to the fine arts, such as paintings, drawings, prints, photographs, etchings, woodcuts, watercolors, and other works on paper, and also includes the decorative arts of furniture, silver, ceramics, glass, rugs, carpets, and tapestries. All of the foregoing may constitute cultural property. Whereas antiquities are by definition old, even contemporary works of artistic importance may be deemed cultural property and subject to certain export controls.[6]

[B] U.S. Definitions of Cultural Property

Within the fairly limited context of American law, there is a wide variety of definitions of cultural property or works of art. Even the laws that govern possession or movement of archaeological objects or antiquities have inconsistent definitions. For example, the Native American Grave Protection and Repatriation

---

[4] *See, e.g.*, Archaeological Resource Protection Act of 1979, 16 U.S.C. § 470bb(1) (defining material protected by the statute as "any material remains of past human life or activity that are of archaeological interest and which are at least 100 years of age"); Bilateral Agreement with Mali on Archaeological Material from the Niger River Valley and Bandiagara Escarpment, Sept. 23, 1997, entered pursuant to the Convention for Cultural Property Implementation Act, 19 U.S.C. § 2600 *et seq.* (restricting, under certain circumstances, the import of certain archaeological material provided such property is at least 250 years old). Both the European Union Council Regulation on the Export of Cultural Goods (EEC No. 3911/92) and the UNESCO Convention on the Means of Prohibiting and Preventing the Illicit Import, Export and Transfer of Ownership of Cultural Property of 1970 refer to objects over 100 years old.

[5] One sometimes hears the phrase "objects of historical importance." This is a colloquial, catch-all phrase that may include any other objects deemed important or valuable to a nation, tribe, or region and which may be subject to export regulation. For example, objects originally known for a utilitarian or commercial purpose, such as historical books, manuscripts, maps, letters and musical scores, as well as such items as scientific or musical instruments, may constitute objects of historical importance.

[6] *See, e.g.*, Export Control laws of India, the Antiquities and Art Treasures Act, 1972 (works of the modern artists Amrita Sher-Gil, Jamini Roy, and Nandalal Bose are all under 100 years old but are nevertheless considered "art treasures" and illegal to export under Indian law); Mexican Patrimony Law, Article 16 of the Federal Law on Artistic, Historic and Archeological Monuments and Areas and Article 32 of the Regulations of the Law on Artistic, Historic and Archeological Monuments (permanent export of works by the following modern artists is prohibited: Jose Maria Diego Rivera Barrientos (Diego Rivera), Frida Kahlo, David Alfaro Siquieros, Jose Clemente Orozco, Saturnino Herran and Geraldo Murillo ("Dr. Atl"); and one nineteenth-century artist, Jose Maria Velasco).

Act defines a "cultural item" as "human remains and associated funerary objects unassociated funerary objects . . . sacred objects . . . [and] cultural patrimony."[7] In contrast, the Archaeological Resource Protection Act of 1979 is limited to the protection of "archaeological resources and sites" located on public and Indian lands and defines "archaeological resource" as any material remains of past human life or activity that are of archaeological interest and at least 100 years of age.[8]

The U.S. Convention on Cultural Property Implementation Act "CCPIA" is limited to regulating the import of certain types of archaeological and ethnological materials. The phrase "object of archaeological interest" refers to objects at least 250 years old and of "cultural significance."[9] An "object of ethnnological interest" is something from a tribal or pre-industrial society which is important to the cultural heritage of a people.[10] The wide variety of definitions should not be surprising given that there has been for decades discussion as to how one defines cultural property, and which items should be subject to export and import restrictions.[11]

[C] A Practical Approach to Defining Cultural Property

Given the existing diversity of definitions of "cultural property," it is often useful to begin an analysis of whether or not objects will be deemed cultural property with a pragmatic approach. To determine if an item is regulated, certain practical, threshold questions should be answered, such as:

- What is the age of the object?
- What are the materials from which it is made?[12]

---

[7] 25 U.S.C. § 3001(3)(A)-(D).

[8] 16 U.S.C. § 470bb(1).

[9] 19 U.S.C. § 2601(2).

[10] *Id.* The item must be important because of "its distinctive characteristics, [its] comparative rarity, or its contribution to the knowledge of the origins, development, or history of that people." Beyond the federal laws addressing issues having to do with archaeological objects, there are numerous state laws governing antiquities, archaeological materials as well as entirely different types of cultural property. For example, the New York Visual Artists Rights Act addresses only fine art, sculpture and limited edition multiples. N.Y. Art & Cult. Aff. § 14.03(1)-(4). N.Y. CLS Art & Cult. Aff. § 14.03(1)-(4). In contrast, the California Resale Royalty Act is restricted to fine art (original painting, sculpture, drawing, or work of art in glass). Cal. Civ. Code § 986.

[11] *See, e.g.*, Bator, An essay on the International Trade in Art, 34 Stan. L. Rev. 275, 284 (1982) *reprinted as* The International Trade in Art, 1981, University of Chicago Press (Bator notes that "art historians, archaeologists and anthropologists differ on what should be called a 'work of art' and what should be called an 'artifact'."); *see also* John Henry Merryman, Two Ways of Thinking About Cultural Property, 80 Am. J. Int'l L., 831, 831-33 (October 1986).

[12] *See* discussion *infra* at note 17 regarding various U.S. laws regulating the different forms of endangered or otherwise protected plants or animals ("endangered species"). If an object is subject to an endangered species law, its sale, export, or import may be regulated or even prohibited.

- What is its value?
- Which artist made it?
- Was the object utilitarian or ceremonial?
- Is it a movable item or from a specific archaeological or historic site?
- Where is it now?
- How recently did it arrive there?
- Where is it being sent?
- Where was it made?
- Where and when was it found?
- Is it of local or national historical importance?
- Is it unique, a multiple or part of a set?

Sensitivity to these questions may assist in evaluating whether an item is likely to be regulated in terms of export, import, or sale. Once armed with as much of the this information as possible, the analysis of whether an object is "cultural property" under applicable law and subject to an international, national, or regional restriction on its movement can begin.

§ 6.03 THE TREATMENT OF CULTURAL PROPERTY UNDER U.S. LAW

[A] U.S "Policy" on Cultural Property

Historically, Congress has been reluctant to legislate widely with respect to regulating private domestic or international movement or ownership of cultural property. To the extent a policy has existed, it has been that the United States will not enforce the export control laws of foreign nations.[13] The general policy of non-interference with private ownership or movement of works of art has

[13] *See* U.S. Customs Directive, Detention and Seizure of Cultural Property, April 18, 1991 ("However, it is important to note that merely because an exportation of an artifact is illegal within a particular country does not necessarily mean that the subsequent importation into the United States is illegal."); Paul M. Bator, An Essay on the International Trade in Art, 34 Stan. L. Rev. 275, 287 (1982) ("The fundamental general rule is clear: *The fact that an art object has been illegally exported does not in itself bar it from lawful importation into the United States; illegal export does not itself render the importer (or one who took from him) in any way actionable in a U.S. court* . . .") (emphasis added); *see also* United States v. McClain, *et al.*, 545 F.2d. 988 (5th Cir., 1977), *appealed after remand*, 593 F.2d. 658 (5th Cir., 1979) (acknowledging this policy).

extended to the area of import taxes. Unlike many other countries, the United States has had an historic policy of little or no taxation on the import of works of art.[14] The policy of non-interference has encouraged importation and collection of great works of art, and as a result the United States is home to some of the world's leading museums. Moreover, the United States is among the minority of countries that do not have a Ministry or Department of Culture.[15] Decisions are left in large part to individual U.S. Customs agents and branch offices of the U.S. Attorney's office to determine which types of cases to prosecute and consequently they have created a de facto cultural property policy, particularly in the application of the U.S. customs laws regarding imports and the scope of the National Stolen Property Act.

Otherwise, what limited federal legislation does exist in the United States tends to be narrowly drafted to address specific problems, such as regulating antiquities and archaeological property discovered on federal or Native American lands or property owned or controlled by museums or institutions receiving federal funding.[16]

---

[14] For nearly 100 years most antiques have entered the United States duty-free. *See, e.g.*, Underwood Tariff Act of 1913 § 652-655, Pub. L. 63-16, 38 Stat. 114, 1913 (exempting works of art from import duties).

[15] In the absence of a federal agency establishing policy in this area, the Pew Charitable Trusts announced in 1999 that it would devote close to $50 million over the next five years to the study of cultural policy in the United States. *See* Judith Dobrzynski, "Heavyweight Foundation Throws Itself Behind Idea of a Cultural Policy," The New York Times, Aug. 2, 1999, at E1 (noting that the United States, unlike most other countries, does not have a formal government body establishing a national cultural property policy).

[16] *See* Antiquities Act of 1906, 16 U.S.C. §§ 431-33m (authorizing the imposition of penalties and possibly imprisonment for any person destroying or damaging historic ruins *on public lands*, or for excavating or destroying ruins, monuments or antiquities *on lands owned or controlled by the Federal government*) (emphasis added); National Environmental Policy Act of 1969, 42 U.S.C. § 4321-70a (*in assessing Federal projects*, the Government must consider cultural and environmental values and the Government must use "all practicable means and measures" . . . (to) preserve important historic, cultural, and natural aspects of the national heritage" 42 U.S.C. § 4331(a); (b)(4)); Archaeological Resources and Protection Act of 1979, 16 U.S.C. §§ 470aa-mm (supplements the Antiquities Act of 1906 and protects archaeological resources *on public or Indian land* from sale, purchase, transport, exchange, or receipt, absent permission); Abandoned Shipwreck Act of 1987, 43 U.S.C. §§ 2101-06 (essentially vests title to abandoned shipwrecks *found in state-owned waters* to the Federal Government, which subsequently transfers such title to the states); Native American Graves Protection and Repatriation Act of 1991, 25 U.S.C. §§ 3001-3013 (requires museums *receiving federal funds* and *federal agencies* to prepare inventories of Native American human remains and associated funerary objects to be provided to the tribal governments and traditional religious leaders, and if an affiliation is established with a Native American tribe or lineal descendants, the property must be returned) (emphasis added).

[B] U.S. Import Restrictions

Excluding import restrictions regarding endangered species[17] or political embargoes,[18] there are few federal laws specifically regulating the import into the United States of cultural property. These laws are exceptions to the broad historic U.S. policy in favor of free imports into the United States of cultural property and of the legitimate goal of furthering the exchange of cultural property.[19] Even

[17] A variety of laws and regulations restrict or prohibit the movement or sale of endangered or otherwise protected plants or animals, such as feathers, corals, ivories, tortoiseshell, walrus, seal, certain types of mahogany, and skins of big cats, such as leopard. For example, not only is the United States a signatory to the Convention on International Treaty of Endangered Species, but it is subject to the much stricter restrictions under the Endangered Species Act of 1973. 16 U.S.C. §§ 1531 *et seq.*, 50 C.F.R. § 17.11. There is, however, an exception in the ESA for "antiques" which are defined as articles that are at least 100 years old. 50 C.F.R. § 14.22. For a complete list of CITEs materials that are regulated in the United States, see 50 C.F.R. § 23.23. *See also* Migratory Bird Treaty Act, 16 U.S.C. § 701 *et seq.* (protecting most birds, bird parts (including feathers) from sale, ownership or transfer within the U.S.); Bald Eagle Protection Act 16 U.S.C. § 668 *et seq.*; Marine Mammal Protection Act, 16 U.S.C. § 1361 *et seq.*; and Lacey Act 18 U.S.C., § 42 *et seq.* (restricting imports of certain injurious mammals, birds, fish, amphibia and reptiles). Thus, it is important to conduct a careful physical examination of the piece, in particular when dealing with decorative works of art, to ascertain if there are any endangered species used as parts or as inlay. A knowledgeable person should examine the piece to look for certain protected types of ivory, bone, coral, animal skins or furs, rosewood, etc., and if the sale, export or import of the item is consequently restricted or prohibited.

[18] Certain types of works of art may not be imported (or sold or owned by U.S. citizens or by foreign subsidiaries or affiliates of U.S. companies depending on which country is at issue) as a consequence of various trade embargoes with countries such as Iraq, Iran, Cuba, North Korea, Libya and the Sudan. *See, e.g.*, Iranian Transactions Regulations, 31 C.F.R. § 560; Iranian Assets Control Regulations, 31 C.F.R. § 535; International Emergency Economic Powers Act, 50 U.S.C. § 1701 *et seq.* (regarding Iraq, Iran, Libya and the Sudan); International Security and Development Co-operation Act, 22 U.S.C. § 2349aa-9 (Iran and Libya); Antiterrorism and Effective Death Penalty Act, 8 U.S.C. § 1189 (regarding Iraq, Iran, Cuba, Libya, North Korea and the Sudan); United Nations Participation Act, 22 U.S.C. § 287c (regarding Iraq); Iraqi Sanctions Regulations, 31 C.F.R. § 575; Iraq Sanctions Act of 1990, Pub. L. No. 101-513, 104 Stat. 1979; Cuban Assets Control Regulations, 31 C.F.R. § 515; Cuban Democracy Act, 22 U.S.C. § 6001 *et seq.*; Cuban Liberty and Democratic Solidarity (Liberated) Act of 1996, 22 U.S.C. § 6021 *et seq.* (commonly referred to as the Helms-Burton Act); Libyan Sanctions Regulations, 31 C.F.R. § 550; Foreign Assets Control Regulations, 31 C.F.R. § 500 (regarding North Korea); Sudanese Sanctions Regulations, 31 C.F.R. § 538; Trading with the Enemy Act of 1917, 50 U.S.C.A. §§ 5, 16 (regarding North Korea and Cuba); Crimes and Criminal Procedures Act, 18 U.S.C. § 3571 (authorizing criminal fines for certain violations of the foregoing laws). *See also* Anne Q. Connaughton, Exporting to Special Destinations: Terrorist-Supporting and Embargoed Countries, Coping With U.S. Export Controls 1998, PLI 383-433.

[19] *See, e.g.*, John Henry Merryman, Two Ways of Thinking About Cultural Property, Am. J. Int'l L., Vol. 80, No. 4, October 1986 at 851-52 (notes the historic U.S. policy of free movement of works of art, in terms of the lack of import duties on most works of art and limited export

certain laws limiting the international movement of smuggled or stolen works of art contain express acknowledgements of the vast and inherent benefits of the legitimate exchange of cultural property. For example, the UNESCO Convention of 1970 on the Means of Prohibiting and Preventing the Illicit Import, Export and Ownership of Cultural Property contains statements acknowledging the legitimate exchange of cultural property as an activity that "increases knowledge of the civilization of many, enriches the cultural life of all peoples and inspires mutual respect and appreciation among nations."[20] The CCPIA also recognizes the "general interest of the international community in the interchange of cultural property among nations for scientific, cultural, and educational purposes" and provides remedies for recovery of illegally exported property in the form of temporary import restrictions under certain limited circumstances.[21]

The laws are generally narrow in scope and for the most part address specific, clearly identified problems, such as those addressed by the National Stolen Property Act, which has been used to restrict the import of stolen works of art into the United States.[22]

[1] The Convention on Cultural Property Implementation Act

The UNESCO Convention of 1970 on the Means of Prohibiting and Preventing the Illicit Import, Export and Ownership of Cultural Property is broadly drafted and seeks to curb the illicit trade in cultural property. One of the most noticeable features of the 1970 UNESCO Convention is that it creates an interna-

---

restrictions, and points out that there have been few import control restrictions implemented since 1970 in the form of the treaties and laws discussed *infra*).

[20] UNESCO Convention of 1970 preamble; *see also* Treaty of Co-operation between the United States of America and the United Mexican States Providing for the Recovery and Return of Stolen Archaeological, Historical and Cultural Properties, Art., 2, 1(d) ("The parties undertake . . . consistent with the laws and regulations assuring the conservation of national archaeological, historical and cultural properties to permit legitimate international commerce in art objects").

[21] 19 U.S.C. § 2602(a)(1)(C), and (D). The CCPIA also prohibits the import of certain stolen items, provided they were documented as inventory to a museum, religious or secular public monument, or similar institution. *See infra* § 6.03[B][1][d] (discussing CCPIA).

[22] The jurisprudential preference in the United States for the free movement of cultural property has raised questions as to whether it is appropriate to apply the National Stolen Property Act to a foreign nation's laws deeming an item "stolen" even if the item was never identified or possessed by the foreign nation. *See, e.g.*, United States v. McClain, 545 F.2d 988 (5th Cir. 1977) (finding that it is appropriate to apply the NSPA based on foreign ownership laws), *reh'g denied*, 551 F.2d 52 (5th Cir. 1977), *aff'd in part, rev'd in part,* 593 F.2d 658 (5th Cir. 1979), *and cert. denied*, 444 U.S. 918 (1979); United States v. An Antique Platter of Gold Known as a Gold Phiale Mesomphalos, c. 400 B.C., 184 F.3d 131 (2d Cir. 1999) (hereinafter "*Phiale*") (Second Circuit refusing to decide whether the scope of the NSPA should include foreign nations claim for recovery of "stolen" property); *see also* Bator, An Essay on the International Trade in Art, 34 Stan. L. Rev. at 347-54. *See* discussion of the NSPA and U.S. cultural property policy *infra* at § 6.03[B][4][c].

tional legal scheme that grants recovery rights for both smuggled and stolen property.[23] Although the United States ratified the 1970 UNESCO Convention in 1972, it was not self-executing, and competing interests delayed implementation.

In 1983, the United States enacted implementing legislation in the United States in the form of the Convention on Cultural Property Implementation Act (CCPIA). The CCPIA is narrower than the Convention and applies to specifically identified cultural material that is in "jeopardy of pillage," when either "less drastic remedies are not available" or the pillage is of "crisis proportions." In such cases, the United States may restrict imports by (1) entering into bilateral or multilateral agreements with other State Parties, or (2) imposing emergency import restrictions. In addition, the CCPIA makes it illegal to import property stolen from a museum or religious or secular public monument.

Before the United States decides either to enter an international agreement or to impose emergency restrictions, a request for such relief must be made by a State Party that is also a signatory to the 1972 UNESCO Convention. To lawfully import property from any of the countries[24] for which special import restrictions are in place, one must establish either that the property at issue is accompanied by a valid export certificate from the country of origin, or the property existed outside of the country of origin as of the effective date of the U.S. import restrictions.[25]

[a] The Cultural Property Advisory Committee

To assist in determining whether to grant requested import restrictions, the President[26] may consider the views of the Cultural Property Advisory Committee. The Committee, established pursuant to the CCPIA, consists of 11 members appointed by the President. By statute, the members must represent museums; the fields of archaeology, anthropology, ethnology, or related areas; specialists

---

[23] *See* discussion of the UNESCO Treaty, *infra* § 6.04[A][2].

[24] For an up-to-date list of the import restrictions in effect pursuant to the CCPIA, see the Web site of the State Department, which is currently http://exchanges.state.gov.

[25] 19 U.S.C. § 2606(a) and (b). Pursuant to § 2604 of the CCPIA, the Secretary of the Treasury or her delegate must produce a list of the protected archaeological or ethnological property that is "sufficiently specific and precise to insure: (1) the import restrictions under section 2606 are applied only to the archaeological and ethnological material covered by the agreement or emergency actions; and (2) fair notice is given to importers and other persons as to what material is subject to such restrictions." For a detailed listing of the various types of property protected under the existing agreements or emergency import restrictions, see http://exchanges.state.gov.

[26] From 1986 to 1999, the President delegated his authority to enter into such agreements to the Director of the United States Information Agency (USIA). In 1999, the USIA was merged into the Department of State, and authority was assumed by the State Department. *See* Executive Order 12555, March 10, 1986; and Pub. L. No. 105-277, tit. XIII, of Division G (Oct. 21, 1998) (incorporating USIA into the U.S. Department of State).

in the international sale of archaeological, ethnological and other cultural property; and the interests of the general public.[27] The committee reviews the requests made by the State Party and submits its recommendations to the President's delegate.[28]

Between 1983 and 1995, the Cultural Property Advisory Committee recommended that the United States impose emergency restrictions with respect to five countries, Bolivia, El Salvador, Guatemala, Mali, and Peru, and entered into one bilateral agreement with El Salvador, which extended and widened the scope of the original emergency restrictions. In 1997-99, six forms of import restrictions were imposed: emergency restrictions were imposed in response to requests from Cambodia and Cyprus, and bilateral agreements were entered into with Canada, Guatemala, Mali, and Peru. As of May 2000, Italy, Bolivia, and Nicaragua are also seeking import restrictions. In part because of the dramatic increase in restrictions over a short time and concern at their broad scope, Senators Roth, Moynihan, and Schumer introduced S. 1696, the Cultural Property Procedural Reform Act (CCPRA), in October 1999.[29]

[b] Bilateral or Multilateral Agreements

Under existing legislation, before entering into a bilateral or multilateral agreement, the President or his delegate must determine that:

---

[27] Three seats on the committee are reserved for persons familiar with the international sale of archaeological, ethnological, or other cultural property. However, there were periods in the late 1990s when only two such slots were filled, and then, due to the resignation of these members, a period in 1999-2000 when there were no members with this special area of expertise. Both resigning members complained that the process followed by the committee was unfair to the interests of the international art market. Their complaints in part contributed to the introduction of S. 1696, discussed *infra*.

[28] According to the CCPIA, the committee must make recommendations to the President or his delegate within 150 days of receiving information regarding a bilateral agreement or within 90 days of receiving a request for emergency restrictions. 19 U.S.C. § 2602(f)(3)(B) and 19 U.S.C. § 2603(c)(2). In reality, the President's delegate has yet to make any decisions or determinations absent receiving a recommendation from the committee, even if such recommendations were well outside of the statutory deadline. In fact, the delegate has consistently followed the committee's recommendations. Thus, although in theory the Committee has no statutory decision-making authority, it appears that, in practice, the implementation power of the CCPIA rests with the committee.

[29] The main goals of the CPPRA are to improve the process followed by CPAC and to restore the delicate balance among the trade, archaeologists, museums, and public that was intended in the enactment of the CCPIA. The legislation in effect requires CPAC to make public information provided by requesting states; increases public participation in the investigative and fact-finding role of the CPAC; restates the principle that across-the-board import restrictions are not permissible under the CCPIA; specifies how the multinational response requirement should be treated; imposes procedural review requirements to satisfy the "continuing review" requirement set forth in the statute; clarifies that committee members serve in a representative capacity on the committee; and authorizes that international sales representatives may independently seek information and data to supplement the information provided by the requesting states. It is unclear if the CCPRA will be

1. the cultural patrimony of the requesting state is in jeopardy from pillage of the archaeological or ethnographical materials;
2. the requesting state has taken steps to protect its cultural patrimony;
3. U.S. import restrictions, with actions by other nations with an import trade in these works, would be of "substantial benefit" in deterring a "serious situation of pillage";[30]
4. less drastic remedies are not available; and
5. the import controls are consistent with "the general interest of the international community in the interchange of cultural property among nations for scientific, cultural and educational purposes."[31]

The law requires that each of these factors be satisfied before the United States may impose import restrictions under the CCPIA.

As of August 1999, the United States has entered bilateral agreements that impose import restrictions with Canada,[32] El Salvador, Guatemala, Mali, and Peru. The import restrictions are theoretically temporary in nature and can be terminated by granting six months' notice of the termination.[33]

[c] Emergency Restrictions

A second form of temporary import controls under the CCPIA is the emergency restriction provision. Provided there is a request from a State Party for

---

enacted into law. However, given the great increase in the number of requests for import restrictions and the broad relief being recommended by the CPAC and accepted by the President's delegate, many believe the procedural reforms are essential to ensure the intended balance of interests.

[30] 19 U.S.C. § 2602(a)(1).

[31] The implementation, or lack thereof, of Subparagraph (c), sometimes referred to as the "multinational response" requirement, has generated substantial controversy. This section has its origins in Article 9 of the 1972 UNESCO Convention, discussed *infra* at § 6.04[A][2]. In short, before entering U.S. import restrictions there must be "similar" import restrictions, comparable in scope to those contemplated by the United States, by other art market nations. Merely ratifying or signing up to the UNESCO or UNIDROIT conventions would not satisfy this standard. Given the flurry of bilateral agreements entered in the last few years and the lack of any similar import controls in other art market nations, there have been concerns that the multinational response requirement of the CCPIA has been overlooked. Indeed, Senator Moynihan expressed concern about the implementation of the multinational response requirement in his introductory remarks for the amendment to the CCPIA and offered the following explanation for the requirement: "The rationale [for the multinational response requirement] is that one cannot effectively deter a serious situation of pillage of cultural properties if the U.S. unilaterally closes its borders to the import of those properties, and they find their way, in an undiminished stream of commerce to markets in London, Paris, Munich, Tokyo or other art importing centers."

[32] There has been considerable criticism of the nature and scope of the Canadian/United States Agreement. *See* James F. Fitzpatrick, Stealth UNIDROIT: Is USIA the Villain?, 31 N.Y.U. J. Int'l L. & Pol. 47 (Fall 1998).

[33] Section 2602(b) of the CCPIA limits the term of any bilateral or multilateral agreement to

implementation of emergency import restrictions under the CCPIA, the President's delegate may impose import restrictions.[34] Such restrictions may be appropriate if it is established that certain archaeological or ethnological material is:

1. a "newly discovered type of material which is of importance for the history of mankind *and* is in jeopardy from pillage, dismantling, dispersal, or fragmentation" (emphasis added);
2. identifiable as coming from any site recognized to be of high cultural significance and such pillage is of "crisis proportions"; or
3. part of a remains of a particular culture or civilization the record of which is in jeopardy from pillage . . . of crisis proportions *and* the import restrictions on a temporary basis would "reduce the incentive for such pillage . . ." (emphasis added).

Emergency restriction measures are limited to an initial period of five years, with a possible single extension of up to three years if "the emergency condition continues to apply."[35] Currently, the only existing emergency import restrictions are on behalf of Cyprus and Cambodia. In the past, El Salvador, Guatemala, Peru, and Mali have all requested and received emergency import restrictions, which were ultimately extended and expanded into bilateral agreements.[36] Bolivia had import restrictions that expired in 1996, although it has reapplied for more expanded import protections.

[d] Inventory Stolen from Museums

Unlike the international agreements or the emergency restrictions provisions, the third form of import restrictions under the CCPIA does not require a specific request by the State Party. Rather, § 2607 of the CCPIA renders it illegal to import stolen cultural property that is "documented as appertaining to the inventory of a museum or religious or secular public monument or similar institution," located in any country that is also a signatory to the UNESCO Treaty. Such property must have been stolen on the later of either: the effective date of the CCPIA

---

five years. Renewal for consecutive periods of five years is granted only if the stringent requirements for imposing the original restrictions are met and no cause for suspension exists.

[34] The CPAC administrative staff advises that its members, and not the requesting countries, determine whether to treat requests as for emergency restrictions or for a bilateral or multilateral agreement.

[35] 19 U.S.C. § 2603(c)(3). To date any country that has sought an extension or expansion of the emergency import restrictions has been accommodated in that the CPAC simply converts the emergency relief into a bilateral agreement that is renewable *ad infinitum*. One questions whether, if the multinational response requirement were strictly applied, the emergency restrictions would have been successfully converted into bilateral agreements.

[36] *See* text *supra* at § 6.03[B][1][b] regarding bilateral agreements.

(January 12, 1983) or a date after the State Party entered the UNESCO Treaty entered into force.

One of the few cases invoking the CCPIA stolen-property provision involved a Fray Junipero Serra manuscript stolen from the Mexican National Archives.[37] In the *Serra* case, the manuscript was documented as comprising part of the Mexican National Archive since 1956.[38] It was also admitted in the litigation that the manuscript had been purchased by a Mexico City dealer at a flea market in Mexico in 1992 for approximately $300 in U.S. dollars and imported into the United States in 1993. The import triggered both U.S. customs laws and the CCPIA.[39] The Mexico City dealer sold the manuscript in 1996 to an American private collector in Chicago for $16,000 in cash.

---

[37] *See* United States of America v. An Original Manuscript Dated November 19, 1778 bearing the signature of Junipero Serra, located at Sotheby's, 1999 WL 97894 (S.D.N.Y.), 96 Civ. 6221 (LAP) (Feb. 19, 1999); *see also* United States v. A Tenth-Century Marble Wall Panel Sculpture of a Guardian from the Tomb of Wang Chuzhi Located at Christie's, 20 Rockefeller Plaza, New York, New York, 00 Civ 2356 (April 2000) (U.S. Attorney requesting forfeiture of wall panel, consigned to Christie's Manson & Woods in New York, which allegedly had been stolen from a site in the People's Republic of China).

[38] The manuscript was documented as having been stolen after the effective date of the UNESCO Treaty in Mexico (April 1, 1973) and after the effective date of the CCPIA on January 12, 1983; therefore, § 2606 of the CCPIA clearly applied. Moreover, the manuscript had been reported as early as 1956 to constitute part of the Mexican National Archives.

Although the Christie's wall panel case referred to in note 37 has not been fully litigated, it contrasts with the *Serra* case in at least one disturbing respect. The wall panel was allegedly stolen from an unexcavated site in 1994. According to the complaint, "Subsequent to the theft, the tomb . . . was excavated by archaeologists." The complaint does not refer to any inventories or listings of the contents of the site existing before the wall mural was allegedly stolen. Rather, the inventory was created *after* the wall mural was allegedly removed. The Government's willingness to adopt this extraordinarily broad definition of the phrase "documented as appertaining to the inventory of . . . a public monument" has the potential to create a vast loophole in the CCPIA. The loophole would allow countries to claim property that was not documented in an inventory . . . until the date the claim is made. *Cf.* Peru v. Johnson, 720 F. Supp. 810 (C.D. Cal. 1989). Adoption of such a policy would be in direct conflict with the decision in *Peru v. Johnson* that in order to pursue recovery of cultural property, the foreign claimant must establish that the specific item was in the relevant country during the relevant time period.

[39] Another option available to Mexico, although not invoked in this instance, is the United States/Mexican Co-operation Treaty (the "Treaty"). Each party to the Treaty may employ legal means to recover stolen Pre-Columbian and colonial cultural property of "outstanding importance to the national patrimony." The manuscript is colonial cultural property. The Treaty does not create a separate criminal cause of action, but grants only a civil forfeiture remedy to the party requesting recovery of cultural property. In addition, it grants to the U.S. attorney general the right to institute a civil action in the United States to effect the return of stolen Mexican cultural property, if the Mexican authorities are otherwise unsuccessful in recovering the property. It is unclear whether the Mexican government would be required to establish that the property it seeks to recover is both stolen and "of outstanding importance to the national patrimony." If so, it may explain why Mexico did not itself pursue recovery of the Serra manuscript. Instead, the U.S. Customs Service led the

The court ordered the return of the manuscript to Mexico and denied the defendant-collector's request for compensation for the loss of the manuscript.[40] Assisting the government in its victory in this instance may have been the varying burdens of proof between the U.S. government and the defendant, the private collector, applicable to a forfeiture proceeding involving cultural property. In the context of a forfeiture proceeding for violations of the CCPIA, the U.S. government need only establish "probable cause," which may be based on hearsay affidavits. In contrast, the private collector was required to establish by a preponderance of the evidence, which evidence had to be admissible at trial, that the property is not subject to forfeiture.[41] Thus, without the benefit of a hearing to determine the relevant witnesses' credibility, in particular that of the Chicago collector, the court ruled against the defendant.

On a motion for summary judgment, the court found that the Chicago collector had not established by a preponderance of the evidence that he was an innocent purchaser. The court relied on the following facts: the meeting between buyer (the collector) and seller (the Mexican dealer) had taken place in a hotel room; the seller did not provide documents other than the invoice to support the provenance he gave for the manuscript; the buyer paid the seller in cash; and the buyer failed to ask sufficient questions regarding the provenance.[42]

It is arguable whether the facts indicate a "willful blindness to the suspicious nature of the transaction" as found by the court.[43] For example, because the seller was a dealer based in Mexico City, not in Chicago, there is at least one plausible

investigation and recovery of the manuscript under the stolen-property provisions of the CCPIA, discussed above. Another explanation as to why Mexico pursued recovery of the manuscript through U.S. Customs is that it is simply cheaper and more efficient for the Mexican government to have the U.S. government pursue its claims.

[40] 19 U.S.C. § 2609 (authorizing compensation to be paid in certain circumstances to purchasers who buy "for value without knowledge or reason to believe [the item] was stolen"). In part because the court concluded that the purchaser in this instance was not "innocent," the defendant was not entitled to compensation. *Serra, supra* note 37, at 14.

[41] *Serra, supra* note 37, at 10-11. Historically, when the U.S. government elected forfeiture proceedings in a cultural property case, an alleged foreign government victim clearly had an advantage over the U.S. defendant. Unlike other cases of theft when the victim and subsequent possessor are from the United States, the foreign governments needed only provide the U.S. government with sufficient information to establish a prima facie case applying a probable-cause-standard of proof. In this case, the government of Mexico did not appear as a party and was not required to obtain counsel or to establish a case, other than to submit affidavits at the request of the U.S. Attorney's office. In contrast, the U.S. purchaser was required to establish by a preponderance of the evidence, without the victim ever appearing in court and without the benefit of a trial or a hearing, that he was an innocent purchaser. The government's standard of proof, however, has recently been raised pursuant to the Civil Asset Forfeiture Reform Act of 2000, discussed *infra* at note 59.

[42] *Serra, supra* note 37, at 5.

[43] *Serra, supra* note 37, at 14.

explanation for meeting in a hotel room. Moreover, the fact that the dealer was a foreigner may explain the cash nature of the transaction. The Mexican dealer may not have wanted an out-of-country check, which would have taken time to clear and incurred bank fees. Additionally, he may have been motivated to accept cash in order to avoid potential Mexican tax liabilities. Indeed, the buyer may have assumed that the seller was trying to avoid Mexican tax law obligations or to keep currency outside of Mexico, given the sometimes volatile nature of their currency. Although such motives are not admirable, purchasers do not have a legal obligation to ensure that sellers pay whatever taxes a seller may owe in connection with a sale.

On the contrary, had the buyer had any suspicion that he had purchased stolen property, he is unlikely to have consigned it to a high-profile international auction house whose catalogues are circulated throughout the world. Another fact that at least raises the possibility that the buyer did not suspect he was purchasing "hot" property at a discount price was that the auction house's published low presale estimate for the manuscript was $20,000, only $4,000 more than the buyer had paid.

Certain additional facts surrounding the purchase also indicate that the Chicago collector may well have been acting in good faith. For example, the purchaser, a private collector (as opposed to a dealer[44]), asked if the seller owned and had authority to sell the manuscript. The seller told the collector that the manuscript had been purchased in the 1970s from a well-known private collection. The collector also consulted with an attorney before making the purchase, and he asked for and received a bill of sale, on which he incorporated the representations made by the seller regarding provenance. Still, the court found these facts insufficient to establish an innocent-owner defense.[45]

In a case such as this, one would have preferred to have had the court or the jury benefit from the testimony of live witnesses in order to make a better informed decision. Instead, the art market is left with a problematic decision in which taking the following actions was deemed insufficient to determine the good faith of the buyer: consulting a lawyer; inquiring about provenance, incorporating into the purchase invoice the provenance information provided; purchasing an item within the reasonable range of its fair market value; and subsequently acting in a way that advertises the existence of the piece.

---

[44] It may be argued that as a private collector purchasing from a dealer, the purchaser was entitled to rely on the seller's representations without independently verifying their accuracy, unless there was some reason to believe this seller could not transfer title. *See* U.C.C. § 2-103(1)(b); *see also* Hrandi v. Ancell (City Court, White Plains, N.Y.), N.Y.L. J., Friday July 25, 1997 (purchaser deemed good-faith purchaser, despite the fact that he did not ask provenance questions, apparently in reliance on low, but fair, price paid and the fact that the purchaser met with the dealer in his gallery); *see also* Chapter 5, "Stolen Art."

[45] *Serra*, *supra* note 37, at 5.

[2] The Pre-Columbian Monumental Law

The Pre-Columbian Monumental or Architectural Sculpture or Murals Law of 1972[46] authorizes the U.S. Customs Service to seize a monumental or architectural sculpture or mural made by a Pre-Columbian Indian culture of Mexico, Central America, South America or the Caribbean Islands, unless the importer or the owner can establish that the item was lawfully removed from the country of origin or was outside the relevant jurisdiction prior to implementation of the Pre-Columbian Monumental Law.[47]

[3] U.S. Customs Powers to Seize Illegally Imported Goods

The Customs Service has broad criminal authority to seize and forfeit cultural property illegally brought into the United States.[48] The forfeiture provision of 19 U.S.C. § 1595 provides Customs with authority to obtain a warrant to search for and seize property *otherwise* subject to forfeiture.[49] In other words, § 1595 must be based on another provision of law, whether criminal or civil. Although there are numerous statutory predicates for Customs to exercise its forfeiture powers under § 1595,[50] to date the two most common sections on which Customs has

---

[46] 19 U.S.C. §§ 2091-2095.

[47] 19 U.S.C. § 2092(a), (b)(2). In the early 1970s the United States entered into several treaties with individual Central American countries regarding recovery of stolen, as opposed to illegally exported, archaeological and historical cultural properties. *See* Agreement between the United States of America and the Republic of Peru for the Recovery and Return of Stolen Archaeological, Historical and Cultural Properties, signed, Lima, Peru, September 15, 1981, TIAS. No. 10136; Agreement for Recovery and Return of Stolen Archaeological, Historical and Cultural Properties, United States-Guatemala, TIAS, May 21, 1984; Agreement for Recovery and Return of Stolen and Archaeological, Historical and Cultural Properties, United States-Ecuador, November 17, 1983; and Treaty of Co-operation between the United States of America and the United Mexican States Providing for the Recovery and Return of Stolen Archaeological, Historical and Cultural Properties, July 17, 1970. Although available as remedies, in some cases for more than 25 years, these treaties are very rarely invoked to recover property.

[48] *See, e.g.*, 18 U.S.C. §§ 542, 545 and § 983, (1999); 19 U.S.C. §§ 1497, 1595 (1999). In 1991, the U.S. Customs Service set forth a general statement of its powers, and attempted to clarify how claims of illegal import of cultural property should be addressed. U.S. Customs Directive, "Detention and Seizure of Cultural Property," Apr. 18, 1991. The Customs Service announced in 1999 that it intended to revise or clarify its position and a new directive is expected to be published in 2001.

[49] 19 U.S.C. § 1595 (1999). Although the Civil Asset Forfeiture Reform Act of 2000 does not apply to Title 19 seizures, it does apply to a § 545 seizure, discussed *infra* at note 59. *See* 18 U.S.C. § 983(i)(2).

[50] *See, e.g.*, 18 U.S.C. § 541 (authorizing Customs to seize property that is underdeclared); 18 U.S.C. § 1001 (allowing Customs to seize property that is misclassified). The fact that most works of art may enter the United States duty-free is not in any way a defense to underdeclaring or misclassifiying an imported item. Although a particular violation may not be a loss of revenue to the government, it may nevertheless be prosecuted because any incorrect import data skews the trade statistics on which the government relies in international trade negotiations. *See, e.g.*, Jack

based its forfeiture of cultural property are §§ 542 and 545 of Title 18, the Crimes and Criminal Procedure Act. Section 542 sets forth the elements required to establish the crime of entering goods into the United States by means of false statements. This section is directed primarily at errors made in the entry process, that is, when there is an error or omission on the import declarations made to U.S. Customs. Section 545 has a broader scope and applies to any import that is "contrary to law."

[a] Entry of Goods by Means of False Statement in Violation of 18 U.S.C. § 542

Section 542 of the Crimes and Criminal Procedures Act provides:

> Whoever enters or introduces into the commerce of the United States any imported merchandise by means of any fraudulent or false invoice, declaration affidavit, letter, paper or by means of any false statement, written or verbal . . . or makes [or procures the making of] any false statement in any declaration *without reasonable cause to believe the truth* of such statement . . . shall be fined for each offence under this title or imprisoned not more than two years or both.[51]

Section 542 addresses situations in which a false statement is made in the entry process and permits Customs to prosecute the importer of any property if such person makes a false statement "without reasonable cause to believe the truth" of such statement.[52] The case law interpreting § 542 has imposed a requirement that the false statement be material.[53] The potential criminal liability pursuant to § 542 extends to the importer as well as the freight forwarder.

Lucentini, Journal of Commerce, Customs takes importer to court for allegedly overvaluing goods, http://www.joc.com (reporting on a trial in which importer was prosecuted for overvaluing goods and the government argued that the overvaluation "skewed trade statistics which the government uses to establish foreign policy").

[51] 18 U.S.C. § 542 (emphasis added).

[52] For example, U.S. Customs law requires that an importer or exporter disclose in which country an item is or was manufactured or made. This designation of country of origin may cause Customs to conduct a further investigation. *See Phiale*, *supra* note 22, at __; *see also* discussion of *Phiale infra* at § 6.03[B][4][b]. In *Phiale*, the importer represented that the country of origin for an antiquity was Switzerland, which was problematic because there is little basis to believe that an antiquity was originally made within the modern borders of Switzerland. The country-of-origin requirement (as opposed to the country-of-export requirement) can be troublesome when trying to attribute an accurate modern-day country of origin to an item that was made hundreds if not thousands of years ago. To comply with U.S. law, it is important to have "reasonable cause to believe" that the designated modern-day country could have been a location in which the item was originally made.

[53] There are two different tests for determining materiality in this context: the "but for" test followed by the Fifth and Ninth circuits, and the "natural tendency test" followed by the First and Second circuits. For a discussion of the materiality requirement, *see Phiale*, *supra* note 22, at __.

[b] Smuggling Goods Into the United States in Violation of 18 U.S.C. § 545

Section 545 of the Crimes and Criminal Procedure provisions of the United States Code provides:

> Whoever fraudulently or knowingly imports or brings into the United States, any merchandise *contrary to law*, or *receives, conceals, buys, sells, or in any manner facilitates* the transportation, concealment or sale of such merchandise after importation, *knowing the same to have been imported or brought into the United States contrary to law* . . . shall be fined under this title or imprisoned not more than five years, or both. (emphasis added)[54]

Section 545 extends the authority of Customs to pursue criminal cases against individuals beyond importers and their agents to include subsequent possessors, purchasers, and sellers of such property provided they knew that the property was illegally imported. The high standard set in § 545, that a subsequent possessor must know that an import was illegal, means the government is unlikely to prosecute a subsequent possessor, buyer, or seller who innocently possesses property that was smuggled into the United States. Such persons nevertheless run the risk of having their property seized and forfeited to the U.S. government if the *importer* knowingly illegally imported an item.[55] Subsequent possessors are not necessarily entitled to compensation from the Government, and may be compelled to pursue a claim against the seller.[56]

[c] Forfeiture Provisions

In addition to the forfeiture right based on § 545 discussed above,[57] the Government's general authority to seize property is set forth in § 1595(a) of the

---

The natural-tendency test provides that the misstatement is material if it has the potential significantly to affect the integrity or operation of the importation process. *Id.*

[54] 18 U.S.C. § 545.

[55] The actual importer in *Phiale* was not a party to the forfeiture proceeding and refused to testify in his deposition, pleading the Fifth Amendment. Hence the court was permitted to draw the adverse inference that he had knowledge of the illegal import. Obviously, this greatly eased the government's burden of proof. The dealer/importer did, however, articulate his position in a statement published in The Art Newspaper in which he alleged that he in fact did not *know* what representations his broker/shipper made when the property was imported. The Art Newspaper, Vol. X, No. 93, June 1999, cover. Instead, he claimed to have simply followed his standard procedure: sending the broker/shipper the invoice of sale with a request to clear it through U.S. Customs.

[56] The subsequent possessor in *Phiale* is pursuing recovery of his damages from the U.S. attorney general. *See* Steinhardt Seeks $1.2 Million Refund, Wall St. J., March 3, 2000.

[57] If the forfeiture is based on § 545, as opposed to a Title 19 forfeiture, then the recently enacted Civil Asset Forfeiture Reform Act of 2000 applies. *See infra* note 59 (discussing the Civil Asset Forfeiture Reform Act).

Customs Duties Act.[58] The Government is free to use its broad prosecutorial discretion in deciding whether to become involved in a foreign government's patrimony claim, to pursue forfeiture proceedings, or simply to interplead civilly a case and compel the interested parties to establish their respective claims before a U.S. court of law. Forfeiture of works of art imported into the United States may be appropriate if the property is stolen, as further discussed below in § 6.03[B][4], or if the property is imported either without reasonable cause to believe the truth of the import representations or otherwise "contrary to law" in violation of §§ 542 and 545.

Forfeiture versus Interpleader. In situations involving claims initiated by foreign governments to recover cultural property allegedly imported illegally but in the hands of a subsequent possessor or purchaser, forfeiture may in many cases inappropriately favor a foreign government over a potentially innocent U.S. buyer/owner.[59] In such cases, the foreign government is not required to participate as a party to the litigation, and the U.S. government in effect does that government's prosecutorial work for it. In fact, by soliciting such assistance from the U.S. government, the foreign government may completely avoid ever itself having to establish the underlying, substantive violation of the law. Moreover, the U.S. defendant is often faced with litigating facts and circumstance of a prior theft abroad or a foreign illegal export about which he is likely to have no first hand knowledge.

The Roman Torso Case. A recent example may be useful to illustrate the practical effect of a policy preference for forfeiture over interpleader.[60] On December 17, 1996, an American private collector purchased a Roman Torso ("the Torso") at public auction in New York from Sotheby's.[61] After the sale was

[58] 19 U.S.C. § 1595. The relevant portions of § 1595a (1)(c) provide: "If any officer . . . authorized to make searches and seizures has probable cause to believe that . . . any merchandise has been . . . brought into the United States unlawfully; [such person] may make application, under oath, to search for and seize such merchandise."

[59] There have in the past been concerns, even in contexts outside cultural property claims by foreign governments, about the U.S. government's exercise of its forfeiture powers. *See, e.g.*, Forfeitures and Fairness, The New York Times, opinion page, Feb. 28, 2000 ("There is widespread agreement that the forfeiture rules tilt too far in favor of government power."). The response to these concerns was the enactment of the Civil Asset Forfeiture Reform Act of 2000. The Civil Asset Forfeiture Reform Act of 2000 includes fundamental changes that would apply to a § 545 forfeiture procedure, such as an increase in the government's burden of proof from probable cause to a preponderance-of-the-evidence standard; a right to an innocent-owner defense; and the potential to recover attorney fees in the event there was no reasonable cause for the seizure. 18 U.S.C. § 983 *et seq.*

[60] A warrant seizure was filed in this case, United States v. Torso of Apollo, 98 Mag. 2354 (S.D.N.Y.), listed by the U.S. Customs Agency in its correspondence as Notice of Intent to Forfeit Case No. 99-1001-000055.

[61] In the ordinary course of business, the auction catalogue was sent prior to the sale to the Art

concluded, the Italian government claimed that the Torso had been stolen in 1984 from a private family in Italy. Based on these allegations and on the allegation that the Torso was imported into the United States in 1989 by means of a false statement, U.S. Customs seized the Torso. The purchaser at the 1996 sale was not involved with either the allegedly illegal import or the alleged theft. Moreover, there was strong evidence to indicate that the seller in the 1996 auction had acquired good title to the Torso. The 1996 seller had acquired the Torso in 1988 in good faith at another auction in the United Kingdom. Under §§ 3 and 4 of the United Kingdom's Limitations Act of 1980, title to stolen property passes to a good-faith purchaser at the expiration of six years from the date of the purchase.

The Assistant U.S. Attorney was fully aware that the 1988 auction purchaser may have had good title and right to possession of the Torso based on English law. In addition, it was obvious from the facts that the current U.S. possessor was not involved with any wrongdoing. Nevertheless, the U.S. government pursued a forfeiture proceeding. Facing protracted litigation with the American government, the 1996 purchaser simply chose not to contest the forfeiture and instead sought recovery from the auctioneer. The dealer who had originally consigned the piece was no longer in existence. The auctioneer canceled the sale and refunded the 1996 purchaser the purchase price of approximately $100,000. Thus, both an American company and an American private collector were required to relinquish possession of an object and suffer financial loss without the Italian family or the Italian government ever having to prove their case in a U.S. or Italian court.

Compelling the U.S. possessor to establish a prior right to possession before the alleged victim has established its case turns standard American jurisprudence on its head. Forfeiture simply makes no sense in this context. Such claims could more appropriately be addressed, as with most other title disputes, in a civil interpleader action between the Republic of Italy or the original theft victim and the U.S. possessor/owner. Italy, like any other alleged victim of theft, would be the plaintiff and have to prove its right to possession before the U.S. participant would be put to its proof.

When the U.S. government elected instead to use its extraordinary forfeiture powers, after satisfying a minimum reasonable-cause standard, the burden of the litigation fell on a good-faith American purchaser who was left litigating against the virtually limitless resources of the U.S. government.[62] For practical reasons—

Loss Register to ascertain whether the item had been listed as lost or stolen. No claims were made prior to the sale.

[62] This situation is of particular concern given the Southern District of New York's criticism of art buyers for including standard title representations, warranties and indemnities in purchase contracts involving works of art. *See, e.g., Phiale, supra* note 22, at __. Certainly, courts do not infer bad faith on the part of buyers in other contexts simply because they include standard purchase clauses in their contracts. If such clauses justified finding a buyer suspicious, then any real estate

such as the low monetary value of an item or, as in the Torso case, the buyer being asked to engage in international discovery to prove matters well beyond his knowledge or experience—the possessor may choose not to assume the expense and burden of litigating with the U.S. government. In the U.S. government's efforts to accommodate foreign governments, domestic possessors may become innocent victims of international politics.

It would be more prudent and fair for the U.S. government to have a presumption in favor of civil interpleader, unless either the U.S. government intends independently to pursue a criminal case regarding the relevant violation or there is credible evidence, based on a preliminary investigation, that the possessor had actual knowledge that the property was stolen or imported contrary to law. Indeed, the U.S. Customs Service acknowledges in its 1991 directive the legitimate option of pursuing interpleader in cases involving the illegal import of cultural property.[63] For the United States to compel foreign governments to pursue their own claims to property, rather than exercising its forfeiture power, harms no one because a foreign government with a legitimate claim is free to pursue it in court.

[4] National Stolen Property Act, 18 U.S.C. §§ 2314-15

The National Stolen Property Act (NSPA) provides that "[w]hosoever transports, transmits, or transfers in interstate or foreign commerce any goods, wares, merchandise . . . of the value of $5,000 or more, knowing the same to have been stolen, converted or taken by fraud . . . shall be fined under this title or imprisoned not more than ten years or both."[64]

There is no debate that the NSPA applies to domestically stolen cultural property (in the traditional meaning in the United States of the word "stolen").[65] Nor is there any debate that the NSPA applies to property stolen in the traditional sense of the word within the borders of a foreign nation and subsequently imported into the United States.[66] The NSPA has been applied to cases in which property

---

purchaser requesting full representations, warranties and indemnities against environmental or superfund problems would be in trouble.

[63] *See* Customs Directive, *supra* note 48, at 11. Interestingly, the directive offers this option only in cases in which there is insufficient evidence to sustain a U.S. violation. One could argue that in such cases, the foreign government claimant should not benefit from the U.S. Government commencing an interpleader, but should be compelled, like any other alleged theft victim, to itself assume the obligations and risks of being a plaintiff.

[64] 18 U.S.C. § 2314.

[65] *See* Chapter 5, "Stolen Art."

[66] *See, e.g.*, United States of America v. Hollinshead, 495 F.2d 1154 (9th Cir. 1974) ("overwhelming evidence that the defendants knew that it was contrary to Guatemalan law to remove the stele, and that the stele was stolen").

was never physically possessed by a foreign institution, museum, or nation but has nevertheless been deemed by such nation to be owned by it simply by operation of foreign local law, such as a finder's law or export control law.[67] There continues to be a debate about whether it is appropriate to use the NSPA in the context of cultural property claims based in essence on export control laws.

The Customs Service also expressly acknowledges the U.S. policy of not enforcing the export control laws of foreign countries, except in limited circumstances.[68] Customs accepts that there is an open question of whether the definition of "stolen" NSPA should be extended to apply to all cultural property claims made by foreign governments.[69] In its 1991 Directive on Cultural Property, Customs explained that as of 1991, U.S. courts had "only determined that [one country's] laws claiming ownership of cultural artifacts are sufficient for a successful criminal prosecution."[70] Courts have refused to enforce the cultural property laws of Peru, Croatia, and Hungary for a variety of reasons in connection with cultural property claims.[71]

There are fundamental concerns about the government applying the NSPA to cultural property claims. It creates the problem of the U.S. government basing its actions on foreign patrimony laws that may be entirely contrary to U.S. concepts of ownership and private property[72] or being in a position of enforcing laws that

---

[67] *See, e.g.,* United States v. McClain, 593 F.2d 658 (5th Cir. 1979), *cert. denied*, 444 U.S. 918 (1979); and *Phiale, supra* note 22.

[68] The U.S. Customs Directive on Cultural Property states, "[I]t is important to note that merely because an exportation of an artifact is illegal within a particular country does not necessarily mean that the subsequent importation into the United States is illegal." The Directive goes on to note that there are two federal laws that permit the seizure upon import into the United States based on an illegal export from a foreign country: the Pre-Columbian Monumental and Architectural Sculpture and Murals Statute and the CCPIA. Directive, *supra* note 48, at 1 and 3.

[69] The courts have in other contexts refused to extend the concept of "stolen" in the NSPA beyond its common understanding. *See* United States v. Carman, 577 F.2d 556 (9th Cir. 1978) (in the context of an NSPA prosecution in the area of interstate transfer of money knowing such funds were taken by fraud, the court followed *McClain,* quoting that "Section 2314 should not be expanded at the government's will beyond the connotation—depriving an owner of its rights in property—conventionally called to mind"); and United States v. Rogers, 786 F.2d 1000 (10th Cir. 1986) (the court refused to expand the definition of stolen to include the defendant's taking his own property which had not yet been declared forfeited).

[70] The Directive notes that U.S. courts have accepted claims by Mexico, while the cultural property claims of ownership by "Peru, Guatemala and Ecuador [are] more open to challenge." Directive, *supra* note 48, at 11.

[71] *See* The Republic of Croatia v. The Trustee of the Marquess of Northampton 1987 Settlement, 610 N.Y.S.2d 263 (1st Dep't 1994), *leave to appeal denied,* 84 N.Y.S.2d 85 (1994) (Croatia and Hungary failed to satisfy their burden of proof supporting their respective claims of title to a collection of ancient Roman silver. The original plaintiff, the Republic of Lebanon, withdrew its claim shortly before the trial); *Peru v. Johnson, supra* note 38 (Government of Peru unable to establish its claim for recovery of 89 artifacts it alleged had originated in Peru).

[72] *See infra* § 6.03[B][4][c].

are poorly understood or not enforced by the government involved.[73] There are also concerns (discussed above) about the U.S. government using forfeiture proceedings to pursue cultural property cases. When the U.S. government's primary reason for pursuing a matter is not the domestic-law violation but the foreign patrimony claim and potential international diplomacy benefit, expanding the scope of the NSPA is particularly troublesome.

As a practical matter, application of the NSPA to cultural property has resulted in expensive, difficult, and protracted domestic litigation. These cases have largely been based on complicated, contradictory, and inconsistently applied foreign law, which results in the U.S. court system and litigants devoting extensive resources to understanding and applying such laws.[74] It is worth asking why the U.S. courts and citizens should be required to enforce such laws, which are often fundamentally inconsistent with American concepts of private property rights and ownership, such as the basic principle that one legitimately owns objects found on one's own land.

[a] United States v. McClain[75]

The Fifth Circuit has held that the NSPA applies to the internal laws of foreign countries claiming title to cultural property within their borders that is subsequently illegally exported from such country. Although the procedural history of the *McClain* case is long and complicated, the relevant facts are fairly simple. Five defendants were accused of violations of the NSPA and of conspiracy based on a scheme in which they apparently systematically smuggled out of Mexico various pre-Columbian artifacts for resale in the United States.[76] As a result of a Federal Bureau of Investigation sting operation, the court was provided evidence establishing that one of the defendants had "five squads working in various Mexican archaeological zones and that the objects were passed, a few at a time, 'by contraband' " to the defendant's store.[77] The defendant explained that "the

---

[73] *See infra* note 94 (citing articles concerning foreign governments or armies participating in illegal export).

[74] *See, e.g.,* United States v. McClain, 545 F.2d 988 (5th Cir. 1977) *cert. denied*, McClain v. U.S., 100 S. Ct. 234 (1979); Government of Peru v. Johnson, 720 F. Supp. 810 (C.D. Cal. 1989); Republic of Lebanon v. Sotheby's and the Trustee of the Marquess of Northampton Settlement and The Socialist Federal Republic of Yugoslavia, 167 A.D. 2d 142 (N.Y. App. Div. 1 1990); Republic of Croatia v. Trustee of the Marquess of Northampton Settlement, 203 A.D. 2d 167 (NY App. Div. 1 1994); Republic of Turkey v. OKS Partners, 797 F. Supp. 64 (D. Mass. 1992).

[75] 545 F.2d 988 (5th Cir. 1977), *appealed after remand*, 593 F.2d 658 (5th Cir. 1979).

[76] *McClain* was a criminal prosecution, requiring the government to show beyond a reasonable doubt that the defendants had the requisite intent to commit a crime. In the cases discussed in the prior section, the Government's burden in the forfeiture context was to show probable cause to believe that the defendant had the requisite intent to violate the law.

[77] *McClain*, 593 F.2d at 660.

prices had gone up as a result of the February 1972 presidential agreement between the United States and Mexico [and he] now had to give more money to the people who were passing the objects to him."[78]

The Fifth Circuit addressed the issue of whether the NSPA should apply to a claim of ownership based on a foreign sovereign's internal laws that vest in that sovereign ownership of property within its borders. The court expressly repeated the fundamental rule of U.S. law that "it is not a violation of law to import an item of art or anything else simply because it has been illegally exported from another country."[79] The Fifth Circuit also held that the NSPA could be applied in the context of foreign law but that "a declaration of ownership is necessary before illegal exportation of an article can be considered theft, and the exported article considered 'stolen', within the meaning of the NSPA."[80] The court reached this conclusion despite numerous arguments by defendants and *amici curiae* that the NSPA should not be expanded to include claims of ownership by a foreign sovereign that never established prior possession of the object in question.[81]

[b] United States of America v. An Antique Platter of Gold (*Phiale*)[82]

This case provided the Second Circuit with a clear opportunity to follow the *McClain* court's interpretation of the applicability of the NSPA to claims of property purportedly "stolen" from a foreign sovereign. However, the Second Circuit expressly declined to reach the issue. In *United States vs. An Antique Platter of Gold*, the lower court held that the NSPA did apply because the U.S. government's undisputed expert opinion indicated that under Italian law a Phiale allegedly found in Italy and illegally exported belonged to the Italian government.[83]

---

[78] *Id.*

[79] *McClain*, 593 F.2d at 663 (citing *McClain*, 545 F.2d at 996).

[80] *McClain*, 545 F.2d at 1000, *affirmed by* 593 F.2d at 663.

[81] *See also* United States v. Hollinshead, 495 F.2d 1154 (9th Cir. 1974) (finding that the trial court judge's failure to make clear whether the defendants knew that Guatemalan law transfers title to illegally exported property to the government "may have been error" but was not prejudicial because the defendants clearly knew the property was stolen) and *United States v. Pre-Columbian Objects*, 845 F. Supp. 544 (N.D. Ill. 1993) (discussing NSPA on motion to dismiss, and finding that Guatemalan law granting title to the Republic of Guatemala upon illegal export was sufficient to defeat a motion to dismiss).

[82] 98 Civ. 10537 (BSJ) (S.D.N.Y. 1998), *aff'd*, 184 F.3d 131 (2d Cir. 1999). *See also supra* note 22.

[83] For purposes of a motion of summary judgement, the Southern District of New York accepted the undisputed opinion submitted by the U.S. government's expert that Italy's domestic cultural property law is sufficient to pursue a claim pursuant to the NSPA. However, this district court opinion is not binding precedent. *See* United States v. Santos, 1996 WL 617329 (S.D.N.Y. 1996) (Senior District Judge Haight noting that "District Courts are free to disagree with one another")

However, on appeal, Chief Judge Winter of the Second Circuit specifically provided that "[w]e need not address whether the NSPA incorporates concepts of property such as those contained in the Italian patrimony laws."[84] In the context of deciding whether the misstatement regarding the country of origin on the U.S. Customs form was material, the court reiterated that "regardless of whether *McClain*'s reasoning is ultimately followed as a proper interpretation of the NSPA, a reasonable customs official would certainly consider the fact that *McClain* supports a colorable claim to seize the Phiale as having possibly been exported in violation of Italian patrimony laws."[85]

[c] The NSPA and Cultural Property Policy

A policy of applying the NSPA broadly to the domestic patrimony laws of foreign governments risks placing U.S. courts in the difficult position of interpreting and accepting foreign jurisprudence that is in direct conflict with our own. In addition, it places an onerous burden on U.S. citizens, that of trying to decipher complicated cultural property laws of other countries around the world. The implications of extending the application of the NSPA to foreign patrimony law are disturbing. If a foreigner legally owned a work of art in a country from which it could not be legally exported, that person would suffer a material financial loss if the domestic value of the object is a fraction of the international value. Assume

---

(citing IBM Credit Corp. v. United Home for Aged Hebrews, 848 F. Supp. 495, 497 (S.D.N.Y. 1994)).

[84] *Phiale*, *supra* note 22, at 134. It is often extremely confusing to ascertain the meaning and the effectiveness of foreign domestic laws regarding cultural property. The courts in *McClain* and *Johnson* expressly pointed out the difficulty in determining the nature and scope of the foreign domestic laws governing cultural property at any given point in time. *See* United States v. McClain, et al., 593 F.2d 659 (5th Cir. 1979) (court acknowledges that although expert testimony of various Mexican legal scholars consistently held that illegal exportation of Mexican artifacts amounted to theft under Mexican law, the court noted, "It may well be, as testified so emphatically by most of the Mexican witnesses, that Mexico has considered itself the owner of all pre-Columbian artifacts for almost 100 years. If so, however, it has not expressed that view with sufficient clarity to survive translation into terms understandable by and binding upon American citizens.") *McClain*, 593 F.2d at 670; and *Peru v. Johnson*, *supra* note 38, at 814 (quoting the *McClain* court and stating "I find the same comment to be applicable here").

Were the Southern District to be faced with deciding a case in which the litigants challenged the meaning, interpretation and application of domestic Italian cultural property law, it is unclear whether it would reach the same conclusion. Indeed, when a foreign government, as opposed to the U.S. government, has pursued a claim based on foreign cultural property laws, they have rarely been successful. *See, e.g.*, *Peru v. Johnson*, *supra* note 38; Republic of Croatia v. Trustee of the Marquess of Northampton Settlement, *supra* note 74; and United States v. The Republic of France, 95 Civ. 1470 (S.D.N.Y. 1995) (France failed to pursue a claim to a painting by Jacques Joseph Tissot).

[85] *Phiale*, *supra* note 22, at 137.

such person were nevertheless to export the item illegally for sale in the United States, and that the NSPA's scope is expanded to include foreign cultural property claims. The U.S. government would then be required to recover from the actual owner an item merely exported illegally. The U.S. would be in the awkward position of enforcing a law that violates one of its own fundamental notions of the rights of owners of personal property to transport, sell, and export their private property.

For another potential consequence of expanding the scope of the NSPA, consider the following scenario. Assume a foreign country exists where it becomes illegal for individuals to own private property based on their religious beliefs, ethnic background, sex, or sexual preference. Further assume that such persons attempt to flee the jurisdiction and export "their" property, and that title to the property is consequently deemed automatically to transfer to the foreign nation. Does the U.S. government want its courts to be deciding the meaning of such laws, and, worse yet, to be applying them? Surely the answer must be no.

It is inconsistent with U.S. jurisprudence to automatically transfer title to items found in the ground on one's private property to the government. In the United States, private citizens own objects found in the ground on the land they own. Elsewhere, the government may pre-empt this private property right and deny private ownership rights to property found on one's own land by granting title to the foreign government, by imposing sale restrictions, or by imposing export controls.

One could argue that the U.S. government should not be in the business of upholding foreign patrimony laws that offend our sense of the right to own, sell or export private property or property found on privately owned land. Just as we may not want to impose the U.S. sense of private property ownership on other countries, it may be prudent to refrain from entering the world of interpreting and supporting foreign laws that are fundamentally potentially inconsistent with our own.

§ 6.04 INTERNATIONAL LAWS AND TREATIES

[A] Treaties

[1] UNIDROIT

The International Institute for the Unification of Private Law (UNIDROIT) is an organization originally set up as part of the League of Nations, whose purpose is to promote the international acceptance and adoption of uniform private law treaties. On June 24, 1995, UNIDROIT succeeded in having signed a Convention on the International Return of Stolen or Illegally Exported Cultural Objects.[86]

[86] For the complete text of the UNIDROIT Convention, the signatories to it and a list of which

The UNIDROIT Convention basically provides a legal basis for the return of stolen or illegally exported cultural objects. Although perfectly well intentioned in its efforts to curb the illicit trade in art, the UNIDROIT Convention contains a variety of fundamental problems, such as the provisions governing the return of illegally exported property. Such provisions make it unlikely that a sufficient number of art market nations will sign or ratify it to make it effective.[87] As of July 14, 1999, 22 countries have signed the Convention, but only 12 countries have ratified it.[88]

Chapter III of the UNIDROIT Convention, entitled "Return of Illegally Exported Cultural Objects," is most relevant,[89] and states that the requesting

---

countries have ratified it, see http://www.unidroit.org. For a constructive critique of the UNIDROIT Convention, see Pierre Valentin, The UNIDROIT Convention on the International Return of Stolen or Illegally Exported Cultural Objects, 4 Art, Antiquity and the Law 107 (September 1999).

Chapter One of the Convention sets forth the scope of the Convention and defines "cultural objects" as religious or secular objects which are "of importance for archaeology, prehistory, history, literature, art or science" and are enumerated in further detail in the Annex to the Convention. The descriptions contained in the Annex to the Convention are particularly broad and unlimited by either minimum values or age criteria.

[87] Shortly after the UNIDROIT Convention was signed in Rome, there was much enthusiasm that so-called art market countries would sign. However, because many of the Convention's provisions are inconsistent with numerous art market countries' internal laws or policies, it now appears that the art market countries will not sign or ratify the Convention. Recently, after re-evaluating the Convention, the United Kingdom decided that it would not become a signatory. *See* Letter of MP Chris Smith to the House of Commons, February 2000. Other art market countries that have not signed the Convention include such countries as the United States, France, and Germany. Switzerland and the Netherlands signed, but have decided not to ratify the Convention. All these countries have, however, expressed their support for the goal of suppressing the illicit trade in works of art.

[88] The 12 countries are: Lithuania, Paraguay, Romania, Peru, Hungary, Bolivia, Finland (with declarations), Italy, the People's Republic of China (with declarations), Ecuador, Brazil, and El Salvador. For an up-to-date listing of countries that have ratified the Convention, see http://www.unidroit.org.

[89] The other main substantive provision of the Convention is contained in Chapter II, entitled "Restitution of Stolen Cultural Objects." Specifically, Chapter II sets forth the parameters for a claim to recover property stolen from a private person or a public institution. Whether an item claimed to be recovered is stolen or illegally exported, the alleged victim has a minimum of 50 years and possibly indefinitely to make a claim for recovery. For example, if an item is stolen from a public institution, there is a three year statute of limitation that begins to run from the time the claimant "knew the location of the cultural object and the identity of its possessor." UNIDROIT Convention, Ch. II, art. 3(4). This statute of limitations may be extended further by any Contracting State to a time limitation of "75 years or longer" consistent with local law. Ch. II, art. 3(5). Such extended statutes of limitation lend great uncertainty to the art market and perhaps more importantly directly conflict with many domestic laws on recovery of stolen property. *See, e.g.*, France (statute of limitations of three years from the date of theft against a possessor in good faith); England (standard six-year statute of limitations with a fifteen-year maximum); Switzerland (five-year statute of limitations). Of course, the statute of limitations presumes innocence or good faith of the buyer. Indeed, a recent case before the High Court of England provides that if good faith is lacking, the

country shall be entitled to have an illegally exported cultural object ordered returned to it by the courts of the addressed country, provided that the loss of the object "significantly impairs" at least one of the following interests:

- the physical preservation of the object or of its context
- the integrity of a complex object
- the preservation of information, for example, of a scientific or historical character
- the traditional or ritual use of the object by a tribal or indigenous community

or

- it is established that the object is of "significant cultural importance" for the requesting state.[90]

A possessor of the object may be entitled to "fair and reasonable compensation"[91] but only if such person "neither knew nor ought reasonably to have known at the time of the acquisition that the object had been illegally exported."[92]

Chapter III requires countries to enforce the export control laws of foreign countries, and thereby violates a common legal principal.[93] One reason not to enforce another country's export control laws is that such laws may be inconsis-

relevant statute of limitations may be suspended. *See*, City of Gotha and Federal Republic of Germany v. Sotheby's and Cobert Finance SA [reported in The Times (of London) on 8 October 1998, TLR 8/10/98.]; *see also* Paul Lomas & Simon Orton, Potential Repercussions from the City of Gotha Decision, 4 Art, Antiquity and the Law 159 (June 1999).

[90] UNIDROIT Convention, Ch. II, art. 5(3). Understanding or defining what constitutes "significant" is problematic in itself. The market tends to define significance by an object's rarity, aesthetic qualities, art historic importance or possibly even its history of ownership. These characteristics are often, but not always, reflected in the financial value of an object. In contrast, archaeologists seem to have an entirely different understanding of what "significant" means. Recently, an archaeologist on the U.S. Cultural Property Advisory Committee asked one of the persons providing testimony in opposition to Bolivia's request for import restrictions if he would like to have a presentation made to him explaining why "every $100 pot" is significant to archaeologists.

[91] The terms "fair and reasonable" are undefined and the cause of concern to many. A beneficiary of an estate or the recipient of a gift are not entitled to "fair and reasonable compensation" if such compensation would put the beneficiary or recipient of the gift in "a more favourable position than the person from whom it acquired the cultural object." *See* UNIDROIT Convention, Ch. III, art. 6(5).

[92] UNIDROIT Convention, Ch. II, art. 6(1).

[93] *See infra* note 13 discussing U.S. policy of not enforcing the export control laws of foreign nations. Whereas the countries of the European Union were willing to agree to enforce the export control laws of the other Member States of the European Union, they do not seem willing to enforce the export control laws of every country that may happen to sign on to the Convention. *See infra* discussion of EU 1993 Directive at § 6.04[B].

tently applied, or not applied at all by the foreign nation. In addition, there are concerns about either tacit consent of the foreign authorities of violations of the law, or even government corruption supporting the illegal exports through bribes or otherwise. Indeed, there are regular reports of governmental involvement in the illegal trade in cultural property.[94] Although the possibility of foreign government corruption does not in any way suggest that the problems of smuggling and looting should be ignored, it may mean that repeated pursuit of international conventions is simply not the most productive solution to this complex problem.[95]

[2] UNESCO

On November 14, 1970, the UNESCO Convention on the Means of Prohibiting and Preventing the Illicit Import, Export and Transfer of Ownership of Cultural Property was adopted.[96] As of December 1999, 91 countries have ratified the UNESCO Convention,[97] including the United States in 1972.[98] The provisions of the 1970 Treaty that are most relevant to this discussion include: Article 9, the "crisis" provision; Article 6, the illegal export provision; Article 7(a), regarding museums and illegally exported property; and Article 7(b) regarding property inventoried as part of a museum and subsequently stolen. The 1970 Treaty was

---

[94] *See* Elizabeth Rosenthal, China's Fierce War on Smuggling Uproots a Vast Hidden Economy, N.Y. Times, Mar. 6, 2000 ("Some foreign and Chinese experts estimate that half of all Chinese customs officials in some areas are involved in smuggling, and add that the corruption extends far up the chain of command."); Jonathan Napack, Chinese Policy on Cultural Property; Turning a Blind Eye, Art Newspaper, v. 101, Mar. 2000 ("The scale of this corruption, as well as the seriousness of the crackdown, only became apparent when investigators publicly announced that Xiamen, one of China's wealthiest cities, had essentially become a criminal syndicate under Party figurers including politburo member Jia Qinglin."); Elizabeth Helman Minchilli, Antiquities Gang Busted, Art & Auction, Feb. 15, 1999 at 8 (noting that a chief magistrate in central Sicily is under official investigation on suspicion of illegal trafficking in antiquities); Khasab Oman, A Phoenician Statue for my Coffee-Table, Economist, Apr. 3, 1999, at 39 ("Until recently, the [Lebanese] antiquities officials were themselves part of the problem: indeed, the police raids arose from an investigation into their department."); Michael Sheridan, Looters Strip Cambodia of its Art, Sunday Times (of London), Apr. 11, 1999 (noting that Cambodian soldiers participated in looting and were reported to have delivered "pieces in six black pick-up trucks at a dawn rendez-vous").

[95] *See infra* at § 6.04[A][3] for a discussion of alternatives to international treaties as possible solutions to these problems.

[96] UNESCO 823 U.N.T.S. 231(1972). *See* John Henry Merryman, Two Ways of Thinking about Cultural Property, 80 Am. J. of Int'l L., 831, 842-45 (October 1986) (discussing the UNESCO Convention and its basic purpose).

[97] For an up-to-date list of the countries that have ratified the UNESCO Convention, *see* http://www.unesco.org.

[98] The withdrawal of the United States from membership in UNESCO in 1985 did not alter the commitment to carry out its obligations under the Convention.

not self-executing, thus each country is able to adopt only those provisions that are consistent with its national jurisprudence.[99]

[3] Alternatives to Treaties

Endless hours and inordinate amounts of money have been spent in the negotiation and ratification of these two Conventions.[100] However, only two major art-market countries have entered into force the UNESCO Convention and no major art-market country has ratified the UNIDROIT Convention.[101] The enormous amount of time, money and energy put into these conventions is thus of little benefit.[102] The repeated attempts to have art-market countries enforce international conventions regarding illegal exports that are inconsistent with their internal laws, jurisprudence and polices is not the best use of time or resources to combat the serious problems of smuggling and looting. Rather, perhaps the solution to the problems of looting, pillaging, and smuggling are better addressed by means other than international legal conventions.[103]

The focus should shift from trying to persuade art-market countries to enforce export laws of foreign nations, which often are poorly understood or inconsistently enforced, to developing alternative solutions such as:

---

[99] For example, in the United States the provision regarding recovery of property that constituted "documented inventory" of a museum or public monument was incorporated into the Convention on Cultural Property Implementation Act, discussed *supra* at § 6.03[B][1], but the provisions regarding the broad enforcement of the export control laws of other State Parties to the Convention were greatly limited and modified.

[100] For a detailed discussion of the process of drafting the UNESCO Convention, *see* Paul Bator, The International Trade in Art, 34 Stan. L. Rev. at 370.

[101] France and the U.S. have entered the UNESCO Convention into force. However, the U.S. implementing legislation, in the form of the CCPIA discussed earlier in this chapter, is much more limited in scope. Recently, the United Kingdom reconsidered whether it would become a signatory to the UNESCO Convention. Although Her Majesty's Government expressed support for the goals and principles of the Convention, it ultimately concluded that it would not sign. Letter of MP Chris Smith to the House of Commons, February 2000.

[102] In the case of the UNESCO Convention's implementation in the United States, it took over ten years of debating the scope of the legislation for it finally to become law in 1983. Since 1983, there have been seven instances of emergency restrictions imposed, five bilateral agreements and few cases filed pursuant to the provisions protecting documented inventory of museums or public monuments. *See supra* at § 6.03[B][1] (discussing CCPIA). Although some of these agreements and treaties are open to criticism, one could also argue that given the limited number of requests (as compared with the large number of countries who complain about the loss of their antiquities during discussions of international conventions), serious consideration should be given to pursuing alternate solutions to the problem of illegal export.

[103] The need for further legislation or conventions in this field is also questionable in that in addition to the existing international conventions, there exist numerous domestic laws regulating and prohibiting export and theft.

1. commit resources of staff and money to assist in staffing and training foreign and domestic customs and law enforcement officers in methods to prosecute and understand issues of art theft and smuggling;
2. encourage enactment and enforcement of anti-corruption laws in art-source countries, followed by training in anti-corruption investigation and prosecution techniques by those governments which are less burdened by governmental corruption in favor of those governments with the greater problem;
3. promote the revision of tax laws regarding ownership, donation, and inheritance of works of art in those countries with an active black market, which would create incentives for citizens in these countries to report finds, collect their own heritage, and donate their collections back to the source countries;
4. increase criminal and civil penalties, within the context of countries' existing legal systems, for looting, art theft, and smuggling of cultural patrimony;
5. benefit from the dramatic improvements in modern technology to develop publicly and internationally available registries that would include items of truly outstanding cultural patrimony (including archaeological sites);
6. develop publicly available, sophisticated, private or governmental art loss registries that would accept descriptions and photographs of stolen items, whether from archaeological digs, churches, museums or private collections;
7. maintain a publicly available registry requiring archaeologists excavating in source countries to provide photographs and descriptions of objects found on the digs within a short and reasonable time from the date of each find;
8. research method to support prompt completion of archaeological digs and to make mandatory publication of the finds without delay;
9. investigate the possibility of privatizing archaeological sites and public monuments, subject to certain restrictions, to ease the funding burden on governments of such activities as excavation, research, preservation, and publication; and
10. create a task force among government representatives of art-market countries, source countries, archaeologists, members of the art market, and financial specialists to explore creative ways to fund the above activities, possibly through favorable tax treatment or other benefits in exchange for funding.

The argument that the art-source countries lack sufficient funds to engage in the above described types of activity is the often-repeated response to any suggestion other than international enforcement of all foreign export control laws. This response is an easy avoidance of the shared responsibility of all nations to preserve and protect heritage and was more persuasive before the explosion in technological advancements of our era.

If a financially troubled government makes a true commitment to this cause, it would seem possible to find funds, through international loans, revising tax or duty laws or other creative methods.[104] Moreover, many of the art-rich countries, such as Italy and China, are today economically strong and have taken important steps toward reducing these problems domestically. If international agencies or governmental organizations shift their focus to attracting world-class financial minds to consider the complex question of funding, it is hard to imagine that better solutions would not be found.

[B] THE EUROPEAN UNION

[1] Treaty of Rome

The European Community Treaty of Rome essentially requires the harmonization of European internal laws.[105] For purposes of this chapter, the relevant provisions of the Treaty of Rome include Articles 23, 28, 29 and 30. Articles 23, 28 and 29 effectively require the removal of prohibitions of export and import restrictions and taxes within the European Union, including "quantitative restrictions" on exports and imports. However, an exception to these rules is set forth in Article 30, which provides that the three earlier articles shall not preclude "prohibitions or restrictions on imports, exports or goods in transit justified on grounds of . . . the protection of national treasures possessing artistic, historic or archaeological value. . . ." The treaty limits such patrimony-protection measures by stating that any "such prohibitions or restrictions shall not, however, constitute a means of arbitrary discrimination or a disguised restriction on trade between

[104] There is no question that the favorable charitable donation laws in the United States and the potential tax benefits to donating inherited works of art to the governments of France and England have greatly benefited each of these nations. A willingness to re-evaluate rigid export control laws, burdensome inheritance tax laws and restrictive ownership laws is worth considering. It simply cannot be denied that those countries with less restrictive export laws, equitable tax rates and limited restraints on the market seem to have less of a black market. The fact that many of these countries are also art market countries does not negate the reality. *See infra* note 141, citing articles that encourage the consideration of managed antiquities markets to help source countries fund protection of their cultural heritage; *cf.* Bator, *supra* note 11, at 324 ("even in countries where the looting of sites and monuments is a virulent problem, over-inclusive export embargoes on large categories of antiquities and archaeological materials are self-defeating and undesirable.").

[105] Countries currently comprising the European Union include Austria, Belgium, Denmark, Finland, France, Germany, Greece, Ireland, Italy, Luxembourg, the Netherlands, Portugal, Spain, Sweden, and the United Kingdom. For general information on the European Union, visit http://www.europa.eu.int.

Member States." Unfortunately, there is no definition in the Treaty of Rome as to what constitutes "national treasures."[106]

Several European Member States have national laws regulating with fairly strict controls the export of works of art even within the EU.[107] Some of these export controls are without regard to limits on age or value and fail to make any effort to articulate standards for determining which objects constitute "national treasures."[108] Such strict export controls may arguably violate the Treaty of Rome. To date, none of these laws has been challenged as "arbitrary discrimination" or "disguised restrictions on trade between Member States." Thus, although the internal economic barriers in the EU have been greatly reduced over the last 20 years, there remain numerous restraints on the free flow of works of art even within the EU. One could argue that in response to the real progress made in the European Union toward harmonization in areas such as finance, economics, and employment standards, certain countries more fiercely cling to a nationalistic identity with respect to cultural property or defend more vigorously their rights to retain nationalistic borders in the case of cultural objects. [109]

[2] European Union Laws Regarding Movement of Cultural Property

There are two main laws within the European Union specifically addressing movement of cultural property. One deals with imposing a standard licensing system for export of cultural goods outside of the EU[110] ("1992 Council Regulation") and the second grants to Member States a method of recovering from one

[106] Logical resources to consult to ascertain what may be meant by "national treasures" in the European context are arguably the Council Regulation (3911/92) of Dec. 9, 1992, regarding the export of cultural goods outside of the European Union, and the Council Directive 93/7/EEC of Mar. 15, 1993, regarding return of illegally removed cultural objects from one Member State located in another Member State, both of which are discussed below.

[107] For a detailed discussion of the laws governing the free trade of works of art in the EU, *see* Thomas von Plehwe, Dr. jur., Rechtsanwalt, Cologne, European Union and the Free Movement of Cultural Goods, European L. Rev., v. 20 No. 5 (October 1995).

[108] European countries with relatively more restrictive export control laws include Italy, Greece, and Spain.

[109] There may be cause for concern at the seeming increase in cultural nationalism and the assumption that all objects in any way connected with a culture or country should reside within the borders of the modern-day country. For a thought-provoking critique of cultural nationalism as opposed to cultural internationalism, *see* John Henry Merryman, Two Ways of Thinking about Cultural Property, Am. J. Int'l L., vol. 80, No. 4 (October 1986).

[110] *See* Council Reg. 3911/92, December 9, 1992, on the Export of Cultural Goods: Commission Reg. 752/93, Mar. 30, 1993 (regarding implementation of the 1992 Council Regulation by creating a licensing system); and Council Reg. 2469/96, Dec. 16, 1996 (amending the annex to 1992 Council Regulation regarding gouaches, water colors and pastels).

another a cultural object that was "unlawfully removed" from the requesting Member State[111] ("1993 Directive").[112]

Since 1992, there has been within the European Union a two-tiered analysis required for exporting works of art outside of the EU. The 1992 Council Regulation imposes an EU requirement that, in addition to any national export control laws, certain types of cultural goods are subject to further EU export controls and require an EU license.[113] The 1992 Council Regulation refers to the licensing for "cultural goods," which are defined in an annex to the regulation. Most, but not all, items are subject to age limits and financial minimum thresholds ranging from 0 to 150,000 euros.

The 1993 Directive governs movement of cultural objects within the European Union and grants the right to a Member State to bring an action in another Member State for recovery of an item that was unlawfully removed from the requesting Member State's territory. The 1993 Directive required each Member State to enact laws allowing enforcement within the EU of the various Member States' export control laws. The directive is somewhat limited in scope because it applies only to "cultural objects" that constitute "national treasures" of the requesting Member State and that otherwise satisfy the definition in the 1993 Directive of cultural objects.[114] The right to commence an action in another Member State is granted only to Member States and not to private individuals.[115] The 1993 Directive also resolves the thorny issue of conflict of laws by establishing that questions of title shall be governed by the law of the requesting Member State.[116]

The 1993 Directive has essentially codified a key feature of the UNIDROIT and UNESCO Conventions by granting to Member States the right to have their export control laws enforced or respected by another Member State. Despite the availability of this option, there have been only seven instances in which any Member State has requested the return of an item.[117] From the very few instances

[111] Council Directive on the Return of Cultural Objects Unlawfully Removed from the Territory of a Member State, No. 93/7/EEC of March 15, 1993, as amended by Directive 96/100/EU of the European Parliament and of the Council of 17 February 1997 (amending the Annex to Directive 93/7/EEC).

[112] In the European Union, a "Regulation" is specifically addressed to the Member States and enters into force automatically on a specified date. A "Directive" sets forth the goal or standard of what is to be achieved but requires specific national legislation by each Member State in order to implement the Directive.

[113] *See* Form 6-1.

[114] The Annex to the Directive describes the categories of property covered as well as any age and value thresholds.

[115] Directive 93/7/EEC, art. 1(3).

[116] Directive 93/7/EEC, art. 12.

[117] *See* Annexe III, Report from the Commission to the Council, the European Parliament and the Economic and Social Committee on the Implementation of Council Regulation (EEC) n 3911/92 on the export of cultural goods, and Council Directive 93/7/EEC on the return of cultural objects

in which the 1993 Directive has been invoked, one might conclude that the Member States are apparently unwilling to undertake the cost and effort necessary to exercise this right. In contrast, certain Member States have not hesitated to seek assistance from the U.S. government to recover objects unlawfully removed from their territory.[118] The explanation for this may be purely a matter of ease and economics. If the U.S. government is willing to litigate recovery of cultural property on behalf of a foreign government, the foreign government has little incentive to itself expend the time, money or effort necessary to recover objects that are unlawfully removed.

§ 6.05 LIMITATIONS IMPOSED ON THE EXPORT OF CULTURAL PROPERTY

Specific countries' export restrictions take as many forms as there are countries and are too varied to summarize here.[119] The types of foreign restrictions can broadly be categorized as unrestrictive, moderately restrictive, and restrictive. There are entrenched views as to whether one or another form of export control law helps or hinders the illegal export of works of art. Archaeologists or others in favor of each country retaining all examples of its own heritage tend to argue that unrestrictive import laws in art-market countries encourage looting and smuggling in art-source countries. In contrast, others who believe in the benefits of the international exchange of cultural property and perceive it as "world heritage" tend to argue that the overly restrictive export control laws defy human nature and fuel the illicit market.

[A] Unrestrictive Export Control Laws: Singapore; Switzerland; United States

Certain countries, such as Singapore, Switzerland, and the United States, have very limited restrictions on the export of cultural property from their borders. The United States and Switzerland are often referred to as art-market countries,[120]

---

unlawfully removed from the territory of a Member State, Brussels, May 25, 2000, COM (2000) 325 final.

[118] *See supra* discussion of the Roman Torso case and *Phiale* at § 6.03[B][3][c] and § 6.03[B][4].

[119] Two resources that are somewhat outdated, but that provide listings of export control laws as of the date of publication are: Handbook of National Regulations Concerning the Export of Cultural Property (1988), prepared for UNESCO by Lyndel V. Prott, Reader in International Law and Jurisprudence, and Patrick J. O'Keefe, Associate Professor of Law, both University of Sydney; and The Protection of Cultural Property, Handbook of National Legislations, Bonnie Burnham, International Council of Museums (1974).

[120] The argument has been made that limited export controls on cultural property indicates a willingness of the subject country to tolerate or support smuggling, looting or pillaging. This is a tenuous argument given that the U.S. policy to encourage free export and import of works of art existed long before the United States was even a contender for the title "art-market country."

whereas Singapore has not historically been considered a leading art-market country in Asia. In any event, none of these countries have federal regulations precluding the export of cultural property.

In each of these three countries, if a work of art is legally owned, the owner generally is free to export or sell the work of art[121] and no export taxes are due. Export of such property is limited only in rare circumstances, such as with respect to stolen property or certain endangered species.[122] Additionally, the exporter must properly and accurately declare the object upon export and pay any export duties or taxes that may be due.[123]

Of the three countries, only Singapore requires an exporter to obtain a permit to legally export a work of art in addition to making proper customs and export declarations. A permit is required for personal property and movables valued at S$400 (approximately $234 in U.S. dollars) or more, subject to certain limited exceptions. A permit is also required to export any item of property that is a "controlled substance." Exports to "prohibited countries" are strictly prohibited.[124] The Singapore Trade Development Board (TDB) has authority to issue permits. Although the TDB does not publish criteria for issuing permits, the informal practice is that permits are routinely granted.

Although not a member of the European Union, Switzerland has adopted many of the EU regulations and practices. However, the Swiss do not require either a national cultural property export license or anything similar to an EU cultural license to export works of art. There are no export taxes. One can purchase, sell, exhibit, and import works of art freely in Switzerland.

Similarly, there is no federal or state cultural property license requirement to export a work of art from the United States based on a claim that it constitutes the cultural patrimony of the United States. There are restrictions in the United States on the export of endangered or otherwise protected species,[125] but as with Switzerland and Singapore, there is no legal basis to retain an item within the country's borders simply because it is important to U.S. history or culture.

---

[121] Of the laws of 65 countries that have been reviewed for this chapter, unrestrictive export laws tend to be the exception rather than the rule. In many countries, even if one is free to own a work of art within the nation's borders, the owner's rights to domestic movement, title transfer, or export are generally restricted in some form.

[122] *See supra* at § 6.03[B][4] and note 17.

[123] *See* Form 6-2. U.S. Customs has prepared and makes available to the public instructions regarding how to prepare the U.S. Customs form, commonly referred to as a CF 7501.

[124] In Singapore, a "controlled substance" includes such items as Singapore-made textiles, garments or textiles for export to Canada, Norway, the European Union, or the United States; articles of clothing intended as protection against attack (*i.e.*, bulletproof vests), toy guns, handcuffs, etc. Regulation of Imports and Exports Act (Cap. 272A). The "prohibited" countries are Iraq, Libya, Angola, Rwanda, Liberia, and Sierra Leone.

[125] *See supra*, note 17.

In the United States, the free export rule applies even if a work of major importance becomes available for sale and is at risk of being exported to another country. In the 1990s, two very different but important items were made available for sale by private owners: (1) a Declaration of Independence, and (2) the skeleton of a Tyrannosaurus Rex. The *T.rex* is a good example of an important item, found in the ground on private property, on which the government could not impose any restrictions regarding export, sale, exhibition, or other use. Although some in this country felt the *T.rex* was too important to be put up for sale and possibly exported out of the country, there was no legal means to interfere with the private property rights of the owners.[126]

[B] Moderately Restrictive Export Control Laws: Japan; Venezuela; United Kingdom

Numerous countries, such as Japan, Venezuela, and the United Kingdom, have what may be termed "moderately restrictive" export control laws. All three entirely forbid the export of some individual items of cultural property in certain limited circumstances; allow other items to be exported with a form of export permit from a non-customs agency, such as a heritage or cultural property ministry; and allow other types of property to be freely exported. The system for granting licenses operates fairly predictably and promptly and has a public aspect.

For example, in Japan, if a work of art is designated as a "National Treasure" or "Important Cultural Property" by the Minister of Education, it is virtually impossible to obtain an export permit for sale abroad.[127] Such works of art must be "of fine make and valuable in terms of Japanese cultural history" and are usually of Japanese origin. A work not of Japanese origin but nevertheless deemed a National Treasure or Important Cultural Property, generally is one brought to Japan from abroad more than 100 years ago and having a significant impact on Japanese culture. Although these objects may be owned privately within Japan

---

[126] The *T. rex* was purchased by the Field Museum of Natural History, with assistance from The Walt Disney Company and McDonald's. Similarly, the Declaration of Independence was purchased by an American private collector and has remained in the United States. However, had either item been purchased by a foreign museum or collector, there are arguments to support the export of such items outside of the United States. Given that we already have over 20 examples of the Declaration of Independence in this country, there is no reason precluding one version of this significant historical document to be located abroad for others to see and appreciate firsthand. One can make a similar argument for the export of the *T. Rex*. A foreign country would make a perfectly good home for the *T. Rex*, and could facilitate greater understanding of prehistory in the Americas and possibly stimulate tourism to this country, as no doubt the great antiquities collections in our museums promote understanding of foreign cultures and result in travel abroad.

[127] *See* Japanese Law for the Protection of Cultural Properties (Law No. 214 of 1950, as amended); Japanese Customs Law (No. 61 of 1954).

and purchased and sold domestically, it is highly unlikely that they would be granted an export permit. If a work of art has been designated as a National Treasure or as Important Cultural Property it is published in an official gazette, known as the "kanpou." In addition, a 13-volume publication provides a complete listing of objects that have been declared National Treasures or Important Cultural Property since 1950, when the Law for the Protection of Cultural Properties first went into effect.[128] Although a purchaser is not entitled to financial compensation if the item is not allowed out of the country, the parameters for what will not be allowed out are clear, predictable and limited to items that are truly significant.

Similarly, in Venezuela, objects deemed to constitute "cultural patrimony" are those items bound to the nation's identity and determined to be of exceptional historical value by the Venezuelan Cultural Patrimony Institute. Such items may not be exported. There is a national registry listing all such objects, which comprises mostly items in public institutions. However, if the property does not meet this fairly high standard of national importance, it may be exported without a special permit from the Cultural Patrimony Institute and would require only compliance with the standard customs formalities.[129]

The export license review process in the United Kingdom is unusually open and interactive.[130] In the United Kingdom, the Department of Culture, Media and Sport (DCMS), "aims to preserve nationally important cultural items for future generations, whilst striking a balance between the need to protect the art trade and the rights of private owners." The basic process is similar to those of Venezuela and Japan, in that there is a reviewing body (the DCMS) that considers cultural property export licenses.

An export license application is referred to an expert advisor who makes a recommendation as to whether a license should be granted. The expert advisor is guided by what have come to be known as the "Waverly Criteria," which include the following questions:

- Is the property so closely connected with the U.K.'s history and national life that its departure would be a misfortune?

---

[128] Law for the Protection of Cultural Properties, *supra* note 127.

[129] The standard in Brazil is similar to that articulated in Venezuela and Japan in that there is an emphasis on the concept that the object was somehow important to the history or identity of Brazil. The National Historical and Artistic Patrimony Institute of Brazil, known domestically by its acronym "IPHAN," generally grants export permits provided that the property was not made in Brazil or Portugal before 1889 or, if made elsewhere before 1889, does not "relate" to Brazil. *See* Federal Decree Law No. 25 of Nov. 30, 1937; *see also* Brazilian Federal Constitution, art. 23, items III and IV.

[130] A detailed explanation of the process, identifying specific individuals within the government and their responsibilities, is available on the internet. *See* www.culture.gov.uk.

- Is the property of outstanding aesthetic importance?
- Is the property of outstanding significance for the study of some particular branch of art, learning or history?

Although the Waverly Criteria could be read quite broadly, the reality is that the expert advisors annually review applications for approximately 7,000 to 8,000 works of art and recommend deferral of approximately 30 each year.[131] The open, interactive nature of the process seems to promote the efficient balancing, "as fairly as possible, between the various interests concerned . . . the protection of the national heritage; the rights of the owner selling the goods; the exporter or overseas purchaser; and the position and reputation of the U.K. as an international art market."[132]

If the expert advisor believes that an export license should not be granted, she must submit a report to a reviewing committee in support of the position. A copy is provided to the applicant, who then has an opportunity to submit a report explaining why an export license should be granted. A meeting follows, of the applicant, the Reviewing Committee on the Export of Works of Art, and three independent advisors.

During the meeting both the expert advisor and the applicant (and any advisors he chooses to bring) may ask and answer questions about the license application. If the committee believes the object should not be exported based on the Waverly Criteria, a decision whether or not to grant an export license is deferred. A press release is subsequently circulated by the DCMS notifying relevant museums and the public of the export application and in essence inviting public institutions or private persons to make an offer to purchase the item. If there is an offer to purchase at the fair market value (considering among other factors, the applicant's purchase price, the sale price, if any, and recent auction sales, if relevant) and the owner refuses to sell, it is likely that the export license application will be denied.[133] If there are no reasonable purchase offers with an agreement to

---

[131] *See* DCMS Report on the Export of Works of Art 1998-99, at 8. If the expert advisors do not refer the requested export to the committee, an export license is usually received within four weeks after the application is submitted.

[132] U.K. Export Licensing for Cultural Goods, Procedures and Guidance for Exporters of Works of Art and other Cultural Goods, dated June 3, 1997.

[133] For a better understanding of the types of cases in which an export license has been denied, read the annual report submitted by the Reviewing Committee to Parliament, which includes the various policy discussions and an analysis of the cases considered. For a copy of the report, contact the Stationery Office Publications Centre in London or visit http://www.culture.uk. One case in which the delayed export process drew considerable attention was the attempted export by the Getty Museum of Antonio Canova's "Three Graces." *See, e.g.*, Carol Vogel, The Getty and the Graces, N.Y. Times, Oct. 1, 1993; and George Goldner, Learn to let go gracefully, The Independent (London), Dec. 21, 1994.

provide public access to the item and no reasonable prospect of funds being raised to purchase the item at fair market value,[134] the export license is generally granted within three to nine months of the application.

As the United Kingdom is part of the European Union, there are two additional questions that must be asked prior to exporting works of art from it. First, one needs to determine, based on the description and value of the item, whether an E.U. export license, in addition to the U.K. license, is needed, in light of the different value thresholds.[135] Second, if the property has come directly or indirectly from another European Union member state into the United Kingdom, one must determine whether it was exported properly from the originating member state.[136]

[C] Restrictive Export Control Laws: India; Egypt; Guatemala

Finally, certain export control regulations such as those in India, Egypt, and Guatemala seem restrictive in comparison with the various systems described above, whether by the stated scope of the law or in its application. Since 1972, the law in India provides that "antiquities," whether or not of Indian origin, may not be exported without the authorization of the central government. "Antiquities" include paintings and sculpture more than 100 years old, manuscripts more than

---

[134] Both France and Italy have a requirement that under certain circumstances, the government must pay reasonable compensation to the owner if an export license is denied. In France, there is the famous case of Jacques Walter, who was denied an export license for a Van Gogh painting. After years of litigation, he was awarded by the Court FF 422,187,693. *See* Timothy P. Ramier, Agent Judiciaire du Tresor vs. Walter, Fait du Prince and a King's Ransom, Int'l J. of Cultural Property, V. 6, No. 2, 337 (1997) (discussing the 15 years of legal process between the French government and Walter). Similarly, the Court of European Justice decided that a Swiss dealer who purchased a painting located in Italy and was subsequently denied an export license, was entitled to compensation from the Italian government. *See* Anna Somers Cocks, The European Court of Human Rights Decides for Dealer Ernst Beyeler and against the Italian State over Van Gogh, The Art Newspaper, Jan. 14, 2000.

[135] Whether the individual member states' value thresholds match the EU value thresholds varies from member state to member state. *Compare* France (which has simply adopted the EU descriptions and value thresholds) *with* Italy (has no value thresholds and thereby requires every object to be exported to a non-EU country, to apply for both an Italian and an EU export license).

[136] *See supra*, discussion of the 1993 Directive. An interesting feature of several countries' cultural property export control laws is a requirement that the property must have been in the country for a certain minimum period of time, before the cultural property export restrictions may apply. *See, e.g.*, United Kingdom (if property has been in the United Kingdom for less than 50 years, the export application will generally not be referred to an expert advisor); Argentina (if the property has been in the country for less than 15 years, then the National Secretary of Culture cannot deny the export license); France (if property has been in France for less than 50 years, an export license should be granted); and Japan (unless an item made by a non-Japanese has been in the country for 100 years and is important to the history of Japan, it is likely to be granted an export license).

75 years old, any object of "historical significance," and any object declared to be an antiquity by the central government.[137] In reality, export authorization for any of these categories is granted in very rare circumstances, such as for an international exhibition.[138] Although private ownership of antiquities is permitted in India, the owner must register with the central government and give the government notice of transfer or sale of the item within 15 days.[139]

In Egypt it is generally prohibited to export or sell any "antiquities," defined as "any object of art, science, literature of religion more than 100 years old, which is of archaeological or historical value and any human or animal remains."[140] As in India, in Egypt antiquities must be registered with the government[141] and such items are then photographed, measured, and drawn, and an effort is made to identify the location of the find.[142]

The Guatemalan laws are a classic example of a blanket prohibition on the export of antiquities and "cultural assets," which are broadly defined.[143] "Cultural

---

[137] *See* Antiquities and Art Treasures Act 1972. As noted earlier, even works created in the last 100 years may be designated by the Central Government as an "Art Treasure," and thereby precluded from legal export. Such "contemporary" works may be so designated depending on their artistic or aesthetic value and only if the artist is deceased. The artists are Rabindranath Tagore, Amrita Sher-Gil, Jamini Roy and Nandala Bose. Interestingly, export restrictions do not seem to apply to textiles, unpainted ceramics, jewelry, silver and uncarved furniture.

[138] In such instances, the director general of the Archaeological Survey of India would be the appropriate authority to grant permission.

[139] *See* Indian Antiquities and Art Treasures Act of 1972 and Indian Antiquities and Art Treasures Rules of 1973.

[140] In the past, it was legal to own and sell antiquities in Egypt. It is rumored that when it was legal to own antiquities in Egypt, the authorities knew where all the great finds and collections were. After it became illegal in 1983 to export such items, citizens no longer shared this information with the authorities. This is also allegedly true in Jordan.

[141] In some limited circumstances under Egyptian law, a private person may own an antiquity. For example, the Egyptian Antiquities Authority may grant title to antiquities to private persons as when a similar antiquity has been discovered and registered. In addition, prior to 1983, the law permitted a limited trade in antiquities and when the law changed, such dealers were authorized to dispose of the antiquities they possessed. *See* Egyptian Law on the Protection of Antiquities 117 (1983).

[142] *Id.*

[143] *See* Political Const. of the Republic of Guatemala; Decree No. 425, Congress of the Republic of Guatemala: Law of Protection and Preservation of Monuments, Archaeological, Historic, Typical and Artistic Objects, Sept. 19, 1947, modified by Decree Law No. 437 of the Head of a Provisional Government, March 24, 1966; Decree No. 26-97, Congress of the Republic of Guatemala: Law for the Protection of the Cultural Property of the Nation, Apr. 29, 1997, modified by Decree 38-98, Congress of the Republic of Guatemala, May 26, 1998.

Since the end of the Civil War, Guatemala has been making a concerted effort to protect and preserve its heritage. However, there is an admitted shortage of funds to preserve the multitude of sites. One potential solution might be to modify the export control and ownership regime to authorize the export of certain lesser examples of objects. As in Egypt, such sale or ownership would be

assets" include architectural monuments and their elements as well as movable cultural assets that for religious or nonreligious reasons are important to paleontology, architecture, anthropology, history, literature, art, science, or technology. In addition, objects of living cultural heritage and urban landscapes may be deemed to be cultural assets. Guatemalan cultural assets may not be sold, exported or altered in any form.

Although attempting to serve a nationalistic and scientific goal of preserving a nation's archaeological heritage, blanket export restrictions based on broad definitions arguably lead to economic suffering, and fuel, or even cause, black markets.[144] Moreover, many of the countries with restrictive export control laws are rich in archaeological heritage but either have strong, if not compelling, modernization needs or do not have the resources to excavate, study, or preserve their heritage. For example, in Egypt, in order to build Alexandria's new library, concern for the archaeological history of Alexandria has overridden by the need for modernization, but objects to be destroyed cannot be legally exported.[145]

The allure of objects from other cultures seems to be nearly as innate to humans as the instinct of self-preservation, as humans have collected interesting or beautiful objects for centuries. This is fortunate because it is from some very old collections that we have learned so much today.[146] Accepting this basic human characteristic would move the debate from whether people should collect to how can we best preserve cultural property. Rather than supporting restrictive export control laws that deny this reality and repeatedly pursuing international treaties, it may be time to begin thinking more creatively about how modifying overly

---

allowed only after the items have been measured, photographed and drawn. It may be possible to require the purchaser to pay a duty or fee to a restoration project in Guatemala in exchange for receiving a certificate of export for the item. Various authors have suggested that serious consideration should be given to encouraging art source countries to revise their laws to allow limited controlled sales and exports of cultural property. *See* William G. Pearlstein, Claims for the Repatriation of Cultural Property: Prospects for a Managed Antiquities Market, Law & Pol'y Int'l Business, V. 28, No. 1 (1996); Jason C. Roberts, Comment: The Protection of Indigenous Populations' Cultural Property in Peru, Mexico and the United States, 4 Tulsa J. Comp. & Int'l L. 327 (1997).

[144] *See, e.g.*, Bator *supra* note 11, 34 Stan. L. Rev. at 317.

[145] *See* Joel Swerdlow, The Tale of Three Cities: Alexandria, Cordoba and New York, 196 National Geographic, 2, at 41 (" 'Unfortunately, destroying ancient artifacts is the only way to build anything,' an architect working on the new library explains"); Stephen Kinzer, Newly Found, a '2nd Pompeii' Is in Peril Again, N.Y. Times, May 7, 2000 (reporting on the imminent destruction of an unexcavated ancient city located in modern Turkey, filled with archaeological treasures, in the interests of a vast irrigation project to generate electrical power). In addition to being destroyed for public or private works, many antiquities in underfinanced public collections suffer a similar fate of neglect, theft, and destruction.

[146] The drive to collect existed well before the art market and before items had important financial value. *See* Werner Muensterberger, Collecting an Unruly Passion: Psychological Perspectives, (Princeton University Press, 1994) (arguing that the urge to collect originates in childhood).

restrictive export control laws can benefit preservation of cultural property (including the archaeological context), and to reconcile the realities of poor economies and the ageless interest of humankind in owning and collecting objects from other cultures.

FORMS

FORM 6-1

EU Cultural Goods Export Application

European Community – Cultural Goods

1 Application 1

1 Applicant (Name and address)	**2. Export Licence** No Valid until / / / Definitive ☐ Temporary ☐ Date for reimportation / / /
3 Applicant's Representative (Name and address)	**4 Issuing Authority** (Name and address)
5A Country of Destination or of Temporary Stay	**6 Member State of Consignment**
5B Consignee	

7 Description in Terms of the Annex to EC Regulation (EEC) No 3911/92 Category of the Cultural Goods

8 Description of Cultural Object or Objects	**9 Commodity Code**
	10 Mass
If the space is insufficient you may continue on one or more supplementary pages which should be copied in triplicate and should contain the information required in boxes 8 to 18 (see note in box 23)	**11 Estimated Value**

Criteria to be used for identification

12 Measurements	**13 Title or Subject**	**14 Dating**	**15 Other Characteristics**

16 Artist, Period or Workshop	**17 Medium or Technique**

18 Documents submitted/specific indications relating to identification

☐ photograph ☐ list ☐ bibliography ☐ catalogue

Application **19A** I hereby apply for an export licence in respect of the cultural object described above and declare in good faith that the information in this application and the supporting documents is true. Place and date Signature	**20** Signature and stamp of issuing authority Place and date

EC ELA
March 1993

Designed by the Information Design Team for the Department of National Heritage

European Community – Cultural Goods

2 Holder's Sheet 2

1 Applicant (Name and address)

2. Export Licence

No

Valid until / /

Definitive ☐ Temporary ☐

Date for reimportation / /

3 Applicant's Representative (Name and address)

4 Issuing Authority (Name and address)

5A Country of Destination or of Temporary Stay

5B Consignee

6 Member State of Consignment

7 Description in Terms of the Annex to EC Regulation (EEC) No 3911/92 Category of the Cultural Goods

8 Description of Cultural Object or Objects

9 Commodity Code

10 Mass

If the space is insufficient you may continue on one or more supplementary pages which should be copied in triplicate and should contain the information required in boxes 8 to 18 (see note in box 23)

11 Estimated Value

Criteria to be used for identification

12 Measurements

13 Title or Subject

14 Dating

15 Other Characteristics

16 Artist. Period or Workshop

17 Medium or Technique

18 Documents submitted/specific indications relating to identification

☐ photograph ☐ list ☐ bibliography ☐ catalogue

19B Endorsement by Competent Customs Office

Customs office

SAD No

Member State

Date of issue

Signature and stamp

20 Signature and stamp of issuing authority

Place and

date

Designed by the Information Design Team for the Department of National Heritage

European Community – Cultural Goods

3 Sheet for Office of Clearance 3

1 Applicant (Name and address)

2. Export Licence

No

Valid until / / /

Definitive ☐

Temporary ☐

Date for reimportation / / /

3 Applicant's Representative (Name and address)

4 Issuing Authority (Name and address)

5A Country of Destination or of Temporary Stay

6 Member State of Consignment

5B Consignee

7 Description in Terms of the Annex to EC Regulation (EEC) No 3911/92 Category of the Cultural Goods

8 Description of Cultural Object or Objects

9. Commodity Code

10 Mass

11 Estimated Value

If the space is insufficient you may continue on one or more supplementary pages which should be copied in triplicate and should contain the information required in boxes 8 to 18 (see note in box 23)

Criteria to be used for identification

12 Measurements	13 Title or Subject	14 Dating	15 Other Characteristics

16 Artist, Period or Workshop

17 Medium or Technique

18 Documents submitted/specific indications relating to identification

☐ photograph ☐ list ☐ bibliography ☐ catalogue

19B Endorsement by Competent Customs Office

Customs office

SAD No

Member State

Date of issue

Signature and stamp

20 Signature and stamp of issuing authority

Place and

date

Designed by the Information Design Team for the Department of National Heritage

European Community – Cultural Goods

21 Photograph of Cultural Object

(minimum 8cm x 12cm)

22 Customs Office of Exit:

Stamp:

23 This form is accompanied by ______ supplementary pages

Note

Any unused space in box 8 or on accompanying supplementary pages shall be duly barred by the competent authorities

Designed by the Information Design Team for the Department of National Heritage

European Community – Cultural Goods

21 Photograph of Cultural Object

(minimum 8cm x 12cm)

22 Customs Office of Exit:

Stamp:

23 This form is accompanied by ______ supplementary pages

Note

Any unused space in box 8 or on accompanying supplementary pages shall be duly barred by the competent authorities

Designed by the Information Design Team for the Department of National Heritage

European Community – Cultural Goods

21 Photograph of Cultural Object

(minimum 8cm x 12cm)

22 Customs Office of Exit:

Stamp:

23 This form is accompanied by ______ supplementary pages

Note

Any unused space in box 8 or on accompanying supplementary pages shall be duly barred by the competent authorities

Designed by the Information Design Team for the Department of National Heritage

FORM 6-2

Export Declaration Form

DEPARTMENT OF THE TREASURY
UNITED STATES CUSTOMS SERVICE

ENTRY SUMMARY

1. Entry No.	2. Entry Type Code	3. Entry Summary Date
4. Entry Date	5. Port Code	
6. Bond No.	7. Bond Type Code	8. Broker / Importer File No.

9. Ultimate Consignee Name and Address	10. Consignee No.	11. Importer of Record Name and Address	12. Importer No.
		13. Exporting Country	14. Export Date
		15. Country of Origin	16. Missing Documents
	STATE	17. I.T. No.	18. I.T. Date
19. B L or AWB No.	20. Mode of Transportation	21. Manufacturer I.D.	22. Reference No.
23. Importing Carrier	24. Foreign Port of Lading	25. Location of Goods/G.O. No.	
26. U.S. Port of Unlading	27. Import Date		

28. Line No.	29. Description of Merchandise: 30. (A) T.S.U.S.A. No. B. ADA CVD Case No.	31. (A) Gross Weight B. Manifest Qty.	32. Net Quantity in T.S.U.S.A. Units	33. (A) Entered Value B. CHGS C. Relationship	34. (A) T.S.U.S.A. Rate B. ADA/CVD Rate (C) I.R.C Rate D. Visa No.	35. Duty and I.R. Tax: Dollars	Cents

36. Declaration of Importer of Record (Owner or Purchaser) or Authorized Agent

I declare that I am the

☐ importer of record and that the actual owner, purchaser, or consignee for customs purposes is as shown above. OR ☐ owner or purchaser or agent thereof.

I further declare that the merchandise

☐ was obtained pursuant to a purchase or agreement to purchase and that the prices set forth in the invoice are true. OR ☐ was not obtained pursuant to a purchase or agreement to purchase and the statements in the invoice as to value or price are true to the best of my knowledge and belief.

I also declare that the statements in the documents herein filed fully disclose to the best of my knowledge and belief the true prices, values, quantities, rebates, drawbacks, fees, commissions, and royalties and are true and correct, and that all goods or services provided to the seller of the merchandise either free or at reduced cost are fully disclosed. I will immediately furnish to the appropriate customs officer any information showing a different state of facts.

Notice required by Paperwork Reduction Act of 1980. This information is needed to ensure that importers/exporters are complying with U.S. Customs laws, to allow us to compute and collect the right amount of money, to enforce other agency requirements, and to collect accurate statistical information on imports. Your response is mandatory.

U.S. CUSTOMS USE		TOTALS	
A. Liq. Code	B. Ascertained Duty	37. Duty	
	C. Ascertained Tax	38. Tax	
	D. Ascertained Other	39. Other	
	E. Ascertained Total	40. Total	

41. Signature of Declarant, Title, and Date

PART 1-RECORD COPY

Customs Form 7501 (030984)

DEPARTMENT OF THE TREASURY
UNITED STATES CUSTOMS SERVICE

ENTRY SUMMARY

(1.) Entry No.	(2.) Entry Type Code	3. Entry Summary Date
4. Entry Date	(5.) Port Code	
6. Bond No.	7. Bond Type Code	8. Broker / Importer File No.

9. Ultimate Consignee Name and Address	10. Consignee No.	(11.) Importer of Record Name and Address	(12.) Importer No.
		(13.) Exporting Country	14. Export Date
		(15.) Country of Origin	16. Missing Documents
	STATE	(17.) I.T. No.	(18.) I.T. Date
(19.) B L or AWB No.	20. Mode of Transportation	21. Manufacturer I.D.	22. Reference No.
(23.) Importing Carrier	24. Foreign Port of Lading	25. Location of Goods/G.O. No.	
26. U.S. Port of Unlading	(27.) Import Date		

(28.) Line No.	(29.) Description of Merchandise			33. (A.) Entered Value B. CHGS C. Relationship	34. (A.) T.S.U.S.A. Rate B. ADA/CVD Rate (C) I.R.C Rate D. Visa No.	(35.) Duty and I.R. Tax	
	30. (A) T.S.U.S.A. No. B. ADA CVD Case No.	31. (A) Gross Weight B. Manifest Qty.	(32.) Net Quantity in T.S.U.S.A. Units			Dollars	Cents

(36.) Declaration of Importer of Record (Owner or Purchaser) or Authorized Agent

I declare that I am the

☐ importer of record and that the actual owner, purchaser, or consignee for customs purposes is as shown above. OR ☐ owner or purchaser or agent thereof.

I further declare that the merchandise

☐ was obtained pursuant to a purchase or agreement to purchase and that the prices set forth in the invoice are true. OR ☐ was not obtained pursuant to a purchase or agreement to purchase and the statements in the invoice as to value or price are true to the best of my knowledge and belief.

I also declare that the statements in the documents herein filed fully disclose to the best of my knowledge and belief the true prices, values, quantities, rebates, drawbacks, fees, commissions, and royalties and are true and correct, and that all goods or services provided to the seller of the merchandise either free or at reduced cost are fully disclosed. I will immediately furnish to the appropriate customs officer any information showing a different state of facts.

Notice required by Paperwork Reduction Act of 1980. This information is needed to ensure that importers/exporters are complying with U.S. Customs laws, to allow us to compute and collect the right amount of money, to enforce other agency requirements, and to collect accurate statistical information on imports. Your response is mandatory.

U.S. CUSTOMS USE		TOTALS	
A. Liq. Code	B. Ascertained Duty	(37.) Duty	
	C. Ascertained Tax	(38.) Tax	
	D. Ascertained Other	(39.) Other	
	E. Ascertained Total	(40.) Total	

(41.) Signature of Declarant, Title, and Date

PART 2-CASHIER

Customs Form 7501 (030984)

FORM 6-2

DEPARTMENT OF THE TREASURY
UNITED STATES CUSTOMS SERVICE

ENTRY SUMMARY

(1.) Entry No.	(2.) Entry Type Code	3. Entry Summary Date
4. Entry Date	(5.) Port Code	
6. Bond No.	7. Bond Type Code	8. Broker / Importer File No.

9. Ultimate Consignee Name and Address	10. Consignee No.	(11.) Importer of Record Name and Address	(12.) Importer No.
		(13.) Exporting Country	14. Export Date
		(15.) Country of Origin	16. Missing Documents
	STATE	(17.) I.T. No.	(18.) I.T. Date
(19.) B L or AWB No.	20. Mode of Transportation	21. Manufacturer I.D.	22. Reference No.
(23.) Importing Carrier	24. Foreign Port of Lading	25. Location of Goods/G.O. No.	
26. U.S. Port of Unlading	(27.) Import Date		

(28.) Line No.	(29.) Description of Merchandise			33. (A) Entered Value B. CHGS C. Relationship	34. (A) T.S.U.S.A. Rate B. ADA/CVD Rate (C) I.R.C Rate D. Visa No.	(35.) Duty and I.R. Tax	
	30. (A) T.S.U.S.A. No. B. ADA CVD Case No.	31. (A) Gross Weight B. Manifest Qty.	(32.) Net Quantity in T.S.U.S.A. Units			Dollars	Cents

(36.) Declaration of Importer of Record (Owner or Purchaser) or Authorized Agent

I declare that I am the

☐ importer of record and that the actual owner, purchaser, or consignee for customs purposes is as shown above. OR ☐ owner or purchaser or agent thereof.

I further declare that the merchandise

☐ was obtained pursuant to a purchase or agreement to purchase and that the prices set forth in the invoice are true. OR ☐ was not obtained pursuant to a purchase or agreement to purchase and the statements in the invoice as to value or price are true to the best of my knowledge and belief.

I also declare that the statements in the documents herein filed fully disclose to the best of my knowledge and belief the true prices, values, quantities, rebates, drawbacks, fees, commissions, and royalties and are true and correct, and that all goods or services provided to the seller of the merchandise either free or at reduced cost are fully disclosed. I will immediately furnish to the appropriate customs officer any information showing a different state of facts.

U.S. CUSTOMS USE		TOTALS	
A. Liq. Code	B. Ascertained Duty	(37.) Duty	
	C. Ascertained Tax	(38.) Tax	
	D. Ascertained Other	(39.) Other	
	E. Ascertained Total	(40.) Total	

Notice required by Paperwork Reduction Act of 1980. This information is needed to ensure that importers/exporters are complying with U.S. Customs laws, to allow us to compute and collect the right amount of money, to enforce other agency requirements, and to collect accurate statistical information on imports. Your response is mandatory.

(41.) Signature of Declarant, Title, and Date

PART 3-STATISTICAL

Customs Form 7501 (030984)

DEPARTMENT OF THE TREASURY
UNITED STATES CUSTOMS SERVICE

ENTRY SUMMARY

1. Entry No.	2. Entry Type Code	3. Entry Summary Date
4. Entry Date	5. Port Code	
6. Bond No.	7. Bond Type Code	8. Broker / Importer File No.

9. Ultimate Consignee Name and Address	10. Consignee No.	11. Importer of Record Name and Address	12. Importer No.
		13. Exporting Country	14. Export Date
		15. Country of Origin	16. Missing Documents
STATE		17. I.T. No.	18. I.T. Date
19. B L or AWB No.	20. Mode of Transportation	21. Manufacturer I.D.	22. Reference No.
23. Importing Carrier	24. Foreign Port of Lading	25. Location of Goods/G.O. No.	
26. U.S. Port of Unlading	27. Import Date		

28. Line No.	29. Description of Merchandise: 30. (A) T.S.U.S.A. No. B. ADA CVD Case No.	31. (A) Gross Weight B. Manifest Qty.	32. Net Quantity in T.S.U.S.A. Units	33. (A) Entered Value B. CHGS C. Relationship	34. (A) T.S.U.S.A. Rate B. ADA/CVD Rate (C) I.R.C Rate D. Visa No.	35. Duty and I.R. Tax: Dollars	Cents

36. Declaration of Importer of Record (Owner or Purchaser) or Authorized Agent

I declare that I am the

☐ importer of record and that the actual owner, purchaser, or consignee for customs purposes is as shown above. OR ☐ owner or purchaser or agent thereof.

I further declare that the merchandise

☐ was obtained pursuant to a purchase or agreement to purchase and that the prices set forth in the invoice are true. OR ☐ was not obtained pursuant to a purchase or agreement to purchase and the statements in the invoice as to value or price are true to the best of my knowledge and belief.

I also declare that the statements in the documents herein filed fully disclose to the best of my knowledge and belief the true prices, values, quantities, rebates, drawbacks, fees, commissions, and royalties and are true and correct, and that all goods or services provided to the seller of the merchandise either free or at reduced cost are fully disclosed. I will immediately furnish to the appropriate customs officer any information showing a different state of facts.

U.S. CUSTOMS USE		TOTALS	
A. Liq. Code	B. Ascertained Duty	37. Duty	
	C. Ascertained Tax	38. Tax	
	D. Ascertained Other	39. Other	
	E. Ascertained Total	40. Total	

Notice required by Paperwork Reduction Act of 1980. This information is needed to ensure that importers/exporters are complying with U.S. Customs laws, to allow us to compute and collect the right amount of money, to enforce other agency requirements, and to collect accurate statistical information on imports. Your response is mandatory.

41. Signature of Declarant, Title, and Date

PART 4-MULTIPLE USE

Customs Form 7501 (030984)

FORM 6-2

DEPARTMENT OF THE TREASURY
UNITED STATES CUSTOMS SERVICE

ENTRY SUMMARY

(1.) Entry No.	(2.) Entry Type Code	3. Entry Summary Date
4. Entry Date	(5.) Port Code	
6. Bond No.	7. Bond Type Code	8. Broker / Importer File No.

9. Ultimate Consignee Name and Address STATE	10. Consignee No.	(11.) Importer of Record Name and Address	(12.) Importer No.
		(13.) Exporting Country	14. Export Date
		(15.) Country of Origin	16. Missing Documents
		(17.) I.T. No.	(18.) I.T. Date
(19.) B L or AWB No.	20. Mode of Transportation	21. Manufacturer I.D.	22. Reference No.
(23.) Importing Carrier	24. Foreign Port of Lading	25. Location of Goods/G.O. No.	
26. U.S. Port of Unlading	(27.) Import Date		

(28.) Line No.	(29.) Description of Merchandise 30. (A) T.S.U.S.A. No. B. ADA CVD Case No.	31. (A) Gross Weight B. Manifest Qty.	(32.) Net Quantity in T.S.U.S.A. Units	33. (A) Entered Value B. CHGS C. Relationship	34. (A) T.S.U.S.A. Rate B. ADA/CVD Rate (C) I.R.C Rate D. Visa No.	(35.) Duty and I.R. Tax Dollars	Cents

(36.) Declaration of Importer of Record (Owner or Purchaser) or Authorized Agent

I declare that I am the

☐ importer of record and that the actual owner, purchaser, or consignee for customs purposes is as shown above. OR ☐ owner or purchaser or agent thereof.

I further declare that the merchandise

☐ was obtained pursuant to a purchase or agreement to purchase and that the prices set forth in the invoice are true. OR ☐ was not obtained pursuant to a purchase or agreement to purchase and the statements in the invoice as to value or price are true to the best of my knowledge and belief.

I also declare that the statements in the documents herein filed fully disclose to the best of my knowledge and belief the true prices, values, quantities, rebates, drawbacks, fees, commissions, and royalties and are true and correct, and that all goods or services provided to the seller of the merchandise either free or at reduced cost are fully disclosed. I will immediately furnish to the appropriate customs officer any information showing a different state of facts.

U.S. CUSTOMS USE		TOTALS
A. Liq. Code	B. Ascertained Duty	(37.) Duty
	C. Ascertained Tax	(38.) Tax
	D. Ascertained Other	(39.) Other
	E. Ascertained Total	(40.) Total

Notice required by Paperwork Reduction Act of 1980. This information is needed to ensure that importers/exporters are complying with U.S. Customs laws, to allow us to compute and collect the right amount of money, to enforce other agency requirements, and to collect accurate statistical information on imports. Your response is mandatory.

(41.) Signature of Declarant, Title, and Date

PART 5-MULTIPLE USE

Customs Form 7501 (030984)

CHAPTER 7

INTERNATIONAL TRANSACTIONS IN THE ART MARKET

Van Kirk Reeves*

* The author would like to express his gratitude to his partner, Timothy P. Ramier, *avocat* admitted in Paris and attorney at law, Louisiana, for his assistance; Olivier de Baecque, *avocat* admitted in Paris and attorney at law, New York, for his work in preparing § 7.11, "Auctions"; and Nili Safavi, researcher, for her review of art law issues.

§ 7.01 INTRODUCTION

Purchases and sales in the art market usually involve a unique object. The passion, pride, and enthusiasm concerning the object create tensions among the negotiating parties. With high stakes and prestige involved, one would expect a careful review of the transaction and detailed documentation, but often this is not the case.[1]

The enthusiasm to acquire a rare work sometimes leads parties to abandon the due diligence review that should be made before the transaction closes. Unscrupulous sellers and their intermediaries often encourage such behavior by limiting access to the object sought, threatening that another buyer is in the offing, and asserting that the seller is not prepared to deal with a buyer who is not prepared to trust him. These practices lead to problems, particularly in international transactions where a party may be dealing in a different cultural environment, a different legal system, and often a different language.

At the planning stage, it is essential that each party know what he wants, and what redress will be sought if the transaction goes awry. Local counsel should be consulted early on so that the agreement provides redress in a jurisdiction where the other party has assets and is amenable to suit. Where a party accepts a standard form agreement, he should study what rights are given him with the aid of seasoned advisors so that the risks can be weighed.

This chapter highlights the major issues that parties must consider when transacting art-related business in the international arena. The subject matter is worthy of a full treatise in its own right; this discussion is limited to the most frequently occurring problems, with references primarily to English and French law.

§ 7.02 PRINCIPAL TYPES OF INTERNATIONAL TRANSACTIONS

[A] Buying and Selling

A buyer should want an agreement for the sale of an art work to give him all possible rights to return the work or obtain damages in the event that he is

---

[1] A. H. Hudson, Agency and the Sale of Paintings, in Art, IV Antiquity & L.2, 169-73 (June 1999), analyzes the case Nahum v. Royal Holloway and Bedford New College, C.A., Nov. 12, 1998. This litigation exemplifies how the art market often works on the basis of oral understandings done with minimal or no documentation. Peter Nahum, an experienced English art dealer, agreed to represent the Royal Holloway and Bedford New College as their agent for the sale of three works, based on a telephone call whereby he was offered a 2.5% commission if he found buyers for the works. He found a buyer for one work, and then the same buyer bought a second work directly from the seller. Nahum was paid a commission on the first sale, but his claim for a commission on the second sale was refused. He sued and was awarded his commission on the basis that he had originally put the buyer and seller together. A major suit was required to settle this issue, as the parties had not put their agreement into writing.

unsatisfied with the work for any reason, including flaws in title and questions as to attribution or condition. He should want such rights exercisable in a jurisdiction where the laws are favorable to him.

The buyer should have the following provisions in the agreement for sale of the object:

- the right to inspect the work
- the right to return or exchange the work
- when payment is by installments, ownership upon the first payment, to avoid future difficulties with the seller
- guarantee of title
- guarantee of authenticity
- guarantee of condition
- the right to rescind in the event of a breach of warranty
- the right to damages in the event of a breach of warranty
- the right to claim loss of economic opportunity in the event of a breach of warranty
- his choice of law and forum in the event of litigation

The seller, on the other hand, should want to sell the object with no rights of recourse against her. She wants to exercise the principle of Roman law, *caveat emptor*. Her position would be that it is the buyer's duty to obtain information about the work to be acquired and her only duty is to deliver the object. The seller would like the following provisions placed in the agreement for sale of the object:

- cash against delivery or even prior thereto
- no guarantees whatsoever—"what you see is what you get"
- no transfer of title, even if there is delivery of the work, until full payment
- limitation to the greatest extent permitted by law of rights of recourse by the buyer
- her choice of law and forum in the event of litigation

In the absence of a written agreement, a court may be called upon to establish the rights of the parties and which law should apply to the transaction. A properly written agreement will address most of the legal and procedural issues, though public policy may limit the provisions that can be included in the agreement.[2]

[1] Right to Inspect the Work

A buyer should not purchase a work of art without seeing it, even where there is a condition report by a reliable expert, the authenticity of the work is clear, and its provenance is impeccable. There is magic about a work of art that can be perceived only by viewing it. No photograph can convey the visual impact of the work itself. The right to inspect the work prior to accepting title and making payment is essential.

A buyer should insist that the agreement for sale give the right of inspection for himself and for his advisors. A buyer and his advisors may need to visit more than once to confirm their views and conduct scientific tests. Specific times and places for inspection should be agreed upon.

[2] Right to Return for Cash or to Exchange the Work

Money-back guarantees are not a customary feature of art transactions, nor is the right to return a work for a work of equivalent value a legal right. These rights must be established by contract. Many galleries that do not offer refunds for returned works of art may be prepared to offer other works in exchange. In the absence of an agreement, this is merely a commercial policy decision.

[3] Payment by Installments

Installment payments can easily cause problems. If title is transferred before all payments are made, the buyer is free to sell the work and the original seller may only have a right to sue her buyer, who may have absconded or be in financial difficulty.

The buyer who does not take title allows his seller to find another buyer in his place, which would leave the buyer only with a claim for money damages. In many jurisdictions the passage of title can be established by contract. However, failure to make a provision in this regard may leave one with a suit under the laws where the transaction took place, which may not be the place where the defaulting party has assets.

---

[2] As an example of public policy intervening in a transaction, see Otto Sandrock, Foreign Laws Regulating the Export of Cultural Property: The Respect Due to Them by the Judge of the Lex Fori, in International Sales of Works of Art 457-82 (Inst. Int'l Bus. L. & Practice, Int'l Chamber of Commerce and Faculté de Droit de Genève 1985). If an object of cultural property is situated within an export regulating state, any contract breaching export regulations may be null and void. Example of France: Law n° 92-1477 of Dec. 31, 1992 governing the export of art objects.

[4] Guarantees

[a] Guarantee of Title

This guarantee is often provided as a matter of law, but the applicable law or laws governing the seller must be verified.[3] Even if a guarantee is provided as a matter of law, the guarantee should also be given in writing. Buyers should attempt to get an absolute guarantee for as long a period as possible, although dealers are very reluctant to provide a guarantee of more than two years. Guarantees of six months or a year are more common. Sellers have little opportunity to avoid this guarantee, although a carefully drafted waiver may be possible in certain jurisdictions in a transaction, particularly between professionals.

Under English law, a person who does not own an object cannot give good title to that object by selling it, even to a bona fide purchaser for value.[4] Nonetheless, a buyer may acquire good title by the passage of time or due to the failure of the true owner to pursue his rights.[5]

Under French law, the general proposition is found in Article 2279 of the Civil Code: "*En fait de meubles, la possession vaut titre*" (in the case of chattels, possession constitutes title). Thus, the good-faith purchaser is presumed to be the owner in the absence of proof of the rights of the original owner. Chattels, by their very nature, pass from person to person, usually with little or no written record, and therefore French law chooses to give some protection to the buyer who has bought in good faith, laying greater fault with the careless owner rather than the innocent purchaser.

---

[3] A recurring theme is the principle of *nemo dare potest quod non habet*: a person who does not himself possess good title to an object cannot give good title to the person to whom he tries to sell that object. As an example, the English law is contained in § 21(1) of the Sale of Goods Act (SGA) (1979): "Subject to this Act, where goods are sold by a person who is not their owner, and who does not sell them under the authority or with the consent of the owner, the buyer acquires no better title to the goods than the seller had, unless the owner of the goods is by his conduct precluded from denying the seller's authority to sell." The buyer can be sued by the true owner for recovery of the work, even though he is a bona fide purchaser for value. *See infra* § 7.03[A].

[4] There was an English exception of sale in market overt, SGA § 22 (1) (1979): "Where goods are sold in market overt, according to the usage of the market, the buyer acquires a good title to the goods, provided he buys them in good faith and without notice of any defect or want of title on the part of the seller." This exception of sale in market overt was abolished by the Sale of Goods (Amendment) Act of 1994 with regard to transactions concluded after Jan. 3, 1995, but it must still be applied to claims involving the purchase of works of art in market overt before that date. A market overt was an open, public and legally constituted market. The sale had to be in accordance with the usage of that market, that is, opening hours, opening days, and so on, had to be respected. The innocent purchaser had to prove that the sale took place within the market overt.

[5] Ruth Redmond Cooper, Limitation Periods in Art Disputes, Title and Time in Art and Antiquity Claims, Institute of Art and Law (hereinafter "IAL"), Nov. 13, 1995 (all written reports on IAL seminars cited herein are available from the Institute of Art and Law, Bank Chambers, 121 London Road, Leicester LE2 0QT, England). Ralph E. Lerner & Judith Bresler, Art Theft and the Statute of Limitations, Art Law 220 (2d ed. PLI).

Where the chattels have been lost or stolen, there are elements of *nemo dare potest quod non habet* (no one can sell what is not his) in French law. The owner who has lost an object or from whom an object was stolen has the right to reclaim it from the possessor for a period of three years from the date of such loss or theft. This rule applies against even the good-faith purchaser, although he may have recourse against the owner for the price paid for the object. However, if the possessor did not buy the object in good faith, the three-year time limit does not apply; rather, he may be sued up to thirty years following the loss or theft, and he will have no right to compensation from the rightful owner.[6]

Swiss law also favors the bona fide purchaser. In general, if the owner of an object has been deprived of his possession against his will, as in a case where the object is lost or stolen, the acquirer is generally not protected and the dispossessed owner can claim the object within five years of the loss or theft. A bona fide acquirer can demand that the owner reimburse him for the price at which the object was acquired.[7] After five years, the dispossessed owner is barred from claiming back the stolen work of art from the bona fide acquirer, and the acquirer becomes the owner.[8] Swiss law contains strict rules relating to the proof of good faith that are found in Article 3 of the Swiss Civil Code: "No person can plead bona fide in any case where he has failed to exercise the degree of care required by the circumstances." This has been interpreted by the Swiss Supreme Court to mean that "whenever the circumstances raise doubts as to the quality of the seller, the purchaser may no longer content himself with the mere appearance constituted by possession; the purchaser must inquire into the seller's capacity to convey property right."[9]

Under Italian law, the bona fide acquirer of a stolen work of art usually does not have to return it to the dispossessed owner, whether he acquired it from a merchant or from a private person.[10] This rule does not apply to works of art belonging to public collections. The possession of such objects, even in good faith, has no effect, since they are public property and as such are *extra commercia*.[11]

---

[6] Jacques Ghestin, Le Droit Interne Français de la Vente d'Objets d'Art et de Collection, *in* International Sales of Works of Art (Inst. of Int'l Bus. L. & Prac., Int'l Chamber of Commerce & Faculté de Droit de Genève 1985).

[7] Art. 954 II Civ. C.

[8] Art. 934, 936, 714 II Civ. C.

[9] Paul-Henri Steinhauer, L'Acquisition d'Objets d'Art selon le Droit Privé Suisse, in International Sales of Works of Art, *supra* note 2. *See also* Marc-André Renold, Summary of Holding: Swiss Supreme Court, Second Civil Division, Decision of March 5, 1996, "Insurance X versus A.M.", Cultural Property Roundtable, Ass'n of the Bar of the City of New York, Comm. on Art Law, Nov. 12, 1996.

[10] Art. 1153 Civ. C.

[11] Art. 1145 Civ. C. and art. 23 *et seq.* of the Law of June 1, 1939, n° 1089, modified by the Law of Aug. 8, 1972, n° 487. Francesco Galgano, Aspects Juridiques du Commerce de l'Art en Italie, in International Sales of Works of Art, *supra* note 2.

German law, as a matter of principle, does not allow good-faith acquisition of stolen or lost property. However, good title may be acquired on a stolen good or lost property. The possessor must have been in good faith when the object was passed to him, and possessed the object and behaved like an owner in good faith for 10 years without interruption. However, German law is similar to Swiss law in that the possessor cannot acquire good title if he was negligent as to the provenance of the object.[12]

In the event of a successful claim by the owner against the buyer, the buyer will want the right to be compensated by the seller and to receive the full measure of damages, including compensation for all expenses and the loss of economic opportunity. The existence of a title guarantee in an agreement may give the buyer more time to recover from a seller than would be allowed under the statute of limitations. Owners and their successors may have a cause of action without a statute of limitations,[13] or with a longer statute of limitations, if the work has been the subject of despoliation as part of a crime against humanity,[14] or if it is

---

[12] § 935 I BGB. Hans Hanisch, Aspects Juridiques du Commerce International de l'Art en République Fédérale d'Allemagne, in International Sales of Works of Art, *supra* note 2.

[13] *See infra* § 7.09.

[14] *See generally* Recovery of Stolen and Looted Works of Art, December 10, 1998 Seminar, IAL, and Art, Law and the Holocaust, Oct. 5, 1999 Seminar, IAL, and in particular the statement of Charlotte van Rappard Boon, Chief Inspector, Ministry of Education, Science and Culture, Inspectorate of Cultural Heritage, the Netherlands, indicating that in litigation on ownership of works seized in the Holocaust and now held by the state, the statute of limitations should be waived. The French answer is partly reflected by the creation of a special commission—Edict of Sept. 10, 1999—creating a commission to examine individual claims emanating from victims or their families.

See also U.S. Dept. of State, Washington Conference on Holocaust-Era Assets, which poses the following Principles with Respect to Nazi Confiscated Art that should be respected by the participant nations within the context of their own law:

1. Nazi-confiscated art has to be identified;
2. relevant archives and records for researchers must be accessible;
3. resources and personnel must be provided to facilitate the identification of Nazi-confiscated art;
4. in establishing that a work is Nazi-confiscated, the passage of time and the circumstances of the Holocaust must be taken into consideration (if there are unavoidable gaps);
5. confiscated works must be published in order to locate pre-War owners;
6. a central register must be established;
7. pre-War owners and heirs must be encouraged to claim the works;
8. if pre-War owners or their heirs are identified, an adequate solution for the specific case has to be found;
9. if the pre-War owner or his heirs cannot be identified, a just and fair solution has to be found;
10. membership of the commissions and bodies that identify confiscated art has to be balanced; and

located in a country that has ratified the UNIDROIT Convention,[15] which provides for a 50-year statute of limitations.

[b] Guarantee of Authenticity

Buyers should have it clearly in writing that authenticity is guaranteed and remedies spelled out in the event of breach.[16]

In many jurisdictions a sales invoice from a professional dealer without limiting language using the full name of the artist constitutes a declaration by the seller that the work is by the hand of the artist.[17] Where the seller is not willing to give such a guarantee, the rights of the buyer should be confirmed under the law of the jurisdiction applicable to the seller so that risk can be appreciated. Where the seller is a private person, however, such a guarantee may not be implicit except if it is so stated, unless the circumstances and the consideration paid show clearly that such a guarantee was contemplated by the parties.

Authenticity issues include dealing with fakes and forgeries, and establishing the identity of the artist who did the work.[18] Many dealers and auction houses seek explicitly in their contractual terms to limit their liability by stating that authenticity is not warranted, but is merely an "opinion."[19] Weighed against such self-serving statements are the rights as established in different jurisdictions to hold a seller responsible under differing terms for the authenticity of the work sold.[20]

---

11. participating nations must be encouraged to implement these principles within national processes.

For more detailed information on the issue, see Chairman's concluding statement, Washington Conference on Holocaust-Era Assets, Dec. 3, 1998.

[15] UNIDROIT Convention on the International Return of Stolen or Illegally Exported Cultural Objects June 24, 1995 (hereinafter UNIDROIT Convention).

[16] *See* Form 7-1, Purchase Agreement, art. 9.

[17] Under French law, Decree n° 81-255 of March 3, 1981, J.O. March 20, 1981, on the Control of Fraud in Transactions in Works of Art and Collection Items, art. 3 provides that "when the name of the artist is followed immediately by the name of the work, unless exception is expressed on authenticity, there is a guarantee that the work stated is effectively by the artist."

[18] A "fake" is a work in the style of the artist in question, the authenticity of which is often supported by forged signatures and/or documents. Fakes can also consist of altered art, or art that has later been completed by another artist. "Forgeries" are replicas of genuine works of art, which are deliberately created to deceive, or innocently created and then later passed off as originals. As copying masterpieces has been traditional exercise for the training of artists, there is a great deal of material available.

[19] Christie's "Conditions of Business," art. 14a: "Statements by us in the catalogue or condition report, or made orally or in writing elsewhere, regarding the authorship, origin, date, age, size, medium, attribution, genuineness, provenance, condition or estimated selling price of any lot are merely statements of opinion, and are not to be relied on as statements of definitive fact."

[20] Marie Zelinger de Balkany and Christie Manson & Wood Limited, Defendant, High Court

The buyer has the burden of proof to show that the work is not authentic, even where the seller has given an unequivocal guarantee of authenticity. Common law courts use expert witness testimony on authenticity. The court then weighs the credibility of the expert opinions, even though the court may not have the requisite expertise to make such a judgment.[21]

In France, authenticity is treated as a question of *fact*, to be determined by an expert appointed as a *master*. The expert so appointed often defers to the opinions of the acknowledged authorities in the field and/or the holders of the moral rights.

The buyer and seller will propose different periods of effectiveness. Sellers will want their guarantees to end in short order so that they will not be subject to claims when new experts have established their authority and where the marketplace has evolved. Buyers will want to hold sellers responsible for issues of title, authenticity and condition for the greatest period possible so as to limit their risks.

[c] Guarantee of Condition

Works of art are generally considered to be sold "as is," particularly where the buyer has had the opportunity of inspection. A guarantee as to condition would normally give only a right of restitution because quantifying the damages that would be due for breach of this guarantee is difficult. However, a court might well accept testimony on this issue.

A full and accurate description of the work and its condition in a contract for its sale is particularly valuable to avoid a dispute regarding the guarantee. The guarantee becomes particularly important where there has been a major restoration or even a reconstitution of the work.[22]

[5] Remedies

[a] Rescission

Rescission is often an inequitable remedy for either the buyer or the seller due to conditions in the market after the sale. Rescission is an inadequate remedy

---

of Justice, Queen's Bench Division, 1993 D No. 1089. This case ruled that a major reconstitution constituted a forgery so that Christie's disclaimer of liability did not protect it from liability.

[21] Greenberg Gallery, Inc. v. Bauman, 817 F. Supp. 167 (D.D.C. 1993), *aff'd*, U.S. App. LEXIS 27175 (1994). The trial court was not satisfied with the testimony of Klaus Perls, a leading expert on the work of Alexander Calder, that a sheet metal mobile was a forgery. The opposing party introduced evidence from Linda Silverman, a longtime dealer in Impressionist and early twentieth-century art, that the object was authentic. The court concluded that "it is more likely than not that the mobile is not a forgery." The decision was affirmed without comment. This decision provides legal authentication for a work that, according to Perls, may be without value in the marketplace.

[22] *Cf. supra* note 20.

for the buyer where works of art have increased in value or where the artist has become more prominent subsequent to the sale of the work. The buyer's remedy is limited because sellers normally wish to offer the buyer only a right of rescission without interest. Rescission is an inadequate remedy for the seller where the art market has suffered serious losses in values due to economic circumstances, or where tastes in the market have evolved so that the work is not as popular as it was when purchased.

[b] Damages

Damages to compensate the injured party for his loss should be an attractive remedy, but proof of amount can be difficult, particularly as courts do not like to award damages where they cannot be established with certainty. What is the loss of value where a canvas has been torn and restored? How can that loss be established? Comparisons are difficult to make and opinions can vary widely.

[c] Loss of Economic Opportunity

Buyers who have purchased an object that is unsatisfactory would like compensation for the increase in value that would have occurred if the object had been good. Proving such loss by citing the rise in value of similar works, so that a court will not consider such a claim for damages to be speculative, is a challenging task.

A seller will resist such a proposal. The consideration is established as the value at the time of sale, and such a right is an incitement to litigation based on changes in the market that the parties could not have predicted when they made their agreement.

Compensation on the basis of what the purchase price would have earned in interest during the period is easy to prove, but the buyer is unlikely to deem the result to be adequate recompense.

[6] Choice of Forum for Litigation

Buyers will want the convenience of litigating in a jurisdiction best known to them, where the seller can be compelled to pay a successful judgment. Neither party will wish to be put to the expense of litigating in foreign jurisdictions. A buyer should be warned that if the jurisdiction of the litigation is not the jurisdiction where the seller has assets, the buyer, in the event of a successful judgment, may have to seek enforcement of his judgment in a foreign jurisdiction.

The rules by which a court in one forum enforces the judgment of a court in another forum are based on comity, that is, the natural respect that courts should have for each other. The court called upon to enforce a judgment from another forum can look into all aspects of the foreign judgment to see if its notions of public policy and fundamental principles of justice have been respected. The court may conduct an extensive investigation into all the circumstances surrounding the initial judgment.[23] Thus counsel should weigh carefully whether to sue in a convenient jurisdiction and then seek to enforce that judgment in a jurisdiction where the defendant has assets, or to bring the initial suit in a jurisdiction where the defendant has assets.

In considering choice of forum, American counsel should keep in mind the differences in European legal practice. European courts do not force an adverse party to submit to interrogatories and do not make discovery available to a plaintiff. European countries also have antidisclosure statutes to protect against economic espionage from the use of depositions and discovery documents.[24] Such statutes limit the plaintiff to the rights and sanctions under the Hague Convention, which does not permit interrogatories or forced disclosure. Foreign counsel conducting interrogatories on foreign soil may be committing a criminal offense,[25] unless such interrogatories are taken and depositions made at an embassy where such a party cannot be compelled to give testimony except in exceptional circumstances.

[B] Consignments and Loans

An owner risks a work when it is placed in the hands of another. Owners can take such safety precautions as they choose, and if their property is not protected adequately, only the owner is to blame.

When property is placed in the hands of a third party, the work may be damaged or destroyed due to civil insurrection, war, hostilities, riots or natural forces such as earthquakes, floods and high winds. The object may be stolen, or may deteriorate due to changes in climate and humidity. The third party may be negligent.[26] Owners want the third party to protect their property to the greatest extent possible.[27] However, where objects are consigned without a written agree-

---

[23] Bernard Audit, L'Effet des Jugements Etrangers, in Droit International Privé (Economica 2d ed. 1997).

[24] French anti-disclosure statutes: Law n° 80-538, July 16, 1980, shields French corporations from giving information to foreign antitrust and other foreign public authorities, and prevents the taking of depositions in France other than depositions specially authorized by the Hague Evidence Treaty of 1970.

[25] *Cf.* note 24. Sanctions are two-to-six month imprisonment and/or 10,000- to 20,000-franc fines.

[26] *See* Antony F. Anderson, A Collector's View of the Art Loan Process, Lessons from the Denney Collection, 4 Art, Antiquity & Law 23 (1999). In this case a well-known collector lent a collection to the Dallas Museum of Art. After his death, a forged letter instructed the museum to transfer the collection to the Museum of Modern Art in Toulouse, France, where it was accepted by the city as a gift from the widow in spite of claims by the decedent's children that the collection was theirs. In subsequent litigation the court of the decedent's domicile ruled in favor of the widow.

[27] *See generally* Norman Palmer, Art Loans, Kluwer Law Int'l and Int'l Bar Ass'n, 1997.

ment, the owner may be without proper protection. Alternatively, a consignee without a written agreement may, under the law of the jurisdiction that governs the consignment, be liable for a higher level of care than the consignee feels is reasonable.[28]

A well-thought-out consignment agreement will establish the rights of the parties so that they know the risks that they are undertaking. But even with the most carefully drafted agreement, parting with property creates risks that the owner may never have envisioned and may place responsibilities upon the consignee that should not be accepted. The consignment agreement should address the following issues:

- Does the owner or the consignee bear the risk of the work's destruction or damage in the event of a *force majeure*?
- Where a consignee is liable only for reasonable care, how is such care defined, and what activities or actions go beyond such care?
- In the event of damage and a right against the consignee, how is such damage established?
- In a consignment agreement, to what extent can the consignee limit his liabilities or limit the period during which the owner may assert his rights? How may the owner obtain an enforceable judgment that will compensate him for his loss where the consignee is in a foreign jurisdiction?
- To what extent do insurance contracted in that foreign jurisdiction, letters of credit, or other guarantees satisfy the owner for the risks undertaken in consigning the work?
- May a consignment agreement executed by a consignee in a foreign jurisdiction contain provisions that are unenforceable under the terms of the law of that jurisdiction?

[C] Gifts, Legacies, and Inheritances

[1] Taxation

Transfer of title without consideration normally calls for a tax on such transfer, whether called a gift, estate, or succession tax, or a tax on unrealized capital gain. Such a tax generally applies to all gifts, legacies, and inheritances.

---

[28] The English rule was established in Coggs v. Bernard (1703) 2 Ld Raym 909, holding that a loan without payment requires the borrower to exercise "the strictest care and diligence" at 915, but this rule can be defeated by an agreement that establishes what the standard of care should be, subject to the applicability of a number of laws dealing with fairness. Contract Terms Act 1977, Unfair Terms in Consumer Contracts Regulations, effective July 1, 1995, et al.

Such tax may be sought to be assessed where the transferor is resident, domiciled or is a citizen; where title is transferred; or where the beneficiary is resident.[29] Whether such tax is assessed on the donor or the recipient varies from country to country and the object itself may be subject to a lien by the tax administration seeking to collect such tax.[30]

Gifts and legacies to charitable organizations are often excluded from taxation. Different jurisdictions have very different rules as to what organizations are qualified to receive tax exemptions and what portion of the gift, legacy, or inheritance may be subject to tax.[31]

[2] Interdiction of Transfers

Many jurisdictions forbid or limit transfers of title without consideration. In many civil law countries, children, parents, and spouses are entitled to receive a stated percentage of a decedent's estate. Transfers without consideration that defeat such rights may be set aside, whether or not the beneficiaries knew of the existence of such transfers at the time they were made.[32]

In certain jurisdictions, charities may not receive more than a certain percentage of a testator's estate. Local law also may have classes of beneficiaries who are not entitled to accept gifts.[33] Even today, the issue is still being debated as to the extent to which gifts to charity should be exempt from tax on the transfer of assets to them.[34]

---

[29] The French tax law, Article 750 ter 3 of the Code Général des Impôts calls for taxes similar to an estate tax rates to be paid by a French resident who receives a gift, inheritance, or legacy from a foreign jurisdiction. Such gift, inheritance, or legacy may also be subject to tax in another jurisdiction where the donor or testator was domiciled.

[30] Under French law, in the absence of special language in the will of the donor, a donee is liable for gift tax and a legatee or heir is liable for estate tax. Such transfers are taxed at 60% where there is no blood relationship between the parties. This can place the new owner in the difficult position of having a valuable illiquid gift or legacy without the funds to cover the tax. Code Général des Impôts, art. 777.

[31] For example, under French law a charity, where a member of its board receives compensation of any kind, would be subject to normal gift or legacy taxes on donations and legacies to it.

[32] French Civ. C. art. 731-767.

[33] In France, gifts of real property to charity are subject to approval by the Ministry of the Interior. The origin of this law comes from the view developed during the French Revolution that real property deeded to religious organizations too great an economic control of the nation's assets.

[34] *See* Matignon s'intéresse aux Associations, Le Figaro, Feb. 22, 1999, at 6. This article discussed the reaction of the French Prime Minister to the Secretary of State for the Budget, who had called for limiting strictly the tax advantages of charities. The debate concerns what activities should be considered charitable and what criteria should be used to judge them. The article foresees that many French charities may lose their tax-privileged status, and those that retain their tax-privileged status will be subject to tax on their "commercial" activities.

§ 7.03 ISSUES RELATING TO TITLE

[A] Claims of Previous Owners and Part Owners

[1] Theft

Art theft is a serious issue.[35] A theft in the chain of title can lead to lengthy disputes between the original owner and the bona fide purchaser for value.[36] A thief cannot give good title and the possessor of a stolen work may be liable to return the work to the true owner, even if he is a bona fide purchaser for value. The possessor normally retains a right of action against the thief,[37] but such individuals are often elusive, and indeed when caught, are usually unable to pay damages.

Many times, owners allow themselves to be prime targets for theft and do not pursue diligently their remedies. Often stolen works are not registered with the Art Loss Register[38] which, for a small charge, will register and publicize the theft of a work. Buyers also do not take advantage of these research facilities, thus encouraging the traffic in stolen art. Buyers also are often lax in seeking to

---

[35] The magnitude of art theft in recent years is shown in statistics by Interpol (thefts in Czechoslovakia have increased sixteen fold since 1989), Lloyds of London (a billion pounds' worth of art is stolen each year), and the Italian government ($50 million worth of art is stolen in Italy every year).

[36] Ashton Hawkins, Richard A. Rothman, David B. Goldstein, A Tale of Two Innocents: Creating an Equitable Balance between the Rights of Former Owners and Good Faith Purchasers of Stolen Art, 64 Fordham L. Rev. 49 (1995).

[37] Kunstsammlung zu Weimar v. Elicofon, 678 Fed. 1150 (2d Cir. 1982). The KZW filed suit in 1966 to recover two portraits by Albrecht Dürer that had been illegally removed from Germany during World War II. The defendant, Elicofon, bought the paintings in 1946 from an American serviceman. His innocence as to knowledge of the origin, identity, and value of the paintings remained undisputed. The court suggested that Germany's contacts with the case were irrelevant, and therefore applied the New York common law of personal property. According to New York law a bona fide purchaser cannot acquire good title from a thief (Stanton Motor Corp. v. Rosetti, 11 A.D.2d 296, 298, 203 N.Y.S. 2d 273, 276 (1960)). This common law principle is restated by the Uniform Commercial Code, adopted by New York (N.Y.U.C.C., §§ 1-101 to 1-105).

See Winkworth v. Christie Manson & Woods Ltd & Another, 2 W.L.R. 937 (1980). In that case, the plaintiff was the original owner of art works stolen from him in England, and which had then been taken to Italy where they had been resold by a third party, the second defendant, who delivered them to England for sale there by Christie's. The plaintiff brought an action in England seeking the return of the art works. The judges had to decide whether English or Italian law should be applied to determine the ownership of the art works. According to the principle of the *lex situs*, the court decided that Italian law applied. According to Italian law, good faith is presumed; therefore the second defendant would have acquired title to the art works. The application of English law might have resulted in the opposite conclusion: according to English law, a bona fide purchaser may acquire good title from one who is not the owner if the title of the transferor is voidable. In the case in issue, the works being acquired from a thief, the title of the transferor would be void.

[38] Art Loss Register, discussed *supra* in Chapter 5.

document ownership prior to purchase, and buyers can be very casual about seeking knowledge as to the previous ownership of a work.

[2] Fraudulent Conveyance

The most common type of fraudulent conveyance arises where the owner has let a third party have apparent authority to deal with his property or has given possession of the property to a third party. Where the third party sells the property to a buyer, the buyer may have good title to it. The court must decide between a bona fide purchaser for value and an owner who has allowed the purchaser to think that the third party was authorized to sell the property.[39] Where the buyer is found not to be in good faith, his rights are reduced against the original owner.[40]

The rights of a buyer in such circumstances are different in each jurisdiction in accordance with the assessments of the relative merits of the two innocent parties. An owner risks his art work where he gives the work to be framed, particularly where the framer then asks if he can exhibit the work with its new frame in its shop window, or hands the work over to a restorer, an appraiser, or an expert for his leisurely contemplation and study of the work. The owner and the third party taking possession of his work should enter into an agreement so that the third party's duties and responsibility are clear.

Not all insurance covers the loss arising while the object is in the possession of a third party. The owner's best course of action is to review his insurance coverage and see if a special rider is needed.

[3] Claims of Previous Owners

Because of art theft and fraudulent conveyances, disputes arise regularly between bona fide purchasers for value and victims who have lost possession of their works. Some jurisdictions give extensive rights to previous owners by requiring that the previous owner must give notice to the present possessor before a statute of limitations can commence.[41] Other jurisdictions favor certainty in commerce by providing that ownership cannot be contested after a given number of years. Others adopt positions between the two.

---

[39] Norman Palmer, The Appendix: Some Modern Cases Taking Security over Art, seminar sponsored by IAL in association with Mishcon de Reya's art law group, June 16, 1997, takes the reader through litigation after litigation where the owner is at risk for not properly protecting his property.

[40] Article 2262 of the French Civil Code provides for a 30-year statute of limitations, where for many actions a three-year statute would have been applicable from the date of the theft if the buyer had been in good faith.

[41] Solomon R. Guggenheim Foundation v. Lubell, 569 N.E.2d 426 (N.Y. 1991).

The accident of where a work may be held at any moment may give the original owner substantially different rights. For this reason, the loan of a work which places the work in another jurisdiction may bring forth litigation that was barred in the jurisdiction of the possessor of the work.[42]

[4] Claims of Owners of a Partial Interest in a Work

In order for ownership to be transferred, all the present owners must consent to the sale so that one cannot transfer full title of a work over which one does not have full ownership. One can transfer only one's own share of interest in the work. This is a special aspect of fraudulent conveyance, in that one of a group of owners may seek to sell a work and can transfer his individual part of the title, but without the agreement of the other owners, the work cannot change hands. This issue becomes particularly important where several legatees or heirs share ownership in a work of art, or where a work has been bought in partnership.[43]

[B] Other Liens

[1] Liens of State

A work may be seized by a state and sold where the state has a claim against the owner.[44] The state may also erroneously seize and sell works in the hands of a possessor, and the steps needed to disentangle such a seizure are complex and difficult. The right of the original owner to recover the work may be difficult to assert, particularly against a buyer in a state-sponsored auction.

[2] Liens of Private Parties

In the United States, the Uniform Commercial Code (UCC)[45] gives clear rules as to how to place an effective lien on personal property. Under most foreign rules, however, there is little possibility of asserting a security interest or privileged debt position against personal objects, unless such objects are retained by the creditor.[46] Foreign law has nothing comparable to the UCC rules and no equivalent

---

[42] *See infra* § 7.02[A][4] for discussion of English, French, Swiss, Italian and German rules.

[43] Judith Hill, Co-Ownership in Art, Transacting in Art IAL seminar, July 6, 1995.

[44] Under French law, where taxes have not been paid, upon notice, the tax authorities may seize property belonging to the taxpayer. Such property is then sold at a judicial auction. LPF art. R. 258-1.

[45] U.C.C., art. 9.

[46] French law is typical in requiring that the security holders keep the asset in order to maintain their security interest. *See* French Civ. C. art. 2071 *et seq. See also* J. Mestre, E. Pulman, M. Billian, La Notion d'Hypothèque Mobilière in Droit Civil—Droit Spécial des Sûretés Réelles 459-63.

of a UCC filing. Possession is normally the only way that a party may protect his rights in an object pledged to secure such rights.[47]

[3] Violation of Export Rules

[a] General Rules

Most countries other than the United States,[48] and even the United States for certain cultural property,[49] have rules forbidding or requiring an export license for the exportation of art objects and objects of historical, archaeological, religious, anthropological, or cultural interest. Such rules and the rigor of their application

---

[47] *Cf. supra* note 39, IAL seminar, June 16, 1997.

[48] English rule: A significant cultural asset may not leave the United Kingdom upon its sale for a six-month period during which an attempt can be made to find a British buyer prepared to pay the same price. These rules are discussed by Michael Clint of the U.K. Department of National Heritage, in Export Controls and the International Art Market, Transacting in Art, The Legal Pitfalls, IAL seminar in association with The Art Newspaper, Oct. 29, 1996. In extreme cases, such as that of Antonio Canova's sculpture "Three Graces," this six-month rule has been extended in a manner some thought arbitrary. In 1990, the British government did not grant an export license for the work. When the Getty Museum tried to purchase the work, British buyers could not match the purchase price until Nov. 5, 1994, when Baron Thyssen-Bornemisza pledged the final £1.2 million needed to keep the "Three Graces" in Britain.

French rule: France's rules on the export of art objects (Law n° 92-1477, Dec. 31st, 1992 and Decree n° 93-124, Jan. 29, 1993) provide that for paintings with a value of more than 150,000 euros and sculptures with a value of more than 50,000 euros, an export certificate must be requested. If refused, the request cannot be re-submitted for three years. It can then be refused again only if the work is declared a National Treasure. As such, under the leading case of *Walter*, the owner should be compensated in the amount of the difference between the value of the work in the French market and its value on the international market. The owner has the right to this indemnity and retains the object. Agent Judiciaire du Trésor v. Walter, Cass. Civ. 1, Feb. 20, 1996, Bulletin de la Cour. This case established the right under French law to compensation when an export license is refused. *See* Timothy P. Ramier, Agent Judiciaire du Trésor v. Walter, Fait du Prince and a King's Ransom, Int'l J. Cultural Property, V. 6, No. 2 (1997).

Italian rule: In Italy, all works over 150 years old require an export license. Such licenses are discretionary, and in the event of a refusal, the work may not leave Italy. No compensation is offered if the license is refused.

European rule: The Treaty of Rome creating the European Economic Community, now the European Union, provides for the free commerce in goods, but Articles 28 and 29 provide an exception to such rules permitting each member state to establish its own rules for the protection of "national treasures possessing artistic, historic and archaeological value." *See also* John H. Merryman, The Retention of Cultural Property, 21 U.C. Davis L. Rev. 477 (1988). *See also supra* Chapter 6, discussing cultural property rules and treaties at length.

[49] *See* Cultural Property Implementation Act (CPIA) 19 U.S.C. §§ 2601-2613 (1983) implementing the 1970 UNESCO Convention on the Means of Prohibiting and Preventing the Illicit Import, Export and Transfer of Ownership of Cultural Property (UNESCO Convention), discussed in § 6.04[A].

vary greatly from country to country,[50] but one should assume that they exist, and that a buyer may have significant difficulties if they have not been observed. International conventions have strengthened enforcement of these rules.[51]

[b] Violation as Criminal Act in Another Jurisdiction

A growing body of authority asserts that there is a flaw in title where export rules have not been respected. Such flaw in title may subject owners to a claim of receipt of stolen goods,[52] may allow exporting states or importing states to seize such objects, and may subject owners to significant adverse publicity.

The UNIDROIT rules are applicable not only to stolen property, but to property that has been illegally exported, requiring the return of such property to the country of export. The statute of limitations is 50 years, which can, in certain instances, be extended.[53]

[c] Reduction in Market Value

As nations whose export laws are violated have increased remedial rights, objects exported in violation of the rules may have a reduced value in the marketplace.

[4] Violation of Import Rules

Moreover, customs regulations[54] and criminal rules on receiving stolen prop-

---

[50] *See, e.g.*, Canadian law: The Cultural Property Export & Import Act (June 1997).

[51] UNESCO Convention—UNIDROIT Convention.

[52] *See* United States v. McClain, 593 F.2d 658 (5th Cir. 1979), 545 F.2d 988 (5th Cir. 1977). Transporting of stolen foreign cultural property in the United States is a federal crime under the National Stolen Property Act (NSPA), if it can be established that the accused knew the property was stolen. *McClain* involved pre-Columbian artifacts from Mexico that had been smuggled by persons who were aware of the Mexican law concerning ownership of excavated and unexcavated materials and of Mexican export regulations. The Fifth Circuit in the first *McClain* decision found that the NSPA could apply to the *illegal exportation* of artifacts, but only if Mexican law clearly declared that the state owned all such property.

[53] UNIDROIT Convention. The European Union Cultural Objects Law, formally known as Council Directive 93/7, 1993 O.J. (L74).

[54] United States v. An Antique Platter of Gold Known as a Gold Phiale Mesomphalos, c. 400 B.C., 95 Civ. 10537 (BSJ), 1997 U.S. Dist. LEXIS 18899. An art collector (defendant *in rem*) bought an ancient gold plate from a Swiss art dealer with whom he had been doing business for many years. The customs declaration stated the value and origin inaccurately. The collector did not know about the provisions of the customs declaration. After receiving a complaint from the Italian government, United States Customs Agents removed the plate from the collector's apartment A United States District Court ordered the artifact to be returned to Italy. For additional analysis of this case, see *supra* §§ 6.03[B][1] and 6.03[B][4][b].

erty[55] require buyers to verify the status of property in the country from which the works originated and whether export rules have been respected.

[5] State Property

Where property is held by the state, title to it may be contested if it is lent for exhibition in another country. The claimants or other interested parties may attempt to litigate title in the country to which the work has been lent. Different nations have different legislation seeking to discourage claimants from using their courts to assist such claims.[56]

State property that has been converted or stolen is subject to special rules.[57] In certain jurisdictions,[58] state property cannot be alienated, and there is no statute of limitations terminating the right of the state under its own law to recover such items. Even where there are appropriate statutes of limitations, the pressure that a state may bring to bear can make quiet possession of such property problematic.

Many countries provide that archaeological and ethnological objects that have yet to be discovered remain the property of the state. Such countries are becoming more prepared to bring criminal or civil charges[59] to recover such property.

[6] Particular Rules for Antiquities

Many states provide that antiquities that are unidentified and have not been excavated are the property of the state in which they are found,[60] and that the

---

[55] *Cf. McClain, supra* note 52 (the first case in which it was found that the NSPA was applicable to the illegal exportation of artifacts); United States v. Hollinshead, 495 F.2d 1154 (9th Cir. 1974) (This case was the first criminal conviction in the United States under the NSPA for the illegal transport of cultural property. An art dealer was charged with the illegal transport of a Mayan stele. The behavior of the dealer showed that he had known that the stele was stolen, and therefore it did not have to be proved that the dealer knew that the law of Guatemala vested title to the stele in the state); United States v. Pre-Columbian Artifacts and the Republic of Guatemala, 845 F. Supp. 544 (N.D. Ill. 1993) (the NSPA was applied to a violation of Guatemalan export laws).

[56] The Chtchoukine family unsuccessfully sought title in France to paintings seized from their family by the Soviet Union after the Russian Revolution. These paintings were on loan for exhibition in France. To avoid such litigation in the future, the Law of August 8, 1994, was passed, providing that cultural objects lent by foreign powers for exhibition may not be seized.

[57] United States v. An Original Manuscript Dated Nov. 19, 1778, Bearing the Signature of Junipero Serra, located at Sotheby's, 1999 WL 97894 96 Civ. 6221 (LAP) (Feb. 19, 1999).

[58] In France, property declared "monument historique" cannot be transferred through the operation of a statute of limitations. Law of Dec. 13, 1913, art. 12.

[59] In Republic of Turkey v. Metropolitan Museum of Art, 762 F. Supp. 44 (S.D.N.Y. 1990), a civil action was brought in the State of New York by the government of Turkey to recover possession of artifacts that were allegedly excavated in Turkey in 1966 and exported to the United States in contravention of Turkish law. An out-of-court settlement resulted.

[60] *E.g.*, Mexico (art. 40 & 41 Crim. C.). *See generally* Chapter 6.

excavation or export of such works is a criminal act. United States courts have accepted this premise and its corollary, that such property therefore is stolen property and that criminal sanctions are appropriate for the thief and also for the recipient as a receiver of stolen property.[61] Needless to say, in the country of origin, such acts are criminal and incur sanctions as such. Not only is the United States now considering such looting as a crime for which U.S. courts are prepared to offer redress, and handling such property is considered to be dealing in stolen property.

The U.S. Customs Service is now taking the philosophy one step further in holding that false declarations made in a Customs form permit the Customs Service to seize such property and have it forfeited, so as to be able to return it to the country of its origin.[62] Those in the antiquities market must therefore pay rigorous attention to the export laws of the country where antiquities are initially excavated.

[C] Rights of the Artist and His Heirs

In American law, works of art are generally treated as chattels that can be transferred from party to party. Nonetheless this concept has been eroded, principally by ideas that have their origin in Europe and in particular France, and are enshrined in the Universal Declaration of Human Rights[63] and are codified in the Berne Convention.[64]

Copyright gives limited defined rights to artists, while the *droit d'auteur* in French law literally means the "rights of a creator."[65] This concept is far broader and includes pecuniary rights and moral rights, as discussed below. Many other jurisdictions have adopted certain moral rights.[66]

In a tradition of law which at its most extreme is exemplified by French law,[67] a work of art has almost a legal personality, and the artist, his assignees and his legatees and heirs may assert substantial rights. To be able to advise his client, an attorney working on an international transaction must know which rights are retained by the artist and which should be negotiated at the time of transfer of a work. In particular, reproduction rights should be included with the transfer of the object and simultaneously acquired as part of the purchase. Failure to include such rights can give the owner only the right to the physical object without

---

[61] *Cf.* notes 52, 54-56.

[62] *Cf.* note 54. *See also* § 6.03[B][3].

[63] 6 U.N. Bull. 6, 8 (Jan. 1, 1949).

[64] Berne Copyright Convention, 1928.

[65] Law n° 57-298 of March 11, 1957 on literary and artistic ownership (J.O. 2723 Mar. 14, 1957, Dalloz Législation 102), and corrections thereto April 19, 1957.

[66] Subsequent to the enactment of the Copyright Designs and Patents Act 1988, England recognizes the right of paternity.

[67] Law n° 57-298, Mar. 11, 1957 (*op. cit.*).

the right to reproduce it. Similarly, the seller of a work needs to check the law as to whether there is a *droit de suite*, that is, the artist's right to receive compensation in a stated percentage when one of his works is resold.

Other rights, often called "moral rights" in French law, are retained by the artist, and in France are inalienable, but the use of these rights may require payments to the injured party.

[1] Economic Rights

[a] Reproduction Rights

Usually the most important pecuniary right retained by the artist under the laws of France (unless expressly transferred) is the right to reproduce the work. Reproduction license fees paid to popular artists or their estates can exceed U.S. $500,000 per year. Under French law, the artist retains the reproduction right but may transfer it with or without consideration to any third party. The owner may make no reproduction of the work if this right has not been transferred.

*[b] Participation in Future Sales of Works (***Droit de Suite***)*

The *droit de suite* is the right of an artist to be compensated with a percentage of the sales proceeds of any subsequent sale of his works during his lifetime and for the 50 years following his death.[68] In France, rights associations such as the *Société Dans les Arts Graphiques et Plastiques* (Society of Visual and Graphic Artists, or ADAGP) are often given authority to enforce such rights and collect such payments. This agency is also used to collect reproduction royalties where the artist has retained such rights.[69]

Such *droit de suite* rights vary according to the legislation of different countries in an amount between 3 percent and 5 percent.

Most European countries have one or more active artists' rights societies able to police art sales. Where there are no such organizations, often these rights are ignored even though they exist at law.[70]

[2] Moral Rights

French law contains the most important protection of artists' rights. They are not assignable.[71]

---

[68] *Id.*

[69] For debate on the utility of the *droit de suite*, see U.K. Minister Opposes Droit de Suite, The Art Newspaper, July-Aug. 1998.

[70] California Resale Royalties Act, Cal. Civ. Code § 986 (West 1982 & Supp. 1997). This law appears to be largely ignored in California, except for public auction sales.

[71] Reeves, Bauer & Lieser, Retained Rights of Authors, Artists and Composers under French Law of Literary and Artistic Property, J. Arts Mgmt. & L., V. 14, No. 4 (Winter 1985).

[a] The Right to Create

The right to create and the freedom and latitude allowed in so doing is one of the Rights of Man.[72] There are limits on the right to create. In every society there are certain taboos. Figures such as the Queen of England and the President of France, representations of religion, or representations of nationality such as the American flag can be the subject of legislation and are a permanent incitement to certain creative artists. The battle between these icons and artists is continuous, whether it is defined as free speech or unfettered creativity.

Works of art can be considered obscene, and their display subject to police and court action, but incidents of prosecution are less common in Europe than in the United States. The standards of obscenity vary greatly among nations and localities. An unveiled face may arouse more revulsion in one jurisdiction than an unveiled couple would in another.

[b] The Right to Disclosure and Completeness

Only the artist can determine when his work has been achieved.[73] His failure to achieve his work may place him in breach of contract if he has contracted to deliver the work to a purchaser. A court will require, however, that the buyer be reimbursed in the event that the artist does not complete the work, and damages may be granted where the court is convinced that the artist's refusal to complete the work is in bad faith.[74]

[c] The Right to Withdraw

The artist, even after he has completed the work and divulged it, may, if he has second thoughts about it, withdraw it, taking it back from the owner. This right is seldom exercised because of the damages that the artist is required to pay.[75]

---

[72] *Cf.* 6 U.N. Bull. 6, 8 (Jan. 1, 1949). French law also protects the honor and reputation of an artist against the mistreatment of his work. This right to honor and reputation is sometimes referred to as a moral right, but this is incorrect.

[73] Law n° 57-298 of Mar. 11, 1957 (*op. cit.*), art. 19.

[74] Eden c. Whistler (1898) Judgment of Mar. 14, 1900, Cass. Civ. (1900) Dalloz Périodique et Critique, I 497. In this case, the artist refused to deliver a portrait and painted another face on the sitter. The artist was not required to deliver the work, but he was subject to damages which possibly were increased for his willfulness.

[75] Law n° 57-298 Mar. 11, 1957 (*op. cit.*), art. 32.

[d] The Right of Paternity

The artist is entitled to be recognized as the creator of the work,[76] and where a work is done by several parties, recognition must be given to them all.[77]

[e] The Right of Integrity

The right of integrity is very broad and has occasioned much litigation. The right of integrity is designed to protect against the destruction of the artist's meaning by alterations in size or attributes, or other unauthorized tampering. Attributing such an altered object to an artist may damage his honor and reputation.[78]

§ 7.04 AUTHENTICITY

[A] Various Issues Involving Authenticity

There are different issues involving the authenticity of an artwork. A fake or forgery is an object created with the intention of deceiving.[79] False attribution

[76] Law n° 57-298 Mar. 11, 1957 (*op. cit.*), art. 6. Guille c. Colmant (1967), Gaz. Pal. 1.17 (Cour d'Appel, Paris). The contract to have an artist use a pseudonym was void.

[77] Law n° 57-298 Mar. 11, 1957 (*op. cit.*), art. 14 *et seq.*

[78] A simple case embodying this principle is that of the well-known Bernard Buffet refrigerator painted by the artist as an undividable unit. The artist was able to stop the sale of dismantled parts. Buffet c. Fersig (1962).

Recueil Dalloz (D. Jur.) 570 (Cour d'Appel Paris), note Desbois, *aff'd,* (1965) Gaz. Pal. II126). The dispute between Jean Dubuffet and the Régie Renault shows the broadness of the protection that French law accords to an artist's work. In this case, Jean Dubuffet was asked to design a garden for one of the factories of the car manufacturer, Renault. The artist created the model, which was approved by the Régie Renault, and construction of the garden commenced but was subsequently abandoned. The artist sued claiming his moral rights were violated; the Appeals Court held that the artist had no rights to be asserted as to the garden that was to be created from his model, but the Highest Court ruled that the artist's moral rights existed in the garden that Renault had agreed to have built from the model, and on rehearing the Court ruled that Renault was required to fulfill its obligations to complete the garden in accordance with the form of the model. However, having been vindicated, the artist took no further action. TGI Paris, 23 Mar. 1977, RIDA July 1977, note Desbois; CA, Paris, 2 June 1978, Dall. 1979 J. 14, note Colombet; Gaz. Pal. 1978 III, note Franck; Cass. Civ. 8 Jan. 1980, *JCP* 1980-19336, note Lindon, Dall. 1980-83, note Edelman, RIDA April 1980, p. 154, observations Francon; Versailles, 8 July 1981, Dall. 1982; IR 45, observations Colombet; Cass. Civ. 16 Mar. 1983, RIDA July 1983, p. 80.

[79] The attempt to sell a fake or a forgery may be a crime, and under the more rigorous laws of France the creation of such an object is a crime. French Code de la Propriété Littéraire et Artistique, Art. L. 335-2.

occurs when the work itself is a genuine work of creativity, but the work is attributed to another artist.[80]

The sale of a fake may constitute a criminal act, and in certain continental jurisdictions, such as France, an aggrieved party may join a civil suit to a criminal proceeding.[81] The aggrieved party gives the public prosecutor control of the lawsuit. The advantage of joining the proceedings is that a public prosecutor has more access to information than does a private plaintiff. However, the private plaintiff has less control over the proceedings than in a purely civil case.

Sometimes an issue of attribution arises to determine whether a named artist created the work.[82] False attribution may give rise to tort claims for negligence, and breach of duty or breach of contract.

[1] Authenticity in the Marketplace

Certain persons are considered to have a sufficiently definitive view as to whether a master did a work that the market will accept their judgments. However, there is no legal definition of what an art expert is, nor is there certainty as to his responsibilities. Experts may be professors of fine arts, dealers, holders of moral rights, or persons with a long association with the artist's work. Generally in Europe, major auction houses request the opinion of experts, but seek to avoid giving a warranty for the opinion of the expert. In France, *commissaires-priseurs* relying on experts are required to refund the sale price if the expert who authenticated an auction item is proved to be wrong. Experts may change their opinions, and in the absence of a showing of negligence in acting as experts, they are not subject to damages where their opinions change.[83]

---

[80] The French often refer to a controversy as an "affaire." In the "affaire" of the false Latapie, 141 drawings were authenticated by the artist's son. The artist's daughter felt that the works were fakes, and the lower court agreed with her. On appeal the court held that the works were not by the artist, but by another artist. They were misattributed. As the works were not fakes, they were not destroyed as is customary in France when an object is held to be a fake or a forgery. The court required that the signature or studio seal of the atelier be suppressed and that on the back there should be a seal indicating the true artist. Tribunal de Grande Instance, Paris, 1st Chamber, 1st Section, (Apr. 23, 1997); Ct. App. Paris, 1st Chamber, Sec. B, (Mar. 12, 1999).

[81] Brian W. Harvey, Fakes and Forgeries in the Salesroom, Transacting in Art, IAL seminar, July 6, 1995. According to Harvey, "it is the civil law which is in issue but all should bear in mind that descriptions in auctioneers' catalogues clearly come within the Trade Description Act 1968 and the old myth that this aspect of the criminal law does not apply to the 'art world' in general and auctioneers in particular has long since been exposed as mythological."

[82] Harlingdon & Leinster Enterprises Ltd v. Christopher Hull Fine Arts Ltd. I All E.R. 737 (1990). This case held that as the seller said that he did not know whether the work was by the artist and the buyer examined the work with care before deciding to purchase it, the sale would not be rescinded nor damages given.

[83] *Cf. supra* note 19. SCP Perrin-Royere-La Jeunesse c. Daniel Guillard, Cour de Cassation, Civ. 1, Nov. 21, 1995. Here the auction house (*commissaire-priseur*) and the expert were held

[2] Judicially Determined Authenticity

There is a substantial difference between the way authenticity is established in a court of common law as in England or the United States, and a court of civil law as in continental Europe.

[a] Common Law

In the common law jurisdictions, plaintiff and defendant provide their own evidence, including witnesses who may be qualified as expert witnesses, and present these to the jury, or the judge in the absence of a jury. The jury or judge determines whether the plaintiff has met his burden of proof, by weighing the evidence and testimony.[84]

[b] Civil Law

In France, the court customarily appoints an expert to determine the issue of authenticity. The court-appointed expert hears the witnesses and evidence of the parties, and makes his decision on the issues. The court either accepts the opinion of this expert, or requires new court-appointed experts to reassess the issue.[85]

[c] Liability of Experts

It is well accepted in the marketplace and by courts that the determination as to whether a work is by a given artist is a question of opinion, and in the absence of negligence or a failure of due care, the expert is not liable for errors, except to the extent where he has given his own guarantee. The failure of an expert conscientiously to make his study can give rise to damages.[86]

[B] Provenance

Provenance is the chain of title of owners of a work. The provenance may add to the value of the work if it has been owned by a well-known connoisseur,

---

liable, not because the work was a fake, but because they had failed in their duty of diligence to ascertain whether the work was by the artist or not. Their liability was in tort for a failure of due diligence. If a guarantee of title had been the issue, then liability would have been involved even if the *commissaire-priseur* had fulfilled its professional duties of diligence, but the expert would have been liable in contract only if he had given a guarantee of authenticity. Experts do not usually give such a guarantee.

[84] *See* Greenberg Gallery, Inc. v. Bauman, 817 F. Supp. 167 (D.D.C. 1993), *aff'd*, U.S. App. LEXIS 27175 (1994).

[85] The burden of proof is usually on the plaintiff in such suits. *See* French Civ. C. art. 1315.

[86] *Cf. supra* § 7.04[A][1].

an authority on the artist, or a celebrity. Both the value and the importance of a work may also increase if the work has been exhibited in well-known institutions, or has been sold by a major auction house or well-known dealer. Provenance is also used as an indication of authenticity.

The absence of a documented provenance causes concern as to whether there is a flaw in title. A reliable provenance may not be obtainable. Many owners do not wish to publicize that they own certain art works, fearing that publicity may encourage theft of the work or collection.

Lack of provenance for a work raises questions of whether the work may have been stolen. For example, lack of provenance for the World War II years may indicate that the work was looted.[87]

Many artists do not document their work and private owners may be quite casual as to the curating of their collections. In such cases one may have to rely upon oral statements or the memory of elderly people to establish provenance.

[C] Defenses of Good Faith and Due Diligence

Where title to a work is challenged, an owner is in a much stronger position to defend his ownership if he has exercised good faith and due diligence in reviewing the material available about the work. When the seller offers a "bargain" and/or is not prepared to give any guarantees or information about how the work was acquired, a potential buyer should be concerned: is the possessor the owner, and is the work by the hand of the purported artist? Where courts must allocate a financial loss between the buyer and seller, they favor the party who has shown good faith and due diligence over the one who has made no effort to verify title and authenticity.[88] By the same token, the original owner is more likely to be able to recover his work if he is able to show due diligence in searching for his property.

§ 7.05 WARRANTIES

[A] Warranty as to Title

A warranty of title is practically always provided in a sale. However, failing to document the sale may make it difficult for a buyer to prove that the work in

---

[87] *See infra* § 7.09 [B].

[88] As an excellent example of heightened concern for good practice, see the Codes of Due Diligence for Dealers and Auctioneers Trading in Fine Art, Antiques, Antiquarian Books, Manuscripts and Collectors Items proposed by the Council for the Prevention of Art Theft (CoPAT), drawn up with the cooperation of the Antiquarian Booksellers' Association, the British Antique Dealers' Association, the Library Association, the Rare Book Group, the Incorporated Society of Valuers and Auctioneers, and the Royal Institution of Chartered Surveyors (Appendix 7-A).

dispute was the work he acquired. Generally, a seller's denial that he has a duty to guarantee title to the work is unlikely to succeed.

[B] Warranty as to Authenticity

The sale of an object does not normally include a warranty of the object's authenticity, although the facts surrounding the sale may show sufficiently the intention of the parties to give such a warranty,[89] for instance, giving a receipt which uses the artist's name in the description of the work.[90] Nevertheless, a suit brought to rescind a sale or for damages on the basis of a warranty of authenticity causes the buyer to meet a burden of proof that the work is not authentic.

[C] Warranty as a Matter of Law

In civil law jurisdictions, a warranty is more likely to be assumed as a matter of law where a professional, that is, a person accustomed to dealing in a type of goods, is selling to a private person, someone not in the business of dealing in such goods.[91] Such a warranty may also be established in common law jurisdictions, and indeed, such warranties have a long history in law.[92] However, a court may feel that both parties have sufficient knowledge to make their own transactions in accordance with their own decisions as to the nature and condition of the item.[93]

§ 7.06 TRANSFER OF TITLE

[A] Effects of Transfer

Each country has its own rules as to when title passes. The sale agreement between the parties may also address when title passes. In an international transaction, the law of the seller, the law of the buyer, the law applicable where the

---

[89] A leading English case, Leaf v. International Galleries 2 K.B. 86 (1950) found a Bench of Appeal Judges in disaccord over the rights of buyer and seller concerning a forgery purporting to be "Salisbury Cathedral" by J. Constable. One judge found that the buyer could not repudiate his purchase but only had a right to damages, another felt that, as the painting was of Salisbury Cathedral, no redress was needed; a third was concerned that critics of great eminence varied in their views as time went by. A judgment of this nature after a lower court case and an appeal is a clear warning to those who litigate authenticity.

[90] *Cf. supra* note 17.

[91] For warranties in the context of U.S. law, see generally Chapter 10.

[92] In Great Britain, damages might be awarded either under § 2 (1) of the Misrepresentation Act, 1967, or for the tort of negligent misstatement under Hedley Byrne & Co. Ltd v. Heller & Partners Ltd. (1964, A.C. 465). In French law the courts are given wide discretion to void a contract where there has not been a proper description of the object sold. In appropriate cases such an act is criminal. Civ. C. art. 1116.

[93] Harlingdon & Leinster Enterprises Ltd v. Christopher Hull Fine Art Ltd., *supra* note 82.

object was located, the law of the place of payment, and the law applicable where the object was transferred may be very different, and the first duty of litigants is to establish what law is applicable and then to determine the rights of the parties.

Title to a work does not necessarily change hands at the same time as does the work itself or consideration for the work, so a seller who hands over an artwork can find himself without the purchase price and without ownership of the work. Where title has passed, the new owner may resell the work, leaving the original owner with only a claim for money damages if payment is not made.

[B] Reversion of Title

A true rescission of a transaction should place the parties where they had been prior to the transaction. The original owner should have title, and the original buyer should have his consideration, but it is important to establish who shall bear the cost of a rescission, that is, the cost of the money that was for a time in the original seller's possession and the other costs. Such costs are often stated in a claim for damages brought together with a complaint seeking rescission.

A rescission is most commonly granted for an essential error in the substance of the agreement. That error may be as to the authenticity, title, or other elements of the work, but a rescission will not be granted normally for minor variations unless there are very specific provisions to that effect in the sales agreement.

[C] Restitution

In English law, a plaintiff may not be able to obtain damages or the return of the object but may be able to sue in restitution, that is, a claim for the benefit or the enrichment that the defendant obtained wrongly.[94] The practitioner in civil law jurisdictions may be dealing in similar concepts when he chooses to make a claim in tort rather than seek a recovery based on a breach of contract.[95]

§ 7.07 ACTIONS AGAINST SELLERS

The right to rescind and the right to damages may be based on a claim of negligence in the work of an auction house, expert or the co-contractant. The most likely ground for seeking an action in regard to a sale is when the object sold is not the work that the parties had in mind.

---

[94] This issue is well analyzed by Jane Ulph in her presentation, Tracing and Restitution, IAL seminar, "Is It Mine?", Mar. 31, 1998.

[95] SCP Perrin-Royere-La Jeunesse c. Daniel Guillard, *supra* note 83.

[A] Fraud

Where the seller has sold a fake, forged, or misattributed work with the intent to deceive, a claim of criminal or civil fraud can be appropriate. Other actions on the part of a seller or other co-contractant may assert that the transaction has been induced by fraud.

As fraud and wrongdoing, particularly in another jurisdiction, may be difficult to prove, counsel for the victim may wish to consider remedies where proof of wrongdoing is unnecessary.

[B] Failure of Consideration and Inadequate Consideration

Sometimes a work sold in a transaction is not the work contemplated by the parties. This error is referred to as a failure of consideration, because the parties had contemplated a genuine work by a given artist, and the failure to deliver such a work given the price paid constitutes a failure of consideration. This error can also be considered as inadequate consideration in that if the parties contemplated an original work by a particular artist, the sale of a work by a lesser artist would be inadequate consideration for the amount paid.

[C] Unconscionable Transactions

In a number of jurisdictions, particular remedies are provided so as to give a right of claim to victims of bad practices. The classic complaint is that a dealer has underestimated the value of a work of art when buying from an uninformed, often elderly seller. Sometimes the victim has limited understanding of the language in which the transaction is conducted. The court will find a transaction unconscionable when it is shocked by the result.[96]

Even without proof of fraud or misrepresentation, courts may find the transaction to be inherently unfair. In so doing they may find that the party proposing the transaction had some type of fiduciary duty toward his co-contractant. The attorney should consider broadly different legal approaches: fraud, misrepresentations, breach of fiduciary duty, and the like, so as to offer the court the widest grounds for a favorable resolution for the victim.

---

[96] Sir Anthony Mason, A.C., K.B.E., Exploiting the Weaker Party; Unconscionable, Unequal and Disadvantageous Transactions in Art; When Will the Courts Intervene?, IAL Seminar on Transacting in Art I, July 6, 1995.

In French law, broad powers are given to French judges to rescind an agreement where a seller has acted in a manner that resulted in a transaction being concluded which would not have happened if the seller had behaved properly. Civ. C. art. 1116.

§ 7.08 VALUATION

Valuation is a vexatious problem, particularly for works of art, because no one work is the equivalent of another. The Internal Revenue Service defines valuation as "the price which property will bring when offered for sale by a willing seller to a willing buyer, neither being obligated to buy or sell."[97] In most art sales, there is an intermediary, whether a dealer or an auction house, so the first issue is whether one is talking of replacement value, that is, the price to be paid from a dealer or the price paid including commission when buying at auction, or the price at which an owner may sell his goods to a dealer or through an auction house after deduction of the commission payable to such auction house. Usually, private parties lack the resources to find buyers, so art sales generally require them to incur significant selling expenses.

When a unique art object must be valued but no sale is contemplated, value must be established by analogy to other sales, with a subjective appreciation as to how close the comparison is and how the adjustment should be made between the valued object and other objects used as comparisons.[98]

§ 7.09 STATUTES OF LIMITATION FOR CLAIMS

[A] Generally

International statutes of limitation vary so greatly that they should be verified in each case.[99] A court called on to apply the statute of limitations of another jurisdiction must consider whether the foreign jurisdiction's rules violate notions of fairness.[100]

---

[97] I.R.C. § 1.1001-1.

[98] Marie Cornu, La Question de l'Importance et de l'Evaluation de la Valeur d'une Oeuvre d'Art; Dominique Dujon-Rémy, Jean-Louis Denard, La Détermination de la Valeur des Oeuvres d'Art par Recours à l'Expertise, Association Art & Droit, Lyon, France, Seminar of May 15, 1997.

[99] *Cf.* note 5. For the applicable limitation period in English law for conversion and theft, see §§ 2, 3 and 4 of the Limitations Act, 1980. Section 2 provides a general limitation period of six years in tort, beginning on the date when the cause of action occurred. Section 3 attempts to elaborate and clarify the position of goods which are the subject of successive conversions. Section 4 gives special rules related to theft. There is a single six-year limitation period in the case of conversion, even though a work may have changed hands many times since the original theft and been subject to successive acts of conversion. However, as provided in Section 4, the theft cannot benefit from the six-year limitation period. The six-year time limit applies only to conversion and not to theft.

In favor of long statutes of limitation is the UNIDROIT Convention and the European Union Cultural Objects Law (*op. cit.*). The latter gives 70 years as the period for thefts from public collections and 30 years for private collections.

[100] Paul Lomas & Simon Orton, Potential Repercussions from the *City of Gotha* Decision, IV Art, Antiquity & Law, 2, at 159 (June 1999).

The question whether German limitation law was contrary to English public policy under the Foreign Limitation Periods Act 1984 was considered by Moses J. as *obiter dicta*. He identified the

[B] Holocaust and Crimes Against Humanity Exceptions

The claim that victims and their families who have lost property due to the Holocaust should not be subject to the same statutes of limitation as ordinary plaintiffs is actively being reviewed at this time. Claims are often settled in negotiation,[101] but recent litigation,[102] as well as a heightened sense of justice,[103] is causing a more generous reappraisal of the rights of victims than was granted before, and a recognition that standard rules of statutes of limitation are not appropriate for dealing with the recovery of works of art looted by the Nazis.[104]

§ 7.10 ESCROW ARRANGEMENTS; ACCESS TO WORKS PRIOR TO SALE

There is a conflict between sellers who do not want works to leave their hands before receiving payment or its equivalent, and buyers who do not want

---

following principles:

(a) Public policy should be invoked to disapply a foreign limitation period only in exceptional circumstances.

(b) Foreign law should be disapplied only where it is contrary to a "fundamental principle of justice," meaning where it "outrages [the Court's] sense of justice or decency" (*e.g.*, a law that is discriminatory on the basis of race, religion or nationality).

(c) The fundamental principle of justice with which the foreign law conflicts must be clearly identifiable. It must not depend upon the judge's notion of fairness or expedience, but must be recognizable with clarity from English limitation law or some other recognized principle of policy. The foreign law must be "manifestly" incompatible with that policy.

(d) English limitation law serves the purpose of providing protection for defendants against stale claims, encouraging claimants to institute claimings without unreasonable delay and conferring on a potential defendant confidence that after the lapse of a specific period of time he will not face a claim.

(e) A foreign limitation period will not be disapplied merely because it is less generous than the comparable English provision. There must be some reason other than mere length.

[101] French Relent over War Loot: A Monet Returned, A Bonnard, Léger and Matisse still Claimed, The Art Newspaper, Vol. X, N° 93, June 1999, at 1. The article discusses the return to a daughter and a daughter-in-law of Paul Rosenberg, a leading pre-World War II art dealer, of a work of Monet held by France as part of the MNR (Musées Nationaux Récupération) since the War. The article also discusses that a Léger is not being returned as it is claimed that the work belonged to Paul Rosenberg's brother, and so his heir is the sister of the other brother.

[102] Subsequent to an unfavorable ruling on June 2, 1999, by the Court of Appeals in Paris in an action brought by the heirs of Gentili di Giuseppe, the Louvre has agreed to hand over paintings it had been holding. *See generally* Recovery of Stolen and Looted Works of Art and Art, Law and the Holocaust (*op. cit*). *See also* Leila Anglade, Art, Law and the Holocaust, the French Situation, 4 Art, Antiquity and Law 301 (1999).

[103] *Cf. supra* note 14.

[104] The Edict of September 10, 1999, created in France a new commission to establish the rights of victims and their families. This commission will not be bound by statute-of-limitation rules, and

to part with consideration or give a guarantee without having first seen the works, or until the works are in their hands.

One solution is for the buyer to provide a guarantee to the seller, but this is far from perfect; sellers have used such guarantees to seek another buyer at a higher price, while holding the guarantee of the first buyer. Where the guarantee is provided through the funding of a bank account, there have been enough fraudulent transactions so that buyers are wary of giving such guarantees. The more distant the buyer is from the seller, and the greater the number of intermediaries, the greater the complexities of the transaction.

Letters of intent are helpful in confirming the interest of a buyer, but buyers are often reluctant to give them, fearing that a written expression of interest may be used for an improper purpose, or to incite another potential buyer to complete the purchase of the same work.

An escrow arrangement often provides the solution to the need for a seller to have his consideration and the need of the buyer to have access so as to inspect the work before payment.[105] Unfortunately, banks, lawyers and other responsible parties are often reluctant to act as escrow agents. In the event of conflict between buyer and seller, escrow agents may be made parties to the suit as well, requiring the escrow agent to defend itself in court. Sometimes, due to facts not contemplated at the time of the transaction, the escrow agent can be held liable for a loss.

As an alternative, many warehouses will accept the seller's work and, under the seller's instructions, allow the buyer access to the work in a supervised, controlled environment. Shipping and insurance costs must be negotiated between the parties. Such arrangements do not prevent an unethical dealer from selling the work to a buyer other than the one who thought he had sole rights to view with an option to buy. Often rights of recourse are complex because of the different jurisdictions of the parties.

§ 7.11 AUCTIONS

[A] Auction Houses and *Commissaires-Priseurs*

Auction rules vary from country to country, including the terms for the acceptance of objects at auctions and the responsibility of the auction house to the buyer and the seller. British auction houses seek to limit their responsibilities through their conditions of sale.[106] Subject to such terms being reasonable, the conditions of sale define the rights of the parties.

---

its powers are broad to hear parties and witnesses, investigate on its own, and consult. *See also* § 5.05.

[105] *See* Form 7-4.

[106] *Cf. supra* note 19.

French auctioneers (hereinafter "*commissaires-priseurs*") are responsible for the authenticity of the objects that are auctioned. In order to protect customers and the *commissaire-priseur*, an expert is appointed for each sale where works of art of a certain importance are sold to give his opinion on authenticity. Where a fault in the title of an object is discovered or the object does not comply with its description, the *commissaire-priseur* is liable to the buyer.[107] The buyer, however, will need to prove the error of the expert on whom the *commissaire-priseur* relied.

The statute of limitations for English and Dutch auction houses is rather short; however, the *commissaires-priseurs* are subject to a 30-year statute of limitations during which aggrieved buyers can initiate proceedings against them.

In accordance with European Union regulations calling for the free movement of providers of goods and services, the EU has determined that *commissaires-priseurs* should relinquish their monopoly, and laws have been drafted to this effect, including provisions to compensate *commissaires-priseurs* for the loss of their monopoly. At this writing, that legislation has not been passed, much to the frustration of auction houses in other countries of the European Union, but the French Parliament is discussing a bill and is expected to vote on it soon. It is therefore important to underline its major features and the changes it will entail, knowing, however, that modifications may still be made.[108]

[B] Reserve Price

The reserve price is the price below which the seller will not sell. In practice, the reserve price is mutually agreed between the seller and the auctioneer. In order to obtain a fair auction, the reserve price cannot be disclosed. A bidder with knowledge of the reserve price will influence the auction. Therefore, in most jurisdictions, the auctioneer is under an obligation to keep the reserve price confidential.

Certain countries have specific rules regarding the reserve price. The bill on auctions currently being discussed before the French Parliament holds that the reserve price cannot be superior to the low estimate provided by the auction house.[109]

[C] Right to Be a Principal

The auctioneer is a principal when he sells his own objects. Such a sale is likely to alter the fairness of the auction, because the auctioneer will seek to

---

[107] *Cf. supra* note 83.

[108] Bill adopted by the *Sénat* on rules for nonjudicial public auction sales, recorded at the Assemblée Nationale on June 11, 1999.

[109] Art. 10.

influence buyers in order to obtain a better price for his own objects. Therefore, this situation is generally governed by a contract or legislation. British auction houses have stated in their conditions of sales that they do not sell their own objects.

Commissaires-priseurs are prohibited from selling their own objects. The bill on auctions, however, sets forth one exception to this rule: a *commissaire-priseur* can guarantee to a seller that his object will reach a mutually agreed upon price and that if such a price is not reached, he will pay this price himself and keep the object. In this case, the *commissaire-priseur* will have the option of selling the object on his own behalf at a subsequent auction.[110]

[D] Liability for Statements in Catalogues

As buyers and sellers tend to rely heavily on statements in catalogues, an auctioneer can be liable for statements included in such catalogues in certain jurisdictions. The legal definitions included in catalogues can be derived from contracts or from law. British auction houses explain the meaning of terms in the catalogues themselves. Under French law, terms such as "signed by" or "school of" are defined by decree.[111]

[E] Online Auctions

European states are now considering new legislation to deal with online auctions. It is perceived that serious abuses are possible, but there is not yet any consensus on how such auctions should be regulated.

§ 7.12 TAXATION

[A] On Transfer

[1] Ordinary Income

Normal rules for the taxation of income generally apply to art dealers. Dealers' profits may be taxed as ordinary income; they may be required to maintain inventories and to keep records and file reports regarding value-added tax reports.

When a collector occasionally deals in art, there is a question as to whether he is subject to the rules on the taxation of a business[112] or whether he is subject

[110] Art. 11.

[111] Decree No. 81-255 of March 3, 1981.

[112] Bénéfice Industriel et Commercial, Produit d'Exploitation, Memento Pratique Francis Lefèbvre 620 (Fiscal 1999) (French law).

only to the rules applicable to private citizens who buy and sell art as collectors.[113] Collectors actively selling items from their collection should exercise care to avoid being taxed as dealers.[114]

[2] Capital Gains

The tax on the gain on the sale of works of art varies widely when the seller is not considered to be a dealer. In France, the taxpayer is subject to a 5 percent tax on the sale of works of art. A seller who has held a work for more than two years may elect to treat the gain under the general rules applicable to capital gains, which allow a 5 percent discount on the tax to be paid after the first two years on each additional year that the work is held, so that where the taxpayer can prove that he has held the work for more than 21 years, no capital gains tax is due.[115] Other jurisdictions also have reduced taxation or no tax on the profits from the occasional sale of works of art.

[3] Value-Added Tax

In most countries that have value-added tax (VAT), dealers in art objects are required to pay VAT on the sale of art objects.[116] It is difficult to assess the impact of VAT on the sale of works of art.[117]

[4] Gift and Inheritance Taxes

In most jurisdictions, tax is assessed on gifts of works of art and on works of art in an estate. Each jurisdiction has its own notions as to how valuation should be established, and also its own rules as to whether the tax on a gift or legacy or inheritance of a work of art is taxable to the donor or estate, the beneficiary, or both. If the location of the work of art is different from the domicile of the donor or decedent or the residence of the beneficiary, local rules must be verified for all jurisdictions involved. Receiving art as a gift or legacy without funding to cover the taxes due in a jurisdiction where the tax must be paid by the beneficiary constitutes a significant burden. Each jurisdiction will also have

---

[113] French Code Général des Impôts, Art. 150 V*bis et seq.*

[114] British rules on value-added tax; French regulations on being a *commerçant.*

[115] French Code Général des Impôts, Art. 150 V*bis et seq.*

[116] In the United Kingdom, the rate was at 2% under a special concession granted to the United Kingdom under European Union rules, but that exception ended in 1999 and a minimum of 5% VAT is to be assessed, as is the case for the other European Union members.

[117] Works of Art in the European Union, Studies in Art Law, Sept. 27, 1993, Schulthess Polygraphischer Verlag AG Zurich 1994.

its own special rules as to the tax effect of gifts to the state or to a charity.[118] These issues should be reviewed with an experienced local practitioner.

[B] On Entry Into or Departure From a Country

On the entry into a country of a work of art, VAT is assessed, except for transfers within the European Union. Customs duties are usually not charged on the importation of works of art.

When a work of art leaves a jurisdiction, even when no sale or transfer is contemplated, the tax authorities may assess a tax at export so as to be certain that a subsequent capital gains tax on the work's sale will not escape taxation.[119]

[C] Wealth Tax

France, among other jurisdictions that assess an annual tax on wealth,[120] debates regularly whether artworks, which are construed broadly to include antiquities, designer furniture, and book collections, should not be subject to this tax.[121]

---

[118] *See* Blake Bromley & Judith Hill, Passing on the Family Works of Art, Int'l Bar Ass'n 1998 Conference, Vancouver, Canada, Sept. 13-18, 1998.

[119] France taxes works of art that leave the European Union. The taxpayer may elect either to pay 5% of their value, or to pay ordinary capital gains tax on the gain at a descending rate that exempts works that can be shown to have been acquired over 21 years before the export. *See supra* § 7.12[A][2].

[120] French Code Général des Impôts, art. 885 *et seq.*

[121] Les Collectionneurs sous la Menace de l'ISF, Le Figaro, June 19, 1998.

FORMS AND APPENDICES

Form 7-1:	Purchase Agreement
Form 7-2:	Bill of Sale
Form 7-3:	Quitclaim Bill of Sale
Form 7-4:	Escrow Agreement
Appendix 7-A:	CoPAT Codes of Due Diligence

FORM 7-1

Purchase Agreement

PURCHASE AGREEMENT

Agreement made as of ____________________ by and between _______________ ("Seller"), an individual residing at __________________ and _________, an individual residing at __________________ ("Buyer").

WHEREAS, Seller owns a work of fine art entitled ____ by the artist ______(the "Work"), a photograph of which is attached hereto as Exhibit A; and

WHEREAS, Seller desires to sell the Work to Buyer, and Buyer desires to purchase the Work from Seller for the price and on the terms and conditions hereinafter set forth;

NOW, THEREFORE, in consideration of the foregoing, the mutual covenants and agreements hereinafter set forth, and for other good and valuable consideration, the receipt and sufficiency of which are hereby acknowledged, the parties hereto agree as follows:

1. **SALE OF THE WORK.**

Subject to the terms and conditions of this Agreement, at the Closing (as hereinafter defined), Seller shall sell and transfer to Buyer all right, title and interest in and to the Work, including without limitation all rights of Seller, if any, to sue or make claims against any party against whom Seller may have a claim relating to the Work.

2. **CONSIDERATION.**

In consideration for the Work and the agreements of the Seller contained herein, Buyer shall pay to Seller the sum of _______________ at the time of Closing. [One half of this sum shall be held in escrow by Buyer's attorney pending completion of certain scientific tests which, if they fail to confirm the approximate date of the creation of the Work, will be grounds for complete rescission of this transaction.]

3. **INSPECTION.**

At a time and place to be mutually agreed, the Buyer and/or his agents shall have a right to visually inspect the Work for purposes of determining authenticity. [The Buyer may not remove physical samples of the Work.][Notwithstanding any such inspection, the Buyer is relying upon the warranties set forth below with respect to authenticity.] The condition of the Work is "as is".

4. **CLOSING.**

(a) The closing of the transaction contemplated hereby shall take place at 10:30 a.m. on _________________, at the offices of _____________(the "Closing"), unless the parties hereto mutually agree to a different date or place for the Closing. The Closing may be accomplished by facsimile and overnight mail. The "Closing Date" shall be the date on which the Closing takes place.

(b) At the Closing, above Buyer shall pay to Seller the appropriate amounts due under Section 2 above and Seller shall deliver the Work. [The Work shall be held in escrow by Buyer's attorney pending Seller's receipt of full payment specified above.]

(c) At the Closing, Seller shall deliver to Buyer the Bill of Sale for the Transferred Assets, in the form attached hereto as Exhibit A, and other documents of title as may be reasonably requested by Buyer. [The Bill of Sale shall be held in escrow by Buyer's attorney pending Seller's receipt of full payment specified above.]

(d) [Discuss holdback or escrow, for title and other issues, if any.]

4. INSURANCE, SHIPPING, AND RISK OF LOSS.

(a) Seller shall be solely responsible for insurance and risk of loss until the transfer of the Work at the Closing, at which time all risk of loss shall transfer to Buyer, who is nonetheless obligated to maintain insurance on the Work in an amount not less than the purchase price until such time as all monies for the purchase have been release from escrow to the Seller

(b) If the Buyer elects not to take physical possession of the Work at Closing, or if the Closing is held by facsimile and overnight mail, the Buyer shall pay all shipping costs and arrange all paperwork necessary for shipment of the Work, with the reasonable assistance of the Seller. Unless full payment has been received by Seller, Seller shall have an approval right over the manner and mode of shipping, not to be unreasonably withheld.

6. REPRESENTATIONS AND WARRANTIES OF SELLER.

Seller warrants to Buyer that the following statements are true and correct on the date hereof:

(a) Validity of Agreement. Seller has the full right and power to execute and deliver this Agreement and the Bill of Sale and to consummate the transactions contemplated herein. Neither the execution nor the delivery of this Agreement by Seller nor the consummation of the transactions contemplated hereby will conflict with, or result in, a violation of any law, regulation, order, permit, license or decree to which Seller is a party or subject, nor will it result in the imposition of any lien, encumbrance or charge upon the Work. No consent of a third party is required to authorize this Agreement or the performance of any of the transactions contemplated hereby.

(b) The Work.

(i) Seller and/or members of Seller's family have owned the Work since ______. Prior thereto, the provenance of the Work is as follows:

(ii) The Work is an original oil painting on canvas, measuring ___x___. The work is of ________.

(iii) [The Work does not violate or infringe any moral rights, copyrights of others or contain material which is libelous or which may cause harm or injury or which is contrary to law. There is no assertion or claim of any violation or infringement of any copyright of others whether statutory or common law or of any claim of libel.]

(c) Title to the Work. Seller has good right, title and interest in and to the Work free and clear of all liens, including tax liens, claims, pledges, title defects, encumbrances, security agreements, security interests or restrictions of any kind, nature or description.

(d) Pending or Asserted Litigation. There are and have been no material disputes between Seller and any other party concerning the Work. There are no actions, suits or proceedings to which Seller is a party, or which are pending, or to the knowledge of Seller threatened against Seller, which affect the Work, before any court, governmental department, commission, board, agency or instrumentality, and Seller is not subject to any order, injunction or decree of any court, governmental department, agency, commission or instrumentality relating to or affecting the Work. There are no judgments against Seller relating to the Work.

(e) Import. The work has been legally imported to its current location, and will be legally exported by Seller to the location of the Closing.

(f) No Changes in Condition. There have been and will be no changes in the physical condition of the Work from the date of first inspection by Seller until the Closing.

7. COVENANTS OF SELLER.

At the Closing, and from time to time thereafter, Seller shall execute and deliver to Buyer such further instruments and documents and take such other actions as Buyer reasonably may request in order to more fully perfect or further evidence the sale of the Work to Buyer.

8. SURVIVAL OF REPRESENTATIONS, WARRANTIES AND AGREEMENTS.

Each of the representations and warranties made by Seller hereunder shall survive the date of Closing for a period of two (2) years.

9. INDEMNIFICATION.

(a) Seller shall indemnify Buyer, its successors and assigns, and hold them harmless against any and all costs, losses and damages (including reasonable expenses and legal fees), resulting from or arising out of any breach of any representation, warranty or covenant of Seller set forth in this Agreement, or the untruth or inaccuracy thereof. Additionally, in the event of a breach of warranty of title or authenticity, the Buyer may elect, in lieu of all other claims, to rescind the sale in exchange for a full refund of the purchase price [with interest].

(b) Seller's obligations under Subsection (a) above shall be limited to claims first asserted by Buyer against Seller in writing within five (5) years after the Closing Date.

10. EXPENSES.

Each party shall be solely responsible for its own expenses, including without limitation its own attorneys, experts and advisors. For the avoidance of doubt, the parties represent that [Dealer 1] is Seller's agent, and [Dealer 2] is Buyer's agent.

[11. ESCROW AGREEMENT.

Simultaneously with execution of this Agreement, the parties have entered into an Escrow Agreement, which is incorporated herein by reference.]

12. SALES TAX.

Seller and Buyer each believe that the sale of the Work pursuant to this Agreement will not give rise to any liability for sales tax or similar tax. Each party agrees that it will not take any action without the consent of the other party which would jeopardize the right of such other party to claim any applicable exemption from sales tax or similar tax. If a tax is to be paid, it will be paid by the party upon whom the law imposes the primary obligation for such payments.

13. MISCELLANEOUS.

(a) Entire Agreement. This Agreement contains the entire agreement and understanding among the parties and shall be deemed to supersede and cancel all other agreements and understandings, written or oral, relating to the transactions herein contemplated. No amendment or modification to this Agreement shall be valid unless made in writing and signed by all of the parties hereto.

(b) Assignment; Successors and Assigns. This Agreement shall be binding upon and shall inure to the benefit of the parties, their successors and assigns.

(c) Notices. Any notice or other communication required or contemplated by this Agreement shall be deemed to have been given when reduced to writing and mailed, certified or registered mail, return receipt requested, postage prepaid, to the parties at their respective addresses as shown below, or to such other addresses as may be designated in writing from time to time:

To the Seller:

To the Buyer:

The return receipt of the post office shall be prima facie evidence of mailing. Notice shall be deemed given on the date mailed.

(d) Counterparts. This Agreement may be executed in two or more counterparts, each of which, if bearing the signature of all parties, shall be deemed an original, or any two or more of which containing in the aggregate the signatures of all parties shall together constitute but one and the same instrument which shall be deemed an original.

(e) Publicity. No publicity release or announcement concerning this Agreement or the transactions contemplated hereby shall be issued without advance approval of the form and substance thereof by the Seller and the Buyer.

(f) Confidentiality. The Seller and the Buyer agree to keep the terms and conditions of this Agreement confidential except insofar as disclosure may, in the disclosing party's reasonable judgment, be required by law or regulation or legal process. In the event of legal process the party so required to disclose shall provide the other party with prompt notice to enable it to seek a protective order or other appropriate remedy preventing disclosure.

(g) Construction. This Agreement shall be construed and interpreted pursuant to the laws of the State of New York and of the United States as interpreted by the Courts located within the State of New York, without reference to New York's choice of law rules. Any legal action, suit or proceeding arising out of, concerning, or relating to this Agreement or the Exhibits hereto or the breach thereof shall be instituted in a Court of competent jurisdiction in the county in which the defendant maintains its principal place of business and each party hereby consents and submits to the personal jurisdiction of such court and consents to service of process by registered or certified mail, return receipt requested, at the last known address of such party.

IN WITNESS WHEREOF, the parties hereto have executed this Agreement on the day and year first above written.

[SELLER]	**[BUYER]**
By: ______________________	By: ______________________
Name: ______________________	Name. ______________________
Title: ______________________	Title: ______________________

FORM 7-2

Bill of Sale

BILL OF SALE

_________________, an individual residing at __________ ("Seller"), for good and valuable consideration, the receipt and sufficiency of which are hereby acknowledged, does hereby grant, sell, assign and transfer to _______________ ("Buyer"), his successors and assigns, all right, title and interest in and to the work of art by ______ entitled _______ (the "Work", a copy of which is attached hereto as Exhibit A), including without limitation Seller's rights, if any, to sue any third parties for claims relating to the Work, to have and to hold the same him, his successors and assigns, for his and their use, benefit and behalf forever, with full title guarantee and all other warranties and guarantees as set for in the Purchase Agreement dated _____ by and between Seller and Buyer

IN WITNESS THEREOF, Seller, has executed this Bill of Sale as of the ______day of _____, ____.

Seller:

____

STATE OF NEW YORK)
: ss.:
COUNTY OF NEW YORK)

On ___________________ before me, _________________________________, a Notary Public in and for the State of New York, personally appeared _________________, personally known to me (or proved to me on the basis of satisfactory evidence) to be the person whose name is subscribed to the within instrument, and acknowledged to me that he freely executed the within instrument and that, by his signature on the within instrument, he intended to be bound by its terms.

WITNESS my hand and official seal.

Signature __________________________ (Seal)

FORM 7-3

Quitclaim Bill of Sale

QUITCLAIM BILL OF SALE

_______________, an individual residing at _________ ("Seller"), for good and valuable consideration, the receipt and sufficiency of which are hereby acknowledged, does hereby grant, sell, assign and transfer to _____________, his successors and assigns, all of the Seller's right, title and interest in and to the work of art by ______ entitled _______ (the "Work", a copy of which is attached hereto as Exhibit A), including without limitation Seller's rights, if any, to sue any third parties for claims relating to the Work, to have and to hold the same him, his successors and assigns, for his and their use, benefit and behalf forever, without warranties of any kind, including without limitation warranties of title, authenticity, and condition.

IN WITNESS THEREOF, Seller, has executed this Bill of Sale as of the ______day of _____, ____.

Seller:

____

STATE OF NEW YORK)
: ss.:
COUNTY OF NEW YORK)

On __________________ before me, ____________________________, a Notary Public in and for the State of New York, personally appeared ________________, personally known to me (or proved to me on the basis of satisfactory evidence) to be the person whose name is subscribed to the within instrument, and acknowledged to me that he freely executed the within instrument and that, by his signature on the within instrument, he intended to be bound by its terms.

WITNESS my hand and official seal.

Signature ________________________ (Seal)

FORM 7-4

Escrow Agreement

ESCROW AGREEMENT

Agreement made as of ____________________ by and between ________________ ("Seller"), an individual residing at __________________, _________, an individual residing at __________________ ("Buyer"), and ______, an attorney with an office at ___________(the "Escrow Agent").

WHEREAS, prior to the execution of this Escrow Agreement, Buyer and Seller have entered into a Purchase Agreement of even date (the "Purchase Agreement") pursuant to which the Seller is to sell and the Buyer is to purchase a work of art by ____ entitled ______ (the "Work");

WHEREAS, the Purchase Agreement provides that Buyer will deposit with the Escrow Agent at the Closing thereunder the sum of $_______ to be held and applied by the Escrow Agent in accordance with the terms of this Escrow Agreement;

WHEREAS, the Purchase Agreement provides that Seller will deposit with the Escrow Agent at the Closing thereunder a Bill of Sale and the Work pending Seller's receipt of all funds as set forth in the Purchase Agreement;

NOW THEREFORE, in consideration of the premises and of the mutual covenants and agreements hereinafter set forth, the parties hereto agree as follows:

1. Creation of the Escrow Fund. Buyer has delivered to the Escrow Agent contemporaneously with the execution of this Escrow Agreement a certified check in the amount of $_________ (the "Escrow Amount"), the receipt of which is hereby acknowledged by the Escrow Agent.

2. Deposit of the Escrow Amount. The Escrow Agent shall immediately deposit the Escrow Amount in an account with Citibank N.A. at its branch office located at __________ and notify the Buyer and the Seller of the account number. The funds in the account shall be invested solely in Citibank money market funds or Citibank Certificates of Deposit with maturities not to exceed one month. The Escrow Amount and all interest credited to the account in which the Escrow Amount is deposited in are hereinafter referred to as the "Escrow Fund". The Escrow Fund shall continue to be held in such account unless otherwise directed by the Buyer and Seller.

Simultaneously with the deposit of the Escrow Amount, the Escrow Agent shall place the executed Bill of Sale and the Work in secure storage at _____, with full costs and insurance to be paid by Buyer.

3. Distribution of Escrow Fund.

(a) Upon the occurrence of a right of rescission or a breach of a warranty which could give rise to an obligation on the part of the Seller to indemnify the Buyer pursuant to the Purchase Agreement, Buyer shall, on or before ______, deliver notice (a "Claim Notice") to Escrow Agent stating that Buyer has paid or properly accrued such a right or become aware of such a breach, specifying in reasonable detail the basis for such claims At the time of delivery of a Claim Notice to Escrow Agent, Buyer shall deliver a duplicate copy of such Claim Notice to Seller.

(b) In the event Seller disputes the contents of the Claim Notice, Seller shall have thirty days from the date of delivery of the Claim Notice to deliver a notice (a "Dispute Notice") to Escrow Agent stating that Seller disputes all or a portion of the facts claimed in the Claim Notice, and if a portion, stating the amount so claimed that Seller disputes or that Seller intends to contest the Action. At the time of delivery of a Dispute Notice to Escrow Agents, Seller shall deliver a duplicate copy of such Dispute Notice to Buyer.

(c) On the thirtieth day following receipt of a Claim Notice (unless such day is not a business day, in which case on the immediately following business day), provided that Escrow Agent has not received a Dispute Notice with respect thereto, Escrow Agent shall pay to Buyer out of the Escrow Fund the amount claimed in such Claim Notice. In the event Escrow Agent has received a Dispute Notice disputing only a portion of the amount claimed in such Claim Notice, Escrow Agent shall, on such thirtieth day (or such next business day), pay to Buyer out of the Escrow Fund all undisputed amounts claimed in such Claim Notice. Escrow Agent shall retain in the Escrow Fund amounts (not in excess of the then Escrow Fund) which are sufficient to indemnify Buyer for all amounts that are claimed to be disputed by Seller in a Dispute Notice ("Disputed Losses") until such dispute has been resolved by mutual agreement of Buyer and Seller or by award of an arbitrator if the dispute is submitted to arbitration, or by final order, decreed or judgment of a court of competent jurisdiction.

(d) On _______, the Escrow Agent shall pay to Seller on behalf of the Seller the amount, if any, then in the Escrow Fund which exceeds the amount of any unresolved disputed amounts. Upon the resolution of any unresolved claims in the manner described in Section 3(c) above, the Escrow Agent shall pay to Seller, on behalf of the Seller, any funds not directed to be paid to the Buyer and not required to resolve any remaining unresolved claims. Upon final resolution of all claims, Escrow Agent shall either deliver the Bill of Sale and the Work to (1) Buyer, if no grounds for rescission have been presented, or (2) Seller, if the transaction has been rescinded, and the Escrow Fund has been returned to Buyer.

The fact that the Escrow Fund may not be sufficient to pay Buyer's claims pursuant to the Purchase Agreement shall not affect Seller's liability under the indemnification provisions thereunder.

4. Concerning the Escrow Agent

(a) The parties acknowledge that Escrow Agent is acting solely as a stakeholder at their request and for their convenience, that Escrow Agent shall not be deemed to be the agent of any of the parties, and that Escrow Agent shall not be liable to any of the parties for any act or omission on his part unless taken or suffered in bad faith, in willful disregard of this Agreement or involving gross negligence on the part of Escrow agent. Seller and Buyer shall jointly and severally indemnify and hold Escrow Agent harmless from and against all costs, claims and expenses, including reasonable attorneys' fees, incurred in connection with the performance of Escrow Agent's duties hereunder, except with respect to actions or omissions taken or suffered by Escrow Agent in bad faith, in willful disregard of this Agreement or involving gross negligence on the part of Escrow Agent, provided, however, that any fees or disbursements for services rendered as Escrow Agent shall be the sole responsibility of the Buyer. This indemnity shall survive Closing. Notwithstanding the foregoing, the Escrow Agent will be liable for any payment made to any person other than Seller or Buyer except if such payment is made pursuant to (i) the written direction of Seller and Buyer, or (ii) pursuant to the award of an arbitrator or a final order, decree or judgment of a court of competent jurisdiction. The following are the parties' federal taxpayer indemnification numbers:

Seller - ________________

Buyer - ________________

(b) Escrow Agent shall be entitled to rely upon any notice, award, judgment, certificate, demand or other document delivered to him hereunder without being required to determine the authenticity or the correctness of any facts stated therein, the propriety or validity thereof, or the jurisdiction of the arbitrator(s) or Court issuing any such award or judgment. The Escrow Agent may act in reliance upon any document or signature believed by him to be genuine or duly authorized.

(c) Escrow Agent shall have the right but not the obligation to require and receive such written certifications or instructions from either Buyer or Seller as he deems necessary or appropriate before taking any action hereunder. If any dispute arises between Buyer and the Seller, or if he is uncertain as to his obligations hereunder, he shall have the right but not the obligation to refrain from taking action other than to continue to hold in escrow the Escrow Fund or the amount in dispute until otherwise directed by a final judgment of a court of competent jurisdiction or a written agreement signed by Buyer and Seller. Escrow Agent shall not be obligated to, but may, institute legal proceedings of any kind, including but not limited to a legal proceeding or action in a court of competent jurisdiction to determine his obligations hereunder or to seek permission to deposit the Escrow Fund in court and be relieved of all further obligations hereunder.

(d) The Escrow Agent may resign and be discharged from his duties or obligations hereunder by giving notice in writing to Buyer and to the Seller, specifying the date when such resignation shall take effect. The Buyer and Seller acting jointly, may remove the Escrow Agent. In the event of such resignation or removal, or the death or disability of the Escrow Agent, the Buyer shall designate a successor escrow agent reasonably satisfactory to Seller.

5. Notices. Any Claim Notice, Dispute Notice or other communication (or any copy of thereof) which may be required to be given or delivered hereunder shall be in writing, and if to Buyer shall be delivered by hand, mailed by certified mail return receipt requested, sent by overnight courier or sent by facsimile transmission, to:

with a copy to its counsel, ____________________:

and if to Seller, shall be delivered by hand, mailed by certified mail return receipt requested, sent by overnight courier or sent by facsimile transmission, to:

with a copy to its counsel, ____________________:

and if to the Escrow Agent, shall be delivered by hand, mailed be certified mail return receipt requested, sent by overnight courier or sent by facsimile transmission, to:

Any notice so given shall be deemed to have been given on the date of delivery, if hand delivered, on the date of mailing is sent by certified mail and on the date of sending if sent by overnight courier or facsimile transmission, except any notice to the Escrow Agent shall be deemed given only when actually received by the Escrow Agent. Any party hereto may change the address to which notice shall be sent by giving written notice to all of the other parties hereto of such address.

6. Entire Agreement: Amendments and Waiver. This Escrow Agreement is intended to be read together with the Purchase Agreement, which together with this Escrow Agreement, supersede all prior agreements, understandings, negotiations and discussions, whether oral or written, of the parties. No supplement, modification or waiver of this Escrow Agreement shall be binding unless executed in writing by the party to be bound thereby. No waiver of any of the provisions of this Escrow Agreement shall be deemed or shall constitute a waiver of any other provision hereof (whether or not similar), nor shall such waiver constitute a continuing waiver unless otherwise expressly provided. This Agreement may be executed in or more counterparts, each of which shall be deemed an original, and all of which taken together shall constitute one instrument. Each such counterpart may contain one or more signature pages.

7. Governing Law. This Escrow Agreement shall be construed and enforced

in accordance with, and the rights of the parties shall be governed by, the laws of the State of New York as if wholly entered into and performed in the State of New York.

8. Benefit and Binding Nature of the Agreement. This Agreement shall inure to the benefit of, and be binding upon, the parties hereto and their respective heirs, personal representatives, successors and assigns.

9. Headings. The headings in this Agreement are for convenience of reference only and shall not limit or otherwise affect any of the terms or provisions hereof.

IN WITNESS WHEREOF, this Agreement has been executed by the parties hereto as of the day and year first above written.

BUYER:

____

SELLER:

____

ESCROW AGENT:

____

APPENDIX 7-A

CoPAT Codes of Due Diligence

Courts are, increasingly, referring to codes of practice and codes of ethics to establish whether or not due diligence was exercised in particular cases. In the context of buying art objects, exercising due diligence has been defined as taking care by all reasonable means available that you do not knowingly purchase an item which has been reported as stolen property or which by its very nature, may have been illegally obtained.

In recent years the concept of due diligence has become more clearly established through decisions in various court cases concerning personal property. In 1996, the Council for the Prevention of Art Theft (CoPAT) undertook to establish the principle of 'due diligence' in all transactions by art and antique dealers and auctioneers by providing them voluntary codes of conduct.

The codes have been produced by the Trades and Professions Committee of CoPAT, on which are represented organisations representing art and antique dealers, appraisers of fine art, and auctioneers. These organisations include the Incorporated Society of Valuers and Auctioneers, the Royal Institution of Chartered Surveyors, the Antiquarian Bookseller's Association, the British Antique Dealers' Association, the London and Provincial Antique Dealers' Association, the Library Association, and the Society of Fine Art Auctioneers.

In developing the codes, the committee asked the opinions of dealers, auctioneers, collectors, lawyers, police officers, customs and excise, and government departments. As part of this information gathering exercise the Committee conducted a questionnaire survey (published by the Antiques Trade Gazette). The findings of the consultations were then used to inform the drafting of the Code.

The codes have been adopted by The British Antique Dealers' Association, the Incorporated Society of Valuers and Auctioneers, the Royal Institution of Chartered Surveyors, the Antiquarian Booksellers Association, the Library Association, the Rare Books Group the Society of Fine Art Auctioneers. They are also strongly supported by key heritage bodies, including English Heritage, the Museums and Galleries Commission, the National Trust (England and Scotland), and the Historic Houses Association. In addition, the UK's Association of Chief Police Officers (ACPO) has supported the codes by recommending that every police service in England and Wales should have an officer with responsibility for due diligence. Each force has now appointed a "due diligence officer", responsible for liaison with the art trade and with other police intelligence and investigative resources at local, national, and international levels.

Council for the Prevention of Art Theft (CoPAT)

CODE OF DUE DILIGENCE FOR AUCTIONEERS
TRADING IN FINE ART, ANTIQUES, ANTIQUARIAN BOOKS, MANUSCRIPTS AND COLLECTORS ITEMS.

In order to prevent the illicit trade in stolen art and antiques , CoPAT recommends that auctioneers endeavour to:

1. **Request a vendor to provide their name and address and to sign a form identifying the item for sale and confirming that it is the unencumbered property of the vendor and that they are authorised to sell it, and this form will be dated.**

2. **Verify the identity and address of new vendors and record the details.**

3. **Be suspicious of any item whose asking price or requested reserve does not equate to its market value.**

4. **Pay particular attention to late sale entries.**

5. **If there is reason to believe an item may be stolen:**
   a) Attempt to retain the item while enquiries are made.
   b) Contact the officer with responsibility for art and antiques within the local police force area, or, in an emergency dial 999.
   c) Check with relevant stolen property register(s).
   d) Pass to the police any information which may help to identify the person(s) in possession of such items.
   e) If still uncertain, refuse to buy, sell or value it.

6. **Submit relevant catalogues to the appropriate stolen property register(s).**

7. **If requested, submit catalogues to the officer with responsibility for art and antiques within the local police force area.**

8. **Look critically at any instance when requested to pay cash** and avoid doing so unless there is a strong and reputable reason to the contrary. In the absence of such a reason, pay by cheque or other method that provides an audit trail.

9. **Send cheques by post.**

10. **Be aware of money laundering regulations.**

11. **Appoint a senior member of staff to whom employees can report suspicious activities.**

12. **Ensure that all staff are aware of their responsibilities in respect of the above.**

This code has been drawn up with the co-operation of:
Incorporated Society of Valuers and Auctioneers
The Royal Institution of Chartered Surveyors
Antiquarian Bookseller's Association
British Antique Dealers Association
Library Association
Rare Books Group

APPENDIX 7-A

Council for the Prevention of Art Theft (CoPAT)

CODE OF DUE DILIGENCE FOR DEALERS
TRADING IN FINE ART, ANTIQUES, ANTIQUARIAN BOOKS, MANUSCRIPTS AND COLLECTORS ITEMS.

In order to prevent the illicit trade in stolen art and antiques, CoPAT recommends that dealers endeavour to:

1. **Request a vendor to provide their name and address and to sign a form identifying the item for sale and confirming that it is the unencumbered property of the vendor and that they are authorised to sell it, and this form will be dated.**

2. **Verify the identity and address of new vendors and record the details.**

3. **Be suspicious of any item whose asking price does not equate to its market value.**

4. **If there is reason to believe an item may be stolen:**
   a) Attempt to retain the item while enquiries are made.
   b) Contact the officer with responsibility for art and antiques within the local police force area, or, in an emergency dial 999.
   c) Check with relevant stolen property register(s).
   d) Pass to the police any information which may help to identify the person(s) in possession of such items.
   e) If still uncertain, refuse to buy, sell or value it.

5. **If requested, submit catalogues to the officer with responsibility for art and antiques within the local police force area.**

6. **Look critically at any instance when requested to pay cash** and avoid doing so unless there is a strong and reputable reason to the contrary. In the absence of such a reason, pay by cheque or other method that provides an audit trail.

7. **Be aware of money laundering regulations.**

8. **Appoint a senior member of staff to whom employees can report suspicious activities.**

9. **Ensure that all staff are aware of their responsibilities in respect of the above.**

This code has been drawn up with the co-operation of:
Incorporated Society of Valuers and Auctioneers
The Royal Institution of Chartered Surveyors
Antiquarian Bookseller's Association
British Antique Dealers Association
Library Association
Rare Books Group

CHAPTER 8

ARTIST-DEALER RELATIONS

Steven Johnson*

* This chapter was written with the able assistance of Jennifer Shmulewitz, an associate at Paul Hastings Janofsky & Walker.

* Available on companion CD-Rom.

§ 8.01 INTRODUCTION

Relationships between artists and dealers are by nature complex. The typical arrangement involves issues of payment, schedules, copyright, taxes, consignment, insurance, costs, and accounting. These relationships are also intensely personal. Whether due to the personal aspects, lack of knowledge, or resistance to the more formal ways of the business world, the fact is that although artists and dealers should reduce the terms of their relationships to writing, they rarely do, and more often than not they rely on little more than an informal conversation concerning the division of sales proceeds as the basis for their relationship. Given this reality, a body of common law and statutory law has been adopted or created to address this void. This chapter will discuss the laws that apply in the absence of a contract and propose contractual language that can help protect artists and dealers in their relationships if they choose to reduce the terms of their relationships to writing.

In the absence of a written agreement between an artist and dealer, the law grants certain basic rights to an artist who tenders artworks to a dealer for sale and imposes stringent obligations upon the dealer who takes possession of artworks for the purpose of selling them. The arrangement by which a dealer is given an artist's artwork for the purpose of sale is referred to under law as a consignment, and a majority of states in recent years have enacted specific legislation governing the consignment relation between artists and dealers. In addition, many court decisions address the rights and obligations of the artist and dealer in a consignment relation that is not governed by a written contract or statute.

§ 8.02 CONSIGNMENT STATUTES

In the past 30 years, more than half of the states have enacted legislation governing the consignment of artworks.[1] These statutes, which seek to avoid

[1] *See* Alaska Stat. §§ 45.03.326, 45.65.200 (Michie 1999), Ariz. Rev. Stat. Ann. §§ 44-1772, 44-1775, 44-1776 (West 1999), Ark. Code Ann. § 4-73-207 (Michie 1999), Cal. Civ. Code §§ 1738.5-1738.6 (West 1999), Colo. Rev. Stat. Ann. § 6-15-102 (West 1999), Conn. Gen. Stat. Ann. §§ 42-116l, 42-116m (West 1999), D.C. Code Ann. § 28:8-114 (1999), Fla. Stat. Ann. Title XXXIX § 686.503 (West 1999), Ga. Code Ann. §§ 10-1-522, 10-1-523, 10-1-524 (1999), Idaho Code §§ 28-11-102, 28-11-103 (1999), 815 Ill. Comp. Stat. Ann. 320/2, 302/5 (West 1999), Iowa Code Ann. §§ 556D.2, 556D.3, 556D.4 (West 1999), Ky. Rev. Stat. Ann. §§ 365.855, 365.860 (Banks-Baldwin 1999), Md. Code Ann., Com. Law § 11-8A-02 (1999), Mass. Gen. Laws Ann. ch. 104A, §§ 2, 3 (West 1999), Mich. Comp. Laws Ann. § 442.312 (West 1999), Minn. Stat. Ann. §§ 324.01, 324.02, 324.03 (West 1999), Mo. Ann. Stat. §§ 407.902, 407.904, 407.905 (West 1999), Mont. Code Ann. §§ 22-2-502, 22-2-503 (1999), N.H. Rev. Stat. Ann. § 352:4 (1999), N.J. Stat. Ann. §§ 12A:2-332, 12A:2-333, 12A:2-334, 12A:2-336 (West 1999), N.M. Stat. Ann. § 55-326 (Michie 1999), N.Y. Arts & Cult. Aff. Law § 12.01 (McKinney 1999), N.C. Gen. Stat. § 25C-2 (1999), Ohio Rev. Code Ann. §§ 1339.72, 1339.75 (West 1999), Or. Rev. Stat. § 359.205, 359.225 (1998), 73 Pa. Cons. Stat. Ann. § 2123 (West 1999), Tenn. Code Ann. §§ 47-25-1003, 47-25-1004 (1998), Tex. Civ.

alleged abuses of artists at the hand of dealers, make clear the obligations of the dealer to the artist and, in many instances, impose severe penalties in the event the law is not followed. For purposes of economy, this chapter will discuss four of these statutes. Three of these statutes—New York, California, and Illinois—are similar in approach, if not in all details, and have been included because they govern relations in three of the top U.S. art markets. The fourth, Florida, is included both as an example of a different type of statute, and in recognition of southern Florida's growing importance as an art market.

[A] New York

New York was an early enactor of artist-dealer consignment legislation and, as such, many other states have used the New York statute to model their own legislation. Under the New York law, a consignment occurs when

> an artist or craftsperson, or his heirs or personal representatives, delivers or causes to be delivered a work of fine art, craft or a print of his own creation to an art merchant for the purpose of exhibition and/or sale on a commission, fee or other basis of compensation, the delivery to and acceptance thereof by the art merchant establishes a consignor/consignee relationship.[2]

The New York State statute then sets forth the duties of the dealer who has received works of art on consignment. Specifically, the statute provides that the consignee (art dealer) is

> deemed to be the agent of such consignor [artist typically] with respect to the said work; such work is trust property in the hands of the consignee for the benefit of the consignor [artist]; any proceeds from the sale of such work are trust funds in the hands of the consignor; such work shall remain trust property notwithstanding its purchase by the consignee for his own account until the price is paid in full to the consignor . . . [and] no such trust property shall be subject or subordinate to any claims, liens or security interest of any kind.[3]

The statute makes clear that upon delivery of the artwork to the dealer, a consignment relation is established between the artist and dealer and that the artwork, and any sales proceeds from the sale of the consigned artwork, are to be held in trust by the dealer for the benefit of the artist.[4] Significantly, although

---

Stat. Ann. art. 9018 (West 1999), Wash. Rev. Code Ann. §§ 18.110.020, 18.110.030 (1999), Wis. Stat. Ann. §§ 129.02, 129.05, 129.06 (West 1999).

[2] N.Y. Arts & Cult. Aff. Law § 12.01(1)(a) (McKinney Supp. 1999). *See* Appendix 8-A.

[3] *Id.* § 12.01(1)(a)(i)-(v)

[4] *See* Lazarevic v. Sindin Galleries, Inc., Oct. 27, 1997, N.Y.L.J. at 29, col. 2 (as a matter of law, a fiduciary relationship between the artist and the dealer was formed when the artist delivered his work to the dealer.), *see* N.Y. Arts & Cult Aff. Law § 12.01(1)(b) (McKinney Supp. 1999).

an artist may waive the requirement that his or her dealer hold the proceeds from the sale of a consigned work of art in trust for the artist, no other provisions of this statute can be waived, and any contract to the contrary will be held to be void as a matter of law.

In addition, the statute provides that any proceeds from the sale of the artwork may be used only for the benefit of the artist, and the dealer may not retain possession of an artist's work to ensure the repayment of money or any claims that the dealer claims to have against the artist.[5] Most recently, this issue was raised when an art gallery refused to return artworks, claiming that it was entitled to retain the artwork as collateral until the artist repaid monies he allegedly owed to the gallery.[6] The gallery argued that the legislature never intended to protect artists who defaulted on their personal debts, but rather, the statute was intended to prohibit seizure of innocent artists' consigned works by creditors of art dealers.[7] The court rejected the gallery's argument on the grounds that the language of the statute was clear and unambiguous in prohibiting the gallery from retaining artwork as collateral to ensure repayment of a debt.[8] Thus, under the statute, any claimed security interest in an artist's consigned works by an art dealer is void.[9]

Another issue that has engendered litigation is who constitutes an "Art Merchant" subject to the statute. Under New York law, an "Art Merchant" is defined as

> a person who is in the business of dealing, exclusively or non-exclusively, in works of fine art or multiples, or a person who by his occupation holds himself out as having knowledge or skill peculiar to such works, or to whom such knowledge or skill may be attributed by his employment of an agent or other intermediary who by his occupation holds himself out as having such knowledge or skill. The term "art merchant" includes an auctioneer who sells such works at public auction, and except in the case of multiples, includes persons, not otherwise defined or treated as art merchants herein, who are consignors or principals of auctioneers.[10]

Courts have broadly interpreted this statute for the benefit of the artist. In *Wesselmann v. International Images, Inc.*,[11] a printer argued that it was not subject to the fiduciary requirements imposed on art merchants as he did not meet the

---

[5] N.Y. Arts & Cult. Aff. Law § 12.01(1)(a) (McKinney Supp. 1999).

[6] Zucker v. Hirschl & Adler Galleries, Inc., 648 N.Y.S.2d 521, 523, 170 Misc. 2d 426, 428 (Sup. Ct. N.Y. Co. 1996).

[7] *Id.* at 525-26, 170 Misc. 2d at 432.

[8] *Id.* at 526, 170 Misc. 2d at 433.

[9] *Id.*

[10] N.Y. Arts & Cult. Aff. Law § 11.01(2) (McKinney Supp. 1999).

[11] 169 Misc. 2d 476, 479, 645 N.Y.S.2d 263, 265 (Sup. Ct. N.Y. County 1996).

definition of an art dealer. In that case, the artist had allegedly not consigned his work to the printer, but rather, the works were created by the printer at its place of business.[12] In recognition of the statute's broad intent, the court rejected the printer's argument and held that the artist's signature on the prints constituted delivery to the printer and that the printer was subject to the fiduciary requirements of New York's Art and Cultural Affairs Law.[13]

[B] California

California's consignment statute was enacted more recently, but is similar in content to New York's:

> [W]henever an artist delivers or causes to be delivered a work of fine art of the artist's own creation to an art dealer . . . for the purpose of exhibition or sale, or both, on a commission, fee or other basis of compensation, the delivery to and acceptance of such work of fine art by the dealer shall constitute a consignment unless the delivery to the art dealer is pursuant to an outright sale for which the artist receives or has received full compensation for the work of fine art upon delivery.[14]

California's law, like New York's, imposes upon the dealer the duty to hold consigned works and the proceeds from sales thereof in trust for the artist.[15] However, California's law also imposes an additional responsibility on dealers: it makes them responsible for any loss or damage to works that they have received on consignment.[16] In one case, an artist recovered the fair market value of his paintings from an art gallery after nine of the ten paintings he consigned to the gallery were destroyed or damaged in a gallery fire.[17] This decision was particularly favorable to artists because the California Court of Appeals also held that the proper measure of damages for the lost works of art was the fair market value of the paintings rather than the paintings' wholesale value (fair market value discounted by the percentage of commission due to the dealer under the consignment contract).[18] The court explained that the California statute imposes absolute liability upon the art dealer, regardless of the terms of the consignment contract,

---

[12] *See* Wesselmann v. International Images, Inc., 172 Misc. 2d 247, 250, 657 N.Y.S.2d 284, 287 (Sup. Ct. N.Y. County 1996), *aff'd*, 687 N.Y.S.2d 339 (1st Dep't 1999).

[13] *Id.*, 172 Misc. 2d at 252, 657 N.Y.S.2d at 288.

[14] Cal. Civ. Code § 1738.5 (West 1999). *See* Appendix 8-B.

[15] *See id.* § 1738.6(b), (d).

[16] *See id.* § 1738.6(c).

[17] Pelletier v. Eisenberg, 177 Cal. App. 3d 558, 561, 223 Cal. Rptr. 2d 84, 85 (Cal. Ct. App. 1986).

[18] *Id.* at 567, 223 Cal. Rptr. 2d at 89-90.

because the destruction of art works results in a unique loss to the artist such as a loss of his or her reputation.[19]

The California statute also provides that the dealer's obligation to hold the art consigned to him in trust for the artist terminates when the price is paid in full to the dealer/consignor, "notwithstanding the subsequent purchase thereof by the [dealer] directly or indirectly for the [dealer's] own account."[20]

To protect the artist from a dealer buying a work for its own account as inventory to resell at a higher price and retain the difference, the California statute also provides that if, after a dealer purchases a work on consignment from an artist, but before the artist is paid in full for the work, the dealer resells the work to a third party, the dealer must hold the funds from the sale of the work to a third party in trust for the artist until the dealer has paid the artist in full for the work.[21]

Finally, California's law provides that an artist who consigns work to a dealer may not waive any of the provisions of the statute.[22]

[C] Illinois

The Illinois Consignment Statute largely mirrors those of New York and California. The statute states, in relevant part, as follows:

> (1) Whenever an artist delivers or causes to be delivered a work of fine art of the artist's own creation to an art dealer in this State for the purpose of sale, exhibition, or both, on a commission, the delivery to and acceptance of the work of fine art by the art dealer is deemed to place the work of fine art on consignment, unless the delivery is pursuant to an outright sale for which the artist receives or has received full compensation for the work of fine art upon delivery.

---

[19] *Id.*

[20] Cal. Civ. Code § 1738.7 (West 1999). *See* Appendix 8-B.

[21] *See id.*

[22] *See id.* § 1738.8. In addition to the artist-dealer consignment law discussed above, California also provides (on paper at least), one of the more controversial provisions of the laws of certain European jurisdictions, the Artist Resale Royalty Act (Cal. Civ. Code § 986). This act, which is largely ignored even in California except by brick-and-mortar auction houses, provides:

> Whenever a work of fine art is sold and the seller resides in California or the sale takes place in California, the seller or the seller's agent shall pay to the artist of such work of fine art or to such artist's agent 5 percent of the amount of such sale. The right of the artist to receive an amount equal to 5 percent of the amount of such sale may be waived only by a contract in writing providing for an amount in excess of 5 percent of the amount of such sale.

Cal. Civ. Code § 986(a) (West 1999). *See* Appendix 8-B.

> (2) Such art dealer shall thereafter, with respect to the work of fine art, be deemed the agent of the artist.
>
> (3) Such work of fine art is trust property and the art dealer is trustee for the benefit of the artist until the work of fine art is sold to a bona fide purchaser or returned to the artist.[23]

Unlike New York and California, the Illinois statute imposes a 30-day deadline on the dealer to pay the proceeds of a sale to the artist after receiving them, and requires that the artist is to be paid first in the event of installment sale by the gallery. Specifically, the statute reads:

> the proceeds of the sale of a work of fine art are trust property and the art dealer is trustee for the benefit of the artist until the amount due the artist from the sale is paid in full. Except for customer deposits, these trust funds shall be paid to the artist within 30 days of receipt by the art dealer unless the parties expressly agree otherwise in writing. If the sale of the work of fine art is on installment, the funds from the installment shall first be applied to pay any balance due to the artist on the sale, unless the parties expressly agree in writing that the proceeds on each installment shall be paid according to a percentage established by the consignment agreement. Customer deposits shall be used to pay the amounts due the artist within 30 days after such deposits become part of the payment for the work. Any agreement entered into pursuant to this subsection (4) must be clear and conspicuous.[24]

Additionally, the Illinois statute makes the dealer strictly liable for any loss or damage to the artwork unless the artist has failed to remove the artwork within 30 days following an agreed-to removal date or notice to remove the artwork.[25]

[D] Florida

Florida's consignment statute differs substantially from those discussed above, in that it mandates that a written agreement be entered into between the artist and dealer. The language of the statute is as follows:

> Whenever a consignee accepts a work of art for the purpose of sale, or exhibition and sale, to the public on a commission, fee, or other basis of compensation, there shall be a written contract or agreement between the consignor and consignee which shall include, but not be limited to, the following provisions . . .

[23] 815 Ill. Comp. Stat. 320/2(4) (West 1999). *See* Appendix 8-C.

[24] 815 Ill. Comp. Stat. 320/2(4) (West 1999).

[25] *See id.* at (4)-(5).

(1) The proceeds of the sale of the work of art shall be delivered to the consignor at a schedule agreed upon by the consignor and consignee.

(2) The consignee shall be responsible for the stated value of the work of art in the event of the loss of or damage to such work of art while it is in the possession of such consignee.

(3) The work of art shall only be sold by the consignee for an amount at least equal to the amount agreed upon by the consignor in writing.

(4) The work of art may be used or displayed by the consignee or others only with the prior written consent of the consignor and only if the artist is acknowledged in such use or display.

(5) A work of art delivered to an art dealer by an artist for the purpose of exhibition or sale and the artist's share of the proceeds of the sale of the work by the dealer, whether to the dealer on his or her own account or to a third person, shall create a priority in favor of the artist over the claims, liens, or security interests of the creditors of the art dealer, notwithstanding any provisions of the Uniform Commercial Code.[26]

Pursuant to this statute, the burden falls on the artist and dealer to make certain that the terms of their agreement are reduced to writing.[27] Yet in the absence of any written agreement, it is unclear under the statute what happens when the artist and dealer have failed to enter into a written agreement. Presumably, however, the mandated terms of the artist-dealer contract would still apply.

§ 8.03 COMMON LAW CLAIMS

In addition to the statutory laws enacted by a majority of the states, there is a body of case law clarifying the duties and rights of the artist and dealers to each other when they have failed to enter into an agreement defining their rights. These common law rules often supplement the relevant state statutes.

---

[26] Fla. Stat. Ann. Title XXXIX § 686.503 (West 1999). *See* Appendix 8-D.

[27] The burden also falls upon the artist to comply with other provisions of the consignment statute, including § 686.502(2), requiring the artist-consignor to affix a sign or tag to his or her artwork to indicate to the public that the artwork is being sold subject to a contract of consignment. Failure to comply with the statute brings harsh results. In Shuttie v. Festa Restaurant, Inc., 566 So. 2d 554, 556 (Fla. Dist. Ct. App. 1990), an art dealer "unexplainedly departed" after giving artworks to a restaurant as security for loans and for display purposes. The court held that because the artist failed to affix any notation as to ownership as required by the consignment statute, the restaurant had a superior possessory interest in the paintings. *Id.* at 558.

[A] Agency

Under common law, as with the statutory law discussed above, upon delivery of an artwork by an artist to a dealer, the dealer becomes the artist's agent and the laws of agency govern.[28] In one case, an artist's widow agreed to sell, transfer and assign all of the decedent artist's works in her possession to an art dealer, absolutely and forever, in consideration of one-half of the realized sale prices.[29] After the widow's death, her estate demanded the return of all artwork in the dealer's possession, and upon his refusal, litigation ensued.[30] The court, acknowledging that consignments of art, not sales, are the most prevalent business arrangement between artists and art dealers, determined that the agreement was a consignment agreement rather than a sale agreement.[31] Based on the foregoing, the court construed the agreement as a consignment and held that the agreement terminated upon the principal's death in accordance with the principles of consignment law.[32]

[B] Fiduciary Duty

An agent, such as an art dealer, has a fiduciary obligation, and the law requires that the dealer (1) work with the artist in an honest and fair manner; (2) prudently manage the consigned artwork; (3) account to the artist on a periodic basis with respect to the sale of the artworks; and (4) provide the artist with all relevant information relating to the subject of the agency.[33] A dealer who breaches his fiduciary duties is liable to the artist for damages resulting from that breach. Moreover, a dealer could be criminally liable for such breaches if the dealer knowingly seeks to defraud the artist.

A fiduciary also owes the artist a duty of loyalty and must avoid conflicts of interest, which compromise this duty. In the infamous case *In re Estate of Mark Rothko*,[34] the court held that the three fiduciaries for the estate of Mark Rothko acted improperly by entering into contracts disposing of the estate's paintings through sales and consignment that were neither fair nor in the best interests of the estate.[35] The court determined that two of the executors had a

---

[28] *See* Britton v. Ferrin, 171 N.Y. 235, 243-44, 63 N.E. 954, 956-57 (N.Y. 1902); In re Friedman, 64 A.D.2d 70, 83, 407 N.Y.S.2d 999, 1006-07 (2d Dep't 1978).

[29] *Friedman*, 64 A.D.2d at 74-75.

[30] *Id.* at 82, 407 N.Y.S.2d at 1006.

[31] *Id* at 83. Although the agreement was entered into prior to the enactment of the New York Arts and Cultural Affairs Law, the court noted that the statute was enacted "to clarify the inherently fiduciary nature of the 'consignment arrangement' in the artist-art dealer relationship." *Id.* (citation omitted).

[32] *Id.* at 78.

[33] Restatement (Second) of Agency §§ 379, 381, 382, 394 (1958).

[34] 43 N.Y.2d 305, 314, 401 N.Y.S.2d 449, 451 (1977).

[35] *Id.* at 319, 401 N.Y.S.2d at 454.

direct conflict of interest because one held a position as a director and officer of the gallery they had contracted with and the other executor was an artist under contract with the gallery.[36] The court held that both executors had violated their duty of loyalty because their personal interests conflicted with the interest of the estate.[37] As for the third executor, the court found that although he did not act in bad faith or to further his self-interest, he failed to exercise the ordinary prudence and diligence required of a fiduciary.[38]

As the court stated, a fiduciary is required to "employ such diligence and prudence to the care and management of the estate [or trust] assets and affairs as would prudent persons of discretion and intelligence."[39] Thus, good faith alone is insufficient to defeat a claim for breach of fiduciary duty, and a fiduciary cannot "remain passive or move with unconcern in the face of the obvious loss to be visited upon trust assets."[40] As a result of their breach of the duty of loyalty, the court found that the fiduciaries were required to make the estate whole and awarded the estate the appreciated value of the paintings rather than the value of the paintings at the time of the dispositions.[41]

§ 8.04 ARTIST-DEALER CONTRACTS

Although the law will impose certain rights and duties on the artist and dealer even in the absence of a written agreement, and oral contracts may be enforced, a written contract is always advisable. It makes clear the parties' intentions and provides a means of avoiding disputes over issues that are likely to arise.

[A] Oral Agreements

The utility of a written contract is illustrated by cases concerning attempts by artists or dealers to enforce the terms of the alleged oral agreement. For example, art dealers seeking to enforce the terms of oral exclusivity arrangements

---

[36] *Id.*

[37] *Id.*

[38] *Id.* at 320, 401 N.Y.S.2d at 455.

[39] *Id.*

[40] *Id.*

[41] *Id.* at 322, 401 N.Y.S.2d at 456. There are other examples of artists claiming that a dealer misappropriated funds and/or breached its fiduciary duties. For example, in a suit between the art dealer Ronald Feldman Fine Arts, Inc. and the artist Ilya Kabakov, Kabakov claimed that Ronald Feldman failed to pay him money from the sale of seven works, commingled funds from the sale of Kabakov's paintings with the gallery's funds, and deducted funds from the sales of Kabakov's paintings without authorization. Ronald Feldman Fine Arts, Inc. v. Kabakov, No. 96-604348 (Sup. Ct. N.Y. County filed Nov. 17, 1997). For a sample complaint for a claim by an artist against a gallery brought under the relevant New York statute and common law, see Form 8-6.

have run into various obstacles, including the statute of frauds. In one case, renowned artist Georgia O'Keefe sued her commissioned sales agent for the return of artworks and to account for monies owed on the sale of her works.[42] The agent asserted several counterclaims based upon oral promises made by O'Keefe, including the artist's promise to make the agent her exclusive sales agent during and after her lifetime; to create a trust guaranteeing the agent an income of at least $50,000 a year should she outlive O'Keefe; and to appoint the agent as executor of O'Keefe's estate.[43]

Under New York's statute of frauds, agreements that cannot be performed before the conclusion of a lifetime must be in writing.[44] Thus, the court held that the alleged oral promises for a lifetime exclusive agency and to create a trust in recognition of the agent's services rendered during O'Keefe's lifetime were barred by the statute of frauds in the absence of a written agreement.[45] The court also held that the alleged oral promises to make the agent O'Keefe's executor and to empower her to act as sales agent after O'Keefe's death were unenforceable because promises to make a testamentary disposition must also be in writing.[46]

In another case involving the artist Jean Michael Basquiat, an art dealer alleged that the artist orally agreed to give the dealer the exclusive right to buy all of his artwork and to pay the dealer 50 percent of all realized sale prices.[47] The dealer further alleged that after the artist died, his father, also the administrator of the estate, orally agreed to abide by this arrangement. Relying on these assurances, the dealer allegedly expended considerable time and money promoting the artist's work. When the dealer learned that the artist's father had contracted with another gallery to handle the artwork, the dealer sought to enjoin him from selling any of the artwork. Because the agreement was not in writing to support the dealer's claim that it had a contract to purchase the artist's work, the court characterized the agreement as a consignment and concluded that the agreement terminated upon the artist's death.

[B] Written Agreements

[1] Drafting Artist-Dealer Contracts

Art dealers often fear that their reputation and standing in the art community may be irreparably harmed by the defection of a well-known artist. Artists, on the other hand, may feel frustrated if their needs are not being met in their

---

[42] O'Keefe v. Bry, 456 F. Supp. 822, 824 (S.D.N.Y. 1978).

[43] *Id.* at 828, 830.

[44] *Id.* at 827.

[45] *Id.* at 830.

[46] *Id.*

[47] Estate of Basquiat, N.Y.L.J., Sept. 3, 1991, p. 25, col. 2 (Sur. County, N.Y. County).

relationship with a gallery. A written agreement defines the duties that each party owes to the other, and in the event that the relationship deteriorates, the agreement clarifies these rights and duties.

An agreement between an artist and dealer need not be lengthy or complicated. In fact, a consignment agreement can be a single page and merely refer to works consigned, the selling price, and the duration of the consignment. A contract concerning an ongoing relationship, however, should include several other terms which define the nature of the relationship and the apportionment of risks.

[2] Terms

The following comments address various terms that should be considered when drafting an artist-dealer agreement. These comments correspond to the numbered paragraphs in Form 8-1, an annotated artist-gallery agreement, provided by St. Louis Volunteer Lawyers and Accountants for the Arts, an organization that is by its nature "pro-artist." By way of comparison, we have also included references to an artist-gallery agreement prepared for dealers in Form 8-2 ("The Dealer Form").

1. Agency: Fiduciary Duty of Gallery. This provision basically affirms the fact that the dealer acts as a fiduciary for the artist and puts the dealer on notice of its responsibilities to the artist. The Dealer Form is silent on this issue. While the law may impose a fiduciary duty, most galleries would not choose to explain this to artists, nor concede the point in a litigation.

2. Consignment. For the artist, the artworks that are being consigned to the gallery for sale should be described accurately and in detail on the consignment sheet. The parties must decide whether all works by the artist in every medium are to be consigned or merely selected works in a particular medium. For example, an artist may wish to designate a particular gallery as the exclusive agent for dealing with his or her works on paper, yet may desire to have another gallery act as agent for dealing with his or her paintings or sculptures. The gallery will typically seek output rights on all works in all media in which it has experience, and perhaps in all other media as well, so as to avoid contact between the artist and a competitor.[48]

Option 1: Gallery as Exclusive Agent and Option 2: Gallery as Exclusive Seller. The agreement must state whether the gallery is being given the right to act as the exclusive agent of the artist or whether the relationship is a limited agency. If the gallery is not granted an exclusive relationship with the artist, it

---

[48] Form 8-2, Clause 3(a).

is a good idea to explain in the agreement what priority, if any, the gallery has in relation to other agents in selecting the artist's works. Also, if the gallery is granted the exclusive right to represent the artist, the agreement should make clear the geographic area for which exclusivity is granted, if any. Moreover, if the gallery is to act as the exclusive agent for the artist, the parties may want to clarify whether the artist will be allowed to barter works for services, or make any sales from his or her studio, and what commission, if any, the gallery will be entitled to in the event of studio sales by the artist.[49]

3. Duration; Termination. The artist and the gallery should agree on the initial term of the agreement. An artist may not want to enter into an agreement which would tie him or her to a single gallery for too long a period of time; the gallery, on the other hand, may desire an agreement which is long enough to provide it with the incentive to promote the artist's work and benefit from what it hopes will be an increased reputation for the artist over a period of years. One way to deal with these competing interests is to agree to a moderate initial term such as three years, with the possibility of an automatic renewal.[50] Alternatively, the agreement could provide for termination on 90 days' notice, thereby allowing for an orderly termination of the relationship.

Additionally, the parties may want to specify the timing of the return of the artist's work in the event of termination, when the payment of any remaining monies due the artist will be made, and whether the artist will be provided with slides, transparencies, and other materials previously prepared or maintained by the gallery.

4. Delivery. Delivery of the artworks and the costs related thereto should be apportioned between the parties as they deem fit.

5. Title; Copyright. It may be important to the gallery, particularly when dealing with artworks which incorporate third party images and logos, for the artist to warrant not only that they created the work but also that the works do not infringe the rights of any third parties. Also, the gallery will typically want written confirmation of its implied license to make copies of the artwork for its own purposes, and possibly the right to seek third-party licenses for the works.[51]

6. Insurance. Typically, the dealer assumes the cost of insuring the works in its possession. Although certain states impose liability on the gallery in the event of damage or loss of consigned works, it is still a good idea to specify

---

[49] *Compare* Form 8-1, Option 1, *with* Form 8-2, Clauses 3(a) and (c).

[50] Form 8-2, Clause 7.

[51] Form 8-2, Clauses 4 and 5.

in the contract who bears the responsibility for insurance so that there is no misunderstanding.[52] Additionally, the parties should specify how the damages will be measured in the event of a loss (market value vs. wholesale value).[53] The dealer's agreement will often leave this issue silent. If work insured for retail cost is destroyed in a fire, the dealer could reasonably want to pay only the artist's share to the artist, and retain the profit. The artist may also desire to be named in the insurance policy as the beneficiary or as an additional insured.

7. Exhibition; Promotion; Costs. The artist may want to specify the number of individual and group exhibitions that the gallery is required to provide the artist over the duration of the contract, as well as the duration of the shows, and the exhibition space allocated to the artist's work. For its part, the gallery may choose silence with respect to a commitment to a certain number of exhibits, or provide that it has sole discretion with respect to the issue in order to maintain flexibility.[54]

It may also be prudent to address the degree of control the artist will have over the exhibitions at the gallery. For example, the artist may want a provision giving him or her complete control over the installation of the exhibitions or to require the gallery to consult with the artist before installing an exhibition. In the event the gallery does not agree to assume the cost of advertising, framing, promotion, shipping, and storing the artist's work, the agreement should specify how these costs are to be apportioned.

8. Sales; Prices; Commissions. An important element of the artist-dealer agreement is what portion of the selling price of the work of art is to be retained by the gallery and what percentage is to be paid to the artist. Although a 50/50 arrangement is most common, gallery commissions can range from as low as 25

---

52 *See, e.g.*, Alaska Stat. § 45.65.200(5) (Michie 1999), Ariz. Rev. Stat. Ann. § 44-1772(4) (West 1999), Cal. Civ. Code § 1738.6(c) (West 1999), Colo. Rev. Stat. Ann. § 6-15-102(4) (West 1999), Fla. Stat. Ann. § 686.503(2) (West 1999), Ga. Code Ann. § 10-1-524(3) (1999), Idaho Code § 28-11-103(3) (1999), 815 Ill. Comp. Stat. Ann. 320/2(5) (West 1999), Iowa Code Ann. § 556D.2(2) (1999), Ky. Rev. Stat. Ann. § 365.860(3) (Banks-Baldwin 1999), Mass. Gen. Laws Ann. ch. 104A, § 3(c) (West 1999), Minn. Stat. Ann. § 324.03(3) (West 1999), Mo. Ann. Stat. § 407.902 (West 1999), Mont. Code Ann. § 22-2-503(3) (1999), N.H. Rev. Stat. Ann. § 352.4 (1999), N.J. Stat. Ann. § 12A:2-335 (West 1999), Ohio Rev. Code Ann. § 1339.72(d) (West 1999), Tenn. Code Ann. § 47-25-1004(3) (1999), Wash. Rev. Code Ann. § 18.110.020(4) (1999), Wis. Stat. Ann. § 129.02(4) (West 1999).

53 For example, a California appellate court ruled that despite the fact that an artist would only receive 60 percent of the actual purchase price of an art work with the remainder going to the gallery in the form of a commission, the artist was entitled to receive the full market value for works that had been damaged or destroyed in a fire. *See* Pelletier v. Eisenberg, 177 Cal. App. 3d 558, 566, 23 Cal. Rptr. 84, 89 (Cal. Ct. App. 1986).

54 Form 8-2, Clause 1(a).

percent for an artist of substantial reputation with significant selling prices to over 50 percent for an unknown artist. In considering the commission rate, the artist should take into account the benefits of having the gallery promote his or her work. Conversely, an artist of substantial reputation may bring a much needed *cachet* to a gallery's reputation and therefore a gallery would be willing to accept a lower commission rate in return for being able to represent a well-known artist. Also, where the production of the work has entailed significant expense, for example, bronze casting, the parties should consider adopting the common practice of calculating the commission based on the amount in excess of the artist's direct costs to create the work. Under such an arrangement, the artist supplies the gallery with a statement of direct costs before the work is placed on sale and only that portion of the sale price that exceeds the production costs is used to calculate the gallery's commission.

The prices for the works to be sold by the gallery may be jointly established by the artist and the dealer, in which case the contract should specify the initial prices at which the artist's works are to be offered. A provision for the periodic review of prices in consideration of the artist's reputation and conditions of the market may be included. Additionally, the issue of discounts to be offered to collectors should be addressed by specifying the amount of discount which the gallery may provide without consultation with the artist (typically 10 percent), and whether the discount is to be absorbed by the gallery or split between the artist and the gallery.

9. Payment. The agreement should specify when the gallery will pay the artist after receiving payment from the purchaser (such as 30 days after receipt of payment by the gallery), or, if the buyer pays in installments, whether the artist or dealer will be given priority.

It is also common for the artist to be paid on regular time intervals, such as monthly or quarterly. To the extent that the artist is to be paid a set amount on a regular time interval, the agreement should specify the amount of the payment and, if the regular payments exceed the amount generated by the sales of the artist's work, when and if the advance is repayable by the artist with future sales.

10. Rentals; Other Uses of Work. Artists may wish to be consulted before their works are rented or lent. The dealer prefers the opposite rule.

11. Assignment. Because the relationship between the gallery and the artist is an intensely personal one, the artist may want a provision in the contract that prohibits the gallery from transferring or assigning any of its rights to any third party without the artist's prior written approval. This will reduce the value of the gallery in connection with a sale or transfer of ownership, so galleries contemplating sale will resist this clause.

12. Bills of Sale. Mutual approval for Bills of Sale transferring artwork will help with respect to record keeping, and can be used effectively to control rights other than possession, such as copyrights.

13. Records. A provision concerning the maintenance of good records should help avoid conflicts over the number of works sold and the amount due the parties.

14. Security. This provision seeks to protect the artist from gallery creditors who could attempt to seize the artist's works to satisfy or collateralize the debts of the gallery. Scrupulous galleries have little to lose by this language.

15. Amendments. Unless a provision prohibiting oral amendments is contained in the agreement, either party could potentially seek to avoid its obligations by claiming that it had orally agreed to terms in conflict with the terms of the written agreement. This is a particularly prevalent situation in personal relationships between artists and dealers.

16. Integration. This provision seeks to avoid either party claiming that they had agreed to terms not embodied in the written agreement.

17. Mediation/Arbitration. Artists are advised to include an arbitration provision in the contract specifying that any disputes that arise will be decided by an arbitration tribunal. The benefits of an arbitration provision are a quicker, and typically less costly, adjudication of the dispute than if the parties were to seek to enforce their rights in court. In addition, since an arbitration is private, the parties may be able to avoid adverse publicity. Mediation is also an option, but unlike arbitration, it is not binding on the parties.

Many galleries prefer litigation. This is because galleries are generally holding the assets in dispute (cash or artwork), and the expense of litigation may be harder for the artist to bear than for the dealer. Additionally, arbitration is not generally subject to appeal, so a party trying to rely on favorable, if somewhat unfair, contractual language will often prefer a court over the more equitably based judgments of an arbitral tribunal.[55]

18. Governing law. The governing law should be that of the state in which the parties reside or, if they reside in different states, the state in which the consigned artworks are located.

[55] *See* Form 8-2, Clause 9(d).

FORMS AND APPENDICES

* Included on companion CD-Rom.

FORM 8-1

Template Artist-Gallery Agreement (Artist Form)

Agreement: another word meaning contract

ARTIST-GALLERY AGREEMENT

This section identifies the parties to the contract and why each party has entered into the contract.

This agreement is made and entered into on the _____ day of ___________, 20__ by and between _____________________ ("Artist"), of ____________________________ and ___________________________ ("Gallery"), located at _____________________.

WHEREAS, Artist has created, expended time and labor on, and does rightfully own and possess certain __(medium)__, and desires to sell the same; and

WHEREAS, Gallery is engaged in the business of exhibition, display, public distribution and sale of Works of Art, and desires to represent and assist Artist under the terms of this agreement;

Covenant: a promise by one of the parties to a contract to do a specified thing

NOW, THEREFORE, in consideration of the foregoing premises and conditions, mutual covenants, and promises contained herein, and for other valuable considerations, the parties have agreed as follows:

As an agent for the Artist, the Gallery acts as the Artist's public representative for the business at hand. This clause outlines the Gallery's duties in broad strokes; subsequent clauses explicitly define the Gallery's duties.

Agency: a legal relationship where one has the authority to act for another

Fiduciary: a person who acts primarily for another's benefit

1. **AGENCY; FIDUCIARY DUTY OF GALLERY.** Artist appoints and establishes Gallery as agent for the purpose of exhibition and sale of the consigned Works of Art in _(location)_ . The parties agree that Gallery, as agent for Artist, has a fiduciary relationship to Artist and owes a duty to Artist to deal fairly and honestly, to care prudently for and to manage the business affairs for Artist on sales and commissions, to account periodically and disclose promptly all information relevant to Gallery's representation of Artist. Parties agree that Gallery has a legal obligation to act only in the interest of Artist and to forego all advantages aside from proper compensation.

Consignment: the physical transfer of possession of goods to an agent for sale; right of ownership does not pass

This clause lays out the method of consignment and the procedure to add other works not originally consigned. Options 1 and 2, following this main clause, may be added to explicitly spell out the rights of both parties concerning Works of Art that have not been consigned.

2. **CONSIGNMENT.** Artist shall consign to Gallery, and Gallery shall accept consignment of, all Works of Art described in the Consignment Sheet (Schedule A), for the full term of the agreement. The parties shall each have a copy of Schedule A. All modifications or additions to Schedule A shall be in writing, signed by both parties, and attached to this Agreement.

Artist shall not exhibit or sell any Works consigned to Gallery without the prior written approval of Gallery. If consent is given, Gallery shall receive ____ percent of the sale as commission. Artist and Gallery specifically agree that Artist shall be free to exhibit and sell any Work of Art not consigned to Gallery or otherwise included under this paragraph.*

In addition, Artist and Gallery may mutually covenant that the following Works of Art will become part of this Agreement if agreed to in writing, signed by both parties, and attached to this Agreement:

___All FUTURE works created by Artist in the following media:

____

___Any or all EXISTING Works of Art by Artist which Gallery shall select.

___Not less than ____ NEW Works of Art per year in the following media:

____

All NEW Works of Art in all media created by Artist:

____

The following options are mutually exclusive. Only one should be used. Option 1 limits the Artist's right to sell already consigned works, but allows the Artist to sell works that are not consigned. The Gallery is made the exclusive agent of the Artist — the Artist is not allowed to consign any other works to a second gallery or agent. As an exclusive agent, the Gallery asserts a right to collect on its advertising and promotion of the Artist, and would collect commission on works sold through other agents. Option 1 should be used if the parties desire to establish an **exclusive agency** for the duration of the consignment. If used, Option 1 should replace the last sentence ("Artist and Gallery specifically agree . . .") of the paragraph ending with an asterisk on page 6.

Option 1: Gallery as exclusive agent. Artist may not, without Gallery's written consent, sell or consign any Works of Art of Artist to any other Gallery or agent in the ________________ area ("exclusive territories") for the duration of this Agreement. Artist warrants that none of the Works of Art are at present consigned to, located or exhibited in, or being sold at any other Gallery or by any other agent in the exclusive territory except as otherwise agreed by the parties and specifically set forth.

In the event of such consent to and sale of a Work of Art either included in Schedule A or under an exclusive agency agreement, Gallery, as Artist's exclusive agent, shall receive a commission of ____ percent.

Option 2 outlines the duties and rights of the Gallery as **exclusive seller**. As exclusive seller, the Gallery would collect commission whenever a work by the Artist is sold — whether by the Gallery, another agent, or the Artist herself. This is a very far-reaching clause. If the parties decide to incorporate Option 2, it should replace the last sentence ("Artist and Gallery specifically agree . . . ") of the paragraph ending with an asterisk on page 6.

Option 2: Gallery as exclusive seller. Gallery is the exclusive seller of Artist's Works in the ________________________ area ("exclusive territories") for the duration of this Agreement. Artist may not sell in the exclusive territory any Works of Art without the prior written approval of Gallery. In the event of such consent and subsequent sale, Gallery shall receive ____ percent of the sale as commission.

The power to terminate the agreement is an important and useful right. For instance, if a party is dissatisfied with the other's performance of its duties, the agreement may be terminated. The clause gives the right to termination to both parties, only if the non-terminating party also agrees to end the relationship. The subsequent options eliminate the termination "agreement" requirement thus, one party may void the agreement without the other's consent.

3. **DURATION; TERMINATION.** This Agreement shall commence upon the date of signing and shall continue in effect until the ____ day of _____________, 20___. Neither party may terminate this Agreement without the prior written consent of the other party. The Agreement shall continue in force for _____ days after such consent is given.

If the parties decide to include a power of termination that does not depend on getting the other party's consent, the second to last sentence of clause 3 should be deleted ("Neither party . . .") and **Option 1** should replace it.

Unilateral: one-sided; not dependent on the other party

Option 1: Unilateral termination. Either party may terminate this Agreement by giving ____ days written notice.

The parties also might want to extend the duration of the agreement if a sale is in progress. **Option 2** should then be added.

Option 2: Extension of agreement while sale is in progress. The consignment period shall be extended for a period of ____ days if a bona fide sale or negotiation for sale is in progress.

Clause 4 places the responsibility of getting the works to the Gallery on the Artist; however, the costs of transporting the works can be apportioned between the Gallery and the Artist.

4. **DELIVERY.** Artist shall be solely responsible for delivering the consigned Works of Art to Gallery at the above address and agrees to accept delivery of the property, if not sold, at Artist's address on the expiration or termination of this Agreement.

Costs of delivery (including transportation and insurance) to Gallery and costs of delivery (including transportation and insurance) for return to Artist shall be paid by the parties according to Schedule B.

This clause has three functions. First, it asserts that the Artist owns the works outright, i.e., no one else has any claim to them. Secondly, it retains rights of title for the Artist until someone purchases the work **and** the Artist is paid in full. This is very important in a consignment agreement, especially in cases where third parties (usually creditors of the Gallery) claim ownership. Finally, it preserves the Artist's copyright and the work itself from alteration.

Title: right to ownership and superior right to possession

Copyright: the exclusive right to copy or authorize others to reproduce, distribute copies, prepare derivative works, and display work publicly

5. **TITLE; COPYRIGHT.** Artist warrants and represents that he/she created the Works of Art, possess unencumbered title and full copyright to each and all Works of Art consigned to Gallery under this Agreement.

This Agreement is not intended nor does it transfer any rights of title or copyright to Gallery. Title to the consigned Works shall remain in Artist's name until delivery to purchaser and Artist is paid in full. No work may be reproduced by Gallery without the prior written approval of Artist. If written permission is given, then all approved reproductions in catalogues, brochures, advertisements and other promotional literature shall carry the following notice: © by _______________ 20__.

Gallery shall not attempt to or actually modify or alter the artistic or structural integrity of any Work consigned under this Agreement.

The works are to be **insured by the Gallery** while in its possession for their full value. This is one of four necessary elements the statute has laid out. Both parties should be careful in their assessment of the value of the works. If they are destroyed or damaged, the Artist will seek full compensation. If the works are undervalued, the Artist will not receive their true value from the Gallery's insurance company. If they are overvalued, the insurance company will only pay a fraction of the value. The Gallery would then need to pay the Artist out of its own funds to meet the full stated value. The last sentence of clause 6 clearly addresses this provision.

Possession: actual physical control over property

6. **INSURANCE.** Gallery shall be responsible for all loss of, or damage to, the consigned Works of Art while in its possession; specifically from the date of delivery to Gallery until the date of delivery to a Purchaser, repossession by Artist, or return delivery to Artist. Gallery warrants and represents that it has an insurance policy with __________, which insures all of Artist's work against loss, theft, fire, and destruction of any kind. Gallery agrees to indemnify and hold harmless Artist from any loss resulting from lapse of coverage, error, or failure by Gallery to have the insurance coverage warranted.

Indemnify: to secure against hurt, loss or damage

Clause 7 outlines the exhibition, opening, and promotion of the Artist's works. For the protection of both the Artist and the Gallery, every cost should be spelled out and put in writing before anything is contracted for or purchased. The apportionment of costs need not be equal.

7. **EXHIBITION; PROMOTION; COSTS.** Gallery agrees to exhibit the consigned Works of Art beginning on the ___ day of _________, 20___, and continuously thereafter until ________ or the expiration or termination of this Agreement. Gallery agrees to exhibit the consigned Works of Art within the limits of its available space and the commitments for other exhibits which it may have from time to time. Artist's Works shall not be interspersed with any other displays or Works, or included in any group exhibition, without Artist's prior written approval.

Gallery shall consult Artist on all decisions relating to the exhibition and reproduction of the Works.

Good Faith: honesty of purpose, freedom from intention to fraud, and being faithful to one's duty or obligation

Gallery agrees to make all reasonable and good faith efforts to promote Artist and sell the consigned Works.

Gallery agrees to sponsor and to hold an "Opening," or reception, for Artist to be held during the first week of the exhibition on the ____ day of ___________, 20__. The "Opening" shall be specifically advertised and notices shall be sent to all members or patrons of Gallery and to a list of persons, not more than ____ in number, to be supplied by Artist.

Costs for the exhibition and "Opening" shall be apportioned by Gallery and Artist as provided on Schedule B, and shall include specifically photography, printing, postage, shipping, publicity, refreshments, and any special framing, construction, catalogs, signage and other costs. The Parties agree that they shall put in writing prior to incurring any cost or expense, each item consented to, how much shall be paid for these expenses, and how much they each will pay in advance of the exhibition.

The Gallery will not sell work for less than an agreed price that is found on Schedule A. This is another statutory requirement. The Gallery may want to have the power to ask for more than the agreed price. However, the Artist should carefully consider before agreeing to the power to vary the price. The Parties also should consider whether the Gallery should receive commission on total sales, or a specific commission for each piece, i.e., a definite amount regardless of the actual sale price.

8. **SALES PRICES; COMMISSIONS.** Gallery shall sell the consigned Works at the prices mutually agreed to by both parties as specified in writing on Schedule A. The Works shall be sold only for an amount at least equal to the price agreed upon by Artist as specified in writing on Schedule A. Gallery shall receive a commission according to Schedule A.

Gallery shall have discretion to vary the agreed price only by ___ percent.

This clause has three functions. First, it ensures that the Artist will be paid within a certain amount of time after a sale is made. Secondly, it ensures that the Artist will get paid before the Gallery receives its share. Thirdly, it is required by statute. The Artist can agree to modify this stipulation and pro-rate payments. However, any modification must follow the requirements stated in the last paragraph ("Waiver of proceeds in trust").

9. **PAYMENT.** The parties agree that Gallery shall hold the proceeds from sales of the consigned Works in trust for the benefit of Artist. Gallery shall get written consent from Artist before any installment sales are made. Payments shall be made to Artist as follows:

a. On outright sales, Gallery shall pay Artist's share within _____ days from receipt of payment from purchaser;

b. On installment sales, Gallery shall first apply the proceeds of installment payments to Artist's share. Artist's share shall be completely satisfied before Gallery may deduct its commission. Payment to Artist shall be made within _____ days from the receipt of any installment payment.

Waiver: the intentional relinquishment of a known right.

Pro-rated: proportioned according to a certain rate or percentage.

Waiver of proceeds in trust. Parties may agree in writing by special stipulation that installment payments will be pro-rated between them. The waiver of proceeds in trust must be clear, conspicuous, in writing and signed by Artist. No waiver shall apply to Gallery purchases of Works initially received on consignment.

Clause 10 limits the uses of the Artist's Works by the Gallery. In addition, it requires the Gallery to obtain written consent from the Artist for any display or use. This is the last statutory requirement.

10. **RENTALS; OTHER USES OF WORK.** The Works of Art may be used or displayed by Gallery only with the prior written consent of Artist. Gallery may not rent or lend any consigned Work without the prior written consent of Artist. If Gallery should desire to enter any of the consigned work in any art show or other exhibition, Gallery shall obtain written consent of Artist on any entry form used for the purpose, or in the event there is no entry form, to obtain the written consent of the Artist prior to the entry in any display, art show, or other exhibition.

This clause protects the Artist by preventing the Gallery from giving someone else the rights to display the Works. The Artist retains control over whom she is dealing with. Notice on the change of management also serves to inform the Artist.

Assignment: the transfer of one's interest or rights

ASSIGNMENT. This Agreement may not be assigned by Gallery to another person or gallery without the prior written consent of the Artist. Gallery shall notify Artist in advance of any change in personnel in charge of Gallery or of any change in ownership of Gallery.

This clause, in conjunction with the next, is intended to facilitate bookkeeping. The Bill of Sale should contain and explain all information that the Artist desires or needs to know.

Bill of Sale: legal document or form recording purchase of property

12. **BILLS OF SALE.** Gallery shall use a standard bill of sale or other form approved in advance by Artist for any sale of the consigned Works of Art.

13. **RECORDS.** Gallery agrees to keep accurate records of, together with payments made, for the Works of Art on Consignment by Artist. Gallery agrees that it will send Artist an accounting every _____ months. The accounting shall include:

(1) the number of Artist's works which have been sold;

(2) the amount of sales price for each work;

(3) the amount of sales price collected by the Gallery to the date of the accounting;

(4) the amount of Gallery's commission on payments received;

(5) the amount of money paid and the amount due to Artist from Gallery;

(6) the list and location of all unsold works covered by the Consignment sheet.

This clause protects the Artist from the Gallery's creditors, and is supported by the "consignment" statute. However, to be extremely safe, the Artist may want to file a "security interest" claim; it is a straight-forward form and is inexpensive. It should be filled out if the Artist has consigned a very expensive or valuable work. This also will protect the Artist if the Gallery removes the Works out-of-state. Consult an attorney for more information.

Uniform Commercial Code: a statute adopted by the state that governs the sale of goods

14. **SECURITY.** The consigned Works of Art shall be held in trust for the benefit of Artist and shall not be subject to any claim by a creditor of Gallery. In the event of any default by Gallery or any claim made against the consigned Work by any creditor of Gallery, Artist shall have all the rights of a secured party pursuant to the Uniform Commercial Code.

This clause emphasizes that any changes to the Agreement must meet certain criteria.

15. **AMENDMENTS.** This Agreement may be amended, waived, discharged, modified or terminated only by an instrument in writing signed by both parties and attached to this Agreement.

The following clause simply protects parties from misunderstandings and unscrupulous business partners. The clause limits the Agreement to the **written** contract – ensuring that both parties have at all times the sum and substance of their agreement in front of them. Any modifications – if in writing, signed and attached – are considered part of the "integrated" agreement.

Integration: total agreement, and not alterable unless certain requirements are met

Inure: to take effect; benefit

16. **INTEGRATION.** This Agreement embodies and contains the entire Agreement and understandings of the parties and shall be binding upon and inure to the benefit of and be enforceable by their respective heirs, legal representatives, successors and assigns.

Compared to litigation, mediation and arbitration are much quicker and less costly methods of resolving problems that may arise. **The following options are mutually exclusive. Only one should be used.**

Mediation: an informal dispute resolution process in which a neutral third party helps the disputants arrive at their own solution

17. **Option 1: MEDIATION.** All disputes arising out of this Agreement shall be submitted to mediation in accordance with the rules of the Arts Resolution Services, a program of the St. Louis Volunteer Lawyers and Accountants for the Arts.

Arbitration: alternative dispute resolution forum in which a neutral third party hears both sides of the problem then decides what the solution should be

Option 2: ARBITRATION. In the event a dispute arises under this Agreement, the parties shall confer with all reasonable dispatch and endeavor to arrive at a solution; failing agreement, the dispute shall be submitted to a single arbitrator either agreed to by the parties, or appointed by the American Arbitration Association, who shall decide the dispute under the rules of the Association; and any decision by an arbitrator shall be final and binding upon both parties.

18. **GOVERNING LAW.** This Agreement is entered into in the State of Missouri (or Illinois), contains covenants to be performed within the State of Missouri (or Illinois) and shall be construed in accordance with and governed by the laws of the State of Missouri (or Illinois). All performance by both parties shall be in accordance to Missouri Civil Code §§407.900-910 (Illinois Rev. Stat. Ch. 121 _ Sec 1400-1408).

IN WITNESS THEREOF, the parties have signed this Agreement.

____

ARTIST DATE

____

GALLERY DATE

CONSIGNMENT RECORD
(SCHEDULE A)

[Should identity Title of the Work, Creation Date, Medium, Dimensions, Slide or Other Identification Number, Suggest Price, Allowed Discounts, Commission, Division of Discounts, Any Unique Terms]

APPORTIONMENT OF COSTS
(SCHEDULE B)

[Costs may include shipping, framing, insurance, catering, publicity, advertising, promotional material (including layout and production costs), postage, printing, manufacturing, and handling]

FORM 8-2

Template Artist-Dealer Agreement (Gallery Form)

AGREEMENT

Agreement made as of the _ day of ____, ___ between ____, an individual ("Artist"), and ______, a New York Corporation doing business at ________ ("Gallery"), with respect to Gallery's representation of Artist.

WHEREAS Artist creates unique works of art (the "Artworks") through the expenditure of time and effort; and

WHEREAS Gallery is in the business of the sale, exhibition, display and public distribution of art and would like to promote the distribution of the Artworks on an exclusive basis except as noted below;

NOW THEREFORE, the parties hereto agree as follows:

1. Gallery's Duties

a. Gallery agrees to represent Artist as its agent for the sale of the Artworks, to promote Artist's artistic career, to show the Artworks in its exhibition space, to attempt to sell the Artworks to collectors, museums, and/or others who the gallery deems appropriate.

b. Gallery shall be solely responsible for transporting finished Artworks from Artist's current address, and delivering them to galleries or customers as appropriate.

c. Gallery shall keep accurate records of all purchasers of Artworks both to enable Gallery to make accurate payments to Artist, and to enable Gallery to maintain a record of the provenance of Artist's genuine Artworks.

2. Artist's Duties

Artist shall deliver all finished Artworks to Gallery. Artist is under no obligation to create a minimum number of Artworks. Sale of Artworks by Artist directly to customers may be made under the terms set forth below, but Artist shall use reasonable efforts to retain records of such sales to enable Gallery to maintain a record of the provenance of Artist's genuine Artworks, and to enable Artist to fulfill his obligations under this Agreement.

3. Scope of Agency

a. Gallery shall have the exclusive worldwide right to sell, rent, lend or otherwise dispose of all Artworks created by Artist, in any media. This includes, but is not limited to, the right but not the obligation to sell Artworks directly to the public, to display the Artworks publicly, and to authorize others, including other galleries, to do the same.

b. Gallery shall market, sell and distribute the Artworks in such manner and at such prices as Gallery may choose in its professional discretion.

c. Artist retains the right to make and sell Artworks subject to 6(b) below. Additionally, Artist shall have the right to exchange Artworks in barter directly for goods and services.

4. Copyrights

Artist shall retain all copyrights and all other intellectual property rights in all Artworks. Notwithstanding the foregoing, Gallery shall have the non-exclusive, royalty-free right to make a reasonable number of copies for advertising and promotional purposes designed to promote the name of the Artist and/or the sale of the Artworks. Artist warrants to Gallery that all works are original and do not infringe upon the rights of others.

5. Licenses

Gallery shall have the exclusive right to seek third party licensees for the Artworks for merchandising or similar purposes. Any such license shall be subject to Artist's prior approval. Gallery's commission for each license shall be the subject of mutual agreement between Artist and Gallery and will be set forth in an addendum hereto.

6. Fees

a. Gallery shall be entitled to 50% of its net receipts for the sale or rental of Artworks, including without limitation sales by Gallery or any third party acting under Gallery's authority. Notwithstanding the foregoing, Artist will be entitled to a minimum payment of ____ per Artwork sold by Gallery itself or through a third party acting under Gallery's authority.

b. Pursuant to 3(c) above, in recognition of Gallery's efforts to develop Artist's career and cataloguing responsibilities, Gallery shall be entitled to 20% of Artist's net receipts for Artworks sold by Artist directly or through third parties authorized by Artist.

c. "Net receipts" shall mean all revenues actually received by Gallery or Artist for sale or rental of Artworks, less taxes, shipping, disbursements, and framing (unless the frame was provided by Artist, in which case it shall be included). Thus, for example, if Gallery sells an Artwork directly to a customer for $800.00, Gallery will be entitled to $400.00, and Artist will receive $400.00. If Gallery authorizes another dealer to sell an Artwork, and that dealer sells it for $800.00 and retains a $400.00 commission, Gallery and Artist are each entitled to $200.00.

7. Term

The initial term of this Agreement shall be three (3) years. Thereafter, this Agreement shall renew automatically for additional terms of three (3) years each unless either party notifies the other of its desire to terminate this Agreement at the end of the initial or any renewal term upon at least thirty (30) days but not more than sixty (60) days prior written notice before the end of that term. Either party may terminate this Agreement early upon written notice to the other party in the event that the other party is or becomes bankrupt or is declared insolvent. Notwithstanding termination, this Agreement shall continue if full force with respect to any Artworks which are then subject to negotiation for sale or rental as of the effective date of termination.

8. Quarterly Statement and Payments

Gallery shall collect all money for the sale, rental, or license of the Artworks, or any other income relating thereto. Gallery shall pay any sums due to Artist under this or any other Agreement on a quarterly basis. In the event that Artist is paid directly by a third party for the sale of Artworks, he shall pay the sum due to Gallery hereunder on a quarterly basis. Each party shall keep records of all sales or other income related to this Agreement and shall make the records available to the other on an annual basis.

9. General

a. The parties hereto are independent contractors and nothing herein shall be deemed to create a joint-venture, partnership, or employment relationship between Artist and Gallery.

b. This Agreement contains the entire agreement between the parties relating to the subject matter hereof, and is not subject to change or modification except in a writing signed by both parties.

c. This Agreement may not be assigned by either party without the prior written consent of the other party.

d. This Agreement shall be construed and interpreted in accordance with the internal laws of the State of New York. Any action, suit or proceeding arising out of or relating thereto shall be commenced in a court of competent jurisdiction in the State of New York, County of New York, and each party hereto consents to the propriety of the jurisdiction and venue of such court.

AGREED AND ACCEPTED

ARTIST

____

GALLERY

____

By:
Title:

FORM 8-3

Letter Agreement for Co-Production of Exhibit Between Two Commercial Galleries

Dear ____:

This Letter Agreement, when signed by you and returned to me shall constitute a binding Agreement between you and ___________ ("Gallery") pursuant to which we will co-produce a gallery exhibition (the "Exhibition") of the artworks of _______ (the "Artist"), an artist exclusively represented by Gallery.

The Exhibition will be presented at your gallery [name], from [date] to [date]. Your gallery will be open Tuesdays through Sundays, [hours].

I. Gallery's Responsibilities

A. In consultation with you, Gallery will select _ artworks for the Exhibition, will arrange for and advance the costs of framing, and will pack and arrange for shipping of the artworks by [specify type of courier] from Gallery's premises on [date], for delivery to your gallery on or around [date].

B. Gallery will make low cost travel arrangements for its owner, _____ ("Owner") and the Artist.

C. Gallery will provide transparencies and other production materials for the preparation of press kits and mailings.

D. Gallery will, at its own expense, mail invitations to collectors, dealers, and members of the media on its own lists who Gallery reasonably believes may be interested in the Exhibition.

E. Gallery will provide the services of Owner as consultant. Owner will also work in your gallery up to _ hours during the Exhibition from [date] to [date].

[F. Gallery will arrange for corporate co-sponsorship of the Exhibition].

II. Your Responsibilities

A. You will provide exhibition space at your gallery and insurance coverage while the artworks are within your control.

B. You will arrange for catering for the opening reception.

C. You will be responsible for arranging the production of press kits and mailings.

D. You will be responsible for local publicity, and will mail invitations to collectors, dealers, and members of the media on your lists who you reasonably believe may be interested in the Exhibition.

E. You will provide staff for the gallery at all times set forth above.

F. You will arrange for shipping of the artworks back to Gallery by [courier] insured for their full retail cost at the end of the Exhibit.

III. Financial Arrangements

A. Gallery will be solely responsible for all costs and expenses incurred with respect to items I.D., I.E. and I.F.

B. Gallery will forward Owner's travel expenses, and all costs and expenses incurred with respect to items I.A. and I.C.

C. You will be solely responsible for Artist's travel costs and all costs and expenses incurred with respect to items II.A., II.D., and II.E.

D. You will forward all costs and expenses incurred with respect to items II.B., II.C., and II.F.

E. Thirty days after the close of the Exhibition, you will prepare an accounting of all expenses forwarded by Gallery pursuant to III.B. (as provided to you by Gallery within one week of the close of the Exhibition), and all expenses forwarded by you pursuant to III.D., which expenses are to be divided evenly between the parties. The accounting should include any sums claimed by Gallery which you dispute, with a clear statement identifying the disputed sums. Gallery will have 15 days to accept or reject the accounting. If accepted, you or Gallery shall pay to the other the money owed. If rejected, the undisputed sums shall be paid, and the parties will negotiate a resolution in good faith, provided that if they do not resolve the dispute within 15 days, the accounting shall be submitted to a mutually acceptable CPA, whose decisions shall be final.

F. Thirty (30) days after the close of the Exhibition, you will pay to Gallery and Artist their respective shares, as follows: 10% from the sale of each Artwork shall be paid to Gallery as reimbursement for the frames. The remaining money shall be split 50% for Artist, 25% for you, and 25% for Gallery. Any payment plans for the purchases of Artworks extending beyond the thirty (30) day period following the close of the Exhibit are subject to the prior written approval of Gallery and Artist.

G. You guarantee the purchase of at least three artworks with a retail price of not less than _____. In the event that three artworks are nor sold during the Exhibition, you agree to purchase the deficiency and to pay Gallery and Artist their respective shares pursuant to III.F. above.

H. Any shared expense in excess of $_ must be approved in writing by you and Gallery.

IV. Miscellaneous

A. This letter constitutes the entire Agreement with respect to the subject matter hereof, and may not be modified except in writing signed by both parties.

B. This letter Agreement may not be assigned by either party without the written consent of the other.

C. All payments and correspondence relating to this letter Agreement shall be mailed to the addresses of the parties set forth above.

D. This Letter Agreement shall be interpreted in accordance with the internal laws of the State of New York. Any lawsuit or claim arising out of or relating to this Letter Agreement shall be commenced in a court of competent jurisdiction in the State of New York, City of New York, and each party hereto consents to the jurisdiction of such courts, waives objections to venue therein, and consents to service of process by first class mail.

Please signify your acceptance of these terms by signing on the line below provided for such purpose.

Sincerely,

[Owner]

AGREED AND ACCEPTED

By: ____________________

Name: __________________

Date: ___________________

FORM 8-4

Independent Sales Representative Agreement for Art Gallery

AGREEMENT made this ___day of___, 2000, by and between ___________, a New York Corporation with offices at ___________ ("Gallery") and ______, an individual residing at _______ ("Sales Representative").

1. Sales Representative's Duties. Gallery hereby appoints Sales Representative as a non-exclusive sales representative for the sale of works by artists represented by Gallery (the "Artworks"). To this end, Sales Representative shall have the right to broker sales of the Artworks with Sales Representative's clients in exchange for the commission set forth below. In order to receive a commission, Sales Representative is responsible for showing the Artworks to prospective clients, and for all aspects of completing the sale, including arranging for framing, packing, framing, billing and collection.

2. Commission. In consideration of the services to be performed by Sales Representative hereunder, Gallery shall pay to Sales Representative a commission of 20% of Gallery's share from sales of Artworks by Sales Representative to her clients. "Gallery's share" shall be defined as the amount gallery receives for the Artwork, net of artist's commission, taxes, shipping, framing, or other costs. Sales Representative is entitled to request information about the amount of her commission prior to making a sale. Sales Representative is entitled to and expected to charge collectors separately for the costs of frames (except where the frame is part of the Artwork, in which case it shall be included in the sale), shipping, taxes, and other third party expenses. If Sales Representative does not complete the sale or if Gallery is required to forward any expenses in connection with the sale, Gallery shall be entitled to deduct the direct costs from commission payments due Sales Representative hereunder, and may charge personnel time as set forth in Attachment A hereto.

Gallery shall make payments to Sales Representative within 30 days of Gallery's receipt of full payment for the Artworks. Gallery will not transfer possession of any Artwork until Gallery has been paid in full for that Artwork.

3. Gallery's Duties. Gallery will work with Sales Representative and will be reasonably available for private exhibitions of artists, visits to artists' studios, and to answer general inquiries from Sales Representative's clients about the artists. Gallery will provide Sales Representative with promotional material concerning the artists upon request, and will extend a reasonable number of invitations to Sales Representative's clients for openings, previews, and other special events, if any. Gallery will allow Sales Representative's clients to pay by credit card.

4. Confidentiality. In performing its obligations under this Agreement, each party may receive confidential information from the other and its customers or artists, which may be oral or written.

Such information includes, but it is not limited to, the terms and conditions of this Agreement and information pertaining to sales, customers, marketing, exhibition, and business plans, and all information that by the nature of the circumstances surrounding the disclosure, ought in good faith to be treated as confidential. Each party shall use such confidential information solely to perform its obligations pursuant to this Agreement and for no other purpose whatsoever. Each party shall protect all such information from disclosure to other parties with the same degree of care as that which is accorded to its own proprietary information. Gallery agrees that it shall not directly solicit sales to clients it learns of solely from Sales Representative, but may sell to clients of Sales Representative who contact it directly. Sales Representative agrees that it will only purchase artworks by Gallery's artists through Gallery, but shall not be prevented from purchasing such works elsewhere upon termination of Gallery's representation of said artists.

5. Term and Termination. This Agreement shall commence upon the date first written above and shall extend until either party terminates this Agreement, such termination to take effect four (4) months following delivery of written notice to the non-terminatory party unless sooner terminated as provided below.

Either party may terminate this Agreement immediately upon written notice to the other in the event (a) the other party becomes bankrupt, insolvent or enters into voluntary or involuntary bankruptcy proceedings, or (b) the other party breaches any provision of this Agreement.

6. Independent Contractors. This Agreement creates neither an employment relationship between the parties (or between any party or the other party's employees) nor a joint venture. At no time may either party represent itself as an agent of the other without the express written consent of the other. Sales Representative may not bind Gallery to any agreement without Gallery's express written approval.

7. Indemnity. Sales Representative covenants and agrees to indemnify and hold Gallery free and harmless from and on account of any claim, demand or judgment arising out of or relating to Sales Representative's performance under this Agreement. Sales Representative shall not pledge the credit of Gallery in any way.

Gallery covenants and agrees to indemnify and hold Sales Representative free and harmless from and on account of any claim, demand or judgment arising out of or relating to Gallery's performance under this Agreement.

8. Assignment. This Agreement and the rights hereunder granted to Sales Representative are not assignable nor may the obligations imposed be delegated without the prior written consent of the Gallery. Subject to the foregoing, this Agreement shall be binding upon and inure to the benefit of the parties, their successors and assigns.

9. Force Majeure. Neither party shall be liable to the other for a failure to perform any of its obligations under this Agreement where such failure is due to any event of force majeure. An event of force majeure shall be defined as any event reasonably outside the control of either Gallery or Sales Representative which, without prejudice to the generality of this Agreement, shall include any accident, fire, explosion, casualty, epidemic, act of god, official labor dispute, lock-out, labor condition, unavailability of materials, transportation, riot, war or armed conflict or enactment of the law. Where such event of force majeure delays performance for more than one month, either party shall have the right to terminate this Agreement by notice in writing to the other party.

10. Notices. All notices to be given by either party hereunder shall be in wring and shall be sent be certified mail, postage prepaid, or by courier service to the parties at the addresses set forth above.

11. Complete Agreement. This Agreement sets forth the complete understanding of the partiesand supersedes all prior agreements or negotiations between the parties with respect to the subject matter of this Agreement. This Agreement shall not be subject to change or modification, in whole or in part, unless in writing, signed by both parties. Any failure to assert a right or waiver of any term, condition, or breach of this Agreement shall not be deemed a waiver of any other term, condition, or breach of this Agreement or any part thereof.

12. Governing Law. This Agreement shall be construed and interpreted pursuant to the laws of the State of New York. Any legal action, suit or proceeding arising out of or relating to this Agreement or the breach thereof shall be instituted in a court of competent jurisdiction in the State of New York, County of New York, and each party hereby consents and submits to the personal jurisdiction of such court and waives any objection to venue in such court.

ACCEPTED AND AGREED:

GALLERY	SALES REPRESENTATIVE
By:____________________	By:____________________
Name:__________________	Name:__________________
Title:__________________	Title:__________________
Date:__________________	Date:__________________

FORM 8-5

Private Commissioned Artwork Agreement

AGREEMENT

AGREEMENT made as of this _ day of , 1995, between _______ ("Artist"), residing at _________ and _______ ("Commissioning Party"), located at ___________.

WHEREAS, Artist is a well-known professional artist who has received wide critical acclaim; and

WHEREAS, Commissioning Party wishes to commission Artist to create a work of art ("the Work") in his own unique style; and

WHEREAS, the parties wish to have the creation of the Work governed by the mutual obligations, covenants and conditions herein;

NOW, THEREFORE, in consideration of the foregoing premises and mutual covenants hereafter set forth, and other valuable consideration, the parties hereto agree as follows:

1. Intended Work.

a. The Work. Artist shall create the Work according to the following specifications:

(i) Theme: __________

(ii) Medium: Oil on canvas;

(iii) Size: Approximately ________, exact size to be mutually agreed upon by the date of approval by Commissioning Party of the preliminary drawing;

(iv) Price: Between ______ and ________, exact price to be mutually agreed upon by the date of approval by Commissioning Party of the preliminary drawing;

b. Preliminary Drawings. Artist shall commence the Work by creating a preliminary drawing. Commissioning Party shall pay a fee of ________ for the preliminary drawing upon the signing of this Agreement. Artist shall develop the preliminary drawing of the intended work in accordance with the theme set forth above. Artist shall deliver the preliminary drawing to Commissioning Party no later than ____________. Commissioning Party may, within two (2) weeks of receipt of the preliminary drawing, request changes which shall be,upon the agreement of the parties, incorporated in the Work. Commissioning Party shall pay _________ for each subsequent preliminary drawing requested by Commissioning Party. Upon payment of the required amount, Commissioning Party shall own any such preliminary drawing.

c. Completion of the Work. Upon written approval of the preliminary drawing, Artist shall commence the Work. Commissioning Party shall have the right to inspect the Work in progress upon reasonable notice to Artist. Artist shall complete the Work by _____________.

2. Obligations of Commissioning Party. Payment for the Work. Upon Commissioning Party's giving written approval of the preliminary drawing, Artist shall proceed with creation of the Work, and Commissioning Party shall pay the price for the Work, as determined under Paragraph l(a)(iv) of this Agreement, as follows: 50% at approval with the balance due on completion. Commissioning Party shall pay the applicable sales tax with the final payment.

3. Reproductions of the Work. Artist shall provide Commissioning Party with a limited edition photo-offset lithograph of the Work (the "Lithograph"), in an edition of 300 lithographs (the "Reproductions"). The Reproductions may be sold or otherwise distributed by Commissioning Party at its sole discretion. In addition, ten printer's proofs shall go to Commissioning Party.

Artist shall have the right to approve the color quality of the Lithograph before the edition is printed. Each individual Lithograph shall be numbered, authenticated, and signed by Artist for an additional fee of $30.00 per signature. The dimension of the Lithograph shall be __________. The cost of the edition shall be determined at the time the size of the Work is determined, and shall not exceed _______ . Artist shall arrange for delivery of the Reproductions and the artist's proofs for receipt by Commissioning Party on or before ___________. The Reproductions and artist's proofs shall be shipped via _______ at the expense of Commissioning Party to the following address: ________.

4. Insurance and Shipping. Artist shall keep the Work fully insured against fire and theft and bear any other risk of loss until delivery of the Work to Commissioning Party. In the event of loss caused by fire or theft, Artist shall use the insurance proceeds to recommence the making of the Work. Upon completion of the Work, it shall be shipped via ________ at the expense of Commissioning Party to the following address: ______________

5. Termination. This agreement may be terminated on the following conditions:

(a) If Commissioning Party does not approve the preliminary drawing pursuant to Paragraph 1.

(b) Commissioning Party may, upon payment of any payment due pursuant to Paragraph 2, or upon payment of an amount agreed in writing by Artist to represent the pro rata portion of the price in relation to the degree of completion of the Work, terminate this Agreement. Artist shall give a good faith estimate of the degree of completion of the Work if requested by Commissioning Party to do so.

(c) Artist shall have the right to terminate this agreement in the event Commissioning Party is more than sixty days late in making any payment due pursuant to Paragraph 2.

(d) Commissioning Party shall have the right to terminate this Agreement if Artist fails to complete the Work by August 1, 1996.

(e) This Agreement shall automatically terminate on Artist's death or incapacity, provided, however, that in the case of death, Artist's estate shall retain any payments already made pursuant to paragraphs 1 and 2.

(f) The exercise of a right of termination under this Paragraph shall be written and set forth the grounds for termination.

6. Ownership. Artist shall retain title to the Work until he has been paid in full. In the event of termination of this Agreement pursuant to Subparagraphs (a), (b), (c) or (d) of Paragraph 5, Artist shall retain all rights of ownership in the Work and shall have the right to complete, exhibit and sell the Work if he so chooses, provided that no connection is made or implied between Commissioning Party and Artist with respect to the Work. In the event of termination of the agreement pursuant to Paragraph 6(e), Commissioning Party shall own the Work, in whatever degree of completion, and shall have the right to complete, exhibit, and sell the Work if it so chooses. Artist's name may be associated with the Work as the Artist if the Work is approved by his Estate. Pursuant to Paragraph 1, Commissioning Party shall own any preliminary drawings upon completion and delivery to Commissioning Party.

Artist shall retain all rights of ownership in any incidental works such as sketches, studies and mock-ups, made in connection with the Work. However, prior to sale of such incidental works, Artist shall first offer to sell the incidental works to Commissioning Party, which shall have the right of first refusal.

7. Copyright. Artist shall retain all rights of copyright in the Work, the preliminary drawings, and any incidental works made in the creation of the Work. Notwithstanding the foregoing, Artist shall grant to Commissioning Party a nonexclusive, royalty-free license to (a) display the Work and (b) reproduce the work as follows:

[Specify Uses]

Furthermore, in consideration of Commissioning Party's commissioning of the Work, Artist shall not, nor license any other party to, commercially exploit the copyright in the Work, including, but not limited to, make copies, create derivatives, or reproduce the Work for exhibition or sale, except that Artist may reproduce the Work as part of his portfolio, or in exhibition catalogs, monographs, and the like.

8. Attribution, Non-Destruction, Alteration and Maintenance. Artist Shall receive authorship credit in connection with the Work or any reproductions of the Work, including, but not limited to, the uses set out in sections 3 and 7. Commissioning Party shall not intentionally destroy, damage, alter, modify, or change the Work in any way whatsoever as long as the Work is owned by Commissioning Party.

9. Possession. For as long as Commissioning Party is the owner of the Work, Commissioning Party agrees that Artist shall have the right to possession of the Work up to ___ days every 5 years for the purpose of exhibition of the Work to the public, at no expense to Commissioning

Party. Artist shall give Commissioning Party written notice at least 90 days prior to the opening of any such exhibition and provide proof of sufficient insurance and prepaid transportation.

10. Time is of the Essence. Delivery of the final Work will occur by ________ as time is of the essence.

11. Non-Assignability. Neither party shall have the right to assign this Agreement without the prior written consent of the other party. However, Artist shall have the right to assign money due to him under the terms of the Agreement.

12. Heirs and Assigns. This Agreement shall be binding upon the parties hereto, their heirs, successors, assigns, and personal representatives, and references to Artist and Commissioning Party shall include their heirs, successors, assigns, and personal representatives.

13. Integration. This Agreement constitutes the entire understanding between the parties and its terms can be modified only by an instrument in writing signed by both parties .

14. Waiver. A waiver of any breach of any of the provisions of this Agreement shall not be construed as a continuing waiver of other breaches of the same or other provisions hereof.

15. Notices and Change of Address. All notices shall be addressed as follows:

To Artist:

To Commissioning Party:

Each party shall give written notification of any change of address prior to the date of said change.

16. Governing Law. This Agreement shall be governed by the laws of the United States and the State of New York.

IN WITNESS WHEREOF, the parties hereto have signed this Agreement as of the date first set forth above.

Artist

____

Commissioning Party

FORM 8-6

Complaint for Artist-Dealer Dispute

SUPREME COURT STATE OF NEW YORK
NEW YORK COUNTY
---x

NICE ARTIST, :

Index No.

Plaintiff, :

-against- :

COMPLAINT

BIG GALLERY, INC. and :
JANE DEALER,

:

Defendants.

:

---x

Plaintiff, Nice Artist ("Artist") by her attorneys, LAW FIRM, as and for her complaint against Defendants Big Gallery, Inc. (the "Gallery") and Jane Dealer ("Dealer"), alleges as follows:

PRELIMINARY STATEMENT

The within complaint sets forth the disturbing account of how Plaintiff, an internationally acclaimed and award winning artist, has been deceived and defrauded out of ____ dollars by an art gallery and its owner. Defendants' conduct is not only reprehensible, it violates the express provisions of New York's Arts & Cultural Affairs Law ("ACAL"). Artist is one of America's preeminent artists. Her unique work has been featured in a solo exhibition at the

__________________ and collected by _________ and other equally prestigious institutions. For over ___ years, Artist was represented by the Big Gallery. Recently, Artist discovered, to her shock and dismay, that Defendants not only credited themselves with over _____ in commissions they were not entitled to, they misappropriated hundreds of thousands more in unreported sales, improper deductions and other means of financial chicanery. As will be set forth below, Defendants brazenly disregarded their statutory and fiduciary obligations to Artist by, among other things, (i) failing to pay Artist for sales and transfers which were conducted without her knowledge or consent, (ii) failing to provide Artist with the services required to entitle them to a commission; (iii) failing to furnish regular and accurate account statements, (iv) commingling Artist's trust funds with the Gallery's own accounts, (v) failing to safeguard Artist's work from loss, damage or theft; and (vi) breaching their fiduciary duty to hold Artist's works and the sale proceeds thereof as trust property for her benefit.

Even more damning, as set forth below, Defendants have ignored Artist's pleas to return unsold pieces – the bulk of her available work – and, instead, are holding them "hostage" and demanding an outrageous ransom for their return.

Through the claims asserted herein, Artist seeks to redress these grievous wrongs.

THE PARTIES

1. Plaintiff Artist is a resident of ____, New York and earns her livelihood through the sale of works of fine art and craft of her own creation.

2. Artist is an "Artist" within the meaning of ACAL § 11.01(1).

3. Upon information and belief, Defendant Gallery is a corporation organized

and existing pursuant to the laws of the State of New York, with its principal place of business located at ______, New York, New York.

4. Upon information and belief, Defendant Jane Dealer is an owner, director and officer of the Gallery.

5. Upon information and belief, Dealer resides in the State of New York.

6. The Gallery and Dealer are each engaged in, among other things, the business of exhibiting and selling on a commission basis works of fine art created by others and, as such, act as an "Art merchant" within the meaning of ACAL § 11.01(2).

BACKGROUND

7. Commencing in or around ____ and at various times thereafter, Artist agreed to consign and caused to be delivered to Defendants hundreds of works of "Fine art" and "Craft" of her own creation, as those terms are defined in ACAL § 11.01(8)(9) (the "Consigned Artwork"), which the Gallery, acting through its principal Jane Dealer, undertook to exhibit and/or sell. Those works which were delivered to Defendants but neither sold nor returned to Artist are referred to as the "Unsold Consigned Artwork."

8. N.Y. Arts & Cultural Affairs Law § 12.01(1) provides in pertinent part:

> 1. *Notwithstanding any custom, practice or usage of the trade*, any provision of the uniform commercial code or any other law, statute, requirement or rule, or any agreement, note, memorandum or writing to the contrary:
>
> (a) Whenever an artist or craftsperson, his heirs or personal representatives, *delivers or causes to be delivered* a work of fine art, craft or a print of his own

> creation to an art merchant for the purpose of exhibition and/or sale on commission, fee or other basis of compensation, the delivery to and acceptance thereof by the art merchant *establishes a consignor/consignee relationship* as between such artist or craftsperson and such art merchant with respect to the said work, and
>
> (i) such consignee shall thereafter be deemed to be the agent of such consignor with respect to the said work;
>
> (ii) such work is *trust property* in the hands of the consignee for the benefit of the consignor;
>
> (iii) any proceeds from the sale of such work are trust funds in the hands of the consignee for the benefit of the consignor;
>
> * * *
>
> (v) *no such trust property or trust funds shall be subject or subordinate to any claims, liens or security interest of any kind or nature whatsoever*. (Emphasis supplied.)

N.Y. Arts & Cult. Aff. Law § 12.01(1) (McKinney Supp. 1997) (emphasis added).

9. In addition to the Consigned Artwork, Artist caused to be delivered to Defendants photographs, videos, slides, transparencies, catalogues and other materials relating to her work which belonged to her but were stored in the Gallery's files along with its records regarding Artist's work (i.e., various invoices, consignment forms, inventory cards and computerized records) which identify and track the disposition of Artist's work . (The above materials are collectively referred to herein as the "Inventory Records.")

10. For a prolific artist like Artist, without access to and control of her Inventory Records, her studio operations are literally paralyzed – she cannot adequately respond to inquiries regarding her work, determine which pieces are available or which have been sold, to whom and for how much.

11. Pursuant to the ACAL, Defendants became an agent of Artist, with a duty to hold the Consigned Artwork and the Inventory Records as trust property and to hold the proceeds from sales of Artist's work as trust funds for the benefit of Artist. In addition, Defendants were expressly prohibited from subordinating Artist's work or the proceeds thereof to any claims, liens or security interest of any kind or nature whatsoever.

12. As trustee of Artist's property and funds, Defendants owed Artist the duty of undivided loyalty and the duty to (a) skillfully, diligently and carefully account for the sale or other disposition of the Consigned Artwork, (b) keep honest, accurate and correct accounts of all affairs relating to Artist's work, (c) keep and render true and accurate accounts, (d) furnish information in a timely manner, (e) segregate trust property, and all other obligations fundamental to the trustee/beneficiary relationship, and (f) safeguard Artist's works from loss, damage or theft.

13. At all times relevant herein and as more fully set forth below, Defendants failed to carry out these responsibilities.

14. At all times relevant herein, Dealer committed or participated in the fiduciary and statutory breaches and other unlawful acts perpetrated by the Gallery and, therefore, is individually liable for her conduct.

15. Artist relied on Defendants' maintenance of an account for her benefit and on Defendants' timely reporting of the status of her works and any sales thereof.

16. Defendants breached their obligations to Artist and defrauded Artist of property that Defendants were obliged to hold in trust solely for her benefit. Upon information and belief, rather than maintain a trust account for the benefit of Artist, Defendants wantonly

commingled the trust funds belonging to Artist with the Gallery's own accounts, purposefully failed to pay any interest thereon and refused demands to tender amounts due and owing to Artist. Upon information and belief, Defendants earned interest which they credited to themselves on the trust funds belonging to Artist that they commingled with their own accounts.

17. Upon information and belief, the Gallery acting through its principal Dealer, secretly sold numerous works for which it received in excess of $______ (the "Secret Sales"). The Gallery, and Dealer in particular, failed to disclose to Artist that these sales and transfers were made and refused to respond to repeated requests for information regarding the status of these works. Defendants never paid to Artist her share of the agreed upon retail value of these works.

18. Upon information and belief, the Gallery acting through its principal Dealer, secretly transferred works for which it received cash and/or other forms of consideration (the "Secret Transfers"). The Gallery, and Dealer in particular, failed to disclose to Artist that these transfers were made and refused to respond to repeated requests for information regarding the status of these works. Defendants never paid to Artist her share of the agreed upon retail value of these works.

19. In addition, Defendants, without Artist's prior knowledge or written authorization, improperly deducted exhibition and fabrication expenses purportedly incurred by them from the proceeds of the sales of Artist's works made by them in an amount exceeding $______.

20. Defendants otherwise abused Artist's account when they granted "discounts" in connection with a sale without Artist's knowledge or consent which were then improperly deducted from Artist's share of the sale proceeds. Upon information and belief, many of these discounts were never, in fact, given and Defendants kept this money for themselves.

21. As consignee of Artist's works, Defendants were responsible for ensuring the integrity of works during the period of consignment. Defendants failed to fulfill their duties. To wit, numerous works have been lost, damaged or stolen and, yet, upon information and belief, Defendants have not taken any meaningful action to recover, repair or report these losses.

22. In addition to breaching their fiduciary and statutory obligations, Defendants were required — but failed — to perform certain services in order to be entitled to a commission on the sale of Artist's work.

23. Finally, Defendants violated, and continue to violate New York law by refusing to return the Unsold Consigned Artwork and Inventory Records to Artist despite her repeated demands therefor.

AS AND FOR A FIRST CAUSE OF ACTION
(Violation of Section 12.01 of Arts & Cultural Affairs Law)

24. Artist repeats, realleges and reiterates the allegations of paragraphs 1 through 23 hereof with the same force and effect as though more fully set forth hereat.

25. Artist caused the Consigned Artwork to be delivered to Defendants for purposes of exhibition and/or sale on a commission basis, thereby consigning such works to Defendants.

26. The Consigned Artwork were, until their sale to bona fide purchasers, trust property in the hands of Defendants for the benefit of Artist pursuant to the terms and restrictions of the ACAL.

27. From 1982 to the present, Defendants breached their statutory obligations to Artist by, among other things:

a. unlawfully commingling the trust funds belonging to Artist with the Gallery's own accounts, failing to segregate Artist's funds and failing to pay her any interest accumulated thereon;

b. failing to provide accurate statements of account on a regular basis;

c. failing to provide the services they were required to perform to be entitled to over $____ in commissions which Defendants collected on the sale of her works;

d. engaging in Secret Sales and Secret Transfers which they failed to report or pay her for despite repeated demands therefor;

e. failing to safeguard her works from loss, damage or theft and failing and refusing to repay to Artist for such losses despite repeated demands therefor;

f. improperly deducting "discounts" from the agreed upon retail price without Artist's knowledge or consent and refusing to account for such deductions or reimburse Artist for same despite repeated demands therefor;

g. unlawfully deducting exhibition and fabrication expenses in an amount greater than $_______ from Artist's account without Artist's knowledge or consent and failing to reimburse Artist on account of these improper deductions despite repeated demands therefor;

h. failing to return Unsold Consigned Artwork and the Inventory Records to Artist despite her repeated demands therefor;

i. failing to respond correctly, if at all, to inquiries from third parties regarding the availability of Artist's work; and

j. upon information and belief, Defendants committed other acts of misconduct which are not currently known to Artist but will be learned upon further discovery.

28. Defendants' conduct as set forth above constitutes a violation of the ACAL.

29. At no time did Artist waive, whether orally or in writing, the trust fund status of the Consigned Artwork, the proceeds from the sale of these works or the Inventory Records.

30. As a result of Defendants' repeated breaches of the fiduciary and statutory duties they owed to Artist, they should not be permitted to profit from their wrongful conduct by retaining any of the commissions previously collected by them in connection with the sales of Consigned Artwork.

31. By reason of Defendants' blatant violations of Artist's statutory rights, Artist has been damaged in an amount to be determined at trial, but not less than $_______, plus interest from the date of each violation along with punitive and exemplary damages in a sum to be determined at trial and attorneys' fees and costs.

AS AND FOR A SECOND CAUSE OF ACTION
(Action for Recovery of Chattel under CPLR Article 71)

32. Artist repeats, realleges and reiterates the allegations of paragraphs 1 through 23 and 25 through 30 hereof with the same force and effect as though more fully set forth hereat.

33. Defendants held the Consigned Artwork and the Inventory Records as consignees in trust for Artist's benefit.

34. Defendants produced public exhibits of, or otherwise offered for sale, the

Consigned Artwork at various times from ____ to, upon information and belief, the present On more than one occasion Defendants sold one of more works of art created by Artist to a customer.

35. Defendants' last show of Artist's work was held in ____. After that show closed, Defendants retained and continue to hold over ___ pieces of the Consigned Artwork which had not been sold — the Unsold Consigned Artwork. A list of the Unsold Consigned Artwork which Artist, upon information and belief, believes are still within the possession and control of the Gallery is annexed hereto as Exhibit "A" and incorporated by reference herein This list is not meant to be complete or exhaustive. To the contrary, upon information and belief, Defendants are in possession and control or have consigned to undisclosed third-parties other works the which can only be identified after full and complete discovery.

36. By letter dated ______, Artist's counsel issued a formal demand for the return of the Unsold Consigned Artwork and Inventory Records. Defendants have refused, without cause or explanation, to return them. Instead, they have falsely asserted that Artist owes the Gallery money on account of certain unpaid fabrication costs which they assert must be paid in order to secure the release of the work and records.

37. Defendants' conduct, as set forth above, violates Arts & Cultural Affairs Law § 12.01(1). Accordingly, Artist has an unconditional right to the return and possession of any and all of the Consigned Artwork and Inventory Records that remain in Defendants' possession, custody or control.

AS AND FOR A THIRD CAUSE OF ACTION
(Declaratory Judgment)

38. Artist repeats, realleges and reiterates the allegations of paragraphs 1 through

23, 25 through 30 and 33 through 37 hereof with the same force and effect as though more fully set forth hereat.

39. The Consigned Artwork and the Inventory Records are unique and irreplaceable.

40. Artist is entitled to an order of this Court directing Defendants to return all Unsold Consigned Artwork and the Inventory Records to her.

41. Artist has no adequate remedy at law.

AS AND FOR A FOURTH CAUSE OF ACTION
(Breach of Fiduciary Duties)

42. Artist repeats, realleges and reiterates the allegations of paragraphs 1 through 23, 25 through 30, 33 through 37, 39 and 40 hereof with the same force and effect as though more fully set forth hereat.

43. The ACAL imposes upon art merchants such as Defendants fiduciary obligations towards artists who consign their works of fine art to them.

44. Defendants wrongfully and intentionally breached their fiduciary obligations to Artist by, among other things:

a. unlawfully commingling the trust funds belonging to Artist with the Gallery's own accounts, failing to segregate Artist's funds and failing to pay her any interest accumulated thereon;

b. failing to provide accurate statements of account on a regular basis;

c. failing to provide the services they were required to perform to be entitled to over $______ in commissions which Defendants collected on the sale of her works;

d. engaging in Secret Sales and Secret Transfers which they failed to report or pay her for despite repeated demands therefor;

e. failing to safeguard her works from loss, damage or theft and failing and refusing to repay to Artist for such losses despite repeated demands therefor;

f. improperly deducting “discounts” from the sales price without Artist’s knowledge or consent and refusing to account for such deductions or reimburse Artist for same despite repeated demands therefor;

g. unlawfully deducting exhibition and fabrication expenses in an amount greater than $______ from Artist’s account without Artist’s knowledge or consent and failing to reimburse Artist on account of these improper deductions despite repeated demands therefor;

h. failing to return Unsold Consigned Artwork and the Inventory Records to Artist despite her repeated demands therefor;

i. failing to respond correctly, if at all, to inquiries from third parties regarding the availability of Artist’s work; and

j. upon information and belief, Defendants committed other acts of misconduct which are not currently known to Artist but will be learned upon further discovery.

45. By reason of Defendants’ breaches of their fiduciary obligations, Artist has been damaged in an amount to be determined at trial, but not less than $_______ plus interest from the date of each breach, along with punitive and exemplary damages in a sum to be determined at trial and attorneys’ fees and costs.

AS AND FOR A FIFTH CAUSE OF ACTION
(Conversion)

46. Artist repeats, realleges and reiterates the allegations of paragraphs 1 through 23, 25 through 30, 33 through 37, 39, 40, 43 and 44 hereof with the same force and effect as though more fully set forth hereat.

1. Notwithstanding the consignment of the Consigned Artwork to Defendants, Artist retained all right, title and interest therein.

47. Defendants converted to their own use (a) the proceeds from the Secret Sales and Secret Transfers, (b) the Unsold Consigned Artwork and Inventory Records which they refused to return to Artist, (c) a sum in excess of $_______ from Artist's account deducted for exhibition and fabrication expenses; and (d) the amounts improperly deducted from Artist's account for unauthorized "discounts" and unearned commissions.

48. Defendants have refused to return to Artist any of her property that they have converted, although due demand has been made therefor.

49. By reason of Defendants' conversion of Artist's property entrusted to the Gallery, Artist has been damaged in an amount to be determined at trial, but not less than $______ plus interest from the date of each conversion along with punitive and exemplary damages in a sum to be determined at trial and attorneys' fees and costs.

AS AND FOR A SIXTH CAUSE OF ACTION
(Accounting)

50. Artist repeats, realleges and reiterates the allegations of paragraphs 1 through 23, 25 through 30, 33 through 37, 39, 40, 43, 44 and 47 through 49 hereof with the same force and effect as though more fully set forth hereat.

51. Artist is entitled to an accounting by Defendants of the sale, transfer or other disposition of all of the Consigned Artwork and Inventory Records.

52. Artist has suffered, is suffering and will continue to suffer irreparable harm absent the grant of relief sought herein.

53. Artist has no adequate remedy at law.

AS AND FOR A SEVENTH CAUSE OF ACTION
(Breach of the Gallery's Obligations)

54. Artist repeats, realleges and reiterates the allegations of paragraphs 1 through 23, 25 through 30, 33 through 37, 39, 40, 43, 44, 47 through 49 and 52 through 54 hereof with the same force and effect as though more fully set forth hereat.

55. In consideration for Artist's obligation to pay the Gallery a commission on the sale of artwork, the Gallery was required to perform certain services in connection therewith. Specifically, among its other duties, the Gallery was required to field inquiries and handle correspondence from prospective purchasers, galleries, museums, and other cultural and educational institutions, maintain an archive of the artist's work (including, but not limited to, reviews, magazine articles, catalogues, etc.), promote and support the artist's work, coordinate consignments to other art galleries and loans to museums, and insure accurate record keeping and labeling of artworks.

56. Defendants failed to perform the above duties. In fact, Artist was required

to hire employees (whose engagement continues to date), at her own expense, to perform the tasks that the Gallery should have — but did not —provide to earn its commission. As such, Defendants are not entitled to any commissions on account of works sold.

57. By reason of Defendants' breaches of their obligations, Artist has been damaged in an amount to be determined at trial, but not less than $______ plus interest from the date of each breach, along with punitive and exemplary damages in a sum to be determined at trial and attorneys' fees and costs.

WHEREFORE, Plaintiff Artist demands judgment as follows:

(1) On the First Cause of Action, granting Artist judgment against the Gallery and Gladstone, jointly and severally, in the sum of at least $_______ plus interest thereon from the date of each violation along with punitive and exemplary damages in a sum to be determined at trial;

(2) On the Second Cause of Action, an order, pursuant to CPLR 7101 that Artist has the right to possession of all Unsold Consigned Artwork and the Inventory Records and directing Defendants immediately and unconditionally to return any such works in their possession, custody or control to Artist at Defendants' sole cost and expense;

(3) On the Third Cause of Action, a judgment declaring that Defendants have no right of possession in the Unsold Consigned Artwork or Inventory Records and that Artist retains sole right, title and interest therein;

(4) On the Fourth Cause of Action, granting Artist judgment against the Gallery and Gladstone, jointly and severally, in the sum of at least $_______ plus interest thereon from the date of each breach along with punitive and exemplary damages in a sum to be determined at trial;

(5) On the Fifth Cause of Action, granting Artist judgment against the Gallery and Gladstone, jointly and severally, in the sum of at least $________, plus interest thereon from the date of each sale along with punitive and exemplary damages in a sum to be determined at trial;

(6) On the Sixth Cause of Action, directing Defendants to prepare an accounting an accounting of the artwork described herein and a declaration of Artist's rights with respect to the commissions owed her pursuant to the Agreement;

(7) On the Seventh Cause of Action, granting Artist judgment against the Gallery and Gladstone, jointly and severally, in the sum of at least $_______ plus interest thereon from the date of each sale along with punitive and exemplary damages in a sum to be determined at trial; all together with costs and disbursements of this action, including attorneys' fees.

Dated: New York, New York
_______, 20__

LAW FIRM

By:______________________
Attorney
Attorneys for Plaintiff

FORM 8-7

Artist-Agent Agreement*

Agreement, this _____ day of __________ between

____

(hereinafter referred to as the "Artist"), residing at

____

____

and ____

(hereinafter referred to as the "Agent"), residing at

____

____

Whereas, the Artist is an established artist of proven talents; and

Whereas, the Artist wishes to have an agent represent him or her in marketing certain rights enumerated herein; and

Whereas, the Agent is capable of marketing the artwork produced by the Artist; and Whereas, the Agent wishes to represent the Artist;

Now, therefore, in consideration of the foregoing premises and the mutual covenants hereinafter set forth and other valuable consideration, the parties hereto agree as follows:

1. Agency

The Artist appoints the Agent to act as his or her exclusive representative: (A) in the following geographical area:

____

____

(B) for the markets listed here (specify publishing, advertising, etc.):

____

____

The Agent agrees to use his or her best efforts in submitting the Artist's work for the purpose of securing assignment for the Artist. The Agent shall negotiate the terms of any assignment that is offered, but the Artist shall have the right to reject any assignment if he or she finds the terms thereof unacceptable.

2. Promotion

The Artist shall provide the Agent with such samples of work as are from time to time necessary for the purpose of securing assignments. These samples shall remain the property of the Artist and be returned within thirty (30) days of termination of this Agreement. The Agent shall take reasonable efforts to protect the work from loss or damage, but shall be liable for such loss

*This agreement, prepared by the Graphic Artists Guild, was drafted primarily for use by an agent representing an artist's intellectual property rights. It is easily adapted to other uses.

or damage only if caused by the Agent's negligence. Promotional expenses, including but not limited to promotional mailings and paid advertising, shall be paid _____% by the Agent and _____% by the Artist. The Agent shall bear the expenses of shipping, insurance and similar marketing expenses.

3. **Term**

This Agreement shall take effect on the day of _____, 20_, and remain in full force and effect for a term of one year, unless terminated as provided in Paragraph 9.

4. **Commissions**

The Agent shall be entitled to the following commissions: (A) On assignments secured by the Agent during the term of this Agreement, twenty-five (25%) per cent of the billing. (B) On house accounts, ten (10%) per cent of the billing. For purposes of this Agreement, house accounts are defined as accounts obtained by the Artist at any time or obtained by another agent representing the Artist prior to the commencement of this Agreement and are listed in Schedule A attached to this Agreement. It is understood by both parties that no commission shall be paid on assignments rejected by the Artist or for which the Artist fails to receive payment, regardless of the reason payment is not made. Further, no commissions shall be payable in either (A) or (B) above for any part of the billing that is due to expenses incurred by the Artist in performing the assignment, whether or not such expenses are reimbursed by the Client. In the event that a flat fee is paid by the Client, it shall be reduced by the amount of expenses incurred by the Artist in performing the assignment, and the Agent's commission shall be payable only on the fee as reduced for expenses.

5. **Billing**

The ☐ Artist ☐ Agent shall be responsible for all billings.

6. **Payments**

The Party responsible for billing shall make all payments due within ten (10) days of receipt of any fees covered by this Agreement. Late payments shall be accompanied by interest calculated at the rate of _____% per month thereafter.

7. **Accountings**

The party responsible for billing shall send copies of invoices to the other party when rendered. If requested, that party shall also provide the other party with semiannual accountings showing all assignments for the period, the Clients' names, the fees paid, expenses incurred by the Artist, the dates of payment, the amounts on which the Agent's commissions are to be calculated, and the sums due less those amounts already paid.

8. **Inspection of the Books and Records**

The party responsible for the billing shall keep the books and records with respect to commissions due at his or her place of business and permit the other party to inspect these books and records during normal business hours on the giving of reasonable notice.

9. **Termination**

This Agreement may be terminated by either party by giving thirty (30) days written notice to the other party. If the Artist receives assignments after the termination date from Clients originally obtained by the Agent during the term of this Agreement, the commission specified in Paragraph 4 (A) shall be payable to the Agent under the following circumstances. If the Agent has represented the Artist for six months or less, the Agent shall receive a commission on such assignments received by the Artist within ninety (90) days of the date of termination. This period shall increase by thirty (30) days for each additional six months that the Agent has represented the Artist, but in no event shall such period exceed one hundred eighty (180) days.

10. Assignment

This Agreement shall not be assigned by either of the parties hereto. It shall be binding on and inure to the benefit of the successors, administrators, executors, or heirs of the Agent and Artist.

11. Arbitration

Any disputes in excess of $_____ (maximum limit for small claims court) arising out of this Agreement shall be submitted to binding arbitration before the Joint Ethics Committee or a mutually agreed upon Arbitrator pursuant to the rules of the American Arbitration Association. The Arbitrator's award shall be final and judgment may be entered in any court having jurisdiction thereof. The Agent shall pay all arbitration and court costs, reasonable attorney's fees, and legal interest on any award or judgment in favor of the Artist.

12. Notices

All notices shall be given to the parties at their respective addresses set forth above.

13. Independent Contractor Status

Both parties agree that the Agent is acting as an independent contractor. This Agreement is not an employment agreement, nor does it constitute a joint venture or partnership between the Artist and Agent.

14. Amendments and Merger

All amendments to this Agreement must be written. This Agreement incorporates the entire understanding of the parties.

15. Governing Law

This Agreement shall be governed by the laws of the State of _______________.

In witness whereof the parties have signed this Agreement as of the date set forth above.

FORM 8-7

SCHEDULE A: HOUSE ACCOUNTS

Date ________ *(remove all italics before using this form)* ________

1 . ________ *(name and address of Client)* ________

2. ________

3. ________

4. ________

5. ________

6. ________

7. ________

8. ________

9. ________

10. ________

11. ________

12. ________

____

ARTIST

____

AGENT

FORM 8-8

Public Buildings Sevice Contract for Fine Arts Services

GENERAL SERVICES ADMINISTRATION
PUBLIC BUILDINGS SERVICE CONTRACT FOR FINE ARTS SERVICES

On this _____ day of __________, 20__, the United States of America (hereinafter referred to as the Government), acting by and through the General Services Administration, and __________ (hereinafter referred to as the Artist), an individual whose address is __________, do hereby mutually agree as follows:

ARTICLE 1. Definitions

(a) The term "head of the agency" as used herein means the Administrator of General Services, and the term "his duly authorized representative" means any person or persons or board (other than the Contracting Officer) authorized to act for the head of the agency.

(b) The term "Contracting Officer" as used herein means the person executing this contract on behalf of the Government and includes a duly appointed successor or authorized representative.

ARTICLE 2. Scope of Services

(a) The Artist shall perform all services and furnish all supplies, material and equipment as necessary for the design, execution and installation of _______________ (hereinafter referred to as "the work") to be placed in _______________ at the location shown on Contract Drawing No. __________ attached hereto. The Artist shall execute the work in an artistic, professional manner and in strict compliance with all terms and conditions of this contract.

(b) The Artist shall determine the artistic expression, subject to its being acceptable to the Government. The Artist shall submit to the Government a sketch or other document which conveys a meaningful presentation of the work which he/she proposes to furnish in fulfillment of this contract; he/she shall allow _____ calendar days for the Government to determine acceptability of the proposed artistic expression.

(c) The work shall be of a material and size mutually acceptable to the Government and to the Artist.

(d) The Artist shall install the work, in the location shown on the attached drawings.

(e) The Artist shall be responsible for prepayment of all mailing or shipping charges on sketches, models or other submissions to the Government.

(f) Upon installation the artist is to provide written instructions to the contracting officer for appropriate maintenance and preservation of the artwork. The Government is responsible for the proper care and maintenance of the work.

(g) The Artist shall furnish the Government with the following photographs of the finished work as installed:

1. One black and white negative 4" x 5"
2. One color negative 4" x 5"
3. Two black and white prints 8" x 10"
4. Two color prints 8" x 10"
5. One color transparency 4" x 5"
6. Five representative 35mm color slides

ARTICLE 3. Changes

(a) The Artist shall make any revision necessary to comply with such recommendations as the Contracting Officer may make for practical (non-aesthetic) reasons.

(b) If the Contracting Officer makes any recommendations within the scope of paragraph (a) above, after approval of any submission by the Artist, the Artist's fee shall be equitably adjusted for any increase or decrease in the Artist's cost of, or time required for, performance of any services under this contract; the contract shall be modified in writing to reflect any such adjustment. Any claim of the Artist for adjustment under this clause must be asserted in writing within 30 days from the date of receipt by the Artist of the recommendation, unless the Contracting Officer grants a further period of time before the date of final payment under the contract.

(c) If the Contracting Officer makes any recommendations within the scope of paragraph (a) above, prior to the approval of any submission by the Artist, the Artist shall make the revisions necessary to comply with these recommendations, at no additional cost to the Government.

(d) No services for which an additional cost or fee will be charged by the Artist shall be furnished without the prior written authorization of the Contracting Officer.

ARTICLE 4. Inspection and Care

(a) The Artist shall furnish facilities for inspection of the work in progress by authorized representatives of the Contracting Officer. The Government will contact the Artist in advance of any inspection to arrange a mutually convenient time.

(b) The Artist shall be responsible for the care and protection of all work performed by him/her until completion of the installed work and acceptance by the Contracting Officer and shall repair or restore any damaged work; provided, however, that the Artist shall not be responsible for any damage which occurs after installation is complete and before acceptance by the Contracting Officer which is not caused by any acts or omissions of the Artist or any of his/her agents or employees.

(c) The Artist shall give the Contracting Officer at least 10 days advance written notice of the date the work will be fully completed and ready for final inspection. Final inspection will be started within 10 days from the date specified in the aforesaid notice unless the Contracting Officer determines that the work is not ready for final inspection and so informs the Artist.

ARTICLE 5. Time for Completion

The Artist shall complete all work as follows:

(a) The preliminary submittal as required by Article 2.(b): _____ calendar days after the receipt of notice to proceed.

(b) The completed work in place: _____ calendar days after receipt of notice to proceed.

ARTICLE 6. Ownership

All designs, sketches, models, and the work produced under this Agreement for which payment is made under the provisions of this contract shall be the property of the UNITED STATES OF AMERICA. All such items may be conveyed by the Contracting Officer to the National Collection of Fine Arts-Smithsonian Institution for exhibiting purposes and permanent safekeeping.

The Artist shall neither publicly exhibit the final work, nor shall he/she make exact reproductions or reductions of the finished work except by written permission of the Contracting Officer.

ARTICLE 7. Fee and Payment

In consideration of the Artist's performance of the services required by this contract, the Government shall pay the Artist a fixed fee not to exceed $_____. The fee shall be paid in installments as follows:

(a) $_____ upon approval of the proposed artistic expression as required by Article 2.(b).

(b) $_____ when the work is completed, approved and ready for installation.

(c) $_____ upon completion, and acceptance by the Government, of all services required under this contract. The Contracting Officer shall advise the Artist in writing of the approval or reasons for disapproval within 30 days after (i) receipt of the document(s) showing the artistic expression, (ii) receipt of the notice that the work is completed and ready for installation, or (iii) after inspection of the installed work.

Upon approval and/or acceptance (whichever is applicable) of the work performed under this contract, the amount due the Artist shall be paid as soon as practicable after receipt of a correct billing from the Artist. Prior to the final payment, the Artist shall furnish the Government with a release of all claims against the Government under this Agreement, other than such claims as the Artist may except. The Artist shall describe and state the amount of each excepted claim.

ARTICLE 8. Travel

All travel by the Artist and his/her agents or employees as may be necessary for proper performance of the services required under this contract is included in the fee amount set out in Article 7, above, and shall be at no additional cost to the Government.

ARTICLE 9. Responsibility of the Artist

(a) Neither the Government's review, approval or acceptance of, nor payment for, any of the services required under this contract shall be construed to operate as a waiver of any rights under this contract or of any cause of action arising out of the performance of this contract, and the Artist shall be and remain liable to the Government in accordance with applicable law for all damages to the Government caused by the Artist's negligent performance of any of the services furnished under this contract.

(b) The rights and remedies of the Government provided for under this contract are in addition to any other rights and remedies provided by law.

(c) The Artist guarantees all work to be free from defective or inferior materials and workmanship for one year after the date of final acceptance by the Government. If within one year the Contracting Officer finds the work in need of repair because of defective materials or workmanship, the Artist shall, without additional expense to the Government, promptly and satisfactorily make the necessary repairs.

ARTICLE 10. Suspension of Work

(a) The Contracting Officer may order the Artist in writing to suspend all or any part of the work for such period of time as he may determine to be appropriate for the convenience of the Government.

(b) If the performance of all or any part of the work is for an unreasonable period of time, suspended or delayed by an act of the Contracting Officer in the administration of this contract, or by his failure to act within the time specified in this contract (or if no time is specified, within a reasonable time), an adjustment shall be made for any increase in cost of performance of this contract (excluding profit) necessarily caused by such unreasonable suspension or delay, and the contract modified in writing accordingly. However, no adjustment shall be made under this clause for any suspension or delay to the extent (1) that performance would have been suspended or delayed by any other cause, including the fault or negligence of the Artist or (2) for which an equitable adjustment is provided for or excluded under any other provision of this contract.

(c) No claim under this clause shall be allowed (1) or any costs incurred more than 20 days before the Artist shall have notified the Contracting Officer in writing of the act or failure to act involved (but this requirement shall not apply as to a claim resulting from a suspension order), and (2) unless the claim, in an amount stated, is asserted in writing as soon as practicable after the termination of such suspension or delay, but not later than the date of final payment. No part of any claim based on the provisions of this clause shall be allowed if not supported by adequate evidence showing that the cost would not have been incurred but for a delay within the provisions of this clause.

ARTICLE 11. Termination

(a) The Contracting Officer may, by written notice to the Artist, terminate this contract in whole or in part at any time, either for the Government's convenience or because of the failure of the

Artist to fulfill his/her contractual obligations. Upon receipt of such notice, the Artist shall immediately discontinue all services affected (unless the notice directs otherwise).

(b) If the termination is for the convenience of the Government, the Artist shall at his/her option have the right to either:

(1) An equitable adjustment in the price (without allowance for anticipated profit on unperformed services) in which event the Government shall have the right to possession and transfer of title to all sketches, designs, models, the work (whether completed or uncompleted) and all other items produced by the Artist in the course of performing the contract prior to the date of termination, which right may be exercised or not at the sole discretion of the Contracting Officer; or

(2) The possession of all sketches, designs, models or other documents or materials produced and submitted to the Government in the course of the Artist's performance of the work prior to termination, in which case the Artist shall remit to the Government a sum equal to all payments (if any) made pursuant to this contract prior to the termination.

(c) If the termination is due to the failure of the Artist to fulfill his contract obligations, the Government shall return to the Artist all sketches, designs, models or other documents or materials produced and submitted to the Government in the course of the Artist's performance of the work prior to termination, in which case the Artist shall remit to the Government a sum equal to all payments (if any) made pursuant to this contract prior to the termination.

(d) If, after notice of termination for failure to fulfill contract obligations, it is determined that the Artist had not so failed, the termination shall be deemed to have been effected for the convenience of the Government. In such event, the provisions of paragraph (b) of this Article shall be deemed applicable.

United States of America	Artist
By: __________________	By: __________________
Title: __________________	Title: __________________

APPENDIX 8-A

New York Consignment Statute

New York State Consolidated Laws Arts and Cultural Affairs

ARTICLE 11 DEFINITIONS

§ 11.01. Definitions.

§ 11.01. Definitions. As used in this title:

1. "Artist" means the creator of a work of fine art or, in the case of multiples, the person who conceived or created the image which is contained in or which constitutes the master from which the individual print was made.

2. "Art merchant" means a person who is in the business of dealing, exclusively or non-exclusively, in works of fine art or multiples, or a person who by his occupation holds himself out as having knowledge or skill peculiar to such works, or to whom such knowledge or skill may be attributed by his employment of an agent or other intermediary who by his occupation holds himself out as having such knowledge or skill. The term "art merchant" includes an auctioneer who sells such works at public auction, and except in the case of multiples, includes persons, not otherwise defined or treated as art merchants herein, who are consignors or principals of auctioneers.

3. "Author" or "authorship" refers to the creator of a work of fine art or multiple or to the period, culture, source or origin, as the case may be, with which the creation of such work is identified in the description of the work.

4. "Creditors" means "creditor" as defined in subdivision twelve of section 1-201 of the uniform commerical code.

5. "Counterfeit" means a work of fine art or multiple made, altered or copied, with or without intent to deceive, in such manner that it appears or is claimed to have an authorship which it does not in fact possess.

6. "Certificate of authenticity" means a written statement by an art merchant confirming, approving or attesting to the authorship of a work of fine art or multiple, which is capable of being used to the advantage or disadvantage of some person.

7. "Conservation" means acts taken to correct deterioration and alteration and acts taken to prevent, stop or retard deterioration.

8. "Craft" means a functional or non-functional work individually designed, and crafted by hand, in any medium including but not limited to textile, tile, paper, clay, glass, fiber, wood, metal or plastic; provided, however, that if produced in multiples, craft shall not include works mass produced or produced in other than a limited edition.

9. "Fine art" means a painting, sculpture, drawing, or work of graphic art, and print, but not multiples.

10. "Limited edition" means works of art produced from a master, all of which are the same image and bear numbers or other markings to denote the limited production thereof to a stated maximum number of multiples, or are otherwise held out as limited to a maximum number of multiples.

11. "Master" when used alone is used in lieu of and means the same as such things as printing plate, stone, block, screen, photographic negative or other like material which contains an image used to produce visual art objects in multiples, or in the case of sculptures, a mold, model, cast, form or other prototype, other than from glass, which additional multiples of sculpture are produced, fabricated or carved.

12. "On consignment" means that no title to, estate in, or right to possession of, the work of fine art or multiple that is superior to that of the consignor vests in the consignee, notwithstanding the consignee's power or authority to transfer or convey all the right, title and interest of the consignor, in and to such work, to a third person.

13. "Person" means an individual, partnership, corporation, association or other group, however organized.

14. "Print" in addition to meaning a multiple produced by, but not limited to, such processes as engraving, etching, woodcutting, lithography and serigraphy, also means multiples produced or developed from photographic negatives, or any combination thereof.

15. "Proofs" means multiples which are the same as, and which are produced from the same masters as, the multiples in a limited edition, but which,whether so designated or not, are set aside from and are in addition to the limited edition to which they relate.

16. "Reproduction" means a copy, in any medium, of a work of fine art, that is displayed or published under circumstances that, reasonably construed, evinces an intent that it be taken as a representation of a work of fine art as created by the artist.

17. "Reproduction right" means a right to reproduce, prepare derivative works of, distribute copies of, publicly perform or publicly display a work of fine art.

18. "Sculpture" means a three-dimensional fine art object produced, fabricated or carved in multiple from a mold, model, cast, form or other prototype, other than from glass, sold, offered for sale or consigned in, into or from this state for an amount in excess of fifteen hundred dollars.

19. "Signed" means autographed by the artist's own hand, and not by mechanical means of reproduction, after the multiple was produced, whether or not the master was signed or unsigned.

20. "Visual art multiples" or "multiples" means prints, photographs, positive or negative, sculpture and similar art objects produced in more than one copy and sold, offered for sale or consigned in, into or from this state for an amount in excess of one hundred dollars exclusive of any frame or in the case of sculpture, an amount in excess of fifteen hundred dollars. Pages or sheets taken from books and magazines and offered for sale or sold as visual art objects shall be included, but books and magazines are excluded.

21. "Written instrument" means a written or printed agreement, bill of sale, invoice, certificate of authenticity, catalogue or any other written or printed note or memorandum or label describing the work of fine art or multiple which is to be sold, exchanged or consigned by an art merchant.

ARTICLE 12 ARTIST-ART MERCHANT RELATIONSHIPS

Section 12.01. Artist-art merchant relationships.

§ 12.01. Artist-art merchant relationships. 1. Notwithstanding any custom, practice or usage of the trade, any provision of the uniform commercial code or any other law, statute, requirement or rule, or any agreement, note, memorandum or writing to the contrary:

(a) Whenever an artist or craftsperson, his heirs or personal representatives, delivers or causes to be delivered a work of fine art, craft or a print of his own creation to an art merchant for the purpose of exhibition and/or sale on a commission, fee or other basis of compensation, the delivery to and acceptance thereof by the art merchant establishes a consignor/consignee relationship as between such artist or craftsperson and such art merchant with respect to the said work, and:

(i) such consignee shall thereafter be deemed to be the agent of such consignor with respect to the said work;

(ii) such work is trust property in the hands of the consignee for the benefit of the consignor;

(iii) any proceeds from the sale of such work are trust funds in the hands of the consignee for the benefit of the consignor;

(iv) such work shall remain trust property notwithstanding its purchase by the consignee for his own account until the price is paid in full to the consignor; provided that, if such work is resold to a bona fide third party before the consignor has been paid in full, the resale proceeds are trust funds in the hands of the consignee for the benefit of the consignor to the extent necessary to pay any balance still due to the consignor and such trusteeship shall continue until the fiduciary obligation of the consignee with respect to such transaction is discharged in full; and

(v) no such trust property or trust funds shall be subject or subordinate to any claims, liens or security interest of any kind or nature whatsoever.

(b) Waiver of any provision of this section is absolutely void except that a consignor may lawfully waive the provisions of clause (iii) of paragraph (a) of this subdivision, if such waiver is clear, conspicuous, in writing and subscribed by the consignor, provided:

(i) no such waiver shall be valid with respect to the first two thousand five hundred dollars of gross proceeds of sales received in any twelve-month period commencing with the date of the execution of such waiver;

(ii) no such waiver shall be valid with respect to the proceeds of a work initially received on consignment but subsequently purchased by the consignee directly or indirectly for his own account; and

(iii) no such waiver shall inure to the benefit of the consignee's creditors in any manner which might be inconsistent with the consignor's rights under this subdivision.

(c) proceeds from the sale of consigned works covered by this section shall be deemed to be revenue from the sale of tangible goods and not revenue from the provision of services to the consignor or others, except that the provisions of this paragraph shall not apply to proceeds from the sale of consigned works sold at public auction.

2. Nothing in this section shall be construed to have any effect upon any written or oral contract or arrangement in existence prior to September first, nineteen hundred sixty-nine or to any extensions or renewals thereof except by the mutual written consent of the parties thereto.

12.03. Exemption from seizure.

§ 12.03. Exemption from seizure. No process of attachment, execution, sequestration, replevin, distress or any kind of seizure shall be served or levied upon any work of fine art while the same is enroute to or from, or while on exhibition or deposited by a nonresident exhibitor at any exhibition held under the auspices or supervision of any museum, college, university or other nonprofit art gallery, institution or organization within any city or county of this state for any cultural, educational, charitable or other purpose not conducted for profit to the exhibitor, nor shall such work of fine art be subject to attachment, seizure, levy or sale, for any cause whatever in the hands of the authorities of such exhibition or otherwise.

APPENDIX 8-B

California Consignment Statute

986. (a) Whenever a work of fine art is sold and the seller resides in California or the sale takes place in California, the seller or the seller's agent shall pay to the artist of such work of fine art or to such artist's agent 5 percent of the amount of such sale. The right of the artist to receive an amount equal to 5 percent of the amount of such sale may be waived only by a contract in writing providing for an amount in excess of 5 percent of the amount of such sale. An artist may assign the right to collect the royalty payment provided by this section to another individual or entity. However, the assignment shall not have the effect of creating a waiver prohibited by this subdivision.

(1) When a work of fine art is sold at an auction or by a gallery, dealer, broker, museum, or other person acting as the agent for the seller the agent shall withhold 5 percent of the amount of the sale, locate the artist and pay the artist.

(2) If the seller or agent is unable to locate and pay the artist within 90 days, an amount equal to 5 percent of the amount of the sale shall be transferred to the Arts Council.

(3) If a seller or the seller's agent fails to pay an artist the amount equal to 5 percent of the sale of a work of fine art by the artist or fails to transfer such amount to the Arts Council, the artist may bring an action for damages within three years after the date of sale or one year after the discovery of the sale, which ever is longer. The prevailing party in any action brought under this paragraph shall be entitled to reasonable attorney fees, in an amount as determined by the court.

(4) Moneys received by the council pursuant to this section shall be deposited in an account in the Special Deposit Fund in the State Treasury.

(5) The Arts Council shall attempt to locate any artist for whom money is received pursuant to this section. If the council is unable to locate the artist and the artist does not file a written claim for the money received by the council within seven years of the date of sale of the work of fine art, the right of the artist terminates and such money shall be transferred to the council for use in acquiring fine art pursuant to the Art in Public Buildings program set forth in Chapter 2.1 (commencing with Section 15813) of Part 10b of Division 3 of Title 2, of the Government Code.

(6) Any amounts of money held by any seller or agent for the payment of artists pursuant to this section shall be exempt from enforcement of a money judgment by the creditors of the seller or agent.

(7) Upon the death of an artist, the rights and duties created under this section shall inure to his or her heirs, legatees, or personal representative, until the 20th anniversary of the death of the artist. The provisions of this paragraph shall be applicable only with respect to an artist who dies after January 1, 1983.

(b) Subdivision (a) shall not apply to any of the following:

(1) To the initial sale of a work of fine art where legal title to such work at the time of such initial sale is vested in the artist thereof.

(2) To the resale of a work of fine art for a gross sales price of less than one thousand dollars ($1,000).

(3) Except as provided in paragraph (7) of subdivision (a), to are sale after the death of such artist.

(4) To the resale of the work of fine art for a gross sales priceless than the purchase price paid by the seller.

(5) To a transfer of a work of fine art which is exchanged for one or more works of fine art or for a combination of cash, other property, and one or more works of fine art where the fair market value of the property exchanged is less than one thousand dollars ($1,000).

(6) To the resale of a work of fine art by an art dealer to a purchaser within 10 years of the initial sale of the work of fine art by the artist to an art dealer, provided all intervening resales are between art dealers.

(7) To a sale of a work of stained glass artistry where the work has been permanently attached to real property and is sold as part of the sale of the real property to which it is attached.

(c) For purposes of this section, the following terms have the following meanings:

(1) "Artist" means the person who creates a work of fine art and who, at the time of resale, is a citizen of the United States, or a resident of the state who has resided in the state for a minimum of two years.

(2) "Fine art" means an original painting, sculpture, or drawing, or an original work of art in glass.

(3) "Art dealer" means a person who is actively and principally engaged in or conducting the business of selling works of fine art for which business such person validly holds a sales tax permit.

(d) This section shall become operative on January 1, 1977, and shall apply to works of fine art created before and after its operative date.

(e) If any provision of this section or the application thereof to any person or circumstance is held invalid for any reason, such invalidity shall not affect any other provisions or applications of this section which can be effected, without the invalid provision or application, and to this end the provisions of this section are severable.

(f) The amendments to this section enacted during the 1981-82 Regular Session of the Legislature shall apply to transfers of works of fine art, when created before or after January 1, 1983, that occur on or after that date.

CIVIL CODE SECTION 1738

1738. As used in this title:

(a) "Artist" means the person who creates a work of fine art or, if that person is deceased, that person's heir, legatee, or personal representative.

(b) "Fine art" means a painting, sculpture, drawing, work of graphic art (including an etching, lithograph, offset print, silk screen, or a work of graphic art of like nature), a work of calligraphy, or a work in mixed media (including a collage, assemblage, or any combination of the foregoing art media).

(c) "Art dealer" means a person engaged in the business of selling works of fine art, other than a person exclusively engaged in the business of selling goods at public auction.

(d) "Person" means an individual, partnership, corporation, limited liability company, association or other group, however organized.

(e) "Consignment" means that no title to, estate in, or right to possession of, fine art, superior to that of the consignor shall vest in the consignee, notwithstanding the consignee's power or authority to transfer and convey to a third person all of the right, title and interest of the consignor in and to such fine art.

1738.5. Notwithstanding any custom, practice or usage of the trade to the contrary, whenever an artist delivers or causes to be delivered a work of fine art of the artist's own creation to an art dealer in this state for the purpose of exhibition or sale, or both, on a commission, fee or other basis of compensation, the delivery to and acceptance of such work of fine art by the art dealer shall constitute a consignment, unless the delivery to the art dealer is pursuant to an outright sale for which the artist receives or has received full compensation for the work of fine art upon delivery.

1738.6. A consignment of a work of fine art shall result in all of the following:

(a) The art dealer, after delivery of the work of fine art, shall constitute an agent of the artist for the purpose of sale or exhibition of the consigned work of fine art within the State of California.

(b) The work of fine art shall constitute property held in trust by the consignee for the benefit of the consignor, and shall not be subject to claim by a creditor of the consignee.

(c) The consignee shall be responsible for the loss of, or damage to, the work of fine art.

(d) The proceeds from the sale of the work of fine art shall constitute funds held in trust by the consignee for the benefit of the consignor. Such proceeds shall first be applied to pay any balance due to the consignor, unless the consignor expressly agrees otherwise in writing.

1738.7. A work of fine art received as a consignment shall remain trust property, notwithstanding the subsequent purchase thereof by the consignee directly or indirectly for the consignee's own account until the price is paid in full to the consignor. If such work is thereafter resold to a bona fide purchaser before the consignor has been paid in full, the proceeds of the resale received by the consignee shall constitute funds held in trust for the benefit of the consignor to the extent necessary to pay any balance still due to the consignor and such trusteeship shall continue until the fiduciary obligation of the consignee with respect to such transaction is discharged in full.

1738.8. Any provision of a contract or agreement whereby the consignor waives any provision of this title is void.

1738.9. This title shall not apply to a written contract executed prior to the effective date of this title, unless either the parties agree by mutual written consent that this title shall apply or such contract is extended or renewed after the effective date of this title.

The provisions of this title shall prevail over any conflicting or inconsistent provisions of the Commercial Code affecting the subject matter of this title.

APPENDIX 8-C

Illinois Consignment Statute

Illinois Compiled Statutes
Business Transactions
Consignment of Art Act
815 ILCS 320/
Sec. 0.01. Short title. This Act may be cited as the Consignment of Art Act.
(Source: P.A. 86-1324.)

(815 ILCS 320/1)

Sec. 1. As used in this Act, unless the context otherwise requires:

(1) "Art dealer" means a person engaged in the business of selling works of fine art, other than a person exclusively engaged in the business of selling goods at public auction.

(2) "Artist" means the creator of a work of fine art or, if such person is deceased, the creator's heir, legatee, or personal representative.

(3) "On consignment" means that no title to, estate in, or right to possession of the work of fine art superior to that of the consignor shall vest in the consignee, notwithstanding the consignee's power or authority to transfer and convey all of the right, title, and interest of the consignor in and to such work of fine art to a third party.

(4) "Commission" means the fee, compensation, or percentage of the actual selling price of a work of fine art agreed upon by the artist and art dealer which the art dealer may retain after the sale of the artist's work to a third party.

(5) "Creditor" includes, but is not limited to, those persons embraced by the definition of "creditor" in Section 1-201 of the "Uniform Commercial Code", approved July 31, 1961, as amended.

(6) "Bona fide purchaser" means a person who in good faith makes a purchase without notice of any outstanding rights of others.

(7) "Work of fine art" means:

(a) A visual rendition including, but not limited to, a painting, drawing, sculpture, mosaic, videotape, or photograph.

(b) A work of calligraphy.

(c) A work of graphic art including, but not limited to, an etching, lithograph, serigraph, or offset print.

(d) A craft work in materials including, but not limited to, clay, textile, fiber, wood, metal, plastic, or glass.

(e) A work in mixed media including, but not limited to, a collage, assemblage, or work consisting of any combination of paragraphs (a) through (d).
(Source: P.A. 84-683.)

(815 ILCS 320/2)

Sec. 2. Any custom, practice, or usage of the trade notwithstanding:

(1) Whenever an artist delivers or causes to be delivered a work of fine art of the artist's own creation to an art dealer in this State for the purpose of sale, exhibition, or both, on a commission, the delivery to and acceptance of the work of fine art by the art dealer is deemed to place the work of fine art on consignment, unless the delivery is pursuant to an outright sale for which the artist receives or has received full compensation for the work of fine art upon delivery.

(2) Such art dealer shall thereafter, with respect to the work of fine art, be deemed the agent of the artist.

(3) Such work of fine art is trust property and the art dealer is trustee for the benefit of the artist until the work of fine art is sold to a bona fide purchaser or returned to the artist.

(4) The proceeds of the sale of a work of fine art are trust property and the art dealer is trustee for the benefit of the artist until the amount due the artist from the sale is paid in full. Except for customer deposits, these trust funds shall be paid to the artist within 30 days of receipt by the art dealer unless the parties expressly agree otherwise in writing. If the sale of the work of fine art is on installment, the funds from the installment shall first be applied to pay any balance due to the artist on the sale, unless the parties expressly agree in writing that the proceeds on each installment shall be paid according to a percentage established by the consignment agreement. Customer deposits shall be used to pay the amounts due the artist within 30 days after such deposits become part of the payment for the work. Any agreement entered into pursuant to this subsection (4) must be clear and conspicuous.

(5) The art dealer shall be strictly liable for the loss of or damage to the work of fine art while it is in the art dealer's possession. The value of the work of fine art is, for purposes of this subsection, the value established in a written agreement between the artist and art dealer prior to the loss or damage or, if no written agreement regarding the value of the work of fine art exists, the fair market value of the work of fine art. Any reimbursement due the artist from the dealer as a result of the loss of or damage to a work of fine art shall not exceed the amount which would have been due to the artist if the work had been sold at the stated purchase price in the agreement.

(6) The art dealer shall not be held liable for loss or damage to the work of fine art if the artist fails to remove the work of fine art within a period of 30 days following the date agreed upon for removal of the work of fine art in a written contract between the artist and art dealer or, if no written agreement regarding a removal date exists, 30 days after notice to remove the work of fine art is sent by registered mail to the artist's last known address.

(Source: P.A. 84-683.)

(815 ILCS 320/3)

Sec. 3. (1) If a work of fine art is trust property under Section 2 when initially received by the art dealer, it remains trust property notwithstanding the subsequent purchase of the work of fine art by the art dealer directly or indirectly for the art dealer's own account until any balance due to the artist from the sale is paid in full.

(2) If the art dealer resells a work of fine art to which subsection (1) applies to a bona fide purchaser before the artist has been paid in full, the work of fine art ceases to be trust property and the proceeds of the resale are trust funds in the hands of the art dealer for the benefit of the artist to the extent necessary to pay any balance due to the artist. The trusteeship of any of the proceeds continues until the fiduciary obligation of the art dealer with respect to the transaction is discharged in full.

(Source: P.A. 84-683.)

(815 ILCS 320/4)

Sec. 4. No property which is trust property under Section 2 or Section 3 is subject to the claims, liens or security interests of the creditors of the art dealer.

(Source: P.A. 84-683.)

(815 ILCS 320/5)

Sec. 5. (1) An art dealer may accept a work of fine art for commission on consignment from an artist only if prior to or within seven days of acceptance the art dealer enters into a written contract with the artist which shall include but not be limited to the following provisions:

(a) The value of the work of fine art.

(b) The time within which the proceeds of the sale are to be paid to the artist if the work of fine art is sold.

(c) The commission the art dealer is to receive if the work of fine art is sold.

(d) The minimum price for the sale of the work of fine art, and any discounts ordinarily given by the art dealer in his regular course of business.

(2) An art dealer who accepts a work of fine art for commission on consignment from an artist may use or display the work of fine art or a photograph of the work of fine art or permit the use or display of the work of fine art or a photograph of the work of fine art only if notice is given to users or viewers that the work of fine art is the work of the artist.

(3) If an art dealer violates this Section 5, the artist may seek relief in a court of competent jurisdiction by having the obligation of the artist voided with respect to that art dealer or to his successors or assigns.

(Source: P.A. 84-683.)

(815 ILCS 320/6)

Sec. 6. Any portion of an agreement which waives any provision of this Act is void.

(Source: P.A. 84-683.)

(815 ILCS 320/7)

Sec. 7. Any art dealer who violates Section 5 is liable to the artist in an amount equal to:

(1) $50; and

(2) The actual damages, if any, including the incidental and consequential damages, sustained by the artist by reason of the violation and reasonable attorneys' fees.

(Source: P.A. 84-683.)

(815 ILCS 320/8)

Sec. 8. (1) This Act shall not apply to a written contract executed prior to the effective date of this Act, unless either the parties agree by mutual written consent that this chapter shall apply or such contract is extended or renewed after the effective date of this Act.

(2) The provisions of this Act shall prevail over any conflicting or inconsistent provisions of the "Uniform Commercial Code", approved July 31, 1961, as amended, affecting the subject matter of this Act.

(Source: P.A. 84-683.)

APPENDIX 8-D

Florida Consignment Statute

1999 Florida Statutes

Title XXXIX COMMERCIAL RELATIONS	Chapter 686 Sales, Distribution, and Franchise Relationships

686.502 Consignment relationship; notice; proceeds of sales held in trust; contract requirements.—

(1) Whenever a consignor delivers, or causes to be delivered, a work of art to a consignee for the purpose of sale, or exhibition and sale, to the public on a commission, fee, or other basis of compensation, the delivery to and acceptance thereof by the art dealer is deemed to be "on consignment"; and, with respect to the work of art, such consignee shall thereafter be deemed to be the agent of such consignor.

(2) Whenever a consignor delivers or causes to be delivered a work of art to a consignee, such consignor shall give notice to the public by affixing to such work of art a sign or tag which states that such work of art is being sold subject to a contract of consignment, or such consignee shall post a clear and conspicuous sign in the consignee's place of business giving notice that some works of art are being sold subject to a contract of consignment.

(3) The proceeds of sale of a work of art shall be held in trust by the consignee for the benefit of the consignor. Such proceeds shall be applied first in payment of any amount due to the consignor.

(4) Any provision of a contract or agreement whereby the consignor waives any of the provisions of this section is void.

History.—s. 2, ch. 86-118.

686.503 Contract provisions.—Whenever a consignee accepts a work of art for the purpose of sale, or exhibition and sale, to the public on a commission, fee, or other basis of compensation, there shall be a written contract or agreement between the consignor and consignee which shall include, but not be limited to, the following provisions:

(1) The proceeds of the sale of the work of art shall be delivered to the consignor at a schedule agreed upon by the consignor and consignee.

(2) The consignee shall be responsible for the stated value of the work of art in the event of the loss of or damage to such work of art while it is in the possession of such consignee.

(3) The work of art shall only be sold by the consignee for an amount at least equal to the amount agreed upon by the consignor in writing.

(4) The work of art may be used or displayed by the consignee or others only with the prior written consent of the consignor and only if the artist is acknowledged in such use or display.

(5) A work of art delivered to an art dealer by an artist for the purpose of exhibition or sale and the artist's share of the proceeds of the sale of the work by the dealer, whether to the dealer on his or her own account or to a third person, shall create a priority in favor of the artist over the claims, liens, or security interests of the creditors of the art dealer, notwithstanding any provisions of the Uniform Commercial Code.

History.—s. 3, ch. 86-118; s. 744, ch. 97-102.

APPENDIX 8-E

Annotated Agreement for Commission of Public Art

Commissioning a Work of Public Art: An Annotated Model Agreement*

Federal, state and municipal governments, as well as private corporations and real estate developers, have become more active in commissioning works of fine art for temporary or permanent exhibition in public places. Such commissions have become larger in terms of scale, cost and complexity of fabrication and installation. Artists have been asked to participate, often in collaboration with other design professionals, in developing innovative solutions to public design problems in such areas as building design and park development. It is thus not surprising that the experience and skills of lawyers have been increasingly called upon in the preparation of the contractual documents governing these projects.

Each project is necessarily unique in its particular public/private sector involvement, matching funds participation, timing and scheduling, formalities for review and acceptance of the proposed work and the finished, installed work, not to mention the apportionment of the burdens of obtaining and paying for materials, labor (including labor union involvement at installation), site preparation work and insurance coverage, to name a few common considerations. Thus it would be folly to propose that a single form of agreement be used for all projects.

Nevertheless, all public art projects do have certain aspects in common. They all involve creative work by an artist under circumstances in which the integrity and authenticity of the artist's creation must be assured throughout the often lengthy and costly process of fabrication and installation, and beyond installation to exhibition, maintenance and repair of the work of fine art.

In addition, the high visibility of public art has led, in some instances, to community reaction and strong controversy, particularly as the contemporary public artist uses new forms and symbols unfamiliar to the taste and culture of the community served. As George Segal, a noted sculptor, stated in discussing the difference between private and public commissions: "Now I have to take public feelings into account. . . . The question is whether you can maintain the density of your subject matter at a decently high level of thinking and still be accessible to a lot of people." Partners for Livable Places, Art in Public Places, 1981 at 75.

Because the considerations of reconciling artistic integrity and public accommodation are not commonly found in other public works construction agreements, they often give rise to concern on the part of attorneys and their clients who are unfamiliar with them.

The Model Agreement is proposed in the hope that it will elucidate some of these issues, both for legal practitioners and their clients. Thus, the accompanying

---

annotations are intended to be as valuable as the specific agreement language which serves as their framework.

The Model Agreement incorporates those aspects of public art contracts that have already acquired a history in negotiation and utilization in actual case situations. The objective has been to strike a balance of fairness between the legitimate concerns of an artist who desires to obtain a commission and realize a work that enhances the artist's reputation and the concerns of a commissioning body conscious of its responsibility to ensure that a project of quality is realized.

In the interest of clarity, the typical situation posited in the Model Agreement is one of the simplest: an agreement between a municipality that wishes to commission a work of art and an individual artist who will be responsible for all aspects of the conception, creation, fabrication and installation of the finished work. Nevertheless, the issues raised and annotated in the Model Agreement are also applicable when a private or public foundation, a private corporation, or a real estate developer commissions a work of art for a public space.

The Model Agreement assumes that a municipality, subject to a "percent for art" requirement that a certain percentage of capital construction costs for public buildings be dedicated to fine arts, wishes to retain an individual artist to conceive, propose, fabricate and install a particular work of art. The commission method, as distinct from the direct purchase of an existing art work or the selection of the artist on the basis of the submission of a competitive proposal, entails selecting the artist to create a new work after evaluation of the artist's portfolio. The commission method affords the advantage of creative participation and involvement for the construction project architect, the contracting agency, the arts commission and the public, since no product exists at the time of the commission; on the other hand, the commission method involves the hazards inherent in communication and the creative process.

The Model Agreement also assumes, for purposes of simplicity, that the artist will fabricate the major part of the work in a studio or foundry. It does not provide for an elaborate construction phase, which would involve the artist in on-site supervision in order to insure that the work is executed in a professional and workmanlike manner and in accordance with the original design.

In order to maintain its focus upon aspects unique to the commissioning process, the Model Agreement does not address many common situations. Three such areas not covered are:

1. An artist's use of a corporation to undertake some or all of the responsibilities of carrying out a public art project. For instance, a commissioning body concerned that an individual artist may die or become physically incapacitated during the fabrication and installation phases of a project might require that the artist establish or retain a corporation or provide for some other successor to assume the fabrication and installation obligations after the artist's death or inca-

pacitation. Similarly, an artist concerned about individual contractual or tort liability in case of loss or damage to the work in process or injury caused to others by materials or fabrication/installation activities may wish to avail himself of the limited liability of the corporate form, at least with regard to the non-conceptual aspects of the artist's services.

Some artists have joined together in corporate or partnership form to produce collaborative works of public art and, in an increasing number of cases, artists' tax situations will suggest the appropriateness of using a corporation to carry out the bulk of a complicated public art project. Since the decision of whether, or how, to use a corporation to participate in a public art project will depend on the circumstances, the Model Agreement does not suggest any apportionment of services between an artist and a corporation to fulfill the artist's role in the project described in the Model Agreement.

2. An artist's role as a subcontractor. A major public or private construction project will delegate to the architect, engineer, general contractor or landscape architect of the entire project the task of selecting and integrating into the project design a significant work of fine art by an outside artist. In such cases, the artist is customarily retained as a consultant under a contract entered into between the artist and the architect, engineer or landscape architect, which contract is made subject to the various prior agreements in force between the overall project developer and the professional retaining the artist. Although the structure of such a contract will vary from the Model Agreement, many of the issues reflected in the Model Agreement annotations will be relevant.

3. The commissioning body's active involvement in implementing the artist's design. Some public art projects have involved commitments of resources (materials, labor, organization and scheduling) beyond those available to the artist retained to conceive the work of art. In such instances, the role of the artist (or the artist's corporation) is often limited to one of conception, design, site supervision and consultation to insure that the construction of the art work conforms to the artist's design; preparation of the site, acquisition and transportation of materials, and supervision of installation labor are essentially performed by the commissioning body. Such a situation may be vastly simpler, or substantially more complicated, than the prototypical public art project described in the Model Agreement.

Even the simple "model" public art situation posited here must contain alternative texts for certain items, such as the system of providing compensation to the artist. The Model Agreement, recognizing the always unique character of the issue of insurance coverage, does not address either the form or the substance of insurance coverage requirements to be imposed on either the commissioning body or the artist.

As indicated above, the Model Agreement incorporates clauses of public art contracts that have already acquired a history in negotiation and utilization. In drafting the Model Agreement, the members of the Committee on Art Law have reviewed numerous commission agreements, discussed the Model Agreement with other lawyers, art administrators and artists, and relied on their own experience and expertise in order to arrive at a balanced agreement which takes into consideration the needs of the artist, the public and the commissioning body. Given the diversity of contemporary public art projects and the varying character and goals of commissioning bodies, it is clear that not every clause in the Model Agreement is essential or appropriate to every situation. Further, some clauses will become elements in the bargaining process, and whether they are included or modified will become largely a function of the price paid for the art work. The clauses placed in brackets are most likely to change as a function of the nature of the work, the nature of the project and the bargaining process.

It should be kept in mind that there is no substitute for sound legal advice, and that the Model Agreement has been drafted only for use by or in conjunction with an attorney. The Committee would be most interested in receiving comments and experiences from readers, especially those who have used the Model Agreement in negotiating a commission for a work of public art. Comments and experiences should be directed to Barbara Hoffman, c/o Committee on Art Law, The Association of the Bar of the City of New York, 42 West 44th Street, New York, New York 10036.

The Committee would like to express its gratitude to those who took time to comment on the Agreement, as well as to the law firm of Paul, Weiss, Rifkind, Wharton & Garrison, which provided crucial word processor support for this project.

Committee on Art Law, The Association of the Bar of the City of New York, Neale M. Albert, Chair, Barbara Hoffman, Chair, Subcommittee on Public Art—Stanley M. Ackert III,* Robert Anthoine, Elizabeth D. Bauman, Catherine A. Bostron,* Ronald Wellington Brown, Tatyana Doughty, Robert A. Feldman, Gary N. Horowitz, Ricky Dale Horton, Theodore N. Kaplan, Barry Mitchell Koch, Gregory K. Marks, Edward C. Marschner,* Steven B. Miller, Rex W. Mixon, Jr., Hanno D. Mott, Robert L. Poster, Susan Berggren Rothschild, Arlene Shuler, William S. Sterns III, Beverly M. Wolff, Carl L. Zanger.

---

* Member, Subcommittee on Public Art.

FORM 9.06-1 Agreement for Commission of Public Art Work

AGREEMENT BY AND BETWEEN THE CITY OF .... AND ....

THIS AGREEMENT, entered into this .... day of ...., 20.., by and between the City of .... (the "City"), acting by and through the .... Art Commission (the "Commission") and .... (the "Artist") residing at ....

WHEREAS, the City is implementing a public art program pursuant to [local ordinance or funding source] by allocating certain funds for the establishment of artworks in public places and authorizing the making of payments for the design, execution, fabrication, transportation and installation of works of art and the support of an artist-selection process; and

WHEREAS, [City Department] percent-for-art funds have been allocated for the selection, purchase and placement of art work; and

WHEREAS, the Artist was selected by the City through the procedures duly adopted by the Arts Commission to design, execute, fabricate and install a [three-dimensional] work of art (the "Work") in a public space located at [locality] described as set forth in Exhibit .... hereto (the "Site"); and

WHEREAS, both parties wish to promote and maintain the integrity and clarity of the Artist's ideas and statements as represented by the Work;

NOW, THEREFORE, the City and the Artist, for the consideration and under the conditions hereinafter set forth, agree as follows:

Article 1. Scope of Services.

1. 1 *General*

a. The Artist shall perform all services and furnish all supplies, material and equipment as necessary for the design, execution, fabrication, transportation and installation of the Work at the Site.

b. The Artist shall determine the artistic expression, scope, design, color, size, material, texture, [and location on the Site] of the Work, subject to review and acceptance by the City as set forth in this Agreement.

Annotation

Paragraph (a) of this Section describes the more tangible aspects of the Artist's services. If the Artist is to perform only some, and not all, of these services, the interaction between the Artist and others should be specified. For example, this provision could define the roles of the architects, engineers or landscape architects retained by the commissioning body and the manner in which the commissioning body will assure that those professionals coordinate effectively with the Artist to avoid delay or confusion.

Similarly, if any of the supplies, material, equipment, fabrication, transportation or installation work is to be provided by the commissioning body or agents or contractors designated by it (or by another participant in the project), the respective roles of all participants should be clearly defined and linked.

A provision like paragraph (b) reserves to the Artist the artistic, aesthetic aspects of the services, subject in each instance to the review and acceptance prerogatives of the commissioning body. The Model Agreement includes location on the Site as one of the artistic elements. While the Site will be predetermined by the commissioning body, artists are increasingly being asked to collaborate in the design of the space for their artwork. For example, the design for New York's 3-1/2-acre waterfront plaza project at Battery Park City was a collaborative effort among the architect Cesar Pelli, landscape architect M. Paul Friedberg, and artists Siah Armajani and Scott Burton. " 'We wanted to redefine the traditional role of artist and architect in the design of public spaces,' said Richard A. Kahan, Chairman of the Battery Park City Authority. 'We wanted artists to actually design space and not be assigned spaces in which to do pieces of art.' " N.Y. Times, Dec. 1, 1983, at C28.

1.2 *Proposal*

a. As promptly as possible after the execution of this Agreement, the Artist shall carry out such reasonable site inspections, interviews and research as may be necessary, including meetings with the [City Department] and the project architect, in order to prepare a design proposal for the Work (the "Proposal"). The City shall make available to the Artist the necessary background materials and information on matters affecting the Site and installation of the Work including, where applicable, a written program of requirements and specifications for the Work and the plans for the underlying capital project (the "Project"). It is the intent of the parties that the City and the Artist shall establish a close and cooperative consultation throughout the duration of this Agreement.

b. The City will arrange for the Artist to meet with representatives of the community in order for the Artist to learn of their concerns.

c. [If the inspections, interviews, research and meetings provided for in paragraphs (a) and (b) require more than [three (3)] trips by the Artist to the [locality] before approval of the Proposal, the City shall promptly reimburse the Artist's reasonable expenses for travel and lodging on additional trips.]

d. Within ninety (90) days after the execution of this Agreement, the Artist shall prepare and submit the Proposal to the City. The Proposal shall specify such materials, dimensions, weight, finish and preliminary maintenance recommendations and proposed installation method and include such [drawings and other documents and models] as are required to present a meaningful representation of the concept and design of the proposed Work. [The Proposal shall include a budget, not to exceed $ . . . ., that includes estimated costs for design, execution, fabrication, transportation and installation and the Artist's fee.]

e. The City shall, within thirty (30) days following the next regularly scheduled Commission meeting after the Artist's submission of the Proposal, notify the

Artist whether it approves or disapproves the Proposal. During this period the Artist shall be available as reasonably required to meet with the City to discuss the Proposal.

f. If the City shall determine that the Proposal is disapproved, it shall provide the Artist with a statement in writing of its reasons for such disapproval. In such event, the Artist shall be afforded an opportunity either to submit a second Proposal for the Work within a reasonable period of time specified by the City, or to terminate this Agreement. Within thirty (30) days following such submission by the Artist, the City shall notify the Artist in writing whether it approves or disapproves the Proposal. If the City shall determine that the second Proposal is disapproved, it shall provide the Artist with a statement in writing of its reasons for disapproval, whereupon this Agreement shall terminate.

g. In the event of termination of this Agreement pursuant to paragraph (f), the Artist shall retain the Proposals and all compensation theretofore paid and neither party shall be under any further obligation to the other in respect of the subject matter thereof.

Annotation

The most important practical contribution of a written contract for public art is found here: the clear, step-by-step description of the process for the conception and approval of the design of the proposed Work.

Experience suggests that the following elements should receive special attention:

(a) The need for close cooperation and a full exchange of information regarding the Site, the Project, all scheduling and the respective roles of all participants in the Project. To the extent possible, the Model Agreement attempts to provide close interaction between the architect and the Artist and, where appropriate, a true collaboration in the design process at the earliest time.

(b) The manner in which the Artist is expected to familiarize himself with community and user concerns. Any specific representations regarding the way in which those concerns are to be reflected in the proposed Work should be stated here. Much of the public controversy surrounding public art has occurred because of inadequate communication between the Artist and his clients, i.e., the Commission, the relevant City Department and the community. One of the unresolved issues in public art is the definition of that community. Since much contemporary art is based on an iconography that is not widely shared, it is suggested that only with public involvement and participation from inception to dedication can the art become accessible to the public it serves. The success of public art must be related, in part, to the power of art work to generate public response and a dialogue over its meaning. The public should be invited to experience and discuss a given project.

(c) The number of visits to the Site the Artist is obligated to make when engaged in studying and preparing a creative proposal. At this stage, he should not be required to spend inordinate time and resources in repeated meetings and trips to a distant city. A provision for the commissioning body to bear the expenses incurred by the Artist (or even to pay a per them for his time), beyond an agreed reasonable number of meetings and trips, would be normal.

(d) The content of the Proposal to be submitted. The commissioning body may wish to develop a standard proposal format. A Proposal can be a simple paragraph describing the Work, or it can be an elaborate combination of budget, three-dimensional scale model, engineering drawings, artist's renderings, environmental impact statements, and other expensive features designed to assist the commissioning body in presenting the Proposal to its own constituents (e.g., a city council, a corporate board of directors, or a community hearing). For the usual public art project, the initial Proposal includes merely schematic drawings (not drawn to scale), perhaps a simple maquette for three-dimensional works and, as regards a budget, rough estimates of materials costs, labor expense, and transportation, installation and insurance costs, with the remainder of the total estimated compensation allocated as the so-called "Artist's fee."

It should be kept in mind that the Proposal submitted is the complete focus of the approval process. This means that the finished Work must faithfully reflect the Proposal unless the areas of subsequent creative leeway reserved for the Artist are clearly reflected in the Proposal itself.

It is extremely useful for the commissioning body and for the Artist that the Proposal include a written description of the aspects of the Proposal that may change as fabrication and installation go forward. For example, the Proposal should, if appropriate, contain a caveat that the colors, texture, dimensions, materials and scale of the finished Work may depart significantly from those indicated in the Proposal. Providing such a caveat permits both parties to avoid disagreements in the future regarding elements of the Work that the commissioning body deems to be essential to its approval of the Proposal. The Artist should also specify in his Proposal any elements of the Work he considers as integral elements which may not be readily apparent to the commissioning body, such as lighting for the Work or Site.

(e) The need for a reasonable period of time for the commissioning body to consider the Proposal. The commissioning body is required to state in writing its acceptance or disapproval of the Proposal and, in the case of disapproval, to specify its reasons. The time allotted for consideration of the Proposal by the commissioning body will depend on how unwieldy the commissioning body's internal procedures are. The Model Agreement contemplates an active art commission with a regular schedule of meetings to review proposals for public art projects. In other circumstances, a fixed time period of 30, 60 or 90 days is usually adopted, so that the Artist will not be left waiting for a response to a Proposal in which he has invested a great deal of time and expense.

(f) The course of events if the Proposal is disapproved. In the event of disapproval of the Proposal, the Artist is offered a second (and sometimes third) opportunity to resubmit either the same Proposal or an entirely new Proposal to take account of the reasons for the earlier refusal. Usually the time periods for the Artist's submission of the revised Proposal, and for the commissioning body's review of it, are shorter than the time periods provided for the initial submission.

Unless the Artist has received an installment on his fee at the time of submission of the initial Proposal, the Artist during this period is working from the initial installment of compensation. This means that he will have to anticipate, while preparing the first

Proposal, that he may have to go through the time and expense of preparing a second Proposal if the first is refused. The Artist should have the right to decline to prepare a second Proposal, thereby causing termination of the agreement, if he feels that it would be too costly or that, based on the reasons stated by the commissioning body in its refusal, a new Proposal would not be accepted either. The commissioning body should not have the right to prevent a second Proposal, but it should not be required to spend a very long period of time waiting for it and then reviewing it, since the commissioning body may wish to offer the public art project to another artist if it finds the first Proposal entirely unacceptable.

(g) The consequences of acceptance and refusal of the Proposal at each step should be clearly set forth.

1.3 *Structural Design Review.*

a. Within .... days after the City approves the Proposal, the Artist shall[, after consultation and collaboration with the project architect,] prepare and submit to the City detailed working drawings of the Work and the Site, together with such other graphic material as may reasonably be requested by the City in order to permit the City to carry out structural design review and to certify the compliance of the Work with applicable statutes and ordinances. Upon request by the Artist, the City [and the project architect] shall promptly furnish all information, materials and assistance required by the Artist in connection with said submission.

b. The City may require the Artist to make such revisions to the Proposal as are necessary for the Work to comply with applicable statutes, ordinances or regulations of any governmental regulatory agency having jurisdiction over the project.

c. The City may also request revisions for other practical (nonaesthetic) reasons.

d. The Artist's fee shall be equitably adjusted for any increase or decrease in the Artist's cost of, or time required for, performance of any services under this Agreement as a result of revisions made under this Section 1.3. Any claim of the Artist for adjustment under this paragraph must be asserted in writing within thirty (30) days after the date of the revision by the Artist.

e. Within .... days after its receipt of the Artist's submission pursuant to this Section 1.3, the City shall notify the Artist of its approval (or disapproval) of such submission and of all revisions made in the Proposal as a result thereof. Revisions made pursuant to this Section 1.3 become a part of the Proposal.

Annotation

It is time consuming and expensive for an Artist to prepare the initial Proposal. It is usually too burdensome to ask the Artist at that stage, when the Proposal has not yet been accepted even in principle, to engage the additional expense involved in preparing engineering drawings drawn to scale, so as to permit the commissioning body to evaluate in detail the problems of integration of the Work into the Site and to coordinate the installation work with schedules for site preparation and other adjacent construction.

The Model Agreement reflects the common requirement that such detail work be reserved for after approval of the Proposal, when the Artist has presumably received a second installment of his fee to help him meet the expenses of detailed planning.

The compensation provisions of the Agreement should be generous enough in the early installments to permit the Artist to pay his professional architect and engineer advisors for their services in preparing detailed drawings.

The schedule for submissions of detailed drawings and specifications should clearly delineate the deadlines to be respected by both the Artist and the commissioning body.

The consultation with the project architect initiated in the preliminary design phase should continue. In projects where the commissioning body will be primarily responsible for implementing construction of the Work, the Artist will not be responsible for the preparation of detailed structural drawings, but will only be required to approve the documents prepared by the engineer and architect to assure that the final construction conforms to his design.

1.4 *Execution of the Work*

a. After written approval of the submissions and revisions made pursuant to Section 1.3, the Artist shall furnish to the City a tentative schedule for completion of fabrication and installation of the Work, including a schedule for the submission of progress reports, if any. After written approval of the schedule by the City, the Artist shall fabricate, transport and install the Work in accordance with such schedule. Such schedule may be amended by written agreement between the City and the Artist.

b. The City shall have the right to review the Work at reasonable times during the fabrication thereof. The Artist shall submit to the City progress reports in accordance with the schedule provided for in Section 1.4(a).

c. The Artist shall complete the fabrication and installation of the Work in substantial conformity with the Proposal.

d. The Artist shall present to the City in writing for further review and approval any significant changes in the scope, design, color, size, material or texture of the Work not permitted by or not in substantial conformity with the Proposal. A significant change is any change in the scope, design, color, size, material, texture or location on the Site of the Work which affects installation, scheduling, site preparation or maintenance for the Work or the concept of the Work as represented in the Proposal.

Annotation

The importance of the completion schedule referred to in paragraph (a) above cannot be overemphasized. Any time parameters within which the schedule must fit should be clearly specified in the commission agreement. All other parties involved (such as the architect) should be consulted in the formulation of the schedule. The Artist should send copies of the schedule to all parties involved.

Many commissioning bodies will not require written progress reports or the right to visit the Work during fabrication, as provided in paragraph (b). If requested, however, these are reasonable requirements if they do not so unduly burden the Artist as to delay his completion of the Work.

Paragraphs (c) and (d) reflect the need for leeway to the Artist as the creative process goes forward, while assuring the commissioning body that the Proposal is executed as approved. The Artist must execute the Work in substantial conformity with the Proposal. Minor changes as the Work progresses are permitted; however, significant changes which affect installation scheduling, site preparation and maintenance for the Work and the concept of the Work require further written approval of the commissioning body.

An example of the type of controversy with which paragraphs (c) and (d) are concerned is that surrounding the creation of a public art commission in San Francisco in 1981. Robert Arneson was chosen in a competitive process to execute a bust of the assassinated Mayor George Moscone for the Moscone Convention Center. All of the nationally known artists who competed were asked to submit a sketch "sufficiently detailed so that judgment can be made." Arneson's preliminary design showed a broadly smiling head on an unadorned pedestal. In the final work, the artist embellished the pedestal with biographical notes. Most controversial were the imprinting of a Smith and Wesson revolver, bloodlike splatters of red glaze, and the inscription "Twinkie," referring to a novel defense raised by the assassin. There was uniform approval of the design and execution of the portrait likeness, but strong criticism regarding the references to the murder and the murderer's defense. The Art Commission rejected the work as inappropriate to the site after receiving a letter from Mayor Feinstein stating that Arneson's pedestal did not reflect the "spirit of non-violence to which the City committed itself when it claimed for itself the name of St. Francis." Mayor Feinstein also argued that "an artist must be held accountable to his or her maquette" and that there must be "assurance that guidelines will not be spurned and standards disregarded." Arneson, upon advice of counsel, returned the compensation he had received for the commission. The bust was returned to him and subsequently sold to a private collector. Controversial Public Art from Rodin to di Suvero, Milwaukee Art Museum, 1983.

The Model Agreement seeks to provide a mechanism for resolving the type of controversy raised by the Arneson situation by delimiting the creative discretion to be allowed the Artist after approval of the Proposal. In this connection, Arneson might have noted in his Proposal the nature of his previous work, and that the spirit of that work often evoked social and political commentary which would be an integral part of the Work not subject to subsequent review by the commissioning body. Finally, to the extent possible, all parties should refrain from actions which inhibit the Artist in reaching creative solutions to the design problems the Artist has been commissioned to solve. The Artist, on his part, must be sensitive to the unique qualities of public art and to the guidelines and parameters upon which the parties have agreed.

1.5 *Delivery and Installation.*

a. The Artist shall notify the City in writing when fabrication of the Work is completed and he is ready for its delivery and installation at the Site.

b. The Artist shall deliver and install the completed Work at the Site in compliance with the schedule approved pursuant to Section 1.4.

c. The City shall be responsible for all expenses, labor and equipment to prepare the Site for the timely installation of the Work, including landscaping, footings, plumbing, public access, public security, and area and spot lighting of the Work.

Annotation

Where the size or scope of the Work or the fee compensation schedule make it appropriate, final approval of the fabricated Work, as being in conformity with the Proposal should be made before delivery and installation, in order to facilitate modifications in design and avoid unnecessary costs of transportation and installation. When the commissioning body is responsible for site preparation, the Artist should coordinate closely with it to ascertain that the Site is prepared to receive the Work.

In those projects in which the Artist is a member of the design team and the Work is constructed on the Site as an integral part of the environment, a more detailed description of the Artist's role in site supervision, construction and installation may be provided.

1.6 *Post-Installation.*

a. Within days after the installation of the Work, the Artist shall furnish the City with the following photographs of the Work as installed:

(i) two sets of three 35 mm. color slides of the completed Work, one taken from each of three different viewpoints;

(ii) two sets of three different 8" × 10" glossy black and white prints of the Work and negatives; and

(iii) a set of three color transparencies of the completed Work.

b. At the City's expense, the Artist shall be available at such time or times as may be agreed between the City and the Artist to attend any inauguration or presentation ceremonies relating to the transfer of the Work to the City. The City shall use its best efforts to arrange for publicity for the completed Work in such art publications and otherwise as may be determined between the City and the Artist as soon as practicable following installation.

c. Upon installation of the Work, the Artist shall provide to the City written instructions for appropriate maintenance and preservation of the Work.

Annotation

Public art projects usually require photographic documentation for archival purposes. The photographic documentation requested will, of course, depend on the requirements of the commissioning body. In rare instances it may be more appropriate to require the commissioning body to pay for and provide for photographic documentation.

Paragraph (b) of this section continues the dialogue previously encouraged between the community and the Artist. Even with a work conceived, approved and installed, the dialogue is not complete. The dedication often sets the tone for initial public reaction and, to the extent that the Work may evoke controversy, the Artist should be a participant in the debate.

The Artist should specify any special requirements for maintaining and preserving the Work. This section should be read in conjunction with the warranty section of Article 4 and the section on maintenance in Article 7.

1.7 *Final Acceptance.*

a. The Artist shall advise the City in writing when all services required prior to those described in Section 1.6(b) have been completed in substantial conformity with the Proposal.

b. The City shall notify the Artist of its final acceptance of the Work.

c. Final acceptance shall be effective as of the earlier to occur of (1) the date of the City's notification of final acceptance or (2) the 30th day after the Artist has sent the written notice to the City required under Section 1.7(a) unless the City, upon receipt of such notice and prior to the expiration of the 30-day period, gives the Artist written notice specifying and describing the services which have not been completed.

Annotation

The purpose of this provision is to provide a method of determining with some degree of certainty when the Work has been finally accepted by the commissioning body, since this a signal event for the creating or shifting of obligations between the parties. Final acceptance is usually referred to in the Section 2.1 schedule of payments due the Artist; it is expressly referred to in the succeeding Sections 1.8 through 1.11 as a factor in determining title, ownership of documents, risk of loss and indemnity.

While the mechanism for final acceptance starts with the assumption that the commissioning body will, in due course, notify the Artist of its acceptance of the Work, it also recognizes that the Artist necessarily exercises an artistic judgment as to when the Work is complete, and that the Artist should therefore initiate the acceptance process.

Final acceptance is based upon completion of the artistic services referred to generally under Section 1.1. Failure to complete or comply with obligations or requirements under the contract which are independent of and clearly ancillary to the performance of the artistic services should not provide grounds for denial of final acceptance. Thus, failure to have obtained a performance bond, if required, should not prevent final acceptance once performance is completed.

However, final acceptance could be reasonably conditioned upon the Artist's certification that all obligations incurred by the Artist, pursuant to Section 1.1, for "supplies, material and equipment as necessary for the design, execution and installation of the Work" have been fully satisfied. Since final acceptance triggers a general indemnity, the commissioning body may wish to add to the agreement a provision requiring the Artist either to disclose any outstanding or disputed claims against the Artist arising out of the Work, or to certify that no such claims exist. Such a provision would go further than the general warranty against liens contained in Section 4.1(d). Since not all claims become liens, the commissioning body might be subject to nuisance suits brought by individuals who have provided materials or services to the Artist, the warranty of Section 4.1(d) notwithstanding.

1.8 *Risk of Loss.* The risk of loss or damage to the Work shall be borne by the Artist until final acceptance, and the Artist shall take such measures as are necessary to protect the Work from loss or damage until final acceptance; except that the risk of loss or damage shall be borne by the City prior to final acceptance during such periods of time as the partially or wholly completed Work is in the custody, control or supervision of the City or its agents for the purposes of transporting, storing, installing or performing any other ancillary services to the Work.

Annotation

This provision sets forth the standard practice of leaving the risk of loss or damage to the work-in-progress with the Artist until final acceptance. The question of insurance for loss or damage is one which is left entirely to the Artist's judgment under the circumstances.

It is recognized, however, that the Artist increasingly functions as an element of a larger project, and that portions of the Artist's work may have to be performed outside the confines of the studio. Site preparation, transportation, storage and installation may be responsibilities undertaken by the Artist, but they are often performed by the commissioning body or its agencies and contractors. Under these circumstances, while the Work is substantially removed from the Artist's continuing dominion and control the risk of loss will shift accordingly.

The *force majeure* provision under Section 3.4 contemplates only an extension of time for performance in the event that the Work is damaged or destroyed; however, substantial damage or destruction of the Work may permit either party to invoke the termination provisions of Article 10.

1.9 *Indemnity.* Upon final acceptance of the Work, the City shall, to the extent permitted by law, indemnify and hold harmless the Artist against any and all claims or liabilities then existing or arising thereafter in connection with the Work, the Site, the Project or this Agreement, except claims by the City against the Artist and claims which may occur as a result of the Artist's breach of the warranties provided in Article 4.

Annotation

This provision may vary depending upon the statutory limitations affecting the ability of state or municipal agencies and bodies to enter into indemnity agreements.

This section is keyed to the final acceptance process. The possibility that the commissioning body may find itself indemnifying the Artist against the claims for the Artist's suppliers and subcontractors is reduced considerably if final acceptance is conditioned upon certification by the Artist that all such underlying claims, liens and encumbrances have, been or will be satisfied. Similarly, bonding and insurance provisions may be included in the agreement to protect against such claims.

1. 10 *Title.* Title to the Work shall pass to the City upon final acceptance.

1.11 *Ownership of Documents, Models.* Upon final acceptance, all studies, drawings, designs, maquettes and models prepared and submitted under this Agreement shall be returned to the Artist and shall belong to the Artist. The City may select and the Artist shall convey to the City [one] of the original drawings submitted pursuant to Section 1.2 as part of the Proposal, the City representing that such drawing(s) will be used by it solely for exhibition and held by it in permanent safekeeping.

Annotation

Most public art commissions give ownership of all maquettes, drawings and other designs prepared in connection with the commission to the Artist. One notable exception is the present General Services Administration Art in Architecture Contract, where such items are retained by the government for the National Museum of American Art of the Smithsonian Institution.

It generally should not be presumed that the commissioning body has purchased the maquettes and models. At best, the artist usually only breaks even financially on public art commissions, and the ability to sell the maquettes, sketches, drawings, etc., produced in connection with the project often provides an essential source of income.

In many respects the artist as a provider of design services can be analogized to the architect. The American Institute of Architects standard form owner-architect contract provides that all drawings, models and maquettes remain the property of the architect, but gives the owner the right to copies of the drawings and plans.

The commissioning body and the public do have legitimate interests in documenting the history and evolution of the Work. In those instances in which the commissioning body intends to exhibit the sketches and keep them for documentation and archival purposes, the second sentence in Section 1.11 may be added.

The exact language should be keyed to the specific requirements adopted for the Proposal. In some circumstances the commissioning body may wish to negotiate for ownership of all drawings, maquettes and models prepared and submitted in connection with the Proposal. This may be appropriate when museum and other exhibition spaces are available.

In certain exceptional situations, the commissioning body may require acquisition of all drawings and maquettes prepared and submitted in connection with the Proposal as part of the fixed Artist's fee. This position may not be justified if the only intention of the commissioning body is resale. In no event should the commissioning body, without further adjustment in price, obtain ownership of documents prepared by the Artist subsequent to the Proposal.

The question of ownership of the documents under this Section does not affect copyright in the sketches, models and maquettes, which remains with the Artist, except as modified in Article 6. The commissioning body may wish to retain the right to the photographic reproduction of the Proposal for public information and exhibition purposes.

Article 2. Compensation and Payment Schedule.

2.1 *Fixed Fee.* The City shall pay the Artist a fixed fee of $............. , which shall constitute full compensation for all services and materials to be performed and furnished by the Artist under this Agreement. The fee shall be paid in the following installments, expressed as percentages of such fixed fee, each installment to represent full and final, nonrefundable payment for all services and materials provided prior to the due date thereof:

a. . . . . percent (%) upon the execution of this Agreement, recognizing that the Artist has already invested time and expense in preliminary design coordination with the City and other interested parties;

b. . . . . percent (%) within ten (10) days after the City notifies the Artist of its approval of the Proposal;

c. . . . . percent (%) within ten (10) days after the City notifies the Artist of its approval of the submission of detailed working drawings required under Section 1.3.

d. . . . . percent (%) within ten (10) days after the Artist notifies the City that the Work is fabricated and ready for installation at the Site.

e. . . . . percent (%) within ten (10) days after final acceptance.

Annotation

This traditional installment system for payment of compensation usually contemplates payments of a percent of a fixed fee upon readily defined dates such as the following: the execution of the agreement, submission of the Proposal, notice of approval of the Proposal, submission of detail drawings, arrival of materials at the Artist's fabrication facilities or at the Site, notice by the Artist that installation is ready to begin, similar notice that installation is completed, and final acceptance.

If reasonable persons may differ as to the occurrence of a specified event, the installment should be payable upon notice given to one or the other that the event has occurred, or the definition of the occurrence should be modified to make it readily determinable in an objective manner. For example, installments should be paid on completion of defined phases, not when the work is "half complete."

In public art projects where the commissioning body and the Artist are sharing the expense of materials or labor, the installments are sometimes calculated and paid ratably as the expenses of materials and labor are incurred. This is done either on a percentage basis or dollar-for-dollar against vouchers for expenses incurred or soon to be incurred for materials and labor.

In some commissions, particularly in those in which the Artist is retained as a design consultant, the Artist will receive a fee for design and supervision, with out-of-pocket expenses paid against vouchers and all other costs of construction, installation, insurance and the like paid for by the commissioning body.

2.2 *Sales Taxes.* Any sales, use or excise taxes, or similar charges relating to services and materials shall be paid by the City.

2.3 *Artist's Expenses.* The Artist shall be responsible for the payment of all mailing or shipping charges on submissions to the City, the costs of transporting the Work to the Site and the costs of all travel by the Artist and the Artist's agents and employees necessary for the proper performance of the services required under this Agreement.

Annotation

Sections 2.2 and 2.3 merely allocate those related expenses which are reimbursable to the Artist and those which are costs to be paid from the fixed fee.

Alternative Article 2

Article 2. Compensation and Payment Schedule.

2.1 *Preliminary Design Proposal.* Upon the execution of this Agreement by the City, the City shall pay to the Artist an initial fee of $ .... for the preparation of the Proposal as set forth in Section 1.2. The initial fee may be retained by the Artist, and no part of it shall be refunded, provided the Artist submits the Proposal to the City as provided in Section 1.2(c). If the Proposal is not so submitted, the City may by notice to the Artist require the initial fee to be refunded to the City, whereupon this Agreement shall terminate and there shall be no further obligations between the parties.

2.2 *Further Agreement.* Acceptance of the Proposal shall be contingent upon agreement between the City and the Artist upon a second fee, not expected to exceed $ .... for execution, fabrication, transportation and installation of the Work.

2.3 *Addendum.* The payments for the Artist's services for the execution, fabrication, transportation and installation of the Work shall be made at intervals specified by addendum to this Agreement, signed by the Artist and the City, upon approval of the Proposal by the City.

[Sections 2.2 and 2.3 of usual Article 2 become Sections 2.4 and 2.5 if this Alternative Article 2 is used.]

Annotation

The alternative compensation language is offered for situations in which the scale and cost of the final project will not be known until after the Proposal is approved.

In this circumstance, it is usual to pay the Artist for preparing the Proposal and to postpone until after acceptance of the Proposal the fixing of the further fee due to the Artist (or a fabrication and installation corporation designated by him) for completion of the post-approval aspects of the project.

The disadvantage of this approach is the uncertainty of a commitment of either the Artist or the commissioning body to proceed with the project even after a Proposal is approved, since later negotiations over compensation and scheduling may sometimes defeat an otherwise worthwhile project.

Article 3. Time of Performance.

3.1 *Duration.* The services to be required of the Artist as set forth in Article 1 shall be completed in accordance with the schedule for completion of the Work as proposed by the Artist and approved by the City pursuant to Section 1.4, provided that such time limits may be extended or otherwise modified by written agreement between the Artist and the City.

3.2 *Construction Delays.* If, when the Artist completes fabrication or procurement of the Work in accordance with the approved schedule and notifies the City that the Work is ready for installation, the Artist is delayed from installing the Work within the time specified in the schedule as a result of the construction of the Site not being sufficiently complete reasonably to permit installation of the Work therein, the City shall promptly reimburse the Artist for reasonable transportation and storage costs incurred for the period between the time provided in the schedule for commencement of installation and the date upon which the Site is sufficiently complete reasonably to permit installation of the Work.

3.3 *Early Completion of Artist Services.* The Artist shall bear any transportation and storage costs resulting from the completion of his services hereunder prior to the time provided in the schedule for installation.

3.4 *Time Extensions.* The City shall always grant a reasonable extension of time to the Artist in the event that there is a delay on the part of the City in performing its obligations under this Agreement or in completing the underlying capital project, or if conditions beyond the Artist's control or Acts of God render timely performance of the Artist's services impossible or unexpectedly burdensome. Failure to fulfill contractual obligations due to conditions beyond either party's reasonable control will not be considered a breach of contract; provided that such obligations shall be suspended only for the duration of such conditions.

Annotation

The provisions of the Model Agreement providing for careful coordination of schedules between the commissioning body and the Artist, and responsibility for the coordination with other participants in related work, cannot be over-emphasized. More unsuccessful public art projects have come to grief through poor coordination than for any other reason.

The Model Agreement attempts to provide rigor in the establishment of a schedule and equitable flexibility in the procedures for maintaining communication necessary to modify the schedule as required. The objective is the maintenance of cooperation to ensure that the Work will be realized.

Article 4. Warranties.

4.1 *Warranties of Title.* The Artist represents and warrants that: (a) the Work is solely the result of the artistic effort of the Artist; (b) except as otherwise disclosed in writing to the City, the Work is unique and original and does not infringe upon any copyright; (c) that the Work, or a duplicate thereof, has not been accepted for sale elsewhere; and (d) the Work is free and clear of any liens from any source whatever.

4.2 *Warranties of Quality and Condition.* The Artist represents and warrants, except as otherwise disclosed to the City in writing in connection with submission of the Proposal pursuant to Section 1.2, that: (a) the execution and fabrication of the Work will be performed in a workmanlike manner; (b) the Work, as fabricated and installed, will be free of defects in material and workmanship, including any defects consisting of "inherent vice" or qualities which cause or accelerate deterioration of the Work; and (c) reasonable maintenance of the Work will not require procedures substantially in excess of those described in the maintenance recommendations to be submitted by the Artist to the City hereunder.

The warranties described in this Section 4.2 shall survive for a period of one year after the final acceptance of the Work. The City shall give notice to the Artist of any observed breach with reasonable promptness. The Artist shall, at the request of the City, and at no cost to the City, cure reasonably and promptly the breach of any such warranty which is curable by the Artist and which cure is consistent with professional conservation standards (including, for example, cure by means of repair or refabrication of the Work).

Annotation

Section 4.1 recognizes that the Artist is responsible for assuring that the Work is original and free of liens, does not infringe any copyright and has not previously been sold.

Section 4.2 reflects the Artist's responsibility for fabricating the Work in quality materials, in accordance with professional, "workmanlike" standards and with a sensitivity to the nature and longterm behavior of materials and methods used, the conservation goals of the commissioning body and the conditions of the installation site (including weather, temperature, type and density of audience, and other environmental and architectural features of the site).

By permitting written disclosure of factors at odds with these concerns, and excluding such disclosed factors from the Artist's warranties, the Agreement also recognizes that the Artist's aesthetic choices and goals may sometimes be antithetical to—and of paramount importance to—concerns of maintenance and conservation. For example, the Artist may choose to work with materials that are intended to change in appearance over time or exposure to the elements, or the Artist may wish to try experimental techniques and materials that do not age in a traditional way or the conservation impact of which is not yet fully known. Such inventiveness should not be discouraged so long as these artistic choices are disclosed at a time when the commissioning body can make an informed evaluation of the impact of such choices on the standard warranties, i.e., upon submission of the Proposal pursuant to Section 1.2.

The Artist's warranties relating to defects and "inherent vice" (a term used by conservators to describe a quality of a work of art which causes or accelerates physical deterioration of the work) are particularly important to a potential owner of an art work in view of the fact that most standard fine arts insurance policies will not cover damage or loss of value sustained as a result of a defect or inherent vice in a work. Defects in design and materials can result in a decrease or total loss in value of the art work, expenses for conservation work to rectify defects, and even liability for personal injury.

Costs of conservation and maintenance undertaken as a result of normal "wear and tear" on an art work are also not reimbursable under an insurance policy but are rather continuing expenses of upkeep of a work. A purchaser of a commissioned art work should be aware of any extraordinary conservation procedures or any high-cost maintenance factors.

The Artist's warranties relating to the condition and quality of the Work are limited to a period of one year, since most instances in which serious defects have become evident in public art have occurred within that time. The length of the warranty should, however, be set in light of the nature of the Work, the type of materials and methods used with respect to the Work, the conservation record relating to similar works, the period of time during which defects are likely to manifest themselves, the cost of the Work and the potential liability involved.

The Artist is required to cure, at the request of the commissioning body, defects resulting from substandard workmanship, if such cure is consistent with professional conservation standards.

If a breach of a warranty is not curable by the Artist, the Artist may then be responsible for reimbursing the commissioning body for damages, expenses and loss incurred by the commissioning body as a result of a breach of or inaccuracy in a warranty or representation.

Other responsibilities, warranties and remedies may arise under applicable law, in addition to those expressly provided for by contract.

In view of the probable importance of conservation considerations to the commissioning body, the limitation on certain of the Artist's warranties and the likely failure of insurance coverage to respond to these issues, it may be desirable for the commissioning body to obtain an independent expert evaluation of the materials and techniques used in the Work prior to acceptance.

Article 5. Insurance

5.1 *General.* [ ]

Annotation

No model clauses are provided with respect to liability insurance, since appropriate provisions would vary greatly in different circumstances, depending on state or local requirements, the size of the project, whether extensive or prolonged fabrication and installation will be performed at the Site, and other factors.

The person who is responsible for obtaining and paying for insurance coverage—whether the Artist, the commissioning body, or another person such as a general contractor, if the project also involves building construction—will also vary, depending on the nature of the activities of the persons involved in the project and the availability and cost of coverage to each such person.

For example, if the Artist is primarily responsible for designing a Work that will be installed by others at the Site, it is unlikely that the Artist would be responsible for obtaining liability insurance coverage.

Normally, insurance would cover claims and losses for both personal injury and property damage arising from performance under the agreement, and would cover subcontractors and employees of the insured. Workmen's compensation insurance and automobile liability insurance, as well as public liability insurance, may also be required.

Regardless of who is responsible for obtaining coverage, each of the other parties among the Artist, the commissioning body, and the landowner, if different, should be named in the policy as an additional insured with respect to the coverage. The party contracting the insurance is usually required to provide a certificate of insurance or other evidence of adequate coverage to the others. Such certificate would also likely provide for at least ten days' prior notice of change or cancellation of the policy.

5.2 Performance Bonds. The Artist shall not be required by the City to post any performance bonds or similar undertakings, and any requirement of any other authority for performance bonds shall be the responsibility of the City.

Annotation

Contractors on usual public works construction projects are routinely required to obtain bonds guaranteeing performance of the contract and proper payment to all subcontractors, materialmen and suppliers. Public art commissions customarily do not require artists to obtain performance bonds; however, when artists are given design responsibility for an entire site, and as projects shift from the isolated art object to artwork integrated with its environment, administrators may feel compelled to request performance bonds.

A recent opinion by a county attorney construed a state statute which required a performance bond for a "work" or "improvement" on public property as including an artwork commissioned for the county jail. The artwork involved extensive on-site construction. The Sacramento Metropolitan Arts Commission had never required a performance bond for an art project with the city but was asked by the county to handle a public art project for it: an aquarium serving as a wall, and a seating area, to be designed by Doug Hadlis as part of a jail construction project. The bond was required because the artist was not known to the county and because the administrator thought the work resembled "construction" rather than "a work of art." The premium cost of the bond was ultimately added to the project budget, relieving the artist of the additional expense.

The Miller Act, 40 U.S.C.A. § 270a, requires a performance bond on all federal construction contracts over $25,000. To avoid this problem in connection with a federal art commission in Seattle, Washington, the project director of the Art Program at the National Oceanic and Atmospheric Agency chose to negotiate professional services contracts rather than construction contracts with the artists involved, even though the projects resembled construction more than studio pieces. An identical contract was used for architects, construction managers, and researchers on the project.

Architects and engineers are typically exempt from bonding requirements. The Oregon Court of Appeals explained, "[s]ince performance of a contract involving esthetic judgment cannot be measured objectively, it would not be reasonable to require an architect to post a performance bond." Mongiovi v. Doerner, 24 Or. App. 639, 546 P.2d 1110, 1113 (1976).

The analogy to the architect is appropriate for the public artist. Since the artist is a provider of professional services which are unique, the performance bond seems unsuitable as a mechanism for assuring performance. The artist's performance is best assured by a contract (such as the Model Agreement) with payments in installments on completion of phases of the project and, if appropriate, an invoice for final payment which is accompanied by a statement from each subcontractor that the financial obligation has either been met in full or has been settled to the subcontractor's satisfaction. If a performance bond is required, it should cover only that percentage of the artist's fee which represents on-site fabrication.

Article 6. Reproduction Rights.

6.1 *General.* The Artist retains all rights under the Copyright Act of 1976, 17 U.S.C. §§ 101 et seq., and all other rights in and to the Work except ownership and possession, except as such rights are limited by this Section 6. 1. In view of the intention that the Work in its final dimension shall be unique, the Artist shall not make any additional exact duplicate, [three]-dimensional reproductions of the final Work, nor shall the Artist grant permission to others to do so except with the written permission of the City. The Artist grants to the City and its assigns an irrevocable license to make two-dimensional reproductions of the Work for non-commercial purposes, including but not limited to reproductions used in advertising, brochures, media publicity, and catalogues or other similar publications, provided that these rights are exercised in a tasteful and professional manner.

6.2 *Notice.* All reproductions by the City shall contain a credit to the Artist and a copyright notice substantially in the following form: © [Artist's name], date of publication.

6.3 *Credit to City.* The Artist shall use his best efforts to give a credit reading substantially, "an original work owned and commissioned by [City]," in any public showing under the Artist's control of reproduction of the Work.

6.4 *Registration.* The City shall at its expense cause to be registered, with the United States Register of Copyrights, a copyright in the Work in the Artist's name.

Annotation

Copyright is a property right which allows the Artist (or one to whom he transfers the right) to prevent unauthorized copying, publishing or other use of his copyrighted work. In effect, the copyright law gives the initial owner of the copyright the exclusive right to reproduce the work and to prepare derivative works.

A new federal copyright law, the Copyright Act of 1976, 17 U.S.C. §§ 101 et seq., became effective in 1978.

Under the new law the owner of the rights protected by copyright is the creator of the work unless the work is a "work made for hire." A work made for hire is defined as (1) "a work prepared by an employee within the scope of his or her employment" or (2) "a work specially ordered or commissioned" for certain uses specified in the statute. 17 U.S.C. § 201(b). A work of art commissioned for a public space would not normally constitute such a use. It is generally accepted, therefore, that the Artist initially owns the copyright in the work. Unless there is a written agreement that transfers the copyright to the purchaser of a work of art, the creator automatically retains the copyright. Not only is copyright completely separate from ownership of a physical work of art, but each of the exclusive rights of copyright can be subdivided.

The Model Agreement does not provide for a blanket assignment of copyright ownership to the commissioning body. A blanket transfer to the commissioning body of copyright control in the Work would give the commissioning body more than it reasonably needs and, more importantly, probably more than it has paid for, given the fact that the Artist's fee is not usually sufficient to reflect compensation for reproduction rights; as noted previously, public commissions are rarely financially rewarding for the Artist. Article 6 of the Model Agreement strikes a balance to permit the commissioning body to utilize reproductions in connection with publicity about the Work, and protects its legitimate interest in not having the Artist reproduce identical works for others. At the same time, the Artist controls the important right to derivative utilization of the Work in ways which do not deprive the commissioning body of the unique quality of its purchase and its potential symbolic effect. The Artist is thus free to use the Work or the themes embodied therein, in future works—an important right for artists developing a continuing body of work.

The image of a work of public art may often become a symbol for a locality. For example, the Alexander Calder piece "La Grande Vitesse" has given a sense of place to the square in Grand Rapids, Michigan, in which it is located, and the image of the sculpture is reproduced on city vehicles and on the mayor's stationery. Article 6 does not prohibit such use, unless such use would interfere with an Artist's trademark or constitute unfair competition with prior works of the Artist.

However, the language of Article 6 prohibits the commissioning body from reproducing the work on tee shirts, post cards and posters, or making other commercial use of the image. Of course, additional language can be negotiated by which the Artist transfers an exclusive or non-exclusive license to the commissioning body, presumably for a royalty or some other additional compensation.

The Oregon Arts Commission in a recently adopted contract provided the following alternative language:

The WORK created under this agreement shall be the property of the CITY. Any rights of copyright shall be in the CITY after completion and transfer of the WORK to the CITY. ARTIST shall deliver a bill of sale or other appropriate evidence of transfer to the CITY of all rights, including copyright, upon payment of ARTIST's fee.

ARTIST shall not make any type of reproductions of the finished work except by written permission of the CITY. However, ARTIST shall have the right to include photographs or other representation of the WORK in ARTIST's portfolio, catalogues or other similar publications, provided there is prominent reference to the fact that the WORK is installed in the building under the CITY's One Percent for Art Program, administered by the Metropolitan Arts Commission. ARTIST shall also have the right to reproduce the maquette for ARTIST's personal collection.

Similarly, the CITY shall not make any type of reproductions of the finished work except by written permission of ARTIST. However, the CITY shall have the right to include photographs or other representation of the WORK in the CITY's portfolio, catalogues or other similar publications, provided there is prominent reference of the fact that the WORK was created by ARTIST.

The rationale raised by the Oregon Arts Commission for this complex transfer and retransfer (which may deprive the Artist of the valuable right to make derivative works) was that the Commission would have the right to proceed against infringing third parties only if it were the copyright holder. While this is correct as a matter of copyright law, the artist would normally have an even more compelling interest in preventing unauthorized reproductions.

Section 6.2 serves to protect the copyright of the Artist by requiring that the appropriate notice appear on all copies of the Work. Further, even if the commissioning body were to breach its agreement and omit the notice, under the Copyright Act of 1976 the omission of notice does not cause the work to fall into the public domain if the notice was left off copies against written instructions (here set forth in the Model Agreement) that the notice appear on the Work. 17 U.S.C. § 405(a)(3).

Registration is not necessary to gain copyright protection but does have important advantages. Registration must occur before an infringement in order to obtain an award of statutory damages and attorneys' fees. If the only rights provided to the commissioning body are those in the Model Agreement, the commissioning body may be unwilling to register the copyright in the Artist's name. Registration by the commissioning body may encourage the Artist to protect his own rights from infringement if statutory damages and attorneys' fees are available.

Section 6.2 should probably be omitted if the Artist retains *all* rights to copyright; in such case, the Artist should register the Work.

Article 7. Artist's Rights.

7.1 *Identification.* The City shall, at its expense, prepare and install at the Site, pursuant to the written instructions and subsequent approval of the Artist, a plaque identifying the Artist, the title of the Work and the year of completion, and shall reasonably maintain such notice in good repair against the ravages of time, vandalism and the elements.

Annotation

Article 7 of the Model Agreement provides for certain limited artist's rights originally found in the civil law doctrines of *droit moral*, or moral rights.

Droit moral is distinct from copyright. Copyright protects the artist's right to exploit a work—a property right. The right of *droit moral* is a personal right protecting an artist's reputation, personality and expression.

Under the doctrine of *droit moral*, the creator of a work of art retains a legally protected interest in the treatment of his work notwithstanding the transfer of ownership. The moral rights doctrine primarily protects two fights: the right of paternity and the right of integrity. The right of paternity is the artist's right to be recognized by the public as the creator of a particular work of art (Section 7.1), and, under certain circumstances, to be able to disclaim authorship. The right of integrity is the right of the artist, even after he relinquishes title to a work, to prevent the alteration, mutilation or distortion of the work [Section 7.4].

The traditional American value of the free alienability of property conflicts with this civil law concept. In the past, the concept of *droit moral*, if recognized at all, was recognized under theories of contract, libel, privacy and unfair competition law. Gilliam v. ABC, 538 F.2d 14 (2d Cir. 1976); Granz v. Harris, 198 F.2d 585 (2d Cir. 1952).

Recently, however, several states have enacted statutes that grant artists significant moral rights protection (Section 7.8 and Annotation). In addition, the rights contained herein have already acquired a history in public art commission agreements.

Section 7.1 incorporates certain aspects of the right of paternity: the Artist has the right to be recognized by the public as the creator of the Work.

7.2 *Maintenance.* The City recognizes that maintenance of the Work on a regular basis is essential to the integrity of the Work. The City shall reasonably assure that the Work is properly maintained and protected, taking into account the instructions of the Artist provided in accordance with Section 1.6(c), and shall reasonably protect and maintain the Work against the ravages of time, vandalism and the elements.

Annotation

When an art work is first installed no one can be sure how it will hold up. Someone must assume the responsibility for maintenance and security. It is usually the responsibility of the commissioning body to maintain the art work.

The standard of care imposed on the commissioning body is one of reasonable care.

7.3 *Repairs and Restoration.*

a. The City shall have the right to determine, after consultation with a professional conservator, when and if repairs and restorations to the Work will be made. During the Artist's lifetime, the Artist shall have the right to approve all repairs and restorations, provided, however, that the Artist shall not unreasonably withhold approval for any repair or restoration of the Work. If the Artist unreasonably fails to approve any repair or restoration, the City shall have the right to make such repair or restoration. To the extent practical, the Artist, during the Artist's lifetime, shall be given the opportunity to make or personally supervise significant repairs and restorations and shall be paid a reasonable fee for any such services, provided that the City and the Artist shall agree in writing, prior to the commencement of any significant repairs or restorations, upon the Artist's fee for such services.

b. All repairs and restorations shall be made in accordance with recognized principles of conservation.

Annotation

Many artists are adamant about having the right of first refusal if repairs are necessary. The Model Agreement supports this view but requires that all repairs be carried out in accordance with professional conservation standards. The important point is that a professional conservator should be consulted for any repair or restoration. Section 7.3 and Section 7.4 not only protect the legitimate interest of the Artist in his artistic and intellectual creation but also reflect the public interest in preserving cultural and artistic creations.

7.4 *Alteration of the Work or of the Site.*

a. The City agrees that it will not intentionally damage, alter, modify or change the Work without the prior written approval of the Artist.

b. The City shall notify the Artist of any proposed alteration of the Site that would affect the intended character and appearance of the Work and shall consult with the Artist in the planning and execution of any such alteration and shall make a reasonable effort to maintain the integrity of the Work.

c. Nothing in this Section 7.4 shall preclude any right of the City (1) to remove the Work from public display or (2) to destroy the Work [*limiting conditions*]. If the City shall at any time decide to destroy the Work, it shall by notice to the Artist offer the Artist a reasonable opportunity to recover the Work at no cost to the Artist except for an obligation of the Artist to indemnify and reimburse the City for the amount by which the cost to the City of such recovery exceeds the costs to the City of the proposed destruction.

Annotation

(a) Section 7.4(a) is the classic expression of the right of integrity. The commissioning body's obligation under this section need not extend to alteration of the Site unless the Artist has specifically provided that the Site is an integral part of the Work. As to remedies for a breach of this section, equitable relief may be appropriate when damages are inadequate or difficult to ascertain and when the wrong can be cured. This may compel the commissioning body to cure the wrong by restoration since in many cases alteration may occur before preventive remedies such as injunctive relief are available. Damages for breach of this contractual obligation may be more difficult to establish but presumably would encompass the resulting injury to the Artist's reputation.

(b) Even in situations in which the Site is not an integral part of the Work so as to make alterations of the Site fall within the parameters of paragraph (a) of this Section, to the extent that alterations of the Site affect the Work, the commissioning body under the terms of Section 7.4(b) must consult with the Artist.

(c) Most foreign jurisdictions do not, under the doctrine of *droit moral*, prohibit the destruction of art work, on the ground that once a work of art no longer exists, an artist's reputation cannot be injured. It is a matter of heated debate whether a public art commission agreement should restrict the right to destroy the work of public art. Notwithstanding any strong public interest in the preservation of works of public art, it appears that, in the end, any limitations placed on this right of the commissioning body must be left to the negotiating process. For example, limitations of the right to destroy a work of public art might permit the commissioning body to destroy the Work only if the Site was needed for other purposes and the Work could not be removed without significant alteration. Similarly, a limitation negotiated by the Artist on the right to remove the Work from public display might require that the Work shall remain on public display for a period of at least a specified time after completion unless liquidated damages of an agreed amount of money are paid to the Artist for every month that the period of such public display is shortened.

It is generally thought advisable that commissioning bodies engaged in programs of public art develop a procedure which details the conditions under which a work of art can be removed from public display or destroyed.

7.5 *Permanent Record.* The City shall maintain on permanent file a record of this Agreement and of the location and disposition of the Work.

Annotation

It is important for archival and notice purposes to maintain a record of works of art commissioned by public bodies. This requirement may sometimes be omitted in private commissions.

7.6 *Artist's Address.* The Artist shall notify the City of changes in his address. The failure to do so, if such failure prevents the City from locating the Artist, shall be deemed a waiver by the Artist of the right subsequently to enforce those provisions of this Article 7 that require the express approval of the Artist. Notwithstanding this provision, the City shall make every reasonable effort to locate the Artist when matters arise relating to the Artist's rights.

Annotation

The Artist will not be able to enforce his rights under Article 7 if he does not keep the commissioning body informed as to his whereabouts.

7.7 *Surviving Covenants.* The covenants and obligations set forth in this Article 7 shall be binding upon the parties, their heirs, legatees, executors, administrators, assigns, transferees and all their successors in interest, and the City's covenants do attach and run with the Work and shall be binding to and until twenty (20) years after the death of the Artist. However, the obligations imposed upon the City by Sections 7.3(a) and 7.6 shall terminate on the death of the Artist. The City shall give any subsequent owner of the Work notice in writing of the covenants herein, and shall cause each such owner to be bound thereby.

Annotation

The Model Agreement provides that the covenants other than the right to make repairs (which is clearly a personal right) survive until twenty years following the Artist's death. (In Europe, the *droit moral* is perpetual, surviving the death of the Artist.)

7.8 *Additional Rights and Remedies.* Nothing contained in this Article 7 shall be construed as a limitation on such other rights and remedies available to the Artist under the law which may now or in the future be applicable.

Annotation

California, Massachusetts and New York have enacted statutes to protect the Artist's rights of authorship and integrity. The California and Massachusetts statutes differ substantially from the New York law in their approach.

The California Art Preservation Act, Cal. Civ. Code § 987 (West 1985) (the "California Act"), and Chapter 231 of the Massachusetts General Laws, Section 85S, are aimed directly at preventing the destruction and alteration of works of art of recognized quality, while the New York Artist's Authorship Rights Act, N.Y. Arts and Cultural Affairs Law §§ 14.51-14.59 (McKinney's 1984) (the "New York Act"), is aimed at preventing damage to an artist's reputation.

The New York Act borrows from the law of libel and misrepresentation and reflects an interest in the personal rights of the artist rather than the public's interest in the physical preservation of artwork. Thus the New York Act does not prevent the destruction of an artwork, but instead prevents the knowing public display or publication of a work of fine art of an artist "or a reproduction thereof in an altered, defaced, mutilated or modified form if the work is displayed, published or reproduced as being the work of the artist or under circumstances under which it would reasonably be regarded as being the work of the artist, and damage to the artist's reputation is reasonably likely to result therefrom."

The New York Act is primarily concerned with the right of paternity, but a limited right of integrity may be implied since the New York Act empowers the artist to prevent the display of his work in an altered form with his name or in circumstances in which it would reasonably be assumed to be the artist's work.

It is too early to determine how the New York Act will be interpreted and enforced since its effective date was January 1, 1984. In some respects its application may be broader than the California Act, which protects against only the physical alteration of the work and does not apply to the context in which the work is displayed.

For example, in one of the early cases filed under the New York Act, the artist Larry Rivers alleged a violation of the Act when an illustration prepared by him was used to illustrate what he termed "offensive doggerel." Rivers v. Conde Nast Publications, Inc , Index No. 84 Civ. 5571 (MP) (S.D.N.Y. 1984).

Injunctive relief is available under both laws—in New York to prevent or terminate prohibited displays and publications, and in California to prevent intentional alteration or destruction of the work. Restoration of an altered work may also be compelled under the California Act. Both statutes provide for actual damages but provide little guidance in computing such damages.

In a recent New York case, Newmann v. Delmar Realty Co., Index No. 2955/84 (Sup. Ct., N.Y. County), a Supreme Court judge granted the artist Robert Newmann preliminary injunctive relief while the Court considered the issue of whether the new owner of a building was obligated by either property or contract law to display a Newmann mural which the previous owner had contracted to display. The Court held that under the New York Act, the artist had the right to finish the work so long as it was publicly displayed during the period of the injunction despite the fact that if the new owner prevailed, he would be entitled to destroy the work.

Section 7.8 makes clear that the contractual rights provided herein are in addition to, and do not constitute a waiver of, any rights or remedies created by statutes like those of California, Massachusetts and New York.

Optional

[7.9 *Resale Royalty.* If, during the life of the Artist, the City sells or otherwise disposes of ownership of the Work, the City shall pay the Artist a sum equal to fifteen percent (15%) of the appreciated value of the Work. For the purpose of this Agreement, appreciated value shall mean the sales price of the Work less the original fixed fee stipulated in this Agreement, as amended. Nothing in this Agreement shall be construed to impose any obligation on the City as to the method of sale or disposal. The choice of such method of sale or disposal shall be the sole right of the City.]

Annotation

Recognizing that *droit de suite* clauses have not received widespread utilization, we offer for consideration the Section 7.9 provision as one for which the Artist may wish to negotiate.

The basic goal of the *droit de suite*, or art resale royalty right, is to provide greater economic security for artists. Only California has enacted the resale royalty right into law. Cal. Civ. Code § 986 (West 1985). It is beyond the scope of this Annotation to discuss the arguments for and against the right. However, one of the arguments occasionally made by some opponents of proceeds rights statutes is that they are unnecessary because the artist can contract for such a right as one element in a bargaining process. Proponents argue that the artist has often sacrificed monetary gain for the public exhibition of his work, an advantage which is lost if the work is sold to a private collector for private exhibition. The proceeds right is offered as an optional provision because of its controversial nature.

Article 8. Artist as Independent Contractor.

The Artist shall perform all work under this Agreement as an independent contractor and not as an agent or an employee of the City. The Artist shall not be supervised by any employee or official of the City nor shall the Artist exercise supervision over any employee or official of the City.

Annotation

This provision of the Model Agreement reaffirms that the Artist is not an employee of the commissioning body. The Artist's status as an independent contractor is not only significant for copyright law purposes, but also has tax consequences; for example, the commissioning body will not withhold income taxes. In addition, the Artist will not be entitled to vacation, sick leave, retirement or other benefits afforded the commissioning body's employees.

Article 9. Assignment, Transfer, Subcontracting.

9.1 *Assignment or Transfer of Interest.* Neither the City nor the Artist shall assign or transfer an interest in this Agreement without the prior written consent of the other, provided, however, that claims for money due or to become due from the City under this Agreement may be assigned to a financial institution without approval.

9.2 *Subcontracting by Artist.* The Artist may subcontract portions of the services to be provided hereunder at the Artist's expense provided that said subcontracting shall not affect the design, appearance or visual quality of the Work and shall be carried out under the personal supervision of the Artist.

Annotation

A material element of the Model Agreement is the personal skill, judgment and creativity of the Artist. The Artist is not permitted to assign or transfer the creative and artistic portions of the Work to a stranger without the prior written approval of the commissioning body. Similarly, the Artist should have the right to approve any transfer of the commissioning body's rights and responsibilities under the Agreement.

Article 10. Termination. If either party to this Agreement shall willfully or negligently fail to fulfill in a timely and proper manner, or otherwise violate, any of the covenants, agreements or stipulations material to this Agreement, the other party shall thereupon have the right to terminate this Agreement by giving written notice to the defaulting party of its intent to terminate specifying the grounds for termination. The defaulting party shall have thirty (30) days after receipt of the notice to cure the default. If it is not cured, then this Agreement shall terminate. In the event of default by the City, the City shall promptly compensate the Artist for all services performed by the Artist prior to termination. In the event of default by the Artist, all finished and unfinished drawings, sketches, photographs, and other work products prepared and submitted or prepared for submission by the Artist under this Agreement shall at the City's option become its property, provided that no right to fabricate or execute the Work shall pass to the City, and the City shall compensate the Artist pursuant to Article 2 for all services performed by the Artist prior to termination. Notwithstanding the previous sentence, the Artist shall not be relieved of liability to the City for damages sustained by the City by virtue of any breach of this Agreement by the Artist, and the City may reasonably withhold payments to the Artist until such time as the exact amount of such damages due the City from the Artist is determined.

Annotation

The normal remedies for breach of contract are damages and, in certain circumstances, specific performance. Article 10 provides that the Agreement may be terminated for cause provided the breaching party is afforded 10 days to cure the breach and fails to do so. It also provides the commissioning body with the option of acquiring the maquettes and models as an offset to its damage claim, since under the Agreement the commissioning body would not be entitled to such drawings, maquettes and models if the Artist were not in breach.

In some situations, particularly where the underlying capital improvement project so provides, the commissioning body may require that the Agreement give the commissioning body the right to terminate for convenience as well as for cause. Construction contracts often include provisions permitting termination for convenience where the owner finds after entering into a contract that funding is unavailable or needs have changed. Ordinarily, where a contract is terminated for convenience, the contractor is entitled under the contract to receive full payment for all work performed. Without such a provision, most circumstances which would cause an owner to want to terminate a contract would not be sufficient to constitute impossibility, frustration of purpose or other grounds which would relieve the owner of contractual obligations.

Large-scale collaborative projects may require a termination for convenience clause. If the right to terminate for convenience is provided to the commissioning body, the Artist should also have the right.

A clause that combines both convenience and cause is as follows:

(a) The services to be performed under this Agreement may be terminated by either party, subject to written notice submitted thirty (30) days before termination, provided that attempts to reconcile the reason for termination have been undertaken but failed. The notice shall specify whether the termination is for convenience or cause.

(b) If the termination is for the convenience of the City, the Artist shall have the right to an equitable adjustment in the fee (without allowance for anticipated profit on unperformed services), in which event the City shall have the right at its discretion to possession and transfer of title to the sketches, designs and models already prepared and submitted or prepared for submission to the City by the Artist under this Agreement prior to the date of termination, provided that no right to fabricate or execute the Work shall pass to the City.

(c) If termination is for the convenience of the Artist, the Artist shall remit to the City a sum equal to all payments (if any) made to the Artist pursuant to this Agreement prior to termination.

(d) If either party to this Agreement shall willfully or negligently fail to fulfill in a timely and proper manner, or otherwise violate, any of the covenants, agreements or stipulations material to this Agreement, the other party shall thereupon have the right to terminate this Agreement by giving written notice to the defaulting party of its intent to terminate specifying the grounds for termination. The defaulting party shall have thirty (30) days after receipt of the notice to cure the default. If it is not cured, then this Agreement shall terminate. In the event of default by the City, the City shall promptly compensate the Artist for all services performed by the Artist prior to termination. In the event of default by the Artist, all finished and unfinished drawings, sketches, photographs, and other work products prepared and submitted or prepared for submission by the Artist under this Agreement shall at the City's option become its property, provided that no right to fabricate or execute the Work shall pass to the City, and the City shall compensate the Artist pursuant to Article 2 for all services performed by the Artist prior to termination. Notwithstanding the previous sentence, the Artist shall not be relieved of liability to the City for damages sustained by the City by virtue of any breach of this Agreement by the Artist, and the City may reasonably withhold payments to the Artist until such time as the exact amount of such damages due the City from the Artist is determined.

Article 11. Contract Administrator. The Contract Administrator for this Agreement shall be the [Executive Director of Arts Commission]. Wherever this Agreement requires any notice to be given to or by the City, or any determination or action to be made by the City, the [Executive Director] shall represent and act for the City.

Annotation

It is always important to identify the person authorized to give approvals, authorize changes and take all other actions on behalf of the commissioning body.

Article 12. Non-Discrimination. In carrying out the performance of the services designated, the Artist shall not discriminate as to race, creed, religion, sex, age, national origin or the presence of any physical, mental or sensory handicap, and the Artist shall comply with the equality of employment opportunity provisions of Ordinance . . . . as presently existing or hereafter amended.

Annotation

Non-discrimination (and often anti-bribe, as well) clauses are usually required by local laws for public authority contracts.

Article 13. Compliance. The Artist shall be required to comply with Federal, State and City statutes, ordinances and regulations applicable to the performance of the Artist's services under this Agreement.

Article 14. Entire Agreement. This writing embodies the entire agreement and understanding between the parties hereto, and there are no other agreements and understandings, oral or written, with reference to the subject matter hereof that are not merged herein and superseded hereby.

Article 15. Modification. No alteration, change or modification of the terms of the Agreement shall be valid unless made in writing and signed by both parties hereto and approved by appropriate action of the City.

Article 16. Waiver. No waiver of performance by either party shall be construed as or operate as a waiver of any subsequent default of any terms, covenants and conditions of this Agreement. The payment or acceptance of fees for any period after a default shall not be deemed a waiver of any right or acceptance of defective performance.

Article 17. Governing Law. This Agreement, regardless of where executed or performed, shall be governed by and construed in accordance with the laws of the State of ....

Article 18. Heirs and Assigns. This Agreement shall be binding upon and shall inure to the benefit of the City and the Artist and their respective heirs, personal representatives, successors and permitted assigns.

Article 19. Arbitration. All disputes or controversies that may arise between the parties with respect to the performance, obligations or rights of the parties under this Agreement, including disputes as to the physical acceptability of the work or any alleged breach thereof, shall be settled by arbitration to be held in in accordance with the then current Rules of Commercial Arbitration of the American Arbitration Association; however, consideration of artistic merit being a matter for the exclusive determination of the Artist, no dispute or controversy may arise with respect thereto.

The dispute shall be referred to a panel of three arbitrators, one to be selected by the Artist, one to be selected by the City and the third to be selected by the first two. If an agreement on the third arbitrator cannot be reached within thirty (30) days after the appointment of the second arbitrator, such arbitrator shall be appointed by ....

The decision and award of the arbitrators, or that of any two of them, shall be final and binding on the parties, and judgment may be entered upon it in any court having jurisdiction thereof.

Annotation

In addition to the usual arguments favoring arbitration over court litigation of disputes (i.e., that it is quicker, less expensive and permits more flexible and informal rules of evidence and construction), there is also the consideration that disputes over public art works may be too controversial to risk submitting to a jury or any sort of public trial. The arbitration clause also provides the Artist with the assurance of being able to select a strong advocate for his position on the arbitral panel.

As a general proposition, states, municipal corporations and governmental agencies are competent to enter into agreements to arbitrate as a consequence of their power to enter into contracts. Exceptions to this rule arise either by reason of a specific restriction in a charter, statute or enabling document, or under circumstances where the dispute submitted to arbitration involves review of what amounts to executive acts which, as a matter of public policy, may only be reviewed through mandamus proceedings. In contrast to the general proposition, agencies of the Federal Government have no implied authority to enter into arbitration agreements and may do so only under express statutory authority.

This arbitration clause removes from the scope of arbitration disputes as to "artistic merit." Since, as a rule, the arbitrators decide the question of whether or not the dispute is covered by the arbitration clause, it may be expected that in many disputes the threshold issue to be addressed by the arbitrators will be whether or not the dispute is really over "artistic merit."

The Artist or commissioning body must take care to assert any claim in a timely fashion, since most statutory limitations for asserting claims against states and municipalities apply to arbitration as well as court litigation. In this regard, determination of when the claim arises may implicate the various notice and time provisions in the contract.

Further consideration must be given to whether the Artist is a prime contractor of the state or municipal agency or a subcontractor. The problem may arise that, even though a statutory prohibition against state or municipal arbitration may not extend to the arbitration provision in a subcontract, an arbitration award under the subcontract may not be recognized in settling claims between the prime contractor and the state or municipal agency.

Article 20. Notices. All notices, requests, demands and other communications which are required or permitted to be given under this Agreement shall be in writing and shall be deemed to have been duly given upon the delivery or receipt thereof, as the case may be, if delivered personally or sent by registered or certified mail, return receipt requested, postage prepaid, as follows:

a. if the City, to: ....

b. if to the Artist, at the address first above written with a copy to: [address of Artist's attorney]

IN WITNESS WHEREOF the parties hereto have executed this Agreement on the day and year first written above.

[CORPORATE SEAL]

Attest:

	CITY:
Clerk	By its Arts Commission
By:... Deputy Clerk	By:... Executive Director
	ARTIST:
.... Witness	.... (Name)
Approved as to form and legal sufficiency:	.... (Signature)

CHAPTER 9

E-COMMERCE

Benjamin Strouse

§ 9.01 THE ART SITE

Advancements in technology have meant that Web sites, which once consisted largely of text-based content, now usually feature multimedia elements, such as photographs, graphic design, music, animation, movies, and so on, all, of course, in digital form.[1] This expanded palette has contributed to an explosion of art and art-related sites devoted to artists displaying their work, galleries promoting their artists' work, auction houses selling their merchandise, museums extending location-based exhibits or exhibiting online, and academic and professional art institutions providing resources. Accordingly, this section focuses on the legal and business issues of creating and managing Internet art sites such as these. (For the basics on art, new media, and the law, refer to Chapter 4.)

[A] Creating an Art Site

Like other Web sites, art sites consist of certain fairly distinct parts. We shall analyze them in no particular order.

The first component is the content, such as graphics and other media, which is the substance of the site. Some or all of the content may be created, or modified from existing content, specifically for the Web site. Web site content is usually maintained physically as a group of related files, subject to copyright law.[2] Where someone other than the owner of the site performs this work, it may raise questions of ownership, discussed below.

The second element of an art site is the design and layout, which is part of its look and feel, and which may be protected under copyright and trademark laws.[3]

Third are the trademarks and service marks themselves, which contribute to the identity of the site. If the Web site is related to an existing business, such marks probably exist independent of the Web site as well and are, of course, protected under trademark law.[4] The domain name of the Web site may also be included in this third category.

The fourth component includes certain software applications and instructions,[5] which make the site perform and interact with the user.[6] All software may

---

[1] *See generally supra* § 4.01[A].

[2] *See supra* Chapter 1 and § 4.02[A][1] for general discussions of copyright.

[3] The site may also include unique methods of doing business, which may be protected under patent law. While a discussion of patents for business processes is beyond the purview of this chapter, one good source for learning more about the subject is the Patent Practice Handbook by Peter Canelias.

[4] *See* Chapter 1 and § 4.02[A][2] for general discussion of trademarks.

[5] Web sites today are based on versions of Hypertext Markup Language (HTML), which turns standard ASCII text into multimedia Web documents, with graphics, sound, video and links connecting content.

[6] Software runs on computer hardware. For the Web site administrator, the hardware such as

be protected under patent and trade secret law as well as copyright. It is more likely that a smaller Web site will use software that has not been created specifically for it, but is off-the-shelf or licensed from the company developing or hosting it.[7]

Like any Web site, an art site can be simple or complex. The artist may develop it herself or hire others to do so. Regardless, all art sites are constituted of these several basic elements.[8] As a result, creating an art site implicates certain issues of ownership and management.

[1] Development and Ownership

The development of a Web site usually affects who owns and controls it and its component parts.[9] In particular, this section discusses the transfer of rights between Web site developers and their clients, and the sharing of ownership among multiple parties.

[a] Transferring, Licensing, and Retaining Ownership

The creator of copyrightable work, content or software, generally owns the work product.[10] If the creator is an employee, and the creation is within the scope of employment, than the employer owns the work product on a work-for-hire basis.[11] Ownership of copyright can only be transferred through a written agreement. Absent such a document, the most that the law will infer is a nonexclusive

---

the server (*see* § 4.01[A][2]) is frequently fungible. However, sophisticated Web sites may require custom hardware configurations, which might be considered to be part of the Web site as well.

[7] These constituents of the site are loaded onto the computer server, which is connected to the Internet via data lines. At that point, visitors with an Internet connection and basic browser software (a program that serves as a window onto the Web, rendering text and visual media, playing sounds and movies, and enabling visitors to surf among Web sites by selecting links and entering URLs) can visit and interact with the site at the domain name address selected for it.

[8] Of course, the act of combining these elements into a coherent Web site usually has discrete value as well, so the sum of the site may be greater than the parts.

[9] Other basic development issues include selecting a domain name and hosting services for the site. The Web site administrator or an agent can select and register a domain name at the Web site of an Internet registration agency such as Network Solutions (www.networksolutions.com). The registration of a domain name also requires consent by the registrant, in an electronic click-through agreement, to terms and conditions governing the administration of the URL and the process for resolving any third-party disputes over it. Likewise, a hosting service (most of which will also register domain names on behalf of their clients) will require consent by the customer to additional terms and conditions, such as indemnification for violation of laws and third-party rights and limitations of liability for loss of data. The forms at the end of this section contain examples of the foregoing.

[10] *See* Chapter 1 and § 4.02[A][1].

[11] *Id.*

license to use the work, which would leave ownership of the work, including the remainder rights, under the control of the creator.[12]

Web site development firms base their business on these basic rules. These development firms often employ graphic artists and programmers on a work-for-hire basis, and the work product of those employees belongs entirely to the firm.[13] Where graphic artists and programmers are consultants and not employees, the firms usually retain them under a consulting agreement, the primary purpose of which is to transfer ownership of the work product to the firm.[14] At the same time, the firm is in the business of creating these works for its clients. A client generally prefers to own all rights in a work it has commissioned, but the developer may want to retain ownership, or at least certain rights,[15] enabling it to reproduce the work for other customers.

Because the rights in a work product can be finely parsed, usually based on certain basic categories of scope, term, media, and usage, the issue of determining what rights in the work product are to be transferred from the developer to the client is a heavily negotiated one.[16] Ultimately, the agreement usually expresses the licensee's[17] rights in the work product[18] (1) on an exclusive, semi-exclusive,

---

[12] Courts have recognized that the modern copyright law assures that the creator of the work will not give away a copyright inadvertently, and the law forces parties who want to use the work to negotiate with the creator to determine precisely what rights are being transferred and at what price. Effects Assocs., Inc. v. Cohen, 908 F.2d 555 (9th Cir. 1990), *cert. denied*, 498 U.S. 1103 (1991). The language of § 101 of the statute specifically removes nonexclusive licenses from the writing requirement of § 204. 17 U.S.C.A. § 101 (West 1996); *see also*, I.A.E., Inc. v. Shaver, 74 F.3d 768 (7th Cir. 1996) (holding that even though the statute invalidates any transfer that is not in writing, the Copyright Act also explicitly removes the nonexclusive license from the writing requirement). A nonexclusive license can therefore be implied absent a written instrument.

[13] If a party is developing a Web site using its own employees, and is not outsourcing it to a development firm, the same work-for-hire rules govern ownership.

[14] See Appendix 9-C, which sets forth major issues to be negotiated.

[15] For example, a developer who creates a unique visual environment for a client's Web site and transfers all ownership rights in it might be precluded from using basic signature elements of the design in future work for other clients. This is the primary concern that usually motivates developers to retain rights, and its implications are sometimes unexpected. For instance, where a developer produces a digital work mimicking a three-dimensional environment (such as through the use of virtual reality modeling language), that designer would conceivably be precluded from later using a physical structure like a column in architectural blueprints, because such a use would be a derivative of the "original" work created for the client and therefore be included within the bundle of rights controlled by the owner of the copyright.

[16] As noted in the following footnote, for clients receiving a full transfer of copyright in a work product, the same issues will apply in reverse by virtue of a license-back arrangement.

[17] The "licensee" can be either party. While the licensee is usually the client, it is not uncommon for the client to bargain for a complete transfer of ownership in the work product, and then to license back to the developer certain rights to reuse it.

[18] Where an agreement does not purport to transfer copyright in the work product, but only a license to use it, the agreement will often contain general retainer-of-rights language, such as:

or nonexclusive basis; (2) forever or for a fixed term; (3) in all media, only in certain categories of media (such as "interactive electronic media"), or in a single medium; and (4) within a particular industry or some small part of one.[19] For example, a typical license may look something like this:

> Subject to Licensee's compliance with the terms and conditions of this Agreement, upon Completion of the Project, Licensor agrees to grant to Licensee a license to use the Work within the Licensee's business (a) on a non-exclusive basis in perpetuity throughout the world over the Internet and (b) on an exclusive basis for one year and thereafter on a non-exclusive basis for four additional years within the [defined] Territory in all media whatsoever.

This kind of grant of rights is the central provision in development agreements, but other terms also affect the owner's control over the work product, such as noncompete covenants, confidentiality provisions, reservations of rights and prior works, and even dispute-resolution procedures. For instance, while a noncompete covenant does not transfer the rights away from the licensor, it nevertheless has an indirect impact on ownership rights because it prevents a competitor of the licensee from exploiting them during the covenant's term.[20] The following is one simple example of such a noncompete provision:

> During the term of the Agreement and for one (1) year after its termination or expiration, Licensor agrees not to license the rights in the Work to any other party except Licensee that directly or indirectly develops, manufactures, procures, markets or sells art over the Internet.

In the process of working together, parties may share or unintentionally disclose confidential information that becomes part of the work product. Unlike

---

> The Deliverables and all products of the Developer services performed hereunder, and all elements thereof, and all other Developer intellectual property used or created in the course of its performance under the Agreement, inventions conceived or reduced by Developer to practice during the performance of the Agreement, Developer creations, designs, trademarks, works of any kind (including, by way of example only, movies and audio or visual works), masks, models, and works-in-process ("Work Product") shall be exclusively owned by Developer and shall not be considered works-made-for-hire for purposes of copyright ownership, and Client acknowledges that the Work Product and all the elements thereof and all rights relating thereto are the sole and exclusive property of Developer, its successors and assigns, absolutely and for all copyright terms and renewal terms thereof throughout the world, in all media, and for all uses and purposes whatsoever.

[19] The scope of the license might also include the transferability of the license to third parties, and whether or not it is revocable in the event of a subsequent material breach of the agreement, among other terms.

[20] The licensor, however, retains a present interest in the future exploitation of the rights, assuming the provision lapses after some period of time.

expression that is fixed in a tangible medium and therefore subject to copyright law,[21] such confidential information may be subject to the law of trade secrets,[22] and the parties may want to exclude it from the literal application of license grants and noncompete provisions. One mechanism for doing so is a confidentiality provision, such as the following example:

> "Confidential Information"[23] shall include information in any form regarding either party's business plans, customer data, business forecasts, marketing strategies, financial information, account information, products or services under development, computer software, related documentation, and any other nonpublic materials or information that is identified by the disclosing party as confidential at or promptly following disclosure. Notwithstanding the foregoing, Confidential Information does not include any information: (1) that was in the possession or under the control of a party prior to the Agreement, (2) that was made available to either party free of any confidentiality obligation at the time of disclosure, (3) that is or becomes available to the public on or after the date of the Agreement (other than through prohibited disclosure), or (4) that is developed or discovered by either party independently of such Confidential Information.

Additionally, the parties (but especially the developer) may also wish to explicitly carve out any rights in the process of creating the work product, also referred to as "residual information" and "know-how." The following is one example of a residual information clause clarifying the retention of certain rights:

> During the course of Developer's performance of services hereunder, Developer or its employees or agents may acquire or develop or become acquainted with general and expressive ideas, concepts, programming techniques, data processing skills, and general know-how ("Residual Information"), and shall be entitled to use freely and otherwise employ such Residual Information in the furtherance of its respective business activities, including the provision of services to its other customers. Nothing herein shall be construed to permit either party to use the other's Confidential Information.

Similarly, the developer may also wish to carve out rights in prior work that is or may be incorporated into the work product to be transferred. While such a "Prior Work" clause can be combined with a provision retaining rights in residual

---

[21] *See* Chapter 1 and § 4.02[A][1].

[22] Trade secrets can be thought of as confidential information that if revealed would confer to others an unfair competitive advantage in the marketplace. *See* 1 Roger M. Milgrim, Milgrim on Trade Secrets §§ 1.03-.04 (1996). Some states have additional requirements for trade secrets, such as novelty, continuous use in the plaintiff's business, or concreteness.

[23] While this example clause is bilateral, unilateral clauses are also appropriate, but will also be subject to greater scrutiny by the party that is not protected.

information, the following alternative examples are presented independently for precision:

> Developer hereby grants Client and its affiliates a royalty-free, nonexclusive, nontransferable and revocable license to use pre-existing work that Developer incorporates into the services performed pursuant to the Agreement [set forth in the attached Exhibit] ("Prior Work") in connection with the use of the Deliverables hereunder. Client may not transfer or sublicense the Prior Work [or the Deliverables] without the prior written consent of Developer, except to any entity that acquires Client or substantially all of its assets, and Developer retains all right, interest, and title thereto.

Or:

> Nothing contained in this agreement shall prevent Developer from using any work product produced for other parties prior to this Agreement whether or not substantially similar to the Work Product, and Client waives any claim against Developer or any third party that it may otherwise have for infringement of any such prior work product based on the subject matter of this agreement.

Finally, disputes arising out of the agreement are likely to implicate ownership issues. While not directly affecting the transfer or retention of rights in the work product, dispute resolution directly affects the processes of resolving ownership and ultimately enforcing the transfer of rights. Significantly, a good dispute resolution provision should also provide a mechanism of forestalling disputes. The following is one example:

> In the event of any controversy or claim arising out of this Agreement raised by either party, the party raising the dispute will promptly notify the other party in writing of the nature of the dispute and the factual background. Within a seven calendar day period following such notice, the parties will initiate an attempt in good faith to reach a reasonable solution to the dispute, including escalation to the vice-president (or a senior executive) of each party responsible for the subject matter of the dispute. If the dispute cannot be amicably resolved within fifteen calendar days of written notification, then either party may seek to resolve said dispute by arbitration before a single arbitrator knowledgeable in the technology and the Art industry in accordance with the commercial arbitration rules of the American Arbitration Association. The arbitrator shall also promptly resolve any dispute as to the interpretation of this section. The place of arbitration shall be [the locale of the responding party]. Each party shall provide to the arbitrator, no later than fifteen calendar days following the date of the arbitrator's appointment, a statement, including any supporting documents or other evidence on which such party relies, as to why it believes that the dispute should be resolved in its favor, and all such materials and any other materials provided to the arbitrator by either party shall simultaneously be provided by such party to the other party. Within fifteen calendar days after

the submission of such statements by all parties, the arbitrator shall hold a hearing with respect to the dispute. At such hearing, the arbitrator may, in his or her sole discretion, allow the parties to call and cross-examine witnesses, make any additional arguments, or submit any additional materials to support the position taken in their respective statements. The arbitrator shall enter an award within fifteen calendar days following conclusion of the foregoing hearing. Nothing shall preclude either party from making an application to the arbitrator, for good cause, to expedite the proceedings, nor restrict the arbitrator from granting such an application. In addition to such other relief as the arbitrator may award, the arbitrator shall be vested with jurisdiction and may award to the prevailing party in his or her discretion its reasonable attorney's fees and expenses, and all other costs associated with the arbitration. The award rendered by the arbitrator shall be final, immediately binding on the parties, and judgment may be entered upon it in accordance with applicable law in any court having jurisdiction thereof.

[b] Sharing Ownership

Ownership issues become more complicated where several persons have an interest in the art site and must begin to think through all the details of their business relationship. Determining how to divide assets may take care of some concerns but does not address others, for example, whether one person can commit the whole company or project to costly obligations such as development and marketing deals.

If the persons are each owners of a corporation or partners in a formal partnership, then the corresponding agreement among them[24] will most likely govern their interest in the art site. However, if no formal entity owns the site, it would be prudent to formalize the interests and responsibilities of the parties using a relatively simple short-form agreement. The following are examples of certain key provisions:

Individual Responsibilities

Each party shall have the following general responsibilities commencing upon the Effective Date:

- *Jones.* Jones shall pay any and all maintenance costs associated with the Site up to $100/month ("Monthly Maintenance").
- *Wilson.* Wilson shall oversee technical issues associated with site opera-

[24] For example, the membership agreement of a limited liability company would most likely be the document controlling the interests of parties in the assets of the corporation in the absence of another agreement.

tions. The URL(s) for the Site shall be held in the name of Wilson, subject to the following section.

- *Smith.* Smith shall be responsible for generating and/or providing all text-based content.
- *Rogers.* Rogers shall be responsible for generating and/or providing all non-text based content, including graphics and photographs.
- *Unspecified.* All other responsibilities, costs and fees, including further Site development, maintenance in excess of Monthly Maintenance, operations, legal and administrative costs and taxes ("Operations"), shall be shared equally, or otherwise as mutually agreed in writing, among the parties.

First Priority. Each party shall make herself available on a first-priority basis as necessary to satisfactorily perform her obligations under the Agreement.

Ownership

Equal Site Ownership. All services, deliverables and other materials, undertaken, developed or prepared for any of the parties pursuant to the subject matter of this Agreement and/or in anticipation thereof, including without limitation photographs, graphics, text, audio, video, plans, diagrams, notes, program images, and any HTML code relating thereto, or any program code or scripting created by or at the request of any of the parties ("Work(s)"), and derivatives of the Works, are and shall be the joint and several property of the parties, and shall be deemed to be works made for hire, and all title and interest therein shall vest in the parties jointly and severally. To the extent that title to any such Work(s) may not, by operation of law, vest in the parties jointly and severally, or such Work(s) may not be considered Works made for hire, the owner of said Works hereby irrevocably and unconditionally assigns, conveys and transfers all rights, title and interest in the Work(s), and all copyright interests therein, for the entire term of copyright protection of the Work(s), as now existing or as hereinafter may be enacted, in the United States and throughout the world, jointly and severally to and among the parties.

Equal Trademark Ownership. To the extent that any trademarks, service marks or any other forms of identity (including domain names) are or shall be associated with the Site ("Marks"), whether or not registered, the same shall be owned jointly and severally by and among all of the parties to the same extent that said Mark(s) is owned by any of the parties.

Operations, Profits, and Sale

Prior Approval. The assumption or expenditure of any discretionary expenses, fees or costs in excess of [five hundred dollars] related to the Site shall be subject to the mutual agreement of all parties in advance.

Disbursement of Revenues. All income, including all revenue, receivables and the like, related to the Site and its Operations shall be distributed:

- *Operations.* First, to pay all fees, costs and other expenses related to Operations and otherwise incurred by the parties jointly under the Agreement, and
- *Remainder.* Second, any remainder thereafter distributed among the parties as follows: twenty percent (20%) to Jones, fifteen percent (15%) to Wilson, fifty-five percent (55%) to Smith, and ten percent (10%) to Rogers ("Distribution Formula").

Sale of Site. Any proceeds from the sale or license of the Site, or any assets related thereto, shall be distributed according to the Distribution Formula.

[2] Administration and Operations

This subsection discusses basic issues of administering an art site, such as copyright protection online, which differs somewhat from other media; evolving rules for the acceptability of Web site privacy policies; and linking among Web sites, which can be a basis of third-party intellectual property rights violations.

[a] Copyright Notice and Privacy Policy

As discussed elsewhere in this book, copyright protection for works created after March 1, 1989, requires no formal notice. However, adhering to simple registration and notice requirements gives the copyright holder a greater arsenal for enforcing its copyright against infringers.[25]

Administrators of art sites should simply post a copyright notice at the bottom of every page rendering that has copyrighted material on it.[26] Valid copyright notice need contain only the copyright symbol "©," followed by the year(s) of the creation and modifications of any of the contents of the site, followed by the individual or corporate names of the copyright owner(s)—for example, "© 2000, 2001 by Kaufman Creations, Inc."

It is advisable for art site administrators to post in addition a more comprehensive copyright policy, which is frequently included as part of a more general "site use" policy. The following is one example of a copyright policy:

> All content and graphics on this site ("Content") are protected by U.S. copyright and international treaties, and may not be copied without the express permis-

---

[25] *See generally* Chapter 1. The most up-to-date copyright registration procedures are discussed in depth at the copyright site at the Library of Congress (www.loc.gov/).

[26] This kind of posting can be efficiently accomplished online with a simple code that automatically repeats the appropriate footnote on each page that is generated.

> sion of Kaufman Creations, Inc., which reserves all rights. Re-use of any of the Content online or elsewhere for any purpose is strictly prohibited. Permission to use the Content is granted on a case-by-case basis, and we welcome requests. Please direct your inquiries to caleb@kaufmancreations.com.

If an administrator intends to use the Web site to collect information from the general public, he or she should institute a cohesive and consistent privacy policy[27] to govern how or whether such information can be reused. Current Federal Trade Commission issued recommendations[28] stress principles of notice, choice, access, and security as the basis of an acceptable Web site privacy policy,[29] and European laws on the subject—such as legislation based on EU Directive 95/46/EC—are strict. Anytime personally identifying information is collected, the site administrator should prominently point to the clear privacy policy detailing the collection and use of customer information.

[b] Linking and Framing

The operation of the Web is based on linking among different Web sites, Web pages, and content.[30] Administrators routinely provide hyperlinks that send visitors to specific areas elsewhere on the Internet or call up specific content from elsewhere and play or render it within the Web site. Art sites employ hyperlinks to promote art works, to provide additional resources, and even to create new art. However, when executed in violation of another's rights, these practices can constitute a new kind of "information age" intellectual property infringement.[31]

If the link is important to the art site, it may be prudent to seek to secure written permission from the administrator of the targeted information before establishing it.[32] Technical and administrative contacts of Web sites are currently

---

[27] The FTC and its parent the Commerce Department have been consistently vocal in suggesting that Web sites adhere strictly to the privacy rules they publish. *See* http://www.ftc.gov/opa/1998/9808/geocities.htm.

[28] Privacy Online: A Report to Congress, Federal Trade Commission, June 4, 1998. Available online at http://www.ftc.gov/reports/privacy3/toc.htm.

[29] "Notice" refers to clear and conspicuous notice of the policy; "choice" refers to the ability of the user to effectively accept or reject the activity that is associated with the collection of the information; "access" refers to the ability of the user to have access to her information, such that she can make any changes to it to preserve its accuracy; and "security" refers to the obligation to keep the personally identifying information safe. *See* http://www.ftc.gov/opa/1998/9808/geocities.htm.

[30] *See* § 4.01[A][2].

[31] *See* § 4.02[B][2][b].

[32] There is no protocol for requesting permission to link. The following terms are simple examples of such a request:

> We would like to provide a link from our site at www.linkingsite.org to the page on your site at www.targetsite.com/picture.html through a banner ad for your site on our home page.

listed by registration agents such as Network Solutions under the corresponding domain name.[33] Likewise, the administrator may have the right to object to links to the art site from third parties, and either prevent them or bargain for appropriate consideration.[34]

Linking between or among Web sites is often the basis of joint business ventures. In these cases, the joint venturers recognize that the hyperlinking offers

---

Of course, it would be necessary to request permission to use proprietary information, such as the logo of the targeted party, as the indication of the hyperlink:

> We would like to use your logo of the target's bull's eye as the indicator of the link to your site, and request your permission to do so. We only promote reputable goods/ services, and would be pleased to tell you more about our Web site and business.

If the link is an icon or banner, its size can be described in terms of pixels:

> The link shall consist of a prominent promotional banner displayed to users without any scrolling or navigation ("above the fold") on the home page of the site, which shall appear as an object no less than 90 x 30 pixels or 70 x 70 pixels in size.

Links can also be a basis of exploring more comprehensive business relationships:

> We would be willing to negotiate a more comprehensive agreement governing the link, but until we can create and sign a more formal document, we request that this series of e-mails serve as your permission for us to maintain the link.

In all events, the administrator of the targeted information may wish to assert some control over the quality of the linking site:

> Okay to your request, provided that you confirm that Targeted Company has the right to notify Linking Company to promptly remove any Offers or other materials on or around Linking pages that contain content judged by Targeted Company in its sole discretion to be objectionable or in other ways offensive in a manner that would negatively affect Targeted Company.

[33] On the Internet today, while it is true that unauthorized linking might have serious consequences if the linking party breaches the targeted party's rights, it is equally true that preventing certain kinds of unwanted links may not be worth the trouble and expense, even where the entity controlling the targeted information may value the privilege of linking to it. For example, in one incident involving the author of this chapter, the representative of a software industry Web magazine that published a favorable review of a design product refused the product designer's request to link from the page on his site describing the product to the online magazine's review of it. The basis for the rejection was that the link would permit visitors to bypass valuable advertising on the magazine's home page. Nevertheless, the designer established and maintained the unauthorized link for months without protest, until it became out of date.

[34] For example, like other specialized Web sites, art sites may be portals to useful information that reflects industry expertise or sophisticated tastes. In such cases, while the portal site desires to maintain continuous and up-to-date links with the targeted art sites, the administrators of those targeted sites are eager for the traffic that the portal delivers. In cases like these, even if no money changes hands, establishing privity of contract in an area of business, like cross-linking, where the law is unsettled provides desired consistency.

mutual value, so they have an incentive to establish their respective rights and obligations. Appropriate marketing agreements will usually address issues such as how the links are to be displayed on each Web site in terms of graphics and placement on pages; the maintenance of the performance of the links; the control over the destination information; the integrity of the information associated with the links; and linking-related issues like upselling of goods and services.

In all events, the targeted party may wish to protect against the possibility of its own liability for indirect infringement of third-party rights or applicable laws by the linking party. The following language is an example of such preventative terms:

> Linking Company shall indemnify, defend, and hold harmless Targeted Company, its directors, officers, employees and agents, with respect to any claim, demand, cause of action, debt or liability, including reasonable attorney fees, to the extent that the same is based upon a claim that any of the content on the Linking Site infringes or violates any patents, copyrights, trademarks, trade secrets, licenses or other property rights of any third party, as well as laws or regulations of any kind.[35]

[B] Art Exhibitions and Museums Online

Internet museums (there are literally thousands) are virtual institutions devoted to exhibiting collections of works; they may or may not have traditional physical counterparts. Some Internet museums are largely conventional representations of their onsite facilities, exhibitions, and other physical assets;[36] others use the Web to explore wholly new forms of art.[37] Yet by and large all Internet museums must address certain basic issues of clearing rights for online exhibitions and protecting their digital assets.[38]

---

35 Complementary terms of use should also reside on the Web site of each party. For example:

> This Site contains links and pointers to the other related Web sites, resources, and sponsors of the Site. Links to and from any site to other third-party sites do not constitute an endorsement by Company of any third-party resources or their contents, nor shall Company be responsible in any way for any third party. As a visitor to this Site, you acknowledge that any reliance upon any third-party Web site opinion, advice, statement, memorandum, or information shall be at your sole risk.

36 For example, see the Israel Museum's online tour (http://www.imj.org.il).

37 See www.rhizome.org, for example, exploring various and evolving forms of Web art.

38 In addition to third-party rights violations, online art exhibits may run the risk of violating obscenity statutes. While there is ample case law relating to obscenity in more conventional contexts (discussed in Chapter 3), there is currently little guidance as to what content on the Internet would be likely to draw the attention of government authorities as illegally obscene. In particular, it remains to be seen whether the locally based definition of "community standards" for determining whether materials are obscene will remain workable in a worldwide milieu. In brief, the Communications Decency Act (CDA), part of the Telecommunications Act of 1996, was enacted to encourage Internet

[1] Releases and Clearances of Rights

In a typical online exhibition, a living artist has created works that a curator wishes to exhibit on the Web. The exhibitor may be entitled to assurance that the exhibition will not violate the rights (including copyrights and moral rights) of the artist or of any third party (including violations of publicity and privacy rights of third parties depicted in the works), and that the appropriate party will indemnify the exhibitor from such third-party rights violations. Therefore, before an electronic image of the work is created or an existing image is displayed on the museum site, it is prudent for the exhibitor to obtain appropriate releases from the creator (as well as the owner of the work, if it is not the same person).[39]

Proper releases will also include representations that the art is original (or at least noninfringing), and that it is owned and controlled solely by the artist (or the appropriate party), and the explicit right to display it in the chosen medium and manner. A portion of one detailed example of such a grant includes the following language:

> Artist grants Exhibitor the non-exclusive right to make a high-quality digital image of Work ("Image") and display said Image within the Exhibitor site located at www.museumsite.com ("Site") in a manner within Exhibitor's good faith discretion but in no case less prominently than the "featured works" in any other primary exhibition on the Site. Accordingly, Artist releases Exhibitor from any misuse of the Image by any third party, provided, however, that Exhibitor displays and maintains all necessary copyright management information, such as copyright notices, name of the Artist as the creator of the work, name of Artist as the owner of the copyright, restrictions on any further use of the work in conjunction with the Image, and related site usage information and guidelines in conjunction with the Web page on which it is displayed.

---

development by shielding service providers from tort liability, and to restrain Internet pornography. However, members of the Internet community objected to portions of the CDA, such as those sections punishing pornographic transmissions accessible to juveniles, on the grounds that the measures unfairly interfered with free speech. The courts agreed, and eventually the Supreme Court struck down some of those measures as unconstitutional in an opinion, Reno v. American Civil Liberties Union, which is still the leading decision defining the role of the Internet as a protected communications medium. Currently, a number of parties, including several from the art world such as www.artnet.com, a leading vendor of fine art online, are also challenging the Children's Online Privacy Act (COPA), which restricts the display of items on the Internet "harmful to minors.' *See* COPA (to be codified at 47 U.S.C. § 231(e)(6)).

[39] For both the artist and the exhibiting institution, reproduction of a work of art in a new medium may be a sensitive issue, and the process of obtaining a proper release may create an opportunity to address questions about how the work is to be displayed online. For instance, among other issues, the parties may wish to discuss whether the work is to be publicized in a particular manner, reproduced using a certain level of scanning technology, displayed at a certain size, and positioned within the site in a specific fashion.

Other than the electronic reproduction and posting of the Image, Exhibitor may not modify the Image in any way whatsoever, including by alteration (except for size) or combination with any other image. Subject to the foregoing, Artist irrevocably waives her moral rights under the laws of the United States, every state and other locality, and any foreign countries, including without limitation any provision of law known as "droit moral" or any similar law that may now or hereafter be recognized in any country or place (including without limitation any rights of attribution, integrity, withdrawal and/or publication).

[2] Protecting and Sharing Electronic Assets

The prominence of the Internet has made most museums much more aware of the value of their electronic assets, and likewise, that the establishment of a presence on the Internet places those same assets at some risk of misappropriation by visitors.[40] Copyright law, of course, forbids unauthorized taking of protected material (except where such taking qualifies as "fair use");[41] yet copyright restrictions are not always paramount in the minds of visitors. There is no technological solution today that prevents such unauthorized taking, but there are methods such as digital watermarking[42] for impeding it.

Digital watermarks[43] can be embedded within electronic images using several technologies.[44] Most digital watermarks enable proprietors of the copyrighted

[40] For example, using a "screen-capture" program (many of which are available free of charge at Web sites devoted to publishing shareware) or even certain standard browser features permitting, a visitor would be able to quickly capture, and later manipulate and redistribute if so inclined, any static image that is displayed online.

[41] *See* Chapter 1 and § 4.02[A][1].

[42] Etymologically derived from the faintly visible watermarks imprinted on stationery that identify the manufacturer, watermarking is a pattern of bits inserted into a digital file that can identify its copyright information (author, rights, etc.). Unlike printed watermarks, which are intended to be somewhat visible, digital watermarks may be designed to be completely invisible, or in the case of audio clips, inaudible to the unaided ear. Moreover, the actual bits representing the watermark may be scattered throughout the file in such a way that they cannot be identified and manipulated.

[43] In addition to digital watermarking, software encryption is also a means of protecting electronic content. Both are technical measures, not legal doctrines of intellectual property. With encryption, for instance, that a work is in the public domain does not imply that it will be available free from a non-encrypted source—which is to say that the legal concept of public domain and the marketplace reality of public access are not the same. Unlike digital watermarks, however, encryption schemas work best for information that is not intended for general public consumption or is intended for public consumption at relatively modest prices (so that the act of defeating the encryption schema becomes an intellectual exercise that is not worth the time and trouble for most people). *But see* Paul Goldstein, Copyright and Its Substitutes, 45 J. Copyright Soc'y U.S.A., 151, 154 (1997). The European Commission's Legal Advisory Board has observed that "[e]ncryption mechanisms [could] gradually replace copyright as the principal means of protecting information." Legal Advisory Board Reply to the Green Paper on Copyright and Related Rights in the Information Society, www.2.echo.lu/legal/en/ipr/reply/techport.html#HD_NM_5.

works to use standard search methodologies to track down copyright violations that have been posted on a public network (like the Internet).[45] If the infringing copies can be traced to the source, then the infringing parties can be prosecuted under the copyright law. Second, visible electronic watermarks make it more difficult to reuse unauthorized copies,[46] because the infringer must either include the watermark (which is frequently an attribution or identifier of the source of the content), include a blemish from the removal of it, or go through the effort of repairing the unauthorized copy.[47]

As museums and other institutions have become increasingly sophisticated in managing electronic assets, the Internet has become a tool for pooling resources for archival and loan purposes.[48] Setting up online programs like these for the sharing of art works requires membership and loan agreements,[49] which differ

---

[44] The Multimedia Watermarking and Data Hiding Research & Technology site lists about 20 companies and dozens of other institutions and individuals actively engaged in watermarking technology research, development and licensing (www-nt.e-technik.uni-erlangen.de/~hartung/watermarkinglinks.html).

[45] Watermark software may enable the owners of the protected works to automatically compare the location of found objects bearing the watermarks to the location information associated with outstanding licenses.

[46] For example, the Smithsonian Institution, which earns revenues by selling publication rights to its photographs, places an electronic watermark in the corner of high-resolution photographs it displays online.

[47] As contrasted with digital watermarking, some groups have more recently begun to explore systems of identifying copyright ownership online as a means of protecting the works. One of the bases of this kind of schema is a third-party registry that identifies copyrightable works and their perpetual network locations with particularity. The model is intended to foster public acceptance of an alternative computer-network infrastructure for copyright within which infringing copies would be not be registerable, so that (if the paradigm catches on with the public) unauthorized works on the network would be prevented from masquerading as originals. One institution that has been working in this area to develop a standard for the identification of copyrightable works is the International Digital Object Identifier Foundation (www.doi.org), which is creating an international standard for the identification of all types of media and the means of resolving links that can lead to multiple formats of a work.

[48] Leading examples of such resources include the Art Museum Image Consortium (www.amico.org), the Museum Loan Network (www.loanet.mit.edu/Web/index.htm), and the Museum Digital Library Collection (www.museumlicensing.org). AMICO members include 26 of the nation's top art museums, including New York's Metropolitan Museum of Art, the Art Institute of Chicago, the Museum of Fine Arts in Boston, and the Museum of Contemporary Art, San Diego. In part it arose from the Museum Educational Site Licensing Project (MESL), which was a three-year collaboration undertaken between seven universities and seven museums to define terms and conditions for the educational use of digitized museum images and related information on educational networks. Mirapaul, Museums Turn to Internet to Share Collections, N.Y. Times, Jan. 28, 1999. The Museum Loan Network was created to capitalize on the fact that most museums are able to display only 5% of their permanent collections at any one time, and awards grants to facilitate the temporary transfer of art works from one institution to another. Philanthropy News Digest, Feb. 10, 1999.

[49] *See* the forms section accompanying this chapter.

depending on the nature of the venture (commercial versus not-for-profit), whether the assets being shared are electronic or in multiple formats, the extent of sharing permissible, and so on. Questions to be addressed include:

- How are the works to be presented?
- How are they to be transferred?
- Can more than one participant exhibit identical works online simultaneously?
- Is advertising in conjunction with presentation of shared works restricted?
- Can fees be charged to viewers, and if so, are they to be shared among participants?
- Is there a governing body for settling disputes among participants?

Once these kinds of questions are answered, lawyers can begin to prepare the appropriate agreements.

§ 9.02 SELLING ART ON THE INTERNET

Professional Web sites devoted to selling art, once a rarity, today number in the thousands, ranging from galleries that promote their on-site brick-and-mortar exhibitions[50] to aggregators of multiple galleries, Web-based art auctions, and even sales of art forms native to the Web. E-commerce art sites are coalescing and evolving and their business models are changing, but the process of selling art on the Internet usually begins[51] with the process of executing and managing transactions online.[52]

---

[50] Gallery owners note that benefits of an online presence include higher traffic at their physical exhibitions, and that the Internet attracts bidders on a worldwide basis. John Labate, Financial Times, Mar. 11, 1999.

[51] The development of an e-commerce art site, generally speaking, does not vary in kind from development of other Web sites, so the previous section addressing basic Web site development is relevant here too. E-commerce sites may, however, be larger or more complex than noncommercial Web sites, and the development agreements for them (*see* the forms section) rely on "statements of work" (or "schedules"), which define the details of the characteristics and functionality: What is the overall layout of the site? Are there performance standards? How is art to be compressed and exhibited? Do visitors retain control over viewing the art, and how so? Are the images going to be encrypted or watermarked, and how? Is information collected from visitors, and how? The statement of work is therefore an integral part of the agreement, which usually exists as an attachment to it. Unwisely, parties sometimes enter into a heavily negotiated agreement that references statements of work that have not been prepared or completed, with the expectation that these documents will take shape during the development process.

[52] This book discusses elsewhere other issues related to selling art in any environment, including the Internet, such as copyright restrictions, authenticity and fraud regulations, moral rights of artists, and jurisdictional concerns, among other issues. This subsection, however, focuses on the sale transaction per se.

[A] E-Commerce and Art

The electronic "click-through"[53] contract is the basis of selling art online.[54] On June 30, 2000, the federal government, in response to the fractured and diverse attempts of the states to address the issue, enacted legislation to govern electronic transactions,[55] which partially pre-empts the states' laws. The recent legislation is currently untested, and at present the law concerning the validity of the nearly ubiquitous click-through agreement is sparse and evolving. An overview of it follows.

[1] Click-Through Agreements

Click-through agreements are roughly analogous to so-called "shrink-wrap"[56] agreements for off-the-shelf software, and court decisions adjudicating the latter help us to understand the former agreements as well. Generally, shrink-wrap agreements have been held to be enforceable provided that the consumer has the opportunity to read their terms and to return the product for a full refund if she finds the terms unacceptable.[57]

By analogy, click-through contracts should also be written to provide conspicuous notice of the terms and conditions as well as a simple mechanism for accepting or rejecting them. With electronic agreements, however, satisfying these requirements is also a matter of the logistics of how the document is presented in the commercial process. The requirement of a mechanism for clearing obtaining

[53] This kind of agreement is sometimes also called a "click-wrap" contract, based on the more familiar "shrink-wrap" concept associated with sales of off-the-shelf software.

[54] As set forth more fully in the form agreements, in addition to the basic terms of the transaction, click-through sales contracts may include diverse terms such as disclaimers of liability and implied warranties, linking disclaimers, framing prohibitions, designations of governing law, and even designation of a specific jurisdiction for the adjudication of disputes arising out of it.

[55] S. 761, signed by President Clinton June 30, 2000. *See also* Jeri Clausing, Signatures on Cyperspace's Dotted Line, N.Y. Times, Nov. 11, 1999, at C2 (explaining how forms of "digital signatures," including encryption, fingerprint readers, and stylus pads that are used to verify identity online in order to certify contracts, are accepted as legally binding in some states and localities, but not in all). Congressional legislation that was meant to create a uniform federal law recognizing the validity of digital signatures as a basis of electronic contracts ran into the quagmire of state and local laws requiring institutions like banks and insurance companies to keep certain paper records and to notify customers by mail of certain situations, including default on their credit-card debts or loans; changes in the terms of a financial agreement, like increases in a monthly payment; foreclosure of a home mortgage; or cancellation of an insurance policy.

[56] These are the detailed agreements within or attached to sealed boxes of off-the-shelf software that dictate the permissible uses of the product inside.

[57] *See* ProCD Inc. v. Zeidenberg, 86 F.3d 1447 (7th Cir. 1996) (the court held that a software shrink-wrap license is binding on the software's purchaser and that enforcement of such a license under state law was not preempted by Copyright Act).

knowing consent from the counter-party, for instance, is usually satisfied with a simple and conspicuous description of the terms and conditions in conjunction with an option to opt-into the transaction (such as with a button stating "I Agree" or the like that must be selected to indicate assent).

Nevertheless, alternative click-through contract formats are not uncommon. For instance, many companies make terms and conditions of a sale accessible only via a link (usually at the bottom of the sales pages),[58] and do not require that the consumer view the agreement before agreeing to its terms. These types of click-through agreements may be less likely to withstand legal scrutiny than those that present the terms and conditions in conjunction with the opt-in consent mechanism and full disclosure.[59] Regardless of presentation, however, click-through contracts are becoming more comprehensive, even for relatively minor transactions that traditionally have few terms and conditions.[60]

[2] Foreign Jurisdictions

Notably, the issue of which jurisdiction interprets the agreement according to its laws is also an area of uncertainty. The Internet transcends geographical boundaries and reaches a global audience, so Web sites conducting business online must be concerned about the exercise of foreign jurisdiction over any of their activities.

For assertions of jurisdiction by foreign entities within the United States (that is, a state other than the home state of the Web site company),[61] traditional due process considerations and a state's long-arm statute[62] determine whether

[58] Many consider this form of presentation, which involves less upfront text, to be more user-friendly.

[59] *See* ProCD Inc. v. Zeidenberg, 86 F.3d 1447 (7th Cir. 1996); Hotmail Corp. v. Van$ Money Pie Inc., No. C 98-20064, 1998 WL 388389 (N.D. Cal. Apr. 16, 1998). However, legislation and case law are evolving too rapidly, as of this writing, to make firm pronouncements on the validity or invalidity of particular formats.

[60] As of this writing, a court has yet to fully address the concept that conceivably the adequacy of disclosure can vary in proportion to the length or scope of the online agreement, at least in certain kinds of transactions where short-form agreements are traditional. But if successful, this kind of argument—that cramming too many terms into a single electronic agreement makes it unintelligible in certain circumstances online—would undercut the apparent convenience to the seller of substituting long-form click-through contracts for traditionally brief terms and conditions.

[61] As of this writing, there are no notable instances of non-U.S. jurisdictions attempting to assert jurisdiction over a U.S. company or person based solely on Web site activity

[62] For example, New York's long-arm statute provides in part that acts which are the basis of jurisdiction over any non-domiciliary include those that arise from the transaction of any business within the state or contracts anywhere to supply goods or services in the state; the commission of a tortuous act within the state; or the commission of a tortuous act outside of the state that causes injury to person or property within the state, only if the entity either regularly solicits business, engages in persistent conduct, or derives substantial revenue from goods or services in the state,

jurisdiction can be successfully asserted, and e-commerce activities are susceptible. However, if history is to be a guide, it is worth noting that with few exceptions courts have not exercised personal jurisdiction over Web sites that merely post information and maintain no other contact with a forum state.[63] On the other hand, where contractual relations or other direct contact exists with a state, courts have exercised jurisdiction.[64]

One difficulty of this paradigm is ascertaining the location where a click-through agreement, entered into online, is executed and performed. Relatively few decisions have addressed whether entering into a contract over the Internet, and nothing more, is sufficient to subject a party to the jurisdiction of a foreign state.[65] Instead, courts address traditional issues, such as prior dealings with the state, the future consequences of the activities (for instance, deliveries of goods or services),[66] and whether a choice-of-law clause is part of the contract.[67]

---

or should reasonably expect the act to have consequences in the state and also derives substantial revenue from interstate or international commerce. N.Y. Civ. Prac. L. & R. § 302(a)(1)-(3) (Consol. 1978 & Supp. 1997).

[63] Web v. Jolly Hotels, 977 F. Supp. 327 (D.N.J. 1997); Bensusan Restaurant Corp. v. King, 937 F. Supp. 295 (S.D.N.Y. 1996, *aff'd*, 1997 U.S. App. LEXIS 23742 (2d Cir. Sept. 10, 1997); McDonough v. Fallon McElligott, 40 U.S.P.Q.2d (BNA) 1826 (S.D. Cal. 1996). A Web site alone, and nothing more, has been analogized to a plain advertisement in a national publication, which may not meet the requirements of a state's long-arm statutes. Hearst Corp. v. Goldberger, No. 96 Civ. 3620, 1997 U.S. Dis. LEXIS 2065 (S.D.N.Y. 1997). Courts also liken Web sites to national magazine or television ads, which are insufficient by themselves to subject an advertiser to personal jurisdiction in a state in which it otherwise does not do business or have contact. Animation Station, Ltd. v. The Chicago Bulls, LP, 992 F. Supp. 382 (S.D.N.Y. 1998) (unauthorized use of plaintiff's animated video; downloads could reasonably be expected to occur in Illinois, so suit could have been brought there). *See also* Panavision International, L.P. v. Toeppen, 141 F.3d 1316 (9th Cir. 1998) (suit could be brought in California because defendant had "engaged in a scheme to register Panavision's trademarks as his domain names for purpose of extorting money from Panavision" there, where it was reasonable to anticipate that the "effects" of his activity could be felt.)

[64] *See* Zippo Manufacturing Co. v. Zippo Dot Com, Inc., 952 F. Supp 1119 (W.D. Penn. 1997), CompuServe, Inc. v. Patterson, 89 F.3d 1257 (6th Cir. 1996).

[65] Normally, merely entering into a contract is not in itself sufficient to assert foreign jurisdiction. Burger King Corp. v. Rudzewicz, 471 U.S. 462, 105 S. Ct. 2174 (1985).

[66] The activities associated with selling art online, such as capturing personal information, fielding customer queries, and taking and fulfilling orders, are the kinds of activities that can expose a Web site to foreign jurisdiction.

[67] Bensusan Restaurant Corp. v. King, 126 F.3d 25 (2d Cir. 1997) (passive Web site in forum not enough to establish personal jurisdiction without more); Cody v. Ward, 954 F. Supp. 43 (D. Conn. 1997) (telephone calls and e-mails to forum, along with committing tortious act in forum, sufficient to establish personal jurisdiction); CompuServe, Inc. v. Patterson, 89 F.3d 1257 (6th Cir. 1996) (personal jurisdiction established because defendant's acts were purposefully directed to forum, cause of action arose out those contacts sufficient to establish "minimum contacts"); Cybersell, Inc. v. Cybersell, Inc., 130 F.3d 414 (9th Cir. 1997) (single act of trademark infringement not enough to establish personal jurisdiction on nonresident); Playboy Enterprises v. Chuckleberry

Although it is by no means foolproof, for this reason it is prudent to include conspicuous disclaimers in click-through agreements and Web site policies (repeated where appropriate in contracts, e-mails, and newsletters) stating that the visitor agrees to submit to the exclusive jurisdiction of the courts of the home state to resolve any disputes that may arise if she continues to use the Web site or its services.

[B] Art Auctions on the Internet

As discussed elsewhere in this book, state and local laws regulate traditional art auctions. But an Internet auction is different from a traditional auction: there is no auctioneer acting as the seller's agent, the transfer of title occurs directly between the seller and the buyer, and the question of where the auction takes place is not easily resolved.[68] For these reasons, while state or local laws today may not recognize a distinction,[69] an Internet auction can be thought of as a forum, provided as a service, for buying and selling.

[1] Describing the Auction Process

Because laws governing online auctions are unsettled, operators of auction sites should give participants an appropriate sense of expectation about the online auction process[70] to help avoid fraud and similar claims. For instance, processes such as proxy bidding[71] can be confusing, and bidders must be offered a careful explanation before being allowed to commit money to an irrevocable offer.[72]

Publishing, Inc., 939 F. Supp. 1032 (S.D.N.Y. 1996) (prohibition of distribution or sale of magazine in U.S. extended to distribution or sale through Internet Web page); Smith v. Hobby Lobby Stores, Inc., 968 F. Supp. 1356 (W.D. Ark. 1997) (advertisement not sufficient contact to establish personal jurisdiction over nonresident defendant); Zippo Mfg. Co. v. Zippo Dot Com, Inc., 952 F. Supp. 1119 (W.D. Pa. 1997) ("electronic commerce" on Internet established "minimum contacts").

[68] *See* § 9.02[A][2] on foreign jurisdictions.

[69] As of this writing, however, states have not sought to regulate the conduct of Internet auction sites according to local rules.

[70] There are several types of online auctions: English auctions are the most common type, where users bid on individual items and the high-bidding winner pays the price bid. In Vickrey auctions, the highest bidder obtains the item at the price offered by the second-highest bidder. Dutch and Yankee auctions are special formats designed to handle a situation in which a seller wishes to sell multiple identical items. Gregory S. Shatan & Johanna L. Werbach, Going, Going, Gone, Legal Issues To Ponder In Running Online Auctions, Multimedia & Web Strategist, July 1999.

[71] In proxy bidding, the software on the Web site can be instructed to increase a prospective buyer's bids as necessary right up until it reaches either the seller's private and predetermined maximum (which cannot be changed once the process has begun) or the highest bid.

[72] Likewise, operators of auction Web sites should be careful to disclose key details of the transaction that occur even after the bidding process. For example, some auction sites suggest that sellers describe their shipping requirements in the description of the item that they provide: Where will the seller ship? Who will pay shipping costs? How much will shipping cost, and will insurance

Posting conspicuous rules that instruct users in selling and placing bids on the auction site may be valuable for curtailing liability to users and is easily accomplished.

Many auction sites, such as eBay, also provide a feedback mechanism for their users to provide post-transaction commentary about other users. This user commentary is meant to keep the bidding process open if not honest, and to allow customers to communicate their satisfaction or dissatisfaction with the seller and its goods. However, user feedback on an auction Web site can also be the basis of libel claims,[73] and other user-generated content, such as descriptions of products, can potentially create liability for the operator based on other causes of action, such as intellectual property infringement and false advertising. Therefore, the auction operator should post appropriate indemnity language where it gathers user input.

[2] Compliance

Auction Web sites usually require bidders and sellers to submit personally identifying user information, including name, address, telephone number, and e-mail address, as part of a registration process before participating. As discussed previously, anytime personally identifying information is collected online, the site administrator should prominently display a clear privacy policy, detailing the collection and use of customer information, in accordance with current and evolving standards.[74]

Like other key terms and conditions of site usage, the privacy policy should be conspicuous to visitors, especially at the point where information is collected. The auction site should continue to provide the users with access to their information so that it can be modified, even by an exchange of e-mails. The operator must also maintain personally identifying information in a secure fashion.[75]

Finally, online auction houses should investigate the application of local auction regulations. For example, many states require an auctioneer to be licensed or to receive accredited training, or for the auction house to post a bond. Conceiv-

---

be provided for shipping? Auction Web sites may also wish to recommend that bidders and sellers use an escrow service that will not release the item to the seller until the bidder confirms delivery. *See* Shatan & Werbach, *supra* note 70.

[73] *See* Fed. Liquidation Trustee Inc. v. Specialty Car Sales Inc., 1:99 CV 1021 (D.D.C. Apr. 26, 1999); David Segal, E-Buse Alleged in Online Auction, Washington Post, Apr. 28, 1999 at E01.

[74] Privacy Online: A Report to Congress, Federal Trade Commission, June 4, 1998. Available online at http://www.ftc.gov/reports/privacy3/toc.htm.

[75] *See* http://www.ftc.gov/opa/1998/9808/geocities.htm.

ably, an auction company conducting business online may be subject to the regulations of foreign jurisdictions[76] including venues outside the United States.[77]

[C] Web Art

In contrast to static or printed art (increasingly sold online), Web art is an art form that is native to the Internet. It can be understood as real-time kinetic experiences or performances (or an account of past ones), generally accessible publicly from an art site. Also known as "net.art,"[78] this art form raises interesting new issues of transfer of rights, because it is digital, public by nature, and frequently reliant on a certain level of continued public interaction to achieve its intended effect.[79]

Net.art may also be contrasted with discrete multimedia products,[80] which generally consist of "content"—that is, the text, audio, video, photographs, animation and graphics; the software that manipulates and renders the content; and the hardware "platform"—proprietary gaming platforms (such as Sega's, Nintendo's and Sony's), CD-ROM, and DVD[81] players. The creation of any of these products

---

[76] *See* § 9.02[A][2].

[77] One way to avoid the potential application of non-U.S. auction regulations is to limit participation in online auctions to U.S. residents.

[78] Web art is also referred to as "new media art" and "digital art," although the term "net.art" is adopted for this chapter.

[79] Of course, there are different definitions of net.art; some call it an exercise in pure Web aesthetics, others classify it as merely another form of multimedia. One observer terms it "work that not only employs new technologies such as computers, networks, digital production, but also takes advantage of the potential for 'interactive' art that these technologies offer. . . . This interactive potential means that art can no longer be seen as beginning and ending with the individual artist, but rather, involving a larger public." Katarina Soukup, http://www.rhizome.org/query/ Mar. 24, 1997. Another defines it in broader terms "includ[ing] CD-ROM, Web art and other hypermedia projects in this definition, as well as [streaming media] performances and robotic work (which is often computer driven or relies on media technologies)." Laura McGough, http://www.rhizome.org/query/ Mar. 19, 1997.

[80] A discussion of multimedia products, which mix graphics, sounds, text and moving images on a proprietary format requiring specialized hardware and software, is beyond the purview of this chapter. Suffice to say, however, that one defining difference between multimedia products and multimedia on the Web is that multimedia products are manufactured as discrete physical objects, usually en masse. The processes can be expensive, and therefore the profit models can be both sophisticated and complicated. The complex nature of the business of designing, marketing and distributing various kinds of multimedia products deserves exclusive attention elsewhere. One good source is Michael D. Scott, Scott on Multimedia Law, 2d Ed. (Aspen Law & Business 1997). Of course, this distinction between multimedia products and Web content may fade with time: as the connections among computers on the Internet grow more robust, and users can process increasingly large volumes of information at increasingly rapid speeds, platform-specific multimedia products may exist online as well.

[81] The CD-ROM storage media can hold between 600 to 700 megabytes of data, equal to 500

for popular consumption requires an enormous investment, sometimes as much as several million dollars of development, and more money to market the product, and sophisticated rights clearances.[82]

Net.art, on the other hand, presents the challenge of making money for art in new ways, such as user-access fees or royalty payments.[83] Net.art also tests traditional notions of ownership, as transfer of these works could conceivably be nothing more than a transfer of title and rights in profits ("transfer" of the net art may not even require switching servers), and therefore invites new approaches to crafting art agreements to reflect new business models.

[1] Assuring Ownership

Unlike the majority of artworks, net.art emphasizes the cooperative aspect of the Internet. For instance, artists directing the development of works of net.art that are joint products of multiple individuals may have to acquire rights from each contributor who may be a copyright owner in the whole of the final (or ongoing) collective product.[84] In this context, click-through agreements, discussed above, become potentially very useful: where the producer of a piece of net.art invites public contribution to the work, she can position a click-through agreement licensing necessary rights in it, consent to which would be a pre-condition for participation.

Moreover, as with all forms of multimedia, producers of net.art must consider clearing rights of privacy and publicity[85] if the work product makes use of images

high-density floppy diskettes, while a DVD-ROM can presently hold between 4,000 and 10.000 megabytes (4 to 10 gigabytes), enough for full-length feature films.

[82] For a single multimedia product, for example, it may be necessary to acquire licenses for graphics, illustrations, synching and public performances of music, photographs and cartoons, merchandising, and celebrity identities (which implicate publicity as well as privacy issues), as well as licenses for any existing art that may be included in the final product in any form. For one example of the failure to clear rights, see Ringgold v. Black Entertainment Television, Inc., 126 F.3d 70 (2d Cir. 1997).

[83] Blanket annual royalty payments are more familiar in the music business than in art. Paying on a per-use basis is something that the American Society of Composers, Authors and Publishers (ASCAP) has advocated for artists since its formation in 1913. The right to collect licensing fees on for-profit performances was established with the unanimous decision of the Supreme Court in Herbert v. Stanley Co., 242 U.S. 591 (1917). ASCAP and Broadcast Music Incorporated (BMI) may license some organizations and institutions by collecting a relatively small yearly fee, which serves to cover the performance of any and all licensed works. It is conceivable that this kind of royalty scheme could exist for net.art as well, perhaps through the Visual Artists and Galleries Association or the Artists Rights Society.

[84] *See, e.g.*, Margaret Chon, New Wine Bursting from Old Bottles: Collaborative Internet Art, Joint Works, and Entrepreneurship, Symposium: Innovation and the Information Environment. Or. L. Rev., Spring 1996.

[85] A live person whose image is used may have rights of privacy and possibly of publicity that would need to be waived. If the person is deceased, the publicity rights may continue to reside

of real people, and of pre-existing art works or other copyrightable content as well as moral rights that other artists may have if use is made of underlying works. The rights clearance process begins with the identification and location of the owner of the rights, and then the negotiation of a license to use the underlying work within the net.art. The process of rights acquisition can be complicated, however, because chains of title may not be clear and prior agreements granting rights in the work may be ambiguous.[86]

These licenses should state the subject, and attach representations of the work to be incorporated (if possible) or describe it with specificity. It should list the restrictions, if any, on the use to be made of the work with respect to criteria such as media (for instance "HTML-based Web uses" or "all electronic media"), the duration of the grant (for instance "90 days" or "in perpetuity"), the exclusivity of the grant ("nonexclusive" or "exclusive"), and its territory ("solely on the Company's intranet"[87] or "throughout the world").[88]

[2] Transferring Works

Although there is not yet a strong market for net.art among private collectors, museums are beginning to collect and pay for it, and such transfers for value require an agreement.[89] The following issues should be carefully addressed in contracts transferring a work of net.art:

---

with her estate, as many states including California recognize a right of publicity even after the death of an individual. *See generally* Appendix 3-A.

[86] In addition, the rights to incorporate a single work may be controlled by more than one entity. For instance, the rights to a movie clip may reside in the film company, the author of the underlying screenplay, the author of the book on which the screenplay was based, and the composer of the soundtrack, as well as the lyricist, arranger, performer, music publisher and record company; waivers of rights of privacy and publicity may also be needed if actual events and people are represented. The film company alone may not be able to grant the bundle of rights by itself based on the deal struck with the other entities.

[87] An "intranet" is a computer network that is restricted to a particular entity or entities and not generally accessible to the public.

[88] In all events, the grant must be precise as to rights conveyed and scope of use. The grant may also be made "revocable," meaning that it is terminable by the grantor in the event of material breach of the agreement. The grantor should also reserve all other rights to avoid any implied grants beyond those specifically delineated. *See supra* § 9.01[A][1][a]. In addition, for the limited kinds of underlying works of art that are covered by the Visual Artists Rights Act, *see supra* § 4.02[A][1] note 55, the acquisition of the right to reproduce a digital image should include a waiver of the right to assert moral rights claims based on that use.

[89] To date, corporate funding, from Altoids to Absolut, has been an unlikely but important source of net.art. For instance, the Japanese cosmetics firm Shiseido maintains an online art gallery, CyGnet, which is an offshoot of the company's own art collection. Mirapaul, Times Arts at Large, Aug. 5, 1999.

- Describe the rights of each party, before and after the transfer.[90] Is copyright being transferred or just certain rights?
- Describe the obligations of each party. Is the new owner responsible for maintenance and bug fixes of the software and/or graphics? For maintaining access to all necessary plug-ins, even if they become outdated, or a portion of the underlying technology is no longer available? For keeping sufficient server space available? Where does the server reside, and who is responsible for its maintenance?
- Describe the nature of the contract. Is it a "sale" or "license," and to what extent can the art be resold or sublicensed?
- Describe the consideration. Is the new "owner" committed to a particular revenue scheme? Are royalties included? How are they to be paid? If the host site is a prestigious institution, is mere name recognition plus upkeep sufficient compensation for the artist?
- Describe any restrictions on the party transferring the work. Must the artist agree not to compete?[91] To make herself available for free to fix breaks in the code and other upkeep of the work?
- Sort out the joint obligations of the parties. How far does obligation to maintain site extend? Best efforts? Reasonably commercial? Does anyone take over

[90] The following dialogue from the online net.art gallery of Art.Teleportacia highlights some of the legal issues implicated in the transfer of net.art:

> [Q:] How can I really own the artwork which I've bought?
>
> [A:] Property is a fiction. And even more in time of Internet. So, Art.Teleportacia in alliance with artists sells the access to the artwork. As soon as you bought an artwork, you can decide about its accessibility. By the way, it is the same as with off-line world: the owner of the painting has mainly the right to choose, whether this artwork is shown publicly, whether it remains only in private or company rooms, whether it is hidden in cellar.
>
> [Q:] Who controls the access to the artwork?
>
> [A:] Accessibility of a sold artwork is checked by a special script, which runs on art.teleportacia server. Art.Teleportacia arranges the purchase of the artwork, Art.Teleportacia arranges for every artwork a special contract, which regulates the further accessibility, and it guarantees to keep this contract. http://art.teleportacia.org/art-ie4.html.

[91] One net.art artist contractually binds himself not to keep a copy of the "site" or to duplicate it elsewhere. As he points out, this commitment makes him the only person in the world *unable* to do so, as was demonstrated by the entire duplication of the site during a public event. http://www.wired.com/news/news/culture/story/11678.html.

maintenance obligations in the event of failure? Are there other reversion rights?

- Describe restrictions on modifying the work. What are the limits of modifications that can be made to the art, either in the discretion of the owner, for reasons of upkeep, or to keep up with new technologies?[92]

[92] Art.Teleportacia also offers some preliminary contract terms—"a wide range of ways to own a piece of net.art"—to prospective purchasers of net.art: the buyer-to-be may express a preference for future access to the work—"free" (free access for all), "limited" (access only from owner's home page), or "private" (viewable only inside the owner's intranet). http://art.teleportacia.org/art-ie4.html.

FORMS AND APPENDICES

Registration Agreements

Appendix 9-A: Domain Name Registration Agreement (Network Solutions)

Appendix 9-B: Domain Name Dispute Policies (Network Solutions)

Hosting Agreements

Form 9-1: Standard Web Site Hosting Agreement (Pro-ISP)

Form 9-2: Web Site Hosting Agreement

Web Site Copy

Form 9-3: Online Copyright Protection Terms

Form 9-4: Copyright Protection Terms (Permitting Noncommercial Sharing of Assets)

Form 9-5: Copyright Protection Terms (As a Condition of Access)

Form 9-6: Museum Web Site Terms of Use

Form 9-7: Terms of Use of Online Images

Form 9-8: Privacy Policy

Form 9-9: Commercial Web Site Terms of Use (E-Commerce Site)

Form 9-10: Web Site Terms of Use (Commercial Services Site)

Form 9-11: Net.Art Web Site Terms of Use

Web Site Development and Ownership Agreements

Appendix 9-C: Negotiation Guidelines for Art Site Development (Favorable to Client)

Form 9-12: Proof-of-Concept Web Site Development Agreement

Form 9-13: Web Site Co-Ownership Agreement (Multiple Parties, Short Form)

Form 9-14: Museum Web Site Development Agreement (Pro-Museum)

Form 9-15: Commercial Web Site Development Agreement

Form 9-16: Commercial Web Site Development Agreement (Ongoing or Multiple Projects)

Form 9-17: Development Agreement for Web Site Technology (IP-Management Software)

Form 9-18: Short-Form Waiver and Release for Commercial Use of Images Online

Administration and Operation Agreements

Form 9-19: E-Commerce Linking Agreement

Form 9-20: E-Commerce Linking Agreement (Short Form)

Form 9-21: Art Consortium Membership Agreement

Form 9-22: Auction Rules and Web Site Terms of Use Policies

Form 9-23: Auction Participation Agreement

Form 9-24: Online Gallery Co-Marketing Agreement

Form 9-25: Net.Art Download Agreement

Form 9-26: Net.Art Hosting and Sales Agreement

Form 9-27: Art E-Newsletter Subscription Agreement

APPENDIX 9-A

Domain Name Registration Agreement (Network Solutions)

1. INTRODUCTION. In this Service Agreement ("Agreement"), "you" and "your" refer to each customer ("Customer") and "we", "us" and "our" refer to Network Solutions, Inc. ("Network Solutions"). This Agreement explains our obligations to you, and your obligations to us in relation to your use of our services. By selecting Network Solutions' service(s) you have agreed to establish an account with us for such services. When you use your account or permit someone else to use your account to purchase or otherwise acquire access to additional Network Solutions' service(s) or to modify or cancel your Network Solutions' service(s) (even if we were not notified of such authorization), this Agreement covers any such service or actions. Any acceptance of your application(s) for our services and the performance of our services will occur at our offices in Herndon, Virginia, the location of our principal place of business.

2. SECURITY. When you register a domain name with us through our e-mail application process, you are responsible for selecting a security option to protect your domain name registration records (including your contact records and host records) from unauthorized changes. There are three levels of security available for domain name registration records, contact records and host records: (i) Mail From; (ii) Encrypted Password (CRYPT-PW); and (iii) Pretty Good Privacy (PGP). Please review our Website at http://www.networksolutions.com/help/guardian.html for an explanation of each security option and select the option that best serves your requirements.

3. VARIOUS SERVICES. Paragraphs 1 through 25 are applicable to any and all of the services you have chosen. The terms and conditions set forth in paragraphs A through D at the end of this Agreement apply only to customers who have selected Network Solutions' services other than our domain name registration services.

4. FEES, PAYMENT AND TERM OF SERVICE. As consideration for the services you have selected, you agree to pay Network Solutions the applicable service(s) fees set forth on our Website at the time of your selection. All fees are due immediately and are non-refundable. Network Solutions may take all remedies available to collect fees owed. If you qualify, we may extend payment terms to you under our Business Account Credit Program. Unless otherwise specified, each Network Solutions' service is for a two-year initial term and renewable thereafter for successive one-year terms. Any renewal of your services with us is subject to our then current terms and conditions and payment of all applicable service fees at the time of renewal and in the case of domain name re-registration, the domain

name registry's acceptance of your domain name registration. You agree that you may not transfer your domain name registration to another domain name registrar during the first sixty (60) days from the effective date of your initial domain name registration with us.

5. ACCURATE INFORMATION. As further consideration for the Network Solutions service(s), you agree to: (1) provide certain current, complete and accurate information about you as required by the application process; and (2) maintain and update this information as needed to keep it current, complete and accurate. We rely on this information to send you important information and notices regarding your account and our services. Our privacy statement, located on our Website at http://www.networksolutions.com/legal/privacy-policy.html and incorporated herein by reference sets forth your and our rights and responsibilities with regard to your personal information. You agree that we, in our sole discretion, may modify our privacy statement. We will post such revised statement on our Website at least thirty (30) calendar days before it becomes effective. You agree that, by using our services after modifications to the privacy statement become effective, you have agreed to these modifications. You acknowledge that if you do not agree to any such modification, you may terminate this Agreement. We will not refund any fees paid by you if you terminate your Agreement with us. We will not process the personal data that we collect from you in a way incompatible with the purposes and other limitations described in our privacy statement and we will take reasonable precautions to protect your personal data from loss, misuse and unauthorized access, disclosure, alteration or destruction. You represent and warrant that you have provided notice to, and obtained consent from, any third party individuals whose personal data you supply to us as part of our services with regard to: (i) the purposes for which such third party's personal data has been collected, (ii) the intended recipients or categories of recipients of the third party's personal data, (iii) which parts of the third party's data are obligatory and which parts, if any, are voluntary; and (iv) how the third party can access and, if necessary, rectify the data held about them. You further agree to provide such notice and obtain such consent with regard to any third party personal data you supply to us in the future. We are not responsible for any consequences resulting from your failure to provide notice or receive consent from such individuals or for your providing outdated, incomplete or inaccurate information. Even if you intend to license the use of our domain name registration services to a third party, you will remain our customer and you are responsible for complying with all terms and conditions of this Agreement. Subject to the requirements of our privacy statement, in order for us to comply with the current rules and policies for the domain name system, you hereby grant to Network Solutions the right to disclose to third parties through an interactive publicly accessible registration database the following mandatory information that you are required to provide when registering or

reserving a domain name: (i) the domain name(s) registered by you; (ii) your name and postal address; (iii) the name(s), postal address(es), e-mail address(es), voice telephone number and where available the fax number(s) of the technical and administrative contacts for your domain name(s); (iv) the Internet protocol numbers of the primary nameserver and secondary nameserver(s) for such domain name(s); (v) the corresponding names of those nameservers; (vi) the original creation date of the registration; and (vii) the expiration date of the registration. We, as are all accredited domain name registrars, are also required to make this information available in bulk form to third parties who agree not to use it to (a) allow, enable or otherwise support the transmission of mass unsolicited, commercial advertising or solicitations via e-mail (spam) or (b) enable high volume, automated, electronic processes that apply to our systems to register domain names.

6. MODIFICATIONS TO AGREEMENT. Except as otherwise provided in this Agreement, you agree, during the term of this Agreement, that we may: (1) revise the terms and conditions of this Agreement; and/or (2) change part of the services provided under this Agreement at any time. Any such revision or change will be binding and effective immediately upon posting of the revised Agreement or change to the service(s) on Network Solutions' Websites, or upon notification to you by e-mail or United States mail. You agree to periodically review our Websites, including the current version of this Agreement available on our Websites, to be aware of any such revisions. If you do not agree with any revision to the Agreement, you may terminate this Agreement at any time by providing us with notice by e-mail or United States mail addressed as follows, Attention: Registrar Business Affairs, P.O. Box 525, Herndon, Virginia 20170. Notice of your termination will be effective on receipt and processing by us. Any fees paid by you if you terminate your Agreement with us are nonrefundable, but you will not incur any additional fees. By continuing to use Network Solutions' services after any revision to this Agreement or change in service(s), you agree to abide by and be bound by any such revisions or changes. We are not bound by nor should you rely on any representation by (i) any agent, representative or employee of any third party that you may use to apply for our services; or in (ii) information posted on our Website of a general informational nature. No employee, contractor, agent or representative of Network Solutions is authorized to alter or amend the terms and conditions of this Agreement.

7. MODIFICATIONS TO YOUR ACCOUNT. In order to change any of your account information with us, you must use the Account Number and the Password that you selected if you opened your account with us through our online application process, or the security authentication option that you selected if you opened your account with us through our e-mail application process. Please safeguard your Account Number and Password or security authentication option from any

unauthorized use. In no event will we be liable for the unauthorized use or misuse of your Account Number or Password or security authentication option.

8. DOMAIN NAME DISPUTE POLICY. If you reserved or registered a domain name through us, you agree to be bound by our current domain name dispute policy that is incorporated herein and made a part of this Agreement by reference. The current version of the dispute policy may be found at our Website: http://www.networksolutions.com/legal/dispute-policy.html. Please take the time to familiarize yourself with that policy.

9. DOMAIN NAME DISPUTE POLICY MODIFICATIONS. You agree that we, in our sole discretion, may modify our dispute policy. We will post any such revised policy on our Website at least thirty (30) calendar days before it becomes effective. You agree that, by maintaining the reservation or registration of your domain name after modifications to the dispute policy become effective, you have agreed to these modifications. You acknowledge that if you do not agree to any such modification, you may terminate this Agreement. We will not refund any fees paid by you if you terminate your Agreement with us.

10. DOMAIN NAME DISPUTES. You agree that, if your use of our domain name registration services is challenged by a third party, you will be subject to the provisions specified in our dispute policy in effect at the time of the dispute. You agree that in the event a domain name dispute arises with any third party, you will indemnify and hold us harmless pursuant to the terms and conditions set forth below in this Agreement. If we are notified that a complaint has been filed with a judicial or administrative body regarding your use of our domain name registration services, you agree not to make any changes to your domain name record without our prior approval. We may not allow you to make changes to such domain name record until (i) we are directed to do so by the judicial or administrative body, or (ii) we receive notification by you and the other party contesting your registration and use of our domain name registration services that the dispute has been settled. Furthermore, you agree that if you are subject to litigation regarding your registration and use of our domain name registration services, we may deposit control of your domain name record into the registry of the judicial body by supplying a party with a registrar certificate from us.

11. AGENTS. You agree that, if your agent (e.g., an Internet Service Provider, employee, etc.) purchased our service(s) on your behalf, you are nonetheless bound as a principal by all terms and conditions herein, including the dispute policy. Your continued use of our services shall ratify any unauthorized actions of your agent. By acting on your behalf, your agent certifies that he or she is authorized to apply for our services on your behalf, that he or she is authorized to bind you to the terms and conditions of this Agreement and that he or she has apprised

you of the terms and conditions of this Agreement. In addition, you are responsible for any errors made by your agent. We will not refund fees paid by you or your agent on your behalf for any reason, including, but not limited to, in the event that your agent fails to comply with the terms and conditions of this Agreement, your agent incorrectly provides information in the application process or if your agent changes or otherwise modifies your domain name record incorrectly.

12. NOTICES AND ANNOUNCEMENTS. You authorize us to notify you as our customer of information that we deem is of potential interest to you. Notices and announcements may include commercial e-mails and other notices describing changes, upgrades, new products and services or other information pertaining to Internet security or to enhance your identity on the Internet and/or other relevant matters. If you do not wish to receive bulk email solicitation notices or announcements please send us an email at remove@networksolutions.com.

13. LIMITATION OF LIABILITY. You agree that our entire liability, and your exclusive remedy, with respect to any Network Solutions' service(s) provided under this Agreement and/or for any breach of this Agreement is solely limited to the amount you paid for such service(s). Network Solutions and its contractors shall not be liable for any direct, indirect, incidental, special or consequential damages resulting from the use or inability to use any of the Network Solutions' services or for the cost of procurement of substitute services. Because some states do not allow the exclusion or limitation of liability for consequential or incidental damages, in such states, our liability is limited to the extent permitted by law. We disclaim any and all loss or liability resulting from, but not limited to: (1) loss or liability resulting from access delays or access interruptions; (2) loss or liability resulting from data non-delivery or data mis-delivery; (3) loss or liability resulting from acts of God; (4) loss or liability resulting from the unauthorized use or misuse of your Account Number, Password or security authentication option; (5) loss or liability resulting from errors, omissions, or misstatements in any and all information or service(s) provided under this Agreement; (6) loss or liability relating to the deletion of or failure to store e-mail messages; (7) loss or liability resulting from the development or interruption of your Website; (8) loss or liability from your inability to use our dot com mail service; (9) loss or liability that you may incur in connection with our processing of your application for our services, our processing of any authorized modification to your domain name record or your agents failure to pay any fees, including the initial registration fee or re-registration fee; or (10) loss or liability as a result of the application of our dispute policy.

14. INDEMNITY. You agree to release, indemnify, and hold Network Solutions, in our capacities as the registry and a registrar, and our contractors, agents, employees, officers, directors, shareholders, affiliates and assigns harmless from

all liabilities, claims, damages, costs and expenses, including reasonable attorneys' fees and expenses, of third parties relating to or arising under this Agreement, the Network Solutions services provided hereunder or your use of the Network Solutions' services, including without limitation infringement or dilution by you, or someone else using our service(s) from your computer, of any intellectual property or other proprietary right of any person or entity, or a violation of any of our operating rules or policies relating to the service(s) provided. When we are threatened with suit or sued by a third party, we may seek written assurances from you concerning your promise to indemnify us; your failure to provide those assurances may be considered by us to be a material breach of this Agreement.

15. BREACH. You agree that your failure to abide by any provision of this Agreement, any Network Solutions operating rule or policy, the dispute policy, or your willful provision of inaccurate or unreliable information as part of the application process, or your failure to update your information to keep it current, complete or accurate, or your failure to respond for over fifteen (15) calendar days to inquiries from us concerning the accuracy of the contact details associated with your domain name registration may be considered by us to be a material breach and that we may provide a written notice, describing the breach, to you. If within ten (10) calendar days of the date of such notice, you fail to provide evidence, which is reasonably satisfactory to us, that you have not breached your obligations under the Agreement, then we may delete the registration or reservation of your domain name and/or terminate the other Network Solutions' service(s) you are using without further notice. We will not refund any fees paid by you if we terminate your Agreement due to your breach. Any such breach by you shall not be deemed to be excused simply because we did not act earlier in response to that, or any other breach, by you.

16. NO GUARANTY. You agree that, by registration of your chosen domain name, such registration does not confer immunity from objection to either the registration or use of your domain name.

17. REPRESENTATIONS AND WARRANTIES. You agree and warrant that: (i) the information that you or your agent on your behalf provide to us during the application process to register your domain name or to apply for other Network Solutions' service(s) is, to the best of your knowledge and belief, accurate and complete, and that any future changes to this information will be provided to us in a timely manner according to the modification procedures in place at that time, (ii) to the best of your knowledge and belief neither the registration of your domain name nor the manner in which you intend to use such domain name will directly or indirectly infringe the legal rights of a third party, (iii) you have all requisite power and authority to execute this Agreement and to perform your obligations hereunder, (iv) you have selected the necessary security option(s) for your domain

name registration record, and (v) you are of legal age to enter into this Agreement. You agree that your use of our service(s) is solely at your own risk. You agree that all of our services are provided on an "as is," and "as available" basis.

18. DISCLAIMER OF WARRANTIES. WE EXPRESSLY DISCLAIM ALL WARRANTIES OF ANY KIND, WHETHER EXPRESS OR IMPLIED, INCLUDING BUT NOT LIMITED TO THE IMPLIED WARRANTIES OF MERCHANTABILITY, FITNESS FOR A PARTICULAR PURPOSE AND NON-INFRINGEMENT. WE MAKE NO WARRANTY THAT OUR SERVICE(S) WILL MEET YOUR REQUIREMENTS, OR THAT THE SERVICE(S) WILL BE UNINTERRUPTED, TIMELY, SECURE, OR ERROR FREE; NOR DO WE MAKE ANY WARRANTY AS TO THE RESULTS THAT MAY BE OBTAINED FROM THE USE OF THE SERVICE(S) OR AS TO THE ACCURACY OR RELIABILITY OF ANY INFORMATION OBTAINED THROUGH OUR DOT COM MAIL SERVICE. YOU UNDERSTAND AND AGREE THAT ANY MATERIAL AND/OR DATA DOWNLOADED OR OTHERWISE OBTAINED THROUGH THE USE OF OUR DOT COM MAIL SERVICE IS DONE AT YOUR OWN DISCRETION AND RISK AND THAT YOU WILL BE SOLELY RESPONSIBLE FOR ANY DAMAGE TO YOUR COMPUTER SYSTEM OR LOSS OF DATA THAT RESULTS FROM THE DOWNLOAD OF SUCH MATERIAL AND/OR DATA. WE MAKE NO WARRANTY REGARDING ANY GOODS OR SERVICES PURCHASED OR OBTAINED THROUGH ANY OF OUR SERVICES OR ANY TRANSACTIONS ENTERED INTO THROUGH SUCH SERVICES. NO ADVICE OR INFORMATION, WHETHER ORAL OR WRITTEN, OBTAINED BY YOU FROM US OR THROUGH OUR DOT COM MAIL SERVICE SHALL CREATE ANY WARRANTY NOT EXPRESSLY MADE HEREIN. TO THE EXTENT JURISDICTIONS DO NOT ALLOW THE EXCLUSION OF CERTAIN WARRANTIES, SOME OF THE ABOVE EXCLUSIONS MAY NOT APPLY TO YOU.

19. REVOCATION. You agree that we may terminate your contractual right to use our service(s) if the information that you are obligated to provide to register your domain name or register for other Network Solutions service(s), or that you subsequently modify, contains false or misleading information, or conceals or omits any information we would likely consider material to our decision to register your domain name or to continue to provide you domain name registration services. You agree that we may terminate our service(s), including our domain name registration services, in the event that you use such service(s) for any improper purpose, as determined in our sole discretion. Furthermore, you agree that we may suspend, cancel or transfer your domain name registration services in order to: (i) correct mistakes made by us or the registry in registering your chosen domain

name, or (ii) to resolve a dispute under our dispute policy. We will not refund any fees paid by you if we terminate your services.

20. RIGHT OF REFUSAL. We, in our sole discretion, reserve the right to refuse to register your chosen domain name or register you for other Network Solutions' service(s), or to delete your domain name within the first thirty (30) calendar days from receipt of your payment for such services. In the event we do not register your domain name or register you for other Network Solutions' service(s), or we delete your domain name or other Network Solutions' service(s) within such thirty (30) calendar day period, we agree to refund any applicable fee(s) you have paid. You agree that we shall not be liable to you for loss or damages that may result from our refusal to register, the deletion your domain name or refusal to register you for other Network Solutions' service(s).

21. SEVERABILITY. You agree that the terms of this Agreement are severable. If any term or provision is declared invalid or unenforceable, that term or provision will be construed consistent with applicable law as nearly as possible to reflect the original intentions of the parties, and the remaining terms and provisions will remain in full force and effect.

22. ENTIRETY. You agree that this Agreement, the rules and policies published by us, the dispute policy and the privacy statement are the complete and exclusive agreement between you and us regarding our services. This Agreement, our rules and policies, the dispute policy and the privacy statement supersede all prior agreements and understandings, whether established by custom, practice, policy or precedent.

23. NON-ASSIGNMENT. Your rights under this Agreement are not assignable. Any attempt by you to assign your rights shall render this Agreement voidable at our option. Any attempt by your creditors to obtain an interest in your rights under this Agreement, whether by attachment, garnishment or otherwise, shall render this Agreement voidable at our option.

24. GOVERNING LAW. You agree that this Agreement and any disputes hereunder shall be governed in all respects by and construed in accordance with the laws of the Commonwealth of Virginia, United States of America, excluding its conflict of laws rules. Except for disputes concerning or arising from your use of a domain name registered with us, you and we each submit to exclusive subject matter jurisdiction, personal jurisdiction and venue of the United States District Court for the Eastern District of Virginia, Alexandria Division. If there is no jurisdiction in the United States District Court for the Eastern District of Virginia, Alexandria Division, then jurisdiction shall be in the Circuit Court of Fairfax County, Fairfax, Virginia. Only for disputes concerning or arising from your use of a domain name registered with us, you agree to submit to subject matter jurisdiction, personal

jurisdiction and venue of the United States District Court for the Eastern District of Virginia, Alexandria Division and the courts of your domicile.

25. AGREEMENT TO BE BOUND. By applying for a Network Solutions' service(s) through our online application process or by applying for and registering a domain name as part of our e-mail template application process or by using the service(s) provided by Network Solutions under this Agreement, you acknowledge that you have read and agree to be bound by all terms and conditions of this Agreement and any pertinent rules or policies that are or may be published by Network Solutions.

This is Network Solutions Service Agreement Version Number 5.1.

Reprinted by permission.

APPENDIX 9-B

Domain Name Dispute Policies (Network Solutions)

1. Purpose. This Uniform Domain Name Dispute Resolution Policy (the "Policy") has been adopted by the Internet Corporation for Assigned Names and Numbers ("ICANN"), is incorporated by reference into your Registration Agreement, and sets forth the terms and conditions in connection with a dispute between you and any party other than us (the registrar) over the registration and use of an Internet domain name registered by you. Proceedings under Paragraph 4 of this Policy will be conducted according to the Rules for Uniform Domain Name Dispute Resolution Policy (the "Rules of Procedure") and the selected administrative-dispute-resolution service provider's supplemental rules.

2. Your Representations. By applying to register a domain name, or by asking us to maintain or renew a domain name registration, you hereby represent and warrant to us that

a. the statements that you made in your Registration Agreement are complete and accurate;

b. to your knowledge, the registration of the domain name will not infringe upon or otherwise violate the rights of any third party;

c. you are not registering the domain name for an unlawful purpose; and

d. you will not knowingly use the domain name in violation of any applicable laws or regulations.

It is your responsibility to determine whether your domain name registration infringes or violates someone else's rights.

3. Cancellations, Transfers, and Changes. We will cancel, transfer or otherwise make changes to domain name registrations under the following circumstances:

a. subject to the provisions of Paragraph 8, our receipt of written or appropriate electronic instructions from you or your authorized agent to take such action;

b. our receipt of an order from a court or arbitral tribunal, in each case of competent jurisdiction, requiring such action; and/or

c. our receipt of a decision of an Administrative Panel requiring such action in any administrative proceeding to which you were a party and which was conducted under this Policy or a later version of this Policy adopted by ICANN. (See Paragraph 4(i) and (k) below.)

We may also cancel, transfer or otherwise make changes to a domain name registration in accordance with the terms of your Registration Agreement or other legal requirements.

4. Mandatory Administrative Proceeding. This Paragraph sets forth the type of disputes for which you are required to submit to a mandatory administrative proceeding. These proceedings will be conducted before one of the administrative-dispute-resolution service providers listed under Providers.

a. Applicable Disputes. You are required to submit to a mandatory administrative proceeding in the event that a third party (a "complainant") asserts to the applicable Provider, in compliance with the Rules of Procedure, that

i. your domain name is identical or confusingly similar to a trademark or service mark in which the complainant has rights; and

ii. you have no rights or legitimate interests in respect of the domain name; and

iii. your domain name has been registered and is being used in bad faith.

In the administrative proceeding, the complainant must prove that each of these three elements is present.

b. Evidence of Registration and Use in Bad Faith. For the purposes of Paragraph 4(a)(iii), the following circumstances, in particular but without limitation, if found by the Panel to be present, shall be evidence of the registration and use of a domain name in bad faith:

i. circumstances indicating that you have registered or you have acquired the domain name primarily for the purpose of selling, renting, or otherwise transferring the domain name registration to the complainant who is the owner of the trademark or service mark or to a competitor of that complainant, for valuable consideration in excess of your documented out-of-pocket costs directly related to the domain name; or

ii. you have registered the domain name in order to prevent the owner of the trademark or service mark from reflecting the mark in a corresponding domain name, provided that you have engaged in a pattern of such conduct; or

iii. you have registered the domain name primarily for the purpose of disrupting the business of a competitor; or

iv. by using the domain name, you have intentionally attempted to attract, for commercial gain, Internet users to your Website or other online location, by creating a likelihood of confusion with the complainant's mark as to the source, sponsorship, affiliation, or endorsement of your Website or location or of a product or service on your Website or location.

c. How to Demonstrate Your Rights to and Legitimate Interests in the Domain Name in Responding to a Complaint. When you receive a complaint, you should refer to Paragraph 5 of the Rules of Procedure in determining how your response should be prepared. Any of the following circumstances, in particular but without limitation, if found by the Panel to be proved based on its evaluation of all evidence presented, shall demonstrate your rights or legitimate interests to the domain name for purposes of Paragraph 4(a)(ii):

i. before any notice to you of the dispute, your use of, or demonstrable preparations to use, the domain name or a name corresponding to the domain name in connection with a bona fide offering of goods or services; or

ii. you (as an individual, business, or other organization) have been commonly known by the domain name, even if you have acquired no trademark or service mark rights; or

iii. you are making a legitimate noncommercial or fair use of the domain name, without intent for commercial gain to misleadingly divert consumers or to tarnish the trademark or service mark at issue.

d. Selection of Provider. The complainant shall select the Provider from among those approved by ICANN by submitting the complaint to that Provider. The selected Provider will administer the proceeding, except in cases of consolidation as described in Paragraph 4(f).

e. Initiation of Proceeding and Process and Appointment of Administrative Panel. The Rules of Procedure state the process for initiating and conducting a proceeding and for appointing the panel that will decide the dispute (the "Administrative Panel").

f. Consolidation. In the event of multiple disputes between you and a complainant, either you or the complainant may petition to consolidate the disputes before a single Administrative Panel. This petition shall be made to the first Administrative Panel appointed to hear a pending dispute between the parties. This Administrative Panel may consolidate before it any or all such disputes in its sole discretion, provided that the disputes being consolidated are governed by this Policy or a later version of this Policy adopted by ICANN.

g. Fees. All fees charged by a Provider in connection with any dispute before an Administrative Panel pursuant to this Policy shall be paid by the complainant, except in cases where you elect to expand the Administrative Panel from one to three panelists as provided in Paragraph 5(b)(iv) of the Rules of Procedure, in which case all fees will be split evenly by you and the complainant.

h. Our Involvement in Administrative Proceedings. We do not, and will not, participate in the administration or conduct of any proceeding before an Administrative Panel. In addition, we will not be liable as a result of any decisions rendered by the Administrative Panel.

i. Remedies. The remedies available to a complainant pursuant to any proceeding before an Administrative Panel shall be limited to requiring the cancellation of your domain name or the transfer of your domain name registration to the complainant.

j. Notification and Publication. The Provider shall notify us of any decision made by an Administrative Panel with respect to a domain name you have registered with us. All decisions under this Policy will be published in full over the Internet, except when an Administrative Panel determines in an exceptional case to redact portions of its decision.

k. Availability of Court Proceedings. The mandatory administrative proceeding requirements set forth in Paragraph 4 shall not prevent either you or the complainant from submitting the dispute to a court of competent jurisdiction for independent resolution before such mandatory administrative proceeding is commenced or after such proceeding is concluded. If an Administrative Panel decides that your domain name registration should be canceled or transferred, we will wait ten (10) business days (as observed in the location of our principal office) after we are informed by the applicable Provider of the Administrative Panel's decision before implementing that decision. We will then implement the decision unless we have received from you during that ten (10) business day period official documentation (such as a copy of a complaint, file-stamped by the clerk of the court) that you have commenced a lawsuit against the complainant in a jurisdiction to which the complainant has submitted under Paragraph 3(b)(xiii) of the Rules of Procedure. (In general, that jurisdiction is either the location of our principal office or of your address as shown in our Whois database. See Paragraphs 1 and 3(b)(xiii) of the Rules of Procedure for details.) If we receive such documentation within the ten (10) business day period, we will not implement the Administrative Panel's decision, and we will take no further action, until we receive

i. evidence satisfactory to us of a resolution between the parties;

ii. evidence satisfactory to us that your lawsuit has been dismissed or withdrawn; or

iii. a copy of an order from such court dismissing your lawsuit or ordering that you do not have the right to continue to use your domain name.

5. All Other Disputes and Litigation. All other disputes between you and any party other than us regarding your domain name registration that are not brought pursuant to the mandatory administrative proceeding provisions of Paragraph 4 shall be resolved between you and such other party through any court, arbitration or other proceeding that may be available.

6. Our Involvement in Disputes. We will not participate in any way in any dispute between you and any party other than us regarding the registration and use of your domain name. You shall not name us as a party or otherwise include us in any such proceeding. In the event that we are named as a party in any such proceeding, we reserve the right to raise any and all defenses deemed appropriate, and to take any other action necessary to defend ourselves.

7. Maintaining the Status Quo. We will not cancel, transfer, activate, deactivate, or otherwise change the status of any domain name registration under this Policy except as provided in Paragraph 3 above.

8. Transfers During a Dispute.

a. Transfers of a Domain Name to a New Holder. You may not transfer your domain name registration to another holder

i. during a pending administrative proceeding brought pursuant to Paragraph 4 or for a period of fifteen (15) business days (as observed in the location of our principal place of business) after such proceeding is concluded; or

ii. during a pending court proceeding or arbitration commenced regarding your domain name unless the party to whom the domain name registration is being transferred agrees, in writing, to be bound by the decision of the court or arbitrator.

We reserve the right to cancel any transfer of a domain name registration to another holder that is made in violation of this subparagraph.

b. Changing Registrars. You may not transfer your domain name registration to another registrar during a pending administrative proceeding brought pursuant to Paragraph 4 or for a period of fifteen (15) business days (as observed in the location of our principal place of business) after such proceeding is concluded. You may transfer administration of your domain name registration to another registrar during a pending court action or arbitration, provided that the domain name you have registered with us shall continue to be subject to the proceedings commenced against you in accordance with the terms of this Policy. In the event that you transfer a domain name registration to us during the pendency of a court action or arbitration, such dispute shall remain subject to the domain name dispute policy of the registrar from which the domain name registration was transferred.

9. Policy Modifications. We reserve the right to modify this Policy at any time with the permission of ICANN. We will post our revised Policy at least thirty (30) calendar days before it becomes effective. Unless this Policy has already been invoked by the submission of a complaint to a Provider, in which event the version of the Policy in effect at the time it was invoked will apply to you until the dispute is over, all such changes will be binding upon you with respect to any domain name registration dispute, whether the dispute arose before, on or after the effective date of our change. In the event that you object to a change in this Policy, your sole remedy is to cancel your domain name registration with us, provided that you will not be entitled to a refund of any fees you paid to us. The revised Policy will apply to you until you cancel your domain name registration.

Additional information regarding the Uniform Domain Name Dispute Resolution Policy & Rules may be found at http://www.icann.org/udrp/udrp.htm.

Reprinted by permission.

FORM 9-1

Standard Web Site Hosting Online Agreement (Pro-ISP)

Provider Service Agreement

1. All services provided by Provider may be used for lawful purposes only. Transmission or storage of any information, data or material in violation of any law or administrative regulation is prohibited, including without limitation copyrighted material, material legally judged to be threatening or obscene, or material protected by trade secret and other statue. The subscriber agrees to indemnify and hold harmless Provider from any claims resulting from the use of the service that damages the subscriber or any other parties. The following is strictly prohibited on the Provider server, and Provider shall be the sole arbiter as to what constitutes a violation of this provision: pornography and sex-related merchandising; and spamming, or the sending of unsolicited email, and/or using an email address or domain name in a spam that is maintained on a Provider machine.

2. Payment is due immediately after date of invoice. All setup fees are non-refundable once setup has been completed. All payments must be in US dollars and withdrawable from a US bank. The subscriber is responsible for providing up-to-date payment information. Provider will not be held responsible should the subscriber's payment information become out-of-date and Provider terminates service for nonpayment.

2.1. If payment is by credit card, the subscriber authorizes Provider to charge the credit card listed for those charges for Provider services that may accrue from month to month, or for any past-due balances, in order to bring the account to current status. Credit card payments will be billed and charged automatically, and Provider may charge the amount due to the provided card at any time.

2.2. Accounts are in default if payment is not received within 20 days after date of invoice. If a subscriber's check is returned by the bank as unredeemable, the subscriber will be deemed to be in default, and will be liable for a "returned check" charge. Accounts unpaid 20 days after date of invoice may have their service interrupted. Such interruption does not relieve the subscriber from the obligation to pay the monthly charge and Provider will not be liable therefor. Only a written request to terminate your service relieves you of your obligation to pay the monthly account charge. Accounts in default are subject to a late payment charge and an interest charge of 1.5% per month on the outstanding balance. If the subscriber's state law does not allow an interest rate of 1.5% per month, the maximum allowable rate for the subscriber's state will be charged. If the subscriber defaults, the subscriber agrees to pay Provider its reasonable expenses, including attorney and collection agency fees, incurred in enforcing its rights under these Terms and Conditions.

2.3. All files, information and mail under the account will be preserved for 15 days from the date the payment is due. If the payment is not received after 15 days, all files, information and mail under the account will be deleted. If the subscriber wishes to use the service again, the subscriber must re-apply as a new subscriber. For this, an activation fee will be required.

3. The subscriber agrees that the company has the right to delete all data, files or other information that is stored in the subscriber's account if the subscriber's account with the company is terminated, for any reason, by either Provider or the subscriber.

4. System accounts cannot be transferred or used by anyone other than the subscriber.

5. Provider shall have the right to suspend service to the subscriber at any time, and for any reason, without notice. If such a suspension is to last for more than 30 days, the subscriber will be notified as to the reason.

6. Service provided by Provider may be cancelled in writing at any time with no penalty. Login Id and domain name must be included in the cancellation request. Cancellation will take effect only when the receipt of the cancellation request is confirmed by Provider.

7. The subscriber certifies that he or she is at least 18 years of age.

8. If the subscriber requests that Provider provide services not delineated herein at any time during the 30 day period and thereafter, the subscriber agrees to pay Provider's price for such services in effect at the time such service was rendered.

9. Provider exercises no control whatsoever over the content of the information passing through Provider.

10. Provider makes no warranties of any kind, whether expressed or implied, for the service it is providing. Provider also disclaims any warranty of merchantability or fitness for a particular purpose. Provider will not be responsible for any damage suffered. This includes loss of data resulting from delays, nondeliveries, misdeliveries, or service interruptions caused by Provider's negligence or the subscriber's errors or omissions. Use of any information obtained via Provider is at your own risk. Provider specifically denies any responsibility for the accuracy or quality of information obtained through its services.

11. ANY LIABILITY OF THE COMPANY, INCLUDING WITHOUT LIMITATION ANY LIABILITY FOR DAMAGES CAUSED OR ALLEGEDLY

CAUSED BY ANY FAILURE OF PERFORMANCE, ERROR, OMISSION, INTERRUPTION, DELETION, DEFECT, DELAY IN OPERATION OR TRANSMISSION, COMMUNICATIONS LINE FAILURE, THEFT OR DESTRUCTION OF OR UNAUTHORIZED ACCESS TO, ALTERATION OF, OR USE OF RECORDS, WHETHER FOR BREACH OF CONTRACT, TORTUOUS BEHAVIOR, NEGLIGENCE, OR UNDER ANY OTHER CAUSE OF ACTION, SHALL BE STRICTLY LIMITED TO THE AMOUNT PAID BY OR ON BEHALF OF THE SUBSCRIBER TO THE COMPANY FOR THE CURRENT MONTH.

12. Should any provision of this agreement be held to be illegal, invalid, or unenforceable by a court law, the legality, validity and enforceability of the remaining provisions of this agreement shall remain unaffected thereby unless otherwise stated.

13. These Terms and Conditions supersede all previous representations, understandings or agreements and shall prevail notwithstanding any variance with terms and conditions of any order submitted. Use of Provider service constitutes acceptance of these Terms and Conditions.

If the authorized representative of Subscriber agrees with the foregoing terms and conditions, select the "I Agree" button. Otherwise select the "I don't Agree" button.

→ [button] <u>I agree.</u> → [button] <u>I don't agree.</u>

FORM 9-2

Web Site Hosting Agreement

The following terms and conditions (these "Terms") govern the provision by Company, Inc. ("Company") of the services and/or products (referred collectively herein as "Services and Products") described on the Server Order Form and Contract attached hereto ("Order Form") and defined in Company's product support listing, to Customer, Inc. ("Customer"). The Order Form, these Terms and the attachments hereto, which are identified on the Order Form, executed with respect to the Services and Products are referred to herein, collectively, as this "Agreement."

1. Obligations of Company. Company shall install within ten business days after execution by Company of the Order Form, unless otherwise specified in the Order Form, and maintain the Services and Products which are designated in the Order Form (as such may be supplemented pursuant to Section 5, below). Company will use its best efforts to assure that Customer's Internet server will be available 24 hours a day, seven days a week. If the Customer's Internet server is unavailable for more than a total of 4 hours in any week, other than as a result of the maintenance activities described in Section 4, below, fees for that week will be waived and the applicable monthly invoice will be adjusted accordingly. For the purposes of this Agreement, a week shall be considered to run from Sunday to Saturday. Customer's Internet server shall be deemed to be not available for purposes of this Section 1 if Company's standard hardware, software, or operating system is functioning in a manner that prevents access to the Internet server ("Unavailability"). For purposes of this Section 1, Unavailability shall not be deemed to occur hereunder as a result of Customer action or inaction, including, but not limited to, Customer utilization of Customer owned, non-standard, or unsupported hardware and/or software installed by the Customer or Company at the Customer's request. Company shall provide 24x7x365 customer support, unless modified by Company to new, different or improved similar support structure.

2. Obligations of Customer. Customer shall comply with all of the terms of this Agreement, including, but not limited to, the Acceptable Use Policy attached hereto (the "Use Policy"), as the Use Policy may be modified from time to time. Upon notice from Company, Customer promptly shall eliminate any hazard, interference or service obstruction that any hardware or software used by Customer, whether or not provided by Company ("Customer Materials"), is causing, or is likely to cause. If Customer requests Company to assist it in removing any hazards, interference or service obstruction that Customer Materials are causing or are likely to cause, Company may, but is not required to, assist in such removal. The

charges for Company's services in connection with such assistance shall be at rates determined by Company at the time such services are requested and payment with respect thereto shall be made in accordance with Section 3, below. In the event that the primary function(s) of Customer's Website is impaired during non-business hours or holidays, and Company has been unable to successfully locate and/or contact an authorized representative of Customer, Company may take reasonable steps to restore the functionality of Customer's Website without prior Customer approval. Any necessary work that is performed by Company to restore functionality that was impaired by Customer design flaws or errors is billable to Customer. Customer understands that Customer shall pay to Company a billable rate for time and materials, as indicated on the Order Form under Time and Materials Order. These charges are in excess of the monthly recurring charges.

3. Payment.

3.1. Generally. Charges for the Services and Products (including the charges described in the balance of this Section 3.1, the "Charges") are set forth on the Order Form. Charges shall commence to accrue on the date that Company provides access codes to Customer ("Operational Date"). All payments for Charges shall be made in U.S. Dollars. Customer may pre-pay the Charges for the entire term of this Agreement or may pay this Agreement or applicable law with respect to the collection of a Payment Default, including, but not limited to, reasonable attorney's fees and the fees of any collection agency retained by Company.

3.2. Taxes. Customer shall be liable for, and shall reimburse Company and indemnify and hold Company harmless from, all local, state, federal and non-United States taxes or similar assessments or charges (including any interest and penalties imposed thereon), other than taxes based on the net income of Company, arising out of, or relating to this Agreement or the sale of the Services and Products hereunder.

3.3. Pass Through Items and Other Expenses. Company will have the right at any time during any term of this Agreement to pass through and invoice to Customer any new or increased fees, assessments, taxes or other charges imposed on or required to be collected by Company by any governmental agency or any new or increased charges upon the Services and Products hereunder by any carrier, which charges pass through any such governmental agency fees, assessments, taxes or other charges, that affect Company's costs in providing Services and Products to Customer. Customer also will be responsible for paying any sales, license and use taxes, fees, or assessments levied by any local, state or federal government or governmental agency with respect to the provision of Services and Products under this Agreement. Customer will pay and be solely responsible for all taxes, fees and charges levied directly upon it.

4. Maintenance. Company designates time periods ("Scheduled Maintenance Windows") during which it may limit or suspend the availability of the hardware and/or software involved in providing its Services and Products (an "Outage") to perform necessary maintenance or upgrades. If planned maintenance has the possibility of making the server or servers, as the case may be, utilized by Customer inaccessible to the Internet during a Scheduled Maintenance Window, Company will provide not less than seventy-two (72) hours prior electronic mail or other notice to Customer of the Scheduled Maintenance Window during which the Outage is planned. In addition, Company reserves the right to perform any required (emergency) maintenance work outside of the Scheduled Maintenance Window with twenty-four (24) hours prior notice to Customer.

5. Additional Products or Services. With Company's concurrence, Customer may request in writing service or products ("Additional Item") then offered by Company in addition to the Services and Products (a "Written Request"). A Written Request may only be made by the Individual(s) listed as the authorized customer upgrade contact on the Order Form. Customer will have five (5) business days after making the Written Request to cancel the Additional Item in writing. As soon as practicable after receiving the Written Request, Company will begin the installation process with respect to the Additional Item. Customer will be charged Company's then current list price for the Additional Item. If Customer cancels the Written Request, Customer shall pay all applicable charges of Company with respect to the installation of the Additional Item. An Additional Item shall be subject to this Agreement as "Services and Products."

6. Term and Termination. The initial term of this Agreement shall be two (2) years and shall commence on the Operational Date and upon expiration shall automatically renew for successive ninety (90) day terms at the Charges in effect at the commencement of such terms (which Charges shall have been communicated to Customer in writing forty five (45) days prior to the end of the preceding term) or until written notice of non-renewal by either party is delivered to the other party at least thirty (30) days prior to the end of the then current term.

6.1. Termination by Company. In addition to any other rights it may have under this Agreement or applicable law, Company may, at its option, immediately terminate this Agreement, upon (i) a Payment Default which breach is not cured by Customer within ten (10) business days of Customer's receipt of notice of such breach, (ii) Customer's failure to comply with any other obligation of Customer under this Agreement which breach is not cured by Customer within ten (10) business days of Customer's receipt of notice of such breach (iii) Customer's failure to comply with any of the terms of the Use Policy which is not cured by Customer within two (2) business days of Customer's receipt or notice of such breach, (iv) Customer ceasing to do business in the normal course, becoming or being declared insolvent or bankrupt, being the subject of any proceeding relating to liquidation or insolvency which is not dismissed within 90 calendar days or making an assignment for the benefit of its creditors, or (v) any attempt by Customer to derive any source code from the Services or Products.

6.2. Termination by Customer. Customer may terminate this Agreement with respect to all, and not less than all of the Services and Products in the event of (a) a material breach by Company of its obligations under this Agreement which breach is not cured within ten (10) business days after written notice thereof is received by Company, or (b) otherwise in the first sixty (60) days of the initial term hereof (such section 6.2 (b) termination hereinafter referred to as a "Permissible Termination"). In the event or a Permissible Termination, Customer shall pay (i) installation Charges, (ii) a pro-rated Charge based on the number of days Company provided Services and Products prior to the date of termination of this Agreement by Customer under this Section 6.2, and (iii) if the Services and Products include software for which Company does not then provide general customer support (products not in Company's product catalog), Customer shall pay to Company an amount equal to Company's cost of such software for the entire term. If Customer terminates this Agreement other than in a Permissible Termination, Customer shall pay to Company an amount equal to all unpaid Charges for the remainder of the then-current term of this Agreement.

6.3. Rights and Obligations on Termination. Upon termination of this Agreement, Company and Customer shall have no obligations to each other except as provided in this Agreement. Upon termination of this Agreement, Customer shall (i) pay all amounts due and owing to Company, (ii) remove from Company's premises all property owned by Customer, and (iii) return to Company within a reasonable time all software, access keys and any other property provided to Customer by Company under this Agreement, and Company shall return to Customer all property or copies of software, if any, within a reasonable time after termination unless Customer requests a specific return delivery date. The nights and obligations of both parties, which by their nature would continue beyond the termination of this Agreement (including, without limitation, those relating to confidentiality, payment of Charges, limitations of liability and indemnification), shall survive such termination.

7. Proprietary Rights. Company hereby grants Customer a non-exclusive, non-transferable license to use the Services and Products provided hereunder during the term of this Agreement. All rights with respect to the Services and Products, including, but no limited to, intellectual property or similar rights with respect therefore belong exclusively to Company, whether or not they are embedded in any Service or Product. Notwithstanding the foregoing, Customer shall not

be obligated to make any royalty or other payments with respect to the Services and Products other than as provided in this Agreement.

8. Proprietary Rights Indemnification.

8.1. By Customer. Customer agrees to indemnify and hold harmless Company, all individuals or entities controlling, controlled by or under common control with Company (each, a "Company Affiliate"), and the officers, directors, attorneys and employees of Company and each Company Affiliate (a "Section 8 Indemnified Party") against any losses, claims, damages, liabilities, penalties, actions, proceedings or judgments (collectively, "Losses") to which a Section 8 Indemnified Party may become subject related to or arising out of any infringement or misappropriation or alleged infringement or misappropriation of any United States, copyright, trade secret or other proprietary right related to any hardware or software not provided by the Company and utilized by Customer in connection with any of the Services or Products and will reimburse a Section 8 Indemnified Party for all legal and other expenses, including disbursements, reasonable attorneys' fees and court costs (including and allocation for in-house counsel fees) incurred by such Section 8 Indemnified Party in connection with investigating, defending or settling any Loss whether or not in connection with pending or threatened litigation in which such Indemnified Party is a party.

8.2. By Company. Company agrees to indemnify and hold harmless the Customer against any Losses to which the Customer may become subject related to or arising out of infringement or misappropriation of any United States copyright, patent, trade secret or other proprietary right related to the equipment and software provided by the Company to the Customer, and will reimburse the Customer for all legal and other expenses, including without limitation, disbursements, reasonable attorney's fees and court costs (including an allocation for in-house counsel fees) incurred in connection with investigating, defending, or settling any such loss, claim, damage, liability, action or proceeding whether or not in connection with pending or threatened litigation in which the Customer is a party. This indemnification does not relate to the Customer's content or matters that arise from Customer's content or conduct. The provisions of this Agreement relating to indemnification shall survive termination of Customer's account. If any such Products and Services, or any part thereof, is an infringement or a misappropriation, then Company will, at no additional charge to the Customer, use commercially reasonable efforts to either (i) procure for Customer the right to using such Products and Services or part thereof; or (ii) replace such Products and Services with non-infringing Products and Services; or (iii) modify the same so as to make it non-infringing; or (iv) the Agreement as to the infringing Products and Services will terminate, and Company shall refund to Customer any and all unused portion of the fees paid for such Products and Services.

9. Indemnification. In addition to other indemnification provided herein, Customer agrees to indemnify and hold harmless Company, each Company Affiliate and the officers, directors, employees and agents of Company and each Company Affiliate (each an "Indemnified Party") against any losses, claims, damages, liabilities, penalties, actions, proceedings or judgments (collectively, "Losses") to which an Indemnified Party may become subject and which Losses arise out of Customer's use of the Services and Products in violation of law or the legal rights of third parties, and will reimburse an Indemnified Party for all legal and other expenses, including reasonable attorney's fees incurred by such Indemnified Party in connection with investigating, defending or settling any Loss whether or not in connection with pending or threatened litigation in which such Indemnified Party is a party.

10. Limitation on Company Liability. The parties acknowledge that the limitations set forth in this Section 10 are integral to the amount of fees levied in connection with this Agreement, and that, were Company to assume any further liability other than as set forth herein, such fees would of necessity be set substantially higher. Company does not monitor or exercise control over the content of the information transmitted through its facilities. Use of the Services and Products or any information that may be obtained therefrom is at Customer's own risk. Company shall have no responsibility or liability for the accuracy or quality of information obtained through its Services and Products. Company shall not be deemed to be in default of any provision of this Agreement or be liable for any delay, failure of performance or interruption of the provision of Services and Products to Customer resulting, directly or indirectly, from any (i) weather conditions, natural disasters or other acts of God, (ii) action of any governmental or military authority, (iii) failure caused by telecommunication or other Internet provider, or (iv) other force or occurrence beyond its control. Notwithstanding the foregoing, Customer may immediately terminate this Agreement should such foregoing delay, failure of performance or interruption of the provision of Services and Products to Customer continues for a period of forty-eight (48) hours or more, but Customer shall pay an amount equal to all unpaid Charges for hardware and software for the remainder of the then current term of this Agreement, and all other payments and fees shall be waived.

11. Remedies. The exclusive remedy against Company for any damages whatsoever to Customer arising out of or related to this Agreement shall be the refund of the fees paid by Customer to Company with respect to the then current term of this Agreement. COMPANY SHALL NOT BE LIABLE FOR (i) ANY INDIRECT, INCIDENTAL, SPECIAL OR CONSEQUENTIAL DAMAGES, OR FOR ANY LOSS OF PROFITS OR LOSS OF REVENUE RESULTING FROM THE USE OF THE COMPANY'S SERVICES AND PRODUCTS BY CUSTOMER

OR ANY THIRD PARTIES EVEN IF COMPANY HAS BEEN ADVISED OF THE POSSIBILITY THEREOF, OR (ii) ANY LOSS OF DATA RESULTING FROM DELAYS, NONDELIVERIES, MISDELIVERIES OR SERVICE INTERRUPTIONS. COMPANY PROVIDES THE SERVICES AND PRODUCTS AS IS, WITHOUT WARRANTY OF ANY KIND, WHETHER EXPRESS OR IMPLIED. COMPANY DISCLAIMS ALL IMPLIED WARRANTIES, INCLUDING, BUT NOT LIMITED TO, THE IMPLIED WARRANTIES OF MERCHANTABILITY OR FITNESS FOR A PARTICULAR PURPOSE. CUSTOMER SHALL BE SOLELY RESPONSIBLE FOR THE SELECTION, USE AND SUITABILITY OF THE SERVICES AND PRODUCTS AND COMPANY SHALL HAVE NO LIABILITY THEREFORE. The limitations of liability provided in Section 10 of this Agreement shall inure to the benefit of Company and all Company Affiliates and to all of the respective officers, directors, attorneys, employees and agents of Company and such other entities ("Limited Liability Parties"). The limitations of liability afforded Company in this Agreement shall apply whether (i) the action in which recovery is sought is based in contract, tort (including, but not limited to, negligence or strict liability), statute or otherwise or (ii) a Limited Liability Party is alleged to be liable jointly with one or more parties or otherwise.

12. Other Customer Assurances. During any time period when Customer is provided access to any facilities, hardware or other property owned or leased by, or otherwise under the control of Company (collectively "Company Property") pursuant to this Agreement, Customer shall (i) maintain liability insurance, covering any damage or destruction to Company Property (collectively "Damage") and (ii) reimburse Company for all expenses incurred by Company in replacing or repairing, as the case may be, any Damage caused by Customer.

13. Limited Company Liability. Neither Company nor any of its officers, directors, employees, and agents shall be liable for any damage or destruction of equipment or other materials belonging to, leased by, or otherwise under the control of Customer ("Customer Property"), whether or not any such equipment or materials are at any time located in facilities owned or operated by Company, except where such damage or destruction is a direct result of the negligence, recklessness or willful misconduct of Company or any of its officers, directors, employees, and agents. Company shall maintain liability insurance covering any such damage or destruction of Customer Property.

14. Confidentiality.

14.1. Confidentiality. The parties recognize that they will have access to confidential proprietary information and/or trade secrets of the other party. Customer specifically acknowledges that the Services and Products constitute valuable trade secrets of Company. Accordingly, the parties agree that (i) the provisions of this Agreement, (ii) any information whatsoever with respect to the Services and Products, (iii) the course of dealing between Company and Customer hereunder and (iv) all other non-public information relating to the foregoing, including but not limited to user information submitted through Customer's web forms, and the number of such web forms submitted (collectively, the "Confidential Information") shall be treated by parties on a confidential basis and shall not be reproduced, reduced to writing, disclosed to any employees of the parties (except on a need to know basis and then only if the employee is subject to an obligation of confidentiality) or any other person or entity without the prior written consent of the disclosing party. Upon termination of this Agreement, any documentation or data reflecting any Confidential Information shall be promptly returned to the disclosing party. Disclosure of information pursuant to applicable statutes or regulations (collectively, "Laws") shall be excepted from this provision; provided, however, that prior to any disclosure pursuant to any Laws, the recipient will assert the confidential nature of the Confidential Information and will cooperate fully with the disclosing party, at disclosing party's expense, in protecting against any such disclosure including, but not limited to, obtaining a protective order or similar order narrowing the scope of such disclosure of the Confidential Information. In the event such protection is not obtained, the recipient shall disclose the Confidential Information only to the extent necessary to comply with the Laws.

14.2. Tampering. The parties agree that they will not attempt to copy in any way, alter, re-engineer or otherwise tamper with any of the Confidential Information of the other party.

14.3. Injunctive Relief. The parties acknowledge that violation of the provisions of Sections 14.1 or 14.2, above, could cause irreparable harm to the disclosing party and adequately compensable by monetary damages. In addition to other relief, it is agreed that injunctive relief shall be available to the disclosing party in the event of such violations without necessity of posting bond to prevent any actual or threatened violations of such sections.

15. Transfer and Assignment. Neither party may sell, assign or transfer any of its rights or obligations under this Agreement without the prior written consent of the other party. Notwithstanding the foregoing, Customer may assign this Agreement to an affiliate and Customer may assign this Agreement to any financially responsible third party with the Company's prior written consent, which consent shall not be unreasonably withheld, provided that such assignee shall assume in writing Customer's obligations hereunder and Customer shall remain liable hereunder.

16. Use of Customer's or Company's Name With Customer's prior written consent. Company shall be permitted to use Customer's name in connection with proposals to prospective customers and otherwise in print or electronic form for marketing or other purposes, including, but not limited to, use in connection with (i) compliance with applicable laws or regulations; and (ii) the protection of any rights relating to Company or its business. Customer may use the name "COMPANY" in connection with the Services and Products or otherwise only with Company's prior written consent.

17. No Third Party Beneficiaries. Except as otherwise specifically provided herein, this Agreement inures to the benefit of Company and Customer only and no third party shall enjoy the benefits of this Agreement or shall have any rights hereunder.

18. Notices. Unless otherwise specified herein, any notices or other communications required or permitted hereunder shall be sufficiently given if in writing and delivered personally or sent by facsimile transmission, internationally recognized overnight courier, registered or certified mail (postage prepaid with return receipt requested), to the address or facsimile number of Customer as set forth in the Order Form or Company as set forth below. Such notices or other communications shall be deemed received (i) on the date delivered, if delivered personally, (ii) on the date that return confirmation is received, if sent by facsimile, (iii) on the business day (or, if international, on the second business day) after being sent by an internationally recognized overnight air courier or (iv) five days after being sent, if sent by first class registered mail, return receipt requested.

19. Survival of Claims. Any claims arising out of or related to this Agreement must be brought no later than one year after it has accrued.

20. Independent Contractor Status. Nothing in this Agreement or in the course of dealing between Company and Customer pursuant hereto shall be deemed to create between Company and Customer (including their respective directors, officers, employees and agents) a partnership, joint venture, association, employment relationship or any other relationship other than that of independent contractors with respect to each other.

21. Governing Law. This Agreement shall be governed by and construed in accordance with the laws of the State of New York, without regard to choice of law provisions that would cause the application of the law of another jurisdiction.

22. Dispute Resolution.

22.1. Mutual Discussions; Mediation. If a dispute or difference of any kind whatsoever (a "Dispute") shall arise between Company and Customer in connection with, relating to or arising out of this Agreement, including the interpretation, performance, non-performance, or termination hereof, the parties shall attempt to settle such Dispute in the first instance by mutual discussions. If such Dispute has not been resolved within thirty (30) days by mutual discussions, the parties shall endeavor to settle the Dispute by mediation under the Mediation Rules of the American Arbitration Association prior to any recourse to arbitration pursuant to Section 22.2, below.

22.2. Arbitration. If such Dispute cannot be settled within thirty (30) days after submission to mediation pursuant to Section 22.1, above, such Dispute shall be settled by an arbitral tribunal (the "Tribunal") under the Arbitration Rules of the American Arbitration Association (the "Arbitration Rules"). Each party shall appoint an arbitrator within thirty (30) days after the expiration of the aforementioned thirty-day period, which arbitrators shall then jointly appoint a third arbitrator within thirty (30) days after the appointment of the second arbitrator, to act as president of the Tribunal. Arbitrators not so appointed shall be appointed pursuant to the Arbitration Rules. The costs of the arbitration shall be borne by the parties as determined by the Tribunal. The award rendered in any arbitration commenced hereunder shall be final and conclusive and judgment thereon may be entered in any court having jurisdiction for its enforcement. Neither party shall (i) appeal to any court from the decision of the Tribunal or (ii) have any right to commence or maintain any suit or legal proceeding concerning a Dispute until such Dispute has been determined in accordance with the arbitration procedure provided for herein and then only for enforcement of the award rendered in such arbitration. All mediation and arbitration proceedings pursuant to this Agreement shall take place in New York City.

23. Headings. The section and subsection headings have been used in this Agreement as a matter of convenience only and shall not be used in the interpretation of any provision of this Agreement.

24. Non-Waiver, Waiver and Amendment. Failure by either Company or Customer to enforce any of the provisions of this Agreement or any rights with respect hereto or the failure to exercise any option provided hereunder shall in no way be considered to be waiver of such provisions, rights or options, or to in any way affect the validity of this Agreement. No waiver of any rights under this Agreement, no any modification or amendment of this Agreement shall be effective or enforceable unless in writing and signed by both parties, except as provided by Section 5, above.

25. Severability. If one or more of the provisions contained in the Agreement are found to be invalid, illegal or unenforceable in any respect, the validity, legality and enforce ability of the remaining provisions shall not be affected.

26. Entire Agreement. This Agreement constitutes the entire agreement of the parties and supersedes all oral negotiations and prior writings with respect thereto. When used in this Agreement, the terms "hereof", "herein" and "hereunder" refer to this Agreement in its entirety, including any attachments to this Agreement and not to any particular provisions of this Agreement, unless otherwise indicated.

27. Counterparts. This Agreement may be executed in any number of counterparts, each of which shall be deemed an original, but all which together shall constitute one and the same instrument.

28. USE OF COMPANY SERVICES AND PRODUCTS CONSTITUTES ACCEPTANCE OF THESE TERMS AND CONDITIONS.

IN WITNESS WHEREOF, the parties have executed this Agreement as of the day and year first written above.

Company	Customer
By:______________________	By:____________________

FORM 9-3

Online Copyright Protection Terms

All content and graphics on this site are protected by U.S. copyright and international treaties, and may not be copied without the express permission of Operator, which reserves all rights. Re-use of any of Operator content and graphics for any purpose is strictly prohibited. Permission to use Operator content is granted on a case-by-case basis. Please direct your inquiries to info@operator.com.

FORM 9-4

Copyright Protection Terms (Permitting Noncommercial Sharing of Assets)

Access to and use of the Museum's image files and data is subject to the following terms and conditions:

1. The Museum retains all rights, including copyrights, in data, image, text, and any other information contained in these files.

2. The material contained in this website is copyrighted by the Museum or by third parties from whom we have obtained permission to publish their materials on the Museum's website and whose credit line appears in association with their copyrighted information. Any commercial use or publication of any material from the Museum's website is strictly prohibited.

3. The Museum's image and text files on this website are made available for noncommercial, educational, and personal use only. Copyright or redistribution in any manner for commercial use is not permitted. Commercial publication or exploitation of the Museum's website files is specifically prohibited. Users may download these files for their own use, subject to any additional terms or restrictions that may be provided with the individual file or program. Fair educational use of the contents of this website is permitted. Specifically, an Internet user may download images and text files and share them with others for limited noncommercial and educational purposes only.

4. Anyone wishing to use any of these files or images for publication, commercial use, or any purpose not permitted herein must request and receive prior written permission from the Museum, which retains the right to grant permission for such use in its sole discretion. [*Insert contact information*] All requests for permission to reproduce images must be submitted in writing and should include the following information: the artist and title of the art work, the format desired (including color or black-and-white), and the author's name, title, and publisher of the publication in which the work will be reproduced.

→ [button] I understand and agree.

FORM 9-5

Copyright Protection Terms (As a Condition of Access)

Museum presents these images as a catalogue of our collections. Because we respect the right of every artist represented in the collection to make a living, we must remind you that you may not reproduce, alter or transmit any artwork in the catalogue without written permission, and that we will prosecute anyone who violates this rule.

→ [button] <u>I understand and agree.</u>

[*Note that this click-through agreement must be placed at a strategic point in the viewing process. Its efficacy will also be connected with the back-end database administration and tracking of each user, and so appears deceptively simple.*]

FORM 9-6

Museum Web Site Terms of Use

Your access to and use of the site ("Site") is subject to the following terms and conditions ("Terms and Conditions") and all applicable laws. By accessing and browsing the Site, you accept, without limitation or qualification, the Terms and Conditions and acknowledge that any other agreements between you and the Museum concerning the issues covered herein are superseded and of no force or effect.

1. Unless otherwise noted, you may download material displayed on the Site for non-commercial, personal use only provided that you retain all copyright and other proprietary notices contained on the materials. You may not, however, distribute, modify, transmit, reuse, repost, or use the content of the Site for public or commercial purposes, including the text, images, audio, and video without the Museum's written permission. The Museum neither warrants nor represents that your use of materials displayed on the Site will not infringe rights of third parties not owned by or affiliated with the Museum.

2. Images of people or places displayed on the Site are either the property of, or used with permission by the Museum. The use of these images by you, or anyone else authorized by you, is prohibited unless specifically permitted by these Terms and Conditions or specific permission provided elsewhere on the Site. Any unauthorized use of the images may violate copyright laws, trademark laws, the laws of privacy and publicity, and communications regulations and statutes.

3. The trademarks, logos, and service marks (collectively the "Trademarks") displayed on the Site are registered and unregistered Trademarks of the Museum and others. Nothing contained on the Site should be construed as granting, by implication or otherwise, any license or right to use any Trademark displayed on the Site without the written permission of the Museum or such third party that may own the Trademarks displayed on the Site. Your misuse of the Trademarks displayed on the Site, or any other content on the Site, except as provided in these Terms and Conditions, is strictly prohibited. You are also advised that the Museum will aggressively enforce its intellectual property rights to the fullest extent of the law, including the seeking of criminal prosecution.

4. Your use of and browsing in the Site are at your risk. Neither the Museum nor any other party involved in creating, producing, or delivering the Site is liable for any direct, incidental, consequential, indirect, or punitive damages arising out of your access to, or use of, the Site. Without limiting the foregoing, everything on the Site is provided to you "AS IS" WITHOUT WARRANTY OF ANY KIND, EITHER EXPRESSED OR IMPLIED, INCLUDING, BUT NOT LIMITED TO,

THE IMPLIED WARRANTIES OF MERCHANTABILITY, FITNESS FOR A PARTICULAR PURPOSE, OR NON-INFRINGEMENT. Some jurisdictions may not allow the exclusion of implied warranties, so some of the above exclusions may not apply to you. Check your local laws for any restrictions or limitations regarding the exclusion of implied warranties. The Museum also assumes no responsibility, and shall not be liable for, any damages to, or viruses that may infect, your computer equipment or other property on account of your access to, use of, or browsing in the Site or your downloading of any materials, data, text, software, images, video, or audio form the Site.

5. The Museum has not reviewed all of the sites linked to the Site and is not responsible for the content of any off-site pages or any other sites linked to the Site. Your linking to any other off-site pages or other sites is at your own risk.

6. The Museum makes no warranties or representations as to the accuracy of any information on the Site and assumes no liability or responsibility for any errors or omissions in the content of the Site.

7. Although the Museum may from time to time monitor or review discussions, chats, postings, transmissions, bulletin boards, and the like on the Site, it is under no obligation to do so and assumes no responsibility or liability arising from the content of any such locations nor for any error, defamation, libel, slander, omission, falsehood, obscenity, pornography, profanity, danger, or inaccuracy contained in any information within such locations on the Site. You are prohibited from posting or transmitting any unlawful, threatening, libelous, defamatory, obscene, scandalous, inflammatory, pornographic, or profane material or any material that could constitute or encourage conduct that would be considered a criminal offense, give rise to civil liability, or otherwise violate any law. The Museum will fully cooperate with any law enforcement authorities or court order requesting or directing the Museum to disclose the identity of anyone posting any such information or materials.

8. Any communication or material you transmit to the Site by electronic mail or otherwise, including any data, questions, comments, suggestions, or the like is, and will be treated as, nonconfidential and non-proprietary. Anything you transmit or post may be used by the Museum or its affiliates for any purpose, including, but not limited to, reproduction, disclosure, transmission, publication, broadcast and posting. Furthermore, the Museum is free to pursue any ideas, concepts, know-how, or techniques contained in any communication you send to the Site for any purpose whatsoever including, but not limited to, developing, manufacturing and marketing products using such information.

9. The Museum may at any time revise these Terms and Conditions by updating this posting. You are bound by any such revisions and should therefore periodically visit this page to review the then current Terms and Conditions.

10. For purposes of the Digital Millennium Copyright Act (DMCA), 17 U.S.C. Sec. 512 (c)(2), the Museum has designated an agent for notification of claimed infringement as follows: [Name, contact information]. The museum provides the above contact information for purposes of the DMCA only and reserves the right to respond only to correspondence that is relevant to this purpose.

USE OF MUSEUM SITE, SERVICES OR PRODUCTS CONSTITUTES ACCEPTANCE OF THESE TERMS AND CONDITIONS.

FORM 9-7

Terms of Use of Online Images

Access to and use of museum image files and data is subject to the following terms and conditions:

1. Software, documentation, electronic image files, and other materials ("Materials") may be covered by restrictions, and/or copyright. The Museum's image files are made available for non-commercial, personal use. Copying or redistribution in any manner for personal, corporate or commercial gain is not permitted. For questions about whether a particular use is permissible contact the Museum at [contact information].

2. The museum specifically retains any rights, including possible copyright, which it may have in data, files, and/or the images they contain.

3. Users may download these files for their own use, subject to any additional terms or restrictions that may be provided with the individual file or program.

4. All parties posting, obtaining and/or using these Materials represent and warrant to the museum that the submission, installation, copying, distribution, and use of such Materials will not violate any other party's proprietary rights.

5. The museum is not responsible for any errors created in or damage to the Materials as a result of their use. All Materials maintained are provided "as is" with no warranties of any kind.

6. THE MUSEUM DISCLAIMS ALL EXPRESS WARRANTIES INCLUDED IN ANY MATERIALS, AND FURTHER DISCLAIMS ALL IMPLIED WARRANTIES, INCLUDING WARRANTIES OF MERCHANTABILITY, FITNESS FOR PARTICULAR PURPOSES, AND NON-INFRINGEMENT OF PROPRIETARY RIGHTS.

7. Materials may not be used for any purpose requiring fail-safe performance, or as to which defects in or failure of Materials could cause death, personal injury, or property or environmental damage ("High Risk Activities"). THE MUSEUM DISCLAIMS ALL EXPRESS AND IMPLIED WARRANTIES WITH RESPECT TO HIGH RISK ACTIVITIES. MUSEUM SHALL NOT BE LIABLE FOR ANY DAMAGES OF ANY KIND, INCLUDING CONSEQUENTIAL OR INCIDENTAL DAMAGES, ARISING FROM THE SUBMISSION, INSTALLA-

TION, MAINTENANCE, TRANSMISSION, COPYING, MODIFICATION, DISTRIBUTION OR ANY USE OF ANY MATERIALS.

If the User agrees with the foregoing terms and conditions, select the "I Agree" button. Otherwise select the "I don't Agree" button.

→ [button] I agree. → [button] I don't agree.

FORM 9-8

Privacy Policy

Privacy Statement

At ArtInfoCo., protecting your privacy is very important. We want to make your experience on the Internet as comfortable and rewarding as possible, and we want you to make use of the Internet's vast array of information, tools and opportunities with complete confidence.

A. User information. When users visit the pages of the ArtInfoCo. Websites, they may be asked to give us contact information, such as their names and email addresses. Financial information that is collected is used to bill the user for products and services.

B. Our sites use order forms for customers to request information, products and services. Contact information from the order forms, such as a user's email address, is used to send orders and information about our company to our customers.

C. Our online surveys ask users for contact information (such as their email addresses) and demographic information (such as zip codes, age, or income levels). We use contact data from our surveys to send information about our company to our users. We use demographic and profile data to tailor our sites and display content according to our users' interests and preferences. This information is shared with advertisers only on an aggregate basis. We do not share any personal information about our users. We run contests on our sites in which we ask users for contact information, such as their email addresses. The customer's contact information is used to contact the user when necessary. In all cases above, users may opt out of receiving future mailings that may result from providing email addresses. See the Choice to Opt Out section, below.

D. Our sites may also record the user's IP address, which helps us diagnose problems with our server and administer our Website. Your IP address also is used to gather broad demographic information. If you are a member of any of the ArtInfoCo. programs, we will use a "cookie" to save your settings and provide your own personalized information. Cookies are tiny data files that are placed on your hard drive when you visit some Websites. Only information that you specifically supply, such as a user ID, will be included in the cookie.

E. Public Forums. Please remember that any information that you disclose in ArtInfoCo. public areas of the Internet becomes public information. You should exercise caution when deciding to disclose personal information.

F. Security. Our sites have security measures in place to protect the loss, misuse and alteration of the information under our control.

G. Children's Guidelines. We do not collect online contact information without prior parental consent or parental notification, which will include an opportunity for the parent to prevent use of the information and participation in the activity. Without prior parental consent, online information will only be used to respond directly to the child's request and will not be used for other purposes without prior parental consent. We do not collect personally identifiable offline contact information without prior parental consent. We do not distribute to third parties any personally identifiable information with out prior parental consent. We do not give the ability to publicly post or otherwise distribute personally identifiable contact information without prior parental consent. We do not entice by the prospect of a special game, prize or other activity, to divulge more information than is needed to participate in the activity.

H. Choice to Opt Out. Our sites provide users the opportunity to opt out of receiving communications from us and our partners at the point where we request information about the user.

I. Change/Modify. Our sites give users options for changing and modifying information previously provided. To make or inquire about such changes, send email to Webmaster@ArtInfoCo.com.

FORM 9-9

Commercial Web Site Terms of Use (E-Commerce Site)

These terms and conditions of use apply to and govern your use of the Company Website (the "Site"). Your use of the Site signifies your agreement to be bound by these terms and conditions. If you do not agree to be bound by these terms and conditions of use, you may not access or otherwise use the Site. Company's then-current privacy policy which addresses Company's use and release of information collected from your use of the Site is available at www.Company/about/privacy.html.

1) License to Use the Site. Company grants you a non-exclusive, non-transferable, limited right to access, use and display the Site and the materials thereon for your personal use only, provided that you comply fully with these terms and conditions of use. You shall not interfere or attempt to interfere with the operation of the Site in any way through any means or device including, but not limited to, spamming, hacking, uploading computer viruses or time bombs, or the means expressly prohibited by any provision of these terms and conditions of use.

2) Changes to Terms and Conditions. Company reserves the right, at its sole discretion, to change, modify, add or remove any portion of these terms and conditions of use, in whole or in part, at any time. Changes in these terms and conditions of use will be effective when posted. You agree to review these terms and conditions of use periodically to be aware of any changes. Your continued use of the Site after any changes to these terms and conditions of use are posted will be considered acceptance of those changes.

3) Ownership; Restrictions. Company owns, controls, licenses or has the right to use and provide the Site and all material on the Site, including without limitation text, images, articles, photographs, illustrations, audio and video clips, (collectively the "Art Works"). The Site is protected by copyright as a collective work and/or compilation, pursuant to U.S. copyright laws, international conventions, and other copyright laws. Company is the owner of the copyright in the entire Site. Company owns a copyright in the selection, coordination, arrangement and enhancement of the Site. You agree to abide by any and all copyright notices, information or restrictions displayed on the Site. You may not modify, create derivative works from, participate in the transfer or sale of, post on the World Wide Web, or in any way exploit the Site or any portion thereof for any public or commercial use without the express written permission of Company. You may download one (1) copy of the Art Works from the Site for your personal use, provided that you maintain all copyright, attribution and other notices contained in such Art Works, including without limitation trademarks and service marks of Company

and its affiliates or the copyright holder identified in the individual Art Work's copyright notice. You acknowledge that you do not acquire any ownership rights by downloading copyrighted material. You are responsible for complying with all applicable laws, rules and regulations regarding your use of any such downloaded Art Works. In the event of any permitted copying, redistribution or publication of material from the Site, no changes in or deletion of author attribution, trademark, legend or copyright notice shall be made. You may obtain more information on the copyrights, trademarks, and service marks of Company and its affiliates and Art Works owners by viewing the copyright and trademark notices posted on the Site.

4) Change to Site or Art Works. Company shall have the right for any reason, in its sole discretion, to terminate, change, suspend or discontinue any aspect of the Site, including but not limited to Art Works, features, or hours of availability. Company may also impose limits on certain features and services or restrict your access to parts or all of the Site without notice or liability.

5) Monitoring, Editing and Disclosure of User Material. You agree that Company has the right, but not the obligation, to monitor all material on the Site at any time for any reason in its sole discretion to determine compliance with these terms and conditions of use and any other operating rules that Company may establish from time to time. Notwithstanding this right of Company, Company does not and cannot review all materials posted to the Site by users, and Company is not responsible for any such materials posted by users. Company reserves the right at all times to edit, disclose, refuse to post, request removal of or remove any material or information as may be necessary to comply with any law, regulation or government or agency request or if, in Company's sole discretion, such materials are objectionable or in violation of these terms and conditions of use.

6) Indemnification. You shall indemnify, defend and hold harmless Company, and all its officers, directors, owners, agents, employees, Art Works providers, affiliates, licensors and licensees (collectively, the "Indemnified Parties") from and against any and all losses, damages, liabilities, and claims and all fees, costs, expenses, of any kind related thereto (including, without limitation, reasonable attorneys' fees) incurred by the Indemnified Parties in connection with any claim arising out of, based upon or resulting from your use of the Site. Company reserves the right, at its own expense, to assume the exclusive defense and control of any matter otherwise subject to indemnification by you and you shall not in any event settle any matter without the written consent of Company.

7) Links to Other Website. The Site contains links and pointers to the other World Wide Web Internet sites, resources, and sponsors of the Site. Links to and from any site to other third party sites, maintained by third parties, do not constitute an endorsement by Company or any of its subsidiaries and affiliates of any

third party resources or their contents. Links do not imply that Company or the Site sponsors are affiliated or associated with or are legally authorized to use any trademark, trade name, logo or copyright symbol displayed in or accessible through the links, or that any linked sites are authorized to use any trademark, trade name, logo or copyright symbol of Company or any of its affiliates. You should direct any concerns regarding any external link to its site administrator or Webmaster. Company does not represent or endorse the accuracy or reliability of any advice, opinion, statement, or other information displayed or distributed through the Site. You acknowledge that any reliance upon any such opinion, advice, statement, memorandum, or information shall be at your sole risk. Company reserves the right, in its sole discretion, to correct any errors or omissions in any portion of the Site.

8) Disclaimer of Warranties and Damages; Limitation of Liability. THE SITE, INCLUDING ALL CONTENT, SOFTWARE, FUNCTIONS, MATERIALS AND INFORMATION MADE AVAILABLE ON OR ACCESSED THROUGH THE SITE, IS PROVIDED ON AN "AS IS" "AS AVAILABLE" BASIS WITHOUT REPRESENTATIONS OR WARRANTIES OF ANY KIND WHATSOEVER EXPRESS OR IMPLIED, INCLUDING WITHOUT LIMITATION, NON-INFRINGEMENT, MERCHANTABILITY OR FITNESS FOR A PARTICULAR PURPOSE. NEITHER COMPANY NOR ITS CONTENT PROVIDERS WARRANT THAT THE FUNCTIONS, FEATURES OR CONTENT CONTAINED IN THE SITE WILL BE UNINTERRUPTED OR ERROR FREE, THAT DEFECTS WILL BE CORRECTED, OR THAT ANY OTHER SITE OR THE SERVER THAT MAKES IT AVAILABLE IS FREE OF VIRUSES OR OTHER HARMFUL COMPONENTS; NOR DO THEY MAKE ANY WARRANTY OR REPRESENTATION AS TO THE ACCURACY OR RELIABILITY OF THE SITE, THE CONTENT THEREOF, THE MATERIALS, INFORMATION AND FUNCTIONS MADE ACCESSIBLE BY THE SOFTWARE USED ON OR ACCESSED THROUGH THE SITE, ANY PRODUCTS OR SERVICES OR HYPERTEXT LINKS TO THIRD PARTIES OR FOR ANY BREACH OF SECURITY ASSOCIATED WITH THE TRANSMISSION OF SENSITIVE INFORMATION THROUGH THE SITE OR ANY LINKED SITE. COMPANY AND ITS SUBSIDIARIES AND AFFILIATES MAKE NO WARRANTIES AND SHALL NOT BE LIABLE FOR THE USE OF THE SITE, INCLUDING WITHOUT LIMITATION, THE CONTENT AND ANY ERRORS CONTAINED THEREIN UNDER ANY DIRECT OR INDIRECT CIRCUMSTANCES, INCLUDING BUT NOT LIMITED TO COMPANY'S NEGLIGENCE. IF YOU ARE DISSATISFIED WITH THE SITE OR ANY MATERIALS ON THE SITE, YOUR SOLE REMEDY IS TO DISCONTINUE USING THE SITE. CERTAIN CONTENT MAY BE CONSIDERED OBJECTIONABLE BY INDIVIDUAL USERS AND USERS MUST EXERCISE

THEIR DISCRETION IN USING AND ALLOWING MINORS OR OTHERS TO USE THE SITE. UNDER NO CIRCUMSTANCES SHALL COMPANY, ITS SUBSIDIARIES, AFFILIATES OR CONTENT PROVIDERS BE LIABLE FOR ANY SPECIAL, INCIDENTAL OR CONSEQUENTIAL DAMAGES THAT ARE DIRECTLY OR INDIRECTLY RELATED TO THE USE OF, OR THE INABILITY TO USE, THE CONTENT, MATERIALS AND FUNCTIONS IN THE SITE, INCLUDING WITHOUT LIMITATION LOSS OF REVENUE OR ANTICIPATED PROFITS OR LOST BUSINESS, EVEN IF SUCH ENTITIES OR AN AUTHORIZED REPRESENTATIVE THEREOF HAVE BEEN ADVISED OF THE POSSIBILITY OF SUCH DAMAGES. SOME STATES DO NOT ALLOW THE EXCLUSION OR LIMITATION OF INCIDENTAL OR CONSEQUENTIAL DAMAGES, SO THE ABOVE LIMITATION OR EXCLUSION MAY NOT APPLY TO YOU. IN NO EVENT SHALL THE TOTAL LIABILITY OF COMPANY, ITS SUBSIDIARIES AND AFFILIATES TO YOU FOR ALL DAMAGES, LOSSES, AND CAUSES OF ACTION (WHETHER IN CONTRACT OR TORT, INCLUDING, BUT NOT LIMITED TO, NEGLIGENCE OR OTHERWISE) ARISING FROM THESE TERMS AND CONDITIONS OF USE OR YOUR USE OF THE SITE EXCEED, IN THE AGGREGATE, $100.00.

9) Company's Rights to Materials Provided by Users. Company welcomes your comments regarding our merchandise and services, including the Site. However, any or all material and information provided by you to the Site may be included in a database owned by Company and its subsidiaries and affiliates in which we have rights and interest, including but not limited to, the compilation copyright. We reserve the right to use any information or materials you provide to us or that we obtain through your use of the Site to the fullest extent permitted by law. By posting messages, uploading files, inputting data or engaging in any other form of communication (individually or collectively "Communications") to or within the Site, you grant to Company a perpetual, worldwide, irrevocable, unrestricted, non-exclusive, royalty-free license to use (including use for promotional and advertising purposes), copy, license, sublicense, adapt, distribute, display, publicly perform, reproduce, transmit, modify, edit and otherwise exploit such Communications and any ideas or original materials contained in such Communications, in all media now known or hereafter developed. This grant shall include the right to exploit any and all proprietary rights in such Communications including, without limitation, any and all rights under copyright, trademark. service mark or patent laws under any relevant jurisdiction. You waive all rights you may have to inspect and/or approve of any use by Company of any material or idea submitted by you in any Communications or receive any compensation for such use. You waive all rights to any claim against Company for any alleged or actual infringements of any proprietary rights, rights of privacy and publicity, moral rights, and rights of attribution in connection with such Communications. You

agree and understand that Company is under no obligations to use any material or ideas submitted by you in any Communications in any way whatsoever.

10) No Responsibility for Transmitted Material. You acknowledge that transmissions to and from this Site are not confidential and your Communications may be read or intercepted by others. You acknowledge that by submitting Communications to Company or the Site, no confidential, fiduciary, contractually implied or other relationship is created between you and Company or any Company affiliate or subsidiary other than pursuant to these terms and conditions of use. Company shall not be responsible for the payment of any monies to any party in connection with Company's use of Communications submitted by you to the Site.

11) Non-United States Residents. Company makes no representation that materials in the Site, including merchandise offered for sale on the Site and their copyrights, trademarks, patents, and licensing arrangements, are appropriate or available for use in locations other than the United States. Those who choose to access this Site from other locations outside of the U.S. do so on their own initiative and are responsible for compliance with local laws, if and to the extent local laws are applicable. With respect to shipments of merchandise to consumers, wherever they may reside, title to the merchandise shall pass to the buyer upon delivery of the merchandise to the common carrier.

12) General Provisions. These terms and conditions of use shall be governed by and construed in accordance with the laws of the State of New York, without regard to conflicts of laws provisions. The sole and exclusive jurisdiction for any action or proceeding arising out of or related to these terms and conditions of use shall be an appropriate State or Federal court located in New York County in the State of New York and you hereby irrevocably consent to the jurisdiction of such courts. If for any reason a court of competent jurisdiction finds any provision of these terms and conditions of use, or portion thereof, to be unenforceable, that provision shall be enforced to the maximum extent permissible so as to effect the intent of these terms and conditions of use, and the remainder of these terms and conditions of use shall continue in full force and effect. These terms and conditions of use constitute the entire agreement between you and Company with respect to the subject matter hereof, and supersede all previous written or oral agreements between the parties with respect to such subject matter. No waiver by either you or Company of any breach or default hereunder shall be deemed to be a waiver of any preceding or subsequent breach or default. The section headings used herein are for convenience only and shall not be given any legal import.

FORM 9-10

Web Site Terms of Use (Commercial Services Site)

Our Website is intended solely for the use of persons who agree to be bound by these Company terms of use ("Terms"). Please read these Terms carefully. By using the Company Website, you agree to be bound by these Terms. If you do not agree with these Terms, do not use this Website.

1. Acceptance of Terms

The Terms are agreed to by and between Company and you. Company provides the services and information accessible on and through the Company site (the "Services") to you subject to the Terms. In addition to the Terms, any other Company terms specific to any other transaction between you and Company shall apply to that transaction, including a separate written license or other agreement with Company that is currently in effect. If there is a conflict with the Terms, then the transaction-specific terms or separate agreement governs. If your agent uses the Company site on your behalf, you nonetheless agree to be bound by these Terms as a Principal, and your continued use of the Company site will ratify any unauthorized actions of your agent.

2. Your Obligations

In consideration of your use of the Services, you agree to be solely responsible for: (a) providing true, accurate, current, and complete information about yourself or your agents as prompted by any Service registration form (the "Registration Data"), and (b) maintaining and promptly updating the Registration Data to keep it true, accurate, current and complete. You are solely responsible for the security of any password provided to you by Company. If you provide any information that is false, inaccurate, out of date, or incomplete, or Company has reasonable grounds to suspect that such information is false, inaccurate, not current, or incomplete, Company may suspend or terminate your account (as described in section 8) and refuse any and all current or future use of the Services (or any portion thereof). You are responsible for all costs and charges, including without limitation, phone charges and telecommunications equipment, that you incur in order to use the Services.

3. Confidentiality of Company Information

In order to gain access to the Services, you agree to these confidentiality provisions:

3.1 You acknowledge that you may obtain direct access to certain Company confidential information via the Website, including Company databases containing confidential information of Company and its suppliers, such as technical, marketing, and other valuable information ("Information"). You must hold Information in strict confidence and may provide Information to your employees only on a need-to-know basis. You may use the Information from the Website solely for the purpose of purchasing, maintaining and supporting Your Company products and equipment. Title to and ownership of Information remains with Company. You agree, either as an individual or on behalf of your agent(s) and/or principal(s), to be bound by the provisions of this section 3.

3.2 You do not acquire any rights in Information, except the limited right to use Information as described above.

3.3 Any breach of the Terms will result in irreparable harm to Company for which damages would be an inadequate remedy and, therefore, in addition to its rights and remedies otherwise available at law, Company will be entitled to equitable relief, including both a preliminary and permanent injunction, if such a breach occurs. You waive any requirement for the posting of a bond or other security if Company seeks such an injunction.

3.4 Your obligations regarding Information expire five (5) years after the date of disclosure, although such expiration (or early termination of these Terms) shall not otherwise affect the confidential nature of the Information. Upon termination of the Terms or Company's written request, you must cease use of Information and return or destroy all Information.

3.5 The Terms impose no obligation upon you with respect to Information that you can establish by legally sufficient evidence: (a) you possessed, or knew, prior to your receipt from Company, without an obligation to maintain its confidentiality; (b) is or becomes generally known to the public through no act or omission by you, or otherwise without violation of the Terms; (c) you obtained from a third party who had the right to disclose it, without an obligation to keep such information confidential; (d) you independently developed without the use of Information and without the participation of individuals who have had access to Information, or (e) in response to a valid order by a court or other governmental body, as otherwise required by law, or as necessary to establish the rights of either party under these Terms and as disclosed after prior notice to Company adequate to afford Company the opportunity to object to the disclosure.

4. Your Conduct

4.1 You understand that all information, data, text, software, music, sound, photographs, graphics, video, messages, or other materials ("Content"), whether publicly posted or privately transmitted, are the sole responsibility of the person from whom such Content originated. This means that you, and not Company, are entirely responsible for all Content that you upload, post or otherwise transmit via the Services. Company does not control the Content posted via the Services and, as such, does not guarantee the accuracy, integrity or quality of such Content. You understand that by using the Services, you may be exposed to Content that is offensive, indecent or objectionable.

4.2 While it is not our intent to monitor your online communications, Company reserves the right to edit or remove content that we become aware of and determine to be harmful, offensive or otherwise in violation of these Terms. Violation of these restrictions ("Restrictions") may also result in the termination or suspension of your account. These Restrictions apply to all content provided to or through the Services, including email messages, newsgroup postings, chat, and personal or business web pages.

4.3 You agree not to post or store on Company or any of its affiliated sites any Content that violates or infringes anyone's intellectual property rights (including copyrights, trademarks, trade secrets, patents, publicity rights or (to the extent protectable) confidential ideas) or that is obscene, defamatory, racist, lewd, excessively violent, harassing or otherwise objectionable ("Objectionable").

4.4 You agree not to use the Services in any way for spamming or to transmit chain letters, junk email or bulk communications. You agree not to transmit through the Services any Material that is Objectionable. You agree not to use any Company domain name as a pseudonymous return email address for any communications that you transmit from another location or through another service; and you may not pretend to be someone else when using the Services. Furthermore, you agree not to transmit unsolicited or bulk communications to any Company account holder or to any Company or affiliated email address (regardless of whether you use the Services to transmit any such communication).

4.5 You agree not to use the Services for any unlawful activities not otherwise covered above, including (without limitation) attempting to compromise the security of any networked account or site. Additionally, you agree not to use the Services to: (a) impersonate any person or entity, including, but not limited to, a Company official, or falsely state or otherwise misrepresent your affiliation with a person or entity; (b) forge headers or otherwise manipulate identifiers in order to disguise the origin of any Content transmitted through the Services or develop hidden pages or images (those not linked to Company from another accessible page); (c) upload, post or otherwise transmit any Content that you do not have a right to transmit to the public under any law or under contractual or fiduciary relationships (such as inside information, proprietary or confidential information learned or disclosed as part of employment relationships or under nondisclosure agreements); (d) upload, post or otherwise transmit any material that contains software viruses or any other computer code, files or programs designed to interrupt, destroy or limit the functionality of any computer software or hardware or telecommunications equipment; (f) violate any applicable local, state, national or international law, or any regulations having the force of law; or (g) collect or store personal data about other users.

5. Content Submitted to Company

5.1 Company does not claim ownership of the Content you place on any part of Company. By submitting Content to Company for inclusion on Company, you grant Company a worldwide, royalty-free, and nonexclusive license to reproduce, modify, distribute, transmit, display, perform, adapt, and publish the Content (including in digital form) solely for the purposes relating to the Company Website.

5.2 You acknowledge that Company does not pre-screen Content, but that Company and its designees have the right (but not the obligation) in their sole discretion to block or restrict access to or the availability of, or to disable, any Content that is available via the Services. Without limiting the foregoing, Company and its designees may disable, restrict access to or the availability of, any Content that violates the Terms or is otherwise objectionable. You must evaluate, and bear all risks associated with, the use of any Content, including any reliance on the accuracy, completeness, or usefulness of such Content.

5.3 Unless otherwise explicitly stated, any "Materials" (defined below) provided by you in connection with this Website shall be deemed to be provided on a nonproprietary and nonconfidential basis. Company shall have no obligation of any kind with respect to such Materials and shall be free to use or disseminate such Materials on an unrestricted basis for any purpose. You acknowledge that you are responsible for the Materials that you submit, and you, not Company, have full responsibility for the Materials, including their legality, reliability, appropriateness, originality and copyright.

6. Spam Email and Postings

You agree that Company would be irreparably harmed by the use, by you or others, of Company's Services or facilities in connection with the transmission of spam newsgroup postings or unsolicited email in violation of these Terms, and that Company is entitled to obtain injunctive relief against any such transmission (in addition to all other remedies available at law or in equity). Company reserves the right to block, filter or delete unsolicited email.

7. Indemnity

You agree to indemnify and hold Company, and its subsidiaries, affiliates, officers, agents, co-branders, alliance members, or other partners, and employees, harmless from any claim or demand, including reasonable attorneys' fees, made by any third party due to or arising out of your Content, your use of the Services, including any use by your employees (including as described in Section 3.1), your connection to the Services, your violation of the Terms, or your violation of any rights of another.

8. Notices; Modification and Termination of Terms, Services

8.1 Company may send notices to you via either email or regular mail. Company reserves the right at any time and from time to time to revise, modify or discontinue, temporarily or permanently, the Terms and/or Services (or any part thereof) with or without notice. Any such revision or change will be binding and effective immediately upon posting of the revised Terms or change to the Services on the Company Website, or upon notification to you by e-mail or United States mail. You agree to periodically review our Website, including the current version of these Terms, to be aware of any such revisions. If you do not agree with any revision to the Terms or Services, you may discontinue use of the Website and/or Services. If such changes affect your continuing obligations and/or Information within your possession or control, you agree to return or destroy the Information and certify to us that you have done so, and to provide us with notice of discontinuance by e-mail or United States mail addressed as follows, Attention: Legal Affairs, [address]. Notice of your rejection of the Terms and/or Services will be effective on receipt and processing by us. By continuing to use the Website and/or Services after any revision to these Terms and/or Services, you agree to abide by and be bound by any such revisions or changes.

8.2 Company, in its sole discretion, may terminate any password provided to you, or your use of the Services, and remove and discard any Content within the Services, for any reason, including, without limitation, for lack of use or if Company believes that you have violated or acted inconsistently with the letter or spirit of the Terms. Any termination of your access to the Services under any provision of the Terms may be effected without prior notice, and Company may immediately de-activate or delete any account provided for your benefit and all related information and files and/or bar any further access to such files or the Services. Further, Company will not be liable to you or any third-party for any termination, modification, or suspension of the Services.

9. Links

9.1 The Services may provide, or third parties may provide, links to other Internet sites or resources. Because Company has no control over such sites and resources, you acknowledge and agree that Company is not responsible for the availability of such external sites or resources, and does not endorse and is not responsible or liable for any Content, advertising, products, or other materials on or available from such sites or resources. Company will not be responsible or liable, directly or indirectly, for any damage or loss caused or alleged to be caused by or in connection with use of or reliance on any such Content, goods or services available on or through any such site or resource.

9.2 This Website may be linked to other websites that are not under the control of and are not maintained by Company. Company is not responsible for the content of those sites. Company is providing these links to you only as a convenience, and the inclusion of any link to such sites does not imply endorsement by Company of those sites.

10. Company Proprietary Rights

10.1 The Services and any software used in connection with the Services ("Software") contain proprietary and confidential information that is protected by applicable intellectual property and other laws. Content contained in third-party advertisements or information presented to you through the Services or advertisers is protected by copyrights, trademarks, service marks, patents, publicity rights, or other proprietary rights and laws. Except as expressly authorized by Company or advertisers, you agree not to modify, rent, lease, loan, sell, distribute or create derivative works based on the Services or the Software, in whole or in part.

10.2 You must not modify, decompile, or reverse engineer any Software Company discloses to you, and must not remove, overprint, or deface any notice of copyright, trademark, logo, legend, or other notice of ownership from any originals or copies of Software or Information from the Services.

10.3 "Company Trademarks" means all names, marks, brands, logos, designs, trade dress and other designations Company uses in connection with Company products ("Products") or Services. Customer may refer to Products and Services by the associated Company Trademarks, provided that such reference is truthful and not misleading. Customer may not remove or alter any Company Trademarks, nor may it co-logo Products or material associated with Customer's services. Customer acknowledges Company's rights in Company Trademarks and agrees that any and all use of Company Trademarks by Customer shall inure to the sole benefit of Company. Customer agrees not to incorporate any Company Trademarks into Customer's trademarks, service marks, company names, Internet addresses, domain names, or any other similar designations.

11. Disclaimer of Warranties

11.1 YOUR USE OF THE SERVICES IS AT YOUR SOLE RISK. THE SERVICES AND INFORMATION (AS DEFINED IN SECTIONS 1.2 AND 3.1) ARE PROVIDED ON AN "AS IS" AND "AS AVAILABLE" BASIS. UNLESS OTHERWISE EXPLICITLY STATED, THE MATERIALS ON THE WEBSITE ARE PROVIDED "AS IS", AND ARE EXPERIMENTAL. COMPANY DISCLAIMS

ALL EXPRESS OR IMPLIED CONDITIONS, REPRESENTATIONS, AND WARRANTIES OF ANY KIND, INCLUDING ANY IMPLIED WARRANTY OF MERCHANTABILITY, FITNESS FOR A PARTICULAR PURPOSE, OR NONINFRINGEMENT. COMPANY MAKES NO REPRESENTATIONS, WARRANTIES, OR GUARANTIES AS TO THE QUALITY, SUITABILITY, TRUTH, ACCURACY OR COMPLETENESS OF ANY OF THE MATERIALS CONTAINED ON THE WEBSITE. ANY QUESTIONS REGARDING THE MATERIALS SHOULD BE DIRECTED TO THE PROVIDERS OF SUCH MATERIALS. IN NO EVENT WILL COMPANY OR ITS SUPPLIERS BE LIABLE FOR THE ACCURACY OR COMPLETENESS OF THE INFORMATION FROM COMPANY.

11.2 COMPANY MAKES NO WARRANTY THAT: (I) THE SERVICES WILL MEET YOUR REQUIREMENTS, (II) THE SERVICES WILL BE UNINTERRUPTED, TIMELY, SECURE, OR ERROR-FREE, (III) THE RESULTS THAT MAY BE OBTAINED FROM THE USE OF THE SERVICES WILL BE ACCURATE OR RELIABLE, (IV) THE QUALITY OF ANY PRODUCTS, SERVICES, INFORMATION, OR OTHER MATERIAL PURCHASED OR OBTAINED BY YOU THROUGH THE SERVICES WILL MEET YOUR EXPECTATIONS, OR (V) ANY ERRORS IN THE SOFTWARE WILL BE CORRECTED.

11.3 ANY MATERIAL DOWNLOADED OR OTHERWISE OBTAINED THROUGH THE USE OF THE SERVICES IS DONE AT YOUR OWN DISCRETION AND RISK AND YOU ARE SOLELY RESPONSIBLE FOR ANY DAMAGE TO YOUR COMPUTER SYSTEM OR LOSS OF DATA THAT RESULTS FROM THE DOWNLOAD OF ANY SUCH MATERIAL.

11.4 NO ADVICE OR INFORMATION, WHETHER ORAL OR WRITTEN, OBTAINED BY YOU FROM COMPANY OR THROUGH OR FROM THE SERVICES WILL CREATE ANY WARRANTY NOT EXPRESSLY STATED IN THE TERMS. COMPANY'S EMPLOYEES ARE NOT AUTHORIZED TO VARY THESE TERMS.

12. Limitation of Liability

12.1 TO THE EXTENT NOT PROHIBITED BY APPLICABLE LAW, COMPANY IS NOT LIABLE FOR ANY DIRECT, INDIRECT, INCIDENTAL, SPECIAL, CONSEQUENTIAL, PUNITIVE, OR EXEMPLARY DAMAGES, INCLUDING BUT NOT LIMITED TO, DAMAGES FOR LOSS OF PROFITS, REVENUE, GOODWILL, USE, DATA, ELECTRONICALLY TRANSMITTED ORDERS, OR OTHER ECONOMIC ADVANTAGE (EVEN IF COMPANY HAS BEEN ADVISED OF THE POSSIBILITY OF SUCH DAMAGES), HOWEVER CAUSED AND REGARDLESS OF THE THEORY OF LIABILITY, ARISING

OUT OF OR RELATED TO: (I) THE USE OF OR THE INABILITY TO USE THE SERVICES; (II) THE COST OF PROCUREMENT OF SUBSTITUTE GOODS AND SERVICES RESULTING FROM ANY GOODS, DATA, INFORMATION OR SERVICES PURCHASED OR OBTAINED OR MESSAGES RECEIVED OR TRANSACTIONS ENTERED INTO THROUGH OR FROM THE SERVICES; (III) UNAUTHORIZED ACCESS TO OR ALTERATION OF YOUR TRANSMISSIONS OR DATA; (IV) LOSS, CORRUPTION OR DELAY OF YOUR DATA OR THE DATA OF ANY THIRD PARTY; (V) LOSS OF COMMUNICATIONS WITH OR CONNECTION TO THE WEBSITE OR ANY MATERIAL, PRODUCT OR SERVICES PROVIDED THROUGH IT; (VI) STATEMENTS OR CONDUCT OF ANY THIRD PARTY ON THE SERVICES AND COMPANY; OR (V) ANY OTHER MATTER RELATING TO THE SERVICES.

12.2 YOU HAVE SOLE RESPONSIBILITY FOR ADEQUATE PROTECTION AND BACKUP OF DATA AND/OR EQUIPMENT USED IN CONNECTION WITH THE WEBSITE AND WILL NOT MAKE A CLAIM AGAINST COMPANY FOR LOST DATA, RE-RUN TIME, INACCURATE OUTPUT, WORK DELAYS OR LOST PROFITS RESULTING FROM THE USE OF THE MATERIALS.

12.3 YOU AGREE TO HOLD COMPANY HARMLESS FROM, AND YOU COVENANT NOT TO SUE COMPANY FOR, ANY CLAIMS BASED ON USING THE WEBSITE. Some jurisdictions do not allow the exclusion or limitation of incidental or consequential damages, so the above limitation or exclusion may not apply to you.

13. Intellectual Property Rights

13.1 Company is committed to respecting others' intellectual property rights, and we ask our users to do the same. Company may, in its sole discretion, terminate the accounts or access rights of users who infringe or otherwise violate others' intellectual property rights.

13.2 All information, documents, products, software, and services (the "Materials") provided on this Website were provided by or to Company by their respective manufacturers, authors, developers and vendors (the "Third Party Providers") and are the copyrighted work of Company and/or the Third Party Providers. Except as stated herein, none of the Materials may be copied, reproduced, distributed, republished, downloaded, displayed, posted or transmitted in any form or by any means, including, but not limited to, electronic, mechanical, photocopying, recording, or otherwise, without the prior express written permission of Company or the Third Party Provider. No part of the Website, including logos, graphics, sounds or images, may be reproduced or retransmitted in any way, or by any means, without the prior express written permission of Company. You also may not, without Company's prior express written permission, "mirror" any Material contained on this Website on any other server.

13.3 Nothing on this Website shall be construed as conferring any license under any of Company's or any Third Party Provider's intellectual property rights, whether by estoppel, implication, or otherwise. You acknowledge sole responsibility for obtaining any such licenses.

13.4 Permission is granted to display, copy, distribute and download Company's Materials on this Website provided that: (1) both the copyright notice identified below and this permission notice appear in the Materials, (2) the use of such Materials is solely for personal, non-commercial and informational use and will not be copied or posted on any networked computer or broadcast in any media, and (3) no modifications of any of the Materials are made. This permission terminates automatically without notice if you breach any of these terms or conditions. Upon termination, you must immediately destroy any downloaded and printed Materials.

13.5 Any unauthorized use of any Materials contained on this Website may violate copyright laws, trademark laws, the laws of privacy and publicity, and communications regulations and statutes.

13.6 Materials provided by Third Party Providers have not been independently authenticated in whole or in part by Company. Company does not provide, sell, license, or lease any of the Materials other than those specifically identified as being provided by Company.

14. General Information

14.1 The Terms constitute the entire agreement between you and Company and govern your use of the Services, superseding any prior agreements between you and Company (including, but not limited to, any prior versions of the Terms). You also may be subject to additional terms and conditions that may apply when you use other Company services, third-party content or third-party software. You must not assign or otherwise transfer the Terms nor any right granted hereunder. Sections 4.5, 11, and 12 survive termination of the Terms.

14.2 New York law and controlling U.S. federal law govern any action related to the Terms. No choice of law rules of any jurisdiction apply. The parties specifically disclaim the U.N. Convention on Contracts for the International Sale of Goods. You and Company agree to submit to the personal and exclusive jurisdiction of the courts located within the county of New York, New York for any disputes arising out of this Agreement or your use of the Website.

14.3 Company controls and operates this Website from its headquarters in various locations in the United States of America and makes no representation that these Materials are appropriate or available for use in other locations. If you use this Website from other locations, you are responsible for compliance with applicable local laws including but not limited to the export and import regulations of other countries.

14.4 You acknowledge and agree that Materials are subject to the U.S. Export Administration Laws and Regulations. Diversion of such Materials contrary to U.S. law is prohibited. You agree that none of the Materials, nor any direct product therefrom, is being or will be acquired for, shipped, transferred, or re-exported, directly or indirectly, to proscribed or embargoed countries or their nationals, nor be used for nuclear activities, chemical biological weapons, or missile projects unless authorized by the U.S. Government. Proscribed countries are set forth in the U.S. Export Administration Regulations. Countries subject to U.S. embargo are: Cuba, Iran, Iraq, Libya, North Korea, Syria, Serbia, and the Sudan. This list is subject to change without further notice from Company, and you must comply with the list as it exists in fact. You certify that you are not on the U.S. Department of Commerce's Denied Persons List or affiliated lists or on the U.S. Department of Treasury's Specially Designated Nationals List. You agree to comply strictly with all U.S. export laws and assume sole responsibility for obtaining licenses to export or re-export as may be required.

14.5 This Website could include inaccuracies or typographical errors. Company and the Third Party Providers may make improvements and/or changes in the products, services, programs, and prices described in this Website at any time without notice. Changes are periodically made to the Website. Company may amend these Terms at any time by posting the amended terms on this site. If you are a registered user of Company, Company will notify you of changes to these Terms when you log-in after such changes have been made, thus giving you an opportunity to review the Terms.

14.6 The failure of Company to exercise or enforce any right or provision of the Terms does not constitute a waiver of such right or provision. If a court of competent jurisdiction finds any provision of the Terms to be invalid, the parties nevertheless agree that the court should endeavor to give effect to the parties' intentions as reflected in the provision, and the other provisions of the Terms remain in full force and effect. Regardless of any statute or law to the contrary, any claim or cause of action arising out of or related to use of the Services or the Terms must be filed within one (1) year after such claim or cause of action arose or be forever barred. The section titles in the Terms are for convenience only and have no legal or contractual effect.

14.7 These Terms represent the entire understanding relating to the use of the Website and prevail over any prior or contemporaneous, conflicting, or additional, communications.

FORM 9-11

Net.Art Web Site Terms of Use

The Artist's acceptable use policy ("Use Policy") has been formulated with the following goals in mind:

- Ensure security, reliability and privacy of Artist's systems and network for you, the user;
- Avoid situations that may cause Artist to incur civil liability;
- Maintain the image and reputation of Artist as a responsible provider;
- Preserve the value of Internet resources as a conduit for free expression; and
- Preserve the privacy and security of individual users.

The Use Policy below defines the actions which Artist considers to be abusive, and thus, strictly prohibited. The examples named in this list are non-exclusive, and are provided solely for guidance to users. If you are unsure whether any contemplated use or action is permitted, please send mail to info@theArtist.com and we will assist you.

General Conduct

Users are prohibited from transmitting on or through any of Artist's services, any material that is, in Artist's sole discretion, unlawful, obscene, threatening, abusive, libelous, or hateful, or that encourages conduct which would constitute a criminal offense, give rise to civil liability, or otherwise violate any local, state, national or international law.

Artist services may only be used for lawful purposes. Transmission, distribution, or storage of any information, data or material in violation of United States or state regulation or law, or by the common law, is prohibited. This includes, but is not limited to, material protected by copyright, trademark, trade secret, or any other statute. Artist reserves the right to remove such illegal material from its servers.

System and Network Security

Users may not attempt to circumvent user authentication or security of any host, network, or account ("cracking"). This includes, but is not limited to, accessing data not intended for the customer, logging into a server or account the customer is not expressly authorized to access, or probing the security of other networks.

Users may not attempt to interfere with service to any user, host, or network ("denial of service attacks"). This includes, but is not limited to: "flooding" of networks, deliberate attempts to overload a service, and attempts to "crash" a host.

Users may not use any kind of program/script/command, or send messages of any kind, designed to interfere with a user's terminal session, via any means, locally or by the Internet.

Users who violate systems or network security may incur criminal or civil liability. Artist will cooperate fully with investigations of violations of systems or network security at other sites, including cooperating with law enforcement authorities in the investigation of suspected criminal violations.

APPENDIX 9-C

Negotiation Guidelines for Art Site Development (Favorable to Client)

I. Product Description and Functional Specifications

Early in the negotiation process, the commissioning party and the developer should agree upon a detailed description of the final website, which can be appended to the contract as an exhibit. In addition, the commissioning party should attempt, where possible, to secure a functional specification for the website, as required by the RFP, prior to entering into the contract. In some cases, however, it will not be possible to obtain the document in advance because of the labor involved in preparing comprehensive functional specifications. In such cases, the functional specifications should be the first contract deliverable. The description should address the following questions:

- Is the website description (which will be attached to the contract) sufficiently detailed and specific to describe the purpose and features? The goal is to develop a detailed and unambiguous document which will safeguard against any disagreements as the development process evolves.

- If the commissioning party plans for its website to be portable within a variety of competing technological platforms, does the website description specifically refer to them?

All components of the finished website must be considered. If the developer will be providing the user's guide, documentation, or help files these items must be identified in the description.

During negotiations the commissioning party should also discuss how any changes to the description or functional specifications during the development of the product will be handled.

II. Ownership

Ownership can mean many things: ownership of the website as a compilation, ownership of the content, or ownership of copyright, trade secret rights, or patents in the software. A website may incorporate an existing software engine owned by the developer or off-the-shelf software licensed for use in the website. Accordingly, the commissioning party must pay particular attention to the question of ownership early in its negotiations. While obtaining the entire copyright may be more expensive, ownership will ensure complete exclusivity as well as the unfettered right to update and revise the website and prepare derivative works. In cases where ownership is not feasible, the commissioning party must take great care to ensure that it obtains all necessary distribution and development rights as well as the degree of exclusivity necessary to preserve its investment.

If the developer wishes to reserve any rights in software which the commissioning party is paying to have developed, the commissioning party should consider the feasibility of owning the copyright and licensing back to the developer the specific rights which the developer wants. For example, if necessary, the commissioning could license back the rights to prepare and publish the developer's own derivative works or improvements provided that all the commissioning party's content is removed. The commissioning party might also require developer to provide free source code updates and/or a royalty-free license to use such developer-owned works.

If it is clear, however, that the developer must own the copyright, the commissioning party must resolve the following issues:

- Will the commissioning party's rights be exclusive or non-exclusive?
- Will the commissioning party's rights be limited to a particular market segment?
- Will the commissioning party's rights be limited to a fixed term (e.g., three years)?
- Will the commissioning party have the right to modify the website or develop platform conversions? Is the commissioning party obliged to work with the original developer or may it use a third party developer? Does it have access to the necessary source code?
- Will the commissioning party have access to the source code for any purpose (e.g., to fix bugs or update the website)? Is it in a usable, annotated format? Will the developer provide support in using the source code?
- What rights will the developer retain? Will these rights affect the commissioning party's ability to compete in a given market? Has the commissioning party negotiated the best possible non-compete provisions, if necessary?

III. Hardware and Software Specifications

Are there hardware specifications to use the commissioning party's product? Additional bells and whistles may require more capacity than most computers have. Will the website require "plug-ins" that are difficult to load or require a lot of memory? The commissioning party needs to understand its market and the market's sophistication.

IV. Delivery and Acceptance

The commissioning party must negotiate a clear, explicit schedule for the delivery of work in progress as well as the finished website. It is advised that the commissioning party require delivery of complete functional specifications, prototype and beta versions in advance of the final version. The schedule should take into account the time necessary for the commissioning party to evaluate deliverables and the time reasonably required for the developer to accommodate any changes proposed by the commissioning party as well as its target release date for the website. If the commissioning party will be supplying any content or other components of the product, the schedule will need to address this process as well. Finally, the commissioning party may wish to include in the schedule a requirement for regular status reports or face-to-face meetings.

The commissioning party must negotiate appropriate acceptance standards. Wherever possible, the commissioning party should require that all deliverables be "complete and satisfactory" to it. If the commissioning party simply cannot persuade a developer to accept these terms (for example, by explaining that it is the commissioning party's standing policy to insist upon a "complete and satisfactory" standard and that the law, as well as its own principles, require it to exercise good faith in the evaluation process even when making subjective judgments), the commissioning party may have to accept some objective constraints on the acceptance process.

Developers sometimes insist, for example, that deliverables which conform to functional specifications be deemed acceptable. This is not unreasonable, particularly for a website that is not critical to your business. In cases in which the functional specifications will not be agreed upon until after the contract is signed, however, the commissioning party should reserve the right to evaluate these subjectively even if the commissioning party agrees that subsequent deliverables will be deemed acceptable if they conform in all respects to the functional specifications. Bear in mind that any such constraints may hinder the commissioning party's ability to reject a product and that the commissioning party should do as much as it possibly can to avoid paying for work it cannot use. At a bare minimum, it should reserve the right to contract with third parties to "fix" software which it is required to accept but cannot use in its present form. In any event, if the commissioning party does agree to such constraints on its acceptance criteria, it is particularly important to negotiate a "no-fault" termination provision which limits exposure (see section VI below).

V. Financial Terms

A developer's compensation may consist of an hourly fee (in which case the commissioning party should insist upon a maximum or "cap" on fees for completion of the project), a fixed development fee (which may be paid out in stages tied to acceptance, not merely delivery, of interim deliverables), royalties or a combination thereof. In negotiating fees, the commissioning party should try to minimize "front-loading" or payment of large amounts in advance of delivery of the finished product. Any amounts paid up front should also be taken into account when negotiating termination provisions including "kill" fees and "no-fault" termination rights. In addition, the commissioning party may wish to structure the development fee to include incentives or penalties with respect to timely delivery.

If the commissioning party is going to pay a royalty to the developer, the commissioning party should try to structure some or all of the development fee as an advance. The commissioning party should try to establish the proper balance between the projected royalties and the size of the advance, remembering that its own risk increases and the developer's risk declines as the amount of the advance increases. In formulating a royalty structure, the commissioning party must take into account the ways in which the website will actually generate revenue. Is the website:

- a specific product, such as a publication?
- an auction or other facilitator of transactions?
- a venue for the sale of add space?

Obviously, not all websites are appropriate for royalties.

Finally, if the website will incorporate any third party or "off-the-shelf" software, the commissioning party needs to consider whether it or the developer will negotiate and pay for the necessary licenses. Often, developers receive volume discounts which can be passed on to the commissioning party. If the licenses in question are of fixed duration, be sure to negotiate an adequate term. The commissioning party should also consider whether such licenses will allow it to revise the website as needed.

VI. Termination Rights

Although no one wishes to dwell on the possibility of disappointment at the outset of promising negotiations, it is essential that the commissioning party agree upon appropriate termination provisions with the developer. A carefully negotiated, well-drafted contract can enable the commissioning party to dissolve an unsuccessful relationship without rancor and, better yet, without involving lawyers and legal threats.

The commissioning party will certainly need to reserve the right to terminate the agreement in the event the developer fails to deliver timely and acceptable deliverables (see Section IV above). The commissioning party must consider, however, whether it will be required to give the developer an opportunity to correct deficiencies before it can terminate the agreement. If the commissioning party does agree to such an arrangement, the developer must agree upon a reasonable time limit for delivery of corrected materials. The commissioning party should also consider whether the delivery dates for subsequent deliverables will be extended in view of the time spent "curing" an earlier deficiency. If the commissioning party does allow such an extension, however, it should set a fixed period of time beyond which the final delivery date for the completed project will not be extended.

The commissioning party must consider the financial consequences of termination for failure to deliver timely and acceptable materials. The developer may be required to refund all or part of the fees paid to date, depending on the payment schedule for the project (see Section V above). The more money the developer receives up front, the greater the obligation to refund money should be.

From a practical standpoint, however, it may be more important to focus on the commissioning party's rights to complete or correct work in progress as of the time of termination. Even where there is a legal right to a refund, it may be difficult to obtain cash from a disgruntled or insolvent developer. In such cases, the right to complete a work in progress may be the best means of salvaging investment in a project.

Finally, the commissioning party should consider demanding a "no-fault" termination provision which will enable it to terminate a project even if the developer has met all of its obligations. This is particularly useful where the development process is likely to be lengthy; in such cases, the anticipated market needs may change during the development process and termination may become quite attractive. The financial consequences of "no-fault" termination are often quite different from those of termination for cause. In some instances, the commissioning party may even agree to pay a "kill" fee (for example, a percentage of the balance due the developer upon completion of the next deliverable or of the final project) in exchange for the opportunity to walk away from a project that no longer looks promising.

VII. Warranties and Liabilities

The limitations on liability are often the hardest part of a negotiation with a developer. As a general rule, developers have their own form agreements designed to protect their interests. For the commissioning party, it is always better to prepare a new draft. The warranty and liability clauses provide a good example of the truth of this statement. Developer's contracts are notoriously deficient (from the commissioning party's perspective, of course) with respect to warranties. A typical developer's form agreement will contain virtually no warranties and many disclaimers. The commissioning party, on the other hand, should require reasonable warranties of:

- non-infringement;
- accurate processing of millennial dates and leap years;

- no harmful statements or instructions;
- no viruses, time bombs, Trojan horses, etc.;
- full and complete source code;
- full performance in accordance with specifications; and
- full authority to sign agreement.

A responsible developer will usually agree to most of the above referenced warranties, but will often require a disclaimer of warranties of fitness for a particular purpose. Developers will also often try to limit their liability for a breach of warranty to the contract value. Whether to accept this limitation requires an evaluation of the risks involved. Consideration should be given to whether the developer has been sued before, and of course, how much money is involved. For a million dollar contract, one million dollars might be adequate to compensate for any loss, although, as a practical matter, it is easier to get concessions from a developer in a million dollar contract. Additionally, different limits on liability can sometimes be negotiated with respect to different warranties.

VIII. Other Development Issues

• Authoring System and Programming Language. It is important to ascertain in advance what authoring system and programming language the developer proposes to use. These issues bear directly on the ability to modify, correct or complete the project itself in the event the relationship with the developer breaks down. Access to the source code for the product will be meaningless if the programming language or authoring system is arcane. The choice of authoring system may also limit the ability to modify the finished website.

• Licenses and Fees. Are there any licensing fees for the authoring system and other tools used to develop this product, or any other permissions required? If so, who is responsible for obtaining the licenses and paying the fees?

• Content. Who will obtain any required multimedia assets, such as video, audio, and animations and who will pay for them?

• Beta Testing. Will the developer be responsible for complete beta testing? Will beta test reports be submitted? Does the beta testing include evaluation of network compatibility?

• Errors and Bugs. The commissioning party should be sure that the developer will provide a warranty that the final version of the product will be free of errors and programming bugs for an adequate term (generally at least twelve months). Confirm that error corrections will be done in a timely manner at no cost.

• Technical Support. Negotiations should also address the subject of technical support. How will the developer support the completed website? Does the developer maintain telephone support services? Will there be a charge for technical support? Who will support any third party software used?

• Confidentiality. Be certain that the developer understands that work in progress must be treated as highly confidential.

FORM 9-12

Proof-of-Concept Web Site Development Agreement

WHEREAS, Developer is in the business of designing, developing and supporting Internet Services; and

WHEREAS, Client desires to acquire certain Internet services from Developer, including the development of a proof-of-concept Website, pursuant to the terms and conditions set forth below; and

WHEREAS, Developer desires to provide such services to Client;

NOW, THEREFORE, in consideration of the mutual promises set forth herein, Developer and Client hereby agree as follows:

1. Definitions.

For purposes of this Agreement, the following terms shall have the indicated meanings:

1.1 "Client Art Works" means certain existing online content of Client, as well as design structure, imagery, text-based and any audio and audiovisual material, photographs, logos, trademarks, and other materials provided to Developer by Client to the extent such information is copyrightable. Developer shall have no rights in any Client Art Works.

1.2 "Correction" means the elimination of programming errors or defects that cause the Website to fail to function in accordance with the Functional Specifications and are reproducible under analogous conditions on the Test Site.

1.3 "Deliverable" means any item to be delivered by Developer to Client in accordance with the Statement of Work attached as *Exhibit A* hereto.

1.4 "Functional Specifications" means the detailed written description of the Website's functional and aesthetic aspects that Developer shall develop and deliver as provided in the Statement of Work attached as *Exhibit A* hereto.

1.5 "Documentation" means instructions that are necessary to assist an entity with a high level of web-site maintenance skills in maintaining the Website, including without limitation all written materials developed pursuant to the Statement of Work, such as all templates, specifications, programmers' notes, technical documentation and a listing of any Utilities required to maintain the Website.

1.6 "Intellectual Property Rights" means any and all now known or hereafter existing rights associated with works of authorship or inventions throughout the universe, including but not limited to copyrights, patents, trademarks, service marks, know-how, "look and feel" and all other intellectual and industrial property and proprietary rights (of every kind and nature throughout the universe and however designated) relating to intangible property.

1.7 "Revisions" means any changes or additions to the Website which give the Website features or capabilities not described in the Functional Specifications.

1.8 "Scheduled Final Completion Dates" mean the dates scheduled for delivery of the final Deliverable for each Phase as set forth in the Statement of Work in *Exhibit A* attached hereto.

1.9 "Service Fee Schedule" means the schedule attached hereto as *Exhibit B* of the fees payable to Developer for services rendered under the Statement of Work.

1.10 "Source Code" means the computer programs in the original development formats, including programmers' comments, data files and structures, header and include files, macros, object libraries, programming tools not commercially available, technical specifications, flowcharts and logic diagrams, schematics, existing annotations and documentation reasonably required or necessary to enable an independent third party programmer with a high level of programming skills to create, maintain, modify or enhance the Website.

1.11 "Statement of Work" means the written description attached hereto as *Exhibit A* of the work to be performed by Developer in the development of the Website, including without limitation the description of the milestones and Deliverables to be delivered and the dates by which each milestone is to be completed and each Deliverable is to be delivered to Client.

1.12 "Test Site" means the parallel Website maintained solely by Developer at its facilities or facilities under its control on the same host operating system as the Website (to be jointly designated in writing hereafter), comprised of the approved Deliverables, any Corrections, Revisions and executed Change Requests.

1.13 "Utilities" means the compiled versions of all development tools or other technology used in the development of the Website that are written by Developer during this Agreement.

1.14 "Website" means a proof-of-concept Website consisting of a so-called HTML "home page" and other linked pages and all portions thereof, capable of running in a satisfactory manner on a host operating system designated by the parties in writing, including without limitation, all HTML or other formatted text files, all related graphics files, data files, modules, routines and objects, and the computer software and all other script or program files required to exploit such materials and that collectively control the display of and user interaction with the Website and have the features and capabilities described in the Functional

Specifications, together with all Corrections thereto. Without limitation of the foregoing, "Website" includes the complete Source Code for the Website and all portions thereof, all material created by Developer, its employees, consultants, contractors or other personnel working directly for Developer hereunder and all existing related data or information required to enable an entity with a high level of web-site maintenance skills to maintain it.

1.15 "Work Product" means any and all existing or to-be-developed parts, work-in-progress, components, elements, portions or aspects of the Website that are developed, created or contributed to by or on behalf of Developer under this Agreement.

2. Services and Deliverables.

2.1 Services. Developer shall develop, produce, complete and deliver the Deliverables to Client. Developer shall develop the Website using state-of-the-art software tools and development hardware. Except for Client Art Works to be provided by Client, Developer shall provide, at its expense, all necessary programming and graphic production services in order to implement the Functional Specifications. Notwithstanding the foregoing, Client shall be solely responsible for purchasing and/or licensing all third-party content to be integrated into the Website. Art Works from third parties shall be incorporated by Developer into the Website only with Client's prior written consent, which shall be provided in Client's sole discretion. The Website will perform optimally under either Netscape Communicator version 4.06 or Internet Explorer version 4.01, as the parties jointly designate in writing, and satisfactorily under the other browser. *Exhibit A* may be modified from time to time during the term of this Agreement but only by written instrument signed by both parties. Developer shall directly render all services to be performed by Developer under this Agreement exclusively through its employees, consultants, contractors or other personnel working directly for Developer on behalf of Client.

2.2 Change Requests. If either party desires to alter the Statement of Work the following procedures will apply:

(i) The person who requests the change (the "Originator") will forward to the other party (the "Recipient") a proposal for an alteration to the Statement of Work ("Change Request") which will include (i) the date of the Change Request, (ii) a description of the Proposed Change, and (iii) the reason for the Proposed Change or other relevant background information.

(ii) Developer will assign a number to and log each Change Request.

(iii) Upon receipt of the change request, Developer will make reasonable efforts to investigate the impact of the proposed alteration on the price, timetable,

Statement of Work, Functional Specifications and relevant obligations under this Agreement (the "Impact Study"). Developer shall report the results of such impact study to Client promptly.

(iv) Developer shall document the number of man-hours devoted to each Impact Study. Developer shall notify Client in writing if Developer estimates that any Impact Study will require in excess of sixteen (16) man-hours prior to undertaking such an Impact Study. For each man-hour in excess of sixteen (16) man-hours devoted to any impact study, Developer shall, at its sole discretion, have the right to postpone, defer or continue any contractual deadline for any Developer obligation whatsoever, without penalty or prejudice, for an equivalent duration, at any time during this Agreement ("Discretionary Time"), for which it shall provide written notice to Client of the origin and amount of the time in question at the time it elects such postponement, deferment or continuance. For each man-hour in excess of sixteen (16) man-hours devoted to any Impact Study wherein Client is the Originator of the Change Request, upon completion of said Impact Study, Developer shall invoice Client, and Client shall pay Developer, __ hundred dollars per man-hour, in addition to any and all monies due or owing to Developer under this Agreement, provided that Client shall have sole discretion to approve Impact Studies wherein Client is the Originator of the Change Request upon notice by Developer that said Impact Study may exceed sixteen (16) man-hours. Notwithstanding the foregoing, Developer shall have an obligation to undertake only a reasonable number of Impact Studies wherein Client is the Originator.

(v) At the conclusion of each Impact Study, Client and Developer shall each approve in writing within two (2) days the alteration proposed in the Change Request if they mutually agree to implement the Change Request. In the event that the parties shall approve the alterations as reflected in the Impact Study, then Developer shall promptly implement such alterations, and the Statement of Work shall thereby be deemed amended to reflect such alterations. For each man-hour devoted to implementing such alterations, Developer shall, at its sole discretion, have the right to postpone, defer or continue any contractual deadline for any Developer obligation whatsoever, without penalty or prejudice, for an equivalent duration, at any time during this Agreement, for which it shall provide written notice to Client of the origin and amount of the time in question at the time it elects such postponement, deferment or continuance.

(vi) The failure of Client to approve the proposed alteration or any Impact Study within five (5) days of its receipt thereof shall operate as a disapproval of such alteration or Impact Study. For each hour beyond two days following receipt of notice by Client for its approval of an Impact Study, Developer shall, at its sole discretion, have the right to postpone, defer or continue any contractual deadline for any Developer obligation whatsoever, without penalty or prejudice, for an equivalent duration, at any time during this Agreement, for which it shall provide written notice to Client of the origin and amount of the time in question at the time it elects such postponement, deferment or continuance. For purposes of computing time under this agreement, a day shall be defined as any and every day of the week, exclusive only of federal holidays, and as consisting of the hours between 9am and 6pm E.S.T.

2.3 Consultation; Project Liaisons. Developer shall consult with Client throughout the development of the Website. Client shall have the right, at Client's expense, from time to time, to send Client personnel to Developer's place of business upon reasonable notice during normal business hours for reasonable consultation with respect to the Website's development. Unless and until otherwise designated in writing by Developer or Client, as the case may be, the project liaison for Developer is ________ and for Client is _________. All discussions involving the Website shall be conducted by these persons, or their designees.

2.4 Website Deliverables. Developer shall deliver to Client without limitation: (a) all HTML or other formatted text files, all existing and related graphics files, data files, modules, routines, objects, computer software, all Utilities developed, and all other script or program files required for an entity with a high level of website operation skills to operate the Website, (b) the complete Source Code for the Website and all portions thereof, and (c) all existing and related data or information required to enable an entity with a high level of web-site maintenance skills to maintain the Website, including without limitation, Utilities and other programs necessary to generate any Website reports set forth in the Statement of Work. Deliverables will in all cases conform to the Functional Specifications and/or any modifications thereto in accordance with Section 2.2 hereof. Developer agrees to develop the Documentation and to deliver the Documentation to Client for approval upon Completion of the Agreement (as hereinafter defined).

2.5 Client Training. During the term of this Agreement, and upon written request from Client, Developer will train Client personnel in the development, maintenance and operation of the Website so that such personnel will be able to perform such activities without consultation by Developer, at a rate of ____ hundred dollars per man-hour. In addition, for each man-hour devoted to training, Developer shall, at its sole discretion, have the right to postpone, defer or continue any contractual deadline for any obligation whatsoever, for an equivalent duration, at any time during this Agreement, for which it shall provide written notice to Client of the origin and amount of the time in question at the time it elects such postponement, deferment or continuance.

2.6 Corrections. Notwithstanding Client's approval of the Website hereunder, during the term of this Agreement, Developer shall make, at its own expense, whatever Corrections are necessary with respect to the Website. Developer shall promptly notify Client of any claimed or suspected defect in any aspect of the Website or any Deliverable. Developer shall make such Corrections promptly after receipt of written notice from Client specifying the nature of the defect with particularity. Any nonconformity whatsoever with the Functional Specifications, Revisions or Change Requests, deserving of Corrections or otherwise, shall be deemed to exists if and only if such nonconformity is reproducible on the Test Site. The Test Site software shall, at Client's discretion, be destroyed or transferred to Client "AS IS" in a form and manner entirely at the discretion of Developer, upon final termination of this Agreement and any warranty period thereafter.

2.7 Updates and Enhancements. Developer shall promptly notify Client of any Updates and Enhancements (as defined in this section) to the Utilities or other programs which are developed by Developer or licensed to Client pursuant to Sections 5.2 and 5.3 below. For purposes of this Agreement, "Updates" shall mean any revisions, updates, "bug" fixes and corrections of the Utilities or any part thereof, and "Enhancements" shall mean any further developments, extensions, improvements or modifications of the Utilities, or any part thereof. Developer will provide all Updates free of charge during the term of this Agreement, and will make available all Enhancements at the same standard published rates as it charges its other customers.

3. Delivery and Acceptance.

3.1 Firm Project Deadlines. The parties agree that "Week 1" described in the Section II of the Statement of Work entitled "Process Outline and Schedule" will commence on the first Sunday immediately following the date of this Agreement, and the dates of all subsequent weeks described in such section shall be determined in accordance therewith and with the terms of this Agreement. Developer shall deliver to Client all of the items listed in the Statement of Work in a timely manner. Client agrees to provide Developer with access to all people, data, content, systems and all other things relating to the Statement of Work as requested by Developer, in a timely and reasonable manner, subject to the accrual to Developer of Discretionary Time for unreasonable delay by Developer. In addition to other provisions governing delivery of Deliverables under this Agreement, if either party's delay in performance of its obligations hereunder directly causes delay in provision of a Deliverable, the parties promptly will evaluate with each other the impact of such delay on Developer's ability to deliver the next Deliverable and assess the appropriate delivery date for the next Deliverable based on the needs of the then-current situation. After adjusting for any Discretionary Time, in the event Developer fails to meet the Scheduled Final Completion Date for any phase, Client may impose a ____ hundred dollars per day late fee for each day the final Deliverable set forth in the Statement of Work is not complete beginning one week after said Scheduled Final Completion Date, and ____ hundred dollars per day late fee for each day beginning two weeks after the Scheduled Final Completion Date. After adjusting for any Discretionary Time, in the event Developer completes delivery of pertinent Deliverables prior to the Scheduled Final Completion Date for any phase, in addition to all other monies paid or payable to Developer under this Agreement, Developer shall invoice Client, and Client shall pay Developer ____ hundred dollars per day early fee for each day prior to the scheduled date that the final Deliverable set forth in the Statement of Work is complete beginning one week prior to said Scheduled Final Completion Date, and ____ hundred dollars per day early fee for each day beginning two weeks prior to the Scheduled Final Completion Date. Developer's maximum liability for late fees and entitlement to early bonus shall not exceed ____ thousand dollars.

3.2 Approval of Client; Client Modifications to Website. Client has the final decision on whether to use or license the Website once development is completed. Client may also modify, change or alter the Website in any respect at any time, whether before, at or after the Website goes online. To the extent any such modification by Client delays the fulfillment of any obligation by Developer under this Agreement, Developer shall, at its sole discretion, have the right to postpone, defer or continue any contractual deadline for any Developer obligation whatsoever, without penalty or prejudice, for an equivalent duration, at any time during this Agreement, for which it shall provide written notice to Client of the origin and amount of the time in question at the time it elects such postponement, deferment or continuance. For each such additional man-hour, Developer shall invoice Client, and Client shall pay Developer, ____ hundred dollars per man-hour, in addition to any and all monies due or owing to Developer under this Agreement.

3.3 Delivery; Acceptance. Deliverables shall in all cases conform to the Functional Specifications and Statement of Work and/or any modifications thereto mutually agreed upon in writing by the parties. Delivery shall occur when Client receives a Deliverable from Developer accompanied by a written statement listing the items delivered and stating that such Deliverable is ready for Client's approval. Client shall have seven (7) days after receipt of each Deliverable in a form mutually agreed upon by the parties to review and test each Deliverable (the "Approval Period"). At Client's request, Developer will demonstrate that the relevant Deliverable is complete and satisfies the applicable portion of the Functional Specifications. Acceptance or rejection by Client of Deliverables shall occur as follows: During the Approval Period, Client shall indicate its acceptance or rejection of a Deliverable by executing and delivering to Developer a signed writing expressly referring to the Deliverable and acknowledging Client's acceptance or rejection thereof. Absent such notice from Client, acceptance of each Deliverable shall not be deemed to occur automatically upon expiration of the Approval Period, but shall be deemed to occur automatically upon thirty (30) days after receipt of each Deliverable, absent written rejection by Client. For time in excess of said seven (7) days and prior to said thirty (30) days, Developer shall, at its sole discretion, have the right to postpone, defer or continue any contractual deadline for any Developer obligation whatsoever, without penalty or prejudice, for an equivalent duration, at any time during this Agreement, for which it shall provide written notice to Client of the origin and amount of the time in question at the time it elects such postponement, deferment or continuance. Furthermore, Client shall reimburse Developer for non-cancelable costs and expenses actually incurred by Developer as a result of such delay in providing rejection or approval to the extent such costs and expenses were (i) approved by Client in advance prior to delivery of the Deliverable to Client, and/or (ii) within categories of expenses specifically included in budgets for the Website previously approved in writing by Client where the rates for such categories of expenses were also previously approved in writing by Client, in each case subject to Developer providing Client written documentation evidencing Developer's performance of such work and incurrence of such non-cancelable costs and expenses.

3.4 Rejection. Client may reject Deliverable(s) solely for a non-conformity with the Functional Specifications that is reproducible under analogous conditions on the Test Site, and any notice of rejection must set forth with particularity such nonconformity. In the event that Client identifies in writing any such alleged nonconformity, Developer will use its best efforts to correct such nonconformity within ten (10) days. Client will then have five (5) days after delivery of such corrections by Developer to notify Developer of any continuing nonconformity. If at the expiration of any such five (5) day period, the parties disagree as to the existence of a nonconformity after having negotiated in good faith regarding the same during such five (5) day period, the parties hereby agree to submit the dispute to binding arbitration as set forth in Section 13. Developer's obligation for alleged non-comformities that are not reproducible on the Test Site shall be as set forth in Paragraph 3.2.

4. Compensation and Payment Terms.

4.1 Invoices; Payments. Upon submission of an invoice by Developer, Client shall make the payments to Developer set forth in the Service Fee Schedule within ten (10) days after receipt of invoice. Developer shall submit an invoice for payment to be made in conjunction with any Deliverable, to Client upon delivery of such Deliverable. All payments due hereunder shall be made in U.S. dollars by wire transfer of immediately available funds to___ . Except as expressly otherwise provided in this Agreement, Client shall have no obligation with respect to Developer's services hereunder in excess of the Maximum Fee specified in the Service Fee Schedule.

4.2 Acquisition of Hardware, Software and Art. Client acknowledges that hardware, third-party software, and licensed or commissioned art, including without limitation, photographs and illustrations, related to the development and/or hosting of the Website are not included in the fees set forth in the Service Fee Schedule. Developer will notify Client in writing of requirements for such hardware and/or software. At Client's sole option and upon written notice to Developer, Client will either purchase such hardware and/or software itself or request that Developer purchase such hardware and/or software on Client's behalf. If Client elects to have Developer make such purchases, or to license or commission art, such costs will be payable in full by Client in advance of such purchases or expenditures. Unreasonable delays in purchasing such hardware or software attributable to Client shall be treated by the parties as Developer Discretionary Time.

4.3 Expenses. Developer shall submit invoices to Client for reasonable travel and lodging expenses incurred in the course of this Agreement, and Client shall reimburse Developer for said expenses within thirty (30) days of receipt of said invoices; provided, however, that Developer shall obtain approval from Client prior to incurring estimated travel and lodging expenses in excess of ___ hundred dollars per person per trip and ____ thousand dollars for the entire project.

4.4 Late Payment Interest. In addition to any other remedy of Developer, any late payment shall bear interest from the date due until paid in full at one and one-half percent (1–1/2%) per month.

5. Proprietary Rights.

5.1 Ownership Rights to Website. Subject to Section 5.2 below, Developer shall transfer and assign to Client all rights in and to the Website, the Work Product, Deliverables, all value and goodwill accruing in connection with the Website and all results and proceeds of Developer's services hereunder, including without limitation the name and URL associated therewith, and all Intellectual Property Rights therein and thereto, upon Completion of the Agreement (as defined). At the time of transfer and assignment, with respect to any so-called "moral rights," Developer shall unconditionally waive such rights and the enforcement thereof, and Client may thereafter register the copyright for the Website (and each element thereof) and any Work Product or derivative work in its own name or that of any of its designees for the full term of copyright and all renewals and extensions thereof.

5.2 Developer License Rights. To the extent any Utilities or pre-existing intellectual property owned or licensed by Developer are used in connection with development or maintenance of the Website pursuant to Section 2, upon transfer and assignment of the Website, Developer will grant Client a non-exclusive, perpetual, irrevocable, fully paid-up, royalty-free, worldwide right and license, including the right to grant and authorize sublicenses, to use such Developer intellectual property in connection with the Website.

5.3 Trademark Rights. Developer shall not, and shall not allow or assist any other party (other than Client or its designee) to, register or attempt to register, any trademark, service mark, trade name or other Intellectual Property Right related to the Website or any Work Product with any public or private authority without the prior written consent of Client. Developer shall not, and shall not allow or assist any other party to, attach any additional trademarks, logos or trade designations to the Website or any Work Product without Client's prior written approval.

5.4 Possession of Work Product. Upon transfer and assignment of the Website by Developer, Client shall have the sole and exclusive right to possession and custody of all Work Product. Thereafter, possession by Developer or any third party of any Work Product is solely for the purpose of fulfilling Developer's obligations under this Agreement and in no way shall be deemed or construed to grant, license or otherwise convey any rights to Developer or any other party in the same, by any means, including without limitation, any insolvency, creditor or other laws of any jurisdiction. Developer shall retain no rights to use the Work Product and agrees not to challenge the validity of the ownership by Client of rights in the Work Product after transfer and assignment of the Website.

5.5 Proprietary Notices. Client shall provide Developer with appropriate notices of copyright, trademark and other proprietary rights in Client's name, and Developer shall place such notices in such a manner as Client shall direct. In no event shall Developer alter, remove, obscure, erase or deface or otherwise hide from view, any copyright, trademark or other proprietary rights notice of Client contained on or incorporated in the Website. Client shall have the right to develop and implement any method or mechanism Client deems appropriate to prevent or protect against unauthorized copying of the Website, the HTML code for the Website, or any materials on the Website. To the extent any such modification by Client delays the fulfillment of any obligation by Developer under this Agreement, Developer shall, at its sole discretion, have the right to postpone, defer or continue any contractual deadline for any Developer obligation whatsoever, without penalty or prejudice, for an equivalent duration, at any time during this Agreement, for which it shall provide written notice to Client of the origin and amount of the time in question at the time it elects such postponement, deferment or continuance. For each such additional man-hour, Developer shall invoice Client, and Client shall pay Developer, ___ hundred dollars per man-hour, in addition to any and all monies due or owing to Developer under this Agreement.

5.6 Further Assurances. Developer shall, and shall cause every party acting under it in relation to this Agreement to, execute any and all documents and do such other acts requested at any time by Client as may be required to evidence, perfect, confirm and/or further effect the rights granted Client under this Section 5.

5.7 Client Goodwill. Developer acknowledges and agrees that, as between Developer and Client, all Client Art Works is owned by Client.

6. Term and Termination.

6.1 Term. The term of this Agreement shall commence on the date of this Agreement and continue in full force and effect until Client has (i) provided final written acceptance of the Website and all Work Product including without limitation each and every Deliverable and (ii) paid all outstanding invoices ("Completion").

6.2 Termination for Breach. In the event of a material breach of the Agreement, upon written notice by either party to the other of said breach, the breaching party so notified shall have a fifteen (15) day period to cure said breach (the "Cure Period").

6.3 Termination for Insolvency. Each party shall have the right to terminate this Agreement upon written notice to the other in the event that said other party makes any assignment for the benefit of creditors or files a petition in bankruptcy or is adjudged bankrupt or becomes insolvent or is placed in the hands of a receiver or if the equivalent of any of the proceedings or acts referred to in this clause, though known and/or designated by some other name or term, shall occur.

6.4 Effect of Termination. Upon termination of this Agreement and payment by Client of all outstanding invoices, Developer will immediately deliver to Client all intellectual property, Source Code and object code of software, materials and other elements of the Website necessary for an entity with a high level of web-site development skills to continue the development of the Website. In addition, Developer will provide Client with reasonable assistance in transitioning the Website to an alternate party for an additional ___ hundred dollars per man hour. Notwithstanding other payment terms, in the event of any termination of this Agreement prior to its completion, Developer shall, within ten (10) days of such termination, submit an invoice to Client for all the services provided and expenses incurred through and including such termination date, and Client shall, within ten (10) days of receipt, pay said invoice.

6.5 Survival of Terms. Sections 5, 6.4, 6.5, 7, 8, 9, 11, 12, 13 and 14 shall survive the expiration or termination of this Agreement. Following payment by Client of all outstanding invoices, in no event shall Developer have any right to recover or obtain any Intellectual Property Rights in or to the Website or any Work Product, or enjoin or otherwise interfere with Client's development, provision or other exploitation of the Website (or any element thereof), or any Work Product.

7. Confidentiality.

7.1 Confidential Information. Each party may, during the performance under this Agreement, have access to and acquire knowledge from, material, data, systems and other information concerning the operation, business, financial affairs, products, customers and Intellectual Property Rights of the other party that may not be accessible or known to the general public (referred to as "Confidential Information"). "Confidential Information" also includes (a) the terms of this Agreement, (b) all Client Art Works, (c) any information or materials that Client obtains from any third party that Client treats as proprietary or designates as Confidential Information, whether or not owned by Client and (d) all Developer intellectual property licensed to Client pursuant to Section 5.3. "Confidential Information" does not include information that a party can document in reasonable detail: (i) is known by such party at the time of receipt from the other party and is not subject to any other non-disclosure agreement between the parties; (ii) is now, or hereafter becomes, generally known to the public through no fault of such party; or (iii) is otherwise lawfully and independently developed by such party, or lawfully acquired from a third party without any obligation of confidentiality.

7.2 No Disclosure or Use. Each party acknowledges that it will receive Confidential Information of the other party. All Confidential Information of the other party shall be held in strict confidence and shall not be disclosed or used without express written consent of the other party, except as may be required by law, court order or subpoena, or in accordance with this Agreement. Each party shall use reasonable measures and reasonable efforts to provide protection for Confidential Information, including measures at least as strict as those such party uses to protect its own Confidential Information.

7.3 No Confidential Information of Other Parties. Developer represents and warrants that it shall not use in the course of its performance hereunder, and shall not disclose to Client, any confidential information of any third party (including competitors of Client or Developer) unless Developer is expressly authorized in writing by such third party to do so.

7.4 Website Confidential. Until the public availability of the Website, Developer shall not, and shall have no right to, release, distribute or disclose to any third party the Website or any Work Product or any portion thereof or any of the materials provided by Client hereunder. Developer will not provide advance access to the Website or any portion thereof to any person or entity without the prior written consent of Client, which consent may be granted or withheld by Client in its sole discretion. All so-called "test pages" for the Website that Developer may make available on the Internet for review by Client shall be password protected.

8. Warranties.

8.1 Developer represents and warrants that (a) it has the right, power and authority to enter into this Agreement and to perform fully its obligations under this Agreement; (b) the making of this Agreement by it does not violate any agreement existing between it and any other person or entity; (c) it owns or has acquired all necessary license rights in and to all materials it contributes to the Website; and (d) it complies, and at all times shall comply, with all applicable laws, rules and regulations in effect at the time services are performed pursuant to this Agreement, including without limitation all professional registration requirements and technical specifications pertaining to any aspect of the Website, provided, however, that Developer shall in no way be responsible for conformity or compliance in any way with governmental or other authority governing web-site content, including, without limitation, financial information, individual privacy, or the handling of other information.

8.2 Developer represents and warrants that (a) subject to the provisions of Sections 5.2 and 5.3 thereof, the Website and all Work Product therein that is not supplied by Client, as delivered by Developer, is original, has not been previously published in any form and is not in the public domain; (b) the Website and all Work Product are delivered free and clear of any liens, charges, encumbrances or restrictions, including those of Developer's suppliers; (c) all HTML or other formatted text files, Source Code and object code as delivered by Developer is complete and accurate; and (d) all Source Code is and shall be properly commented to industry standard.

8.3 Developer represents and warrants that the Website and all Work Product, including without limitation any images or graphics contained therein that are not supplied by Client, do not violate or infringe any right of privacy or publicity or any other Intellectual Property Right, or contain any libelous, defamatory, obscene or unlawful material, or otherwise violate or infringe any other right of any person or entity, and that Developer will not exercise any of the rights granted to it under or pursuant to this Agreement in a manner that will violate any applicable law, rule or regulation.

8.4 Developer represents and warrants that the Website (a) will be of high quality and free of defects in material and workmanship in all material respects, (b) as delivered by Developer, shall be free of any willfully introduced computer virus or any other similar harmful, malicious or hidden program or data or software device or code which will prevent Client from accessing or using the Website or any portion thereof and (c) for a period of six (6) months following acceptance by Client of the final Deliverable set forth in the Statement of Work (the "Warranty Period") shall operate and perform in accordance with the Functional Specifications, as measured against the Test Site. During the Warranty Period,

Developer shall correct any such errors at Developer's expense within forty-five (45) days of written notification of such errors, or within a mutually agreed upon timetable signed by both parties.

8.5 Client represents and warrants that (a) it has the right, power and authority to enter into this Agreement and to perform fully its obligations under this Agreement; (b) the making of this Agreement by it does not violate any agreement existing between it and any other person or entity; and (c) it has all necessary rights in and to the Client Art Works and any other materials it contributes to the Website. Client further represents and warrants that such materials contributed by Client do not violate or infringe any Intellectual Property Rights of any other person or entity.

8.6 THE EXPRESS REPRESENTATIONS, WARRANTIES AND COVENANTS SET FORTH IN THIS AGREEMENT ARE THE ONLY WARRANTIES MADE BY EITHER PARTY HEREUNDER. NEITHER PARTY MAKES ANY IMPLIED WARRANTIES WHATSOEVER, INCLUDING ANY IMPLIED WARRANTY OF MERCHANTABILITY OR FITNESS FOR A PARTICULAR PURPOSE. WITHOUT LIMITING THE GENERALITY OF THE FOREGOING, NEITHER PARTY MAKES ANY WARRANTIES WHATSOEVER, WHETHER EXPRESS OR IMPLIED, WITH REGARD TO ANY SOFTWARE SUPPLIED BY THIRD PARTIES.

9. Limitation of Liability.

IN NO EVENT WILL EITHER PARTY, OR ITS RESPECTIVE AFFILIATES, OFFICERS, DIRECTORS, EMPLOYEES, CONSULTANTS AND AGENTS, BE LIABLE FOR INCIDENTAL, SPECIAL OR CONSEQUENTIAL DAMAGES (INCLUDING BUT NOT LIMITED TO LOST PROFITS) SUFFERED BY THE OTHER PARTY, EVEN IF IT HAS PREVIOUSLY BEEN ADVISED OF THE POSSIBILITY OF SUCH DAMAGES, OR THE DAMAGES WERE OTHERWISE FORESEEABLE. DEVELOPER'S LIABILITY TO CLIENT SHALL BE LIMITED TO DIRECT DAMAGES AND IN NO EVENT EXCEED ________________.

10. Notices.

All notices that one party gives to the other pursuant to this Agreement shall be in writing and sent by registered or certified mail or overnight courier service, postage prepaid, return receipt requested, to the parties at the address provided below and shall be effective as of the date of receipt:

11. Indemnification.

11.1 Except as provided in Paragraph 9, Developer agrees to, and shall, indemnify, defend and hold harmless Client and its directors, shareholders, officers, agents, employees, affiliates, successors and assigns from and against any and all claims, demands, suits, actions, judgments, damages, costs, losses, expenses (including attorneys' fees and expenses) and other liabilities arising from (a) any breach of any of the representations, warranties, undertakings or agreements made by it under this Agreement, or (b) any of its subcontractors of any portion of the Client Art Works or the Website.

11.2 Client agrees to, and shall, indemnify, defend and hold harmless Developer, and its directors, shareholders, officers, agents, employees, affiliates, successors and assigns from and any and all claims, demands, suits, actions, judgments, damages, costs, losses, expenses (including attorneys' fees and expenses) and other liabilities arising from, in connection with or related in any way to, indirectly or indirectly, a breach or alleged breach of the representations and warranties set forth in Section 8.6 hereof, Client's acceptance and/or use of the Deliverables and/or Website, its content and/or any linked sites and their content. Developer shall promptly notify Client of any such claim, and Client shall bear full responsibility for the defense of such claim (including any settlements).

12. Use of Name; Publicity.

Client acknowledges that performance of Developer's services under this Agreement may require that Developer include Client's name in registrations and administrative filings, which are available to the public. Developer shall inform Client of any such registrations and filings in advance thereof.

13. Governing Law; Arbitration.

This Agreement shall be governed by and construed in accordance with the substantive laws of the State of New York and the United States, regardless of its place of execution or performance, and without regard to choice of law principles. Any dispute or claim arising out of or in relation to this Agreement, or the interpretation, making, performance, breach or termination thereof, shall be finally and exclusively settled by binding arbitration in New York City, New York under the commercial arbitration rules (the "Rules") of the Center for Public Resources ("CPR"). Within twenty (20) days of giving or receiving of notice of arbitration, Client on the one hand and Developer on the other hand shall appoint one independent arbitrator, and within twenty (20) days thereafter, the two arbitrators shall appoint a third arbitrator. If the two cannot agree upon a third arbitrator, the CPR shall appoint a third. The arbitration hearing shall be commenced within sixty (60) days of the third arbitrator's appointment. The arbitral proceedings and all pleadings and written evidence shall be in the English language. Any written evidence originally in a language other than English shall be submitted in English translation accompanied by the original or a true copy thereof. Judgment on the award rendered by the arbitrators may be entered in any court having jurisdiction thereof. The prevailing party (plaintiff or defendant, as the case may be) shall be entitled to recover, in addition to any other relief awarded, its reasonable costs and expenses, including without limitation attorneys' and expert witness fees, incurred in the proceeding.

14. Independent Contractor.

14.1 This Agreement does not constitute and shall not be construed as constituting an agency, partnership or joint venture between Developer and Client. Developer is an independent contractor. Neither Developer nor Developer's employees, consultants, contractors, or other personnel are agents, employees, or joint venturers of Client, nor do they have any authority to bind Client by contract or otherwise to any obligation. They shall not represent to the contrary, either expressly, implicitly, by appearance or otherwise.

14.2 Personnel supplied by Developer shall work exclusively for Developer and shall not, for any purpose, be considered employees or agents of Client. Developer assumes full responsibility for the actions of such personnel while performing services hereunder and shall be solely responsible for and shall indemnify Client and hold it harmless from their supervision, daily direction and control (including without limitation Developer's and such personnel's compliance with all applicable laws, regulations and ordinances), compensation, benefits (including without limitation any pension or welfare plans and workers' compensation program) and taxes (including without limitation all withholding taxes, payroll taxes, disability insurance payments, unemployment taxes, and other similar taxes and charges on the payments made or required to be made by Developer to such personnel). Developer shall file all returns and reports that may be required by any governmental or professional agency with respect to any of the foregoing.

14.3 Client shall have no obligation whatsoever to compensate Developer on account of any damages or injuries which Developer or any person or entity engaged by Developer may sustain as a result or in the course of the performance of Developer's or such employee's services under this Agreement other than personal injury or property damage proximately caused by Client's gross negligence or willful misconduct.

15. Assignment; Binding Effect.

The services rendered by Developer are personal in nature, and neither party may assign its obligations or this Agreement without the prior written consent of the other, including any assignment by operation of law or pursuant to any change of ownership control. Subject to the foregoing, this Agreement shall inure to the benefit of the parties and their successors and assigns.

16. Waiver of Provisions.

The terms and conditions of this Agreement may be waived only by a written instrument executed by the party waiving compliance.

17. Invalidity.

If any provision of this Agreement is held by a court of competent jurisdiction to be contrary to law, then the remaining provisions of this Agreement shall remain in full force and effect.

18. Counterparts.

This Agreement may be executed in counterparts, each of which shall be deemed an original and all of which, taken together, shall constitute one and the same instrument.

19. Captions.

All headings in this Agreement are inserted for convenience only and are not intended to affect the meaning or interpretation of this Agreement or any clause contained herein.

20. Entire Agreement.

This Agreement contains the entire agreement of the parties relating to the subject matter hereof and supersedes and cancels any and all prior agreements between them. This Agreement may only be modified by a writing signed by both parties.

Accepted and Agreed:

Developer	Client
By:______________________	By:______________________
[Name]	[Name]
Date: ____________________	Date: ____________________

FORM 9-13

Web Site Co-Ownership Agreement (Multiple Parties, Short Form)

This Website agreement ("Agreement") is entered into as of [DATE] (the "Effective Date") by and between SMITH at [address] ("Smith"), KLINE at [Address] ("Kline"), and BEETCHUM [Address] ("Beetchum]") regarding the Website located at www.thequickbrownfox.com (the "Site"), and successor and affiliated Web addresses.

1. SERVICES.

1.1. Scope. The parties have jointly developed the Site, and shall jointly own, operate and maintain the Site, and all contents thereof, subject to the terms of the Agreement.

1.2. Prior Arrangements. It is hereby acknowledged that each of the parties has contributed various services, monies and other resources in consideration of the Agreement and/or its subject matter, and no monies or other compensation is or shall be due or owing between or among any of them as of the Effective Date, except as expressly set forth herein.

2. RESPONSIBILITIES.

2.1. Each party shall have the following general responsibilities commencing upon the Effective Date:

> 2.1.1. Smith. Smith shall pay any and all maintenance costs associated with the Site up to $100/month ("Monthly Maintenance").
>
> 2.1.2. Kline. Kline shall oversee technical issues associated with site operations. The URL(s) for the Site shall be held in the name of Kline, subject to section 3.
>
> 2.1.3. Beetchum. Beetchum shall be responsible for generating and/or providing all text-based content.
>
> 2.1.4. Unspecified and Shared Obligations. All other responsibilities, costs and fees, including without limitation of any kind, the acquisition of other content, further Site development, maintenance in excess of Monthly Maintenance, operations, legal and administrative costs and taxes, shall be shared equally among the parties, unless mutually agreed among all parties otherwise. Any discretionary expenses, fees or costs in excess of five hundred dollars ($500) hereunder shall be subject to the mutual of agreement of all parties in advance.

2.2. First Priority. Each party shall make himself available on a first-priority basis as necessary to satisfactorily perform his obligations under the Agreement.

3. OWNERSHIP.

3.1. Equal Site Ownership. All services, works, deliverables and other materials, products, modifications developed or prepared for any or all of the parties pursuant to the subject matter of this agreement and/or in anticipation thereof, including without limitation photographs, graphics, text, audio, video, plans, diagrams, notes, program images and, any HTML code relating thereto, or any program code created by or at the request of any of the parties ("Work(s)"), and derivative Works therefrom, are and shall be the joint and several property of the parties, and shall be deemed to be works made for hire and made in the course of the Services rendered hereunder, from the time of inception and regardless of any acceptance, completion or other circumstances, and all title and interest therein shall vest in the parties jointly and severally. To the extent that title to any such Work(s) may not, by operation of law, vest in the parties jointly and severally, or such Work(s) may not be considered Works made for hire, the owner of said Works hereby irrevocably and unconditionally assigns, conveys and transfers all rights, title and interest in the Work(s), and all copyright interests therein, for the entire term of copyright protection of the Work(s), as now existing or as hereinafter may be enacted, in the United States and throughout the world, jointly and severally to and among the parties.

3.2. Equal Trademark Ownership. To the extent that any trademarks, service marks or other forms of identity are or shall be associated with the Site ("Marks"), whether or not registered, the same shall be owned jointly and severally by and among all of the parties to the same extent that said Mark(s) is owned by any of the parties.

4. PROFITS AND SALE.

4.1. Disbursement of Revenues. All income, including all revenue, receivables and the like, related to the Site and operation thereof shall be distributed first to pay all fees, costs and other expenses incurred by the parties jointly, and thereafter distributed among the parties as follows: twenty percent (20%) to Smith, twenty percent (20%) to Kline, and sixty percent (60%) to Beetchum ("Distribution Formula").

4.2. Sale of Site. Any proceeds from the sale of the Site, or any assets related thereto, shall be distributed according to the Distribution Formula.

5. TERM AND TERMINATION.

5.1. Term. This Agreement shall be effective until terminated in accordance with this section.

5.2. Termination. This Agreement may be terminated at any time by any of the parties individually upon ninety (90) days written notice to each of the others; upon the abandonment of the Site; or upon the bankruptcy of any of the parties.

5.3. Actions upon Termination. Upon termination of the Agreement for any reason, the Site and all assets relating thereto that are subject to the Agreement shall be divided equally among the parties.

6. ASSIGNMENT.

6.1. No party shall have any right to assign the Agreement or his interest herein.

7. ENTIRE AGREEMENT.

7.1. This Agreement constitutes the sole and entire agreement of the Parties, and merges and supersedes all prior discussions, agreements, contracts and understandings relating to the subject matter hereof.

Accepted and Agreed:

R. Smith	C. Kline	M. Beetchum
By:__________	By:__________	By:__________
Date:__________	Date:__________	Date:__________

FORM 9-14

Museum Web Site Development Agreement (Pro-Museum)

AGREEMENT (the "Agreement") made as of DATE (the "Effective Date") by and between Museum located at [address] and Designer located [address].

Whereas the Museum desires to establish a museum on the World Wide Web portion of the Internet to promote its materials and products and Designer provides design and production services in connection with creating Websites and desires to design, develop and update such a museum as set forth in this Agreement. Therefore, in consideration of the mutual covenants herein, the Museum and Designer agree as follows:

1. Services.

1.1. Scope of Services. Subject to the terms and conditions of this Agreement, Designer shall perform the services and deliver the materials set forth or described in this Agreement and/or as otherwise subsequently agreed to in writing by the parties (collectively, the "Services"), in order to design, develop and update a Museum-branded virtual Museum on the Word Wide Web portion of the Internet (the "Internet Museum") in accordance with the Specifications (as hereinafter defined). Designer acknowledges and agrees that the Internet Museum will be accessible by users of the Internet solely and directly through a URL designated and owned by the Museum. Designer acknowledges that additional services will be required to implement the Internet Museum and Designer hereby agrees to work closely with all contractors hired by the Museum with regard to the Internet Museum project in order to implement the Internet Museum.

1.2. Specifications and Schedule. Designer shall prepare and deliver to the Museum specifications for the Internet Museum, which shall detail the design, technical and functional capabilities, look and feel and other attributes of the Internet Museum including Museum's objective, schedule, constraints and criteria (the "Specifications"). The Specifications shall contain certain materials and services, which shall be due and owing to the Museum (the "Deliverables"). A portion of Designer's fee shall be contingent upon the Museum's acceptance of each Deliverable as further detailed below. Designer's services as described in the Specifications shall be performed as expeditiously as is consistent with professional skill and care and the orderly progress of the project. The Designer shall submit for the Museum's approval a schedule for the performance of the Services including the submission of the Deliverables (the "Schedule") that may be adjusted as the project proceeds if subsequently agreed to in writing by the parties. This schedule shall include allowances for periods of time required for the Museum's review and approval of work submitted.

1.3. Delivery of Specifications. Designer shall deliver to the Museum the Specifications as described in the Schedule. If Designer fails to timely deliver the Specifications, or if the Museum does not provide Designer with written notice of acceptance of the Specifications within thirty (30) days after the Museum's receipt thereof, the Museum shall have the right to terminate this Agreement without further obligation to Designer.

1.4. Acceptance. Within thirty (30) days after the receipt of the Specifications or as soon as practicable thereafter, the Museum will test and evaluate Designer's submission. The Museum shall determine to the Museum's sole satisfaction that the submission of the Specifications (including, when applicable, the Deliverables) appears and functions in accordance with the Museum's requirements (collectively, the "Museum Requirements"). In the event that the Specifications meet the Museum's Requirements, the Museum shall notify the Designer that such submission is acceptable ("Acceptance"). In the event the submission fails to meet the Museum's standards, The Museum will advise Designer in writing as to which aspects of the submission failed. Designer shall, at no cost to the Museum, remedy such failure and deliver the corrected Specifications to the Museum for review within thirty (30) days following receipt by Designer of notice of the failure. This process will be repeated until the Specifications (including, when applicable, the Deliverables) meet the Museum's Requirements and achieves Acceptance, or until the Museum exercises its right to terminate this Agreement due to the continued failure of the Specifications to meet Museum's Requirements, which right is hereby conferred upon the Museum.

1.5. Museum Responsibilities. Museum shall provide full information in a timely manner regarding work submitted by Designer; requirements for and limitations on the project, including an approval in writing of the Schedule and Specifications submitted by Designer. Museum shall provide Designer, within fifteen (15) days of a written request, information necessary and relevant for the Designer to complete further evaluation, development or refinement of the Schedule and Specifications. Museum shall keep Designer informed of any revisions to the project in a timely manner and shall be responsible for hiring the services of consultants when such services are reasonably required by the Specifications. Museum shall provide prompt written notice to the Designer if the Museum becomes aware of any fault or defect in the Internet Museum (including, where applicable, the Deliverables) including any errors, omissions or inconsistencies in the work delivered to the Museum by the Designer. Designer remains solely responsible for the work it provides to Museum.

1.6. Continuing Services. Designer's Services, including feasibility of implementation of any aspect of the project with respect to availability and compatibility of software, bandwidth, types of servers, equipment or networks, Internet provider or end user, shall represent the Designer's judgment as a design professional familiar with current industry standards. The Designer shall attempt to use and accommodate the most current technology that is viable and commercially available and shall be responsible for revising and updating the Internet Museum over the term of this Agreement plus twelve (12) months. The Designer agrees to cooperate with the Museum and any other consultant or third party developers including but not limited to software and code writing consultants, website management services and host service providers to ensure that the Internet Museum is implemented, maintained and updated according to the Specifications in a timely fashion. Designer agrees to act as a lull time consultant to any third parties the Museum determines, in its sole discretion, are necessary to implement the Internet Museum.

1.7. Designer represents and warrants that all Services shall be performed so that the Internet Museum, when operated on the Host Server will function and perform in accordance with the Specification. Designer shall, at no cost to the Museum, promptly provide any updates, revisions, necessary patches, fixes, workarounds, modifications and replacements necessary for the Internet Museum to function and perform in accordance with the Specifications when operated on the Host Server by the Hosting Service Provider. The Museum reserves the right to designate an alternative Host Server and Hosting Service Provider, and such designation shall not relieve Designer of its obligations under this Section 3.2. At no cost to the Museum, Designer shall fully cooperate with the Museum and the Hosting Service Provider including but not limited to consulting with regard to the implementation of the Internet Museum on the Host Server and identifying and correcting any errors with regard to the design aspects (including look and feel) of the Internet Museum.

1.8. Following implementation of the Internet Museum, Designer shall periodically update (as defined in the Specifications) the Internet Museum as requested by the Museum for the term of this Agreement plus six (6) months. All such updates shall become part of the Internet Museum and shall be governed by the terms and conditions of this Agreement. Updates shall be subject to the acceptance process outlined in Section 2.2 of this Agreement.

1.9. Designer represents and warrants that during the Initial Term (as that term is hereinafter defined) and any renewal period, Designer shall continually use and integrate the most current and up-to-date technology commercially available into the Internet Museum and any Specifications, subject to the prior approval of the Museum.

2. In consideration of Designer entering into this Agreement and performing all requirements hereunder, the Museum shall pay to Designer a total of [$AMOUNT], subject to acceptance by the Museum as follows: (i) an initial payment of [$AMOUNT] upon Designer's execution of this Agreement; and (ii) fur-

ther payments to be determined by a schedule attached hereto as exhibit 1 which shall become owing upon the receipt by Museum of a portion of the Deliverables as further outlined in exhibit 1. The amount paid by the Museum to the Designer each month shall be based on the Designer's invoice, which shall also include reimbursable expenses. Expenses shall be reimbursed (any particular expense in excess of $100.00 must be approved in writing) for the following: long distance telephone charges, delivery and messenger services, postage, long distance travel and accommodations when required by the Museum, reproduction and binding costs associated with presentations ordered by the Museum as well as duplication of films, videos, tapes, CDs and other forms of media when requested or approved by the Museum. Any consultant services or third party software obtained with the approval of the Museum shall also be reimbursed. In the event the Museum rejects the Specifications, and if mutual agreement cannot be reached on modifications thereto within thirty (30) days after the Effective Date, Designer shall refund the Initial Payment and this Agreement shall automatically terminate. Designer shall have no right to any royalties, revenues, fees or other payments in connection with, or as a result of the Services or the Internet Museum, or with respect to products or services promoted on or by the Internet Museum, except as expressly provided in this Agreement.

3. The Museum shall have exclusive artistic and editorial control over the Internet Museum, including, without limitation, integration of all Content, and the Design and look and feel of the Internet Museum. Designer shall not publish, or otherwise display the Internet Museum or any portion thereof without the prior written approval of the Museum. The Internet Museum shall be designed to attract repeat user visits and promote the most current Content, assets and properties identified by the Museum.

4. Ownership.

4.1. Except for the Designer Materials, all materials, products, and modifications developed or prepared for the Museum by Designer under this Agreement, including, without limitation, the Museum Materials, are and shall remain the property of the Museum, and all right, title and interest therein shall vest in the Museum and shall be deemed to be a "work made for hire" and made in the course of the Services rendered hereunder. To the extent that title to the Museum Materials does not, by operation of law, vest in the Museum or the Museum Materials are not considered works made for hire, all right, title and interest therein are hereby irrevocably assigned to the Museum. All such materials shall belong exclusively to the Museum with the Museum having the right to obtain and to hold in its own name copyrights, registrations or such other protection as may be appropriate to the subject matter, and any extensions and renewals thereof. Designer agrees to give the Museum and any person designated by the Museum any reasonable assistance required to perfect the rights.

4.2. All right, title and interest in and to the Content (as provided by the Museum and as digitized or otherwise reformatted by Designer or consultants for the Internet Museum, in all media now known or hereafter developed), the Specifications, Confidential Information (as hereinafter defined), the Internet Museum and any trademarks, trade names, logos, characters and other materials provided by the Museum, and the look and feel of the Internet Museum, including, without limitation, all copyrights, trademarks, trade names and other proprietary rights inherent therein or appurtenant thereto (collectively the "Museum Materials") are owned and retained exclusively by the Museum.

4.3. Designer shall not use the Museum Materials or any portion thereof for any purpose other than that of fulfilling Designer's obligations under this Agreement. The Museum Materials and any portion thereof may not be used, disclosed, transmitted, transferred, sold, assigned, leased or otherwise disposed of or made available for access by third parties, or be commercially exploited by or on behalf of Designer, its employees or agents, except as expressly provided in this Agreement.

4.4. Subject to the Museum's ownership of all right, title and interest in and to the Museum Materials and the Internet Museum, all techniques, algorithms and methods not in the public domain or licensed by Designer from any third party and rights thereto owned by Designer as of the Effective Date of this Agreement are and shall remain the property of Designer (collectively, the "Designer Materials").

4.5. The Museum hereby grants to Designer a non-exclusive, non-transferable, limited license, solely during the Initial Term of this Agreement and any renewal period, to use the Content solely for the benefit of the Museum in accordance with the terms and conditions of this Agreement. Designer may make such copies of the Content as may be necessary to perform its obligations under this Agreement, including back-up copies of the Content.

4.6. The Designer shall have the right to include representations of the design of the project among the Designer's promotional and professional materials. The Designer's materials shall not include the Museum's confidential or proprietary information if the Museum has previously advised the Designer in writing of the specific information considered by the Museum to be confidential or proprietary. Any use of the Museum name or trademark by Designer must be approved in advance by the Museum. The Museum shall provide professional credit for the Designer as part of any demonstration or display of the Internet Museum (provided the Internet Museum has not been materially re-designed). If requested by the Designer in writing, the Museum shall delete Designer's name from mention with regard to the project including all promotional materials.

5. Unless otherwise agreed in writing by the Museum, Designer shall maintain the strict confidentiality and shall not disclose to any third party the existence

of; or terms and conditions of; this Agreement. In addition, Designer, in performing the Services for the Museum hereunder, will have access to or be exposed to, directly or indirectly, Museum Materials, user information, data, knowledge, information about the marketing, product and/or business affairs of the Museum, and proprietary and trade secret information of the Museum, in oral, graphic, written, electronic or machine readable form (collectively, the "Confidential Information"). All Confidential Information shall be held in strict confidence by Designer and shall not be disclosed or used by Designer without the prior written consent of the Museum, except as provided in this Agreement, or as may be required by law. Designer shall hold Confidential Information in strict confidence and shall use its best efforts to provide protection for Confidential Information.

6. Designer agrees that it shall not, without the prior written consent of the Museum, disclose, distribute or release to any third party, in any manner or medium, directly or indirectly or through its representatives: (i) the Internet Museum, or any advertising, publicity or promotion materials (including, without limitation, distribution through the Internet) related to the Internet Museum or which include the name of the museum or its affiliates or subsidiaries or any trademark, trade name, or any abbreviation, contraction, or other embodiment thereof, and (ii) any materials or properties owned, controlled, licensed or otherwise proprietary to the Museum, whether or not such materials are incorporated into the Internet Museum, prior to the "public" release of such materials.

7. Warranties.

7.1. Designer represents and warrants that: (i) all of the Services to be performed hereunder will be rendered using sound, professional practices and in a competent and professional manner by knowledgeable, trained and qualified personnel; (ii) the Internet Museum will appear and operate in conformance with the Specifications; (iii) Designer has full authority to enter into this Agreement; (iv) all obligations owed to third parties with respect to the activities contemplated to be undertaken by Designer pursuant to this Agreement are or will be fully satisfied by Designer, so that the Museum will not have any obligations with respect thereto; (v) Designer is the owner of or otherwise has the right to use and distribute the Designer Materials, and any other materials and methodologies used in connection with providing the Services hereunder; (vi) Designer will comply with all applicable federal, state and local laws in the performance of its obligations hereunder; (vii) the Designer Materials and other materials and methodologies used by Designer in fulfilling its obligations under this Agreement (except the Content) shall not infringe upon any third party copyright, trademark, patent, trade secret or other third party right and Designer has the right to freely transfer the Designer Materials to the Museum; (viii) Designer, in providing Services hereunder, shall not alter the Museum Materials in any manner, unless agreed to in advance by the Museum; and (ix) Designer agrees that it shall not, without prior written consent of the Museum, design and/or create a Internet Museum for any other organization for a period of twelve (12) months after the public launch of the first phase of the Museum Museum's Internet Museum.

7.2. The Museum represents and warrants that: (i) it has full authority to enter into this Agreement; (ii) all obligations owed to third parties with respect to the activities contemplated to be undertaken by the Museum pursuant to this Agreement are or will be fully satisfied by the Museum, so that Designer will not have any obligations with respect thereto; and (iii) the Museum has provided Content for the Internet Museum that does not infringe or violate copyright, patent, trademark, trade secret or other proprietary rights of any third party.

7.3. The warranties set forth in this Agreement are limited warranties and are the only warranties made by the respective parties. The parties expressly disclaim, and hereby expressly waive, all other warranties, express or implied, including, without limitation, warranties of merchantability and fitness for a particular purpose. The Museum makes no warranties or guarantees as to the accuracy or completeness of any content published or made accessible on the Internet Museum.

8. Indemnities.

8.1. Designer shall indemnify, defend, and hold harmless the Museum, its directors, officers, employees and agents, with respect to any claim, demand, cause of action, debt or liability, including reasonable attorneys' fees, to the extent that the same is based upon a claim that: (i) if true, would constitute a breach of any of Designer's representations, warranties, or obligations hereunder; (ii) arises out of the negligence or willful misconduct of Designer; or (iii) any of the Designer Materials, or Services or the Internet Museum or any portion thereof infringes or violates any patents, copyrights, trademarks, trade names, trade secrets, licenses, or other rights of any third party. If any of the Designer Materials or Services or Internet Museum or any portion thereof provided pursuant to this Agreement are alleged to be infringing, Designer agrees to provide new materials so as to remedy the alleged infringement in a timely manner. The Museum reserves the right to terminate this Agreement and receive a full refund all fees paid by it pursuant to this Agreement if the Museum is unable to use any materials provided by Designer due to an alleged infringement.

8.2. The Museum shall indemnify, defend, and hold harmless Designer, its directors, officers, employees and agents, with respect to any claim, demand, cause of action, debt or liability, including reasonable attorneys' fees, to the extent that the same is based upon a claim that any of the Content provided by the Museum infringes or violates any U.S. patents which have issued as of the Effective Date, copyrights, trademarks, trade secrets, licenses or other property rights of any third party.

9. The initial term of this Agreement shall commence on the Effective Date set forth above, and shall continue until the third anniversary thereof ("Initial Term"). Thereafter, the Agreement may be renewed by mutual agreement of the Parties, in writing, for such periods as the Parties may agree.

10. Expiration, Termination.

10.1. The Museum may terminate this Agreement upon thirty (30) days written notice to Designer. Designer shall be entitled to fees earned prior to the termination. Either Party may terminate this Agreement at any time upon written notice to the other Party in the event the other Party materially breaches any of its representations, warranties, obligations or agreements hereunder, and such breach, if capable of being cured, is not cured within thirty (30) days following receipt of written notice of such breach from the non-breaching Party.

10.2. In the event of a termination of this Agreement for any reason, the Museum shall own all Work completed by Designer pursuant to this Agreement as of the date of termination.

10.3. Upon expiration or termination of this Agreement, or upon request by the Museum, Designer shall immediately cease using and return to the Museum all copies of Museum materials, if any, in its control or possession, in addition to all other property belonging to and/or received from the Museum.

10.4. Upon expiration or termination of this Agreement, all provisions comprising the Parties' express warranties provided herein shall survive.

10.5. Upon termination or expiration of this Agreement for a period of six (6) months, Designer shall, at no cost to the Museum, provide reasonable assistance to the Museum and any third parties authorized by the Museum in assuming performance of those Services necessary for the continued and uninterrupted operation of the Internet Museum.

11. General.

11.1. The Parties agree and acknowledge that the relationship of the Parties is in the nature of an independent contractor. This Agreement shall not be deemed to create a partnership or joint venture and neither Party is the other's agent, partner, employee or representative.

11.2. Neither Party shall be deemed in default of this Agreement to the extent that performance of its obligations or attempts to cure any breach are delayed or prevented by reason of any act of God, fife, natural disaster, or act of government provided that such Party gives the other Party written notice thereof promptly upon discovery thereof and uses its best efforts to cure the delay.

11.3. Should any provision of this Agreement be held to be void, invalid or inoperative, the remaining provisions of this Agreement shall not be affected and shall continue in effect and the invalid provision shall be deemed modified to the least degree necessary to remedy such invalidity.

11.4. The failure of either Party to partially or fully exercise any right or the waiver by either Party of any breach shall not prevent a subsequent exercise of such right or be deemed a waiver of any subsequent breach of the same or any other term of this Agreement.

11.5. Designer shall not assign this Agreement or any of its rights or obligations under this Agreement.

11.6. Any notice required or permitted under this Agreement shall be in writing. Notices shall be sent to the addresses first set forth above.

11.7. This Agreement, including any Exhibits annexed hereto, sets forth the entire agreement between the Parties on this subject and supersedes all prior negotiations, understandings and agreements between the Parties concerning the subject matter.

11.8. This Agreement shall be governed and interpreted in accordance with the laws of the State of New York without regard to principles of conflict of laws. The Parties agree to submit all disputes hereunder to the appropriate federal or state courts in the State of New York located in New York County.

Whenever possible, Designer shall name the Museum as an additional insured for the duration of this Agreement.

ACCEPTED AND AGREED:

Museum	Designer
By:______________________	By:____________________
[Name]	[Name]
Title:_____________________	Title:___________________
Date: ____________________	Date: ____________________

FORM 9-15

Commercial Web Site Development Agreement

This Development Services Agreement ("Agreement") is entered into as of DATE ("Effective Date") by and between Developer, Inc. ("Developer"), and Client, Inc. ("Client"), regarding the acquisition by Client of certain Website development and related services.

WHEREFORE, in consideration of the mutual promises and covenants contained herein, and other good and valuable consideration, the sufficiency of which is hereby acknowledged, the Parties agree as follows:

1. SERVICES.

1.1. Scope. Developer agrees to perform for Client the various Internet-related design, development, programming, implementation, warranty, management, migration and other services ("Services") as set forth in individual tasking documents issued hereunder from time-to-time and signed by the Parties hereto ("Schedules"), under the direction of authorized personnel as may be designated by Client from time-to-time.

1.2. Art Works. Developer shall use commercially reasonable efforts to secure for Client the broadest possible rights to any third party content provided or to be provided by Developer, on either an ownership or a license basis, subject to Client's final approval. Client shall be responsible for any costs or fees thereof, either directly to such third party or as a reimbursable expense of Developer.

2. TIMELINE AND NOTICE. Developer shall use commercially reasonable efforts to provide the Services in the most efficient manner feasible. Developer agrees that it shall be responsible for promptly notifying Client in writing as it becomes aware of any delays or potential delays, and for documenting with specificity the duration and reasons for said delays. Undocumented delays of which Developer is or should reasonably be aware shall be attributable solely to Developer. In the event of slippage attributable to Developer, and in addition to any other rights and remedies of Client hereunder, Developer shall assign additional personnel, retain personnel beyond the original deadline for completion of a milestone or significant deliverable, or some combination thereof, at the sole reasonable discretion of Client.

3. FEES. Fees and the payment thereof shall be as set forth in the attachment, subject to the following:

3.1. Expenses. Client shall reimburse Developer for all reasonable out-of-pocket and material expenditures incurred and properly documented by Developer and, for amounts in excess of five hundred ($500) dollars, authorized in advance by Client.

3.2. Taxes. Any levies, fees, charges or taxes placed upon any transaction, linkage or service conducted at or provided by Client' Website or application, or resulting from Developer's hosting or technical support of such Website or application, shall be the sole responsibility of Client.

4. OWNERSHIP.

4.1. Work For Hire. All Services, works, deliverables and other materials, products, modifications developed or prepared for Client by Developer under and/or in anticipation of this Agreement and its subject matter, including without limitation plans, diagrams, notes, program images and text viewable on the Internet, any HTML Code relating thereto, or any program code created at the request of Client ("Work(s)"), and derivative Works therefrom, are the sole property of Client, and shall be deemed to be works made for hire and made in the course of the Services rendered hereunder, from the time of inception and regardless of Acceptance, completion or other circumstances, and all title and interest therein shall vest in Client. Developer shall have no right to assert any interest, lien or encumbrance in such Works, nor may it use such Works for any other purpose except for the benefit of Client.

4.2. Residuals. Developer and Client acknowledge and agree that during the course of Developer's performance of Services hereunder, both Parties and their respective employees and agents may acquire or become acquainted with Residuals. "Residuals" means general data processing ideas and concepts, programming facility and techniques, and general know-how and skills. Notwithstanding the foregoing sentence, "Residuals" shall not mean or include, but shall expressly exclude, any information or documentation protected or protectable under law as trade secret(s) of any kind. Subject to the provisions of this section 4 and subsection 9.1.9, Developer and Client shall be entitled to use freely and otherwise employ such Residuals in the furtherance of their respective business activities, including the provision of services by Developer to its other customers. Nothing herein shall be construed to permit either Party to use the other's Confidential Information, as such is described below.

4.3. Transfer. To the extent that title to any such Work(s) may not, by operation of law, vest in Client, or such Work(s) may not be considered Works made for hire, in consideration of the Agreement, Developer hereby irrevocably and unconditionally assigns, conveys and transfers all rights, title and interest in the Work(s) to Client, and all copyright interests therein, for the entire term of copyright protection of the Work(s), as now existing or as hereinafter may be enacted, in the United States and throughout the world, with Client having the right to obtain and to hold in its own name, all copyright registrations or such other protection as may be appropriate to the subject matter, and any extensions and renewals thereof. Developer agrees to give Client reasonable assistance at Client's expense required to perfect the rights defined herein, and hereby agrees, at the request of Client, to execute and deliver such documents as in the opinion of Client are necessary to evidence Client's ownership interest. If Developer engages person(s) that are not current and valid "employees" (as that term is used by the IRS) to create all or part of the Work(s), Developer will cause said person(s) to agree in writing to assign all rights as set forth in this paragraph to Client.

4.4. Developer Programs. Any Developer-created or owned programming, software, source code or scripts developed or prepared outside of this Agreement and used in any project hereunder ("Custom Programming") shall remain the exclusive property of Developer, subject to a worldwide, perpetual, non-exclusive and non-revocable license to Client to use, display, perform and modify (including to maintain and update), such Custom Programming ("Developer License") in accordance with the subject matter of the Agreement. Commencing on the Effective Date, Developer shall identify all Custom Programming in writing to Client prior to the commencement of Services hereunder relating to the same.

4.5. Trademarks. Each Party reserves all rights in its respective trademarks and each Party agrees that any use of a Party's trademarks and all related good will shall inure to the benefit of the owner of such trademark.

4.6. Domain Names. To the extent any product of this Agreement is associated with a domain name chosen by Client and registered in Client's name by Developer, all right, title and interest in the domain name for the product shall vest exclusively in Client.

5. TERM AND TERMINATION.

5.1. Term. This Agreement shall become effective upon the date written above for a term of two (2) years, and shall automatically renew for additional one (1) year terms thereafter, unless and until terminated in accordance herewith.

5.2. Termination. This Agreement, or any Schedule issued or project undertaken pursuant to it, may be terminated by Client upon ten (10) days written notice, and Developer shall be paid for all Services performed, and expenses incurred, for or on behalf of Client through the effective date of any such termination. Either Party may terminate this Agreement within thirty (30) days of the end of the then-current term, or if the other is in material breach thereof and has not cured said material breach within thirty (30) days of written notice specifying the same.

5.3. Actions upon Termination. Upon termination of this Agreement, each Party (the "Receiving Party") shall promptly return to the other (the "Providing Party") (or, at the request of the Providing Party, destroy) all copies of business information, data, records or property, including without limitation Confidential Information, which belong to the Providing Party.

6. CONFIDENTIALITY. "Confidential Information" means any and all information, regardless of form, regarding a Party's intellectual property, trade secrets, customer data, business forecasts, marketing strategies, financial information, account information, products or services under development, computer software, source codes, object codes, documentation and programmer commentary, analytical techniques and processes, and any other nonpublic materials or information created, developed or owned by such Party. Confidential Information also includes the terms of this Agreement. Confidential Information does not include information that: (1) was made available to a Party free of any confidentiality obligation to the other Party at the time of disclosure; (2) is or becomes available to the public on or after the date of this Agreement (other than through prohibited disclosure by a Party); (3) is developed or discovered by a Party independently of such Confidential Information; or (4) is required by valid legal process to be disclosed by such Party, provided that the Party subject to legal process or any claim thereof shall provide immediate notice and reasonable cooperation in any attempt by the other Party to oppose the same. The Parties acknowledge the likely disclosure to each other during this Agreement of Confidential Information, the secrecy of which provides the disclosing Party an important commercial benefit. During the term of this Agreement and thereafter, each Party shall protect the secrecy of such Confidential Information, shall use it only for purposes of this Agreement, and shall not disclose such Confidential Information to any other person or entity, other than to its employees or agents who strictly need such access, without the written consent of the other Party. All Confidential Information shall remain the exclusive property of the disclosing Party.

7. REPRESENTATIONS & WARRANTIES.

7.1. By Developer. Developer represents and warrants that:

7.1.1. all of the Services to be performed by it hereunder will be rendered using sound, professional practices and in a competent and professional manner by knowledgeable and qualified personnel;

7.1.2. the software deliverables as developed and delivered by Developer hereunder will operate in conformance with the relevant terms of this Agreement and/or the applicable specifications as set forth in the applicable Schedule for the period as set forth in the applicable Schedule (if any);

7.1.3. Developer is the owner of or otherwise has the right to use and distribute all materials and methodologies used in connection with providing the deliverables;

7.1.4. Developer will comply with all applicable federal, state and local laws in the performance of its obligations hereunder;

7.1.5. Client shall receive good title free and clear of all liens, claims and encumbrances to all Works produced under this Agreement;

7.1.6. the software deliverables as developed and delivered solely by Developer hereunder are free of any virus, defect, disabling device, knowingly-inserted "time bomb" or remote control mechanism by Developer that might, or might be utilized to, impede the Service operation, damage Client's computer systems environment or software in any respect, or compromise the integrity of any of Client's files or data;

7.1.7. all deliverables hereunder will be compatible and operate in conjunction with all software and hardware previously delivered under this Agreement, excepting software and hardware that is expressly not recommended by Developer or to the extent that said deliverables have been expressly designed otherwise (with the approval of Client);

7.1.8. the software deliverables as developed and delivered by Developer hereunder shall have the ability successfully to maintain their functionality while processing, accepting, calculating, writing and output times or dates, or both, whether such dates are before, on or after 12:00 a.m. January 1, 2000 and any time periods determined or to be determined based on any such times or dates or both ("Y2K Compliant"); and

7.2. Both Parties.

7.2.1. Each Party represents and warrants that (i) it is an organization validly existing under law, and has all necessary powers and authorities to enter into and perform this Agreement; (ii) the execution and performance of this Agreement does not and will not conflict with its charter or by-laws, or any law or regulation, and will not breach or constitute default under any agreement, instrument or order to which it is subject, (iii) it is the owner of, or has a valid license to use, any intellectual property, content or Confidential Information provided hereunder, and any such use does not infringe, misappropriate, unfairly compete with or violate any right of any third party, and (iv) it shall not, during the term of this Agreement and for six (6) months thereafter, directly or indirectly solicit (except solely through advertisements directed to the general trade) for employment or retention as an independent contractor any employee, former employee or independent contractor of the other who provided Services pursuant to this Agreement.

7.2.2. EXCEPT AS SPECIFICALLY PROVIDED HEREIN, NEITHER PARTY MAKES ANY OTHER REPRESENTATIONS OR WARRANTIES, EXPRESS OR IMPLIED, INCLUDING WITHOUT LIMITATION ANY WARRANTY OF MERCHANTABILITY OR FITNESS FOR A PARTICULAR PURPOSE.

8. INDEMNIFICATIONS AND LIMITATIONS.

8.1. By Developer. Developer agrees to indemnify and hold harmless Client, its directors, officers, employees and agents, and defend any action brought against same with respect to any claim, demand, cause of action, debt or liability, including court costs and reasonable attorneys' fees (including an allocation for in house counsel fees), to the extent that it is based upon a claim that: (i) if true, would constitute a breach of any of Developer's representations or warranties hereunder; or (ii) any of Developer materials, deliverables or Services to be provided by Developer hereunder infringes or violates any patents, copy-rights, trade secrets, licenses, or other property rights of any third party.

8.2. By Client. Client agrees to indemnify and hold harmless Developer, its directors, officers, employees and agents, and defend any action brought against same with respect to any claim, demand, cause of action, debt or liability, including court costs and reasonable attorneys' fees (including an allocation for in house counsel fees), to the extent that it is based upon a claim that: (i) if true, would constitute a breach of any of Client's representations or warranties hereunder; or (ii) any of the content provided by Client hereunder and used by Developer as contemplated in this Agreement infringes or violates any patents, copyrights, trade secrets, licenses, or other property rights of any third party.

8.3. Notice of Claim. In claiming any indemnification hereunder, the indemnified Party shall promptly provide the indemnifying Party with written notice of any claim which the indemnified Party believes falls within the scope of the foregoing subsections. The indemnified Party may, at its own expense, assist in the defense if it so chooses, provided that the indemnifying Party shall control such defense and all negotiations relative to the settlement of any such claim and further provided that any settlement intended to bind the indemnified Party shall not be final without the indemnified Party's written consent, which shall not be unreasonably withheld.

8.4. IN NO EVENT SHALL EITHER PARTY BE RESPONSIBLE FOR ANY INDIRECT, SPECIAL, CONSEQUENTIAL, INCIDENTAL OR PUNITIVE DAMAGES, INCLUDING WITHOUT LIMITATION, LOST PROFITS OR LOSS OR DAMAGE TO DATA ARISING OUT OF THE USE, PARTIAL USE OR INABILITY TO USE THE RESULTS OF THE SERVICES. EXCEPT AS PROVIDED IN THIS PARAGRAPH, IN NO EVENT SHALL EITHER PARTY'S LIABILITY ARISING OUT OF THIS AGREEMENT, WHETHER IN CONTRACT, TORT OR OTHERWISE, EXCEED THE AMOUNT PAID OR OWING OR TO BE PAID TO DEVELOPER BY CLIENT FOR THE SERVICES UNDER THIS AGREEMENT; PROVIDING, HOWEVER, THAT SAID LIMITATION SHALL NOT APPLY TO ANY CLAIMS AND/OR DAMAGES RESULTING FROM ANY BREACH BY ONE PARTY OF THE OTHER PARTY'S INTELLECTUAL PROPERTY RIGHTS, OF SECTION 8 ("CONFIDENTIALITY"), OR FOR ANY MATTERS OF INDEMNIFICATION UNDER THE AGREEMENT.

9. NOTIFICATION. Any notice or other correspondence required or permitted to be given pursuant to this Agreement shall be in writing and shall be deemed to have been given (a) immediately if served personally, (b) immediately if sent to a designated FAX number (with confirmation of receipt), and simultaneously via first-class mail, postage pre-paid and addressed to the persons set forth below, (c) three (3) business days after posting if sent by certified or registered mail return receipt requested, postage prepaid, and addressed to the persons set forth below, (d) on the next business day if sent via internationally recognized carrier such as FedEx or U.P.S. and addressed to the persons set forth below.

10. DEVELOPMENT CREDIT. Client shall acknowledge Developer as the site developer of the Site in text in an "acknowledgments page" of the Internet Display, which will include a hyperlink to Developer's site on the World Wide Web. The format of such development credit shall be at the sole discretion of Client. It shall be the sole responsibility of Developer to provide Client with sufficient information to create and update such hyperlink. Such development credit will remain on the Site for until two (2) years from the Initial Display Date (as defined herein) or the termination of this Agreement, whether or not the Site is transferred in-house to facilities at the premises of Client. Such development credit shall not give Developer any trademark, copyright or other proprietary interest or rights in the Internet Display. Nothing herein shall be construed to require the Client to promote the Site and the level of effort and spending in promotion of the Site, if any, shall be in Client's sole discretion.

11. INSURANCE. Developer shall purchase and keep in force at its own cost and expense the minimum coverages including: (a) Worker's Compensation and Employer's Liability Insurance; (b) Commercial General Liability Insurance,

including Contractual Liability, completed operations, personal injury coverage, broad form property damage; (c) Errors and Omission Insurance; and (d) Umbrella coverage for (b) and (c) above at minimum coverage amounts for (a), (b) and (c) to be no less than one million ($1,000,000) dollars and (d) to be no less than four million ($4,000,000) dollars. Each and every policy and certificate shall contain an endorsement stating that the insurance company will not, prior to the expiration or termination of this Agreement or any policy expiration date shown on the policy and certificate, terminate the policy or change any coverage below that provided in this Section 12 without giving written notice to Client. This notice shall be provided by certified mail to Client and shall arrive at least fifteen (15) days prior to the termination or change.

12. RELATIONSHIP. The Parties to this Agreement are independent contractors. Neither Party is an agent, representative, or partner of the other Party. Neither Party shall have any right, power or authority to enter into any agreement for or on behalf of, or incur any obligation or liability of, or to otherwise bind, the other Party. This Agreement shall not be interpreted or construed to create an association, agency, joint venture or partnership between the Parties or to impose any liability attributable to such a relationship upon either Party.

13. GOVERNING LAW AND JURISDICTION.

13.1. Law. This Agreement shall be construed and enforced in accordance with the laws of the State of New York, without giving effect to the principles of conflicts of law.

13.2. Jurisdiction. The Parties consent and agree that all legal proceedings arising out of or relating to this Agreement deemed beyond the scope of this Section 15 shall be exclusively maintained in either the federal courts or the state courts located in New York, New York, and each hereby consents to the personal jurisdiction of said courts.

14. FORCE MAJEURE. In any case where either Party is required to do any act, delays caused by acts of nature, war or other emergency, civil commotion, fire, accident, flood or other casualty, strike, lockout, labor difficulties, breakdown, failure of supply or shortages of labor, materials or equipment, government orders or regulations, unusually severe weather or other causes beyond such Party's reasonable control shall not be counted in determining the time during which such work shall be completed, whether such time be designated by a fixed date, a fixed time or a "reasonable time" and such time shall be deemed to be extended by the period of such delay; providing, however, that no additional rights shall otherwise be granted hereby, nor shall this section abridge, limit or amend any rights, remedies or power of either Party.

15. ASSIGNMENT. Client shall have the right, without the prior written consent of Developer, to assign this Agreement in whole. Neither this Agreement nor any rights or obligations hereunder shall be transferred or assigned by Developer without the prior consent of Client. Notwithstanding the above, Developer may, upon written notice to Client, assign this Agreement in whole, including all of its rights and obligations hereunder, to any entity acquiring all or substantially all of the stock or assets of Developer.

16. NO WAIVER. No delay or omission by either Party hereto to exercise any right or power hereunder shall impair such right or power or be construed to be a waiver thereof. A waiver by either of the Parties hereto of any of the covenants to be performed by the other or any breach thereof shall not be construed to be a waiver of any succeeding breach thereof or of any other covenant herein contained.

17. PUBLICITY. Developer may include Client's name in its published client lists and may issue to the general public announcements and written statements concerning the existence of this Agreement and the general substance of projects to be performed and performed hereunder, provided that Developer maintains the confidentiality of all proprietary and Confidential Information.

18. SEVERABLE. In the event any one or more of the provisions of this Agreement or any Schedule is deemed by the final decree of a court of competent jurisdiction to be invalid or unenforceable, the enforceability of remaining provisions shall be unimpaired.

19. HEADINGS. The headings of the articles and sections used in this Agreement are included for convenience only and are not to be used in construing or interpreting this Agreement.

20. ENTIRE AGREEMENT. This Agreement constitutes the sole and entire agreement of the Parties, and merges and supersedes all prior discussions, agreements, contracts, and understandings. Any waiver, modification or amendment to this Agreement must be in writing and executed by each Party. Waiver of any provision or any breach hereof shall not be deemed a waiver of any other breach or non-compliance herewith. If any provision of this Agreement shall be held to be invalid, illegal or unenforceable, it shall be severed and the other provisions shall remain valid and fully enforceable.

21. SURVIVAL. Sections ______shall survive termination of this Agreement, regardless of cause.

22. COUNTERPARTS. This Agreement may be executed in two counterparts, each of which shall be an original; but such counterparts shall together constitute one and the same instrument.

Accepted and Agreed:

Developer	Client
By:____________________ [Name]	By:__________________ [Name]
Title:____________________	Title:__________________
Date: __________________	Date: __________________

FORM 9-16

Commercial Web Site Development Agreement (Ongoing or Multiple Projects)

AGREEMENT (the "Agreement") made as of DATE (the "Effective Date") by and between Museum located at [address] ("Museum") and consulting designer ("Consultant") located at [address].

1. Services.

1.1. Consultant agrees to perform for the Museum the various software-related design, development, programming, implementation, maintenance, management, migration, training and other services ("Services") set forth in the schedules, attached and to be attached from time-to-time hereafter, each bearing a head-note referencing this Agreement and the unique title of the schedule running page-to-page throughout, and signed by the parties hereto not in counterpart ("Schedules").

1.2. Each Schedule shall include a corresponding statement of work, containing a description of the tasks to be performed by Consultant, together with such other descriptors as the parties see fit to include, such as designation of deliverables, documentation, milestones, acceptance criteria, warranty periods, performance schedules, payment schedules, general functional descriptions, detailed software specifications, relationships of software to hardware, terminal response time, data conversion responsibility, programming languages, Consultant staffing, staff qualifications, etc.

1.3. Consultant agrees to perform the Services in a professional manner, including without limitation the delivery of functional software, under the direction of the Museum personnel designated from time-to-time by the Museum.

1.4. To the extent any Services whatsoever are negotiated or performed by or between the parties, including in the absence of corresponding Schedules, all such Services shall be governed by the terms of this Agreement, unless otherwise agreed to in writing by the parties with specific reference to this subsection.

2. Payments

2.1. UNLESS OTHERWISE PROVIDED IN WRITING WITH SPECIFIC REFERENCE TO THIS SECTION: Prior to "Testing Notification" (defined below) and subject generally to the terms of the Agreement, for Services rendered during the then-current calendar month, Consultant will invoice the Museum the following month, and payment shall be net thirty (30) calendar days. The Museum shall reimburse Consultant for all reasonable out-of-pocket and material expenditures incurred and properly documented by Consultant and, for amounts in excess of Two Hundred Fifty ($250) Dollars, authorized in advance by the Museum.

2.2. For Services rendered by Consultant for which fees have not been delineated with particularity, Consultant shall invoice the Museum as set forth in the "Time & Material Rates" in Attachment A hereto and incorporated herein, as amended by mutual written consent of the parties from time-to-time hereafter. Without limiting the foregoing, nothing in this subsection shall be construed to affect Services performed for a fixed-price.

2.3. If the Museum disputes any amount(s) payable, the Museum shall pay that portion of the amount(s) not in dispute, if any, and either party may submit the disputed sum(s) to dispute resolution hereunder.

2.4. Fixed-price project fees associated with software development services only shall be payable in equal installments of twenty-five percent (25%) upon the occurrence of each of the following conditions: (i) commencement of the project, (ii) the halfway point as determined with reference to the applicable time-line, (iii) "Acceptance" (defined below) (or waiver thereof) of the final Deliverable of the project, and (iv) operation without any material program errors impairing functions of the project as it is designed to perform ("Material Program Errors") for ninety (90) consecutive days following the commencement of Live Operation (defined in section 8).

2.5. Subject generally to the terms of the Agreement, Museum shall have no obligation to pay Consultant, and Consultant shall assume all responsibility, for all fees and costs associated with any and all overruns related to fixed-price projects, except for any addition, unanticipated work resulting from rework caused by government changes to standards or from the failure of Museum to perform its obligations hereunder, in which event Museum shall be solely responsible for the fees and costs corresponding thereto.

2.6. Museum shall pay Consultant seventy-five (75%) percent of time-and-material fees set forth in "Time & Material Rates" (subsection 2.2) for any and all unapproved slippage of delivery dates related to time and materials projects.

3. Ownership and Property. Notwithstanding anything to the contrary, and except as provided below: All Services and work performed by the Consultant under this Agreement, including without limitation all materials, products, "Deliverables" (defined below) and derivative works therefrom, are the property of the Museum, and shall be deemed to be works made for hire and made in the course of the Services rendered hereunder, from the time of inception and regardless of Acceptance, completion or other circumstances. All title and interest therein shall vest in the Museum and may not be used by Consultant for any other purpose except for the benefit of the Museum. To the extent that title to any such Services or work may not, by operation of law, vest in the Museum or such work may not be considered works made for hire, all rights, title and interest therein are

hereby irrevocably assigned to the Museum by Consultant, with the Museum having the right to obtain and to hold in its own name, copyrights, registrations or such other protection as may be appropriate to the subject matter, and any extensions and renewals thereof. The Consultant agrees to give the Museum reasonable assistance at the Museum's expense required to perfect the rights defined in this section, and hereby appoints the Museum as its agent and attorney-in-fact to sign in its name any such instruments or other documents which have not been duly signed by it and received by the Museum within five (5) calendar days following the Museum's request therefor. Consultant shall not be precluded from performing similar services for others even where such services shall produce similar results, subject to this subsection 3.1 and sections 10 and 11.

4. Project Meetings/Progress Reports. Unless otherwise provided by Schedule or by the Museum at any time, the Consultant's project manager(s) shall present one or more written report(s) to the Museum with respect to the status and progress of all existing or ongoing Services on a weekly basis. Such report(s) shall include a summary of the accomplishments and difficulties during the prior reporting period, the anticipated results during the next reporting period, and estimated time and cost to complete, where applicable. In addition, if requested by the Museum during the prior reporting period, Consultant agrees to submit time sheets in a form to be proposed by the Museum and approved by the Consultant (such approval not to be unreasonably withheld, conditioned or delayed), and to itemize the services rendered by individual, rate and days-hours worked during the weekly period. Project meetings involving the Consultant's project manager(s) and personnel designated by the Museum shall occur as provided in the corresponding Schedule or (absent such provisions) as reasonably required by the Museum.

5. Modification of Services

5.1. The Museum may at any time modify the scope of the existing Services agreed to between the parties, specifying the desired modifications to the same degree of specificity as in the original specifications. The Consultant may at its own discretion agree to investigate modified Services, and will notify the Museum of its decision within five (5) business days following receipt of such notice. Consultant will reasonably attempt to manage these conditions without impacting project plans and requirements. If Consultant agrees to investigate such modified Services, it will submit to the Museum, along with the notice of its decision to undertake the work, an estimate of the time and cost to effect such modification ("Estimate"). Whether or not the Museum accepts Consultant's Estimate, the Museum will pay Consultant for reasonable costs incurred by Consultant in investigating and preparing such Estimate, not to exceed two thousand ($2,000) dollars without prior Museum consent in each instance. The Museum shall respond to Consultant's Estimate within three (3) business days. Nothing herein shall relieve

Consultant of its obligations hereunder to maintain up-to-date time-lines and to advise the Museum on a contemporaneous basis of any changes thereto and the reasons therefor.

5.2. Notwithstanding anything to the contrary herein, at any time and for any reason, the Museum may in its sole discretion, pursuant to this subsection on thirty (30) calendar days notice, terminate any Schedule(s). Subject to the terms of the Agreement, the Museum thereupon shall reimburse Consultant for incurred costs on either a time-and-material or pro-rata basis, except to the extent that Consultant staff working on the terminated Schedule(s) can be reassigned to other Museum projects, for which reassignment Consultant shall provide its full cooperation.

6. Timeliness of Performance

6.1. Consultant understands that prompt performance of all Services hereunder is required by the Museum in order to meet its schedules and commitments, and the parties shall agree in writing with specificity on time-lines to apply to all Services, including without limitation to Deliverables such as projects, systems and their component parts, from commencement through final delivery and Acceptance.

6.2. It is understood that the Museum must cooperate in the furnishing of appropriate information, facilities and other resources to the Consultant, and that, if the Museum fails to cooperate, through no fault of Consultant, in the furnishing of such information, facilities or other resources, Consultant shall promptly deliver to Museum a written notice, giving specific itemization of information, facilities or other resources required to be delivered to Consultant for the timely performance of Services.

6.3. Consultant agrees that it shall be responsible for promptly notifying Museum in writing as it becomes aware of any delays or potential delays, and for documenting the duration and reasons for said delays with specificity. Undocumented delays of which Consultant is or should reasonably be aware shall be attributable solely to Consultant, excluding the exceptions identified in subsection 2.5. In the event of slippage attributable to Consultant, Consultant shall assign additional personnel, retain personnel beyond the original deadline for completion of a milestone or significant Deliverable, or some combination thereof, at the sole reasonable discretion of the Museum and in accordance with section 2.

7. Acceptance

7.1. UNLESS PROVIDED ELSEWHERE TO THE CONTRARY IN WRITING WITH SPECIFIC REFERENCE TO THIS SUBSECTION, the Museum shall have the right to review and test any and all new or additional software and software modifications, upgrades, bug fixes and migrations (including without limitation the design, development, programming, implementation, installation and re-installation thereof, as applicable), as well as other Services designated by the parties as deliverables ("Deliverables"). Consultant shall perform its own unit and system testing of Deliverables to its satisfaction, and thereafter notify the Museum in Consultant's weekly project reports or otherwise in writing of the availability of said Deliverable(s) for formal review and testing by the Museum, which notification shall be deemed to certify to the Museum that the corresponding Deliverable is functionally sound ("Testing Notification"). The Museum shall accept or decline in its discretion and in a timely fashion to perform such review and testing. Where no acceptance test has been defined to govern the review and testing of a specific Deliverable, the Museum may, in its discretion, review and test said Deliverable in a reasonable and timely manner as it sees fit ("Acceptance Test").

7.2. The Museum shall provide the Consultant written notification in a timely manner of the results of the Acceptance Test. If a Deliverable is deemed by the Museum to fail Acceptance Testing, subject to section 2, Consultant shall thereafter make any corrections necessary for the Deliverable to pass the Acceptance Test. If any Deliverable does not pass the Acceptance Test within sixty (60) calendar days of Museum's initial notification of testing results, the Museum may require Consultant to continue to attempt to correct the Deliverable at Consultant's sole expense, reserving the right to terminate the corresponding Schedule without notice or any further obligation or liability of any kind.

8. Maintenance. The Museum may in its sole discretion commence the live transmission and processing of Museum's operational data in standard, peak and other functional modes using any Deliverable, or any system comprised of Deliverables, and all related systems ("Live Operation"), following the passing or waiver of Acceptance Testing. For ninety (90) calendar days following the commencement of Live Operation, Consultant shall perform maintenance on the Deliverable(s) and related systems, free of charge, to assure that such are in conformance with the specifications and other obligations of this Agreement, including without limitation the furnishing of such materials and services as shall be necessary to correct any defects in the operation of the Deliverable(s) or other products in Museum's possession, and maintain them in good working order in accordance with the specifications for same ("Maintenance"). Maintenance shall also include correction of errors or malfunctions. Consultant shall have no Maintenance obligations as set forth herein with respect to any specific Deliverable(s) for which the Museum did not perform Acceptance Testing, provided that Consultant's warranty obligations (below) shall be unaffected by any waiver of Acceptance Testing, and Consultant shall still be responsible for cor-

recting, free of charge, any Material Program Errors directly caused by said Deliverable(s) in related systems. Irrespective of any Maintenance obligations or lack thereof, if any Deliverable(s) and all systems affected directly thereby are not free of all Material Program Error(s) within ninety (90) calendar days of the commencement of Live Operation, the Museum may require Consultant to continue to attempt to correct said Material Program Errors at Consultant's sole expense, reserving the right to terminate the applicable Schedule without notice or any further obligation or liability of any kind.

9. Documentation and Training. Consultant shall provide all applicable documentation with Testing Notification for each Deliverable, which could include detailed design specifications, system flow charts, program flow charts, file layouts, report layouts, screen layouts, program source code, and all other documentation as specified in the appropriate Schedule, RFP or Museum proposal ("Documents" and "Documentation"). Thereafter, Consultant's project manager(s) shall review all applicable Documentation with personnel designated by the Museum, to the satisfaction of Museum, whereupon the Museum shall release Consultant from any further obligation to provide Documentation in connection with the corresponding Deliverable(s) or project(s). Documentation shall not be defined more narrowly than herein provided without specific written reference to this section.

10. Confidentiality/Injunctive Relief

10.1. Museum and Consultant acknowledge that each may come into the possession of confidential information of the other relating to employee's, customers, operations, activities, intellectual property (including without limitation trade secrets and know-how), products and/or services, that such information is property valuable to the party that has developed it, and that the party that has developed it desires to retain it in confidence and withhold it from publication to others. Consultant further acknowledges that the services which the Museum performs for its clients are confidential; that to enable the Museum to perform these services, its clients furnish to the Museum confidential information concerning their business affairs, finances, properties, methods of operation and other data; that the good will of the Museum depends, among other things, upon its keeping such services and information confidential and that unauthorized disclosure of the same would irreparably damage the Museum; and that by reason of its duties hereunder, the Consultant may come into possession of information concerning the services performed by the Museum for its clients or information furnished by its clients to the Museum, even though the Consultant does not itself take any direct part in or furnish the services performed by those clients. Excepting information which is or becomes publicly available through no breach of this Agreement, or information which is independently developed or received by a party under no obligation of confidentiality, all information described in this subsection is hereinafter collectively referred to as "Confidential Information".

10.2. Each party agrees that any and all Confidential Information of the other, and any information or knowledge which may be imparted through receipt and examination of Confidential Information of the other, will not be copied or communicated to any third party, or used by a party, its employees, servants or agents except as may be necessary for fulfilling the terms of this Agreement or upon prior written approval of the other party. Each party agrees to return all written or other tangible Confidential Information of the other, including all extracts and copies thereof, upon the other's request, or to dispose of such Confidential Information in accordance with the other's written instructions. Each party agrees that it will not at any time during or for a period of three (3) years after the term of this Agreement disclose any Confidential Information of the other to any person whatsoever, or permit any person whatsoever to examine and/or make copies of any reports or any documents it has prepared or which it has come to possess or control by reason of the Services. If either party is required to disclose Confidential Information pursuant to legal process, said disclosing party shall provide the other party with prompt written notice of the same and shall cooperate with the other party in any reasonable effort to oppose such process, at the expense of the opposing party. Each party acknowledges that its disclosure of any Confidential Information of the other will give rise to irreparable injury to the other, or the owner of such information, inadequately compensable in damages. Accordingly, each party, or the owner of such information, may seek and obtain injunctive relief against the breach or threatened breach of the foregoing undertakings, in addition to any other legal remedies which may be available without requirement of posting bond or other security.

11. Non-Compete

11.1. In recognition of the fact that Consultant's personnel provided to Museum under the Agreement and prior agreements may perform similar services from time-to-time for others, this Agreement shall not prevent Consultant or its employees from performing such similar services or restrict it from using personnel provided to Museum under this Agreement, subject to confidentiality and other Consultant obligations hereunder. Consultant shall make every effort consistent with sound business practice to honor the specific requests of the Museum with regard to the assignment of its employees and other personnel; however, Consultant reserves the right to determine the assignment of its employees. Notwithstanding the foregoing, Consultant agrees that, for this period of providing Services to Museum and continuing for one (1) year after the termination of this Agreement, Consultant will not, unless approved by Museum in its sole discretion in each instance, render similar services for [named competitors]. Without limiting the Agreement in any way, this section shall apply to all affiliates, subsidiaries and/or successors-in-interest of the Consultant.

11.2. The Consultant further acknowledges and agrees that in the event of the termination of this Agreement, its experience and capabilities are such that it can obtain a consulting arrangement or employment in business activities which are either (1) of a different or non-competing nature with its activities as a consultant for the Museum, or (2) are carried on outside the United States; and that the enforcement of a remedy hereunder by way of injunction will not prevent it from operating its business or earning a reasonable livelihood. The Consultant further acknowledges and agrees that the covenants contained herein are necessary for the protection of the Museum's legitimate business interests and are reasonable in scope and content.

12. Hiring. Neither Museum nor Consultant shall solicit, attempt to solicit, hire or employ, without the prior written consent of the other, employees of the other party during the term of this Agreement, and for a period of one (1) year following its termination.

13. Indemnity and Insurance

13.1. Consultant agrees to indemnify the Museum for any liability or expense due to breach of this Agreement, negligence of Consultant, claims for personal injury or property damage arising out of Consultant's performance of the Services, as well as from any claim for payment of compensation or salary asserted by an employee of Consultant. Museum agrees to indemnify Consultant for any claim for payment of compensation or salary asserted by an employee of Museum. Consultant will, at its own expense, defend any action brought against it or the Museum to the extent that such action is based on a claim relating to Services or systems used within the scope of this Agreement or infringement of any patent, copyright, license or trade secret; provided that Consultant is promptly notified in writing of such claim. In no event shall Consultant settle any such claim, lawsuit or proceeding without the Museum's prior written approval. If, as a result of any such claim, litigation or threat thereof, the Museum or the Consultant is permanently enjoined from using any product of Consultant's Services by final, non-appealable decree, at the discretion of the Museum, Consultant at its sole expense may procure for the Museum the right to continue to use said product(s) or replace or modify said product(s) so as to settle such claim, litigation or threat thereof. Notwithstanding the foregoing, Consultant shall not have any obligation to indemnify or defend Museum to the extent any claim, damage, cost or expense is caused by the Museum's modification of any product.

13.2. Consultant agrees to maintain for itself and its employees all insurance coverages as required by federal and/or state law, including worker's compensation insurance, General Liability and Automobile Liability. Consultant shall upon request, furnish the Museum with a certificate of insurance showing the amount of coverage and naming the Museum as an additional insured as its interests may appear. Such certificate shall include a provision whereby fifteen (15) calendar days notice must be received by the Museum prior to coverage cancellation by either Consultant or insurer.

14. Limitation of Liability. Neither party shall be liable to the other for any special, indirect or consequential damages or lost profits. Consultant's liability hereunder for damages with respect to work performed under a particular Schedule, regardless of the form of action, shall not exceed the total amount paid to Consultant for its Services pursuant to the applicable Schedule attached to this Agreement. Other than for indemnification under subsection 13.1, no action, regardless of the form thereof, arising out of the Services under this Agreement, may be brought by either party more than two (2) years after the cause of action has accrued, and no action for non-payment may be brought after eighteen (18) months of the date of the last payment.

15. Independent Contractor. Consultant is an independent contractor. Neither Consultant nor Consultant's employees are or shall be deemed for any purpose to be employees of the Museum. The Museum shall not be responsible to Consultant, Consultant's employees or any governing body for any payroll-related taxes related to the performance of the Services.

16. Assignment. This Agreement is not assignable, in whole or in part, by operation of law or otherwise, including without limitation, by merger, acquisition, consolidation or sale of assets or securities, by either party without the prior written consent of the other party, such consent not to be unreasonably withheld, delayed or conditioned. Notwithstanding the foregoing, Museum is permitted to assign this Agreement to affiliates as part of any operating reorganization without the approval of Consultant; Consultant may utilize from time-to-time non-supervisory independent contractors in the performance of Services hereunder, with the prior written consent of the Museum.

17. Term. The term of this Agreement shall commence on the date set forth in the caption and, unless earlier terminated in accordance herewith, shall terminate on DATE, and shall be automatically renewed for successive six (6) month periods thereafter.

18. Termination. Notwithstanding anything to the contrary herein, the Museum may terminate this Agreement at any time for any reason upon written notice to Consultant of One Hundred Twenty (120) calendar days. Consultant shall have no right to terminate this Agreement until DATE, at which time Consultant may terminate this Agreement upon written notice to the Museum of One Hundred

Twenty (120) calendar days. Either party may terminate the Agreement after DATE, upon sixty (60) calendar days written notice. In the event of such termination, the Museum is obligated to pay only for costs incurred and actual services rendered by the Consultant prior to the termination. Upon termination or expiration of this Agreement for any reason, Consultant shall deliver to the Museum all Confidential Information and other materials relating to the Museum or this Agreement, and return the Museum Resources, at Museum's expense (unless termination is due to breach by Consultant, in which case Consultant shall bear the associated expenses).

19. Warranties. Consultant warrants that: (a) each of its employees assigned to perform services under any Schedule shall have the proper skill, training and background so as to be able to perform in a competent and professional manner and that all work will be performed in accordance with the applicable Schedule; (b) Museum shall receive good title free and clear of all liens, claims and encumbrances to all materials, Deliverables and products developed under this Agreement; (c) each and every Deliverable, including all software, contemplated by any Schedule, shall conform to the specifications for the same as mutually agreed to in writing by Museum and Consultant, and, furthermore, shall conform to the highest relevant industry standards of quality; and (d) the Deliverables shall maintain their functionality, taking into account any processing, accepting, calculating, writing and outputting of times or dates, or both, whether before, on or after 12:00 a.m. January 1, 2000 and any time periods determined or to be determined based on any such times or dates or both. This subsection 19(d) shall apply solely to code developed and delivered by Consultant hereunder, and shall not be deemed to apply to (i) Consultant software developed prior to this Agreement to process a number of characters insufficient to achieve Y2K compliance at the specific request of the Museum (collectively, "Noncompliant Software") or (ii) any third-party software embedded within a Deliverable or (iii) any Museum Resources, which Noncompliant Software Consultant shall identify with particularity at the expense of the Museum. Consultant disclaims all other warranties except those expressly provided for in this Agreement or in any Schedule.

20. Force Majeure. In any case where either party is required to do any act, delays caused by acts of nature, war or other emergency, civil commotion, fire, accident, flood or other casualty, strike, lockout, labor difficulties, breakdown, failure of supply or shortages of labor, materials or equipment, government orders or regulations, unusually severe weather or other causes beyond such party's reasonable control shall not be counted in determining the time during which such work shall be completed, whether such time be designated by a fixed date, a fixed time or a "reasonable time" and such time shall be deemed to be extended by the period of such delay, subject to subsection 6.3.

21. Dispute Resolution

21.1. In the event of any controversy or claim arising out of this Agreement raised by either party, the party raising the dispute will promptly notify the other party in writing of the nature of the dispute and the factual background. Within the fifteen (15) day period following such notice, the parties will initiate an attempt in good faith to reach a reasonable solution to the dispute, including escalation to the vice-president of each company responsible for the subject matter of the dispute. If the dispute cannot be amicably resolved within thirty (30) calendar days of written notification, then either party may seek to resolve said dispute by arbitration before a single arbitrator in accordance with the commercial arbitration rules of the American Arbitration Association, and judgment upon the award rendered by the arbitrator may be entered in any court having jurisdiction thereof. The place of arbitration shall be Springfield, MA. Each party shall provide to the arbitrator, no later than fifteen (15) calendar days following the date of the arbitrator's appointment, a statement, including all supporting documents or other evidence on which such party relies as to why it believes that the dispute should be resolved in its favor, and all such materials and any other materials provided to the arbitrator by either party shall simultaneously be provided by such party to the other party. Within twenty (20) calendar days after the submission of such statements by all parties, the arbitrator shall hold a hearing with respect to the dispute. At such hearing, the arbitrator may, in his or her sole discretion, allow the parties to call and cross-examine witnesses, make any additional arguments or submit any additional materials to support the position taken in their respective statements. The arbitrator shall enter an award within fifteen (15) calendar days following the hearing provided for herein. Nothing shall preclude either party from making an application to the arbitrator, for good cause, to expedite the proceedings, nor restrict the arbitrator from granting such an application. In addition to such other relief as the arbitrator may award, the arbitrator shall be vested with jurisdiction and shall award to the prevailing party its reasonable attorney's fees and expenses, and all other costs associated with the arbitration. The award rendered by the arbitrator shall be final, and judgment may be entered upon it in accordance with applicable law in any court having jurisdiction thereof.

21.2. This Agreement and performance hereunder shall be governed by and construed in accordance with the laws of the State of New York but conflict of law rules shall not apply. Any and all proceedings relating the subject matter deemed beyond the scope of subsection 21.1 shall be maintained in the courts of the State of New York or the Federal District Court sitting in New York County, which court shall have exclusive jurisdiction for such purpose.

22. Complete Agreement. This Agreement constitutes the complete agreement and understanding between the parties unless modified in writing, signed by

both parties, or modified by a change in Schedules initialed by both parties. Where there is any conflict, redundancy, intersection of terms or other overlap whatsoever between this Agreement and any agreement between the parties, or where this Agreement could reasonably be applied to govern any conduct, performance or other aspect of the parties' relationship in any circumstance, including current circumstances arising under existing agreements, this Agreement shall take precedence and govern the parties conduct, rights and obligations. This Agreement shall not otherwise be deemed to alter, change or affect Consultant's warranty, maintenance or support obligations with respect to any software delivered prior to the date hereof, which shall be governed solely by the terms of any prior agreements under which such software was developed or delivered.

23. Survival. The following sections will survive the termination of this Agreement: 3 (Ownership and Property), 7 (Acceptance), 8 (Maintenance), 10 (Confidentiality/Injunctive Relief), 11 (Non-Compete), 12 (Hiring), 13 (Indemnity and Insurance), 14 (Limitation of Liability), 19 (Warranties), 21 (Dispute Resolution), 23 (Survival), 24 (Severable), 25 (No Waiver), 26 (Binding) and 27 (Notice).

24. Severable. In the event any one or more of the provisions of this Agreement or any Schedule is deemed by the final decree of a court of competent jurisdiction to be invalid or unenforceable, the enforceability of remaining provisions shall be unimpaired.

25. No Waiver. The failure of either party to exercise in any respect any rights provided for herein shall not be deemed a waiver of any right hereunder.

26. Binding. This Agreement is binding on and shall inure to the benefit of the respective parties, their successors-in-interest, affiliates, subsidiaries, agents and permitted assigns.

27. Notice. Any notice of communication required to be given by either party pursuant sections 13 (Indemnity and Insurance), 18 (Termination) or 21 (Dispute Resolution) shall be hand delivered; sent by registered mail, return receipt requested; or delivered by internationally recognized carrier (*e.g.*, FedEx, UPS) to the party receiving such communication at the address specified by each party as it principal office or such other address as either party may in the future specify in writing to the other party; and (if to the Museum) to the attention of both of (1) the Vice President of Operations or the Chief Technical Officer, and (2) the General Counsel. All other notices under this Agreement shall be delivered in the same manner, or by both facsimile and electronic mail; and (if to the Museum) to the attention of both of (1) the person designated by the Museum for purposes of receiving the corresponding type of notice or, if no such person exists, a Museum project manager familiar with the subject matter of the notice, and (2) the Vice

President of Operations or the Chief Technical Officer. Notices shall be deemed given and received upon the latest date of the receipt(s) confirming delivery.

28. Captions. The various captions in this Agreement are inserted for convenience only and shall not affect the meaning or interpretation of this Agreement or any provision hereof.

IN WITNESS WHEREOF, the parties have executed this Agreement as of the day and year first written above.

Consultant	Museum
By:____________________	By:____________________
[Name]	[Name]
Title: ________________	Title: ________________

FORM 9-17

Development Agreement for Web Site Technology (IP-Management Software)

This Development Agreement ("Agreement") is made as of the ___ day of _______________, (the "Effective Date") by and between CLIENT ("Client"), and DEVELOPER ("Developer").

WHEREAS, Developer has certain expertise relating to the design, development, creation, testing, and delivery of administrative support and presentation automated systems incorporating image capture, management, support and presentation of images and artwork; and

WHEREAS, Client desires to obtain from Developer, and Developer wishes to provide to Client, Developer's services.

NOW, THEREFORE, in consideration of the mutual promises, representations, and covenants set forth herein and for other good and valuable consideration, the receipt and sufficiency of which are hereby acknowledged, the parties agree as follows:

1. Definitions.

a. Code: computer programming/formatting code, any files necessary to create and operate the System, the database, maintenance and other support systems, image maps function, and any server code necessary to make forms, buttons, check-boxes, and the like function.

b. Deliverables: all Code, Documentation, reports, production, programming, designs, test results and other materials developed by Developer in the course of its performance of the Services pursuant to this Agreement, as well as any and all other items necessary for the operation of the System, excluding third-party operating system software, third-party networking software and hardware, as amended by the parties from time to time.

c. Developer Materials: any and all materials owned and/or controlled by Developer that are incorporated into or necessary for the utilization by Client of the System and/or any Deliverables, alone or in combination with other materials owned by Client or by third parties.

d. Documentation: written or typed materials that relate to the System and Code, including materials useful for design such as logic manuals, flow charts, and principles of operation that may be developed by Developer in the course of its performance under this Agreement.

e. Services: the services provided by Developer to Client in the design and establishment of the System as described in Attachment A, attached hereto and made a part hereof.

f. System: the consolidated bibliographic database and maintenance system of artwork containing database entry, maintenance, query and report software, "tiny images," high true-color resolution images, on-screen presentation of bibliographic and image data, automated synchronization of the systems in Client's offices, high quality true-color image print, and high resolution image capture facilities, including, but not limited to, software applications, Code, database architecture, content conversion processes and security processes.

2. Scope of Services. Developer will perform the Services described on Attachment A. Developer shall perform the Services in accordance with the Schedule attached hereto as Attachment C. Notwithstanding any specific delivery or completion dates set forth in Attachment C, Client and Developer acknowledge that such dates may be dependent upon the timely provision by Client of information or feedback to Developer, and any delay in providing such information or feedback may delay the dates set forth in Attachment C.

3. Fees for Services and Time of Delivery. As compensation to Developer for the Services, Client shall pay Developer the fees and expenses at the rates described on Attachment B, attached hereto and made a part hereof, upon receipt of Developer's invoice. Such fees and expenses shall be computed based on the actual number of hours spent by Developer and the actual expenses incurred.

4. Term. Unless terminated sooner in accordance with the provisions herein, this Agreement shall continue for a period of five years from the Effective Date and shall be automatically extended for successive four-year terms upon the expiration of the initial term or any renewal terms; provided, however, that the party seeking to renew is not in material breach of this Agreement. There shall be no fees payable by reason of such renewal.

5. Acceptance of Deliverables. Client will inform Developer in writing within ten days of receiving a Deliverable whether Client accepts or rejects that Deliverable, and, if rejected, the specific reasons for rejection of the Deliverable, which reasons must constitute material non-compliance with the Specification Document referenced in Attachment A. If Client fails to notify Developer within the specified time, Client will be deemed to have accepted the Deliverable. If Client rejects a Deliverable, Developer shall, within 30 days of notice of such rejection, revise the Deliverable and resubmit such Deliverable for Client's re-examination and approval. Developer shall continue to submit a new sample of the Deliverable to Client for Client's examination and approval up to a total of three times and after such Deliverable is rejected in accordance with the standards and

process set forth in this paragraph. After the third such rejection Client may, at its option, terminate the Agreement. Client shall use its reasonable judgment in approving Deliverables. Client and Developer acknowledge that certain aspects of the Deliverables involve aesthetic issues, the determination of which is highly subjective. Developer and Client agree that issues related to color calibration and other aesthetic matters shall not constitute material non-compliance with Specification Document, and Client and Developer shall use good faith efforts to resolve such issues, and failure to resolve such issues shall not constitute a material breach of this Agreement for so long as the parties continue to use good faith efforts to attempt to resolve such issues.

6. Reports. Developer will report to Client on the status of each Deliverable at reasonable intervals. On reasonable notice, Client may inspect Developer's work in progress with respect to any Deliverable and receive copies of it where applicable. Developer shall notify Client promptly of any factor, occurrence, or event coming to its attention that may affect Developer's ability to meet the requirements of this Agreement, or that is likely to occasion any material delay in delivery of Deliverables including, without limitation, any loss or reassignment of key employees, threat of strike, or major equipment failure.

7. Termination.

a. Either party may terminate this Agreement immediately upon written notice to the other party in the event that: (I) a party attempts to assign this Agreement (whether voluntarily or involuntarily, by operation of law or otherwise) without the other party's express prior written consent; or (II) the other party has materially breached this Agreement.

b. This Agreement may be terminated automatically upon the filing of an infringement action, proceeding or claim against either party because of either party's use of a Deliverable.

c. If this Agreement is terminated for any reason, Developer shall be entitled to payment for work done up to the date of termination.

8. Independent Contractor Status.

a. Developer is an independent contractor. Developer understands and agrees that Developer is not an employee of Client, that Developer is ineligible for any Client employee benefits and that no employment relationship is created by this Agreement. This Agreement does not create the relationship of partner, principal and agent, or joint venturer between the parties. Neither party has the right or authority to incur obligations of any kind in the name of or for the account of the other party nor to commit or bind the other party to any contract or other obligation.

b. Developer shall supply all equipment and supplies necessary for the satisfactory completion of the Services required of Developer under this Agreement. Developer shall have no right to use any Client equipment.

c. Developer shall report as income to the appropriate government agencies all compensation received pursuant to this Agreement and shall pay all applicable taxes. Client shall not make deductions from its payments to Developer for taxes, insurance, bonds, or any other * of any kind.

9. <u>Content Provided to Developer; Client Intellectual Property</u>.

a. Solely for purposes of developing the System and providing the Services hereunder, during the Term Client grants to Developer a nonexclusive, royalty-free license to use and make derivative works from all information, images and artwork provided by Client, regardless of the form of such information or images, including a license to modify such content as appropriate for use on a video display monitor and other video devices. Client shall indemnify and hold Developer harmless from liability for claims made by third parties for infringement of copyright, rights of publicity or other violations of law arising out of or relating to from the use of content as provided by Client to Developer for inclusion in the System.

b. Developer acknowledges and agrees that, except as expressly provided herein, no right, property, license, permission, or interest of any kind in or to the Licensed Trademarks is or is intended to be given or transferred to or acquired by Developer by the execution, performance, or non-performance of this Agreement or any part hereof.

10. <u>Developer Materials</u>.

a. Developer hereby grants Client and its subsidiaries and affiliates a royalty-free, nonexclusive, nontransferable license to use the Developer Materials and the System in connection with its use of the System and the Deliverables. Client may not transfer or sublicense the Developer Materials, the System or the Deliverables without the prior written consent of Developer, except as provided in the immediately succeeding sentence. Client may transfer or sublicense the Developer Materials, the System and/or the Deliverables to any entity that acquires or administers at the direction of the owner all or substantially all of the artwork produced by Client, provided that: (i) such transfer or sublicense is limited in application to the artwork, images and information subject to the System pursuant to this Agreement; and (ii) such transferee or sublicensee agrees in writing to be bound by the terms of this Agreement.

b. Developer retains all right, interest, and title in and to the System and the Developer Materials, including any patents, copyrights, trademarks, and other intellectual property rights therein, subject to the licenses granted to and by Client pursuant to this Section 10 and Section 9.

11. Ownership of Work Product.

a. Except as provided herein, the System, the Deliverables, the Developer Materials and all elements thereof, including but not limited to, all notes, reports, Documentation, drawings, computer programs (source code, object code, and listings), graphics, text, logos, taglines, logotype, and all other intellectual property that will be used by Developer in the course of performing under this Agreement, derivatives of pre-existing copyrighted works of Developer, inventions conceived or reduced to practice during the performance of work under this Agreement, creations, designs, trademarks, works of any kind (including, by way of example only, movies and audio or visual works), masks, models, and works-in-process (for purposes of this Section 11, the "Work Product") shall be exclusively owned by Developer and shall not be considered works-made-for-hire for purposes of copyright ownership. Client acknowledges that the Work Product and all the elements thereof and all rights relating thereto are the sole and exclusive property of Developer, its successors and assigns, absolutely and for all copyright terms and renewal terms thereof throughout the world, in all media, and for all uses and purposes whatsoever. Developer's ownership of the Deliverables, the Developer Materials and all elements thereof does not extend to any interest in any information, artwork or images provided by Client, and Developer disclaims all interest therein.

b. Except as provided herein, all information, images and artwork provided by Client to Developer pursuant to the Agreement shall be exclusively owned by Client. Developer acknowledges that the information, images and artwork provided by Client to Developer pursuant to this Agreement and all the elements thereof and all rights relating thereto are the sole and exclusive property of Client, its successors and assigns, absolutely and for all copyright terms and renewal terms thereof throughout the world, in all media, and for all uses and purposes whatsoever.

c. During and after this Agreement, Client shall provide reasonable assistance to Developer, at Developer's sole cost and expense, to secure, maintain, and defend for Developer's benefit all copyrights, trademarks, patent rights, mask work rights, trade secret rights, and other proprietary rights in and to the Work Product.

12. Warranties.

a. Developer represents and warrants to Client that:

(i) The Services provided by Developer pursuant to this Agreement, including, but not limited to, the System, Deliverables, Developer Materials, and any and all elements thereof, do not and will not infringe upon any patent rights, copyrights, mask work rights, trademark rights, rights of publicity, or property right of any third person, firm, corporation, or other entity whatsoever. Should Client or Developer receive notice of any claim that any element of the System is infringing, Developer shall replace the infringing material with non-infringing material with the same functionality, and shall do so in a timely manner and at Developer's expense.

(ii) Developer has full power to enter into this Agreement, to carry out its obligations under this Agreement, and to grant the rights and/or licenses granted to Client herein, including without limitation, ownership or control of all copyrights, trademarks, and all other necessary rights, if any, in and to any or all pre-existing images, Code, Deliverables, icons, characters, graphics, sounds, music, and/or other data in the form of photographs, recordings, video, film, animation, cartoons, illustrations, accompanying text captions, scripts, skits, or related materials, owned and/or in the possession, custody, or control of Developer including, but not limited to, all Developer Materials.

(iii) The Services provided in connection with this Agreement and all Deliverables are, and at all times will be, in compliance with all applicable federal, state, and local laws and regulations, including without limitation, all advertising and employment laws.

b. Client represents and warrants to Developer that:

(i) Any materials provided by Client pursuant to this Agreement, including, but not limited to, the artwork and images of such artwork, do not and will not infringe upon any patent rights, copyrights, mask work rights, trademark rights, rights of publicity, or property right of any third person, firm, corporation, or other entity whatsoever. Should Client or Developer receive notice of any claim that any material provided by Client is infringing, Client shall replace the infringing material with non-infringing material with the same functionality, and shall do so in a timely manner and at Client's expense.

(ii) Client has full power to enter into this Agreement, to carry out its obligations under this Agreement, and to grant the rights and/or licenses granted to Developer herein, including without limitation, ownership or control of all copyrights, trademarks, and all other necessary rights, if any, in and to any or all preexisting images, Code, Deliverables, icons, characters, graphics, sounds, music, and/or other data in the form of photographs, recordings, video, film, illustrations, accompanying text captions, scripts, or related materials, owned and/or in the possession, custody, or control of Client including, but not limited to, all artwork.

(iii) Client has obtained or shall obtain in writing prior to delivery of any and all materials under this Agreement, all necessary rights, including without limitation any and all display, reproduction, distribution, derivative work, duplication, performing, publicity, recording, and/or synchronization rights on any and all third-party copyrighted and/or non-public domain items included in the materials to be provided by Client pursuant to this Agreement, and will obtain prior to the delivery under this Agreement, all necessary releases, including without limitation, the releases of all persons or organizations whose name, voice, likeness, portrayal, impersonation, or performance is included in the materials delivered by Client pursuant to this Agreement, as may or shall be required to enable Developer to create and develop the Deliverables.

(iv) Client shall notify Developer in writing of any allegation of intellectual property infringement within three days of learning of such allegation.

13. Indemnification:

a. Developer hereby agrees at all times to defend, indemnify, hold and save harmless Client, its affiliates, franchisees or subsidiaries and directors, officers, employees and agents of each, from and against all damages, liabilities, suits, losses, claims, fines, penalties, obligations, costs and expenses (whether based on tort, breach of contract, product liability, patent, trademark or copyright infringement, or otherwise), including reasonable attorneys' fees of whatever kind or nature (collectively, "Loss"), resulting from or arising out of: (i) a breach or any alleged breach of this Agreement by Developer; (ii) the negligence, gross negligence, or willful misconduct of its officers, directors, affiliates, licensees, subcontractors, employees, and agents; and (iii) any use by Client or any third party of the Developer Materials and/or the Deliverables pursuant to this Agreement.

b. Client hereby agrees at all times to defend, indemnify, hold and save harmless Developer, its affiliates, franchisees or subsidiaries and directors, officers, employees and agents of each, from and against all Loss resulting from or arising out of: (i) a breach or any alleged breach of this Agreement by Client; (ii) the negligence, gross negligence, or willful misconduct of its officers, directors, affiliates, licensees, subcontractors, employees, and agents; and (iii) any use by Developer or any third party of materials provided by Client pursuant to this Agreement.

c. Neither party may settle any claim or action on the other party's behalf without a party's prior written permission. In the event Client and

Developer agree to settle a claim or action, a party agrees neither to disclose the settlement nor to permit the opposing party to disclose the settlement without first obtaining the other party's written permission.

d. Neither party shall in any case be liable to the other party for lost profits or for consequential or punitive damages.

e. The provisions of this Section 13 shall survive the expiration or sooner termination of this Agreement.

14. Maintenance and Upgrades. Developer shall provide routine maintenance of the Deliverables for a period of six months from acceptance of the last Deliverable by Client. Such maintenance shall include consulting and training service with respect to the maintenance, use and operation of the Deliverables. The hourly fees for such maintenance services shall be as set forth on Attachment B. After such six month period the parties may enter into a mutually agreeable maintenance agreement. For so long as Developer is providing maintenance services to Client (whether during the six month period referenced above or pursuant to a maintenance agreement), Developer shall provide Client with any upgrades applicable to the System. Such upgrades shall be at no charge to Client, other than such fees or costs as Developer is obligated to pay to unaffiliated third parties (i.e., license fees and costs of hardware necessary for such upgrades.)

15. Miscellaneous.

a. Assignment. Neither party may assign or delegate its rights or obligations under this Agreement without the other party's prior written consent.

b. Attorneys' Fees. If any legal action is necessary to enforce this Agreement, the prevailing party shall be entitled to reasonable attorneys' fees and expenses in addition to any other allowable relief.

c. Governing Law; Dispute Resolution. This Agreement shall be construed and enforced according to the laws of the State of Wyoming without regard to principles of conflicts of law.

d. Severability. If any provision of this Agreement is found by a court of competent jurisdiction to be unenforceeble for any reason, the remainder of this Agreement shall continue in full force and effect.

e. Entire Agreement; Modification. This Agreement and the attached exhibits constitute the full and complete understanding and agreement of the parties relating to the subject matter hereof and supersede all prior understandings and agreements relating to such subject matter. Any waiver, modification, or amendment of any provision of this Agreement shall be effective only if in a writing and signed by the parties.

16. Counterparts. This Agreement may be executed in two or more counterparts, each of which shall be deemed an original, but all of which shall constitute one and the same instrument.

Developer	Client
By:____________________	By:____________________
[Name]	[Name]
Title:____________________	Title:____________________
Date:____________________	Date:____________________

FORM 9-18

Short-Form Waiver and Release for Commercial Use of Images Online

WAIVER AND RELEASE. I,________________, for valuable consideration received, hereby grant to ART ENTERPRISES, LLC ("AE"), with respect to the photographs, or other recordings taken of me (the "Photos"), the perpetual, world-wide right, for all purposes relating to AE's products and/or services, to:

Reproduce, display, distribute, copy, use and/or modify the Photos (in combination with or as a composite of other matter), in any media or embodiment, now known or to become known, including, but not limited to, all electronic and/or computer-readable formats, and use my name in connection therewith.

I release AE from any claim or cause of action (whether now known or unknown), for infringement of copyright, trademark or other intellectual property rights, defamation, invasion of right to privacy, publicity or personality or any similar matter, or based upon or relating to the use and exploitation of the foregoing.

I also understand that the Works on the Internet cannot be adequately protected from unauthorized use by third-parties and agree to hold harmless AE from any such misuse. I waive all my rights to inspect and approve the finished Photos or their use. I agree that there shall be no obligation to utilize the authorization granted by me hereunder.

I warrant and represent that I am over the age of twenty-one (21) years and that I am free to enter into this agreement.

NAME	AE
By:____________________	By:__________________

FORM 9-19

E-Commerce Linking Agreement

AGREEMENT ("Agreement") as of DATE (the "Effective Date") between Website 1 ("Company A") and Website 2 ("Company B"). Company B wishes to offer Company A services on its Website located at www.Company-B.com and replacement and successor addresses thereto (the "Company B Site") in order to earn commissions.

1. Art Offerings.

1.1. Art Materials. Company A shall provide Company B with Company A logo and graphics, copies of Art represented on the Company A Site, Art graphics, banners, offer copy, offer elements and other copy, all of which may be updated in the discretion of Company A from time-to-time (collectively, the "Presentation Materials"), for promotion of the Art offers on the Company B Site. Company A will transmit updated Art Materials to Company B via email or FTP from time to time, and will promptly notify Company B upon transmission.

1.2. Art Offers. Using the Presentation Materials, Company B will market and offer to Company B Site visitors ("Offer(s)"), in accordance with the terms and conditions of the Agreement, Art materials from a choice set forth in Exhibit A hereto as updated from time to time hereafter with the consent of Company A which will not be unreasonably withheld, conditioned or denied ("Arts").

2. Offer Placement.

2.1. Company A Store. Subject to the approval of Company A not to be unreasonably withheld, conditioned or denied, Company B shall design, build, host and operate at its sole expense a premium, branded section of the Company B Site to be known as the Company B Art store, which store shall be devoted entirely to Offering and selling the Arts and shall feature state-of-the-art e-commerce functionality and features ("Art Store"), which shall be a part of, and subject to the same conditions as, the Company B Site.

2.2. Art Offer Links. Company B shall place links to the Art Store, and references to Art Offers outside the Store, on top-level pages of the Company B Site, in conspicuous locations that are also visible to customary users upon initial receipt of the pages without any scrolling or navigation.

2.3. Site Coordination. Company A and Company B shall jointly coordinate all elements of the placement of Art Materials on the Company B Site.

2.4. Changes. Company B agrees to execute any and all changes in the Art Materials within five (5) business days of receipt of the same. Upon notice by

Company A, Company B shall promptly remove any Art Offers or other materials on pages that contain content judged by Company A in its sole discretion to be objectionable or in other ways offensive in a manner that would negatively affect Company A.

3. Rights Granted.

3.1. License to Company A Marks. Subject to all the terms and conditions of this Agreement, Company A grants Company B the non-exclusive, non-transferable, non-sublicensable, revocable right to use the Presentation Materials during the term of the Company B Agreement for the sole purpose of generating Art sales through the Company B Site. In additional to other rights and remedies herein. Company A reserves all of its rights, and those of the other respective rights owners, in the Presentation Materials, and Company B claims no rights whatsoever in the Presentation Materials. All good will attributed to the Company A logo(s), tradename(s) and trademarks ("Company A Marks") will inure to the benefit of Company A exclusively.

3.2. License to Company B Marks. Company B grants Company A the non-exclusive, non-transferable, non-sublicensable, revocable right during this Agreement to use its logo(s), tradename(s) and trademark(s) ("Company B Marks") on the Company A Site, and to construct any links from the Company B Marks to the Company B Site for purposes of promotion of the subject matter of this Agreement, in the sole discretion of Company A. All good will attributed to the Company B Marks will inure to the benefit of Company B exclusively.

4. Orders, Fulfillment and Support.

4.1. Company B-Customer Agreements.

4.1.1. Company A may provide Company B with a copy of certain terms and conditions binding upon customers to which the sale of Arts are subject ("Sales Agreements"), and prior to the completion of any order, Company B will require customers to agree to said terms and conditions as a condition of purchasing said Arts. Company A may change any provision of Sales Agreements from time to time on thirty (30) days notice to Company B.

4.1.2. Company B shall place a toll-free telephone number and e-mail address to be provided by Company A on the Art Store in conjunction with all orders, to enable customers to contact Company A directly for customer service and to cancel Art orders.

4.2. Order Information. Company B will deliver to Company A on a weekly basis via secure electronic transmission in a file format reasonably designated by Company A all Art order information for each and every customer, including (i) full first and last names and complete mailing address(es) for both billing and shipping, (ii) one or more valid email address(es), (iii) one or more valid telephone number(s), (iv) the quantity and titles of Art, and the corresponding Art code supplied by Company A, (v) the order date and any price information associated with the order, and (vi) and complete credit card information, including a valid credit card number, expiration date and name of credit card holder (Visa, MasterCard, American Express and Discover Card only) (collectively, "Order Information"). Company B will be solely responsible for collecting and transmitting to Company A in accordance with the terms and conditions of the Agreement all Order Information.

4.3. Cancellations. Company A will process cancellations of orders in accordance with the Company A cancellation policy as set forth on the Company A Website and Company modified by Company A from time-to-time. Company B shall promptly transmit to Company A all cancellation information, with reference to the corresponding Order Information, upon receipt of the same and in accordance with the terms of the Agreement. Company A shall determine, in its sole discretion, the validity of cancellations, and shall be solely responsible for the refund of any fees.

4.4. Records. Company B shall maintain records of each customer order, including Order Information, for a period of at least two (2) years from the date of each such order.

4.5. Order Fulfillment. Company A shall be solely responsible for fulfillment of orders and all expenses directly associated therewith.

5. Customer Responsibility. Company B agrees that customers who purchase Art through the Art Offers on the Company B site will be deemed to be customers of Company A as well, for all purposes, including without limitation information management and direct marketing, subject to the Company A rules, policies and operating procedures concerning customer orders, and customer service in connection therewith.

6. Art Commissions and Payments.

6.1. Qualifying Orders. Orders shall qualify for the payment of commissions to Company B and Company A fulfillment solely as follows: (i) orders shall be received online through the Company B Site, and include valid credit card information guaranteeing payment of the order fee in full; (ii) Company B shall have delivered to Company A in accordance with the Agreement all corresponding Order Information; (iii) orders shall be subject to Company A fulfillment requirements and limitations; and (iv) fees must be paid to Company A for the Art ("Qualifying Orders").

6.2. Payments. Company A shall pay Company B fifteen (15%) percent of each Qualifying Purchase ("Commissions"). Company A shall pay Commissions less any taxes required by law to be withheld within sixty (60) days after the end of each month in which such Commissions accrue.

6.3. Reports. Company B shall deliver to Company A weekly reports via email representing estimated gross order of Arts through the Company B Site.

6.4. Renegotiate. Company A and Company B agree to use their best efforts to renegotiate a lower Commission rate if after six (6) months from the Effective Date: (a) there are fewer than one hundred (100) Qualifying Orders per month for more three (3) or more consecutive months, or (b) the rate of cancellation of orders placed through the Company B Site is greater than twenty-five percent (25%).

6.5. Non-Compete. During the term of this Agreement, Company B will not offer through or on the Company B Site the Art materials of any company other than Company A, nor shall it offer such services itself, directly or indirectly, nor shall Company B allow any advertisements, promotions or content from an Art commerce company, links to any Art websites or links to any websites with Art services to appear on the Company B Site, other than Company A.

7. Term and Termination

7.1. Term. The term of this Agreement shall commence on the date of execution by Company A and Company B ("Effective date") for one (1) year ("Initial Term"), and shall be automatically renewed thereafter for subsequent one (1) year periods (collectively, "term").

7.2. Termination. Either party shall have the right to terminate this Agreement:

7.2.1. if the other party commits a material breach and fails to cure such breach within thirty (30) days following written notice describing such breach;

7.2.2. during the first year of the term upon sixty (60) days written notice, and thereafter upon ninety (90) days written notice;

7.2.3. immediately by written notice upon the insolvency, or the voluntary or involuntary bankruptcy, of the other party, or if the other party makes an assignment for the benefit of creditors, or has a receiver or trustee appointed; and

7.3. Actions upon Termination. Upon termination or expiration of this Agreement for any reason whatsoever, Company B's rights hereunder to market, promote, offer or otherwise act pursuant to this Agreement shall immediately cease, and Company B shall immediately and completely cease any such activity. Within five (5) days after such termination or expiration Licensee shall return to

Company A all Presentation Materials and other materials provided to Company B under this Agreement, and all copies thereof, or upon request by Company A destroy the same, and certify in writing that the foregoing and all copies thereof have either been so returned to Company A or destroyed at the end of the termination.

8. Representations and Warranties.

8.1. COMPANY A MAKES NO REPRESENTATIONS OR WARRANTIES TO ANY PERSON OR ENTITY WITH RESPECT TO ANY SERVICES PERFORMED OR ANY INFORMATION, CONTENT OR OTHER MATERIALS PROVIDED OR MADE AVAILABLE BY IT HEREUNDER, AND DISCLAIMS ALL IMPLIED WARRANTIES, INCLUDING WITHOUT LIMITATION WARRANTIES OF MERCHANTABILITY, FITNESS FOR A PARTICULAR PURPOSE OR ANY IMPLIED WARRANTIES ARISING OUT OF A COURSE OF PERFORMANCE, DEALING OR TRADE USAGE. COMPANY A DOES NOT REPRESENT THAT THE OPERATION OF ITS SERVICES WILL BE UNINTERRUPTED OR ERROR-FREE, AND IT WILL NOT BE LIABLE FOR THE CONSEQUENCES OF SUCH INTERRUPTIONS, ERRORS OR NON-FULFILLMENT OF ORDERS.

8.2. Company B represents and warrants:

> 8.2.1. it is solely responsible for the development, operation, and maintenance of the Company B Site and all portions thereof. Company B agrees to accurately display and maintain the Art Materials, including offer terms, in good working order, and not to alter or modify them in any way without obtaining the prior written consent of Company A. Under no circumstance shall Company B vary the authorized prices by implicitly or expressly offering discounts, premiums or any other incentives. Company B agrees to make any imperative changes to Art Materials, such as changes to price, within two (2) business days;
>
> 8.2.2. any and all content and materials, other than the Presentation Materials, which are posted on, or accessible directly through, the Company B Site, do not violate or infringe upon the rights of any third party, and are not libelous or otherwise illegal;
>
> 8.2.3. Company B shall maintain the Art Store in good working Order and, under all circumstance, with a level of complete support no less favorable than the complete support it provides to the primary parts of the Company B Site; and
>
> 8.2.4. it shall use best efforts at all times to maximize Art sales through the Art Store.

8.2.5. SUBJECT TO THE FOREGOING COMPANY B MAKES NO REPRESENTATIONS OR WARRANTIES TO ANY PERSON OR ENTITY WITH RESPECT TO ANY SERVICES PERFORMED OR ANY INFORMATION, CONTENT OR OTHER MATERIALS PROVIDED OR MADE AVAILABLE BY IT HEREUNDER, AND DISCLAIMS ALL IMPLIED WARRANTIES, INCLUDING WITHOUT LIMITATION WARRANTIES OF MERCHANTABILITY, FITNESS FOR A PARTICULAR PURPOSE OR ANY IMPLIED WARRANTIES ARISING OUT OF A COURSE OF PERFORMANCE, DEALING OR TRADE USAGE. COMPANY B DOES NOT REPRESENT THAT THE OPERATION OF ITS SERVICES WILL BE UNINTERRUPTED OR ERROR-FREE, AND IT WILL NOT BE LIABLE FOR THE CONSEQUENCES OF SUCH INTERRUPTIONS, ERRORS OR NON-FULFILLMENT OF ORDERS.

9. Indemnification. Each party (the "Indemnitor") shall indemnify and hold harmless the other (the "Indemnitee") against and from all claims, liabilities, suits, damages, costs, including without limitation, attorney's fees, disbursements and court costs (including an allocation for in-house counsel fees), if any, arising out of any of the foregoing, which, if true, would constitute a violation of the Indemnitor's representations and warranties; provided that (a) the Indemnitor is promptly notified in writing of such claim or suit, (b) the Indemnitor shall have the sole control of any defense and/or settlement thereof, (c) the Indemnitee furnishes to the Indemnitor, on request, information available to the Indemnitee for such defense, and (d) the Indemnitee reasonably cooperates in any defense and/or settlement thereof as long as the Indemnitor pays all of the Indemnitee's reasonable out of pocket expenses and attorneys' fees. The Indemnitee shall not admit any such claim without prior consent of the Indemnitor and the Indemnitor shall not enter into any settlement or compromise, which would require the Indemnitee to make any payment or bear any obligation other than those set forth herein without the Indemnitee's prior written consent.

10. Limitations of Liability. EXCEPT AS OTHERWISE PROVIDED, NEITHER PARTY SHALL BE LIABLE OR OBLIGATED UNDER ANY SECTION OF THIS AGREEMENT OR UNDER CONTRACT, NEGLIGENCE, STRICT LIABILITY OR OTHER LEGAL OR EQUITABLE THEORY FOR ANY SPECIAL, INDIRECT, INCIDENTAL OR CONSEQUENTIAL DAMAGES OR LOST PROFITS OR COST OF PROCUREMENT OF SUBSTITUTE GOODS OR SERVICES.

11. Confidentiality. Each party (the "Disclosing Party") agrees that all information concerning the other (the "Receiving Party"), including without limitation business and financial data, vendor lists, pricing and sales information, and the

terms of this Agreement, shall remain strictly confidential and shall not be disclosed to third parties, with the sole exception of the Receiving Party's accountants and attorneys on a confidential basis, or pursuant to valid legal process, of which the Receiving Party shall provide immediate notice to the Disclosing Party and cooperation in any attempt by the Disclosing Party to oppose said process.

12. Relationship. Each party may identify the other as an "affiliate" or "partner" and participant the nature of services that are the subject matter of the Agreement. Under no circumstances shall this Agreement, nor either party's activities under it, create any agency, franchise, sales representative or employment relationship between Company B and Company A, and neither party has any authority to make or accept any offers on behalf of the other without prior written consent.

13. Force Majeure. Neither party shall be liable for nonperformance or delay in performance (other than of obligations regarding confidentiality) caused by any event reasonably beyond the control of such party including, but not limited to wars, hostilities, revolutions, riots, national emergency, strikes, lock-outs, unavailability of supplies, epidemics, fire, flood, earthquake, force of nature, explosion, embargo, or any other Act of God, or any law, proclamation, regulation, ordinance, or other act or order of any court, government or governmental agency.

14. Assignment. Either party may assign this Agreement, and its rights, licenses and obligations hereunder, without the prior written approval of the other, solely to any acquiror of all or of substantially all of its equity securities, assets or business relating to the subject matter of this Agreement, or pursuant to any internal re-organization in the sole discretion of the re-organizing party. Any attempted assignment in violation of this Section will be void and without effect. Subject to the foregoing, this Agreement will benefit and bind the parties' successors and assigns.

15. Survival.

The following shall survive any expiration or termination of this Agreement: (a) sections (and subsections thereof) numbers ———; (b) any accrued payment obligations; (c) except as otherwise expressly provided herein, any right of action for breach of this Agreement prior to termination, and (d) Company A's rights, and obligations to customers, relating to existing Art and fulfillment services.

16. Severable. In the event that any of the provisions of this Agreement shall be held by a court or other tribunal of competent jurisdiction to be unenforceable, such provisions shall be limited or eliminated to the minimum extent necessary so that this Agreement shall otherwise remain in full force and effect and enforceable.

17. Waiver. The failure to enforce any provision of the Agreement will not be a waiver of our right to subsequent enforcement of the provision or any other provision of the Agreement.

18. Notice. Any notice or other correspondence required or permitted to be given pursuant to this Agreement shall be in writing and shall be deemed to have been given (a) immediately if served personally, (b) immediately if sent to a designated FAX number (with confirmation of receipt), and simultaneously via first-class mail, postage pre-paid and addressed to the persons set forth below, (c) three (3) business days after if sent by certified or registered mail return receipt requested, and addressed to the persons set forth below, (d) on the next business day if sent via internationally recognized carrier such as FedEx or U.P.S. and addressed to the persons set forth below:

19. Headings. Headings and captions are for convenience only and are not to be used in the interpretation of this Agreement.

20. Choice of Law, Dispute Resolution and Jurisdiction.

20.1. Choice of Law. This Agreement shall be construed and enforced in accordance with the laws of the State of New York, without giving effect to the principles of conflicts of law.

20.2. ADR Procedures. In the event of any controversy or claim arising out of this Agreement raised by either party, the party raising the dispute will promptly notify the other party in writing of the nature of the dispute and the factual background. Within the fifteen (15) calendar day period following such notice, the parties will initiate an attempt in good faith to reach a reasonable solution to the dispute, including escalation to the vice-president of each company responsible for the subject matter of the dispute. If the dispute cannot be amicably resolved within thirty (30) calendar days of written notification, then either party may seek to resolve said dispute by arbitration before a single arbitrator in accordance with the commercial arbitration rules of the American Arbitration Association, and judgment upon the award rendered by the arbitrator may be entered in any court having jurisdiction thereof. The place of arbitration shall be New York, NY. Each party shall provide to the arbitrator, no later than fifteen (15) calendar days following the date of the arbitrator's appointment, a statement, including all supporting documents or other evidence on which such party relies as to why it believes that the dispute should be resolved in its favor, and all such materials and any other materials provided to the arbitrator by either party shall simultaneously be provided by such party to the other party. Within twenty (20) calendar days after the submission of such statements by all parties, the arbitrator shall hold a hearing with respect to the dispute. At such hearing, the arbitrator may, in his or her sole discretion, allow the parties to call and cross-examine witnesses, make any additional arguments or submit any additional materials to support the position taken in their respective statements. The arbitrator shall enter an award within fifteen (15) calendar days following the hearing provided for herein. Nothing shall preclude either party from making an application to the arbitrator, for good cause, to expedite the proceedings, nor restrict the arbitrator from granting such an application. In addition to such other relief as the arbitrator may award, the arbitrator shall be vested with jurisdiction and shall award to the prevailing party its reasonable attorney's fees and expenses, and all other costs associated with the arbitration. The award rendered by the arbitrator shall be final, and judgment may be entered upon it in accordance with applicable law in any court having jurisdiction thereof.

20.3. Consent to Jurisdiction. The parties consent and agree that all legal proceedings arising out of or relating to this Agreement deemed beyond the scope of the prior subsection shall be exclusively maintained in either the federal courts or the state courts located in New York, New York, and each hereby consents to the personal jurisdiction of said courts.

21. Complete Agreement.

This Agreement (including the attached exhibits) constitutes the entire agreement between the parties with respect to the subject matter hereof and supersedes all prior discussions, documents, agreements and prior course of dealing, and shall not be effective until signed by both parties.

22. Counterparts.

This Agreement may be executed in two counterparts, each of which shall be an original; but such counterparts shall together constitute one and the same instrument.

Company A	Company B
By:____________________	By:____________________
[Name]	[Name]
Title:____________________	Title:____________________
Date:____________________	Date:____________________

FORM 9-20

E-Commerce Linking Agreement (Short Form)

The following outlines the terms under which SITE A and its affiliates ("Seller") will participate in Online Art Site promotion of the SITE B Marketing Network ("Marketer").

1. Seller agrees to provide the following offer to Marketer visitors from ____ through the termination or expiration of this short form agreement and successor agreement(s).

2. Marketer will provide a continuous and prominent link from the Marketer Connections home page on the Internet via a banner exhibiting Seller logo and offer copy to a non-specific storefront residing on Seller-controlled server(s) where all further product transactions and fulfillment shall occur.

3. Seller agrees to fulfill requests that come directly from Marketer visitors beginning ____. Fulfillment of such a request should be in accordance with Seller standard policies for its goods.

4. Seller agrees to provide information to Marketer on the number and dollar value of orders placed by Marketer visitors in relation to the promotion by providing a summary at the conclusion of the program.

5. Seller grants Marketer the right to use its name, logos, trademarks or other copyrighted or licensed material in connection with this promotion, subject to its prior approval, not to unreasonably withheld. Seller grants Marketer the right to use any promotional materials that Seller shall provide hereunder and which Seller may modify in its discretion from time to time.

6. Marketer is responsible for ensuring that the promotional materials comply with all applicable laws and do not infringe upon the rights of any third party. Notwithstanding the foregoing, Seller shall have a right of approval over all materials related to this short form agreement, not to be unreasonably withheld.

7. Seller will not use the Marketer name, logo, trademarks or other copyrighted or licensed material without written consent from Marketer.

8. Marketer agrees to include the name and/or description of the Seller offer in communications related to the Monthly Statement Marketing promotion and as mutually agreed by Seller and Marketer.

9. Marketer will not promote competing goods offered by any merchant other than Seller.

10. Seller agrees to pay Marketer 40% of the sale price for all net sales derived from this promotion, subject to its standard terms and conditions for payment and cancellations.

11. Except as required by law or to inform affiliates, neither party shall disclose this Agreement to third parties without the other's approval. To protect Customer and other confidential information developed during the term of this Agreement and for a period of three (3) years thereafter, each party shall (i) keep such information in strict confidence, (ii) prevent its disclosure to third parties (except for authorized employees and agents with a need-to-know), (iii) promptly notify the other of any loss or unauthorized use or disclosure of or access to it, and (iv) promptly notify the other upon receipt of a request or demand pursuant to law to disclose the information, so that the appropriate party may seek a protective order or similar remedy.

12. Each party shall indemnify and hold harmless the other, its subsidiaries and affiliates, their respective directors, officers, employees, agents, attorneys, affiliates, successors, and assigns from all claims, losses, liabilities, damages, suits, actions, government procedures, taxes, penalties or interest, associated auditing and legal expenses and other costs incurred (including reasonable attorneys' fees and costs of suit) arising from the other party's; its agents; its subcontractors; or their personnel: (a) performance of its obligations under this Agreement; (b) misrepresentation or breach of any representation, warranty, obligation or covenant of this Agreement; and (c) unauthorized use of the other party's trademarks or other intellectual property.

13. The parties intend to negotiate a more comprehensive agreement governing the subject matter of this short-form agreement and related marketing initiatives. However, until such time as a more formal document is signed, this short-form agreement shall reflect the entire agreement between the parties regarding the services, payments and other obligations described herein.

Accepted and Agreed:

Marketer	Seller
By:______________________	By:______________________
Date______________________	Date______________________

FORM 9-21

Art Consortium Membership Agreement

INTRODUCTION

1. The Art Network, a nonprofit corporation, manages and maintains its database of regularly updated art works (collectively, the "Art Works"). This membership agreement ("Agreement") sets forth the terms and conditions under which a qualified institution may become a member of The Art Network ("The Art Network Member"), subject to the approval of The Art Network. Criteria and parameters for qualifying institutions, incorporated by reference, are available online at The Art Network Website. The Agreement is by and between The Art Network and ________________ and shall be deemed effective upon execution by The Art Network (the "Effective Date").

2. **The Art Network Membership**

By accepting all of the terms of this Agreement and paying the requisite fees a qualified institution may become a The Art Network Member entitled to all of the benefits and subject to all of the responsibilities of The Board of Directors of The Art Network (the "Board") shall establish or amend the policies and procedures governing membership from time to time. The Art Network Members also agree to review the membership terms and conditions periodically for revisions. Continued acceptance of all of the terms and conditions of this Agreement as it may be amended from time to time is a condition of being a The Art Network Members.

a. **Benefits**

Certain benefits that a The Art Network Member is entitled to include:

i. using of The Art Network database of art (the "System") under the terms and conditions of this Agreement,

ii. participating in the governance of The Art Network by voting for Members of the Board and on various issues, and

iii. recommending one or more representatives (if desired) to certain of The Art Network working committees through which policy recommendations are made (the Board shall retain the authority to appoint and remove committee members in its discretion).

b. **Responsibilities**

Duties and obligations that a The Art Network Member is responsible for include:

i. complying with The Art Network bylaws, all of the terms and conditions of this Agreement, and the policies governing The Art Network membership that the Board adopts from time to time,

ii. as soon after electronic publication as reasonably practicable, making periodic contributions to the System of Art Works ("Contributed Art Works"),

iii. ensuring that such Contributed Art Works conform to The Art Network technical documentation standards,

iv. using commercially reasonable efforts to link to The Art Network Site from Web pages of Member Websites related to Enabled Art Works ("Related Sites"),

v. nominating business, billing and technical contact, for purposes of The Art Network administration, and keeping the relevant contact information up to date,

vi. promptly paying all membership dues and any charges or fees, as established by the Board from time to time and set forth on The Art Network Site, and

vii. not deleting or modifying any of The Art Network's copyright notices on documents, electronic text or programs that The Art Network may prepare or enable for the use or display of The Art Network Members.

3. **Specific Obligations**

In addition to other membership terms and conditions, The Art Network Members agree to abide by the following rules:

a. **No Advertising**

The Artwork Members designated Art Work pages may not contain or generate any advertising unless it also contains the full and complete Art Work described, in which case it may contain or generate sponsorship copy (*i.e.*, "art brought to you by . . .") banner advertising that does not reasonably interfere with the accessibility of non-advertising information or as adjacent interstitial advertising (*e.g.*, using new browser window or Flash functionality) (information about how to purchase or access the Art Works shall not be considered advertising for purposes of this subsection).

b. **No Framing**

As part of the Artwork Network Service, The Art Network Member may not frame any third-party site or content (other than pursuant to an independent agreement between the necessary parties) in a manner that, in the discretion of The Art Network, suggests an association between that The Art Network Member and any other party.

c. **No Fees**

Each The Art Network Member shall control access to its systems, and shall have discretion to establish pricing and other terms of access to its Art Works that are not part of the System. Notwithstanding the foregoing, The Art Network Members may not charge fees for linking from within the Artwork Network.

d. **Original Works**

Deposited Art Work must include links to substantially non-derivative copyrightable works of intellectual property ("Original Works").

e. **Third-Party Art Works**

Art Works that belongs to a third party and is not lawfully acquired independently is "Proprietary Art Works". Members may not use Proprietary Art Works obtained through The Art Network. Members may not provide or transfer for value any Proprietary Art Works to any third party.

4. **Intellectual Property Rights**

a. **Proprietary Rights**

As between The Art Network and The Art Network Member, The Art Network Member retains all right, title and interest in the Art Works submitted to The Art Network, except as expressly provided in this Agreement. Likewise, except as set forth herein, The Art Network shall make no use of Proprietary Art Works.

b. **Warranty**

Each party warrants and represents that it has the full power and complete authority to enter into this Agreement, that it has conducted a review of the rights granted herein according to documented internal policies and procedures, and that the rights granted herein will not infringe the rights of any third party. The Art Network Member agrees only to deposit or register Art Works in the System for Art Works to which it has electronic rights including the right to use such Art Works as part of the System and the Artwork Network Service.

c. **Grant of Rights**

Subject to the terms and conditions of this Agreement, The Art Network Member hereby grants to The Art Network and its agents a fully-paid, non-exclusive, worldwide and perpetual license to use, reproduce, transmit, distribute, display and sublicense the Contributed Art Works in connection with the System, the Artwork Network Service, and related services. Subject to applicable law, The Art Network Member reserves all other rights in the Contributed Art Works, and acknowledges that nothing shall enlarge or restrict the rights of The Art Network or its agents to develop and/or maintain collective rights in its own Art Works.

d. **Disputes**

The Art Network has the right but not the obligation to enforce the terms of this Agreement against any Member, including without limitation for misuse of Proprietary Art Works. The Art Network shall not be obligated to take any action with respect to any Art Works that is the subject of an intellectual property dispute, but nonetheless reserves the right, in its sole discretion, to remove or suspend access to it, or to take any other action it deems appropriate. The Art Network Members shall be responsible for promptly notifying The Art Network of any claim, dispute or action related to their Contributed Digital Identifiers or Contributed Art Works. The Art Network from time to time may in its discretion establish and amend dispute resolution and other procedures relating to the subject matter of this section ("Dispute Policies"), and The Art Network Members agree to abide by the terms and conditions of such Dispute Policies at all times.

e. **Injunctive Relief**

The Art Network Member acknowledges that the Proprietary Art Works is unique property of extreme value and the unauthorized use thereof would cause The Art Network irreparable harm that could not be compensated by monetary damages. The Art Network Member agrees that The Art Network may seek injunctive and preliminary relief to remedy any actual or threatened unauthorized use of said Art Works without the posting of a bond, in addition to and without limitation of any other remedies.

f. **Enforcement**

By signing the Agreement, The Art Network Members agree that any The Art Network Member contributing Art Works ("Contributing Member") may bring and maintain a cause of action directly against any other The Art Network Member to enforce rights and seek available remedies for misuse of the Contributing Member's Contributed Art Works, in addition to and not in limitation of any and all other rights and remedies available to the Contributing Member at law or in equity. The Art Network Member may not seek to impel The Art Network to act against any other Member, and agrees not to join The Art Network in any action between The Art Network Members or to bring any related cause of action against The Art Network directly or indirectly for such purpose(s). The Art Network agrees, however, to use commercially reasonable efforts to seek to enforce any final judgment of a competent tribunal that The Art Network reasonably believes to be enforceable, subject to the receipt of sufficient indemnities by The Art Network Member seeking enforcement. Nothing in this section shall limit a The Art Network Member's actions against The Art Network for a direct violation of this Agreement.

g. **Acknowledgment of Ownership**

As between The Art Network and The Art Network Member, The Art Network Member acknowledges that The Art Network has all right, title and interest in and to the System and the Artwork Network Service, including all related copyrights, database compilation rights, trademarks, trade names, and other intellectual property rights, currently in existence or later developed, except as expressly provided herein (such as with respect to Proprietary Art Works).

5. **Indemnification**

To the extent authorized by law, and subject to section 4f (Enforcement), The Art Network Member agrees to indemnify and hold harmless The Art Network, and its agents and affiliates, and their directors, officers and employees ("The Art Network"), as well as other The Art Network Members, from and against any and all liability, damage, loss, cost or expense, including reasonable attorney's fees, costs, and other expenses arising out of any activity undertaken by The Art Network Member, its agent(s) or representatives, pursuant to this Agreement or its subject matter, or which if true would be a violation of any Member obligation or of any third-party intellectual property right of any kind. Without limiting the foregoing, The Art Network reserves the right to eliminate or restrict access by The Art Network Member to the System and related services, and by third parties to the corresponding Contributed Digital Identifiers and Contributed Art Works, for just cause as determined in the good faith discretion of The Art Network, and the Art Network Member agrees to hold harmless The Art Network from any consequences.

6. **Limitations of Liability**

a. NONE OF THE PARTIES SHALL BE LIABLE TO THE OTHER FOR ANY INDIRECT, SPECIAL, INCIDENTAL, PUNITIVE, CONSEQUENTIAL DAMAGES OR LOST PROFITS ARISING OUT OF OR RELATING TO THIS AGREEMENT, EVEN IF IT HAS BEEN INFORMED IN ADVANCE OF THE POSSIBILITY OF SUCH DAMAGES.

b. NEITHER PARTY SHALL BE LIABLE TO THE OTHER FOR (I) ANY LOSS, CORRUPTION OR DELAY OF DATA OR (II) FOR ANY LOSS, CORRUPTION OR DELAY OF COMMUNICATIONS WITH OR CONNECTION TO RELATED PRODUCT OR CONTENT.

7. **Term and Termination**

a. **Term**

This Agreement shall commence upon the Effective Date and shall continue through the end of the then-current calendar year ("Initial Term"), and thereafter shall automatically be renewed for consecutive calendar years (each a "Term") unless terminated in accordance with the Agreement.

b. **Termination**

The Art Network Member may terminate this Agreement upon at least ninety (90) days' prior written notice, but shall not be entitled to a refund of any fees that have been paid or waiver of any fees that have accrued. Termination shall have no adverse effect on The Art Network's intellectual property rights in any Art Works or upon any related licenses then in effect.

8. **Miscellaneous Provisions**

a. **Notices**

The Art Network may give written notice to The Art Network Members under this Agreement by electronic mail, by facsimile transmission (with receipt confirmed), or by standard postal service. In the case of electronic mail, notice shall be deemed to have been given on the day of the delivery of the transmission. In the case of standard post, notice shall be deemed to have been given on the fifth business day following the day of mailing if mailed postage prepaid.

b. **Promotion**

Both The Art Network and The Art Network Member may use the other's name and mark to identify the other as a member of The Art Network. Notwithstanding the foregoing, The Art Network reserves the right to reasonably regulate or restrict use of The Art Network name or mark by The Art Network Members in press releases, advertising, client lists, or marketing materials from time to time. The Art Network Members shall use commercially reasonable efforts to place the mark and link "Artwork Network Enabled," in electronic form supplied by The Art Network, in a prominent location on the Websites of Related Sites.

c. **No Waiver**

The parties agree that no delay or omission by either party hereto, or by any The Art Network Member, to exercise any right or power hereunder shall impair such right or power or be construed to be a waiver thereof. A waiver by either of the parties of any of the covenants to be performed by the other or any breach thereof shall not be construed to be a waiver of any succeeding breach thereof or of any other covenant contained herein.

d. **Headings**

The headings of the sections and subsections used in this Agreement are included for convenience only and are not to be used in construing or interpreting this Agreement.

e. **Taxes**

The Art Network Member is responsible for all sales and use taxes imposed with respect to the services rendered or products provided to The Art Network Member hereunder, other than taxes based upon or credited against The Art Network's income.

f. **No Partnership**

Neither party to the Agreement is an agent, representative, or partner of the other party, except insofar as The Art Network rules and regulations expressly provide that The Art Network may act on behalf of The Art Network Member. The Art Network Member shall not have any right, power or authority to enter into any agreement for or on behalf of, or incur any obligation or liability of, or to otherwise bind, The Art Network.

g. **No Assignment**

The Art Network Member may not assign, subcontract or sublicense this Agreement without the prior written consent of The Art Network, which consent shall not be unreasonably withheld.

h. **No Third-Party Beneficiaries**

Except as set forth herein, each party intends that this Agreement shall not benefit, or create any right or cause of action in or on behalf of, any person or entity other than The Art Network or The Art Network Member.

i. **Choice of Law**

This Agreement shall be interpreted, governed and enforced under the laws of New York, without regard to its conflict of law rules. A federal court located in

New York, New York shall be the sole venue for resolving any claims or disputes arising out or relating to this Agreement.

j. **Entire Agreement**

The terms and conditions of this Agreement and any exhibits supersede all prior oral and written agreements between the parties with respect to the subject matter of this Agreement and shall constitute the entire agreement between the parties with respect to the matters contained herein. This Agreement shall not be modified or amended except by writing duly executed by authorized representatives of the parties.

IN WITNESS THEREFORE, the Parties have caused this Agreement to be executed as the first day and year written first above.

The Art Network	Member
By:______________________ [Name]	By:______________________ [Name]
Title:______________________	Title:______________________
Date:______________________	Date:______________________

FORM 9-22

Auction Rules and Web Site Terms of Use Policies

1. TIME. At the seller's option, auctions last varying numbers of days and amounts of time. Bidding automatically terminates at the end of the auction. When the auction ends, the seller and high-bidder are notified via email. Auction results are also available for everyone to examine. These results indicate the final bid price and the seller's and high-bidder's email addresses. The complete bidding history is also available as a link from the page showing the art's description. The high-bidder and seller should contact each other within 3 business days of the end of the auction. A seller may contact the next-highest bidder if the seller is unable to conclude the transaction with the high-bidder within 3 business days. Therefore, high-bidders may lose their place as winning bidder if the high-bidder does not contact the seller within 3 business days of the end of the auction.

2. BIDDING. By placing a bid, the bidder is placing a legally-binding and irrevocable offer to purchase the art at any price up through the bidder's maximum bid amount. If the bid is accepted by the seller, then the bidder is legally obligated to complete the transaction. The bidder's failure to complete the transaction is a breach of the User Agreement and may be legally actionable by the seller. The bidder must provide a valid email address or User ID with the bidder's bid. Before the bidder makes a bid, the bidder should verify the art he or she is bidding on and the seller's honesty as best the bidder can. If the bidder has any questions about the art, email the bidder's questions to the seller. Make sure the bidder clearly understands the shipping terms (who pays?), payment terms (can the bidder pay by personal check? credit card? and so on) and other details. Look at the seller's feedback and see how others have interacted with this seller in the past. Always check the feedback of the seller first before buying the bidder's art and read the descriptions of the feedback in addition to simply looking at the seller's feedback score. The bidder can place a bid when the bidder is viewing the art the bidder would like to bid on. Please bid the maximum amount the bidder is willing to pay for the art (the amount is kept secret). If necessary, bids will be automatically made on the bidder's behalf as other bidders increase the bid price, up to the bidder's maximum amount or the necessary preset bid increment to outbid other bidders. (All bidding is done with bid increments, which vary from art to art based on the current price.) This process is different for Dutch Auctions. In the case of a tie for the highest bid, the earlier bid takes precedence. Once the bidder makes and confirm a bid, the bidder cannot retract it except in exceptional circumstances. Exceptional circumstances include the seller materially changing the description of the art after the bidder's bid and clear typographical errors. Exceptional circumstances do not include bidding or winning a bid on another (perhaps similar)

art, not having the budget to pay for the bidder's art, changing the bidder's mind, and so on.

3. Buying Art. The bidder should call or email the seller to clarify the terms of shipping and insurance if he or she has not done so before the bid. Negotiate with the seller for escrow, sales tax, shipping fees, and payment terms.

4. Selling Art. After entering the seller's area, provide a short, descriptive title and provide a complete description of the art in the appropriate space. The seller cannot use HTML tags in the title, but the seller may use HTML in the seller's description. This means that the seller can link to pictures if the seller chooses. All content linked to the art description must comply with the User Agreement. The seller might want to consider setting the minimum bid for the seller's art a little lower than the seller think the art will eventually be sold for, just to get the auction going. If the seller's minimum bid is too high, people may not bid. However, keep in mind that the minimum price the seller specifies indicates the minimum amount the seller will accept to sell the art. The software automatically specifies the bidding increment. The increment is kept low to encourage more people to bid. By auctioning the seller's art, the seller is irrevocably (except as described below) and legally committing to accept the high bid for the art (or the highest-bidder who does not renege). If the seller receives one or more bids above the minimum price the seller stated the seller would be willing to accept, then the seller are legally obligated to complete the transaction. The seller's failure to complete the transaction is a breach of the User Agreement and may be legally actionable by one or more of the bidders. The seller has the right to cancel the transaction with any user with whom they are uncomfortable completing a transaction with. The seller may place any merchandise up for auction that the seller have the right to sell, so long as it complies with the User Agreement. Please list the seller's art in an appropriate category. In the description of the seller's art, the seller should clarify any additional terms or expenses associated with the art, such as who will bear shipping and insurance expenses.

5. Notice of End of Auction/Account Status. Once the auction is over, the bidder will be notified via email. However, if the bidder is bidding, the bidder is responsible for checking back at Auctioneer to see if the bidder has won. If the bidder does not receive notice and thinks he or she is the top bidder, the bidder must check the auction status at Auctioneer for the auction results. After the auction has ended, the top bidder needs to contact the seller within three days. Likewise, the bidder can check the bidder's account at any time online. The notice is a courtesy. If the bidder's account is past due, the bidder may incur late fees or find the bidder's account on hold, so keep on top of the bidder account balance.

6. Pricing. Some guidelines regarding pricing: First, we encourage sellers to set the minimum bid for their auction at the lowest fair price at which they are willing to sell their art. Second, a seller may employ a reserve price auction. This allows the seller to set a price below which he or she does not agree to sell the art. Third, a seller may not bid on his or her own auction. If the seller starts an auction and decides they no longer wish to sell his or her art, the seller should cancel all bids on the auction and then end the auction.

7. Reserve Prices. Auctions may be run with reserve prices. The reserve price is the lowest price at which a seller is willing to sell the art. The reserve price is not disclosed to bidders. A seller might specify a reserve price if he or she is unsure of the real value of the art and would like to be able to refuse to sell the art if the market value is below a certain price. During an auction, an annotation will be displayed in the art information screen if the seller has specified a reserve price. The seller specifies the reserve price when he or she lists the art. This price should be above the minimum bid price. The auction begins at the minimum bid price. When a bidder's maximum bid is equal to or greater than the reserve price, the art's current price is raised to the reserve price. At this time, the art information will indicate the reserve price has been met. The bidder is also notified that his or her bid met the reserve. Please note that reserve price auctions are not available for Dutch auctions, and arts with reserve prices are not displayed in the hot arts section.

8. Private Auctions. A seller may specify that an auction will be a private auction. This means bidders' email addresses will not be disclosed on the screen or bidding history screen. Only the seller and the high-bidder will be notified via email when the auction is over. This option is useful when the seller realizes that potential bidders may not want their identities disclosed to the general public. This option is not available for Dutch auctions.

9. Dutch Auctions. Dutch auctions are a special auction format where a seller has multiple, identical arts he or she wishes to sell. The seller specifies the minimum price (the starting bid) and the number of arts available. Bidders bid at or above that minimum for the quantity they are interested in purchasing. At the close of the auction, the highest bidders purchase the arts at its lowest successful bid. For example, imagine there are 10 prints being sold at $100. 25 people bid $100 for one print each. In this case, only the first 10 people will be the successful bidders, since the bid amounts are the same, and earlier bids take precedence. Now, say that one of those people bid $150 for one print. Since her bid is higher than all the others, she will certainly be one of the successful bidders. The other 9 prints will be claimed by the earliest bidders who bid $100, and the final price for each print will be $100. If enough people bid above the minimum bid, the final price of the art will increase as well. On the other hand, if less than 10 people bid

in our example, then only that number of prints will be sold at the opening price of $100. For the selling price to increase past the opening price specified by the seller, there must be an equal or higher level of demand than the supply indicated. In our example, the selling price would only increase if 11 or more prints were bid upon, no matter what the amount of each bid. In the case of multiple quantities bid for by a bidder, the lowest bidder may not earn the right to purchase the complete quantity, since there may only be one left by the time the higher bidders have been processed. In other words, if the lowest bidder requested a quantity of 3 photographs, she might only be entitled to one photograph, since 9 other photographs could be allocated to higher bidders. The only way around this problem is to ensure that you are not the lowest bidder. In some cases, a bidder may reserve the right to refuse purchase of a partial quantity. In that case, the seller may skip that bidder and move on to the next one, if any.

10. Feedback. We encourage all users to leave feedback about their trading partners, but not to abuse the privilege of posting feedback about others.

11. Fraud. Please contact members before beginning a transaction. Most fraud complaints tend to be misunderstandings about the product, shipping terms, or shipping addresses. Users should clarify all of these elements before bidding, and definitely before sending money. However, fraud is a reality of doing business, both on and off the Web, and users should report it to the authorities if it happens in our community.

12. Defamation. Please be careful of what you say about other people online. Postings on the discussion board or in the feedback forum cannot be erased or deleted.

If the User agrees with the foregoing terms and conditions, select the "I Agree" button. Otherwise select the "I don't Agree" button.

→ [button] I agree. → [button] I don't agree.

FORM 9-23

Auction Participation Agreement

1. Agreement. Any person who wants to access the Site to buy, sell or bid for goods or to use the other services we provide (collectively, the "Services") must accept the terms and conditions of this Participation Agreement without change. BY REGISTERING FOR AND USING THE SERVICES, YOU AGREE TO BE BOUND BY ALL TERMS AND CONDITIONS OF THIS AGREEMENT AND ALL POLICIES AND GUIDELINES INCORPORATED BY REFERENCE.

2. Changes. Auctioneer reserves the right to change any of the terms and conditions contained in this Agreement or any policies or guidelines governing the Site or Services, at any time and in its sole discretion. Any changes will be effective upon posting of the revisions on the Site. All notice of changes to this Agreement will be posted on the Site for thirty (30) days. You are responsible for reviewing the notice and any applicable changes. Changes to referenced policies and guidelines may be posted without notice to you. YOUR CONTINUED USE OF THIS SITE AND THE SERVICES FOLLOWING AUCTIONEER'S POSTING OF ANY CHANGES WILL CONSTITUTE YOUR ACCEPTANCE OF SUCH CHANGES OR MODIFICATIONS. IF YOU DO NOT AGREE TO ANY CHANGES TO THIS AGREEMENT, DO NOT CONTINUE TO USE THE SERVICES OR THIS SITE.

3. Eligibility. Use of the Services is limited to parties that lawfully can enter into and form contracts under applicable law. For example, minors are not allowed to use the Services. To register, you must provide your real name, address, phone number, email address, and valid credit card information.

4. Sellers' Fees and Payment Terms. Click here for the Fee Schedule and Payment Terms, which are incorporated into this Participation Agreement by reference. All fees are in U.S. Dollars unless stated otherwise. The Fee Schedule and Payment Terms may vary in the future. The Fee Schedule and Payment Terms in effect on the date of listing the item shall govern the transaction. You should check the fees and terms each time you participate. All fees are payable upon demand on a VISA, MasterCard, American Express, or Discover credit card. By listing an item for fixed price sale or auction on the Site, you authorize Auctioneer to charge your credit card for amounts due.

5. Applicable Policies and Guidelines. You agree to abide by the procedures and guidelines for conducting fixed price sales and auctions contained in the Help Section, which are incorporated by reference into, and made part of, this Participation Agreement. The procedures and guidelines contained in the Help Section explain the processes and set out acceptable conduct and prohibited prac-

tices. These procedures and guidelines may be changed by us in the future, but unlike the Participation Agreement, these changes will be effective immediately upon posting without notice to you. You should regularly refer to the Help Section to understand the current procedures and guidelines for participating and to be sure that the goods you offer for sale or want to buy can be auctioned or purchased on the Site.

6. Auctioneer's Role. Auctioneer provides a venue for Sellers and Buyers to negotiate and complete transactions. Auctioneer is not involved in the actual transaction between Sellers and Buyers and is not the agent of and has no authority for either for any purpose. As a Seller, you may "list" any item on the Site unless it is a prohibited item as defined in the procedures and guidelines contained in the Help Section. Specifically, you may not list any item, link or post any related materials, or purchase any item that (a) infringes any third-party intellectual property rights (including copyright, trademark, patent, trade secrets), or other proprietary rights (including rights of publicity or privacy); or (b) is counterfeited, illegal, stolen, or fraudulent. It is up to the Seller to accurately describe the item for sale or auction. Auctioneer cannot and does not know whether any listing is accurate, complete, misleading or deceptive or if the Seller and Buyer will perform as promised so you should always take due care in entering into any agreement with another person. Buyers and Sellers use the Site and the Services at their own risk.

7. Auctioneer Payment Services

7.1. Buyers may pay Sellers registered with Auctioneer Payment, Inc. ("Auctioneer Payments") by purchasing an Auctioneer Payments electronic credit ("Electronic Money") for the full amount owed. Buyers may purchase Electronic Money with a VISA, MasterCard, American Express, or Discover. Buyers will be notified of this option in the winning email notification. After the credit card charge is approved, Auctioneer will direct Seller to ship the item to Buyer. Buyer is bound by any Electronic Money purchase request he or she authorizes. The Auctioneer Payments service is the purchase of Electronic Money and not the purchase of the Seller's goods. Buyer will resolve any dispute directly with Seller, and not through attempting to revoke an Electronic Money purchase transaction.

8. Auctioneer Reservation of Rights

8.1. Auctioneer retains the right to immediately halt any auction or fixed price sale, prevent or restrict access to the Site or the Services or take any other action to restrict access to or availability of objectionable material, any inaccurate listing, any unlawful items or any items otherwise prohibited by the procedures and guidelines contained in the Help Section.

8.2. Auctioneer retains the right to seek reimbursement from Seller if we, in our sole discretion, decide to reimburse Buyer or we receive a chargeback from Buyer's credit card issuer for the amount of Buyer's purchase from Seller.

8.3. Auctioneer Auctions is a licensed and bonded auction company under the laws of the State of Wyoming. Auctioneer itself may participate in auctions or fixed price sales from time to time. When Auctioneer offers goods for fixed price sale or auction, it is no different than any other seller engaged in a transaction and will abide by the same procedures and guidelines contained in the Help Section as any seller on this Site, notwithstanding any other terms and conditions of this Participation Agreement. In addition, employees of Auctioneer are permitted to participate in their personal capacity (i.e., not as Auctioneer employees, representatives or agents) in the transactions conducted through this Site (unless they have confidential information about a particular item). Auctioneer employees, when participating in any transaction in their personal capacity, are subject to this Participation Agreement and the same procedures and guidelines contained in the Help Section as any buyer or seller on this Site.

9. Your Transactions

9.1. Fixed Price Sales. Bidders, Buyers, and Sellers create different obligations by accessing the Site and using the Services. For sales where a Seller lists goods at a fixed price ("Fixed Price Sales"), the Seller is obligated to sell the goods at the listed price to Buyers who meet the Seller's terms. By listing an item in a Fixed Price Sale or by auction, you represent and warrant to prospective Buyers that you have the right and ability to sell, and that the listing is accurate, current and complete and is not misleading or otherwise deceptive.

9.2. Auction Sales. For auctions, the obligations of the Seller and Buyer are different. Unless a Seller specifies a "reserve price," all auction items are "without reserve", i.e., the Seller must sell the auctioned item to the highest bidder that meets or exceeds the minimum price. If a Seller sets an undisclosed "reserve price," the Seller is not obligated to sell unless the reserve price is met or exceeded. For Bidders, a bid is a legal offer to buy the auction item. Once the auction closes, both the Buyer and Seller are obligated to complete the transaction.

9.3. Your Obligation. By entering into this Agreement and (a) posting a listing for auction or Fixed Price Sale or (b) bidding on an auctioned item or making an offer in a Fixed Price Sale, you agree to complete the transaction as described by this Agreement. You acknowledge that by not fulfilling these obligations, your action or inaction may be legally actionable.

9.4. Sales/Use Taxes. You agree that it is the Seller's and the Buyer's responsibility to determine whether sales or use taxes apply to the transactions and to collect, report and remit the correct tax to the appropriate tax authority. You also agree that Auctioneer is not obligated to determine whether sales or use taxes apply and is not responsible to collect, remit or report any sales or use taxes arising from any transaction.

9.5. Refund Obligation. Sellers must provide a full refund directly to any Buyer who remits payment, either directly or through Auctioneer Payments, if the item cannot be shipped at the close of the sale. Seller must provide the refund promptly, but in no case later than thirty (30) days following the close of the sale. Any Buyer who believes he/she may be entitled to a refund on this basis should contact the Seller directly.

10. Password Security. Your password may be used only to access the Site, use the Services, electronically sign your transactions and review your completed transactions. You are solely responsible for maintaining the security of your password. You may not disclose your password to any third party (other than third parties authorized by you to use your account) and are solely responsible for any use of or action taken under your password on this Site. If your password is compromised you must change your password.

11. Illegal Activity

11.1. Compliance with Laws; Fraud. The Site and Services only may be used for lawful purposes and in a lawful manner. You agree to comply with all applicable laws, statutes and regulations regarding use of the Services, including in regard to bidding, listing, purchasing and selling items. You may not register under a false name or use an invalid or unauthorized credit card. You may not make bids under a false name, impersonate any participant, or use another participant's password(s). Such fraudulent conduct is a violation of federal and state laws. Fraudulent conduct may be reported to law enforcement, and Auctioneer will cooperate to ensure that violators are prosecuted to the fullest extent of the law.

11.2. Investigation. Auctioneer has the right, but not the obligation, to monitor any activity and content associated with this Site. Auctioneer may investigate any reported violation of its policies or complaints and take any action that it deems appropriate. Such action may include, but is not limited to, issuing warnings, suspension or termination of service, denying access and/or removal of any materials on the Site, including listings and bids. Auctioneer reserves the right and has absolute discretion, to remove, screen or edit any content that violates these provisions or is otherwise objectionable.

11.3. Disclosure of Information. Auctioneer also reserves the right to report any activity that it suspects violates any law or regulation to appropriate law enforcement officials, regulators, or other third parties. In order to cooperate with governmental requests, to protect Auctioneer's systems and customers, or to ensure the integrity and operation of Auctioneer's business and systems, Auctioneer may access and disclose any information it considers necessary or appropriate, including, without limitation, user contact details, IP addressing and traffic information, usage history and posted content.

12. Privacy. Auctioneer is committed to protecting your privacy. Click here for our general Privacy Policy. The Privacy Policy may be changed by us in the future. You should check the Privacy Policy frequently for changes. Unless otherwise authorized or consented, you agree not to use any information regarding other participants which is accessible from the Site or disclosed to you by Auctioneer except to enter into and complete transactions. You agree not to use any such information for purposes of solicitation, advertising, unsolicited e-mail or spamming, harassment, invasion of privacy or otherwise objectionable conduct.

13. No Warranties. THE SITE AND THE SERVICES ARE PROVIDED ON AN "AS IS" BASIS. AUCTIONEER MAKES NO OTHER REPRESENTATIONS OR WARRANTIES OF ANY KIND, EXPRESS OR IMPLIED, INCLUDING WITHOUT LIMITATION:

13.1. THE IMPLIED WARRANTIES OF MERCHANTABILITY, FITNESS FOR A PARTICULAR PURPOSE, TITLE, AND NON-INFRINGEMENT;

13.2. THAT THE SITE OR THE SERVICES WILL MEET YOUR REQUIREMENTS, WILL ALWAYS BE AVAILABLE, ACCESSIBLE, UNINTERRUPTED, TIMELY, SECURE OR OPERATE WITHOUT ERROR;

13.3. THE INFORMATION, CONTENT, MATERIALS OR PRODUCTS INCLUDED ON THE SITE WILL BE AS REPRESENTED BY SELLERS, AVAILABLE FOR SALE AT THE TIME OF AUCTION OR FIXED PRICE SALE, LAWFUL TO SELL, OR THAT SELLERS OR BUYERS WILL PERFORM AS PROMISED;

13.4. ANY IMPLIED WARRANTY ARISING FROM COURSE OF DEALING OR USAGE OF TRADE; AND

13.5. ANY OBLIGATION, LIABILITY, RIGHT, CLAIM OR REMEDY IN TORT, WHETHER OR NOT ARISING FROM THE NEGLIGENCE OF AUCTIONEER.

14. TO THE FULL EXTENT PERMISSIBLE UNDER APPLICABLE LAW, AUCTIONEER DISCLAIMS ANY AND ALL SUCH WARRANTIES.

15. General Release BECAUSE AUCTIONEER IS NOT INVOLVED IN TRANSACTIONS BETWEEN BUYERS AND SELLERS OR OTHER PARTICIPANT DEALINGS, IF A DISPUTE ARISES BETWEEN ONE OR MORE PARTICIPANTS, EACH OF YOU RELEASE AUCTIONEER (AND ITS AGENTS AND EMPLOYEES) FROM CLAIMS, DEMANDS AND DAMAGES (AC-

TUAL AND CONSEQUENTIAL) OF EVERY KIND AND NATURE, KNOWN AND UNKNOWN, SUSPECTED AND UNSUSPECTED, DISCLOSED AND UNDISCLOSED, ARISING OUT OF OR IN ANY WAY CONNECTED WITH SUCH DISPUTES.

16. Limitation of Liability AUCTIONEER WILL NOT BE LIABLE FOR ANY DAMAGES OF ANY KIND INCLUDING WITHOUT LIMITATION DIRECT, INDIRECT, INCIDENTAL, PUNITIVE AND CONSEQUENTIAL DAMAGES, ARISING OUT OF OR IN CONNECTION WITH THE PARTICIPATION AGREEMENT, THE SITE, THE SERVICES, THE INABILITY TO USE THE SERVICES OR THOSE RESULTING FROM ANY GOODS OR SERVICES PURCHASED OR OBTAINED OR MESSAGES RECEIVED OR TRANSACTIONS ENTERED INTO THROUGH THE SERVICES.

17. Applicable Law. The Site and the Services are arranged, sponsored, or managed by Auctioneer in State, and its laws govern this Participation Agreement and all of its terms and conditions, without giving effect to any principles of conflicts of laws. You agree that any action at law or in equity arising out of or relating to these terms and conditions shall be filed only in state or federal court located in State, and you hereby irrevocably and unconditionally consent and submit to the exclusive jurisdiction of such courts over any suit, action or proceeding arising out of these terms and conditions.

18. Disputes. Because Auctioneer is not involved in the actual transaction between Sellers and Buyers and is not the agent of either for any purpose, Auctioneer will not be involved in resolving any disputes between participants related to or arising out of any transaction. Auctioneer urges Sellers and Buyers to cooperate with each other to resolve such disputes.

19. Licenses

19.1. Your Grant. By entering into this Participation Agreement and listing an item, you grant Auctioneer a non-exclusive, world-wide, royalty-free, irrevocable, right to exercise all copyright and rights of publicity over the material displayed in your listings, bids, or purchases in any existing or future media, known or unknown, now or at any later date.

19.2. Auctioneer's Grant. Auctioneer grants a limited license to each participant to make personal use only of the Site and the Services. This license expressly excludes, without limitation, any resale or commercial use of the Site and the Services, making any derivative of the Site or the Services, the collection and use of participant email addresses or other participant information, ratings or listings, or any data extraction or data mining whatsoever.

20. Termination. Auctioneer, in its sole discretion, may terminate this Participation Agreement, access to the Site or the Services, or any current auctions or fixed price sales immediately without notice for any reason.

21. General Provision

21.1. Entire Agreement. This Agreement constitutes the entire agreement of the parties with respect to the subject matter hereof and supersedes and cancels all prior and contemporaneous agreements, claims, representations and understandings of the parties in connection with the subject matter hereof.

21.2. No Agency; Third-Party Beneficiary. Auctioneer is not the agent, fiduciary, trustee or other representative of you. Nothing expressed or mentioned in or implied from this Agreement is intended or shall be construed to give to any person other than the parties hereto any legal or equitable right, remedy or claim under or in respect to this Agreement. This Agreement and all of the representations, warranties, covenants, conditions and provisions hereof are intended to be and are for the sole and exclusive benefit of Auctioneer, you, and relying Buyers or Sellers.

21.3. Severability. If any provision of this Agreement shall be deemed unlawful, void, or for any reason unenforceable, then that provision shall be deemed severable from these terms and conditions and shall not affect the validity and enforceability of any remaining provisions.

22. No Waiver. Auctioneer's failure to enforce the strict performance of any provision of this Agreement will not constitute a waiver of Auctioneer's right to subsequently enforce such provision or any other provisions of this Agreement.

If the User agrees with the foregoing terms and conditions, select the "I Agree" button. Otherwise select the "I don't Agree" button.

→ [button] <u>I agree.</u> → [button] <u>I don't agree.</u>

FORM 9-24

Online Gallery Co-Marketing Agreement

AFFILIATE AGREEMENT ("Agreement") between Gallery.com ("Gallery"), and Syndicate.com, Inc. ("Syndicate").

Syndicate wishes to maintain and facilitate links to the Gallery Website located at www.GalleryWebSite.net and replacement, successor and affiliate addresses thereto (the "Gallery Site") from and through its Website located at www.SyndicateProgram.com and replacement, successor and affiliate addresses thereto (the "Syndicate Site") as well as independent Gallery and Art Websites controlled by Syndicate affiliates (collectively, "Syndicate Affiliates") in relation to and conjunction with the facilitation and execution of electronic commerce transactions (collectively, the "Links"), and thereby earn commissions payable on sales of Art that are realized through the Links.

1. The Links.

a. Form of Links. Gallery shall provide Syndicate with distinctive Gallery logo and graphics, images of current Gallery Art represented on the Gallery Site and at Gallery, and offer copy and other offer elements (the "Presentation Materials"), as well as HTML code containing unique Syndicate and Syndicate Affiliate identifications.

b. Presentation to Syndicate Affiliates. In conjunction with Gallery, Syndicate shall design, develop and implement pages and links thereto throughout the Syndicate Site, and in its electronic and other communications with Syndicate Affiliates, detailing the offers for Syndicate Affiliates to take advantage of the Presentation Materials and such other activity under the Agreement as is appropriate, and instructions for accepting and implementing the same.

c. Placement. Syndicate shall place the Presentation Materials on the Syndicate Site and use commercially reasonable efforts to facilitate the placement of the Presentation Materials on Syndicate Affiliate Websites, in the manner hereinafter described, such that visitors may link from any of the Presentation Materials to Syndicate Purchase Area(s).

i. Conspicuous. Presentation Materials shall be placed on top-level pages within the aforementioned Websites, in conspicuous locations that are also visible to users upon initial receipt of the pages without any scrolling or navigation.

ii. Maintenance. Syndicate agrees to display and maintain the Presentation Materials in good working order, and not to alter or modify them in any way without obtaining the prior written consent of Gallery.

iii. Compliance. Upon written notice, Syndicate agrees to promptly remove any Presentation Materials on pages under its direct or indirect control that contain content judged by Gallery in its sole discretion to be objectionable or in other ways offensive in a manner that would negatively affect Gallery.

d. Syndicate Affiliate Compliance. Syndicate shall require Syndicate Affiliates using Links, or otherwise participating in the subject matter of the Agreement, to be bound in writing or by opt-in click-through to terms substantially similar hereto, and as set forth in Exhibit A (Affiliate Terms & Conditions).

2. Trademark Licenses.

a. Gallery Marks. Gallery grants Syndicate the non-exclusive, non-transferable, non-sublicensable, revocable right to use the Presentation Materials during the term of the Syndicate Agreement for the sole purpose of generating sales on the Gallery Site, subject to Gallery's quality control.

i. Reservation of Rights. Gallery reserves all of its rights, and those of the other respective rights owners, in the Presentation Materials, and Syndicate claims no rights whatsoever in the same.

ii. Good Will. All good will attributed to the Gallery logo(s), tradename(s) and trademarks ("Gallery Marks") will inure to the benefit of Gallery exclusively.

b. Syndicate Marks. Syndicate grants Gallery the non-exclusive, non-transferable, non-sublicensable, revocable right during this Agreement to use its logo(s), tradename(s) and trademark(s) ("Syndicate Marks"), to co-brand the Syndicate Purchase Area(s), to construct any links from the Syndicate Marks to the Syndicate Site, or to otherwise promote the Gallery-Syndicate relationship, in the sole good-faith discretion of Gallery, subject to Syndicate's quality control.

i. Reservation of Rights. Syndicate reserves all of its rights in the Syndicate Marks, and Gallery claims no rights whatsoever therein.

ii. Good Will. All good will attributed to the Syndicate Marks will inure to the benefit of Gallery exclusively.

3. Sales, Commissions and Payments.

a. Qualifying Purchases. Purchases shall qualify for the accrual of commissions to Syndicate ("Qualifying Purchases") as follows:

i. Online. Qualifying Purchases must be made on the Internet at the purchase areas on the Gallery Site, accessed through the Syndicate Purchase Area(s).

ii. Information. Qualifying Purchases must include valid, chargeable credit card numbers, full customer names, mailing addresses, email addresses, and other basic contact information.

b. Commissions. Commissions shall accrue only on Qualifying Purchases, and otherwise as follows ("Commissions"): The rate of Commissions on Qualifying Purchases shall be ___ percent of the fee paid.

c. Syndicate Payment. Gallery shall pay accrued Commissions to Syndicate, less any taxes required by law to be withheld, within thirty (30) days after the end of each month in which both the Gallery full-refund period ("Refund Period") expires, and the fee has been collected and retained in full by Gallery.

4. Reports.

a. By Gallery. Syndicate shall receive monthly reports from Gallery via email representing gross sales generated through the Syndicate Purchase Area(s) by Syndicate Affiliates and estimated Commissions due, the form, content and frequency of which may vary in the sole good faith discretion of Gallery.

b. By Syndicate. Syndicate shall provide Gallery with reports in a form reasonably required by Gallery on a weekly basis, detailing the number of impressions and impression levels from click-throughs, as well as conversion rates among Syndicate Affiliates using Links, and such other information from the Syndicate Site and Syndicate Affiliate Websites that is reasonably specified by Gallery relating to the Presentation Materials and sales.

5. Gallery Administration Policies.

a. Approval over Copy. Syndicate acknowledges the sensitivity of promotional and attribution language, and agrees that any copy that is on the same electronic page or otherwise adjacent to any offer copy hereunder must be approved in advance by Gallery, and shall remain subject to Gallery approval, for conformance with appropriate legal and publishing guidelines as such are currently interpreted and enforced.

b. Refunds. Gallery may modify its customer refund policies at any time and for any reason and without prior notice to Syndicate.

c. Customer Responsibility. Customers who purchase through the Gallery Site will be deemed to be customers of Gallery for all purposes, including without limitation information management and direct marketing, and will be subject to the Gallery rules, policies and operating procedures concerning customer orders, and customer service.

d. Customer Service. Gallery is responsible for all processing, fulfillment and customer service related to orders, and Syndicate shall neither have nor retain any responsibility for customers ordering through the Gallery Site, except as expressly set forth in the Agreement.

6. Site Maintenance.

a. Gallery. Gallery shall be exclusively responsible for the maintenance and operation of its Site, and all programs, content and programming associated therewith, subject to the terms of the Agreement, including maintenance and control of all elements of the Syndicate Purchase Area(s), including its functionality and appearance.

b. Syndicate. Syndicate is solely responsible for the maintenance and operation of the Syndicate Site, and all programs, content and programming associated therewith, including for the proper maintenance and display of the Presentation Materials, which shall not be modified in any way without the prior written consent of Gallery.

7. Term and Termination.

a. Terms. The initial term of this Agreement shall commence upon execution by Gallery for one (1) year, and shall be automatically renewed thereafter for subsequent one (1) year periods.

b. Termination without Cause. Either party may terminate the Agreement during the initial term upon sixty (60) days prior written notice, and thereafter upon ninety (90) days prior written notice.

c. Termination for Cause. Gallery supports honest business practices and may in its sole discretion require Syndicate to terminate the subject matter of this Agreement with any Syndicate Affiliate that Gallery determines at any time to be unsuitable for inclusion hereunder for reasons such as, without limitation of any kind, the submission to Gallery of false or misleading information; the promotion of content that is in any way defamatory, discriminatory, obscene, violent, or otherwise objectionable; business practices that Gallery deems in its sole discretion to be improper; and for any alleged material breach of this Agreement.

d. Actions upon Termination/Expiration. Upon termination or expiration of the Agreement, Syndicate shall immediately delete the Presentation Materials and all copies thereof from the Syndicate Site, and all other media directly or indirectly under its control, or return them to Gallery (upon prior request of Gallery), and promptly affirm in a signed writing that it has so complied with the provisions of this subsection.

8. Promotion. The parties shall promote the subject matter of the Agreement as mutually agreed.

9. Warranties and Representations.

a. By Gallery. Gallery represents and warrants as follows:

i. Gallery Site. The Gallery Site, the contents thereof, and the activity thereon or related directly thereto shall not infringe the rights of any third party.

ii. Presentation Materials. The Presentation Materials shall not infringe the rights of any third party.

iii. Reservation of rights. Gallery reserves the right to change the selection of its art and their prices at any time without notice in its sole discretion, and may reject any orders that do not comply with its requirements as interpreted in its sole discretion.

iv. Disclaimers. Gallery does not represent that the operation of the Gallery site and ordering pages will be uninterrupted or error-free, and it will not be liable for the consequences of such interruptions, errors or non-fulfillment of orders.

v. No Other Warranties. GALLERY MAKES NO WARRANTIES TO ANY PERSON OR ENTITY WITH RESPECT TO ANY SERVICES PERFORMED OR ANY INFORMATION, CONTENT OR OTHER MATERIALS PROVIDED OR MADE AVAILABLE BY IT HEREUNDER, AND DISCLAIMS ALL IMPLIED WARRANTIES, INCLUDING WITHOUT LIMITATION WARRANTIES OF MERCHANTABILITY, FITNESS FOR A PARTICULAR PURPOSE OR ANY IMPLIED WARRANTIES ARISING OUT OF A COURSE OF PERFORMANCE, DEALING OR TRADE USAGE.

b. By Syndicate. Syndicate represents and warrants as follows:

i. Syndicate Site. The Syndicate Site, the contents thereof, and the activity thereon or related directly thereto shall not infringe the rights of any third party.

ii. Presentation Materials, Prices. Syndicate shall not modify, reproduce or distribute the Presentation Materials, or vary the authorized prices by implicitly or expressly offering discounts, premiums or any other incentives, but shall use best efforts to immediately adopt any modifications thereto upon the request of Gallery.

iii. Carry Out. Syndicate shall carry out the terms and conditions of the Agreement to the best of its ability, and shall use all commercially reasonable efforts to maximize sales hereunder.

10. Limitations.

EXCEPT AS OTHERWISE PROVIDED, NEITHER PARTY SHALL BE LIABLE OR OBLIGATED UNDER ANY SECTION OF THIS AGREEMENT OR UNDER CONTRACT, NEGLIGENCE, STRICT LIABILITY OR OTHER LEGAL OR EQUITABLE THEORY FOR ANY SPECIAL, INDIRECT, INCIDENTAL OR CONSEQUENTIAL DAMAGES OR LOST PROFITS OR COST OF PROCUREMENT OF SUBSTITUTE GOODS OR SERVICES. WITHOUT LIMITING THE FOREGOING, GALLERY SHALL IN NO EVENT BE LIABLE FOR ANY AMOUNT IN EXCESS OF THE ACCRUED COMMISSIONS PAYABLE AND PAID HEREUNDER.

11. Confidentiality.

Each party agrees that all information concerning the other party, including without limitation business and financial data, customer and vendor lists, and pricing and sales information, and the terms of this Agreement, shall remain strictly confidential and shall not be disclosed to third parties, with the sole exception of Syndicate's accountants and attorneys on a confidential basis, or pursuant to valid legal process, of which the party subject to said process shall promptly notify the other party, and cooperate in any attempt by, and at the expense of, the other party to oppose said process.

12. Indemnification.

a. By Gallery. Gallery shall at all times indemnify, defend and hold Syndicate, its subsidiaries, affiliated companies, directors, officers, employees, agents and representatives harmless from and against any and all claims, damages, liabilities, disbursements, costs and expenses, including reasonable attorneys' fees (including an allocation for in-house counsel and expert fees), arising out of Gallery's (1) unauthorized use of the Syndicate Marks; (2) violation of a third party's intellectual property rights with respect to the Gallery Marks, Presentation Materials; (3) breach of warranties; (4) breach of confidentiality; and (5) willful misconduct or gross negligence.

b. By Syndicate. Syndicate shall at all times indemnify, defend and hold Company, its parent(s), subsidiaries, affiliated companies, directors, officers, employees, agents and representatives harmless from and against any and all claims, damages, liabilities, disbursements, costs and expenses, including reasonable attorneys' fees (including an allocation for in-house counsel and expert fees), arising out of Syndicate's (1) unauthorized use of Gallery Marks, the Presentation Materials (2) violation of a third party's intellectual property rights with respect to the Syndicate Marks; (3) breach of warranties; (4) breach of confidentiality; (5) Site or services offered thereon whether within or beyond the scope of the Agreement, and (6) willful misconduct or gross negligence.

13. Relationship.

Gallery may identify Syndicate as an "Syndicate" or "Partner", and participant in the Affiliate Program without Syndicate's additional consent. Neither this Agreement nor Syndicate's participation in the Affiliate Program is intended to create any agency, franchise, sales representative, partnership, or employment relationship between Syndicate and Gallery, and neither party has any authority to make or accept any offers on behalf of the other without prior written consent.

14. Force Majeure.

Neither party shall be liable for nonperformance or delay in performance (other than of obligations regarding confidentiality) caused by any event reasonably beyond the control of such party including, but not limited to wars, hostilities, revolutions, riots, civil commotion, national emergency, strikes, lock-outs, unavailability of supplies, epidemics, fire, flood, earthquake, force of nature, explosion, embargo, or any other Act of God, or any law, proclamation, regulation, ordinance, or other act or order of any court, government or governmental agency.

15. Assignment.

Either party may assign this Agreement, and its rights, licenses and obligations hereunder, without the prior written approval of the other, solely to any affiliate or other acquiror of all or of substantially all of its equity securities, assets or business relating to the subject matter of this Agreement, or pursuant to any internal re-organization in the sole discretion of the re-organizing party. Any attempted assignment in violation of this Section will be void and without effect. The issuance of or trading in any securities that are registered under the Securities Act of 1933, as amended, or in conjunction with any transaction that is registered under the Securities and Exchange Act of 1934, as amended, shall not be deemed to violate the provisions of this Section. Subject to the foregoing, this Agreement will benefit and bind the parties' successors and assigns.

16. Notice.

Any notice or other correspondence required or permitted to be given pursuant to this Agreement shall be in writing and shall be deemed to have been given (a) immediately if served personally, (b) immediately if sent to a designated FAX number (with confirmation of receipt), and simultaneously via first-class mail, postage pre-paid and addressed to the persons set forth below, (c) three (3) business days after posting if sent by certified or registered mail return receipt requested, postage prepaid, and addressed to the persons set forth below, (d) on the next business day if sent via internationally recognized carrier such as FedEx or U.P.S. and addressed to the persons set forth below.

17. Severability.

In the event that any of the provisions of this Agreement shall be held by a court or other tribunal of competent jurisdiction to be unenforceable, such provisions shall be limited or eliminated to the minimum extent necessary so that this Agreement shall otherwise remain in full force and effect and enforceable.

18. Waiver.

The failure to enforce any provision of the Agreement will not be a waiver of our right to subsequent enforcement of the provision or any other provision of the Agreement.

19. Headings.

Headings and captions are for convenience only and are not to be used in the interpretation of this Agreement.

20. ADR Procedures.

In the event of any controversy or claim arising out of this Agreement raised by either party, the party raising the dispute will promptly notify the other party in writing of the nature of the dispute and the factual background. Within the fifteen (15) calendar day period following such notice, the parties will initiate an attempt in good faith to reach a reasonable solution to the dispute, including escalation to the vice-president of each company responsible for the subject matter of the dispute. If the dispute cannot be amicably resolved within thirty (30) calendar days of written notification, then either party may seek to resolve said dispute by arbitration before a single arbitrator in accordance with the commercial arbitration rules of the American Arbitration Association, and judgment upon the award rendered by the arbitrator may be entered in any court having jurisdiction thereof. The place of arbitration shall be New York, NY. Each party shall provide to the arbitrator, no later than fifteen (15) calendar days following the date of the arbitrator's appointment, a statement, including all supporting documents or other evidence on which such party relies as to why it believes that the dispute should be resolved in its favor, and all such materials and any other materials provided to the arbitrator by either party shall simultaneously be provided by such party to the other party. Within twenty (20) calendar days after the submission of such statements by all parties, the arbitrator shall hold a hearing with respect to the dispute. At such hearing, the arbitrator may, in his or her sole discretion, allow the parties to call and cross-examine witnesses, make any additional arguments or submit any additional materials to support the position taken in their respective statements. The arbitrator shall enter an award within fifteen (15) calendar days following the hearing provided for herein. Nothing shall preclude either party from making an application to the arbitrator, for good cause, to expedite the proceedings, nor restrict the arbitrator from granting such an application. In addition to such other relief as the arbitrator may award, the arbitrator shall be vested with jurisdiction and shall award to the prevailing party its reasonable attorney's fees and expenses, and all other costs associated with the arbitration. The award rendered by the arbitrator shall be final, and judgment may be entered upon it in accordance with applicable law in any court having jurisdiction thereof.

21. Choice of Law.

Any disputes arising under the Agreement outside the purview of section 20 will be governed by New York law and settled by a court situated in the county of New York, New York, without reference to conflict of law principles, and the parties hereby consent to the exclusive jurisdiction of the federal courts located in New York County, New York therefor.

22. Survival.

Sections _______, and any accrued payment obligations and, except as otherwise expressly provided herein, any right of action for breach of this Agreement prior to termination shall survive any termination of this Agreement. Furthermore, upon termination or expiration of this Agreement, the licenses and obligations hereunder shall immediately cease.

23. Complete Agreement.

This Agreement (including any exhibits that may be attached with the written consent of both parties) constitutes the entire agreement between the parties with respect to the subject matter hereof and supersedes all prior discussions, documents, agreements and prior course of dealing, and shall not be effective until signed by both parties.

Accepted and Agreed:

Gallery	Syndicate Client
By:______________________	By:______________________
[Name]	[Name]
Title:______________________	Title:______________________
Date______________________	Date______________________

Exhibit A

Affiliate Terms & Conditions

Syndicate Affiliates adopting any Presentation Materials shall agree substantially as follows:

1) The Links.

Presentation Materials. Syndicate Affiliate(s) shall use the Presentation Materials on the Syndicate Affiliate(s) Site, and agrees to display and maintain the same in good working order, and not to alter or modify them in any way without obtaining the prior written consent of Gallery. Upon written notice, Syndicate Affiliate(s) agrees to promptly remove any Presentation Materials on pages under its direct or indirect control that contain content judged by Gallery in its sole discretion to be objectionable or in other ways offensive in a manner that would negatively affect Gallery.

2) Trademark Licenses.

a) Gallery Marks. Gallery grants Syndicate Affiliate(s) the non-exclusive, non-transferable, non-sublicensable, revocable right to use the Presentation Materials during the term of the Syndicate Affiliate(s) Agreement for the sole purpose of generating sales on the Gallery Site.

i) Reservation of Rights. Gallery reserves all of its rights, and those of the other respective rights owners, in the Presentation Materials, and Syndicate Affiliate(s) claims no rights whatsoever in the same.

ii) Good Will. All good will attributed to the Gallery logo(s), tradename(s) and trademarks ("Gallery Marks") will inure to the benefit of Gallery exclusively.

3) Gallery Administration Policies.

a) Selection of Art. Gallery may change its selection of art their prices at any time in its sole good-faith discretion.

b) Refunds. Gallery may modify its customer refund policies at any time and for any reason and without prior notice to Syndicate Affiliate(s).

c) Customer Responsibility. Customers who purchase art through the Gallery Site will be deemed to be customers of Gallery for all purposes of information management and direct marketing, and will be subject to the Gallery rules, policies and operating procedures concerning customer orders, and customer service.

d) Customer Service. Gallery is responsible for all processing, fulfillment and customer service related to orders, and Syndicate Affiliate(s) shall neither have nor retain any responsibility for customers ordering through the Gallery Site, except as expressly set forth in the Agreement.

4) Site Maintenance.

Syndicate Affiliate(s) is solely responsible for the maintenance and operation of the Syndicate Affiliate(s) Site, and all programs, content and programming associated therewith, subject to the terms of the Agreement, including for the proper maintenance and display of the Presentation Materials, which shall not be modified in any way without the prior written consent of Gallery.

5) Termination.

Actions upon Termination. Upon termination or expiration of the use of the Presentation Materials, Syndicate Affiliate(s) shall immediately delete the same and all copies of thereof from the Syndicate Affiliate(s) Site, and all other media directly or indirectly under its control, or return them to Gallery (upon prior request of Gallery), and promptly affirm in a signed writing that it has so complied with the provisions of this subsection.

6) Warranties and Representations.

a) Syndicate Affiliate(s) Site. The Syndicate Affiliate(s) Site, the contents thereof, and the activity thereon or related directly thereto shall not infringe the rights of any third party.

b) Presentation Materials, Prices. Syndicate Affiliate(s) shall not modify, reproduce or distribute the Presentation Materials, or vary the authorized prices by implicitly or expressly offering discounts, premiums or any other incentives, but shall use best efforts to immediately adopt any modifications thereto upon the request of Gallery.

7) Choice of Law.

Any disputes arising under the Agreement will be governed by New York law and settled by a court situated in the county of New York, New York, without reference to conflict of law principles, and the parties hereby consent to the exclusive jurisdiction of the federal courts located in New York County, New York therefor.

FORM 9-25

Net.Art Download Agreement

IMPORTANT - READ CAREFULLY: You should carefully read the following terms and conditions before downloading this application. Unless you have a separate license agreement signed by Artist governing your use of this art product specifically YOUR DOWNLOADING AND/OR USE OF IT INDICATES YOUR ACCEPTANCE OF THE TERMS AND CONDITIONS OF THIS END USER LICENSE AGREEMENT AND WARRANTY.

This Artist ("Artist") End User License Agreement ("Agreement") is a legal agreement between you and the Artist. This Agreement accompanies the application known as ____, and the associated media (individually and collectively "Software" or "Software Product"). The terms "Software" and "Software Product" shall also include any related explanatory materials, upgrades, modified versions or updates of the Software licensed to you by the Artist. Please read this Agreement carefully. At the end, you will be asked to accept this agreement and continue to install or, if you do not agree to the terms of this Agreement, to decline this agreement, in which case you are not authorized to use the Software. BY INSTALLING, COPYING OR OTHERWISE USING THE SOFTWARE, YOU AGREE TO BE BOUND BY THE TERMS OF THIS AGREEMENT.

While Artist continues to own the Software, the Artist grants to you a nonexclusive license to use the Software, provided that you agree to the following:

1. Use of the Software.

The Artist grants to you the right to copy and use the Software on the hard disk or other storage device of as many personal computers as you own, but not over a network. If you are an entity, such as a corporation, and not an individual, you may use the Software on a network, provided that you have a licensed copy of the Software for each computer/workstation that can access the Software over that network and a separate Agreement for each individual who uses the Software. If your agent uses the Software on your behalf, you nonetheless agree to be bound by this Agreement as a principal, and your continued use of the Artist Software will ratify any unauthorized actions of your agent.

2. Restrictions. You agree not to:

(i) copy the documentation which accompanies the Software;

(ii) sublicense, rent or otherwise share for value any portion of the Software;

(iii) reverse engineer, decompile, disassemble, modify, translate, make any attempt to discover the source code of the Software, or create derivative works from the Software;

(iv) remove any copyright notices on the Software; or

(v) distribute copies of the Software to third parties.

3. Copyright and Trademark Rights. All rights, title and copyrights in and to the Software is owned by the Artist, and its structure, organization and code are the valuable trade secrets of the Artist. The Software also is protected by United States Copyright Law and International Treaty provisions. This Agreement does not grant you any intellectual property rights in the Software. The Software is licensed, not sold.

4. No Warranty. THE SOFTWARE IS BEING DELIVERED TO YOU 'AS IS'. BECAUSE OF THE VARIOUS HARDWARE AND SOFTWARE ENVIRONMENTS INTO WHICH THE SOFTWARE MAY BE INSTALLED, NO WARRANTY OF FITNESS FOR A PARTICULAR PURPOSE IS OFFERED. TO THE MAXIMUM EXTENT PERMITTED BY APPLICABLE LAW, THE ARTIST HEREBY DISCLAIMS ALL WARRANTIES AND CONDITIONS, EITHER EXPRESS OR IMPLIED, INCLUDING, BUT NOT LIMITED TO, IMPLIED WARRANTIES OF MERCHANTABILITY, NONINFRINGEMENT OF THIRD PARTY RIGHTS, FITNESS FOR A PARTICULAR PURPOSE, TITLE, THE PERFORMANCE OR RESULTS YOU MAY OBTAIN BY USING THE SOFTWARE AND/OR DOCUMENTATION. SOME STATES OR JURISDICTIONS DO NOT ALLOW THE EXCLUSION OF IMPLIED WARRANTIES OR LIMITATIONS ON HOW LONG AN IMPLIED WARRANTY MAY LAST, SO THE ABOVE LIMITATIONS MAY NOT APPLY TO YOU. GOOD DATA PROCESSING PROCEDURE DICTATES THAT ANY PROGRAM BE THOROUGHLY TESTED WITH NON-CRITICAL DATA BEFORE RELYING ON IT. THE USERS MUST ASSUME THE ENTIRE RISK OF USING THE PROGRAM.

5. No Liability. TO THE MAXIMUM EXTENT PERMITTED BY APPLICABLE LAW, IN NO EVENT SHALL THE ARTIST BE LIABLE FOR ANY SPECIAL, SIMILAR, INCIDENTAL, PUNITIVE, INDIRECT OR CONSEQUENTIAL DAMAGES WHATSOEVER (INCLUDING, WITHOUT LIMITATION, DAMAGES FOR LOSS OF PROFITS, LOSS OF SAVINGS, BUSINESS INTERRUPTION, CORRUPTION OF FILES, LOSS OF BUSINESS INFORMATION, LOSS OF DATA, OR ANY OTHER PECUNIARY LOSS) REGARDLESS OF CAUSE OR FORM OF ACTION, INCLUDING CONTRACT, TORT OR NEGLIGENCE, ARISING OUT OF THE USE OF OR INABILITY TO USE THE SOFTWARE PRODUCT, EVEN IF THE ARTIST HAS BEEN ADVISED OF THE POSSIBILITY OF SUCH DAMAGES. BECAUSE SOME STATES

AND JURISDICTIONS DO NOT ALLOW THE EXCLUSION OR LIMITATION OF LIABILITY OF CONSEQUENTIAL OR INCIDENTAL DAMAGES, THE ABOVE LIMITATION MAY NOT APPLY TO YOU. GOOD DATA PROCESSING PROCEDURE DICTATES THAT ANY PROGRAM BE THOROUGHLY TESTED WITH NON-CRITICAL DATA BEFORE RELYING ON IT. THE USER MUST ASSUME THE ENTIRE RISK OF USING THE PROGRAM.

6. Limitation of Liability. THE ARTIST'S ENTIRE LIABILITY AND YOUR EXCLUSIVE REMEDY UNDER THIS AGREEMENT SHALL NOT EXCEED ONE DOLLAR (US $1.00).

7. Governing Law and General Provisions. This Agreement will be governed by the laws of the State of New York, U.S.A., excluding the application of its conflicts of law rules. This Agreement will not be governed by the United Nations Convention on Contracts for the International Sale of Goods, the application of which is expressly excluded. You and the Artist agree to submit to the personal and exclusive jurisdiction of the courts located within the county of New York, New York for any disputes arising out of this Agreement or your use of the Software. If any part of this Agreement is found void and unenforceable, it will not affect the validity of the balance of the Agreement, which shall remain valid and enforceable according to its terms. You agree that the Software will not be shipped, transferred or exported into any country or used in any manner prohibited by the United States Export Administration Act or any other export laws, restrictions or regulations. The failure of the Artist to exercise or enforce any right or provision of the Agreement does not constitute a waiver of such right or provision. If a court of competent jurisdiction finds any provision of the terms of the Agreement to be invalid, the parties nevertheless agree that the court should endeavor to give effect to the parties' intentions as reflected in the provision, and the other provisions of the Agreement remain in full force and effect. This Agreement shall automatically terminate upon failure by you to comply with its terms and/or notice of termination by the Artist. This Agreement may only be modified in writing signed by an authorized officer of the Artist that specifically references this agreement.

Copyright (c) 2000 The Artist. All rights reserved

FORM 9-26

Net.Art Hosting and Sales Agreement

1. General Information

The ArtCo. NetArchive (the "NetArchive") is an online archive of net-based art projects. The NetArchive is assembled and maintained by ArtCo., Inc. ("Company"). Company intends the NetArchive to be used as resource for curators, critics, artists and others who are interested in net-based art. As such, one of the main goals of the NetArchive project is to preserve net-based art projects that may be historically significant. This agreement sets out the terms and conditions by which you agree to provide the art project identified below ("your Art Project") for use in the NetArchive. If you agree to the terms and conditions set out herein, please fill in your Art Project's Title and current URL, and replace the words "Provider's Name" with your name, at the end of this agreement.

2. Company's Rights to Your Art Project

You grant Company the non-exclusive, worldwide, royalty-free right to reproduce, store, modify, distribute in digital form, perform and display your Art Project in connection with, or to promote, the NetArchive. You also agree that Company may use your name on the Company Website, or in connection with promoting the NetArchive.

Company reserves the right to make changes to your Art Project as may be necessary to promote, distribute or maintain the NetArchive, including for the purpose of adapting it to changing technologies, to index your Art Project within the NetArchive, to remove your Art Project from the NetArchive at any time or to discontinue the NetArchive. Company will consider your requests to modify or update your Art Project, but will not be required to make any such changes.

Company reserves the right to charge fees to third parties for access to the NetArchive, in which case Company will not owe you any royalties, commissions or other fees. Company will not, however, charge third parties fees specifically for access to your individual Art Project.

3. Representations; Disclaimer of Warranties; Limitation of Liability

You represent that the NetArchive does not infringe the intellectual property rights of any other person, that you have the rights to provide your Art Project to Company and that you are authorized to enter into this agreement. Neither Company nor its officers, directors, employees, agents, representatives, information providers or licensors ("Affiliates") represent or warrant that the NetArchive will be available or will be uninterrupted or error free, or that access to the NetArchive will be secure.

The NetArchive is provided on an "as is" basis without warranties of any kind, either express or implied, including but not limited to warranties of title or implied warranties of merchantability or fitness for a particular purpose. In no event shall Company or any of its Affiliates be liable for any direct, indirect, incidental, special or consequential damages arising out of the use of or inability to use the NetArchive or the presentation or availability of your Art Project.

4. Indemnification

You agree to defend, indemnify and hold harmless Company and its Affiliates from and against all claims and expenses (including attorneys' fees) arising out of your Art Project, including, but not limited to, any breach of any of your representations.

5. Termination

You may terminate this Agreement at any time upon sixty (60) days written notice to Company and, upon termination, Company will remove your Art Project from the NetArchive, as made available on line.

6. Survival

Section 4 shall survive termination of this Agreement.

7. Miscellaneous

This agreement constitutes the entire agreement between Company and you and may only be amended in writing by mutual agreement. No waiver by either party of any breach or default hereunder shall be deemed to be a waiver of any preceding or subsequent breach or default. This agreement shall be construed in accordance with the laws of the State of New York, without regard to its conflict of laws rules.

Project Title: ____

Current URL: ____

Signature: ____

Name: ____

FORM 9-27

Art E-Newsletter Subscription Agreement

1. General Information.

Art E-News is an e-mail service operated by ArtCo., Inc. ("ArtCo.") in connection with its Website located at http://www.___.org (the "ArtCo. Website"), and is dedicated to fostering communication and community in the field of new media art. To this end, it is critical that all subscribers to Art E-News be sensitive to the rights of others. Accordingly, each subscriber must agree to comply with all the terms and conditions in this agreement. IF THE TERMS OF THIS AGREEMENT ARE UNACCEPTABLE TO YOU, DO NOT CLICK ACCEPT.

Your right to use and receive Art E-News is personal to you and is not transferable. You are responsible for all postings contributed from your e-mail address by any person.

ArtCo. may modify these terms and conditions from time to time, and such modifications will be effective upon notice posted to Art E-News.

2. Subscriber Submissions

By sending or posting material to Art E-News you agree to grant ArtCo. the nonexclusive, worldwide, perpetual, royalty-free right to reproduce, modify, edit, publish, sub-license, make derivative works from and distribute such material in any form or media, including posting such material on Art E-News or the ArtCo. Website. ArtCo. reserves the right, in its sole discretion, to edit any subscriber posting, and to chose to include or not include such posting in Art E-News or the ArtCo. Website.

You must own all rights to any material that you submit to Art E-News or, if you have the right to post works copyrighted by another, you must include with your posting a statement describing where you obtained the work. In no event may you post to Art E-News any material protected by copyright without the permission of the copyright owner.

Although we encourage thoughtful criticism, you may not post any material that defames any person, invades their privacy, infringes their right of publicity, infringes their trademark or other rights, or which is otherwise unlawful.

3. No Commercial Use

Postings to Art E-News may not include any advertising or commercial solicitation. You may not distribute any material posted to Art E-News for any commercial purposes.

4. Permitted Use

The contents of Art E-News are copyrighted under United States copyright laws. You may download any of the postings from Art E-News for your own personal, non-commercial use, provided that you agree to abide by any copyright notice or other restriction contained in any individual posting and include any author attribution, copyright or trademark notice or restriction in any materials that you download.

5. Third-Party Art Works

Art E-News is an unfiltered, unmoderated and unedited mailing list consisting of contributions from subscribers. Subscriber postings are distributed automatically to all subscribers on the list, without any review or editing whatsoever by ArtCo. Certain content from Art E-News and other sources is compiled into a single weekly message. ArtCo. is not responsible for screening, monitoring or verifying the content of Art E-News, including with respect to such content's accuracy, reliability, or compliance with copyright and other laws. Without limiting the foregoing, ArtCo. reserves the right, but does not have the obligation, to monitor, edit and delete any material on Art E-News.

ArtCo. does not endorse any opinion, statement or other material posted on Art E-News. Any opinions, statements or other material expressed by third parties (including other subscribers) are those of the respective author(s) or distributor(s) and not of ArtCo.

6. Disclaimer of Warranty; Limitation of Liability

NEITHER ARTCO. NOR ITS EMPLOYEES, AGENTS, REPRESENTATIVES, INFORMATION PROVIDERS OR LICENSORS ("AFFILIATES") REPRESENT OR WARRANT THE ACCURACY, RELIABILITY, TIMELINESS OR COMPLETENESS OF ANY OPINION, STATEMENT OR OTHER MATERIAL POSTED ON ART E-NEWS OR THAT THE SAME IS NON-DEFAMATORY, NON-INFRINGING OF COPYRIGHT OR OTHER RIGHTS, OR OTHERWISE LAWFUL. YOU ACKNOWLEDGE THAT ANY RELIANCE ON OR USE OF SUCH OPINION, STATEMENT OR MATERIAL SHALL BE AT YOUR SOLE RISK.

NEITHER ARTCO. NOR ITS AFFILIATES WARRANT THAT ART E-NEWS WILL BE AVAILABLE ON A TIMELY BASIS, OR WILL BE UNINTERRUPTED OR ERROR FREE. ART E-NEWS IS PROVIDED ON AN "AS IS" BASIS WITHOUT WARRANTIES OF ANY KIND, EITHER EXPRESS OR IMPLIED, INCLUDING BUT NOT LIMITED TO WARRANTIES OF TITLE OR IMPLIED WARRANTIES OF MERCHANTABILITY OR FITNESS FOR A PARTICULAR PURPOSE.

IN NO EVENT SHALL ARTCO. OR ITS AFFILIATES BE LIABLE FOR ANY DIRECT, INDIRECT, INCIDENTAL, SPECIAL OR CONSEQUENTIAL DAMAGES ARISING OUT OF THE USE OF OR INABILITY TO USE ART E-NEWS.

7. Indemnification

You agree to defend, indemnify and hold harmless ArtCo. and its Affiliates from and against all claims and expenses (including attorneys' fees) arising out of any posting to Art E-News by you or anyone using your e-mail account or any breach by you of the terms of this agreement.

8. Right to Terminate Subscription

ArtCo. reserves the right to terminate your subscription to Art E-News at any time in the event that it considers, in its sole discretion, any conduct by you to be in violation of the terms of this agreement or otherwise in violation of the spirit of Art E-News.

9. Miscellaneous

This agreement constitutes the entire agreement of the parties with respect to such subject matter of this agreement. No waiver by either party of any breach or default hereunder shall be deemed to be a waiver of any preceding or subsequent breach or default. This agreement shall be construed in accordance with the laws of the State of New York, without regard to its conflict of laws rules.

Accepted and Agreed:

By: ______________________________

CHAPTER 10

AUTHENTICATION AND APPRAISAL OF ARTWORK

Steven Mark Levy

Forms and Appendices

§ 10.01 INTRODUCTION

Is it real? How much is it worth? In the world of art, no two questions come up as often, or lead to as many disputes. Forgeries and misattributions abound even as record prices in the tens of millions of dollars are paid for what are believed to be authentic artworks.

Until recently, *caveat emptor*—let the buyer beware—was the guiding principle with respect to issues of authenticity and value in the largely unregulated art market. Much of that has changed. The purpose of this chapter is to provide an overview of the growing body of law that now governs the authentication and appraisal of fine art.

The chapter begins with a discussion of authentication, authenticity, the authentication expert, and the *catalogue raisonné*. The next section concerns the appraisal expert, appraisal methods, and special rules for IRS valuations. The chapter concludes with an overview of the liability of the authenticator and appraiser, including a discussion of the most common theories of liability and affirmative defenses.

§ 10.02 AUTHENTICATION

[A] General Considerations

[1] Authentication Defined

To authenticate a work of art is to establish that it is what it claims to be. Authentication can concern the identity of the artist (a painting by Wassily Kandinsky), the place and period of origin (a Chinese vase from the Sung Dynasty), the artwork's connection to historical events (a gold disk belonging to a Spanish galleon sunk in 1622), or any other claimed attribute.

Authentication must be based on evidence, such as scientific testing, expert opinions (including connoisseurship), historical facts, documents, and chain of custody.

[a] Compare: Provenance

The provenance of an artwork is the "chain of ownership from the original artist to the present owner."[1] The art world considers it to be "persuasive evidence" of authenticity,[2] but the two are not synonymous. "Provenance supports the authenticity of a work, thereby enhancing its value."[3]

---

[1] Greenberg Gallery, Inc. v. Bauman, 817 F. Supp. 167, 173 (D.C. 1993) .

[2] *Id.*

[3] Peters v. Commissioner, 36 T.C.M. (CCH) 552 (1977).

The distinction between "authentication" and "provenance" is sometimes blurred by the courts. In one case the terms "certificate of authenticity" and "provenance" were used interchangeably.[4] In another case, a sale of a Picasso drawing was "conditional upon receipt of absolutely convincing provenance." The court defined this to mean "*proof* of authenticity."[5]

Provenance is only *evidence* of authenticity, and can be rebutted. Forged provenances supporting fake works of art are not uncommon in the art world.[6] In one recent incident, a con man named John Drewe used his charm and a $32,000 donation to gain access to the archives of the Tate Gallery in London. There he changed and fabricated the official records of provenance, using antique paper, period ink, and an old typewriter. He even forged a Tate Gallery stamp, which he used on the backs of documents. Unsuspecting experts later relied on the altered records to authenticate his fakes.[7]

In *Duchossois Industries Inc. v. Stelloh*,[8] involving an allegation of negligently prepared provenance, the parties disagreed over the meaning of "provenance." Plaintiff asserted that a provenance is routinely relied upon, and intended to be relied upon, to establish authorship. Defendant suggested that only through physical authentication can one be certain as to a painting's authorship. The court held that there was a triable issue of fact as to whether people in the trade rely on the provenance to establish the authorship.

Even when a provenance traces an artwork from the present owner back to the artist himself, and is supported by reliable records, it must be determined whether the subject artwork is the one referred to or a substitution.

[b] Compare: Appraisal

An appraisal is an informed opinion of the value of an artwork. Unlike authentication, an appraisal does not purport to confirm provenance or authenticity, although these are important factors.[9] An appraisal by itself is not a warranty of authenticity.[10]

---

[4] Jafari v. Wally Findlay Galleries, 741 F. Supp. 64, 65 (S.D.N.Y. 1990) .

[5] McCloud v. Lawrence Gallery, Ltd., 1991 U.S. Dist. LEXIS 9631 (S.D.N.Y. 1991) (emphasis added).

[6] *See* Greenberg Gallery, Inc. v. Bauman, 817 F. Supp. 167, 173 (D.C. 1993).

[7] Landesman, A 20th-Century Master Scam, N.Y. Times, July 18, 1999, sec. 6, at 31; Mosely, Genius Forgery Scheme Sends Shockwaves Through World of Art, Chicago Tribune, Feb. 16, 1999, at 1.

[8] 1988 U.S. Dist. LEXIS 178 (N.D. Ill. 1988).

[9] Foxley v. Sotheby's, Inc., 893 F. Supp. 1224, 1235 (S.D.N.Y. 1995).

[10] Rosen v. Spanierman, 894 F.2d 28 (2d Cir. 1990) .

The U.S. Tax Court frequently decides the value of donated artwork whose origins are in doubt while expressly declining to decide their authenticity.[11] Doubt about authenticity is subjectively factored into the value.[12]

Although an appraisal does not constitute an authentication, the fact remains that authenticity is the factor that largely determines the value of a work of art.[13] Probably for that reason, the Internal Revenue Service warns taxpayers that the authenticity of a donated painting or other art object "must" be determined by the taxpayer's appraiser.[14] Thus, for tax purposes, an appraisal submitted to the IRS constitutes a representation of authenticity.

[c] Compare: Commentary

A Sotheby's auction catalogue stated that a painting represented to be by Mary Cassatt would be accompanied by a copy of a letter "discussing" the work from Adelyn Dohme Breeskin, who was considered an authority on Cassatt. The court held that this statement did not constitute a representation that the Breeskin letter authenticated the painting.[15]

[2] Why Authenticity Matters

Occasionally a defendant is able to persuade the court that what matters most is the quality or aesthetic appeal of the particular work of art, not its authenticity. The plaintiff, so the argument goes, is as well off with a good fake as with a mediocre original, and should not complain.

In one case, plaintiffs paid $36,200 for Salvador Dali prints and wall sculptures that turned out to be counterfeit.[16] The court rejected the plaintiffs' claim against the seller for breach of the implied warranty of merchantability under UCC § 2-314, holding that "the ordinary purpose to which artwork is put is to be displayed for its aesthetic appeal." The court said that with respect to this ordinary use, "a counterfeit will have satisfied that purpose equally with an original."[17]

---

[11] *E.g.*, Peters v. Commissioner, 36 T.C.M. (CCH) 552 (1977) .

[12] *Id.*

[13] In re Donald S. Austin, 138 B.R. 898, 914 (N.D. Ill. 1992) ("Authentic lithographic prints by well-known artists such as Dali, Chagall, Miro and Picasso can be worth hundreds or thousands of dollars, while inauthentic reproductions of works by these artists may be worth no more than fifty dollars.").

[14] I.R.S. Pub. 561 Determining the Value of Donated Property 4 (1996).

[15] Foxley v. Sotheby's Inc., 893 F. Supp. 1224, 1229 (S.D.N.Y. 1995). Note that it seems that a representation of authenticity was implicit.

[16] Balog v. Center Art Gallery-Hawaii, Inc., 745 F. Supp. 1556, 1563 (D. Haw. 1990).

[17] *Id.* Plaintiffs fared better on their express warranty claim.

In another case the plaintiff purchased as a gift for her daughter a painting "guaranteed" to be by John Singer Sargent.[18] The plaintiff sued the seller for fraud, professional negligence, and other torts when the work turned out to be a fake. The court denied recovery, reasoning that a fake was as good as the original to the plaintiff:

> [Plaintiff] made a gift with no expectation of repayment. Thus, from a legal standpoint, [she] is in no worse position than if the painting had been authentic. She parted with $15,000 in exchange for the gratitude that accompanied a gift. She is no worse off if the painting is not an original.[19]

In most cases, however, the court has no trouble understanding that authenticity matters a great deal, affecting both market value and the buyer's natural desire to possess the real thing. It also matters because original artworks are like historical documents. They provide insights into artists and their times, and our cultural past. A forgery, no matter how aesthetically appealing, is by definition historically incorrect. It promises fact and delivers fiction.

[B] Seller's Representations of Authenticity

Many responsible dealers, auctioneers and private sellers stand behind the works they sell, and offer to refund the purchase price if the buyer discovers a problem with authenticity. Often, however, sellers impose time limits or other conditions. Moreover, some legitimate sellers, and most scam artists, refuse to make guarantees or to agree to rescind transactions. In those situations a disappointed buyer must look to his legal remedies under the Uniform Commercial Code (UCC), special state arts laws, or common law remedies such as fraud.

[1] Uniform Commercial Code

The sale of goods is governed by the Uniform Commercial Code. Artwork is considered "goods" within the meaning of the UCC.[20]

When artwork is sold, the seller often gives the buyer a bill of sale or invoice that specifically states that the artwork is authentic. This generally constitutes an express warranty under UCC § 2-313, which provides that "any affirmation of fact . . . made by the seller to the buyer which relates to the goods and becomes

---

[18] Rosen v. Spanierman, 894 F.2d 28 (2d Cir. 1990).

[19] *Id.* at 33-34. *See also* Harlingdon ua Leinster Enterprises Ltd. v. Christopher Hull Fine Art Ltd., 1 All E.R. 737 (C.A. 1989), which held that a painting is not unmerchantable simply because it is a forgery. "It could still have been hung on a wall somewhere and been enjoyed for what it was, albeit not for what it might have been."

[20] Firestone & Parson, Inc. v. Union League Club of Philadelphia, 672 F. Supp. 819 (E.D. Penn. 1987), *aff'd*, 833 F.2d 304 (3d Cir. 1987).

part of the basis of the bargain creates an express warranty that the goods shall conform to the affirmation."[21] Thus, for example, a bill of sale stating "that the painting is an authentic original oil painting by the renowned artist Francis Bacon" constitutes an express warranty.[22]

In some situations the buyer has knowledge at the time of purchase that the warranty of authenticity is not true. Does that knowledge bar him from recovery for breach of warranty? Not necessarily. According to the Second Circuit, if his knowledge comes from third parties, or if it is "common knowledge," he can still recover. "In these cases, it is not unrealistic to assume that the buyer purchased the seller's warranty 'as insurance against any future claims,' and that is why he insisted on the warranties in the bill of sale."[23] On the other hand, if his knowledge comes from the seller, he is foreclosed from asserting breach of warranty unless he expressly reserves his rights under the warranties, because "it cannot be said that the buyer . . . believed he was purchasing the seller's promise as to the truth of the warranties."[24]

If the seller's assurances as to authenticity lack specificity or are made in an equivocal manner, they will be deemed not to be a warranty but merely the seller's opinion, pursuant to UCC § 2-213(2).[25]

In addition to the express warranty in § 2-313, the UCC provides for implied warranties under §§ 2-314 (warranty of merchantability) and 2-315 (warranty of fitness for particular purpose). The cases are split as to whether these warranties apply to inauthentic artwork.

In *Balog v. Center Art Gallery-Hawaii, Inc.*,[26] the court said that the warranty of merchantability does not apply to lithographs and wall sculptures purportedly by Salvador Dali because "the ordinary purpose to which an artwork is put is to be displayed for its aesthetic appeal" and because "a counterfeit will have satisfied that purpose equally with an original."[27] It also held that the warranty of fitness for a particular purpose does not apply, because artwork is never created for a particular purpose, only for the ordinary purposes of investment or display.[28]

In *McKie v. R.H. Love Galleries, Inc.*,[29] on the other hand, the court allowed plaintiffs to proceed with the breach-of-implied-warranty claims against the defen-

---

[21] U.C.C. § 2-313(1)(a).

[22] *See* Rogath v. Siebenmann, 941 F. Supp. 416, 420-22 (S.D.N.Y. 1996).

[23] Rogath v. Siebenmann, 129 F.3d 261, 264-65 (2d Cir. 1997).

[24] *Id.*

[25] Keith v. Buchanan, 173 Cal. App. 3d 13, 21-22, 200 Cal. Rptr. 392 (1985). Under § 2-313(2), "an affirmation merely of the value of the goods or a statement purporting to be merely the seller's opinion or commendation of the goods does not create a warranty."

[26] 745 F. Supp. 1556 (D. Haw. 1990).

[27] *Id.* at 1563.

[28] *Id.*

[29] 1990 U.S. Dist. LEXIS 14748 (N.D. Ill. 1990).

dant art gallery with respect to an oil painting by William Merritt Chase that did not conform to the affirmations in the defendant's Authentication and Appraisal Report. The court held that if the painting could not pass muster under the Report, it was unmerchantable. Furthermore, a claim for breach of the warranty for a particular purpose was supported by the plaintiffs' allegation that at the time of purchase they informed the defendant of their interest in acquiring "high quality works of art with excellent potential for price appreciation."

[2] State Statutes Governing Dealer Representations

Some states have enacted special arts laws that govern an art dealer's representations of authenticity. For example, an arts law statute in New York provides:

> Whenever an arts merchant, in selling or exchanging a work of fine art, furnishes to a buyer of such work who is not an art merchant a certificate of authenticity or any similar instrument it: (a) shall be presumed to be part of the basis of the bargain; and (b) shall create an express warranty for the material facts stated as of the date of such sale or exchange.[30]

This statute eliminates any argument by the defendant that his representations as to authenticity were merely expressions of opinion and not a warranty.[31]

As for whether the warranty has been breached, it is not enough to show that the item in question is not authentic. Rather, the standard to be applied is whether the defendant's representations "can be said to have had a reasonable basis in fact, at the time that these representations were made, with the question of whether there was such a reasonable basis in fact being measured by the expert testimony provided at trial."[32]

Michigan has a similar statute, which provides:

> When an art merchant, in selling or exchanging a work of fine art, furnishes to a buyer of such work who is not an art merchant, a written instrument which, in describing the work, identifies it with any author or authorship, the description shall be presumed to be part of the basis of the bargain and shall create an express warranty of the authenticity of the authorship . . . .[33]

However, under the Michigan statute, if the warranty was made in "good faith," the purchaser may not recover consequential damages but is limited to recovery of the purchase price.[34]

---

[30] N.Y. Arts & Cult. Aff. Law § 13.01(1) (McKinney Supp. 1995).

[31] Dawson v. G. Malina, Inc., 463 F. Supp. 461, 465 (S.D.N.Y. 1978).

[32] *Id.* at 467.

[33] Michigan Warranty in Fine Arts Statute, Mich. Comp. Laws Ann. § 442.322(a).

[34] Mich. Comp. Laws Ann. § 442.324(3); Lawson v. London Arts Group, 708 F.2d 226 (6th Cir. 1983).

Similar statutes have been enacted in Florida[35] and Iowa.[36]

[3] Disclaimers

The seller of artwork often includes in the bill of sale or other sales document a written disclaimer with respect to authenticity. Whether or not the disclaimer is valid highly depends on the facts of the particular case.

Generally speaking, if the seller gives a warranty of authenticity that is part of the basis of the bargain, and also includes a general disclaimer of warranty liability, the warranty prevails over the disclaimer where the two cannot be reasonably reconciled.[37]

With respect to implied warranties (to the extent, if any, they even apply to authenticity),[38] they may be excluded "only by conspicuous language or other circumstances which protect the buyer from surprise."[39]

In *Weisz v. Parke-Bernet Galleries, Inc.*,[40] the trial court, in reasoning that was rejected on appeal, held that the following disclaimer in the auction catalogue, which at least one plaintiff was aware of, did *not* absolve the defendant auctioneer from liability for selling paintings that turned out to be forgeries:

> The Galleries has [sic] endeavored to catalogue and describe the property correctly, but all property is sold "as is" and neither the Galleries nor its consign [sic] warrants or represents, and they shall in no event be responsible for, the correctness of description, genuineness, authorship, provenance or condition of the property, and no statement contained in the catalogue or made orally at the sale or elsewhere shall be deemed to be such a warranty or representation, or an assumption of liability.

The court pointed out that the disclaimer was not given special prominence and that the rest of the catalogue "was clearly designed to emphasize the genuineness of the works to be offered." Moreover, the very fact that an exceedingly well-known gallery like Parke-Bernet was offering an artwork was enough to

---

35 Fla. Stat. Ann. § 686.504.

36 Iowa Code Ann. §§ 715B.2-4.

37 *See* Consolidated Data Terminals v. Applied Digital Data Systems, Inc., 708 F.2d 385, 391 (9th Cir. 1983) (applying New York law); Hauter v. Zogarts, 14 Cal. 3d 104, 119, 120 Cal. Rptr. 681 (1975) (disclaimer gives way to express warranty unless clear agreement between the parties dictates contrary intention).

38 *See* text *supra* at notes 26-29.

39 U.C.C. § 2-316, official comment 1.

40 67 Misc. 2d 1077, 325 N.Y.S. 2d 576 (1971), *rev'd*, 77 Misc. 2d 80., 351 N.Y.S. 2d 911 (1974).

"inspire confidence that it was genuine and that the listed artist in fact was the creator of the work."[41]

In *Kelly v. Brooks*,[42] on the other hand, the court held that a very similar disclaimer *did* absolve an auctioneer from liability to the buyers for representations of authenticity of the paintings:

> All property is sold "AS IS", and neither State Line Auctions nor the Consignor(s) make any guarantees, warranties or representations, expressed or implied, with respect to property purchased, and in no event shall the seller nor the consignor be responsible for genuineness, nor deemed to have made any representation of genuineness, authorship, attribution, provenance, period, cultural, source, origin, or condition of the purchased property and no verbal statements made regarding this property either before or after the sale of the stated property, or in this bill of sale, or invoice or catalogue or advertisement or elsewhere shall be deemed such a guarantee of genuineness.[43]

The court emphasized that one of the buyers signed the disclaimer, and said that a reasonable purchaser would have investigated the paintings more thoroughly before purchasing them.[44]

[4] Consumer Statutes

Some jurisdictions have adopted special consumer statutes to provide buyers with protection from certain types of counterfeit or forged art.

For example, under California's Fine Arts Multiples Statue,[45] an art dealer who sells or consigns a fine art multiple must furnish to a purchaser or consignee a written certificate of authenticity containing certain details and descriptive information as prescribed by the statute. The term "multiples" includes prints, photographs, sculpture casts, collages, and similar objects produced in more than one copy and offered for sale for $100 or more exclusive of any frame. The statute provides that in certain situations the information conveyed creates an express warranty.

Somewhat similar statutes exist in New York,[46] Illinois,[47] Maryland,[48] and Hawaii.[49] To further illustrate what these statutes provide, Appendix 10-A reproduces a "Guide to the California Fine Art Multiples Act."

---

[41] *Id.*, 325 N.Y.S. 2d at 581.

[42] 1993 U.S. Dist. LEXIS 3385 (S.D.N.Y. 1993).

[43] *Id.*

[44] *Id.* In the words of the court: "Caveat emptor—particularly when so advised by the seller."

[45] Cal. Civ. Code §§ 1740-1745.5.

[46] N.Y. Arts & Cult. Aff. Law §§ 15.01 *et seq.* (McKinney 1984 and Supp. 1997).

[47] Ill. Rev. Stat. ch. 121-1/2, §§ 361-69.

[48] Ann. Code of Maryland, Commercial Law § 14-501 *et seq.*

[49] Haw. Rev. Stat. §§ 481F-1-481F-9.

A few states have criminal statutes prohibiting misrepresentations of the authenticity of American Indian arts and crafts that are offered for sale.[50]

At the federal level, the Indian Arts and Crafts Act of 1990[51] prohibits the "offering or displaying for sale or selling a good . . . in a manner that falsely suggests it is Indian produced, an Indian product, or the product of a particular Indian or Indian tribe or Indian arts and crafts organization . . . ."[52]

[C] The Authentication Expert

[1] Licensing and Regulation

Some 30 years ago a court said of art authenticators:

> We know of no governmental control of this profession, or requirement that a diploma or other authorization from any seat of learning must . . . [be] held.[53]

That is as true today as it was then. Unlike other professions, such as law, medicine, and even cosmetology, "art expert(ise)" entails no licensing, regulations, or minimum requirements whatsoever. If a person claims to be an art expert, and can find a court or client to believe him, that makes him one. Of course, whether he is a good expert or a bad one depends on his knowledge, experience, study, and cleverness in applying what he has learned.[54]

[2] Qualifications

The usual qualifications to authenticate art include a degree in art history, museology, or art science; job experience as an art dealer, museum curator, auctioneer, or art professor; publications; membership in professional organizations; and prior authentication experience in the relevant area. Depending on the circumstances, however, almost anyone can be called upon to assist in authenticating art.

In one case,[55] involving the authenticity of two purportedly antique Asian Indian sandstone sculptures, the experts included:

- two experts in antique Asian arts and stylistic analysis
- an expert in conservation science, a technique that analyzes an artifact's

---

[50] *See, e.g.*, Ariz. Rev. Stat. Ann. § 44-1231.01; Colo. Rev. Stat. Ann. §§ 12-44.5-101 *et seq.*; Okla. Stat. Ann. tit. 78, §§ 71-75.

[51] 25 U.S.C. § 305e.

[52] *See* Ho-Chunk Nation v. Nature's Gifts, Inc., 1999 U.S. Dist. LEXIS 3687 (N.D. Ill. 1999).

[53] Porcella v. Time, Inc., 300 F.2d 162, 166 (7th Cir. 1962).

[54] Hahn v. Duveen, 133 Misc. 871, 875, 234 N.Y.S. 185, 190 (1929).

[55] Pritzker v. Krishna Gallery, 1995 U.S. Dist. LEXIS 8778 (N.D. Ill. 1995).

weathering and accretions to determine whether they are consistent with the object's attributed age

- an expert in the iconometric rules and proportional systems employed by ancient Indian sculptors
- an expert in geology, geophysics and radiocarbon dating, who employed techniques of radiocarbon dating and microscopic analysis to date the sculptures
- an expert in geology, hydrology and petrographic analysis

Opinion testimony from a lay witness was held admissible to prove the authenticity of Salvador Dali's signature on artwork because the witness, although not a handwriting expert, had been a longtime associate of Dali and was familiar with Dali's signature.[56]

The general test regarding the admissibility of expert testimony in a court of law is whether the jury can receive "appreciable help" from such testimony.[57] The trial court has broad discretion to admit or exclude expert testimony,[58] subject to its "gatekeeping" obligation to ensure that the testimony "both rests on a reliable foundation and is relevant to the task at hand."[59]

Not all experts qualify under the above standards. For example, in an unpublished case having to do with whether certain sculptures qualified as "original" Salvador Dali art, the Ninth Circuit held that a Dali archivist who was an expert in Dali prints was properly excluded as an expert at trial because he had not concentrated on Dali's sculpture.[60]

It would seem logical that the artist himself, if he is alive and not blind, is the most qualified expert on authenticity. According to an affidavit by André Emmerich, who was twice president of the Art Dealers Association of America and a prominent art dealer himself, it is "self evident [that] the artist is the definitive expert on what is his/her own work. When a living artist repudiates a work as a forgery or a fake, the work becomes unmerchantable and unsaleable."[61]

---

[56] United States v. Wiseman, 1993 U.S. App. LEXIS 8787 (9th Cir. 1993).

[57] United States v. Gwaltney, 790 F.2d 1378, 1381 (9th Cir. 1986), *cert. denied*, 479 U.S. 1104 (1987).

[58] United States v. Aguon, 851 F.2d 1158, 1171 (9th Cir. 1988).

[59] Daubert v. Merrell Dow Pharmaceuticals, Inc., 509 U.S. 579, 597, 113 S. Ct. 2786, 2799, 125 L.Ed.2d 469 (1993) (scientific expert testimony); *and see* Kumho Tire Co., Ltd. v. Carmichael, 526 U.S. 137, 119 S. Ct. 1167 (1999) (*Daubert* gatekeeping obligation applies not only to testimony based on "scientific" knowledge but also to testimony based on "technical" and "other specialized" knowledge).

[60] United States v. Wiseman, 1993 U.S. App. LEXIS 8787 (9th Cir. 1993).

[61] Arnold Herstand & Co., Inc. v. Gallery, 211 A.D.2d 77, 78-79, 626 N.Y.S.2d 74, 75 (1995).

Like everyone else, however, artists sometimes forget or don't tell the truth. In the same case[62] the court held that there was a triable issue of fact regarding a drawing's authenticity despite a sworn affidavit by the artist himself, the renowned European artist Balthus, that the work was an obvious forgery. The artist's statement was inconsistent with his prior conduct and with the provenance of the work. Moreover, there was the suggestion that Balthus had a history of repudiating some of his artworks "to punish former lovers or dealers with which he has had disagreements."[63]

The next most logical person to authenticate an artwork would be the artist's dealer, especially if the dealer has had a longstanding, exclusive relationship with the artist, as is often the case.[64] Thus, for example, a court relied on the testimony of art dealer Ivan C. Karp to hold that an artwork was an authentic Andy Warhol because "Karp represented Warhol for many years throughout Warhol's career and was exceedingly familiar with the quality and characteristics of Warhol's artistic work."[65]

The dealer not only has the advantage of knowing the artist's work well, but he also has the sales records and other documents relating to provenance. On the other hand, the fact that he has an inventory of the artist's work, and perhaps even a financial interest in the item in question, could taint his opinions.

Art historians, museum curators, and college professors are often called upon to express opinions on authenticity. They are normally motivated not by any financial interest but by a scholarly interest to define correctly an artist's body of work,[66] and tend to be cautious in their attributions because their academic reputations are at stake.

[3] Authority Under *Droit Moral*

In France and other European countries, there exists a doctrine known as "moral rights," or *droit moral*, which provides an artist with certain protections

---

[62] *Id.*

[63] *Id.*, 626 N.Y.S.2d at 78. Equally troubling are the examples of artists such as Giorgio De Chirico who have forged their own works. Robert Rosenblum, De Chirico's Long American Shadow, 84 Art in America 7 (July 1996).

[64] *See, e.g.*, Greenberg Gallery, Inc. v. Bauman, 817 F. Supp. 167, 174 (D.C. 1993) ("the best way to determine the authenticity of an artist's work is to have it examined by someone who knows the artist's work well or by the artist's gallery dealer").

[65] Estate of Robert C. Scull v. Commissioner, 67 T.C.M. (CCH) 2953 (1994).

[66] Note that many of the largest museums do not allow their curators to consult on third-party works. Also note that even scholars can have financial conflicts of interest. Frederick Hartt, one of the world's leading Renaissance scholars, caused a controversy when he authenticated a plaster statue as a long-lost model by Michelangelo without revealing that he gave his opinion in exchange for a cash payment of 5% of the gross proceeds at an auction sale. *See* Hartt v. Newspaper Publishing P.L.C. and Others (LEXIS Enggen library, Cases file) (Q.B. Dec. 6, 1989).

with respect to his work. Those rights include, among others, the right to withdraw or disavow the work, and the right to paternity, that is, to have his name associated with the work. The rights are hereditary. When the artist dies, an heir or designee by will is given authority to assert them.[67]

The person who holds the *droit moral* for the artist will often claim the right to authenticate works attributed to the artist. For example, Marguerite Duthuit, the daughter of the great French painter Henri Matisse, issues certificates of authenticity for Matisse's works pursuant to the French law of *droit moral.*[68] She is said to be "the last word" on authenticity of works attributed to her father.[69] Similarly, Claude Laurens holds the *droit moral* for prominent French painter Georges Braque. When a question arose as to the authenticity of a Braque pastel sold by Christie's at auction, Christie's had the pastel flown to France for examination by Laurens or his son.[70] Their refusal to issue a certificate of authenticity allegedly made the work unsaleable.[71]

A somewhat similar right to claim or disclaim authorship is provided in the federal Visual Artists Rights Act[72] and in several state statutes,[73] although with the exception of the California statute the right belongs only to the artist and is not hereditary.

An opinion on authenticity by the person who holds the *droit moral* of an artist may carry tremendous weight in the art market, but neither the French law nor the U.S. statutes contain any provision making it conclusive on the trier of fact in any legal proceeding. As far as the law is concerned, the holder of the *droit moral* is just another expert whose opinion is only as good as his qualifications and the arguments he puts forward. Specific factors to be considered in assessing the validity of the *droit moral* holder's opinions include:

- whether the individual has the training, experience, and scholarship necessary to qualify as a legitimate expert in his own right
- whether the art community accepts the individual as an expert and relies on his opinions on authenticity
- whether the individual personally examined the artwork in question
- whether the individual has a financial conflict of interest[74]

---

[67] *See* §§ 1.04[B], 7.03[C][2].

[68] Findlay v. Duthuit, 86 A.D.2d 789, 446 N.Y.S.2d 951 (1982).

[69] *Id.*, 446 N.Y.S.2d at 952.

[70] Greenwood v. Koven, 880 F. Supp. 186 (S.D.N.Y. 1995).

[71] *Id.*

[72] 17 U.S.C. § 106A.

[73] *E.g.*, Cal. Civ. Code § 987; N.Y. Arts & Cult. Aff. Law § 14.03, art. 14-A.

[74] Findlay v. Duthuit, 86 A.D.2d 789, 791, 446 N.Y.S.2d 951, 954 (1982). In this case, the court noted that Duthuit was not only the holder of the *droit moral* for Henri Matisse but a major collector

- whether the individual is mentally and physically competent to authenticate works by the artist
- whether the individual's opinions are consistent with the opinions of other qualified experts and published works

[4] Authentication Committees

Sometimes committees or authentication boards are set up to authenticate the work of a particular artist. For example, a group of art experts and members of the artist's family formed the *Comite Picasso* to make a definitive assessment of the authenticity of works purportedly produced by Pablo Picasso.[75] Similarly, Jackson Pollock's widow Lee Krasner organized the Pollock-Krasner Authentication Board to authenticate Pollock's works.[76]

An authentication committee's refusal to authenticate a work can make the work unmarketable at the major auction houses and galleries. However, a committee's pronouncements have no conclusive legal force or effect. Like other experts, the opinions are only as good as the qualifications, experience and reasoning of their members.

Authentication committees tend to come and go, which makes them less accountable than other experts. The *Comite Picasso* broke up when Picasso's daughter Maya refused to participate any longer.[77] The Pollock-Krasner Authentication Board dissolved because of lawsuits claiming antitrust violations.[78] The lawsuits were eventually dismissed, but the board incurred some $200,000 in legal fees and concluded that the risk of further lawsuits was too great.[79]

[5] Conflict of Interest

The fact that so much money can be at stake based on a given expert's attribution of a work of art makes it imperative that the expert avoid even the appearance of a financial conflict.

Some years ago the College Art Association of America promulgated the following ethical guideline, which still has relevance:

---

and seller of his works, which created a potential conflict of interest with respect to Matisse works sold by rival dealers.

[75] *See* McCloud v. Lawrence Gallery, Ltd., 1991 U.S. Dist. LEXIS 9631 (S.D.N.Y. 1991).

[76] *See* Kramer v. Pollock-Krasner Foundation, 890 F. Supp. 250 (S.D.N.Y. 1995).

[77] Grant, The Real Problems of Authenticating Modern Art, Pittsburgh Post-Gazette, May 23, 1999 at G-2.

[78] *See, e.g.*, Kramer v. Pollock-Krasner Foundation, 890 F. Supp. 250 (S.D.N.Y. 1995).

[79] Grant, *supra* note 77.

> Art historians, when consulted on such matters as scholarly attribution, can avoid the suggestion of self-interest by establishing in advance fees which bear no relation to the monetary value of any work of art in question and which do not otherwise relate to the monetary effect of any research, investigation, opinion or statement by the art historian.[80]

The mere fact that an expert owns a number of works by the same artist is not sufficient to show bias. "It is natural that one knowledgeable about a prolific modern artist would own that artist's work; to the extent that mere ownership is evidence of bias, virtually any modern art expert would be suspect."[81] On the other hand, if the expert not only owns the artwork, but sells it in the national or international arena in competition with other dealers and owners, a potential conflict of interest exists.[82]

[6] "Monopoly" Power

For each artist there is often a single expert or authentication board whose opinion on authenticity is considered by the art market to be the most authoritative. Their certificates of authentication, or refusal to issue them, can literally make or break artworks in terms of market value. One might say such experts or boards "monopolize" the market for such works. Can such a "monopoly" rise to the level of a Sherman Antitrust Act violation?

That question was answered in the affirmative in *Vitale v. Marlborough Gallery*.[83] Plaintiff owned a painting purportedly signed by Jackson Pollock. When she tried to sell it in New York, she was told by Parke-Bernet Gallery, Christie's Gallery, and 10 other galleries that they could not sell the painting for her without a letter of authentication from the Pollock-Krasner Authentication Board, despite the fact that other qualified experts were willing to authenticate the painting. The plaintiff brought an antitrust action against the board and others, alleging that the board's control of the process of authentication and sale of Pollock paintings constituted an unlawful restraint of trade in violation of the Sherman Antitrust Act.

Under the Act, a plaintiff must allege a relevant product market in which trade was unreasonably restrained or monopolized. The plaintiff alleged that the relevant market was the market for the sale of contemporary and modern paintings, and that Jackson Pollock paintings constitute a distinct and independent submarket. The court agreed, holding that Pollock paintings may constitute a submarket, the

---

[80] College Art Association of America, A Code of Ethics for Art Historians and Guidelines for the Professional Practice of Art History, Guidelines § 11(e) (1975).

[81] United States v. Burke, 718 F. Supp. 1130, 1138 (S.D.N.Y. 1989).

[82] Findlay v. Duthuit, 86 A.D.2d 789, 791, 446 N.Y.S.2d 951, 954 (1982).

[83] 1994 U.S. Dist. LEXIS 9006 (S.D.N.Y. 1994).

monopolization of which may be unlawful under the Act. Unfortunately for the plaintiff, the court found that the action was barred under the applicable statute of limitations.[84]

In *Kramer v. Pollock-Krasner Foundation*,[85] the plaintiff sued the authentication board and the two major New York auction houses, Christie's and Sotheby's, for antitrust violations after the auction houses refused to auction his purported Jackson Pollock painting without authentication by the board, which refused to authenticate it. The plaintiff contended that the relevant product market was the sale of paintings *at auction* by modern and contemporary artists, with a submarket for Pollock paintings. The court dismissed the lawsuit on the ground that Pollock works sold *at auction* did not constitute a valid submarket, because plaintiff could have sold his painting through dealers, galleries, or private sales.

[7] Selecting an Authentication Expert

Auction houses and art musuems are good sources of recommendations for authentication experts, although internal rules prevent many museum curators from doing the work themselves. The *Official Museum Directory*, published annually by the American Association of Museums, lists more than 8,000 museums in the United States and describes their areas of specialization. It is available at libraries or from the American Association of Museums, 1575 Eye Street, N.W., Suite 400, Washington, D.C. 20005; telephone, (202) 289-1818.

Another source is the International Foundation for Art Research (IFAR), 500 Fifth Avenue, Suite 1234, New York, N.Y. 10010; telephone, (212) 391-6234. This nonprofit, tax-exempt organization offers an artwork authentication service through its network of art historians and other scholars. For illustrative purposes only, a copy of IFAR's standard consultation agreement is included in Form 10-1.

[D] The Authentication Process

[1] Checklist of Common Techniques

The authentication process generally includes some or all of the following techniques. If a given technique is applicable to the work in question, but has not been used by the expert, he or she is open to impeachment.

- examining the work from a stylistic standpoint, also known as connoisseurship (The idea is for someone with expertise in the artist's work to compare the

[84] *Id.*

[85] 890 F. Supp. 250 (S.D.N.Y. 1995).

subject piece with known genuine works to see if they are consistent in terms of artistic quality, style, use of colors, subject matter, type of paint and canvas, brushstrokes and so on. The expert should be able to express clearly in words what his eye observes.)

- verifying the genuineness of the signature, if any (Keep in mind that the presence of a forged signature on a work does not necessarily mean that the work is not an original. Phony signatures are sometimes added to unsigned authentic works to increase their value or appeal.)
- reviewing the *catalogue raisonné* and other published books and articles for mention of the work
- searching sales records, correspondence, exhibition and auction catalogues, the artist's archives and other available documentation of the history of ownership or provenance (The courts consider provenance to be "a weighty consideration in the process of authentication,"[86] although care must be taken to ensure that the provenance has not been altered or forged.)
- scientific testing, when appropriate, to determine such things as the age and composition of the work; common tests include x-rays, ultraviolet and infrared light exams, and pigment analysis[87]
- eyewitness testimony from the artist, the artist's family or dealer, prior owners, or anyone else who professes to know the artwork in question
- weighing the probabilities of a forgery; for example, if the subject work is known to have existed at a given time when the artist's works were not fetching high prices, the odds are low that a forger was involved[88]
- weighing the probabilities of a copy; certain types of art, such as Chinese painting, have a tradition of legitimate contemporary copying that makes attribution difficult

[2] Reliance on Photographs

Many authentications are done on the basis of photographs alone, without inspecting the work itself. Except where the forgery is patently obvious, this is not a good practice, and can subject the expert to possible malpractice liability.

---

[86] Arnold Herstand & Co., Inc. v. Gallery, 211 A.D.2d 77, 80, 626 N.Y.S.2d 74, 76 (1995).

[87] Horgan, But it is Art, Scientific American, October 1987, at 48, 52. Care must be taken to ensure not only that the tests are done properly, but that the results are interpreted correctly. In one instance, an expert concluded that an early eighteenth-century American painting was a fake, based on laboratory tests showing the presence of a modern pigment, zinc white. It was later discovered that the painting merely had been retouched.

[88] *See* Arnold Herstand & Co., Inc., v. Gallery, 211 A.D.2d 77, 80, 626 N.Y.S.2d 74, 76 (1995).

Three-dimensional artworks are especially difficult to authenticate based on photographs alone. In one case, the question was whether a certain mobile was the original long-lost work entitled "Rio Nero" by Alexander Calder.[89] The plaintiff's expert compared the subject mobile with a photograph of the "Rio Nero" taken 23 years earlier, and concluded it was not authentic because the blades were not identical. The court held that this testimony was insufficient to carry the plaintiff's burden of proof, "given the distortions all experts conceded are involved in photographing Calder mobiles, as well as the inherent difficulties involved in comparing a two-dimensional photograph to a three-dimensional moving piece."[90]

[3] Risks of Entrusting Artwork to the Expert

Inspection of the artwork usually requires shipping it to the expert, who may be in Paris, New York, or some other distant location. Apart from the risk that the artwork may be damaged or lost in transit, there is also the risk that the expert will not send it back.

If you send the artwork to Paris for authentication by the holder of the artist's *droit moral*, and he concludes (rightly or wrongly) that it is a fake, he will likely summon the local police superintendent to seize the artwork and deposit it with the clerk of the court. He will then ask the court to rule that it is a counterfeit, and to order that it be destroyed and costs assessed against the owner.[91] The owner, if he hopes to get the artwork back or ever plans to show his passport in France someday, must hire local counsel and his own experts at great expense to attempt to establish authenticity and to oppose the assessment of costs.

Bringing the artwork to an expert in New York also entails some risk. In one case, the owner of a painting purportedly signed by Jackson Pollock brought it to Pollock's widow for authentication, and left it overnight. Upon arriving the following day, the owner was met by three men from the Manhattan District Attorney's Office, who questioned her and then confiscated the painting as evidence in an ongoing art forgery case. It took the owner five-and-a-half years to get it back.[92]

Another risk is the entrustment doctrine. Under UCC § 2-403, an owner who entrusts artwork to a dealer, for authentication or for any other purpose, gives him the power to transfer the artwork to a buyer in the ordinary course of

---

[89] Greenberg Gallery, Inc. v. Bauman, 817 F. Supp. 167 (D.D.C. 1993).

[90] *Id.*, 817 F. Supp. at 174. *See also* Sammons v. Commissioner, 838 F.2d 330 (9th Cir. 1988) (authenticity of Indian artifacts could not be determined based on photographs).

[91] Unlike in the United States, where fake works are allowed to circulate again and again like proverbial bad coins, France considers a fake artwork to be a serious infringement of the moral rights of the artist or his beneficiaries, justifying confiscation and destruction. *See* Articles L21-1 and L 335-7 du Code de la Propriété Intellectuelle and Article 1382 du Code Civil.

[92] Vitale v. Marlborough Gallery, 1994 U.S. Dist. LEXIS 9006 (S.D.N.Y. 1994).

business. Such a buyer in the ordinary course will prevail over the claim of the party who entrusted the artwork.[93]

[E] The *Catalogue Raisonné*

A *catalogue raisonné* is an annotated, illustrated book of a particular artist's works usually prepared by art historians, scholars or dealers. The intent is to be definitive and all-inclusive. Thus, inclusion of an artwork in a *catalogue raisonné* is evidence of authenticity, while non-inclusion suggests that the work is not genuine.[94]

An example of a *catalogue raisonné* is the one recently published on Dutch abstract painter Piet Mondrian: two fat volumes, 1,151 pages, weighing over 20 pounds, listing 1,280 works, and selling for $250. Written by two art historians, it required more than 30 years of tedious research.[95]

Catalogues are intended to be definitive, but subsequent scholarship or new technology may reveal that certain works should or should not have been included. Nevertheless, the inclusion of an artwork in an authoritative catalogue by itself is sufficient evidence of authenticity to establish a triable issue of material fact in a case challenging authenticity.[96] Moreover, while a catalogue constitutes hearsay, it is admissible in evidence to the extent that it falls into the learned treatise hearsay exception under Federal Rule of Evidence 803(18). To qualify under the exception, an expert witness must be called to testify as to the authoritativeness of the catalogue.[97]

A catalogue prepared by a dealer may be viewed with skepticism because of a perceived conflict of interest and lack of objectivity. After all, some of the works on which he is passing judgment are in his own inventory for sale, and others are owned by rival dealers. On the other hand, few people are more knowledgeable about an artist's work than the dealer, and the dealer often has sales records and access to the artist's own archival papers.

Catalogues prepared by friends, heirs, or relatives of the artist who are not also experts may be unreliable.

---

[93] *See, e.g.*, Deweldon, Ltd. v. McKean, 125 F.3d 24, 26-27 (1st Cir. 1997). If the buyer is another art dealer, he may be required to show that he took reasonable steps to investigate the provenance of the artwork, in accordance with commercial standards, in order to qualify for the protection of § 2-403. Graffman v. Espel, 1998 U.S. Dist. LEXIS 1339 (S.D.N.Y. 1998).

[94] Kirby v. Wildenstein, 784 F. Supp. 1112, 1113 (S.D.N.Y. 1992).

[95] Blotkamp, Review of Piet Mondrian Catalogue Raisonné, Art in America, May 1, 1999, at 41.

[96] Pilliard v. Sotheby's, Inc., 1997 U.S. Dist. LEXIS 9725 (S.D.N.Y. 1997) (wooden jar purportedly sculpted by the artist Paul Gauguin).

[97] *Id.*

Another potential problem is the anxious collector who, having spent thousands or even millions of dollars on a painting, may offer money or other inducements to the author of the catalogue to ensure a favorable ruling on the artwork.

A party's failure to consult the *catalogue raisonné* can constitute negligence or lack of diligence. In one case, the question was whether a plaintiff claiming ownership of a stolen Claude Monet painting had used due diligence in locating the painting in order to postpone the running of the statute of limitations in her suit against a good-faith purchaser. In holding that she had not, the court stated that plaintiff's failure to consult the *catalogue raisonné* "is particularly inexcusable." The catalogue listed the painting and contained a provenance that easily could be used to identify the current owner.[98]

In recent years, the scholarly authors of learned catalogues have come in for a rude shock in the form of lawsuits. The claims have included product disparagement, violation of the Lanham Act,[99] unauthorized publication, unjust enrichment, interference with advantageous business relationships, and others. The defendants tend to win these lawsuits, but only after expending much time and money.

In one case, the plaintiff owned a painting by the nineteenth-century French artist Jean Beraud which was to be listed in the forthcoming *catalogue raisonné* as authentic but described as damaged by "an abusive restoration and cleaning."[100] The painting failed to sell at a Christie's auction. The plaintiff sued the Foundation Wildenstein, under whose auspices the catalogue was being prepared, for product disparagement. The plaintiff's facts were not strong, and the court entered summary judgment against him for lack of evidence of causation and special damages.

In another case, the Yale University Press published a *catalogue raisonné* on Jackson Pollock that categorized as a forgery a painting owned by the plaintiff[101] Unable to sell the painting, the plaintiff sued the persons who supplied the allegedly false information in the catalogue concerning her painting, alleging violation of the Lanham Act and various state law claims. The court held that her Lanham Act claim was barred by the statute of limitations and declined to exercise jurisdiction over the remaining state law claims. However, the court refused to impose Rule 11 sanctions on the plaintiff or her attorney, holding that the claims were not frivolous.

---

[98] DeWeerth v. Baldinger, 836 F.2d 103, 112 (2d Cir. 1987) (decided under New York law). Note that the New York Court of Appeals rejected the due diligence requirement with respect to the running of the statute of limitations in actions for repossession of lost or stolen art, although there remains a laches defense against nondiligent plaintiffs. *See* Solomon R. Guggenheim Foundation v. Lubell, 567 N.Y.S.2d 623, 569 N.E.2d 426 (1991).

[99] 15 U.S.C. § 1125(a) (false designation of origin or false description or advertisement).

[100] Kirby v. Wildenstein, 784 F. Supp. 1112 (S.D.N.Y. 1992).

[101] Vitale v. Marlborough Gallery, 1994 U.S. Dist. LEXIS 9006 (S.D.N.Y. 1994).

To help protect against lawsuits, many catalogue authors now require art owners who submit a work for possible inclusion in the catalogue to sign a release agreement. As an illustration, Form 10-2 contains a copy of the "Release, Waiver and Indemnity Agreement" that the Mary Cassatt *Catalogue Raisonné* Committee requires from every owner.

Another prudent measure is to include in the catalogue a disclaimer of responsibility for decisions with respect to authenticity. Sample disclaimer language is attached in Form 10-3.

[F] Effect of a Judicial Authenticity Ruling

The fact that an artwork has been adjudicated in a court of law as being authentic or inauthentic is conclusive only with regard to the parties to the lawsuit. It does not constitute a definitive pronouncement on authenticity binding on the art market at large or on future generations, because in a court of law, the trier of fact must make a decision based upon a preponderance of the evidence, and can consider only such evidence as the parties choose (or can afford) to offer.

"Preponderance of the evidence" does not mean absolute or mathematical certainty.[102] It does not even mean that the fact finder's conclusion must be the only one that logically can be reached.[103] All it means is that the evidence on one side has more convincing force than that opposed to it.[104] If the evidence is evenly balanced, the issue must be decided against the party who had the burden of proving it (usually the plaintiff).[105] Thus, a court could rule that a painting is not authentic even if the evidence is equally strong that it is a genuine original.

In addition, lawsuits are often decided on extraneous factors, such as sympathy for one side or the other, or a disparity in the lawyers' trial skills or personal charm. If a judicial finding on authenticity were binding on the art market, a great work of art could be lost to posterity simply because juror number five had a crush on one of the lawyers.

As a practical matter, of course, a judicial decision unfavorable to the artwork can cast a dark cloud over it that can last for years. In fact, even a ruling *favorable* to the artwork can do irreparable damage, as happened in *Greenberg Gallery, Inc. v. Bauman*.[106] The plaintiffs claimed that a mobile for which they paid $500,000 was not a genuine Alexander Calder. To support their position, they retained one of the world's leading experts on Calder, Klaus Perls, to testify that the mobile

---

[102] Standard Civil Jury Instruction No. 2-8 (burden of proof), quoted in The Greenberg Gallery, Inc. v. Bauman, 817 F. Supp. 167 (D.D.C. 1993).

[103] Kridler v. Ford Motor Co., 422 F.2d 1182, 1884 (3d Cir. 1970).

[104] Cal. Jury Inst. Civ., BAJI No. 2.60 (8th ed. 1994).

[105] *Id.*

[106] 817 F. Supp. 167 (D.D.C. 1993).

was an extremely good forgery. The court concluded that it was authentic. Not only were the plaintiffs stuck with the mobile and a huge legal bill, they suffered as victims of their own expert's testimony, which the defendant's expert said would render the "authentic" mobile unmarketable.[107]

In light of such risks, it is not surprising that most disputes over authenticity are settled quietly out of court and kept highly confidential.

§ 10.03 APPRAISAL

[A] General Considerations

[1] "Appraisal" Defined

The term "appraisal" has no specific legal definition. An appraisal is merely someone's opinion or estimate as to the monetary value of an item of property. It can range from an informal oral opinion, with little or no supporting research or data, to a detailed written report prepared by a highly experienced valuation expert and based on extensive research.

Notwithstanding the lack of a legal definition, a proper appraisal of artwork generally means:

1. A signed written report
2. regarding a clearly identified piece of art,
3. prepared by a person with the necessary training and experience
4. who is impartial and disinterested,
5. stating an opinion as to the market value
6. as of a given date, and
7. setting forth the facts and analysis supporting the opinion.

[2] Purpose of Appraising Artwork

The general purpose of appraising a work of art is to determine its value as of a particular time.[108]

The specific purpose of appraising a work of art is usually one of the following:

[107] *Id.* at 174 n.8.

[108] There are numerous types of value, including fair market value, defined as "the price at which the [artwork] would change hands between a willing buyer and a willing seller, neither being under any compulsion to buy or sell and both having reasonable knowledge of the relevant facts," (Section 1.170A-1(c)(2), Income Tax Regs), replacement value (used primarily in the insurance context), marketable cash value, and liquidation value.

- to determine a purchase or sales price
- for tax purposes (charitable deduction, gift tax, estate tax)
- for insurance purposes (premiums are usually set, and claims paid, based on replacement value)
- in the dissolution of a marriage
- to obtain a loan secured by the artwork
- to calculate damages in litigation or other contexts
- to establish jurisdictional minimums (for example, the National Stolen Property Act[109] criminalizes the trafficking in stolen property in interstate commerce valued at more than $5,000)
- to satisfy the curiosity of the owner

[3] Special Difficulties in Appraising Artwork

Original artwork is one of the most difficult things to value. Unlike fungible property, such as corporate stocks and pork bellies traded daily in organized markets at publicly disseminated prices, original works of art are unique, change hands only rarely and not always publicly, and are often the subject of debate as to their relative quality and value.[110]

Artwork is also difficult to appraise because the value often depends on external factors that are difficult to quantify. In one case, for example, the Tax Court found that the value and merit of various pieces of artwork had been enhanced by the sophisticated art dealer's expertise as a salesman.[111] Demand for the paintings collapsed when the dealer was sent to federal prison for tax fraud and could not be on hand to run the sales.

[4] Judicial Discretion on Questions of Value

Few courts relish the prospect of adjudicating the value of artwork. Settlement is always encouraged. As the U.S. Tax Court has said on more than one occasion:

> Too often in valuation disputes the parties have convinced themselves of the unalterable correctness of their positions and have consequently failed successfully to conclude settlement negotiations—a process clearly more conducive to the proper disposition of disputes such as this. The result is an overzealous effort, during the course of the ensuing litigation, to infuse a

---

[109] 18 U.S.C. §§ 2314-2315. *See* United States v. Tobin, 576 F.2d 687 (5th Cir. 1978) (stolen sculpture, although a fake, still valued by expert at more than $5,000).

[110] *See* Furstenberg v. United States, 219 Ct. Cl. 473, 595 F.2d 603, 605 (Ct. Cl. 1979).

[111] Andrew Crispo Gallery, Inc. v. Commissioner, 86 F.3d 42, 44 (2d Cir. 1996).

> talismanic precision into an issue which should frankly be recognized as inherently imprecise and capable of resolution only by a Solomon-like pronouncement.[112]

The valuation cases that do go to trial involve a battle of the experts. Each side's expert advocates a valuation formula that should be used, and testifies that the approach used by the other side's expert is incorrect.[113] The court is not bound to accept the experts' opinions. In weighing the persuasiveness and helpfulness of the expert testimony the court may adopt some portions and reject other portions. In some cases, it may reject both sides' valuations as defective and reach its own independent valuation determination.[114]

The court's discretion in determining value is very broad. Among the factors it considers are:

> "Whether the appraiser's experience and testimony entitle his opinion to more or less weight."
>
> "Whether an alleged comparable sale fairly approximates the subject property's market value."
>
> "The overall cogency of each expert's analysis."[115]

When each side presents equally persuasive (or unpersuasive) expert testimony, the court may split the difference between the two valuations. But don't count on it. In one case, for example, the value of a donated rock sculpture was put at $500,000 by the taxpayer's expert, and $30,000 by the expert for the IRS.[116] The court was not convinced of the correctness of either expert's valuation, but found the IRS's valuation to be more credible. Instead of picking a number somewhere in between, the court valued the sculpture at exactly $30,000.

[B] The Appraisal Expert

[1] Licensing and Regulation

The appraisal of artwork falls within the category of general personal property appraising.[117] Personal property appraising is not regulated by the federal or state

---

112 Doherty v. Commissioner, 63 T.C.M. (CCH) 2112 (1992), quoting from Messing v. Commissioner, 48 T.C. 502, 512 (1967).

113 Murphy v. Commissioner, 61 T.C.M. (CCH) 2935 (1991).

114 Estate of Robert C. Scull v. Commissioner, 67 T.C.M. (CCH) 2953 (1994).

115 Doherty v. Commissioner, 16 F.3d 338, 340 (9th Cir. 1994).

116 Murphy v. Commissioner, 61 T.C.M. (CCH) 2935 (1991).

117 The category also includes furniture, antiques, automobiles, jewelry, coins, stamps and carpets, among other things.

government and there are no licensing or certification requirements.[118] Anyone may call himself a personal property appraiser, whether he has had formal training or not. Thus, the burden is on the client to ascertain the appraiser's qualifications and suitability.

Real estate appraisers, by contrast, are generally licensed and certified by the state.[119]

[2] Qualifications and Objectivity

There are no particular qualifications required to appraise artwork. Completion of an appraisal studies program or an art history program is one way to enter the profession. Membership in one of the major appraisal organizations, and certification by the organization in one or more specialty areas, are common credentials. Teaching experience and published works relating to appraising are also a plus. On the negative side, one appraisal organization asks new applicants if they have ever been convicted of a felony related to business practices or ethics, or expelled from any professional organization.[120]

The main qualification is experience in the particular area of specialization, either as an appraiser or as someone, such as an art dealer or auctioneer, who makes daily aesthetic and economic judgments about works of art. From the client's standpoint, the more focused the specialization, the better. A specialty in "painting" is better than one in "art," and "contemporary American painting" is better than "painting." On the other hand, from the appraiser's standpoint, the economics of the appraisal business are such that he cannot afford to be too narrow in his focus. The wider the net he casts, the more potential clients he has.

The appraiser, of course, must be financially disinterested. His fee must not be based on a fixed percentage of the value of the item, or on the financial outcome from the use of the appraisal.[121] He should not have an ownership interest in the item appraised, or acquire one after the appraisal. One jury returned a fraud verdict against an appraiser who appraised a plaintiff's Civil War artifacts at $88,800, purchased them at that price after winning the plaintiff's trust, and then quietly resold them a few weeks later for $880,000.[122]

---

[118] However, the Appraisals Standards Board of the Appraisal Foundation (www.appraisalfoundation.org) promulgates a uniform code of practice entitled the Uniform Standards of Professional Appraisal Standards (USPAP). The three major trade associations all follow USPAP.

[119] *See, e.g.*, California Business and Professions Code §§ 11300 *et seq. See also* Title XI of the Financial Institutions Reform, Recovery and Enforcement Act of 1989, as amended (FIRREA), 12 U.S.C. 3331.

[120] International Society of Appraisers, Application for Membership (1999).

[121] *See* Code of Ethics, Appraisers Association of America (1999); Code of Ethics and Professional Conduct, International Society of Appraisers (1998). *See also*, Treas. Reg. § 1.70A-B(c)(6)(i).

[122] Pickett v. American Ordnance Preservation Association, 1999 U.S. Dist. LEXIS 13726 (E.D. Pa. 1999).

Another requirement is objectivity. Where the record indicates that the taxpayer and the taxpayer's expert are close friends and long time business associates, the expert's valuation must be "substantially discounted" despite his considerable experience as an art dealer and appraiser.[123] On the other hand, another court saw no lack of objectivity in a case where the valuation expert for the IRS in a lawsuit over the value of a donated painting had served on the particular Art Advisory Panel that had originally valued the painting for the IRS.[124] "There is no reason to assume that, because an expert has expressed an opinion during confidential deliberations of a particular panel and has heard the views of the other experts, he will give anything other than his best independent expert judgment if called as a witness on the question of valuation."[125]

The appraiser should never allow his personal feelings to interfere with his objectivity. In one case the issue was the fair market value of certain donated paintings by noted nineteenth-century African-American artists.[126] The taxpayer's expert "obviously [had] a wealth of knowledge of nineteenth-century black American art and artists. He has taught at numerous universities, served on advisory panels at several museums, and published extensively." Yet the court totally rejected his opinions. "We are concerned that his figures reflect his personal opinion of what the artworks should be worth when consideration is given to the circumstances faced by the black artists in the nineteenth century."[127]

The expert's qualifications count for nothing if his opinion is not backed by fact and analysis. In one case involving the value of four donated watercolor paintings, the taxpayer's expert had the more impressive credentials.[128] He had been an art dealer for some 14 years, and had sold, purchased, and appraised a number of works by the same artist. He had the buying and selling experience that the IRS expert lacked. Nevertheless, the court rejected his opinion, and adopted the IRS valuation, because the taxpayer's expert presented his conclusions without offering an adequate explanation of how they were reached.

[3] Selecting an Appraiser

Not all people who hold themselves out as fine arts appraisers have the necessary qualifications and experience to provide a meaningful appraisal. Inter-

---

[123] *Id.*, 595 F.2d at 609.

[124] Furstenberg v. United States, 595 F.2d 603, 605 (Ct. Cl. 1979). The Art Advisory Panel is a group of art experts who, on a voluntary basis, advise the IRS concerning the value of artwork claimed as a tax deduction.

[125] *Id.*

[126] Frates v. Commissioner, 53 T.C.M. (CCH) 96 (1987).

[127] *Id.*

[128] Reynolds v. Commissioner, 43 T.C.M. (CCH) 115 (1981).

viewing the appraiser and asking questions is a must. Here are some of the questions to ask:

- Does the appraiser have substantial experience with artwork that is similar and in the same price range? The more focused the specialty, the better.
- Does the appraiser's experience include doing commercial evaluations, as opposed to being limited to scholarly or academic study?[129] A museum curator, for example, might be the right person to *authenticate* an Old Master drawing, but may lack the market knowledge to determine its current market value.
- If the appraisal is being prepared in connection with litigation, is the appraiser sufficiently articulate and knowledgeable to be a convincing expert?
- What type of formal appraisal education or training does the appraiser have? Has he published books or articles, or lectured in his field? Is he a member of a recognized appraisal organization and subject to its code of ethics and continuing education requirements?
- Is the appraiser independent, unbiased, and free of any financial conflict of interest? The appraisal fee must not be based on a contingency or upon the value of the property.
- Will the appraiser supply references?
- Does the appraiser have professional liability insurance coverage?
- Does the appraiser have sample reports to examine?

To locate a suitable appraiser, any of the following organizations may be contacted:

- Appraisers Association of America, Inc., 386 Park Avenue South, Suite 2000, New York, N.Y. 10016; telephone (212) 889-5404.
- International Society of Appraisers, 16040 Christensen Road, Suite 102, Seattle, Wash. 98188; telephone (206) 241-0359.
- American Society of Appraisers, 555 Herndon Parkway, Suite 125, Herndon, Va. 20170; telephone (703) 478-2228.
- Art Dealers Association of America Appraisal Service, 575 Madison Avenue, New York, N.Y. 10022; telephone (212) 940-8590.

---

[129] *See, e.g.*, Ashkar v. Commissioner, 61 T.C.M. (CCH) 1657 (1991) (appraisals of ancient Biblical fragments rejected because the appraisers presented academic rather than commercial valuations); Perdue v. Commissioner, 62 T.C.M. (CCH) 845 (1991) (referencing a case where the court gave less weight to testimony of a tenured professor and art museum curator than to coin dealers in deciding the value of ancient Greek coins).

- Private Art Dealers Association, P.O. Box 872, Lenox Hill Station, New York, N.Y. 10021; telephone (212) 572-0772.
- Christie's Estates & Appraisals, 20 Rockefeller Plaza, New York, N.Y. 10022; telephone (212) 636-2400.
- Sotheby's Appraisals, 1334 York Avenue, New York, N.Y. 10021; telephone (212) 894-1126.

[4] The Appraisal Agreement

Many appraisers use their own preprinted appraisal agreements, which are designed mainly to ensure payment of fees and to limit the appraiser's legal liability. An example of an appraisal agreement currently used by one large organization is Form 10-4. If a more comprehensive agreement is desired, the "Agreement for Conservation Services" in Form 12-1 can be readily modified and adapted for use in connection with appraisal services.

[C] Basic Appraisal Methods

There are several possible methods or approaches to the appraisal of artwork. The specific method used by an appraiser will depend on the purpose of the appraisal and the goals of the party retaining the appraiser.

[1] Market Comparison Approach

This is the most common method of appraising artwork and other personal property. The appraiser locates other, similar works of art by the same artist or by another artist of equal reputation and stature that have sold within a reasonable time of the valuation date. He then analyzes to what extent these comparable sales are indicative of the value of the subject item.[130] Consideration must be given to whether the sale prices of the comparable items truly reflect market value or were determined mainly by family relationships, tax considerations, or distress sales. The appraiser must also determine the most appropriate marketplace where the subject item would be sold, through art galleries, public auction, private sale, or another venue.

[2] Cost Approach

This method, also known as the reproduction or replacement cost approach, values an object based on the cost of reproducing or recreating an identical item,

---

[130] In determining whether the works are similar, the appraiser should take into account such factors as the quality and condition of the items, the amount of restoration, inclusion in catalogues and museum showings, provenance supporting the authenticity of the works, size, subject matter, and "glamour" factors such as prior ownership by a prestigious collector.

if possible. It does not apply to most artwork. The cost of the canvas, paint and varnish, for example, is usually a negligible consideration when it comes to the value of a painting.

On the other hand, this method might be applicable where, say, the value of an artwork made of precious metals or gems depends largely on the raw materials, or in the case of the decorative arts where the cost of manufacture is the main factor in determining its value.

[3] Income Approach

This method may be appropriate where the artwork produces income, such as artwork in the stock of someone in the business of renting out artwork, or a master image used to produce signed and numbered prints or commercial products such as posters and t-shirts. Under this method, the stream of income is capitalized and used as the basis for estimating value.

[4] Intuitive Approach

This approach is not officially recognized by any of the major appraisal organizations or the IRS, but it is commonly used in the art world.[131] This approach was implicitly used by Sotheby's in valuing a recently discovered painting by the thirteenth-century Italian artist Cimabue. When commenting on why a painting originally valued by Sotheby's at £2 million was being sold to London's National Gallery in a Sotheby's-brokered deal for £6½ million, an executive of the auction house stated that, "[w]e put out a marker at two million pounds originally . . . but as time went by, it became clear the price would be nearer ten million pounds."[132]

In one case involving a donated sculpture of John Wayne, the taxpayer's appraiser considered the history of the sculpture and the media attention that it had received and arrived at a value that was 17 times the value determined by the IRS.[133] The court rejected the IRS's contention that the taxpayer's appraisal was unreliable, holding that an appraiser can rely on the "romantic appeal and glamour" of an artwork because of the publicity surrounding it, even if the value according to more traditional valuation methods is considerably less.

In another case, an arbitration panel likely used this approach to value the 26-second John F. Kennedy assassination film by Abraham Zapruder at $16 million for purposes of awarding compensation to Zapruder's family for the

---

[131] Some appraisers would argue that it is not a separate approach, but an extreme version of the market-comparison approach.

[132] London's National Gallery Acquires Cimabue in Lieu of Tax, TheArtNewspaper.com (July 2000).

[133] Murphy v. Commissioner, 1993 U.S. App. LEXIS 26485 (9th Cir. 1993).

government's seizure of the film.[134] The award was for the physical film only, not for the copyright, which was still owned by the family. Zapruder had sold the film in 1963 for $150,000 to Time-Life Inc., which later gave it back to the family for $1. That was evidence that its value was largely symbolic. But the family argued that the original film was comparable to a DaVinci manuscript or a Van Gogh painting. The market-comparison approach, which yielded vastly different appraisals from the parties, provided only limited assistance.

[D] Authenticity or Title in Doubt

[1] Appraiser's Duty to Consider

A work of art whose authenticity is in doubt "will change hands at a lower price than one for which authenticity is undisputed."[135] The fact that authenticity is in doubt "acts as a depressant on value."[136] Such doubt constitutes a "blemish" whose effect should be taken into account in determining value.[137]

An appraiser's failure to take into account questions raised by other experts about a painting's authenticity constitutes "at a minimum, gross negligence."[138]

Similarly, doubt over title can seriously depress the value of an artwork. In one instance, there was a cloud over title to a painting by Matisse due to suspicions that it had been exported from Italy clandestinely, without an export permit.[139] The appraised value dropped from $750,000 to zero because, in the opinion of the appraiser, "no reputable auction house or dealer would be prepared to handle it."[140]

If an appraiser suspects that an artwork may be stolen, he should check with the Art Loss Register and/or other relevant registers to see whether it has been reported missing.[141] If so, he has an ethical obligation to decline the assignment and to inform the appropriate authorities.[142]

---

[134] Lichblau, U.S. Ordered to Pay $16 Million for Film of JFK, Las Vegas Review-Journal, August 4, 1999, 1A.

[135] Doherty v. Commissioner, 16 F.3d 338, 340 (9th Cir. 1994).

[136] Peters v. Commissioner, 36 T.C.M. (CCH) 552 (1977).

[137] Mathias v. Commissioner, 50 T.C. 1994 (1968).

[138] Foxley v. Sotheby's, 893 F. Supp. 1224, 1236 (S.D.N.Y. 1995) (finding that it would have been a gross negligence if a painting purportedly by Mary Cassatt had been appraised at $650,000 despite knowledge that the Cassatt Committee had questioned its authenticity, potentially rendering it worthless).

[139] Jeanneret v. Vichey, 693 F.2d 259 (2d Cir. 1982).

[140] *Id.* at 263.

[141] The Art Loss Register, created in 1991, is the largest private database of stolen and missing works of art in the world, and has an office at 666 Fifth Avenue, New York, N.Y. 10103, telephone (212) 262-4831. For more information, see *supra* Chapter 5, Form 5-2, and Appendix 5-C.

[142] *See* Appraisers Association of America Code of Ethics (1999).

Doubts over authenticity or title must be factored into the appraisal even if the doubts do not surface until *after* the valuation date—for instance, when the work is donated to charity. "It is enough that the facts that formed the basis of the doubt that later arises were in existence at the time of the [charitable] contribution, and would have affected the bid of a willing buyer."[143] In other words, the doubts must be factored in if they "were known or reasonably should have been known to [the owner] and his appraisers at the critical date," and appraisers have an affirmative duty of due diligence to investigate these doubts.[144]

[2] Compare: Insurance Appraisal Clause

Most fine arts policies have insurance schedules with mutually agreed-upon values based on appraisals. If not, the typical homeowner's insurance policy contains an appraisal clause which provides that if the insured and the insurer cannot agree on the amount of a loss, a panel of three "competent and disinterested" appraisers shall be selected to appraise the loss.[145] Under such a clause, the panel does *not* have the duty, or even the power, to consider doubts as to authenticity or title. It must assume that the insured lost exactly what he claimed to have lost, and appraise the property accordingly.[146]

[E] The Appraiser's Report

Some appraisals are oral, or in the form of a brief letter. A more comprehensive written appraisal report, which should conform to Uniform Standards of Professional Appraisal Standards (USPAP) standards, would include the following information:[147]

- the identity of the client
- the identity and qualifications of the appraiser, and a statement of his disinterest in the item appraised and that his fees are not contingent upon the outcome of the appraisal
- the purpose of the appraisal
- the date of the appraisal and the date as of which the valuation is effective, such as the date of charitable contribution

---

[143] Doherty v. Commissioner, 16 F.3d 338, 340 (9th Cir. 1994).

[144] Mathias v. Commissioner, 50 T.C. 994, 998-999 (1968).

[145] *E.g.*, Cal. Ins. Code § 2071 (standard form of fire insurance policy).

[146] Safeco Insurance Co. v. Sharma, 160 Cal. App. 3d 1060, 207 Cal. Rptr. 104 (1984) (panel exceeded its powers by determining that 36 stolen miniature paintings described by the insured as a *matched* set from the Bundi School, India, late eighteenth century, were an *unmatched* set).

[147] *See supra* note 118.

- a complete description of the artwork and its physical condition, according to Object ID parameters[148]
- the provenance, exhibition history and publication history of the artwork, if any, and a brief biography of the artist
- assumptions and conditions, such as that the artwork is authentic and that the owner has good title; some appraisers always preface the appraisal with the phrase "if the work is authentic, it would likely bring a price of x"
- a statement that the artwork was personally inspected by the appraiser or, if he relied solely on photographs, an explanation why (reliance on photographs is risky; for example, an examination of a photograph may not reveal that a painting has been heavily restored or overpainted, adversely affecting its value)[149]
- the appraisal method used, a brief description of the method, and a description of the market used as the basis for the valuation
- supporting data, such as comparable sales, test results, catalogues consulted, income data, and so on
- the appraised value, expressed as a specific dollar amount or a range of values
- signature of the appraiser[150]

[F] Online Appraisals

A recent development is the appearance of online art-appraisal Web sites, which perform valuations based on digital photographs and other information submitted by the client online. They offer convenience and low cost, and are readily accessible to the general public. Such electronic appraisals, however, like their real-world counterparts, are only as good as the methods and experts they use, and should be approached with caution. The following factors are among those a prospective client should consider.

Some online appraisal sites use anonymous experts. Not knowing the expert's identity, qualifications and experience makes it impossible for the client to assess the validity of a valuation opinion, and renders the appraisal useless for insurance, tax and other purposes.

Online appraisals are done without inspection of the actual item. That makes it difficult or impossible to determine the condition of the item, its authenticity, and other factors that affect value.

---

[148] *See* Appendix 5-A.

[149] *See* Posner v. Commissioner, 35 T.C.M. (CCH) 943 (1976) (very poor condition of 300-year-old Venetian painting not apparent to Art Advisory Panel from examination of a photograph).

[150] These and other items are published in Elements of a Correctly Prepared Appraisal, published by the Appraisers Association of America.

The written opinions provided by online appraisers vary in quality, and do not always provide enough information to support the conclusions reached.

Some online sites include broad disclaimers which seem to defeat the very purpose of purchasing an appraisal. One site, for example, states that appraisals are only "hypothetical in nature," are provided "solely for educational purposes," may not be used for tax, insurance, or other real-world purposes, and do not constitute a representation as to valuation!

[G] Valuation for IRS Purposes

The one area where appraisers and appraisals are subject to government rules and regulations is in the tax arena.

Regulations have been promulgated by the IRS that govern the determination of fair market value for measuring the income tax deduction for non-cash charitable contributions, such as artwork.[151] Among other things, the regulations contain specific requirements with respect to appraisals used to substantiate the deduction. There are separate regulations governing fair market value determinations for purposes of the estate tax[152] and gift tax.[153]

Whenever the donated property's claimed value exceeds $5,000, the taxpayer must:

- get a "qualified appraisal" for the property made by a "qualified appraiser"[154]
- attach an "appraisal summary" to the return on which the deduction is first claimed[155]
- maintain "reliable written records" containing certain specific information regarding the property[156]

Unless the taxpayer substantially complies with these rules, no tax deduction is allowed.[157]

[1] Qualified Appraisal

A "qualified appraisal" is an appraisal document that:

[151] Treas. Reg. § 1.170A-1(c).
[152] Treas. Reg. § 20.2031-6.
[153] Treas. Reg. § 25.2512-1.
[154] Treas. Reg. § 1.170A-13(c)(2)(i)(A).
[155] Treas. Reg. § 1.170A-13(c)(2)(i)(B).
[156] Treas. Reg. § 1.170A-13(c)(2)(i)(C).
[157] *See, e.g.*, D'Arcangelo v. Commissioner, 68 T.C.M. (CCH) 1223 (1994).

1. relates to an appraisal made not earlier than 60 days prior to the date of contribution of the appraised property;
2. does not involve a prohibited appraisal fee, that is, a fee based on a percentage of the property's appraised value, unless the fee is based on a sliding scale and is paid to a generally recognized association that regulates appraisers;
3. includes certain information; and
4. is prepared, signed and dated by a qualified appraiser.[158]

The information required to be included in the qualified appraisal is specified in the regulations.[159] Among other things, it includes a description of the property, its physical condition, the date and terms of the contribution, the identity and qualifications of the appraiser, the date on which the property was valued, the appraised fair market value on the date of contribution, the method of valuation used, and the specific basis for the valuation, such as any specific comparable sales transaction.

IRS Publication 561, Determining the Value of Donated Property (Rev. Nov. 1996), gives the following example of information that should be included in a description of a donated painting:

1. A complete description of the object, indicating the:
   - size,
   - subject matter,
   - medium,
   - name of the artist (or culture), and
   - approximate date created
2. The cost, date, and manner of acquisition
3. A history of the item, including proof of authenticity
4. A photograph of a size and quality fully showing the object, preferably a 10x12-inch print
5. The facts on which the appraisal was based, such as:
   - sales or analyses of similar works by the artist, particularly on or around the valuation date
   - quoted prices in dealer's catalogues of the artist's works or works of other artists of comparable stature
   - a record of any exhibitions at which the specific art object had been displayed
   - the economic state of the art market at the time of valuation, particularly with respect to the specific property

[158] Treas. Reg. § 1.170A-13(c)(3)(i).
[159] Treas. Reg. § 1.170A-13(c)(3)(ii).

- the standing of the artist in his profession and in the particular school or time period

Unless the total value of the artwork exceeds $20,000, the "qualified appraisal" itself is not submitted to the IRS. Rather, the taxpayer submits with his tax return an "appraisal summary," which is a separate statement prepared on a form prescribed by the IRS.[160]

[2] Qualified Appraiser

Unlike other personal property appraisals, where the appraiser is not required to meet any particular qualifications, a "qualified appraisal" for tax purposes must be prepared only by a "qualified appraiser."

A "qualified appraiser" is an individual who:

1. holds himself out to the public as an appraiser or performs appraisals regularly;
2. is qualified by background, experience, education, and professional appraisal association memberships to make appraisals of the type of property being valued; and
3. understands that a false or fraudulent overstatement of the property's value may subject the appraiser to a civil penalty and may result in future appraisals being disregarded by the IRS.[161]

The IRS regulations provide that certain persons who may have a conflict of interest cannot be qualified appraisers, for example, the donor, the donee, or anyone employed by or related to either of them.[162]

[H] Determining "Recognized Stature" under the Visual Artists Rights Act (VARA)

Appraisers and other art professionals are occasionally called upon to provide expert opinion as to whether a given work of visual art is of "recognized stature" pursuant to the Visual Artists Rights Act (VARA).[163] It's a tough assignment, because there are so few standards.

VARA was enacted by Congress in 1990 to provide certain protections for artists' moral rights.[164] Among other things, VARA recognizes the right of a living

---

[160] Treas. Reg. § 1.170A-13(c)(4). *See* IRS Form 8283, Non-Cash Charitable Contributions—Appraisal Summary.

[161] Treas. Reg. § 1.170A-13(c)(5)(i).

[162] Treas. Reg. § 1.170A-13(c)(5)(iv).

[163] 17 U.S.C. § 106A. The statute is part of the Copyright Act, but the rights are independent of copyright.

[164] *See* S.M. Levy, Artists' Moral Rights: Will Federal Legislation Have Any Real Impact in Deterring the Mutilation and Destruction of Artworks? Los Angeles Lawyer, March 1988, at 11.

author of a work of visual art "to prevent any destruction of a work of recognized stature." This right endures even after title has been transferred from the author.

What this means is that if you spend good money for a painting of "recognized stature," and take it home as your property, you are not free to destroy it. If you do, the artist can sue you for monetary damages for the harm done to his reputation, plus costs and attorney fees. Similarly, if you purchase an office building with a mosaic of "recognized stature" embedded in the floor of the lobby, you should learn to like the mosaic because the law does not allow any removal that would cause its destruction. Your private property rights are deemed less important than the "dignity" of the artist and the public interest in preserving our culture.[165]

The phrase "recognized stature" is not defined in VARA. One court has stated that the artwork need not be a Picasso or a Chagall to qualify, nor aesthetically pleasing to the trier of fact, but it must at least be something more substantial than a five-year-old's fingerpainting.[166] How much more substantial is a question for the experts to debate at trial.

In *Carter v. Helmsley-Spear, Inc.*,[167] the three artist-plaintiffs installed "a variety of sculptural elements" in the lobby of defendant's building pursuant to a contract. The defendant later decided it didn't want the artwork, and announced plans to remove it. The plaintiffs sued under VARA for an injunction and for monetary damages. The court granted a permanent injunction prohibiting defendant from mutilating or destroying the artwork during the lifetimes of the three plaintiffs.

One of the key issues in the *Carter* case was whether the artwork was of "recognized stature." Based on the opinions of plaintiffs' experts who testified at trial, the court held that it was. The experts included a professor who testified that the sculpture was "a work of art like almost nothing I have ever seen before"; the president of the municipal art society, who testified that people who had toured the artwork were "very, very excited" about it; and a professor who echoed the belief that it was "a very exciting piece."

The defendant's expert testified that the work was "a pastiche of recognized clichés" and "so lacking in merit that I believe that it serves no useful purpose to retain it." The court gave this opinion no weight whatsoever, because it appeared that the expert had a disdain for contemporary art in general.

In *Martin v. City of Indianapolis*,[168] the standards were further relaxed. The plaintiff artist used a welding torch to erect a huge metal sculpture on land owned by a private individual. Later, the city purchased the land and demolished the

---

[165] *See, e.g.*, Martin v. City of Indianapolis, 1999 U.S. App. LEXIS 20886 (7th Cir. 1999).

[166] Carter v. Helmsley-Spear, Inc., 851 F. Supp. 303, 325 (S.D.N.Y. 1994), *aff'd in part, vacated in part, rev'd in part*, 71 F.3d 77 (2d Cir. 1995).

[167] *Id.*

[168] 1999 U.S. App. LEXIS 20886 (7th Cir. 1999).

sculpture without prior notice to the plaintiff. The plaintiff brought suit under VARA and prevailed on summary judgment. The court of appeals affirmed.

The plaintiff produced no expert witnesses with respect to "recognized stature." His evidence consisted solely of certain newspaper and magazine articles and various letters, all in support of the sculpture, and an award a model of the sculpture had won. The court, rejecting the defendant's hearsay objection, held that this evidence established the "recognized stature" of the artwork. One of the appellate judges dissented, stating that VARA was designed to protect only "great" works of art and that "recognized stature" cannot be demonstrated by old newspaper articles.

It is clear that a more objective and rigorous definition of "recognized stature" is needed to achieve the proper balance between private property rights and the public interest in preserving the nation's culture. At the very least, there should be some jurisdictional minimum value, expressed in dollars, for a work to qualify for protection—say, $20,000. Jurisdictional minimums are quite common in the law to weed out the trivial and to allocate scarce judicial resources.

§ 10.04 LIABILITY OF THE AUTHENTICATOR OR APPRAISER

Major financial decisions are often based on the opinions of those who authenticate and appraise art. An erroneous opinion can cause a client to buy too high or sell too low, incur tax penalties for an overstated charitable deduction or an understated estate tax calculation, insure the property for too much or too little, or be taken in by a con artist. When things go wrong, clients are increasingly looking to the professional for compensation.

Fine arts authenticators and appraisers have been sued under a variety of legal theories, discussed below. The most dramatic change in recent years has been the recognition of a "standard of care" applicable to art professionals.[169] Reliance on instinct and educated guesses, unsupported by methodical research, fact-gathering and analysis, is no longer an acceptable method of practice.

[A] Personal Jurisdiction

Given the small number of qualified experts in any given art specialty, the opinions expressed by these experts frequently travel across state lines or even international borders. An art collector in California, for example, might seek the opinion of an expert in New York as to the authenticity of a French nineteenth-century painting he wishes to buy. If the expert gives him the wrong advice, and the owner decides to sue him in California, the question arises whether the expert

[169] *See* S.M. Levy, Liability of the Art Expert for Professional Malpractice, 1991 Wis. L. Rev. 595 (1991).

is subject to personal jurisdiction in that state. That is, does the California court have the power to render an effective judgment against the expert, who is a nonresident?

Many states have "long-arm" statutes, some of which sweep so broadly that they authorize their courts to exercise jurisdiction over nonresidents on any basis not inconsistent with state or federal constitutional due process.[170] That means that the court may exercise jurisdiction over a nonresident where "minimum contacts" exist between the nonresident and the forum state such that the exercise of jurisdiction will not offend "traditional notions of fair play and substantial justice."[171]

In the following cases, contacts were deemed insufficient under state long-arm statutes:

- A single telephone call from an appraisal association in New York to the daughter of Henri Matisse in Paris, in which the daughter expressed the opinion that plaintiff's Matisse painting was a fake, was insufficient to subject the daughter to personal jurisdiction in New York.[172]
- A Tennessee art collector who sold an inauthentic painting to an Illinois art gallery, which he allegedly misrepresented as an original, was not subject to personal jurisdiction in Illinois despite various interstate telephone conversations and mail correspondence regarding the transaction, the collector's contract with the Illinois gallery whose portion of the contract was performed in Illinois, and two visits by the collector to the gallery.[173]

In the following cases, the contacts were held sufficient:

- The single act by a Louisiana art dealer of shipping to an Illinois buyer four paintings and a "provenance" purporting to authenticate them was sufficient to confer personal jurisdiction in Illinois, although the dealer had no other contacts with or presence in the state.[174]
- A nonresident who never set foot in Montana was subject to jurisdiction there because she mailed certificates of authenticity to Montana where the owner and the paintings were located, telephoned the owner 10 to 12 times annually to offer advice about the purchase of art in general, and telephoned him to assure him that the specific Dali paintings in question were genuine.[175]

---

[170] *E.g.*, Cal. Civ. Proc. Code § 410.10.

[171] International Shoe Co. v. Washington, 326 U.S. 310, 316, 66 S. Ct. 154, 158 (1945).

[172] Findlay v. Duthuit, 86 A.D.2d 789, 446 N.Y.S.2d 951 (1982).

[173] Maurice Sternberg, Inc. v. James, 577 F. Supp. 882 (N.D. Ill. 1984) .

[174] Duchossois Industries, Inc. v. Stelloh, 1988 U.S. Dist. LEXIS 178 (N.D. Ill. 1988) .

[175] Deshaw v. Bellette Hofmann Fine Art, Inc., 1998 U.S. App. LEXIS 10215 (9th Cir. 1998) (unpublished opinion).

- A New York art gallery that solicited an Ohio collector through telephone calls and mailings to purchase a drawing purportedly by Picasso, and shipped the drawing to Ohio with a certificate of authenticity, was subject to personal jurisdiction in Ohio although it was a "one-shot affair" and the gallery had no other contacts with or presence in Ohio.[176]

[B] Theories of Liability

The following is an overview of the most common causes of action asserted against persons who authenticate or appraise art.

[1] Professional Malpractice

Art expert malpractice is the negligent rendering of a professional opinion relating to a painting, sculpture or other work of art. The plaintiff must prove (1) the duty to possess and exercise ordinary skill and knowledge, (2) a breach of that duty, (3) a causal connection between the negligent conduct and the resulting injury, and (4) actual loss or damage.

Expert testimony is normally required to prove the standard of care and its breach. The plaintiff can also refer to pronouncements by relevant professional organizations, including the USPAP standards, as evidence of the standard of care. For example, each of the three major appraisal organizations has a code of ethics and professional conduct with which its members are expected to comply.

Perfection is not required. An art expert is not automatically negligent because he arrives at a conclusion that later is challenged by other experts or ultimately proves to be wrong. He is negligent only if the error is due to a failure to use the care and skill ordinarily used by other experts in the same or similar locality under similar circumstances.[177]

As an illustration, in June 1996 the grandson of a woman who died conducted an estate sale at her home, after hiring an appraiser. Among the items that sold were two flower paintings, for $60. Later, the buyer took them to his own expert and learned they were by the nineteenth-century American artist Martin Johnson Heade. The paintings sold at a Christie's auction in December 1996 for more than $1 million. Needless to say, the grandson made a claim against his appraiser for not recognizing the value of the paintings. The appraiser settled for an undisclosed sum.[178]

---

[176] McCloud v. Lawrence Gallery, Ltd., 1991 U.S. Dist. LEXIS 9631 (S.D.N.Y. 1991).

[177] *See, e.g.*, Cal. Jury Inst. Civ., BAJI No. 6.37.

[178] Kinsella, Seller Beware: $60 Tag-Sale Paintings Bring $1.1 Million, Wall St. J., Dec. 11, 1998, at W16.

A very similar situation occurred in *Luxmoore-May v. Messenger May Baverstock.*[179] The plaintiffs sold two small paintings of foxhounds for £840 after having them examined by an expert, who told them they were "dirty" and "ill-drawn" and not worth much. Five months later, to the plaintiffs' chagrin, the two foxhounds sold at Sotheby's for £88,000 as originals by the celebrated animal painter George Stubbs. Plaintiffs sued the expert for professional malpractice and were awarded the full auction value, the court concluding that "no competent practitioner could have missed the signs of merit in these painting and failed to recognize that they were worthy of further investigation."[180]

[2] Breach of Contract

The elements of a claim for breach of contract are (1) a contract, (2) performance of the contract by one party, (3) breach of the contract by the other, and (4) damages.[181]

Few actions against art professionals are for breach of express or written contract, because the written contract, if there is one, is unlikely to contain any promises or guaranties. More likely, it will be filled with disclaimers and denials of responsibility.

On the other hand, implicit in every contract is the promise to exercise ordinary skill and knowledge in rendering professional services.[182] Since that is the same thing as the standard of care, the plaintiff has the option to sue for negligence or breach of the implied contractual undertaking of due care, or both. Negligence often suffices, unless the plaintiff can benefit by the contract measure of damages or by the longer statute of limitations that usually applies to a breach-of-contract claim.

[3] Breach of Express or Implied Warranty

These theories are typically asserted against a dealer, auctioneer or other seller who, as part of a sales transaction, renders advice as to authenticity or value. See the discussion at § 10.02[B][1] and [2], above.

[4] Breach of Fiduciary Duty

A "fiduciary" is a person who is in a special relationship of trust and confidence with another. An example is the lawyer-client relationship. The advan-

---

179 04 E.G. 115 (Q.B. 1988) (LEXIS, Comcas library, All file), *rev'd*, 1 All E.R. 1067 (C.A. 1989).

180 *Id.*, 04 E.G. at 115.

181 *See, e.g.*, Nordic Bank PLC v. Trend Group, Ltd., 619 F. Supp. 542, 561 (S.D.N.Y. 1985).

182 *See, e.g.*, Bucquet v. Livingston, 57 Cal. App.3d 914, 129 Cal. Rptr. 514 (1976); Saveca v. Reilly, 111 A.D.2d 493, 488 N.Y.S.2d 876 (1985).

tage of pleading breach of fiduciary duty is that it opens up the prospect for punitive damages and damages for emotional distress, in addition to compensatory damages. However, art experts are rarely found to be fiduciaries unless special circumstances show a relationship of trust and confidence.

Thus, for example, an expert does not, solely by virtue of his expertise, have a fiduciary responsibility toward his clients.[183] Allegations of superior knowledge or expertise in the art field are *per se* insufficient to establish the existence of a fiduciary relationship.[184] The fact that the defendants sold numerous pieces of art to the plaintiffs over the course of two years, held themselves out as nationally recognized art experts, and provided appraisals of the artworks does not make them fiduciaries.[185] Similarly, evidence that an art consultant advised her clients as to which artists' paintings were good investments, assisted them in locating and selecting suitable artworks at the "best prices," purchased the selected artworks for her own account, and then resold them at a profit to the clients without indicating the amount of the original purchase price, is insufficient to prove a fiduciary relationship.[186]

An art expert will be held to be a fiduciary if he is found to be an agent of his client. An agent is one who represents another, called a principal, in dealing with third persons.[187] As an illustration, an auctioneer is a fiduciary of persons who consign works for auction, and can be liable for breach of fiduciary duty for misrepresenting the sum the artwork was expected to bring at auction or failing to disclose the risks inherent in auction sales.[188] There is no fiduciary relationship, however, between the auctioneer and the purchaser.[189]

[5] Fraud

While the elements of fraud may vary from state to state, plaintiff is generally required to prove that (1) defendant made a material false representation of fact, (2) the representation was made with the intent to deceive, (3) plaintiff reasonably relied on the representation, and (4) plaintiff was damaged as a result.[190] Most jurisdictions require fraud to be pled with particularity.[191]

---

183 Hutton v. Klabal, 726 F. Supp. 67, 73 (S.D.N.Y. 1989).

184 Mechigian v. Art Capital Corp., 612 F. Supp. 1421, 1431 (S.D.N.Y. 1985).

185 Granat v. Center Art Galleries-Hawaii, Inc., 1993 U.S. Dist. LEXIS 14092 (S.D.N.Y. 1993).

186 Fenton v. Freedman, 748 F.2d 1358 (9th Cir. 1984).

187 *E.g.*, Cal. Civ. Code § 2295.

188 Cristallina S.A. v. Christie, Manson & Woods Int'l, Inc., 117 A.D.2d 284, 502 N.Y.S.2d 165 (1986).

189 Foxley v. Sotheby's, Inc., 893 F. Supp. 1224, 1232 (S.D.N.Y. 1995).

190 *See* Flickinger v. Harold C. Brown & Co., 947 F.2d 595, 599 (2d Cir. 1991).

191 *See, e.g.*, Fed. R. Civ. P. 9(b).

For example, if an appraiser knows, or should know, that there is significant doubt as to the authenticity of a painting, an appraisal that assumes the painting is genuine constitutes fraud.[192]

When the person making the statement about the value of an artwork is the seller, the statement is often treated as a mere expression of opinion.[193] However, if the seller holds himself out as an expert art appraiser, his representation that the artwork has a given fixed market value may be found by the trier of fact to be a representation by one possessing knowledge rather than mere opinion, giving rise to a claim for fraud.[194]

The requirement that plaintiff reasonably relied on the fraudulent representation is much easier to prove if the plaintiff is a novice art collector with no experience in buying fine art, as opposed to a museum, major collector or other experienced, sophisticated party who should have known better.[195]

"Intent to deceive" is required for a fraud claim. Because it is rarely susceptible to direct proof, fraudulent intent is normally established by circumstantial evidence and the reasonable inferences that can be drawn from it. As an example, the following circumstantial evidence was held sufficient to support a finding that written appraisals of two paintings by an art dealer were intentionally false: (1) the appraisals were four times higher than the fair market value as found by at least one other expert; (2) the dealer received a commission on the sale of the paintings, giving him an inducement to inflate the value; and (3) the dealer held himself out as an expert appraiser, from which a jury could reasonably infer that he did know the true market values.[196]

An authentication of a painting purportedly by Spanish artist Manolo Millares was found to be a fraudulent authentication based on the following evidence: (1) the author of the *catalogue raisonné* for Millares, and Millares's widow, both testified that the painting was not an original; (2) the defendant paid $2,200 for the painting only two months before he resold it for $180,000; and (3) the defendant disappeared after a lawsuit was filed.[197]

---

[192] Foxley v. Sotheby's, Inc., 893 F. Supp. 1224, 1237 (S.D.N.Y. 1995). The court demonstrated its point with the following hypothetical: "If an appraiser knew that an alleged family heirloom diamond ring was made of cubic zirconium, then a $100,000 appraisal is simply fraudulent. One cannot *presume* authenticity in the face of facts to the contrary."

[193] McKie v. R.H. Love Galleries, Inc., 1990 U.S. Dist. LEXIS 14748 (N.D. Ill. 1990).

[194] Goldman v. Barnett, 793 F. Supp. 28, 31 (D. Mass. 1992).

[195] Balog v. Center Art Gallery-Hawaii, Inc., 745 F. Supp. 1556, 1564 (D. Haw. 1990).

[196] Goldman v. Barnett, 793 F. Supp. 28, 31 (D. Mass. 1992).

[197] Artcurial, S.A. v. Lowenthal, 763 F. Supp. 768 (S.D.N.Y. 1991).

[6] Negligent Misrepresentation

The elements of a cause of action for negligent misrepresentation vary from state to state, but generally include an untrue representation of a material fact, made without any reasonable ground for believing it to be true, with intent to induce the plaintiff to rely on it, justifiable reliance by the plaintiff, and resulting damages.[198]

New York imposes an additional requirement that there be some special relationship of trust from which the defendant's duty to the plaintiff arises.[199] An arm's-length business relationship is not enough.[200] The relationship must be of a fiduciary nature.[201] In a case concerning a counterfeit Mary Cassatt painting, the sale of that work at auction, where the catalogue guaranteed the authenticity of the painting and stated that the painting would be accompanied by a copy of a letter discussing the work from an authority on Cassatt, did not give rise to a negligent misrepresentation claim under New York law, because the special relationship was absent.[202]

[7] Violation of Consumer Statutes

Most states have their own special consumer protection statutes. For example, the Illinois Fraud and Deceptive Business Practices Act prohibits deception or fraud in the conduct of any trade or commerce, and gives consumers standing to sue. A violation of the act is easier to prove than proving common law fraud.[203] The act has been held to protect purchasers of artwork who were given an allegedly false authentication and appraisal report.[204]

Occasionally, suit is also brought under the federal Magnuson-Moss Warranty Act,[205] which regulates written warranties on consumer goods manufactured after July 4, 1975, and distributed in interstate commerce. The term "consumer goods" includes artworks.[206]

[8] Defamation and Product Disparagement

Defamation and disparagement are the classic art law torts. Some truly legendary cases have come down over the years involving art experts who publicly

---

[198] *E.g.*, Cal. Jury Inst. Civ., BAJI No. 12.45.

[199] City of Amsterdam v. Goldreyer, Ltd., 882 F. Supp. 1273, 1283 (E.D.N.Y. 1995).

[200] Foxley v. Sotheby's, Inc., 893 F. Supp. 1224, 1232 (S.D.N.Y. 1995).

[201] *Id.*

[202] *Id.*

[203] Perlman v. Time, Inc., 64 Ill. App. 3d 190, 380 N.E.2d 1040 (1978).

[204] McKie v. R.H. Love Galleries, Inc., 1990 U.S. Dist. LEXIS 14748 (N.D. Ill. 1990).

[205] 15 U.S.C. §§ 2301 *et seq.*

[206] *See* Stenger v. R.H. Love Galleries, Inc., 1983 U.S. Dist. LEXIS 12738 (N.D. Ill. 1983).

questioned the authenticity or value of important works of art, only to be hauled into court.[207]

Defamation is an invasion of an individual's *personal reputation*. It is defined as a false and unprivileged communication that "tends so to harm the reputation of another as to lower him in the estimation of the community or to deter third persons from associating or dealing with him."[208] Disparagement, by contrast, is an invasion of a person's *interest in property*. It is defined as an intentional falsehood that degrades the quality or authenticity of the plaintiff's property and results in pecuniary damages.[209]

Perhaps the most famous case is *Hahn v. Duveen*,[210] a product disparagement case. The plaintiff intended to sell a painting to the Kansas City Art Museum which had been authenticated by a respected French art expert as a genuine Leonardo da Vinci. The defendant, world-renowned art dealer Sir Joseph Duveen, denounced the painting as a fake. His remarks, published in the New York World, caused the museum to back down and allegedly rendered the painting unsaleable anywhere in the world. A four-week trial ensued in 1929, with each side calling numerous trial experts to testify as to whether the painting was genuine. The jury deadlocked 9-3 in favor of the plaintiff, agreeing that the defendant had maliciously and intentionally wrecked the sale, but disagreeing as to whether the painting was authentic. The defendant settled by paying a huge sum before the case could be retried.

In *Milkovich v. Lorain Journal Co.*,[211] decided in 1990, the U.S. Supreme Court held that statements of opinion on matters of public concern are protected under the First Amendment as long as they do not contain a provably false factual connotation. Also protected are "statements that cannot reasonably be interpreted as stating actual facts about an individual."[212]

Whether or not an art expert's statements give rise to liability depends on the answers to a number of questions, including but not limited to:

- Are the statements absolutely privileged under the U.S. Constitution pursuant to *Milkovich*?[213]

---

[207] *See generally* L. Adams, Art on Trial: From Whistler to Rothko (1976).

[208] Prosser & Keeton on Torts (5th ed. 1984) § 111 at 774, citing Restatement (Second) of Torts, § 559 (1976).

[209] Prosser & Keeton, *supra* note 208, § 128, at 962-66. *See* Restatement (Second) of Torts, § 626 (1976); Kirby v. Wildenstein, 784 F. Supp. 1112, 1115 (S.D.N.Y. 1992).

[210] 133 Misc. 871, 234 N.Y.S. 185 (Sup. Ct. 1929). *See* L. Adams, *supra* note 207, at 253.

[211] 497 U.S. 1, 110 S. Ct. 2695, 111 L.Ed.2d 1 (1990).

[212] *Id.*, 110 S. Ct. at 2706.

[213] If defendant's alleged defamatory statements are privileged, the privilege defeats not only a defamation cause of action but other causes of actions such as intentional interference with contract, product disparagement, and so on. *See, e.g.*, Jefferson County School District v. Moody's Investors Services, Inc., 175 F.3d 848, 857 (10th Cir. 1999).

- If not, are they absolutely privileged under the broader protections afforded by some state constitutions?
- If not, is there a qualified privilege? For example, under New York law a nonmalicious statement is privileged if made in good faith on a matter in which the party making the statement has an interest or a duty, and in which the party about whom the statement is made has also a corresponding interest or duty.[214]
- Is plaintiff a public figure,[215] or a "limited purpose" public figure,[216] in which case liability would require proof of malice?

[9] Lanham Act

Claims that are essentially for defamation or product disparagement under state law can, in some circumstances, also be asserted as federal Lanham Act claims. Section 43(a) of the Act[217] provides, among other things, that any person who, in a commercial setting, misrepresents the nature, qualities or characteristics of a plaintiff's goods or services shall be liable in a civil action for damages.

Ordinary consumers don't having standing to sue, because they don't have a commercial interest.[218] However, for example, an art collector who owns a significant percentage of the extant works attributed to one artist, has taken steps to promote his collection, and has contracted to sell a substantial number of those works, does have a sufficient commercial interest at stake to give him standing.[219]

In *Boule v. Hutton*,[220] the plaintiffs brought a Lanham Act lawsuit against various defendants, including an expert who purportedly issued certificates of authenticity for 16 of the plaintiffs' Lazar Khidekel paintings and later disparaged the plaintiffs' collection and disputed its authenticity, interfering with the plaintiffs' ability to sell the works. The defendant expert was the son of the artist, and had available for sale his own inventory of Khidekel paintings which he had inherited. A catalogue advertising the defendant's paintings contained two statements that the plaintiff claimed were false: (1) "We present for the first time anywhere the work of Lazar Markovich Khidekel," and (2) neither "[Khidekel] nor his family ever [sold] or parted with any of his works." The court held that these statements

[214] McNally v. Yarnall, 764 F. Supp. 838, 850 (S.D.N.Y 1991).

[215] New York Times Co. v. Sullivan, 376 U.S. 254, 84 S.Ct. 710, 11 L.Ed. 2d 686 (1964).

[216] Lerman v. Flynt Distributing Co., 745 F.2d 123 (2d Cir. 1984), *cert. denied*, 471 U.S. 1054 (1985).

[217] 15 U.S.C. § 1125(a).

[218] *See, e.g.*, PPX Enters., Inc. v. Audio Fidelity, Inc., 746 F.2d 120, 125 (2d Cir. 1984).

[219] Boule v. Hutton, 1999 U.S. Dist. LEXIS 15731 (S.D.N.Y. 1999).

[220] *Id.*

implied that the defendant was the only source of authentic Khidekel paintings and, if untrue, would support the plaintiffs' Lanham Act claim.

[C] Affirmative Defenses

While the law in each jurisdiction may vary, the following affirmative defenses are commonly raised in lawsuits against art authenticators and appraisers.

[1] Contributory or Comparative Negligence

The plaintiff has a duty within reason to look after his own affairs and protect his own interests. In this regard, a plaintiff's relative knowledge and sophistication about art is admissible in evidence and is "highly relevant to the question of his diligence and prudence."[221]

It has been said that an art collector who spends a "considerable" sum of money for a painting has a duty not to rely on the seller's authentication and appraisal but to obtain an opinion from an independent expert.[222] On the other hand, if the total consideration given for seven pieces of art is "only" $36,000, plaintiff has no duty to undertake an "extensive investigation" into the truth of the defendant's claims that the artwork was genuine.[223]

Other conduct by the plaintiff that might constitute contributory or comparative negligence could include failing to provide the expert with complete or truthful information about the artwork, failing to heed the expert's advice, and failing to make reasonable inquiries. Of course, contributory negligence is not a defense to an intentional tort, such as fraud.[224]

[2] No Standing to Sue

The plaintiff must be the "real party in interest," that is, the person who owns or holds title to the claim involved, as opposed to others who may be interested in or benefit from the litigation.[225] For example, where a plaintiff purchased a painting for her daughter and son-in-law, and the gallery made

---

221 Waller v. Scheer, 175 Ga. App. 1, 4-5, 332 S.E. 2d 293, 297 (1985).

222 Rosen v. Spanierman, 894 F.2d 28 (2d Cir. 1990) (holding that the U.C.C. statute of limitations, § 2-725, was not tolled because the painting's lack of authenticity would have been "readily apparent to the trained eye of an art expert").

223 Balog v. Center Art Gallery-Hawaii, Inc., 745 F. Supp. 1556, 1566 (D. Haw. 1990). *See also* Pickett v. American Ordnance Preservation Ass'n, 1999 U.S. Dist. LEXIS 13726 (E.D. Pa. 1999) (whether plaintiff should have obtained a second opinion on value is a jury issue).

224 AMPAT/Midwest, Inc. v. Illinois Toolworks, Inc., 896 F.2d 1035, 1041 (7th Cir. 1990) ("That a more curious buyer . . . might have smelled a rat does not defeat liability.")

225 *E.g.*, Gantman v. United Pacific Insurance Co., 232 Cal. App. 3d 1560, 1566, 284 Cal. Rptr. 188 (1991).

representations to the son-in-law but not to the plaintiff that the painting was an authentic John Singer Sargent portrait, the plaintiff had no standing to sue the gallery for fraud. The cause of action belonged to the son-in-law and the daughter.[226]

[3] Failure to Mitigate Damages

Generally, an injured party has a duty to exercise reasonable care and diligence to avoid or minimize his damages, and to the extent he fails to do so he cannot recover. Thus, for example, if the plaintiff purchases a painting of waterlilies in reliance on an expert's opinion that the artist is Claude Monet, and if the painting later turns out to be by Joe Smith, the plaintiff has a duty to preserve the artwork in good condition and take advantage of any opportunity to sell it at an advantageous price.

[4] Assumption of Risk

Under the doctrine of "assumption of risk," a plaintiff is precluded from recovery if he knew of and appreciated the danger involved and voluntarily accepted the risk.[227] For example, if the plaintiff takes a sculpture, intended as a charitable donation, to four different appraisers, gets three low values and one high one, and uses the high appraisal for his tax deduction, he assumes the risk that the appraisal was in error. Similarly, if he takes the sculpture for authentication but refuses to spend the money for scientific tests recommended by the expert, or provides the expert with an incorrect provenance, he assumes the risk of an erroneous opinion.

[5] Privilege

As already discussed,[228] privilege is a defense to an action for defamation or product disparagement.

Privilege is also a defense in another context. Art experts are frequently retained by trial lawyers to testify in court as expert witnesses with respect to the authenticity or the value of a work of art. If the expert performs his duties in a negligent or tortious manner, and is sued, a doctrine known as the "judicial proceedings" or "litigation" privilege may be available as a defense.

The privilege varies from state to state, but generally protects lawyers, judges, jurors, and witnesses from liability for any communication made in the course of a judicial proceeding, both inside and outside the courtroom.

---

[226] Rosen v. Spanierman, 894 F.2d 28, 33-34 (2d Cir. 1990).

[227] Prescott v. Ralphs Grocery Co., 42 Cal. 2d 158, 162, 265 P.2d 904 (1954).

[228] *See* § 10.04[B][8].

The privilege protects an expert from any subsequent suit for defamation or for any other tort brought by the opposing party or by third persons.[229] It also protects him from liability to the parties who retained him if he is hired jointly by adverse parties as a neutral, dispute-resolving participant.[230] However, authority is split as to whether the expert is protected from suit brought by the party who hired and paid him if the expert was retained by only one side.[231]

[6] Exculpatory Release

Most art experts attempt to avoid liability by including in their standard contract a full release of all claims. Such an agreement is void and unenforceable to the extent it seeks to exonerate the expert from liability for willful and grossly negligent acts.[232] To the extent it seeks to protect against claims of simple negligence, it is enforceable in many jurisdictions if two conditions are met: the release must be clearly and explicitly drafted, and it must not affect the "public interest."[233] The question has not yet been decided, but it is unlikely the services performed by art experts involve the public interest as that term is defined in this context. Thus, a properly drafted exculpatory release should be enforceable.

[7] Moral Rights

Under the federal moral rights statute, the author of a work of visual art has the right to claim authorship of that work and to prevent the use of his name as the author of any work of visual art that he did not create.[234] The French law of *droit moral* grants similar rights and, in addition, provides that the rights are "transferable at death to the heirs or legatees of the author."[235] There is no express requirement in either law that the holder of these rights exercise them reasonably or responsibly.[236] Thus, although no case has yet addressed the issue, the holder of the *droit moral* who authenticates or denounces works purportedly attributed

---

229 Mattco Forge v. Arthur Young & Co., 5 Cal. App. 4th 392, 6 Cal. Rptr. 2d 781 (1992).

230 Gootee v. Lightner, 224 Cal. App. 3d 587, 274 Cal. Rptr. 697 (1990).

231 *Compare* Bruce v. Byrne-Stevens & Associates Eng., 113 Wash. 2d 123, 776 P.2d 666 (1989) (expert immune from suit) and *Mattco Forge*, *supra* note 229 (expert not immune).

232 Gross v. Sweet, 49 N.Y.2d 102, 106, 400 N.E.2d 306, 308, 424 N.Y.S.2d 365, 367 (1979); Cal. Civ. Code § 1668; *see also* Restatement of Contracts § 575.

233 *E.g.*, Tunkl v. Regents of University of California, 60 Cal. 2d 92, 101-04, 383 P.2d 441, 452-54, 32 Cal. Rptr. 33, 44-46 (1963) (hospital release affects public interest).

234 17 U.S.C. § 106A(a)(1).

235 Damich, The New York Artists' Authorship Rights Act, 84 Colum. L. Rev. 1733, 1748 (1984).

236 Compare the California moral rights statute, Cal. Civ. Code § 987(d), which requires "just and valid reason" for disclaiming authorship.

to the artist should have a complete defense to any lawsuit arising out of his pronouncements.

[8] Opinion Conforming to Prevailing View

The world's inventory of art is always undergoing scrutiny and re-evaluation by art scholars. Opinions about authenticity or value that are generally accepted today may be universally rejected tomorrow as erroneous. For example, in 1989, 39 paintings in the Louvre and other great museums that had always been considered Rembrandts were denounced by the influential Rembrandt Research Project, "sending shockwaves through the art world."[237]

The art expert is not responsible for failing to anticipate future shifts in opinion based on new scholarship, changing fashion, or advanced scientific technology, any more than the physician is required to guarantee the correctness of his diagnosis[238] or an attorney the infallibility of his legal judgment concerning unsettled propositions of law.[239] The art expert who has and uses ordinary care and skill in formulating his opinion in accordance with then-current knowledge as to what is or is not a Rembrandt will not be guilty of malpractice if later on, in hindsight, he is deemed to be wrong.[240]

[9] Statute of Limitations

Statutes of limitations are intended to encourage prompt filing of claims "while parties are alive" and "before papers are lost and witnesses die."[241] They vary from state to state and from tort to tort, with the time usually ranging from one to six years and accrual ranging from the date of the wrongful act (or the date that damage occurs) through the date of discovery of the facts constituting the cause of action.

---

[237] Art Experts Say 39 Rembrandts Not Genuine, Reuter newswire report, Dec. 8, 1989. For a discussion of the Rembrandt Research Project, *see* Hochfield, Rembrandt: The Unvarnished Truth? Artnews, Dec. 1987, at 103.

[238] Dewitt v. United States, 593 F.2d 276, 280 (7th Cir. 1979); Christianson v. Downs, 90 Wis. 2d 332, 337, 279 N.W.2d 918, 921 (1979).

[239] Smith v. Lewis, 13 Cal. 3d 349, 358, 540 P.2d 589, 600, 118 Cal. Rptr. 621, 630 (1975).

[240] *See* Firestone & Parson, Inc. v. Union League of Philadelphia, 672 F. Supp. 819 (E.D. Pa. 1987) (seller not responsible if, due to shift in prevailing opinion after sale, painting no longer generally accepted as a Bierstadt); Nataros v. Fine Arts Gallery of Scottsdale, Inc., 126 Ariz. 44, 612 P.2d 500 (Ariz. Ct. App. 1980) (overly high appraisal of paintings not negligent because it conformed with the prevailing view at the time and place of the auction sale).

[241] Glenn v. Cuttle, 48 Pa. 524 (1853).

[10] Laches

Regardless of whether or not the statute of limitations has run, a plaintiff's claim may be time-barred by the equitable doctrine of laches. Laches is based on the basic rule of law that one who sleeps on his rights loses them. However, it is not enough simply to show the passage of time. The defendant must also show that the plaintiff's delay was unreasonable and that the defendant was prejudiced as a result.[242]

[D] Criminal Liability

Preparing forged or counterfeit documents relating to the authenticity or provenance of a work of art can lead to criminal prosecution under state forgery statutes.

Some states have criminal-simulation statutes declaring it a crime to make or alter an object (including an artwork) so that it appears to have an antiquity, rarity, source, or authorship that it does not in fact possess.[243] The rationale for such laws is that "the existence of non-genuine objects undermines confidence in the genuine and thus constitutes a burden on this branch of commerce."[244]

The federal mail and wire fraud statutes, 18 U.S.C. §§ 1341 and 1343, have been used to prosecute art dealers for knowingly buying and selling counterfeit works of art.[245]

Finally, being caught with artwork that constitutes a health or safety hazard can lead to criminal charges. For example, a well-known Manhattan art dealer was arrested, jailed, and charged with unlawful distribution of ammunition after exhibiting a sculpture of firearms and a vase full of live 9-millimeter cartridges for the public to take away.[246]

---

[242] Hutchinson v. Spanierman, 1999 U.S. App. LEXIS 21643 (7th Cir. 1999).

[243] *E.g.*, N.Y. Penal Law § 170.45.

[244] People v. Hafif, 128 Misc. 2d 713, 714, 491 N.Y.S.2d 226, 228 (1985).

[245] *E.g.*, United States v. Amiel, 889 F. Supp. 615 (E.D.N.Y. 1995); United States v. Austin, 54 F.3d 394 (7th Cir. 1995).

[246] Stewart, Charges Dropped in Dealer's Bullet Exhibit, N.Y. Times, Dec. 7, 1999, at A21.

FORMS AND APPENDICES

FORM 10-1

Standard Consultation Agreement—International Foundation for Art Research (IFAR)

REPRESENTATIONS AND AGREEMENTS FOR CONSULTATION

To: International Foundation for Art Research, Inc.:

I, ____, do hereby represent that I am the owner, (authorized agent of ______________________________, Owner) of the work of art described on the reverse of this page. At the request of the Foundation, I shall submit documents in proof thereof.

I acknowledge that you have advised me that the Foundation does not carry any insurance against damage to, or loss of, works of art in its custody.

In consideration of your willingness to examine the aforementioned object, it is agreed as follows:

1. I have made a non-refundable deposit to cover your fees in the amount of ______. I agree to pay on demand such total fees of the Foundation as may be determined by the Foundation to be appropriate for the examination and report on this work of art. The Foundation agrees to advise me, in advance, of the estimated fees in each case.
2. I hereby expressly waive all present or future claims against, and release the Foundation, its directors and officers, the members of its advisory council, members of its staff and any other individuals who are assigned to do work under this agreement on the work of art herein described (hereinafter collectively referred to as "its personnel") from all liability arising from damage to, or loss of such works by fire, theft, vandalism or other accidents, including any alleged or actual deficiency of workmanship, while in the custody of the Foundation or its personnel. I agree to hold the Foundation and its personnel free of harm from all claims which an insurer of the undersigned may assert against the Foundation or its personnel by way of subrogation.
3. I hereby give you permission to take photographs, to make X-rays or any other tests which you may deem necessary or desirable in connection with your examination. I grant the Foundation, or an expert used by the Foundation, the right to publish any photographs or other reproduction of the work of art in its custody, made during examination, as well as any data, findings, conclusions, or the final report resulting from its investigation. I agree to refrain and desist from instituting against the Foundation or its personnel, any claim, action or proceeding arising from such publication. I further agree to indemnify and hold harmless the Foundation and its personnel, experts and consultants from any

claim, action or proceeding arising from such publication or examination. I understand that provenance research may uncover problems in ownership history, and, if so, appropriate people may have to be notified.

4. I agree that I have furnished all information including copies of documents and reports, and have not withheld or misrepresented any facts or opinions that I have regarding this work, e.g., provenance and history, attributions, condition and technical data, ownership and sales.

5. I hereby understand and agree that the names of the consultants and facilities used by the Foundation in any way related to my work will not be disclosed to me. I agree that I shall not subpoena, call as a witness, or use any administrative or judicial process to compel the attendance or testimony of any of its personnel in any arbitration, administrative or court proceeding.

6. I agree that I shall, at my own expense, at the time or times designated by the Foundation, make the work of art available at the Foundation's office or at any other place designated by the Foundation for the purpose of its examination, and I agree upon notification to collect the work of art from the designated place. If I fail to collect such work of art within ten days after notification from the Foundation, the Foundation shall have the right to deliver the work to any warehouse company to be stored for my account at my expense.

7. I understand that the opinion of the Foundation or any of its experts or consultants may be negative or may question the authenticity of the object submitted to the Foundation. I expressly assume any and all claims against the Foundation and its personnel from any liability for libel, slander, or any other claim with respect to the work which may be deemed to arise resulting from the rendition of such opinion.

8. This document sets forth the entire agreement between me and the Foundation. There is no oral understanding, arrangement, or commitment relating to the Foundation's willingness to examine the work. No amendment shall be made to this agreement except by another instrument, in writing, executed by both me and the Foundation.

Signed:____

(Owner or authorized agent)

FORM 10-1

INTERNATIONAL FOUNDATION FOR ART RESEARCH, INC.
500 FIFTH AVENUE, SUITE 1234 NEW YORK, NY 10110
Tel: (212) 391-6234 Fax: (212) 391-8794

REQUEST FOR CONSULTATION

Date: ______________________________

Name of Applicant: ____

Business Address: ____

________________ Tel. No.______________________

Home Address: ____

________________ Tel. No.______________________

How referred to Foundation: ____

When was ownership acquired and under what circumstances: ____________

____

Reason for Request: ____

____

____

____

____

DESCRIPTION OF WORK OF ART:

- ATTRIBUTION* (Artist, Period, etc.):
- TITLE:
- MATERIAL OR MEDIUM:
- DIMENSIONS:
- SIGNATURE, INSCRIPTIONS, STAMPS:
- PRESENT LOCATION:
- PROVENANCE (Previous Owners, Collections, etc.):

PLEASE NOTE: For a proper evaluation of this request, we ask that the applicant furnish all information including copies of documents and reports and not withhold or misrepresent any facts or opinion that you have regarding this work, e.g., provenance, history, attributions, conditions and technical data, ownership and sales.

*The attributions given are those supplied by the applicant and are not to be taken as an expression of opinion by IFAR.

FORM 10-2

Release, Waiver and Indemnity Agreement—Mary Cassatt *Catalogue Raisonné* Committee

RELEASE, WAIVER AND INDEMNITY AGREEMENT, dated as of __________________ by and between the Mary Cassatt Catalogue Raisonné Committee (the "Committee") and __________________________________, the owner (the "Owner") of a painting/pastel/watercolor/drawing (circle one) entitled ______________________________ _________________, measuring __________________________________, (the "Work"). [Please measure the Work, in both inches and centimeters. If a painting, give the outside dimensions of the stretcher from the back. If a Work on paper, give the full sheet size if possible. If the measurements are sight dimensions, please indicate.]

WHEREAS, the Mary Cassatt Catalogue Raisonné Committee (the "Committee") has been established for the purpose of the preparation and publication of a revised and expanded catalogue raisonné of the works of Mary Cassatt; and

WHEREAS, the Owner expressly acknowledges and understands that one or more members of the Committee may be in the business of buying and selling art, including works by Mary Cassatt; and

WHEREAS, the Owner has requested that the Committee consider the Work for inclusion in the forthcoming publication of the Catalogue Raisonné of the works of Mary Cassatt (which publication is herein called the "Catalogue Raisonné" and which term as used herein shall include all editions of the publication); and

WHEREAS, the Committee has agreed to consider the Work for inclusion in the Catalogue Raisonné on the terms and conditions set forth herein and in the accompanying cover letter of even date, which cover letter is annexed hereto and made a part hereof as if fully set forth herein;

NOW THEREFORE, the parties hereto agree as follows:

1. The Committee agrees to examine a transparency or professional quality photograph ("photograph") of the Work or the Work itself for purposes of determining whether or not to include the Work in the Catalogue Raisonné. After such consideration and research as the Committee, in its sole discretion, shall deem appropriate, the Committee shall advise the Owner in writing as to whether or not it intends to include the Work in the Catalogue Raisonné.

MARY CASSATT CATALOGUE RAISONNÉ Founded by Adelyn Dohme Breeskin Jay E. Cantor, *Director*
Adelson Galleries The Mark Hotel 25 East 77th Street New York, NY 10021 Tel 212 439-0946 Fax 212 439-6870

2. The Owner expressly understands and agrees that (i) none of the Committee or its individual members warrants or guarantees the correctness of the Committee's opinion or decision and (ii) the only obligation of the Committee and each of its individual members with respect to the Work is for the members of the Committee to exercise reasonable judgment in formulating a decision to include or not to include the Work in the Catalogue Raisonné. Accordingly, the Owner hereby:

(a) waives and relinquishes the right to sue or assert any claim against the Committee and each of the individual members thereof, his or its heirs, executors, administrators, legal representatives, successors and assigns, arising out of, based upon or resulting from (i) the Committee's examination of a transparency or photograph of the Work or the Work itself, (ii) the decision of the Committee of its intention to include or not to include the Work in the Catalogue Raisonné, or (iii) the inclusion or non-inclusion of the Work in the Catalogue Raisonné; and

(b) releases and discharges the Committee and each of the individual members thereof, his or its heirs, executors, administrators, legal representatives, successors and assigns, from and against any and all claims, liabilities, losses and damages, and all costs and expenses related thereto, including, but not limited to, reasonable attorneys fees, arising out of, based upon or resulting from (i) the Committee's examination of a transparency or photograph of the Work or the Work itself, (ii) the decision of the Committee of its intention to include or not to include the Work in the Catalogue Raisonné, or (iii) the inclusion or non-inclusion of the Work in the Catalogue Raisonné; and .

3. The Owner represents and warrants to the Committee that he is the owner of the Work and that the Owner has sole title thereto and right to possession thereof. The Owner further represents, warrants and agrees that the Committee has the Owner's permission and authorization to publish the Work in the Catalogue Raisonné.

4. The Owner hereby agrees to defend, indemnify and hold harmless the Committee and each of the individual members thereof, his or its heirs, executors, administrators, legal representatives, successors and assigns, from and against any claims, liabilities, losses and damages, and all costs and expenses related thereto, including reasonable attorneys fees, by any third party arising out of, based upon or resulting from (a) the Committee's examination of a transparency or photograph of the Work or the Work itself, (b) the decision of the Committee of its intention to include or not to include the Work in the Catalogue Raisonné, or (c) the inclusion or non-inclusion of the Work in the Catalogue Raisonné; and

5. This Release, Waiver and Indemnity Agreement shall be binding upon and inure to the benefit of, the parties hereto, their respective heirs, executors, administrators, agents, representatives, successors and assigns and upon any subsequent purchaser of the Work. This Release, Waiver and Indemnity Agreement shall be governed by and construed in accordance with the law of the State of New York and any action commenced hereunder or pertaining to the Committee or the Catalogue Raisonné shall be subject to the exclusive venue and jurisdiction of the federal and state courts in the County, City and State of New York.

6. In the event that any provision of this Release, Waiver and Indemnity Agreement or the annexed cover letter, or the application of any such provision, is held invalid, the remaining provisions of this Release, Waiver and Indemnity Agreement and the annexed cover letter, shall not be affected thereby.

7. Any waiver, modification or amendment of any term, provision or condition of this Release, Waiver and Indemnity Agreement or related documents, shall not be enforceable unless it is in writing and signed by the party that is charged with waiver, modification or amendment. Such waiver, modification or amendment shall not be deemed a waiver, modification or amendment of any other term, provision or condition.

8. This Release, Waiver and Indemnity Agreement and the annexed cover letter contain the full and complete understanding of the parties with respect to The Mary Cassatt Catalogue Raisonné Committee and supersede any and all prior written or oral agreements or understanding among the parties hereto.

IN WITNESS WHEREOF, the parties have executed this Release, Waiver and Indemnity Agreement as of the date first above written.

THE MARY CASSATT CATALOGUE RAISONNÉ COMMITTEE. By ____________________

OWNER ____________________________________ Date __________________________

In the event that the Committee determines to include the Work in its forthcoming Catalogue Raisonné, the Committee shall describe the ownership of the Work as follows (check one):

_____ The Committee may use my name as owner of the Work.

_____ The Committee shall describe the Work as property of a private collection.

rev 10/16/97

FORM 10-3

Sample *Catalogue Raisonné* Disclaimers

While the Publisher and cataloguers of this *Catalogue Raisonné* have made their best professional efforts to identify all genuine artworks by [artist] for inclusion, authentication of artwork is necessarily a subjective effort, and the information contained herein is not meant as a guarantee of authenticity, nor should it be relied upon as the sole basis of a determination of authenticity when contemplating the purchase of an artwork by [artist]. Similarly, the exclusion of an artwork from this *Catalogue Raisonné* does not necessarily indicate that the excluded artwork is not authentic. Any decisions with respect to authenticity of an artwork should be made by specially retained, qualified experts. The Publisher and cataloguers hereby expressly disclaim any liability arising from any use of the information contained in this book.

FORM 10-4

Standard Appraisal Agreement—Sotheby's

SOTHEBY'S
Founded 1744

Appraisal Agreement

July 23, 1999

Dear Mr.

This letter agreement (the "Agreement") will confirm your request that Sotheby's, Inc. furnish you with a written appraisal of the *fair market* or *insurance* value of the items of property described as .... and located at ..... (collectively, the "Property").

It is agreed that the appraisal, including without limitation, all copies, summaries and drafts thereof (collectively, the "Appraisal"):

(i) represents our best judgment and opinion as to the current *fair market* or *insurance* value and any other matters covered therein, and is not a statement or representation of fact;

(ii) is not to be deemed a representation or warranty with respect to the authenticity of authorship, period of creation, description, genuineness, attribution, provenance, title or condition of the Property and to the extent that any item of Property is appraised from a photograph, it is presumed in providing a value that the item is in good condition;

(iii) is not to be deemed a representation or warranty that the Property will bring the appraised value if offered for sale at public auction or otherwise;

(iv) except as is stated in (v) below, is not furnished and will not be used or relied upon, by you or any third party in connection with any transaction involving the Property, including but not limited to any purchase, sale, loan, donation or exchange; and

(v) is requested by the undersigned solely for [estate tax or family division] or [insurance] purposes.

In consideration of our furnishing the Appraisal, you hereby release Sotheby's, Inc., its parent, subsidiaries and affiliated entities and the officers, directors, employees and agents of each of them (collectively, "Sotheby's") from any liability or damages whatsoever arising out of or related to the Appraisal or the Property and agree to indemnify and hold Sotheby's harmless from any claims, actions, liabilities, damages or expenses (including reasonable attorney's fees) incurred as a result of claims based on or related to the Appraisal or the Property. You further agree that Sotheby's will not be required by subpoena or otherwise to appear in any legal proceeding, including deposition, relating to the Appraisal

1334 York Avenue, New York, New York 10021
Telephone 212 606 7000

SOTHEBY'S

and that you will not at any given time commence any action, assert any claim or make any demand of Sotheby's in connection with the Property or Appraisal.

You represent and warrant that you own the Property free and clear of any claims, liens, encumbrances or interests of others. You agree that Sotheby's may consult others in connection with its Appraisal. Your representations, warranties and indemnity shall survive completion of the transactions contemplated herein.

Upon receipt of the Appraisal, you agree to pay Sotheby's a fee of __.

If you consign any of the Property to Sotheby's within one year from the date of the Appraisal, Sotheby's will refund at the time of settlement of the sale of the consigned property, a pro rated portion of the appraisal fee based on the appraised value of the consigned property. For example, if the Property is appraised at $100,000, and items appraised at $50,000 are consigned, one-half of the appraisal fee (excluding out-of-pocket expenses) will be credited to the selling commission.

[This Agreement may be executed in two or more counterparts, each of which shall be deemed an original, but all of which together shall constitute one and the same instrument.]

This Agreement will be governed by and construed and enforced in accordance with the laws of the State of New York. In the event of a dispute hereunder, you agree to submit to the jurisdiction of the state and federal courts in the State of New York. This Agreement shall be binding upon your heirs, executors, beneficiaries, successors and assigns, but you may not assign this Agreement without our prior written consent.

Please confirm your agreement with the foregoing by signing and dating this letter.

Very truly yours,
SOTHEBY'S, INC.

By: ______________________

ACCEPTED AND AGREED:

____
Mr.

____
Date

APPENDIX 10-A

Guide to the California Fine Arts Multiples Act

Los Angeles

San Francisco

San Diego

Sacramento

San Bernardino

Costa Mesa

Lewis, D'Amato, Brisbois & Bisgaard LLP
221 North Figueroa, Suite 1200
Los Angeles, California 90012
(213) 250-1800

Lewis,
D'Amato,
Brisbois
& Bisgaard LLP

artist

dealer

disclosure

authenticity

value

scarcity

injunction

compliance

counsel

advice

auctioneer

Guide to the California Fine Art Multiples Act

INTRODUCTION

The California Sale of Fine Art Multiples Act, passed two decades ago in 1970, still mystifies many art dealers. Indeed, some dealers are unaware of its existence. Yet the Act's provisions are mandatory, and their violation can lead to significant financial liability and civil penalties. The purpose of this guide is to provide an overview of the law's requirements.

WHAT IS THE MULTIPLES ACT?

The Multiples Act is a state law (Calif. Civil Code §§1740 et seq.) that requires art dealers to disclose to purchasers of fine art multiples certain details relevant to scarcity and authenticity. The purpose is to enable purchasers to make informed decisions as to the value of the artwork. The law requires disclosure of such matters as the identity of the artist, the artist's signature, the medium, whether the multiple is a reproduction, and the number of multiples in a "limited edition", among other things.

WHAT IS A FINE ART MULTIPLE?

A fine art multiple is any engraving, etching, lithograph, serigraph, photograph (positive or negative), sculpture cast, collage or similar art object produced in more than one copy. It also includes pages or sheets taken from books and magazines and offered for sale as art objects. The Act applies to any multiple offered for sale at wholesale or retail for $100 or more, exclusive of any frame.

WHO IS AN ART DEALER?

An "art dealer" is anyone who is in the business of dealing in fine art multiples or anyone who by occupation holds himself or herself out as having knowledge or skill peculiar to these works. The term also includes an auctioneer who sells these works at public auction. A dealer must comply with the Act even if multiples are only a part of his business.

WHAT DOES THE ACT REQUIRE?

Generally speaking, the Act requires the following:

- Before sale or consignment of a fine art multiple, the dealer must furnish to the purchaser or consignee a written certificate of authenticity setting forth certain information about the multiple.
- With certain exceptions, the dealer must include the same information in any catalog, prospectus, flyer or other written advertisement which solicits a direct sale of a specific multiple.
- The dealer must post a conspicuous sign in his place of business which informs buyers of their right to receive the information.

WHAT MUST BE DISCLOSED IN THE CERTIFICATE OF AUTHENTICITY?

With certain exceptions, the required information includes the following:

- The name of the artist.
- If the artist's name appears on the multiple, a statement whether the multiple was signed by the artist.
- A description of the medium or process.
- If the multiple is a certain type of reproduction of an image produced in a different medium, for a purpose other than the creation of the multiple, a statement of this information. In addition, if the multiple is not signed, a statement whether the artist authorized the multiple or the edition.
- Whether the artist was deceased at the time the master was made and/or at the time the multiple was produced.
- Whether the multiple was made from a master which produced a prior limited edition.
- For multiples produced after 1949, the year the multiple was produced.
- Whether the edition is being offered as a limited edition and, if so, the authorized number of impressions.
- Whether the master has been destroyed, effaced, altered, defaced or cancelled after the current edition.

WHAT IF THE PURCHASER IS ANOTHER ART DEALER?

A certificate of authenticity must be furnished to the purchaser even if he is another knowledgeable art dealer.

DO THE DISCLOSURE REQUIREMENTS APPLY TO ARTISTS?

Yes. Whenever an artist sells or consigns a multiple of his or her own creation or conception, the artist must disclose the same information.

WHAT IF THE DEALER DOESN'T KNOW SOME OF THE INFORMATION?

An art dealer may disclaim knowledge as to an item, but the disclaimer must be clearly, specifically and categorically stated and contained in the physical context of the other disclosures.

WHAT ARE THE PENALTIES FOR NONCOMPLIANCE?

If the dealer fails to comply with the Act, he is liable to the purchaser for the purchase price plus interest, upon return of the multiple in its original condition. If the violation is willful, the dealer is liable for triple the amount. In addition, the court may require the dealer to pay the purchaser's costs, attorneys' fees and expert witness fees (which, in this day and age, can be considerable).

The Act also empowers the Attorney General or any district attorney to prosecute the dealer for an injunction and civil penalties of up to $1,000 for each violation. The dealer may also be liable for a penalty surcharge of up to $1,000 per violation.

ARE THERE OTHER PROVISIONS?

Yes. The Act contains a number of other provisions and nuances, some of which are rather technical. A knowledgeable lawyer can assist the dealer in setting up the necessary forms and procedures.

ANY QUESTIONS?

For further information regarding this Guide, please contact Steven Mark Levy at the Los Angeles office of Lewis, D' Amato, Brisbois & Bisgaard at (213) 580-7933 or levy@ldbb.com.

ABOUT LEWIS, D'AMATO, BRISBOIS & BISGAARD

Established in 1979, Lewis, D'Amato, Brisbois & Bisgaard is a full-service law firm comprised of some 200 attorneys with offices in Los Angeles, San Diego, San Francisco, Costa Mesa, Sacramento and San Bernardino, California. The firm's art law department can provide artists, private collectors, art galleries, museums, art publishers, appraisers, conservators, insurers and others in the art community with the highest-quality legal advice and representation.

GUIDE TO CALIFORNIA FINE ART MULTIPLES ACT

CHAPTER 11

AUCTION LAW

Jonathan A. Olsoff*

* The author thanks the following individuals for their helpful comments on this chapter: John R. Cahill, Rena J. Moulopoulos, Peter R. Stern, Donaldson C. Pillsbury, and Mitchell Zuckerman.

§ 11.01 THE LAW OF AUCTIONS

[A] Introduction

The sale of art and antiques at auction is largely unregulated by federal or state statutes. However, certain key jurisdictions, including New York City,[1] do have laws regulating auctions. New York City is both the largest market in the world for the sale of works of art at auction (excluding, perhaps, at sometime in the future, cyberspace) and the forum of most litigation on this subject. Set out below is a detailed summary of the auction regulations promulgated by the New York City Department of Consumer Affairs (hereinafter "the Regulations"),[2] which is applicable to all auctions occurring within New York City, along with reference to the relevant provisions of the Uniform Commercial Code ("UCC").

[B] The New York City Auction Regulations

[1] The Requirement of a Written Consignment Agreement

Section 2-122 of the Regulations prohibits the sale of personal property at auction unless a written contract has been executed between the auctioneer and the consignor or the consignor's agent.[3] The Regulations require that a consignment agreement include two specific provisions. First, "to the extent practicable," the consignment agreement must specify "all fees, commissions and charges to be paid by the consignor to the auctioneer . . . ."[4] To comply with this provision, the standard consignment agreements used by both Christie's, Inc. and Sotheby's, Inc. include detailed provisions setting forth the selling commission and expenses that will be charged to the consignor.[5]

Section 2-122(2) also requires that consignment agreements include a warranty from the consignor that "he or she has complete and lawful right, title, and interest in the property auctioned" and specifies that "an intended beneficiary of this warranty is the ultimate purchaser at auction." The consignor must also agree to "indemnify" the "auctioneer, his or her agents, principals, employees, employers, or assigns in the event of any defect in title." This warranty of title parallels the implied warranty of title that applies to the sale of goods pursuant to the UCC.[6]

---

[1] Several other states have laws regulating the conduct of auctions. *See, e.g.*, the Illinois statutes, Auction License Act, 99 Ill. ALS 603.

[2] Subchapter 13 of Title 20 §§ 20-278 to 20-290 *et seq.*; Subchapter M of Title 6, Rules of the City of New York §§ 2-121 to 2-125, *et seq.*

[3] A written consignment agreement is not required when the property is being sold "pursuant to an order of a court of competent jurisdiction." New York City Auction Regulations § 2-122(a).

[4] New York City Auction Regulations § 2-122(b)(1) .

[5] *See* Appendices 11-A and 11-B (Sotheby's and Christie's standard consignment agreements).

[6] U.C.C. § 2-312 ("there is in a contract for sale a warranty by the seller that (a) the title conveyed shall be good, and its transfer rightful").

Section 2-124 prohibits an auctioneer from disclaiming the warranty of title.[7] In the event that a purchaser does not acquire "transferable title" to a work sold at auction, the auctioneer must return to the purchaser the amount paid for the object, including the buyer's premium.[8]

[2] Required Disclosures By Auction Houses

[a] Guarantees

The Regulations require auction houses to make certain public disclosures. Most importantly, if an auctioneer "has any interest, direct or indirect, in an article, including a guaranteed minimum, other than the selling commission, the fact [that] such interest exists must be disclosed" in the auction catalogue or other printed material distributed regarding the sale.[9] This provision applies, for example, when the auction house has an ownership interest in a work of art offered for sale at auction, or, as specifically set forth in the Regulations, if the auction house has guaranteed the consignor a minimum amount, regardless of the amount for which the work is actually sold.[10] The auction house, however, is not required to disclose the nature and extent of the interest, including the amount of the guarantee.

[b] Bidding by Consignors

The consignment agreements used by the major auction houses typically prohibit consignors from bidding on their own property. There are circumstances, however, in which consignors or other interested parties do want to bid on consigned property, as in the cases of trustees, executors, or beneficiaries of an estate or trust. In those instances in which consignors or other interested parties are permitted to bid, the Regulations require auction houses to disclose that consignors

---

[7] New York City Auction Regulations § 2-124(a). In contrast, U.C.C. § 2-312(2) permits a seller to disclaim the implied warranty of title.

[8] The buyer's premium is a set percentage of the hammer price that the successful bidder pays to the auction house. *Id.* As can be seen on Forms 1 and 2, the Conditions of Sale of most major auction houses limit the liability of the auction house to the purchase price of the lot (including the buyer's premium).

[9] New York City Auction Regulations § 2-122(d). Such disclosure is not required in advertisements in newspapers or periodicals.

[10] Christie's current auction catalogue, for example, states that (1) when lots are offered in which Christie's has an ownership interest, each such lot is offered subject to a reserve and is identified with the symbol Δ next to the lot number; (2) when lots are offered in which Christie's has a financial interest such as a guaranteed minimum, or an advance has been secured on the property, such property is subject to a reserve and is identified by the symbol ° next to the lot number; and (3) when Christie's has an interest in every lot, it is noted on the front of the catalogue. Sotheby's current auction catalogue includes similar language.

or interested parties will be permitted to bid.[11] Similarly, UCC § 2-328 provides that if an auctioneer will accept bids from the consignor, notice must be given to the buyer. In the event that bids on behalf of the consignor are accepted without notice that such bidding will be permitted, the buyer may "avoid the sale or take the goods at the price of the last good faith bid prior to the completion of the sale."[12]

[c] Loans and Advances

It is not unusual for an auction house to loan or advance funds to a consignor prior to the auction. In such cases, the property typically serves as the collateral for the loan. If it is the practice of an auction house to make such loans or advances, the Regulations require that "this fact must be conspicuously disclosed in the auctioneer's catalogue or printed material."[13] The New York City Department of Consumer Affairs does not require that this disclosure be made on a lot-by-lot basis; instead, the obligation to disclose is satisfied by a general statement in the auction catalogue that the auction house does offer loans or advances to its consignors.

[d] Reserves

Works of art sold at auction are typically sold subject to a "reserve." A "reserve" is the confidential minimum price established between the consignor and the auctioneer, below which an object will not be sold. When objects are subject to a reserve, Section 2-122(f)(1) of the Regulations requires the auctioneer to disclose the fact that the sale is subject to a reserve. In the event that every lot in an auction is subject to a reserve, as is generally the case in sales by the major auction houses, the obligation to disclose the existence of reserves is satisfied by a general statement in the auction catalogue that all lots are being offered subject to a reserve unless otherwise designated. If the bidding on a lot does not reach the reserve, the auctioneer may withdraw the lot from sale by announcing that the lot has been "passed," "withdrawn," "returned to owner" or "bought in."[14]

To implement the reserve, the Regulations permit the auctioneer to place consecutive or successive bids on behalf of the seller up to the amount of the reserve.[15] If an auction house intends to bid on behalf of the seller up to the

---

[11] *Id.* § 2-122(e).

[12] U.C.C. § 2-328(4).

[13] New York City Auction Regulations § 2-122(h).

[14] *Id.* § 2-123(a); *see also* U.C.C. § 2-328(3).

[15] New York City Auction Regulations § 2-123(b).

reserve, this practice must be disclosed in the auction catalogue.[16] Once bidding has reached the reserve, the auctioneer is prohibited from bidding on behalf of itself or the consignor and may accept bids only from persons other than the auction house or the consignor, with the exception of absentee, telephone, order, or other agents' bids.[17]

Over the last several years, legislation has been suggested in New York that characterizes bidding by the auctioneer up to the amount of the reserve as "sham" or "chandelier" bidding, which should be prohibited. In opposing such legislation, the auction houses have taken the position that such bidding is necessary to protect the confidentiality of the reserve since, if all prospective buyers knew in advance the consignor's minimum price, there would be no incentive for anyone to make an opening bid. Instead, prospective buyers would hope that the property would remain unsold and available for private purchase following the auction. This could also encourage the illegal practice of collusive bidding. In the face of these arguments, the suggested legislation has never been enacted.[18]

In addition, the Regulations prohibit auction houses from setting reserves in an amount greater than the low estimate on the property.[19]

§ 11.02 THE CONSIGNMENT AGREEMENT

[A] The Legal Relationship between the Consignor and the Auction House

As the auction house acts as the agent of the consignor in offering property for sale at auction, the relationship between an auction house and a consignor is governed by basic principles of agency law. As the agent of the consignor, the auction house owes a fiduciary duty to the consignor. The scope of an auction house's fiduciary duty to a consignor, and the extent to which those duties may be modified by contract, has been the subject of important reported decisions, first in 1986 in *Cristallina S.A. v. Christie, Manson & Woods, International,*

---

[16] *Id.* For example, Sotheby's auction catalogues include the following notice:

> It is important for all bidders to know that the auctioneer may open the bidding on any lot by placing a bid on behalf of the seller. The auctioneer may further bid on behalf of the seller, up to the amount of the reserve, by placing consecutive bids for a lot . . . . The auctioneer will not place consecutive bids on behalf of the seller above the reserve.

Sotheby's Guide For Prospective Buyers. Christie's catalogues include a similar statement.

[17] *Id.*

[18] On approximately six occasions since 1991, New York State Assembly Member Richard L. Brodsky has introduced a bill that would prohibit successive bidding.

[19] New York City Auction Regulations § 2-123(d). Until 1992, the Regulations provided that the reserve could not exceed the *high* estimate.

Inc.,[20] and subsequently in *Greenwood v. Koven*.[21] These two decisions, and their implications, are discussed below.

[1] *Cristallina S.A. v. Christie, Manson & Woods, International, Inc.*

Cristallina is perhaps the most dramatic of the cases involving disputes between consignors and auction houses. Indeed, the facts revealed during the litigation led the New York City Department of Consumer Affairs to suspend the licenses of two of Christie's auctioneers and the resignation of its president.[22] Cristallina S.A., a Panamanian company, had consigned eight Impressionist paintings to Christie's. Cristallina's principal, Dimitri Jodidio, first met with David Bathurst, Christie's president at the time, in February 1981.[23] After Bathurst inspected eleven paintings, he recommended that eight of them be offered for sale at auction.[24] Cristallina accepted Bathurst's recommendations and consigned the paintings to Christie's.[25] Before the sale, the total value of the paintings was estimated at $8.5 million to $12.6 million.[26]

Following execution of the consignment agreement, Bathurst began to discuss with Cristallina the appropriate reserves for the paintings.[27] Bathurst initially recommended a total reserve of $9.3 million.[28] Cristallina, however, sought a reserve of $10 million.[29] In light of this difference, Bathurst and Cristallina agreed to delay the final decision on reserves until just before the auction.[30] Upon the arrival of the paintings in New York in March 1981, Christopher Burge, the head of Christie's Impressionist department, began to research the paintings.[31] Burge, in contrast to Bathurst, believed that these paintings were "tough" and would be difficult to sell at auction.[32] Indeed, while Bathurst had placed a high estimate on a Cézanne of $3.2 million, Burge believed such a figure to be "unobtainable."[33] A painting by Van Gogh entitled "Rats" was, in Burge's view, "pretty horrible."[34]

---

[20] 117 A.D.2d 284, 502 N.Y.S.2d 165 (1st Dep't 1986).

[21] 880 F. Supp. 186 (S.D.N.Y. 1995).

[22] 502 N.Y.S.2d at 173.

[23] *Id.* at 167.

[24] *Id.*

[25] *Id.*

[26] *Id.*

[27] *Id.* at 168.

[28] *Id.*

[29] *Id.*

[30] *Id.*

[31] *Id.*

[32] *Id.*

[33] *Id.*

[34] *Id.*

Cristallina contended that Burge's view of the market appeal of the paintings at auction was never disclosed to it by Christie's.[35]

By May 4, 1981, Christie's had revised its high presale estimates for Cristallina's paintings to $8.55 million, a figure approximately $4 million lower than Christie's original high presale estimate. Christie's now recommended a total reserve of $8.5 million, just $50,000 less than the *high* estimate. Additionally, Christie's violated its own policy of prohibiting reserves higher than the high presale estimate for certain specific works.[36] For example, although the high estimate on a work by Van Gogh was $2 million, the reserve on that work was set at $2.3 million.

On May 12, 1981, just one week before the May 19 auction of the paintings, Christie's public relations officer, based on information she received from Burge, informed the media that Christie's expected the Cristallina paintings to sell for between $5 million and $9 million. This amount, the court observed, was *less* than the estimates Christie's had provided Cristallina only a week earlier.

As the auction approached, Cristallina and Christie's continued to discuss the appropriate level of the reserves. Although Bathurst believed that the public had reacted favorably to the paintings during the presale exhibition, he nevertheless wanted to lower the reserves based on "negative" feelings he had about the sale. The day before the auction, Bathurst recommended that Cristallina reduce the reserves to $9.25 million. This reserve, the court noted, was "inconsistent with Christie's prior advice to the media that the paintings would earn between $5 million and $9 million and the fact that the bidding public had already been given high presale estimates, figures which were lower than the reserves Bathurst was recommending."[37]

At the May 19 auction, seven of the eight paintings failed to sell. One of the paintings, a Gauguin, appeared to have been sold for $1.3 million, a figure equal to the reserve agreed to by Christie's and Cristallina. Christie's, however, claimed that the painting in fact had failed to sell because Bathurst had raised the reserve to $1.35 million, based on an alleged "floating" reserve of $150,000 that Cristallina agreed could be applied by Christie's. Despite this, immediately after the sale, Bathurst informed Christie's press office that three of the eight paintings had been successfully sold and, on June 1, 1981, Christie's issued a press release confirming the sale of three of the Cristallina paintings. Bathurst subsequently admitted the falsity of the press release, but sought to justify it by claiming it was for "the benefit of [Cristallina] and the art market."[38]

---

[35] *Id.*

[36] Christie's policy was consistent with the Regulations which, at the time, prohibited setting reserves in excess of the high estimate.

[37] *Id.* at 170.

[38] *Id.*

Shortly after the auction, Cristallina brought suit against Christie's, asserting claims of fraudulent misrepresentation, negligence, breach of contract, and breach of fiduciary duty. Although the trial court granted Christie's motion for summary judgment, the appellate court reinstated the crux of Cristallina's complaint. Starting from the basic premise that an auction house "ha[s] a fiduciary duty to act in the utmost good faith and in the interest of Cristallina, its principal," the appellate court found that Cristallina had stated viable causes of action against Christie's for breach of contract, negligence, breach of fiduciary duty, and fraud.[39] The court's decision was prompted by the apparent falsity of several of Christie's statements to both Cristallina and to the public regarding the value of the paintings, Christie's failure to disclose material information to Cristallina, and Christie's violation of its own internal policies. The court wrote:

> Cristallina also argues that Christie's and Bathurst failed to inform it of the information Christie's released in May 1981 to members of the public and the media shortly before the time Bathurst and [Cristallina] met to set the final reserves. Christie's, a self-avowed expert, inexplicably advised the public and the media that the values of the paintings were less than what it knew the reserves to be. Besides prejudicing Cristallina, those actions also violated a policy set by Christie's that reserves were not to exceed the high estimates. Based on the public and media disclosures, Christie's and Bathurst knew or should have known that it would be virtually impossible to sell the paintings unless the reserves were lowered. Yet, at his May 18th meeting with [Cristallina], Bathurst failed to recommend that the reserves be substantially lowered below those recommended in February. Instead, he recommended that certain of the reserves be increased, which was done, with the result, Cristallina claims, that the paintings were bought in and their value thereby adversely affected.[40]

With respect to the fraud claim, the court found sufficient evidence to support a finding that Bathurst had induced Cristallina to consign the paintings to Christie's by assigning a value to them that he knew could not be achieved.[41] The court rejected Christie's contention that Bathurst's statements were not actionable because they were simply opinions and not representations of existing fact.[42] Instead, the court reasoned that even if Bathurst's statements were mere "opinions," he nevertheless had "an obligation to render such opinion truthfully."[43] Furthermore, the court held that "[a]n expression or prediction as to some future event, known by the author to be false or made despite the anticipation that the event will not

[39] *Id.* at 171.

[40] *Id.* at 172.

[41] *Id.* at 172.

[42] *Id.* at 172-73.

[43] *Id.*

occur, 'is deemed a statement of material existing fact, sufficient to support a fraud action.' "[44]

Given the court's findings that Bathurst had made false statements, that Christie's had violated its own internal policies, and that Christie's had informed the public that the paintings would likely sell for less than Cristallina's reserves, the court had no difficulty in holding that Christie's had not satisfied its duties as agent. The court, holding Christie's, as Cristallina's agent, to a high standard of professionalism, explained that "[w]hen an agent is selected because of its special fitness for the performance of the duties to be undertaken, the principal is entitled to rely on the agent's judgment and integrity."[45] And, while the court properly recognized that an auction house does not guarantee the results of an auction, it nevertheless concluded that an auction house, in providing consignors with estimates of value, must provide those estimates in good faith.[46]

The court concluded that Christie's could not possibly have acted in good faith, because it essentially orchestrated the failure of the sale by setting reserves in excess of what it told the media the paintings were likely to sell for. What is not evident in the decision, however, is any explanation for this conduct. The interests of the auction house and the consignor are obviously aligned in that unless the auction house can sell the consigned property, it earns no commissions. Why, then, would Christie's in this case have taken actions which seem inimical not only to the interests of its consignor, but to its own interests as well? Whether this was simply a question of negligence on the part of the auction house or whether there was some other explanation for the auction house's conduct is not evident from the decision. But, there is no question that it was the series of misstatements by Christie's officials to Cristallina and to the public, coupled with its violations of its own internal policies, that ultimately persuaded the court that Christie's had not acted with the standard of care appropriate to an international auction house.

[2] *Greenwood v. Koven*

The principal issues in *Cristallina* concerned the duties and responsibilities owed by an auction house to a consignor. Given the egregiousness of the allegations against Christie's, the issues were fairly clear cut. However, almost 10 years after *Cristallina*, the court in *Greenwood v. Koven*[47] was asked to sort out a far more subtle problem, namely, how to balance the fiduciary duty an auction house owes

---

[44] *Id.* at 173.

[45] *Id.* at 172.

[46] *Id.* at 172-73.

[47] 880 F. Supp. 186 (S.D.N.Y. 1995).

to its consignor with the corresponding duties it owes to purchasers of works offered for sale by auction houses.

[a] The Facts in Greenwood

Greenwood arose out of the consignment by Jane Koven to Christie's of a pastel by Georges Braque. Prior to offering the pastel for sale, Christie's did not consult any outside experts regarding authenticity because the pastel had an impeccable provenance: Koven had purchased it in 1948 from A.P. Rosenberg & Co., one of the most important of the Impressionist dealers, and Christie's own specialists had reviewed the work and concluded that it was authentic.[48] The pastel was purchased at auction by Barbara Lee Diamonstein for $600,000.

Shortly after the sale, Diamonstein raised questions regarding the authenticity of the pastel.[49] To allay Diamonstein's concerns, Christie's confirmed with the Rosenberg Gallery the provenance of the pastel and assured her that its own view that the pastel was authentic remained unchanged.[50] Christie's also assured Diamonstein that it guaranteed the authenticity of the pastel.[51] Diamonstein, undeterred, demanded that Christie's provide her with a statement from a scholar that the pastel was authentic.[52]

In response to Diamonstein's demand, Christie's turned to Claude Laurens, the holder under French law of the *droit moral* for Braque.[53] Christie's contacted Quentin Laurens, the son of Claude Laurens, and delivered the pastel to France for his review. After examining the pastel, Quentin Laurens notified Christie's that he did not believe the work to be authentic and that he would not issue a certificate of authenticity.[54] As a result, Christie's rescinded the sale of the pastel and refunded the purchase price to Diamonstein. However, when Christie's sought to recover the sales proceeds from Koven, Koven refused the request. As a result, Christie's, through its insurers, commenced an action against Koven, alleging that she had breached her consignment agreement with Christie's by refusing to return the sale proceeds.

In response, Koven alleged that Christie's acted improperly in rescinding the sale despite its own belief that the pastel was authentic. Koven also alleged that Christie's had erred in relying on the opinion of Quentin Laurens, rather than

---

[48] *Id.* at 188-89.

[49] *Id.* at 189.

[50] *Id.*

[51] *Id.*

[52] *Id.*

[53] *Id.* at 189. Under French law, after an artist's death, "an heir or designee by will is given authority to assert the artist's 'moral rights', including the right to authenticate which works are done by the artist." *Id.*; *see generally*, § 7.03[C][2].

[54] *Id.* at 189.

his father, Claude Laurens, and that Christie's had rescinded the sale solely as a "favor" to Diamonstein, an important client of Christie's who allegedly felt she had overpaid for the pastel in a falling market.[55]

[b] The Contractual Provisions at Issue

In *Greenwood,* the court was asked to construe several provisions in Christie's standard consignment agreement. The first provision at issue was paragraph 1 of the consignment agreement pursuant to which Koven expressly agreed that Christie's would offer the Pastel for sale subject to Christie's Conditions of Sale and Limited Warranty. Paragraph 1 provided as follows:

> 1. CONSIGNMENT: Seller hereby consigns to Christie's the property . . . which Christie's, as the Seller's agent, will offer for sale at public auction . . . subject to the provisions set forth below and Christie's standard CONDITIONS OF SALE and LIMITED WARRANTY . . .[56]

The Limited Warranty referred to in paragraph 1 provided that Christie's warranted "for a period of six years from the date of the sale that any article . . . which is unqualifiedly stated to be the work of a named author . . . is authentic and not counterfeit . . ."[57]

In paragraph 15 of the consignment agreement, Koven agreed that Christie's had the right to rescind the sale under the terms of the Limited Warranty:

> 15. RESCISSION OF SALE: Christie's, as Seller's agent, is authorized to accept the return and rescind the sale of any property at any time *if Christie's in its sole judgment determines that the offering for sale of any property has subjected or may subject Christie's and/or Seller to any liability, including liability under warranty of authenticity or title.* In such event, Christie's is fully authorized to refund or credit to the buyer the purchase price of such returned property.[58]

[c] The Decision in Greenwood

Whether Christie's Acted Disloyally. In ultimately rejecting Koven's claims against Christie's, the court first rejected Koven's theory that Christie's, in investigating Diamonstein's claim that the pastel was inauthentic, had acted disloyally to her in breach of its fiduciary obligations. The starting point for the court's analysis was § 387 of the Restatement (Second) of Agency which provides that

---

[55] *Id.* at 190.

[56] *Id.* at 192.

[57] *Id.*

[58] *Id.* at 192 (emphasis added).

"[u]nless otherwise agreed, an agent is subject to a duty to his principal to act solely for the benefit of the principal in all matters connected with his agency." Focusing on the prefatory language to this section—"unless otherwise agreed"—the court explained that an agent and principal are allowed to modify by contract the common law principles that would otherwise govern their relationship.[59] Section 391 of the Restatement, the court next observed, explicitly permits the modification of the agent's common law duty of undivided loyalty: "*Unless otherwise agreed*, an agent is subject to a duty to his principal not to act on behalf of an adverse party in a transaction connected with his agency without the principal's knowledge" (emphasis added).[60]

In light of the above, the court next turned to the question of whether Koven's consignment agreement permitted Christie's to investigate Diamonstein's allegations. The court concluded that it did. First, the court explained, pursuant to the first paragraph of the consignment agreement, Koven explicitly agreed that Christie's would guarantee the authenticity of the pastel.[61] In so agreeing, Koven acknowledged that "Christie's loyalty to her was subject to a conflicting loyalty to the buyer."[62] Koven argued, however, that this provision alone did not authorize Christie's to actually assist Diamonstein in establishing her right to rescission. The court rejected this argument in light of a provision in the consignment agreement pursuant to which Koven granted Christie's absolute discretion in consulting experts.[63] The court also rejected Koven's contention that Christie's right to consult experts was limited to "the pre-sale environment":

> [I]f, as Koven alleges, her interests in consummating a final sale of her product are furthered by Christie's taking no action to uncover potentially unfavorable information, that interest is similarly implicated by pre-sale inquiries, which are equally capable of rendering Koven's pastel unsalable. Thus, the Court does not perceive any reasonable explanation as to why, given the entire Consignment Agreement, Koven would not have bargained for this particular limitation, other than that on the facts of this case, it appears to Koven in hindsight that such a restriction would have been beneficial to her.
>
> Conversely, it is quite clear that Christie's would have bargained for the authority to consult experts post-sale, given its warranties to the buyer, and the prospect that rescission of the contract might be necessary.[64]

---

[59] *Id.* at 194.

[60] The court in *Greenwood* correctly noted that while *Cristallina* did hold that an auction house owes fiduciary duties to its consignors, it did not hold that such duties could not be contractually modified. *Id.* at 195.

[61] *Id.* at 196.

[62] *Id.*

[63] *Id.*

[64] *Id.* In concluding that Christie's had the right to investigate Diamonstein's claims, the court also relied on paragraph 15 of the consignment agreement, which authorized Christie's to rescind a sale if it determined, "in its sole judgment," that a sale might subject it to liability under its

Hence, the court concluded that Christie's acted properly in investigating Diamonstein's allegations that the pastel was not authentic.

Whether Christie's Breached Its Duty of Care. Having determined that Christie's had the right to investigate Diamonstein's claims, the court in *Greenwood* next turned to whether Christie's investigation was consistent with its duty of care. To determine the proper standard of care, the court looked to paragraph 15 of the consignment agreement, which gave Christie's the right to rescind the sale if it determined in "its sole judgment" that the sale might subject it to liability. Analogizing this provision to a "satisfaction clause," the court held Christie's to a standard of "subjective good faith."[65] That standard, however, did not completely "insulate" Christie's decision from judicial scrutiny as Christie's was still obligated to act in "good faith," that is, "that Christie's honestly believe[d] it might be subject to litigation prior to rescinding" the sale.[66]

The court, in applying this standard, found that Christie's had acted with subjective good faith. In so holding, it relied upon the following undisputed facts:

- Christie's responded to Diamonstein's initial complaints by confirming authenticity
- the rescission of the sale caused Christie's to lose its commissions, including the buyer's premium
- Diamonstein requested written confirmation of authenticity following the sale
- Claude Laurens, who under French law had authority to issue certificates of authenticity for works by Braque, informed Christie's that no certificate would be issued for the pastel
- Christie's did not rescind the sale until Laurens refused to issue a certificate of authenticity[67]

The court found that these undisputed facts overcame Koven's speculation that Christie's had rescinded the sale only to accommodate an important client who regretted her purchase. In conclusion, the court explained:

> Christie's contractual arrangements between its buyers and sellers appear to be a sensible resolution of a complex commercial problem, recognizing important duties to different parties. The buyer of artwork is protected by a warranty; the seller is protected not only by the covenant of good faith, but by the fact

guarantee of authenticity. *Id.* Given that Christie's was obligated to exercise this right in good faith, it necessarily had the right to consult the experts necessary to determine whether the work sold was authentic. *Id.*

[65] *Id.* at 199.

[66] *Id.*

[67] *Id.* at 201.

> that an auction house earns its money by consummating final sales of artwork. Thus, the broad discretion to rescind afforded Christie's by the Consignment Agreement is tempered by the fact that Christie's own interest is that such rescission not occur.[68]

In so holding, the court recognized that although the auction house clearly owes fiduciary duties to its consignor, it also has obligations to its purchasers with respect to issues such as authenticity.

[B] The Conduct of the Auction

The consignment agreement sets out those issues on which an auction house must seek direction from its consignor and those issues on which the auction house has discretion to make decisions itself. As a general matter, the auction house and the consignor must reach a specific agreement on the reserves, but the consignment agreements of the major auction houses typically have a "default" provision requiring, in the absence of an agreement to the contrary, that reserves be fixed at a certain percentage of the low estimate.

Other matters relating to the conduct of the auction, such as the experts the auction house will consult, the research the auction house will conduct, the manner

---

[68] *Id.* at 203.

A similar issue arose in Kohler v. Hindman, 80 F.3d 1181 (7th Cir. 1996). In that case, the Kohlers had consigned a work to Leslie Hindman, Inc., an Illinois auction house, believing it to be an authentic work by Theodore Rousseau, a Barbizon school painter. *Id.* at 1183. Hindman, in contrast to auction houses such as Christie's and Sotheby's, offers all works on an "as is" basis, with no guarantee of authenticity. *Id.* at 1184. Prior to the sale, Richard Thune expressed interest in the painting, but had concerns over its authenticity. To allay those concerns, Hindman, without informing Kohler, made a verbal "side deal" with Thune in which it agreed to rescind the sale if Thune could not have the painting authenticated within approximately 30 days of the sale. *Id.* Thune was the successful bidder on the painting. However, because Thune was unable to have the painting authenticated, Hindman rescinded the sale.

As a result, Kohler sued both Hindman and Thune. As to Hindman, Kohler contended that Hindman had breached its fiduciary duties to him, because the auction house lacked the authority to enter into a "side deal" with Thune and, instead, had only the right to sell the painting on an "as is" basis, with no guarantee of authenticity. *Id.* at 1185. In response, Hindman relied on paragraph 14 of its consignment agreement with Kohler, which, like the consignment agreement at issue in *Greenwood*, permitted Hindman to rescind a sale if it determined, in its "sole discretion," that it or its consignor was subject to liability under a warranty of authenticity. *Id.* The United States Court of Appeals for the Seventh Circuit adopted the reasoning of the court in *Greenwood*, finding that, pursuant to this provision, Hindman only had to prove that it had acted in "good faith" in rescinding the sale. *Id.* at 1187. Applying this standard, the court found that Hindman had acted with subjective good faith, because its actions were taken solely to benefit Kohler by maximizing the chances that Thune would bid at the auction. *Id.* For this reason, the court also concluded that Hindman's failure to disclose to Kohler its side agreement with Thune was not evidence of a "consciousness of guilt." *Id.*

in which the property will be described in the auction catalogue, the ordering of the lots in the auction catalogue, the scheduling of the auction, and the conduct of the sale are left to the "absolute" discretion of the auctioneer. Most of these issues, of course, can be the subject of specific negotiation between the auctioneer and the consignor if the consignor is unwilling to grant the auction house discretion on these issues.

There are relatively few decisions arising out of disputes between auction houses and consignors relating to the conduct of the sale. The most notable decision, of course, is the *Cristallina* case, described in detail above.

More recently, a lawsuit was commenced against Sotheby's by Gene Reale, in which Reale made a variety of claims concerning the manner in which Sotheby's offered for sale his collection of 74 rare American coins.[69] Although the *Reale* action is pending, two of Reale's claims have been dismissed. The first of these alleged that Sotheby's had fraudulently induced him to enter into a consignment agreement by representing that a particular coin dealer would not have any involvement with the auction or in establishing the presale estimates. Reale alleged that Sotheby's, in breach of this representation, had consulted with this expert. The court dismissed this claim on the basis of the provision in the consignment agreement giving Sotheby's the absolute right to consult with any expert of its choice.[70]

Reale also alleged that Sotheby's had breached its fiduciary duties by referring in the auction catalogue to the grades given Reale's coins by William Noyes, whom Reale characterized as a "notoriously harsh grader" of coins. These references, Reale claimed, caused his coins to sell for lower prices than they might have otherwise. In dismissing this claim, the court relied both on the provision of the consignment agreement giving Sotheby's "absolute discretion" in consulting experts and on the exculpatory clause in the consignment agreement providing that Sotheby's would not be liable for "any errors or omissions in the catalogue or other descriptions of the Property with respect to its authenticity, condition or value."[71] The court's decision was also informed by its apparent disbelief of Reale's claims: "[i]t strains credulity to believe that Sotheby's would undermine its own financial interest in the outcome of the auction, since it was to be paid a commission of 5% of the successful bid price."[72]

[C] The Consignor's Representations and Warranties

Most major auction houses, including Sotheby's and Christie's, require consignors to make certain representations and warranties as a condition to offering

---

[69] Reale v. Sotheby's, Inc., Index No. 604890/98 (Sup. Ct. N.Y. County Nov. 9, 1999).

[70] *Id.*

[71] *Id.*

[72] *Id.*

property for sale. The most important of the representations and warranties concerns title. Specifically, and in accordance with the Regulations, auction houses require consignors to represent and warrant that, as of the date of the auction, he or she has "complete and lawful right, title, and interest in the property auctioned" and that good title shall pass to the successful bidder at the auction.[73] The consignor must also represent and warrant that, in the event there is any defect in title, he or she will indemnify the auctioneer.[74]

Although not mandated by the Regulations, auction houses also require consignors to make additional representations and warranties. For example, given the increasing number of claims to property lodged by foreign states based on patrimony laws,[75] many auction houses now specifically require consignors to represent and warrant that the consigned property has been lawfully imported into the United States from any country in which it had previously been located.[76] Auction houses also require consignors to affirmatively represent and warrant that the consignor has no reason to believe that the work is inauthentic, and to provide all information regarding the provenance of the property.[77] This latter requirement has become increasingly important in light of claims concerning art looted during World War II, in which the provenance can be a key factor in determining whether a work might have been looted.[78]

The consignor's representation of title and indemnity are particularly important to auction houses, because courts have generally held auction houses strictly liable when they have offered property to which the consignor lacked title. The most notable decision on this point was *Brownstone v. Pyzel,*[79] in which an action was brought against Sotheby's for having sold works worth $2,790,955 that allegedly had been stolen by Sotheby's consignor from her aunt, Ethel Brownstone, an elderly woman who had been stricken with Alzheimer's. Sotheby's consignors were Roberta Pyzel, who had been appointed as co-conservator for Mrs. Brownstone, and Eileen Grosso, a friend of Pyzel. When the plaintiff discovered that Pyzel and Grosso had stolen the works and Sotheby's had sold them, she, through her conservator, sued Pyzel, Grosso, Sotheby's, and the fidelity company that had bonded Pyzel as a conservator.[80]

The court in *Brownstone* denied Sotheby's motion to dismiss the negligence claim on several grounds. The court first held that Sotheby's alleged failure "to

---

73 New York City Auction Regulations § 2-122(b)(i).

74 *Id.*

75 *See* Chapter 6, "Cultural Property."

76 *See* Appendices 11-A and 11-B.

77 *Id.*

78 *See* Chapter 5, "Stolen Art."

79 Slip Op., Index No. 13713/91 (Sup. Ct. New York County July 24, 1996).

80 Pyzel and Grosso were both convicted of grand larceny and sentenced to prison terms and restitution. *Id.* at 2.

make even the most elementary inquiry into the bona fides" of the consignor, such as seeking verification of her name, address, and telephone number, adequately set forth a claim of negligence.[81] Sotheby's also contended that the negligence claim should be dismissed as there was no privity between it and Brownstone. In rejecting this argument, the court found that a conversion claim could be stated against an auctioneer regardless of whether privity existed. Relying on two New York cases decided in 1924,[82] the court held that an auctioneer who sold stolen property could be liable for conversion regardless of whether the auctioneer acted in good faith and without knowledge of the theft, following the statement of the New York Court of Appeals in *Island Trading Co.* that "[a]s between two innocent victims of the fraud . . . , the one who makes possible the fraud on the other should suffer."[83] Thus, the court in *Brownstone* explained, "[s]ince Sotheby's was the agent of [Grosso] and in the best position to discover the fraud, there existed a duty of care which will support a claim of negligence based on nonfeasance."[84]

In *Parker v. P & N Recovery of New York, Inc.,*[85] the court, though not referring to *Brownstone,* reached the same conclusion. In *Parker*, the plaintiff filed an action against a towing company that had consigned the plaintiff's car for sale at auction after the car had been seized by the New York City Marshal due to unpaid parking tickets. After the car had been sold, the plaintiff also commenced an action against the auctioneer for conversion. The auctioneer alleged that it could not be liable for conversion because it sold the automobile in good faith without any knowledge of alleged defects in the liens against the car. The court in *Parker* rejected these arguments, finding that "an auctioneer may be held personally liable for conversion where the auctioneer sells property in [sic] behalf of a principal who, as it turns out, never actually had title to, or the authority to

---

[81] As a general matter, auction houses rely on the representations and indemnity of the consignor, and the public nature of the auction process, to ensure that there is no defect in title to consigned property. In addition, most auction houses send their auction catalogues to the Art Loss Register (ALR) for review prior to sale. The ALR is the world's largest private database of stolen and missing works of art. Since its inception in 1991, the ALR reports that it has identified and assisted in the recovery of over 1,000 items, valued at $80 million to $90 million. *See* www.artloss.com. In the event that the ALR identifies a lot in an auction catalogue as stolen or missing, the ALR will notify the auction house, the claimant and, if appropriate, the relevant law enforcement agency. In addition, since 1997, the ALR has substantially expanded its database to include works that were looted during World War II. *See supra* Chapter 5, Form 5-1.

[82] Levy Bros. & Adler, Rochester, Inc. v. Karp, 124 Misc. 901, 902 (Sup. Ct. Monroe County 1924); Island Trading Co. v. Berg Brothers, Inc., 239 N.Y. 229, 233 (1924).

[83] *Brownstone,* Slip Op. at 5 (quoting *Island Trading Co.,* 239 N.Y. at 233).

[84] *Id.* at 5. The court also found that Sotheby's had violated § 2-121 of the Regulations, which provides that an "auctioneer will be held responsible for the truth of any statement contained in any catalogue." As Sotheby's had "explicitly or implicitly" represented to the public that its consignor had good title, the court found a violation of this regulation.

[85] N.Y.L.J., QDS:26701455 (August 23, 1999) (Supreme Court).

dispose of, the property." The court concluded that "the true owner would have a viable cause of action against both the principal and the auctioneer."[86]

The court in *Parker* offered the following justification for the "harshness" of this rule:

> Although the foregoing rule of law, imposing as it does apparent strict liability upon auctioneers for conversion, may appear to be harsh, it is, as a matter of public policy, "designed to discourage larceny and the reckless sale of personal property," and thus properly protects, as much as possible, the only truly innocent party in the equation—the true owner. Significantly, the auctioneer can attempt to insulate itself from liability, or minimize its liability, by exercising extreme caution to ensure that its principal has proper title to, or the authority to sell, the property which the principal seeks to have the auctioneer sell . . . Auctioneers are essentially charged with knowing that possession does not equate with, and does not confer upon the possessor-principal, ownership of, or title to, the possessed property.[87]

In light of the potential strict liability auction houses face for selling property with defective title, typically auction houses are cautious in offering property for sale when they are provided with notice of a good-faith claim of title by a third party.[88] Hence, if an auction house receives a good-faith claim of title prior to offering property for sale, often the house will withdraw the property from sale.[89]

---

[86] *Id.*

[87] *Id.* The court in *Parker* noted that an auctioneer can avoid liability in conversion if "it can be said that the true owner constructively or expressly consented to, or acquiesced in, the sale of the property, or otherwise engaged in negligent or intentional conduct which misled the principal." *Id.* (citing Pease v. Smith, 61 N.Y. 477, 486 (1875); Spraights v. Hawley, 39 N.Y. 441, 447 (1868)). In *Parker*, the court found that a material issue of fact existed as to the viability of the defense as the plaintiff's failure to have sought to recover the car for 10 months after its seizure by the marshal could demonstrate "constructive consent" to the sale or an intent to abandon the automobile.

[88] While auction houses generally will decline to sell property when a good-faith claim of title has been made by a third party, that is not to say that just any claim will suffice. Indeed, in 1997, Christie's offered for sale a manuscript by Archimedes despite a claim by the Patriarchate of Jerusalem that that manuscript had been stolen from its monastery. Christie's did not believe the claim of the Archpatriarch to be legally sustainable and hence refused to withdraw the manuscript from sale. As a result, the Archpatriarch sought a preliminary injunction to halt the auction, but was unsuccessful. *See* Greek Orthodox Patriarchate of Jerusalem v. Christie's, Inc., 1999 WestLaw 673347 (S.D.N.Y. 1999).

[89] On occasion, the property at issue will be offered for sale pursuant to an agreement among the parties that title to the disputed property will pass to the successful purchaser and that the third party's claim of title will be satisfied out of the proceeds of the sale. For example, in Denver Art Museum v. DeMenil, Civ. No. 98-3153(NRB) (S.D.N.Y.), the Denver Art Museum (DAM) made a claim of title to a classic Navajo blanket which was being offered for sale by Sotheby's on behalf of Adelaide de Menil. After negotiations, Sotheby's, the DAM and de Menil entered into an agreement that allowed Sotheby's to sell the blanket and hold the net proceeds until the DAM and de Menil reached a settlement or title was judicially determined. Ultimately, a settlement was not

In such circumstances, auction houses typically retain possession of the property until title is determined. If the parties will not consent to the retention of the property by the auction house, the auction house may commence an interpleader action. Not surprisingly, the decision of an auction house not only to withdraw property from sale, but to retain possession of it, has led to litigation. In *Garcia v. Sotheby's, Inc.*,[90] Sotheby's refused to return six Old Master paintings to its consignor, Sandra Garcia, after receiving notice from the attorneys for the Republic of the Philippines that the Philippines was the rightful owner of the paintings. Garcia commenced an action against Sotheby's in Virginia, and Sotheby's, in turn, commenced an interpleader action in New York, naming as parties both Garcia and the Republic of the Philippines. In denying a motion by Garcia to stay the action that Sotheby's had commenced, the court in *Garcia* endorsed Sotheby's commencement of an interpleader action, finding that it was "not required to evaluate the merits of conflicting claims at its peril; rather it need only have a good faith concern about duplicitous litigation and multiple liability if it responds to the requests of certain claimants and not to others."[91] In perhaps the only judicial comment on what constitutes a sufficient claim to justify an auction house's retention of disputed property, the court in *Garcia* noted that a letter from counsel asserting ownership on behalf of the Philippines was a sufficient claim to justify the commencement of an interpleader action.[92]

[D] When the Purchaser Fails to Pay

Auction houses, as a general rule, do not guarantee payment by the purchaser. Instead, the consignment agreements of the major auction houses typically provide that the auction house is not obligated to enforce payment against a defaulting purchaser and will pay to the consignor only such amounts as the auction house actually receives. In *DeBruno v. Sotheby Parke Bernet, Inc.*,[93] the successful bidder refused to pay as a result of his concerns over the authenticity of the lot. Upon learning of this, the auction house informed the consignor that it had no obligation to enforce payment, but advised the consignor of his right to enforce the sale directly against the successful bidder. The auction house also offered to attempt

---

reached; following a trial, the court found that Sotheby's consignor, de Menil, had good title to the blanket, and thus awarded to her the proceeds of the sale, which had been held in escrow by Sotheby's. Slip Op., 98 Civ. 3153 (S.D.N.Y. June 1, 1999).

[90] 802 F. Supp. 1058 (S.D.N.Y. 1992).

[91] *Id.* (citing Bache Halsey Stuart Shields, Inc. v. Garmaise, 519 F. Supp. 682, 684-85 (S.D.N.Y. 1981). The same result was reached in both John v. Sotheby's, Inc., 141 F.R.D. 29 (S.D.N.Y. 1992) and Koons v. Christie, Manson & Woods, International, Inc., 1999 WestLaw 38195, 1999 Copr. L. Dec. ¶ 27,867 (S.D.N.Y. 1999).

[92] *Garcia, supra* note 90, at 1065.

[93] Slip Op., Civ. No. 84-3021 (D.N.J. Nov. 8, 1984).

to resell the painting. The consignor, however, commenced an action against Sotheby Parke Bernet for breach of contract. The court dismissed this claim in light of the standard provisions in the consignment agreement absolving the auction house from responsibility for defaulting purchasers.[94]

A more difficult issue was posed in *Dembeck v. Sotheby's, Inc.*[95] In that case, it was Louise Dembeck, the consignor, who sought to cancel the sale when the purchaser's payment was late. When Sotheby's refused to cancel the sale, Dembeck commenced an action against Sotheby's alleging breach of contract. In denying cross-motions for summary judgment, the court set out certain principles that govern payment disputes between consignors and auction houses. First, as in *DeBruno*, the court held that the auction house is not obligated to pay the consignor for the property when the purchaser is in default.[96] The court also held that although a consignor has all of the rights set forth in the UCC against defaulting buyers, it cannot exercise those rights "so as to deprive the auctioneer altogether of its right to cancel."[97] Instead, under the consignment agreement, the consignor is obligated to determine, in conjunction with the auction house, the remedies that should be pursued against a defaulting purchaser and must provide the auctioneer with a reasonable time within which to cancel the sale.[98] If the auctioneer failed to cancel the sale within a reasonable period, the consignor would itself then have the right to cancel the sale.[99] The court ultimately denied the motions of both Dembeck and Sotheby's on the basis that it did not have before it sufficient facts to determine whether the consignor had afforded Sotheby's a reasonable period to decide whether to cancel. In so holding, the court almost certainly erred, because the auction house did receive payment within 60 days of the auction. Given that Sotheby's consignment agreement with Dembeck gave Sotheby's, in the event the property was unsold, the absolute right to sell the property privately for a period of 60 days at an amount at least equal to the reserve, the court had no reason not to find that Sotheby's had, as a matter of law, acted reasonably in refusing to cancel the sale.[100]

---

[94] *Id.*

[95] Slip Op., Index No. 120424/95 (Sup. Ct. New York County, July 30, 1996).

[96] No. 120424/95 (Sup. Ct. New York County, July 30, 1996).

[97] *Id.*

[98] *Id.*

[99] *Id.*

[100] In Nass v. Sotheby's, Inc., Slip Op. Index No. 11229/91 (Sup. Ct. New York County 1991), a telephone bidder sought to cancel a sale, claiming that she had bid on the wrong object. When Sotheby's agreed to cancel the sale, Sotheby's consignor, Herbert Nass, commenced an action against Sotheby's for breach of contract, negligence, and breach of fiduciary duty. The court granted Nass's motion for summary judgment, finding that Sotheby's did breach its contract with Nass because nothing in the consignment agreement authorized the auction house to rescind a sale based on a claim by a purchaser that it had bid on the wrong lot. Interestingly, had the purchaser simply refused to pay, Sotheby's could have cancelled the sale since, as discussed above, the auction house

§ 11.03 THE PURCHASER AT AUCTION

[A] The Legal Relationship

The relationship between an auction house (and the consignor) and the purchaser is governed by the "Conditions of Sale" that appear in the auction catalogue. The Conditions of Sale have uniformly been held to constitute an enforceable contract entered into by the auction house, the consignor, and the purchaser.[101] The Conditions of Sale typically address a variety of issues, including payment terms, the extent of any guarantee of authenticity or condition, and the rules relating to the bidding process.[102]

In addition to the terms set forth in the Conditions of Sale, the relationship between an auction house and a purchaser is governed by the UCC as the sale and purchase of a work of art has been found to constitute the sale of goods.[103]

[B] The Bidding Process

Relatively few conflicts have arisen concerning the conduct of the bidding process at auction. The relevant sources of law concerning the bidding process include the New York City Auction Regulations, § 2-328 of the UCC and the Conditions of Sale governing the auction. The Regulations, discussed in detail above, address issues such as reserves, required disclosures by auction houses, and consecutive bidding.[104]

Section 2-328 of the UCC provides that a sale by auction is complete when "the auctioneer announces by the fall of the hammer or in other customary manner." In the event that a bid is made while the hammer is falling, the auctioneer has

---

is not obligated to enforce payment against a defaulting purchaser. In that case, however, Nass himself would have been entitled to bring an action against the purchaser in order to obtain payment.

[101] *See*, e.g., T.T. Exclusive Cars, Inc. v. Christie's, Inc., 1996 WestLaw 737204 (S.D.N.Y. 1996); Marx v. Sotheby Parke Bernet, Inc., Index No. 7561/81 (Sup. Ct. New York County June 2, 1983).

In Weisz v. Parke-Bernet Galleries, Inc., 67 Misc. 2d 1077, 325 N.Y.S.2d 576 (N.Y. Civ. Ct. 1971), the trial court refused to enforce the Conditions of Sale where a purchaser claimed that he was not aware of their existence. This decision was reversed on appeal and the Appellate Court found that the Conditions of Sale were enforceable. 77 Misc. 2d 80, 351 N.Y.S.2d 911 (1st Dep't 1974).

[102] The Conditions of Sale are fixed and generally are not subject to negotiation by purchasers. The only provision that can be altered is the timing of payment by the buyer; auction houses, with the consent of the consignor, will at times grant purchasers extended payment terms.

[103] *See, e.g.*, Foxley v. Sotheby's, Inc., 893 F. Supp. 1224, 1232 (S.D.N.Y. 1995); *see also* Firestone & Parson, Inc. v. Union League Club of Philadelphia, 672 F. Supp. 819, 821-22 (E.D. Pa.), *aff'd*, 833 F.2d 304 (3d Cir. 1987).

[104] *See supra* § 11.01[A][2].

the discretion to either reopen the bidding or declare the goods sold under the prior bid.[105]

In *Marx v. Sotheby Parke Bernet, Inc.*,[106] Sotheby's found itself in a dispute with an unhappy bidder. In that case, Leonard and Virginia Marx claimed that the auctioneer had improperly reopened the bidding on a sofa after he had acknowledged Virginia Marx as the successful bidder. According to a tape recording of the auction, the auctioneer initially acknowledged Virginia Marx's bid of $22,000 as the high bid. However, only seconds after doing so, the auctioneer noticed that he had missed a bid in the back of the tent in which the auction was being conducted and he therefore reopened the bidding. Virginia Marx continued to bid and was ultimately the high bidder at $34,000. Following the auction, she did not complain about the bidding process and attempted to arrange for delivery of the sofa. Subsequently, however, she refused to pay $34,000 for the sofa and tendered a check to Sotheby's for only $24,200 ($22,000 hammer price plus the 10 percent buyer's premium). Sotheby's rejected the check and insisted on payment of $34,000 plus the buyer's premium. The Marxes sued Sotheby's, seeking to enforce what they contended was a contract to purchase the sofa for $22,000.

The court in *Marx* found that Sotheby's acted appropriately in reopening the bidding. In so holding, the court relied on (1) the provision in Sotheby's Conditions of Sale giving the auctioneer discretion to reopen the bidding in the event of a dispute between bidders or doubt as to the validity of any bid, and (2) on the authority granted the auctioneer by UCC § 2-328(2) to reopen bidding when a bid is made while the hammer is falling. The court explained:

> UCC 2-328(a) was not intended to restrict reasonable and fair Conditions of Sale. The plaintiffs . . . were engaged not only in collecting antiques for themselves but also for purposes of resale and were sophisticated and experienced individuals. The court concludes that paragraph "5" of the Conditions of Sale is a fair and reasonable condition and was applied in this case in a fair and reasonable manner.
>
> The court also concludes that by not protesting to [Sotheby's] at the reopening of bidding at the time of that event; by participating in the reopened bidding; and by taking possession of the Sofa prior to making such protest, they are estopped from challenging the propriety of the reopening of the bidding.[107]

[C] The Purchaser's Obligation to Pay

Sotheby's and Christie's Conditions of Sale both provide that title to the property passes to the successful bidder upon the fall of the hammer, subject to

---

105 U.C.C. § 2-328(2).

106 Slip Op., Index No. 7561/81 (Sup. Ct. New York County June 2, 1983).

107 *Id.* at 13.

payment.[108] In the event that a purchaser fails to pay, the Conditions of Sale provide the auction house and the consignor with a variety of remedies, including (1) holding the purchaser liable for the total purchase price (including late payment charges and the costs of collection); (2) canceling the sale; and (3) re-offering the property for sale and holding the purchaser liable for any deficiency.[109]

[1] Defects in Condition

As discussed above, the Conditions of Sale published in an auction catalogue constitute the contract among the consignor, the auction house and the purchaser. It is extremely important that purchasers carefully inspect any property on which they intend to bid because the Conditions of Sale usually include a disclaimer as to the physical condition of the property and such sales are thus on an "as is" basis.

The importance of inspecting property prior to bidding was underscored in a recent case involving Christie's. In that case, *T.T. Exclusive Cars, Inc. v. Christie's, Inc.*,[110] the plaintiff, T.T. Exclusive Cars, Inc., a wholesaler and dealer of classic cars, had purchased a 1962 Mercedes-Benz 300 SL Roadster from Christie's for $239,000. Christie's auction catalogue stated that the Roadster's "total mileage was 24,000 miles, and that it had original paint and chrome and factory fitted hose clips." After successfully bidding on the Roadster, the plaintiff had it appraised and learned that, in contrast to the description published in Christie's auction catalogue, the Roadster had "mileage in excess of 100,000 miles, had been repainted, had new hoses, screw clamps, brush touch-up under the hood and a creased and dirty interior." The plaintiff, in light of these discoveries, sought to cancel the sale.

The U.S. District Court for the Southern District of New York dismissed T.T.'s complaint. Most significantly, the court concluded that, even assuming that Christie's description of the Roadster included specific representations of fact creating an express warranty, any such warranty was effectively disclaimed by the provision of Christie's Conditions of Sale stating that all property is sold on

---

[108] The Conditions of Sale in an auction catalogue typically provide that, by bidding at auction, the purchaser submits to the jurisdiction where the auction is being conducted. *See* Csaky v. Meyer, 1995 WestLaw 494574 (S.D.N.Y. 1995). In addition, telephone bidders who default on their purchases are subject to the jurisdiction of the courts of the state where the auction was held. *See* Parke-Bernet Galleries, Inc. v. Franklyn, 26 N.Y.2d 13, 308 N.Y.S.2d 337 (1970) (applying New York long-arm statute).

[109] *See, e.g.*, Christie's v. Bretal, 1996 WestLaw 660906 (S.D.N.Y. 1996) (holding defaulting purchaser liable for deficiency where painting was resold privately for less than hammer price following bidder's default, as well as for interest, storage charges, and costs); *Csaky*, 1995 WestLaw 494574 (S.D.N.Y. 1995).

[110] 1996 WL 737204 (S.D.N.Y. Dec. 24, 1996).

an "as is" basis. Consequently, the court dismissed T.T.'s contract claim.[111] The conclusion of the court in *T.T. Exclusive Cars* was consistent with § 2-316 of the UCC, which permits the use of language like "as is" to disclaim express and implied warranties.

The court in *Giusti v. Sotheby's*[112] reached the same result. The plaintiff was the successful bidder on a diamond ring at Sotheby's. Prior to the auction, a Sotheby's employee had told Giusti that the ring was "E" color, was "flawless," weighed over nine carats, and was accompanied by an original certificate issued by the Gemological Institute of America (GIA). Sotheby's statements were premised on representations that had been made to it by its consignor, Lee Vandervelde. Following the sale, it was determined that there was no GIA certificate ascribing these attributes to the ring and that the certificate Vandervelde had provided to Sotheby's was not genuine, but was instead a composite of two different certificates issued by the GIA. Giusti therefore sought to rescind the sale. When Sotheby's refused to do so, Giusti sued both Sotheby's and Vandervelde.

The court in *Giusti* found that Sotheby's had not made any negligent or reckless misrepresentations to Giusti and that Giusti had not relied on any such statements. Underlying this finding was the court's determination that Giusti, in deciding to purchase the ring, had bid on the ring because "he liked it after having looked at it," and did not "attach any significance" to the certificate until after he had purchased the ring. The court also found that even if Giusti had relied on the representations by Sotheby's and Vandervelde, such reliance would be unjustified in light of the notices in the Conditions of Sale that all property is sold "as is." The court explained:

> [Giusti] is bound by the terms of the sale and the limitations clearly imposed thereon and his claimed lack of actual knowledge of them '. . . through negligence or inexcusable trustfulness' will not relieve him of his contract.
>
> Giusti's reliance upon the Uniform Commercial Code is likewise unavailing. Any express or implied warranties imposed upon this transaction by

[111] *Id.* at *2. T.T. advanced several additional causes of action in an effort to avoid Christie's disclaimer as to condition. For example, T.T. alleged that Christie's had negligently misrepresented the condition of the Roadster. The court, however, rejected this claim because no fiduciary duty exists between an auction house and a purchaser. *Id.* at *3. The court also rejected this claim because T.T. failed to demonstrate that Christie's possessed any material information unavailable to T.T. or knew that T.T. was acting on the basis of mistaken knowledge. *Id.* In so holding, the court emphasized that T.T. "had every opportunity to view the Automobile and arrange for its own inspection." *Id.* at *4.

T.T. also claimed that Christie's was guilty of fraud, alleging "that when Christie's advertised the Automobile, it knew that its representations were false and concealed the truth from T.T." *Id.* at *4. The court, however, dismissed this claim as well because T.T. was unable to allege any specific facts, as required by Fed. R. Civ. P. 9(b), to support its allegations of fraud.

[112] Slip Op., Index No. 6843/76 (New York County July 1, 1982).

virtue of the provisions of UCC 2-313 are effectively modified or excluded as provided in UCC 2-316, by the conspicuously placed "as is" disclaimers.[113]

[2] Disputes Over Authenticity

Although there have been very few cases involving disputes over the physical condition of artwork sold at auction, disputes over authenticity have provided a far more fertile ground for controversy. Major auction houses generally warrant the authenticity of works of art they offer for sale, but such warranties are limited in duration and vary widely based on the nature of the merchandise. Prospective purchasers at auction must therefore carefully review the "Terms of Guarantee" in auction catalogues so that they fully understand the nature of the guarantee being offered by the auction house.

To rescind a sale, the Terms of Guarantee typically require the purchaser to provide the auction house with the opinions of two generally recognized experts in the relevant field, mutually acceptable to the auction house and the purchaser, that the work is not authentic. The auction houses will often provide purchasers with the names of acceptable experts. In addition, the purchaser must return the work to the auction house in the same condition as it was at the time of sale.[114]

[a] Disclaimers Relating to Authenticity

The disclaimers published by auction houses relating to authenticity have generally been upheld. In *Weisz v. Parke-Bernet Galleries*,[115] two purchasers of works attributed by Parke-Bernet Galleries, Inc. to Raoul Dufy sought to rescind their purchases after the works were determined to be inauthentic. Parke-Bernet Galleries argued that the sales were not subject to rescission in light of the provision in its Conditions of Sale providing that all works were sold on an "as is" basis and disclaiming "the correctness of description, genuineness, authorship, provenance, or condition of the property."[116] The trial court found Parke-Bernet's disclaimer unenforceable. The trial court first observed that, notwithstanding the disclaimer of authenticity, Parke-Bernet expected that bidders would rely on the accuracy of the descriptions in the auction catalogue and on its reputation for expertise. In contrast to this expectation, the trial court noted, the auction catalogue contains "highly technical and legalistic words of disclaimer in a situation in which plain and emphatic words are required" and that the disclaimer was "in

[113] Slip Op. at 8-9 (citations omitted).

[114] *See* Form 9-1 (Limited Warranty) and Form 9-2 (Terms of Guarantee, Paragraph 2).

[115] 67 Misc. 2d 1077, 325 N.Y.S.2d 576 (Civ. Ct. New York County 1971), rev'd, 77 Misc. 2d 80, 351 N.Y.S.2d 911 (1st Dep't 1974).

[116] 67 Misc. 2d at 1080, 325 N.Y.S.2d at 579.

no way given the special prominence that it clearly requires."[117] Hence, the court found the disclaimer unenforceable and entered judgment in favor of the purchasers.[118]

Parke-Bernet Galleries successfully appealed this decision. In contrast to the trial court, the First Department found the disclaimer in the Conditions of Sale fully enforceable. The First Department disagreed with the trial court's conclusion that the disclaimer was not sufficiently prominent and was too "technical" to be enforced:

> [D]efendant's auction-sale, catalogue listing, describing and illustrating these paintings gave leading and prominent place, in its prefatory terms of sale (explaining and regulating the conduct of the auction) to a clear, unequivocal disclaimer of any express or implied warranty or representation of genuineness of any paintings as products of the ascribed artist.[119]

The First Department also found that among the variables which affected the competitive bidding for the paintings was the degree of certainty that the works were authentic. Absent evidence of any intent by the auctioneer to deceive its purchasers, the First Department noted that "the purchasers assumed the risk that in judging the paintings as readily-identifiable, original works of the named artist, and scaling their bids accordingly, they might be mistaken."[120] As in *T.T. Exclusive Cars*, the decision of the appellate court is consistent with § 2-316 of the UCC.[121]

---

[117] 325 Misc. 2d at 1082; 325 N.Y.S.2d at 581-82; *accord* Kelly v. Brooks, 1993 WestLaw 88259 (S.D.N.Y. 1993).

[118] This case was decided under New York's former Sales Act, the predecessor to the U.C.C. The trial court suggested that its decision would have been the same under the U.C.C. *Id.* The trial court also found the Conditions of Sale unenforceable against one of the purchasers who testified that he was unaware of its terms, finding that Parke-Bernet Galleries had not done enough to bring this disclaimer to the attention of an unsophisticated purchaser, particularly, since, in the trial court's view, the disclaimer was inconsistent with the catalogue's presentation of the information as "certain[ ] and reliab[le]." *Id.*

[119] 77 Misc. at 80, 351 N.Y.S.2d at 912.

[120] *Id.*

[121] Issues relating to the enforceability of a disclaimer can also arise regarding the descriptive material included in an auction catalogue. Auction houses generally do not warrant the accuracy of all of the descriptive information printed in the auction catalogue about a particular work; the guarantee usually extends only to the portion that is set off from the general description, typically by the use of bold print or all capital letters. This issue arose in a suit brought against Sotheby's by William C. Foxley, a prominent collector of American paintings who had purchased at auction a painting attributed to Mary Cassatt. Foxley v. Sotheby's, Inc., 893 F. Supp. 1224 (S.D.N.Y. 1995). Foxley alleged, among other things, that Sotheby's had misrepresented the provenance of the painting by not disclosing the identity of the consignor, Michael Altman. Foxley contended that Altman was not "a trustworthy dealer" and that he would not have purchased the painting had he known the identity of the consignor. The court in *Foxley* dismissed this claim and enforced the disclaimer in Sotheby's Conditions of Sale, which provided that neither Sotheby's nor the consignor "make any representations or warranties of the correctness of the catalogue or other descriptions [including]

[b] The Time Frame within which Authenticity Claims Must Be Made

When disputes have arisen with respect to the authenticity of a work of art, the most common area of contention has been the time frame within which a claim can be brought. Although the major auction houses typically guarantee the authenticity of works for five years from the date of the sale, purchasers have brought claims when the sale occurred more than five years before the request for rescission. As explained below, the courts, almost without exception, have enforced the five-year limitation on the guarantee of authenticity.

The starting point for the analysis of the enforceability of the five-year guarantee of authenticity is the UCC, which, as explained above, governs the relationship between the auction house and the purchaser.[122] With respect to the accrual of actions, UCC § 2-725(2) provides:

> A cause of action accrues when the breach occurs, regardless of the aggrieved party's lack of knowledge of the breach. A breach of warranty occurs when tender of delivery is made, except where a warranty explicitly extends to future performance of the goods and discovery of the breach must await the time of such performance the cause of action accrues when the breach is or should have been discovered.

Thus, the key question is whether the guarantee provided by auction houses extends to "future performance." The courts have generally found with respect to works of art that the guarantee is not one of future performance and that any breach of the guarantee accrues at the time of the sale, regardless of whether the purchaser was aware at that time that the work was not authentic. In *Rosen v. Spanierman*,[123] for example, the plaintiffs had purchased a painting in 1968 that the defendant art gallery "fully guaranteed . . . to be an original work by John Singer Sargent."[124] In 1987, however, when the plaintiffs attempted to sell the painting at Christie's, they were informed that it was inauthentic. Consequently, they commenced a breach of contract action against the defendant art gallery. To avoid the dismissal of their claim pursuant to UCC § 2-725(2), the plaintiffs contended that in the case of paintings, "a warranty of authenticity necessarily extends to future performance."[125] The Second Circuit rejected this argument and

---

. . . provenance . . . and no statement anywhere, whether written or oral, shall be deemed such a warranty or representation." *Id.* at 1230-31. The court also found that Sotheby's had, as a matter of fact, not misrepresented the provenance of the painting and that it is common practice for auction houses to not disclose the identity of consignors. *Id.*

[122] *See supra* § 11.01.

[123] 894 F.2d 28 (2d Cir. 1990).

[124] *Id.* at 30.

[125] *Id.* at 31.

found that § 2-725's "explicitness requirement" applied even when the warranty concerned an "immutable quality" of the goods:

> [Plaintiffs] are, in essence, asking us to create an exception to section 2-725's explicitness requirement when the warranty concerns an immutable quality. We decline this invitation to invade what is properly the domain of the state legislature. As the district court recognized, subdivision 2 of Section 2-725 is itself an exception to the general statute of limitations on breach of warranty claims. It would be inappropriate to expand this exception beyond its plain terms by dispensing with the condition that, to take advantage of the exception, the warranty *explicitly* extend to future performance.[126]

The Second Circuit also rejected the plaintiff's contention that the statute of limitations should have been tolled because they could not have "discovered" that the painting was not authentic until they attempted to sell the painting in 1987. Instead, the Second Circuit held that it is not unreasonable to require a purchaser of valuable art to obtain a second opinion on authenticity at the time of the purchase:

> But section 2-725(2) makes clear that it only applies where discovery of a defect necessarily awaits future performance. If the defect is discoverable as soon as the good is purchased, section 2-725(2) simply does not apply. While we would hesitate to deem the alleged defect here readily discoverable if extraordinary measures were required to detect the flaw, a painting's lack of authenticity is readily apparent to the trained eye of an art expert. A purchaser who spends a considerable sum of money for a painting, undoubtedly will, as the Rosens did here, obtain appraisals for insurance purposes. Requiring a purchaser to obtain that appraisal from an expert other than the seller is not an onerous burden.

Although *Spanierman* arose in the context of a sale by a dealer rather than an auction house, the same analysis has been applied with respect to sales at auction, most recently in *Nacht v. Sotheby's, Inc.*[127] Eva Leclair Nacht filed an action against Sotheby's in 1999 after learning that a painting she had purchased from Sotheby's in 1981 which had been attributed to Francis Picabia had been rejected as an authentic work by the recently formed Picabia Committee, notwithstanding the fact that three different members of the Picabia family had written letters confirming the authenticity of the painting. Sotheby's motion to dismiss Nacht's breach-of-contract claim was granted by the court, which held that "[w]here, as here, delivery occurred in 1981, and the warranty did not extend to

[126] *Id.*

[127] Slip Op., Index No. 100938-98 (Sup. Ct. New York County April 14, 1999).

future performance, the warranty claim had to have been brought by 1986, *i.e.*, the statutory four years plus the additional fifth year afforded by Sotheby's express warranty."[128] The court reached this conclusion despite the fact that the Picabia Committee was not formed until several years after Nacht purchased the painting. This is important because scholarly opinion on the authenticity of works of art does change from time to time.

Because the time limit on auction houses' guarantees has withstood court challenges, purchasers who find themselves with time-barred claims have tried to pursue their claims by invoking tort and fraud law. These theories, for the most part, have been unsuccessful.

The most prevalent of the tort claims raised by purchasers seeking to avoid the five-year limitation is a negligent misrepresentation claim in which the purchaser alleges that the auction house was negligent in representing a work to be authentic when, in fact, the work was not authentic. These claims have generally proved unsuccessful because a prerequisite to a negligent misrepresentation claim is that a "special relationship" exist between the parties. To establish a "special relationship" the plaintiff must show more than an "arms-length" business relationship and must demonstrate that a fiduciary duty existed between the auction house and the purchaser.[129] This standard is quite high and, in the *Foxley* action, the court found that Foxley lacked the requisite relationship with Sotheby's despite his allegations of a 20-year relationship with the auction house which included personal visits, viewings of his personal collection, introductions to key Sotheby's personnel, and private luncheons.[130]

The other common vehicle employed by purchasers in an attempt to avoid the time limit on authenticity claims is a fraud action. These claims, like claims sounding in tort, have generally been unsuccessful. In *Kim Yoon v. Sotheby's*,[131] for example, Kim Yoon sought to rescind his purchase of a Korean screen he

---

[128] *Id.* at 6. There are several additional decisions enforcing the five-year limitation on the guarantee of authenticity offered by auction houses. *See, e.g., Foxley, supra* note 121; Kim Yoon v. Sotheby's, Inc., Slip Op., Index No. 107652-96 (Sup. Ct. New York County July 17, 1997).

[129] *See, e.g., Foxley, supra* note 121, at 1232 (citing American Protein Corp. v. AB Volvo, 844 F.2d 56, 63-64 (2d Cir.), *cert. denied*, 488 U.S. 852, 109 S. Ct. 136, 102 L.Ed. 2d 109 (1988); United Safety of America, Inc. v. Consolidated Edison Co., 623 N.Y.S.2d 591, 593 (1st Dep't 1995); Stewart v. Jackson & Nash, 976 F.2d 86, 90 (2d Cir. 1992); *Nacht, supra* note 127, at 8-9 (dismissing negligent misrepresentation claim because auction house is the agent of the consignor, not the purchaser, and "does not normally owe a fiduciary duty to the buyer"); *see also* Rosen v. Spanierman, 711 F. Supp. 749, 758 (S.D.N.Y. 1989), *vacated in part and remanded on other grounds*, 894 F.2d 28 (2d Cir. 1990).

[130] 893 F. Supp at 1232.

[131] *Kim Yoon, supra* note 128; *see also* Friedle v. Sotheby's, Inc., Index No. 89-17905 (Sup. Ct. Suffolk County Sept. 17, 1990) (in authenticity action, plaintiff cannot "by adding an allegation of scienter convert his action into one based on fraud and thus invoke a longer period of limitation").

later believed to be inauthentic. Among the causes of action he advanced was a claim that Sotheby's had acted fraudulently in offering the allegedly inauthentic screen for sale. The court in *Kim Yoon* dismissed the fraud claim on the basis that it was identical to the time-barred contractual cause of action:

> Plaintiff's fraud claims asserted in the fourth and fifth causes of action are not viable because they are duplicative of the first cause of action for breach of contract. All three causes of action are predicated on defendant's alleged failure to provide plaintiff with an original work. To state a viable claim sounding in fraud plaintiff must allege a breach of duty which is collateral or extraneous to the contract between the parties. A cause of action for fraud will not arise if the alleged fraud merely relates to the breach of contract.[132]

The court in *Nacht*[133] reached a somewhat different result. *Nacht,* discussed above, involved the plaintiff's attempt to rescind her purchase of a painting attributed to Francis Picabia that she had purchased from Sotheby's 17 years earlier. Nacht alleged that Sotheby's had fraudulently induced her to purchase the painting by means of false representations regarding its authenticity.[134] In this instance, the court denied the auction house's motion to dismiss the complaint, finding that, at the pleadings stage, Nacht's allegations that the auction house "knew of [the painting's] questionable authenticity, yet included it in its catalogue of works for sale without noting the questionable authenticity," stated a cause of action.[135] The court in *Nacht*, however, did note that in order to establish fraud, Nacht would have to prove scienter and the "mere fact that the painting which Sotheby's guaranteed in 1981 was later found to be of questionable authenticity does not in and of itself amount to fraud."[136]

In sum, courts have generally enforced the provisions of an auction house's Conditions of Sale relating to authenticity. In so doing, courts have interpreted the Conditions of Sale as the contract between the auction house and the purchaser and have held both parties to the terms of the contract. The principal litigation relating to authenticity has involved claims that were brought only after the auction

---

132 *Id.* at 2-3 (citing Miller v. Volk & Huxley, Inc., 44 A.D.2d 810 (1st Dep't 1974)).

133 *Nacht, supra* note 127.

134 *Id.*

135 *Id.*

136 *Id.* The court did hold that, if the purchaser succeeded in proving fraud, the purchaser would only be entitled to recover the amount she had paid for the work since "the damages recoverable in a fraud case are designed to compensate the aggrieved party for what she lost due to the fraud, not to compensate her for what she might have gained." *Id.* Hence, the court explained, "there can be no recovery of profits which would have been realized in the absence of fraud." *Id.*

house's warranty had expired. The courts have found that auction houses are not obligated to guarantee in perpetuity the authenticity of works sold at auction and, in the absence of specific factual allegations of fraud, have dismissed claims filed after the expiration of the applicable guarantee period.

FORMS AND APPENDICES

FORM 11-1

Conditions of Sale and Limited Warranty—Christie's

These Conditions of Sale and Limited Warranty, together with any Glossary which may appear elsewhere in this publication, are Christie's and the Consignor's entire agreement with the buyer with respect to the property listed in this catalogue. The Conditions of Sale and Limited Warranty and all other contents of this catalogue may be amended by posted notices or oral announcements made during the sale. The property will be offered by us as agent for the Consignor, unless the catalogue indicates otherwise. By bidding at auction, you agree to be bound by these terms and conditions.

Conditions of Sale

1. The authenticity of property listed in the catalogue is guaranteed only as stated in the Limited Warranty and otherwise all property is sold "AS IS" without any representations or warranties by us or the Consignor as to merchantability, fitness for a particular purpose, description, size, quality, condition, rarity, importance, medium, provenance, exhibition history, literature or historical relevance of any property. No statement set forth in this catalogue or made at the auction or in the bill of sale, or otherwise, whether oral or written, shall be deemed such a warranty, representation or assumption of liability. We and the Consignor make no representations and warranties, express or implied, as to whether the purchaser acquires any copyrights or any reproduction rights in any property. Neither we nor the Consignor are responsible for the errors and omissions in the catalogue, glossary or any supplemental material. Prospective bidders should inspect the property before bidding to determine its condition, size, and whether or not it has been repaired or restored.

2. The purchase price payable by a buyer will be the sum of the final bid price plus the buyer's premium, together with any applicable sales or compensating use tax. The buyer's premium is 17½% of the final bid price up to and including $80,000 plus 10% of any amount in excess of $80,000.

3. We reserve the right to withdraw any property before or at the sale and shall have no liability whatsoever for such withdrawal.

4. We reserve the right to reject any bid. The highest bidder acknowledged by the auctioneer will be the buyer. In the event of any dispute between bidders, or any other issue with respect to the bidder, the auctioneer will have absolute discretion to determine the successful bidder, to continue the bidding, to cancel the sale or to reoffer and resell the article in dispute. If any dispute arises after the sale, our sale record is conclusive.

5. Although in our discretion we will execute absentee bids (written bids left with us prior to sale) or accept telephone bids as a convenience to clients who are not present at auction, we are not responsible for failing to execute such bids or for any errors or omissions in connection therewith.

6. All lots in this catalogue are offered subject to a reserve, which is the minimum price the Consignor is willing to accept and below which the lot will not be sold. This amount is confidential and will not exceed the low pre-sale estimate. If any lots are not subject to a reserve, those lots are identified with the symbol • next to the lot number. Christie's shall act to protect the reserve by bidding through the auctioneer. The auctioneer may open bidding on any lot below the reserve by placing a bid on behalf of the Consignor. The auctioneer may continue to bid on behalf of the Consignor up to the amount of the reserve, either by placing consecutive bids or by placing bids in response to other bidders.

7. Title to the offered lot passes to the buyer upon the fall of the auctioneer's hammer and the announcement by the auctioneer that the lot has been sold, subject to compliance by the buyer with all other Conditions of Sale. The buyer thereupon assumes full risk and responsibility for the lot (including, without limitation, liability for or damage to frames or glass covering prints, paintings or other works) and shall immediately pay the full purchase price or such part as we, in our sole discretion, require. In addition, the buyer may be required to sign a confirmation of purchase. We reserve the right to impose a late charge of 16% per annum of the total purchase price if payment is not made in accordance with this paragraph.

8. No lot may be removed from our premises until the buyer has paid the purchase price in full or has satisfied such terms as we, in our sole discretion, shall require. Subject to the foregoing, all lots are to be paid for no later than 4:30 P.M. on the seventh calendar day following the sale. We may move the property to an off-site warehouse at the risk of the buyer. If a lot has not been collected by 4:30 P.M. of the twenty-eighth calendar day following the sale, the buyer will be liable for administration, handling and insurance charges of at least $30 for each lot so remaining. These charges will increase each day, up to an additional $20 per day per lot, until the lot is collected, and must be settled in full before the lot will be released.

9. We are not responsible for our acts or omissions in the handling, packing or shipping of purchased lots or those of other handlers, packers or carriers of purchased lots. Packing and handling of purchased lots are at the entire risk of the buyer. If Christie's arranges and bills for such services via invoice or credit card, Christie's will include an administrative charge. If we obtain on behalf of the purchaser an export license for an item containing an endangered species, there will be a charge of $150 for each item for which a license is obtained.

10. If the buyer fails to comply with any of these Conditions of Sale, we may, in addition to asserting all remedies available by law, including the right to (i) hold

such defaulting buyer liable for the purchase price, (ii) cancel the sale, (iii) resell the property without reserve at public auction or privately on seven days' notice to the buyer, (iv) pay the Consignor an amount equal to the net proceeds payable in respect of the amount bid by the defaulting buyer and then resell the property to a third party without reserve at public auction or privately on seven days' notice to such buyer, or (v) take such other action as we deem necessary or appropriate. If we resell the property pursuant to clause (iii) or (iv) above, the defaulting buyer shall be liable for the payment of any deficiency between the purchase price and the price obtained upon resale pursuant to clause (iii) or (iv) above and all costs and expenses including administration, handling, insurance, warehousing, the expenses of both sales, reasonable attorneys' fees, commissions, incidental damages and all other charges due hereunder. In the event that such buyer pays a portion of the purchase price for any or all lots purchased, we shall apply the payment received to such lot or lots as we, in our sole discretion, deem appropriate. Any buyer who fails to comply with these Conditions of Sale will be deemed to have granted us a security interest in, and we may retain as collateral security for such buyer's obligation to us, any property in our possession owned by such buyer. We shall have the benefit of all rights of a secured party under the Uniform Commercial Code adopted in the state where the auction is held. Payment will not be deemed to have been made in full until we have collected good funds. In the event the buyer fails to pay any or all of the total purchase price for any lot and Christie's nonetheless elects to pay the Consignor any portion of the sale proceeds, the buyer acknowledges that Christie's shall have all the rights of the Consignor to pursue the buyer for any amounts paid to the Consignor, whether at law, in equity, or under these Conditions of Sale.

11. The respective rights and obligations of the parties with respect to the Conditions of Sale and the conduct of the auction shall be governed and interpreted by the laws of the state in which the auction is being held. By bidding at an auction, whether present in person or by agent, by absentee bid, telephone or other means, the buyer shall be deemed to have consented to the exclusive jurisdiction of the courts of such state and the Federal courts sitting in such state. The buyer expressly agrees that (i) neither we nor the Consignor shall be liable, in whole or in part, for any special, indirect or consequential damages, including, without limitation, loss of profits and (ii) the buyer's damages are limited exclusively to the original purchase price paid for the lot.

Limited Warranty

Christie's warrants the authority of authorship on the terms and conditions and to the extent set forth herein. Subject to the provisions of the last paragraph hereof, Christie warrants for a period of five years from the date of sale that any property described in headings printed in UPPER CASE TYPE in this catalogue (as such description may be amended by any salesroom notice or announcement) which is unqualifiedly stated to be the work of a named author or authorship, is authentic and not counterfeit. The term "author" or "authorship" refers to the creator of the property or to the period, culture, source or origin, as the case may be, with which the creation of such property is identified in the description of the property in this catalogue. Only UPPER CASE TYPE headings of lots in this catalogue (i.e., headings having capital-letter type) indicate the degree of authenticity of authorship warranted by Christie's. If this catalogue has a glossary, the terms used in such headings are further explained therein. Any heading which is stated in the Glossary to represent a qualified opinion is not subject to the warranty contained herein. Christie's warranty does not apply to supplemental material which appears below in UPPER CASE TYPE heading of each lot in this catalogue and Christie's is not responsible for any errors or omissions in such supplemental material.

The benefits of this warranty are not assignable and shall not be applicable to only the original buyer of the lot and not subsequent assigns, purchasers, heirs, owners or others who have or may acquire an interest therein. This warranty is conditioned upon the buyer returning the lot to Christie's, 20 Rockefeller Plaza, New York, New York 10020, in the same condition as at the time of sale.

The buyer's sole and exclusive remedy against Christie's and the Consignor under this warranty shall be the rescission of the sale and the refund of the original purchase price paid for the lot. This remedy shall be in lieu of any other remedy which might otherwise be available as a matter of law, and neither Christie's nor the Consignor shall be liable, in whole or in part, for any special, incidental or consequential damages, including, without limitation, loss of profits.

It is Christie's general policy, and Christie's shall have the right, to have the buyer obtain, at the buyer's expense, the opinion of two recognized experts in the field, mutually acceptable to Christie's and the buyer, before Christie's determines whether to rescind a sale under the above warranty. If the buyer requests, Christie's will provide the buyer with the names of experts acceptable to it.

Except as otherwise specifically provided herein, all property is sold "as is" and neither Christie's nor the Consignor makes any express or implied warranty or representation of any kind or nature with respect to the property. In no event shall Christie's or the Consignor be responsible for the correctness of, or be deemed to have made, any representation or warranty of merchantability, fitness for purpose, description, size, medium, genuineness, attribution, quality, rarity, importance, provenance, exhibition history, literature, historical relevance, or condition concerning the property, and no statement set forth in this catalogue or made at the sale or in the bill of sale or invoice or elsewhere, whether oral or written, shall be deemed such a warranty or representation or an assumption of liability. Christie's and the Consignor make no warranty or representation, express or implied, that the buyer of any work of art or other property will acquire any copyright or reproduction rights thereto.

Christie's limited warranty does not apply to: (i) authorship which on the date of sale was in accordance with the then generally accepted opinion of scholars and specialists; (ii) any lot as to which the catalogue description, or salesroom notice specifically mentions that there is a conflict of scholarly or specialist opinion as to authorship; and (iii) identification of the period or dates of the execution of any property which may be proven inaccurate by means of a scientific process which was not generally accepted for use until after the date of the auction, unreasonably expensive or impractical to use or likely to have caused damage to the property.

FORM 11-2

Conditions of Sale and Terms of Guarantee—Sotheby's

Conditions of Sale

The following Conditions of Sale and Terms of Guarantee are Sotheby's, Inc. and the Consignor's entire agreement with the purchaser relative to the property listed in this catalogue.

The Conditions of Sale, Terms of Guarantee, the glossary, if any, and all other contents of this catalogue are subject to amendment by us by the posting of notices or by oral announcements made during the sale. The property will be offered by us as agent for the Consignor, unless the catalogue indicates otherwise.

By participating in any sale, you acknowledge that you are bound by these terms and conditions.

1. Goods auctioned are often of some age. The authenticity of the Authorship of property listed in the catalogue is guaranteed as stated in the Terms of Guarantee and except for the Limited Warranty contained therein, all property is sold "AS IS" without any representations or warranties by us or the Consignor as to merchantability, fitness for a particular purpose, the correctness of the catalogue or other description of the physical condition, size, quality, rarity, importance, medium, provenance, exhibitions, literature or historical relevance of any property and no statement anywhere, whether oral or written, whether made in the catalogue, an advertisement, a bill of sale, a salesroom posting or announcement, or elsewhere, shall be deemed such a warranty, representation or assumption of liability. We and the Consignor make no representations and warranties, express or implied, as to whether the purchaser acquires any copyrights, including but not limited to, any reproduction rights in any property. We and the Consignor are not responsible for errors and omissions in the catalogue, glossary, or any supplemental material.

2. Prospective bidders should inspect the property before bidding to determine its condition, size, and whether or not it has been repaired or restored.

3. A buyer's premium will be added to the successful bid price and is payable by the purchaser as part of the total purchase price. The buyer's premium is 20% of the successful bid price up to and including $15,000; 15% on the next $85,000 up to and including $100,000; and 10% on any amount in excess of $100,000.

4. We reserve the right to withdraw any property before the sale and shall have no liability whatsoever for such withdrawal.

5. Unless otherwise announced by the auctioneer, all bids are per lot as numbered in the catalogue.

6. We reserve the right to reject any bid. The highest bidder acknowledged by the auctioneer will be the purchaser. In the event of any dispute between bid-

ders, or in the event of doubt on our part as to the validity of any bid, the auctioneer will have the final discretion to determine the successful bidder, cancel the sale, or to reoffer and resell the article in dispute. If any dispute arises after the sale, our sale record is conclusive. Although in our discretion we will execute order or absentee bids or accept telephone bids as a convenience to clients who are not present at auctions, we are not responsible for any errors or omissions in connection therewith.

7. If the auctioneer decides that any opening bid is below the reserve of the article offered, he may reject the same and withdraw the article from sale, and if, having acknowledged an opening bid, he decides that any advance thereafter is insufficient, he may reject the advance.

8. Subject to fulfillment of all the conditions set forth herein, on the fall of the auctioneer's hammer, title to the offered lot will pass to the highest bidder acknowledged by the auctioneer, and such bidder thereupon (a) assumes full risk and responsibility therefore (including, without limitation, liability for or damage to frames or glass covering prints, paintings or other works), and (b) will immediately pay the full purchase price or such part as we may require. In addition to other remedies available to us by law, we reserve the right to impose from the date of sale a late charge of $1^1/_2$% per month of the total purchase price if payment is not made in accordance with the conditions set forth herein. All property must be removed from our premises by the purchaser at his expense not later than 10 business days following its sale and, if it is not removed, (i) a handling charge of 1% of the total purchase price per month from the tenth day after the sale until its removal will be payable to us by the purchaser, with a minimum of 5% of the total purchase price for any property not so removed within 60 days after the sale, and (ii) we may send the purchased property to a public warehouse for the account, at the risk and expense of the purchaser. If any applicable conditions herein are not complied with by the purchaser, the purchaser will be in default and in addition to any and all other remedies available to us and the Consignor by law, including, without limitation for the total purchase price, including all fees, charges and expenses more fully set forth herein, we, at our option, may (x) cancel the sale of that, or any other lot or lots sold to the defaulting purchaser at the same or any other auction, retaining as liquidated damages all payments made by the purchaser, or (y) resell the purchased property, whether at public auction or by private sale, or (z) effect any combination thereof. In any case, the purchaser will be liable for any deficiency, any and all costs, handling charges, late charges, expenses of both sales, our commissions on both sales at our regular rates, legal fees and expenses, collection fees and incidental damages. We may, in our sole discretion, apply any proceeds of sale then due or thereafter becoming due to the purchaser to us or any affiliated company, whether or not intended to reduce the purchaser's obligations with respect to the unpaid lot or lots, to the deficiency and any other

amounts due to us or any affiliated companies. In addition, a defaulting purchaser will be deemed to have granted and assigned to us and our affiliated companies, a continuing security interest of first priority in any property or money of or owing to such purchaser in our possession or in the possession of any of our affiliated companies, and we may retain and apply such property or money as collateral security for the obligation due to us or to any affiliated company of ours. We shall have all of the rights accorded a secured party under the New York Uniform Commercial Code. Payment will not be deemed to be made in full until we have collected good funds. In the event the purchaser fails to pay any or all of the total purchase price for any lot and Sotheby's nonetheless elects to pay the Consignor any portion of the sale proceeds, the purchaser acknowledges that Sotheby's shall have all of the rights for any amounts paid to the Consignor to pursue the purchaser for any amounts paid to the Consignor, whether at law, in equity, or under the Conditions of Sale.

9. All lots in this catalogue are offered subject to a reserve, which is the confidential minimum price acceptable to the Consignor. No reserve will exceed the low presale estimate stated in the catalogue, or as amended by oral or posted notices. We may implement such reserve by opening the bidding on behalf of the Consignor and may bid up to the amount of the reserve, by placing successive or consecutive bids for a lot, or bids in response to other bidders. In instances where we have an interest in the low bid other than our commission, we may bid up to the reserve to protect such interest. In certain instances, the Consignor may pay us less than the standard commission rate where a lot is "bought-in" to protect its reserve.

10. Unless exempted by law, the purchaser will be required to pay the combined New York State and local sales tax, any applicable compensating use tax of another state, and if applicable, any federal luxury or other tax, on the total purchase price. The rate of such combined tax is 8¼% elsewhere in New York.

11. These Conditions of Sale and terms of Guarantee as well as the purchaser's and our respective rights and obligations hereunder, shall be governed by and construed and enforced with the laws of the State of New York. By bidding at an auction, whether present in person or by agent, order bidder, telephone or other means, the purchaser shall be deemed to have consented to the jurisdiction of the state courts of, and the federal courts sitting in, the State of New York.

12. We are not responsible for the acts or omissions in our packing or shipping of purchased lots or of other carriers or packers of purchased lots, whether or not recommended by us. Packing and handling of purchased lots is at the entire risk of the purchaser. If we obtain on behalf of the purchaser an export license for an item containing endangered species, there will be a charge of $150 for each license obtained.

13. In no event will our liability to a purchase exceed the purchase price actually paid.

Terms of Guarantee

Sotheby's warrants the authority to Authorship of each lot contained in this catalogue on the terns and conditions set forth below.

1. Definition of Authority. "Authorship" is defined as the creator, period, culture, source of origin, as the case may be, as set forth in the BOLD TYPE HEADING of a lot in this catalogue, as amended by any oral or written saleroom notices or announcements. If there is a "Glossary" of terms in this catalogue, please note that any such bonding represents a qualified statement or opinion and is not subject to these Terms of Guarantee. Sotheby's makes no warranties whatsoever, whether expressed or implied, with respect to any material in this catalogue other than that appearing in BOLD TYPE HEADING and subject to the exclusion in 5 and 6 below.

2. Guarantee Coverage. Subject to the expulsions in 5 and 6 below, Sotheby's warrants the Authorship (as defined above) of a lot for a period of five years from the date of sale of such lot and only to the original purchaser of record at the auction. If it is determined to Sotheby's satisfaction that the BOLD TYPE HEADING is incorrect, the sale will be rescinded as set forth in 3 and 4 below, provided that lot is returned to Sotheby's at the original selling location in the same condition in which is was at the time of sale. It is Sotheby's general policy, and Sotheby's shall have the right to have the purchaser obtain at the purchaser's expense, the opinion of two recognized experts in the field, mutually acceptable to Sotheby's and the purchaser, before Sotheby's determines whether to rescind a sale under the above warranty. If the purchaser requests, Sotheby's will provide the purchaser with the names of experts acceptable to it.

3. Non-Assignability. The benefits of this warranty are not assignable and shall be applicable only to the original purchase of record and not to any limitation, heirs, successors, beneficiaries or assigns who have, or may acquire an interest in any purchased property.

4. Sole Remedy. It is explicitly understood and agreed that the rescission of sale and the refund of the original purchase price paid (the successful bid price, plus the buyer's premium) is exclusive and in lieu of any other remedy which might otherwise be available as a matter of law, or in equity. Sotheby's and the Consignor shall not be liable for any incidental or consequential damages incurred or claimed.

5. Exclusions. This warranty does not apply to: (i) Authorship of any paintings, drawings or sculpture created prior to 1870, unless the lot is determined to be a counterfeit (a modern forgery intended to deceive) which has a value at the date of claim for rescission which is materially less than the purchase price paid for the lot; or (ii) any catalogue description where it is specifically mentioned that there is a conflict of specialist opinions on the Authorship of a log; or (iii) Authorship which on the date of sale was in accordance with the then generally accepted opinion of scholars and specialists; or (iv) the identification of periods or dates of execution which may be proven inaccurate by means of scientific process not generally accepted for use until after publication of the catalogue, or which were unreasonably expensive or impractical to use.

6. Limited Warranty. As stated in paragraph 1 of the Conditions of Sale, neither Sotheby's nor the Consignor makes any express or implied representations or warranties whatsoever concerning any property in the catalogue. Including without limitations, any warranty of merchantability or fitness for a particular purpose, except as specifically provided herein.

APPENDIX 11-A

Standard Consignment Agreement—Sotheby's

MASTER CONSIGNMENT AGREEMENT

Thank you for consigning property to Sotheby's.

This confirms our agreement under which property which is consigned by you from time to time and which is accepted by us for an auction sale, as evidenced by a confirmation notice, will be offered at auction. All property accepted shall be referred to as "Property". For purposes of determining the selling commission set forth in paragraph 2 below, "Consignment" shall mean all Property listed on the attached Schedule I or on one standard form Property Receipt issued by us. Property will be offered subject to the following terms and our standard Conditions of Sale and Terms of Guarantee to be printed in the catalogue for the sale, by which you hereby agree to be bound. As used herein, "we", "us" and "ours" mean Sotheby's, Inc. and any affiliated company offering Property for sale under this Agreement, and "you" and "your" mean the individual, corporation or other entity listed above.

SOTHEBY'S

1334 York Avenue, New York, New York 10021 Telephone: (212) 606-7000

1. **The Auction.** In connection with any auction, we will have absolute discretion as to (a) consulting any expert either before or after the sale, (b) researching the provenance of the Property, (c) grouping the Property into lots and providing catalogue and other descriptions as we believe appropriate, (d) the date or dates of an auction and (e) the manner of conducting the sale.

2. **Commission.** Your selling commission will be determined by reference to the highest of: (a) the total of the successful bid prices of all Property sold in this Consignment, (b) the total of the successful bid prices for all property sold by you in the calendar year immediately preceding the year of the current Consignment, or (c) the total of the successful bid prices for all property sold by you in the calendar year of the current Consignment. The highest of (a), (b) or (c) above shall be referred to herein as the "Total". In each of (a), (b) and (c), "sold" shall be defined as a lot which sold at auction and for which we have collected good funds. If the sale of any lot has been rescinded under paragraph 10, such lot will not be deemed to have been "sold" for purposes of determining the Total. If we collect good funds, the sale shall be deemed to have taken place on the date of the auction. You agree to pay us a selling commission on each lot sold based on the amount of the Total and at the lowest applicable rate set forth on the Selling Commission Schedule below.

You authorize us to charge the buyer and retain for our account a commission on each lot sold (the "buyer's premium"). The Conditions of Sale in the catalogue for the auction will state the rate at which the buyer's premium will be assessed against the buyer, and such rate will be a percentage of the successful bid price of each lot sold.

3. **Settlement.** On the Settlement Date(s) (as defined below), we will mail to you the sale proceeds we collect and receive, after deducting our selling commission, buyer's premium and reimbursable expenses (the "net sale proceeds"), unless the purchaser has notified us of intention to rescind the sale (as provided in paragraph 10). We may also deduct and retain from the net sale proceeds any other amount you owe us or any of our affiliated entities, whether arising out of the sale of the Property or otherwise. If all of the Property is sold in the same auction, the "Settlement Date" will be the date that is thirty-five days after the last session of the auction. If the Property is to be sold in more than one auction, then the "Settlement Dates" will be the dates that are thirty-five days after the last session of each auction.

We have no obligation to enforce payment by any purchaser. If a purchaser does not pay, and you and we do not agree on another course of action, we reserve the right to cancel the sale and return the Property to you.

Notwithstanding the preceding sentence, if we pay you all or part of the net sale proceeds for any lot of the Property and have not collected from the purchaser of such Property payment of the amount we paid to you, simultaneously with, and to the extent of, any such payment by us to you, you assign to us any and all rights you may have against such purchaser, whether at law, in equity or under the Conditions of Sale. You agree to execute any documents we may reasonably request evidencing this assignment, and you agree that all of your representations, warranties and indemnities set forth in this Agreement shall apply to us or the purchaser, as the case may be, with respect to such item. You authorize us, in our discretion, to impose on any purchaser and retain for our account a late charge if payment is not made in accordance with the Conditions of Sale.

4. **Reserves.** Unless a different reserve has been agreed upon by you and us and confirmed in writing before the auction, the reserve for each lot of the Property will be the following percentage of our latest announced or published low pre-sale estimate: (i) 25% for any lot having a low estimate of less than $300, (ii) 40% for any lot having a low estimate of $300 or more up to $1,000, or (iii) 60% for any lot having a low estimate of $1,000 or more. However, we may sell any lot of the Property at a price below the reserve, provided that we pay you in accordance with paragraph 3 above the net amount which you would have been entitled to receive had such lot of the Property been sold at the reserve (that is, the reserve less our selling commission, reimbursable expenses and any amount you owe us or any of our affiliated entities). No reserve for a lot will exceed its low pre-sale estimate.

You agree not to bid on the Property. Although we shall be entitled to bid on your behalf up to the amount of the reserve, you shall not instruct or permit any other person to bid for the Property on your behalf. If, however, you violate your foregoing commitment and you or your agent become the successful bidder on the Property, you will pay us the selling commission as set forth in paragraph 2 and the buyer's premium on the successful bid price, the Property may be sold without any reserve, and you will not be entitled to the benefit of any warranties under the Conditions of Sale or Terms of Guarantee.

In the event any lot is bought-in, we will make an announcement that such lot has been "passed", "returned to owner", "withdrawn" or "bought-in", and you will be charged a commission in accordance with the Selling Commission Schedule below.

5. **Sotheby's Arcade Auctions.** If we deem it appropriate, we may, in our sole dis cretion, include in a Sotheby's Arcade Aucti any Property with a low pre-sale estimate ir our opinion of $5,000 or less. In such even or if you and we agree to include any proper in a Sotheby's Arcade Auction, we will offer the Property subject to the provisions of this Agreement and our Conditions of Sale f Sotheby's Arcade Auctions printed in the catalogue, except that the Settlement Date will be twenty-one days after the last session of the auction.

6. **Representations and Warranties; Indemnity.** You represent and warrant to u and each purchaser that you have the right to consign the Property for sale; that it is now and through and including its sale will be kept, free of all liens, claims and encumbranc of others including, but not limited to, claim of governments or governmental agencies; tha good title and right to possession will pass to the purchaser free of all liens, claims and encumbrances; that you have provided us wit any information you have concerning the provenance of the Property; that you have no reason to believe that any lot of Property is not authentic or is counterfeit; that where the Property has been imported into the United States, the Property has been lawfully importe into the United States and has been lawfully and permanently exported as required by the laws of any country (including any laws or regulations applicable in the European Union) in which it was located; that required declarations upon the export and import of the Property have been properly made and any duties and taxes on the export and import of the Property have been paid; that you have paid or will pay any and all taxes and/or duties that may be due on the net sale proceeds of the Property and you have notified us in writing of any and all taxes and/or duties that are payable by us on your behalf in any country other than the United States; and that there are no restrictions on our right to reproduce photographs of it. We retain the exclusive copyright to all catalogue and other illustrations and descriptions of the Property created by us.

You agree to indemnify and hold us and each purchaser harmless from and against any and all claims, actions, damages, losses, liabilities and expenses (including reasonable attorneys' fees) relating to the breach or alleged breach of any of your agreements, representations or warranties in this Agreement.

Your representations, warranties and indemnity will survive completion of the transactions contemplated by this Agreement.

7. **Expenses.** You agree to bear the expenses of: (a) purchasing insurance which will insure you for loss or damage to the Property (as further provided in paragraph 8), (b) our standard

fees then in effect for catalogue illustration, (c) packing, shipping and customs duties to our premises, (d) any agreed-upon advertising, (e) the cost of any reproduction rights and (f) other services, such as framing, restoration and gemological tests, approved by you. There will be a 20% service charge on the cost of any services performed by others and paid for by us for your account. In addition to other remedies available to us by law, we reserve the right to impose a late charge of 1½% per month on any amount due us or any of our affiliated entities and remaining unpaid for more than fifteen days after we notify you.

8. **Insurance for Loss or Damage.** Unless, at the time you deliver the Property to us, you provide us with a certificate of insurance with a waiver of subrogation each in form acceptable to us, by executing this Agreement, you authorize us to purchase insurance to cover the risk of loss or damage to the Property from the time of our receipt of such Property until it ceases to be in our custody or control, or until 60 days after the sale, whichever occurs first, in the amount set forth in the paragraph below, Insurance Amount. Such insurance will automatically be arranged by us and you authorize and instruct us, whether or not the Property is sold, to pay insurance premiums on your behalf. The insurer's and our combined liability to you resulting from loss or damage to any lot of Property shall not exceed the Insurance Amount of such Property. The premium will be 1% of the Insurance Amount described below for Property receipted by us at our auction premises or warehouse in New York City, or 1½% if the Property is receipted at a branch office or any other location.

Insurance Amount. The amount of the insurance we are purchasing on your behalf and to which you agree is: (a) for Property which has been sold, the successful bid price (excluding buyer's premium), (b) for Property which has failed to sell at the auction, the reserve, or (c) for Property not yet offered for sale, the mean of our latest pre-sale estimates. In the event of a total loss (Property which has been lost, or Property which has been damaged and has depreciated in value, in the insurer's opinion, by more than 50%), the insurer will pay you the foregoing amount, less in any case the selling commission and expenses payable by you under this agreement, and the Property will belong to the insurer. In the event of a partial loss (Property which has been partially damaged or lost and has depreciated in value, in the insurer's opinion, by less than 50%), the insurer will either (i) pay you the amount of depreciation and such Property will be offered for sale or returned to you or (ii) pay you the "Insurance Amount" for the Property as set forth in the preceding sentence, and the Property will belong to the insurer. Neither the insurer nor we will be liable for damage to frames or glass covering prints, paintings or other works, or for damage occurring in the course of any process undertaken by independent contractors employed with your consent (including restoration, framing or cleaning), or for damage caused by changes in humidity or temperature, inherent conditions or defects, normal wear and tear, war, nuclear fission or radioactive contamination.

9. **Withdrawal.** You may not withdraw any Property from sale after the date on which we issue a receipt or you sign this Agreement, whichever is earlier. Regardless of whether we have previously issued a receipt, published a catalogue including the Property or advertised its sale, we may withdraw any Property at any time before sale if in our sole judgment (a) there is doubt as to its authenticity or attribution, (b) there is doubt as to the accuracy of any of your representations or warranties, or (c) you have breached any provision of this Agreement. If we withdraw any Property under (b) or (c) of this paragraph 9, you must within ten days of our notice to you of withdrawal pay us a withdrawal fee equal to 20% of the mean of our latest pre-sale estimates for the withdrawn Property, as well as all out-of-pocket expenses incurred by us up to and including the date of withdrawal (the "Withdrawal Fee"). If any Property is withdrawn under (a) above, you will not be charged a Withdrawal Fee and, subject to any liens against or claims to the Property, such Property will be returned to you at your expense.

10. **Rescission.** You authorize us to rescind the sale of any Property in accordance with the Conditions of Sale and Terms of Guarantee, or if we learn that the Property is inaccurately described in the catalogue, or if we learn that the Property is a counterfeit (a modern forgery intended to deceive), or if we determine in our sole judgment that the offering for sale of any lot of Property has subjected or may subject us and/or you to any liability, including liability under the warranty of title or warranty of authenticity included in the Terms of Guarantee. If we receive from a purchaser notice of intention to rescind and we determine that a lot of the Property is subject to rescission under the Terms of Guarantee or as otherwise set forth above, we will credit the purchaser with the purchase price, you will return to us on ten days' notice to you any sale proceeds for such Property paid by us to you or to a third party as directed by you, and we will return the Property to you upon your reimbursing us for expenses incurred in connection with the rescinded sale, and paying us any other amounts you owe us or any of our affiliated entities.

11. **Private Sales.** If any lot fails to reach its reserve and is bought-in for your account, you authorize us, as your exclusive agent, for a period of 60 days following the auction, to sell the lot privately for a price that will result in a payment to you of not less than the net amount (after our selling commission and expenses) to which you would have been entitled had the lot been sold at a price equal to the agreed reserve. In such event, your obligations to us hereunder with respect to such lot are the same as if it had been sold at auction.

12. **Treatment of Unsold Property.** If any Property remains unsold for any reason after the auction, we will notify you. If such Property has not been sold privately pursuant to paragraph 11, and if it is not reconsigned to us for sale on mutually agreed-upon terms or picked up within 60 days after such notification, we may (a) return it to you at your expense, (b) sell it at public auction without reserve at a place and date determined by us or (c) transfer it to a third-party warehouse. The proceeds of any sale pursuant to (b) above will be applied to any amount you owe us or any of our affiliated entities, including, but not limited to, our commissions and expenses, and any excess will be remitted to you. In the event of the transfer of any unsold Property to a third-party warehouse, you shall bear all cost and risk thereof and shall be liable to such warehouse for the payment of all storage and insurance charges at such warehouse's standard rates.

You shall not be entitled to reclaim any unsold Property until all commission, expenses and other amounts owed to us or any of our affiliates have been paid in full. Unless and until we reoffer and sell such Property or return it to you, we will hold it without charge for a period of 30 days after the auction in which it is offered but not sold. Thereafter a handling charge of 1% per month of the mean of our pre-sale estimates will be payable by you to cover our costs of handling.

13. **Estimates; Catalogue Descriptions** Pre-sale estimates, if any, are intended as guides for prospective bidders. We make no representations or warranties of the anticipated selling price of any Property and no estimate anywhere by us of the selling price of any Property may be relied upon as a prediction of the actual selling price. Estimates included in receipts, catalogues or elsewhere are preliminary only and are subject to revision by us from time to time in our sole discretion.

We will not be liable for any errors or omissions with respect to the auction or in the catalogue or other descriptions of the Property and make no guarantees, representations or warranties whatsoever to you with respect to the Property, its authenticity, condition, value or otherwise.

14. **Use of Name.** We may use your name as owner of the Property as set forth on the first page of this Agreement or we may designate the Property as indicated by you below (please print your instructions and initial the box next to it), when we offer the Property for sale, advertise or otherwise promote the sale, both before or after the auction. If you do not want us to use your name or otherwise designate the Property, please initial the box below.

You may designate the Property as follows:

________________________________[ ]

You may not use my name: [ ]

15. **Legal Status.** If you are acting as a fiduciary in executing this Agreement and in the transactions contemplated hereunder, please initial "Fiduciary" and sign and return to us our standard "Fiduciary Agreement".

Fiduciary [ ]

If you are acting as an agent for someone who is not signing this Agreement, you and your principal jointly and severally assume your obligations and liabilities hereunder to the same extent as if you were acting as principal.

16. **Term of Agreement; Amendment.** Either you or we may terminate this Agreement at any time upon 30 days' prior written notice to the other. No such termination shall permit you to withdraw from sale any Property previously delivered to us or relieve either you or us of any obligations or liabilities incurred prior to the effective date of such notice.

Neither you nor we may amend, supplement or waive any provision of this Agreement other than by means of a writing signed by both parties except that if at any time we propose by written notice to amend or supplement any provision of this Agreement, or provide additional terms or conditions as to your future consignments, you will be deemed to have agreed thereto with respect to any property received by us at any time after such notice, unless you advise us in writing to the contrary before such property is received by us.

17. **Miscellaneous.** *This Agreement shall be governed by and construed and enforced in accordance with the laws of the State of New York. In the event of a dispute hereunder, you agree to submit to the exclusive jurisdiction of the state courts of and the federal courts sitting in the State of New York.* This Agreement shall be binding upon your heirs, executors, beneficiaries, successors and assigns, but you may not assign this Agreement without our prior written consent. Neither party shall be liable to the other for any special, consequential or incidental damages. This Agreement, including the Schedules hereto, and the Conditions of Sale and any Terms of Guarantee, constitute the entire agreement between the parties with respect to the transactions contemplated hereby and supersede all prior or contemporaneous written, oral or implied understandings, representations and agreements of the parties relating to the subject matter of this Agreement. You agree that you will not disclose the terms of this Agreement to any third party without our prior written consent, except to attorneys and accountants on a need-to-know basis, or as a result of valid legal process compelling the disclosure, provided you first give us prompt written notice of such service of process and allow us, if we deem it appropriate, to obtain a protective order. Any notices given hereunder to you or us shall be in writing to the respective address indicated on the first page of this Agreement (or to such other address as you or we may notify the other in writing) and shall be deemed to have been given five calendar days after mailing to such address or within one business day of delivery by hand or telecopier. The paragraph headings contained in this Agreement are for convenience of reference only and shall not affect in any way the meaning or interpretation of this Agreement.

Please confirm your agreement with the foregoing by dating, signing and returning to us the duplicate copy of this Agreement.

SOTHEBY'S, INC.

By:________________________________

ACCEPTED AND AGREED TO:

SIGN HERE

____

Consignor

Dated:________________

SELLING COMMISSION SCHEDULE

If the sold Total is less than $100,000, the commission rate is on a per lot basis, subject to a minimum commission of $100 on each lot sold, and $75 per lot in Arcade sales, as follows:

HAMMER PRICE PER LOT (IN U.S. DOLLARS)	SELLING COMMISSION RATES
0–$1,999	20% of the successful bid price of each lot sold
$2,000–$7,499	15% of the successful bid price of each lot sold
$7,500–$99,999	10% of the successful bid price of each lot sold

If the sold Total is equal to or greater than $100,000, the lowest applicable commission rate on the amount of the Total based on each lot sold is as follows:

SOLD TOTAL (IN U.S. DOLLARS)	SELLING COMMISSION RATES
$100,000–$249,999	9% of the Total
$250,000–$499,999	8% of the Total
$500,000–$999,999	6% of the Total
$1,000,000–$2,499,999	5% of the Total
$2,500,000–$4,999,999	4% of the Total
$5,000,000–or more	2% of the Total

The commission for any lot which has failed to sell will be 5% of the reserve, subject to a minimum handling charge of $75 on each unsold lot.

APPENDIX 11-B

Standard Consignment Agreement—Christie's

Date: ___ - ___ - ___

Client Number: ________

CLIENT

CHRISTIE'S

CONSIGNMENT AGREEMENT BETWEEN

CONSIGNOR	AND	CHRISTIE'S INC. ("CHRISTIE'S")
Title/initials/first name or company name:		
Family name or company name:		
Building/Street:		502 PARK AVENUE
Subdistrict:		NEW YORK, NY 10022
Town/City:		TEL: (212) 546-1000
County/State:		
Post/Zip code:		219 EAST 67th STREET
Country:		NEW YORK, NY 10021
Business Tel:		TEL: (212) 606-0400
Home Tel:		
Mobile/Car Tel:		
Fax/e-mail		
Re Sale Number:		FOR CHRISTIE'S USE ONLY MCC: ____
Commission Type:		

	FOR AND ON BEHALF OF:	CHRISTIE'S REGIONAL REPRESENTATIVE (IF RELEVANT)
Name:		
Building/Street:		
Subdistrict:		
Town/City:		
County/State:		
Post/Zip code:		
Country:		
Business Tel:		
Home Tel:		
Mobile/Car Tel:		
Fax/e-mail		

Thank you for consigning your property to Christie's. The terms and conditions of the consignment are as follows:

1. CONSIGNMENT

You (the "Consignor") hereby consign to Christie's the property identified on the attached schedule, as amended from time to time, (the "Property") which Christie's, as the exclusive agent for Consignor, will offer for sale at public auction, unless otherwise agreed, subject to the provisions set forth below and Christie's standard Conditions of Sale and Limited Warranty in effect at the time of the auction. In the event of a conflict between the Conditions of Sale and Limited Warranty, on the one hand, and this Agreement, on the other hand, the terms of this Agreement shall control.

2. COMMISSION

(a) Subject to subparagraph (c) below, for its services, Christie's will receive and retain from the proceeds of the sale of the Property a commission from Consignor based upon the aggregate final bid price of all Property sold during any calendar year as follows:

TOTAL PROPERTY SOLD:	COMMISSION RATE PER LOT:
$5,000,000 or more	2% of the final bid price
$2,500,000 – $4,999,999	4% of the final bid price
$1,000,000 – $2,499,999	5% of the final bid price
$500,000 – $999,999	6% of the final bid price
$250,000 – $499,999	8% of the final bid price
$100,000 – $249,999	9% of the final bid price

(b) Subject to subparagraph (c) below, if the aggregate final bid price of all Property sold during any calendar year is less than $100,000, Christie's will receive and retain from the proceeds of sale a commission based upon the final bid price of each lot sold as follows:

FINAL BID PRICE:	COMMISSION RATE PER LOT:
$7,500 – $99,999	10% of the final bid price
$2,000 – $7,499	15% of the final bid price
less than $2,000	20% of the final bid price

(c) If Consignor has sold property through Christie's during the prior calendar year, the commission rate payable shall be the lesser of (i) the rate to be charged pursuant to subparagraph (a) or (b) above or (ii) the rate that would have been paid by Consignor during the prior calendar year under the commission scale outlined above.

(d) Christie's shall also receive a premium to be collected from the buyer of 15% of the final bid price up to and including $50,000 plus 10% of the final bid price above $50,000.

(e) There will be a minimum commission charge of $100 per lot for each lot sold at Christie's Park Avenue galleries and $50 per lot for each lot sold at Christie's East.

3. EXPENSES

Except as set forth in the attached Schedule, Consignor agrees to pay all costs relating to:

(a) packing and shipping the Property to Christie's;
(b) packing and shipping the Property from Christie's if any Property is returned to Consignor;
(c) insurance, as provided in paragraph 4 below;
(d) transit insurance, as provided in paragraph 4 below;
(e) all applicable customs duties and customs user fees;
(f) catalogue illustration up to a maximum of $900 per lot for color illustration and $300 per lot for black and white illustration;
(g) restoration;
(h) framing;
(i) tests or procedures that Christie's deems necessary or desirable to verify authenticity, attribution or quality of any Property and any fees in connection therewith;
(j) any special marketing costs;
(k) storage of the Property after the sale, including in a third-party warehouse, as provided in paragraph 8(e) below;
(l) an unsold property charge in the event that any lot fails to sell, as provided in paragraph 8(e) below;
(m) such additional costs and expenses not set forth above as may be agreed to by Consignor.

Expenses incurred by Christie's for Consignor's account pursuant to this paragraph shall include a 10% service charge.

4A. CHRISTIE'S INSURANCE

(a) Unless Christie's and Consignor agree otherwise, each lot of Property will be insured at Consignor's expense from the time of receipt by Christie's until it ceases to be in Christie's custody for an amount equal to (i) the mean of the pre-sale estimates prior to sale, (ii) the amount of the final bid price if sold, or (iii) the amount of the reserve if unsold (in each case, the "Insured Value").

(b) Insurance for Property received at Christie's auction premises will be charged to Consignor at a rate of 1% of the Insured Value for all Property other than breakables, such as porcelain or glass, and 2% of the Insured Value for all breakable property. Insurance for Property received at one of Christie's regional offices or at any location other than its auction premises will be charged to Consignor at an additional rate of 0.5% of the Insured Value to cover transit to Christie's auction premises. Whenever Consignor is responsible for packing and shipping charges, Christie's shall have no liability whatsoever to Consignor in connection therewith, even when Christie's has recommended a carrier.

(c) Each lot of Property will remain insured until 30 days after the sale. If any such lot has not been sold, there will be an additional charge for insurance after that date.

Form Ref: NYC50. Issue: 1 (4/97)

(d) Christie's liability to Consignor resulting from loss of or damage to any lot of Property shall not exceed the Insured Value of such Property. While Christie's undertakes to exercise reasonable care in handling the Property, we shall not be responsible for any damage to any Property caused by climatic or atmospheric conditions or for any damage to picture frames or to glass therein.

4B. CONSIGNOR'S INSURANCE

If Consignor has instructed Christie's not to insure the Property, it will be insured at Consignor's expense under Consignor's insurance policy from the time of receipt by Christie's until it ceases to be in Christie's custody. Christie's shall have no liability to Consignor whatsoever resulting from loss of or damage to any Property. Consignor shall execute and deliver to Christie's an insurance waiver letter in form and substance satisfactory to Christie's or shall deliver to Christie's a certificate of insurance naming Christie's as an additional named insured.

5. CONSIGNOR'S REPRESENTATIONS AND WARRANTIES, COVENANTS AND INDEMNIFICATION

(a) Consignor represents and warrants to Christie's that: (i) Consignor has the right and title to consign the Property for sale; (ii) the Property is, and until the completion of sale by Christie's will be, free and clear of all liens, claims and encumbrances of others or restrictions on Christie's right to offer and sell the Property; (iii) upon sale, good and marketable title and right to possession will pass to the buyer free of any such liens, claims, encumbrances or restrictions; (iv) Consignor has no reason to believe that any lot of Property is not authentic or is counterfeit; (v) the Property is not "confiscated Property" within the meaning of any United States federal or state laws; (vi) Consignor's consignment to and authorization of Christie's to sell the Property is in full compliance with all United States federal and state laws; (vii) the exportation, if any, of the Property from any foreign country has been in full conformity with the laws of such country and the importation of the Property into the United States has been or will be in full conformity with the laws of the United States; and (viii) there are not, and until the completion of sale by Christie's there will not be, any restrictions on Christie's right to photograph, reproduce photographs of or exhibit the Property.

(b) Consignor agrees that such representations and warranties are for the benefit of Christie's and buyers of the Property and that such representations and warranties shall survive the completion of the transactions contemplated hereby. Consignor agrees to notify Christie's promptly in writing of any events or circumstances that may cause the foregoing representations and warranties to be inaccurate or breached in any way.

(c) If Consignor is acting as an agent for a principal, Consignor and principal, jointly and severally, assume all of Consignor's obligations set forth in this Agreement.

(d) Consignor grants to Christie's the right to illustrate and photograph the Property and to use such photographs, illustrations or images at any time before or after the sale and for such purposes as Christie's deems appropriate. Consignor agrees that all catalogue and other photographs, illustrations and descriptions of the Property created by or for Christie's are not "works made for hire" on behalf of Consignor under copyright law, and that Christie's shall own the exclusive copyright and all other rights relating to all such photographs, illustrations and descriptions.

(e) Consignor shall defend, indemnify and hold harmless Christie's from and against any and all losses, damages, liabilities and claims, and all fees, costs and expenses of any kind related thereto (including, without limitation, reasonable attorney's fees), arising out of, based upon or resulting from (i) any act by or omission of Consignor or Consignor's agents (other than Christie's) or representatives relating to or affecting the Property or (ii) any inaccuracy or alleged inaccuracy, asserted by Christie's or any third party in a court action, of any representation or warranty made by Consignor pursuant to this Agreement.

6. SALE ARRANGEMENTS

(a) Christie's shall have complete discretion as to (i) the place and date of sale and the manner in which such sale is conducted, including the Conditions of Sale then in effect, (ii) the illustration, if any, and the description of the Property in our catalogues and other literature, (iii) seeking the views of any expert, either before or after the sale, and (iv) the combination or division of the Property into such lots and/or separate auctions as Christie's in our sole judgement may deem appropriate.

(b) Any written or oral appraisal, estimate or other statement of Christie's or our representatives with respect to the estimated or expected selling price of any lot of Property is a statement of opinion only and shall not be relied upon by Consignor or any third party as a prediction or guarantee of the actual selling price. Christie's makes no representations or warranties to Consignor with respect to the Property, its authenticity, condition or otherwise. Christie's shall not be liable for any errors or omissions in catalogue or other descriptions of the Property. Printed pre-sale estimates shall not include the buyer's premium or taxes.

(c) No Property may be withdrawn from sale after the date of this Agreement without Christie's consent. If Christie's consents to a withdrawal, a lot of Property may be withdrawn upon payment of 20% of the reserve price or 20% of the mean of the pre-sale estimates if the reserve has not yet been set plus all out-of-pocket expenses incurred by Christie's.

(d) Christie's reserves the right to withdraw any Property at any time before sale if in Christie's sole judgment (i) there is doubt as to its attribution or authenticity, (ii) there is doubt as to the accuracy of any of Consignor's representations or warranties set forth herein, (iii) Consignor has breached any provision of this Agreement or (iv) other just cause exists. There shall be no charge to Consignor, other than Christie's out-of-pocket expenses, for a withdrawal pursuant to clause (i) or (iv). In the event of a withdrawal pursuant to clause (ii) or (iii), Consignor shall be liable for the withdrawal charges and other expenses set forth in subparagraph (c) of this paragraph 6.

7. CONDUCT OF THE SALE

(a) ***Reserves.*** Unless otherwise agreed, each lot of Property will be sold subject to a reserve (the confidential minimum price below which such Property will not be sold) which shall not exceed the low pre-sale estimate therefor and shall not include the buyer's premium or taxes. Unless the reserve is mutually agreed upon and confirmed by Consignor in writing before the sale, the reserve will be determined by Christie's in our sole discretion. Any reserve set in an amount other than a bidding increment will be rounded down to the next bidding increment.

(b) ***Selling Below Reserve.*** Christie's may sell any lot below the reserve if Consignor receives the amount, less Consignor's commission and any sale-related expenses, which Consignor would have received had such lot been sold at the reserve.

(c) ***Christie's Acting to Protect Reserve.*** As Consignor's agent, Christie's shall act to protect the reserve by bidding through the auctioneer.

(d) ***No Bidding by Consignor.*** Under no circumstances shall Consignor (as agent or principal), its representatives, employees or agents, if any (other than Christie's acting as Consignor's agent in accordance with paragraph 7 (c) above), enter or cause to be entered a bid on any lot of Property being offered for sale.

(e) ***Limited Liability.*** In no event shall Christie's be liable for the failure of any lot of Property to be sold at or within its estimate range or to reach the reserve.

8. AFTER THE SALE

(a) ***Settlement of Account.*** Provided Christie's has received payment in full from the buyer, and subject to the next sentence hereof, 35 calendar days after the sale (the "Settlement Date"), Christie's will pay Consignor the net proceeds (the final bid price less Consignor's commission payable to Christie's pursuant to paragraph 2 above, any reimbursable expenses and any other amounts due Christie's or any of our affiliates, whether arising out of the sale of the Property or otherwise) received and collected from the sale of the Property. Christie's will not make such payment if Christie's shall have received notice of the buyer's intention to rescind the sale or of any other bona fide claim relating to the Property or its sale prior to the Settlement Date. In the event that Consignor has agreed to arrangements for payment by the buyer which extend beyond the Settlement Date, such date and the amount payable to Consignor thereon shall be adjusted accordingly.

(b) ***Non-Payment by Buyer.*** Christie's shall have no obligation to enforce payment by the buyer. However, in the event of non-payment by the buyer, Christie's in our sole discretion, as Consignor's agent or on our own behalf, may cancel the sale and return the Property to Consignor, enforce payment by the buyer or take any other actions permitted by law. Christie's shall not, under any circumstances, be liable for any consequential damages to Consignor as a result of non-payment by the buyer.

(c) ***Recision of Sale.*** Christie's, as Consignor's agent, is authorized to accept the return and rescind the sale of any lot of Property at any time if Christie's in our sole judgment determines that the offering for sale of any Property has subjected or may subject Christie's and/or Consignor to any liability, including liability under warranty of authenticity or title. In such event, Christie's is further authorized to refund or credit to the buyer the purchase price of such returned Property. If Christie's has already remitted to Consignor any proceeds of the rescinded sale, Consignor forthwith shall pay Christie's upon request an amount equal to the remitted proceeds.

(d) ***Post-Auction Sales.*** If any lot is bought-in for failure to reach its reserve, Christie's as Consignor's exclusive agent is authorized for a period of 30 days following the auction to sell the lot privately for a price that will result in payment to Consignor of an amount at least equal to the amount, after deduction of Consignor's commission and Christie's reimbursable expenses, that Consignor would have received if the lot had been sold at the reserve, or for such lesser amount as Christie's and Consignor shall agree. In such event, all other provisions of this Agreement shall remain in full force and effect.

(e) ***Unsold Property.*** For each lot offered but not sold, Consignor shall pay Christie's a service charge of 5% of the reserve. Property remaining unsold following the auction or the expiration of the 30-day period referred to in paragraph 8 (d) above and not reconsigned to Christie's for sale must be collected by Consignor at Consignor's expense within 35 days following the date on which Christie's offered such Property for sale. Thereafter, Consignor will incur a storage charge of $10 per day per lot. Consignor shall not be entitled to reclaim any unsold Property until all commission, expenses and other amounts owed to Christie's or any of our affiliates have been paid in full. In Christie's sole discretion, any Property not picked up or reconsigned for sale within 60 days following the date on which Christie's offered such Property for sale may be returned to Consignor at Consignor's expense, transferred to a third-party warehouse or sold at public auction by Christie's at Christie's standard commission rates and charges with a reserve, if any, set in Christie's sole discretion. The proceeds of such sale shall first be applied to the expenses of such sale, then to any indebtedness owing to Christie's or any of our affiliates and any excess shall be remitted to Consignor. In the event of transfer of any unsold Property to a third-party warehouse, Consignor shall bear all cost and risk thereof and shall be liable to such warehouse for the payment of storage and insurance charges of at least $10 per day per lot.

9. ADDITIONAL CONSIGNMENTS

Christie's agrees that prior to December 31 of this calendar year, Christie's may, upon Consignor's request, offer for sale at appropriate auctions to be held during this calendar year any additional property of Consignor that Christie's considers suitable for sale at such auction. Such additional property will be offered for sale by Christie's upon the same terms and conditions as those which govern this Agreement. Christie's will mail to Consignor a property Schedule for such additional property. The return of such Schedule signed by Consignor shall be evidence of, and shall constitute Christie's and Consignor's agreement with respect to, the consignment to Christie's of the property listed on such property Schedule upon such terms and conditions. Such property shall thereupon constitute "Property" under the terms of this Agreement.

10. OTHER MATTERS

(a) This Agreement constitutes the entire agreement and understanding between the parties with respect to the transactions contemplated hereby and supersedes all prior agreements relating to the Property.

(b) This Agreement shall be governed by and construed in accordance with the laws of the State of New York. In the event of any dispute hereunder, (i) the parties hereby consent to the exclusive jurisdiction of the courts of the State of New York and the Federal courts of the United States of America located in the Southern District of New York and (ii) neither party shall be liable to the other for any special, consequential or incidental damages.

(c) This Agreement shall be binding upon Consignor's heirs, distributees, executors, legal representatives, successors and assigns.

(d) Consignor may not assign its rights and/or obligations under this Agreement without the prior written consent of Christie's.

THE PARTIES AGREE TO THE FOREGOING BY SIGNING IN THE SPACES PROVIDED BELOW:

CONSIGNOR: ______________________ CHRISTIE'S INC: ______________________

Print Name: ______________________ By: ___ - ___ - ___ Date Signed: ___ - ___ - ___

Licensed by the New York City Department of Consumer Affairs

Status: ______________ duly authorised Date Signed: ___ - ___ - ___

Principal Auctioneer, Christopher J. Burge: License #761543

Form Ref: NYC50. Issue: 1 (4/97)

APPENDIX 11-C

Selected New York City Auction Regulations

Subchapter 13
Auctioneers

§ 20-278 License required. It shall be unlawful for any person to engage in the business of auctioneer without a license therefor.

* * *

§ 20-280 Requirements for auctioneers. Each auctioneer shall cause his or her name and license number to represent or to be conspicuously displayed at any place where he or she shall conduct an auction sale during such sale.

§ 20-281 Persons acting as auctioneers. It shall be unlawful for any person not licensed as an auctioneer to represent or circulate or place before the public any announcement, or to insert or cause to be inserted in any city, business or telephone directory, any notice that he or she is conducting the business of auctioneering.

§ 20-282 Advertising. Every auctioneer in his or her own name, shall give notice in one or more of the public newspapers printed in the city, of every auction sale to be conducted by him or her. In the event that such auctioneer shall be connected with any firm or other person his or her name shall in all cases precede the name of such firm or other person.

* * *

§ 20-284 Sale of jewelry.

a. Each auctioneer shall cause to be delivered to the purchaser of diamonds, precious stones or other jewelry, a signed document containing a description of the article sold and the representations made in regard thereto at the time of the sale.

b. Each article of jewelry sold at public auction shall have affixed thereto a tag, on which shall be printed or written a correct description of such article.

* * *

§ 20-288 False or fraudulent representations. Any auctioneer who shall have knowledge of any false or fraudulent representations or statements or who makes or causes any such statements to be made in respect to the character of any sale, or the party authorizing the same, or the quality, condition, ownership, situation, or value of any property, real or personal, exposed, put up, or offered by him or her for sale at public auction, shall be deemed guilty of a misdemeanor, and, upon conviction thereof, shall be punished by imprisonment not exceeding one year or by a fine not exceeding one thousand dollars.

§ 20-289 Complaints.

a. The commissioner may take testimony, under oath, relating to and upon the complaint of any person who claims he or she has been defrauded by any auctioneer, his or her clerk, agent or assignee, or relating to and upon the complaint of any person who has consigned real or personal property for sale and to whom such auctioneer shall not have accounted fully. The license of each such auctioneer may be revoked and his or her bond declared forfeited if, in the opinion of the commissioner, such charge is sustained. Any such person whose license has been revoked for cause shall not be granted another such license.

b. The commissioner may take testimony, under oath, relating to and upon the complaint of any person who claims that any auctioneer, his or her clerk, agent or assignee, has been guilty of misconduct relating to the business transacted under such auctioneer's license, and if such charge, in his or her opinion, shall be sustained, the commissioner may suspend such license for a period not to exceed six months.

Subchapter M
Auctioneers

§ 2-121 Standards, Licenses and Applications of Regulations.

(a) The auctioneer will be held responsible for the truth of any statement contained in any catalogue, advertisement, announcement, press release or other public statement made by the auctioneer relating to any auction.

(b) The auctioneer shall be held responsible for full compliance by his employer or principal with all rules and regulations of the Department and pertinent provisions of law.

(c) Each application for a license shall be accompanied by the Affidavits of three citizens who are residents of New York City and who have known the applicant not less than two years.

(d) The fee for a permit to auction publicly after 8 P.M. the goods or any of them specified in § 20-283 of the Administrative Code shall be ten dollars for the first permit in any license year. Subsequent permits issued during the same license year may be issued without fee.

(e) Each applicant for a permit to auction publicly after 8 P.M. shall furnish with the application for the permit a catalogue of the articles to be auctioned, and a copy of the advertisement to be published in connection with said auction. In the case of an auction of fruit, vegetables or other farm products, the catalogue shall be filed as soon as it is printed.

(f) All licensed auctioneers and auction houses must include their Department of Consumer Affairs license number, or the license number assigned to their auction house or principal auctioneer and identify it as such in all advertisements in any medium, and on all written contracts, catalogues and announcements, relating to the auction activity in New York City.

(g) The rules and regulations do not apply to auction sales of real property.

§ 2-122 Requirements and Obligations of Licensees.

(a) *Contracts Required.* No personal property may be auctioned except pursuant to a written contract between the consignor or his or her agent or authorized representative and the auctioneer, unless auctioned pursuant to an order of a court of competent jurisdiction.

(b) Every contract required pursuant to § 2-122(a) must contain the following provisions:

(1) All fees, commissions and charges to be paid by the consignor to the auctioneer or his or her agents, principals, employees, employers or assigns shall:

(i) to the extent practicable, be itemized and specified as to amount (which may be stated as a percentage of the reserve price or any final bid), and

(ii) if such itemization and specification as to amount is not practicable, be described with sufficient particularity to inform the consignor of the nature of the services for which such fees, commissions and charges will be imposed.

(2) That as of the date of the auction the consignor warrants that he or she has complete and lawful right, title and interest in the property auctioned, and that the consignor shall indemnify the auctioneer, his or her agents, principals, employees, employers or assigns in the event of any defect in title, and that an intended beneficiary of this warranty is the ultimate purchaser at auction.

(c) Where articles are referred to by catalogue or advertisement as having been obtained from any specific person, place or source, such articles must be separately enumerated and identified.

(d) If an auctioneer or public salesroom has any interest, direct or indirect, in an article, including a guaranteed minimum, other than the selling commission, the fact such interest exists must be disclosed in connection with any description of the article or articles in the catalogue or any other printed material published or distributed in relation to the sale. Such notice may be denoted by a symbol or letter which will refer the reader to an explanation of the nature of the interest the symbol or letter denotes. For the purpose of this subdivision (d), advertisements in newspapers or other periodicals shall not constitute printed material. Where no printed material is provided in connection with an auction, the auctioneer shall have available during the advertised inspection period, information of as to whether such an interest exists with relation to a particular item and shall announce before he or she commences the auction that such information is available upon request.

(e) Where a consignor is to receive a rebate commission in whole or in part or where he or she will be permitted to bid upon and to buy back his or her own article at the sale, disclosure of such a condition must be made in connection with any description of the item or items so affected in the catalogue or any other printed material published or distributed in relation to the sale. The existence of such a condition may be denoted by a symbol or letter which will refer the reader to an explanation of the nature of the interest the symbol or letter denotes. For the purpose of this subdivision (e), advertisements in newspapers or other periodicals shall not constitute printed material. Where no printed material is provided in connection with the auction, the auctioneer shall have available during any advertised inspection period information of whether such condition exists with relation to a particular item and shall announce before he or she commences the auction that such information is available upon request.

(f) (1) If the consignor has fixed a price below which an article will not be sold, the "reserve price," the fact that the lot is being sold subject to reserve must be disclosed in connection with the description of any lot so affected in the catalogue or any other printed material published or distributed in relation to the sale. The existence of a reserve price may be denoted by a symbol or letter which will refer the reader to an explanation of reserve price. For the purpose of this subdivision (f), advertisements in newspapers or other periodicals shall not constitute printed material. Where no printed material is provided in connection with the auction an auctioneer shall have available during the any advertised inspection period information as to whether a particular lot is to be sold subject to reserve and shall announce before he or she commences the auction that such information is available upon request.

(2) When a lot is not subject to a reserve price, the auctioneer shall not indicate in any manner that the lot is subject to a reserve price.

(g) The auctioneer shall:

(1) Provide information as to the number of jewels, approximate number of carats, number of points (diamond), principle metal content, and manufacturer's name, if known, for all articles of jewelry, including watches. The information required by this subdivision (g) shall be provided either in the catalogue description of such items or by attaching to each such item a tag or marking containing the information.

(2) Issue or cause to be issued to each purchaser an invoice which shall contain all the following information:

(i) The auctioneer's name, business address and license number;
(ii) The name and address of the auctioneer's employer or principal;
(iii) The date of sale;
(iv) The lot number, description, quantity and selling price of each lot;
(v) The total amount of purchase with a separate statement of sales tax;
(vi) All deposits made against the purchase price.

This does not apply to the auction sale of fruit, vegetables or other farm products.

(3) Notify the department ten days in advance regarding the name and address of a new employer or the new location of activity.

(4) [*Reserved*]

(5) Advertise each auction sale at least once in the seven-day period immediately preceding the auction.

(6) Notify the person whose property is being auctioned (and any other person entitled to be notified according to law) as to the date, place and time of sale.

(7) Permit (prior to the start of the auction) prospective purchasers to inspect each and every article to be offered for sale.

(8) Furnish to any buyer, consignor or owner of an article, upon request, information as to the whereabouts of that article that comes into his or her possession or that is sold or offered for sale by him or her.

(9) Send check for net amount received on all sales to persons entitled to the proceeds thereof within fourteen days of date of sale (except as otherwise agreed in writing or otherwise provided by law) together with a complete detailed statement including lot number, quantity, description and selling price of each lot; total amount received on sale; and disbursements listing commission, cost of advertisement, labor, charges and allowances, and sundry expenses.

(10) Report to the Department of Consumer Affairs the date and place of any sale of merchandise which includes a scale, in time to permit the Department to have an inspector present at the sale.

(11) Notify the department in advance if he or she is unable because of sickness or other valid reason to conduct a duly advertised auction; and then a licensed auctioneer may act as his or her substitute.

(12) When an auctioneer has a number of the same kind of articles to be sold and intends to dispose of each of them at the amount at which the first is sold, he or she shall make an announcement to that effect prior to opening the sale of the first article.

(h) If an auctioneer makes loans or advances money to consignors or prospective purchasers, this fact must be conspicuously disclosed in the auctioneer's catalogue or printed material. If the auctioneer does not provide any such printed material, he or she shall make the disclosure, either by conspicuously posting a sign, or in another similarly conspicuous manner, at the time of any advertised inspection periods prior to the auctions. For the purpose of this subdivision (h) advertisements in newspapers or other periodicals shall not constitute printed material.

(i) Except to implement a reserve price, and subject to § 2-123(b), no auctioneer, his or her consignor, employee, employer, assignee or agent for any of them may bid for his or her own account at any auction if any of them shall have access to information not otherwise available to the public regarding reserves, value or other material facts relating to the articles which are the subject of the auction, unless their "insider" status and intended participation is disclosed in the auctioneer's catalogue and any printed material and on signs posted at the auction.

(j) Wherever an estimate or estimated value of an item or lot is published in a catalogue or any other printed material published or distributed in relation to an auction sale, a general description of the estimate and its meaning and function must be included in such printed material. For the purpose of this subdivision (j), advertisements in newspapers or other periodicals shall not constitute printed material. Where no printed material is provided, and an estimate or estimated value is announced or disseminated in any manner, a general description of the estimate and its meaning and function must be available for distribution and its availability must be announced at the commencement of the auction.

(k) In any advertisement indicating an auction sale due to a business' loss of lease or liquidation, the auctioneer must include the name of the consignor or business authorizing the auction. In any sale advertised as pursuant to a security agreement, the name of the debtor shall be indicated conspicuously.

(l) The following newspapers published in the City of New York hereby designated as newspapers in which auctioneers shall advertise as required by §§ 20-282 and 20-283 of the Administrative Code:

New York Times
New York Journal of Commerce
New York Post
New York Daily Fruit Reporter
Newsday
Staten Island Advance
New York Daily News
New York Law Journal
American Banker
Action
Il Progresso
China Post
China Times
Chinese Journal
France-Amerique
Aufbau
National Herald
Novoye Russkoye Slovo
El Diario
El Mirador
Svoboda
Jewish Daily Forward
Barbininkas

§ 2-123 Reserves.

(a) If the reserve price is not bid, the auctioneer may withdraw a lot from sale. At the time of such withdrawal, and before bidding on another lot begins, the auctioneer shall announce that the withdrawn lot has been "passed," "withdrawn," "returned to owner" or "bought-in."

(b) *Affirmative disclosure.* Before bidding on any lot has reached its reserve price no auctioneer may make or place consecutive or successive bids, or place bids in response to bids from others, on behalf of the consignor, unless the fact that the auctioneer will or may bid in such a manner is clearly and conspicuously disclosed in any catalogue and any other printed material published or distributed in connection with the sale. For the purpose of this subdivision (b) advertisements in newspapers or other periodicals shall not constitute printed material. This disclosure must also be made on signs prominently displayed in the auction room and at the entrance thereto, and must be announced by the auctioneer immediately prior to the commencement of any auction.

The sign required by this subdivision (b) must be at least 12 inches by 18 inches in dimension with letters at least one inch high, and must read as follows, or convey a substantially similar disclosure:

> The Auctioneer may open bidding on any lot by placing a bid on behalf of the seller. The auctioneer may further bid on behalf of the seller, up to the amount of the reserve, by placing successive or consecutive bids for a lot, or by placing bids in response to other bidders.

(c) After bidding has reached the reserve price of a lot:

(1) the auctioneer may not bid on behalf of the consignor or the auction house; and

(2) the auctioneer may only accept bids from persons other than the consignor or the auction house except absentee telephone, order or other agent's bids;

(3) This subdivision (c) shall not apply to auction sales conducted pursuant to an order of a court of competent jurisdiction, including an order of a bankruptcy judge or trustee, or a sale of a secured property pursuant to the Uniform Commercial Code, or the sale of property which is subject to a lien or assignment pursuant to the laws of the State of New York.

(d) In no event shall the reserve price for any lot exceed the minimum estimated value of the lot as published in any catalogue or other printed material distributed by the auctioneer.

§ 2-124 Prohibited Practices.

(a) An auctioneer may not disclaim warranty of title of any item sold at auction. The auctioneer shall reimburse any purchaser in an amount equal to the successful bid at auction plus any buyer's commission paid in the event it is determined that the purchaser has not acquired transferable title to the item.

(b) At the auction sale premises only exterior signs may be displayed advertising the auction sale but the same shall not be excessive in size.

(c) An auctioneer may not:

(1) Offer more than one article for sale at any one time unless the combining of articles or lots is so indicated prior to the initial bid.

(2) Represent an article to be guaranteed by the manufacturer or the owner unless a manufacturer's or owner's guarantee accompanies the article.

(3) Offer an article contained in a carton, package or other container commonly known as a blind article unless prior to the offer it is announced that the highest bidder may reject the article if not satisfactory to him or her. This provision does not refer to an auction of articles in bulk where a sample is displayed and balance of articles are represented to conform with the sample.

(4) Use a loudspeaker outlet located within ten feet of any entrance or exit or which is beamed in any direction except away from said entrance or exit. In any event loud-speaker apparatus must not attract attention from outside auction premises.

(5) Accept as payment or exchange any article previously knocked down or sold to a successful bidder. The article knocked down or sold must be delivered to the bidder or, if the auctioneer is willing and at the bidder's election, the purchase price refunded in full. No other article may be offered to said bidder as a substitute or replacement. Such refund shall take place within a reasonable time or may be applied as part payment or payment for any other article purchased at auction by the same bidder.

§ 2-125 Records; Miscellaneous.

(a) An auctioneer must keep a written record of all details of each sale including copies of advertisements; lot number, quantity, description and selling price of each lot; record of disbursement; and net amount sent to persons entitled to proceeds of sale for a period of six years form the date of the auction.

(b) *Exceptions.* § 2-122(c) through (e) inclusive above shall not apply to:

(1) Any auction sale involving a printed catalogue when all of the following conditions are met:

- (i) the printed catalogue is distributed and available for a reasonable period of time prior to the auction being held;
- (ii) said catalogue contains a precise, detailed description of the items to be auctioned and the terms used to describe the items have a widely accepted, standardized usage in the field;
- (iii) the value of the items described in said catalogue can be verified by reference to standard recognized reference sources commonly known of and utilized in the field; and
- (iv) the sale of the item at the auction is not final until the purchaser has had a reasonable opportunity to verify independently that the item purchased was accurately described in said catalogue.

(2) Any auction sales conducted for primarily commercial purposes where all of the bidders at such auction can reasonably be anticipated to be purchasing for use in a commercial endeavor and not for use by the purchaser, or the purchaser's family, as consumer goods as that term is defined in the Consumer Protection Law of 1969 of The City of New York (Administrative Code of the City of New York § 20-700 et seq.).

Historical Note: Amended by Local Law No. 44 for 1970, August 10. Subchapter 13 is amended by adding 20-279(c) and Section 279.1 Local Law No. 66 for 1989, eff. October 10, 1989.

Historical Note: Amended by Local Law No. 172 for 1939, November 20; Local Law No. 20 for 1973, June 5.

Historical Note: Amended by Local Law No. 20 for 1973, June 5.

Historical Note: Amended by Local Law No. 20 for 1973, June 5.

Historical Note: Amended by Local Law No. 172 for 1939, November 20; Local Law No. 20 for 1973, June 5.

Historical Note: Subdivision b as amended by Law, Chapter 83 for 1947, March 8.

Historical Note: Auctioneers were licensed by the Department of Licenses (since 1968, the Department of Consumer Affairs) beginning in 1938.

CHAPTER 12

CONSERVATION AND RESTORATION OF ARTWORK

Steven Mark Levy

§ 12.01 INTRODUCTION

Not many decades ago, most art restorations were done by self-taught "restorers" or by artists who needed the extra money. The main goal of these individuals was to improve the aesthetic appearance of the artwork. Some approached the task with sensitivity. Others might simply take a stiff brush and soapy water and rub every which way until the dirt was gone.

Today, conservators tend to be highly trained specialists with knowledge of chemistry, physics, computer science, art history and studio art. The focus is on preserving the artwork in its originally intended form for future generations. Professionalization is growing.

This chapter will discuss the increasing number of legal requirements and potential liabilities that have accompanied this recent growth in professionalization. After definition of terms and an overview of the controversy that surrounds restorations, the discussion will consider the role of the conservation professional, conservation contracts and fees, the restoration process, and the relationship between restorations and market value, followed by a description of selected laws that affect conservation practice. In conclusion we discuss the liability of the conservation professional for malpractice and other torts and the issue of defamation.

§ 12.02 GENERAL CONSIDERATIONS

[A] Conservation and Restoration Defined

The term "conservation" refers to the examination and analysis of cultural objects to determine whether and to what extent they have deteriorated or been damaged, and the preservation and maintenance of such objects, including preventative measures to retard future loss. Cultural objects include paintings, prints, sculpture and other fine arts, as well as anthropological artifacts, historic buildings, furniture, old books, and other items of cultural significance.

Restoration, a subcategory of conservation, is direct action carried out on the cultural object to bring back its original aesthetic appearance and physical characteristics to the extent practicable. In the case of an oil painting, for example, restoration might include removing dirt, grime and yellowed varnish, removing or reducing previous restorations, replacing deteriorated lining fabric, and adding new paint to areas where the original paint has been lost.

The terms "conserve" and "restore" are given special definitions in some state artists' rights statutes. The Pennsylvania Fine Arts Preservation Act,[1] for example, contains the following definitions:

---

[1] 73 Pa. Stat. § 2102. A somewhat similar definition appears in the California Art Preservation Act, Cal. Civ. Code § 987(b). *See also* La. Rev. Stat. § 51:2152.

> "Conserve". To preserve a work of fine art by retarding or preventing deterioration or damage through appropriate treatment in accordance with prevailing standards in order to maintain the physical integrity of a work of fine art.
>
> "Restore". To return, as nearly as feasible, a deteriorated or damaged work of fine art to its original state or condition in accordance with prevailing standards.

Some artists' rights statutes combine both terms into a single definition. For example, the New York Arts and Cultural Affairs Law[2] defines conservation to mean "acts taken to correct deterioration and alteration and acts taken to prevent, stop or retard deterioration."

[B] The Controversy Over Art Restorations

The British art historian Ernst Gombrich remarked that the word restoration is generally a misnomer, because "we can never turn back the wheels of time."[3] In fact, as Goya observed in 1801, even if the original artist were alive, he could not retouch a painting perfectly "because of the aged tone given the colors by time."[4] Some critics charge that many restorations are unnecessary, or are carried out overzealously, resulting in needless injury to the artwork and the falsification of art history.

The cleaning of Michelangelo's ceiling frescos in the Sistine Chapel between 1980 and 1990 illustrates the controversy. Critics allege that the restorers went too far, removing subtle shadings, destroying the seasoned, aged aspect of the work, called the patina, and presenting brighter-than-bright colors that are inconsistent with descriptions of the ceiling by Michelangelo's contemporaries.[5]

Another recent example is Leonardo da Vinci's "Last Supper," a 500-year-old wall painting in Milan, the latest restoration of which lasted 20 years and was completed in 1999. Referring to it as the "Lost Supper," critics maintain that as little as 20 percent of the original remains and that by removing previous repaintings and touch-ups added by people who were closer to Leonardo, the restorers have destroyed the historical continuity of the painting and turned it into a twentieth-century Leonardo.[6]

---

[2] N.Y. Art & Cult. Aff. § 11.01(7). Identical definitions appear in R.I. Gen. Laws § 5-62-2(2); 27 Me. Rev. Stat. § 303.

[3] Foreword by Ernst Gombrich to S. Walden, The Ravished Image 3 (1985).

[4] J. Beck & N. Daley, Art Restoration: The Culture, the Business and the Scandal 142 (1993).

[5] *See, e.g.*, D. Alberge, Art Expert Attacks Restoration Works, The Independent (London), Nov. 2, 1993, at 9; E. Gibson, Painting a Dark Picture of Art Restoration, Wash. Times, April 3, 1994, at B-7.

[6] *See, e.g.*, F. Kennedy, Leonardo's Lost Supper, The Independent (London), May 26, 1999, at 1, 8; C. Endean, Restoration of da Vinci's Last Supper an Affront to Art Lovers, Sunday Telegraph (London), May 23, 1999, at 28.

Most conservators bristle at such criticism. Their job as they see it is merely to retrieve the authentic condition of the artwork to the extent humanly feasible, aided by research, science and technology, and with respect for the artist's original intentions. They consider many of the critics to be uninformed. As the chief restorer of the Vatican put it with regard to the Sistine Chapel frescoes:

> I don't know how these people can draw conclusions if they don't know anything about the techniques of fresco and fresco restoration. From reading some of the protests, you'd think that Michelangelo had wanted to paint the ceiling dark. And that we were up here scraping his work off with sandpaper.[7]

The problem is not limited to priceless masterpieces. The art dealer or private collector with an aging painting for sale may understand the need to preserve artistic integrity but may also desire to present the work as attractively as possible, in accordance with the modern tastes of potential buyers. The tension between these competing interests can lead to misunderstandings and legal disputes.

§ 12.03 THE CONSERVATION PROFESSIONAL

[A] Licensing and Regulation

No licensing or certification is required to be a conservator. Anyone can hang out his shingle. Neither the government nor any private agency checks qualifications, administers examinations, or regulates the practice of persons holding themselves out as conservators.

The American Institute for Conservation of Historic and Artistic Works (AIC) is a national organization of conservation professionals in the United States.[8] It promulgates a Code of Ethics and Guidelines for Practice.[9] However, membership in the AIC, and adherence to its standards, are entirely voluntary.

[B] Qualifications

Many art conservators learn their trade on the job, as apprentices to established conservators in private practice or as employees of large museum conserva-

---

[7] K. Shulman, Anatomy of a Restoration: The Brancacci Chapel, 184-85 (1991).

[8] The AIC is located at 1717 K Street, N.W., Suite 200, Washington D.C. 20006; telephone (202) 452-9545. Similar organizations exist in other countries, including the Canadian Conservation Institute in Ottawa, Ontario; the International Institute for Conservation of Historic and Artistic Works in London, England; the European Confederation of Conservator-Restorers' Organizations in Brussels, Belgium; and the Australian Institute for the Conservation of Cultural Material in Canberra, Australia.

[9] The AIC Code and Guidelines are reprinted with permission in Appendix 12-A. They are supplemented by highly detailed "Commentaries" which may be accessed through the AIC's Web site at http://aic.stanford.edu.

tion departments. Some are artists, but being an artist is not a prerequisite. Replacing lost paint is only part of the job. One other way to become a conservator is to enroll in a university art conservation graduate program, which takes two to four years of study and leads to a master's degree.[10]

The most important qualification is hands-on experience, particularly in the conservator's chosen specialty, such as paintings, sculpture, textiles or works on paper. A dose of humility is also a plus, because the best restoration is one that no one notices.[11]

[C] Selecting a Conservator-Restorer

Local art museums can provide a list of private restorers, or refer you to their own in-house conservators. Another source is the AIC, which provides computer-generated lists of conservators grouped by location, specialization and type of service provided. Art dealers and private collectors can also make referrals. Finally, there are 13 regional conservation centers in the United States which can provide expertise and referrals. These are listed in Appendix 12-B.

An interview of the conservator is a must. The conservator should be asked about his or her background, training, experience in working with the type of artwork in question, membership in conservation organizations, whether conservation is his or her principal occupation, the estimated cost of the treatment, the names and telephone numbers of references and previous clients, and whether he or she maintains malpractice insurance. Show the artwork to the conservator and try to assess whether he or she seems knowledgeable about it.

§ 12.04 CONTRACTS AND FEES

Unless there is some emergency that requires immediate intervention to preserve the artwork, there should always be a written contract for conservation services. The contract may be nothing more than an informal letter of agreement that includes the scope of the work, time deadlines, fees and costs, and signatures of both parties. Some conservators prefer such an informal document so that the relationship will begin in a relaxed and friendly manner. The better practice,

---

[10] Among the schools offering graduate degrees in conservation are State University of New York-Buffalo; the University of Delaware in Newark, Del.; Columbia University and New York University both in New York City; the University of Pennsylvania, Philadelphia, Pa.; and the University of Texas at Austin.

[11] As one Italian restorer colorfully put it: "You've got to wake up every morning and kick yourself in the butt and say, 'YOU'RE NOBODY! YOU'RE NOBODY!' . . . Otherwise, a restorer might get the idea that he's somebody. That he's a painter, too. He might start to think he's good. And the moment he says to himself that he's good, he's finished as a restorer." K. Shulman, Anatomy of a Restoration: The Brancacci Chapel 212-14 (1991).

however, is to enter into a more formal contract that covers all of the key aspects of the transaction.

[A] Contractual Terms: A Checklist

The law of contracts varies from jurisdiction to jurisdiction, and a lawyer should always be consulted, but in general the following provisions should be considered for inclusion in the agreement. A sample Agreement for Conservation Services is included as Form 12-1 for use as a starting point.

1. Date of the Agreement.
2. Names of the conservation professional and the client.
3. The client's representation that he owns the artwork or has authority to contract. This is important. In one case, the General Services Administration in Washington, D.C. delivered to the restorer six large mural paintings for restoration. The restorer, believing the paintings belonged to the federal government, performed a massive restoration project and billed over half a million dollars. The government later disclaimed any interest in the murals and refused to pay, asserting that the murals belonged to someone else.[12]
4. Identification of the art object and description of its condition.
5. Description of the services to be performed. This a key term, without which the contract may not be valid.[13] If desired, the initial condition report and treatment proposal can be attached and incorporated by reference. If the conservator intends to delegate or subcontract some of the work, or will not accept subcontracting, the agreement should so specify.
6. Documentation to be prepared by the conservator. Typically, the conservator will prepare a condition report and treatment proposal at the outset of the engagement, and a final report detailing what treatment was performed. He or she may also provide photographic documentation of the conservation process.
7. Time periods, including the start date and estimated completion date.
8. Transportation and shipping. The contract should indicate who is responsible for packaging the art object and transporting it to and from the conservator's laboratory, and what shipping options are acceptable, such as U.S. Postal Service registered mail, air freight or air express, UPS,

---

12 Hoelzer v. City of Stamford, Conn., 972 F.2d 495 (2d Cir. 1992).

13 Anderson v. Schwegel, 118 Idaho 362, 796 P.2d 1035 (Ct. App. 1990) (oral agreement to restore antique car invalid because no meeting of minds as to meaning of "restore"); Doane v. Stadele, 190 Wis. 2d 468, 528 N.W.2d 91 (Ct. App. 1994) (no agreement absent a meeting of the minds as to the level of the restoration to be performed on an antique car).

or personal delivery. Transit insurance should be required unless the conservator has a fine arts policy that covers objects in transit to and from the studio.

9. Disclosure of risks. The conservator should describe the risks involved in the proposed treatment, such as the potential for loss of some original paint or the unpredictability of repairing torn canvas.
10. Disclaimer of guarantee. Sample language: "Nothing in this agreement, and nothing that the conservator has stated to the client, shall be construed as a guarantee or a promise about the outcome of the treatment. The conservator does not make any such guarantees or promises. Any comments by the conservator about the outcome of the treatment are expressions of opinion only."
11. Client's duties. The client should agree to provide the conservator with truthful information about the art object, its provenance, and its prior restorations; to abide by the agreement; to pay the conservator's bills on time; and to keep the conservator informed of the client's current address and telephone number.
12. Confidentiality. The conservation profession recognizes an ethical duty to keep relationships with clients confidential unless the client waives the confidentiality in writing.[14] Therefore, the agreement should specify whether and to what extent the conservator may publish or otherwise divulge the treatment and its results. For example, it should state whether the conservator may use the examination and treatment records for educational and scholarly purposes and whether, if the artwork changes hands, the conservator may reveal the treatment to the new owner.
13. Fees, costs and other charges. The contract should specify whether the fees are by the hour, the day or the project, and whether there is a separate charge for materials or for reports and documentation. For example, the conservator may charge a nonrefundable flat fee for the condition report and treatment proposal and then, if the client decides to proceed, an hourly rate plus cost of materials.
14. Terms of payment. If the fee is a lump sum, the contract might provide for a certain percentage to be paid upon approval of the treatment proposal and the balance upon completion of the project. If the fee is by the hour, a common practice is for the conservator to bill monthly for the actual time spent and, in addition, take an initial deposit for security.
15. Interest charges. The contract may provide that if a billing statement is not paid when due, interest will be charged on the principal balance.

[14] Guidelines for Practice of the American Institute for Conservation of Historic and Artistic Works, ¶ 7 (hereinafter AIC Guidelines).

16. Unclaimed artwork. The parties should agree on what should happen if the artwork is not claimed within a stated period of time after the owner is notified that the job is completed. For example, the conservator might be given the right to charge a storage fee and/or to sell the artwork and apply the proceeds toward unpaid billings.
17. Arbitration clause. If the parties wish, they can agree to have any and all disputes decided only by binding arbitration and not by court action. Contractual arbitration is generally faster and cheaper than litigation, but there are a number of disadvantages. There is no right to appeal, no right to discovery, the rules of evidence do not apply, and the arbitrator generally is not required to make a decision strictly in accordance with the law.[15]
18. Governing law. Specify the state whose law governs the agreement. The conservator will usually prefer to specify the state in which he performs his services.
19. Attorney fee clause. The contract may provide that the prevailing party in any action or proceeding arising out of the agreement will be awarded reasonable attorney fees and costs. In the absence of such a provision, each side normally pays its own attorney fees. This type of clause is good if you win the case, but not so good if you lose, especially because you have no control over how much the other side "reasonably" runs up in fees. Also keep in mind that the inclusion of this clause makes it easier for a plaintiff to find a lawyer to represent him and thus increases the likelihood of litigation.
20. Entire agreement. An entire agreement clause, also known as an "integration clause" or a "merger clause," typically provides that the contract constitutes the entire understanding of the parties and supersedes all prior negotiations, agreements and understandings. Such a clause prevents a party later attempting to contradict or change the contract by introducing evidence of alleged prior or contemporaneous oral or written negotiations, stipulations, representations, or promises.[16]
21. Modification by subsequent agreement. Sample language: "This agreement may be modified by subsequent agreement of the parties only by an instrument in writing signed by both of them or an oral agreement only to the extent that the parties carry it out."
22. Signatures and addresses.

[15] Mercury Insurance Group v. Superior Court, 19 Cal. 4th 332, 79 Cal. Rptr. 2d 308 (1998).

[16] *See* Alling v. Universal Manufacturing Corp., 5 Cal. App. 4th 1412, 1433-37, 7 Cal. Rptr. 2d 718 (1992).

[B] Exculpatory Clauses

Many conservators include an exculpatory clause in their standard contracts, or require the client to sign a separate document called an "Exculpatory Agreement," "Release Form," "Waiver of Liability," or similar document to relieve the conservator from legal liability for his own negligence.

Some states are more receptive to these clauses than others. In New York the courts are "reluctant" to enforce exculpatory agreements and have developed an "exacting standard" by which to measure their validity.[17] In Ohio, on the other hand, a clear and unambiguous exculpatory provision will be enforced even if the parties were in unequal bargaining positions and the clause does not specifically refer to negligence, is not conspicuous, and was not read or understood by the plaintiff.[18]

In California, a clearly and explicitly drafted exculpatory clause protecting against claims of simple negligence is enforceable if the agreement does not affect the "public interest."[19] A court considers several factors in determining whether defendant's activity affects the public interest, including whether the type of business engaged in by the defendant is suitable for public regulation and whether defendant's services are of great importance or necessity to the public.[20] No case has yet decided whether art conservation or other types of art expertise affect the public interest, but it seems unlikely that they do in this context.

In most jurisdictions, exculpatory agreements are enforceable only to the extent they exempt someone from liability for his or her ordinary negligence. An agreement that seeks to exempt a person from liability for his own fraud, willful injury to the person or property of another, or violation of the law is against public policy and therefore unenforceable.[21]

A release clause that purports to absolve the actor from liability for conduct more culpable than ordinary negligence, including gross negligence and wanton or willful misconduct, is invalid in its entirety, even as to ordinary negligence, unless it is obvious from the language of the contract that the parties intended each contractual provision to be severable.[22]

---

[17] Gross v. Sweet, 49 N.Y.2d 102, 107, 400 N.E.2d 306 (1979) (parachute training school).

[18] Hall v. Woodland Lake Leisure Resort Club, Inc., 1998 Ohio App. LEXIS 4898 (1998) (use of resort facilities).

[19] Tunkl v. Regents of Univ. of Cal., 60 Cal. 2d 92, 101-04, 383 P.2d 441, 32 Cal. Rptr. 33 (1963) (government-operated hospital agreement affects public interest, invalidating release).

[20] *See* Guido v. Koopman, 1 Cal. App. 4th 837, 841, 2 Cal. Rptr. 2d 437 (1991) (horseback riding not within the "public interest" category).

[21] *See, e.g.*, Cal. Civ. Code § 1668; Restatement (Contracts) §§ 574-575 (1932); Gross v. Sweet, 49 N.Y.2d 102, 106, 400 N.E.2d 306 (1979); Davis v. Commonwealth Edison Co., 61 Ill. 2d 494, 500-01, 336 N.E.2d 881 (1975).

[22] Farina v. Mount Bachelor, Inc., 66 F.3d 233 (9th Cir. 1995) (ski facility).

[C] Fees

[1] Ethical Considerations

The AIC recognizes the following ethical guidelines with respect to fees:

- fees should be "commensurate with services rendered"
- fees must not be based on the value of the cultural property
- paying or requesting a referral fee, broker's fee or finder's fee is improper
- dividing the fee is appropriate only when based on the division of service or responsibility
- "price fixing" is improper, but so is the "consistent undercutting of local or regional markets"[23]

[2] Without a Formal Agreement

Suppose the owner requests restoration work but there is no valid written or oral agreement because there was no meeting of the minds as to an essential term, such as the level of restoration to take place. In that case, the restorer is entitled to payment on the basis of *quantum meruit*, that is, the reasonable value of the services rendered.[24] This is true even if the restorer's efforts have not actually enhanced the value of the property.[25]

On the other hand, if the restoration work was not requested by the property owner but was undertaken by the restorer by mistake or as a volunteer, the measure of recovery is the enhanced value of the property, if any. That is, the owner is not liable for the services performed by the restorer except to the extent they actually resulted in economic value to him.[26]

Since *quantum meruit* is an equitable as opposed to a legal remedy, the courts are free to tailor the remedy to fit peculiar facts. In *Hoelzer v. City of Stamford*,[27] six badly damaged murals on canvas belonging to the city found their way into the possession of the federal government without the city knowing they were missing. The federal government turned them over to a noted art restorer who performed $557,200 worth of work on them in the belief that they were federal property. Later the federal government disclaimed any interest in the murals, refused to pay, and told the restorer to resolve the issue with the city.

---

[23] AIC Guidelines, ¶ 4d and Commentary 4d.

[24] Doane v. Stadele, 190 Wis. 2d 468, 528 N.W.2d 91 (Ct. App. 1994) (antique car restoration).

[25] Anderson v. Schwegel, 118 Idaho 362, 796 P.2d 1035 (Ct. App. 1990) (antique car restoration).

[26] *Ibid.*

[27] 972 F.2d 495 (2d Cir. 1992).

The restorer sued the city and won a judgment for the full amount of his services based on *quantum meruit*. The Second Circuit affirmed the judgment, but with one important modification: finding that the city could have had no idea, when it claimed ownership and conceded that the restorer was entitled to some compensation, that the cost of restoring the murals would come to as much as $557,200, the court held that it would be inequitable to compel the city to pay any such amount unless it was willing to do so. Accordingly, it held that the city could pay the judgment or, alternatively, transfer ownership of the murals to the restorer.

§ 12.05 THE RESTORATION PROCESS

[A] Preliminary Condition Report and Treatment Proposal

The restoration process begins with the conservator examining the art object and preparing a condition report and treatment proposal, which the client reviews and approves.

The report identifies the artwork, owner and conservator and describes the artwork's physical condition. In the case of an oil painting on canvas, for example, the report would discuss the condition of the canvas, lining, stretcher, paint, ground layers, and surface layers, and would note any prior restorations. The report then describes the conservation treatment that the restorer recommends, and discloses any anticipated difficulties or risks.

In some cases, the condition report and treatment proposal serves as the contract and includes a price estimate for the treatment and a signature line for the client. The better practice is to use a separate contract form and incorporate the treatment proposal by reference.[28]

[B] Treatment Steps

The conservation work consists of whatever is judged suitable to the preservation of the aesthetic and physical characteristics of the particular artwork. For example, restoring an older oil painting might involve removing of dirt, grime and accretions from the varnish layer, yellowing varnish, and the old lining and adhesives from the reverse of the canvas; replacing the lining materials, and applying new varnish, new paint where the original paint has been lost (inpainting) and/or on top of original paint (overpainting), and a final protective varnish layer.

Professional ethics require that inpainting, overpainting or other compensation for loss be detectable (using visible light, ultraviolet radiation or low power magnification), reversible, and faithful to the artwork's original appearance.[29]

---

[28] *See* § 12.04[A] and Form 12-1.

[29] AIC Guidelines, Commentary 23.

[C] Final Report on Treatment

When the treatment is completed, the conservator prepares a written report describing the materials and procedures used.[30] The report may also contain "before" and "after" photographs of the artwork and recommendations for its continued handling, use, maintenance, storage, and display.

In the event of a claim or dispute, the conservator's final report and other documentation can provide the lawyer with a road map of the artwork's original condition, the conservator's diagnosis and plan of treatment and the actual treatment and scientific testing performed, much like the medical records of a patient in a medical malpractice action. There may even be x rays and laboratory test results.

[D] Owner's Duties

The owner or authorized custodian of the artwork has the duty to review and approve the written preliminary condition report and treatment proposal, and to be available for consultation with the conservator if any major changes in the proposal are required. The owner also has a duty to provide complete and accurate information to the conservator regarding prior restorations, reconstructions and other relevant matters about which the conservator may inquire.[31] Finally, the owner has a duty to follow the conservator's advice regarding the continued care of the artwork;[32] to do otherwise could constitute comparative fault and/or a failure to mitigate damages.

The conservation profession takes the position that the owner bears a joint responsibility with the conservator on the feasibility of a treatment and its outcome.[33] That may be true in some idealistic sense, but as a legal matter the owner is entitled to rely on the professional conservator—the expert—to make the appropriate recommendations and to perform the work properly, without the owner having to supervise, review, inquire, or look over the shoulder of the conservator.[34]

---

[30] Conservators have an ethical obligation to prepare "accurate, complete and permanent records of examination, sampling, scientific investigation and treatment." AIC Guidelines, ¶ 24.

[31] *See* Nika v. Danz, 199 Ill. App. 3d 296, 556 N.E.2d 873 (1990) (client's failure to provide essential information for his representation to his attorney constitutes contributory negligence).

[32] *See* Conklin v. Weisman, 145 N.J. 395, 412-13, 678 A.2d 1060 (1996) (legal malpractice).

[33] Conservation Ethics: An Informal Interview, Western Association for Art Conservation Newsletter, Sept. 1984, at 2-10; *and see* Australian Institute for the Conservation of Cultural Material, Code of Ethics and Guidance for Conservation Practice, § 2(1) ("the care and treatment of cultural material is the shared responsibility of the owner and the conservator").

[34] *See, e.g.*, Theobald v. Byers, 193 Cal. App. 2d 147, 13 Cal. Rptr. 864 (1961) (legal malpractice).

[E] Trade Secrets Protection

Some conservators employ their own special processes and materials for restoration of artwork, developed through years of experience and experimentation. In appropriate circumstances, such processes and materials can be entitled to protection as trade secrets.

A trade secret is defined as:

> Any information that can be used in the operation of a business or other enterprise and that is sufficiently valuable and secret to afford an actual or potential economic advantage over others.[35]

Under this definition, for example, the formulas and chemicals used by the conservator, the know-how necessary to perform a certain restoration, and even the identity and requirements of customers could be entitled to protection if they are secret and valuable enough to provide an economic advantage.[36]

The trade secrets issue most frequently arises in the context of an employee or former employee who uses or discloses the employer's trade secrets in breach of the duty of loyalty. In one case, a nationally prominent art conservation business brought suit for wrongful use of trade secrets against a former employee who had established a competing restoration business.[37] The plaintiff alleged that the former employee wrongfully obtained from its office records the name of a supplier of a unique product that plaintiff used for painting ceramics, and wrongfully used other products used by the plaintiff, including a ceramic glaze (Ceramit) and a filler putty (Duratite). The plaintiff won a favorable jury verdict at trial, but the verdict was set aside by the trial court because the plaintiff had failed to prove the existence of any trade secrets used by the former employee. The Court of Appeals affirmed, holding that although the plaintiff clearly did not reveal to the general public the techniques employed for restoration, the evidence did not establish that these techniques were unique in the trade. In fact, they were either generally known in the trade or obtainable from available publications.[38]

[F] Are Restorations Copyrightable?

The argument has been made that "significant" art restorations constitute an original contribution by the conservator to the artwork itself, and qualify for copyright protection.[39] No reported decision has ever addressed the issue, but it

---

[35] Restatement (Third) of Unfair Competition § 39.

[36] *Ibid.* cmt. d.

[37] Wiebold Studio, Inc. v. Old World Restorations, Inc, 19 Ohio App. 3d 246, 484 N.E.2d 280 (1985).

[38] *Ibid.*, 484 N.E.2d at 285.

[39] R.A. Mandel, Copyrighting Art Restorations, 28 Bulletin Copyright Soc'y U.S.A. 273 (1981).

seems clear that a restoration done in accordance with ethical guidelines could not, by definition, satisfy the legal requirements of copyrightability.

In order to be copyrightable, a work of art "must embody some creative authorship in its delineation or form."[40] In addition, the work must "contain some substantial, not merely trivial originality."[41] The dual requirements of creativity and originality are not satisfied by a mere showing of technical skill, effort and "sweat of the brow."[42] Nor is the requisite creativity supplied through "innovations which are solely utilitarian or mechanical," such as the use of materials that enhance durability or color retention.[43]

Under the conservation profession's ethical guidelines, the goal of art restoration is not to be creative, but to preserve the original "aesthetic, conceptual and physical characteristics" of the artwork.[44] Any inpainting or overpainting must be designed to return the work to the way it was when the artist completed it.[45] Thus, it would be difficult to envision a legitimate art restoration qualifying for copyright status.

§ 12.06 SELECTED LAWS AFFECTING CONSERVATION PRACTICE

Given the thousands of federal and state laws, rules and regulations governing virtually every aspect of human endeavor, it should not be surprising that a variety of legal restrictions affect the practice of art conservation.

[A] Occupational Safety and Health Regulation

Art restoration can involve the use of toxic chemicals, flammable solvents, and other potentially dangerous materials. It can also involve exposure to hazardous materials contained in the original artwork or used in past treatments, including such highly toxic substances as cobalt, manganese, barium, radium, lead, benzene,

---

[40] Gardenia Flowers v. Joseph Markovits, Inc., 280 F. Supp. 776, 781 (S.D.N.Y. 1968) (flower arrangements lacked creativity); John Muller & Co., Inc. v. N.Y. Arrows Soccer Team, Inc., 802 F.2d 989, 990 (8th Cir. 1986) (team logo lacked necessary level of creativity).

[41] L. Batlin & Son, Inc. v. Snyder, 536 F.2d 486, 490 (2d Cir. 1976) (plastic replica of antique cast-iron bank lacked originality despite variations).

[42] Bridgeman Art Library, Ltd. v. Corel Corp., 36 F.Supp. 2d 191, 197 (S.D.N.Y. 1999) (art reproductions lacked necessary originality).

[43] *Gardenia Flowers*, *supra*, note 40, at 781.

[44] AIC Guidelines ¶ 21 and Commentary 23.

[45] *Ibid.*; *and see* L. Kruth & H. Kruth, The Question of Copyrighting Art Restorations, Western Ass'n for Art Conservation Newsletter, Sept. 1981, at 1-2. ("To recognize inpainting or replacement of losses as original artwork in itself and thereby encourage such practices in order to satisfy the requirements of copyright law, is dangerous and contrary to the interests of the profession and art.")

trichlorethylene, silica dust, and asbestos.[46] That implicates federal and state occupational safety and health regulations.

The federal Occupational Safety and Health Act[47] was enacted by Congress in 1970 in order to establish a nationwide floor of health and safety protections in the workplace.[48] The act is administered by the federal Occupational Health and Safety Administration (Fed/OSHA).[49]

Under the federal act, responsibility for occupational safety and health matters is turned over to each individual state if the state submits a plan approved by Fed/OSHA that is "at least as effective as" the corresponding federal regulations.[50] For example, in California the state legislature in 1973 enacted the California Occupational Safety and Health Act, one purpose of which was to adopt a plan to satisfy federal requirements. Once the plan was approved in 1975, Cal/OSHA became responsible to enforce its provisions.[51]

The California act imposes numerous duties on the employer. For instance, the employer must monitor conditions in the workplace to limit or prevent employee exposure to various hazards such as airborne contaminants, confined spaces, noise, cotton dust, asbestos, vinyl chloride, lead and coke oven emissions.[52] Medical surveillance programs or medical examinations are required for exposures to these and such other hazards as ethylene oxide, ethylene dibromide (EDB), formaldehyde, DBCP, lead and carcinogens.[53] Employees exposed to a hazardous substance must be furnished with the information contained in the Material Safety Data Sheet for the substance.[54]

[B] Excavated Objects and Human Remains

The federal Archeological Resources Protection Act of 1979[55] makes it a crime to transport, receive or otherwise traffic in any "archaeological resource" that was unlawfully excavated or removed from public lands or Indian lands.[56]

---

[46] *See generally* M. McCann, Health Hazards Manual for Artists (1985); J. Waller, Safe Practices in the Arts and Crafts: A Studio Guide (1985).

[47] 29 U.S.C. §§ 651 *et seq.*

[48] United Airlines, Inc. v. Occupational Safety & Health Appeals Board, 32 Cal. 3d 762, 772, 187 Cal. Rptr. 387 (1982).

[49] *See* 29 U.S.C. § 553.

[50] 29 U.S.C. § 667(c).

[51] Loskowski v. State Personnel Board, 4 Cal. App. 4th 453, 456, 5 Cal. Rptr. 2d 488 (1992).

[52] *See* 8 Cal. Code Reg. §§ 5097, 5140-5143, 5155, 5158, 5190, 5208, 5210-5211, 5216.

[53] *See* 8 Cal. Code Reg. §§ 5209, 5212, 5216-5217, 5219-5220.

[54] Cal. Labor Code § 6398(b); 8 Cal. Code Reg. § 5194. Material Safety Data Sheets, prepared by the manufacturer, contain information on the ingredients and hazards of the product and precautions that should be taken.

[55] 16 U.S.C. §§ 470aa *et seq.*

[56] 16 U.S.C. § 470ee(b).

Archaeological resources include pottery, basketry, rock paintings, rock carvings, intaglios, graves, human skeletal materials, and other items of archaeological interest that are at least 100 years of age.[57] Any person who knowingly violates the act can be fined up to $20,000 and/or imprisoned for up to two years; for subsequent violations, the penalties increase to $100,000 and five years.[58]

The federal Native American Graves Protection and Repatriation Act[59] penalizes trafficking in Native American human remains and cultural items and creates a felony offense for a second or subsequent violation.[60] "Cultural items" are objects that have ongoing historic, cultural or traditional importance, and are considered inalienable by the tribe by virtue of the objects' centrality in tribal culture.[61]

[C] Endangered Species

The possession of art created from materials obtained from endangered species can violate various federal laws designed to save vanishing wildlife, and lead to civil or criminal penalties, including imprisonment.

- The Endangered Species Act[62] prohibits the possession or transportation of any illegally taken endangered species.[63]
- The Eagle Protection Act[64] prohibits the possession or transportation of any bald eagle or golden eagle, or any part, nest, or egg from such eagles.
- The Migratory Bird Treaty Act[65] makes it unlawful to possess, transport, or carry any migratory bird or "any part, nest or egg of any such bird, or any product, whether or not manufactured, which consists, or is composed in whole or in part, of any such bird, or any part, nest or egg thereof."[66] Violations are treated as strict liability crimes not requiring specific intent or knowledge.[67]
- The Marine Mammal Protection Act[68] prohibits the possession or transportation of any unlawfully taken marine mammal or any product from that mammal.[69]

---

57 16 U.S.C. § 470bb(1). An intaglio is a type of engraving or incised figure in stone.

58 16 U.S.C. § 470ee(d).

59 25 U.S.C. §§ 3001-3013.

60 18 U.S.C. § 1170.

61 25 U.S.C. § 3001(3); United States v. Corrow, 119 F.3d 796, 800 (10th Cir. 1997).

62 16 U.S.C. §§ 1531-1543.

63 16 U.S.C. § 1538.

64 16 U.S.C. §§ 668-668d.

65 16 U.S.C. §§ 701-718.

66 16 U.S.C. § 703.

67 United States v. Corrow, 119 F.3d 796, 805 (10th Cir. 1997) (Navajo masks adorned with protected bird feathers).

68 16 U.S.C. §§ 1361-1407.

69 16 U.S.C. § 1372(a).

[D] Stolen Property

The National Stolen Property Act[70] makes it a criminal offense to transport or transfer in interstate or foreign commerce any goods worth $5,000 or more, or to possess, conceal or sell such goods, with knowledge that the goods were stolen, converted or taken by fraud. "Stolen" goods include not only goods taken from the personal possession of another, but goods such as pre-Columbian artifacts that are "stolen" only in the sense that a Latin American country generally has declared itself the owner of all such artifacts found within its borders.[71]

A New York furniture restorer was charged under 18 U.S.C. § 2315 with possessing and trying to sell stolen art after he discovered a valuable sixteenth-century portrait of Christ in a panel of wood and offered to sell it back to the owner, a German museum.[72] The restorer found the oil painting hidden behind a layer of black paint and an old print glued to a wood panel that had been in his shop for nine years. He cleaned the painting, spent six months researching it, and learned that it had been stolen during World War II. He contacted the museum and offered to return it for a $100,000 finder's fee. The museum refused to pay. The restorer was arrested in 1999 following an undercover sting operation by the U.S. Customs Service in which his telephone conversations with museum officials were recorded.

§ 12.07 RESTORATIONS AND MARKET VALUE

[A] Improper Restorations

An inept or mishandled restoration can lead to a reduction in the value of an artwork. In a case involving a 100-year-old Corot painting of a young woman,[73] the restorer not only inpainted the scratches and abrasions but did a considerable amount of overpainting on top of the artist's original paint in an effort to "prettify" the figure in the painting. The court, noting that the character of the painting was considerably changed, described the restoration as "almost a disaster." There was testimony that the overpainting could be removed through a process of cleaning, but with some risk. The court held that the risk "had a depressing effect on the fair market value."[74]

---

[70] 18 U.S.C. §§ 2314, 2315.

[71] United States v. McClain, 593 F.2d 658 (5th Cir. 1979).

[72] United States v. Vaccaro, No. 99 MAG. 1950 (S.D.N.Y. filed Nov. 4, 1999). *See* B. Weiser, Restorer Who Found Stolen Art Is Prosecuted, N.Y. Times, Nov. 10, 1999, at A22; D. De la Cruz, Long Island Man Arrested For Allegedly Trying To Sell Stolen Painting, Associated Press, Nov. 10, 1999.

[73] Furstenberg v. United States, 595 F.2d 603 (Ct. Cl. 1979).

[74] *Ibid.*, 595 F.2d at 607-08. *See also* Posner v. Commissioner, 35 T.C.M. (CCH) 943 (expert testified that substantial amount of overpainting greatly reduced value of 300-year-old painting).

Even the mere suggestion of an improper restoration can lead to claims of loss of market value. In one case, the owner of a painting by nineteenth-century French artist Jean Beraud alleged that the work had failed to sell at a Christie's auction, and was left "burned" and devalued, as a result of defendants' statement that the painting had been damaged by "an abusive restoration and cleaning."[75]

[B] Proper Restorations

When sudden or accidental damage to an artwork occurs, caused, say, by a flood or by careless handling, the owner may bring a claim against his insurance carrier or against the negligent party for damages. In order to calculate the damages, it must be determined to what extent a competent restoration treatment can restore the lost market value of the artwork. Rarely will it be 100 percent.

In one instance, a wood sculpture entitled "Fulani Mother and Child" fell while on consignment to the Cincinnati Zoo, causing the decapitation of the carved female figure.[76] The artist, claiming the work was his masterpiece, sued the zoo for damages and prevailed. The damage formula used by the trial judge and approved by the Court of Appeal was as follows:

1. Determine the market value of the artwork prior to its damage, based on expert opinion, sales of other pieces by the artist, the artist's asking price, and other relevant evidence ($120,000).
2. Deduct the zoo's commission fee (25%). This yields the value if the undamaged sculpture had been sold for market value through a commissioned sale ($90,000).
3. Determine what percentage of the statue's pre-damage value would be recovered upon proper restoration. (After hearing conflicting expert testimony, the court determined that only 20% of the statue's value, $18,000, could be salvaged by restoration). Reduce the damage award by this "salvage" value ($90,000 minus $18,000 equals $72,000).
4. Add the cost of restoration ($6,000) to arrive at total damages ($78,000).

In another instance, three original oil paintings by artist Aldolf Sehring were damaged in a flood caused by the neighbor's faulty plumbing.[77] The artist sued for damages, claiming that the paintings were irreversibly damaged and that restoring the paintings and putting them back on the market would risk his international reputation as a renowned artist. One expert testified that the paintings had lost all of their value and could not be restored as long as the artist was

[75] Kirby v. Wildenstein, 784 F. Supp. 1112 (S.D.N.Y. 1992). Defendants prevailed on summary judgment because plaintiff produced no evidence of causation or special damages.

[76] Eboigbe v. Zoological Society of Cincinnati, 96 Ohio App. 3d 102, 644 N.E.2d 693 (1994).

[77] Small v. Baloise Ins. Co. of Am., 1998 La. App. LEXIS 634 (1998).

living. Another expert testified that the paintings could be successfully restored. The court concluded that restoration was possible and would restore 50 percent of the paintings' value.

§ 12.08 LIABILITY OF THE CONSERVATION PROFESSIONAL

The objects entrusted to conservators tend to be quite valuable, not only in terms of market value but also in terms of cultural importance. Indeed, the artistic, historic, or social significance of an art object can make it literally invaluable and irreplaceable. That, combined with the fact that most such objects are fragile and easily harmed by maltreatment, creates an ever-present potential for liability.

No one keeps statistics on how many claims or lawsuits have been brought against conservators. Most such claims are resolved quietly and confidentially, because neither the conservator nor the art owner benefits by publicity. The legal theories asserted by claimants include professional malpractice (negligence), breach of contract, and breach of implied warranty.

[A] Who Can Sue?

Only the "real party in interest" can file and prosecute a lawsuit. The "real party in interest" is the person who owns or holds title to the work involved, as opposed to others who may be interested in or benefited by the litigation.[78]

[1] The Owner and Third-Party Beneficiaries

Normally, the real party in interest is the owner of the artwork. It is the owner, or the owner's authorized representative such as a museum curator, who typically contracts with the conservator for the performance of services.

In addition, if the contract was made expressly for the benefit of a third person, such as a collector who has agreed to purchase the artwork or a gallery that intends to exhibit it, that third person might also have standing to sue under third-party beneficiary principles.[79]

[2] The Artist

In some instances, the artist may have the right to sue even if he no longer owns the artwork.

The federal Visual Artists Rights Act (VARA)[80] confers standing on the author of a work of visual art to prevent any "distortion, mutilation or other modification" of his artwork caused by the "gross negligence" of a conservator.

---

[78] *E.g.*, Cal. Civ. Proc. Code § 367; Gantman v. United Pac. Ins. Co., 232 Cal. App. 3d 1560, 1566, 284 Cal. Rptr. 188 (1991).

[79] *E.g.*, Cal. Civ. Code § 1559.

[80] 17 U.S.C. § 106A. For a discussion of VARA generally, see Chapter 1.

A number of states have similar statutes. Massachusetts, for example, gives standing to the artist "or any bona fide union or other artists' organization authorized in writing by the artist" to commence an action for injunctive relief or damages with respect to the mutilation, alteration or destruction of the artist's works of fine art caused "deliberately or through gross negligence."[81] "Gross negligence" is defined as "the exercise of so slight a degree of care as to justify the belief that there was an indifference to the particular work of fine art."[82]

Note that a state statute would be preempted by VARA to the extent the statute and VARA confer equivalent rights.[83]

[3] Can the General Public Sue?

The conservation profession professes that it owes certain obligations not only to the owners, custodians, and authors of cultural property, but also to the general public.[84] Similarly, some state artists' rights statutes proclaim "that there is a public interest in preserving the integrity of cultural and artistic creations."[85] It seems clear, however, that such statements are rhetorical only, and would not be construed as giving the general public a right to sue a conservator for negligently treating, say, a national cultural treasure.

[4] Do Artworks Have Rights?

The short answer is no, but it is worth mentioning that there is a movement, similar to the animal rights movement, to enact legislation that would give artworks certain rights. An organization called ArtWatch International has even formulated a "Bill of Rights" for artworks that includes the right to an "honorable and dignified existence" in a "protected and controlled environment" and, with respect to certain masterpieces, the right to a judicial hearing prior to any conservation treatment.[86]

---

[81] Mass. Ann. Laws ch. 231, § 85 S. *See also* Cal. Civ. Code § 987; Conn. Gen. Stat. § 42-116t; La. R. S. 51:21:52; Nev. Rev. Stat. Ann. § 597.740 (simple negligence); N.J. Stat. § 2A:24A-6 (simple negligence); N.M. Stat. Ann. § 13-4B-3; N.Y. Art & Cult. Aff. Law § 14.03; 73 Pa. Stat. § 2102; R.I. Gen. Laws § 5-62-5 (simple negligence).

[82] Mass. Ann. Laws ch. 231, § 85 S.

[83] Lubner v. City of Los Angeles, 45 Cal. App. 4th 525, 531, 53 Cal. Rptr. 2d 24 (1996).

[84] AIC Code of Ethics, pmbl. ("conservation professionals assume certain obligations to . . . society as a whole"); European Confederation of Conservator-Restorers' Organizations Professional Guidelines (the conservator "has a responsibility to . . . the public and posterity").

[85] Cal. Civ. Code § 989; Mass. Ann. Laws ch. 231, § 85 S.

[86] J. Beck & N. Daley, Art Restoration: The Culture, the Business and the Scandal 176-81 (1993). ArtWatch is located at 931 Schermerhorn Hall, Columbia University, New York, N.Y. 10027; telephone (212) 854-4569.

[B] Professional Malpractice

The conservation professional holds himself or herself out as having superior knowledge and expertise with respect to the examination, scientific analysis, treatment and restoration of cultural property. Thus, the conservator-client relationship carries with it a professional standard of care, the breach of which constitutes professional malpractice.[87]

The elements of a malpractice cause of action against an art conservator or any other professional include: (1) the existence of a relationship creating a duty to possess and exercise ordinary skill and knowledge; (2) a breach of that duty, such as negligence; (3) a causal connection between the negligent conduct and the resulting injury; and (4) actual loss or damage.[88]

The degree of care, skill and knowledge that may be required of a professional is a question of fact for the jury. Normally the jury hears testimony from expert witnesses with respect to the applicable standard of care and its breach.

In a majority of jurisdictions, codes of ethics and other standards and guidelines promulgated by recognized professional organizations are admissible as relevant evidence to show the applicable standard of care.[89] The theory behind this view is that because ethical standards set the minimum level of competence to be displayed by all members of the profession, violation of the standards can be considered evidence of malpractice.[90]

Allowing into evidence standards promulgated by professional organizations creates a potential headache for conservators and a potential windfall for plaintiffs' attorneys. That is because the leading national organization of conservation professionals in the United States, the AIC, [91] has issued a Code of Ethics and Guidelines for Practice that, together with lengthy Commentaries that set forth hundreds of requirements for "minimum accepted practice," is so detailed and so rigorous that it would be difficult to imagine a situation where at least one standard was not violated.

---

[87] *See* LeSueur Creamery, Inc. v. Haskon, Inc., 660 F.2d 342, 348 (8th Cir. 1981) ("Professional persons and those engaged in any work or trade requiring special skill must possess a minimum of special knowledge and ability as well as exercise reasonable care").

[88] *See* S. M. Levy, Liability of the Art Expert for Professional Malpractice, 1991 Wis. L. Rev. 595 (1991).

[89] *See, e.g.*, Diversified Graphics, Ltd. v. Groves, 868 F.2d 293, 296 (8th Cir. 1989) (practice standards adopted by the American Institute of Certified Public Accountants constitute evidence of the standard of care applicable to computer systems consultant); Miami Int'l. Realty Co. v. Paynter, 841 F.2d 348, 352-53 (10th Cir. 1988) (professional ethical standards are relevant to breach of an attorney's duty of care); Pedroza v. Bryant, 101 Wash. 2d 226, 233-34, 677 P.2d 166 (1984) (accreditation standards of the Joint Commission on Accreditation of Hospitals are relevant to a hospital's duty of care).

[90] *See* Sommers v. McKinney, 287 N.J. Super. 1, 13, 670 A.2d 99 (1996).

[91] *See supra* text at notes 8 and 9.

[C] Breach of Contract

The conservator who commits malpractice can be subject to contract as well as tort liability. Implicit in every contract is the promise to exercise ordinary skill and knowledge in the rendition of professional services.[92] Some considerations that might cause a plaintiff to prefer a contract action include the availability of a longer statute of limitations, the potential for greater damages under the benefit of the bargain rule, the fact that a contract claim may be assignable where a tort claim is not, and the fact that a tort claim may not survive the death of one of the parties.[93]

Of course, breach of contract would also be the appropriate claim where some other obligation arising out of the contract is involved.

Every contract for conservation services should be in writing, but an oral agreement is also enforceable if the following essential elements are present: (1) parties capable of contracting, (2) their consent, (3) a lawful object, and (4) a sufficient cause or consideration.[94]

To prevail against a conservator for breach of contract, the plaintiff must prove: (1) the existence of a contract, (2) performance of the contract by the plaintiff, (3) breach of the contract by the conservator, and (4) damages.[95]

[D] Implied Warranties

For historical reasons, warranties are associated primarily with transactions involving the sale of goods, but they are not necessarily confined to such transactions.[96] A contract to supply labor and materials can also give rise to implied warranties, including the warranty of merchantability.[97] The rationale is that the service provider makes implied representations that he has used reasonable skill and judgment in performing his contract.[98]

An implied warranty with respect to conservation services is most likely to arise, if at all, where the contract is for hands-on restoration work involving the provision of labor and materials, such as paint and lining material. By analogy, a Texas court held that an implied warranty to repair tangible goods in a good and workmanlike manner may arise under the state's Deceptive Trade Practices

---

[92] *See, e.g.*, Bucquet v. Livingston, 57 Cal. App. 3d 914, 129 Cal. Rptr. 514 (1976); Saveca v. Reilly, 111 A.D.2d 493, 488 N.Y.S.2d 876 (1985).

[93] W. Page Keeton *et al.*, Prosser and Keeton on the Law of Torts § 92, at 664 (5th ed. 1984).

[94] *E.g.*, Cal. Civ. Code § 1550.

[95] *See, e.g.*, Nordic Bank PLC v. Trend Group, Ltd., 619 F. Supp. 542, 561 (S.D.N.Y. 1985).

[96] Aced v. Hobbs-Sesack Plumbing Co., 55 Cal. 2d 573, 582, 12 Cal. Rptr. 257 (1961) (contract for labor and material for a home heating system).

[97] *Ibid.*

[98] Pollard v. Saxe & Yolles Development Co., 12 Cal. 3d 374, 379, 115 Cal. Rptr. 648 (1974).

Act.[99] A case decided under Kansas law held that there is an implied warranty of workmanlike performance in every contract calling for performance of work or skill.[100]

On the other hand, if the contract is for advice and consultation only, it is possible that no implied warranty would arise. Under New Jersey law, for example, engineers, architects, lawyers, and others who provide professional services must exercise reasonable skill and judgment but do not impliedly warrant that their services will be fit for the intended use because they exercise individual judgment in a situation where unknown and uncontrollable factors are common.[101]

§ 12.09 DEFAMATION

The controversial nature of some art restoration projects, particularly those involving national treasures, tends to provoke statements critical of the work and of the professionals involved. Such statements, when aired in public, occasionally lead to defamation claims.

[A] Libel and Slander Defined

Defamation is the act of harming another person's reputation by libel or slander. While definitions vary from jurisdiction to jurisdiction, libel is generally defined as a false and unprivileged publication *by writing or other permanent form* which exposes any person to hatred, contempt or ridicule, or which causes him to be shunned or avoided or that tends to injure him in his occupation.[102] Slander is a false and unprivileged publication, *orally uttered*, which, among other things, charges a person with a crime or tends to injure him in respect to his profession, trade or business.[103] In sum: slander is spoken, libel is written.

A number of decisions by the U.S. Supreme Court have placed certain constitutional limitations on plaintiffs in defamation lawsuits, which vary depending on whether the plaintiff is a private person as opposed to a public figure or public official.[104] Also, communications made during judicial proceedings are

---

[99] Melody Home Mfg. Co. v. Barnes, 741 S.W.2d 349 (Tex. 1987).

[100] Enfield By and Through Enfield v. Pittman Mfg., 923 F. Supp. 187 (D. Kan. 1996).

[101] R.L. Longo Construction Co., Inc. v. Transit Am., Inc., 921 F. Supp. 1295 (D.N.J. 1996); *and see* Brooks v. United States Fire Ins. Co., 832 F.2d 1378 (5th Cir. 1987) (no implied warranty under Texas law where the essence of the transaction is the exercise of professional judgment rather than the repair or modification of existing tangible goods).

[102] *E.g.*, Cal. Civ. Code § 45.

[103] *E.g.*, Cal. Civ. Code § 46.

[104] *See generally* Milkovich v. Lorain Journal Co., 497 U.S. 1, 110 S. Ct. 2695, 111 L. Ed. 2d 1 (1990); New York Times Co. v. Sullivan, 376 U. S. 254, 84 S. Ct. 710, 11 L. Ed. 2d 686 (1964).

accorded an absolute privilege under the common law[105] as well as under state statutes.[106]

[B] The *Goldreyer* Case

A widely publicized lawsuit by art conservator Daniel Goldreyer against Time, Inc., and the publishers of the Wall Street Journal illustrates how the law of defamation has been applied to public criticism of art restorations.[107] The plaintiff was retained by a museum in Amsterdam to repair and restore a $2 million Abstract Expressionist painting by American artist Barnett Newman which had been repeatedly slashed by a vandal. The restoration, which took three years to complete, was lambasted by some critics, who attacked the quality of the work and accused plaintiff of having ruined a masterpiece. In 1991 Time International and the Wall Street Journal ran stories reporting on the controversy. Goldreyer sued the publications for libel.

An appellate court dismissed the lawsuit as to Time International, holding that the following allegedly defamatory statements were not actionable:

1. "Plaintiff's restoration of Newman's painting, if rehung, should be accompanied by a warning sign, 'Newman according to Goldreyer.' " This statement was entitled to constitutional protection as opinion in the form of "imaginative expression" or "rhetorical hyperbole."
2. "For the burghers of Amsterdam the glow is gone from Newman's once warmly wonderful masterpiece"; and "the painting no longer exists, [and] has become a curiosity with a sad history." These statements were entitled to the same opinion privilege.
3. "After microscopic tests on thirty samples of Newman's work, the [Dutch government forensic] lab concluded that Goldreyer had not matched the original oils. . . . Instead, the lab reported, the restorer had used alkyd, a synthetic paint commonly used on window frames." These statements were not pure opinion, but opinion based upon fact, and therefore actionable because they implied that the lab found that plaintiff used house paint for the restoration. However, the statements were entitled to the absolute privilege as to fair and true reportage of an official proceeding pursuant to New York Civil Rights Law § 74.[108]

---

[105] Briscoe v. LaHue, 460 U.S. 325, 103 S. Ct. 1108, 75 L. Ed. 2d 96 (1983); Restatement, (Second) Torts §§ 585-589.

[106] *E.g.*, Cal. Civ. Code § 47(2).

[107] Daniel Goldreyer, Ltd. v. Van de Wetering, 217 A.D.2d 434, 630 N.Y.S.2d 18 (1995); Daniel Goldreyer, Ltd. v. Dow Jones & Co., Inc., 178 Misc. 2d 308, 678 N.Y.S.2d 453 (1998), *rev'd* 687 N.Y.S .2d 64 (1999).

[108] Daniel Goldreyer, Ltd. v. Van de Wetering, 217 A.D.2d 434, 630 N.Y.S.2d 18 (1995).

The Wall Street Journal article fared less well in court. The article reported that the forensic laboratory had found that the canvas was "completely painted over using an inappropriate type of paint." It further reported, without giving a source, that "some thought [plaintiff] had used a roller to slap house paint on it."[109] The court held that, unlike Time's statements, these statements were *not* privileged as published accounts of official proceedings because, by referring to "house paint" and "roller brushes," they suggested more serious misconduct than that suggested in the official proceeding.[110] However, the publisher ultimately prevailed on summary judgment because plaintiff was held to be a "limited purpose public figure," and therefore was required to prove "with convincing clarity," but was unable to prove, actual malice.[111]

[C] The *Beck* Case

In 1991 a Columbia University art history professor, James Beck, was sued in Italy in four separate venues by an Italian art restorer for "aggravated slander," a criminal offense punishable by up to three years in prison. Italian journalists had quoted Beck as saying that a fifteenth-century sculpture cleaned by the restorer looked "as if it had been treated with acid, cleaned with Spic and Span and polished with Johnson's Wax."[112] The restorer also sought damages in the sum of 60 million lire.[113]

Beck was ultimately acquitted in all four venues, but only after months of anxiety and tens of thousands of dollars in attorney fees.[114]

---

[109] Daniel Goldreyer, Ltd. v. Dow Jones & Co., Inc., 178 Misc. 2d 308, 316, 678 N.Y.S.2d 453 (1998).

[110] Daniel Goldreyer, Ltd. v. Van de Wetering, 217 A.D.2d 434, 436-37, 630 N.Y.S.2d 18 (1995).

[111] Daniel Goldreyer, Ltd. v. Dow Jones & Co., Inc., 687 N.Y.S.2d 64 (1999).

[112] M. Simons, A Restoration Becomes a Criminal Case In Italy, N.Y. Times, May 25, 1999, at 13; D. Lister, Prosecuted for Giving a Critic's Verdict, the Independent (London), Nov. 8, 1991, at 15.

[113] J. Beck & N. Daley, Art Restoration: The Culture, the Business and the Scandal 21 (1993).

[114] *Ibid.* at 4-21.

FORMS AND APPENDICES

Form 12-1: Agreement for Conservation Services

Appendix 12-A: Code of Ethics and Guidelines for Practice—American Institute for Conservation of Historic and Artistic Works (AIC)

Appendix 12-B: Directory of Regional Conservation Centers

FORM 12-1

Agreement for Conservation Services

This Agreement is entered into this ______ day of ______________________, 20__ between ______________________________*[name of client]* (the "Client") and ______________________________ *[name of conservation professional or firm]* (the "Conservator").

OWNERSHIP

1. The Client represents and warrants that he/she:

☐ Is the sole owner of the Art Object described in paragraph 2.

☐ Is the authorized agent of ________________________ *[name and address of owner]*, who is the sole owner of the Art Object described in paragraph 2.

DESCRIPTION OF ART OBJECT

2. The Art Object which is the subject of this Agreement is described as follows:

Artist: ______________________________

Title or Subject Matter: ______________________________

Dimensions: ______________________________

Material or Medium: ______________________________

Approximate Date Created: ______________________________

Present Location: ______________________________

Present Condition: ______________________________

Other: ______________________________

SERVICES

3. ☐ The Conservator agrees to perform the following services: ____
____
____
____________________ *[describe in sufficient detail the nature and extent of conservation services to be rendered.]*

☐ The services to be performed by the Conservator are set forth in the attached Report on Condition and Proposal for Treatment dated _________, 20_____.

4. All services shall be performed in a workmanlike manner, and in accordance with the Code of Ethics and Guidelines for Practice of the American Institute for Conservation of Historic and Artistic Works.

DOCUMENTATION

5. The Conservator shall prepare and provide to the Client the following written documentation *[check boxes which apply]*:

☐ Report on Condition and Proposal for Treatment.

☐ Conservation Report (upon completion of services).

☐ A photographic record of all phases of the treatment in color slides.

☐ Other: ____.

TIME ESTIMATE

6. The estimated start date for the conservation services is ____________, 20_____. The estimated completion date is ______________________, 20_____.

TRANSPORTATION AND INSURANCE

7. Unless otherwise agreed in writing, the Client shall be responsible for transporting the Art Object to and from the Conservator's laboratory, and insuring it for theft, fire, vandalism and other loss or damage.

RISKS

8. The Client understands that there are certain risks involved in performing the services covered by this Agreement, including but not limited to the following:

____

____

____________________________. The Client agrees to assume all said risks.

CLIENT'S DUTIES

9. The Client agrees to provide the Conservator with truthful information about the Art Object, its provenance, and its prior restorations; to abide by this Agreement; to pay the Conservator's bills on time; and to keep the Conservator informed of the Client's current address and telephone number.

CONFIDENTIALITY

10. The relationship between the Client and the Conservator shall be considered confidential. Information obtained from the examination, testing and treatment of the Art Object shall not be published or otherwise made public except as follows: ____ ______________________ *[describe any exceptions, or write "no exceptions"].*

FEES, COSTS AND OTHER CHARGES

11. For services rendered under this Agreement, the Conservator shall be entitled to compensation as follows *[check boxes which apply]*:

☐ A flat fee of ______________________ dollars ($____________), payable as follows: ____ *[e.g., ______________________ dollars ($______________) as an initial nonrefundable retainer and the balance upon completion of the project.]*

☐ An hourly fee at the rate of ________________________ dollars ($______________) for the Conservator and ________________________ dollars ($______________) for the Conservator's assistant(s). The Conservator shall send the Client monthly statements, each payable within _______days of the mailing date. The Client shall pay an initial security deposit in the sum of __________dollars ($________________), to be credited against the last statement. Any unused balance shall be refunded to the Client.

☐ In addition to the above fee, the Conservator shall be entitled to reimbursement for the actual cost of materials and photography, not to exceed a total of ___________________ dollars ($_____________).

INTEREST CHARGES

12. If a billing statement is not paid when due, interest shall be charged on the principal balance shown on the statement. Interest shall be calculated by multiplying the unpaid balance by the periodic rate of 0.833% per month (ten percent annual percentage rate). The unpaid balance shall bear interest until paid.

UNCLAIMED ART OBJECT

13. If the Client fails to claim the Art Object within 30 days after notification by the Conservator, the Conservator may, at his/her option, deliver the Art Object to any commercial storage facility to be stored at Client's expense. If the Client fails to claim the Art Object within one year after notification by the Conservator, the Conservator shall have the right to sell the Art Object at public auction or through other means and apply the proceeds to any unpaid fees, charges, and storage costs.

ARBITRATION

14. By initialing this arbitration provision, the Client and the Conservator agree to have any and all disputes that arise out of or relate to this Agreement decided only by binding arbitration in accordance with the rules of ______________________ *[insert name of arbitration provider, such as the American Arbitration Association]* and not by court action, except as provided by law for judicial review of arbitration proceedings. Judgment upon the arbitration award may be entered in any court having jurisdiction.

In agreeing to this arbitration provision, the Client and the Conservator are specifically giving up:

(a) All rights they may possess to have such disputes decided in a court or jury trial; and

(b) All judicial rights, including the right to appeal from the decision of the arbitrator(s).

If either the Client or the Conservator should refuse to submit to arbitration, either of them may be compelled to arbitrate under applicable law. The Client and the Conservator acknowledge the above, and that this mutual agreement for binding arbitration is voluntary.

____________	___________
(Client initial here)	(Conservator initial here)

GOVERNING LAW

15. The validity of this Agreement or of any of its provisions, as well as the rights and duties of the parties, shall be governed by the laws of the State of __________________.

ATTORNEYS' FEES

16. The prevailing party in any action or proceeding arising out of or to enforce any provision of this Agreement shall be awarded reasonable attorneys' fees and costs incurred in that action or proceeding, or in the enforcement of any judgment or award rendered.

LIABILITY OF CONSERVATOR

17. In performing any of his or her services under this Agreement, the Conservator shall not be liable to the Client or any other person or entity for any claims, damages, losses or expenses, except for gross negligence or willful misconduct on the Conservator's part.

DISCLAIMER OF GUARANTEE

18. Nothing in this Agreement, and nothing that the Conservator has stated to the Client, shall be construed as a guarantee or a promise about the success or effectiveness of any treatment of the Art Object. The Conservator does not make any such guarantees or promises. Any comments by the Conservator about the outcome of the treatment are expressions of opinion only.

ENTIRE AGREEMENT

19. This Agreement contains the entire agreement of the parties. No other agreements, statements or promises made on or before the effective date of this Agreement will be binding on the parties.

MODIFICATION BY SUBSEQUENT AGREEMENT

20. This Agreement may be modified by subsequent agreement of the parties only by an instrument in writing signed by both of them or an oral agreement only to the extent that the parties carry it out.

SEVERABILITY

21. If any provision of this Agreement is held in whole or in part to be unenforceable for any reason, the remainder of that provision and of the entire Agreement shall be severable and remain in effect.

IF THE ARBITRATION CLAUSE IN THIS AGREEMENT HAS BEEN INITIALED, THE CLIENT AND THE CONSERVATOR ARE AGREEING TO HAVE ALL DISPUTES DECIDED BY BINDING ARBITRATION AND ARE GIVING UP THEIR RIGHT TO A COURT OR JURY TRIAL FOR SUCH DISPUTES.

Dated: ______________, 20___ ______________________________

(Client)

Address: ______________________________

____

Telephone: ______________________________

Dated: ______________, 20___ ______________________________

(Conservator)

Address: ______________________________

____

Telephone: ______________________________

APPENDIX 12-A

Code of Ethics and Guidelines for Practice—American Institute for Conservation of Historic and Artistic Works (AIC)

CODE OF ETHICS AND GUIDELINES FOR PRACTICE of the American Institute for Conservation of Historic and Artistic Works

HISTORY

The first formulation of standards of practice and professional relations by any group of art conservators was produced by the IIC-American Group (now AIC) Committee on Professional Standards and Procedures. Formed at the second regular meeting of the IIC-AG, in Detroit, May 23, 1961, the committee worked under the direction of Murray Pease, conservator, Metropolitan Museum of Art; other members of the committee were Henri H. Courtais, Dudley T. Easby, Rutherford J. Gettens, and Sheldon Keck. The Report of the Murray Pease Committee: IIC American Group Standards of Practice and Professional Relations for Conservators was adopted by the IIC-AG at the fourth annual meeting in New York on June 8, 1963. It was published in Studies in Conservation in August 1964, 9(3):116–21. The primary purpose of this document was: "to provide accepted criteria against which a specific procedure or operation can be measured when a question as to its adequacy has been raised."

The first formulation of a code of ethics for art conservators was adopted by the members of IIC-American Group at the annual meeting in Ottawa, Ontario, Canada, on May 27, 1967. It was produced by the Committee on Professional Relations: Sheldon Keck, chair; Richard D. Buck; Dudley T. Easby; Rutherford J. Gettens; Caroline Keck; Peter Michaels, and Louis Pomerantz. The primary purpose of this document was: "to express those principles and practices which will guide the art conservator in the ethical practice of his profession."

These two documents, The Murray Pease Report: Standards of Practice and Professional Relationships for Conservators and the *Code of Ethics for Art Conservators* were published in booklet form by the IIC-AG in May 1968 together with the Articles of Association of IIC and Bylaws of the American Group.

In 1977, the Ethics and Standards Committee (Elisabeth C. G. Packard, chair; Barbara H. Beardsley; Perry C. Huston; Kate C. Lefferts; Robert M. Organ; and Clements L. Robertson) was charged with updating the two documents to reflect changes in the profession. The 1968 format was retained, except that the more general *Code of Ethics* was placed first as Part One, followed by the Standards of Practice as Part Two. These revised versions of the code and standards were approved by the Fellows of AIC on May 31, 1979, at the annual meeting in Toronto. This document was amended on May 24, 1985, at the annual meeting in Washington, D.C., to reflect the addition to the AIC Bylaws of procedures for the reporting, investigation, and review of alleged violations of the code and standards and of mechanisms for appealing such allegations.

Between 1984 and 1990 the Ethics and Standards Committee, responding to further growth and change in the profession, and following on several years of AIC discussion on the issue of certification, was charged by the AIC Board to work on more substantial revisions of the document. This was done by soliciting commentary from the specialty groups and also from the membership via issues sessions at the annual meetings in Chicago (1986) and Cincinnati (1989). Following this, a document consisting of a new simplified *Code*, prepared by the committee, and a revised *Standards*, prepared primarily by the board was presented to the membership for discussion at the 1990 annual meeting in Richmond. The consensus of the membership at the meeting was to continue the revision process. During these important years, the members of the committee were, Elisabeth Batchelor, chair; Robert Futernick; Meg Loew Craft (until 1989); Elizabeth Lunning (from 1987); Carol C. Mancusi-Ungaro; and Philip Vance (until 1986). In 1989, the committee added corresponding members Barbara Appelbaum, Paul N. Banks, Steven Prins, and Elisabeth West FitzHugh.

In 1990, the AIC Board charged a newly appointed committee to assess the role and use of the code and standards and as well to analyze specific difficulties within the documents themselves. The committee first undertook an in-depth comparative analysis of the documents organizing them topically and relating them to other codes of ethics both in conservation and in other professions. Between September 1991 and May 1992, the committee produced five lengthy discussion papers on basic issues as supplements to the *AIC News* (prior to November 1991, the *AIC Newsletter*). From these papers, the committee compiled an extensive body of membership and specialty group commentary, supplementing that obtained previously. It then began the creation of a new revision, the first draft of which was published in the September 1993 *AIC News* following a discussion session at the 1993 annual meeting in Denver. A revised draft was published in the May 1994 *AIC News* and discussed at the 1994 annual meeting in Nashville. A final version of the revised document was prepared and was approved by AIC Fellows and Professional Associates through a mail vote in August 1994.

Besides a new simplified *Code of Ethics* and the creation of *Guidelines for Practice* to replace the *Standards of Practice*, the new document will be supplemented by commentaries, a detailed description of which was published in the November 1993 *AIC News*. The goals and purposes of the committee and the problematic issues it sought to address in creating the revision are described in the committee's columns in the September 1991 *AIC Newsletter* and September 1993 *AIC News*.

Ethics and Standards Committee members during these years and involved in the creation of the revised code and guidelines were: Debbie Hess Norris (chair, resigned 1993); Donna K. Strahan (co-chair 1993–94, chair 1994); Carol Aiken (co-chair from 1993, resigned 1994); Nancy Ash; Dan Kushel; and Robert Espinosa (from 1993).

Elisabeth C. G. Packard, Chair, Ethics and Standards Committee 1977–79

Amended May 24, 1985

Revised August 1994, Dan Kushel, Member, Ethics and Standards Committee

PREAMBLE

The primary goal of conservation professionals, individuals with extensive training and special expertise, is the preservation of cultural property. Cultural property consists of individual objects, structures, or aggregate collections. It is material which has significance that may be artistic, historical, scientific, religious, or social, and it is an invaluable and irreplaceable legacy that must be preserved for future generations.

In striving to achieve this goal, conservation professionals assume certain obligations to the cultural property, to its owners and custodians, to the conservation profession, and to society as a whole. This document, the *Code of Ethics* and *Guidelines for Practice* of the American Institute for Conservation of Historic and Artistic Works (AIC), sets forth the principles that guide conservation professionals and others who are involved in the care of cultural property.

CODE OF ETHICS

I. The conservation professional shall strive to attain the highest possible standards in all aspects of conservation, including, but not limited to, preventive conservation, examination, documentation, treatment, research, and education.

II. All actions of the conservation professional must be governed by an informed respect for the cultural property, its unique character and significance, and the people or person who created it.

III. While recognizing the right of society to make appropriate and respectful use of cultural property, the conservation professional shall serve as an advocate for the preservation of cultural property.

IV. The conservation professional shall practice within the limits of personal competence and education as well as within the limits of the available facilities.

V. While circumstances may limit the resources allocated to a particular situation, the quality of work that the conservation professional performs shall not be compromised.

VI. The conservation professional must strive to select methods and materials that, to the best of current knowledge, do not adversely affect cultural property or its future examination, scientific investigation, treatment, or function.

VII. The conservation professional shall document examination, scientific investigation, and treatment by creating permanent records and reports.

VIII. The conservation professional shall recognize a responsibility for preventive conservation by endeavoring to limit damage or deterioration to cultural property, providing guidelines for continuing use and care, recommending appropriate environmental conditions for storage and exhibition, and encouraging proper procedures for handling, packing, and transport.

IX. The conservation professional shall act with honesty and respect in all professional relationships, seek to ensure the rights and opportunities of all individuals in the profession, and recognize the specialized knowledge of others.

X. The conservation professional shall contribute to the evolution and growth of the profession, a field of study that encompasses the liberal arts and the natural sciences. This contribution may be made by such means as continuing development of personal skills and knowledge, sharing of information and experience with colleagues, adding to the profession's written body of knowledge, and providing and promoting educational opportunities in the field.

XI. The conservation professional shall promote an awareness and understanding of conservation through open communication with allied professionals and the public.

XII. The conservation professional shall practice in a manner that minimizes personal risks and hazards to co-workers, the public, and the environment.

XIII. Each conservation professional has an obligation to promote understanding of and adherence to this *Code of Ethics*.

GUIDELINES FOR PRACTICE

The conservation professional should use the following guidelines and supplemental commentaries together with the AIC *Code of Ethics* in the pursuit of ethical practice. The commentaries are separate documents, created by the AIC membership, that are intended to amplify this document and to accommodate growth and change in the field.

PROFESSIONAL CONDUCT

1. **Conduct:** Adherence to the *Code of Ethics* and *Guidelines for Practice* is a matter of personal responsibility. The conservation professional should always be guided by the intent of this document, recognizing that specific circumstances may legitimately affect professional decisions.
2. **Disclosure:** In professional relationships, the conservation professional should share complete and accurate information relating to the efficacy and value of materials and procedures. In seeking and disclosing such information, and that relating to analysis and research, the conservation professional should recognize the importance of published information that has undergone formal peer review.
3. **Laws and Regulations:** The conservation professional should be cognizant of laws and regulations that may have a bearing on professional activity. Among these laws and regulations are those concerning the rights of artists and their estates, occupational health and safety, sacred and religious material, excavated objects, endangered species, human remains, and stolen property.
4. **Practice:** Regardless of the nature of employment, the conservation professional should follow appropriate standards for safety, security, contracts, fees, and advertising.
   - 4a. **Health and Safety:** The conservation professional should be aware of issues concerning the safety of materials and procedures and should make this information available to others, as appropriate.
   - 4b. **Security:** The conservation professional should provide working and storage conditions designed to protect cultural property.
   - 4c. **Contracts:** The conservation professional may enter into contractual agreements with individuals, institutions, businesses, or government agencies provided that such agreements do not conflict with principles of the *Code of Ethics* and *Guidelines for Practice*.
   - 4d. **Fees:** Fees charged by the conservation professional should be commensurate with services rendered. The division of a fee is acceptable only when based on the division of service or responsibility.
   - 4e. **Advertising:** Advertising and other representations by the conservation professional should present an accurate description of credentials and services. Limitations concerning the use of the AIC name or membership status should be followed as stated in the AIC Bylaws, section II, 13.
5. **Communication:** Communication between the conservation professional and the owner, custodian, or authorized agent of the cultural property is essential to ensure an agreement that reflects shared decisions and realistic expectations.

6. **Consent:** The conservation professional should act only with the consent of the owner, custodian, or authorized agent. The owner, custodian, or agent should be informed of any circumstances that necessitate significant deviations from the agreement. When possible, notification should be made before such changes are made.

7. **Confidentiality:** Except as provided in the *Code of Ethics* and *Guidelines for Practice*, the conservation professional should consider relationships with an owner, custodian, or authorized agent as confidential. Information derived from examination, scientific investigation, or treatment of the cultural property should not be published or otherwise made public without written permission.

8. **Supervision:** The conservation professional is responsible for work delegated to other professionals, students, interns, volunteers, subordinates, or agents and assignees. Work should not be delegated or subcontracted unless the conservation professional can supervise the work directly, can ensure proper supervision, or has sufficient knowledge of the practitioner to be confident of the quality of the work. When appropriate, the owner, custodian, or agent should be informed if such delegation is to occur.

9. **Education:** Within the limits of knowledge, ability, time, and facilities, the conservation professional is encouraged to become involved in the education of conservation personnel. The objectives and obligations of the parties shall be agreed upon mutually.

10. **Consultation:** Since no individual can be expert in every aspect of conservation, it may be appropriate to consult with colleagues or, in some instances, to refer the owner, custodian, or authorized agent to a professional who is more experienced or better equipped to accomplish the required work. If the owner requests a second opinion, this request must be respected.

11. **Recommendations and References:** The conservation professional should not provide recommendations without direct knowledge of a colleague's competence and experience. Any reference to the work of others must be based on facts and personal knowledge rather than on hearsay.

12. **Adverse Commentary:** A conservation professional may be required to testify in legal, regulatory, or administrative proceedings concerning allegations of unethical conduct. Testimony concerning such matters should be given at these proceedings or in connection with paragraph 13 of these *Guidelines*.

13. **Misconduct:** Allegations of unethical conduct should be reported in writing to the AIC president as described in the AIC Bylaws, section II, 12. As stated in the bylaws, all correspondence regarding alleged unethical conduct shall be held in the strictest confidence. Violations of the *Code* and *Guidelines* that constitute unethical conduct may result in disciplinary action.

14. **Conflict of Interest:** The conservation professional should avoid situations in which there is a potential for a conflict of interest that may affect the quality of work, lead to the dissemination of false information, or give the appearance of impropriety.

15. **Related Professional Activities:** The conservation professional should be especially mindful of the considerable potential for conflict of interest in activities such as authentication, appraisal, or art dealing.

EXAMINATION AND SCIENTIFIC INVESTIGATION

16. **Justification:** Careful examination of cultural property forms the basis for all future action by the conservation professional. Before undertaking any examination or tests that may cause change to cultural property, the conservation professional should establish the necessity for such procedures.

17. **Sampling and Testing:** Prior consent must be obtained from the owner, custodian, or agent before any material is removed from a cultural property. Only the minimum required should be removed, and a record of removal must be made. When appropriate, the material removed should be retained.

18. **Interpretation:** Declarations of age, origin, or authenticity should be made only when based on sound evidence.

19. **Scientific Investigation:** The conservation professional should follow accepted scientific standards and research protocols.

PREVENTIVE CONSERVATION

20. **Preventive Conservation:** The conservation professional should recognize the critical importance of preventive conservation as the most effective means of promoting the long-term preservation of cultural property. The conservation professional should provide guidelines for continuing use and care, recommend appropriate environmental conditions for storage and exhibition, and encourage proper procedures for handling, packing, and transport.

TREATMENT

21. **Suitability:** The conservation professional performs within a continuum of care and will rarely be the last entrusted with the conservation of a cultural property. The conservation professional should only recommend or undertake treatment that is judged suitable to the preservation of the aesthetic, conceptual, and physical characteristics of the cultural property. When nonintervention best serves to promote the preservation of the cultural property, it may be appropriate to recommend that no treatment be performed.

22. **Materials and Methods:** The conservation professional is responsible for choosing materials and methods appropriate to the objectives of each specific treatment and consistent with currently accepted practice. The advantages of the materials and methods chosen must be balanced against their potential adverse effects on future examination, scientific investigation, treatment, and function.

23. **Compensation for Loss:** Any intervention to compensate for loss should be documented in treatment records and reports and should be detectable by common examination methods. Such compensation should be reversible and should not falsely modify the known aesthetic, conceptual, and physical characteristics of the cultural property, especially by removing or obscuring original material.

DOCUMENTATION

24. **Documentation:** The conservation professional has an obligation to produce and maintain accurate, complete, and permanent records of examination, sampling, scientific investigation, and treatment. When appropriate, the records should be both written and pictorial. The kind and extent of documentation may vary according to the circumstances, the nature of the object, or whether an individual object or a collection is to be documented. The purposes of such documentation are:

    - to establish the condition of cultural property;
    - to aid in the care of cultural property by providing information helpful to future treatment and by adding to the profession's body of knowledge;
    - to aid the owner, custodian, or authorized agent and society as a whole in the appreciation and use of cultural property by increasing understanding of an object's aesthetic, conceptual, and physical characteristics; and
    - to aid the conservation professional by providing a reference that can assist in the continued development of knowledge and by supplying records that can help avoid misunderstanding and unnecessary litigation.

25. **Documentation of Examination:** Before any intervention, the conservation professional should make a thorough examination of the cultural property and create appropriate records. These records and the reports derived from them must identify the cultural property and include the date of examination and the name of the examiner. They also should include, as appropriate, a description of structure, materials, condition, and pertinent history.

26. **Treatment Plan:** Following examination and before treatment, the conservation professional should prepare a plan describing the course of treatment. This plan should also include the justification for and the objectives of treatment, alternative approaches, if feasible, and the potential risks. When appropriate, this plan should be submitted as a proposal to the owner, custodian, or authorized agent.

27. **Documentation of Treatment:** During treatment, the conservation professional should maintain dated documentation that includes a record or description of techniques or procedures involved, materials used and their composition, the nature and extent of all alterations, and any additional information revealed or otherwise ascertained. A report prepared from these records should summarize this information and provide, as necessary, recommendations for subsequent care.

28. **Preservation of Documentation:** Documentation is an invaluable part of the history of cultural property and should be produced and maintained in as permanent a manner as practicable. Copies of reports of examination and treatment must be given to the owner, custodian, or authorized agent, who should be advised of the importance of maintaining these materials with the cultural property. Documentation is also an important part of the profession's body of knowledge. The conservation professional should strive to preserve these records and give other professionals appropriate access to them, when access does not contravene agreements regarding confidentiality.

EMERGENCY SITUATIONS

29. **Emergency Situations:** Emergency situations can pose serious risks of damage to or loss of cultural property that may warrant immediate intervention on the part of the conservation professional. In an emergency that threatens cultural property, the conservation professional should take all reasonable action to preserve the cultural property, recognizing that strict adherence to the *Guidelines for Practice* may not be possible.

AMENDMENTS

Amendments: Proposed amendments to the *Code of Ethics* and *Guidelines for Practice* must be initiated by petition to the AIC Board of Directors from at least five members who are Fellows or Professional Associates of AIC. The board will direct the appropriate committee to prepare the amendments for vote in accordance with procedures described in Section VII of the Bylaws. Acceptance of amendments or changes must be affirmed by at least two-thirds of all AIC Fellows and Professional Associates voting.

COMMENTARIES

Commentaries: Commentaries are prepared or amended by specialty groups, task forces, and appropriate committees of AIC. A review process shall be undergone before final approval by the AIC Board of Directors.

*Revised August 1994

AIC

American Institute for Conservation of Historic and Artistic Works
1717 K Street, N.W., Suite 301, Washington, D.C. 20006
(202) 452-9545; fax (202) 452-9328; InfoAIC@aol.com

APPENDIX 12-B

Directory of Regional Conservation Centers

1. Balboa Art Conservation Center
   P.O. 3755
   San Diego, CA 92163
   (619) 236-9702
2. Conservation Center for Art and
   Historic Artifacts
   264 South 23rd Street
   Philadelphia, PA 19103
   (215) 545-0613
3. Conservation Center, Society for the Preservation of New England
   Antiquities
   185 Lyman Street
   Waltham, MA 02154
   (617) 891-1985
4. Division for Historic Preservation Collections Care Center
   P. O. Box 219
   Waterford, NY 12188
   (518) 237-8090
5. Gerald R. Ford Conservation Center
   Nebraska State Historical Society
   1326 South 32nd Street
   Omaha, NE 68108
   (402) 595-1180
6. Intermusuem Conservation Association
   Allen Art Building
   83 North Main Street
   Oberlin, OH 44074
   (440) 775-7331
7. Northeast Document Conservation Center
   100 Brickstone Square
   Andover, MA 01810-1428
   (508) 470-1010
8. Rocky Mountain Conservation Center
   2420 South University Blvd.
   Denver, CO 80208
   (303) 733-2712

9. Strauss Center for Conservation
   Harvard University Art Museum
   32 Quincy Street
   Cambridge, MA 02138
   (617) 495-2392
10. Textile Conservation Center
    Museum of American Textile History
    800 Massachusetts Avenue
    North Andover, MA 01845
    (508) 686-0191
11. Textile Conservation Workshop
    3 Main Street
    South Salem, NY 10590
    (914) 763-5805
12. Upper Midwest Conservation Association
    2400 3rd Avenue South
    Minneapolis, MN 55404
    (612) 870-3120
13. Williamstown Art Conservation Center
    225 South Street
    Williamstown, MA 01267-2878
    (413) 458-5741

PART III

DEATH AND TAXES

CHAPTER 13

FEDERAL INCOME TAX CONSEQUENCES OF CREATING, OWNING, SELLING, AND DONATING WORKS OF ART

Richard E. Halperin

§ 13.01 INTRODUCTION

Congress has fashioned federal income tax laws that pervade almost every form of human endeavor. These laws affect most people and entities involved in the art world.

This chapter discusses the deductibility of expenditures incurred by artists and the income tax treatment of the sale or donation of works of art by artists and by art dealers, art collectors, and art investors.

§ 13.02 THE BUSINESS OF BEING AN ARTIST

The income earned and expenditures incurred in being a creative artist are regarded for federal income tax purposes as earned or incurred in a trade or business engaged in by the artist. As a result, most of the tax considerations that would apply to any trade or business apply to the trade or business of being a creative artist.

An artist who sells (or intends to sell) her work must keep proper books and records.[1] This presents some practical difficulty for the artist who begins her artistic endeavor out of creative passion and without regard to whether or not her efforts will produce revenue. Certainly many artists labor for years, finding their voice, and producing no revenue, much less profit. Years later they may regret not having kept proper records from the beginning.

[A] Limitation on Losses Incurred by Persons with Insufficient Profit Motive: The Hobby Loss Rules

The Internal Revenue Code allows some deductions, such as the deduction for taxes[2] and for charitable contributions,[3] whether or not they are connected with the taxpayer's trade or business or activity entered into for profit. On the other hand, other deductions can be taken only if they occur in connection with the taxpayer's trade or business or activity entered into for profit. Common examples of such deductions include ordinary and necessary expenses paid or

---

[1] The artist, like every other taxpayer, must "keep such permanent books of account or records, including inventories, as are sufficient to establish the amount of gross income, deductions, credits, or other matters required to be shown by such person in any [tax or information] return." Treas. Reg. § 1.6001-1(a).

[2] 26 U.S.C. § 164. The types of taxes that are generally deductible are state, local and foreign income taxes and real property taxes, and state and local personal property taxes. Thus for example, if a painter were to use part of her house as a studio, the portion of the real estate taxes attributable to the studio would be deductible regardless of whether the artist was engaged in the business of being a painter.

[3] 26 U.S.C. § 170.

incurred in carrying on a trade or business,[4] depreciation and other methods of recovering the cost of property used in trade or business, or of property held for the production of income,[5] or, in the case of an individual, the ordinary and necessary expenses paid or incurred (1) for the production or collection of income and (2) for the management, conservation, or maintenance of property held for the production of income.[6]

Under statutory rules generally known as the "hobby loss" rules, if an individual, an S corporation, or a partnership[7] engages in an activity and if the activity is not engaged in for profit, the deductions attributable to the activity are limited. Under this limitation, the only deductions allowed are

> (1) the deductions that would be allowable for the taxable year without regard to whether or not the activity is engaged in for profit (such as deductions for state and local personal property taxes on property used in the activity); plus
> (2) a deduction equal to the amount of the deductions that would be allowable for the taxable year only if the activity were engaged in for profit, but only to the extent that the gross income derived from the activity for the taxable year exceeds the deductions allowable under paragraph (1).[8]

The effect of this rule is to allow "hobby" deductions only to the extent of income from that same "hobby," so that the deductions cannot be used to offset other income. Because many artists have not achieved sufficient commercial success to support themselves by their artistic efforts, they may appear to be pursuing art regardless of any intent to earn a profit; the "hobby loss" rules can limit the deductibility of such artists' expenses.

The determination of whether an activity is entered into for profit is entirely subjective, based on all of the facts and circumstances relating to the activity. Although a reasonable expectation of profit is not required, the facts and circumstances must indicate that the taxpayer entered into or continued the activity with

---

[4] 26 U.S.C. § 162(a). These expenses include (1) reasonable compensation for services rendered, (2) traveling expenses (including expenditures for meals and lodging that are not lavish or extravagant under the circumstances) while away from home in the pursuit of a trade or business, and (3) rent for use or possession of property.

[5] 26 U.S.C. §§ 167, 168.

[6] 26 U.S.C. §§ 212(1), (2).

[7] Although 26 U.S.C. § 183(a) refers only to an activity engaged in by an individual or an S corporation, the IRS takes the position that it also applies to the activities of a partnership. Rev. Rul. 77-320, 1977-2 C.B. 78, holds that § 183 is applicable at the partnership level and reflected in the partners' distributive shares. Other authority suggests that § 183 operates with respect to partnership activities as if the taxpayer herself is engaged in an activity as a partner. *See* Treas. Reg. § 12.9 (Temporary), T.D. 7308, 39 FR 9947, Mar. 15, 1974.

[8] 26 U.S.C. §§ 183(a), (b).

the objective of making a profit.[9] In determining whether a profit-making objective exists, it may be sufficient that there is a small chance of making a large profit.[10] Not surprisingly, given the large number of taxpayers who engage in a variety of activities and the factual nature of the inquiry, the courts have considered an enormous number of cases dealing with the profit motive in the context of the hobby loss rules.[11]

The regulations contain a list of nine nonexclusive factors to be considered in determining whether an activity is engaged in for profit. Other factors, not among the nine, may also be taken into account. The regulation cautions that the

---

[9] Treas. Reg. § 1.183-2(a).

[10] For example, under the Regulations, an investor in a wildcat oil well who incurs very substantial expenditures can be in the venture for profit even though the expectation of a profit might be considered unreasonable. Treas. Reg. § 1.183-2(a).

[11] Hobby loss cases involving the arts include Churchman v. Commissioner, 68 T.C. 696 (1977) (losses of artist allowed); Polakof v. Commissioner, T.C. Memo. 1985-197, *aff'd*, 820 F.2d 321 (9th Cir. 1987) (tax shelter film partnership losses disallowed); and Clayden v. Commissioner, 90 T.C. 656 (1988) (tax shelter videotape purchase arrangement losses disallowed). The *Churchman* decision is interesting. The taxpayer was an artist involved in artistic activities for 20 years. She mainly painted but also sculpted, designed, drew, and built; wrote short stories, poems, and songs; performed in films; and made a film. The taxpayer had never derived a net profit from her artistic activities for any of the relevant years. The court noted: "However, such a history of losses is less persuasive in the art field than it might be in other fields because the archetypal 'struggling artist' must first achieve public acclaim before her serious work will command a price sufficient to provide her with a profit." 68 T.C. at 701-02. While the taxpayer's artwork involved recreational and personal elements, her work did not stop at the creative stage but went into the marketing phase of the art business where the recreational element is minimal. The taxpayer designed an art gallery and ran it for a year, she maintained a mailing list and sent announcements of her shows to persons on the list, she went to galleries in San Francisco and New York attempting to have her work shown, and she published a book. Furthermore, when the taxpayer saw that her paintings and other works were not selling well, she adopted new techniques, such as making posters and writing books, in an effort to make her work more available and more salable to the public. Although she did not keep a complete set of books pertaining to her artistic activities, the taxpayer kept all of the receipts for her art expenses and kept a journal recording what she sold and to whom. The court found that these facts indicated that the taxpayer carried on her artistic activities in a businesslike manner for profit. The court stated:

> It is abundantly clear from her testimony and from the objective evidence that petitioner is a most dedicated artist, craves personal recognition as an artist, and believes that selling her work for a profit represents the attainment of such recognition. Therefore, petitioner intends and expects to make a profit. For section 183 purposes, it seems to us irrelevant whether petitioner intends to make a profit because it symbolizes success in her chosen career or because it is the pathway to material wealth. In either case, the essential fact remains that petitioner does intend to make a profit from her artwork and she sincerely believes that if she continues to paint she will do so.

68 T.C. at 702-03.

determination should not be made on the basis of whether the number of factors (whether or not listed in the regulations) indicating a lack of profit objective exceeds the number of factors indicating a profit objective, or vice versa.[12]

The nine factors are:

1. *Manner in which the taxpayer carries on the activity.* The fact that the taxpayer carries on the activity in a businesslike manner and maintains complete and accurate books and records may indicate that the activity is engaged in for profit. Similarly, where an activity is carried on in a manner substantially similar to other activities of the same nature which are profitable, a profit motive may be indicated. A change of operating methods, adoption of new techniques, or abandonment of unprofitable methods in a manner consistent with an intent to improve profitability may also indicate a profit motive.[13]
2. *The expertise of the taxpayer or her advisors.* Preparing for the activity by extensive study of its accepted business, economic, and scientific practices, or consulting with experts in those subjects, may indicate that the taxpayer has a profit motive where the taxpayer carries on the activity in accordance with such practices. However, where a taxpayer has such preparation or procures such expert advice, but does not implement it, that may indicate a lack of intent to derive profit unless it appears that the taxpayer is attempting to develop new or superior techniques which may result in profits from the activity.[14]
3. *The time and effort expended by the taxpayer in carrying on the activity.* The fact that the taxpayer devotes much personal time and effort to carrying on an activity, particularly if the activity does not have substantial personal or recreational aspects, may indicate an intention to derive a profit. A taxpayer's withdrawal from another occupation to devote most of her energies to the activity may also be evidence that the activity is engaged in for profit. The fact that the taxpayer devotes a limited amount of time to an activity does not necessarily indicate a lack of profit motive where the taxpayer employs competent and qualified persons to carry on such activity.[15]
4. *Expectation that assets used in activity may appreciate in value.* The term "profit" encompasses appreciation in the value of assets used in the activity. Thus, the taxpayer may intend to derive a profit from the operation of the activity and may also intend that, even if no profit from current

[12] Treas. Reg. § 1.183-2(b).

[13] Treas. Reg. § 1.183-2(b)(1).

[14] Treas. Reg. § 1.183-2(b)(2). This rule suggests that all art schools should require courses in business practices.

[15] Treas. Reg. § 1.183-2(b)(3).

operations is derived, an overall profit will result when appreciation in the value of property used in the activity is realized.[16]

5. *The success of the taxpayer in carrying on other similar or dissimilar activities.* The fact that the taxpayer has engaged in similar activities in the past and converted them from unprofitable to profitable enterprises may indicate that she is engaged in the present activity for profit, even though the activity, at that time, is unprofitable.[17]
6. *The taxpayer's history of income or losses with respect to the activity.* A series of losses during the initial or startup stage of an activity may not necessarily be an indication that the activity is not engaged in for profit. However, if the activity continues to lose money beyond the customary period needed to bring the operation to profitable status, and the losses cannot be explained by customary business risks or reverses, this may indicate that the activity is not being engaged in for profit. If losses are due to unforeseen or fortuitous circumstances beyond the control of the taxpayer, such as drought, disease, fire, theft, weather damages, other involuntary conversions, or depressed market conditions, such losses would not be an indication that the activity is not engaged in for profit. A series of years in which net income was realized would of course be strong evidence that the activity is engaged in for profit.[18]
7. *The amount of occasional profits, if any, which are earned.* The amount of profits in relation to the amount of losses incurred, and in relation to the amount of the taxpayer's investment and the value of the assets used in the activity, may provide useful criteria in determining the taxpayer's intent. An occasional small profit from an activity generating large losses, or from an activity in which the taxpayer has made a large investment, would not generally be determinative that the activity is engaged in for profit. However, substantial profit, though only occasional, would generally indicate that an activity is engaged in for profit, where the investment or losses are comparatively small. Moreover, an opportunity to earn a substantial ultimate profit in a highly speculative venture is ordinarily sufficient to indicate that the activity is engaged in for profit even though losses or only occasional small profits are actually generated.[19]
8. *The financial status of the taxpayer.* The fact that the taxpayer does not

---

[16] Treas. Reg. § 1.183-2(b)(4). Note, however, that if there is not sufficient operational interrelationship between the holding of the property and the other activity of the taxpayer, they may be considered to be two separate activities for purposes of § 183. Treas. Reg. § 1.183-1(d).

[17] Treas. Reg. § 1.183-2(b)(5).

[18] Treas. Reg. § 1.183-2(b)(6).

[19] Treas. Reg. § 1.183-2(b)(7).

have substantial income or capital from sources other than the activity may indicate that an activity is engaged in for profit. Substantial income from sources other than the activity (particularly if the losses from the activity generate substantial tax benefits) may indicate that the activity is not engaged in for profit, especially if personal or recreational elements are involved.[20]

9. *Elements of personal pleasure or recreation.* The presence of personal motives in carrying on an activity may indicate that the activity is not engaged in for profit, especially where there are recreational or personal elements involved. On the other hand, a profit motivation may be indicated where an activity lacks any appeal[21] other than profit. It is not, however, necessary that an activity be engaged in with the exclusive intention of deriving a profit or with the intention of maximizing profits. For example, the availability of other investments that would yield a higher return, or would be more likely to be profitable is not evidence that an activity is not engaged in for profit. Also, the fact that the taxpayer derives personal pleasure from engaging in the activity is not sufficient to cause the activity to be classified as not engaged in for profit if other factors, whether or not listed in subparagraph (b), indicate that it is.[22]

The Internal Revenue Code contains a presumption in the taxpayer's favor: if the gross income derived from an activity for at least three of the taxable years in the period of five consecutive taxable years ending with the taxable year in question exceeds the deductions attributable to the activity (determined without regard to whether or not the activity is engaged in for profit), then, unless the Internal Revenue Service (IRS) establishes to the contrary, the activity is presumed to be an activity engaged in for profit for that taxable year.[23]

The taxpayer can elect to delay the operation of this presumption in order to have more time to make the activity profitable.[24] Under this election, the determination as to whether the presumption applies with respect to any activity is not made before the close of the fourth taxable year[25] following the taxable year in which the taxpayer first engages in the activity. If the taxpayer makes the

[20] Treas. Reg. § 1.183-2(b)(8). This factor and the following factor seem to be relied upon, more than any other factors, by the IRS and the courts in finding the lack of a profit motive.

[21] Appeal is in the eyes of the beholder. Presumably, the IRS and the courts should not substitute their own views on this subject.

[22] Treas. Reg. § 1.183-2(b)(9).

[23] 26 U.S.C. § 183(d). In the case of the breeding, training, showing, or racing of horses, there need be profit in only two out of seven years.

[24] 26 U.S.C. § 183(e).

[25] In the case of the horse-related activities described *supra* in note 23, the determination is not made before the sixth taxable year.

election, then the presumption applies to each taxable year in the five-taxable-year[26] period beginning with the taxable year in which the taxpayer first engages in the activity, if the gross income derived from the activity for three[27] or more of the taxable years in the period exceeds the deductions attributable to the activity, determined without regard to whether or not the activity is engaged in for profit. The election procedure can be complex and cumbersome[28] and involves the extension of the statute of limitations on the assessment of any deficiency attributable to the activity.[29]

[B] Current Deduction of Expenses of Artists

Most creative artists create *property*—painters and sculptors create paintings and sculptures, composers create scores and writers create manuscripts. In general, when a taxpayer produces property, the costs of producing that property[30] cannot be deducted currently. Rather, in the case of property that is inventory in the hands of the taxpayer, the Internal Revenue Code requires that the costs be included in inventory costs, and in the case of any other property, that the costs be capitalized.[31] The concept of these capitalization rules of § 263A is essentially that the costs incurred in creating a piece of property become part of that property. Under the capitalization rules, a writer could not currently deduct the costs of traveling to research and collect interviews for a book and a sculptor could not currently deduct the costs of marble, bronze, or steel and the costs of operating the sculptor's atelier.

There are two separate rules that mitigate the effect of § 263A with respect to certain costs of certain creative artists. One was enacted by Congress in 1988 in response to controversy engendered by the 1986 enactment of the capitalization rules. The other was promulgated by the IRS earlier in 1988, before Congress enacted its mitigating rule. The two rules are different in scope and effect. In general, the IRS rule benefits more categories of taxpayers engaged in more kinds of creative endeavors; on the other hand, the IRS's rule requires that, with respect to cost incurred in the present year, the deduction of part of those costs be postponed beyond the end of the year. Moreover, the IRS rule is elective and, if

---

26 A seven-taxable-year period applies in the case of the horse-related activities.

27 Or two if horse-related.

28 Treas. Reg. § 12.9 (Temporary), T.D. 7308, 39 FR 9947, Mar. 15, 1974.

29 26 U.S.C. § 183(e)(4).

30 The costs of producing the property include both the direct costs of producing the property (such as materials that become an integral part of specific property, materials that are consumed in producing particular property and labor costs that are associated with particular property), and the property's proper share of those indirect costs (including taxes) part or all of which are properly allocable to the property. 26 U.S.C. § 263A(a)(2). Treas. Reg. § 1.263A-1(e)(2)(i).

31 26 U.S.C. § 263A(a)(1).

elected, must apply to all endeavors and all expenditures covered by the rule. Hence it is important to understand each of the rules to determine which better suits the artist's circumstances.

[1] Special Statutory Rule for Writers, Photographers, and Artists

Congress created a special exception only for freelance writers,[32] photographers,[33] and artists[34] that allows them to deduct "qualified creative expenses" currently rather than being forced to capitalize them. A "qualified creative expense" is any expense paid or incurred by an individual in his or her trade or business (other than as an employee) of being a writer, photographer, or artist (WPA), and which would otherwise be allowable as a deduction for the taxable year. A "qualified creative expense" does not include any expense related to printing, photographic plates, motion picture films, video tapes, or similar items.[35] This can be a severe limitation for artists who do etching, engraving, lithography, or other printmaking or for a photographer who sells original photographic prints.

A WPA whose business is incorporated can also benefit from this exception.[36] In order for the corporate exception to apply, (1) substantially all[37] of the stock of a corporation must be owned by the WPA and members of the WPA's family,[38] (2) the WPA must own, directly or constructively, on any day during the taxable year, at least 10 percent of the outstanding stock of the corporation,[39] and (3) the principal activity of the corporation must be performance of personal services directly related to the activities of the WPA/owner, and those services must be substantially performed by the WPA/owner. The exception applies to any expense

[32] A "writer" is any individual if the personal efforts of the individual create (or may reasonably be expected to create) a literary manuscript, musical composition (including any accompanying words), or dance score. 26 U.S.C. § 263A(h)(3)(A).

[33] A "photographer" is any individual if the personal efforts of the individual create (or may reasonably be expected to create) a photograph or photographic negative or transparency. 26 U.S.C. § 263A(h)(3)(B). Query whether a digital image qualifies as a "negative" or a "transparency."

[34] An "artist" is any individual if his or her personal efforts create (or may reasonably be expected to create) a picture, painting, sculpture, statue, etching, drawing, cartoon, graphic design, or original print edition. However, in determining whether any expense is paid or incurred in the trade or business of being an artist, the following criteria must be taken into account: (1) the originality and uniqueness of the item created (or to be created) and (2) the predominance of aesthetic value over utilitarian value of the item created (or to be created). 26 U.S.C. § 263A(h)(3)(C).

[35] 26 U.S.C. § 263A(h)(2).

[36] 26 U.S.C. § 263A(h)(3)(D).

[37] The Internal Revenue Code does not define "substantially all." The House Ways and Means Committee Report defines it as 95% of the value of the corporation's stock. H.R. Rep. No. 4333, 100th Cong., 2d Sess. 531 (1988).

[38] For this purpose, the family of an individual includes only her brothers and sisters (whether by the whole or half blood), spouse, ancestors, and lineal descendants. 26 U.S.C. § 267(c)(4).

[39] 26 U.S.C. §§ 263A(h)(3)(D)(ii), 269A(b)(2).

of the corporation which directly relates to the activities of the WPA/owner in the same manner as if the expense were incurred by the WPA/owner individually.

[2] IRS Safe-Harbor Rule

In 1988, before Congress enacted the special exception for freelance writers, photographers, and artists, the IRS granted an elective administrative safe harbor that in some ways is more liberal than the statutory rule and in other ways is more limited.[40] The IRS rule is more liberal because it is not limited to WPAs and those corporations owned by WPAs and their families. The IRS rule also can provide deductibility for expense related to printing, photographic plates, motion picture films, videotapes, or similar items. The IRS rule is more limited because it does not permit deduction of 100 percent of the expenditures in the year in which they are incurred.

Under the IRS rule, taxpayers electing the benefit of the rule must aggregate and capitalize all "qualified creative costs" incurred during each taxable year, and then deduct 50 percent of the aggregate costs in the year in which they are incurred, 25 percent of the costs in the first following year, and the final 25 percent of such costs in the second following year.

This three-year safe harbor is available only for the "qualified creative costs" paid or incurred in producing "creative properties" defined as films, sound recordings, videotapes, books (including articles and poems), photographs, plays and other dramatic works, musical and dance compositions (including accompanying words), graphic and pictorial compositions, fine art paintings and sculptures, and other similar fine art products (but not jewelry). This definition provides broader coverage than the statutory rule by including films, sound recordings, and videotapes.

A taxpayer who elects to use the three-year safe harbor in accounting for the costs of producing one creative property must also apply the provision in accounting for the production of any other creative property to which the safe harbor applies. Thus, for example, a taxpayer producing both books and films who elects to apply the three-year safe harbor provision to the books must also apply it with respect to the films. Such a taxpayer should weigh the relative merits of being able to deduct both book and film costs over three years as compared to being able to deduct all book costs currently but being required to capitalize all film costs.

"Qualified creative costs" consist of all costs the taxpayer incurs in creative activity that would otherwise be deductible were it not for the general statutory rule of § 263A, which states that when a taxpayer produces property, the costs of producing that property cannot be deducted currently. Thus, qualified creative

[40] Notice 88-62, 1988-1 C.B. 548.

costs consist of (1) all costs required to be capitalized under § 263A with respect to the production of creative properties, and (2) all other costs incurred and otherwise deductible by the taxpayer in the trade or business of producing creative properties.

Qualified creative costs also include all other costs that would be otherwise deductible in the trade or business of producing creative properties, including the costs of marketing, selling, advertising, and distributing the work. For example, costs incurred by a taxpayer in promoting or selling a finished manuscript or photograph would be qualified creative costs and thus would be subject to the safe harbor. In addition, qualified creative costs include all office overhead, such as general and administrative costs, and all otherwise deductible interest expense incurred in the trade or business of producing creative properties, regardless of whether such costs would be required to be capitalized under § 263A.

Costs can be "qualified creative costs" only if they are incurred by a self-employed individual (or certain partnerships and corporations), in the production of creative properties where the personal efforts of the individual predominantly create such properties. Qualified creative costs do not include the costs paid or incurred by a person in her capacity as an employee, nor costs incurred by an individual in producing creative properties where her personal efforts do not predominantly create such properties—for instance, where the properties are predominantly created by persons other than the individual, such as employees or independent contractors. On the other hand, qualified creative costs do include amounts paid by an individual to employees or independent contractors assisting in the production of the creative properties, if the personal efforts of the individual predominantly create the properties.

Interestingly, qualified creative costs include the costs of producing properties that are sold, or otherwise disposed of in their entirety, by the taxpayer in the same taxable year as the costs are incurred. For example, the costs of writing an article (or producing a photograph) that the taxpayer sells in its entirety to a magazine in the same year that the costs are incurred would be qualified creative costs and thus would be subject to the three-year deduction rather than being deductible in the year of sale.

The three-year safe harbor may be used by a corporation or partnership engaged in the trade or business of producing creative properties (an "eligible corporation" or "eligible partnership"), but only if substantially all of the corporation or partnership is owned by one "qualified employee owner" and the members of her family.[41] A qualified employee owner is deemed to own substantially all of a corporation if she and her family own at least 95 percent (by value) of the

[41] As with the statutory rule, the family of an individual includes only her brothers and sisters (whether by the whole or half blood), spouse, ancestors, and lineal descendants. 26 U.S.C. § 267(c)(4).

stock of the corporation. Similarly, a qualified employee owner is deemed to own substantially all of a partnership if she and her family have an interest in partnership profits and capital of at least 95 percent.

A "qualified employee owner" is an individual employed by an eligible corporation or eligible partnership where the personal efforts of the qualified employee owner produce creative properties for the corporation or partnership. As with the statutory exception, "qualified creative costs" eligible for the three-year safe harbor include only those costs incurred in the production of creative properties where the personal efforts of the qualified employee owner predominantly create the properties, and not where the properties are predominantly created by other persons such as other employees or independent contractors.

Taxpayers may automatically elect to use the three-year safe harbor by determining and reporting their taxable income under the safe harbor on a timely filed (with regard to extensions) federal income-tax return for the first taxable year to which the provisions of § 263A apply to the taxpayer's production of creative properties.

§ 13.03 THE TAX CONSEQUENCES OF OWNING AND SELLING WORKS OF ART

For federal income tax purposes, owners of works of art generally fall into four categories: (1) persons who created the artworks; (2) art dealers; (3) investors in works of art; and (4) all others, who are usually given the respected title of "collectors." The determination of whether an individual falls into a particular category is largely a factual one; in addition, it is possible for a single individual to fall into different categories with respect to different works of art. For example, an art dealer may be a dealer only with respect to her gallery inventory and own her private collection as a collector.

[A] Artists

When an artist sells a work of art he or she created, the gain is ordinary income.[42] The amount of gain is usually the full amount received in the sale.[43] If someone receives a work of art as a gift from the artist who created it, and then sells it, all of the gain is ordinary income.[44]

---

[42] Under 26 U.S.C. § 1221(3)(A), a work of art in the hands of the artist who created it is not a capital asset. Accordingly, capital gain cannot result from its sale.

[43] As discussed *supra* in § 13.02[B], the artist will generally have deducted all of the costs of creating the artwork including the costs of materials so that the artist has no basis or inventory cost in the artwork. Accordingly, the full amount received will be the amount of the gain.

[44] Under 26 U.S.C. § 1221(3)(C), a work of art is not a capital asset in the hands of a person whose basis for the artwork is determined, for purposes of determining gain from a sale or exchange, in whole or part by reference to the basis of the artwork in the hands of the artist who created it.

It is a common practice for artists to swap works with other artists. In such a transaction, each of the artists would realize gain equal to the fair market value of the artworks given or received. If the works are valuable, this can be quite troublesome because the tax could be substantial but the transaction yields no cash with which to pay the tax.

Subject to the "hobby loss" rules discussed in § 13.02[A] of this book, the artist should be able to deduct the ordinary and necessary expenses, such as insurance and storage costs, of holding the artworks that the artist created.

[B] Dealers

A person is a dealer with respect to a piece of property if the person holds the property primarily for sale to customers in the ordinary course of the person's trade or business. In this case, any gain realized on the sale of the property would be ordinary income and any loss would be ordinary loss.[45] A dealer can deduct the ordinary and necessary expenses of operating the business, such as gallery rent, utilities, insurance, security service, advertising and promotion, and gallery staff personnel expenses.[46]

The determination of whether property is held primarily for sale to customers in the ordinary course of the taxpayer's trade or business is essentially factual.[47] In this context, the word "primarily" means "of first importance" or "principally."[48] In resolving this factual question, the courts have examined various factors, including: (1) the purpose for which the property was acquired; (2) the purpose for which it was held; (3) the frequency, continuity, and substantiality of sales; (4) the duration of ownership; (5) the use of the proceeds from the sale of the property; (6) the business of the taxpayer; and (7) the time and effort that the taxpayer devoted to sales activities relating to the asset in question by developing or improving that asset, soliciting customers, or advertising.[49]

---

26 U.S.C. § 1015(a) provides for such "carryover basis" for determining gain on property transferred by gift.

[45] 26 U.S.C. § 1221(1). The purpose of § 1221(1) is to "differentiate between the 'profits and losses arising from the everyday operation of a business' . . . and 'the realization of appreciation in value accrued over a substantial period of time'." Malat v. Riddell, 383 U.S. 569, 572 (1966) (quoting Corn Products Refining Co. v. Commissioner, 350 U.S. 46, 52 (1955), and Commissioner v. Gillette Motor Transport, Inc., 364 U.S. 130, 134 (1960)).

Although losses sustained by individuals are generally limited, a loss incurred by an individual in a trade or business is deductible. 26 U.S.C. § 165(c)(1).

[46] 26 U.S.C. § 162(a).

[47] Pasqualini v. Commissioner, 103 T.C. 1, 6 (1994).

[48] Malat v. Riddell, 383 U.S. at 572.

[49] Thomas B. Drummond v. Commissioner, T.C. Memo 1997-71.

[C] Investors

An individual's status as an investor, as distinguished from a mere "collector," is very valuable for federal income tax purposes.[50] Subject to certain important limitations,[51] the investor may deduct the cost of storing, insuring, and maintaining investment property.[52] Moreover, any loss sustained on the sale of investment property yields a capital loss which may be used to offset capital gains[53] and, to a limited extent, ordinary income.[54] Capital losses not so used may be carried forward for the investor's lifetime to offset future capital gains and, to the same limited extent, ordinary income.[55] Gains from the sale of investment property are taxed at favorable capital gains rates, not at higher ordinary income rates.[56]

Not surprisingly, it has been difficult for individual taxpayers to assert successfully that they hold their collection as investment rather than as personal property.

Under the Internal Revenue Code, an individual taxpayer is permitted to deduct all the ordinary and necessary expenses for the production or collection of income and for the management, conservation, or maintenance of property held for the production of income.[57] However, under the regulations, the expenses of carrying on a transaction are deductible only if the transaction is carried on primarily for the production of income or for the management, conservation, or maintenance of property held for the production or collection of income, rather than primarily as a sport, hobby, or recreation.[58] This test under the regulations

---

[50] It is occasionally preferable for a taxpayer to be a dealer rather than an investor even though ordinary income, rather than capital gain, results from the sale of art at a gain. *See, e.g.*, Drummond v. Commissioner, *supra*, note 49, in which the taxpayer argued (unsuccessfully) that he held a sixteenth-century Italian drawing as a dealer, and realized ordinary income rather than capital gain, because it increased the amount of his retirement plan deduction.

[51] Under 26 U.S.C. § 67, miscellaneous itemized deductions such as investment expenses are generally deductible only to the extent that they exceed 2% of the taxpayer's adjusted gross income for the year. Under 26 U.S.C. § 68, the itemized deductions of individuals with income over certain thresholds, which are quite low in the context of most significant individual art investors, are subject to substantial curtailment.

[52] 26 U.S.C. § 212(2).

[53] 26 U.S.C. §§ 1222(2); 1222(4); 1222(9); 165(c)(2); 165(f).

[54] A taxpayer other than a corporation can deduct up to $3,000 ($1,500 in the case of a married individual filing a separate return) of capital losses against ordinary income. 26 U.S.C. § 1211(b).

[55] 26 U.S.C. § 1212(b).

[56] 26 U.S.C. § 1221, 1(h).

[57] 26 U.S.C. § 212.

[58] "[E]xpenses of carrying on transactions which . . . are not carried on for the production or collection of income or for the management, conservation, or maintenance of property held for the production of income, but which are carried on primarily as a sport, hobby, or recreation are not allowable as nontrade or nonbusiness expenses. The question whether or not a transaction is carried on primarily for the production of income or for the management, conservation, or maintenance of

is frequently relied on by the IRS in denying deductions to persons who say they are art investors but who display their investments in their homes. Particularly illustrative is the case of Charles and Jayne Wrightsman,[59] prominent collectors of eighteenth-century French art and antiques. As stated by the court, Wrightsman believed that

> works of art were an excellent hedge against inflation and devaluation of currencies, that they represented portable international currency, since there were no restrictions on export from the United States, and that works of art were appropriate assets for investment of a substantial portion of this surplus cash being generated.[60]

The court noted that the Wrightsmans were art experts and described the business-like manner in which they acquired and cataloged their collection.

Nevertheless, the court denied the Wrightsmans' expenses for insurance, maintenance, subscriptions and services, shipping, hotel, travel, entertainment, and other miscellaneous expenses. Based on the Treasury Department Regulations, the court held that although the Wrightsmans unquestionably had investment intent, their investment intent was "something less than primary" among the Wrightsmans' purposes for acquiring and holding works of art. The court found that the evidence did not establish investment as the most prominent purpose for the Wrightsmans' acquiring and holding works of art; to the contrary, the record established that the Wrightsmans' personal pleasure or satisfaction was their primary purpose. The court noted that about 77.8 percent of their art and antiques (by insurance value) was in their New York City apartment, 17.7 percent in their Palm Beach home, and 4.5 percent in the Metropolitan Museum of Art in New York. The court also noted that the Wrightsmans' homes had museum-quality air conditioning and humidity controls necessary for the preservation of works of art and that storage facilities for works of art were not then readily available to provide the required atmospheric controls. Nevertheless, the Wrightsmans' display of the art in their homes, and their actual use of their antique furniture, seems to be the fact most relied on by the court in holding in favor of the government.

An individual taxpayer, although not engaged in a trade or business (such as being a dealer) is also permitted to deduct losses incurred in any transaction

---

property held for the production or collection of income, rather than primarily as a sport, hobby, or recreation, is not to be determined solely from the intention of the taxpayer but rather from all the circumstances of the case. For example, consideration will be given to the record of prior gain or loss of the taxpayer in the activity, the relation between the type of activity and the principal occupation of the taxpayer, and the uses to which the property or what it produces is put by the taxpayer." Treas. Reg. § 1.212-1(c).

[59] Wrightsman v. United States, 28 F.2d 1316 (Ct. Cl. 1970).

[60] *Id.*

entered into for profit.[61] Although neither the Internal Revenue Code or the regulations so require, the relevant cases have generally required that profit be the taxpayer's primary motive in entering into the transaction, although other motivations may also be present. [62]

The cases suggest generally that an individual who wishes to treat a work of art as investment property must be prepared to keep it in storage or allow it to be displayed only under circumstances that are likely to enhance its value, such as museum and gallery exhibitions. A scholarly investor may be able to keep the art in the investor's home during a limited period when the investor is studying and writing about the art in an effort to enhance its value.

[D] Collectors

Because a collector lacks the requisite profit motive, she cannot use the losses and expenses incurred in collecting to offset income from other activities. However, a collector may use the costs incurred during the taxable year for storing, insuring, and maintaining the collection to offset any income earned during the taxable year from the collection.[63] This rule requires that both the expenses and the income occur in the same "activity."[64] The eclectic collector may encounter some difficulty in offsetting income from sales of baseball cards with the costs of preserving medieval manuscripts.

If a collector purchases a work of art and then later sells it at a gain, the gain is capital gain.

§ 13.04 CHARITABLE CONTRIBUTION OF ARTWORKS BY ARTISTS, DEALERS, AND COLLECTORS

Painters are often surprised to learn that if they make charitable contributions of their valuable paintings, the amount of the deduction is limited to the cost of the canvas and paint (in fact, if the canvas and paint have been deducted as an expense, the deduction is zero).[65]

---

[61] 26 U.S.C. § 165(c).

[62] *See, e.g.,* Ewing v. Commissioner, 213 F.2d 438 (2d Cir. 1954), *aff'g* 20 T.C. 216 (1958) (loans to a ballet company held to have been primarily motivated by a personal desire to advance the art and only secondarily for profit); Tyler v. Commissioner, 6 T.C.M. 275 (1947) (taxpayer had both personal interest and profit motive in collecting stamps, but the profit motive was primary).

[63] 26 U.S.C. § 183(b). Treas. Reg. § 1.183-1(a) makes it clear that if deductions are not allowable under 26 U.S.C. §§ 162 and 212 (1) and (2), the deductions are nevertheless allowable under 26 U.S.C. § 183(b). The amount of the deduction is also reduced by the amount of any deductions relating to the activity (such as state and local personal property taxes) that would be allowable for the taxable year without regard to whether or not the activity is engaged in for profit.

[64] The term "activity" for this purpose is somewhat loosely defined in Treas. Reg. § 1.183-1(d).

[65] The deduction would also be zero if the painter had made an election under Notice 88-62,

This is one of the more common examples of the rule that a donor of property can deduct no more than her basis in the property if the sale of the property would not have resulted in long-term capital gain to her.[66]

[A] Non-Long-Term Capital Gain Property

Important examples of such non-long-term capital gain property include

- a work of art created by the donor
- a manuscript prepared by the donor
- a copyright, literary, musical, or other artistic composition or other similar property[67] if donated by a taxpayer whose personal efforts created the property
- letters and memorandums or other similar property[68] prepared by or for the donor
- property held by the donor primarily for sale to customers in the ordinary course of the donor's trade or business
- a capital asset held by the donor for not more than one year.[69]

There are some important consequences to these rules with regard to several kinds of donated property, including letters and memorandums prepared by or for the donor. If an artist has an exchange of correspondence with another artist, such letters can be quite valuable to collectors and academics. However, the artists' letters fail to be long-term capital gain property in the hands of either artist because all of the letters were written either by or to[70] both artists.

1988-1 C.B. 548, to deduct the costs of paint, canvas, and turpentine over three years. See the discussion in the text beginning *supra* at § 13.02[B].

[66] 26 U.S.C. § 170(e)(1)(A) provides that the amount of any charitable contribution of property must be reduced by the amount of gain which would not have been long-term capital gain if the property contributed had been sold by the taxpayer at its fair market value (determined at the time of such contribution).

[67] For this purpose, "similar property" includes, for example, such property as a theatrical production, a radio program, a newspaper cartoon strip, or any other property eligible for copyright protection (whether under statute or common law), but does not include a patent or an invention, or a design which may be protected only under the patent law and not under the copyright law. Treas. Reg. § 1.1221-1(c)(1).

[68] For this purpose, "similar property" includes, for example, such property as a draft of a speech; a manuscript; a research paper; an oral recording of any type; a transcript of an oral recording; a transcript of an oral interview or of dictation; a personal or business diary; a log or journal; a corporate archive, including a corporate charter; office correspondence, or a financial record; a drawing, a photograph, or a dispatch. Treas. Reg. § 1.1221-1(c)(2).

[69] Treas. Reg. § 1.170A-4(b)(1).

[70] A letter, memorandum, or property similar to a letter or memorandum, addressed to a taxpayer is considered as prepared or produced for the taxpayer. Treas. Reg. § 1.1221-1(c)(2).

The rules also affect property held by the donor primarily for sale to customers in the ordinary course of trade or business. Specifically, sale by an art dealer of artworks in her inventory result in ordinary income.[71] Accordingly, a charitable gift of artworks from an art dealer's inventory[72] results in a deduction no greater than the dealer's basis in the artworks.[73]

An enterprising taxpayer whose personal efforts created the property or, in the case of a letter, memorandum, or similar property, a taxpayer for whom such property was prepared or produced, might think that she could escape the definition of non-long-term capital gain property by making a gift of the property to someone else who could then take a charitable deduction equal to the full fair market value of the property. This would not work, however, because the Internal Revenue Code provides that in the case of a taxpayer whose personal efforts created the property, or in the case of such a letter, memorandum, or similar property, the property remains non-long-term capital gain property in the hands of the recipient of the gift.[74]

Artwork purchased by a collector is generally a capital asset so that, if the collector donates the art to charity after having held the art for more than one year, the amount of the deduction is not subject to the limitation discussed above. However, the collector's deduction is still limited to the collector's basis in the artwork (generally its cost) unless the use by the donee is related to the purpose or function constituting the basis for the donee's tax-exempt status.[75]

Obviously, a gift of a painting to an art museum that the museum displays or holds for study by art scholars is related to the museum's exempt purpose or function. On the other hand, if the museum were to deaccession the piece immediately after receiving it as a gift, this use would not be related to the museum's exempt function. Accordingly, a collector who donates art should receive a commitment regarding the nature of the use the recipient will make of it.

---

[71] 26 U.S.C. § 1221(1).

[72] Not all artwork owned by a dealer is necessarily inventory. Dealers can be, and often are, art collectors and investors. See the discussion *supra* in text accompanying note 40.

[73] Of course, the amount of the deduction cannot exceed the fair market value of the property. Treas. Reg. § 1.170-1(a)(3).

[74] 26 U.S.C. § 1221(3)(C) provides that such property remains non-long-term capital gain property when held by a taxpayer in whose hands the basis of such property is determined, for purposes of determining gain from a sale or exchange, in whole or part by reference to the basis of such property in the hands of a taxpayer whose personal efforts created the property, or in the case of a letter, memorandum, or similar property, a taxpayer for whom such property was prepared or produced. This rule applies not only in the case of a gift (26 U.S.C. § 1015(a)) but also applies, for example, to a corporation that receives such property from a shareholder in exchange for stock or as a contribution to capital (26 U.S.C. § 362(a)), to a partnership that receives the property as a contribution from a partner (26 U.S.C. § 723) and to a trust that receives the property as a transfer in trust (26 U.S.C. §§ 1015(a),(b)).

[75] 26 U.S.C. § 170(e)(1)(B).

[B] Appraisal Procedures

In order to deduct a contribution of more than $5,000 of property such as art, the donor must obtain a "qualified appraisal." A "qualified appraisal" is a formal appraisal document that must contain specific information required by the regulations.[76] The appraisal can be made not earlier than 60 days prior to the date of contribution of the appraised property nor later than the due date (including extensions) of the return on which a deduction is first claimed for the donated property. The appraisal must be prepared, signed, and dated by a "qualified appraiser."[77] Incentive appraisal fees are generally prohibited by the regulations.[78]

In order to be a "qualified appraiser," the individual appraiser must declare in writing that he or she (1) either holds himself or herself out to the public as an appraiser or performs appraisals on a regular basis; (2) is qualified to make appraisals of the type of property being valued (the appraiser's qualifications must be described in the appraisal); (3) is not disqualified because of a relationship with the donor or the transaction;[79] and (4) understands the legal consequences of making an intentionally false or fraudulent overstatement of the value of the property. These include a civil penalty under § 6701 for aiding and abetting an understatement of tax liability, and may result in the appraisal being disregarded pursuant to 31 U.S.C. § 330(c).[80]

More than one appraiser may appraise the donated property. The donor does not have to use all of multiple appraisals in substantiating the charitable contribution deduction.[81] However, the fact that an appraisal was obtained and then not used is discoverable by the IRS in the event that the valuation is challenged.

---

[76] Among other information that must be set forth are (1) a statement that the appraisal was prepared for income tax purposes; (2) the date (or dates) on which the property was appraised; (3) the appraised fair market value of the property on the date (or expected date) of contribution; (4) the method of valuation used to determine the fair market value, such as the income approach, the market-data approach, and the replacement-cost-less-depreciation approach; and (5) the specific basis for the valuation, such as specific comparable sales transactions or statistical sampling, including a justification for using sampling and an explanation of the sampling procedure employed. Treas. Reg. § 1.170A-13(c)(3)(ii).

[77] Treas. Reg. § 1.170A-13(c)(3)(i). For a thorough discussion of appraisals, see generally § 10.03.

[78] Treas. Reg. § 1.170A-13(c)(6).

[79] The following persons cannot act as a qualified appraiser: the donor; a party to the transaction in which the donor acquired the property being appraised (*i.e.*, the person who sold, exchanged, or gave the property to the donor, or any person who acted as an agent for the transferor or for the donor with respect to such sale, exchange, or gift), unless the property is donated within two months of the date of acquisition and its appraised value does not exceed its acquisition price; the donee of the property; any person related to any of the foregoing; an appraiser who is regularly used by any person described in the first three categories above and who does not perform a majority of his or her appraisals made during his or her taxable year for other persons.

[80] Treas. Reg. § 1.170A-13(c)(5).

[81] Treas. Reg. § 1.170A-13(c)(5)(iii).

The donor must file Form 8283 with the return on which the deduction is claimed, and both the donor and the appraiser must sign the appraisal summary on the form. If the donor's total art contribution deduction for the year is $20,000 or more, a complete copy of the signed appraisal must be filed with the return.

There are a great many other rules governing deductions for charitable contributions that are far beyond the scope of this book that addresses particular issues of artists. A good general description of these rules can be found in IRS Publication 526, "Charitable Contributions." This publication discusses organizations that are qualified to receive deductible charitable contributions, the types of contributions that a donor can deduct, how much can be deducted, what records must be kept, and how to report charitable contributions.

FORMS AND APPENDICES

FORM 13-1

Charitable Gift Agreement Form

(This form is intended to be used by donors. However, many donee institutions may have their own form of gift agreement that may place fewer restrictions on the donee's use of the property.)

[donor's letterhead]

[date]

Name and address of donee

Dear [name of donee]:

I am donating the property described below (the "Property") to [name of donee] ("Donee"). We agree that this gift is subject to the following conditions, and no other conditions:

1. Donee will use the Property in a manner that is related to the purpose or function constituting the basis for Donee's exemption under section 501 of the Internal Revenue Code; provided, however, that, after so using the Property for at least three years,[1] Donee shall be free to make any other use of the Property or to dispose of the Property.
2. I am transferring to Donee all of my right, title and interest in and to the Property and I hereby assign to the Donee any rights and any cause of action that I may have with respect to the Property.[2]
3. Donee will acknowledge this gift in all credits (such as wall labels and catalogs) according to the following credit line: [name of donor as donor wishes it to appear in such credits]

[1] The three-year period is somewhat arbitrary.

[2] If for example, the donor did not receive good title to the Property when the donor purchased the Property, or the Property was damaged by a restorer while it was owned by the donor, the Donee may not be able to collect damages from the seller or the restorer without an explicit assignment to the Donee of any rights and any cause of action that the donor may have with respect to the Property.

I understand that Donee has not promised the public exhibition of the Property and that Donee may loan the Property as Donee deems appropriate.[3]

Very truly yours,

[donor's signature]

[3] Many donee institutions will insist on a provision such as this so that they have freedom to use the property as they see fit.

FORM 13-2

Brandeis University (Rose Art Museum) Gift Agreement

Donor: ____________________________________

Address: __________________________________

____

____

The item(s) described below has been donated by the undersigned to Brandeis University. The undersigned agrees that acceptance of the listed gift(s) by the University is subject to the following conditions:

1. The University cannot promise the permanent exhibition of any object because of limited gallery space and the policy of changing exhibitions.
2. The donor relinquishes all right, title and interest in the described property. Further, the gift shall not be subject to any conditions or limitations set by the donor, including loan arrangements.
3. The University will acknowledge the donor in all credits (wall labels, catalogs, etc.), according to the following credit line designation supplied by the donor:

   ____

   ____

If the donor does not designate a credit line the University will assume that it is the donor's wish that the credit line be the same as the donor's signature supplied on this Gift Agreement form.

Signature of Donor ____

Date ______________________________

Gifts to Brandeis University are deductible for federal income tax purposes in accordance with the provisions of the Internal Revenue Code. Appraisals of donated items are the responsibility of the donor and cannot be performed by the University.

ARTIST: ____

TITLE AND DATE: ______________________________________

MEDIUM: ____

DIMENSIONS: ____

Brandeis University, P.O. Box 9110 Waltham, MA 02254-9110

Please retain the pink copy for your records.

Accepted by the Rose Art Museum ________________________

CHAPTER 14

TRUSTS AND ESTATES

Erik J. Stapper

§ 14.01 INTRODUCTION

After the death in 1890 of Vincent van Gogh, his art dealer brother Theo gave thought to preserving at least 1,700 works of art. Overwhelmed by the task, Theo lost his job, suffered a nervous breakdown and died within six months of Vincent. He had selected the author of Vincent's biography. The author died two years later without having started the biography. If it had not been for the persistence of Theo's wife and son, Vincent's work might have been lost forever[1] and 100 years after Vincent's death the more than 1 million visitors to the Vincent van Gogh Museum in Amsterdam, the Netherlands, would have had to seek other cultural outlets. That year's winning auction bid on van Gogh's "Irises" of $82 million would have had to have been spent on other "investments."

The story of van Gogh, who sold only one painting during his lifetime, is usually told to illustrate what can happen after death to an artist's reputation. It also deserves citation as an example of the need for artists to engage in estate planning and to prepare someone to undertake what can be a Herculean effort.[2]

This chapter is intended to provide guidance for the artist and his or her family members or the artist's advisors by introducing an overview of the state laws affecting the transfer of property during life or at death and describing in some detail the federal tax laws that are important factors in the property transfer decision-making process. This chapter also discusses potential tax traps for the unwary, possible solutions to those problems once created or ways in which the problems can be avoided in the first place. This chapter is not, however, a handbook on the successful post-mortem marketing of an artist's unsold inventory.

§ 14.02 THE ARTIST'S ESTATE

Even if the artist's assets are worth less than the estate tax threshold, the living artist must consider the disposition of the artwork left behind. The law of the jurisdiction of domicile will usually control the disposition of the estate if the artist has no will, or that law determines the validity of the will if one has been written. The location, or "situs," of the artwork at the time of the artist's death may determine how that artwork will devolve. If an artist has a permanent place of work in another jurisdiction, the disposition of the artwork at that location may be subject to the laws of that jurisdiction.

---

[1] Robert Wallace, The World of Van Gogh, 1852-1890, 167 (1969); Cynthia Saltzman, Portrait of Dr. Gachet 52-55 (1998).

[2] *See generally* A Visual Artist's Guide to Estate Planning, Based on a conference co-sponsored by the Marie Walsh Sharpe Art Foundation and the Judith Rothschild Foundation (1998). The Judith Rothschild Foundation supports estates of outstanding but under-recognized American artists in many aspects of estate organization such as cataloguing, preservation, and storage.

Without a will, all the artist's property will go to those persons who are designated by state law. The usual line of succession begins with a spouse and descendants, followed, if none, by parents, siblings, grandparents, and then first cousins or more remote and perhaps unknown family members.[3] These may well be persons unfamiliar with the artist's work or have no interest or ability to promote it.

[A] Probate Procedure

The validity of a will is established in a court proceeding that has the effect of transferring the estate at death to the persons named in the will instead of those designated by the local law. When filed in the court, the will ceases to be a private document and becomes public. At the same time the procedures of most jurisdictions, generally referred to as "probate," require that those persons designated as receiving property at death in the absence of a will (the "statutory heirs") be notified of the will having been offered in probate.[4] The forms currently in use in New York County are included in this chapter's forms as an example of how probate is initiated.

The courts that have jurisdictions over probate are variously referred to as probate or surrogate courts and are either a separate court or a division of the regular civil courts. Federal courts will decline jurisdiction over probate matters even when the diversity of citizenship and other jurisdictional requirements can be satisfied.[5]

In the case of a Holocaust survivor, multiple marriages and divorces, or an unmarried only child not survived by parents or descendants, the requirement to locate possible heirs can be very difficult to satisfy. The advent of DNA makes it easier to establish kinship of distant relatives or children born out of wedlock, but it does not make it easier to find them. Local laws will usually require a showing of a genuine effort to locate heirs before allowing the publication of an official notice in one or more newspapers, an action likely to aid in finding statutory heirs.

In any estate planning discussion, the artist must be asked for a family tree, regardless of estrangement from parents, siblings, or children. This can be a

---

[3] Uniform Probate Code, Part I (Amended 1993) (U.P.C.). The U.P.C. has been adopted in 14 states; except for Florida and Michigan, none of the populous states has adopted it. For a ready reference to the requirements of each state *see* The Wills and Estate Planning Guide, A State and Territorial Summary of Will and Intestacy Statutes, 1995 Edition of the General Practice Section of the American Bar Association, which is to be cited as The Judge Advocate General's School, U.S. Army, JA 262, Legal Assistance Wills Guide (Oct. 1995).

[4] U.P.C. § 3-403(a).

[5] Moore v. Graybeal, 843 F.2d 706 (3d Cir. 1988); Drogan v. Miller, 679 F.2d 712 (7th Cir. 1982).

painful subject, but it cannot be avoided unless steps are taken to avoid probate as is discussed below in § 14.03.

Even after the statutory heirs have been located, local law will probably require, as is the case, for instance, in New York State, that the court must consider the mental capacity of the statutory heirs so that they can effectively consent to the probate of the offered will. If any of the statutory heirs are minors or under some other form of disability, local law may require the appointment of a guardian to protect the interest of those statutory heirs.[6] In New York State a "guardian ad litem," or "GAL," is appointed. The fees of such a guardian are part of the cost of a probate proceeding, as are the court filing fees.

If the incompetent statutory heir has any other rights, such as a spousal right of election against a will, the guardian has the duty of considering the exercise of those rights under the applicable local law. Failure to do so can be malpractice.

A guardian is also appointed in a probate proceeding where the statutory heirs cannot be found. The purpose of the appointment is then to eliminate the rights of any unnamed statutory heirs so that the probate of a will cannot be set aside if statutory heirs finally appear. If there is a significant delay in locating statutory heirs, a named executor may be authorized to collect and preserve, but not distribute, the assets of an estate.[7]

[B] Validity of a Will

Local law prescribes the manner in which a will can be valid. First, the local law's formalities for the signing of a will must have been observed, such as the presence of adult disinterested witnesses and the proving of their signatures. The person who makes a will must be an adult and is usually referred to as the testator or testatrix.[8] A wholly handwritten, or holographic, signed will without witnesses can be valid in the states that have adopted the Uniform Probate Code.[9] New York State does not allow probate of an unwitnessed handwritten will, except under extremely limited circumstances, primarily when death occurs on the battlefield, when a holographic will can be valid.[10]

---

[6] U.P.C., Part 3.

[7] To maintain privacy or to avoid the costs associated with probate, a number of alternatives are available. These are reviewed *infra* in § 14.02[E].

[8] For a general discussion of the execution requirements, see A. James Casner & Jeffrey N. Pennell, Estate Planning § 3.1 (Aspen Law & Business 6th Ed.).

[9] U.P.C. § 2-503.

[10] Other countries and other states have different schemes. For instance, under Norwegian law an oral will made by a person domiciled in Norway is valid even if made elsewhere. After the oral will has been validated in Norway, it may be given effect to pass non-real-estate assets in a jurisdiction that does not recognize the validity of an oral will for its domiciliaries.

After the notice requirements for a probate proceeding are satisfied, the next step is to prove the valid execution of the will by the testator. This frequently requires that the necessary number of witnesses, usually at least two,[11] testify under oath that they saw the testator sign the will in the presence of all witnesses and that the testator made some statement to those witnesses about the signed document being a last will or testament.

The testimony of the witnesses can be by affidavit or by oral evidence given at a judicial hearing. Although an affidavit made either contemporary with the will or as part of the probate proceeding is usually sufficient, the court may direct the witnesses to appear personally where there is concern about the execution or the testator's capacity, particularly when the will was signed shortly prior to death.

After the proponent of a will has established that a will was signed in accordance with the statutory requirements, the presumption is that the will is valid. Any opponent of the will must then show that the testator lacked mental capacity or was influenced to make the will. If an opponent raises sufficient doubt, the proponent of the will must prove mental capacity and/or the absence of undue influence.

As stated above, federal courts will frequently decline to exercise jurisdiction in a probate matter even when all the requirements for jurisdiction are met.[12] The reason for this is that the validity of a will is truly a matter of local law and as long as matters of due process, such as notice requirements, have been observed, there is no substantial federal interest to be served by entertaining jurisdiction in the federal courts.

[1] Mental Capacity

An artist working outside the mainstream of art or leading an alternative lifestyle may leave a will that could be considered an easy target for a contest on the ground of lack of mental capacity to make a will. Even if the testator is a mainstream artist who leaves all his artwork and financial assets to a foundation charged with supporting his reputation, the proponent of the will may well encounter hostility from the surviving family.

Nevertheless, eccentricity, delusions short of insanity, or bad living habits are not sufficient to invalidate a will. The test for the capacity to make a will is not general mental capacity; it is, rather, the ability to make a will at the time it is made.[13] The difference is that a person with severe mental problems may nevertheless be found to have been capable of making a will because testimony

[11] U.P.C. § 2-502.

[12] *See supra* note 5.

[13] *See* the cases cited in William J. Bowe & Douglas H. Parker, Page on Wills § 21 (3d Ed. 1960).

could show that the testator was familiar with the family tree and the earthly possessions forming part of the estate and could make a fully informed decision to benefit one or more persons instead of the statutory heirs. The proponents of the will can satisfy the burden of proof by showing the existence of a lucid moment, in an otherwise disoriented life, sufficient to validate a will made in that moment.[14]

[2] Undue Influence

Unlike the problem of a nonmainstream artist's mental capacity, the question of undue influence is not more prevalent for an artist's estate than for any other testator. Undue influence is found where someone persuades a testator to make a provision in a will for that person or someone related to the persuader that the testator would not have made in the absence of that persuasion.[15]

For example, the will of Georgia O'Keeffe was attacked by her family as having been made under undue influence because it favored a much younger longtime assistant over the family. The court reviewed the length of the association and concluded there had not been any undue influence.

The question of undue influence can also arise if a collection is sought after by a museum to the exclusion of those who might otherwise be the object of the testator's bounty. English common law has a tradition of not allowing excessive bequests to charities, which was, of course, prompted by wills that made large bequests to churches in the expectation of eternal salvation thereby. New York State abolished its remnant of these laws in 1981.[16] Nevertheless, a museum's assiduous courting of a collector can, conceivably, cross over into undue influence.

[3] Disputed Domicile

Another aspect of estate litigation is a dispute over domicile. This issue usually arises in the context of a contest between two or more taxing jurisdictions. It can arise, however, where a relative or friend moves an elderly or otherwise disabled person to a new location and a new will is made there. If the testator did not have the mental capacity to change his or her domicile, the proper jurisdiction to test the validity of the later will is not the place where it was made, but the place from which the person had been moved. Even if a will is admitted to original probate in one state, that does not require the courts of another state to give full faith and credit to that probate with regard to property located in the state of

---

[14] One New York County Surrogate has stated that less mental capacity is required to execute a will than any other legal instrument, Matter of Goldberg, 582 N.Y.S.2d 617, 620 (Sur. Ct. New York County 1992).

[15] *See* the cases cited in Bowe, *supra* note 13, § 15.

[16] Section 5-33 of the New York Estates, Powers and Trusts Law.

domicile.[17] If, however, a party in interest from one state appears in the other and the matter is decided adversely, the doctrine of res judicata bars a suit in the other state.

[4] Ancillary Probate

Once the validity of a will has been established in the place of domicile, it cannot be attacked in another jurisdiction where an artist may own real estate by anyone who appeared in the original probate proceeding.[18] In the absence of a domicile dispute, the decision by the court of domicile is given full faith and credit in all other domestic jurisdiction and will be entitled to comity in other countries. Nevertheless, it may be necessary to have a separate procedure, called "ancillary probate" or "ancillary administration," to transfer property in another jurisdiction.[19]

The validity of a will in the place of domicile does not preclude the application of the law of the place where assets are located. The inheritance of real estate is governed by the law of the state where it is located. The surviving spouse or children may have rights under those laws that cannot be avoided by probate in the place of domicile. For instance, Louisiana has provisions for the mandatory inheritance, or forced heirship, by children. The artist who owns a studio or gallery in the New Orleans French Quarter therefore needs to consult local counsel.

[5] Safekeeping of the Will

After a will has been signed and until it is filed for probate, it must be kept in a safe place where it can be found. If the will is placed in a safe deposit box to which only the testator has access, then after death no one can get to the will and file it for probate. A court order may then be needed for the limited purpose of gaining access to a safe deposit for the purpose of locating a will.

Keeping an original will at home exposes it to the risk of loss in a fire or burglary. If a will had been known to exist and cannot be found, the testator may be presumed to have destroyed it for the purpose of revoking it, which leads to the question of whether the deceased's intention was to die intestate or to reaffirm the validity of a prior will.

The preferred solution is to leave the original will with the artist's attorney for safekeeping and to have a photocopy in the artist's home with a note that

---

[17] In re Estate of Reed, 233 Kan. 531,664 P.2d 824 (1983), *cert. denied,* 52 U.S.L.W. 3385 (1983).

[18] Bowe, *supra* note 13 at § 28.3; In re Wells, 36 Misc. 2d 829, 233 N.Y.S.2d 940 (County Sur. Ct. 1962) (trust beneficiaries who had not appeared in a probate proceeding in Maryland could challenge the validity of a will's exercise of a power of appointment over a New York trust).

[19] U.P.C., art. IV.

identifies the location of the original. The fact that an attorney keeps a will for safekeeping does not mean that the named executor must use that attorney for the probate of the will or the administration of the estate. The executor is free to select his or her own attorney for that work.

[6] Codicil

A codicil is a document by which a will can be amended without revoking the entire will. In the days before electronic word processing a codicil was typically used to make minor changes that did not change an overall estate plan, such as substituting, adding or deleting a beneficiary of an item of personal property or of a dollar amount. A codicil could also be used to change an executor.

The drawback to a codicil is that when it is offered for probate along with the original will, a person adversely affected by the codicil can become a party to the probate proceeding, similar to a statutory heir.

[C] Administration of the Estate

If the deceased leaves no will, the intestate estate is administered by the person designated by the court. The applicable statute lists the priority of potential administrators beginning with the surviving spouse, followed by descendants or siblings. All who are eligible for appointment as well as the other statutory heirs may object to the appointment of an administrator on the ground of the appointee's inability to handle a complex estate or a potential conflict of interest. The deceased artist's wishes are irrelevant because of the absence of a will. The fee to be paid to the administrator is fixed by law or set by the court.

[1] Naming the Executor

If there is a will, the estate is administered by the person or persons named as executor in the will. The naming of an executor is one of the most important reasons for making a will. The naming of an executor should include provisions for requiring or dispensing with a bond and the setting of compensation.

The amount of judicial supervision over the administration of an estate varies greatly from state to state. Some states require prior judicial approval for many important steps such as payment of debts, the sale of real estate, or distributions to beneficiaries. The New York State procedure is much less restricted. The executor can be released at the end of the administration when the beneficiaries sign a receipt and release. When this is not possible, a judicial accounting will complete the administration. In such a proceeding, the beneficiaries can file objections to the handling of the estate.

[2] Conflict of Interest

The selection of an executor is one of the most complex issues for an artist's estate because the bulk of the estate will be made up of artwork and not of traditional financial assets that can be disposed of easily. Although the problems may differ in magnitude or degree, the choice of an executor is as important for the successful artist as for the under-recognized artist.

The decision in *Matter of Rothko*[20] addresses the issue of an executor's self-dealing and breach of fiduciary obligation. The executors of Rothko's estate, which included a director of the Marlborough Gallery and an artist represented by that gallery, agreed to sell paintings to Marlborough Gallery with a 50 percent commission, unless the paintings were sold to or through other dealers, in which case the commission was to be 40 percent. Several of the contract terms were questionable, including the inflated commission (paintings sold during Rothko's lifetime through Marlborough had earned only a 10 percent commission), interest-free installment payments over a twelve-year period, and the sale of so many paintings within a short period of time. All three executors, including the one without conflict of interest, were removed as executors and were fined.

In considering the appointment of a fiduciary, whether executor or trustee, and selecting a qualified attorney, the artist, who is transformed into a "testator" by the act of signing a testament, must be aware of the many opportunities for conflicts of interest. The most obvious conflict situation for an artist arises when the artist selects his or her dealer or publisher as one of the fiduciaries. The tension between earning commissions on the sale of artwork and planning for the long-term welfare of either the artist's survivors or the body of work left behind has led to litigation, a result not avoided by creating a foundation, as is shown by cases other than the Rothko Foundation, such as the Joan Mitchell Foundation, Joseph Cornell Foundation and Warhol Foundation for the Visual Arts, Inc. More important, the selection of a dealer may prevent the dealer from being able to handle the artist's work, thereby removing the person most familiar with the market for the artist's work.

There are, however, many less obvious cases of conflict which can be easily overlooked. The following scenarios are intended to serve as reminders to the artist that one or more individuals or institutions will take over on the artist's death or incapacity, and that those persons may have a conflict of interest in carrying out their fiduciary duties. A conflict can be waived after it has been fully disclosed. Moreover, if the scenarios or multiplicity of cautions here appear overwhelming, the artist must keep in mind the costs and burdens on survivors, whoever they may be, if there is no estate plan.

---

[20] 84 Misc. 2d 830, 379 N.Y.S.2d 923 (Cty. Sur. Ct. 1975), *modified*, 56 A.D.2d 489, 392 N.Y.S.2d 80 (1st Dep't. 1976), *aff'd*, 43 N.Y.2d 309, 401 N.Y.S.2d 449 (1977).

[3] Selection of Spouse, Nonmarital Partner, or Close Friend

If the proposed fiduciary, whether spouse, nonmarital partner or close friend, is also an artist, the appointment may force that appointee to choose between pursuing his or her own artistic career and preserving and advancing the work of the deceased artist. Conversely, if the devoted spouse or acolyte is not an artist, the testator must consider whether there will be a significant financial burden placed on the fiduciary for which the estate's after-tax assets may not be sufficient. Consider for a moment the cost of storing, insuring, or otherwise maintaining the body of artwork left behind. This burden will vary, of course; the deceased may have been a miniaturist, or a creator of giant sculptures.

[4] Selection of Other Family Members

Selecting one person as fiduciary may be more efficient than naming several persons because no time is lost in reaching agreement between co-fiduciaries. For large or complicated estates, co-fiduciaries may be desirable, particularly where each can perform well or has expertise in separate or specific tasks. To do otherwise may create hurt feelings between the artist's surviving children or siblings. An even more difficult situation is created if there is a surviving spouse or nonmarital partner who is not the parent of the child selected as fiduciary. This tension becomes extremely high when the child is forced to select assets that will make up the marital deduction property for a step-parent. For instance, who gets the artwork or other nonincome-producing assets, and who receives the cash and securities? What will the recipient of the former bequest live on?

Even without remarriage, family relations change as the result of intervening deaths. A fiduciary who could work well with the artist's surviving siblings may not be effective when that sibling predeceases the artist so that the fiduciary must now deal with nieces and nephews, or their spouses or children.

[5] Selection of Attorney as Fiduciary

At one time it was not unusual for some New York attorneys to advise their clients that only an attorney could be an executor (in some instances the advice was for two attorneys). This unethical practice is now contrary to a specific provision added in 1995 to New York law.[21] It requires a New York attorney to disclose to all estate planning clients that, subject to limited statutory exceptions, any person, including an attorney, is eligible to serve as executor. Moreover, the attorney must disclose that any person, including an attorney, is entitled to receive a statutory commission, and explain that the statutory fee is payable in the absence

[21] New York State Surrogate's Court Procedure Act, § 2307-a.

of an agreement to the contrary. Finally, the attorney must disclose that an attorney who is named as executor, or an affiliated attorney, will also be entitled to receive just and reasonable compensation for legal services. This is usually referred to as "double dipping."

Most important, the client must confirm the attorney's disclosure in a signed writing. A copy of the statutory model form of acknowledgment of disclosure is included here as Form 14-2. In the absence of the required written acknowledgment, the attorney's commission as executor is limited to half the statutory amount.

To some extent the statutory disclosure is not sufficient because it does not require a disclosure of how the statutory commission is calculated in New York State.[22] The commission is based on the executor *receiving and paying out all sums of money*, including income earned during administration and on the commission paid out. Property that the executor never receives is not included in the computation even if it is part of the taxable estate.

Also not included in the commission calculation base is property specifically identified, or a fixed amount, that is given in the will to a named person, a "specific legacy," and not as part of the balance of the estate referred to as the "residuary estate." Real estate is not included in the calculation even if it is part of the residuary estate, unless the executor is required to take action regarding the property, such as removal of title problems (a "cloud on title"), evicting tenants, or partitioning the property among several beneficiaries of the residuary estate.

Another problem in calculating commissions crops up when the artist is the beneficiary of a trust established by a predeceased spouse, parent, or grandparent and the artist can designate who is to receive the trust assets at his or her own death, which is known as having "power of appointment." Frequently such powers can be used to pay estate taxes. If the power merely directs payment of the tax to the government, that amount does not become part of the calculation base. If it is directed to be paid to the executor for the purpose of having the executor pay the estate tax, then the amount so received and paid out may be included in the calculation.

[6] Selection of Other Professional Advisers

The problem of selecting an appraiser who is independent of the attorney has already been mentioned. Conflicts can also arise between beneficiaries where

[22] The statutory amount now in effect is calculated as follows on commissionable assets:

5% of the first	$ 100,000
4% of the next	200,000
3% of the next	700,000
2 1/2% of the next	4,000,000
2% of the excess over	5,000,000

gifts of artwork are equalized or supplemented by cash legacies. Similarly, if the will provides for an allocation of estate taxes, a conflict can be created among beneficiaries. Moreover, in 1996 the Internal Revenue Service (IRS) announced a new procedure[23] for the advance valuation of artwork for income (charitable contributions), estate, and gift tax purposes. Not all of the estate's beneficiaries may be happy with the result. Nevertheless should the executor use the procedure for all artwork in an estate?

[D] The Probate Estate

The will of an artist can dispose of only the assets that are reached by the will (the "probate estate"). A copyright is an asset that is part of an artist's probate estate. Not included in the probate estate are jointly owned property that includes a right of survivorship, property previously transferred in trust, life insurance that does not name the estate as a beneficiary, and employee retirement or other benefit plans. In most jurisdictions it is possible to designate a financial account as being "in trust for" a named individual.[24] These accounts are referred to as "Totten Trusts" after the case that held the "in trust for" designation removed the account from the probate estate.[25] It is thus possible not to have any probate assets at death, which would make an existing will a nullity without affecting the will's validity. A probate court would normally have jurisdiction to determine whether the joint account or "in trust for" designations were obtained while the person was incompetent or under undue influence. If the court so determines, the designations will be voided and a probate estate will be created.

The New York banking law now also permits a joint account for convenience only. Such an account is in name a joint account so that both designated "owners" can sign checks. Nevertheless, at death this type of joint account is part of the probate estate because the co-owner has neither an ownership interest nor a survivorship interest.

[E] Trusts as Will Substitutes

An artist can avoid probate and maintain privacy by transferring all assets to a trust that is fully revocable. In a number of jurisdictions, such a trust can be established by the artist being both the transferor or the "grantor" of the trust and the trustee who administers the trust.[26] Such a trust has no current tax consequences because it is totally ignored as existing for tax purposes. It is classified as a

---

[23] Rev. Proc. 96-15, 1996-1 C.B. 630.

[24] Casner, *supra* note 8 at § 4.2.2.

[25] Matter of Totten, 179 N.Y. 112 (1904).

[26] See generally the discussion of "merger" in Casner, *supra* note 8, at § 4.2.3, and the sample form at § 4.65 therein.

"grantor trust" or, outside the tax setting, as a "will substitute" because the trust's provisions are substituted for the probate court's jurisdiction.

Obviously, if not all of an artist's assets are placed in the trust that has been set up, there are still probate assets for which a will is needed. Therefore, to establish the trust still requires a will to transfer to the trust after death any probate assets that may not have been transferred during the artist's lifetime. An automobile can be such an overlooked asset.

The problem that the artist faces is that in each subsequent year more works of art are created. To make certain that those assets are treated as part of the trust, the artist should periodically update a listing of the artwork that belongs to the trust.

§ 14.03 TRANSFER TAXES

[A] IRS Code Sections

If both Vincent and Theo van Gogh had lived a normal lifetime, Theo's task as executor or administrator of his brother's estate would have been complicated by having had to deal with the French inheritance tax authorities.[27] French law allows for the payment of death taxes with artwork. Therefore it would have been possible that the van Gogh Museum would have been in France instead of Amsterdam in the same way that the Picasso Museum is in Paris and not in Barcelona.

To continue this historical speculation, the van Gogh brothers as octogenarians could have followed the example of Piet Mondrian by leaving Paris, first for London and then for New York City, where they died. This chain of events would have deprived Theo of the opportunity to pay Vincent's estate tax with artwork, leaving open the further possibilities of the works being left to an American museum that would have changed its name to the van Gogh Museum, or of the works being sold to raise taxes and the Dutch government buying them back many years later.[28]

Subtitle B of the Internal Revenue Code of 1986 (the "Code") is captioned "Estate and Gift Taxes." The subtitle consists of four chapters that continue the numbering started in subtitle A captioned "Income Taxes." As a result the first chapter, on estate tax, is Chapter 11 and includes §§ 2001 through 2209 (there are gaps in the sequence). The gift tax is in Chapter 12 and includes §§ 2501 through 2524. The two remaining chapters are "Tax on Certain Generation-Skipping Transfers" (Chapter 13, §§ 2600 to 2663) and "Special Valuation Rules"

---

[27] *See supra* § 14.01.

[28] In 1998 Mondrian's last and unfinished work, *Victory Boogie Woogie*, was bought from an American collector for $40 million and hung in the Municipal Museum of the Hague, the Netherlands, as a gift to the nation.

(Chapter 14, §§ 2701 through 2704). The reason for referring to these seemingly unimportant matters is that estate planners, like other tax practitioners, fall into the habit of using numbers as short cuts in a discussion that nonspecialists cannot comprehend. For example, the "Tax on Certain Generation-Skipping Transfers" becomes the "GST tax" or the "Chapter 13 tax." A gift for the benefit of a minor becomes a "2503(c) transfer."

Moreover, the separate designation of the estate and gift tax is an historical anomaly. Each once was a separate tax. Since December 31, 1976, the two taxes have been in effect one unified transfer tax that is collected on a cumulative basis (1) during life on gifts (due on April 15 of the year following the year in which a gift was made) and (2) at death on whatever has not been given away (the estate tax return is due nine months after the date of death). To one who is not a tax specialist, the numbering of code sections no longer makes sense because the gift tax numbers are higher than the estate tax, but the gift tax is encountered first in any tax planning, while the estate tax in reality represents the final chapter. The sequence in code chapters and sections is, however, historical because the original estate tax preceded the gift tax by eight years.

The reference to the combination of estate, gift and GST taxes as transfer taxes is constitutionally important. The estate tax is imposed on "the transfer of the taxable estate" (§ 2001(a)). The gift tax is on each year's "transfer of property by gift" (§ 2501(a)). The GST applies to "every generation-skipping transfer" (§ 2601).

When the estate tax was originally attacked in 1921 as unconstitutional on the ground, among others, that it was a direct tax, the U.S. Supreme Court rejected the argument because a tax on the power to transmit property "has always been regarded as the antithesis of a direct tax."[29] The constitutionality of the gift tax was upheld by the Supreme Court in *Bromley v. McCouger.*[30]

> [I]t is a tax laid upon the exercise of a single one of those powers incident to ownership, the power to give the property owned to another. Under the statute all the other rights and powers which collectively constitute property or ownership may be fully enjoyed free of tax.[31]

This analysis is important if an executor is directed to destroy all or part of an artist's output. Under those circumstances is there a transfer that can be taxed? The only reported precedent is the following dictum in *Ahmanson Foundation v. United States*:[32]

---

[29] New York Trust Co. v. Eisner, 256 U.S. 345 (1921).

[30] 280 U.S. 124 (1929).

[31] *Id.* at 136.

[32] 674 F.2d 761, 768 (9th Cir. 1981).

> Thus, for example, if a public figure ordered his executor to shred and burn his papers, and then to turn the ashes over to a newspaper, the value to be counted would be the value of the ashes, rather than the papers.[33]

This language clearly supports the conclusion that a directive in a will to destroy property so as to avoid transferring it to any one should avoid estate tax on the property to be destroyed.

[B] Relationship Between Gift and Estate Taxes

Even though the gift and estate tax constitute a unified transfer tax system, there are advantages to making lifetime gifts over an inheritance. For gift tax purposes a donor may annually make a gift of $10,000 to any donee free of gift tax. The amount of the "annual exclusion" is now indexed for inflation.[34]

A gift of future interest in property (which generally is a gift in trust) does not qualify for the annual exclusion, unless certain powers of withdrawal are included.[35] The exception for gifts of future interests has its own exception for transfers in trust for the benefit of a minor. Such gifts in trust are specifically treated by § 2503(c) as *not* being a gift of a future interest in property provided the property is paid to the beneficiary at age 21 or has been used for the beneficiary's benefit before attaining age 21.[36]

Also excluded from taxable gifts are amounts paid as tuition or for medical care on behalf of another individual. The exclusion is available only if the amounts are paid directly to the educational organization or the medical care provider.

The gift tax provides that a married couple may elect to have their gift to a third party treated as if each spouse had individually made half the gift. Both spouses must signify their consent on a gift tax return. Each spouse can, in any event, make her or his own annual gifts to a third party (for gifts between spouses see the discussion below on the transfer tax marital deduction). The gift-splitting provision is important if one spouse has no assets to give away, or, in the case of an artist, one spouse wants to give away artwork with a value of more than $10,000. In this manner, a married artist with two children, two children-in-law, and four grandchildren can give away each year, free of gift tax, a total of $160,000. The gift tax exclusions will not be allowed if there is an understanding that the other donees then give what they received to one of them.

Another benefit of the gift tax over the estate tax is that it is said to be "tax exclusive" and the estate tax is "tax inclusive." The difference is best demonstrated

[33] *Id.* at 768.

[34] I.R.C. § 2501.

[35] *See infra* § 15.02[C][5][c].

[36] If the beneficiary dies before age 21 the amount must be paid to the beneficiary's estate or as appointed in the beneficiary's will.

by example of an artist who is in the maximum 55 percent transfer tax bracket (amounts in excess of $3 million). A gift of $1 million requires the payment of a tax of $550,000 for a reduction in wealth of $1.55 million of which $1 million ends up in the hands of the beneficiary. The artist who dies owning that $1.55 million must pay an estate tax of $825,000, leaving only $697,500 to go to the beneficiary. Thus, the beneficiary is worse off by $300,500 when the transfer is made by inheritance instead of by gift. The difference is 55 percent of $550,000, the transfer tax not paid on the amount of the gift tax removed from the artist's estate.

[1] Gifts Within Three Years of Death

The differences between the gift tax and the estate tax suggests important benefits for gifts made immediately prior to death. Section 2035 is captioned ominously "Adjustments for Gifts Made Within 3 Years of Decedent's Death" and subsection (a) appears to tax gifts made within three years of death as part of an estate. Paragraph 1 of subsection (d) provides, however, that subsection (a) shall not apply to the estate of a decedent dying after December 31, 1981. Paragraph 2 of that subsection makes it clear that this exclusionary rule does not override a number of other estate tax inclusion sections, such as a revocable transfer with a retained life estate that takes effect at death.

Even though a taxable gift that is made three years before death is not included in a decedent's estate, the gift tax that was paid is added to the value of the estate.[37] This has the effect of collecting the estate tax on the amount of the gift tax. Nevertheless, the exclusion of the gift itself can be beneficial if the transferred property has appreciated in value between the date of gift and the date of death, because that appreciation escapes the application of the transfer taxes.

[2] Gift Tax Statute of Limitations

To compute the estate tax, the value of the estate is added to the value of the decedent's lifetime *taxable* gifts—thus not the annually excluded $10,000 gifts—and the estate tax is tentatively calculated on that total amount. Thereafter the gift tax is calculated on the amount of the included gifts and that gift tax is then deducted from the tentative estate tax to arrive at the actual estate tax due before the application of any credits. In 1990, a divided Tax Court agreed with the IRS that even if the statute of limitations on a gift tax return (usually three years) had run, the property subject to the gift tax could be revalued as of the date of gift for an initially understated value for purposes of determining the

[37] I.R.C. § 2035(c).

estate tax.[38] The Tax Court went on to hold, and the IRS has acquiesced, that it would also be necessary to calculate the gift tax that would have been paid on that revised value and that this amount, although not in fact paid, must be included in the amount of the gift tax deducted from the tentative estate tax.

In 1997, Congress amended the Code to make it more difficult for the IRS to apply this "look back" rule.[39] The change is not, however, a complete ban because the new rule applies only if the gift tax return that was filed adequately disclosed the nature and value of each gift. An artist who gives away a number of artworks may not have made full disclosure of all of his gifts or of the correct values of those gifts that were reported so that the gift tax statute of limitations is no ban to a revaluation.

[C] Transfer Tax Calculation

[1] Unified Credit

The unified transfer tax system does not specifically provide for an amount that is exempt from tax. It does, however, provide for the unified credit against the transfer tax that has the effect of exempting from tax a certain amount of otherwise taxable transfers. From 1981 through 1996 the amount of the credit exempted $600,000 from transfer tax. At that level, the transfer tax began at 37 percent. As a result of changes made in 1997 the "exempt" amount gradually increases so that it reaches $1 million in the year 2006. At that level the applicable transfer tax rate is 41 percent. In a technical change the nontaxable amount was given an official name: the "applicable exclusion amount."

There is a combined exempt amount for gift and estate tax purposes. It can be used all at once with one gift or at death or in pieces over the years. Once the exempt amount has been used up, all excess amounts are subject to either the gift tax or the estate tax unless the gift or death falls in a transition period as is now the case. As the exempt amount increases gradually to $1 million, each year's additional exempt amount becomes available.

The choice of when the transfer tax is paid is up to the artist because the artist can make a gift now of all of his or her artwork, use up the exempt amount, and pay whatever gift tax is due. If the artwork later appreciates in value because the artist's reputation at death has been considerably enhanced, there is no additional transfer tax due on the earlier gifts because the artwork is now outside the artist's estate. If gifts have not been made, the estate will be subject to estate tax if the total value of the estate exceeds that year's "applicable exclusion amount."

---

[38] Smith v. Commissioner, 94 T.C. 872 (1990), *acq.*, 1990-2 C.B.1.

[39] I.R.C. § 2001.

To be certain that the gift artwork is not part of the artist's estate, the artist must have delivered the artwork to the recipients whether they be children, partners or friends. The transfer must be documented and be complete in that the artist cannot retain any right, for instance, to keep it hanging on the wall in his or her studio. If it is to be made part of an exhibition, the catalogue must identify the actual owner.

The increase in the effective applicable rate from 37 percent to 41 percent highlights the need for making lifetime gifts in the appropriate family situation. The married artist who, along with his or her spouse, could have each year given away $160,000 free of gift tax,[40] but who fails to do so, leaves behind an additional estate tax burden of at least $92,496 for each year that gifts were not made. The tax burden could be much heavier if the property has appreciated in value at the time of death.

[2] State Death Tax Credit

For federal estate tax purposes, but not for gift tax purposes, a credit is allowed for a specified amount of state and District of Columbia "estate, inheritance, legacy or succession taxes actually paid."[41] The allowance of the credit does not increase or decrease the total amount of estate tax. The credit is a form of revenue sharing. Nevada does not have an estate tax. Therefore no amount of state death tax credit is allowed and the full amount of the estate tax is paid to the U.S. Treasury.

All other states and the District of Columbia have adopted state death taxes in an amount that is at least equal to the amount of the federal credit. This tax is usually referred to as a "sop" tax because it sops up the amount of the federal credit. In 36 states[42] and the District of Columbia this is the only death tax.

[a] Other State Death Taxes

A number of states have death taxes that exceed the federal credit. Thirteen of these have an inheritance tax.[43] Two states (Ohio and Oklahoma) have their own estate tax. In three states (Mississippi, Montana and New Jersey) the sop tax is limited to spouses and descendants. For other persons a separate inheritance tax remains in effect. (The difference between an estate tax and an inheritance tax is that the estate tax rate is the same regardless of who inherits the property,

---

[40] *See* the example in § 14.04[A].

[41] I.R.C. § 2011.

[42] This number includes New York, where the sop tax becomes effective in case of decedents dying after January 31, 2000.

[43] Delaware, Indiana, Iowa, Kansas, Kentucky, Louisiana, Maryland, Michigan, Nebraska, North Carolina, Pennsylvania, South Dakota and Tennessee.

whereas an inheritance tax applies different rates depending on the family relationship of the beneficiary to the decedent).

[b] State Gift Taxes

New York State repealed its gift tax effective January 1, 2000. This leaves Connecticut, Delaware, Louisiana, North Carolina and Tennessee as the only states with a gift tax.

[3] Credit for Tax on Prior Transfers

For estate tax purposes, but not for gift tax purposes, the Code provides for a full credit of federal estate tax previously paid if the transferee dies within two years of the transferor. The amount of the credit is reduced by 20 percentage points for every subsequent two-year period. Thus no credit is allowed after ten years.

To be eligible for the credit, the estate of the transferee need not include the assets that were taxed in the transferor's estate. For instance, if the transferee was only given a life estate in an asset so that nothing was taxable in the transferor's estate, a credit is nevertheless allowed for the estate tax attributable to the life estate.

[4] Foreign Death Tax Credit

If a decedent's assets are located in a foreign country, those assets may be subject to a death tax in that country. A credit is allowed for that tax, subject to limitations and valuation requirements set forth in § 2014 of the Code. In this context it is important to be aware that the "United States" is defined to mean only the 50 states and the District of Columbia.[44] Puerto Rico, the U.S. Virgin Islands, and other territories are not included and are foreign countries for transfer tax purposes.

Tax treaties. The foreign tax credit does not eliminate all double taxation of estates. This is particularly so since the U.S. estate tax is levied on the basis of citizenship and most other countries base their jurisdiction on residence or domicile. In that event, both countries may tax property located in a third country. The statutory foreign tax credit does not apply, however, because the property is not located in the taxing jurisdiction.

To eliminate double taxation the United States has entered into estate tax treaties with 16 other countries. It has also included in the Canadian income tax treaty a solution for the Canadian tax on capital gains at death. The Tax Court

---

[44] Section 7701(a)(9).

had upheld the Internal Revenue Service position that the Canadian tax could not be taken as a credit against the U.S. estate tax, because the Canadian tax was held to be an income tax and not a tax on transmitting property at death.[45] The income tax treaty now permits the credit.

Most of the estate tax treaties are with Western European countries. The notable exceptions are the absence of treaties with Belgium, Portugal and Spain. Finland and Greece complete the European treaties. Outside Europe the United States has treaties only with Australia (which has abolished its estate tax), Japan, and South Africa. Four of the treaties also deal with gift taxes: those with Denmark, France, Sweden and the U.K. There is a separate gift tax treaty with Australia.

For an artist the most important item to be checked in a treaty is whether maintaining a studio in another country makes it business property that can be taxed there.[46] The other aspect is a "tie breaker" provision for determining domicile where two countries each claim that under their laws the artist is domiciled there.[47]

In cases where a treaty allows a credit, the estate can take the treaty credit or the statutory foreign death credit, whichever is most favorable.[48]

[D] Generation-Skipping Transfer Tax

An artist's estate or gifts can also go to grandchildren, but that requires an election on the estate or gift tax return to take advantage of the generation-skipping transfer tax, or GST tax, exemption of $1 million. The GST tax is in addition to the regular estate tax and is levied at the flat rate of 55 percent on all generation-skipping transfers.

As the name of this tax suggests, it is imposed because a generation is skipped for the purpose of avoiding an estate tax on the immediately following generations (there is an exemption for a transfer to orphans of offspring). For family transfer purposes generations are determined by reference to the grandparents of the transferor and their lineal descendants. For persons who are not lineal descendants an individual who is born not more than 12½ years after the transferor is in the transferor's generation. An individual born more than 12½ but not more than 37½ years after the transferor is in the first generation younger than the transferor. A person who is more than 37½ years younger than the transferor is in the second younger generation.[49]

Thus a person who is 38 years younger is a "skip person" and the transfer to him or her generates a 55 percent generation skipping transfer tax on the amount

[45] Estate of Claire M. Ballard, 85 T.C. 300(1985).

[46] U.S. Model Treaty, art. 6, Tax Treaties (CCH) ¶ 209.06.

[47] *Id.* art. 4, ¶ 209.04.

[48] Reg. § 20.2014-4(a)(i).

[49] I.R.C. § 2651(d).

in excess of $1 million (there is only one exemption of $1 million per transferor). Thus the 88-year-old artist who leaves his or her entire output of artwork to a 50-year-old nonmarital partner is making a generation-skipping transfer.[50] The GST does not apply to a spouse of the artist regardless of the age differential.[51]

A discussion of the full application of the GST tax is outside the scope of this chapter because of the many technical provisions contained in Chapter 13 of the Code and the 50 pages of regulations adopted in 1995.

[E] Special Valuation Rules

Chapter 14 was added to the Code effective October 8, 1990, to provide special valuation rules to transfers made to family members and cases where the transferor retains certain interests in the transferred property. The chapter does not apply to outright gifts of the transferor's entire interest in property or to transfers to persons not family members. Here too there are many detailed technical rules in the Code and the regulations that do not have general application.[52] Nevertheless, it is very important to be aware of one important exception for a "qualified personal residence trust."

[1] Qualified Personal Residence Trust

The important statutory exception to the rules for transfers in trusts for the benefit of family members is the transfer of a personal residence.[53] The statutory exception is implemented by Regulation § 25.2702-5. Paragraph (c) of that regulation sets out the requirements for a qualified personal residence trust (QPRT).

The regulation's definition of "personal residence" refers to two income tax sections: § 1034, which defines a taxpayer's principal residence, and § 280A(d)(1), relating to vacation homes. The regulations specifically include a fractional interest in a principal residence or vacation home.[54] The regulations also include in the definition of "personal residence":

> appurtenant structures . . . and adjacent land not in excess of that which is reasonably appropriate for residential purposes (taking into account the residence's size and location).[55]

---

[50] The GST was added to the Code effective for any generation-skipping transfer made after October 22, 1986. Georgia O'Keeffe died on March 6, 1986 so that the provisions she had made in her will for Juan Hamilton were not affected by the GST. 67 T.C.M. 2700.

[51] I.R.C. § 2651(c)(1).

[52] I.R.C. § 2701(a)(1) & 2702(a)(1).

[53] I.R.C. § 2702(a)(3)(A)(ii).

[54] Reg. § 25,2701-5(c)(2)(i).

[55] Reg. § 25.2702-5(c)(2)(ii).

Most important is the limitation in the regulations that the property must have "its primary use as a residence of the term holder." That primary use is not negated if a portion of the residence is used for business purposes.[56] This concession is, of course, very important for the artist who has a studio at home and deducts for income tax purposes a portion of the residence.

Without discussing here all the limitations on a QPRT, the essential elements are that the residence is transferred to a trust for a period of years during which the transferor continues to occupy the residence. When the term ends, the trust terminates and the property is transferred to the designated family members of the transferor. At that point the transferor can continue occupancy only by paying fair market rent.

When the residence is transferred irrevocably to the trust, the transferor has made a gift of the ownership that takes effect at the earlier of either the transferor's death or the end of a specified term of years. The amount of the gift is reduced by the value of the transferor's right to use the property. The length of that term will be determined depending on the age of the transferor so that the amount of the gift will be kept small.

If the transferor dies during the trust term, then the property is included in the transferor's estate, as if the QPRT did not exist. The only cost will have been the fees for planning the trust and the transfer. If, however, the transferor lives beyond the trust term, the property is then outside the estate at the cost of minimal gift tax payment, if any. The contents of the residence are not affected by the transfer of the residence because the QPRT cannot hold personal property.[57]

The QPRT regulations include a number of other very detailed provisions to cover the possibilities of a sale, destruction and cessation of use, such as a move to a nursing home. All of these contingencies must be provided for in the trust agreement. A QPRT can be used for the benefit of persons other than family members.

[2] Qualified Charitable Trusts

The Chapter 14 regulations also exclude from its rules transfers that qualify for charitable deduction under the gift tax rules of § 2522 or the income tax rules of § 642(c)(5).[58]

[3] Other Estate Freeze Techniques

Chapter 14 was enacted to eliminate the transfer of property to the next generation where the transferor continues to hold an interest in the transferred

---

[56] Reg. § 25.2702-5(c)(2)(iii), which goes on to exclude, for instance, an inn or a bed and breakfast.

[57] Reg. § 25.2702-5(c)(2)(ii) last sentence and Example 4 of 5(d).

[58] The requirements for such trusts are discussed at § 14.04[F][4].

property. The classic case is the example of Regulation § 25.2701-1(a)(3) in which a sole shareholder of a corporation recapitalizes the corporation by exchanging the common shares for new common shares and cumulative preferred stock. Thereafter the common shares are given away and the donor keeps only the preferred shares. Under the valuation rules previously in effect a certain amount of estate value disappeared. The special valuation rules are designed to avoid that result.

The existence of Chapter 14 does not mean, however, that an artist cannot effectively take advantage of other freeze techniques. All of the artist's existing inventory can be transferred to a limited liability company (LLC) of which the artist will be the manager. Thereafter fractional interests in the LLC are given away to the artist's family or nonmarital partner. If the artist's reputation is subsequently enhanced the increased value of the inventory will be out of the artist's estate. Moreover, the value of the gifts of LLC interest would have been very low because the donees cannot control the LLC.[59]

Another technique is the sale on an installment basis of an asset that is expected to appreciate over time. The sale is made to a certain type of trust that has the effect of ignoring the sale for income tax purposes. Again, the intended result is to remove future appreciation from the artist's estate. Here too the technical details are beyond the scope of this publication.

[4] Life Insurance Trusts

An artist or collector who is insurable can take out life insurance and give the policy to a spouse, a partner, or children. Thereafter the artist or collector can make gifts of cash to the new policy owner or owners to allow for the payment of future premiums. These gifts will qualify for the annual gift tax exclusion of $10,000. At the death of the artist or collector, the life insurance is not part of the estate and no estate tax is due. The beneficiaries are now in a position to lend money to the estate to pay estate taxes if they want to. They may not want to do so because the proceeds to which each is entitled is the beneficiary's own money.

To retain a greater amount of control over life insurance proceeds, an artist or collector can set up a life insurance trust that will own the policy. If the gift is of an existing policy, whether in trust or otherwise, the insured must live three years after the gift to have the policy excluded from the insured's estate. If the trust applies for a new policy then there is no three-year rule and the full amount of the life insurance proceeds are excluded from the insured's estate.

The insured must provide the trust each year with the funds to pay the premiums. The annual transfer in trust does not, however, qualify for the annual

[59] Details concerning the use of this and other tax planning structures for the related issue of maintaining control over intellectual property are discussed *infra* in Chapter 15.

gift tax exclusion because it is a future interest. The transfer is made to qualify as a present interest by giving the beneficiaries the power to withdraw $10,000 from the trust within a specified period of time. This can work only if the beneficiaries are notified of their withdrawal rights. Based on a Court of Appeals case that blessed the result, the notifications are known as "Crummey letters."[60] The intention is, of course, that the beneficiaries leave the money in the trust to pay the premiums. The failure to withdraw can then be considered a gift by the beneficiary. To avoid that result, the withdrawal power is limited to the greater of $5,000 or 5 percent of the trust's corpus. A lapse of that power will not be a gift.[61]

The proper drafting of an insurance trust is not a simple matter if the insured wants to be certain of having cash available in the trust at death to help pay estate taxes. The trust must be irrevocable, the insured cannot be a trustee and the insured must not have retained any powers that could cause the trust to be included in the insured's estate.[62]

[F] Relationship Between Transfer Taxes and Income Tax

Section 102(a) of the Code excludes generally from gross income "the value of property acquired by gift, bequest, devise or inheritance." Subsection (b) clarifies that the exclusion does not include the income subsequently received from the property or instances where the gift or inheritance itself is of income from property instead of the property itself. Moreover, since 1986 a transfer by an employer for the benefit of an employee is not excluded from gross income.

The employer exception creates a problem for the artist who wants to provide in a will for a gift of artwork to a longtime assistant. The transfer will be subject to the estate tax and the assistant has to report the amount as income. In either case no money is involved from which the two taxes can be paid. Moreover, the total amount of the two taxes can exceed 100 percent if state and local income taxes are also taken into account. Thus, if an artist wants to give work to a longtime assistant, it is better to do so with a warm hand (assuming an annual value under $10,000) than a cold one. This may have an income tax disadvantage in that the donor's cost basis is assumed by the donee.

[1] Adjustments to Income Tax Basis

The most important relationship between the transfer taxes and the income tax has to do with the cost basis of the transferred property in the event it is sold

---

60 Crummey v. Commissioner, 397 F.2d 82 (9th Cir. 1968).

61 I.R.C. § 2514(e).

62 Among others, beware of I.R.C. § 2042(2).

at a later date. If property is transferred by gift, the recipient's tax cost is that of the donor. If a gift tax has been paid, a portion of it can be added by the donee to the donor's cost. The amount of the gift tax that can be added is, in effect, the gift tax attributable to the appreciation in the value of the property since its purchase by the donor.

When property is received by a transfer at death the recipient's tax cost becomes the fair market value at the date of decedent's death. This rule applies even if no estate tax has been paid either because, for instance, the estate is too small to be subject to estate tax or the transferred property is exempt as qualifying for the marital deduction. The rule applies also if the estate is not a U.S. estate and therefore not subject to U.S. transfer tax. Thus, the U.S. heirs of a foreign artist can inherit the artist's work and value it for tax cost purposes at the date-of-death value, even if the taxable value in the other country is lower than the property's actual fair market value.

The application of the income tax cost basis rule at death in effect erases the decedent's income tax cost and the recipient has a new, or substituted, tax cost. Therefore property that has decreased in value should, in general, be given away before death, to preserve available losses. In contrast, and if there is a choice of assets to be given, property that has appreciated substantially in value should not be given away because death will eliminate the income tax on the appreciation. Property with a very volatile value should probably be sold at opportune times before death and the cash given away, because the income tax to be paid reduces the value of the estate. If the donee of a lifetime gift makes the sale, then the donor's estate is reduced only by the gift tax and the donee must still pay the income tax.

[2] Income Tax Character of a Transferred Asset

As set forth in § 13.03[A], property created by an artist cannot be eligible for capital gain treatment because it is excluded from the definition of a capital asset. Moreover, that character continues when the artwork is owned by a person whose basis for determining gain or loss is made by reference to the basis of the creator of the property. Therefore a recipient of a lifetime gift of art from an artist also cannot qualify for capital gain treatment. The beneficiary of an artist's estate can qualify for capital gains treatment on the inherited assets by reason of the date of death value having established a new tax cost basis.

[3] Income Tax Holding Period and Capital Gains Tax Rate

The sale of inherited property qualifies for long-term capital gain treatment even when sold within one year of the date of death.[63] This rule may have had

[63] Section 1223(11) of the Code.

its origin in making it possible to pay estate tax without also incurring income tax. There is no requirement, however, that the proceeds of the sale must be used to pay estate tax.

The 20 percent capital gains tax rate does not apply to collectibles. Items of property falling into this category are subject to capital gains tax at the rate of 28 percent. The term "collectibles" includes works of art and no distinction is made as to the method or purpose of acquisition. The beneficiary of an artist's estate is treated in the same way as the purchaser of the artist's work (§ 102(h) of the Code).

[4] Fiduciary Income Tax

An estate and a trust, other than a "grantor" trust (a trust which is ignored for income tax purposes), are separate taxpayers and must file annual fiduciary income tax returns. An estate can select its own fiscal year to end on the last day of a month that is not more than 12 months after the decedent's death. A trust must report its income on the basis of the calendar year.

Both an estate and a trust are entitled to a deduction for the amount of income distributed to beneficiaries. The distributed income is then reported as income by the beneficiaries. The estate and trust report as taxable income the undistributed income after deducting the expenses of administering the estate or trust. The undistributed net income is taxed at the rates applicable to individuals but each tax bracket is much more compressed. With adjustments made for inflation the maximum rate of 39.6 percent is already reached in the year 2000 at $8,650.[64]

[a] Election for Administration Expenses

The executor of an estate has the option to deduct all or some of the administration expenses, but not funeral expenses or debts, either on the estate tax return or on the estate's fiduciary income tax return. The executor must calculate on which tax return to take the deductions to save the most taxes.

If an estate is not subject to estate tax the choice is easy. The IRS took the position that where an estate was not subject to estate tax because of either the marital deduction or the charitable deduction, an adjustment had to be made if

---

[64] The rate schedule for 2000 is as follows:

Not over $1,750	15% of taxable income
Over $1,750 but not over $4,150	262.50 + 28% of the excess over $1,750
Over $4,150 but not over $6,300	934.50 + 31% of the excess over $4,150
Over $6,300 but not over $8,650	1,601 + 36% of the excess over $6,300
Over $8,650	2,447 + 39.6% of the excess over $8,650

administration expenses were then deducted for income tax purposes. The U.S. Supreme Court sided with the taxpayer on this issue.[65]

[b] Election for Medical Expenses

Medical expenses that are paid after death are deductible on the estate tax return as a debt of the decedent or as an alternative, they can be deducted on the decedent's final income tax return. Thus, in the case of an estate that bears no estate tax because of, for example, the use of the marital deduction and the credit shelter amount, the income tax deduction still provides a tax benefit. When possible, medical expenses should be paid before death to reduce the estate and to be income tax deductible.

[5] Income in Respect of a Decedent

If an artist's work is, at the time of death, subject to an agreement of sale, the income received by the estate or the beneficiaries falls into the category of "income in respect of a decedent" (IRD). This income is taxed to the recipient in the same way that it would have been taxed to the deceased artist. If no agreement of sale existed at the time of death, then the beneficiaries can sell the artwork without creating IRD.[66] Moreover, the artwork's income tax basis will be adjusted to the date-of-death value.

In contrast, if an artist has made an installment sale of artwork, the installments paid after death are IRD, taxed as ordinary income. There is no adjustment for the date of death value even though the installment sale agreement is included in the artist's estate at its fair market value. The beneficiaries are entitled to an income tax deduction for that portion of the estate tax that is attributable to the installment agreement.

Other examples of IRD are IRA and retirement plan payouts after death. If an artist has licensed the copyright of artwork, as distinguished from selling the work, then there is no IRD.[67] The difference is that at the time of death the artist had not yet earned the income from the exploitation of the copyright and the income tax basis of the copyright is adjusted to its date-of-death value. The distinction is very important because if a sale has occurred, then amounts payable in the future on a contingency basis constitute IRD.

---

[65] Commissioner v. Hubert Estate, 520 U.S. 93 (1997).

[66] Priv. Ltr. Rul. 9043068.

[67] Priv. Ltr. Ruls. 9549023 and 95490001.

§ 14.04 TAX PLANNING

[A] Equalizing Estates of Married Artists

By the year 2006 the amount of the federal exemption will have been increased to $1 million. This has led to the assumption that a husband and wife can leave a $2 million estate tax-free to their children or grandchildren. This conclusion follows only when each spouse has $1,000,000 and does not leave anything to the surviving spouse. If all or most of the property is with only one spouse and the other spouse dies first a $1,000,000 exemption is lost (if the richer spouse dies first, he or she can leave $1,000,000 to the surviving spouse and $1,000,000 to the other members of the family without incurring an estate tax).

To avoid this result and to take the first estate planning step the "have" spouse must make a lifetime transfer to the "have not" spouse. This can be done by outright gift or by making a transfer in trust that qualifies for the marital deduction without giving the spouse property outright. This type of trust is referred to as a Qualified Terminable Interest Property (QTIP) trust, the terms of which must provide that the income is payable only to the surviving spouse for life at least annually and no one has the power during the spouse's lifetime to appoint the property to any person other than the spouse. The purpose of these requirements is that the principal of the trust must be available to be taxed at the death of the surviving spouse.

[1] Transfer to Noncitizen Spouse

A transfer to a spouse can easily qualify for the marital deduction if the spouse is a U.S. citizen. If the spouse is not a citizen, a $100,000 annual marital gift tax exclusion is available (the amount is indexed for inflation) and any trust must satisfy many specific conditions. The regulations that have been issued to define such an eligible trust, or "qualified domestic trust" (QDT), cover 40 pages of fine print.[68] The alternatives to QDT treatment are paying the estate tax or the surviving spouse becoming a U.S. citizen before the estate tax return is filed.

[2] Credit Shelter Trust

If the surviving spouse does not need the income from the other $1 million it can go outright to the children. If the surviving spouse does need the income, then it should be left in trust for the surviving spouse in a "credit shelter trust." The name derives from the amount that is sheltered from tax by the unified credit, the equivalent of $1 million in 2006. The spouse can be given the principal and

[68] Reg. § 20.2056A.

all the income for life at the discretion of the trustee (the surviving spouse should not be a trustee with the power to authorize invasion). At the death of the surviving spouse, the principal and accumulated income goes to the children or continues in trust until they reach a certain age or for life (beware of GST).

The credit shelter trust is taxed neither at the death of the artist nor at the death of the surviving spouse. The QTIP trust is taxable at the death of the surviving spouse. Therefore if the trust instrument allows for invasion of principal for the surviving spouse, the credit shelter trust can be invaded only after the QTIP trust has been exhausted.

[B] Disclaimers

Mistakes in estate planning can be costly to the artist's estate. Post-death disclaimers can be used to correct some of the errors without additional estate or gift tax provided the qualified disclaimers are in writing and received by the transferor within nine months of the transfer (usually by death).[69] No extensions are possible except that a person under 21 can wait until nine months after reaching age 21.

A disclaimer can be used, for example, where the credit shelter trust gives the surviving spouse too much power over that trust with the result that it could become part of the estate of the surviving spouse. The survivor can disclaim that extra power and have the trust remain outside the survivor's estate.

The tax law on disclaimers is found among the gift tax provisions of the Code. This is so because a disclaimer that is not a qualified disclaimer is a gift.

[C] Valuation

For both gift and estate tax purposes, transferred property is valued at the retail value at the date of the gift or the date of death, if it is property that is generally obtained in the retail market.[70] For estate tax purposes the property can be valued six months later, the alternate valuation date, if that reduces the amount of the estate tax. It cannot be used to puff up income tax costs to reduce future capital gains.

The retail value of artwork to be sold at auction can include the buyer's premium.[71] The value of artwork to be sold by a gallery is not reduced by the gallery's commissions unless the sale takes place to pay estate taxes.[72] In that case the commissions actually paid can be deducted by the estate as an administra-

[69] I.R.C. § 2518.

[70] Reg. § 20.2031-1(b) and § 25.2512-l.

[71] Tech. Adv. Mem. 9235005.

[72] Estate of David Smith v. Commissioner, 57 T.C. 650 (1972), *aff'd*, 510 F.2d 479 (2d Cir. 1975).

tion expense on the estate tax return. This deduction would be in addition to a deduction for funeral expenses and debts and other administration expenses, such as executor's commissions and legal or accounting fees.[73]

[1] Valuing an Art Collection

[a] Need for Appraisal and Penalties

Treasury Regulation § 20.2031-6(b) is very specific about how valuable items of personal property are to be appraised and reported for estate tax purposes. There is no similar requirement for the valuation of real estate. The personal property regulation was adopted in 1958. The dollar amount that, in the aggregate, constitutes "a substantial amount of valuable articles" is only $3,000. This low threshold amount has never been increased, even as related provisions of the Code have been indexed for inflation. The risk created for an executor is that the failure to include an appraisal makes the estate tax return incomplete. As a result, either the statute of limitations may not begin to run or the return may be deemed insufficient to place the burden of proof on the IRS.

Even if the appraisal is complete the more important danger is the possibility of penalties for undervaluation. Section 6662(g)(1) of the Code provides for a penalty of 20 percent of the underpaid estate tax if the reported value is 50 percent or less of the value determined to be correct. Section 6662(g)(2) requires that the underpayment of estate (or gift) tax exceed $5,000.

Section 6662(h) increases the 20 percent penalty to 40 percent in case of a gross valuation misstatement. For estate and gift tax purposes a gross valuation misstatement requires a reported value of 25 percent or less of the correct value.

[b] Valuation Standard

The estate and gift tax regulations begin with the well-known general rule that properties are to be appraised for transfer tax purposes at their fair market value either at time of gift or death, and that fair market value is:

> the price at which the [such] property would change hands between a willing buyer and a willing seller, neither being under any compulsion to buy or to sell and both having reasonable knowledge of relevant facts.[74]

---

[73] The sales commissions that were allowed as an estate deduction in the *Smith* case were for those sales needed to pay the decedent's debts, expenses of administration, and taxes.

[74] Reg. §§ 20.2031-1(b) and 25.2512-2. *See also supra* §§ 10.03 and 13.04[B].

[c] Contents of Appraisal

In the case of household and personal effects the estate tax regulations, but not the gift tax regulations, repeat in Regulation § 20.2031-6 the general valuation rule and follow it with more specific instructions:

1. A room-by-room itemization is desirable.
2. All the articles should be named specifically, except that a number of articles in the same room may be grouped if each has a value not in excess of $100.
3. A separate value should be given for each item named.

The same regulation also provides that the itemized list can be dispensed with in favor of an aggregate value if it is made in a written statement under the penalties of perjury by a "competent appraiser" or "appraisers of recognized standing and ability" or by a "dealer in the class of personalty involved."

The $3,000 rule of the regulations exists as a further requirement for such items as jewelry, furs, silverware, paintings, etchings, engravings, antiques, books, statuary vases, oriental rugs, coin or stamp collections. The value of these items must be made in an appraisal by an expert, under oath. The appraisal must be filed with the return. Paragraph (d) of Regulation § 20.2031-6 provides a number of additional detailed requirements, such as, for paintings of "artistic value," the size, subject and artist's name."[75]

In Revenue Procedure 65-19, 1965-2 C.B. 1002, the IRS prescribed conditions for estate tax valuations of tangible personal property that are based on sales as the result of either an advertisement in the classified section of a newspaper or at a bona fide public auction. These results will be presumed to be the retail value for estate tax purposes if the sale is made within a reasonable period following the date of death or the alternate valuation date. The procedure is limited to items of tangible personal property that

> frequently are obtained by members of the general public at a public auction or through sales which result from advertisements placed in the classified section of a newspaper by individual owners who are interested in selling such items.

The auction alternative can apply to artwork,[76] but the classified advertisement alternative is not the customary method of selling art.

---

[75] In the case of income tax charitable deduction valuations, the IRS has issued even more detailed requirements in Rev. Proc. 66-49, 1966-2 C.B. 1257. These requirements do not apply to gift or estate tax valuation.

[76] With the advent of Internet-based auctions, there are increasingly fewer items that do not fit into that category.

Regulation § 20.2031-6(b) provides that with regard to the distribution of household goods and personal effects in advance of an audit, the IRS must be given notice of that intent. The statement of intent must be accompanied by an appraisal made under oath. After that, the IRS informs the executor whether or not one of its representatives will make a personal inspection of the property. The purpose of the procedure is to afford the IRS the opportunity of making the inspection and to give the executor the chance to stop paying rent or storage fees. If the procedure is not followed the executor risks incurring the expense of arranging for an inspection after the property has been distributed.

Effective for requests submitted after January 15, 1996, the IRS has issued Revenue Procedure 96-15, 1996-1 C.B. 630 to provide a mechanism for obtaining an advance ruling on the value of artwork for income, estate, and gift tax purposes with regard to art appraised at $50,000 or more. In addition to paying a fee ($2,500 for the first three items and $250 for each additional item), the taxpayer must submit an appraisal that satisfies a number of detailed requirements, including a "professional quality photograph of a size and quality fully showing the items preferably an 8 x 10 inch color photograph or a clear transparency not smaller than 4 x 5 inches."

The IRS is bound by its advance ruling, although the taxpayer is not. Nevertheless, the taxpayer *must* attach a copy to the relevant tax return, and, in case of disagreement, the taxpayer can attach additional information to support a different value. A taxpayer can withdraw a request for a statement of value at any time before it is issued.

[d] Commissioner's Art Advisory Panel

If an estate tax return is selected for audit and the estate includes "artwork or cultural property with a claimed value of $20,000 or more," the examining agent must refer the valuation to the National Office Art Appraisal Service.[77] This office decides whether or not to refer the appraisal to the Commissioners's Art Advisory Panel. The members of the panel are independent experts. Its two-year charter was renewed on February 13, 1998.[78] The panel meets twice a year to review several hundred items.

The panel's conclusions are then reviewed by the National Office Art Appraisal Service and a detailed report is sent to the examining agent, who sends a copy to the taxpayer. A taxpayer may request reconsideration of a panel adjustment only by providing additional information or new probative evidence. If the staff

[77] Annual Summary Report for 1995 (Closed Meeting Activity), Art Advisory Panel of the Commissioner of Internal Revenue.

[78] Notice filed with Federal Register on Feb. 13, 1998.

of the National Office deems the new information probative, it is submitted for reconsideration at a later meeting of the panel.

If the information is not considered probative, the panel's determination becomes the position of the IRS. If litigation follows, the National Office and the panel will provide assistance at conferences or at trial.

Although there are many cases that have litigated the value of art objects, most of these have been income tax cases involving charitable deductions. The best known estate tax valuation cases relate to the estates of artists whose own works are to be valued. They are discussed in the following section. The only published case involving the estate of an art collector is *Estate of Robert C. Scull v. Commissioner.*[79]

The facts of *Scull* were complicated by Scull having died during a divorce proceeding in which the value and ownership of the collection was also an issue. The estate's appraisals were initially used in the divorce action which went through a series of appeals, the final appeal being decided after Scull's death.[80] On the estate tax return the executors valued Scull's interest in the collection at 65 percent of $6,799,375, or $4,638,411 (the divorce trial court had awarded Mrs. Scull a 35 percent interest). After a review by the Art Advisory Panel, the IRS issued a notice of deficiency on the basis of a total value of $9,305,465.

The Tax Court received into evidence four appraisals and the results of an auction of the Scull collection held 10½ months after Scull's death and before the estate tax return was filed (an initial extension had been obtained, but the return was, nevertheless, filed late and penalties were imposed). The Tax Court decided that the auction results were the best evidence of value, despite publicity and "hoopla" surrounding the auction.[81] That price included the buyer's premium (there was no seller's commission due under the agreement with Sotheby's). Thereafter the Tax Court applied a 15 percent allowance for appreciation since the date of death after the Commissioner conceded that amount.[82]

The Tax Court also had to consider the value of artwork that was not sold, including additional works not reported on the estate tax return but found by the IRS appraiser. The first group the Tax Court considered were 16 works offered at the auction but not sold. The Commissioner's valuation was less than the amount reported on the estate tax return. The next group was for 42 works that were not offered at auction but were included in the divorce action appraisal. The estate had valued them at $178,725 and the Commissioner at $260,925. The expert

---

[79] 67 T.C.M. (CCH) 2953 (1994).

[80] The first appraisal was made by Sotheby's in 1978, covering 215 items. It was updated in 1984 and again in 1985. Scull died Jan. 1, 1986. The collection consisted of over 350 works of art that had not yet been divided between the warring spouses.

[81] 67 T.C.M. at 2957-64.

[82] *Id.*

witness for the IRS lowered the value at trial to $219,800. The Tax Court lowered that to $219,175 to give effect to lower figures on the statutory notice than those arrived at by the expert.

The third group were items not offered for auction and not included in the divorce proceeding. The fourth and final group consisted of the works discovered by the IRS appraiser.

The Tax Court's valuation of Scull's total 65 percent interest in the collection was $7,550,794, including a 5 percent discount for uncertainty about Scull's interest at the time of death when the divorce action's appeal was still pending. This figure was higher than the original statutory notice ($6,298,422), but less than the value asserted by the IRS in an amended Tax Court answer ($8,179,991) and far above the estate's valuation on the return ($4,446,378).

Even though the case is usually cited to support including the buyer's premium in the value of an art object, it is best to remember it as an example of how not to report an art collection on an estate tax return and what not to do on audit. The original deficiency was $710,727.87 plus penalties of $151,303.76. The amended answer in the Tax Court raised these figures to $1,745,589 and $358,276, respectively, for a total increase over the statutory notice of $1,241,835 before interest. The estate tax as finally determined also exceeded the original notice. Finally, the Tax Court rejected the estate's argument that there was reasonable cause for filing the returns late.

The estate based its argument for abatement of penalties on the illness of the estate tax return preparer and the complexities involved in valuing the estate's liabilities in a number of pending lawsuits. The Tax Court held that the illness of an accountant or other agent is not reasonable cause for a healthy executor's failure to file a return.[83] As to contingencies, the Tax Court held that the executors should have filed a return using only tentative values that could be supplemented later by filing an amended return.[84] After the Tax Court identified the executors as experienced professionals, one an attorney, the other a businesswoman, it went on to state:

> Thus, as the deadline for filing the estate tax return drew closer, ordinary business care and prudence required that the executors utilize whatever information had been gathered and prepared to that point to file a timely return and to continue finalizing information for an amended return at a later date. We agree with respondent that the executors were willfully negligent in their failure to take these steps.

[83] 67 T.C.M. 2958.

[84] *Id.*

[2] Valuing an Artist's Own Work

The first issue to be decided in valuing an artist's own work for estate tax purposes is whether it is being valued as a business under Regulation § 20.2031-3 or as tangible personal property under Regulation § 20.2031-6. If the latter, then all the same valuation rules apply as for a collector, subject to the effect of "blockage" for the artist's entire unsold output coming on the market at one time, the date of death.

A valuation of a business requires complete financial data, including accountants' reports and "a fair appraisal" of all the assets of the business, including goodwill and the demonstrated earning capacity of the business.[85] Therefore the artist's reported income and expenses prior to death must be taken into account.

The definition of a trade or business is one of the most litigated issues in the U.S. tax law. Most of the cases arise under the income tax provisions of the Internal Revenue Code. The most important estate tax provision that gives rise to the same issue is § 6161 of the Internal Revenue Code which allows, under specific circumstances, for the payment in installments over a 14-year period of the estate tax attributable to a trade or business. Presumably the income tax tests can be applied for estate tax purposes. Thus the estate of any artist who has reported income from the sale of artwork on Schedule C of Form 1040 (income from a trade or business) should be able to have his unsold inventory valued as business property, the value of which must be reflected in the value of the business.[86]

The value of the artist's business must be based on the stream of income that was earned. If this is not done and the estate tax value is based on a valuation of each individual item of unsold art, then the artist's estate is being valued in the same manner as the estate of an art collector. This result is unwarranted. The collector has acquired his collection through purchase or exchange from the artist, a dealer, or another collector. At one time each of the objects in the collection changed hands. Therefore it is appropriate to consider a valuation of those objects on the basis of comparable sales.

The works the artist owned at death have never been previously sold. One or more of the artist's other works may have been sold, but that which is to be valued is by definition unsold goods of a business. Despite the difference, the decided cases have looked at the artist's estate as being something other than an ongoing business. Two tax cases and one New York Surrogate's Court decision highlight the problem.

---

[85] Reg. § 20.2031-3(a)

[86] Reg. § 20.2031-1(b). For a detailed exposition of this argument, see David Schaengold, Valuation of Artist's Estates: David Smith, Georgia O'Keeffe and Andy Warhol—Have We Missed the Forest for the Trees, 20 Tax Mgmt. (BNA) Est., Gifts & Tr. J. 225 (Nov./Dec. 1995).

The first case was *David Smith Estate v. Commissioner.*[87] At issue was the valuation of 425 unsold, very large sculptures (out of 500 created by Smith during his life), many of them more than seven feet high. The rest of the estate consisted of $210,647.08 in cash and liquid assets. During his 25-year career, Smith had sold only 75 pieces for a total of $218,000. Before his death Smith, with his career finally becoming financially successful, had made an exclusive representation agreement with Marlborough-Gerson Galleries. The gallery was responsible for storage costs and had agreed not to sell the works delivered to it for less than Smith's "listed" price. The gallery's commission was to be one-third of each item's sale price.

Smith's executors valued the unsold works at $714,000. This amount was arrived at by adding up the prices set by Smith ($4,284,000) and reducing that amount, first by 75 percent as a discount for the works coming on the market all at once, and then by one-third for the gallery's commission. The IRS went to trial with the figure of $4,284,000, the total of Smith's asking prices unreduced by potential commissions or any discounts. This approach was consistent with the regulation's requirement that valuation of tangible personal property be based on the retail price.

In a split opinion (five dissents), the Tax Court disagreed with both sides and assigned a value of $2,700,000 to the unsold works. In its decision the Tax Court referred to having to make a "Solomon-like pronouncement." It did not, however, explain how it arrived at the specific amount, but recognized that it was appropriate to allow a discount for an extremely large number of items of the same category being offered for sale at the same time.

In doing so, the court found a "useful analogy" in the blockage rules used in connection with the sale of securities. The analogy is far from perfect because all 425 Smith works were already available for sale immediately before death. Death did not bring them to the market as would be the case in valuing, for instance, a large block of family-owned shares that were not offered for sale just prior to death. Nevertheless, the IRS has acquiesced in the decision. The more appropriate analogy is a quantity discount or bulk sale price for which Smith's executor had argued.

The estate did not appeal the valuation decision. It did appeal the disallowance of the deduction for additional deductions for commissions. It lost on that issue in a two-to-one decision.[88]

The Tax Court dealt again with the valuation of an artist's unsold artwork in *Georgia O'Keeffe Estate v. Commissioner.*[89] Unlike Smith, O'Keeffe was almost

---

[87] 57 T.C. 650 (1972), *acq.* 1974-2 C.B. 4, *aff'd*, 510 F.2d 479 (2d Cir. 1975).

[88] 510 F.2d 479. See the discussion *supra* at note 73 regarding the amount of the allowed deduction.

[89] 63 T.C.M. (CCH) 2699 (1991).

a household name when she died in 1986 at age 98. In 1983 she sold her own paintings at an average price of $631,250.[90] From 1979 through 1986, 145 works of her art were sold by private galleries. Prices ranged from $6,000 for works on paper to more than $1 million for works on canvas. One gallery sold 5 works for prices of more than $1 million and 25 for prices between $500,000 and $1 million. Auctions at Sotheby's and Christie's exceeded $1 million in 1980 and 1984.

O'Keeffe's estate included approximately 400 works of art. The executors reported them at a total value of $18 million. This amount was arrived at by applying a 75 percent discount to the individually appraised total value of $72,759,000 for all 400 works together. The IRS accepted that total. The disagreement lay in the discount factor. The appraiser for the IRS did not allow a discount for works that were specifically bequeathed in O'Keeffe's will. He assigned the other works to one of three categories of value: More than $500,000 (no discount), more than $200,000 but less than $500,000 (20 percent discount), less than $200,000 (50 percent discount). The IRS determined a deficiency of $6,014,493.[91]

In its opinion the Tax Court agreed with the IRS that O'Keeffe's work should be segmented, but not into three categories. Instead the court relied on the estate's experts to divide the works into two categories: works that were saleable within a relatively short period of time and those to be marketed over a long period of years. The court discounted the first category at 25 percent and the second at 75 percent, thereby arriving at a total value at death of $36 million.

The effect of an overall discount on smaller groups of works of art was before the Tax Court in *Louisa J. Calder v. Commissioner*,[92] when Alexander Calder's widow gave away works of his art that she had inherited. In making the gifts she argued that for gift tax purposes she could use the same discount that had been agreed to in settling her husband's estate. The gifts so reported had a total value of $949,750.

The IRS argued that for gift tax purposes the discount should be based on an assumed rate of sale, and arrived at a value of $2.3 million. The Tax Court disagreed with both approaches and based the gift tax discount on actual sales by the donee trusts. The sale demonstrated that a complete liquidation of the artworks would take much longer than the Service had estimated in its appraisal, thereby increasing the allowable discount. The court's value for all the gifts was $1.21 million.

In most states an executor's commission and sometimes an attorney's fees are set at a percentage of an estate. When the artwork qualifies for either the marital or charitable deduction, the valuation of artwork has no tax significance. The valuation will, however, have an effect on value based on commissions and

[90] 63 T.C.M. at 2700.

[91] 63 T.C.M. 2699.

[92] 85 T.C. 713 (1985).

fees. The resulting litigation can be just as difficult as tax litigation. No case demonstrates this better than the litigation to determine legal fees in the Andy Warhol estate.[93]

The appraisal for the executor and the foundation created by the will arrived at a value for the artwork of $265 million. After applying a blockage discount the appraiser, Christie's, arrived at a value of $103,353,000. The appraiser for the attorney came up with $708 million, without discount.

The Surrogate's Court, applying discounts based on the media involved, arrived at a value of $390,979,278, and awarded a legal fee of $7.2 milion. This amount was reduced on appeal to $3.5 million.[94]

[D] Charitable Deduction

For both the art collector and the artist the simple solution to concerns about the estate tax is to leave the artwork to an organization that qualifies for the charitable deduction. Both the estate tax and the gift tax allow such a deduction.[95] Unlike the income tax deduction, the charitable deduction carries no general requirement that the donee organization be a domestic entity. The "domestic" requirement does exist for gifts made by a nonresident, not a citizen of the United States.

In general, entities that qualify for the estate and gift tax charitable deduction are the same entities that are described as being tax-exempt under § 501(c)(3) of the Code. In addition, transfers to fraternal societies operating under a lodge system and to veterans' organizations can also qualify.

Qualifying charitable transfers are not limited to outright transfers. It is possible to give an individual rights to income for life with the remainder going to charities. These transfers can qualify only if certain income tax requirements are satisfied.[96] The income tax rules require that the charity be a domestic entity, eliminating the use of a foreign charity.

Since the enactment of the estate and gift tax laws the "charitable" deduction is not limited to gifts to charities. The permitted estate tax category is much broader and includes

> religious, charitable, scientific, literary, or educational purposes, including the encouragement of art, or to foster national or international amateur sports (but only if no part of its activities involve the provision of athletic facilities or equipment), and the prevention of cruelty to children or animals.[97]

---

[93] In the Matter of the Determination of the Legal Fees Payable by the Estate of Andy Warhol, Deceased, N.Y.L.J., Apr. 18, 1994, at 29, col. 5, No. 824/87.

[94] In re Warhol's Estate, 165 Misc. 2d. 725, 735, 629 N.Y.S.2d 621, 623 (1st Dep't 1995).

[95] I.R.C. §§ 2055 and 2522, respectively.

[96] I.R.C. § 664 and 642(c)(5).

[97] I.R.C. § 2055(a)(2).

The gift tax provision is nearly identical except that it does not include the fostering of amateur sports. Like income tax-deductible gifts, the charitable-deduction gift rules prohibit donations made in an attempt to influence legislation or to participate in political campaigns.

Both the estate and gift tax charitable deductions are unlimited, regardless of whether gifts are made to a public charity or private foundation. The definition of a "private foundation" looks to the sources of funding.[98] In general, a private foundation is an exempt organization that is not supported by the public.

Chapter 42 of the Code imposes a number of restrictions on private foundations, one of which is the prohibition against owning a sole proprietorship (an "excess business holding").[99] This raises the question, on which there is no published authority, of whether the transfer of an artist's entire inventory of unsold artwork to a private foundation created under the artist's will would result in an excess business holding. The Code contains a provision that gives the private foundation five years to dispose of the inventory.[100] One way in which the private foundation can solve the problem is by transferring the sole proprietorship to a partnership[101] and retaining an interest in the partnership of no more than 20 percent after five years.

The preferred way of solving the excess business holding and other private foundation problems[102] is by qualifying the organization as a supporting organization of a public charity.[103] There are very detailed regulations to demonstrate how close a privately formed entity must be to the public entity to qualify as a supporting organization.[104] To qualify for the most loosely connected supporting organization the entity must satisfy a "responsiveness" test and an "integral" part test. The "responsiveness" test is satisfied when

> [T]he officers, directors, or trustees of the supporting organization maintain a close and continuous working relationship with the officers, directors, or trustees of the publicly supported organization.[105]

The "integral part" test is satisfied by either carrying out one of the functions of the public charity or providing it with such financial support as will lead the

---

[98] I.R.C. § 509.

[99] I.R.C. § 4943(c)(6). The special five-year extension of (c)(7) does not apply to gifts of a sole proprietorship.

[100] I.R.C. § 4943(c)(3)(B).

[101] Reg. § 53.4943-10(e).

[102] Certain restrictions on private foundations, not relevant here, are eased if the organization qualifies as a private operating foundation as defined in § 4942(j)(3).

[103] I.R.C. § 509(a)(3).

[104] Reg. § 1.509(a)-4(i)(1)(i).

[105] Reg. § 1.509(a)-4(i)(2)(ii)(c).

public charity to be attentive to the supporting entity.[106] Moreover, "disqualified persons," such as the donor and the donor's spouse, cannot control the supporting organization.[107] The regulations include an example of a five-person board of trustees, two of whom are disqualified persons; if no one has veto power, and thus do not control, this prong of the test is satisfied. The nonmarital partner of a deceased artist is not a disqualified person.[108]

Within the foregoing framework it should not be too difficult to design an organization created by an artist's or collector's will that establishes a connection with a museum or educational organization and avoids private-foundation status.

[E] Estate Tax Deferral for Business Assets

Section 6166 of the Code provides for a complete deferral for four years for the payment of estate taxes on certain business assets. For an additional ten years, the estate must make equal annual payments to pay the estate tax attributable to a *closely held business*. The value of that business must exceed 35 percent of the adjusted gross estate.

In addition, each year the estate must pay interest on the unpaid estate tax balance attributable to these business assets at 45 percent of the regular estate tax interest rate except that a portion of the tax qualified is for the reduced rate of 2 percent. The amount of estate tax that qualifies for the 2 percent rate ("the 2-percent portion") is the estate tax attributable to $1 million (an amount indexed for inflation after 1997) of closely held business assets. The Tax Court has been given jurisdiction to render a declaratory judgment as to an estate's initial or continuing eligibility for the § 6166 election.[109]

[F] Exclusion for Family-Owned Business

For estates of decedents dying after December 31, 1997, § 2057 of the Code provides a deduction for the "adjusted value of the qualified family-owned business interest of the decedent." The deduction cannot exceed $675,000 ($1.3 million less $625,000), but when combined with the applicable exclusion amount, or unified credit shelter amount, the total cannot exceed $1.3 million. Thus if the full $675,000 is elected when the exclusion amount is $1 million, the excludible amount is reduced to $625,000.[110]

---

[106] Reg. § 1.509(a)-4(i)(3)(ii) and (iii).

[107] Reg. § 1.509(a)-4(j).

[108] I.R.C. § 509(a)(3)(C) and § 4946(a)(1).

[109] I.R.C. § 6601 (j). The Code also provides for a special election with respect to installment agreements that were in effect under the prior provisions of § 6166.

[110] I.R.C. § 7479.

The basic definition of a qualified family-owned business carried on as a single proprietorship includes the following requirements:

1. the decedent was a citizen or resident of the United States;
2. the trade or business had its principal place of business in the United States;
3. the adjusted value of the business exceeds 50 percent of the adjusted gross estate;
4. the decedent or member of the decedent's family materially participated in the operation of the business during the eight-year period prior to death for periods aggregating five or more years;[111]
5. not more than 35 percent of the income of the business in the year of death qualified as personal holding company income (a term that includes, subject to limitations, copyright royalties and produced film rents);[112]
6. cash or marketable securities held in the business do not exceed the reasonably expected day-to-day working capital (the excess is disqualified);
7. assets of the trade or business that produce personal holding company income are excluded; and
8. the trade or business is inherited by qualified heirs. The term "qualified heir" includes not only family members but also any active employee[113] of the trade or business who has been employed there for at least ten years prior to the decedent's death. If the "qualified heir" is not a citizen of the United States a trust with special requirements is needed.

The deduction will be available if all of the foregoing requirements have been satisfied. (Many additional requirements apply if the family business is owned by a corporation or partnership.) However, there will be an additional estate tax if within ten years after the date of death and before the date of the qualified heir's death, any of the following occurs:

1. the qualified heir or a member of the heir's family did not materially participate in the business within the already existing farm property rules

---

[111] This requirement can be a problem if the artist had suffered from a debilitating illness or injury and had not been active for a number of years prior to death. The section provides that rules similar to the farm rules for continuous retirement or disability will apply including the definition of disability ("mental or physical impairment which renders him unable to materially participate in the operation of the farm or other business").

[112] This requirement may be troublesome for estates of authors, composers, filmmakers, or illustrators.

[113] The section itself does not include a definition of "active" or "employee." The legislative history refers to "any individual who has been actively employed by the trade or business."

of another section of the Code[114] for at least five years of any eight-year period within ten years following the decedent's death;
2. the qualified heir disposes of any portion of the business;
3. the qualified heir loses U.S. citizenship; or
4. the principal place of business ceases to be located in the United States.

The recapture of estate tax is 100 percent of the estate tax reduction attributable to the deduction if the qualified heir, or members of his or her family, materially participated in the trade or business after the decedent's death for less than six years. If the participation was for more than six years, but less than seven years, the recapture is 80 percent. The recapture is reduced by 20 percentage points for each additional year of material participation until it is at zero after ten years. Interest will be charged on the recaptured amount.

The legislative history includes an example of a brother and sister inheriting a family business from their father. Only the sister is active in the business. Nevertheless, the brother benefits from his sister's material participation because of the family member rule. If the sister ceases to be active within ten years of the father's death, both sister and brother will be subject to the recapture of estate tax unless the brother begins to participate materially.

In connection with the recapture rules it is important to keep in mind that by specific reference material participation includes *active management* of a business. The term "active management" was defined to mean "the making of the management decision." The regulations that have been issued for farm property have produced a significant amount of litigation and in one case, involving a crop share lease, quarterly physical inspection of crops for approximately two hours per inspection was considered sufficient when added to daily attention to farm market reports, monthly telephone calls to the farm tenant (about one hour per month), annual sessions for a crop plan (about one and one-half to two hours per session), annual post-harvest analysis of cash equivalent rental effects (approximately four hours per year) and occasional long-term management decisions.[115]

The Eighth Circuit decision in *Mangels v. United States* suggests that for an artist's estate, a family member who oversees and manages cataloguers, framers, conservators, curators, and dealers with respect to a deceased artist's unsold inventory may be carrying on the deceased artist's trade or business even if there is no further production of new artwork. When further production is present, as in the printing of additional editions or more castings of sculptures from an existing mold, the artist's estate should be allowed to qualify for the exclusion in all parts of the country.

---

[114] The new section is patterned after this provision because much of the impetus for estate tax relief has come from farmers and small business sources. Therefore it may be difficult, but not impossible, to fit an artist's trade or business (or lifestyle) into the requirements for a family farm.

[115] Mangels v. United States, 828 F.2d 1324 (8th Cir. 1987).

One farm valuation rule that has not been carried over to the small business exclusion is a limitation on the step-up in basis at death. For many years the traditional rule has been to make the date-of-death value of property the "cost" for purposes of calculating a future gain or loss on a subsequent sale. If the special "farm" valuation is elected, that special value becomes the income tax cost for calculating gain or loss on a subsequent sale and not the date-of-death value. There is no similar rule for the new small business election. The date-of-death value becomes the new income tax cost. This is probably an oversight that will be corrected by technical amendment.

In considering whether to elect the new family-owned business exclusion, the executor and the family must be conscious of the possibility that when artwork is sold as part of an ongoing family business, profitable sales, measured by reference to date-of-death values, may produce ordinary income which may then also be subject to the self-employment tax. If the election is not made, the profit may qualify for capital gain treatment. In this connection it is important to note that gain on the sale of "collectibles" remains subject to the 28 percent capital gains tax (or 15 percent if that is the applicable bracket), remembering that the term "collectible" means "any work of art" regardless of how it is acquired or who created it.

FORMS AND APPENDICES

FORM 14-1

Probate Petition — New York County

STATE OF NEW YORK
SURROGATE'S COURT: COUNTY OF NEW YORK

PROBATE PROCEEDING, WILL OF

a/k/a

Deceased.

PETITION FOR PROBATE AND:
[ ] Letters Testamentary
[ ] Letters of Trusteeship
[ ] Letters of Administration c.t.a.

File No. ____________

To the Surrogate's Court, County of New York
It is respectfully alleged:

1.(a) The name, citizenship, domicile (or, in the case of a bank or trust company, its principal office) and interest in this proceeding of the petitioner are as follows:

Name: ____________

Domicile or Principal office: ____________ (Street and Number)

____________ (City, Village or Town) (State) (Zip Code)

Mailing Address: ____________ (If different from domicile)

Citizen of: ____________

Name: ____________

Domicile or Principal office: ____________ (Street and Number)

____________ (City, Village or Town) (State) (Zip Code)

Mailing Address: ____________ (If different from domicile)

Citizen of: ____________

Interest(s) of Petitioner(s): (Check one)
[ ] Executor(s) named in decedents Will
[ ] Other (Specify)

1.(b) The proposed Executor [ ] is [ ] is not an attorney.
[NOTE: An Executor-Attorney must comply with SCPA 2307-[a]; also see 207.19G Surrogate's Court Rules]
The death certificate must be filed with this proceeding. If the decedents domicile is different from that shown on the death certificate, attach an affidavit explaining the reason for this inconsistency.

2. The name, domicile, date and place of death, and national citizenship of the above named decedent are as follows:

(a) Name: ____________

(b) Date of death: ____________

(c) Place of death: ____________

(d) Domicile: Street ____________

City, Town, Village: ____________

County: ____________ State: ____________

(e) Citizen of: ____________

3. The Last Will, herewith presented, relates to both real and personal property and consists of an instrument or instruments dated as shown below and signed at the end thereof by the decedent and the following attesting witnesses:

____________ (Date of Will) ____________ (Names of All Witnesses to Will)

____________ (Date of Codicil) ____________ (Names of All Witnesses to Will)

____________ (Date of Codicil) ____________ (Names of All Witnesses to Will)

P-1 (4-98) Petition for Probate edit rev 07-08-98 ms.wpd

Page 1 of 6 Pages

4. No other will or codicil of the decedent is on file in this Surrogate's Court, and upon information and belief, after a diligent search and inquiry, including a search of any safe deposit box, there exists no will, codicil or other testamentary instrument of the decedent later in date to any of the instruments mentioned in Paragraph 3 except as follows: **[Enter "NONE" or specify]**

5. The decedent was survived by distributees classified as follows: (Information is required only as to those classes of surviving relatives who would take the property of decedent pursuant to EPTL 4-1.1 and 4-1-2. State the number of survivors in each class. Insert **"No"** in all prior classes. Insert **"X"** in all subsequent classes].

a. [ ] Spouse (husband/wife). [ ] Divorced **[Attach copy of Divorce Decree]**

b. [ ] Child or children and/or issue of predeceased child or children.
[Must include marital, non-marital, adopted, or adopted-out child under DRL Section 117]

c. [ ] Mother/Father.

d. [ ] Sisters and/or brothers, either of the whole or half blood, and issue of predeceased sisters and/or brothers (nieces/nephews, etc.)

e. [ ] Grandparents. (Include maternal and paternal)

f. [ ] Aunts and/or uncles, and children of predeceased aunts and/or uncles (first cousins). [Include maternal and paternal]

g. [ ] First cousins once removed (children of predeceased first cousins). (Include maternal and paternal]

6. The names, relationships, domicile and addresses of all distributees (under EPTL 4-1.1 and 4-1.2) of each person designated in the Will herewith presented as primary executor, of all persons adversely affected by the purported exercise by such Will of any power of appointment, of all persons adversely affected by any codicil and of all persons having an interest under any other will of the decedent on file in the Surrogate's Court, are hereinafter set forth in subdivisions (a) and (b).

[If the propounded will purports to revoke or modify an inter vivos trust or any other testamentary substitute, list the names, relationships, domicile and addresses of the trustee and beneficiaries affected by the will in subparagraphs (a) and (b) below. **Submit trust agreement]**

(a) All persons and parties so interested who are of **full age and sound mind** or which are corporations or associations, are as follows:

Name and Relationship	Domicile Address and Mailing Address	Description of Legacy, Devise or Other Interest, or Nature of Fiduciary Status

(b) All persons so interested who are persons under disability, are as follows: [Enter "**NONE**" or specify] (Furnish all information specified in **NOTE** following **7b**]

Name and Relationship	Domicile Address and Mailing Address	Description of Legacy, Devise or Other Interest, or Nature of Fiduciary Status

7. (a) The names and domiciliary addresses of all substitute or successor executors and of all trustees, guardians, legatees, devisees, and other beneficiaries named in the Will and/or trustees and beneficiaries of any inter vivos trust designated in the propounded will other than those named in Paragraph 6 herewith are as follows:

Name and Relationship	Domicile Address and Mailing Address	Description of Legacy, Devise or Other Interest, or Nature of Fiduciary Status

(b) All such legatees, devisees and other beneficiaries who are persons under disability are as follows: (Furnish all information specified in **NOTE** below) [Enter "**NONE**" or specify]

Name and Relationship	Domicile Address and Mailing Address	Description of Legacy, Devise or Other Interest, or Nature of Fiduciary Status

(**NOTE**: In the case of each infant, state (a)name, birth date, relationship to decedent, domicile and residence address, and the person with whom he/she resides, (b)whether or not he/she has a court-appointed guardian (if not, so state), and whether or not his/her father and/or mother is living, and (c)the name and residence address of any court-appointed guardian and the information regarding such appointment. In the case of each other person under a disability, state (a)name, relationship to decedent, and residence address, (b)facts regarding his disability including whether or not a committee, conservator, guardian, or any other fiduciary has been appointed and whether or not he/she has been committed to any institution and (c)the names and addresses of any committee, person or institution having care and custody of him/her, conservator, guardian, and any relative or friend having an interest in his/her welfare. In the case of a person confined as a prisoner, state place of incarceration and list any person having an interest in his/her welfare. **In the case of unknowns, describe such person in the same language as will be used in the process.**)

8. (a) **No beneficiary** under the propounded will, listed in Paragraph 6 or 7 above, had a **confidential relationship** to the decedent, such as attorney, accountant, doctor, or clergy person, except: **[Enter "NONE" or indicate the nature of the confidential relationship]**.

(b) No persons, corporations or associations are interested in this proceeding other than those mentioned above.

9. (a) To the best of the knowledge of the undersigned, the approximate total value of all property constituting the decedent's gross testamentary estate is greater than
$__________ but less than $ __________

Personal Property $ __________ Improved real property in New York State $ __________

Unimproved real property in New York State $ __________

Estimated gross rents for a period of 18 months $ __________

(b) No other testamentary assets exist in New York State, nor does any cause of action exist on behalf of the estate, except as follows: **[Enter "NONE" or specify]**

____

____

10. Upon information and belief, no other petition for the probate of any will of the decedent or for letters of administration of the decedent's estate has heretofore been filed in any court.

WHEREFORE your petitioner(s) pray(s) (a) that process be issued to all necessary parties to show cause why the Will and the Codicil(s) set forth in Paragraph 3 and presented herewith should not be admitted to probate; (b) that an order be granted directing the service of process, pursuant to the provisions of Article 3 of the S.C.P.A., upon the persons named in Paragraph (6) hereof whose names or whereabouts are unknown and cannot be ascertained, or who may be persons on whom service by personal delivery cannot be made; and (e) that such Will and Codicil(s) be admitted to probate as a Will of real and personal property and that letters issue thereon as follows: [Check and complete all relief requested.]

[ ] Letters Testamentary to __________

____

[ ] Letters of Trusteeship to __________ f/b/o __________

__________ f/b/o __________

__________ f/b/o __________

[ ] Letters of Administration c.t.a. to __________
and that petitioner(s) have such other relief as may be proper.

Dated: __________

1. __________ (Signature of Petitioner)

2. __________ (Signature of Petitioner)

__________ (Print Name)

__________ (Print Name)

3. __________ (Name of Corporate Petitioner)

__________ (Signature of Officer)

__________ (Print Name and Title of Officer)

COMBINED CORPORATE VERIFICATION, CONSENT AND DESIGNATION
(For use when a petitioner to be appointed is a bank or trust company]

STATE OF NEW YORK
COUNTY OF NEW YORK } **ss.:**

I, the undersigned, a ______________________________ of
(Title)

____
(Name of Bank or Trust Company)

a corporation duly qualified to act in a fiduciary capacity without further security, being duly sworn, say:

1. VERIFICATION: I have read the foregoing petition subscribed by me and know the contents thereof, and the same is true of my own knowledge, except as to the matters therein stated to be alleged upon information and belief, and as to those matters I believe it to be true.

2. CONSENT: I consent to accept the appointment as [ ] Executor [ ] Administrator c.t.a. [ ] Trustee under the Last Will and Testament of the decedent described in the foregoing petition and consent to act as such fiduciary.

3. DESIGNATION OF CLERK FOR SERVICE OF PROCESS: I designate the Clerk of the Surrogate's Court of New York County, and his/her successor in office, as a person on whom service of any process issuing from such Surrogate's Court may be made, in like manner and whenever one of its proper officers cannot be found and served within the State of New York after due diligence used.

____
(Name of Bank or Trust Company)

BY ______________________________
(Signature)

____
(Print Name and Title)

On ______________, 19 ___, before me personally came ______________________________,

to me known, who duly swore to the foregoing instrument and who did say that he/she resides at

______________________________ and that he/she is a ______________________ of

______________________________ the corporation/national banking association described in and which executed such instrument, and that he/she signed his/her name thereto by order of the Board of Directors of the corporation.

____
Notary Public
Commission Expires:
(Affix Notary Stamp or Seal)

Signature of Attorney: ______________________________
(As required by Part 130 of the Rules of the Chief Administrator)

Print Name: ______________________________

Firm Name: ______________________________ Tel. No.: ______________________

Address of Attorney: ______________________________

COMBINED VERIFICATION, OATH AND DESIGNATION
(For use when petitioner is an individual)

STATE OF NEW YORK
COUNTY OF NEW YORK } **ss.:**

The undersigned, the petitioner named in the foregoing petition, being duly sworn, says:

1. VERIFICATION: I have read the foregoing petition subscribed by me and know the contents thereof, and the same is true of my own knowledge, except as to the matters therein stated to be alleged upon information and belief, and as to those matters I believe it to be true.

2. OATH OF [ ] EXECUTOR [ ] ADMINISTRATOR c.t.a [ ] TRUSTEE as indicated above: I am over eighteen (18) years of age and ***A CITIZEN OF THE UNITED STATES*** and I will well, faithfully and honestly discharge the duties of Fiduciary of the goods, chattels and credits of said decedent according to law. I am not ineligible to receive letters and will duly account for all moneys and other property that will come into my hands.

3. DESIGNATION OF CLERK FOR SERVICE OF PROCESS: I hereby designate the Clerk of the Surrogate's Court of New York County, and his/her successor in office, as a person on whom service of any process, issuing from such Court may be made in like manner and with like effect as if it were served personally upon me, whenever I cannot be found and served within the State of New York after due diligence used.

My domicile is: ____
(Street Address) (City/Town/Village) (State) (Zip)

____
(Signature of Petitioner)

____
(Print Name)

On ______________, 19 ___, before me personally came ______________________________,
to me known to be the person described in and who executed the foregoing instrument. Such person duly swore to such instrument before me and duly acknowledged that he/she executed the same.

____
Notary Public
Commission Expires:
(Affix Notary Stamp or Seal)

Signature of Attorney: ____
(As required by Part 130 of the Rules of the Chief Administrator)

Print Name: ____

Firm Name: ______________________________ Tel. No.: ______________

Address of Attorney: ____

P-1 (4-98) Petition for Probate edit rev 07-08-98 ms.wpd

Page 6 of 6 Pages

FORM 14-2

New York Statutory Disclosure Agreement

§ 2307-a. Commissions of attorney-executor

1. Disclosure. When an attorney prepares a will to be proved in the courts of this state and such attorney or a then affiliated attorney is therein an executor-designee, the testator shall be informed prior to the execution of the will that:

(a) subject to limited statutory exceptions, any person, including an attorney, is eligible to serve as an executor;

(b) absent an agreement to the contrary, any person, including an attorney, who serves as an executor is entitled to receive an executor's statutory commissions; and

(c) if such attorney or an affiliated attorney renders legal services in connection with the executor's official duties, such attorney or a then affiliated attorney is entitled to receive just and reasonable compensation for such legal services, in addition to the executor's statutory commissions.

2. Testator's written acknowledgment of disclosure. An acknowledgment by the testator of the disclosure required by subdivision 1 of this section must be set forth in a writing executed by the testator in the presence of at least one witness other than the executor-designee. Such writing may be executed prior to, concurrently with or subsequently to a will in which an attorney is an executor-designee and must be filed in the proceeding for the issuance of letters testamentary to the executor-designee.

3. Models of acknowledgment of disclosure. The following are models of the testator's written acknowledgment of disclosure:

(a) When set forth in a writing executed prior to or concurrently with a will:

(i) subject to limited statutory exceptions, any person, including an attorney, is eligible to serve as my executor;

(ii) absent an agreement to the contrary, any person, including an attorney, who serves as an executor for me is entitled to receive statutory commissions for executorial services rendered to my estate;

(iii) if such attorney serves as my executor, and he or she or another attorney affiliated with such attorney renders legal services in connection with the executor's official duties, he or she is entitled to receive just and reasonable compensation for those legal services, in addition to the commissions to which an executor is entitled.

____________________ ____________________

(Witness) (Testator)

Dated: Dated:

(b) When set forth in a writing executed subsequently to the will:

I, , have designated my attorney, , [a] [an] [executor] [alternate executor] [co-executor] (delete what is inapplicable) in my will dated

Prior to signing my will, I was informed that:

(i) subject to limited statutory exceptions, any person, including an attorney, is eligible to serve as my executor;

(ii) absent an agreement to the contrary, any person, including an attorney, who serves as an executor for me is entitled to receive statutory commissions for executorial services rendered to my estate;

(iii) if such attorney serves as my executor, and he or she or another attorney affiliated with such attorney renders legal services in connection with the executor's official duties, he or she is entitled to receive just and reasonable compensation for those legal services, in addition to the commissions to which an executor is entitled.

____________________ ____________________

(Witness) (Testator)

Dated: Dated:

4. Compliance. The testator's written acknowledgment of disclosure that conforms or substantially conforms to either model in subdivision 3 of this section shall be deemed compliance with subdivision 2 of this section.

5. Effect of absence of acknowledgment. Absent compliance with the requirements of subdivision 2 of this section, the commissions of an attorney who serves as an executor shall be one-half the statutory commissions to which such attorney as executor would otherwise be entitled pursuant to sections 2307 and 2313 of this article.

6. Rents. Notwithstanding the provisions of subdivision 5 of this section, the additional commissions to which an attorney who serves as an executor may be entitled pursuant to subdivision 6 of section 2307 shall not be diminished.

7. Time of determination of compliance. A determination of compliance with the requirements of subdivisions 1 and 2 of this section shall be made in a proceeding for the issuance of letters testamentary to an executor-designee to whom subdivision 1 of this section applies.

8. Definitions. For purposes of this section, the words or phrases hereafter shall be construed as follows:

(a) Affiliated attorney. An attorney who, by reason of partnership, share holding, association or other relationship, express or implied, could participate directly or indirectly, with an executor-designee in fees for legal services rendered.

(b) Executor-designee. An attorney named in a will or codicil, separately or jointly with one or more persons, as a primary, successor, ancillary, or preliminary executor.

9. Application.

(a) This section shall apply to wills executed on or after January 1, 1996 and, irrespective of the date of any will, to estates of decedents dying after December 31, 1996.

(c) With respect to wills executed prior to January 1, 1996:

(i) subdivisions 1 and 2 of this section shall not apply if the testator has acknowledged the disclosure required by subdivision 1 of this section in a writing that conforms or substantially conforms to the model in paragraph (b) of subdivision 3 of this section; and

(ii) the court in its discretion may waive application of subdivisions 1 and 2 of this section for good cause shown; good cause shall include, but not be limited to:

(A) a good-faith effort after the enactment of this statute either to make to the testator the disclosure required by subdivision 1 of this section or obtain from the testator a written acknowledgment substantially conforming to that set forth in paragraph (b) of subdivision 3 of this section, or

(B) otherwise establishing to the satisfaction of the court reasonable grounds to excuse the absence of a written acknowledgment substantially conforming to that set forth in paragraph (b) of subdivision 3 of this section; and

(iii) section 4519 of the civil practice law and rules shall not apply.

FORM 14-3

Form Will for Unmarried Artist

I, also known as , of New York, New York, do make publish and declare this my last will and testament. I intend for this Will to revoke all former wills and codicils of mine.

ARTICLE ONE: I give to my trustee IN TRUST the sum of $, all works of art made by me, in whatever media and including all my copyright interests, (hereinafter sometimes collectively referred to as the "Art Collection") and all my tangible personal property, to hold or to dispose of the same for such exclusively charitable or educational purposes, including the encouragement of art, within the meaning of Sections 170(c) and 2055(a) of the Internal Revenue Code as will qualify the trust for tax exemption under Section 501(c)(3) of said Code in such manner as my trustee may in his discretion determine (hereinafter referred to as the "trust purposes"). It is my wish, but not my direction, that in the event my trustee determines that the trust purposes are best served by selling all or part of the Art Collection, that so much of the net proceeds of sale as my trustee shall in his absolute discretion determine will be distributed to . My trustee may in his discretion terminate the trust at any time by distributing the entire trust corpus whether in works of art or otherwise to such one or more organizations described in Sections 170(c) and 2055(a) of the said Code as he shall in his discretion select. It is my intent to create a trust which is described in Sections 170(c), 2055(a) and 501(c)(3) of the said Code and the provisions of this will shall be interpreted in accordance with this intent.

ARTICLE TWO: If, were it not for the legacies passing under this Article, my residuary estate, as defined in Article THREE hereof, would exceed the amount necessary to fully fund the (non-lapsing) dispositions made under this Article, but not otherwise, I give the following sums to the following persons:

(i) To my friend , now residing at , if he survives me, the sum of $.

(ii) To my friend , now residing at , if he survives me, the sum of $.

(iii) To my friend , now residing at . or, if he does not survive me, to his issue me surviving, *per stirpes*, the sum of $.

ARTICLE THREE: All the rest, residue and remainder of my property and estate, real and personal, of whatever nature and wherever situated (after paying or providing for all my debts and funeral expenses (including the expenses of my last illness) and any administration expenses of my estate and inheritance, estate, transfer, succession or other death taxes or duties payable out of my testamentary

---

estate by reason of my death), including any property hereinbefore mentioned but not effectively disposed of (but excluding any property over which I may have a power of appointment, it being my intention not to exercise any such power), all of which is herein called my "residuary estate", shall be disposed of as follows:

(a) If the legacies under Article TWO do not take effect because of the pre-condition specified therein about the size of my residuary estate, I dispose of my residuary estate as follows:

(i) I give and devise the lesser of (*a*) $ or (*b*) one-quarter of my residuary estate to my said friend, , if he survives me.

(ii) I give and devise the lesser of (*a*) $ or (*b*) one-quarter of my residuary estate to my said friend , if he survives me.

(iii) I give and devise the lesser of (a) $ or (*b*) the balance of my residuary estate after taking into account the amounts passing under clauses (i) and (ii) of this paragraph (a) to my said friend , or, if he does not survive me, to his issue me surviving, *per stirpes.*

Each (non-lapsing) disposition passing under clauses (i) through (iii) of this paragraph shall have allocated to it a pro-rata share of the net income earned by my estate assets (other than income allocable to specific dispositions) but only to the point where the combined principal and income constitutes such disposition equals the fixed dollar amount specified as the maximum amount of such disposition.

(b) In the event my residuary estate (or any part thereof) shall not be effectively disposed of under paragraph (a) of this Article I give and devise such portion or all thereof which is not effectively disposed of to my trustee to be added to the property passing under Article ONE hereof.

ARTICLE FOUR: I direct that my remains be interred in .

ARTICLE FIVE: (a) All transfer, estate, inheritance, succession and other death taxes which shall become payable by reason of my death (including any federal or state generation-skipping transfer taxes), and any interest and penalties thereon, shall be paid out of my testamentary estate as an administration expense, without apportionment. All such taxes (including any federal or state generation-skipping transfer taxes or any taxes imposed by any foreign taxing authority, be it a country or political subdivision thereof) in respect of any property not passing under this will shall be apportioned against and paid by the persons in possession thereof or benefited thereby, in the manner provided by law.

I direct my executor to allocate all or part of my available generation-skipping transfer tax exemption, as defined in the Internal Revenue Code or corresponding provision of state law, first to any property passing under Article TWO or paragraph (a) of Article THREE hereof that would otherwise be subject to any generation-skipping transfer tax, it being my intention that such property shall either pass free of such tax or be subject to the smallest possible amount of such tax. My executor shall have the power to allocate the balance of such generation-skipping transfer tax exemption to any other property as to which I am the transferor, including any property transferred by me during my lifetime or any property passing outside of this will, and to make any elections concerning the tax on generation-skipping transfers in such manner as he shall in his sole discretion determine.

(b) Any income taxes imposed upon or chargeable to the income of my estate shall be apportioned to and deducted from the shares of beneficiaries having an interest in such income, in such equitable manner as my executor shall determine. Any such determination shall be conclusive as to all persons interested in my estate.

ARTICLE SIX: Anything in this will to the contrary notwithstanding:

(a) Whenever any property, whether principal or income, becomes payable to a person hereunder, my executor or trustee, as the case may be, may instead apply the same for the benefit of such person, and in the case of a person under the age of 21 years or under any other legal disability may do so without regard either to the duty of any individual to furnish support for such person or the availability of other funds for such purpose. Applying principal or income for the benefit of a person under a legal disability may take the form of payment to or application for the use of such person directly, or, in the discretion of my executor or trustee, of payment to such person's guardian committee or conservator, in whatever jurisdiction appointed, or to a custodian for such person under any applicable gifts to minors act including a custodian selected by my executor or trustee (who may select one of themselves as such custodian and who may select attaining age 21 years for termination of the custodianship), or to a parent of such person or an individual with whom such person resides, to be held in either case for the benefit of such person, or to anyone authorized by this will to hold the same as donee of a power during minority, and the receipt of the one to whom any such payment or delivery is made shall be a full discharge from accountability to such person.

(b) Whenever any property held under this will vests absolutely and free of trust in a person under the age of 21 years, my executor or trustee, as the case may be, may retain and manage the same in a doneeship as donee of a power during minority with all the powers, discretions and authorities granted to my executor and trustee by this will or by law, and may pay any such property or the income thereof to such person, accumulating any income not so paid, until such person attains the age of 21 years or until such person's prior death, when any remaining principal and accumulated income shall be paid to such person or to his or her estate. Said donee shall be entitled to receive such compensation as he would be entitled to receive if he were holding the property as trustee of a separate trust under this will and shall not be required to render periodic accounts to any court.

(c) In case any beneficiary of this will and I shall die in such circumstances that the order of our deaths cannot be established by proof, it shall be conclusively deemed that such beneficiary predeceased me.

(d) Whenever property passes under this will to or for the benefit of a person's issue living at his or her death, any issue of such person born alive within nine months of his or her death shall be treated as one of such person's issue living at his or her death.

(e) Whenever a distribution of property is to be made under this will to the issue of a person "*per stirpes*", the initial stirpital division shall be at the level of such person's children, whether or not any child of such person is living at the time of such distribution, with the same principle to be applied in any required further division of a share at a more remote generation.

(f) The term "Internal Revenue Code" whenever used herein shall mean the Internal Revenue Code of 1986, as amended, or any successor law thereto, and reference herein to any particular provision of the Internal Revenue Code shall include any corresponding provision of any such successor federal tax law.

ARTICLE SEVEN: I appoint my attorney   to be the executor of this will and trustee of any trust hereby created. If he shall fail to qualify or cease to act in either capacity, I appoint his partner   , to fill the vacancy thereby occasioned.

I authorize any executor or trustee at any time while acting hereunder to appoint one or a succession of individuals, banks or trust companies to act as his successor in the event of any vacancy in his office not otherwise provided for hereinabove in this Article. Any such appointment shall take effect upon the appointee qualifying according to law and may be revoked or changed by the appointor (provided he is still acting hereunder) prior to the appointment becoming effective. Any such appointment, revocation or change shall be by an acknowledged instrument filed in the court wherein this will is probated. In case of conflicting appointments, the appointment by the executor or trustee who was acting as such first shall prevail over appointments made by any executor or trustee acting subsequently.

I authorize any executor or trustee to resign in any capacity by filing written notice of resignation in the court having jurisdiction of my estate, provided, however, that such resignation shall not become effective until the qualification of a successor fiduciary.

My executor and trustee may settle any account of theirs at any time judicially or by agreement. Where a party to any such judicial proceeding or agreement has the same interest as a person under a legal disability, it shall not be necessary to serve the person under a legal disability, or to make such person a party to the agreement.

If it becomes necessary to have ancillary administration of my estate in any jurisdiction, I appoint my executor as my ancillary legal representative or if my executor is not able or willing to accept such office, or if for any reason there is a vacancy in such office, I appoint as such ancillary legal representative such individual as my executor shall designate, in writing. I direct that any balance of my property remaining after such ancillary administration, unless specifically devised or bequeathed, be delivered, to the extent permitted by law, to my executor for disposition in accordance with the terms of this my will.

Unless the context otherwise requires, all powers, discretions and authorities granted to my executor and trustee by this will or by law shall be exercisable by, and reference to any executor or trustee shall include, any other fiduciary acting in any capacity hereunder, including any administrator with the will annexed, and any survivor, substitute, successor or ancillary executor or trustee and any donee of a power during minority, without the necessity of any application to or approval by any court in any jurisdiction.

ARTICLE EIGHT: I authorize and empower my executor with respect to my estate and my trustee with respect to any trust hereby created to exercise from time to time in their absolute discretion and without prior authority from any court, in respect of any property forming part of my estate or of any such trust or otherwise in their possession hereunder, all powers conferred by law upon executors and trustees, or expressed in this will, and I intend that such powers (including the following) be construed in the broadest possible manner:

(1) Power to determine what property is covered by general descriptions contained in this will.

(2) Power to pay my debts and funeral expenses (including the expenses of my last illness, which I direct shall be paid out of my estate) as soon as the convenience of my estate will permit, and to pay or deliver any legacy without waiting the time prescribed by law.

(3) Power to invest in such securities or other property, real or personal (whether within or without the United States), and to retain any property at any time received or held by them hereunder for such periods as they shall in their sole discretion determine, whether or not the same be income-producing (and any aspect of any diversification requirement that would otherwise apply is hereby negated). Notwithstanding any otherwise applicable law, I direct that upon the sale or other disposition of property which has been unproductive or under-productive of income no part of the proceeds received shall be allocated to income.

(4) Power to sell at public or private sale, exchange, mortgage, lease or grant options on (without statutory or other limitation as to duration), partition, alter, improve, demolish buildings, or otherwise deal with any property, real or personal, upon any terms and whether for cash or upon credit.

(5) Power to borrow in the name of my estate or of any trust hereby created from any person, including any executor or trustee in their individual capacities, such sums for such periods and upon such terms as they shall deem necessary or convenient in the administration of my estate or of such trust, and to secure any such loan by mortgage or pledge. No lender shall be bound to see to or be liable for the application of proceeds and no executor or trustee shall be personally liable, but each such loan shall be payable only out of assets of my estate or of such trust.

(6) Power without the consent of any beneficiary to make distributions (including the satisfaction of any pecuniary bequest) in cash or in specific property, real or personal, or an undivided interest therein, or partly in cash and partly in such property. Any distribution of specific property shall be made at its fair market value on the date or dates of distribution and may be made without regard to the income tax basis of specific property allocated to any beneficiary (including any trust) and without any duty to distribute specific property pro rata among beneficiaries or to equalize the tax basis received by such beneficiaries, any provision of this will or rule of law to the contrary notwithstanding.

(7) Power to hold separate shares or trusts in solido.

(8) Power to pay out of my general estate in respect of any real or tangible personal property situated outside the state of my domicile at the time of my death any administration expenses payable under the laws of the state or country where such property is situated.

(9) Power to compromise and adjust all debts or claims due to or made against them.

(10) Power to employ as custodian a bank or trust company located within the United States, and to acquire, hold, register, or dispose of property in the name of such custodian or agent or a nominee thereof without designation of fiduciary capacity, and to employ legal and investment counsel, accountants, legal and clerical assistants or other agents, and to pay out of principal or income or both the charges and expenses of any such custodian, counsel, accountant, assistant or other agent, and to rely and act or decline to rely or act upon any information or opinion furnished by them.

(11) Power to abstain from rendering or filing any inventory or periodic account in any court.

(12) Power to execute and deliver deeds or other instruments, with or without covenants, warranties and representations and with or without consideration, including releases which shall discharge the recipient from responsibility for property receipted for thereby.

(13) Power to improve any real property and to pay the cost out of principal.

(14) Power to permit any person having any interest in the income of any trust hereby created to occupy any real property forming part of such trust upon such

terms as my trustee shall deem proper, whether rent free or in consideration of the payment of taxes, insurance, maintenance and ordinary repairs or otherwise.

(15) Power to charge to principal such sums as they shall determine to be the net loss incurred in operating or carrying any parcel of real property which in their opinion is not producing net income.

(16) Power to continue or to permit the continuation of any business, incorporated or unincorporated, which I may own or in which I may have any interest at the time of my death for such period as they shall determine, or to recapitalize or liquidate the same upon such terms as in their sole discretion they shall determine, including without limiting the generality of the foregoing power (a) to invest additional sums in any business even to the extent that my estate or any trust hereby created may be invested largely or entirely in any such business without liability for any loss resulting from lack of diversification, (b) to act as or to select other persons (including any beneficiary hereunder) to act as directors, officers or other employees of any such business, the same to be compensated without regard to any such person being a fiduciary or beneficiary hereunder, and (c) to make such other arrangements in respect thereof as they shall deem proper.

(17) Power to elect under section 6166 of the Internal Revenue Code (or under a corresponding statute of any state imposing a death tax on my estate), to defer the payment of the federal estate tax or state death tax for such period as my executor may in his sole discretion determine. In the event such an election is made, my executor may in his sole discretion (i) notwithstanding the provisions of Articles TWO, THREE and FIVE of this will, charge interest on the deferred tax to income or principal in such manner as he determines and (ii) elect under section 6324A of said Code (or a corresponding provision of state law) to create a special lien for the deferred estate or death tax (including tax attributable to property not passing under this will) and may subject property belonging to my estate to such lien.

(18) Power to make or refrain from making adjustments among the interests of the persons affected by the exercise of any elections, options and powers available to my executor or trustee under any applicable tax law. Any action taken or omitted to be taken by my executor or trustee under this paragraph shall be conclusive and binding upon all affected persons and shall not be questioned in any court.

ARTICLE NINE: Each executor and trustee acting hereunder shall be exempt from giving any bond or other security in any jurisdiction, including when receiving advance payment on account of commissions. Each executor and trustee shall be deemed to have acted within the scope of his authority, to have exercised reasonable care, diligence and prudence, and to have acted impartially as to all persons interested unless the contrary be proved by affirmative evidence, and in the absence of such proof shall not be liable for loss arising from depreciation or shrinkage in value of any property herein authorized to be held or acquired. The provisions of this Article shall apply to any other fiduciary acting in any capacity hereunder, including any administrator with the will annexed, and any donee of a power during minority.

IN WITNESS WHEREOF, I have hereunto set my hand and seal this day of , in the year two thousand.

______________________________ (L.S.)

SIGNED, SEALED, PUBLISHED AND DECLARED by , the testator above named, as and for his last will and testament, in our presence, and at his request, in his presence and in the presence of each other, have hereunto subscribed our names as witnesses on the day and year last above written.

______________________________ residing at ______________________________

______________________________ residing at ______________________________

____

Acknowledgement of Disclosure

I, have designated my attorney , as the executor and his law partner , as successor executor of my last will and testament dated 2000.

Prior to signing my will, I was informed that:

1. Subject to limited statutory exceptions, any person, including an attorney, is eligible to serve as my executor;

2. Absent an agreement to the contrary, any person, including an attorney, who serves as an executor for me is entitled to receive statutory commissions for executorial services rendered to my estate;

3. If such attorney serves as my executor, and he or another attorney affiliated with such attorney renders legal services in connection with the executor's official duties, he is entitled to receive just and reasonable compensation for those legal services, in addition to the commissions to which an executor is entitled.

In addition to acknowledging the foregoing disclosure I hereby acknowledge that I have placed on loan with my attorney's law firm for the purpose of serving as office decoration a number of works of art created by me. These works of art and the copyrights thereto remain my property and are returnable to me or my executor upon demand.

______________________________	______________________________
(Witness)	(Testator)
Dated: ________________________	Dated: ________________________

APPENDIX 14-A

Treasury Regulation § 20.2031-6

20.2031-6 Valuation Of Household and Personal Effects

(a) General rule. The fair market value of the decedent's household and personal effects is the price which a willing buyer would pay to a willing seller, neither being under any compulsion to but or to sell and both having reasonable knowledge of relevant facts. A room by room itemization of household and personal effects is desirable. All the articles should be named specifically, except that a number of articles contained in the same room, none of which has a value in excess of $100 may be grouped. A separate value should be given for each article named. In lieu of an itemized list, the executor may furnish a written statement, containing a declaration that it is made under penalties of perjury, setting forth the aggregate value as appraised by a competent appraiser or appraisers of recognized standing and ability, or by a dealer or dealers in the class of personality involved.

(b) Special rule in cases involving a substantial amount of valuable articles. Notwithstanding the provisions of paragraph (a) of this section, if there are included among the household and personal effects articles having marked artistic or intrinsic value of a total in excess of $3,000 (e.g., jewelry, furs, silverware, paintings, etchings, engravings, antiques, books, statuary, vases, oriental rugs, coin or stamp collection), the appraisal of an expert or experts, under oath, shall be filed with the return. The appraisal shall be accompanied by a written statement of the executor containing a declaration of the itemized list of each property and as to the disinterested character and qualifications of the appraiser or appraisers.

(c) Disposition of household effects prior to investigation. If it is desired to effect distributions or sale of any portion of the household or personal effects of the decedent on advance of an investigation by an officer of the Internal Revenue Service, information to that effect shall be given to the district director. The statement to the district director shall be accompanied by an appraisal of such property, under oath, and by written statement of the executor, containing a declaration that it is made under the penalties of perjury, regarding the completeness of the list of such property and the qualifications of the appraiser, as heretofore described. If a personal inspection by an office of the Internal Revenue Service is not deemed necessary, the executor will be so advised. This procedure is designed to facilitate disposition of such property and to obviate future expense and inconvenience to the estate by affording the district director an opportunity to make an investigation should one be deemed necessary prior to sale or distribution.

(d) Additional rules if an appraisal involved. If, pursuant to paragraphs (a), (b) and (c) of this section, expert appraisers are employed, care shall be taken to see that they are reputable and of recognized competency to appraise the particular class of property involved. In the appraisal, books in sets by standard authors shall be listed in separate groups. In listing paintings having artistic value, the size, subject and artist's name shall be stated. In the case of oriental rugs, the size, make and general condition shall be given. Sets of silverware shall be listed in separate groups. Groups or individual pieces of silverware shall be weighed and the weights given in troy ounces. In arriving at the value of silverware, the appraisers shall take into consideration its antiquity, utility, desirability, condition, and obsolescence.

APPENDIX 14-B

Revenue Procedure 65-19

26 CFR 601.105: Examination of returns and claims for refund, credit or abatement; determination of correct tax liability. (Also Part I, Section 2031; 20.2031-1.)

Revenue Procedure 65-19.

Procedure with respect to the valuation for estate tax purposes, of items of tangible personal property sold at public auction or through a newspaper advertisement.

Sec. 1. Purpose

The purpose of this Revenue Procedure is to set forth the procedure for determining the retail sales price of certain items of tangible personal property, which are includable in a decedent's gross estate, for the purposes of applying the provisions of paragraph (b) of section 20.2031-1 of the estate Tax Regulations, as amended by T.D. 6826, page 367, this Bulletin, relating to the valuation of such items.

Sec. 2. Background

Paragraph (b) of section 20.2031-1 of the Estate Tax Regulations, as amended by T.D. 6826, provides that in the case of an item of property includible in the decedent's gross estate which is generally obtained by the public in the retail market the fair market value of the item is the price at which it or a comparable item would be sold at retail. In applying this rule it is necessary to determine the retail sales price of certain items of tangible personal property which, while generally available to a member of the general public at a public auction or through sales which result from advertisements placed in the classified section of a newspaper by individual owners who are interested in selling such items.

Sec. 3. Instructions to Taxpayers and Service Personnel

Where there is a bona fide sale of an item of tangible personal property as the result of an advertisement in the classified section of a newspaper and the property is of the type often sold by owners by such means, or there is a bona fide sale of an item of tangible personal property at a public auction, the price for which it is sold will be presumed to be the retail sales price of the item of the sale. Such retail sales price also will be presumed to be the retail sales price of an item on the applicable valuation date if the sale is made within a reasonable period following the applicable valuation date and there is no substantial change in the market conditions or other circumstances affecting the value of similar items between the time of the sale and the applicable valuation date.

Sec. 4. Effective Date

Since the provisions of section 3 of this Revenue Procedure do not represent any change in the administrative practice of the Internal Revenue Service with respect to the valuation of the items of property described therein, this Revenue Procedure shall be applied in the case of the returns of all estates currently under consideration as well as those which will be considered in the future.

APPENDIX 14-C

Revenue Procedure 96-15

Section 1. PURPOSE

This revenue procedure informs taxpayers how to request from the Internal Revenue Service a Statement of Value that can be used to substantiate the value of art for income, estate, or gift tax purposes. A taxpayer that complies with the provisions of this revenue procedure may rely on the Statement of Value in completing the taxpayer's federal income tax, estate tax, or gift tax return that reports the transfer of art.

Section 2. BACKGROUND

.01 Income Tax Charitable Deduction

(1) Section 17(a) of the Internal Revenue Code allows as a deduction any charitable contribution (as defined in 170(c)) payment of which is made during the taxable year.

(2) Section 1.170A-1(c)(1) of the Income Tax Regulations provides that if a charitable contribution is made in property other than money, the amount of the contribution is generally the fair market value of the property at the time of the contribution.

(3) Section 1.170A-1(c)(2) provides that the fair market value is the price at which the property would change hands between a willing buyer and a willing seller, neither being under any compulsion to buy or sell and both having reasonable knowledge of the relevant facts.

(4) Section 1.170A-13 sets forth that record keeping and return requirements for deductions for charitable contributions. For a deduction for a charitable contribution of property in excess of $5,000, 1.170A-13(c) requires a qualified appraisal and an appraisal summary.

(5) Rev. proc. 66-49, 1966-2 C.B. 1257, provides guidelines for review of appraisals of contributed property for purposes of 170. Section 4.01 of Rev. Proc. 66-49 states that the Service will not approve valuations or appraisals prior to the actual filing of the tax return to which the appraisal pertains, and will not issue advance rulings approving or disapproving appraisals.

.02 Estate Tax

(1) Section 2031 provides that the value of the gross estate of a decedent is determined by including the value at the time of death of all property wherever situated.

(2) Section 2031-1(b) of the Estate Tax Regulations provides that the value of the property includible in a decedent's

gross estate is its fair market value at the time of the decedent's death.

(3) Section 2032(a) provides that the executor may elect to determine the value of all the property included in the gross estate as of 6 months after the decedent's death. However, property distributed, sold, exchanged, or otherwise disposed of within 6 months after death must be valued as of the date of distribution, sale, exchange, or other disposition.

(4) Section 20.2031-6(a) provides that the fair market value of a decedent's household and personal effects is the price that a willing buyer would pay to a willing seller, neither being under any compulsion to buy or sell and both having reasonable knowledge of the relevant facts.

(5) Section 20.2031-6(b) provides that if there are included among the household and personal effects articles having marked artistic or intrinsic value of a total in excess of $3,000, the appraisal of an expert or experts, under oath, must be filed with the estate tax return.

(6) Section 20.2031-6(d) provides that if, pursuant to 20.2031-6(a) and (b), expert appraisers are employed, care must be taken to see that they are reputable and of recognized competency to appraise the particular class of property involved. In listing paintings having artistic value, the size, subject, and artist's name must be stated.

.03 Gift Tax

(1) Section 2512(a) provides that if a gift is made in property, the value thereof at the date of the gift is the amount of the gift.

(2) Section 25.2512-1 of the Gift Tax Regulations provides that the value of the property is the price at which the property would change hands between a willing buyer and a willing seller neither being under any compulsion to buy or to sell and both having reasonable knowledge of the relevant facts.

.04 Legislation Authorizing User Fees

Section 10511 of the Revenue Act of 1987, 1987-3 C.B. 1, 166, as amended by 11319 of the Omnibus Budget Reconciliation Act of 1990, 1991-2 C.B. 481, 511, and by 743 of the Uruguay Round Agreements Act, 1995-11 I.R.B. 5, 14, requires the Secretary of the Treasury or delegate to establish a program requiring the payment of user fees for requests to the Service for letter rulings, opinion letters, determination letters, and similar requests. The fees apply to requests made on or after February 1, 1988, and before October 1, 2000. The fees charged under the program (1) vary according to categories or subcategories established by the Secretary; (2) are determined after taking into account the average time for, and difficulty of, complying with requests in each category and subcategory; and (3) are payable in advance.

Section 3. SCOPE

.01 Except as provided in section 3.02, this revenue procedure applies to an item of art that has been appraised at $50,000 or more, and has been transferred (1) as a "charitable contribution" within the meaning of 170(c) (2) by reason of a decedent's death, or (3) by intervivos gift.

.02 The Service may issue a Statement of Value for items appraised at less than $50,000 if (1) the request for the Statement of Value includes a request for appraisal review for at least one item appraised at $50,000 or more, and (2) the Service determines that issuance of such a Statement would be in the best interest of efficient tax administration.

.03 The Service may decline to issue a Statement of Value when appropriate in the interest of efficient tan administration. If the Service declines to issue a Statement of Value under this section 3.03, the Service will refund the user fee.

Section 4. DEFINITIONS

.01 The term "Art" includes paintings, sculpture, watercolors, prints, drawings, ceramics, antique furniture, decorative arts, textiles, carpets, silver, rare manuscripts, historical memorabilia, and other similar objects.

.02 The term "taxpayer" includes an executor or administrator acting on behalf of an estate, and a donor of gift.

.03 The term "valuation date" refers to the date of death, the alternate valuation date (as established under 2032(a)), or the date of the gift.

Section 5. REQUESTING A STATEMENT OF VALUE FOR INCOME TAX CHARITABLE DEDUCTION PURPOSES.

.01 To request a Statement of Value from the Service for an item of art transferred as a charitable contribution within the meaning of 170(c), a taxpayer must submit to the Service a request for a Statement of Value for an item prior to filing the income tax return that first reports the charitable contribution. The request must include the following:

(1) a copy of an appraisal (as described in section 6 of this revenue procedure) of the item of art;

(2) a check or money order payable to the Internal Revenue Service (user fee) in the amount of $2,500 for a request for a Statement of Value for one, two, or three items of art, plus $250 for each additional item of art for which a Statement of Value is requested.

(3) a completed appraisal summary (Section B of Form 8283, Noncash Charitable Contributions) that meets the requirements of 1.170A-13(c)(4); and

(4) the location of the District Office that as or will have examination jurisdiction over the return (not the Service Center where the return is filed).

.02 A taxpayer may withdraw the request for a Statement of Value at any time before it is issued by the Service. The user fee will not be refunded for a request that is withdrawn. When a request is withdrawn, the appropriate District Director will be notified.

.03 If a request for a Statement of Value lacks information essential to the issuance of a Statement of Value for an item of art, the Service will notify the taxpayer that the request will not be processed for that item unless the Service receives the missing information within 30 calendar days after the date of such notification.

Section 6. APPRAISAL FOR INCOME TAX CHARITABLE DEDUCTION PURPOSES

.01 An appraisal submitted to the Service by a taxpayer under section 5 of this revenue procedure must meet the requirements for a qualified appraisal under 1.170A-13(c)(3)(i)-(iii), and must also include the following:

(1) a complete description of the item of art, including:

(a) the name of the artist or culture,

(b) the title or subject matter,

(c) the medium, such as oil on canvas, or watercolor on paper,

(d) the date created,

(e) the size,

(f) any marks, signatures, or labels on the item of art, on the back of the item, or affixed to the frame.

(g) the history (provenance) of the item, including proof of authenticity, if that information is available,

(h) a record of any exhibitions at which the item was displayed,

(i) any reference source citing the item, and

(j) the physical condition of the item;

(2) a professional quality photograph of a size and quality fully showing the item, preferably an 8 X 10 inch color photograph or a color transparency not smaller than 4 X 5 inches; and

(3) the specific basis for the valuation.

.02 The appraisal must be made no earlier than 60 days prior to the date of the contribution of the item of art.

.03 Taxpayers are encouraged to include in the request any additional information that may affect the determination of the fair market value of the item of art.

.04 The requirements of section 6 on this revenue procedure must be met by Subchapter C corporations, even though they would otherwise be exempt under 1.170A-13(c)(2)(ii)(B)(3) from the appraisal requirements.

Section 7. REQUESTING A STATEMENT OF VALUE FOR ESTATE TAX OR GIFT TAX PURPOSES

.01 To request a Statement of Value from the Service for an item of art transferred as part of an estate or as an intervivos gift, a taxpayer must submit to the Service a request for a Statement of Value for the item prior to filing the federal estate tax return that first reports the transfer of the item. The request must include the following.

(1) a copy of an appraisal (as described in section 8 of this revenue procedure) of the item of art;

(2) a check or money order payable to the Internal Revenue Service (user fee) in the amount of $2,500 for a request for a Statement of Value for one, two, or three items of art, plus $250 for each additional item of art for which a Statement of Value is requested.

(3) a description of the item of art;

(4) the appraisal fair market value;

(5) the cost, date, and manner of acquisition;

(6) the date of death (or the alternate valuation date if applicable) or the date of the gift; and

(7) the location of the District Office that has or will have examination jurisdiction over the return (not the Service Center where the return is filed).

.02 a taxpayer may withdraw the request for a Statement of Value at any time before it is issued by the Service. The user fee will not be refunded for a request that is withdrawn. When a request is withdrawn, the appropriate District Director will be notified.

.03 If a request for a Statement of Value lacks information to the issuance of a Statement of Value for an item of art, the Service will notify the taxpayer that the request will not be processed for that item unless the Service receives the missing information within 30 calendar days after the date of such notification.

Section 8. APPRAISAL FOR ESTATE TAX OR GIFT TAX PURPOSES

.01 An appraisal submitted to the service under section 7 of this revenue procedure must include the following:

(1) a complete description of the item of art, including:

(a) the name of the artist or culture,

(b) the title or subject matter,

(c) the medium, such as oil on canvas, or watercolor on paper,

(d) the date created,

(e) the size,

(f) any marks, signatures, or labels on the item of art, on the back of the item, or affixed to the frame,

(g) the history (provenance) of the item, including proof of authenticity, if that information is available,

(h) a record of any exhibitions at which the item was displayed,

(i) any reference source citing the item, and

(j) the physical condition of the item;

(2) a professional quality photograph of a size and quality fully showing the item, preferably an 8 X 10 inch color photograph or a color transparency not smaller than 4 X 5 inches;

(3) a statement that the appraisal was prepared for estate tax purposes or gift tax purposes;

(4) the date (or dates) on which the item of art was appraised;

(5) the appraisal fair market value (within the meaning of 20.2031-6(a) or 25.2512-1); and

(6) the specific basis for the valuation.

.02 The appraisal must be made no earlier than 60 days prior to the valuation date.

.03 Taxpayers are encouraged to include in the request any additional information that may affect the determination of the fair market value of the item of art.

.04 An appraisal must:

(1) be prepared, signed, and dated by an appraiser, and contain a statement by the appraiser that:

(a) the appraiser either holds himself or herself out to the public as an appraiser or performs appraisals on a regular basis;

(b) the appraiser is qualified to make appraisal of the item of art;

(c) the appraiser is not the taxpayer;

(d) the appraiser was not a party to the transaction in which the decedent or donor of the gift acquired the item of art being appraised, unless the valuation date is within 2 months of the date of acquisition and the appraised value is not less than the acquisition price;

(e) the appraiser is not the beneficiary or donee receiving the item of art;

(f) the appraiser is not a person who was employed by the decedent or is employed by the taxpayer.

(g) the appraiser is not related to any of the foregoing persons under 267(b) or married to a person who is in a relationship described in 267(b) with any of the foregoing persons;

(h) the appraiser is not an appraiser who was regularly used by the decedent or who is regularly used by the taxpayer or the beneficiary or donee; and

(i) the appraisal fee is not based on the appraised value of the item of art;

(2) include the name, address, and taxpayer identification number (if a taxpayer identification number is otherwise required by 6109 and the regulations thereunder) of the appraiser. If the appraiser is acting in his or her capacity as a partner in a partnership, an employee of any person (whether an individual, corporation, or partnership), or an independent contractor engaged by a person other than the taxpayer, the appraiser must include the name, address, and taxpayer identification number (if a taxpayer identification number is otherwise required by 6109 and the regulations thereunder) of the partnership or the person who employs or engages the appraiser; and

(3) include the qualifications of the appraiser who signs the appraisal including the appraiser's background, experience, edu-

cation, and membership, if any, in professional appraisal associations.

.05 The appraisal will not satisfy the requirements of this section if the taxpayer has knowledge of facts that would cause a reasonable person to expect the appraiser to overstate or understate the value of the item of art.

Section 9. TAXPAYER'S DECLARATION

.01 A request to obtain a Statement of Value, any factual representations associated with the request, and any amendments to the request must be accompanied by the following declarations: "Under penalties of perjury, I declare that I have examined this request, including the accompanying documents, and to the best of my knowledge and belief, the facts presented in support of this request are true, correct, and complete."

.02 The declaration must be signed by the taxpayer, and not the taxpayer's representative. The person signing for an estate must be the executor or administrator of the estate. The person signing for a trust or partnership must be a trustee or general partner who has personal knowledge of the facts. The person signing for a corporate taxpayer must be an officer of the corporate taxpayer who has personal knowledge of the facts. If a corporate taxpayer is a member of an affiliated group filing consolidated returns, a penalties-of-perjury statement must also be signed and submitted by an officer of the common parent of the group.

.03 A taxpayer that submits additional factual information on several occasions may provide one declaration that refers to all submissions.

Section 10. WHERE TO SUBMIT REQUESTS

Requests for a Statement of Value should be sent to the Internal Revenue Service, POB 120, Ben Franklin Station, Washington DC 20044, Attn: C:AP:AS:ART.

Section 11. NATIONAL OFFICE CONSIDERATION OF REQUESTS

.01 For a completed request for a Statement of Value received after July 15, but on or before January 15, the Service will ordinarily issue a Statement of Value by the following June 30. For a completed request for a Statement of value received after January 15, but on or before July 15, the Service will ordinarily issue a Statement of value by the following December 31. It is the responsibility of the taxpayers to obtain extensions, as necessary, to file the appropriate tax returns.

.02 If the Service agrees with the value reported on the taxpayer's appraisal, the Service will issue a Statement of value approving the appraisal.

.03 If the Service disagrees with the value reports on the taxpayer's appraisal, the Service will issue a Statement of Value with the Service's determination of value, and the basis for its disagreement with the taxpayer's appraisal.

Section 12. ATTACHMENT OF STATEMENT OF VALUE TO RETURN

.01 A copy of the Statement of Value, regardless of whether the taxpayer agrees with it, must be attached to and filed with the taxpayer's income, estate, or gift tax return that reports the transfer of the item of art valued in the Statement of Value. However, if, prior to receiving a Statement of Value, the taxpayer files an income, estate, or gift tax return reporting the transfer of an item of art for which a Statement of Value was requested, the taxpayer must indicate on the return that the Statement of Value has been requested and attach a copy of the request to the return. Upon receipt of the Statement of Value, the taxpayer must file an amended income or gift tax return, or a supplemental estate tax return, with the Statement of Value attached.

.02 If a taxpayer disagrees with a Statement of Value issued by the Service, the taxpayer may submit with the tax return additional information in support of a different value.

Section 13. EFFECT OF STATEMENT OF VALUE

.01 A taxpayer may rely on a Statement of Value received from the Service for an item of art, except as provided in sections 13.02 and 13.03 of this revenue procedure.

.02 A taxpayer may not rely on a Statement of Value issued to another taxpayer.

.03 A taxpayer may not rely on a Statement of Value if the representations upon which the Statement of Value was based are not accurate statements of the material facts.

Section 14. EFFECT ON OTHER DOCUMENTS

Rev. Proc. 66-49 is modified.

Section 15. EFFECTIVE DATE

This revenue procedure applies to a request for a Statement of Value for an item of art if the request is submitted after January 15, 1996.

Chapter 15

STRUCTURES FOR HOLDING AND TRANSFERRING OF COPYRIGHTS*

Richard E. Halperin

* This chapter, in substantially the same form, was originally published in the Columbia-VLA Journal of Law and the Arts (Vol. 22, No. 4, 1998).

§ 15.01 INTRODUCTION

Whether creative artists are authors, composers, lyricists, songwriters, playwrights, screenwriters, photographers, cartoonists, illustrators, or computer jocks, their efforts may produce valuable and protectible copyrights. Most begin their work without any thought of business structures, estate planning, or taxes. However, in the rare instance when an artist achieves commercial success, these issues become relevant.

There would be little need for a business structure if the artist were able to live forever. However, the mortality of the artist as compared to the relative immortality of the artist's work leads to two important questions that the commercially successful artist must consider with respect to the artist's copyrights. First, how will the copyrights be administered and exploited after the artist's death, especially if the artist has more than one heir? Second, what will the estate and gift taxes be on the transfer of the copyrights?

Two relatively recent developments give far greater flexibility in creating a holding structure. The choice of business entities has vastly changed due to the recent enactment by all states of statutes that allow the creation of limited liability companies, or LLCs.[1] Also of enormous significance is the promulgation of the "check-the-box" Treasury Department regulations effective January 1, 1997.[2] These regulations automatically treat a U.S. domestic LLC with more than one member as a partnership, and disregard as an entity separate from its owner a U.S. domestic LLC with only one member.[3] In the latter case, the LLC's activities are treated in the same manner as a sole proprietorship.[4]

This chapter reviews various copyright law and business considerations and federal income, gift, estate, and self-employment tax issues in an effort to find a business entity or trust structure that will solve more of these problems than any other. No one approach solves them all. However, unless the artist has only one heir, some sort of business entity, such as a corporation, partnership, LLC, or alternatively, a trust, is necessary to maintain control over the copyrights after the artist's death.

---

[1] The LLC legislation is generally quite recent. Although Wyoming enacted its statute in 1977, Wyo. Stat. Ann. § 17-15-101 (Michie 1997), Delaware did not enact its LLC law until 1992, Del. Code Ann. tit. 6, § 18-101 (1992), and New York did not enact its law until 1994, N.Y. Ltd. Liab. Co. L. § 101 (McKinney 1998).

[2] T.D. 8697, 61 Fed. Reg. 66584-66593 (1996), promulgating Treas. Reg. §§ 301.7701-1 through 301.7701-3, effective January 1, 1997.

[3] The treatment under the check-the-box regulations is automatic unless the entity elects to be treated for tax purposes as a corporation. *See* Treas. Reg. § 301.7701-3(a) (as amended in 1996).

[4] *See* Treas. Reg. § 301.7701-2(a) (as amended in 1996). A single-member LLC becomes a partnership when one or more additional persons become members. *See* Prop. Treas. Reg. 105162-97, 62 Fed. Reg. 55,768 (1997).

This chapter does not attempt to review considerations generally relevant to the choice of an entity—whether corporation, partnership, or LLC—through which to conduct business or hold property. The chapter is written on the assumption that the reader either has general familiarity with the various forms of entity or has access to an advisor who does.

The forms of business entity discussed in this chapter are:

- sole proprietorships (including, from only a U.S. federal income tax standpoint, Schedule C/LLCs[5])
- partnerships (including, where the distinction is relevant, general partnerships and limited partnerships, and also from only a U.S. federal income tax standpoint, Partnership/LLCs[6])
- LLCs (which have meaning in the context of this chapter only for nontax purposes)
- corporations (including both S and C corporations)

§ 15.02 STRUCTURAL AND COPYRIGHT LAW CONSIDERATIONS

[A] Initial Ownership

The basic details of copyright law are set forth in detail in Chapter 1. For convenience, certain key concepts relevant to this chapter are restated herein.

The copyright in a work vests initially in the artist or artists who created the work.[7] Copyright law refers to these artists as "authors."[8] The authors of a joint work are co-owners of the copyright in the work.[9] In the case of a work made for hire, the employer or other person for whom the work was prepared is considered to be the author for purposes of the copyright law and, unless the parties have agreed otherwise in writing, owns all of the rights in the copyright.[10]

---

[5] An LLC owned by a single individual and treated under the "check-the-box" regulations as a sole proprietorship is referred to as a "Schedule C/LLC." The activities of a sole proprietorship are reported on Schedule C of the individual proprietor's Form 1040, Individual Income Tax Return.

[6] An LLC owned by two or more persons and treated under the "check-the-box" regulations as a partnership is referred to as a "Partnership/LLC."

[7] *See* 17 U.S.C. § 201(a) (1998).

[8] U.S. Const. art. I, § 8, cl. 8.

[9] *See* 17 U.S.C. § 201(a) (1998).

[10] *See* 17 U.S.C. § 201(b) (1998).

A work made for hire is "(1) a work prepared by an employee within the scope of his or her employment; or (2) a work specially ordered or commissioned for use as a contribution to a collective work, as part of a motion picture or other audiovisual work, as a translation, as a supplementary work, as a compilation, as an instructional text, as a test, as answer material for a test, or as an atlas, if the parties expressly agree in a written instrument signed by them that the work shall be considered a work made for hire." 17 U.S.C. § 101 (1994).

[B] Transfer and Fragmentation of Copyright Ownership

[1] Transfer of Copyright Ownership

The ownership of a copyright may be transferred by any written means of conveyance.[11] The owner of a copyright may, for example, sell it, transfer it by gift, transfer it in trust, or transfer it to a partnership, corporation, or LLC. The ownership of a copyright also may be transferred by operation of law and may be bequeathed by will, or else pass as personal property by the applicable laws of intestate succession.[12]

[2] Risks of Fragmented Copyright Ownership

Unless the artist has only one person to whom she wishes to transfer her copyrights upon her death, ownership of the copyrights will become fragmented when transferred to more than one legatee under the artist's will. Similarly, if the artist dies without a will, the ownership of her copyrights will become fragmented unless there is only one surviving intestate distributee of her estate. Intestate distribution laws seem to favor multiple beneficiaries.[13]

Fragmentation of copyright ownership creates very serious administrative problems because it results in fragmentation of control. In the United States, each joint owner of the copyright can, without the consent of the other co-owner or co-owners, exploit the work herself or grant a nonexclusive license to others.[14] This can result in chaotic exploitation of the copyrights.

Moreover, in most foreign countries, a license is not valid unless it is granted by all of the joint owners.[15] This difference between U.S. law and foreign law makes it more important to avoid fragmentation of control when international exploitation of the artistic work is to be undertaken. Even more significant, however, is that for most important transactions it is necessary to grant exclusive rights in the copyrights.[16] A grant of exclusive rights requires the action of all of the co-owners and must be in writing.[17]

---

[11] *See* 17 U.S.C. §§ 201(d)(1), 204(a) (1998).

[12] *See* 17 U.S.C. § 201(d)(1) (1998).

[13] For example, under New York law, if a decedent dies intestate and is survived by both a spouse and issue, the spouse receives $50,000 plus one-half of the residue and the issue receive the remainder *per stirpes*. *See* N.Y. Est. Powers & Trusts § 4-1.1(a)(1) (McKinney Supp. 1998).

[14] *See* 1 Melville B. Nimmer & David Nimmer, Nimmer on Copyright § 6.10 (1997) and the cases cited therein.

[15] *See id.*, § 6.10[C].

[16] The reason for this is simply that a licensee often will not undertake a major publication, advertising campaign or theatrical or motion picture production without exclusive rights.

[17] *See* 17 U.S.C. § 204(a) (1998).

[3] Using Entities or Trusts to Prevent Fragmentation

The artist can prevent splintering of control simply by transferring the ownership of the copyrights to an entity or a trust before her death or to a trust upon her death. However, transfer of the copyrights to an entity or trust does not in all cases permanently prevent fragmentation of control. Under U.S. copyright law, certain transfers or licenses of copyrights are subject to termination. If the termination right is exercised, it could nullify the initial transfer of the copyrights and vest ownership of the copyrights in those persons who have the statutory right of termination.

[4] Termination of Transfers

Any non-testamentary transfer or license of a copyright or any right thereunder, in a work not made for hire, made by its author after 1977, is subject to termination.[18] If the right to terminate is exercised, all rights that were covered by the terminated grants revert to the author or other statutory possessors of the nontransferable termination interest.[19]

In general, the grant can be terminated during the five-year period that begins thirty-five years from the date of the execution of the grant.[20] The right to terminate is vested in the author if the grant was executed by only one author.[21] If the grant was executed by two or more authors of a joint work, termination is effected by a majority of the authors who executed it.[22] Where an author has died, her termination right is exercisable by her surviving spouse if she has no surviving issue and vice versa.[23] If the author is survived by a spouse and also by issue, each owns half of the termination right.[24] Whenever a right is to be exercised on behalf of someone who has died, a majority in interest of the persons standing in the deceased person's stead have the power to exercise that right.[25] The right to terminate is vested in those persons specified in the copyright law, regardless of the artist's estate plan; accordingly, the artist cannot transfer the right to terminate.[26]

The right to terminate a grant is generally regarded as a benefit to artists, enabling them to get back rights that may have changed enormously in value

---

[18] *See* 17 U.S.C. § 203(a) (1998).

[19] *See* 17 U.S.C. § 203(b) (1998).

[20] *See* 17 U.S.C. § 203(a)(3) (1998). If the grant covers the right of publication of the work, the period begins at the end of 35 years from the date of publication of the work under the grant or at the end of 40 years from the date of execution of the grant, whichever term ends earlier.

[21] *See* 17 U.S.C. § 203(a)(1) (1998).

[22] *See id.*

[23] *See* 17 U.S.C. § 203(a)(2) (1998).

[24] *See id.*

[25] *See* 17 U.S.C. § 203(a)(2)(C) (1998).

[26] *See* 17 U.S.C. § 203(a) (1998).

since the time when the original grant was negotiated. However, if the artist has died at the time when the termination right becomes exercisable, it is the copyright law, and not the artist, that determines who has the right to terminate.

[C] Ownership of Copyrights by an Entity or Trust

Copyrights owned by an artist with two or more heirs will be subject to splintered ownership and control upon the death of the artist.[27] This problem can be cured by having the copyrights owned by an entity or a trust, which allows the artist to transfer interests in the copyright at or before death. The ownership of the copyrights by the entity or trust can be effected in one of two ways: by assigning copyrights, or by structuring the initial creation of the copyrighted expression as a work made for hire.

[1] Assignment of Copyrights

One method of vesting ownership of the copyrights in an entity or in a trust is for the artist to assign ownership. As with all grants of copyrights or interests in copyrights made by the author (other than by will), such a transfer is terminable by the artist or, if the artist has died, by the artist's spouse and issue as provided in the copyright law.[28]

[a] Tax Treatment of Copyrights Assigned to Entities

In analogous situations, the Internal Revenue Service (IRS) formerly took the position that the assignee of the copyright was not the true owner of the copyright, but was only the assignee of income earned by the artist.[29] In such a case, the artist would still be subject to tax on the income earned by the entity and the entity's ownership arrangement (stock in the case of a corporation, and income allocation in the case of a partnership or partnership/LLC) would have no effect for income tax purposes.

[b] Royalties Taxable to Transferee

After cases involving copyright transfers were decided in the taxpayer's favor, the IRS issued relevant private letter rulings to the effect that an author can write a manuscript, enter into a publishing contract, and transfer the rights in the contract; as a result, the royalties under the contract are taxable to the

---

[27] As discussed *supra*, the copyrights may pass either under the artist's will or by the laws of intestacy.

[28] *See* 17 U.S.C. § 203 (1998).

[29] *See, e.g.*, Wodehouse v. Commissioner, 8 T.C. 637, 650, 653 (1947).

transferee, rather than the author.[30] This result applies even more clearly when the artist has transferred the copyrights to the entity, which then enters into contractual arrangements with third parties.[31]

[2] Works Made for Hire

In the case of a legal entity such as a corporation, partnership, or LLC,[32] the artist can create the work as a work made for hire,[33] which has both copyright and tax effects that are quite different from those that relate to an assignment of the copyrights by the artist to the entity.[34] The effect on the copyright itself is twofold: duration of the copyright is fixed at the earlier of 95 years from publication or 120 years from creation, rather than the life of the artist plus 70 years;[35] and the right of termination of a grant of a copyright does not apply.[36]

[a] No Termination Rights in Works Made for Hire

The work-made-for-hire procedure prevents the artist (or, if applicable, the heirs) from terminating the entity's rights in the copyrights. This can be detrimental

---

[30] *See* Priv. Ltr. Ruls. 8217037 (Jan. 27, 1982), 8337055 (June 14, 1983), 8444073 (July 31, 1984); *cf.* Priv. Ltr. Rul. 5709235380A (Sept. 23, 1957) (ineffective transfer of corpus precludes transfer of tax liability). A closely analogous case dealing with an inventor and his patent is Heim v. Fitzpatrick, 262 F.2d 887 (2d Cir. 1959).

[31] *See* Rev. Rul. 71-33, 1971-1 C.B. 30. In that ruling, an author made a gift of an unpublished manuscript to a foundation. The foundation thereafter entered into a publishing agreement. The IRS held that the royalties received by the foundation were not income to the author. *See also* Wodehouse v. Commissioner, 177 F.2d 881 (2d Cir. 1949).

[32] A work made for hire would not typically be created for a trust because the artist would not typically be its employee.

[33] If this procedure is followed, there should be a written agreement between the artist and the entity specifying that the works are being created by the artist as an employee of the entity within the scope of the artist's employment. *See* 17 U.S.C. § 101 (1994).

[34] Given the substantive effect under the copyright law, it is unlikely that the IRS would challenge the entity's right to the royalty income in such a work-made-for-hire arrangement. In a somewhat different context, the IRS has stated:

> Provided that the corporate formalities are properly followed and at least one non-tax business purpose exists, the corporate form is generally recognized for both state law and federal law, including federal tax, purposes. Disregarding the corporate entity is generally an extraordinary remedy, applied by most courts only in cases of clear abuse.

Internal Revenue Service, Independent Contractor or Employee?: Training Materials, at 2-23 (Oct. 30, 1996).

The IRS states explicitly that the guide was designed only for training IRS personnel and "[u]nder no circumstances should the contents be used or cited as authority for setting or sustaining a technical position." *Id.* Nevertheless, the guide does give some indication of the IRS's thinking on the subject.

[35] *See* 17 U.S.C. §§ 302(c), (a) (1998).

[36] *See supra* text accompanying note 10.

to the person who would otherwise hold the termination right if the entity has, for example, licensed the copyrights under terms that are no longer favorable to the artist or heirs. In such case, an assignment to the entity would have been preferable, so that the assignment could be terminated, along with the unfavorable license. On the other hand, the work-made-for-hire procedure can be beneficial, for example, in that it enables the artist to transfer ownership in the entity to a friend without fear that some day a surviving spouse or issue would eviscerate the entity by terminating the assignment of the copyrights to the entity.

[b] Income Tax Effects of Works Made for Hire

Compared with an assignment of the copyrights from the artist to the entity, the work-made-for-hire arrangement will tend to draw compensation income out of the entity and into the hands of the artist, and will make that income "wages" for employment tax purposes.[37] Drawing income into the artist's hands will interfere with spreading that income; since spreading income is one of the tax benefits that people often wish to achieve by using a partnership or LLC structure, structuring authorship as a work made for hire may conflict with the artist's desire.[38] On the other hand, drawing income out of the entity results in its lower net income and thus, may result in a lower valuation upon a gift of interests in the entity.[39]

[3] Income Taxes on Sale or Exchange of Interests in an Entity

Although the focus of this chapter is the continued holding of economic interests in the copyright by the artist and her heirs, it is also important to consider the tax consequences of discontinuing those interests. The artist may receive an attractive offer to sell the copyrights. A sale of a copyright by a corporation, partnership, or trust would be a taxable transaction. A sale by a stockholder of stock in a corporation, by a partner of a partnership interest, or by a beneficiary of a beneficial interest in a trust would also be taxable.

However, an exchange by a stockholder of stock in one corporation for stock of another corporation can sometimes be structured as a "tax-free" reorganization,

---

[37] The reason for this is that, under the copyright law, the artist would generally have to be an employee of the entity in order to create a work-made-for-hire relationship. The employment relationship leads to the need for compensation for services and the characterization of that compensation as "wages."

[38] Drawing income out of the entity is helpful with a C corporation. However, as discussed *infra* at §§ 15.03[A][2][b] and 15.03[B][2][a], a C corporation is so ill suited for the holding of copyrights by an artist that it should rarely, if ever, be used.

[39] In this case, lower net income is relevant only with respect to lifetime transfers. The reason, typically, is that the compensation to the artist will cease upon the artist's death. Thereafter, the entity may experience large net income because it is no longer making compensation payments.

the result of which is that the tax is postponed until the sale or exchange of the stock received in the transaction.[40] Such a transaction generally cannot be accomplished with a partnership or a trust. Although transactions of this kind are rarely used to acquire corporations owning copyrights, the technique exists and can be applied in appropriate circumstances.[41]

[4] Gift and Estate Tax Considerations

An artist reaps an enormous gift tax advantage by transferring interests in the entity during the artist's lifetime. If the artist transfers shares of a corporation, a partnership interest, or a membership interest in an LLC, the amount of the gift for gift tax purposes is determined by reference to the interest transferred.[42] This calculation is different from that used for the copyrights owned by the entity.[43]

[a] Tax Benefits of Spreading Minority Interests

Typically, the artist will make gifts over a number of years to various family members. Each such gift will be of a minority interest in the entity.[44] In valuing minority interests in closely-held entities, the courts have generally allowed two discounts, one for the lack of marketability of an interest in a closely-held entity, and the other for the lower values associated with minority positions. Both vary quite widely and the actual discounts ultimately allowed by the courts have much to do with the persuasiveness of the testimony of the competing valuation experts. The combined effect of the discounts usually will result in a reduction of between 30 and 40 percent. There are some indications, however, that courts have been shaving the discounts over the years.[45] Certainly, those who intend to avail themselves of these discounts should engage an expert appraiser who can rationally

---

[40] *See generally* 26 U.S.C. §§ 354(a); 358(a); 361(a); 368(a) (1964).

[41] For example, it is possible that a public entertainment company would be interested in acquiring the stock of a corporation that owned a song catalogue and that the stockholders of that corporation would be interested in owning, and holding, the stock of the public entertainment company.

[42] *See* Rev. Rul. 59-60, 1959-1 C.B. 237.

[43] In general, the value of an entity's assets is only one of the factors considered in valuing an interest in the entity. *See id.*

[44] One important reason to spread gifts over several years is to take advantage of the $10,000 per year per donee gift tax exclusion. *See* 26 U.S.C. § 2503(b) (1994). After 1998, the $10,000 amount is to be increased by a cost-of-living adjustment. *See* 26 U.S.C. § 2503(b)(2) (1994). A gift cannot qualify for the exclusion if it is a gift of a "future interest in property." An outright gift (not in trust) of stock or of a partnership interest generally should be considered to be a "present interest" rather than a "future interest." *See supra* text accompanying note 6 for a discussion of the gift tax annual exclusion.

[45] *See* Melanie J. Earles & Edward E. Milam, Valuations of Closely-Held Businesses and the Tax Court: Are the Discount Percentages Changing?, 75 Taxes 512 (1997).

determine and persuasively defend appropriate discounts. The IRS knows that these discounts are being taken because the gift tax return now requires disclosure, and even conservative discounts are often challenged.[46]

[b] Minority Discounts and the Family-Owned Entity

Much has been written on these discounts, and a review of all of the considerations is beyond the scope of this chapter. However, one issue that continues to draw considerable attention is the applicability of minority discounts in the context of the family partnership or the family-owned corporation. In the prototypical structure, the artist creates the partnership or corporation and then makes gifts of interests in the partnership or corporation during the artist's lifetime to children or other family members. After the gifts, all of the ownership of and control over the partnership or corporation is still owned within the family.

The IRS used to take the position that a minority shareholder discount is not ordinarily allowed with respect to transfers of shares of stock between family members if, based upon a composite of the family members' interests at the time of the transfer, control of the corporation—either majority voting control or de facto control through family relationships—exists in the family unit.[47]

However, after consistently losing in the courts,[48] the IRS officially changed its position in a Revenue Ruling issued in 1993.[49] That ruling considered gifts by a parent who owned all of the single outstanding class of stock of a corporation. The parent transferred all of the parent's shares by making simultaneous gifts of 20 percent of the shares to each of the parent's five children. The IRS concluded that in the case of a corporation with a single class of stock, notwithstanding the family relationship of the donor, the donee, and other shareholders, the shares of other family members will not be aggregated with the transferred shares to determine whether the transferred shares should be valued as part of a controlling interest.

---

[46] The Instructions for Form 709, United States Gift (and Generation-Skipping Transfer) Tax Return (rev. Dec. 1996), at 4, require that, if the value of any gift reported reflects a discount for "lack of marketability, a minority interest, a fractional interest in real estate, blockage, market absorption, or for any other reason," the taxpayer must answer "yes" to a question ("Does the value of any item listed . . . reflect any valuation discount?") on Schedule A to Form 709 and attach to the return an explanation giving the factual basis for the claimed discounts and the amount of the discounts taken.

[47] *See* Rev. Rul. 81-253, 1981-2 C.B. 187.

[48] *See, e.g.*, Estate of Bright v. United States, 658 F.2d 999 (5th Cir. 1981); Propstra v. United States, 680 F.2d 1248 (9th Cir. 1982); Estate of Andrews v. Commissioner, 79 T.C. 938 (1982); Estate of Lee v. Commissioner, 69 T.C. 860 (1978), *nonacq.* 1980-2 C.B. 2.

[49] Rev. Rul. 93-12, 1993-1 C.B. 202.

There have been indications that the IRS has not been content with this position and is attempting to whittle it away.[50] One such attempt has involved the attribution of "swing vote" potential to a block of stock that must be taken into account in valuing the stock.[51] In other situations the IRS has disregarded deathbed transfers to family limited partnerships or corporations in situations where there was no apparent business[52] purpose.[53] In the case of an artist who has formed a partnership or corporation, the business purpose requirement should be met by the desire to maintain management and prevent fragmented legal ownership of the copyrights. This nontax business purpose should enable artists to overcome any IRS argument that there is no substantial business purpose, and thereby should enable artists to obtain the estate and gift tax benefits.[54]

---

[50] One of the more dramatic attempts to limit the use of family partnership for estate and gift tax benefits is the partnership anti-abuse regulations in Treas. Reg. § 1.701-2 (as amended in 1995). As originally promulgated on January 3, 1995, the regulation applied not only to income tax but also to estate, gift, generation-skipping and excise tax. *See* T.D. 8588, 60 Fed. Reg. 23, 24 (1995). On April 13 of that same year, the regulation was amended to provide that it applies solely to income taxes. However, the preamble to the amendment states that "no inference is intended as to the treatment under current law of transactions not covered by the regulation." T.D. 8592, 60 Fed. Reg. 18741 (1995).

[51] *See, e.g.*, Tech. Adv. Mem. 9436005 (May 26, 1994) ("In determining the fair market value of three 30 percent blocks of stock transferred by the donor, the swing vote attributes of each block are factors to be taken into consideration in determining the value of each block."); *see also* Tech. Adv. Mem. 9449001 (Mar. 11, 1994). The swing vote is the ability of one shareholder or partner to join with another and gain control of the business entity. *See* Steven A. Horowitz & Alfred S. Scope, IRS on Minority Interest Discounts: It Don't Mean a Thing If It Still Got That Swing, 73 Taxes 76 (1995).

[52] The partnership anti-abuse rules acknowledge that investment activities are included in the business activities that partnerships can legitimately be used to conduct. *See* Treas. Reg. § 1.701-2(a) (as amended in 1995).

[53] *See, e.g.*, Tech. Adv. Mem. 9725002 (Mar. 3, 1997), in which a family limited partnership was organized less than two months before the decedent's death. The National Office disregarded the partnership for estate tax valuation purposes based, among other theories, on the position that the formation of the partnership and the transfer of the partnership interests in the decedent's will were a single testamentary transaction. *See also* Tech. Adv. Mems. 9723009 (Feb. 24, 1997) and 9719006 (Jan. 14, 1997).

[54] One very important barrier to obtaining the gift tax benefits described above is the "special use valuation" rules of Chapter 14 of the Code. *See* 26 U.S.C. §§ 2701-04 (1994). These rules would reduce the value of the stock or partnership interest retained by the donor and thereby increase the value of the gift. However, the special use valuation rules do not apply "if the retained interest is of the same class of equity as the transferred interest or if the retained interest is of a class that is proportional to the class of the transferred interest. A class is the same class as (or is proportional to the class of) the transferred interest if the rights are identical (or proportional) to the rights of the transferred interest, except for non-lapsing differences in voting rights (or, for a partnership, non-lapsing differences with respect to management and limitations on liability)." Treas. Reg. § 25.2701-1(c)(3) (as amended in 1992). As a result, the kinds of transfers described in this chapter should not implicate Chapter 14.

[c] Control Premiums

The corollary to the minority discount is the control premium. If a block of stock or partnership or LLC interest represents a controlling interest in the enterprise, the value of that stock or interest will be enhanced by the control that it enables the owner to wield. If the artist dies while still owning the controlling interest, her estate may suffer the control premium in valuing the estate for estate tax purposes. On the other hand, if the artist makes enough lifetime gifts of minority interests, the artist can be left with only a minority position at death so that minority discounts can be taken both for gift and estate tax purposes.

[5] Trusts as an Alternative to Entities

The splintering of ownership and control of copyrights can also be prevented by the use of one or more trusts. In the typical pattern, the artist will create a trust, either during her lifetime or under her will, to hold the copyrights. The trustee should be someone with experience in dealing with the type of property involved.[55]

If the copyrights are transferred to the trust upon the artist's death, the full value of the copyrights will be included in the artist's estate for estate tax purposes. At least theoretically, transfers during the artist's lifetime, if carefully structured and drafted, can save both estate and gift taxes.

[a] Fractional Interest Discount

A gift of a fractional interest in a piece of property is subject to a discount analogous to that applied to minority interests in partnerships or corporations.[56] Theoretically, the artist can make gifts of fractional interests in copyrights to one or more trusts for different beneficiaries and thereby obtain a discount with respect to the value of the fractional interest donated. In order to prevent splintering control over the copyrights when separate trusts are used, the same person should be trustee of all the trusts. The IRS could take the position that the separate transfers to the same trustee should be aggregated in determining the minority interest discount;[57] however, based on the authority relating to intra-family gifts of minority interests in partnerships and corporations, the IRS should not prevail.[58]

---

[55] Many artists are tempted to select their agent as trustee because of the agent's familiarity with the artist's work and the market for the work. However, potential conflicts of interests should be carefully considered. In addition, the extent of the trustee's compensation should be considered, *i.e.*, the agent's fee, a trustee's commission, or both. *See generally supra* § 14.02[C].

[56] *See, e.g.*, Propstra v. United States, 680 F.2d 1248 (9th Cir. 1982); Stewart v. Commissioner, (ex rel. Will of Stewart), 31 B.T.A. 201 (1934), *acq.* 1955-2 C.B. 9; Estate of Herter v. Commissioner, 13 T.C.M. (CCH) 298 (1954), all dealing with fractional interests in real estate.

[57] *See, e.g.*, Rev. Rul. 81-253, 1981-1 C.B. 187.

[58] *See* Rev. Rul. 93-12, 1993-1 C.B. 202 and the cases cited therein.

[b] Donor's Control Must Be Limited

If the artist is the trustee, the trust instrument must be carefully drafted so as to avoid giving the artist the types of control over the trust that would cause the inclusion of the trust property in the artist's estate. For example, the power to distribute income to various persons, either alone or in conjunction with another person, will cause the inclusion of the trust property in the artist's estate.[59] The power of the artist to alter, amend, or revoke the trust will also cause the trust property to be included.[60]

[c] The Gift Tax Exclusion and Future Interests in Property

The donor of a gift is entitled to a gift tax exclusion of $10,000 per year per donee.[61] A gift of a "future interest in property" cannot qualify for the exclusion.[62] In general, transfers in trust are "future interests" because the beneficiary of the trust does not have an unrestricted right to the immediate use, possession, or enjoyment of the trust property or the income from the property.[63]

In order for such transfer to qualify for the annual gift tax exclusion, certain rights to withdraw the property that was transferred to the trust may be granted to one or more beneficiaries.[64] This strategy gives the beneficiaries the right to obtain immediate possession of the trust property. However, such a withdrawal would certainly diminish the centralization of control over the copyrights which motivated the artist to use the trust to begin with.

In addition, if the trust owns nothing but one or more copyrights, it may be impractical to make a distribution upon the exercise of the power of withdrawal. Accordingly, the IRS might argue either that the exercise of the right of withdrawal is so fundamentally contrary to the artist's estate plan that there must have been some prearrangement that the right of withdrawal would not be exercised, or that it is merely illusory in view of the impracticality of funding a distribution. The IRS might therefore disregard the right of withdrawal and disallow the annual exclusion. One possible solution is to transfer some relatively liquid assets (in addition to the copyright interests) into the trust so that the beneficiaries have a more credible power of withdrawal.

---

[59] *See* 26 U.S.C. § 2036(a) (1994).

[60] *See* 26 U.S.C. § 2038(a)(1) (1994).

[61] *See* 26 U.S.C. § 2503(b)(1) (1994). After 1998, the amount is to be increased by a cost-of-living adjustment. *See* 26 U.S.C.S. § 2503(b)(2) (1989 & Supp. 1998).

[62] *See id.*

[63] *See* Treas. Reg. § 25.2503-3(a) (as amended in 1983). *Cf. supra* § 14.03[E].

[64] *See* Crummey v. Commissioner, 397 F.2d 82 (9th Cir. 1968).

[d] Inter Vivos *Transfer to Trust Is Generally Disadvantageous*

Notwithstanding the theoretical benefits associated with a lifetime transfer of fractional copyright interests in trust, such transfer of fractional interests is cumbersome at best. A far more practical approach is for the artist to transfer her entire interest in one or more copyrights to an entity, and to then either make direct gifts of minority interests in the entity, or make lifetime transfers of minority interests in the entity to one or more trusts.

§ 15.03 STRUCTURAL AND INCOME TAX CONSIDERATIONS

[A] Basis Step-Up on Death

When a person dies and her property passes to a new owner, the decedent's property tax basis is adjusted to its fair market value on the date of death.[65] Also, the property is deemed to have a sufficiently long holding period to enable the sale or exchange of the property to qualify for long-term capital gain treatment.[66]

[1] Corporate Ownership Prevents Basis Step-Up

Perhaps the most significant disadvantage of an artist's owning copyrights through a corporation (whether a C corporation or an S corporation) is that there is no step-up in the basis of the copyrights at the time of the artist's death. Conversely, if the artist (or the artist's Schedule C/LLC) owns the copyrights, the basis of the copyrights in the hands of a person to whom the copyrights passed from the artist is stepped-up to the fair market value of the copyrights at the date of the artist's death. Similarly, if a partnership (including a Partnership/LLC) owns the copyrights, there can also be a step-up in the partnership's basis in the copyrights as well as a step-up in the the artist's estate's interest in the partnership.[67] With most property, the rule adjusting the basis of property to fair market value is a two-edged sword—if the value of the property declines, the basis is reduced. However, because almost all artists have a zero basis for their copyrights, there is almost always a step-up rather than a step-down in basis.

---

[65] *See* 26 U.S.C. § 1014(a)(1) (1994). If the artist's estate elects to value its property as of the "alternate valuation date," the basis is equal to the fair market value of the copyrights on the date six months after the date of the artist's death, unless the property is disposed of before the end of that six-month period. *See* 26 U.S.C. §§ 1014(a)(2), 2032(a) (1994). *See generally* Chapter 14.

[66] *See* 26 U.S.C. § 1223(11) (1994). I.R.S. Notice 97-59, 1997-45 I.R.B. 7, made clear that this rule extended to the 18-month holding period required for long-term capital gains imposed by the Taxpayer Relief Act of 1997.

[67] *See* 26 U.S.C. § 743 (1994). The adjustment of the partnership's basis in the partnership's property is with respect to the deceased partner only. The adjustment is elective, not automatic. *See* 26 U.S.C. § 754 (1994).

[2] Consequences of Basis Step-Up

There are important consequences to the step-up in basis. Copyrights that could not be depreciated because they had a zero basis become depreciable. Furthermore, the increased basis reduces or eliminates any gain on the sale of the copyrights, and they can be sold at capital gains rates or be eligible for deduction at their full fair market value if they are donated to charity.

[a] Depreciation of Copyrights

The method generally used for the depreciation of copyrights is the "income forecast" method. The IRS has taken the position that this is the correct method for depreciating television films,[68] movies,[69] book manuscripts, patents and master recordings,[70] and copyright interests in musical compositions.[71] The only other method approved by the IRS for property of this kind is the straight-line method, which would rarely be advantageous to the taxpayer.

Under the income forecast method, the depreciation deduction for the first year in which the property is placed in service by the taxpayer is equal to the basis of the property, multiplied by the income from the property for the taxable year, and divided by the estimated total income to be derived from the property.[72] The total income estimated to be derived from the property should be based on conditions known at the end of the taxable year for which the return is made.[73] If the original forecast resulted in faster depreciation than was borne out by experience, it may be necessary to recalculate the depreciation and pay an interest charge.[74]

---

[68] *See* Rev. Rul. 60-358, 1960-2 C.B. 68.

[69] *See* Rev. Rul. 64-273, 1964-2 C.B. 62.

[70] *See* Rev. Rul. 79-285, 1979-2 C.B. 91.

[71] *See* Priv. Ltr. Rul. 8501006 (Sept. 24, 1984).

[72] Until 1996, the income forecast method was used pursuant to IRS rulings but without specific statutory or regulatory guidelines. However, as part of the 1996 Small Business Job Protection Act, Congress added a new § 167(g) to the Code that provides, among other things, that the income from the property to be taken into account in determining the deduction under the income forecast method is equal to "the amount of income earned in connection with the property before the close of the tenth taxable year following the taxable year in which the property was placed in service." *See* 26 U.S.C. § 167(g)(1)(A) (Supp. II 1996). Hence, a total of eleven taxable years (the first taxable year plus the following ten years) is used. Furthermore, the depreciation deduction for the eleventh taxable year is equal to the remaining adjusted basis of the property as of the beginning of that eleventh year. *See* 26 U.S.C. § 167(g)(1)(C) (Supp. II 1996).

[73] *See supra* Rev. Rul. 60-358.

[74] New § 167(g) provides for a "look-back method" under which the taxpayer must pay (or is entitled to receive) interest to the extent that the depreciation claimed differs from the actual experience. The interest is determined with respect to two "recomputation years." *See* 26 U.S.C. § 167(g)(2) (Supp. II 1996).

Except as provided in regulations, "the term 'recomputation year' means the 3d and the 10th

It is common for some kinds of copyrights, such as copyrights in musical compositions that are part of an opera or a musical show, to be licensed in conjunction with each other. Accordingly, it would be difficult to determine a separate value for each copyright, or to determine a separate forecast of the income to be derived from the copyright.[75] Typically, the appraisal of the property in an artist's estate values the artist's works in the aggregate or divides the works into a few clearly defined categories. The courts have approved the aggregation of interrelated intellectual property rights and depreciation of the group as a whole.[76] Given the extraordinary difficulty of calculating depreciation with respect to each individual copyright and the fact that the appraisal of the copyrights (and the forecasts of income used in the appraisal to evaluate the copyrights) typically deals with all of the copyrights in the aggregate, the calculation of depreciation of the copyrights in the aggregate is the only practical method and appears to be permissible.

---

taxable years beginning after the taxable year in which the property was placed in service, unless the actual income earned in connection with the property for the period before the close of such 3d or 10th taxable year" is within 10% of the estimated income that was forecast. 26 U.S.C. § 167(g)(4) (Supp. II 1996).

The interest computed under the look-back method for any recomputation year is determined by

(1) first determining the depreciation for prior taxable years as if the depreciation had been based on the actual income earned plus an estimate of the future income for the remaining portion of the 11-year period (instead of the estimated income from the property);
(2) second, determining (solely for purposes of computing the interest charge) the overpayment or underpayment of tax for each such prior taxable year resulting from the recomputation of the depreciation; and
(3) then using the interest rate applicable to overpayments of tax, compounded daily, on the hypothetical overpayment or underpayment.

26 U.S.C. § 167(g)(2) (Supp. II 1996).

Under an exception, the look-back method does not apply to any property that had a cost basis of $100,000 or less. *See* 26 U.S.C. § 167(g)(3) (Supp. II 1996). Because of the reference to "cost" basis, it is not clear whether this exception applies to inherited property, which does not have a "cost" basis. It is likely that if the copyrights are depreciated in the aggregate (which, as described below, appears to be permissible), it will not be possible to take the position that any of the copyrights has a basis of less than $100,000 unless all of the copyrights together have a basis of less than $100,000.

[75] In fact, the valuation of copyrights is usually based on a projection of future income derived from the exploitation of the copyright. There are rarely sufficient "comparable" sales that an appraiser could use to determine the value.

[76] *See* Lanova Corp. v. Commissioner, 17 T.C. 1178, 1185 (1952), *acq.* 1952-1 C.B. 3; Kraft Foods Co. v. Commissioner, 21 T.C. 513, 590-593 (1954) *acq.* 1954-1 C.B. 5, *rev'd on other grounds*, 232 F.2d 118 (2d Cir. 1956), both dealing with patents.

[b] Gain on Sale or Other Disposition of Copyrights

In the context of the choice of an entity to be used by an artist, the distinction between corporations on the one hand and sole proprietorships and partnerships on the other hand is quite significant. As stated above, a copyright owned by an artist directly or through a partnership of which the artist is a partner, can obtain a stepped-up basis on the artist's death. If the copyright is owned through a corporation (whether a C corporation or an S corporation), there is a step-up in basis only for the stock of the corporation but not for the property owned by the corporation. This is particularly a problem with a C corporation because any disposition by the corporation of the copyrights, whether by sale, dividend[77] or liquidation,[78] would be taxable to the corporation to the extent of the gain realized. In the case of a dividend or a liquidation, the gain realized might well be treated as ordinary income rather than capital gain.[79]

Under the Internal Revenue Code, the definition of "capital asset" specifically excludes a copyright, a literary, musical, or artistic composition, a letter or memorandum, or similar property, held either by the person whose personal efforts created the property, or generally by a person in whose hands the basis of the property is determined by reference to the basis of the creator of the property.[80] Persons whose basis in property is determined by reference to that of the creator include one who receives the property from the artist as a gift,[81] a corporation receiving the property as a contribution to capital[82] or upon incorporation,[83] a

---

[77] *See* 26 U.S.C. § 311(b) (1994).

[78] *See* 26 U.S.C. § 336 (1994).

[79] Section 1239 provides that the gain on the copyrights (which would be depreciable property in the hands of the transferee) is treated as ordinary income if the copyrights are distributed to a person who controls the corporation. 26 U.S.C. § 1239 (1994). In general, a person who owns more than 50% in value of the stock of a corporation is considered to control the corporation for this purpose. *See* 26 U.S.C. § 1239(c)(1) (1994). Under constructive ownership rules, stock owned by the members of a person's family, *i.e.*, brothers and sisters (whether by whole or by half blood), spouse, ancestors and lineal descendants, is considered to be owned by that person. *See* 26 U.S.C. §§ 267(c)(4), 1239(c)(2) (1994). Additional constructive ownership rules apply. For the applicability of § 1239 to the gain recognized under § 311, see Rev. Rul. 75-514, 1975-2 C.B. 116, which addresses language which still appears in the current form of § 311(b) as well as in § 336.

[80] *See* 26 U.S.C. §§ 1221(3)(A), (C) (1994). "Capital asset" also excludes, in the case of a letter, memorandum, or similar property, a person for whom the property was prepared or produced, as well as a person in whose hands the basis of such property is determined, for purposes of determining gain from a sale or exchange, in whole or part by reference to the basis of such property in the hands of the person for whom the property was prepared or produced. *See* 26 U.S.C. §§ 1221(3)(B), (C) (1994).

[81] *See* 26 U.S.C. § 1015(a) (1994). *See supra* § 13.03[A].

[82] *See* 26 U.S.C. § 362(a)(2) (1994).

[83] *See* 26 U.S.C. § 362(a)(1) (1994).

partnership receiving the property as a contribution from a partner[84] and a trust receiving the property as a transfer in trust.[85] If any of these persons sells the property, the gain cannot be taxed as a capital gain.[86] This is of particular interest since long-term capital gains rates were reduced to 20 percent under the Taxpayer Relief Act of 1997.[87] In addition, if any of these persons contributes the property to charity, the amount of the deduction is limited to the artist's basis in the property, which is almost always zero.[88]

[3] Loss of Compensation Deduction by C Corporation

In the case of the C corporation, a critical element for the prevention of the corporate level tax is the deduction of reasonable compensation paid to the artist. When the artist dies, it is usually impossible to justify paying high compensation to the artist's successors.

[B] Foreign Royalty Income

As entertainment, advertising, and communications have become increasingly globalized, U.S. artists have derived a greater amount of their royalty income from foreign sources. Domestic legislation in most countries provides for the withholding of tax on payments of royalties to persons who are not residents of the particular country. Fortunately, the United States has an extensive network of income tax treaties that limit, and in many instances eliminate, the withholding tax on copyright royalties paid to U.S. citizens or residents.

---

[84] *See* 26 U.S.C. § 723 (1994).

[85] *See* 26 U.S.C. § 1015(b) (1994).

[86] *See* 26 U.S.C. § 1222(3) (1994).

[87] *See* 26 U.S.C. § 1(h) (1994), *as amended by* the Taxpayer Relief Act of 1997, Pub. L. 105-34, 26 U.S.C.A. § 1(h) (West Supp. 1998). 26 U.S.C.A. §§ 1(h)(4)(A), 1(h)(5) (West Supp. 1998) provide that "collectibles" as defined in § 408(m) do not qualify for the 20% capital gains rate. "Collectibles" are defined for this purpose as "(A) any work of art, (B) any rug or antique, (C) any metal or gem, (D) any stamp or coin, (E) any alcoholic beverage, or (F) any other tangible personal property specified by the Secretary for purposes of this subsection." 26 U.S.C. § 408(m)(2) (1994), Prop. Treas. Reg. § 1.408-10(b), 49 Fed. Reg. 2794, 2801 (1984). The reference to works of art might be cause for some concern that the 20% rate will not apply to gains realized from the sale of the copyright on a work of art. However, the context of § 408(m) indicates that it is the tangible embodiment of the work of art that is the "collectible." The ownership of the copyright in the work of art is separate from the ownership of the tangible embodiment. *See* 17 U.S.C. § 202 (1994).

[88] *See* 26 U.S.C. § 170(e)(1)(A) (1994), *as amended by* Taxpayer Relief Act of 1997, Pub. L. No. 105-34, 26 U.S.C.A. § 170 (West Supp. 1998). The statutory mechanism for limiting the deduction to the donor's basis is that the amount of the charitable contribution of property is reduced by the amount of gain that would not have been long-term capital gain if the property had been sold by the donor at its fair market value.

[1] International Royalties and Tax Withholding

The withholding on copyright royalties is eliminated under the treaties with some of our most important trading partners such as Canada,[89] France,[90] Germany,[91] the Netherlands,[92] and the United Kingdom.[93] On the other hand, the treaties with

[89] Under Article XII(3)(a) of the income tax treaty between the United States and Canada, there is no Canadian tax on copyright royalties "and other like payments in respect of the production or reproduction of any literary, dramatic, musical or artistic work (other than payments in respect of motion pictures and works on film, videotape or other means of reproduction for use in connection with television)" arising in Canada and paid to a U.S. citizen or resident. The exclusion does not apply to a U.S. citizen or resident who carries on business in Canada through a permanent establishment in Canada, or performs in Canada independent personal services from a fixed base situated in Canada, and the copyright in respect of which the royalties are paid is effectively connected with the permanent establishment or fixed base. Under the Canadian treaty, a copyright royalty is generally regarded as arising in Canada if it is paid by a Canadian resident or if the royalty is for the use of, or the right to use, the copyright in Canada. *See* Income Tax Treaty, Sept. 26, 1980, U.S.-Can., art. XII, *reprinted in* Tax Treaties (CCH) ¶ 1901.12.

[90] Under Article 12.3 of the income tax treaty between the United States and France, there is no French tax imposed on a U.S. resident on royalties arising in France for the use of, or the right to use, any copyright of literary, artistic, or scientific work or any neighboring right (including reproduction rights and performing rights), any cinematographic film, and any sound or picture recording. There is an exception, similar to the one in the Canadian treaty, relating to royalties attributable to a permanent establishment or fixed base situated in France. There is also a rule similar to the rule in the Canada treaty used to determine where a royalty arises. *See* Income Tax Treaty, Aug. 31, 1994, U.S.-Fr., *reprinted in* Tax Treaties (CCH) ¶ 3001.13.

[91] Under Article 12 of the income tax treaty between the United States and Germany, royalties received by a U.S. resident are free of German tax. For this purpose, the term "royalties" includes payments of any kind received as a consideration for the use of, or the right to use, any copyright of a literary, artistic or scientific work (but not including cinematographic films, or works on film, tape, or other means of reproduction for use in radio or television broadcasting). Again, there is an exception, similar to the one in the Canadian and French treaties, relating to royalties attributable to a permanent establishment or fixed base situated in Germany. *See* Income Tax Treaty, Aug. 29, 1989, U.S.-F.R.G., art XII, *reprinted in* Tax Treaties (CCH) ¶ 3249.25.

[92] Under Article 13 of the income tax treaty between the United States and the Netherlands, royalties arising in the Netherlands and beneficially owned by a U.S. resident are not subject to Dutch tax. The term "royalties" includes payments of any kind received as a consideration for the use of, or the right to use, any copyright of literary, artistic, or scientific work (but not including motion pictures or works on film, tape or other means of reproduction used for radio or television broadcasting). As in the Canadian, French, and German treaties, there is an exception relating to royalties attributable to a permanent establishment or fixed base situated in the Netherlands. At the present time, the treaty is not necessary to prevent Dutch withholding tax on royalties because, under Dutch law, the Netherlands does not levy withholding tax on royalties. *See* Income Tax Treaty, Aug. 8, 1986, U.S.-Neth., art. XIII, *reprinted in* Tax Treaties (CCH) ¶ 6103.15.

[93] Article 12 (2) of the income tax treaty between the United States and the United Kingdom exempts from U.K. tax royalties derived and beneficially owned by a U.S. resident. The term "royalties" includes payments of any kind received as a consideration for the use of, or the right to use, any copyright of literary, artistic or scientific work (but not including cinematographic films or films or tapes used for radio or television broadcasting). As in the four treaties mentioned above, there is an exception relating to royalties attributable to a permanent establishment or fixed base

some other trading partners provide for a significant withholding tax on copyright royalties. For example, under the treaties with Australia, China, Japan, Korea, Mexico and New Zealand, the withholding rate on copyright royalties is 10 percent,[94] and under the treaties with Italy and Spain, the rate is 5 percent.[95] Under a few treaties, the rate is 15 percent.[96] There are still some important areas of the world, including virtually all of Central and South America, where there is considerable licensing of U.S. copyrights, but with respect to which there are no effective tax treaties. For example, Brazil has become a major market for U.S. stock photography agencies, but there is no tax treaty between the United States and Brazil.[97]

[2] Tax Credits for Foreign Taxes Paid

Many artists pay quite substantial foreign taxes, and the ability to claim a credit against their U.S. tax is an important consideration in choosing a form of entity in which to do business.[98] Other artists find it too difficult to comply with

---

situated in the U.K. *See* Income Tax Treaty, Dec. 31, 1975, U.S.-U.K., art. XII, *reprinted in* Tax Treaties (CCH) ¶ 10.901.12.

The United States has treaties with many other countries that also provide for no foreign tax on copyright royalties. Some of the more important countries, in terms of volume of activity are: Belgium, the Czech Republic, Denmark, Hungary, Ireland, Norway, Pakistan, Russia, Sweden and Switzerland.

[94] The provisions in the respective treaties addressing the tax on copyright royalties are as follows: Australia, Article 12; China, Article 11; Japan, Article 14; Korea, Article 14(2); Mexico, Article 12; New Zealand, Article 12. With the exception of the treaty with Korea, no special rate is provided for copyright royalties as distinguished from other types of royalties. Some other countries with which the United States has treaties providing for 10% withholding tax on copyright royalties are Israel, Jamaica, Morocco, Poland, and Romania.

[95] Article 12.2(a) of the treaty with Italy limits the 5% rate to royalties for the use of, or the right to use, any copyright of literary, artistic, or scientific work (which does not include motion pictures and films, tapes or other means of reproduction used for radio or television broadcasting). *See, e.g.*, Income Tax Treaty, Apr. 17, 1984, U.S.-Italy, art. XII, *reprinted in* Tax Treaties (CCH) ¶ 4803.25. Similarly, Article 12.2(a) of the treaty with Spain limits the 5% rate to royalties for the use of, or the right to use, any copyrights of literary, dramatic, musical, or artistic work (which does not include cinematographic films, or films, tapes, and other means of transmission or reproduction of image or sound). Under both treaties, the rates on other types of royalties are higher. *See* Income Tax Treaty, Nov. 21, 1990, U.S.-Sp., *reprinted in* Tax Treaties (CCH) ¶ 8403.25.

[96] *See, e.g.*, the treaties with Egypt, India, Indonesia, and the Philippines.

[97] Brazil is now the fifth largest market for some stock photography sales. *See* David Walker, Barbara Roberts: Looking Forward, Looking Back, Photo District News, Dec. 1997, at 20.

[98] 26 U.S.C. § 901 (1994) generally allows a U.S. taxpayer to elect to take a credit against the taxpayer's federal income tax with respect to income taxes paid to foreign countries. A withholding tax, which is collected at a fixed percentage of the gross amount of an item of income such as a dividend, interest or royalty payment, is generally considered to be an "income" tax for this purpose. However, the result is less than clear under the regulations, which impose a requirement that the foreign tax be computed on net income. In theory, net income is calculated by deducting from gross

the requirements for claiming the foreign tax credit and are forced to forgo the credit. One of the principal difficulties that artists encounter is obtaining the requisite information about the source of royalty income and the amount of withholding tax associated with that source.[99] Most major book publishers provide the necessary information, as do the major recording companies, and composers' and authors' royalty collection agencies such as the American Society of Composers, Authors and Publishers (ASCAP) and Broadcast Music Incorporated (BMI). On the other hand, many photographic agencies do not provide appropriate information about the source of royalty income.[100]

[a] Appropriate Vehicles When a Foreign Tax Credit Is Taken

For an artist who intends to take the foreign tax credit, a C corporation is not an efficient vehicle. With a sole proprietorship or Schedule C/LLC, a partnership or Partnership/LLC,[101] or an S corporation,[102] the foreign taxes paid flow through to the artist's (and any co-owners') own tax return. There, the credit can be used to offset the artist's (and any co-owners') U.S. federal income tax liability. However, the amount of credit that a copyright owner can take with respect to foreign taxes imposed on the copyright owner's foreign royalty income cannot exceed the U.S. federal income tax that would be imposed on that income.[103] In the case of a C

---

receipts the significant costs and expenses (including significant capital expenditures) attributable to the gross receipts. The regulations provide that a foreign tax whose base is gross receipts or gross income does not satisfy the net income requirement, except in the rare situation where the foreign tax is almost certain to reach some net gain in the normal circumstances in which it applies because costs and expenses will almost never be so high as to offset gross receipts or gross income, respectively, and the rate of the tax is such that after the tax is paid persons subject to the tax are almost certain to have net gain. *See* Treas. Reg. § 1.901-2(b)(4) (1983). Apparently, in the IRS's view, in the case of dividends, interest and royalties, the expenses incurred in earning the income rarely, if ever, exceed the gross income and even after the withholding tax is paid, the taxpayer is likely to have net income.

[99] Forms 1116 (for individuals, estates and trusts) and 1117 (for corporations) require that the taxpayer set forth the amount of foreign tax paid to each country with respect to which a credit is being claimed.

[100] As of this writing, to the author's knowledge, the software system used by many photo stock agencies does not process the information necessary for the photographers' claiming the foreign tax credit.

[101] *See* 26 U.S.C. § 702(a)(6) (1994).

[102] *See* 26 U.S.C. § 1366(a)(1)(A) (1994).

[103] The mechanism of this limitation is that the total amount of the credit cannot exceed the same proportion of the tax against which the credit is taken which the taxpayer's foreign source taxable income bears to his entire taxable income for the same taxable year. *See* 26 U.S.C. § 904(a) (1994). The limitation is applied separately with respect to different categories or "baskets" of income. *See* 26 U.S.C. § 904(d) (1994). Two relevant baskets are the "passive income" basket, *see* 26 U.S.C. § 904(d)(1)(A) (1994), and the "general limitation" basket, *see* 26 U.S.C. § 904(d)(1)(I) (1994), which picks up all of the other kinds of income not specially set out in § 904(d). Active

corporation, which ordinarily would have no net income at the end of the year, there would be no tax liability against which to take the credit.[104] If the C corporation receives income from both U.S. and foreign sources, it is practically impossible to leave just enough income in the corporation to generate just enough tax to be offset by the credit.

[b] Residency Usually Determines Foreign Treaty Benefits

In general, a U.S. taxpayer obtains the benefits of a tax treaty by being a "resident" of the United States. For example, the treaty with the United Kingdom provides that royalties derived and beneficially owned by a resident of the United States are exempt from tax by the United Kingdom.[105] For purposes of the treaty, the term "resident of the United States" means a U.S. corporation[106] or any person resident in the United States for purposes of U.S. tax. However, a partnership, estate, or trust fulfills the definition of "resident" only to the extent that the income derived by such an entity is subject to U.S. tax as the income of a resident, either in its hands or in the hands of its partners or beneficiaries.[107] A "U.S. corporation" is a corporation (or any unincorporated entity treated as a corporation for U.S. tax purposes) which is created or organized under the laws of the United States or any state or the District of Columbia.[108]

As a result, a U.S. resident individual, a U.S. corporation, a partnership composed of U.S. partners, and a trust which is itself taxable in the United States or whose beneficiaries are taxable in the United States, would all be considered a "resident of the United States" for purposes of the treaty. However, the treaty does not address Partnership/LLCs or Schedule C/LLCs. Under the various state statutes, an LLC is not a "corporation," and certainly a Partnership/LLC or a Schedule C/LLC is not an unincorporated entity treated as a corporation for U.S. tax purposes. A Partnership/LLC is also not a "partnership" under the treaty. The term "partnership" is not defined in the treaty. For purposes of applying the treaty to a U.K. tax, the treaty provides that any term not otherwise defined shall, unless the context otherwise requires, generally have the meaning that it has under U.K.

---

business income generally falls into the general limitation basket. Royalties received in the active conduct of a trade or business are considered active business income for this purpose. *See* 26 U.S.C. §§ 904(d)(2)(A)(i), 954(c)(2) (1994).

[104] If the corporation has no net income, there is no income tax.

[105] *See* Income Tax Treaty, Dec. 31, 1975, U.S.-U.K., art. 12(2), *reprinted in* Tax Treaties (CCH) ¶ 10.901.12.

[106] *See id.*, art. 4(1)(b)(ii).

[107] *See id.*, art. 4(1)(b).

[108] *See id.*, art. 3(1)(b)(i).

law.[109] United Kingdom law would not treat an LLC as a partnership;[110] as a result, a U.S. LLC would not be treated as a partnership under the treaty. Fortunately, in the case of the U.K. treaty, the U.K. Inland Revenue has declared that U.S. LLCs will be treated as partnerships under the treaty even though U.K. law would not treat them as such.[111] This still leaves unanswered the treatment of a Schedule C/LLC, however. A similar issue exists under the German treaty, but appears at the present time not to be formally resolved.[112]

As a result of these issues, the use of an LLC might present problems for an artist with substantial foreign royalty income. However, given the current popularity of LLCs for a broad range of business and investment activities, most countries will likely treat multiple-member LLCs as partnerships.

[c] Employee Benefits

There are many types of retirement and other benefits available that provide significant tax benefits. Most of these benefits are available to both self-employed persons and to persons who are "employees." Therefore, they should not influence the artist's choice of an entity. There are two notable exceptions, however: medical expense reimbursement plans and group term life insurance are available only to employees. To further complicate matters, employee-shareholders of S corporations are not treated as employees for medical expense reimbursement plans, but are considered employees for group term life insurance. The availability of these and other benefits in connection with a variety of structures is set forth in the schedule in Appendix 15-A.[113]

---

[109] *See id.*, art. 3(2).

[110] *See* Patrick Mears, U.K. Clarifies Tax Treatment of U.S. LLCs, 15 Tax Notes Int'l 251 (1997).

[111] *See id.*

[112] *See* Stanley C. Ruchelman et al., European Approaches to Hybrid Entities and Financing Structures: An Introduction, 14 Tax Notes Int'l 1487 (1997).

[113] Schedule 15.1. Details on this and related issues are set forth more fully in Structures for Holding and Transferring Copyrights, 22 Colum.-VLA J.L. & Arts 4 (1998).

FORMS AND APPENDICES

Appendix 15-A: Comparison of Business Entities

APPENDIX 15-A Comparison of Business Entities

	sole proprietorship	Schedule C/LLC	general partnership	limited partnership	Partnership/LLC	C corporation	S corporation	inter vivos trust	testamentary trust
Splintering of control over copyrights upon death of artist	does not prevent splintering	prevents splintering	can be problems on death of any partner	can be problems on death of general partner	prevents splintering	prevents splintering	prevents splintering	prevents splintering	prevents splintering
Can grant of copyright be terminated?	transfer by will cannot be terminated	transfer of copyrights to LLC can be terminated	transfer of copyrights to partnership can be terminated	transfer of copyrights to partnership can be terminated	Transfer of Copyrights to LLC can be terminated	transfer of copyrights to corporation can be terminated	transfer of copyrights to corporation can be terminated	transfer of copyrights to trust can be terminated	transfer by will cannot be terminated
Can be used to spread income	no	no	yes	yes	yes	yes, but with double tax and probable PHCo tax	yes	yes	no
Can there be discounts for lack of marketability and minority interest for estate and gift tax purposes?	no	not while there is only one owner	yes	yes	yes	yes	yes	discounts are available with respect to frac-tional interests in copyrights	no
Is there double tax (tax at entity level plus owner level)?	no	no federal tax but perhaps state or local tax	no	no	no federal tax but perhaps state or local tax	corporate level tax can be prevented by "zeroing out" corporation's net income	no federal tax but perhaps state or local tax	generally no	generally no
Is distribution of property from entity a taxable event?	not relevant	no	generally no	generally no	generally no	yes	yes	not relevant	not relevant
Recognized for tax treaty purposes	yes	uncertain under some treaties	generally yes	generally yes	uncertain under some treaties	yes	generally yes	yes	yes

[Continued on next page]

APPENDIX 15-A (continued)

	sole proprietorship	Schedule C/LLC	general partnership	limited partnership	Partnership/LLC	C corporation	S corporation	inter vivos trust	testamentary trust
Step-up in basis of copyrights on death of artist	yes	yes	yes, to the extent of the artist's interest in the partnership	yes, to the extent of the artist's interest in the partnership	yes, to the extent of the artist's interest in the LLC	no	no	yes, but only to the extent that the artist retains ownership of the copyrights	yes
Foreign tax credit	taken on artist's return	taken on artist's return	taken on partners' returns	taken on partners' returns	Taken on mem-bers' returns	taken on corporation's return	taken on shareholders' returns	on trust's or beneficiaries' re-turns	on artist's return during lifetime, then trust or beneficiaries'
Can artist have a medical expense reimbursement plan?	no	no	no	no	no	yes	no	no	no
Can artist have group term life insurance?	no	no	may be possible	may be possible	may be possible	yes	yes	not relevant	not relevant
Can self-employment tax be reduced?	no	no	no	yes, for limited partners	uncertain	yes, but with double income tax	yes	not relevant	not relevant
Can the entity be acquired in a "tax-free" reorganization?	no	no	no	no	no	yes	yes	no	no

INDEX

Unless otherwise designated, references are to sections.

B

D

F

G

R

U

Y